The contributors

D. N. Ashton

Department of Sociology, University of Leicester

R. K. Brown

Department of Sociology and Social Administration, University of Durham

P. Duncan

Department of Engineering, University of Cambridge

Eric Dunning

Department of Sociology, University of Leicester

S. W. F. Holloway

Department of Sociology, University of Leicester

Geoffrey Hurd

Department of Sociology, University of Leicester

Terence J. Johnson

Department of Sociology, University of Leicester

Mary McIntosh

Nuffield College, Oxford

Sami Zubaida

Department of Politics and Sociology, Birkbeck College, University of London

Human Societies
An introduction to sociology

Geoffrey Hurd

Senior Lecturer in Sociology
Dean of the Faculty of the Social Sciences
University of Leicester

with
D. N. Ashton R. K. Brown
P. Duncan Eric Dunning
S. W. F. Holloway Terence J. Johnson
Mary McIntosh Sami Zubaida

Routledge & Kegan Paul
London, Henley and Boston

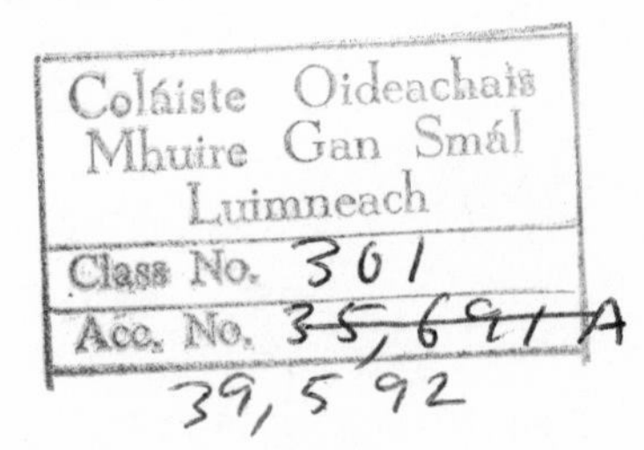

First published in 1973
by Routledge & Kegan Paul Ltd
39 Store Street, London WC1E 7DD,
Broadway House, Newtown Road
Henley-on-Thames, Oxon RG9 1EN and
9 Park Street,
Boston, Mass. 02108, USA
Reprinted 1975 and 1977
Printed in Great Britain by
Billing & Sons Limited, Guildford, London and Worcester

ISBN 0 7100 7611 8 (C)
ISBN 0 7100 7612 6 (P)

Library of Congress Catalog Card Number 73–77041

Contents

Preface

This book has been written for those who are coming to sociology for the first time. No prior knowledge of the subject is assumed but we hope that, in addition to providing an introductory textbook, we have managed to say something of significance about various aspects of the developing structures of human societies. Human societies are full of complexities and we have tried to confront some of these while retaining the clarity needed in a book of this kind. At the end of each chapter we have provided two brief lists of books. Some of these take up in more detail problems raised in the text; others deal with matter which, for the sake of brevity, had to be omitted; others provide a point of view different from that of the authors. Under the heading 'Reading' the majority of the books are clearly written, informative and often comprehensive. The books under the heading 'Further reading' are mostly either more difficult or more detailed studies.

As it is unusual for nine writers to be involved in the production of a unitary book, a word about how it was written may be of interest. For many years there has been an interest at the University of Leicester in the challenges and problems of teaching sociology to newcomers to the field. This interest has been pursued at various times by a number of the authors of this volume and one of them has undertaken research in this area. While collaboration seemed the best way to take advantage of this common interest and of the different specialist interests within the Department of Sociology here, we felt that a book such as this should have a unity of approach and style which would be lacking in a mere collection of essays. The authors therefore agreed to submit their contributions to the ultimate control of the editor, whose task was to ensure the unity of the whole volume and to carry out such revisions and re-writing as this made necessary. Perhaps it would not be out of place for me to express my gratitude for the forbearance of those whose contributions I thought it necessary to alter, and my even deeper gratitude to those whose contributions appear virtually unchanged. Authors of the chapters are as follows:

D. N. Ashton, 'Political aspects of social development'
R. K. Brown, 'Industrial relations'
P. Duncan, 'Socialization'
Eric Dunning, 'Race relations'
S. W. F. Holloway, 'Population'
Geoffrey Hurd, 'Sociology—a way of looking at societies, 'Economic aspects of social development', 'Education', 'Social stratification', 'Religion'
Terence J. Johnson, 'The professions'
Mary McIntosh, 'Urbanization', 'Crime'
Sami Zubaida, 'The family'.

All the authors are, or have been, members of the Department of Sociology at the University of Leicester, and this book tries to reflect something of the comparative and developmental approach to sociology which has developed there under the leadership of Professor Ilya Neustadt. Only those who know the Leicester Department will fully appreciate the huge debt we have all incurred to Professor Neustadt. As long as he remains Head of the Department, to teach sociology at Leicester will continue to be an education of the best and most exciting kind. That so many of the contributors to this book agree about so much is largely due to his influence. The pattern of the book has also been considerably influenced by Professor Norbert Elias, whose introductory course in Sociology inspired his fellow teachers as well as his students.

In the preparation of this book I have incurred many debts, some of which I have forgotten but which are none the less significant for that. Others will forgive me if I single out Audrey Craig and Doreen Butler who typed the various drafts and helped in a number of other ways.

Geoffrey Hurd
University of Leicester

1 Sociology—a way of looking at societies

This is not a book *about* sociology; it is a book about human societies. It is, however, written by sociologists and presents a sociological way of looking at societies. We believe that sociology offers a perspective from which we can gain some understanding of the world in which we live, and of the variety of situations and problems in which men find themselves. There is, however, a great deal of misunderstanding about what sociology is so we have prefaced this book about human societies with a chapter about sociology—what it is, how sociologists go about their work, what kind of assumptions they make, and so on.

The most common short answer to the question 'what is sociology?' is that it is the study of human society. This fails to take us very far: history, too, is the study of human society; so, in their different ways, are many other academic disciplines—especially those we call the social sciences. It is more helpful to say that sociology is a particular way of studying human society; or, better still, a particular way of studying human *societies.* There is little that is distinctive in *what* sociologists study. The most important distinguishing feature of sociology lies rather in the viewpoint from which societies are studied. The distinguishing mark of the sociologist is the *way* he thinks about societies.

Sociology is generally regarded as being a branch of the social sciences and, as its name implies, this group of subjects attempts to bring a scientific attitude to bear upon various aspects of social life. This is not the way most people (even if they are physical or biological scientists) view society. The political revolutionary wants to overthrow society; the reformer wants to change it; the evangelist wants to save it. Everybody looks at society from their own viewpoint. The viewpoint of the sociologist is basically one of curiosity: he wants to find out what a particular society (or some part of it) is like.

A number of points are relevant to this sociological view of societies. The first is that science is morally neutral. It is not the task of a sociologist to say whether a pattern of behaviour or an organization is right or wrong, good or bad. It is his task to find out what the behaviour or organization consists of, to explain how it came about and to demonstrate its consequences. This non-evaluative approach to society is perhaps the characteristic which sets sociology apart from popular views of society more than any other. Second, in industrial societies it is usual to think of society in terms of *individual* people. The sociologist, by contrast, places the emphasis on social relationships and these are by no means exhausted by relationships between individual people. Indeed, sociology is more concerned with the relationships between the major parts of a society, and these can be viewed independently of any one individual in them. Sociology, then, focuses on the interaction between the parts of societies. Third, it is an assumption of sociology (an assumption based on countless observations) that relationships between people, groups of people and social institutions do not occur randomly; that there are regularities in the social life of mankind. The search for these regularities, and their description and explanation is one of the major tasks of the sociologist. Fourth, the way in which sociologists go about their tasks is, in one respect, very similar to the activities of physical scientists. In both fields there is a combination of observation and the formulation of theory. In another way, however, the methods are very different from most (but not all) physical and biological sciences. Because of the nature of his subject matter the sociologist cannot test his theories by experiment. In a laboratory it is possible to control the variables in a situation. Thus water can be turned into ice by lowering the temperature and/or by increasing the pressure, or into steam by raising the temperature and/or reducing the pressure. The variables of temperature and pressure can be altered experimentally and manipulated in such a way as to demonstrate how the substance performs at different temperatures and pressures. Because of the high level of control, theories can be tested experimentally. Such experimentation is not possible in the social sciences; the various aspects of a social situation cannot be isolated experimentally in this way. One cannot experiment to see what England would be like with a Communist government or if Hinduism were the dominant religion. The sociologist has to find other ways of 'controlling' the phenomenon he is investigating and, in particular, he attempts to approximate to a controlled situation through the use of comparison between different societies or between different parts of the same society.

These are the most important ways in which sociologists differ from most other people in their view of society. They form the core of the sociological perspective. Let us now look at them in a little more detail, for to understand them is to go a long way towards understanding what sociologists are trying to do.

The non-evaluative character of sociology

Many of the aspects of a society that are studied by sociologists concern things that ordinary people often have very strong views about—birth control and bureaucracy; revolution and religion; politics and professions; strikes and schooling. Most people have opinions on how human affairs in these matters could (and in their opinion should) be re-arranged so as to make life in some way better and more worth while. Sociology, however. is the study of social situations *as they are*, not as they 'ought' to be. It is not the task of the sociologist to comment on the value or otherwise of what he studies. He is not interested in whether a custom is good or bad, whether a belief is right or wrong. He is concerned with trying to understand it. For example, when we study the class structure of Britain we are not called upon *as sociologists* to say whether we think the system is immoral and should be changed or whether we think it is good and valuable and should be preserved. Rather, we have to discover the character of the relationships between the groups we call classes and how they are changing, to explain how the present system came about, and to find out what its consequences are in other areas of social life. Or again, when we study religion we are not concerned whether the beliefs of any particular religion are true or false, beneficial or otherwise. It is an important social fact that people subscribe to a particular set of beliefs and belong to a certain type of religious organization, a fact which affects both the behaviour of the people concerned and the nature of the whole society.

One of the clearest expressions of this duty of the sociologist to maintain a 'value free' approach to society was that by the great German sociologist Max Weber. Referring, in this instance, to politics, Weber wrote:[1]

> To take a practical political stand is one thing, and to analyze political structures and party positions is another. When speaking in a political meeting about democracy, one does not hide one's personal standpoint; indeed to come out clearly and take one's stand is one's damned duty. The words one uses in such a meeting are not means of scientific analysis but means of canvassing votes and winning over others. They are not ploughshares to loosen the soil of contemplative thought; they are swords against the enemies: such words are weapons. It would be an outrage, however, to use words in this fashion in a lecture or in the lecture room. If, for instance, 'democracy' is under discussion, one considers its various forms, analyzes them in the way they function, determines what results for the conditions of life the one form has as compared with the other . . . But the true teacher will beware of imposing from the platform any political position upon the student, whether it is expressed or suggested.

It is these matters of fact and interpretation we are interested in as sociologists, but sociologists are also people! As individuals and as citizens, sociologists do hold opinions about the beliefs they study and the class structure or political party they observe (and these opinions are, often enough, influenced by their work as sociologists). This is one of the central dilemmas of a sociologist. He has to try to make an impartial analysis of problems about which people (including himself) feel very strongly. He has, to this extent, to try to separate his own opinions about a problem from his investigation of it. Unless he can detach himself from his prior values and beliefs in this way, his values will cause him to misinterpret or distort the very things he is trying to clarify. It is hardly surprising that sociologists are not always entirely successful in this. It is, however, the ideal for which they must strive.

All this, however, is itself something of an evaluation. It assumes that science—in this case sociology—is something worthwhile, something of value; that understanding how societies work is an activity worth spending time, money and energy on. At the level of particular research investigations, every research project involves a similar evaluation of the topic to be investigated. It may be that the researcher's high evaluation of science leads him to choose the type of research that is likely to result in the greatest advance of the discipline of sociology itself. On the other hand—and this is where his other personal values are likely to intrude—he may choose his area of research on the grounds of political or other social values he holds. Thus he may choose to study problems of economic development because of a humanitarian concern for the plight of peoples of the underdeveloped world; or he may study the relationship between social class and educational opportunity because of a feeling that the distribution of educational opportunity is unjust; or he may study race relations because of his disquiet at the exploitation of one group, or his desire to maintain the dominance of another. This is all very well if the non-scientific values of the investigator are not allowed to influence the way in which the research is carried out. To the extent that this is allowed to happen the result will be bad sociology, that is, descriptions and explanations which mislead or distort. (One important check on such distortion is the fact that others are likely to be working in the same field. So colleagues, who may not share the investigator's personal values, can check up on his work.)

There is one other question with regard to values that needs to be raised. One of the more common misconceptions about sociology is that it is concerned with promoting reform. On the contrary, sociology is not concerned with promoting anything except our understanding of human societies. It is not concerned with the making of policy or the advocacy of changes or reforms, with the maintenance of democracy, or with the development of any particular sort of society. But this is not to say that sociology has no practical applications. In the first place, it is possible to use sociological knowledge in the promotion of social reform or, indeed, in the promotion of almost anything. There are many fields of practical decision-making which might draw on sociology for the more efficient implementation of policies, and an increasing number of organizations employ sociologists with this in mind. Sociological insights with regard to the causes of crime may be utilized in the treatment of prisoners; clarification of the social consequences of certain types of urban situations may be used by town planners to avoid what they consider to be undesirable situations; knowledge of the nature of the socialization of children may be used in the execution of educational policy. Individual firms and organizations may also be able to use sociologists or their findings in carrying out the policy of the organization.

At the same time, the growth of sociologicat knowledge may *influence* the policy decisions that are taken by governments and firms—that is to say. it may influence the *objectives* of the policy makers, Thus the objectives of prisons, town plans, education and the like may be defined differently because of the discoveries of sociological research. In other words, the work of the sociologist (or the nuclear physicist, or the astronomer) may have implications for the values that are held by the public at large or at least by significant sections of the public. Changes in scientific knowledge have, in the past, frequently challenged the dominant values of a society in this way. This requires, however, the assimilation of such knowledge by the leaders of public opinion and (in Britain anyway) sociology has, until recently, been unfashionable. Nevertheless, values underlying the creation of new policy have not been unaffected by the findings of sociologists since the second world war.

So sociological knowledge can be of use to policy makers in a variety of fields and may even influence the formulation of policy. The actual determination of policy, however, lies outside the sphere of sociology. The *aims* of applied sociology cannot be determined within the field of sociology, although professional sociologists, since they are also citizens, may be found in the ranks of policy makers.

A study of inter-relationships

'No man is an iland, intire of it selfe; every man is a peece of the continent, a part of the maine. . . .' The well-known words of John Donne serve to illustrate one of the tasks of sociology—namely to show the way in which man is essentially a social animal. Along with the sister discipline of social psychology, sociology has shown how a variety of social factors are involved in the development of an individual person. We have come to see that the life of an individual cannot be understood in isolation from the socio-historical situation in which he finds himself. These disciplines further show something of the way in which individuals interact within a group situation. Thus one of the aspects of a sociological study of the family is the study of the *relationships* between members of the family—the way in which they behave towards each other, who 'wears the trousers', what degree of independence the children have, and so on. Moreover, it is not only at the level of the analysis of small groups like the family that the sociologist places the emphasis on social relationships. What is specifically 'sociological' in the study of a particular feature of a society is the attempt to relate that feature to the rest of the society. The family, for example, is no more 'an island' than are its individual members. The sort of relationships which exist between family members in a given society is closely related to the class structure, the nature of education, the prevailing economic activity and other features of the wider society. Sometimes this interaction helps to maintain the *status quo*. In traditional India, for example, the Hindu doctrine of re-incarnation reinforced the caste system by discouraging social mobility, since only by accepting one's position in this life could one hope for any improvement in the next. Sometimes, however, the interaction between the institutions of a society (or, indeed, interaction between societies) brings about changes. Thus the English educational system owes its present form, and in some ways even its existence, partly to nineteenth-century industrial development, partly to the class system which prevailed throughout its growth, partly to the influence of the churches, partly to changes in the political system. It cannot be understood in purely educational terms, in isolation from the rest of the society. At the same time, the educational developments in England have affected religion, the class structure, the distribution of political power and subsequent industrial developments. And so one could continue for any feature of any society. *Social* changes consist of changes in the relationships between the parts of a society—changes in the *structure* of the society—and the parts influence each other reciprocally. It is far more important to understand this than to ask the often unanswerable question of which changed first.

Many changes occur unintentionally. Others occur as a direct result of human planning, but even such intentional changes invariably have unintended consequences. When, for example, British colonial officials in West Africa at the beginning of the twentieth century used the traditional chiefs to pass on and enforce their demands, the *intention* was to make the administration of the colonies efficient and cheap. Very frequently, however, the unintended consequence was that the performance of this task changed the nature of the relationship between chief and people so that the chiefs were identified with the colonial power and lost much of their influence over their people. Practically every human activity or social organization has unintended consequences of this kind in addition to those which are planned, and it may even be that the intended consequences do not occur. Because of the inter-relatedness of the various institutions of a society, planned changes in one sphere may also have unintended effects on others and on the relationship between the institutions. Thus the implementation of a re-housing policy may alter fundamentally the relationships between family members, or changes in the pattern of recruitment of industrial managers may alter the emphasis on school or college examinations. The fact that such changes are unintended and often unrecognized (and may even be unwanted) does not make them any less significant.

In short, it is the sociologist's way to look for the inter-relationships between social institutions and social processes. Such inter-relationships are perhaps the major element of a society that is brought into focus by the sociological approach.

The search for regularities

This inter-relationship between institutions and processes is systematic: or to put it in other terms, there are regularities in the occurrence of clusters of factors. Textbooks in the physical sciences often speak of physical or chemical laws, by which they mean to imply an invariable relationship between events in a given situation. In the nineteenth century the early sociologists tended to write of social laws in much the same way, but today the term 'regularities' seems preferable since it does not have quite the same ring of inevitability.

Of course, there are many people who would deny that there are *any* regularities in social life, just as there were those in the sixteenth and seventeenth centuries who refused to believe that the earth was not the centre of the universe, and those in the nineteenth century who would not accept the doctrine of evolution. Those of us who have been brought up to believe that the earth revolves around the sun have no difficulty in accepting it, but the idea that there are regularities in social life is one that many are still unfamiliar with. The problem is especially acute where people are brought up to value individualism very highly (as they are in most 'Western' countries). Any suggestion of regularities seems (at first sight anyway) to limit the freedom of the individual and is consequently rejected out of hand. Yet such regularities are demonstrated again and again in the chapters that follow. The number of births and deaths per thousand inhabitants remains constant for a given country *year after year*: some industries *consistently* have more strikes than others; some social groups *regularly* commit more crime than others. Regularities can also be shown in non-statistical terms. Relationships between husband and wife or between doctors and their patients, for example, vary *systematically* in relation to economic factors.

In the past such regularities have rarely been recognized. In Western industrial societies the ethic of individualism has led to a concentration on the position and activities of the individual and to individualistic explanations. People have not seen the regularities in patterns of social behaviour but only the individual differences. In other words, in this respect as well as in the other points we have considered, a sociological way of thinking is not the normal way of thinking in our society. On the contrary most people think individualistically. The tendency is to emphasize the individual's responsibility for his actions, and this is so even in the case of children (in Britain, for example, the age of criminal responsibility is ten). So most people explain crime in terms of individual wickedness or lack of self control; strikes in terms of the personality characteristics of trade union leaders; religious revivals in terms of the personal magnetism of the evangelist. But such explanations, although they may have some relevance to an individual case, cannot explain the amount of crime in a society; why some industries have more strikes than others; what makes a revivalist successful at one time and place but not another. We have suggested that to seek out and explain social regularities is one of the main tasks of sociology; and it is one of the main claims of sociology that these social phenomena cannot be *explained* in individualistic terms.

How the sociologist finds out

(a) Fact and theory

Human societies are extremely complex. There is an almost infinite number of phenomena present to be noticed and no one person, no one investigation, can possibly describe any social situation exhaustively. The result is that all observers, whether social scientists, journalists, politicians or lay participants, select some things from the total situation as being worthy of note and, explicitly or implicitly, reject others. We notice what we want to notice, or what we have been trained to notice, or what we consider to be important for the problem we are interested in. We therefore develop a frame of reference which points our attention to certain aspects of the total situation. The sociological perspective itself draws attention to certain things that are usually neglected. Many of the regularities referred to in the last section are not noticed by a non-sociologist simply because he does not have an orientation which enables him to notice them. So our general observations of society are guided not only by what is there, but also by the sort of questions we ask ourselves. What seems clear and obvious to a person with one set of questions in mind is obscure to those whose focus is on a different set of problems. Part of the training of a sociologist is to learn to ask questions about the regularities of social phenomena and their inter-relatedness. Within this general sociological orientation, however, we select some areas of society to investigate; and in any given area the questions we ask determine to a considerable extent what we observe.

What one selects depends upon what one is trying to do. A politician in a parliamentary debate is likely to select evidence that supports his case. This may be through a conscious rejection of contrary evidence but is more likely to be because he has only been looking for evidence to support his case. This tendency is much more crudely in evidence in everyday arguments, where most of us, at one time or another, 'weight' the evidence we produce in order to make our case more strongly. To the sociologist, however, the point is not to put forward a particular line of argument, not to advocate a particular policy, but to explain the nature and development of social structures. The questions he asks must be subservient to what he observes in the following way. The explanations put forward in the social sciences—especially in the early stages of an investigation—are tentative, hypothetical. A hypothesis may or may not be 'correct', but it focuses attention on those aspects of the situation that are particularly related to that explanation. In other words, a hypothesis sharpens observations of certain aspects of the problem. Where there is a lack of agreement between the hypothesis and the observations, the hypothesis is refined or altered to accommodate the new observations. The new hypothesis may enable yet more elements in the situation to be noticed; elements which may in turn require a further modification of the hypothesis. So the process continues until a hypothesis is formulated which, for the time being at any rate, is adequate to explain the observations. It may be that a particular hypothesis is held to be an adequate explanation of a set of phenomena for many years before it is found wanting and a more adequate explanation is offered. What needs emphasizing is that there are no *final* answers; there is always the possibility of further discoveries that may upset the present position.

Thus one of the essential differences between the procedure of social scientists and that of laymen is that, while the layman is generally trying to 'prove' his point of view, the task of the sociologist is to try to *falsify* his hypothesis. Only when he has tried his hardest to do this and failed can he suggest that his hypothesis is an adequate one in the present state of knowledge. Of course, sociologists, like other people, are rarely saints and sometimes fall short of this ideal. A favourite hypothesis may be clung to grimly in the face of mounting contrary evidence. In the long run, however, science is a product of all its practitioners so even where the individual fails to test his hypothesis adequately someone else will do so.

(*b*) *The uses of comparison*

Comparison is the essence of sociology. The comparison may be historical—a comparison between the same society at different points in time; it may be inter-societal—a comparison between societies; or it may be intra-societal—a comparison between parts of the same society. To a sociologist comparison is important even if he is primarily interested in one specific society. It may be possible to describe social relationships in a given situation by concentrating on that situation alone. If, however, one wants to explain *why* they take one form rather than another, one needs to know under what conditions such relationships prevail elsewhere, and under what conditions the relationships are different.

Thus a man may be interested in, say, what happened in the French Revolution, and he may explain the occurrence of the Revolution in terms of the particular pattern of events in France. This is quite legitimate, but it is unlikely to be sociology. The sociologist may also be interested in the French Revolution, but he is likely to be equally interested in the phenomenon of revolutions. So he may make a comparative study of the French, Russian, Cuban and other revolutions in order to find out what they have in common and how they differ. His interest in any one revolution is primarily the contribution it can make to his understanding of revolutions in general; but at the same time he is interested in the nature of revolutions partly because this general study provides him with intellectual tools with which he can analyse and further understand specific revolutionary movements. In other words, the sociologist is interested both in specific events and in general phenomena; he is interested in the specific for what it tells him about the general, and he is interested in the general for what it tells him about the specific.

In the illustration of the study of revolutions we are comparing phenomena in which we perceive considerable likeness (although what are conventionally labelled revolutions may turn out to be very different social phenomena—for example, the American and the Russian 'revolutions'). It may also be useful to compare unlike phenomena. Thus an understanding of industrial societies is often heightened by comparing them with non-industrial societies; understanding the middle classes is more easily achieved by comparing them with the working classes; an understanding of town life is increased by comparison with rural life. Nor is it possible to assess the consequences for a society of a particular institution unless we make comparison with societies where that institution is different or absent. For example, the effects of colonialism can best be seen by comparing colonies or ex-colonies with societies that are broadly similar except for the absence of a formal colonial relationship. Such a comparison—say, between Sierra Leone and Liberia or Malaysia and Thailand—will enable us better to understand the institution of colonialism and so better to understand countries which have been colonies.

Above all, the proper use of comparison saves us from sweeping statements about 'human nature', by bringing to our notice the infinite variety of arrangements by which human beings conduct their affairs. The Chinese peasant; the international diplomat; the Australian stockman; the Pygmy hunter; the Latin American revolutionary; the French dock labourer; all these and thousands more must be taken into account before we can adequately comment on 'human nature'. Most comments on 'human nature' refer to patterns of behaviour that have been learned in a specific social context and represent only the viewpoint of one small group. One of the salutary experiences of studying sociology is the realization that the customs, habits and patterns of relationships which exist in our own society and which we regard as 'normal' are by no means common to all societies. It is the task of sociology to encompass the variety of the societies of mankind, thereby gaining knowledge which can be used in the analysis of specific societies.

Note

1 Max Weber, 'Science as a Vocation', in H. H. Gerth and C. W. Mills, *From Max Weber: Essays in Sociology*, London: Routledge & Kegan Paul and New York: Galaxy, 1958, p. 145.

Reading

Aron, R., *Eighteen Lectures on Industrial Society*, London: Weidenfeld & Nicolson, 1967, chapter 1. An introductory lecture by a French sociologist.

Berger, P., *Invitation to Sociology*, Harmondsworth: Penguin, 1966. A stylish and often witty commentary upon sociology; what it is and what it is not. Written for those with no previous knowledge of the subject.

Chinoy, E., *The Sociological Perspective*, New York: Random House, 1968. A short and clearly written survey of the field of sociology by an American sociologist.

Neustadt, I., *Teaching Sociology*, Leicester University Press, 1964. A sociologist's view of his subject and how to approach it. Originally delivered as an inaugural lecture.

Further reading

Durkheim, E., *The Rules of Sociological Methods*, Chicago: Free Press, 1950. The characteristics of the sociological approach, viewed by one of the most influential sociologists of all time.

Elias, N., 'Some problems of involvement and detachment', *British Journal of Sociology*, 7, 1956. A discussion of the problems of the sociologist's involvement with his subject matter.

Merton, R. K., *Social Theory and Social Structure*, Chicago: Free Press, 1949, chapters 2 and 3. A plea for a close relationship between the theoretical and empirical aspects of sociological analysis.

Mills, C. Wright, *The Sociological Imagination*, Harmondsworth: Penguin, 1970. An American sociologist's attack upon 'grand theory' and 'abstracted empiricism'; two trends in American sociology which he sees as a threat to the (more fruitful) classical sociology.

Tiryakian, E. A. (ed.), *The Phenomenon of Sociology*, New York: Appleton-Century-Crofts, 1971. A collection of articles and excerpts about sociology—its nature and its growth.

2 Economic aspects of social development

Pre-industrial economic development

One of the most striking things about human societies is their immense variety. There are large societies and small societies; urban societies and rural societies; rich societies and poor societies; industrial societies and agricultural societies. But perhaps an even more significant variation is in the degree of homogeneity within a society. Many societies contain both rich *and* poor; towns *and* villages; industry *and* agriculture; while a few contemporary and many past societies lack such differentiation.

In the simplest societies we know about, life revolves around hunting or some other form of food-getting such as gathering wild fruits. Typically, the men engage in hunting and women in the collection of wild fruits and berries. There are few, if any, comforts or luxuries. Houses are of rudimentary construction and require little labour to build and maintain them; there are virtually no clothes to be made; there are few tools to make or repair. So food-getting is virtually the only economic activity. Only a sparse population can be sustained by 'living on the land' in this way and the roving bands that comprise hunting societies are necessarily small, rarely exceeding thirty or forty members. These bands are made up entirely of kinsmen and their wives and children. Everybody takes part in all the activities of daily life and these are conducted within the context of the whole community. There are no specialist economic tasks and the band is not subdivided in any way. This is what we mean when we refer to such societies as simple societies.

Nowadays, the only surviving band societies are to be found in inhospitable desert or forest areas or on isolated islands (and even these are now changing as a result of their increasing contact with other societies). The pygmy peoples of the Congo and Malaya; the Bushmen of the Kalahari desert; the Aborigines of central Australia; and the inhabitants of the Andaman Islands in the Indian Ocean are the best-known contemporary (or nearly contemporary) examples.

The following description of the Bushmen gives some idea of life in such a society:[1]

> The Bushmen are one of the most primitive peoples living on earth. They dig roots and pick berries because they have no crops. The desert is too dry for anything but desert plants to grow naturally, and the Bushmen, who quickly consume all the wild food available in one place, cannot stay anywhere long enough to tend crops or wait for them to grow. There is not enough water to water livestock, and for this reason Bushmen have no domestic animals. Instead of herding, Bushmen hunt wild antelope with tiny arrows poisoned with a terrible poison extracted from a certain grub. Most of the meat is dried to preserve it, causing it to last at least a few weeks, but sooner or later every last bit of it is eaten, even the mucous lining of the nostrils and the gristle inside the ears. They sometimes eat the hide, sometimes work it into leather to use for clothing, and if the antelope bones are not all cracked for the marrow, pieces are worked into arrow points to shoot another antelope.

> In order to live as they do, Bushmen must travel through the veld, changing their abode every few days in search of food. Because of their way of life, they do not need villages to live in, so they rarely bother to build strong scherms, making small domes of grass for themselves instead, just a little shade for their heads. Sometimes they do not even bother with this, but push little sticks into the ground to mark their places. . . .
>
> The immediate family, a man, his wife, or wives, and children, is the only solid social unit; otherwise the small bands are always breaking up and recombining with other small bands as the structures of single families change, through marriages, divorces, deaths, or as the family decides to pay a prolonged visit to a different group of relatives. Any Bushman will be related by blood or marriage or will be acquainted with all the other Bushmen in his area but this is as far as Bushmen go in their affinities. They do not recognize as their own people strange Bushmen who speak the same language; in fact they suspect and fear them as they do any stranger.

The first human societies to develop were probably very similar to the simplest societies of today. Moreover, the greater part of man's time on earth has been dominated by such societies. With the gradual development of cultivation and the domestication of animals, however, new forms of social organization become possible. These developments represent an important step in man's control over nature. He is no longer passively dependent upon nature's bounty but takes active steps to alter and direct it. The greater productivity per acre allows a greater density of population, and greater productivity per capita releases some people from full-time food production to engage, for part of the time at least, in other tasks. Handicrafts develop, at first as part-time occupations and later, under suitable conditions, as full-time occupations. Religious specialists emerge in the same way. The members of such societies no longer carry out identical tasks.

Such specialization raises trade to the level of an economic necessity. It may take the form of barter—a direct exchange of commodities between the producers, or it may involve the use of money of one sort or another. Usually it involves specialization within the village community, as in medieval Europe where a single village would be likely to contain a blacksmith, herdsmen, and perhaps a miller, a priest, and some weavers, as well as those whose primary task was growing crops. Similarly, in India the majority of villages contain many people who neither own nor work on the land. They engage in a variety of occupations: sweepers; leather-workers; potters; carpenters; washermen; water carriers; merchants; and many more. These specialists are frequently attached to specific households of cultivators for whom they perform their service in exchange for a stipulated amount of grain each year. In addition they engage in reciprocal exchange of services with other specialists—again at stipulated rates of exchange. Such a system is common in all peasant societies. The distinctive feature of the Indian system is that each person is, from birth, tied to his specialized occupation by membership of a particular caste. He is not free to engage in another occupation even if the village has greater need of the alternative service.

More rarely specialization occurs between villages. In these cases each village normally engages in cultivation as well as in one particular craft. A few communities may specialize almost entirely on their craft product. Periodically, the people from the various villages meet at a market-place to exchange their goods and produce. Many areas of rural central America and in the Andes; most of West Africa; and parts of Indonesia (Java for example) are characterized by this kind of specialization and trade. Among the Tiv—a tribe of central Nigeria—markets are held every five days in special market-places and are attended by anything from fifty to over ten thousand people. Essentially, however, market trading is supplementary to the subsistence agriculture of the area —only special foods, luxury items such as clothes, and a few other craft goods are exchanged solely through the market. In addition to supplementing the food a man grows and the goods he makes for family consumption, these regular markets provide places where the leaders of the community discuss their problems and decide the appropriate course of action; where disputes of a legal nature are judged and settled; and where dancing, beer-drinking and other forms of recreation take place. The Tiv market illustrates well the lack of distinction between economic, political and recreational activities and institutions in simpler societies.

The further specialization develops, however, and the more economic productivity increases, the greater is the likelihood that the non-agriculturalists—the craftsmen, the religious specialists, the politicians—may gather together in residential groups, and in this way towns are formed. The process of urbanization is thus closely related to such economic developments.

This *differentiation* of occupations creates a situation in which inequality becomes a possibility. Whereas the simplest societies are egalitarian, as soon as differentiation occurs, wealth, power and prestige are distributed unequally. Some people manage to gain control of crucial resources and so are able to retain for themselves and their families a larger share of goods and services than is available to the rest of the population. In the earliest states of which we have records—the city states of Mesopotamia and Egypt—those who mediated the favours of the gods also controlled the distribution of wealth and commanded general obedience. But in those early state societies, the agricultural surplus was only sufficient to support a tiny minority in non-agricultural activities. This was also the case for the much larger and more complex empires of the ancient world—even for the two largest, Rome in the west and China in the east. With their greater agricultural efficiency, however, and, in the case of Rome, with the military strength to exact tribute in grain from its provinces, these societies were able to support large cities within which very considerable occupational specialization was possible. The relatively high level of complexity of the Roman Empire is reflected in the considerable differentiation of occupations. Rome itself—in the second century A.D. a city of more than one million inhabitants—achieved the highest level of development. Even the task of feeding the inhabitants of the capital depended upon a highly complex system of distribution. Grain—the staple food—came mainly as tribute from Egypt and north Africa and was trans-shipped at Ostia (the port of ancient Rome) into barges for transportation up the river Tiber. The size of the task was immense, as is indicated by the fact that the barge-*owners*' guild at Ostia had a membership of 258. The inscriptions at Ostia indicate, in addition, the presence of thousands of labourers working as measurers, stevedores, bargemen, warehousemen, and record-keepers. Retail distribution was equally complicated. 'Salesmen carried their wares from house to house, peddlers of sulphur matches, retailers of sausages, warm puddings, or pies thronged the streets of Rome, and bakers' boys sold their wares on street corners.'[2] We have no accurate records of how many people were employed in these and similar activities but it must have been a considerable number. Similarly, a large labour force would have been required to maintain buildings and waterworks in effective operation. At one time there were more than seven hundred slaves employed in the Imperial Water Bureau making and laying lead pipes for the distribution of water to baths, palaces, gardens and public fountains. In addition to the slaves there were water gangs divided into several categories of free workmen: overseers, reservoir-keepers, inspectors, pavers, plasterers and other workmen. Rome was also a centre of arts and crafts and numbered among its inhabitants woodcarvers, glassblowers, weavers, carpenters, shoemakers, brickmakers, goldsmiths and many more craftsmen. Within many crafts there was further specialization. In the process of making copper, for example, the metal was melted, mixed with tin or zinc, cast in special moulds that could only be produced by skilled craftsmen, and then finally sent to trained artisans to be polished, carved and forged. Each of these stages was carried out by different groups of workers, each specializing in their task. The whole process implied a far-reaching division of labour within the craft. In addition there were the activities of teachers, doctors, architects and accountants (most of which were carried out by slaves); of commerce and administration; and the upper stratum pastimes of politics and law.

Such a diversified (and in terms of food, unproductive) metropolitan society relied, for its very existence, upon military supremacy. Nothing like a balance of trade was ever achieved, or indeed attempted; the imported food was exacted from conquered or subject territories. As Cicero once remarked of republican Rome: 'if they restored all that belonged to others they would have to return to hovels and lie down in misery and want.'[3] And in the Empire as a whole, of course, the vast majority of the population *was* engaged in agriculture. It was not for more than a thousand years after the fall of the Roman Empire that the technological developments occurred which made it possible for a minority of a population to supply the food for a whole society.

Levels of economic development in the twentieth century

The greater variety of human activities is reflected in the greater complexity of societies. The increasingly specialized activities come to be carried out more and more in specialized institutions; separate organizations of government, trade, religion, family life and education become differentiated. But these specialized institutions do not exist in isolation. They are related to, and in large measure dependent upon, one another. The more there are of them, the more complicated these relationships become; or in other words, the more complex the society becomes. The gradual process of social change from a simpler to a more complex structure of society is known as the process of social development.

On the whole there is a close correlation between the level of social development and the wealth of a society (although, as we shall see later, crude figures of societal wealth can sometimes be misleading). Just as the relative complexity and affluence of ancient Rome is evidenced in the diversity of occupations, so the General Register Office's *Classification of Occupations* for 1960 lists somewhere in the region of 31,000 occupations in contemporary Britain—a far more complex and wealthy society. Related to the multiplication of specialist occupations, however, there occurs a redistribution of the labour force between various types of economic activity. In its early stages, social development invariably involves the movement of labour from agriculture into non-agricultural activities. This movement has continued (with some setbacks) throughout the process of development so far and so the proportion of the population in non-agricultural activities provides a rough and ready guide to a society's level of development. The extent of this movement of labour in selected countries during the last hundred years can be seen in Table 2.1. By the time reasonably accurate figures became available, some three-quarters of the working population of Britain was already engaged in non-agricultural activities—a factor which is related to Britain's early establishment as an industrial and trading country. The greater part of the change had occurred in the previous hundred and fifty years, for in 1688 Gregory King estimated that three-quarters of the working population was wholly or partly engaged in agriculture. The exodus from agriculture in other European countries and in the USA, however, is clearly shown in the table. In these cases, as well as in Britain, the greater part of the redistribution of labour has been associated with the growth of factory production. The proportion of the population employed in non-agricultural activities, however, is not, in itself, a very accurate guide to the degree of industrialization in a country. As the example of metropolitan Rome demonstrates, a non-agricultural population may have other bases than manufacturing industry.

Table 2.1 Percentage of the working population of selected countries engaged in agriculture

	1840	*1850*	*1860*	*1870*	*1880*	*1890*	*1900*	*1910*	*1920*	*1930*	*1940*	*1950*	*1960*	*1970*
Great Britain	22·3	21·9	18·8	15·3	13·3	10·7	9·1	8·8	7·1	6·0	—	5·1	3·6	1·5
USA	—	64·0	59·4	50·2	50·1	42·8	37·6	31·6	27·4	22·0	15·6	11·9	6·5	4·4
Belgium	—	50·9	46·8	44·4	39·5	32·2	27·1	23·3	21·1	17·3	—	12·5	7·4	5·2
New Zealand	—	—	—	—	—	—	32·9	26·1	29·7	25·7	27·2	17·4*	14·4	13·3
Denmark	—	49·4	48·6	47·8	50·4	44·8	46·6	41·7	34·9	35·3	28·5	25·1	17·5	—
France	—	51·8*	—	—	—	46·0*	41·8	41·0	41·5	35·6	36·0*	31·0*	20·0	15·8
South Africa	—	—	—	—	—	—	—	58·8	69·5	—	48·3	32·8	29·8	—
Japan	—	—	—	84·9	82·3	76·1	70·0	63·0	53·5	49·4	44·0	48·3	32·6	17·4
USSR	—	—	—	—	—	58·6	—	—	—	86·1†	—	—	44·3	24·5
Poland	—	—	—	—	—	—	—	—	75·9	65·0	—	57·2	47·7	—
Brazil	—	—	—	—	—	—	—	—	70·5	—	67·4	60·6	51·6	44·2
Mexico	—	—	—	—	—	—	—	63·7	63·0	67·8	65·4	58·3	54·2	—
Greece	—	—	—	—	—	—	—	—	49·6	53·7	—	48·2	55·3	—
UAR	—	—	—	—	—	—	—	69·1	69·2	60·3	70·7	63·7	58·0	49·2
India	—	—	—	—	—	—	67·1	71·9	72·5	67·2	—	73·6	72·9	—

*Interpolated —figures unavailable

†This figure is much higher than most estimates. The more widely supported figure of about 70 per cent is more likely.

Sources: *International Historical Statistics*, vol. 1 (P. Bairoch, director), *The Working Population and its Structure*, Brussels: Editions de l'Institut de Sociologie de l'Université Libre de Bruxelles, 1968; *Yearbook of Labour Statistics 1971*, Geneva: International Labour Office; *British Labour Statistics, Yearbook 1970*, London: HMSO, 1972.

Table 2.2 Occupational distribution of the employed population in selected countries, 1 (per cent)

	Great Britain 1970	*USA 1970*	*Japan 1970*	*Chile 1970*	*Venezuela 1970*	*USSR 1970*	*Brazil 1970*	*UAR 1969*	*Ghana 1960*	*Pakistan 1968*	*Thailand 1960*	*Niger 1960*
Agriculture, etc.	1·5	4·4	17·4	21·2	21·8	24·5	44·2	49·2	61·7	69·1	82·3	96·9
Mining	1·7	0·8	0·4	1·8	2·0	2·0		11·1	1·9	—	0·2	—
Manufacturing	34·8	24·7	27·0	22·9	17·6	25·4	17·8		9·2	9·5	3·4	0·6
Construction	5·3	4·2	7·7	8·0	6·2	8·4		4·2	3·5	2·1	0·5	
Electricity, gas and water services	1·5	5·7	6·9	0·7	1·7	0·6	*	0·7	0·5	0·2	0·1	—
Commerce, banking, etc.	15·1	21·7	22·4	13·2	17·2	5·6	8·9	9·9	14·5	7·8	5·7	0·8
Transport and communications	6·3	5·3	*	8·3	6·1	8·7	4·3	4·1	2·7	3·6	1·2	0·2
Services and administration	24·8	27·4	17·9	23·1	26·0	21·8	19·7	20·8	6·0	6·4	4·8	0·9
Activities not adequately described	9·0	5·8	0·3	0·8	1·4	3·0	5·1	—	—	1·3	1·8	0·6
All occupations	100·0	100·0	100·0	100·0	100·0	100·0	100·0	100·0	100·0	100·0	100·0	100·0

*Included elsewhere

Sources: *International Historical Statistics*, vol. 1 (P. Bairoch, director), *The Working Population and its Structure*, Brussels: Editions de l'Institut de Sociologie de l'Université Libre de Bruxelles, 1968; *Yearbook of Labour Statistics 1971*, Geneva: International Labour Office, Tables 2A and 3; *Annual Abstract of Statistics 1971*, London: HMSO.

The more detailed information on the activities of the labour force shown for contemporary societies in Table 2.2 gives us a more accurate (but also more complicated) guide to industrialization and other economic development, and thus to the nature of social relationships. In Table 2.2 the size of the manufacturing sector, of the commercial sector, and of the 'service' sector (the professions, administration, social services, entertainment, transport and the like) is taken into account. These figures provide some indication of the enormous differences between societies of the contemporary world, from societies like Niger and Thailand to those like Britain and the USA. Differences in the proportion of the labour force engaged in agriculture are striking, but they are of less significance as indices of industrialization than the proportion in manufacturing (although the two are clearly related). Even this, however, can be misleading. The manufacturing sector of the employed population of the USA, for example, is proportionately smaller than that of Britain not because industry is less dominant in America, nor even because agriculture is more important, but rather because the greater productivity of American industry (based upon a higher level of technology, greater specialization and an earlier and more whole-hearted use of mass production and automation) releases labour *from* manufacturing. Thus, a larger proportion of the population is engaged in administration, commerce, and in professional services than is the case in Britain. Moreover, Table 2.2 conceals important differences within its broad categories. The nature of the occupations within the manufacturing sector is rather different in Britain and America. In America, because of the higher level of automation, a greater proportion of the *industrial* labour force is engaged in what are usually called 'non-manual' activities. This greater 'modernity' of American industry is not reflected in these figures. Similarly in Table 2.2 the proportion of the Ghanaian labour force in 'commerce, banking and insurance' is almost as high as for Britain. The more detailed national information from which international statistics are derived, however, shows that the majority of those in 'commerce' in Ghana are engaged in very small-scale retail trade—hawking bread, plantains, yams and nuts with a turnover that does not always even ensure subsistence. In fact nearly 80 per cent are women, and their economic activities are essentially supplementary to those of their menfolk. To compare them with the bankworkers, salesmen, insurance clerks and traders of industrial societies is scarcely realistic. Such are the hazards and limitations of international statistical comparisons.

Nevertheless, simplifications of this sort do show up some general differences between societies in the distribution of their labour force. In Table 2.3 we have presented the figures for these same countries in even more simplified form in order to highlight the differences between industrial and non-industrial countries. To the right of the table are those societies where agriculture predominates; in these societies there is little or no industrial

Table 2.3 Occupational distribution of the employed population in selected countries, 2 (per cent)

	Great Britain 1970	*USA 1970*	*Japan 1970*	*Chile 1970*	*Venezuela 1970*	*USSR 1970*	*Brazil 1970*	*UAR 1969*	*Ghana 1960*	*Pakistan 1968*	*Thailand 1960*	*Niger 1960*
Agriculture	1·5	4·4	17·4	21·2	21·8	24·5	44·2	49·2	61·7	69·1	82·3	96·9
Industry	41·8	29·7	35·1	32·7	25·8	35·8	17·8	15·3	14·6	11·6	4·1	0·6
Commerce, administration	47·7	60·1	47·2	45·3	51·0	36·7	32·9	35·5	23·7	18·0	11·8	1·9
Activities not adequately described	9·0	5·8	0·3	0·8	1·4	3·0	5·1	—	—	1·3	1·8	0·6
All occupations	100·0	100·0	100·0	100·0	100·0	100·0	100·0	100·0	100·0	100·0	100·0	100·0

Sources: *International Historical Statistics*, vol. 1 (P. Bairoch, director), *The Working Population and its Structure*, Brussels: Editions de l'Institut de Sociologie de l'Université Libre de Bruxelles, 1968; *Yearbook of Labour Statistics 1971*, Geneva: International Labour Office, Tables 2A and 3; *Annual Abstract of Statistics 1971*, London: HMSO.

development. To the left of the table are those societies whose labour force is heavily concentrated in services, commerce and industry; these are the societies where industrialization has long been established. Between these extremes are societies with substantial industrial development; with highly articulated commerce and services; and at the same time, with a large proportion of the population in agriculture. These overall and somewhat crude, differences between various types of societies should be borne in mind in the discussions that follow.

The significance of these differences and changes becomes clearer when we consider the nature of industrialization more closely. In many ways the emergence of industry has been the most significant economic development since the domestication of crops. One of the most noticeable changes it has involved has been massive economic growth; wherever there has been industrialization there has also been a sharp increase in income per head—a tendency which, with only a few temporary setbacks, has been a continuous characteristic of successfully industrializing societies. But this is only one of the important factors; industrialization involves not only economic growth but economic *development* as well. It is a new type of economic activity carried out in a new set of economic institutions—factories—under the dominance of machine power. These new activities and institutions co-exist with the older agriculture and handicrafts. It is in this sense that industrialization was 'revolutionary'. It was a fundamental change in the nature of the production process which led to rapid changes in the structure of society—that is to say, to changes in the *relationships* between the different groupings of people and between the various parts of the society concerned.

There were many towns and rural areas in eighteenth-century England in which production was expanding and which were experiencing economic growth. But in most of them—in Birmingham for instance—production continued to be by craftsmen working in small workshops. For the most part they were to remain isolated pockets of manufacturing until they adopted factory production. In many places technical and organizational changes were vehemently resisted by the craftsmen's guilds. The new cotton town of Manchester which emerged during the second half of the eighteenth century was quite different. In place of the domestic textile production of an earlier generation the new textile industry was fairly and squarely based upon factory production and steam power. It thus provides us with the first historical example of industrialization. And far from being a local phenomenon its effects were felt throughout England and, indeed, throughout the world. The changes in social relationships between employer and operative in the textile industry were important enough, but they pale into relative insignificance beside the impact of industry upon the structure of the total society. New organizations emerged; often enough wealth passed increasingly into the hands of people who owed their position to little but their own talent and good fortune; new groups were drawn into the political process. With these changes in the location of power, relationships between social strata changed; new towns sprang up; age-old customs and practices were abandoned or altered beyond recognition. The whole character of the society was transformed.

This has been the fate of all societies which have successfully undergone industrialization and in this, as much as in any quantitative changes in national income or income per capita, lies the importance of industrialization. This can be seen more clearly, and some of the necessary qualifications can be made, if we look in more detail at the economic changes in some specific situations.

The first industrialization process

The early industrialization of Britain was, in many ways, unique. All subsequent industrializers were able to utilize British know-how and copy British industrial technology: Britain had to pioneer such developments. All later comers could make use of capital already accumulated by the British industrialists who were willing and often eager to add overseas investments to those they made at home: Britain's industrialization was based on no such giant capital accumulation. All other countries attempting to industrialize were faced with competition from an established industrial power which could undersell them in markets at home and abroad. The British industrialists' only competition was from craft manufacturers—the handloom weavers of Lancashire and Bengal—who were priced out of the market. In other words, Britain's industrialization was unique because it represented mankind's first excursion into the realm of factory production and the use of inanimate power on a large scale.

In other ways, too, the case of Britain has been atypical. Compared with most other industrializing countries, eighteenth-century Britain was a highly differentiated society. Commerce and trade had grown apace throughout the previous century; considerable urbanization had occurred; and, in general, economic specialization was well advanced. In the nature of landownership (and consequently in agricultural relations), in the importance of trade, in the extensiveness of a money economy, and in her international political position, early eighteenth-century Britain was unusual. Here, perhaps, lies part of the explanation for the development of manufacturing industry. The high degree of concentration of landownership (in 1750, 75 per cent of the land was in the hands of a couple of thousand landlords) not only provided a foundation for the huge surplus food production presupposed by industrialization, but also fashioned in the rural areas, a wage labour force that was potentially mobile. The destruction of the peasantry, as it is sometimes called, created a class of persons who were free of ties to the land and could migrate to the towns in search of the higher levels of industrial wages. Indeed, the rural population growth of the period forced rural workers into the towns. In addition, concentration of landownership, and with it the concentration of profit in the hands of a few landowners, made possible the accumulation of capital for industrial investment. Yet much of the important industrial development took place from small beginnings. The early entrepreneurs were more often artisans or craftsmen than landed gentlemen. The early decades of industrial development saw a good many 'self-made men' achieve positions of wealth. This was possible because of the relatively modest demands made on capital by early manufacturing industry. Cotton manufacture, for example, grew strong on the basis of piecemeal development and relatively cheap machines—the spinning jenny, the water frame, and power looms.

The highly developed system of trade provided another source of wealth for the establishment of the first factories. Most of Britain was already involved in a money market, and British merchants had, with government support, engaged in trade with most parts of the world. The early stages of industrialization were closely tied to overseas trade and so implicated the merchants from the start. Britain had emerged victorious in the struggle for the markets of the world. Her political and naval supremacy in Europe had eliminated effective competition for the trade of the non-European world. And by a policy of vigorous protection of British trading interests local competition outside Europe was crushed. Thus war and colonialism were at the heart of the early British industrialization experience. And economic interests in their turn were to play a part in the development of the British style of colonialism. For, as Macaulay argued before parliament in 1833 when supporting the education of Indians:[4]

> It would be far better for us that the people of India were ruled by their own kings, but wearing our broadcloth, and working with our cutlery, than that they were performing their salaams to English collectors and English magistrates, but were too ignorant to value, or too poor to buy, English manufactures. To trade with civilized men is infinitely more profitable than to govern savages.

Home politics played an important part in Britain's industrialization too. Gradually, throughout the eighteenth century, the commerce lobby was defeated by the manufacturing lobby so that government support was assured.

The cotton industry—the 'leading sector' of British industry for the first few decades—

illustrates these points well: compared with later industrial development it required no expensive capital equipment, no complex skills, and, although oriented towards world trade, its survival depended, in the first instance, upon the political influence of manufacturers in their conflict with the merchants. (Wool manufacturers had managed in the teeth of merchant opposition, to erect tariff barriers against Indian textiles—a factor which allowed Lancashire cotton manufacturers to dominate the home market, ultimately, ironically enough, to the virtual extinction of wool manufacture.) Most important of all, the Lancashire cotton industry stood at the hub of world trade. The importation of raw cotton from the West Indies and the southern part of North America; the export of textiles to many parts of the world but especially (initially) to India; to say nothing of the earlier shipping of slaves from Africa to man the plantations of the New World: all these had their trading centre in Liverpool. The creation and maintenance of British markets in India and the Far East had much to do with the evolution of Britain as the world's major colonial power and was carried out at the expense of the domestic production of textiles in India itself. The Indian handloom weavers were denied the tariff protection which enabled the Lancashire cotton manufacturers to grow strong. Once its strength was achieved, Lancashire could therefore undersell local products in India. To this extent social development in Britain was at the expense of the domestic textile producers of India. A similar fate (and one which is much more widely known) awaited the handloom weavers of Britain. At the other end of the production line, a satisfactory supply of raw cotton was provided by the slave economy of the American south. Thus, the fortunes of vast communities as far apart as the Mississippi and the Ganges were determined by British industrialists. And to a very considerable extent the fortunes of British industry were closely related to particular patterns of social relations in North America and India. When one adds to this the more widely known social conditions in early English factories it is apparent that the early industrial era was marked by (and dependent on) gross inequalities of power and wealth throughout the world.

The control exercised by early industrial Britain over a large part of the world's trade and production has never subsequently been approached by a single country. The wealth it generated and the stirrings of industrialization elsewhere—especially in the USA—provided the basis for the diversification of British industry. The growing population of the industrial towns and the major sea-ports provided a rapidly expanding initial market for coal; the industrialization of the USA and Western Europe demanded iron and steel which, at first, could only be produced in Britain; and, above all, the railways which covered Britain from 1837 (and rapidly spread to other industrializing societies) had a seemingly inexhaustible appetite for iron, steel and coal. On this basis the capital goods industries thrived. By 1850 there were 200,000 miners in Britain; by 1880, half a million; and by 1914 well over one million. The development of the iron ship and the application of steam power to sea transport provided a further stimulus to the basic industries as well as a growth in shipbuilding and heavy engineering.

These developments in the economy had implications that were far wider than their importance for Britain's continued economic growth—significant though that was. It was among miners, dockers, shipbuilders and other workers in heavy industry that working-class politics grew into an organized movement. It was these workers, rather than the earlier organizers of 'craft' unions, who were destined to play an important part in the development of the trade union movement and the formation and growth of the Labour party. The nature of British politics ever since has been affected by the incorporation of these groups into the political process.

Many of the factors we have so far referred to help us to understand the changing position of British industry during the last decades of the nineteenth century. These years brought a new phase in the world economic situation. Britain no longer stood alone. The USA and Germany both surpassed Britain in steel production and, for the first time for over a hundred years, Britain had serious economic competitors. For some time the markets of these competitor-nations had been protected against British goods, but in most of the rest of the world Britain's economic and political hegemony had its reward in a monopoly of trade. Much of the world could sell its products nowhere but in Britain and was allowed no other source of supply for manufactured articles. Even in the markets of the under-developed world, however, there was increasing competition, a fact witnessed by the Treaty of Berlin (1870) at which the as yet little explored continent of Africa was divided into colonies and shared out between the major European powers. No longer was Britain the undisputed leader. Still, the Empire was sufficiently large to provide a satisfactory market for her industrial goods and, when competition from other industrial countries threatened some of her traditional markets, imperial preference provided a cushion which was to last a further half a century. Rather than meeting the challenge of competition with further diversification and with the adoption of new technologies, British industrialists continued to make traditional articles for which they sought new markets. The innovating economic developments of the twentieth century have taken place elsewhere—particularly in the USA.

Dominant among the new industries both in America and elsewhere have been a whole range of electrical industries, the motor industry, a variety of chemical industries, and, more recently, the electronics industry. Mid-twentieth-century industry is not dominated, as was mid-nineteenth-century industry, by coal, iron and steel, and textiles. But it is not only that the products of industry have changed and diversified; but techniques of production are also very different. It is in this field that the Americans have been the pioneers, first in the introduction of mass production and more recently in automation, and it is upon these new technologies, as well as upon her great natural resources, that the economy of the richest nation in the world is based. However, there have been other important consequences than the increased standard of living—changes which are mirrored in other industrial societies in so far as they adopt a similar pattern of industrial organization and technology. In quantitative terms, manual workers have declined as a proportion of the employed population. Moreover, within the working classes the miners, steel workers and dockers—so crucial a part of the occupational structure of all industrial societies at the outbreak of the first world war—are no longer such a dominant occupational group. They are far outnumbered by semi-skilled factory workers producing car components, valves for television sets, machinery parts, and the like. Lacking numbers their power in the labour movement, and thus in society more generally, has also declined relative to other groups of manual workers.

By contrast, in all highly industrial societies 'white collar' occupations have been expanding rapidly, both in absolute terms and as a proportion of the working population. The number of clerks and typists, for example, grew rapidly throughout the first half of the twentieth century and numerically these occupations seem to be surviving the automation of some of their former tasks. Other non-manual occupational groups are growing still faster. This is partly because the growth industries of the twentieth century increasingly demand considerable scientific and technical skills, partly because of the complexity of the product itself, and partly because of the complexity of automated production processes. In the American aircraft industry, for example, technical personnel account for a quarter of the labour force; managerial staff for 10 per cent; lower-grade white collar workers for 23 per cent; and production workers for only 40 per cent. The general pattern of an expansion of 'white collar' staff at the expense of 'blue collar' staff is a common one. In addition, a wide variety of service occupations, from taxi drivers to shop assistants, are still on the increase despite the growth of car ownership and self-service stores. At the more skilled and more remunerative level a plethora of professional occupations grows as the affluence of modern industrial societies and the problems of life they generate produce clients for domestic architects, income tax consultants and heart surgeons.

These changes in the proportions between various occupational groups and the growth of new occupations are merely indicative of the important changes in patterns of life in modern industrial societies, changes which affect all members of society. Levels of consumption rise; leisure-time increases; the average period of education is extended. Changing patterns of employment give new significance and power to some groups, notably women and young people. These are just some of the changing relationships to which we shall return in later chapters.

Industrialization and the state

Britain's industrialization took place in the context of a non-industrial world, and the existence of an industrial Britain fundamentally altered the course of economic development all over the world. Throughout the nineteenth century all economic development occurred under the influence of Britain. The industrialization of Western Europe, of the USA, of Imperial Russia and the USSR, and of Japan followed different courses largely because of the example of Britain and the availability of external sources of investment and technology. The other major difference between the industrialization of Britain and that of most other nations lay in the part played by governments who, aware of the results of industrialization sought to imitate Britain. In this, however, there was more variation. In Britain the part of the government had been restricted to the creation, through diplomacy and military action, of world trading conditions favourable to her own sons. Important as this was it does not compare with more direct government action elsewhere: the government subsidies to industry in Japan; the government-guaranteed railways of Prussia; and the government ownership of mines and factories in both Imperial and Soviet Russia.

The early industrialization of Japan and Russia illustrates the point well. In both cases the initial stimulus to industrialize came from outside, industrialization being seen as a means of achieving political ends as much as economic ones, and being actively promoted by the central government. The defeat of the Russians in the Crimean war and the humiliation of the Japanese in 1853 by American gunboats under Commander Perry both demonstrated the military superiority of industrial powers. The lesson was not lost and important changes followed quickly. The abolition of serfdom in Russia in 1861 was the first, and most important, of the changes which laid the foundation for the rapid industrialization of the 1890s, for prior to this only those who owned serfs were assured of industrial labour. This was one reason for the stagnation of mining and textile manufacture after their establishment by Peter the Great. (Even so it is not always realized that mining and textiles together employed nearly a million workers by the mid-1860s.) The main reason for the great industrial spurt of the 1890s, however, was the fact that the development of industry became the major plank of the Tsar's policy. In particular, the decision to develop railway transport at the government's expense created a demand for iron and steel which first gave Russian industry the concentration on heavy industry which has characterized it ever since. Moreover, the iron and steel industry which was established in the last decade of the nineteenth century was one of the most modern in the world. The technology adopted was that of the efficient German industry rather than the outmoded British; the plants were the largest in the world; and the output per unit of the blast furnaces was second only to that in the USA.

Japan, before 1853, existed virtually in isolation from the rest of the world for no foreigners were allowed there. As in Russia there were legal restrictions on the movement of peasants from the land and there were additional restrictions on travel, trade, and upon changing one's occupation. Under the Treaties of 1858 and 1866 Japan was obliged to allow American and European traders to carry out their business and was forbidden to erect tariffs of more than 5 per cent. This forcible opening up of Japan to world trade under semi-colonial terms caused considerable internal problems. In particular, handicraft production of cotton goods, sugar and paper was virtually extinguished by the foreign industrial competition. These were the conditions in which the Meiji regime undertook its drastic reformation of Japanese society. Most important from the economic point of view, freedom of movement and freedom of trade were restored, and people were allowed to choose their occupation. In addition, primary education with a Western-style curriculum was made compulsory. The government, unable to help infant industries in the usual way through tariff protection, became directly involved in the process of industrialization. Railways, banks, insurance companies and factories often began life as state enterprises. Some of them were later passed over to private owners as going concerns, and many private firms were subsidized—government subsidies to the Mitsibishi Shipping Company, for example, were partly responsible for the important position Japan had achieved in international shipping by the first world war. It was largely by such energetic and direct government support for industry, particularly heavy industry, that Japan achieved the distinction of being the only nation so far to industrialize without significant tariff protection. Subsequently, as her industrial and military strength increased, Japan was able to renounce the unfavourable trade agreements with the Western world and to establish colonies of her own in Korea (1910) and extensions of territory, notably in Manchuria, which provided markets for consumer goods. In addition, however, she captured the markets of established industrial countries. To give a single example: in 1913 Britain supplied 97.1 per cent of India's cotton imports; Japan supplied 0.3 per cent. Twenty years later the Indian market was shared equally between the two industrial nations.

By far the most dramatic instance of industrialization under state control, however, is that of the USSR. The chaos created by the first world war, and by the civil war which followed the Bolshevik seizure of power in 1917, meant that the first task of Soviet economic policy after 1921 was to rebuild the farms and factories which had been destroyed. Because the industrial countries of the world were unwilling to give loans or make investments in the new regime, and often refused to trade as well, reconstruction had to be carried out entirely from internal resources. The pre-war (1913) level of output in both industry and agriculture was reached in 1925–6. Only then could new industrial growth seriously be considered. The distinctiveness (at that time) of the Soviet process of industrialization was that it was not only state controlled but entirely state sponsored. It was the 14th Party Congress, in 1925, that resolved:

> That the Soviet Union be converted from a country which imports machines to a country which produces machines, in order that by this means the Soviet Union, in the midst of capitalist encirclement, should not become an economic appendage of the capitalist world economy but an independent economic unit which is building Socialism.

The influence of political considerations upon economic policy is clear enough. Add to this the fact that it was a primarily political body which was taking the decisions, and the fusion of the political and the economic becomes stronger than anything to be experienced in the 'capitalist' world until after 1945.

The other major distinctive feature of Soviet economic development after 1928 was the establishment of the five year plans. The basic decision was to increase the rate of industrialization, and the keynote of the first five year plans was the high rate of investment. This amounted to between one-quarter and one-third of the national income, and three-quarters of this investment was to be in heavy industry. There was an attempt to plan the development of the whole society. Resources were allocated to areas of shortage and to priority concerns. In the first plans (and in practice) priority was given to heavy industry rather than to consumer industries, and to agricultural developments to feed the growing towns. This was partly because of the need to manufacture their own machinery and industrial plant consequent upon a decision to industrialize quickly; and partly, throughout the 1930s, because of the needs of rearmament created by the expansionist policies of Germany in the west and Japan in the east. In agriculture, what was planned as a gradual spread of farming co-operatives aroused the hostility of a large section of the peasantry (chiefly the richer peasants (Kulaks) and the middle-level peasants). The government reacted to this opposition by wholesale collectivization of farms and widespread deportation of Kulaks so that the Kulaks as an economic group (and a potential political force) were destroyed. The economic cost of collectivization was to be felt for a decade, however, since the chief form of peasant protest was the widespread slaughter of livestock. In 1933 the numbers of livestock were still less than half those in 1928, and the 1928 level was not fully regained until 1953. The other major agricultural change was the establishment of state farms, usually on virgin soil, as a crash programme for providing the food without which the proposed rapid industrialization could not proceed. By 1932, state and collective farms produced 84 per cent of the grain marketed in the Soviet Union and 83 per cent of the cotton.

The years 1928-37—the years of the first and second five year plans—witnessed a major change in the structure of the Soviet economy. In the space of ten years there was a colossal movement of labour out of agriculture—the proportion of the labour force engaged in agriculture declined from about 71 per cent to 54 per cent—and at the same time a substantial increase in agricultural output, which was made possible by increased mechanization. In the same decade industrial output rose from 52 per cent to 69 per cent of the gross national product. All this, moreover, took place in the context of the rapid overall economic growth which was one of the most striking features of the Soviet economy of the period. Between 1928 and 1938 output of iron and steel increased by 400 per cent; coal by 350 per cent; oil by 300 per cent; and electricity by 700 per cent. At the same time many new industries were established, including heavy chemicals (for example, plastics and synthetic rubber), aluminium, nickel and copper. The USSR had become the world's leading producer of tractors (an increase of 600 per cent in the period 1928-32 alone) and railway engines—indicative of two of the priorities of the government planners.

The growth of consumption was much more modest. The world depression (which affected the Soviet Union because it lowered the value of her exports) and armament needs necessitated the revision of the plans from time to time, and in this period it was always the consumption industries which were kept in short supply. The overall estimates of Western economists are that during this decade food consumption rose by about 10 per cent and the output of other consumable goods rose by somewhere between 40 per cent and 50 per cent.

The other area in which there was heavy investment during the 1930s was education. Education, like everything else, was part of the overall plan and its development was related to the economic needs of the country. A major literacy drive had, by 1939, eliminated illiteracy in the population aged under fifty. By 1953 there were nearly two million people who had received higher education compared with a mere 136,000 in 1913. More than two and a half million had, by 1953, been trained as skilled workers in middle-level technical institutes. In 1913 there had been only 54,000. It is this emphasis on technical education that characterizes Soviet education in comparison with that of the Western industrial world. Although enrolment in higher education is much lower than in the USA (about 16 per 1,000 compared with 44 per 1,000) more than half of the Soviet graduates, and less than a quarter of the American graduates, are scientists and engineers. The result is that the number of science and engineering graduates per head of population is strikingly similar (9 per 1,000 in the USSR and 10 per 1,000 in the USA).

The USSR provides us with the most extreme case of state ownership and domination of industry. Yet in all highly industrial societies the state is more and more in evidence in economic affairs. Even in the USA, which, of all industrial societies, at one time came closest to the freedom from state intervention which characterized early industrial England, and which still retains an ideology of non-intervention in economic affairs, the state has become increasingly important.

There are three main reasons for this increasing pervasion of the state in non-socialist industrial countries. The first is that the state has become the largest single employer. Tax-collectors, transport workers, secretaries, policemen, administrators, refuse-collectors and teachers are, more often than not, in direct government employment. In the USA—the closest to a free enterprise economy in the contemporary world—there were in 1969 more than twelve million people directly employed by federal and state governments in addition to the three million men in the armed forces.

Second, the state itself has become the largest single customer of industry. In some fields—armaments and military defence are the obvious examples—it is the only significant customer. The government therefore controls the fortunes of large sectors of industry by its military decisions and by the placement of its contracts. More than 90 per cent of the business of the American aircraft industry is supplied by government defence contracts. The General Dynamics Corporation of the USA is a spectacular example of a company which owes its prosperity entirely to defence contracts, 80 per cent of its work being in this field. It had recorded losses over the preceding years when, in 1962, it was given the contract for the hugely expensive F-111 all-purpose military aircraft. In 1967-8 the Corporation received more arms contracts than any other American company—to the value of two thousand million dollars. In such deals the government maintains close control over all aspects of the industry, including the level of profit or loss. Some indication of the importance of the United States government as a customer of industry can be gauged from the total bill for defence spending, which during the 1960s was running at more than 10 per cent of the gross national product. Government decisions on military matters, then, clearly have considerable impact in the industrial world; re-armament or disarmament are economic as well as political issues. The same is true for government enterprises which are not directly (or solely) military. The decision of the Kennedy administration to send men to the moon before 1970, for example, was an important *economic* decision in that it resulted in important economic changes in American industry and in American life more generally.

Third, the general economic activities of government have expanded, particularly in the years since the second world war. Governments have always been involved in economic matters through the necessity of raising taxes. Even in this field, however, a change has occurred as direct taxation has become increasingly a tool of social as well as economic policy—a means of redistributing part of a nation's income. In other ways, too, governments in Western Europe and North America have attempted to prevent or ameliorate some of the consequences of economic changes. This, of course, has a long history, stretching back to the Factory Acts of early nineteenth-century England. Since the great depression of the early 1930s, however, government intervention has been economic as well as legal, and has been especially important in the attempt to maintain full employment. Today, in all the major industrial nations of the world, governments attempt to *direct* economic changes. Thus, British governments of the 1960s offered inducements to industrial firms to move to 'development areas'; they attempted to reverse the movement of the labour force into tertiary occupations by operating a selective employment tax which was levied on all employers of labour other than manufacturers; they subsidized the aircraft industry in order that it could keep abreast of the rapidly changing aero-technology; and they subsidized airlines so that they could buy the latest products of the aircraft industry. The list could be extended, or could be duplicated for other Western nations. Finally, in most industrial societies—for example, in Sweden, Australia and Italy as well as in the USA and Britain—the State has power to arbitrate, or otherwise intervene, in industrial disputes.

One of the most significant features of this increased state involvement in the economies of non-socialist countries is that it is most intense in the newly-developed industries. In the USA it is marked in the space and missile industries with their reliance on electronics, partly because of the importance of these industries in the defence programme (80 per cent of the spending on armaments goes on aircraft, missiles and electronics). Elsewhere, it is sometimes only the state that has the resources needed to develop these new fields. Whatever the reason, this concentration of government economic activities suggests that the increase in state involvement will continue. Clearly, state involvement in the economy is no longer dependent upon a socialist political ideology. Yet equally clearly there still remains a difference between state ownership, as practised in the USSR, and the United States government's policy of giving contracts to private industry. Both the degree and nature of the involvement differ, although this has less effect upon the strictly economic relations than might at first be expected.

Contemporary modernizing[5] societies

Just as the existence of an industrial Britain affected the course of subsequent economic development in Germany, the USA and elsewhere, so the existence of the industrial world affects the development of the non-industrial world today. The knowledge, techniques and machines of advanced industrial societies can be diffused to the 'under-developed' world enabling 'short cuts' to be taken in the establishment of efficient communications networks and sometimes of factory production. This can, in some instances, enable considerable economic growth to take place; less often, but sometimes, it results in industrialization. Yet it may be that the most advanced industrial technology is not that which is best suited to the resources of a given non-industrial society. The expensive labour-saving devices of modern American industry, for example, were developed in response to a situation of labour scarcity. When applied in India they may use an unnecessary amount of the scarce capital of that country and ignore the abundant supply of labour. The 'modern' also has an attraction of its own that is hard to resist.

However, in the diffusion of technology, as in other things, the relationship between industrial and non-industrial countries is not one between equals. It is one between the economically (and politically) powerful and the relatively powerless. Very often in the last hundred years or more it has taken the form of colonialism (although this has not always been the case and the formality of imperialism is less important than the fact of its existence). We have already noticed something of the effect of colonialism on the economic development of Britain. Its effects upon the colonized were no less dramatic. Sometimes the imposition of colonialism was initially associated with rapid economic growth and development. The exploitation of copper mines in the then Northern Rhodesia and Belgian Congo; the introduction of cocoa to West Africa; the commercial mining of tin and the planting of rubber in Malaya; and the spread of coffee plantations in the south and east of non-colonial Brazil: all this represented major diversification in what had previously been relatively simple economies. Similarly, in each case there was an immediate increase in the gross national product of the countries concerned. The capital accumulation which had occurred in Western industrial countries had been so great that investment in non-industrial countries could proceed without in any way bringing a shortage of capital at home. Furthermore, the requirements of the industrial world for raw materials, and the increasingly urban character of European societies which meant that they were unable to provide their own food, provided a ready market which made such investment very attractive. Thus, the initial impulse for economic diversification came from the already industrializing countries, and capital and skills were diffused from Europe and the USA to Africa, Asia and Latin America.

There were two consequences of this, however, which were crucial to the subsequent structure of modernizing societies. The first of these was that a large part of the profit from these economic

Table 2.4 Major importers of the produce of selected modernizing societies, 1966 (per cent)

	Brazil	*Chile*	*Congo*	*Ghana*	*India*	*Nigeria*	*Senegal*	*Zambia*
Belgium	2·2	3·0	54·4	3·6	1·5	2·6	0·9	1·4
Canada	1·3	0·1	0·1	2·7	2·7	3·5	—	—
France	3·4	4·4	6·9	0·7	1·6	9·3	73·8	8·6
Italy	6·3	5·2	10·5	3·6	1·3	4·9	3·9	8·8
Japan	2·4	10·4	—	5·5	9·2	1·5	1·3	14·1
Netherlands	5·1	13·2	2·7	7·6	1·0	9·4	0·7	0·1
UK	4·3	15·0	8·3	16·9	17·3	37·8	1·1	32·5
USA	33·4	24·9	4·2	16·2	18·8	8·0	0·1	—
West Germany	7·7	9·5	4·3	8·3	2·2	10·0	2·2	14·1
Other countries	33·9	14·3	8·6	34·9	44·4	13·0	16·9	20·4
	100·0	100·0	100·0	100·0	100·0	100·0	100·0	100·0

Source: *International Trade Statistics 1966*, New York: United Nations, 1968.

enterprises went (and still goes) overseas to the investors in the industrial countries. Thus, whereas in the early stages of European industrialization such profits were available for ploughing back into further development, this is less the case in today's modernizing societies. This is a problem that was hardly tackled in Africa until the 'independence decade' of the 1960s. Most independent African states have now attempted to come to terms with this particular problem by limiting the proportion of the profit which may be taken out of the country. Yet, important as political independence may be, it is not the only factor. One estimate of the relations between the USA and the 'developing' world suggests that between 1950 and 1965 the USA (which has never been a significant colonial power) invested some $9.0 billion while there was $25.6 billion profit on investments in the 'under-developed' world.[6] While such figures should not be taken to mean that there is no benefit to modernizing societies—such investment usually stimulates employment and provision of supporting services of one kind or another and may be the necessary first step in further development—they do suggest that aid to, and investment in, the Third World is by no means as altruistic an enterprise as it is sometimes made out to be.

The second consequence of the external source of economic development has been that such development has taken place as part of the much wider process of what is sometimes called the international division of labour. The development which has taken place has been overwhelmingly in primary production; that is, either in agriculture or in mining. Typically, exports consist of raw materials—cotton (Egypt); sugar (the West Indies); coffee (Brazil); bananas (Ecuador); cocoa (Ghana); copper (Zambia and Chile); tin (Malaysia); oil (Libya, Iraq and Venezuela). Occasionally the raw materials are exported after the first stage of processing has been carried out. This pattern of development has resulted in economies which are tied, by international trade, to the economies of industrial societies, sometimes to those of only one or two industrial societies. Thus, in 1966, Belgium provided the market for more than half the exports of the Congo; the United Kingdom bought 40 per cent of Nigeria's exports and a third of Zambia's; a third of the exports of Brazil and a quarter of those of Chile went to the USA (see Table 2.4). This reliance on a restricted market (and if one groups together the two or three major importers the concentration is even more marked) further reduces the freedom of action of modernizing societies. Both investment and sales are controlled from abroad.

Colonialism, or other forms of domination by industrial countries, then, tends to result in initial economic development which usually proceeds no further than the emergence of primary production for the world market. Typically, the colonial economy was frozen at this level of primary production. The economic development of Ghana shows this common pattern (although compared with many modernizing societies Ghana is well endowed and relatively rich and prosperous). Before its formal colonization in 1874 the economy of the Gold Coast had made few responses to the centuries of sporadic contact with Europeans. There was some exporting of forest products—

particularly palm products, rubber and timber, which together accounted for more than three-quarters of the total exports. Earlier, in the eighteenth century, the area had been an important source of supply for the slave trade, exporting about 10,000 slaves per year. In addition to these exports there were, by 1891, some 1,500 persons employed directly by the colonial government; and a little over 2,000 persons employed in the gold mines, where the first attempts at commercial exploitation had been made in the late 1870s. Other than these groups and those employed in construction there was little economic activity except for farming—usually at subsistence level.

In the next twenty years the economy was transformed, principally by diversification in two directions. Firstly, the Gold Coast became a not insignificant producer of gold. In particular, the formation in 1897 of the Ashanti Goldfields Corporation, which has remained an important influence ever since, was associated with important discoveries of gold deposits and their commercial exploitation. By 1901, employment in the mines, and in the construction of a railway to serve them, was over 16,000. Second, and perhaps more important, farmers in the eastern part of the colony had begun to invest in a new crop—cocoa. By 1911 more than 600,000 acres were given over to cocoa production, compared with a mere 500 acres in 1891. The scale on which this new crop, based upon a new rural technology, was taken up is staggering. One estimate[7] puts the labour force involved in cocoa production in 1911 at 185,000 (out of a *total* population for the Gold Coast colony and Ashanti of some one and a half million). The whole economy became dependent upon these two products; together they accounted for 74 per cent of the goods exported from the Gold Coast. The mobilization of these resources, then, implied diversification and resulted in considerable economic growth. But the only other developments in the economy were those which were closely tied to this exportation of primary produce—the construction of roads, railways, harbours and the like. There was little attempt to develop manufacturing industry and one can only find isolated examples of the processing of forest products (for example, sawmills) or the provision of light construction materials (such as brickworks). Even the cocoa was processed in Europe or North America and the Gold Coast remained dependent upon Britain for manufactured consumer goods, machinery and capital goods. It was not until the granting of independence in 1957 that serious efforts were made to introduce manufacturing industry. Indeed, the export figures for 1960 show that gold and cocoa still accounted for 77 per cent of all exports. Real per capita income approximately doubled in the last half-century of colonial rule, but the *structure* of the economy remained essentially the same.

The arresting of economic development at the level of primary production has usually been achieved by indirect processes rather than by legal restrictions upon the development of manufacturing industry. The mechanisms, however, were none the less effective for their informality. The refusal of European governments to allow tariffs barriers against their products—a policy which was often justified by an ideological appeal to the notion of free trade—stultified any growth of manufacturing industries. Other things being equal, embryo industries can rarely compete with established ones. It is very largely for this reason that political independence can be so important in the economic development of modernizing societies. Political independence allows the possibility of tariff protection for infant industries faced with competition from foreign established giants, and so makes further economic development a possibility. Under these conditions, or in time of war when international trade is dislocated, there is an opportunity to substitute home produced goods for those made in the industrial world.

It would, however, be unwise to claim too much in this direction for political independence, for the influence of industrial nations over non-industrial nations does not end with the death of colonialism. The economy frequently remains closely linked to (and sometimes controlled by) the economy of the former colonial power (see Table 2.4). The mechanisms of this economic link are no different in their essentials from those linking colony to colonizer; the most important are the factors of market dependency and foreign ownership that we have already discussed.

It is this *economic* dependence, outlasting the formal political dependence, that is termed neo-colonialism, and it shows that political independence is not always the clean break it is sometimes thought to be. Indeed, one of the most influential of the industrial nations has hardly been a colonial power in the formal sense at all. Yet American influence in the Third World, and especially in Latin America, is very considerable, and even extends to political influence. (The same, of course, could be said of the USSR and her relations with the relatively more industrial nations of Eastern Europe.) Similarly, the most important international relationships of most Latin American countries in the last 150 years have not been with Spain and Portugal, the former colonial powers, but with Britain and the USA.

Take, for example, the case of Brazil: the very process of independence in 1822 was hastened by the British in response to restrictive Portuguese trade policies which hampered the operations of British traders. The all important development of the coffee plantations was dependent upon the world (mostly American) market, and subsequent expansion was closely related to the building of railways—often British-owned or financed by British loans and built with British machinery by British engineers and technicians. For good or ill the economic development of Brazil in the second half of the nineteenth century was inextricably tied to the industrial world. As the Brazilian minister in London noted, somewhat bitterly, in 1854:[8]

> The commerce between the two countries is carried on with English capital, on English ships, by English companies. The profits, the interest on the capital, the payments for insurance, the commissions, and the dividends for the business, everything goes in to the pockets of Englishmen.

It is therefore not surprising that merchants and businessmen favoured the international division of labour. Any reduction of this specialization through diversification of the Brazilian economy was clearly seen to be against the interests of those who profited from trade, commerce and insurance. Yet, at the same time, profits were also being made by Brazilians. In particular, foreigners never controlled the production of the coffee in the way they controlled its transportation. And it was upon the basis of profits made by Brazilian planters (and behind the shield provided by world war) that initial industrial developments were later to proceed. Brazilian-British relations, however, effectively demonstrate that even political intervention does not depend upon a formal colonial relationship. On the question of the abolition of slavery in Brazil in the 1870s and 1880s, nobody (in Britain anyway) seems to have questioned the appropriateness of British intervention. Thus, the British navy not only cut off the supply of slaves by naval blockade (a Bill was introduced in the *British* parliament and entered the statute book in 1845 as the Aberdeen Act, giving the Admiralty the right to treat all *Brazilian* slave ships as pirates), but in 1850 British ships entered Brazilian ports and rivers and seized any ships they found fitted out for the slave trade.

For the last hundred years, then, all economic development in the modernizing world has taken place in the context of world trade and international relations. It is equally clear that, while some aspects of this global situation promote economic growth and development in modernizing societies, other aspects hinder these processes. It is on the basis of such an analysis of the economic aspects of social development that we suggest that any *assumption* of industrialization, or even of substantial and continued economic growth, in modernizing societies in the short run (say the next hundred years) is by no means incontestable. In the last hundred years some countries which were little industrialized have managed to achieve self-sustaining growth and continuing differentiation through industrialization. Japan and the USSR are the most striking examples. They have joined the ranks of industrial societies with all that this implies for the standard of living, the nature of work, the process of government, and so on. It is probable that some of the contemporary modernizing societies will also become increasingly industrial. Countries like Brazil, India and Ghana show some signs of doing so. Others, such as the oil-producing countries, are undergoing substantial economic growth but with less change in the fundamental nature of the society. In all these societies there are enclaves of industrial development, of modern urban life, of bureaucracy, in the midst of a more slowly moving rural society. These are societies of great contrasts—greater, perhaps, than any society has known for a couple of centuries. In many ways the widely used term 'dual societies' is not inappropriate. Still other societies seem unlikely to undergo further significant development in the foreseeable future (unless, that is, they are incorporated into other, more developed, societies by diplomacy or conquest). Their absolute level of poverty is often extreme; high rates of population growth eat up any growth in the total output of the economy; competition from existing industrial nations makes industrial development difficult if not impossible; the interests of powerful nations demand their retention as primary producers . . . . The list is almost endless. Yet one further factor needs to be emphasized. The climate of world opinion today has been forged largely in the presently industrial societies. Standards of health, education, security and comfort have been reached in these rich societies of which the whole world is aware, for modern communications make such standards common knowledge, In this sense, too, the world is now one world. The thirst for education, the desire to live long healthy lives, and the wherewithal to achieve these ambitions have been among the more successful of the exports of the industrial world. Politicians in modernizing societies, often from the noblest of motives, frequently attempt to provide services for their people which the country simply cannot afford, and which may be detrimental to the overall economy. It is this that underlies the basic differences between the occupational differentiation of industrializing societies in the nineteenth century and the contemporary differentiation of modernizing societies. As we noted earlier, substantial development of tertiary (service) occupations in the industrial west is a relatively recent phenomenon. It occurred *after* the huge growth of secondary (manufacturing) occupations and consequently only after high levels of societal wealth had been achieved. The development of the occupational structures of modernizing societies, with their characteristic of movement from primary occupations directly into tertiary occupations, is therefore symptomatic of the dilemma of these societies. It may well be that in this, as in other matters, the example of the development of the industrial world is as much an encumbrance to economic development as it is a help.

Notes

1 E. M. Thomas, *The Harmless People*, Harmondsworth: Penguin, 1969, pp. 20–2.

2 T. Frank, *An Economic Survey of Ancient Rome*, Baltimore: Johns Hopkins Press, 1940, volume V, p. 280.

3 Quoted in F. R. Cowell, *Cicero and the Roman Republic*, Harmondsworth: Penguin, 1956, p. 43.

4 Quoted in Taya Zinkin, *India*, London: Thames & Hudson, 1965, p. 45.

5 This term is chosen, with considerable misgivings, to refer to what are variously called 'developing countries'; 'under-developed countries'; 'countries of the Third World'; 'new nations'; or even 'industrializing countries'. It is open to most of the criticisms one might address to these alternatives and we do not use it with the usual connotation (which is a nuisance but an unavoidable one). In particular we do not argue that 'modernizing societies' are necessarily becoming more like industrial societies. Rather, we use the term 'modernization' to refer to processes of development in predominantly non-industrial societies which are occurring *under the influence of societies which are already industrial*. Thus, in our usage, 'modernization' may involve industrialization or it may not. In short, it does not necessarily mean 'becoming more modern' if, by that, we mean 'becoming like Britain' or 'becoming like the USA'.

6 See Harry Magdoff, 'Economic aspects of US imperialism', *Monthly Review*, 18, 6 November 1966, p. 39.

7 See R. Szereszewski, *Structural Changes in the Economy of Ghana*, London: Weidenfeld & Nicolson, 1965, p. 57.

8 Quoted in Richard Graham, *Britain and the Onset of Modernization in Brazil, 1850–1914*, Cambridge University Press, 1968, p. 73.

Reading

Childe, V. G., *Man Makes Himself*, London: Collins/Fontana, 1966. A deservedly famous study of the emergence of man's earliest civilizations. Based upon archaeological evidence.

Hobsbawm, E. J., *Industry and Empire*, Harmondsworth: Penguin, 1969. A study of Britain's economic development from 1750 to mid-twentieth century. The early part of the book is especially valuable for demonstrating the international character of England's industrialization.

Maddison, A., *Economic Growth in Japan and the USSR*, London: Allen & Unwin, 1969. A short historical summary of the industrialization of two important 'late-comers'.

Mead, M. (ed.), *Cultural Patterns and Technical Change*, New York: Mentor, 1955, ch. 2 (pp. 23–176). Consists of studies of the impact of technical change on post-second-world-war Greece, Burma, Tiv (Nigeria), Palau, and the Spanish Americans of New Mexico.

Thomas, E. M., *The Harmless People*, Harmondsworth: Penguin, 1969. A vivid description, by an anthropologist/traveller, of an expedition to the 'kung Bushmen of the Kalahari desert. Gives an insight into many aspects of Bushman life.

Further reading

Cowell, F. R., *Cicero and the Roman Republic*, Harmondsworth: Penguin, 1956. A social, political and economic history of republican Rome. Lively and readable.

Dobb, M., *An Economic History of Russia since 1917: Soviet Economic Development since 1917*, London: Routledge & Kegan Paul, 1966. A standard, but still highly readable interpretation of Soviet economic development.

Gibbs, P. (ed.), *Peoples of Africa*, New York: Holt, Rinehart & Winston, 1965. Contains short descriptions of the social institutions and way of life of fifteen traditional African societies. Useful for political, religious and family background as well as for economic background.

Kerr, C. *et al.*, *Industrialism and Industrial Man*, London: Heinemann, 1962. Suggests that the 'logic of industrialism' is making industrial societies more alike.

Postan, M. M. (ed.), *The Cambridge Economic History of Europe*, vol. VI, Cambridge University Press, 1966. Provides an authoritative and detailed account of the economic development of Europe.

Robson, P. and Lury, D. A. (eds), *The Economies of Africa*, London: Allen & Unwin, 1968. Brief and informative studies of seven African countries. Each section is written by an economist with personal knowledge of the society.

Wolf, E., *Sons of the Shaking Earth*, London: University of Chicago Press, 1959. A stylish and scholarly account of Middle American Society, tracing the emergence and growth of the Maya and Aztec civilizations and the transformation under the Spanish conquest.

3 Political aspects of social development

Parliaments; dictatorships; presidents; diplomacy; political parties; international assemblies: these are some of the more common pictures aroused in most of us by the term politics. Yet even with their considerable diversity they scarcely begin to cover the very considerable variety of social situation within which the art of politics is practised. They do, however, comprise some of the more important institutions through which law and order are maintained in and between the industrial nations of the twentieth century. And, because industrial nation states dominate the contemporary world, their politics forms the greater part of our subject matter. In industrial nations the majority of the population participates in politics in one way or another. The decisions of political leaders affect everybody in the society. They are discussed, with more or less frankness, in newspapers, on the radio and on television, and are consequently exposed to public scrutiny. In terms of human history, however, all this is very new. Only two hundred years ago 'the people' were not involved in state politics at all. Affairs of state were, in most pre-industrial societies, matters for the king or emperor and for selected members of his court. In earlier and still simpler societies, political organization was even more different from that of industrial societies. And in the simplest, a specialized political organization could not be distinguished from social organization more generally. It is with such societies we must start if we are to reach an understanding of politics.

Politics in simple societies

In the simplest societies of which we have records there are no differentiated political institutions nor persons who specialize in political activities. Take, for example, the Bushmen of the Kalahari desert:[1]

> The social structure of Bushmen is not complicated. They have no chiefs or Kings, only headmen who in function are virtually indistinguishable from the people they lead, and sometimes a band will not even have a headman. A leader is not really necessary, however, because the Bushmen roam about together in small family bands rarely numbering more than twenty people. A band may consist of an old man and his wife, their daughters, their daughters' husbands, perhaps an unmarried son or two, and their daughters' children.

Yet the absence of kings, chiefs, armies, courts, police forces and administrators does not mean that political life is chaotic. On the contrary, political life is the concern of the whole society; political authority is dispersed throughout the society.

In societies where the dominant economic activity is hunting wild animals and gathering wild fruits, the sheer struggle for survival is often such as to reduce physical violence and armed conflict between groups to a mininum. The scarcity of food (at any rate in most *surviving* societies of this type) means that the size of the group is rarely more than a few dozen and even this group often splits up for relatively long periods. This small size also facilitates harmony. Perhaps the most important factor, however, is the uncertainty that is attendant upon a hand-to-mouth existence of this kind. Where food is so hard to come by, the very survival of the group may be dependent upon a hunter's willingness to share his catch. Often, too, success in hunting is dependent upon co-operation between the hunters. These simplest societies, then, far from Hobbes' 'war of every man against every man', provide what is probably the most peaceful and co-operative type of society the world has ever known. Social relationships in such societies are governed by informal group controls and they apply pressures which are none the less effective for their informality. A hunter refusing to share his kill, for example, would probably be excluded from all social contact (although so heinous an offence is all but unthinkable). A punishment like this is virtually a death sentence.

In some societies only a little more complex than the hunting band, however, the potentialities for the outbreak of violence are much greater. There are well-defined customs, rights and obligations which lay down the occasions and conditions justifying the use of force, but no general limitation as to who may use it. Which person or group is empowered to administer a punishment depends very much on the nature of the offence. Kinship ties are particularly important. Often, as for example among the Nuer of the southern Sudan or the Tonga of Zambia, kinship is organized on the basis of lineages. These may be reckoned either through the male line (Nuer), in which case sons and daughters are members of their father's lineage; or through the female line (Tonga), in which case they are members of the mother's lineage. In either case there are solemn obligations to one's lineage—including the duty to protect the property and honour of the lineage. These help to maintain the peace, for the threat of revenge by aggrieved kinsmen is usually a sufficient guarantee of conformity to the customs of the society. Apart from fear of personal injury, it is universally recognized in these small-scale societies that open conflict is too inconvenient to be tolerated. In addition, lineages are invariably exogamous—that is to say, marriage within the lineage is forbidden. There are consequently numerous marriage ties between the lineages; and men think twice about attacking a rival lineage if their daughters are married into the rival group. Thus inter-lineage marriage mitigates conflict between lineages.

Kinship ties, however, are by no means the only obligations of a member of a simple society. There are other important characteristics of 'stateless' societies that intensify the inconvenience of conflict and so militate against it. These provide further ties which bind members of one kinship group to another. Frequently the lineage does not live together in a territorial block but is dispersed among a number of villages. So conflict with a neighbouring village involves conflict with members of one's own lineage; conflict with another lineage is likely to involve conflict with one's neighbours. Among both Nuer and Tonga, lineage and residence are the most important of the 'cross-cutting ties' that reduce the likelihood of resort to violence, for if a dispute does occur there are influential social pressures for a peaceful settlement.

In a number of East African tribes, the Turkana, the Karimojong and the Kikuyu for instance, the most important of these 'cross-cutting ties' is the existence of age grades. All those initiated into adulthood at any one time (or in any one period) are members of the same age grade and are bound together by vows of mutual obligation. Yet the age grade is scattered geographically throughout the society and consequently a dispute with, say, a neighbouring village will involve conflict with one's age mates. Such divided allegiances provide added pressures to resolve disputes peacefully.

In addition there is, in all simple societies, a variety of common features which bind members of the society to one another. A common language; common customs; a common religion; all provide some attachment to the group, however vague. Religion is often the most effective of these. Great rituals and religious festivals have an important unifying effect. This can clearly be seen among the Tallensi—a tribe of northern Ghana. Quarrels, fighting and even warfare were common between the various clans of the Tallensi but all had to come together in peace for the great religious ceremonies. In the words of the foremost student of this society:[2]

> The Great Festivals . . . are periods of ritually sanctioned truce, when all conflicts and disputes must be abandoned for the sake of ceremonial co-operation . . . .
> In this festival cycle, therefore, the widest Tale community emerges . . . . It means the dominance, for a period, of the forces of integration ever present in the social structure—in kinship, clanship, chiefship and tendaanaship (priesthood)—but generally submerged by the sectional interest, springing from these same institutions, that divide Tale society into a multitude of independent corporate units.

As well as this ritual unification, there are supernatural sanctions to command obedience to custom. Thus, among the Turkana, murder is virtually unknown since it is believed to prevent rain; and to a pastoralist people in semi-desert country there can be no greater threat.

These are some of the most important mechanisms that serve to integrate societies which have no centralized political authority. But such societies provide (even in their twentieth-century examples) an almost endless variety. The one thing they have in common is an absence of the specialized political institutions that we call the state (or the government). With the emergence of the state the nature of politics (and of society) changes drastically.

The development of the state

The most important characteristic of the state which distinguishes it from the simpler societies we have so far considered is that it is able to exert power; if necessary it can *force* its members to carry out certain tasks. More accurately one should say that those in control of the state apparatus are able to force others to do their will. Those who control the state monopolize the rightful use of physical force. They use it to maintain order; to protect the state against other states; to enforce the laws of the state (which reinforce the less formal custom): and they forbid its use by private individuals or groups. Violence becomes the prerogative of the officers of the state. In order that this may be achieved, armies, police forces and the like are developed which owe their loyalty to the central authority; courts develop to decide the fate of those who break the law; and kings to whom these organizations are responsible stand at the head of the hierarchy. All this is expensive: so states invariably develop some sort of tax system to centralize resources. This may involve a monetary system of taxation; it may involve gifts in kind to the central authority; it may involve some form of labour tax, either voluntary or forced labour, which at its extreme may resemble slavery. Whatever the details, state formation is characterized by the gradual establishment, within a given territory, of twin monopolies: over the use of physical force, and over taxation. The other major aspect of the process of state formation is a gradual growth in the size of territory. This results from the incessant competition between states and the absorption or conquest of the weaker states by the stronger ones.

We know relatively little about the very early stages of this process as it occurred in Mesopotamia, in Egypt, in the new world Maya and Inca societies, and in the ancient Chinese civilization which centred on the Yellow River. The initial growth of the specialized political institutions of the state in such societies, however, is probably closely linked to the emergence of social stratification. Some groups manage to organize military, administrative and religious affairs in a way which acts to their advantage. The establishment of further state offices of law and taxation furthers this process. Thus (especially in less developed states) the law tends to protect the interests of the ruling group; taxes are paid *by* peasants *to* priests or kings; the army is commanded by the strong at the expense of the weak. The emergence of the political state, then, is one manifestation of the growth in wealth and power of one small section of the population. It presupposes the establishment of surplus production which in turn must (except in an exceptionally favourable area) be based upon the domestication of crops or animals. Yet the emergence of the state is by no means inevitable. We know of many simple agricultural societies which have existed for hundreds of years without developing a state form of organization.

Under certain conditions this administrative complexity, and even the central authority itself, breaks down. With the decay of the administrative system, the king or emperor has less control over his territory and becomes increasingly reliant upon provincial lords for the administration of the land and the provision of revenue. The revenue of the state declines so that the central authority can no longer pay armies, and the decreased power of the ruler often means that he cannot conscript soldiers. He becomes increasingly dependent upon the lords for the military power of the state. Sometimes, as most spectacularly in China, again and again one of the provincial lords rises to pre-eminence and, claiming the mandate of heaven, reinstitutes a new dynasty. Thus, the Chinese Empire lasted for some two thousand years but with many different dynasties.

As the size of the state increases, as the demand for taxes arises, as military and administrative problems multiply, and as the king delegates some of his authority, so the organs of administration expand and become more bureaucratic. The development of literacy is crucial since it makes possible the impersonal promulgation of rules. The establishment of a centralized political authority is but the beginning of the process; it is followed by continual differentiation within the political realm. Some of the authority which initially pertains to the *person* of the king is given to officers of the state. Generals fight wars; judges enforce the law; administrators collect taxes; all in the name of the ruler. This delegation of authority creates a recognizable machinery of state. And the further the specialization of state tasks is taken, the more bureaucratic the administration becomes. So in modern industrial states or the imperial states of China or Rome the administrative machinery becomes very complex. But the process of state formation is not irreversible. Or, to put it another way, political changes are not always in the direction of larger, more highly centralized, more complex units. Sometimes the exercise of power becomes fragmented and decentralized. In the place of the once powerful state there emerges a whole series of smaller units in competition with each other for relatively small territories. From this base, the process of state formation starts again.

It was a process of this kind which followed the decline of the Roman Empire in Europe. In what later came to be called England, a series of invasions by Germanic tribes subjugated the local population with more or less success, and a multiplicity of small kingdoms was established. The rulers of these kingdoms were engaged in a perpetual struggle with the Britons and with each other. In the course of these struggles the warriors formed alliances for the purposes of conquest or defence, and frequently enough, these developed into stable political units. Wessex, for example, is thought to have its origins in a confederation formed to drive the Britons out of the South Midlands. By the seventh century this competition between the Angle and Saxon kingdoms had led to the emergence of the three giants—Northumbria, Mercia, and Wessex—each with a variable group of satellites. For the next three hundred years, the rulers of these three major kingdoms were engaged in a struggle to consolidate their power and to establish control over the whole of England. Fortunes fluctuated. First Northumbria, then Mercia, and finally Wessex established dominance. The smaller kingdoms, such as Essex, Kent, and Sussex were increasingly subordinated to their larger neighbours. But while the units of political organization were growing larger, the techniques of warfare and the methods of raising and organizing an army had remained essentially the same. In Mercia and Northumbria in the ninth century, they proved inadequate in the face of Danish invasions. Faced with the same problem Alfred developed something approaching a standing army, introduced new military tactics based upon the use of fortresses, and established a fleet of sailing ships. These military reforms provided an important part of the basis upon which his descendants were able to consolidate their control over a united Kingdom of England. A similar process of the enlargement and consolidation that is so important a part of state formation was evident in other parts of Europe and, indeed, the process is still continuing. The current tentative and hesitating steps towards the creation of some kind of European union are illustrative.

The early English societies also provide a series of instructive cases in the establishment of the monopolies over the use of force and the raising of revenue. The authority that Alfred's descendants were able to exert over the greater part of England was relatively weak because the development of these monopolies was in its early stages. The kings had no centralized administration through which to rule. They were consequently dependent upon the loyalty of ealdormen—the local lords through whom they ruled. It was the ealdorman who collected the local taxes, dispensed justice, and raised and led the forces of his district in war. The king was unable effectively to monopolize the use of force because of his military dependence on the ealdormen; and he only received a proportion of the taxes which the ealdormen collected. This dispersal of power to the local level constituted a threat to the stability of the kingdom—especially at times when the succession was in dispute. The king's weakness and dependence on his ealdormen severely circumscribed his action, for he could not afford to antagonize them as a group. It was not until a later stage of state formation, when effective monopolies over force and taxation had been established, that the king's authority was increased.

A number of the Kingdoms of East Africa were undergoing a similar process of state formation in the nineteenth century when colonization by the more powerful states of Europe upset the process. (Of course, colonization is itself part of the development of larger political units.) The myths of origin of several of these states—Buganda, Ankole, Nyoro, Toro and Ruanda—suggest that conquest and competition was crucial. The conquering groups were nomadic tribes from the north who, probably because they were nomadic, proved to be militarily superior to the settled agriculturalists. After conquest the defeated agriculturalists were made to provide food for the far smaller numbers of victorious pastoralists. This economic exploitation proceeded in step with political domination. The normal course was for the 'inferior' agriculturalists to be forbidden any form of military service so that military power was monopolized by the upper stratum.

These states were only loosely integrated, with the aristocratic pastoralists paying allegiance to the king and rendering him military service in return for the spoils of war. The king and his court provided a central authority but there was little in the way of a central administration. The authority of the king was mediated through a series of chiefs, each administering a local territory. In their territories, the chiefs controlled the militia, collected the revenue, and administered justice. Their loyalty to the king was dependent upon his continued effective protection. In addition there was continual conflict between states. The stronger states, like Buganda, were expanding at the expense of the smaller and weaker ones, many of which were only able to retain a measure of autonomy by the payment of tribute. So the situation was constantly changing.

One aspect of the further development of the state is the emergence of a specialized central administration and a more specialized (and eventually full-time) army, both directly responsible to the ruler. Inca society, for example, had a military organization that was dependent on the ruler and paid by him. The central administration was staffed by specialists whose sole task was to carry out the ruler's commands. Since they, too, were paid by the ruler and had no other sources of livelihood, they proved relatively easy to control. The existence of a standing army and a permanent administration enables a much more efficient appropriation of surplus wealth through taxation to be effected. As these institutions of state develop, the balance of power between the ruler and his lieutenants is tilted in the ruler's favour, and the inequalities of income and wealth increase. Such inequalities require justification, for no state relies *solely* upon force to command the obedience of its members. There is always an ideology that it is right that the ruling group should rule; that the government is legitimate. Sometimes this is based upon a notion of the 'fitness' of the king or aristocracy to rule; upon the idea that they are natural rulers. Most often in the less developed states, however, the government gained its legitimacy from the dominant religion of the society. Thus, the pharaohs of Egypt were themselves considered to be divine (and divine kingship was common among the simpler states of pre-twentieth-century Africa). In ancient China the emperor ruled with the mandate of heaven; in Mesopotamia the king was also the priest who interpreted the will of God; and in many more recent states the ruler has been viewed as the representative of the god or gods. The ruling group also tends to have a monopoly of knowledge (whether religious or secular) and so is able to control the flow of information to the rest of the population. This helps to secure legitimacy for the state and its major function of concentrating power and so supporting the social, political and economic superiority of some groups at the expense of others.

The huge inequalities in wealth and power meant that politics, which in this type of society centred on the struggle for the establishment and control of the apparatus of state, became the sole preserve of the ruler and his court. It was out of societies of this type that the contemporary industrial nation states developed, so it is to a more detailed consideration of the European manifestation of this type of state that we now turn.

Politics in the dynastic states of Europe

In the sixteenth and seventeenth centuries, European politics were the exclusive preserve of the monarch, his court, and members of the aristocracy. Together they made all the major decisions concerning the maintenance of law and order, and they were the only persons concerned with 'foreign affairs'. The majority of the population had no part in the political process and the hereditary nature of kingship meant that succession to the most powerful office in the land was not contestable. Politics consequently tended to be restricted to preserving the interests of king and aristocracy. This involved two things: the continued subjugation of the mass of the population; and increasing the wealth, power and territory of the kingdom at the expense of other kingdoms.

The exclusion of the mass of the population from participation in the political affairs of the state reflected the huge gap that existed between the wealth and power of rulers and ruled. The monarch invariably owned a large part of the territory he ruled (in one estimate for eighteenth-century Prussia, for example, the royal estates comprised at least a third of the total arable area);

he controlled the administration of justice; he was empowered to collect taxes; and he commanded the obedience of the army. With such a concentration of political and economic power the vast majority of the population had no political significance. In Russia, in the middle of the nineteenth century, the 27 million men and women who were state peasants were regarded as the property of the Tsar and could be moved around like pawns in a giant game of chess. Earlier, between 1762 and 1801, Catherine the Great and her son Paul gave away 1,400,000 of them without seriously depleting the resources of the House of Romanov. Differences in wealth and power between rulers and ruled were reinforced by differences of language, education and style of life.

In such a society the control of the monarch and aristocracy over the peasants was highly effective. The peasants were usually economically dependent upon their social superiors, and they were invariably tied to one locality. This fostered a parochial outlook in which the affairs of state were seen as being of little relevance (apart from the unpleasant necessity to pay 'taxes'). More importantly, however, the peasant is typically isolated from other peasants and this isolation prevents the growth of any permanent political organization based upon their common interests. When, in spite of these factors, conditions were so bad as to prompt some sort of rebellion, the protest either took the form of an appeal (sometimes violent, sometimes peaceful) that the monarch himself should rectify the situation or, alternatively, an appeal to God that he should intervene. In this latter case the protest took on a religious flavour, usually with strong millenarian overtones. In either case, however, the clash of interests was always resolved in favour of the rulers since, in the last analysis, the pitchforks of peasants are scarcely a match for the military might and discipline of professional soldiers. Invariably rebellions that were temporarily successful occurred in remote, mountainous regions where the local knowledge and the nature of the terrain made the struggle more equal.

However, the monarch was not all-powerful. He was dependent upon the support of the aristocracy, very largely because they were the other important landowners. Their power lay primarily in the fact that their wealth and property provided a potential source of independence from and opposition to the king. Furthermore, it was from this group that the king had to recruit trustworthy staff to man his household and administration. Thus, as long as agriculture was the major source of wealth, ownership and control of land were the most important requirements for entry into the ruling group.

Even at this time, however, land was not the only source of wealth. Increasingly, the dynastic states of Europe were affected by commerce. The buying, selling and transport of goods and services increased throughout this period with the spread of a money economy and with the growth of markets. Towns and cities, in which this type of activity was centred, flourished, and the merchants, who controlled trade, grew more wealthy and more powerful. One of the ways in which merchants translated their wealth into political power was by underwriting the expenses of the monarch. Financing day-to-day administration and court life, to say nothing of keeping up with the increasing cost of warfare, was a continual problem, and by turning to the merchants for support many kings were able to avoid excessive reliance on the aristocracy. Thus, the aristocracy as a group, gradually lost some of their power to the new merchant classes. Or to put it another way: political participation extended to include the wealthy merchants.

The struggle for power between these three groups—monarchy, aristocracy and merchants—dominates the political life of this type of society. Its consequences, however, were not identical in all European states. The English aristocracy had the greatest success in curtailing the centralization of power in the hands of the king. One of the reasons for this was that, with the development of the warship, the Tudor monarchs devoted a large part of their resources to the establishment of a strong navy to the neglect of the army. The English kings were thus unable to call upon a large army in their disputes with the aristocracy, and navies, however effective for external defence, are severely limited as a means of maintaining internal control. The aristocracy, through their control of parliament, were gradually able to restrict the power of the king. When a standing army did develop in England, it did so under the financial control of parliament, which, in turn, was dominated by the aristocracy.

By contrast the other European monarchs relied for the defence of their countries on large standing armies, and therefore placed the control and financing of the army high on their list of priorities. Their tighter control over the army gave them a greater power over the aristocracy than the English kings had. Louis XIV of France, for example, was successful in establishing a powerful army and making it responsible solely to himself. It was because of this that he was able to insist on the attendance of the French aristocracy at his court; they were not powerful enough to risk disobedience. Moreover, he was able to reduce aristocratic power still further by appointing a number of non-aristocrats to important positions in his administration.

In both France and England, however, effective internal control was achieved, and this made possible the collection of the relatively large tax income which was necessary to support the armed forces and administration. For the peaceful administration of states the size of seventeenth-century England the eighteenth-century France required a relatively complex and bureaucratic administration. Members of the royal household began to be paid for their service with salaries—the beginnings of modern civil services. While this initially enhanced the power of the king at the expense of the aristocracy, in the long run it brought new forces into the political arena. For officials emerged with some form of specialized training and/or skills and they became more and more indispensable to the central government. They thus abrogated some power to themselves, although in the early days this was strictly limited. At the lower levels of administration there was a similar growth of officials paid by the crown in order to assist in the execution of royal policy. In England the justices of the peace developed in this manner, being appointed by and responsible to the crown and so reducing the king's dependence on the aristocracy who had previously performed these tasks.

In terms of naked power, then, the monarch played one group off against another and, with varying degrees of success, managed to control those groups that threatened his position. Yet since no government relies solely on coercion to ensure the obedience of its subjects, all rulers attempt to establish the legitimacy of their rule. In the dynastic states the right to rule was hereditary; the throne was monopolized by a single family for several generations. Thus in England the Tudors and then the Stuarts were dominant; in France the Bourbons ruled. The 'rightness' of the succession was supported by the dominant religion, a support that was symbolized by the religious nature of the coronation itself. Moreover, not only the succession but the rule itself received ecclesiastical approval and so was made more generally acceptable. At its height this was formalized in the doctrine of the divine right of kings, in which the king was seen to rule on behalf of God and therefore could do no wrong. The close relationship between church and state was further reinforced by the frequent practice whereby the monarch appointed church leaders to positions of secular power. In short, the church and the monarchy were mutually supportive.

The development of the industrial state

The monarchs in the dynastic states were successful in establishing the twin monopolies of physical force and taxation and the beginning of a permanent administrative system. In the industrial state, the problem is no longer how the machinery of state will be established, but in whose interests it will be used. This change is reflected in the gradual development of a more effective administration, in the bureaucratization of the state, and an extension in the tasks it performs. Originally state administrations consist of servants and domestics recruited by the king on the basis of their personal loyalty to him, or often their family connections with him. In industrial states they consist of relatively autonomous bureaucratic organizations which recruit their employees from a wide variety of sections of the population according to impersonal criteria like the educational qualifications they hold.

Already in the European dynastic states many specialized offices of state had developed. In England, for example, the Lord Chamberlain was originally responsible for looking after the king's chamber, a task which included responsibility for the money which the king habitually kept there. By the time of Henry VIII his tasks had been narrowed down until his sole charge was the administration of finance. In this way the king's staff grew large and more specialized—partly because of the increase in size of the territories, which necessitated a larger and more efficient administration. Later the development of colonialism continued this expansion and led to the growth of new aspects of government administration. Other factors, however, were rather more important in the continued and increased expansion of government in nineteenth- and twentieth-century Europe. One particularly important factor is the increasing division of labour in the society as a whole. Old tasks are more and more subdivided and new specialized tasks emerge in the course of technological innovations. As a result of this, more people are required to co-ordinate these specialized tasks. So the growth of government administration reflects the increasing specialization in the society as a whole.

Moreover, with the increase in political participation the activities of the state expand to include the provision of education, health and social security in addition to the maintenance of law and order and external defence. Increasingly, too, the governments of contemporary industrial societies are becoming more directly involved in the field of economic affairs. The governments of some industrial societies have, of course, been directly involved with the management of the economy from the start. This is especially the case in socialist countries, but the Japanese government has shown a similar, though less extreme, concern. Since the great depression of the 1930s, the governments of capitalist countries, too, have taken more action in the direction of the economy, especially with regard to the control of unemployment and the rate of economic growth. The dominance of government contracts (especially military contracts) in many industries brings further government involvement. This expansion of the activities of the state, then, helps us to understand the massive growth in size of government bureaucracies.

There have also been important changes in the nature of state administrations. The personal loyalty to the rulers of the dynastic states was often achieved by appointing relatives or friends to influential positions. But frequently the king did not have the monetary resources to pay all his servants and officials a regular income. (Often his wealth was tied up in immobile assets like land.) There were a number of ways in which this problem was solved. A common solution was to allow officers of state to extract an income from their job: thus the Lord Chief Justice in England was allowed to keep a proportion of the fines he imposed. The subtle distinction between the public income of the office and the private income of the individual had not yet developed. Because many official positions were highly lucrative and could be used as a means of amassing fortunes it was possible to sell them to help fill the exchequer. In this way Louis XIV sold state positions in France to merchants. In England, too, this solution was common. Henry Bishop, the inventor of the post mark, paid £21,500 for the position of Postmaster General—a lucrative post which later cost more than £40,000.

The considerable capital outlay on such an 'investment' severely restricted recruitment to government service which became a highly desirable career for the sons of the aristocracy and landed gentry. The lack of differentiation between 'politician' and 'administrator' allowed gentlemen to combine the opportunity to exercise their 'natural' political leadership with the chance to amass a fortune. The financial gains of office, however, did not only come from taxpayers and offenders against the law. The government itself was a constant source of remuneration—in kind if not always in cash. To take one example, once in office in the England of George III, further offices were often given as an encouragement to vote for the government. Often enough, though, the cash pay-off was substantial: it is said that in a single morning George III paid £25,000 to members of parliament who supported him on the Treaty of Utrecht.

During the nineteenth century the revenue available to the governments of European societies gradually increased, and states were able to pay regular salaries to their personnel. With this development a strict separation was more and more enforced between the salary of the administrator and the wealth he administered in his work. With the nineteenth-century competition between European states it also became evident that competence and ability were crucial to effective administration: and the rise of the middle classes made it increasingly clear that these virtues were not the monopoly of the aristocracy. The second half of the nineteenth century is characterized by a number of important changes. In England these were formalized in a variety of legislative reforms: Haldane's army reforms, Gladstone's reform of the civil service, and a variety of local government reforms. The effect of these was to abolish patronage and the sale of government office, and to make appointment to government service more or less dependent upon success in competitive examinations. This did not radically alter patterns of recruitment into government service, for only the aristocracy and the *nouveaux riches* could afford the education necessary for examination success. Nevertheless, it did mean that the civil service became a full-time career with the possibility of appointment and promotion on merit, rather than a way to get rich quick from the legislative and executive offices of parliament. Being full-time employees largely dependent upon their salary for a livelihood, the behaviour of the 'new' civil servant was more easily controlled by his superiors. He was dependent upon his employment and consequently vulnerable to threats of dismissal or loss of promotion.

These changes in the organization of the civil service also laid the basis for a new and different code of public morality. It became 'wrong' for civil servants (and, by extension, employees of large public or private companies) to use the money they handled at work for their personal gain. It became 'wrong' for a public servant to use his influence to get friends and relatives government jobs. It became 'wrong' for a civil servant to accept bribes for providing a more efficient service or for steering a government contract into certain hands. (Although, of course, all these things do go on in industrial societies, albeit illegally and to a limited extent.) These changes in public morality have only become possible with the distinction between office and office holder.

Class formation and the balance of power

Wherever industrialization has occurred it has been associated with important changes in the relationship between rulers and ruled. In particular, in non-socialist societies at any rate, it has been related to the emergence of social classes and the changing distribution of power between them. The development of commerce had resulted in an increase in the power of the merchants. The growth of manufacturing industry led to the growth of a new middle class whose position was based upon manufacture rather than trade, and who controlled an ever-increasing proportion of the wealth of the country. Although their wealth came from a different source, the political position of the industrialist and the merchant was similar. The rulers were increasingly dependent upon them to finance the international wars of expansion and defence upon which the relative standing of the states of Europe was based. In spite of their increasing wealth, however, the industrialists and businessmen were effectively excluded from important political positions. The disregard of their interests by the ruling élite led to an intense political struggle. The ruling group—particularly the aristocracy—tried to maintain their privileges and their domination of the peasants. The manufacturers and businessmen demanded the abolition of such privilege: the introduction of a rational and 'equitable' tax system; an efficient system of administration; and, more generally, social conditions in which free enterprise could flourish.

In France, where the aristocracy persistently resisted these demands, middle-class political frustration coincided with mounting peasant unrest to produce a violent overthrow of the dynastic state. The French Revolution with its expulsion of the aristocracy and the establishment of some sort of 'peoples' government' (albeit on a very restricted franchise) demonstrated the fragility of the political framework of the dynastic states and the possibility of a sudden extension of political participation. Political power was transferred from the king and aristocracy to the middle classes, although the working classes and the peasantry were excluded from the political community until after 1848.

In England, where as a result of the civil war power had already passed from the king to the aristocracy in parliament, the conflict was eventually resolved through the opening of parliament to members of the middle classes. The extension of political participation, in the form of the franchise, to the middle classes in the reforms of 1832 thus marked the conclusion of a long struggle with the aristocracy. The aristocrats' hereditary right to rule was no longer unquestioned; there were now pressures to allow those who had been economically successful a full share in government. Aristocratic monopoly of political power was broken, and for the rest of the nineteenth century the middle classes gradually increased their representation in parliament (and even in the cabinet) at the expense of aristocratic families. After 1832 the main battleground for the struggle between the landed aristocracy and the manufacturers was parliament itself, and the continued intensity of the conflict can be seen from controversies such as that surrounding the corn laws. Here the conflict of interest between the two groups is clear—the landowners trying to protect their prices through the maintenance of taxes on imported corn, and the industrialists attempting to keep the cost of food (and therefore labour) down by abolishing such protection. That the abolitionists were ultimately successful shows how far the balance of power had already changed by the middle of the nineteenth century.

In addition to increasing the wealth and power of the middle classes, the growth of manufacturing industry created new conditions of work for the mass of the population. The agricultural wage labourers who migrated to the industrial towns found themselves in a very different situation. They were concentrated in large numbers near the factories in which they worked and their increased awareness of their common situation, coupled with the greater ease of communicating with each other, made them more capable of sustained political action. Moreover, the growth of collective action enabled them to halt industrial production and this gave them a powerful weapon in their fight with the enfranchised classes. In short the conditions of an urban, industrial society transformed them into a new class of industrial workers.

By the middle of the nineteenth century the working classes in England already had a history of political protest. Initially they had lent their support to the middle classes in the struggle with the aristocracy but the failure of the 1832 Reform Act to concede anything to the working classes contributed to the growth of the Chartist movement. The Chartists had some success in mobilizing support among the urban population and the movement was significant partly because it illustrated the power potential of the workers. Thereafter, and especially with the emergence of trade unions, working-class organization for political and industrial activities became more efficient and more effective. The formal reflection of this was the succession of Acts of Parliament which gradually extended the franchise to include working-class men. As the franchise was extended to include all adult men in the society (and later women too) so the basis of recruitment into parliament widened. The miners Keir Hardie and Ernest Bevin, the ironworker Arthur Henderson and the insurance clerk Philip Snowden joined the aristocrats, industrialists and businessmen at Westminster.

It was not until after the first world war, however, that the representatives of the working classes were able to achieve any position of real power *within* parliament. Even today professional politicians are, on the whole, drawn disproportionately from some social groups rather than others although there have, of course, been considerable changes in the last hundred years. Government may now claim to be very largely *for* the people; to what extent is it directly *by* the people? Such a question clearly would not have occurred in the dynastic states, ruled as they were by a small élite. But even much later, when wider groups were involved in politics and *influenced* political decisions, those who *took* the decisions were still highly unrepresentative even of the electorate. In mid-nineteenth-century Britain, for example, the landowning classes still provided the majority of members of the cabinet. In the period from 1830 to 1868 there were 103 cabinet members. Fifty-six of them were large territorial Lords or the sons of such Lords; twelve were country gentlemen; twenty-one were from the mercantile and administrative upper class; and fourteen were *hommes nouveaux* of 'no family' (most of them were lawyers).[3] By the middle of the twentieth century the proportion of aristocrats had declined but the cabinet was still somewhat socially exclusive. Thus nearly one half of the cabinet members between 1935 and 1955 were either aristocrats and landowners or had attended one of the seven 'top' public schools. The broadening of the social background of members of the cabinet since that time has been reflected in the declining representation of aristocrats (never, of course, conspicuous in Labour ranks). A large proportion of cabinet members, however, have been ex-public schoolboys (about 40 per cent of Labour members and 90 per cent of Conservative members). Thus, the extension of political participation has resulted in some broadening of the social groups from which political leaders are recruited, although cabinets are by no means representative (in terms of social background) of the population as a whole.

The political scene today then is very different from that in the dynastic states of Europe. In contemporary industrial societies politics is no longer the exclusive province of the king and the aristocracy; rulers of industrial societies do not regard the state as their own property. *All* groups and *all* strata in the society are involved with the affairs of state. Major political decisions—say the provision of more schools or the regulation of the economy—are therefore made not only in terms of the interests of the rulers but also have to take account of the interests of other sections of the population. And even in less important matters governments have to take account of the views of any well-organized groups that will be affected.

In the contemporary situation of international competition and rivalry, the power of each state depends upon economic productivity as well as upon the size and capacity of its armed forces. It is because of this that threats, from any section of the population, to disrupt the economy have such political importance. The ruling group has become dependent upon the performance of the whole population. Thus, the government of General de Gaulle was seriously threatened by the general strike of 1967 and was only able to save itself (and then only temporarily) by meeting some of the demands of the workers. In highly complex societies the refusal (or inability) of any specialized group, be they dockers, doctors, diplomats or dustmen, to continue with their activities can disrupt the working of the whole society.

One of the results of this twin process—the extension of political participation and the growing interdependence of sections of industrial societies—is that governments have had to become more and more concerned with the provision of social welfare. The nineteenth-century involvement of the government with elementary education in England and Wales derived partly from both of these sources. The Reform Acts of 1832 and 1867 were crucial to this involvement as were the increasing requirements of industry for workers with some rudimentary education. The growth of government health services had similar stimuli. Perhaps the nineteenth-century public health measures were primarily based upon what, to the upper classes, must have been a distressing lack of class discrimination on behalf of epidemic diseases as they ravaged the densely populated towns. Public health was consequently in their interests as much as anyone's. The twentieth-century spread of medical care, however, derived chiefly from other changes in the nature of the society. In industry and in warfare, in particular, it became impossible to maximize efficiency because of the poor health of the population. Yet the nature of both modern industry and twentieth-century warfare was such that maximum efficiency from *everybody* was required for success. Thus increased dependence upon the ordinary worker and soldier was important.

So all sections of modern society have become indispensable to the government. Directly, governments are often (but not always) dependent upon votes to remain in office. Economically and militarily they are dependent upon the services of the population. This dependence has been instrumental in the extension of the role of government (which, in turn, makes each individual more dependent upon the state).

Political parties

The gradual widening of the scope of politics has occurred in all industrial societies, but it has taken place within different forms of political organization. In Western Europe the context has been that of multi-party states; in the Soviet Union a similar process has occurred within the framework of a one-party state. In the case of the Soviet Union many of the processes we have already discussed for England have been evident in the years since the second world war. The Soviet government has increasingly had to take into account the interest of the mass of the population, and this has resulted in the provision of better housing, health facilities and pensions, greater security of employment, and, more recently, the decision to devote more of the country's resources to the production of consumer goods. This reorientation from the harsher days of more 'absolute' rule is reflected in the following extract from an anti-China speech made by Nikita Kruschev in 1964:[4]

> There are people in the world who call themselves Marxist-Leninists and at the same time say there is no need to strive for a better life. According to them only one thing is important—revolution. *Communism will achieve little if it cannot give the people what they want*. The important thing is that we should have more to eat, schools, housing, and ballet.

This view, however, is a recent one and the outcome of relative affluence. The earlier development of the Communist party of the Soviet Union (as it later came to be known) similarly reflects the condition of the society as a whole. Originally, the party was only one of forty competing factions that comprised the revolutionary movement in late nineteenth-century Russia. Political power in Russia at this time (as in other dynastic states) was concentrated in the office of the emperor; the mass of the population, including the small but growing industrial middle and working classes, was excluded from positions of power. The collapse of the Russian Empire, and especially the destruction of the army in 1917, provided these revolutionary groups with the chance to seize power. They had enough mass support and were sufficiently well organized to carry out and consolidate the revolution.

Once they had established a monopoly of the use of physical force, the leaders of the Communist party were faced with the task of stabilizing the new state. Territorial integrity had to be preserved against other states, and the various sections of the old Russian state had to be made to live together in peace. The ideology of Marxism fitted well with these requirements, for the further and rapid development of industry would help to provide a technologically more efficient army, and the party provided a means whereby the population could be controlled. The monolithic nature of the party, however, emerged only slowly. The decision that industrialization should be totally controlled by the state was a gradual one and centralization was not fully effected until the late 1920s. In the event, the Communist party became *the* vehicle of transformation, and gradually all spheres of social and economic life were brought under the direct control of the party. This included not only government, industry and commerce, but also agriculture, the trade unions, education, literature and the arts.

Thus, monopoly of political power and a refusal to tolerate any independent organization which might develop as a centre of opposition characterizes the single-party state. Through their control of the mass media the party leaders are able to determine which issues shall come up for public discussion, and this affects the expression of public opinion through the party. The party is also the mechanism through which political leaders are selected and demands are made to the political leaders. Finally, the party organization provides a country-wide framework of supervision, ensuring that the party's policy is correctly interpreted and followed.

The demands for ideological commitment and strict obedience to the leadership result in a party organization which is exclusive and selective in its membership policy. Even in the early 1960s only 7 per cent of the total population was in party membership. So, with their monopoly of political power, the party leaders determine the extent and nature of political participation. In practice, at various times in the history of the Soviet Union some groups—intellectuals for example—have been denied party membership. But the extension of political participation has now resulted in a situation where representatives of all groups are to be found in membership. As in all industrial societies there has been a tendency for persons from professional and other non-manual occupations to be more actively involved in politics than manual workers. In the Soviet Union, however, this has been counteracted to some extent by periodic party recruitment drives among the industrial and agricultural manual workers. The limited effectiveness of these campaigns can be seen in Table 3.1 which shows such groups still to be under-represented in the party.

Elections, although they do not provide the population as a whole with any control over the political leaders, are designed to give all adults a sense of involvement in the political process. They also enable the party to legitimate its position and proclaim its achievements. There are also opportunities for participation in the administration of the state, especially at the local level. The twenty million people who are said to participate in the work of the national, regional and local Soviets include many who are not members of the Communist party. Such activity heightens identification with the state, thereby consolidating the legitimacy of the government.

Table 3.1 Occupational distribution of employed population of the USSR and of members of the Communist party of the Soviet Union (1961) (per cent)

Occupational group	*Distribution of employed population*	*Distribution of C.P.S.U. members*
Workers	47·3	34·5
Peasants	32·0	17·5
Mental workers and intelligentsia	20·7	48·0
Total	100·0 (107,600,000)	100·0 (10,000,000)

Source: Adapted from Z. Brzezinski and S. P. Huntington, *Political Power: USA/USSR*, New York: Viking, 1965, p. 100.

The lack of opposition parties does not necessarily mean the suppression of all opposition to the government or that political conflict is not present. Where there is a single party, then the struggle for power occurs within the party. This means that the struggle for power is restricted to a relatively small circle of interest groups. State industries, police, army, and the various levels of party officials struggle for control of the party, and changes in party policy are the outcome of the changing balance of power between these groups. So the decision of Kruschev to decentralize authority to a local level and to reduce the supervisory functions of the party represented a triumph of these local interests. It led to an alliance between the regional party secretaries, members of the central party organization and members of the state administration, all of whom saw their position threatened by the reforms. In the event, this alliance proved to be powerful enough not only to reverse the reforms but to secure the dismissal of Kruschev himself.

Multi-party states have developed almost exclusively in societies where industrialization has been led by independent entrepreneurs. The growth of the modern party system in England, for example, dates from the extension of political participation, which we have already traced to the broad process of industrialization. Before this, the politicians (that is to say, the aristocracy) were split into two factions, the Whigs and the Tories. As new groups and classes entered the political arena the nature of these factions changed. In order to survive they had to appeal for support to a larger (and still growing) proportion of the population. In order to secure support in elections they were obliged to develop national organizations and more explicit political programmes. In other words, the old aristocratic factions evolved into modern political parties. The Liberal party under Gladstone was the first to develop this new type of organization and was rapidly followed by Disraeli's Conservative party. Equally important, these new political parties represented the interests of the major classes rather than, as formerly, differences of interest within the aristocracy. Initially the Conservative party was largely the representative of the landed classes, but with the decline of the landed interest it has come to represent primarily the industrial and commercial middle and upper classes. In this sense it has taken over the mantle of the nineteenth-century Liberal party. The other major party in contemporary Britain—the Labour party—was founded on the growth of the working classes as a conscious group and so has been from the start, a class-based party. (Throughout Europe socialist parties have emerged in this way from groups whose interests were inadequately served by existing parties.) The major interests represented by the two major political parties in contemporary Britain can be seen quite clearly from the way the parties are financed. Thus industry and commerce is the major source of funds for the Conservative party while the Labour party is largely financed by the trade unions. The class basis of British party politics is also reflected in the way various sections of the population vote. The large Labour majorities exist in the working-class industrial areas such as the Rhondda Valley and the Exchange division of Liverpool, while the Conservatives get their biggest majorities in middle-class suburbs like Solihull in Birmingham and in the country districts of southern England. However, party allegiance is not determined directly by class membership. If this were the case the greater numbers of the working classes would ensure the perpetual return to office of a Labour government. In fact, at most elections between one quarter and one half of the working classes vote Conservative. Ever since Disraeli first won substantial working-class support for the Conservative party, electoral success has depended upon at least some working-class support.

In the United States of America, there is also a tendency for modern party support to follow class lines but the situation is much less clear cut than in Britain. It is broadly true that the Republican party derives its greatest support from the more wealthy middle and upper classes, and the Democratic party relies mainly on electoral support from lower classes. In 1948, for example, nearly 80 per cent of the manual workers voted Democrat. In America, however, religious, ethnic and regional factors are also of considerable importance. America's modern political parties emerged from the Civil War: the Republican party as a refurbishment of the 'Grand Old Party' of the north; the Democratic party as the party of the south. The Republican party therefore represented the northern establishment, and any Democratic success in New England in the nineteenth and first part of the twentieth century was dependent upon an appeal to the newly arrived and relatively underprivileged immigrants. Thus began the association of the Democratic party with the Irish in particular and, through them, with Roman Catholicism. In the southern states, however, the situation developed very differently. After the Civil War the southern establishment remained antagonistic to the victorious north and thus to the Republican party. So, while the Democratic party developed in the north as the party of the underdog, the faction of the 'Southern Democrats' represented the wealthy (and often right-wing) southerners. Historically, then, those black Americans who were involved in politics at all tended to give their support to the Republican party with its image as 'the party of Lincoln'. Since the Democratic president Roosevelt introduced the 'New Deal' with its appeal to underprivileged Americans, however, black Americans have been wooed away from their traditional Republican allegiance. For the Democratic party, as well as being the more attractive proposition for the economically underprivileged, has been the party more favourable to the extension of civil rights to black Americans as, indeed, it had been earlier to non-property-holders and immigrants. (In Britain, too, there are examples of parties that are not simply class-based. The growth of Scottish and Welsh nationalist parties is a response to geographically uneven economic growth and perceived regional disparities. The party structure of Northern Ireland is as much based upon religion as class.)

Such is the political control of the establishment

in some American states that the party of the establishment is the only party in existence. In several southern states there are Democratic candidates returned to Congress unopposed and in some northern states the same is true for Republicans. In this way some states have some of the characteristics of a one-party state whilst in others, and at the Federal level, a two-party system operates—a combination uniquely American.

American political parties are much less centralized and less disciplined than British parties. In Britain the fact that the prime minister and cabinet can only remain in office so long as they command a majority in the House of Commons requires strict and effective party discipline if the the system is to work. By contrast, in America the president is elected separately from the legislature and is free to choose his own administration. He thus has far greater autonomy than the British prime minister and often, indeed, represents a different party from that which dominates the legislature. In this situation, party discipline can be much less rigid and a nationally organized party structure is only in evidence at the time of a presidential election.

In complex multi-party states, then, politics has become a struggle between mass-based parties. But in order to govern effectively, and sometimes even in order to get elected, governments and parties have to deal with a wide range of organizations representing the specific interests of various sections of the population. Some of these may be economically based—the Trade Union Congress or the Confederation of British Industries for example. Others have a very different basis—the Lord's Day Observance Society, the League of Empire Loyalists, a variety of Civil Rights movements, Oxfam and so on. The more powerful of these are often consulted before major government decisions are taken. Thus the TUC and the CBI are powerful enough to force any government to consult them. Yet they are allied chiefly to the Labour and Conservative parties respectively, and they are influential in the formulation of party programmes, particularly at election time. Others are only able to exert pressure when legislation is proposed which threatens the interests of their members. Many of them also number members of parliament among their members who can act in their interests behind the scenes.

The growth of nations

We have reserved the term nation-state for a limited number of contemporary states, for only in the twentieth century have states emerged in which all adult members have been able to take some part in politics. But the concept of nation suggests more than this. It implies that the majority of the population *identify* with the nation; they consider themselves a part of the nation; they are willing to subordinate their own interests to interests of the nation. Loyalty to the nation overrides loyalty to family, class, religion and region.

It is this identification with and loyalty to the idea of nationhood, as distinct from, say, the person of a monarch or president that is new. In the nineteenth century, Prussian or Polish nobles no more identified with the peasants they controlled than with the horses they owned. German and French aristocrats identified themselves more with each other than with the peasants in their own country. The enormous power differentials between aristocracy and peasantry, and the concomitant social barriers, militated against the development of any emotional ties which might lead the two groups to identify with each other. Such patriotism as existed was expressed in personal loyalty to the king and in concern for the furtherance of *his* interests. But while a subject might support his king in a dispute with a rival monarch, this in no way affected any relationships he might have with subjects of the rival king. Thus, while monarchs and their armies waged war their subjects would continue to trade with each other. *They* were not at war.

The mutual identification of all groups in the society initially emerged out of the struggle of the middle classes to gain access to positions of political power. Intellectuals began to distinguish between the monarch, the ruling class and the nation; and the embodiment of the nation, they argued, was not to be found in the person of the king but in 'the people' (by which they meant the property-owning middle class, i.e. themselves). So the concept of nation came to refer to 'the people'; the qualities of the nation to the qualities of 'the people'. It was not until the late nineteenth and early twentieth centuries, however, that the definition of the groups forming the nation was extended to include the working classes. In other words, it was only as the power of the working classes increased and the social barriers segregating them from their 'superiors' began to break down that identification of members of the working class with others as Englishmen, Frenchmen, Germans and so on took precedence over other loyalties. Patriotic loyalty was gradually transferred from the person of the king to the nation—the collective that was formed by all members of the society. The gradual nature of the change, however, can be seen from the mood of England during the first world war when men still fought and died 'for *king* and country'.

As the twentieth century has worn on, it has increasingly been the nationalist sentiment that has evoked a response from all members of the society. In each of the major European states men have regarded their own nation as the greatest and best. Englishmen have sought to spread Anglo-Saxon institutions throughout the world; Frenchmen have believed in the civilizing mission of France; Germans have extolled the supremacy of their *Kultur*. Symbols of nationhood such as national flags and national anthems have become vested with emotional qualities and represent national values and qualities. Nor has this process been confined to Western Europe. In Soviet Russia a similar (although more violent) process of change has destroyed the social barriers which existed between social groups under Tsarist rule, and has provided the basis for a common identification of all members of the society. In the USA the process was considerably helped by the retreat from isolationism, since the idea of a nation always implies the existence and competition of other nations. In these two 'super-nations' of the mid-twentieth century the space race is the most recent symbol of national identity, pride and competition.

Nationalism, then, unites the members of one society in opposition to members of other societies and thus tends to intensify conflict between societies. It also feeds upon international conflict and is at its most intense in times of war or international crisis. Inter*national* relations are different from those between other states. Warfare, to cite the most dramatic example, involves and disrupts all sectors of the society. This is partly because of technological changes which have increased the scale of war, but war also involves the subordination of individual needs to the needs of the nation. Nationalistic sentiment becomes one of the most important means by which the whole population is mobilized for the war effort.

Politics and modernization

It is precisely this nationalistic sentiment that is appealed to by many of the leaders of the 'new' states of Africa and Asia. Thus we can find several examples of speeches from these leaders which parallel anything said by a Churchill or a Hitler. In many of these societies, however, the level of development reached so far is lower than that of the industrial states and identification with the state is relatively low. There are interesting comparisons to be made with the earlier development of the industrial nations, but the different context within which they are developing—and in particular the political subjugation of most of them under colonialism during an important period of their development—has led to important differences as well.

In Africa the differences are particularly sharp. Because of the relative simplicity of most African societies in the late nineteenth century the very boundaries between contemporary African states are more the outcome of competition between European nations than between African states themselves. In some areas the monopolization of the use of force and the establishment of a centralized system of administration first occurred under colonialism. The situation was very varied, however. A country like Nigeria was formed out of a large number of very different societies ranging from those with no differentiated political system at all (such as the Tiv) to the highly centralized and hierarchical Hausa-Fulani Emirates in the north. So the imposition of colonialism throughout tropical Africa resulted in unification of many areas as well as the more widely publicized 'partition' of Africa. One consequence of this has been that the process of political development in Ghana, Guinea, Tanzania, Nigeria and the rest of the societies of tropical Africa has been far more rapid than the process of state formation in Europe. Yet these states do not always command the identification of their subjects. More accurately, they are as yet states rather than nations, and the major political task in the decades after independence is the creation of this sense of nationhood.

In most of Latin America, however, the colonial era ended a century and a half ago, yet identification with the political order is, in most cases, still weak. A more complex level of social development has been reached than in tropical Africa, including, in Argentina and Brazil particularly, some industrialization. Yet the political struggle is still for the most part between industrialists and landowners, with the mass of the population being used as pawns to support the position of one or other. This gives them some influence but little power. In modernizing societies until recently then, the monopoly of the use of force which characterizes the state was held either by a small indigenous minority group or by an alien power. As always, administration was based upon the beliefs and values of the rulers and not those of the mass of the population.

The most clear-cut and dramatic of these situations has been that of formal colonialism. Although colonialism was imposed upon a wide variety of societies it always had important implications for the distribution of power. Sometimes the colonial administrators attempted to govern direct from the European capital. The most powerful colonizer—Britain—however, encouraged a good deal of local autonomy (partly because it was cheaper) and attempted to incorporate traditional rulers into the colonial administration. Even in this case the distribution of power and the nature and basis of authority was radically changed. Where the traditional society was relatively complex (as in most of southern Asia and parts of Africa such as northern Nigeria and Buganda) and had firmly established political institutions and rulers, colonialism undermined the traditional rule. The new administration invariably restricted the traditional rulers' use of the physical force upon which their power had rested and it became increasingly clear that the 'power behind the throne' was the colonial administration (and if necessary the colonial army). By transforming traditional rulers into mere administrators for an alien conqueror their authority, which had rested upon a traditional—often hereditary—right to *rule*, was undermined. In those (predominantly African) societies where there were no separate political institutions as such and where there were no 'rulers', this type of indirect rule created even more disruption. For the colonists' incomprehension of such societies led them to mistake elders and family heads for political leaders and to invest them with a power they had never previously possessed. The legitimacy of this power was rarely conceded by the rest of the society—a factor which resulted in considerable unrest whenever unpopular decisions had to be put into effect. (For example, the lack of ability of the Kikuyu 'chiefs' to control their 'subjects' to the satisfaction of the British during the Mau Mau rebellions in Kenya during the 1950s stemmed largely from this situation.) And on top of this, real power—the effective use of force—always lay with the colonial administration.

So whatever the form of the traditional political system, the impact of colonialism makes radical changes in the distribution of power and in the nature of authority. These changes were enhanced by the non-political accompaniments of colonialism. Christianity; the growth of wage labour and a money economy; urbanization; the gradual extension of Western education: together these changed the conditions under which men lived. Furthermore, they exposed people to new values and beliefs which, in turn, led to a questioning of the old ways of life. These forces of change impinged especially on those who went to the Western style schools and colleges. Frequently, in spite of their educational qualifications, this group was excluded from the most important and best paid positions in the administration. These posts were reserved for colonial officials. The social distance between colonizer and colonized was heightened by its association with race. It was seen to be because of his colour that the African or the Indian was allocated an inferior position; for in settler colonies there was no such discrimination against the white population. It was this educated group, taught to believe in the importance of ability and the irrelevance of race and nationality, and yet in their own country denied the positions for which they were qualified, who first built up modern forms of party organization to aid them in their struggle against both the colonial and traditional rulers.

These educated leaders of the twentieth-century independence movements of Asia and Africa achieved their success by mobilizing the urban population and the more modern of the farmers. Thus, the overthrow of colonialism involved the participation of a substantial proportion, and sometimes a majority, of the total population. It is in this period of the struggle for independence that the modernizing societies of Asia and Africa come closest to nationhood. For the colonial power provides a focus against which all the varied ethnic groups, regional sections and strata can unite in the common objective of independence. Yet the mood is more one of antipathy towards the colonial power than of positive identification with and emotional attachment to the new nation. The highly developed occupational specialization and interdependence, upon which the collective identification of industrial societies is largely dependent simply does not exist.

Only in one sense, then, was independence a triumph of nationalism. The leaders of independence movements owed much of their position to their ability to unite the country to this end. As well as the ideology of nationalism, however, these leaders (especially but not only in Africa) derived much of their support from a *personal* magnetism and a faith in their *personal* ability. Men like Nkrumah of Ghana, Gandhi of India, Banda of Malawi, Sekou Touré of Guinea and Kenyatta of Kenya were followed because they could deliver the goods—the goods in question being independence and the establishment of a more equitable social order. The achievement of independence and the durability of inequality has created enormous problems for the continued unity of many modernizing societies. With the removal of the crisis situation of colonialism, the nationalistic identification with the country as a whole sometimes disintegrates in the face of sectionalism of various kinds. Small farmers, who form the majority of the population, tend to spend the whole of their lives in one locality and, under normal circumstances, are likely to identify with this locality or tribe rather than with the state. Indeed, it was those groups who were most involved in a country-wide (or even world-wide) economy—the traders, businessmen, wage earners and cash croppers—who were most easily recruited to the cause of independence.

This sort of sectionalism may provide the basis for the development of a multi-party system somewhat after the lines of those of Western Europe. The basis for the parties, however, may well be different. Whereas in Europe mass-based political parties had a class basis in Asia or Africa political parties are more likely to have their basis in ethnic or regional differences. Thus, in Nigeria before the military coup of 1966 and the civil war which followed it, the three major political parties represented the three regions dominated respectively by Hausa, Yoruba and Ibo majorities. In other circumstances the political parties represent factions within the ruling élite (not altogether dissimilar to the Whigs and Tories of nineteenth-century England) and are not mass-based at all. This was the situation in Vietnam shortly after independence and a similar position has arisen in Bolivia.

Where a substantial degree of industrialization has occurred, however, and with it some class formation, parties may exist on a basis similar to that in the industrial world. The Communist party of India has, in the last decade, made some headway in the towns as a party of the urban working classes and the unemployed. In Argentina by the time of the military coup of 1943, there were more workers employed in industry than in agriculture and cattle raising. It was, therefore possible for Colonel Juan Perón, who as head of the Secretariat of Labour encouraged the development of trade unions, to rise to power very largely on working-class votes and with the support of the trade unions. In most modernizing societies, however, class formation is in an embryonic state and therefore does not provide a basis for political parties.

The nature of political parties in modernizing societies often reflects a long struggle between the local population and a colonial administration. This sometimes results in fairly permanent unification of the various influential sections of the society. To some extent the success of an independence movement depends upon its ability to unify all the political elements in the colony. At independence, therefore, there is sometimes only one party with anything like a national organization and the capability of ruling. So one-party systems characterize many modernizing societies. While in Western Europe the development of multi-party states reflected the struggle of successive groups to achieve political participation, most of the 'new countries' are created with universal suffrage from the start. The factor which stimulated the growth of several parties in nineteenth-century Europe is consequently absent. Universal suffrage, however, does not give political *power* to groups unless they are politically organized, and, with the majority of the population dispersed through the country as small-scale farmers, this political organization is not present. To this extent the rulers are not (in spite of universal enfranchisement) dependent upon the active co-operation of the mass of the population. In such a social situation a mass-based political party may function less as a means whereby sectional interests can influence a government, and more as a means of controlling the population and mobilizing their support *for* the government. Elections thus become a time at which the legitimacy of the government is re-asserted.

The problem of enforcement of law and order is particularly complex. The rapid urbanization; the lessened ability of rural traditional authorities to control social behaviour; and the changing codes of conduct all combine to make the task a difficult one. Some of the newest states are still engaged in the process of establishing a monopoly of the legitimate use of violence. So the very right to administer the territory of the state is sometimes in dispute; the legitimacy of the state is in question. This complicates what may already be a relatively unstable situation.

These three factors, then—divisive sectional interests, the concentration of power in a small élite controlling a single party, and the special problems of law enforcement in modernizing societies—all affect the legitimacy of the government. Separately or together they may be enough to upset political stability. If a charismatic party leader *fails* to deliver the promised goods; if an ethnic group feels (rightly or wrongly) that it is being discriminated against; if a region thinks it is being neglected in the allocation of development funds; and if the civilian forces of law and order cannot control the subsequent protest: then the government may be overthrown. For, whereas in the 'old' nations the right of the state to ensure law and order and administer its territory is well established and is no longer seriously questioned, in many modernizing societies the problem is still to establish the legitimacy of the state and the enforcement of its authority.

It is in this political context that military intervention has become such a common feature of political life. First in Latin America, then in Asia and Africa, military coups (sometimes with police support) have become a normal occurrence, either to maintain in power a leader whose legitimacy has been questioned, or to restore law and order, or sometimes to support their own sectional interest. The entry of the military into politics is facilitated by the lack of active participation by the mass of the population. If there are few sources of opposition to the government there are also few sources of opposition to the military. Indeed, where opposition parties are banned, the military may be the only possible source of opposition to the government.

The influence of industrial societies upon modernizing societies (often in the form of colonialism) has also influenced the growth of the civil service. We have seen that European civil services were founded on the highly differentiated occupational structures of European societies. There is, as yet, little such differentiation in modernizing societies. The civil services are modelled on those of Western societies, but, because of the differences in social context, they often operate in a very different way. Indeed, although the organization of government service is similar to that in contemporary industrial societies, its operation is often more akin to that of the European dynastic states. Where kinship ties are strong there are pressures to utilize one's office to the advantage of kinsmen; thus, in Aba—an eastern Nigerian town—local politicians habitually used their power on the local council to ensure that those of their relatives who were traders got the best pitches in the market. The distinction between public and private income is often obscure; so one member of Nkrumah's government in Ghana was, in a popular and semi-serious joke, reputed to be the wealthiest man in the country because he had held the most ministerial posts! And where junior service salaries are very low, officials may, as a means of supplementing their salaries, demand payment before providing a service. The point is not that such non-bureaucratic behaviour—'corruption' as it is usually called—is absent in industrial societies, for, of course, it is not. But in industrial societies it is universally disapproved and consequently much less common. In modernizing societies the rules are, as yet, far less clear cut and there are conflicting pressures on the civil servant. The 'Western' type of public morality which we discussed earlier has been transferred to the modernizing societies but has not yet been universally accepted. Until such bureaucratic rules are generally viewed as 'right' they will continue to be broken.

Notes

1 E. M. Thomas, *The Harmless People*, Harmondsworth: Penguin, 1969, p. 22.

2 M. Fortes, 'The Political system of the Tallensi', in M. Fortes and E. E. Evans-Pritchard, *African Political Systems*, London: Oxford University Press, 1940, pp. 263–4.

3 The information on the social background of members of the cabinet is taken from W. L. Guttsman, *The British Political Elite*, London: MacGibbon & Kee, 1963.

4 A. F. K. Organski, *The Stages of Political Development*, New York: Alfred Knopf, 1965, p. 178, our italics.

Reading

Black, C. E., *The Dynamics of Modernization*, New York: Harper & Row, 1967. A survey of political and social development which compares processes in a wide variety of societies—European, Asian and African.

Blondel, J., *Voters, Parties and Leaders*, Harmondsworth: Penguin, 1963. A summary of research on various aspects of contemporary British politics.

Carr, E. H., *Nationalism and After*, London: Macmillan, 1945. Part 1 of this two-part essay consists of an analysis of nationalism in Europe.

Coleman, J. S., 'Nationalism in tropical Africa', *American Political Science Review*, 48, 1954. One of the earliest systematic discussions of the growth of African 'nationalism'.

Hobsbawm, E. J., *The Age of Revolution*, London: Weidenfeld & Nicolson, 1962. Chapters 3, 6, and 7 contain an analysis of the French Revolution and, in general, of the social changes associated with the development of the modern nation States of Western Europe.

Krader, L., *The Development of the State*, Englewood Cliffs, N.J.: Prentice-Hall, 1968. A critical discussion of theories of state formation drawing upon examples from Africa, China, North America and Russia.

Mair, L., *Primitive Government*, Harmondsworth: Penguin, 1962. A survey of political processes in stateless societies and in simple kingdoms with examples from traditional societies of East Africa.

Further Reading

Apter, D., *Ghana in Transition*, New York: Atheneum, 1963. A case study of the overthrow of colonialism and the first years of an independent African state.

Bendix, R., *Nation-Building and Citizenship*, New York: Doubleday, 1969. A comparative analysis of nation-building in the Western and non-Western world, focusing on the transformation of authority relationships.

Butler, D. and Stokes, D., *Political Change in Britain*, Harmondsworth: Penguin, 1971. A detailed analysis of the various forces shaping electoral choice in Britain.

Finer, S. E., *The Man on Horseback*, London: Pall Mall, 1962. An attempt to explain why the military intervenes in politics.

Fortes, M. and Evans-Pritchard, E. E. (eds), *African Political Systems*, London: Oxford University Press, 1940. Anthropological monographs on the political systems of eight African traditional societies, together with an important introduction distinguishing between 'state societies' and 'stateless societies'.

Guttsman, W. L., *The British Political Elite*, London: MacGibbon & Kee, 1963. Discusses changes in the social composition of the British political elite, in the form of political organization, and in the distribution of power since 1832.

Moore, Barrington, Jnr, *The Social Origins of Dictatorship and Democracy*, Harmondsworth: Penguin, 1970. An attempt to explain the parts played by the landed upper classes and the peasantry in the development of one-party and multi-party states.

Smith, A. D., *Theories of Nationalism*, London: Duckworth, 1971. An analysis of different theories of nationalism and of the variety of forms that nationalism takes.

4 Urbanization

The city as we know it in the Western world today is essentially a product of industrialization. Without industry, the cities of the twentieth century would be very different in character and they would not exist on the scale they do. In this chapter we shall show how, in pre-industrial as well as industrial times, there has always been a close and complex relationship between technological development and the growth and growing importance of cities. Sociologists commonly measure the degree of urbanization in a country by the proportion of its population living in cities. (A city is usually defined as a place with more than so many inhabitants, the number depending upon what figures are available from the various census returns of different countries, commonly 100,000 20,000 or 2,500. This variability is a nuisance, but not as bad as it seems because countries with a high proportion living in places of 2,500 or more inhabitants also tend to have a high proportion living in places of 20,000 or more inhabitants, and so on. Thus although one cannot compare between the different measures of urbanization any one of the measures will do equally well for making comparisons over time.) The rate of urbanization is the rate at which this proportion increases over time. So an increase in population can produce an increase in the size of cities without altering their size relative to the whole population and therefore without urbanization. To clarify the relationship between technological level and urbanization it is convenient to divide urbanization as it has occurred in the world as a whole into three stages.

The first stage of urbanization—and historically by far the longest—was that from the first emergence of cities until the eighteenth century, when they were to be found in almost all parts of the world. In this stage the cities never reached a very great size (few had more than 100,000 people), and never housed a large proportion of the population; but where they existed they were of considerable importance and influence in the surrounding area. The actual rate of urbanization during the first stage, then, was slight, but by the end of the period the growth of cities was significant.

The second stage of urbanization was brief but of great importance; it was the stage of the very rapid growth of cities that accompanied early industrialization. There was, of course, an enormous increase in population during this period, so that cities would have grown in size even without urbanization. But to this growth must be added the fact that as industrialization progressed an ever-increasing proportion of the people were living in towns.

In more mature industrial societies, the rate of urbanization began to slow down and the second stage was overtaken by the third stage: that of metropolitanization. Metropolitanization is the process of urban centralization that accompanies the centralization of industry and the economy. The larger cities take on an increasing importance, both in terms of their population and in terms of the functions they serve in the society as a whole. The small town does not grow so fast and tends to become drawn into the orbit of a larger one and become a satellite to it. In this stage the towns and cities continue to gain a large number of people every year but this represents only a small *proportionate* growth because the urban population is so large already. Thus the rate of urbanization is low but the absolute increase in the number of those people living in towns is very considerable.

All the countries that are currently highly industrialized can be said to have passed through these three stages of urbanization. But in the countries that are currently modernizing, urbanization is following a somewhat different path and in many of them rapid urbanization is occurring without substantial industrialization. We shall discuss in detail each of the stages of urbanization as it has occurred in the Western world and then focus on urbanization in modernizing countries as an example of an alternative line of development which it is now possible for urbanization to take. But first we must consider what distinguishes the urban from the non-urban.

The urban way of life

What are the important differences between life in a city and life in the country? In what ways are the social relationships of townsmen different from those of countrymen? These are questions that have puzzled and fascinated men through the ages and in recent decades sociologists, too, have tried to answer them. They have suggested that there are three important characteristics of the city which help us to understand the distinctive nature of urban social life. The city is a relatively large, densely populated place, housing a variety of people: or, put more briefly, it is distinguished by its size, density and heterogeneity.

Size and density create problems of supply, co-ordination and control, the solution of which involves fairly elaborate forms of social organization. The people must be housed, fed and kept healthy; it must be possible for them to come and go safely and in an orderly manner. There must, therefore, be an effective system of production, an efficient system of distribution, and some form of government. This is just as true of the pre-industrial as of the industrial city, though the problems and their solutions will take somewhat different forms. We shall see later how the industrial city developed new techniques and new forms of organization in response to these specific problems. But size and density in themselves open up new and wider possibilities than can exist in rural areas; they open up the possibility of heterogeneity, of wide variations among people in status, occupation, style of life, opinions and attitudes. In the countryside one family or village is rather like the next. In towns there are extremes of wealth and poverty; there are people who spend their days making gloves, others who spend their days keeping financial accounts, and others who live by stealing; some listen to Bach, some to Bartok, some to Billy Holiday and some to The Hollies; some believe in syndicalism and others in spiritualism. At the basis of this variety lies the division of labour that is possible in the city. The very existence of the city represents a division of labour; between the agriculture of rural areas and the manufacturing, commercial, religious, educational and governmental activities of the city. But within the city, too, there is an elaborate division of labour. For when a large number of people are gathered together, it becomes possible for some to specialize in one activity and to exchange their produce or services with others who specialize in complementary activities. In a similar way it sometimes happens that in a class of schoolboys one will specialize in doing the maths homework, another in the French and so on. The happy result is that the homework gets done quicker because each is doing his best subject, and the form's homework marks are better for the same reason. Unfortunately, the system is not thought to be very good educationally because it is felt that schoolboys should be well-rounded and not specialized. And so it is with the division of labour in society: the work gets done quicker and better but some would argue that modern man is over-specialized and incomplete as a result.

The division of labour also transforms people's relationships with one another. In the bustling urban life, they have fleeting contacts with hundreds of other people each day. They meet not as relatives or neighbours, but as people exchanging some goods or services. Look at the day of a shopkeeper, for instance: the bus conductress sells him a ticket, the shop assistant works for him in exchange for wages, the commercial traveller brings him news of new goods and tries to sell them to him, the customer buys his goods if they are a bargain, the landlord rents him his premises or the bank lends him money to buy them, the shopkeeper next door competes with him, the policeman enforces legal closing hours to control this competition and also protects his shop from burglary. Each of these relationships, and there are a hundred more, is very superficial, very specialized. The bus conductress is not expected to inquire or to care about his home, his business or his political views, nor he hers. Each deals with only one minor facet of the other's personality, and their relationship is relatively impersonal and rational. They each talk to the other primarily for a purpose of their own: she uses passengers to earn her living, he uses buses to get to work.

Of course, there are also personal, intimate relationships in urban life, among neighbours, friends, family, workmates and so on. But urban life opens up the possibility, which does not exist in rural communities, of a myriad of impersonal, fragmentary relationships, so that ties of kinship become much less important. As this happens groups based on specific interests and activities play a greater part. Political parties and movements, trades unions and professional associations, Christmas clubs and Masonic Lodges, churches and sects and a whole host of other voluntary societies, interested in anything from judo to jam-making, flourish in the urban environment.

We have been describing the way of life of the industrial city, but in essence it is a way of life that can arise in any city. In the cities of medieval Europe, the old, personal, feudal ties were broken and new, impersonal, calculative, relationships developed. People met, as it were, in the market-place, in the world of economic relationships. Thus it was in the cities of Europe that the first stirrings of capitalism were felt. In many pre-industrial cities, however, relationships of this kind did not predominate. Outside Europe, on the whole, kinship and tribal ties among people remained more important and co-existed with the new less personal relationships. People would not trade exploitatively with their kin, so that although there might be a considerable division of labour it did not go to the lengths of the capitalist system.

Nowadays, those of us who have been brought up in a highly urbanized and industrialized society may feel that this sharp distinction between urban and rural life has been exaggerated. In our experience, rural people often have highly specialized occupations, impersonal relations with others, weak ties with their relatives and strong ties with an angling club or the Women's Institute, with Christian Science or with the British Medical Association. In fact many of the things that have been identified as features of towns and cities are more properly described as features of all parts of industrial societies. But even more important is the fact that in countries like Britain there no longer exist many truly rural areas. The countryside may not have a very dense population (though it is much more dense than in most other countries), but tremendous improvements in transportation and communications have effectively compensated for the more sparse population. People can now move about and get in touch with many others almost as readily in the country as in the towns. And the towns have spread their tentacles of influence, establishing an elaborate division of labour both among themselves and with the intervening countryside. In brief then, many of the social relationships which we describe as typically urban apply to British society as a whole because in a very real sense Britain is an urban society.

Pre-industrial cities

As far as we know, the first cities in the world evolved from villages in Lower Mesopotamia, in the valleys of the Tigris and the Euphrates, around 3500 BC. The city of Ur is probably the best known, though not the earliest of these. They differed from villages not only in size—Ur is variously estimated to have held 10,000 to 34,000 people—but also in the variety of activities they embraced. Whereas in villages at that period everyone was engaged in agriculture, in the cities most worked only part-time as farmers and others were full-time craftsmen, merchants, priests and officials. In physical terms, cities were distinguished by their public buildings, such as temples, palaces and market-places. These characteristics serve to explain why cities emerged so comparatively late in man's history; for cities depend upon being able to extract an agricultural surplus from the surrounding countryside to support a population not engaged in food production. The earliest cities therefore appeared in the most fertile areas: in the valleys of the Tigris and Euphrates, of the Nile, of the Indus, and of the Yellow River in China. In Middle America shortly before the time of Christ, the cities of Maya were supported not by fertile land but by the use of maize, a crop which was peculiarly successful in a poor environment. In all these areas the technology was relatively advanced. The people had moved beyond hunting and gathering to settled agriculture using the plough and animal power. They were making efficient use of their land and their methods were not greatly to be improved upon until the mechanization of agriculture and the use of artificial fertilizers which came with industrialization.

The support of the city depended not only upon the existence of an agricultural surplus, but also upon the availability of means of conveying it to the city. The size and influence of the city was therefore limited by the difficulties of communication and transportation. Many of the earliest cities arose on natural transportation routes, such as rivers; but the later growth and spread of cities owed much to advances in writing (like the development from hieroglyphs on papyrus to alphabetic printing on paper), and to developments in transport (like the improvements in wheeled vehicles and in sailing ships).

In all these places, too, social relations were such that the cities had power over the surrounding rural areas, and they could ensure that the agricultural surplus would flow regularly into the cities. In the simplest societies, all men work at the same tasks and are more or less equal. Cities can only arise when some men become more powerful and are able to exert control over the lives of others.

Historians have disputed, however, as to what was the basis of this control. Some have said that the earliest cities were religious centres: as the sacred authority of religious leaders grew, shrine-villages in Mesopotamia became temple-cities. Others have suggested that they were originally fortresses or garrisons where powerful lords secured themselves against attack and mustered forces to dominate surrounding lands. The acropolis, the castle, the Anglo-Saxon 'burgh' are found as the basis of many early cities and testify to such military origins. Yet other writers, particularly those who have studied the Mediterranean trading cities of Tyre, Sidon and Phoenicia or the European cities of Genoa, Venice, Bruges or the Hanseatic League, have argued that the market is a central feature of the early city and trading one of its prime functions.

Yet none of these three forms of specialization (and the power relations associated with them) can be said to be *the* origin of the city. There have been cities such as Timbuctoo, that were trading cities long before they were graced by mosques and that were never fortified; there have been fortress cities, such as those of ancient Sumer, that survived for centuries before a market-place was added to their other facilities. Most cities have combined the three functions, as religious, military-political and economic centres and taken on other functions, as centres of more peaceable political administration and of education, as well. But every city has needed religious power or political power or economic power, or some combination of these, to enable it to extract the agricultural surplus from the surrounding areas, far or near.

The importance of this factor of social power can be seen very clearly when we come to examine the spread and proliferation of cities after these early beginnings in the most favourable places. In general the fortunes of cities depend upon these power relations: they rise and fall as their power rises and falls. The rulers of ancient cities, for example, depended very heavily on military power; military because they lived in a world where international law was unknown and were surrounded by peoples whose culture was alien and whose level of development was much lower. They could at any time be threatened by these barbarians around them and many of their cities were in the end destroyed by invading hordes.

The city-states of Greece and later of medieval Europe were themselves quite small in area, but each controlled a scattered 'empire' which gave it a wider economic base. Usually this did not involve direct rule over a wide area, but rather control of trade. The Italian city-states of Genoa, Pisa, and Venice, for instance, had small territories and trading depots in the eastern Mediterranean which enabled them to dominate trade between Europe and the Near East. In more recent times, urbanization in Europe has been supported in part by international trade and colonialism which permitted the townsmen of Europe to live off the agricultural surplus of the primary producing countries of the rest of the world. The early empires, too, favoured the spread of cities as well as their growth in size. For the mother-city, or metropolis, controlled its empire through the establishment of colonial cities. Many of the cities of modern Europe were founded in this way, particularly during the period of the Roman Empire; many names of English cities can be traced to Latin roots.

Thus, in the first and longest stage of urbanization, cities spread through much of the world and grew in importance as a social form. They depended for their growth upon the power of some of their inhabitants and in turn they helped increase this power. For in cities there were people with the leisure and literacy to make new inventions; merchants were interested in expanding their trade, rulers and soldiers in extending their dominion, religious leaders in spreading their faith.

Although there are striking similarities among pre-industrial cities there are also notable differences. The German sociologist Max Weber distinguished between what he called the Occidental (Western) city and the Oriental city. It was only in medieval Europe that townsmen—'burghers'—emerged as a separate estate, able to govern themselves independent (to some extent at least) of outside interference and with their own courts and their own partially autonomous law. In Europe there was an association or 'community' of citizens to which a man who came to the city might become affiliated. His status as citizen would then supersede any previous status. Thus a serf who left his manor would, after a certain period of town residence—commonly a year—cease to be a serf. It was said: 'City air makes man free.'

But outside Europe there was no concept of 'burgher' that contradicted that of countryman. To quote Weber:[1]

> The Chinese urban dweller legally belonged to his family and native village in which the temple of his ancestors stood and to which he conscientiously maintained affiliation . . . The Indian urban dweller remained a member of the caste.

Similarly, in Timbuctoo today, the members of different tribes are separate and distinct in their cultural traditions. Often people from the same tribal background live together in the same quarter of the city and, because they have little occasion to meet strangers, their way of life is little different from what it would have been in the country.

In pre-industrial Europe, on the other hand, the townsman was freed from these bonds of tradition and tied in a new way to a new type of community based upon trade and commercial relationships. The European city was thus the seed-bed for new developments that eventually brought about its own destruction. For, in the end, this kind of city community gave rise to industrialization which, in its maturity, made the city too small to survive as the most important unit of social life and gave the larger nation-state primacy.

Urbanization and industrialization

With industrialization comes the second stage of urbanization: a very rapid increase in the proportion of people living in towns. If we compare crude measures of industrialization (e.g. the proportion of the labour force in manufacturing occupations) with the degree of urbanization, we find that as countries become more industrialized they become more urbanized (Table 4.1) and that in general the countries that are most highly industrialized are also most highly urbanized (Table 4.2) The details of the urbanization process, however, have varied from one society to another.

Table 4.1 Urbanization and occupational distribution during industrialization in Belgium and the United States (per cent).

<table>
<tr><th></th><th></th><th>Population living in towns with over 2,500</th><th colspan="3">Distribution of Labour force by sector</th></tr>
<tr><th>Country</th><th>Year</th><th>inhabitants</th><th>Agriculture</th><th>Manufacturing</th><th>Services</th></tr>
<tr><td>Belgium</td><td>1880</td><td>33</td><td>25</td><td>39</td><td>36</td></tr>
<tr><td></td><td>1900</td><td>52</td><td>17</td><td>44</td><td>39</td></tr>
<tr><td></td><td>1930</td><td>61</td><td>14</td><td>49</td><td>37</td></tr>
<tr><td></td><td>1947</td><td>63</td><td>11</td><td>50</td><td>39</td></tr>
<tr><td>USA</td><td>1800</td><td>6</td><td>82</td><td colspan="2">18</td></tr>
<tr><td></td><td>1860</td><td>20</td><td>60</td><td>20</td><td>20</td></tr>
<tr><td></td><td>1900</td><td>40</td><td>38</td><td>28</td><td>34</td></tr>
<tr><td></td><td>1930</td><td>56</td><td>22</td><td>32</td><td>46</td></tr>
<tr><td></td><td>1950</td><td>61</td><td>12</td><td>35</td><td>53</td></tr>
</table>

Source: Simon Kuznets, 'Industrial distribution of national product and labour force', *Economic Development and Cultural Change*, V: 4, Supplement. 1957.

The countries that began to industrialize early—Western European countries and especially England—did so more slowly and urbanized more slowly, whereas Japan and the USSR underwent rapid urbanization in association with rapid planned industrialization and with the fact that they were influenced by the prior urbanization and industrialization of other countries.

Overriding these differences there is a basic interdependence between urbanization and industrialization and the reasons for this are fairly obvious. Industrialization usually involves large-scale production, and particularly the use of the factory system of production which brings a labour force together to work in one place. In addition, anyone who wants to set up a factory is likely to site it near to existing factories so that they can draw upon a common pool of labour and share essential services such as power and transportation and the professional services of bankers, lawyers and the like.

Britain was the first country to become industrial and the first to become highly urbanized; and, as Table 4.2 shows, it is still the most urbanized and by some measures the most industrialized country in the world. In the late eighteenth and early nineteenth century British industry depended heavily upon sources of power which were difficult to move—on coal and on water power. Factories therefore tended to cluster near the coal

Table 4.2 Urbanization and industrialization (25 selected countries—1950 and nearby years)

Country	*Percentage of population living in cities of 20,000 or more*	*Percentage of total active labour force working in manufacturing*
Haiti	5·4	2·0
Pakistan	7·8	1·3
Costa Rica	10·8	8·2
India	12·0	3·4
Philippines	12·7	4·9
Bolivia	14·0	3·8
Malaya	17·0	4·6
Mexico	24·0	8·4
Finland	24·0	18·4
Puerto Rico	27·1	16·2
Egypt	29·1	5·5
Venezuela	31·0	7·1
Switzerland	31·2	33·4
France	31·5	18·9
Sweden	34·5	28·7
Canada	35·1	24·6
Chile	39·5	13·6
Austria	39·8	21·5
Belgium	42·2	33·1
U.S.A.	42·8	26·3
West Germany	45·3	27·6
Argentina	48·3	17·3
Netherlands	56·4	21·1
Australia	56·8	25·2
United Kingdom	67·7	38·6

Source: *Report on the World Social Situation*, New York: United Nations, 1957, chapter VII, table 11, p. 127.

mines. The industry was usually labour-intensive so that each factory needed a large work-force to man it. This was the period of industrialization that produced the rapid growth of the northern cities in England. Blake's 'dark satanic mills'; the 'black country' in the West Midlands; such are the products of this period. Later parallel stages of industrialization brought the Ruhr in Germany and Pittsburgh in the USA.

Socially and physically, these cities were very different from the earlier pre-industrial towns. Instead of small individual workshops, they had great factories and mills powered by steam engines; instead of craftsmen organized into guilds they had an homogeneous and, until the rise of the trade unions, unorganized mass of 'hands'. These were men, women and sometimes children who had left the over-populated countryside to sell their labour in the towns. Charles Dickens gives a vivid picture of such places in his novel, *Hard Times*, written in 1854:[2]

> [Coketown] was a town of red brick, or of brick that would have been red if the smoke and ashes had allowed it; but as matters stood it was a town of unnatural red and black like the painted face of a savage. It was a town of machinery and tall chimneys, out of which interminable serpents of smoke trailed themselves for ever and ever, and never got uncoiled. It had a black canal in it, and a river that ran purple with ill-smelling dye, and vast piles of buildings full of windows where there was a rattling and a trembling all day long, and where the piston of the steam engine worked monotonously up and down like the head of an elephant in a state of melancholy madness. It contained several large streets all very like one another, and many small streets still more like one another, inhabited by people equally like one another, who all went in and out at the same hours, with the same sound upon the same pavements, to do the same work, and to whom every day was the same as yesterday and tomorrow, and every year the counterpart of the last and the next.
>
> These attributes of Coketown were in the main inseparable from the work by which it was sustained; against them were to be set off comforts of life which found their way all over the world. . . .

Paradoxically, as the economy and society in general became more complex, the cities became simpler and more specialized. Many of them grew very rapidly from almost nothing and this meant that they consisted almost entirely of the essentials of the industrial system: vast factories, railways and canals, and row upon row of cramped hastily-built houses for the workers.

It was this concentration on what appeared to be essentials that lay at the root of the frequently condemned features of towns during the period of rapid urbanization. The houses were close to the fumes, filth and noise of the factories in order that the workers could walk quickly to work. There were often no sewers nor any system for disposing of rubbish, so waste accumulated in the streets or was carried away in open drains, spreading disease and polluting the inadequate water supplies. The 1845 *Report on the State of*

Large Towns and Populous Districts paints a grim picture of sanitary conditions in urban areas and tells us, among other things, that 'in one part of Manchester in 1843–4 the wants of upward of 700 inhabitants were supplied by thirty-three necessaries only'—that is, one toilet to every 21.1 people. The houses themselves, as in Birmingham and Bradford, were frequently built back-to-back so that half the rooms had no daylight or ventilation. In the Scottish cities tall tenements were built and they were overcrowded, with many people sleeping in one room; and in Liverpool one-sixth of the population lived in 'underground cellars'. In such conditions, disease-bearing pests—rats, lice and flies—could flourish unchecked. There was no planning and little space was left for 'inessentials' such as public parks or children's playgrounds.

Thus the cities of the Industrial Revolution provided an even poorer environment than the rural slums of a decaying agricultural system. Disease, particularly infectious disease, debilitated the people and produced death-rates among both adults and babies that were higher than those in rural areas. Because of this the urban population could not reproduce itself, yet more and more people streamed in from the countryside to work in the factories and swell the ranks of the town dwellers.

It was in this setting that the early attempts at urban planning were made. There was pressure for some kind of control of the individual manufacturer's and builder's activities in the public interest. But although there was often concern about these problems, there was usually no authority in existence with adequate powers to exercise this control. The first attempts consciously to change the urban environment were therefore piecemeal in nature. Private societies, like the Peabody Trust, built better and more healthy artisans' dwellings during the period after 1840. Throughout the nineteenth and early twentieth century various 'model' villages and towns, designed to avoid the evils of ordinary towns, were established. The congestion in the centres of cities was to some extent relieved by the rapid development of suburbs on their peripheries. Cheaper tram and rail transportation, which appeared at the beginning of the twentieth century, made this possible: in London rows of new houses could be built for middle-class people in places like Clapham and Streatham, and artisans moved into what had before been middle-class areas, like Fulham, Hammersmith and Paddington.

Urban planning by public bodies, however, emerged only gradually. The duties of various local authorities were not well defined, so that it was not always clear, for instance, which body was responsible for the water supply or the enforcement of building regulations in an area. It was not until the last quarter of the nineteenth century that local government was reformed and rationalized, taking on the form that we know today with one authority responsible for many different aspects of life in one unified area: for health, housing, education, recreation facilities, roads, sewage, planning, welfare and so on. Even then, the local government had no powers actually to direct what should be built where. The Town Planning Acts of the twentieth century were to give them these powers, but by the time that this happened the third stage of urbanization had been reached.

Metropolitanization

When we look at modern industrial countries we are dealing with the third stage of urbanization when the rate of urbanization has slowed down considerably or even stopped altogether. In Britain the period of most rapid urbanization occurred between 1811 and 1851; for the next half-century it was very slightly slower; after 1900 it tailed off and by now seems to have stopped entirely. Of course, as the population increases the absolute number of people living in towns increases too, but in the recent period the proportion of the population living in towns has stayed more or less the same. Similar changes in the rate of urbanization are occurring in other industrial countries (see, for example, Table 4.1), though none of them is quite as far along the path as Britain. We shall therefore base our discussion on Britain, though much of what we shall say applies also elsewhere. On the basis of this experience, it seems that urbanization is a once-for-all phenomenon and there seems to be an urban saturation point. In the United Kingdom this was reached when about 70 per cent of the population lived in places of over 20,000 inhabitants, but it is likely that it will be at a lower point in many other countries since few will be able to contribute as little as Britain does to the world's agricultural production.

In the third stage of urbanization, then, the rate of urbanization slows down or even stops. Instead there is a reorganization of the urban population so that larger cities and urbanized areas gain in importance at the expense of smaller ones. This process has sometimes been labelled 'metropolitanization'. We have shown how the second stage of urbanization was closely linked to the development of manufacturing industry, with its rapid growth in the so-called 'secondary' sector of occupations; correspondingly, the third stage is linked to the later growth of the 'tertiary' or service sector of occupations.

During the nineteenth century, and especially during the second half, there developed a new kind of technology, based largely upon new inventions in transport, power, communications and office techniques. The motor car, electric power, cheap postage, the telephone and radio, all came into use for the first time; and office machines for typing, duplicating and calculating were invented. All of these heralded a new phase of industrialism. They made possible the growth of larger and more decentralized industrial organizations. Instead of the unitary firm with its office and factory on the same site, there could now be a complex firm consisting of a number of factories making different things or handling different stages of a process and a central 'home' office to administer the whole firm. This reorganization represents a greater division of labour within the firm, with the bureaucratic headquarters taking over many specialized functions like financing, decision-making and marketing. Another feature of this new industrialism is the emergence of new specialisms, particularly in the field of the service occupations. Activities like accounting, advertising and market research are increasingly separated from production and carried on by specialized firms.

These industrial changes are mirrored in an urban change: where once they were relatively discrete entities, cities became more and more involved in complex relationships with each other. For the cities within an area compete with each other as locations for the new co-ordinating headquarters. In the end one of them will predominate over the others, for it is advantageous for the headquarters of a number of firms to be close together so that they can share ancillary services. Then the other towns in the area take on specialized subordinate roles in relation to the central city. Some may specialize in manufacturing, housing the branch factories that are often run from the centre; others, the 'dormitory towns', specialize in residence; others may specialize to some extent in education (Cambridge), tourism (Stratford-on-Avon), retirement (Bournemouth) or holidays (Blackpool). A whole area becomes dependent upon, and supportive of, its central city or metropolis (which need not necessarily be its seat of government). Each place becomes more specialized in relation to the others. This is often reflected in complaints about the decline of local life in country towns or villages: the village chain store or city department store takes over from the local shop, the city hospital from the cottage hospital, the television from the pub sing-song, the 'Men from the Ministry' from the local council, the big construction consortium from the little local builder and so on. The metropolis comes to monopolize many specialist professions, crafts and retail trades and, outside the big cities, the services, supplies and entertainments are mainly mass produced. This big new city, then, has a high proportion of 'black coated workers', the new middle class who man its offices and services.

Physically, too, the metropolis merges confusingly into the surrounding suburbs, country and satellite towns so that it is difficult to identify meaningful boundaries. In Britain new entities, which cannot quite be called cities, have had a name coined for them in census reports. They are called 'conurbations' and are defined as 'continuously urbanized areas surrounding large population centres'. There are seven of them: Clydeside, Tyneside, West Yorkshire (Leeds and Bradford), Merseyside, the Manchester area, the West Midlands, and Greater London. Each of these great urban complexes dominates the surrounding area, but London dominates the whole country to a greater extent than any of the others. Between them, they contain about 40 per cent of the population and they are growing quite fast, in spite of the fact we have already mentioned that rates of population growth and urbanization in general are quite low.

A brief glance at regional studies such as *The South East Study*, published by the Ministry of Housing and Local Government in 1964, serves to reveal how, with metropolitanization, the region rather than the city alone becomes the important unit of study. In particular there has been concern at the rapid growth rate of the population of the London region. The study estimated that the south-east could expect to receive one million immigrants from the rest of the country and abroad in the period 1961–81. The natural increase in the area would add a further 2.4 millions. If no counter-measures were taken, most of this growth would take place in the areas immediately surrounding London. The population of the zone within about fifteen miles of the centre would not increase very much. In fact this type of zone tends to lose population as offices and shops take over from residential buildings and cramped housing is replaced. It is the belt between fifteen and forty miles from the centre that would bear the brunt of the expansion. For London, as the metropolis of the region and of the country, monopolizes many of the facilities that are so attractive to individuals and to firms.

The planners, however, have felt that this uncontrolled growth at the periphery of the city is a dangerous thing. They have feared that the inexorable spread of suburbs housing more and more office workers will mean the disappearance of any countryside accessible to Londoners; and that the increasing number of people travelling into central London for work would eventually paralyse the traffic system. They therefore put forward plans to decentralize growth in the area by founding three completely new cities to act as counter-magnets for population and by the drastic expansion of existing towns beyond the forty-mile radius.

The interest of this to the sociologist is that it illustrates how new meaningful social units are formed as the organization of production changes. It takes time before these new units are reflected in local government boundaries, but moves are slowly taking place in that direction. Among the signs of this is the formation of the Greater London Council.

We have shown how the modern metropolis comes into being, but what are its main characteristics? Its most striking features relate to its distinctive pattern of residence. The early industrial city could be divided, very crudely, into three areas. In the centre was the factory and business district; surrounding that were the homes of the working people; and further out, almost in the country, were the houses of the few middle-class people, the factory owners and managers, the clerks, the shopkeepers and the professional men. (This, incidentally, is the reverse of the pattern in the pre-industrial city where the wealthy people have their big houses in the centre and the poor live near the edge or even outside the walls.) As the industrial city grows into the metropolis, three things happen; some of the factories move out of the centre into new industrial zones; the business and shopping district spreads, invading the neighbouring residential zone; and most conspicuously, the city grows at the edges, spawning layer after layer of suburb.

The nature of these changes is such as to create an old stock of obsolete housing at the centre of the new metropolis. This problem is particularly acute in the area immediately around the business district, the area sometimes called the 'twilight zone'. The old houses in this zone frequently become slums. They are owned by landlords who do not find it worth their while to keep them in good repair and they are rented, often in single rooms, to people who cannot, for one reason or another, find anywhere 'better' to live. Such people are often the new arrivals in the city, who have come from other parts of the country or from abroad to find work; or they are the so-called 'problem families', especially those without a wage-earner, and the down-and-outs who are no longer struggling to find more comfortable surroundings, or they are the older people who were there when the neighbourhood 'saw better days' and now cannot afford to move away. In this zone, then, there is a concentration of unsettled people with a high proportion of males and of younger people.

A group of sociologists in the 1920s and 30s who have become known as the 'Chicago school' found that many of the problems of society were particularly acute in the twilight zone. They found, for example, that delinquency-rates, divorce-rates, illegitimacy-rates, suicide-rates, illiteracy-rates, and many others were highest in the twilight zone and gradually decreased as one moved out from the centre of the city. Attempts to solve the physical and social problems of the twilight zone, such as the rather draconian measure of pulling down large areas of old housing and replacing them with large new blocks of publicly owned flats have not always been successful. The root cause of the social problems, however, is not the state of the houses but the transience of the population and the consequent weakness of neighbourhood ties; and though the physical environment may be improved by urban renewal at the same time such minimal local community life as existed may be destroyed. Whereas the slum had some kind of loose and informal neighbourhood network, within which people found friendship and help if they needed it, the new housing project brings together people from many different places who have no ties with each other, who are isolated and free from either the interference or the support of their neighbours. In the light of this some people have suggested that it would be more valuable to encourage the development of the rudimentary informal social organization than to break it up completely by changing the physical surroundings. In some cities, and this is particularly so in America, community projects have been launched to stimulate self-help and local responsibility in these areas. These, however, are only successful to the extent that the areas become residentially stable. For the basic reason for the weakness of the local community is the fact that the twilight zone is the receiving area for newcomers to the city. Only when the city stops growing will this kind of transitional social problem disappear completely.

The twilight zone is only one of many distinct areas in the metropolis. In the small city different kinds of people are bound to live in fairly close proximity to one another whereas in the metropolis they tend to become much more segregated. Not only do middle-class and working-class people live in separate areas, but each of a variety of smaller groups within each class tends to cluster together, somewhat apart from other groups. Thus there may be an artists' quarter, a Jewish neighbourhood, a lower-middle-class suburb, an upper-crust district, and so on. The name of each locality conjures up an image of its typical inhabitant: think of the Gorbals, Mayfair, Sparkbrook or Woodford Green. This clustering means that although the population of the city itself is heterogeneous, the population of each neighbourhood tends to be homogeneous. People tend therefore to live among and mix with others who are rather similar to themselves. Usually people seem to prefer this; they would feel 'uncomfortable' and 'out of place' among people who were different. This kind of segregation is one of the factors in the preservation of differences between social class. The wealthy seldom see how the poor live in the slums, so they need not trouble to do anything about it; the poor do not see how extravagantly the rich live, so they do not feel resentful. The result is that people learn to see the world from the point of view of the group they live in.

One of the most conspicuous and extreme developments of this kind is the emergence of the 'ghetto'. The original ghettos were Jewish areas within European towns. Now, in industrial societies, we frequently find 'ghettos' of coloured people. In countries like South Africa this residential segregation is enforced by law. In countries with a predominantly white population it often comes about less formally, simply as a result of the relative poverty and powerlessness of the coloured people and the discriminating practices of house-agents and landlords. In England there are no complete 'ghettos' in the sense of areas that are entirely coloured. But coloured people do tend to be clustered in certain areas—in particular in the twilight zones of cities and in the poorer inner suburbs. The chances for neighbourly contact, for children going to school together and making friends between the races are thus very much restricted. Also, because these neighbourhoods in which coloured people find it easiest to get accommodation are the poorest ones, with the oldest schools, 'worst' accents, highest delinquency-rates and poorest job-opportunities, coloured people are less likely to be able to rise in the social scale. Thus, the way in which the residential pattern of big cities is organized may turn out to be a very important factor in turning the coloured group in Britain from a newly arrived immigrant group just finding its feet into a permanent sub-lower class, cut off from the rest of the community.

In addition to these new specialized areas near the centre of the city, the third stage of urbanization brings another kind of new area that has attracted much attention: the suburb. In terms of the space they occupy and the novel way of life they seem to embody, suburbs are probably the most striking feature of the metropolitan society. In Britain they began to grow during the nineteenth century with the advent of trains and trams to carry residents to their work cheaply. But the heyday of suburban expansion was in the inter-war period. A whole belt of land from five to fifteen miles around London was built up during this period. The housing density, at about 12–14 houses per acre, was much lower than in the central areas and the design of the houses and layout of the streets often more varied and informal in style. The result was that although the population of Greater London increased by 1.2 million (about 17 per cent) during the period from 1921 to 1938, the built-up area increased more than three-fold. The same kind of development has occurred around almost all the metropolitan centres in highly urbanized countries. Some observers deplore it, calling it 'suburban sprawl', predicting that it will engulf the entire countryside and characterizing its way of life as dull, standardized and in-growing. Others—and with them a large number of suburbanites—herald it as a move towards a pleasant, open environment for a life free at once from the inconvenience of the country and the stress and congestion of the city.

There is a popular stereotype of suburbia which is reflected not only in the work of novelists, but also in that of some sociologists. The 'suburban way of life' is described as a life where there is more contact with neighbours, more participation in neighbourhood activities, more concern about what the neighbours think, and more focus on family and domestic activities, on doing things together and on improving the home. But closer consideration casts doubt on whether these things are a characteristic of suburban life *as such* or whether they are not rather characteristic of middle-class life anywhere. Most people's image of the suburb is of middle-class suburbia; daily life in working-class suburbs is more similar to working-class life in the inner city.

The pattern of life in new suburbs, too, is very different from that in old-established ones. For new suburbs tend to have houses of similar size and price, so they are inhabited by families of similar income and at a similar stage in their family cycle. There may be mile after mile of lower-middle-class families with two or three young children. But as the suburb ages, some of these will stay and grow older, others will sell out to younger families. In the early stages the suburb is homogeneous, and common interests, together with the fact that the residents have all broken away from old ties, mean that there may be much neighbourly mixing. In the later stages the population of the suburb becomes more mixed and consequently there are greater opportunities for varied ways of life within it.

Urbanization and modernization

In modernizing societies the situation is rather different from what it was in the industrial nations that we have described so far. They are developing in interaction with more developed societies and, to some extent, after their example. One result is that they can see ahead what the fruits of economic growth will be and their people desire the higher standard of living that they know is available elsewhere. This has been described as 'the revolution of rising expectations' and one of its features is a dissatisfaction with primitive rural life, a dissatisfaction which makes many people move to the towns in search of 'better' things. People in modernizing societies also become aware of the independence and individualism of life in industrial societies. They can see American films in which young people live in their own homes and choose for themselves whom to marry, instead of living under the parental roof and submitting to an arranged marriage. So young people, chafing at the traditional restrictions that surround them in their home village, go to the town partly to escape these bonds.

Contact with industrial societies also introduces a money economy into rural areas, so that even a farmer who grows crops for his own consumption may need cash to pay for some of his supplies and implements and to pay his taxes. Yet employment rewarded in cash may not be available to him in the country, so he, or one of his family, must take an urban job at least occasionally.

In many of these countries the population is increasing very rapidly so there is serious overpopulation of rural areas. People are forced off the land because the land can no longer support them and this too produces a flow of people to the cities. Thus in Africa, Asia and Latin America the proportion of people living in towns is much lower than in the industrial regions of the world but relative to their own level and type of economic development, it is very high.

Table 4.3 illustrates an important difference in this respect between urbanization in industrial societies and urbanization in modernizing societies. In many modernizing countries there have been large movements to the cities without any increase in the proportion of workers in industry. Indeed, in the cases cited in Table 4.3 the proportion of the labour force in industry has actually decreased

Table 4.3 Changes in urbanization and the distribution of the labour force in selected countries (per cent)

Country	Year	Population in localities of 20,000 or more	Labour force in Agriculture	Industry	Services
Chile	1920	28	39	30	31
	1952	40 (1950)	31	30	39
India	1911	4	74	13	13
	1951	12	74	10	16
Mexico	1910	11	70	22	8
	1950	24	61	17	22
Australia	1911	43	25	34	41
	1947	57	17	38	45
France	1906	25	43	30	27
	1954	33	28	37	35
USSR	1928	12 (1926)	80	8	12
	1955	32	43	31	26

Source: *Report on the World Social Situation*, New York: United Nations, 1957, chapter VII, table 10, p. 125.

in India and Mexico and remained constant in Chile while in each case the proportion of the population living in urban areas increased dramatically. In each of the industrial societies cited, however, the urbanization process has been accompanied by an increase in the proportion of industrial workers. In so far as we can take the proportion of industrial workers as an index of a society's level of economic growth we may suggest that in these modernizing societies the distribution of population between town and country does not contribute to economic growth and sometimes even inhibits it.

The figures in Table 4.3, however, probably exaggerate the situation because there is usually a shift from small-scale, craft manufacturing to large-scale, factory production, so that although the same proportion of workers may be involved, their productivity is higher. The increase in the 'service' category with urbanization in modernizing societies is particularly interesting. For these service occupations are not predominantly those connected with education, administration and the professions, as they are in industrial societies, but are the result of a lack of mechanization and rationalization. Porters, messengers and servants do work that in industrial countries is commonly mechanized; thousands of small traders, hawkers and market women do work that would be unnecessary in a rationalized retail system. Many of these people are grossly underemployed, picking up work or trade only occasionally. So these urban occupations contribute very little to the general economy.

Furthermore, because the migrants to the cities are usually driven off the land rather than attracted by job opportunities in the cities, there is a tendency for one or two very large cities in each country to grow disproportionately at the expense of the smaller ones. Such migrants are more likely to have heard about the big cities and are more likely to have relatives there; it is easier to travel to them and when they arrive they find it easier to find some way to earn a living, if only because there are already more people to whom they can offer their services. The result is that although the countries of Africa, Asia and Latin America are mostly not highly urbanized but on the contrary largely rural in character, in 1960 half of the twenty biggest 'urban agglomerations' in the world (with populations of over three million people each) were found in these areas.

These large cities tend to monopolize people and resources, so that the growth of medium-sized cities, which might be better suited to industrial development, is hindered. The absolute growth-rate of the cities is even faster than the urbanization rates would indicate because of the high rates of population increase in these countries. The result is that, in addition to hindering economic growth, such places experience all the social difficulties and health hazards of any rapidly expanding city. Indeed, they occur on an especially large scale because of the low level of per capita income and because of the vast size of the cities. There are fourteen cities in the modernizing, and mainly rural, countries that are larger than either Manchester or Birmingham today: cities like Shanghai, Calcutta, Bombay, Peking, Cairo and Rio de Janeiro. Their rapid growth is entirely unco-ordinated; their people huddle in shanty-towns and slums; and, unlike the cities of earlier industrializing countries at a similar stage, because of their huge size they suffer from acute transportation problems. A description of Calcutta serves to illustrate these tendencies:[3]

> The shanties made of castaway materials that crowd the road from the airport at Dum-Dum and the stench of uncovered drains introduce the visitor to the condition of life of the vast majority of the city's inhabitants. More than three-fourths of the population of the city of Calcutta proper live in overcrowded tenement and bustee (slum) quarters. According to an official estimate 'two-thirds of the people live in kutcha (unbaked brick) buildings. More than 57 per cent of multimember families have one room to live in. For more than half the families cramped into one-room quarters there is only 30 square feet or less per family member.' One study showed that the indigent in the bustees share a single water tap among 25·6 to 30·1 persons and a single latrine among 21·1 to 23. . . . 8·6 per cent of the rooms in bustees are either partly or wholly places of work (as well as dwellings) . . . . Even in the midst of the central commercial and banking districts of the city, the traffic situation is appalling. On an average day 500,000 pedestrians and 30,000 vehicles will cross the Howrah bridge, and the traffic jams at both ends are constant. There are never enough taxis or buses. The progress these vehicles make through the streets is slowed by the rickshaws, which are patronized generously by the citizens of Calcutta, and by

the numerous carts drawn by oxen, water buffaloes or men.

Thus the rate and form of urbanization in many modernizing countries is directly inimical to economic growth. Yet, indirectly, the movement to the towns can stimulate economic development by contributing to other aspects of modernization. For the town represents modern civilization: within it modern institutions develop and through its influence modern ways of life spread to rural areas.

Traditional social structure and forms of relationship may no longer be entirely appropriate in the city. A striking illustration of this can be seen in the way that caste definitions and rituals tend to weaken in Indian cities. The rules of caste define the activities that different people may engage in and the ways in which they may relate to other castes. Yet in the city a man must make his own living as best he can and he lives and works alongside strangers whose caste he does not know. At the local level, too, sub-castes are, to some extent, self-regulating associations. Yet when a man moves to the city he removes himself from the observation and control of his caste group. Caste is fundamentally a local phenomenon: not all castes can be found in any one area. So any geographical mobility puts men outside the local caste rules that they have learned and consequently disrupts the caste system. Finally, caste is a system of stratification in which, on the whole, those born into the higher castes are the richer and more powerful members of society. Yet if he moves to the city, a member of a low caste or even an untouchable may gain wealth or influence through success in trade or in a profession. Such a man is of high status in a new urban class structure where social mobility is possible and a man's status depends on his own achievements in life as well as on his caste origin.

In similar ways, many other traditional patterns of behaviour break down in an urban setting. An African townsman need no longer submit himself to tribal or village authority. The kinship network, such an important institution in all simpler societies, becomes weaker. The urban economy in which incomes are the reward of individual rather than collective effort, encourages self-reliance and self-sufficiency. So the townsman's sense of obligation towards his kin and the extent to which he is able to rely on them when in need diminish.

In the cities of West Africa there is a large number and variety of associations, membership of which is voluntary. These help to adapt migrants to their new situation in various ways. Some of them, in particular the tribal associations, enable the migrant to keep in touch with his own language and culture. But they differ from traditional tribalism in that the urban tribal association is not a corporate group; clear-cut traditional kinship rights and obligations are replaced by a vaguer sense of mutual obligation and of metaphysical brotherhood. Voluntary associations have their rules and regulations and often exercise great authority over their members. Thus they serve as a substitute for traditional agencies of social control. The Mende Dancing Compins of Freetown in Sierra Leone, for instance, fine members for street fighting, provide chaperons for the younger members, expel members convicted of a felony and help to patch up family quarrels. In youth associations, the young control their own behaviour instead of submitting to the authority of their elders. Voluntary associations in the cities also provide social security where traditional forms cannot operate effectively and where the state makes no provision. A common form of this in Ghana and Nigeria is a rota fund, which enables people to save regularly against times when they need money.

As well as providing substitutes for traditional institutions, however, voluntary associations play a part in social change. A peculiar characteristic of West African voluntary associations is the large proportion of their members who hold official positions within the association. Holding office, and, indeed, even ordinary membership in a highly organized association, helps to socialize the new townsman into the ways of urban life: he learns to engage in impersonal relationships revolving round specific tasks; he learns a new concept of time and punctuality; he learns to obey and create formal rules, rather than follow tradition. Such experience can be useful preparation for political action as well as for general participation in town life. Partly because of this and partly because political parties were often banned during the colonial period, voluntary associations were important in the growth of independence movements. An important example of this was the Egba Women's Union in Nigeria, a savings club which took an active part in the formation and support of the National Council of Nigeria and the Cameroons, the leading political party in the Eastern Region at the time of independence.

In the town the migrant also plays new roles which bring him into new relationships with other people. In particular, he is more likely to be employed for a wage, which involves him in a new kind of authority relationship with an employer. He finds that instead of owing deference to village and family elders he now owes it to those who are above him in the occupational structure, whatever their age. Furthermore, if he is employed in industry or commerce, he is likely to work alongside a large number of people, differing in tribal background and status, who are now considered his equals and with whom he has common interests. Thus industrial workers in modernizing countries begin to form trade unions that cut across the old barriers and represent a newly emerging social category, a category analogous to the working class in industrial societies.

The towns are also centres for other activities important in a modernizing society. The main educational and administrative institutions are located in towns. Thus the towns become symbols of modernity and those who live in them either participate in, or at least are affected by, modern literacy and rational bureaucratic control. Most of the people who are engaged in white collar activities—a rapidly expanding group—are gathered together in the towns. They meet in their leisure time as well as in their work and develop a sense that they belong together and have common interests. In embryo they too represent the emergence of a new and distinct social group.

Many of those who go to the towns to work, however, do not settle there permanently. They may retire to their home village at the end of their working life or they may go as migrant workers, taking a town job at times when there is little work to be done on the farm. Such people may not become fully assimilated into modern life, but they do carry certain town ways back with them to the rural areas and they help to spread a money economy and a taste for manufactured consumer goods.

We may conclude that even in the places where urbanization occurs without concomitant industrialization, the towns themselves have an important part to play in the process of modernization. They epitomize a new way of life and their influence is felt throughout the whole society.

Notes

1 Max Weber, *The City*, Chicago: Free Press, 1958, pp. 81–2.
2 Charles Dickens, *Hard Times*, London: Dent, 1907, p. 19.
3 Nirmal Kumar Bose, 'Calcutta: a premature metropolis', in *Cities*, a *Scientific American* book, Harmondsworth: Penguin, 1968.

Reading

Cities, a *Scientific American* book, Harmondsworth: Penguin, 1968. A collection of articles that appeared in the magazine *Scientific American* in 1965. The articles by Davis and Sjoberg give a useful survey of urbanization from earliest times; and others describe varying urban situations in greater detail.

Breeze, Gerald, *Urbanization in Newly Developing Countries*, Englewood Cliffs, N. J.: Prentice-Hall, 1966. An introductory survey of urbanization in relation to the process of modernization.

Jacobs, Jane, *The Death and Life of Great American Cities*, Harmondsworth: Penguin, 1965. A lively attack, by an architectural journalist, on contemporary town planning. A fascinating and highly polemical analysis, rich with examples, leads her to the conclusion that the unplanned patterns of growth which represent the organizational complexity of the city, may be preferable to the simplistic ones imposed by planners.

Nottridge, Harold E., *The Sociology of Urban Living*, London: Routledge & Kegan Paul, 1972. A brief introduction to the study of the city, covering a wide range of research and theories.

Pahl, R. E., *Patterns of Urban Life*, London: Longmans, 1970. An introduction to the sociology of the city, with special reference to Britain. The first two chapters, on pre-industrial urbanism and the emergence of industrial urbanism in Britain, are of especial relevance to the theme of this chapter.

Pahl, R. E. (ed.), *Readings in Urban Sociology*, Oxford: Pergamon, 1968. An interesting collection of articles dealing mainly with non-American material, with a helpful introduction by the editor.

Further reading

Dobriner, W. M. (ed.), *The Suburban Community*, New York: Putnams, 1958. A collection of 24 papers which explore varied aspects of the distinctive nature of suburban life.

Hatt, P. K. and Reiss, A. J. (eds), *Cities & Society: The Revised Reader in Urban Sociology*, Chicago: Free Press, 1957. A large and varied collection of articles covering a wide range. Includes classic contributions by Simmel, Wirth, Davies and Golden, Sjoberg, McKenzie and Miner; but mainly deals with American cities.

McKenzie, R. D., *The Metropolitan Community*, New York: McGraw-Hill, 1933. A pioneering work on the changing nature of cities as urbanization proceeds. Gives special emphasis to ecological factors.

Miner, Horace (ed.), *The City in Modern Africa*, London: Pall Mall, 1967. An interesting collection of recent articles.

Reissman, Leonard, *The Urban Process*, New York: Free Press, 1964. Aims to find 'a theory explaining the industrial city and its development', using a comparative typology more elaborate than the series of stages we have used in this chapter. Includes a valuable critical survey of earlier schools of thought.

Weber, Max, *The City*, Chicago: Free Press, 1958. Weber's classic work on the development of the urban 'community' in the occident, with particular emphasis on urban political structures. Don Martindale's introduction to this edition gives a useful survey of American urban sociology.

5 Population

World population growth

Man or very close kin to man has been in existence for perhaps a million years. Although it is not known precisely when *homo sapiens* first appeared, there is clear evidence of his activities in Europe something like 25,000 to 30,000 years ago. For half a million years or more the human species grew in number very slowly, expanding temporarily in some areas, declining in others, but remaining sparse everywhere. Sustenance was obtained by hunting, fishing, and gathering, which required huge areas for few people. Although the domestication of animals and plants ultimately gave rise to some areas of far greater density of settlement than hitherto, it came so gradually that the rate of population growth was hardly raised at all. The emergence of settled pastoral and agrarian societies did, however, lead to a long-term increase in population from about five million in 8000 BC to eighty-six million in 4000 BC. By the beginning of the Christian era world population probably numbered between 200 and 300 million. By 1750 the population of the world had reached about 790 million. Today it is over 3,500 million. A simple analysis of these numbers reveals that an enormous increase in the rate of world population growth has occurred, especially during the past three centuries. As Philip M. Hauser has pointed out, it took most of the millennia of man's habitation of the earth to produce a population as large as one thousand million people simultaneously alive. This population was not achieved until about 1850. To produce a population of two thousand million required only an additional seventy-five years, for this was the world population by 1925. To reach a population of three thousand million required an additional thirty-seven years, for this was achieved by 1962.

Why has the rate of world population growth increased so greatly? The answer may be found by analysing the rates of population growth in different types of society and examining the reasons for these differences. Although the data are subject to error there are a number of conclusions which may legitimately be drawn.

One of the salient facts is that today population is growing faster in the underdeveloped countries than in the highly developed ones.[1] But this is a recent trend, dating from about 1920. Before the first world war the most rapid gains occurred in the more industrialized societies—in those developing economically and raising their levels of living. After 1920 it has been the non-industrial countries that have shown the more rapid growth.

Why is world population as a whole increasing at an accelerating pace? Why has the fastest growth shifted from the richer to the poorer countries? The major demographic cause of the great acceleration of population growth, first evident in Europe and in areas of European settlement, was the decline in the death-rate, not a rise in the birth-rate. Sharp declines in mortality were experienced while fertility remained at relatively high levels. The case of England and Wales can be taken as an illustration of a pattern experienced by all the now highly industrialized countries. In 1750 the birth-rate in England was about 35 live births per 1,000 persons per year. The death-rate stood at a level of about 32 deaths per 1,000 persons per year. Natural increase, the excess of births over deaths, approximated three persons

Figure 5.1 Demographic characteristics of societies at different levels of economic and social development

Level of social and economic development	*Major demographic characteristics*	*Examples*
Societies with low national income per capita. High percentage of labour force in agriculture. Low levels of urbanization.	HIGH birth-rates. HIGH death-rates. HIGH infant mortality-rates. LOW expectation of life at birth. LOW rate of natural increase. HIGH percentage of children. LOW percentage of old people. LOW percentage of persons 15–64.	All societies before 1700. Contemporary modernizing societies (e.g. India, Egypt, tropical Africa, most of Latin America and Asia before 1950).
Societies undergoing the early stages of industrialization. National income per capita increasing. Percentage of labour force in agriculture declining. Rising levels of urbanization.	HIGH birth-rates at first, gradual decline in later stages. DECLINING death-rates. DECLINING infant mortality-rates. RISING expectation of life at birth. VERY HIGH rate of natural increase at first, gradual decline as birth-rates fall in later stages. VERY HIGH percentage of children at first, declining later.	Britain, 1780–1880 USA, 1870–1910 W. Europe, 1830–1900 USSR, 1910–40 Japan, 1920–50
Societies with high national income per capita. Low percentage of labour force in agriculture. High levels of urbanization.	LOW birth-rates. LOW death-rates. LOW infant mortality-rates. HIGH expectation of life at birth. LOW rate of natural increase. LOW percentage of children. HIGH percentage of old people. HIGH percentage of persons 15–64.	Contemporary Britain, W. Europe, USA, USSR, Japan, Australia, New Zealand, Canada.

per 1,000 per year. A century later the death-rate had declined to a level of 23, while the birth-rate remained at the earlier high level. The natural increase was therefore twelve per thousand producing a rate of population increase nearly four times what it had been a century earlier (see Figure 5.2). As in the case of England and Wales, mortality in Western Europe began its relatively rapid decline at the end of the eighteenth century. It was only after a considerable time-lag that the birth-rate began to fall and, therefore, to dampen rates of population growth.

The decline in the death-rate was at first limited to those countries undergoing industrialization. The improvements in agriculture, transport, and commerce during the eighteenth and nineteenth centuries made better diets possible; the advances in manufacturing made improved clothing, housing, and other amenities more widely available. Technological gains and increased productivity made possible a general rise in levels of living. Moreover, the rise in real income facilitated the growth of public health measures and the development of medical science. During the nineteenth century great strides were made in purifying food and water and in improving personal hygiene, which contributed materially to the elimination of parasitic and infectious diseases. But it was not until the present century and the advent of chemotherapy that medical science had much effect on the death-rate. Economic growth, not medicine, led to the decline in the death-rate in Western Europe, North America and Australasia.

Since 1920, however, the less developed countries have experienced much faster declines in death-rates than European countries ever experienced, and these declines have occurred without a comparable rate of economic growth—in many cases without any noticeable gain in *per capita* income at all. Death-rates have been brought down with amazing speed in the economically backward regions of the world because the latest medical discoveries, produced and financed in the highly industrialized countries, can be applied everywhere. In Europe the advances in medical science were the product of a very gradual process of development; today the underdeveloped nations are suddenly getting the benefit of the accumulated heritage of centuries as well as such new discoveries as are made each year. Death-rates in the Third

World are declining seemingly miraculously, but in reality such declines would be impossible without the previous social development of the now highly industrialized societies.

The most important causes of death being eliminated in Africa, Asia, and Latin America are infectious and contagious diseases. The transfer of medical skills, techniques, personnel and funds from the West, especially under the auspices of international agencies like WHO, UNESCO, UNICEF, FAO, etc., has made possible the conquest of such diseases. Insecticides like DDT, antibiotics like penicillin, vaccines like BCG, drugs like sulfanilamide, and systematic public health campaigns, made it feasible to control widespread diseases like malaria, yellow fever, syphilis, cholera, typhoid, smallpox, tuberculosis and dysentery at very low cost. The case of Ceylon (as it was then known) can be used as an illustration. For centuries the major cause of death and illness in Ceylon was malaria. Endemic malaria prevailed in two-thirds of the island and periodic epidemics occurred at regular intervals. The spread of the disease was favoured and magnified by the gross undernourishment of the population. The crude death-rate averaged 26·9 per 1,000 during 1920–29 and 24·5 during 1930–39. In 1946 it was still as high as 20·3, but in that year the spraying with DDT of sites from which the adult mosquito attacked humans was begun. In one year the death-rate fell by 43 per cent (from 20·3 to 14·3) and by 1950 it was as low as 12·6. The malaria mortality-rate was decreased by 82·5 per cent between 1946 and 1949: this was accompanied by a marked reduction in infant and maternal mortality and in several of the other major causes of death. The costs were very low and even these were partly met from WHO funds. The DDT was imported and the experts involved either originated or were trained outside Ceylon. The Cingalese were not required to change their institutions, to acquire any knowledge of malaria and its control, nor to take any initiative. The spectacular decline in the death-rate was not the consequence of any basic economic or social development in Ceylon.

Similar trends are noticeable elsewhere. The death-rate of the Moslem population of Algeria in 1946–47 was higher than that of Sweden in 1771–80. By 1955 the fall in the death-rate in Algeria was greater in eight years than that experienced in Sweden during the century from 1775 to 1875. Between 1940 and 1960 Mexico, Costa Rica, Venezuela and Malaya were among the societies in which the death-rate decreased by

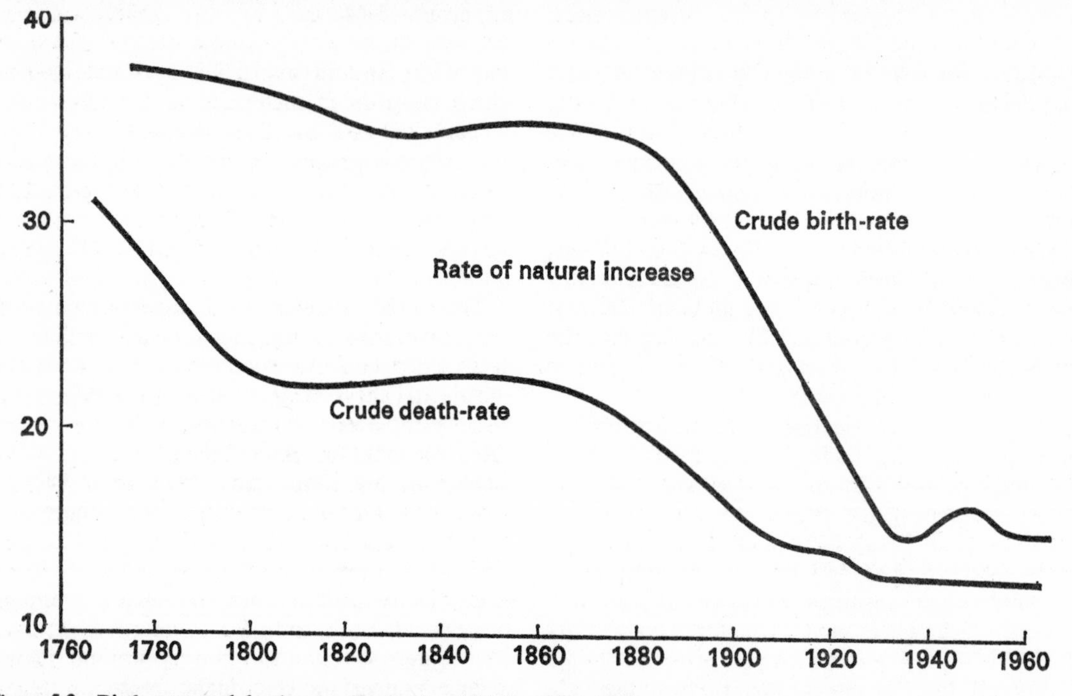

Figure 5.2 Birth-rates and death-rates, England and Wales, 1760–1960

Source: Phyllis Deane & W. A. Cole, *British Economic Growth 1688–1959*, Cambridge University Press, 1962, p. 127; D. V. Glass & E. Grebenik, 'World population 1800–1950', in H. J. Habakkuk & M. Postan (eds), *The Cambridge Economic History of Europe*, vol. VI, part 1, 1965, pp. 68–9.

more than 50 per cent. In 18 under-developed countries the average decline in the death-rate from 1945–9 to 1950–4 was 20 per cent.

Without question this spectacular decline in the death-rates of non-industrial countries has been the most important population phenomenon of the twentieth century. The rate of population growth in these societies today is much higher than that experienced by the economically advanced nations during the period of their rapid population growth. In the history of the highly industrialized societies the decline in mortality was spread out over nearly three centuries during the latter part of which (over periods ranging from fifty years to one and a half centuries) the birth-rate also began to decline. But in present-day non-industrial countries birth-rates remain high. While death-rates have fallen to levels between ten and twenty per thousand per year, birth-rates tend to average forty or more, a level little lower, if any, than it was centuries ago. This difference between the death-rate and the birth-rate gives a natural increase of between twenty and thirty—a population growth-rate of two to three per cent per annum. Moreover, whereas the present industrialized countries experienced falling birth-rates before their sharpest declines in mortality, the under-developed countries of today will do so, if at all, long after their death-rates have reached low levels. It is, as Kingsley Davis has pointed out, this dual fact—the unprecedented conquest of mortality by bringing mid-twentieth-century public health to the Third World, and the continuance of high birth-rates in these backward areas—that explains the extraordinary population growth in the non-industrialized three-quarters of the world. It also explains, along with the rise in birth-rates since the 1940s and continued lowering of mortality in the highly developed nations, the accelerating trend of the total world population.

Mortality

Mortality conditions in all societies once resembled those in the least developed countries of today. As we have seen, since the latter part of the eighteenth century there has been a very impressive reduction of mortality in the now highly industrialized societies. Precise information is not available but in all probability the expectation of life at birth in Egypt, Greece, and Rome around the beginning of the Christian era was not above thirty years. During the period 1650 to 1700 life expectation at birth in Western Europe was about thirty-three years and probably had not changed much during the preceding three or four centuries. By 1900 death-rates had declined to a point where expectation of life in Western Europe and North America had reached a level of forty-five to fifty years. By 1960 life expectation in all highly industrialized societies was about seventy years.

By far the greater part of this increase in expectation of life at birth has been brought about by a decline in infant mortality. The decline in mortality of other age groups is far less impressive. Mortality during the first year of life is extremely sensitive to changes in social conditions. The infant is entirely dependent upon the care of its parents, and that care is itself dependent upon the parents' standard of living (income, housing, level of education and access to medical care). In all societies the infant mortality-rate varies inversely with parents' income. It is highest in the lower income group and lowest in the wealthiest sector of society. Similarly the poorer countries of the world have the highest infant mortality-rates: in Pakistan and India the infant mortality-rate is over 200, in Sweden it is as low as 18. The great decline in mortality brought about by the social changes associated with the process of industrialization can by illustrated by taking the case of France. In the eighteenth century, of every 1,000 infants born, 233 had died before reaching the age of one, 498 had died before twenty, and 786 died before sixty. In contrast, of 1,000 infants born in present-day France only 40 die before reaching the age of one, only 60 before twenty, and only 246 before sixty. In eighteenth-century France of the original 1,000 infants only 214 survived to age sixty: in contemporary France 754 of the original 1,000 are still alive at sixty.

Before the development of modern transportation and industry hunger, malnutrition, and famine were recurrent features of human life. It has been estimated that in Britain between AD 10 and 1846 there were over 2,000 famines. China and India have recorded massive famines even in recent times, with enormous loss of life from hunger and from the disease and violence that hunger often begets. In China between 1876 and 1879 as many as 13 million people may have died from starvation, disease, and violence following a prolonged drought. Before man had developed the necessary techniques to minimize the effects of natural disasters, floods and drought frequently led to famines. Wars that have devastated the land or disrupted the normal routines of cultivation and exchange have also been the cause of famine. The

Thirty Years' War in Germany in the seventeenth century and more recently the internal strife following the breakdown of central government in the Congo and Nigeria led to famine and disease. But more important than the drastic but occasional occurrence of outright starvation in explaining the high mortality of non-industrial societies are the effects of malnutrition and the exigencies of poverty. In the modern world the likelihood of famine has, in any case, sharply diminished. Except in geographically isolated areas or those set apart for political reasons, the threat of famine is now likely to bring quick relief from other regions with agricultural surpluses. But low standards of living still prevail in many parts of the world, and the impact of poverty and low productivity on death-rates can be seen in the great differences still to be found between 'underdeveloped' countries and highly industrialized ones.

The long-term decline in the death-rate in Western Europe was preceded by the achievement of relatively long periods of peace and security as a result of the emergence of powerful and stable central government. This in itself was an essential prerequisite for the rapid expansion of productivity which not only lessened the frequent shortages of basic necessities but also brought with it technological and later medical advances that made possible the prevention and cure of disease. Improved sanitation, purification of water supplies and control of contagious diseases have all contributed greatly to lengthening the normal life span.

Patterns of disease

The recording of sickness and the registration of deaths and their causes present in themselves a significant contrast between societies at different levels of development. Industrial societies have comprehensive systems of registration of vital statistics and produce census data at regular intervals. 'Underdeveloped' societies do not have the administrative resources for collecting the statistics necessary for exact comparison with industrial societies so the data from these countries are based on special surveys and sample areas. But the differences between industrial and non-industrial societies are so great as to leave no doubts about the major contrasts. In highly industrialized societies many deaths are due to diseases whose causes are unknown and which cannot yet be prevented or cured. In less developed societies most deaths are due to diseases which can be controlled by medical science: the fact that they flourish in the face of this knowledge is one facet of the low level of development of these societies.

'Mass diseases' is the term used to describe those diseases which are so widespread and affect so high a proportion of the population that they mask other diseases to the point of making them medically or clinically irrelevant. The mass diseases may be regarded as the undergrowth of disease which has to be cleared before other forms of ill-health even reveal themselves. Mass diseases include: (a) infectious and contagious diseases like malaria, yaws, hookworm, tuberculosis, trachoma, syphilis, gastro-intestinal diseases, pneumonia, leprosy and sleeping sickness; (b) nutritional diseases like kwashiorkor, beri-beri, pellagra, and rickets; (c) pestilential diseases like cholera, smallpox, bubonic plague, typhus, typhoid, and yellow fever.

The term 'degenerative diseases' will be used to refer to those diseases which are associated with the older age groups—diseases of the heart and circulation (like arterio-sclerosis and thrombosis), brain-haemorrhages, organic and glandular disorders (like diabetes, some forms of rheumatism), 'stress' diseases (like gastric and duodenal ulcers), and cancers.

In the 'underdeveloped' countries the great health problem is the problem of mass diseases: this jungle undergrowth of disease has to be cleared before other forms of ill-health reveal themselves. In industrial societies mass diseases have, to a very large extent, been eliminated and the health problem is one of the control of degenerative diseases. Diseases of the heart and circulatory system and cancers and tumours alone now account for over fifty per cent of all deaths in the eight countries with the highest per capita national incomes and the percentage of deaths from these diseases is currently increasing. But it is only when mass diseases have been cleared away that the social and medical significance of degenerative diseases becomes apparent: only when a country has developed so far as to gain effective control of infectious and contagious diseases, when impure water and contaminated food are eliminated, when rodent and insect disease vectors (rats, flies, mosquitoes, etc.) are controlled, only when society reaches a certain stage of social development do degenerative diseases assume significant proportions.

There is a popular tendency to assume that since mass diseases are disproportionately high in the tropical countries, climate is the deciding factor in a society's state of health. But the state of health of a society depends more on the degree of social development than on the degree of latitude. This can be shown in three ways: first, by examining the changes in disease patterns which occur over time as a society industrializes; second, by examining the health conditions of different social groups living in the same area—groups that live side by side but have different standards and levels of living, differing health services, etc.; and third, by correlating indices of health and levels of industrialization *between* societies.

Societies which are now highly developed were once covered by a mantle of mass diseases. The patterns of mortality and morbidity of the now highly industrial societies were once like those current in today's non-industrial societies. We have already observed that the death-rates and more especially the infant mortality-rates of all industrial societies have fallen drastically over the past hundred and fifty years. Before the mid-nineteenth century, plague, cholera, typhus, and smallpox were common causes of death in Europe. Nutritional diseases like rickets and diseases such as tuberculosis, dysentery and syphilis were widespread.

A survey of the changing causes of death in England and Wales during the past hundred years, based on the published mortality statistics of the General Register Office, gives a good picture of the way the disease pattern of a society changes as economic development takes place. After allowance has been made for the changing age structure of the population, the male death-rate at all ages in 1947 was 42 per cent of the rate in 1846–50 and the female rate 35 per cent. Maximum improvement was among girls aged 5–9 years whose death-rate in 1947 was 9 per cent of the rate a hundred years before. The death-rate for boys aged 5–9 in 1947 was 11 per cent of the rate in 1846–50. The reduction in total mortality was such that whereas there were 515,591 civilian deaths registered in England and Wales in 1947, the total would have been over a million had the death-rates of 1848–73 still prevailed. In other words, if there had been no improvement in health conditions over half a million more people would have died.

Table 5.1 summarizes the changes that have taken place in the absolute death-rates from the main groups of diseases over the past hundred years. The figures shown in the table are the rates in 1947 expressed as percentages of the corresponding rates in 1848–72. The tremendous decline in mortality from 'mass diseases' is made clear in this table: the death-rate from infectious diseases for women in 1947 being only 9 per cent of what it had been a hundred years before, and that from tuberculosis being only 12 per cent. At the same time there has been a large absolute increase in the number of deaths attributed to 'degenerative diseases': since 1848–72 there has been a ninefold increase in the number of men dying from cancer and a fourfold increase in the number dying from circulatory diseases.

Table 5.1 Death-rates in 1947 (people of all ages) as percentages of corresponding rates in 1848–72

	Males	*Females*
All causes	58	53
Infectious diseases	13	9
Tuberculosis (all forms)	20	12
Diseases of the nervous system and sense organs	34	46
Diseases of the respiratory system	36	27
Diseases of the digestive system	32	23
Non-venereal diseases of the genito-urinary system	186	231
Diseases of the circulatory system	418	328
Cancer	920	377

Source: W. P. D. Logan, 'Mortality in England and Wales from 1848 to 1947', *Population Studies*, IV, 2, 1950.

Up to now we have considered only the death-rates per thousand of the *total* population, which we have called absolute death-rates: now we wish to look at the death-rates per thousand *deaths* from all causes, which we will call the proportionate death-rates. If we concentrate upon these proportionate death-rates and the relative importance of the various causes of death the same pattern emerges. Table 5.2 shows clearly that in 1848–72 about a third of the total number of deaths at all ages were due to infectious diseases: these were followed by diseases of the respiratory system, of the nervous system and of the digestive system. In 1947, on the other hand, diseases of the circulatory system came first with rather more than one-third of the total and these were followed by cancer.

In 1848–72, then, one death in every three in England and Wales was attributed to infectious disease: by 1947 infectious disease caused one male death in fourteen and one female death in seventeen. Within the group of infectious diseases in 1848–72 the highest individual cause of death

Table 5.2 The leading groups of causes of death in England and Wales in 1848–72 and in 1947 (proportionate rates per 1,000 deaths from all causes)

	1848–72		1947	
	Males	*Females*	*Males*	*Females*
1 Infectious diseases	321	338	71	58
2 Respiratory diseases	148	134	91	68
3 Nervous diseases	129	117	76	101
4 Digestive diseases	83	85	45	36
5 Circulatory diseases	53	63	386	394
6 Cancer	9	22	149	161
All causes	1,000	1,000	1,000	1,000

1 Including typhoid, typhus, smallpox, measles, scarlet fever, whooping cough, diphtheria, influenza, cholera, dysentery, tuberculosis, syphilis.
2 Including bronchitis and all forms of pneumonia.
3 Including cerebral haemorrhage, apoplexy, etc.
4 Including ulcer of the stomach and duodenum, diarrhoea and enteritis, appendicitis, and cirrhosis of the liver.
5 Including heart diseases, diseases of the coronary arteries, and angina pectoris.

Source: W. P. D. Logan, 'Mortality in England and Wales from 1848 to 1947', *Population Studies*, IV, 2, 1950.

was respiratory tuberculosis. Scarlet fever and diphtheria came next, followed, in descending order of importance, by typhus, other forms of tuberculosis, smallpox, whooping cough, measles and cholera. By 1947 there had been a striking decline in the proportionate death-rate from infectious disease. Cholera and typhus had disappeared and smallpox and typhoid had, to all intents and purposes, been eliminated as causes of death. The reduction in mortality from scarlet fever was enormous: in 1848–72 it caused one death in twenty-five, in 1947 less than one in every ten thousand.

As the mass diseases were brought under control so the importance of degenerative diseases became clear. In 1848–72 less than one male death in a hundred was attributed to cancer: in 1947 one in seven was due to that disease. The female rates were one in forty-five in 1848–72 and one in six in 1947. Comparable in magnitude with the increase in cancer has been the rise in mortality from diseases of the circulatory system: in 1947 about one male death in ten and one female death in twenty was attributed to one of the diseases in this group, disease of the coronary arteries, a disease practically unknown as a cause of death at the beginning of this century.

The populations of industrial societies have not always had their present characteristics nor always experienced their current patterns of health and disease. When the present-day advanced economies were less complex the societies had demographic and health patterns, very like those current in contemporary modernizing countries. In nineteenth-century Britain the age structure, birth- and death-rates, and the causes of death, all resembled those now recorded in parts of Africa and other non-industrial countries. The British patterns have changed as the society has developed.

In Britain health and disease patterns characteristic of less developed and highly developed societies were separated in time during which the society became increasingly industrial. However, both patterns may be found existing side by side in those societies where a complex economy has been superimposed and as a result industrial and agrarian sectors co-exist. The Republic of South Africa is one country in which the two distinct patterns of disease can be observed co-existing. White South Africans in the cities enjoy the amenities and the health of an affluent industrial society, while in the tribal areas black South Africans retain the living standards and diseases of a non-industrial society. In Johannesburg the birth-, death- and morbidity-rates of the white population resident in the suburbs are similar to those of the population of a middle-class residential area in England. One such prosperous white suburb in Johannesburg is separated by only a main street from the Alexandra location, entirely populated by black South Africans. A study published in 1954 revealed that in the Alexandra location 10 per cent of the infant population died each summer from gastro-enteritis: tuberculosis was rampant and syphilis widespread. The black South Africans in Alexandra live in extreme poverty in overcrowed slums: in 1953 the average family of five members shared one room and lived on an income of about £3 a week.

This contrasting pattern of disease in adjacent neighbourhoods clearly has nothing to do with climate: it can only be explained in terms of the social development of South Africa. The rapid expansion of industry has greatly elevated the living standards of the politically and economically dominant white people. They form less than one-fifth of the total population but retain the ownership and control of industry and monopolize the better paid and more highly desired occupations. About one-tenth of the cultivable land of South Africa is in the hands of the black people who form four-fifths of the total population. Their reserves are overcrowded and impoverished and at any one time 50 to 70 per cent of the adult men are absent working in the mines and factories of the towns or on the farms owned by whites. This large body of unskilled migrants is the main labour force on which the continued expansion of South African industry depends.

This example illustrates the simple and direct relationship between standards of living and health conditions. Another way of demonstrating the same relationship is shown in Table 5.3. Instead of using data from only one society, we have here taken statistics from seventy-four countries in order to build up a broad comparative picture. The seventy-four countries have first been arranged into six groups by level of per capita national income (column A) and the group averages are given for one other rough indicator of economic development (percentage of male labour force in agriculture, column B) and for five indicators of health conditions. Columns C and D indicate the mortality levels in these societies. Column E gives some indication of the availability of health services. Although the lack of medical services in modernizing countries is underlined by these data, the figures none the less tend to exaggerate the general availability of physicians in the poorer countries. Physicians in these societies tend to concentrate in cities and to be more readily available to the rich than to the poor. Columns F and G are indicators of the levels of nutrition in the societies. Calorie intake is a measure of the quantity of the diet. For the maintenance of physical efficiency the daily calorie intake must be between 2,300 and 2,700. The actual level depends upon age and sex, type of activity, environmental temperature, and body weight. The average calorie supplies fall short of basic requirements in all regions of the world except Europe, North America, Australia, New Zealand, and Japan, that is the industrial societies. The calorie deficit in India may be as much as a quarter of the basic requirement. Column G gives an indication of the quality of the diet. Quality of diet depends on the presence in satisfactory amounts and proportions of vitamins and minerals. Animal protein level is probably the best indicator of quality because foods of animal origin are also good sources of protein and in turn of vitamins and minerals. Where the food supply is sufficient in calories it has usually a high protein content as well, whereas where there is a deficiency in calories the total amount of protein is usually small. Where the proportion of total calorie supply furnished by starchy staples exceeds 60 per cent it affords clear evidence that food supplies are nutritionally unbalanced. Such unbalanced diets (deficient in meat, milk, eggs, fish) have serious effects on health.

We have examined here some of the relationships between economic development and health. We have shown how patterns of disease change in one society over time; we have looked at co-existing but contrasting patterns of health within the same

Table 5.3 Health conditions and social development

	A	*B*	*C*	*D*	*E*	*F*	*G*
	National income per capita (1956–8) (average) US $	*Male labour force in agriculture (mid-1956) (est.) per cent*	*Expectation of life at birth in years (1955–8) (average)*	*Infant mortality-rate (1955–8) (average)*	*Inhabitants per physician*	*Calorie consumption per capita per day*	*Starchy staples as proportion of total calories consumed per cent*
Group 1	1,000+	17	70·6	24·9	885	3,153	45
Group 2	575–999	21	67·7	41·9	944	2,944	53
Group 3	350–574	35	65·4	56·9	1,724	2,920	60
Group 4	200–349	53	57·4	97·2	3,132	2,510	74
Group 5	100–199	64	50·0	131·1	5,185	2,240	76
Group 6	Under 100	74	41·7	180·0	13,450	2,070	77

Source: *Report on the World Social Situation*, New York: United Nations, 1961, p. 41.

country; and, finally, we have seen how, in the world at large, there is a correlation between certain indices of economic development and of mortality, health services and nutrition.

Fertility

Fertility in non-industrial societies[2]

A striking feature of agrarian societies is that all of them have much higher levels of fertility than industrial societies. Practically all of the world's 'underdeveloped' countries today, embracing three-quarters of the world's population, still have high birth-rates, that is, more than 30 live births per 1,000 inhabitants per year and more than four births per woman during her reproductive life (usually reckoned as 14–44). The key to the understanding of this well-documented fact is found, oddly enough, in the death-rate. Until recently, death-rates, especially infant mortality-rates, were extremely high in these areas. Agrarian societies therefore would not have survived had their high mortality not been matched by high fertility levels. This is not to say that parents plan to have children *in order to* maintain the total population, but rather that the *unintended* effect of having large families is to counter the large number of deaths. Probably many societies in the past failed to survive, their members dying faster than they could be replaced. Between 1900 and 1950, for example, it is estimated that nearly a hundred tribes became extinct in Brazil. The Kaingang from the State of São Paulo numbered 1,200 in 1912 but today have dwindled to 80; the Munduruku were 20,000 in 1925—in 1950 they numbered 1,200; the Kayapo of the river Araguaya were 2,500 in 1902 and 10 in 1950. The fate of the North American Indian is well known. The societies we know about today are necessarily the ones that did survive. They did so because they evolved (without any deliberation or planning) a social structure with a built-in system of incentives strong enough to induce their people to reproduce abundantly. If death-rates are very high a society which does not develop such an institutional structure may face extinction.

In analysing the institutional factors responsible for high fertility one must begin with the family, for the family in all human societies performs the functions of bearing, rearing, nourishing, and socializing children. In our society, as in all urban-industrial societies, the typical family consists of parents and their young or unmarried children. We shall call such a structure a 'conjugal' family. Such a family comes into existence with the birth of a first child in marriage; it continues to grow by the birth of other children; it undergoes partial dissolution as the children leave it, perhaps to set up households elsewhere, and comes to an end with the death of the parents. Sometimes, however, parents and children live in the same household or dwelling with other related people. A not uncommon arrangement in our society, particularly in stable working-class areas, is for grandparents to live with a married daughter and her children. In some respects this is paralleled among the Bemba of Zambia where a domestic group consisting of a man and his wife with their daughters and the husbands and children of the latter is found. The group breaks up, and new groups of the same kind are formed, when a man obtains permission to leave his parents-in-law, taking his wife and children with him. Far more prevalent in primitive and agrarian societies is what is sometimes called a patrilocal extended family: this is formed when sons remain in their father's family group bringing their wives to live with them so that their children also belong to the group. The household in all these instances consists of a kinship group larger than the conjugal family. We shall call such a grouping of related people living together as one unit a 'corporate' family. Living together in this way is not simply a matter of dwelling arrangements but also of economic solidarity and social control. One way of looking at the family in simple and agrarian societies is to see the conjugal family as being less independent of the wider kinship structure than it is in industrial societies. Its formation through marriage, its economic position, and the behaviour of its members are all governed to a greater degree by elder relatives. In most pre-industrial societies such control is facilitated by the 'joint-household' which arises when the newly married couple are required to live with the parents of one or the other partner. But a conjugal family may, although not occupying the same household with relatives, share so much of their daily lives that they and their relatives do in effect constitute one domestic unit, one 'composite' family. We use the term corporate family to apply as much to a wider kinship group living together thus as we do to a conjugal family and relatives who are occupying the same household all the time (the 'joint-household'). Again the Bemba provide a good example of the composite family: here the corporate family is composed of separate conjugal families housed in huts in the same village and not fenced off in any way from the rest of the community; but because the daughters' households are so closely linked with that of their mother, it must be reckoned as forming one domestic unit.

Given that in non-industrial societies the corporate family is typical, several consequences follow which are conducive to high fertility. Age at marriage is young because there is no implication that the husband must be able to support a wife and family before he gets married. Marriage is in no way made contingent on the possession of separate property by the newly married pair. In the patrilocal joint-household the bride simply joins her husband's family and the groom continues to live there. The bride can contribute to the joint economy even though young, and the groom is not required to be financially independent. In India in 1891 nearly a fifth of all girls below 15 years of age and 89 per cent of those aged 15–19, had been married. Even in 1951 nearly 10 per cent of Indian girls under 15 and three-quarters of those 15–19 had been married. In countries like Korea and Turkey practically no women between the ages of 20 and 24 are single. Early marriage represents the maximum possible insurance against the possibility of the disappearance of the family line in societies where not only is the annual death-rate high but the danger of sudden catastrophic increases in mortality is ever present. If the age of entry into marriage is late, the potential fertility that is lost may never be recovered: other things being equal, the younger the age at marriage, the higher the ultimate fertility.

In societies where the corporate family system prevails, marriages are usually arranged by the elders who make the arrangements early in the lifetime of the prospective mates. It is not difficult to see why this occurs. If the system is one of patrilocal residence, for example, a grown daughter remaining in her parental home is an anomaly. Her presence runs counter to the normal division of labour by sex which assumes the complementarity of husband and wife. Moreover, she must adjust to the wives of her brothers coming into the household. The daughters, then, must be married off as early as possible. Moreover, the daughter is most in demand as a prospective wife when she is young not only because she then has a greater potential fertility ahead of her and is more attractive sexually but also because she fits more easily into a subordinate status in her husband's parental home.

The corporate family system also encourages the early marriage of sons. The authority of the elders continues after marriage in China, India, rural Africa and many other agrarian areas. The father in China, for example, maintains his authority over his married sons and over the family property until death. The marriage of his sons is not, therefore, a threat to his authority and consequently he has no incentive for postponing the marriage. On the contrary, his authority is extended when his son brings a wife into his household and when she has children. Moreover, a marriage represents an alliance with another family and strengthens the position of the family in the wider community. The necessity of getting one's children married is an essential means of extending one's lineage and is frequently viewed as a religious and moral obligation. Consequently fewer persons go through life without marrying in agrarian than in urban-industrial societies. In India in 1891 a higher proportion of women aged 20–4 had been married (97·3 per cent) than were ever married at all in Western European countries. It is mainly in urban-industrial societies that the proportion of women never marrying by the end of the reproductive period exceeds 10 per cent. In Sweden in 1945 the figure was as high as 20·9 per cent, in Switzerland in 1941 20·1 per cent, in England in 1931 16·8 per cent and in Belgium in 1930 13·3 per cent. In non-industrial societies a very different picture emerges. In India in 1931 it was only 0·6 per cent, in Ceylon in 1946 3·4 per cent, in Malaya in 1947 3·3 per cent.

Once married the young couple in non-industrial societies are motivated to have offspring as early as possible and in considerable number. The economic cost of rearing children does not impinge directly on the parents to the extent it does in those societies where the conjugal family system prevails. With a common household and economy the child draws upon the resources of the kinship group as a whole not upon the parents' income alone. The inconvenience and effort of child care do not fall so heavily on the parents alone. The corporate family enables young mothers to work long hours in handicraft or in the fields while older women or older children look after the infants. The young married woman has every incentive to have children. She arrives in the patrilocal family as a stranger among her husband's relatives; her newness and her youth ensure her a low position in the family hierarchy. The birth of a son proves her contribution to her husband's line, gives her extra standing in her husband's eyes, and improves her status in the family as a whole. The corporate family rewards not only the mother's but also the father's reproduction. Numerous children help to strengthen the family as well as ensuring the continuation of the patrilineage. The household gains economic and political strength by the sheer weight of numbers: further, the more children the parents have the greater the security for their old age.

The roles of men and women tend to be sharply segregated in traditional agrarian societies. Women are confined to the household and to agricultural tasks of a menial kind and their lives revolve around home and children. There are no other careers open to them. The childbearing and rearing role is their main role. Moreover, women have a subordinate status in most agrarian societies. Although they may resent the physical burden and danger of childbearing the husband is unlikely to co-operate in any way to limit the size of the family. The husband usually views reproduction as his prerogative involving simple compliance on the wife's part.

This type of family structure is well adapted to a peasant mode of life. Apart from land, human labour is the main instrument of production. Hence the larger the family, the more labour is available. To learn the skills involved in this work no formal education is required: all that is necessary is observation and practice. Children can start earning a living at a very early age. Women can work in the fields and in the household handicrafts without much hindrance from constant childbearing.

In attempting to explain why fertility is so high in non-industrial societies it has been necessary to focus upon the social structure and in particular the family structure of these societies. It is, of course, true that most agrarian societies do not have the necessary technology to produce effective means of chemical or mechanical birth control. Some of them lack even elementary knowledge of the physiology of reproduction; others do not possess enough knowledge of chemistry to give command over materials. Where techniques of contraception are employed (usually in extra-marital sexual intercourse) the methods tend to be hit-or-miss with folklore, rather than science, guiding the choice of means. Even the methods that would actually accomplish contraception are apt to be clumsy, sexually unsatisfactory, or even unhealthy. The technology and economy of pre-industrial societies are not equal to the task of producing chemical or mechanical contraceptives which would be at once cheap, readily available, effective, and satisfactory. But although techniques like withdrawal, intercourse without penetration, and heterosexual 'perversions', which are not dependent upon scientific and technological progress, are known and practised in nearly all societies, they do not represent major forms of fertility control in underdeveloped areas. The fundamental reason why fertility is so high in agrarian societies is that people are not motivated to limit the size of their families; the institutional structure provides incentives for having many children not for practising birth control.

However, almost all non-industrial societies practise abortion and infanticide as means of reducing the number of children at certain times—for example when food is short and the family is faced with starvation, or when the family is forced to migrate, either to escape from attack or to find new supplies of food, and only those who can be transported can survive. Abortion and infanticide have the advantage over contraception that they are always effective. At time of intercourse there is always the chance that pregnancy will not occur, and if events subsequent to intercourse make the birth of a child undesirable abortion or infanticide are effective remedies. Infanticide, of course, has the especial advantage over contraception that it allows children to be selected. In many underdeveloped societies it was the practice to kill or to allow to die many more female than male children. Infanticide allows offspring to be selected according to physical characteristics, weeding out those with deformities, bad health, or other unacceptable characteristics. Sometimes infanticide is practised when the circumstances of birth are considered abnormal and taboo. Twins, children born by breech birth, or on unlucky days, are typical victims.

The decline of fertility in industrial societies

The contrast between the fertility levels of industrial and non-industrial societies is very marked. This contrast can be illustrated by comparing the crude birth-rates of selected countries around 1955.

(a) Non-industrial societies

Ceylon	37·8
India	40
Malaya	43·5
Burma	45

Egypt	45
Ecuador	45
Mexico	45·9
Venezuela	46·6
Pakistan	50
Philippines	50
Guatemala	50·5

Range 38–50 live births per 1,000 population

(*b*) *Industrial societies*

United Kingdom	15·6
Belgium	16·7
Denmark	17·5
Netherlands	21·6
Australia	22·7
New Zealand	24·6
Norway	18·6
Sweden	14·9
USA	25·2

Range 15–25 live births per 1,000 population

The societies now characterized by low birth-rates formerly had far higher rates. In Scandinavia where birth-rate data are available for the longest period, the birth-rate averaged 31–4 per 1,000 between 1733 and 1800. With minor fluctuations the crude birth-rate was maintained at this level until after 1870. Between 1880 and 1884 the average crude birth-rates in these societies were:

England and Wales	33·82
Belgium	31·09
Denmark	32·26
Netherlands	35·01
Australia	35·09
New Zealand	37·57
Norway	30·83
Sweden	29·35
USA	36

The long-term decline of the birth-rate is one of the most complex problems in the demography of industrialized societies. The decline is known to have begun early in the nineteenth century in both the USA and France. In Sweden a slight downward trend became apparent during the first half of the nineteenth century, and in Ireland the birth-rate seems to have declined since around 1850. In the other industrializing countries the decline probably began later. For most countries it is not possible to determine the exact date at which decline began as the birth-rate fluctuated considerably from year to year and the registration of births was unreliable.

In most of the now industrial countries the level of the birth-rate in the 1870s was around 30 per 1,000 or higher. The downward trend began around 1880 and continued without any significant interruptions up to 1914. This decline proceeded at a rather modest pace up to 1900 but thereafter it became more pronounced. At the outbreak of the first world war the birth-rate had declined to less than 25 per 1,000 in all the now industrialized countries except Finland, Germany, the Netherlands and the countries of Southern Europe. The first world war saw a sharp decline in the birth-rate particularly in countries most directly affected by the war, such as Belgium, France, Germany and Italy where the birth-rate was reduced by 1919 to around 50 per cent of the pre-war level. The separation of men from their homes and families prevented many marriages and many births within existing marriages. In other countries like Finland, Britain, New Zealand and Switzerland, the decline was more moderate but still amounted to around 20–25 per cent. In Australia, Denmark, the Netherlands, Sweden, and the USA, there was only a minor decline.

Immediately after the war a brief period of recovery in the birth-rate was experienced in all countries. The peak rates were experienced in 1920 or 1921: but by 1923–4 the level of the birth-rate in all industrial societies was below the pre-war level. By the early 1930s the crude birth-rates were:

United Kingdom	15·8
Belgium	17·6
Denmark	17·9
Australia	17·6
New Zealand	17·5
Norway	15·7
Sweden	14·4
USA	19·7

The widespread economic depression with its accompanying unemployment and the general political instability of the 1930s acted as a deterrent to marriage and to childbirth. The lowest birth-rates observed between the two world wars in any of the industrialized societies occurred in Austria (12·8 in 1937) and in Sweden (13·7 in 1939). However, in southern Europe, Canada and the Netherlands the birth-rate did not fall appreciably below 20 per 1,000.

The break in the downward trend appeared first in northern Europe and Oceania around 1935: in central and southern Europe and North America the decline in the birth-rate continued until 1936 or 1937 and in Spain and Portugal until

1941. The birth-rates remained fairly stable for several years and even the outbreak of the second world war did not introduce a sharp decline in rates. Indeed rates began to rise noticeably in most European countries even while the fighting continued; the 'recovery' of the birth-rate was well under way by 1942 and 1943. The different patterns of development of the birth-rate during the two war periods were due to the fact that the general level and the underlying long-term trends of the birth-rate were different. Whereas the fluctuations around the first world war were superimposed upon a generally declining trend in an often still very high birth-rate, the trend around the second world war was almost stationary or showed even a slight increase in a very low rate. The average birth-rate for the period 1939–45 was, in most industrial countries, above the pre-war level.

The peak in the 'recovery' of the birth-rate after the 1930s was reached in most advanced societies in 1946 or 1947: the birth-rate at this point had not been as high since the years immediately following the 1914–18 war. Indeed in Finland and New Zealand an equally high rate had not been recorded since before 1914 and for the Netherlands it is necessary to go back to 1900 to find a birth-rate as high as that recorded for the period 1946–50. Since the early post-war years, however, the birth-rate has again declined in most countries: in Denmark, Britain, the Netherlands, and Sweden it declined by 25–30 per cent from the post-war peak of 1947 to 1954. In Australia the birth-rate has fallen from 23·6 per 1,000 in 1946 to 19·4 in 1967. The slight 'recovery' of the birth-rate in industrial societies from some time in the late thirties to about 1947 is likely to be a result of people getting married earlier and of a higher proportion of people getting married rather than of any increase in completed family size.

Why has there been a long-term decline in the birth-rate? Why has the general level of fertility fallen as the societies become increasingly urban and industrial? The answer lies in the ever increasing proportion of the population within these societies adopting the practice of family limitation by contraception. It is, of course, theoretically possible that there has been some decline in the physical capacity of men and women to produce children in industrial societies. It has been suggested that various factors in urban-industrial life have reduced reproductive capacity: increase in alcoholism and in venereal disease, employment of women in factories, excessive practice of sports by women, frequent bathing with soap (an effective spermicide), even bicycle riding (reputed to harm the female reproductive organs) have been mentioned. It has also been alleged that the nervous strain of modern life lowers the intensity of sexual energies and thus reduces the frequency of intercourse. Such arguments need not be taken seriously. All the evidence points to a decline in alcoholism and venereal disease since the eighteenth century: no one has attempted to show how women's sports or employment in factories lessen reproductive capacity. As for bicycle riding, this practice is most common in the Netherlands which has the highest birth-rate in Western Europe. Certain features of modern industrial societies have probably *improved* reproductive potentialities—better health, better nutrition, increased knowledge of the reproductive process, better obstetrical care. Women certainly suffer less from serious deformities of the pelvis than in the past and this must to some extent have increased their capacity to have children. In fact the inquiry into family limitation and human fertility carried out by Dr E. Lewis-Faning for the Royal Commission on Population (1949) demonstrated convincingly that present-day couples in Britain would experience no difficulty in having as many children as Victorian parents had if they so desired. The overwhelming weight of the evidence supports the view that family size has declined in industrial societies as a result of the deliberate use of birth control techniques. The salient factor in the secular decline of the birth-rate over the past hundred years has been a radical change in attitude towards parenthood. People no longer wish to have the large families which were customary in pre-industrial society.

In attempting to explain this phenomenon the experience of England and Wales may be taken as generally illustrative of that of Western Europe, the United States and other industrial societies. It is important to emphasize that the fall in family size has not proceeded uniformly throughout all sections of society. It began first and continued most rapidly among the highest socio-economic groups. The earliest signs of a decline in fertility in England took place among the families of military and naval officers, clergymen, lawyers, doctors, authors, journalists and architects. Not far behind them came civil service officers and clerks, law clerks, dentists, schoolmasters, teachers, professors and lecturers, people employed in scientific pursuits, and accountants. In general the decline in family size in England began as an upper- and middle-class phenomenon at some time in the 1870s. It was not until much later that the decline occurred in less privileged social groups. The inverse relationship between income and fertility is still marked today. Persons in the more highly paid, more desired, and more difficult to enter occupations have smaller families than people in the lower income and status positions: 'the rich get rich and the poor get children'.

During the period 1850–70 there was a very marked increase in the number of middle-class people in England. The number of occupations with middle-range incomes increased enormously. Proportionately more people than in the past were able to afford to live in the middle-class manner. They felt secure and looked forward to ever increasing prosperity and progress. Such optimism gave rise to ever increasing aspirations. The rise in real incomes made higher levels of living possible for the successful and the necessary status symbols of the middle class became increasingly elaborate and expensive. Larger houses, costly food and wine, more servants, carriages, expensive furniture, travel, holidays abroad—these were becoming the marks of middle-class living. This period was also a period of marked social mobility: people from lower-class origins were moving into middle-class occupations. The display of material possessions emphasized the achievement of new status. Then came the so-called great depression of 1870–90. Although the middle-class standard of living was never seriously threatened during this period most people who gained the public ear talked as though it was. The feeling of increasing prosperity, the confidence of the 1850s and 1860s, was shattered. In this situation the members of the middle class chose deliberately to reduce the size of their families rather than give up their newly acquired taste for those material comforts which had become a recognized part of their style of life.

The growing emphasis on personal achievement led to increased preoccupation with the competitive nature of life. It was felt necessary to struggle to keep one's job and one's position in the social hierarchy. Children came to be regarded as a liability, as a severe handicap in the race up the status ladder. The number of children had to be limited, not only because expenditure on them handicapped parents in their own efforts to maintain a middle-class style of life, but also because the fewer the children the more could be spent on each child and the better the start in the competitive struggle the child would have. By 1870 'giving the children a good start in life' was becoming an increasingly expensive affair. It meant providing a long and costly education. The qualifications for entering medicine and the law were tightened. Patronage in the army and the civil service was abolished making entry now by competitive examination. Entrance to the professions thus became more formal and easier to understand. This widened the field and made parents doubly anxious to provide the education necessary for their sons to enter the 'gentlemanly' jobs. It is not surprising that this period marks the great expansion of public school education. Nor is it difficult to see why the idea that children were sent by God gave way to the notion that it was not immoral to prevent them from coming if their future prospects, as members of the middle class, were less bright than those of their parents had been.

Once the process of family limitation got under way it became one of self-sustained momentum. The gap between those with large families and those with small families widened and the advantages of family planning became obvious. For women the advantages were considerable. It freed them from the perpetual risk, burden, and inconvenience of childbirth and child rearing. It enabled them to take advantage of the increasing opportunities to make a career outside the home. The use of birth control was thus a factor in the emancipation of women: at the same time the changing power position of women, and their attainment of greater equality with men, was one of the factors furthering the decline of the birth-rate.

In Britain manual workers were slow to follow the middle classes in adopting family limitation. Although a few skilled workers were enjoying rising wages in the last decade of the nineteenth century, about a third of the total population of the industrial cities was living in poverty. Poverty and overcrowding are not conducive to the foresight and planning which contraception involves: nor are they the conditions which favour a break from tradition and the introduction of new practices. The subordinate role of the manual worker's wife tended to make her feel helpless at the prospect of successive unwanted pregnancies and unable to take the necessary steps to prevent them in the face of opposition from a husband who might regard the use of contraception as a threat to his virility. The separate and largely segregated activities of members of manual workers' families defined children as the wife's responsibility. Husbands paid over a fixed wage to their wives who had to do the best they could with it. The increasing affluence of the manual worker since 1950 has been accompanied by the predictable decline in family size.

Sometimes the fall in family size is explained entirely as the consequence of the improvement and increased dissemination of contraceptives and contraceptive knowledge. Yet sheer knowledge of a technique and its easy availability are not enough to induce people to use it: people will only make use of a technique if it serves their needs. Increased contraceptive knowledge and improved methods of contraception have clearly been a major *means* of limiting fertility since 1870, but the *causes* of family limitation must be sought in the changes in social structure which led to attitudes favourable to smaller families.

Ageing of populations

With few exceptions, every society has persons of all ages in it, but societies differ from one another in their age composition (that is, in the proportion of the total population found in each age group). Where these differences are large they may be of great importance both as factors limiting further demographic changes and also in influencing social and economic development.

Table 5.4 The age structures of different types of society

Country	*Year*	*Age composition of the population (% of total in each age group)* 0–14	15–44	45–64	65+
Non-industrial societies					
Guatemala	1950	44	43	11	2
India	1951	37	46	13	4
Egypt	1947	38	45	14	3
Highly industrialized societies					
Britain	1951	22	43	24	11
Sweden	1950	23	43	23	11
Austria	1951	23	40	26	11
Transitional industrializing societies					
Britain	1851	35	46	14	5
	1901	32	48	15	5
Sweden	1850	33	46	16	5
	1900	33	42	17	8
Austria	1869	34	46	16	4
	1900	34	45	16	5

Source: *The Aging of Populations*, Population Studies, No. 26, New York: United Nations, 1956.

Table 5.4 shows the age distribution of different types of societies in the middle of the twentieth century and of some highly developed countries in the past. By comparison the highly industrialized societies have low percentages of children, high percentages of old people, and a relatively large intermediate age group (sometimes called 'the working age group', 15–64). As far as we know, the age structure of the non-industrial societies has undergone little change in the past hundred years or more. In the now highly developed countries the age structure has, by contrast, undergone marked changes during the last fifty to a hundred years. The direction of this change has been an increase in the proportion of elderly people and a decline in the proportion of children. This process is known as the ageing of the population. In France, for example, the proportion of persons over sixty-five has increased from 6·5 per cent of the total population in 1851 to 11·8 per cent in 1950; Belgium the increase has been from 5·9 per cent in 1846 to 10·7 per cent in 1947; and in the United States the percentage has changed from 3·4 per cent in 1880 to 8·1 per cent in 1950. The present differences between the industrial and non-industrial countries can be put in this way: in France one person in eight is over sixty-four, in Sweden and Britain one in ten and in the United States one in twelve; whereas in Guatemala only one person in fifty is as old as that and in Ghana only one in sixty-six. In France, England, and Sweden half of the population is over thirty-three, thirty-six and thirty-seven respectively: in Pakistan, on the other hand, half of the population is under eighteen, in Brazil under nineteen, and in the Congo under twenty.

What accounts for these differences and these trends in the age distribution of populations? The age structure of a population is governed by demographic factors alone, at least directly. Although it is true that demographic variables are themselves influenced by the social structure, it is through the demographic variables that the social structure affects the age composition. Or to put it a different way, it is only to the extent that changes in social structure produce changes in births, deaths, or migrations that they modify the age structure. The demographic variables—fertility, mortality, migration—may be regarded as independent, at least within a certain range of variation. Changes in fertility may take place without any variation in mortality, and vice versa. Similarly, changes in reproductive behaviour may occur without affecting migratory movements. It is evident, however, that all these variations are independent only within certain limits. If the death-rate in a country with a high level of fertility declines steadily, there will be an increase in population such that sooner or later fertility will decline in turn. Accordingly it may be said that this decline in fertility is not independent of the decline in mortality. It is easy to conceive of situations in which variations in mortality and fertility would ultimately give rise to migratory movements. However, before the stage is reached at which movements are necessarily interdependent, there will be a period when mortality, fertility and migrations may vary independently of one another.

The problem to be solved may therefore be stated as follows: if two of the three factors are held constant, what effect will the variations of the third have on age structure? Let us confine ourselves to a particular example, the population of Britain. There is a long series of good censuses, equally spaced in time, which provide the necessary data. In the last hundred years both fertility and mortality have declined substantially. Mortality has declined since the end of the eighteenth century, though the decline has been most rapid since 1900. Fertility declined from 1870 to the 1930s, then rose slightly, and now appears to be at a level slightly above the 1930s' point. Migration can be ignored here since it has not occurred on a scale large enough to affect significantly the age structure of Britain. The influence of fertility on age composition must now be separated from that of mortality. This can be done by first taking the actual age structure of Britain in 1861 and in 1951, as revealed by the census. Two hypothetical populations are then calculated. The first is the population of Britain in 1951 as it would have been had fertility remained constant at the 1861 level while mortality followed its actual course between 1861 and 1951. The second projection is based on the assumption that mortality remained constant at the 1861 level while fertility followed its actual course.

The resulting age structures are shown in Table 5.5. From this it is clear that the main factor responsible for the ageing of populations is declining fertility. The fall in the birth-rate from the 1870s, if experienced without any change in death-rates, would have led to a trend in age structure following somewhat closely that which actually occurred (cf. columns 4 and 2). Had the mortality decline of the last hundred years been experienced without any change in fertility the proportion of children in the population would have remained much higher and the proportion of aged persons would have been much lower (cf. columns 3 and 2). The effect of a decline in mortality alone would have been to keep the age structure much as it was in 1861 (cf. columns 3 and 1). The reduction of mortality, to which ageing of populations has so often been attributed, does in fact lead to rejuvenation not ageing. The reason for this is that the decline in mortality has been very much a decline in infant and childhood mortality, with relatively little improvement at older ages. Thus the population of Britain has become older since 1861 because of falling fertility; but falling mortality (with its tendency to produce a younger population) has prevented it from becoming older still.

Table 5.5 Age structures of Great Britain, 1861 and 1951 (per cent)

Age	*Actual 1861 census*	*Actual 1951 census*	*Hypothetical 1951: projected from 1861 on assumptions of (a) fertility constant at 1861 level (b) actual mortality 1861–1951*	*Hypothetical 1951: projected from 1861 on assumptions of (a) mortality constant at 1861 level (b) actual fertility 1861–1951*
0–14	35·68	22·38	39·07	20·87
15–59	56·83	61·93	53·71	63·85
60+	7·49	15·69	7·22	15·28

Source: N. H. Carrier, 'Demographic aspects of the ageing of the population', in A. T. Welford *et al.*, *Society*, London: Routledge & Kegan Paul, 1962, pp. 457–68.

Every individual inexorably gets older as time passes. How old he gets depends on how long he avoids death. Populations, on the other hand, can get older or younger. They get older primarily as the result of declining fertility, and younger primarily as the result of rising fertility. It is the small number of children born per woman that explains the high average age found in industrial countries and the high birth-rate of non-industrial countries that accounts for their young populations.

There has been a widespread tendency to exaggerate the effects of ageing of populations.[3] The increase in the proportion of old people in highly developed societies has been considered the cause of many social problems which are, in fact, the result of other changes in social structure. Much of the alarm about ageing is unjustified. The recent rise in the birth-rate in all industrial societies will lead gradually to a decline in the proportion of old people, unless some epoch-making discovery, like a cure for cancer, reduces mortality in the old age groups. The talk about 'the crippling burden of old age' ignores the fact that the youthful age structure of non-industrial societies entails a very high rate of population growth and is concomitant with a large dependent child population.

Whether the aged constitute a problem depends not so much upon their number as on their social situation. All societies assign status, ascribed rights and duties, according to age. In simple societies and in agrarian societies the aged command great respect and power. In traditional societies like ancient China and India, the old had greater authority and prestige than any other age group. In an illiterate society where knowledge depends on memory and habit, the old are the wise ones. In a relatively static society where learning is traditional the old are more proficient than the young: their accumulated knowledge is not displaced by new techniques, new theories, new facts. 'With the ancient is wisdom, and in length of days understanding.' In a society in which the corporate family is the norm the head of the family has great authority. His authority extends over a wide kinship group and is buttressed by his close and long association with other members of the family since their infancy. This creates in them ingrained habits of respect and subordination towards him. In ancient China the family religion (incorporating so-called ancestor-worship) also bolstered the position of the aged. Respect for the aged while alive was closely akin to worship of them after death. In traditional agrarian societies the aged are no problem: they are not pitied or shoved aside, and are not treated as objects of charity and special concern. Their status is very high. An old Chinese proverb puts the matter clearly, 'My father is all-wise but my father's father is even wiser.'

It is only in a changing, mobile, urban, industrial society that birth-rates fall so markedly as to produce ageing of the population. At the same time this type of society also alters the status of the aged. It makes them obsolescent, useless, insecure. For in highly industrialized societies the emphasis is on change, innovation, new ideas, new techniques, new knowledge, new skills. The sheer speed of social change puts a premium on flexibility, on the recency of what has been learnt: and hence the whole emphasis is on youth. The old, with habits and fundamental notions acquired forty years or more ago are out-of-date. What was new and revolutionary forty years ago is regarded as antiquated and conservative today.

An important feature of industrial societies which helps to make the aged a social problem is the conjugal family system—the type of family in which husband, wife, and children live apart as a separate unit and have a high degree of independence from parents and other relatives. This conjugal family structure excludes aged parents because by the time the parents have reached an advanced age the children have gone out to found independent homes of their own. Aged parents must therefore live by themselves or with other old people. In the United States in 1940 only 9·4 per cent of men, and only 20·7 per cent of women aged 70–4 were living in the home of a son or daughter. In interpreting this data it must be realized that, on the average, each old person has more than one grown-up offspring with whom he could live. Even if all persons aged seventy or over lived with a son or daughter, this would still mean that relatively few married couples would have an older person living with them. The spatial and mental separation of parents from children is heightened in industrial society by the fact that the fertile period in each woman's life is tending to begin and end earlier. Women have their first child earlier than was usual in the nineteenth century, and they tend to have all they are going to have at an earlier age, usually before they reach thirty. Thus not only are parents having fewer children but they are experiencing a longer period of life after their children have become independent. The isolation of aged parents from their children is aggravated by the high level of geographical mobility, which often separates parents and children by hundreds of miles, and by the high degree of social mobility which often places parents and children in different social worlds. This high degree of geographical and social mobility is a concomitant of a high degree of industrialization.

Bureaucratization and the shift to large-scale organizations also affect the status of the aged. In farming and in small businesses the owner, as he gets older, can gradually reduce the amount of his work and confine himself increasingly to a supervisory role. He can ease off at his own discretion; he can retire gradually. But in the large enterprise emphasis is placed on efficiency, on standardized bureaucratic rules, and on impersonality. Such conditions preclude gradual retirement. A rigid retirement age is fixed and the change is abrupt and taken without regard to individual capacity. An individual is suddenly separated from his work. Despite a lifetime's experience, he is of no more use. Even before retiring age, the speed of economic change in highly industrial societies creates difficulties for the older worker. Structural changes in industrial employment, a necessary and fundamental feature of highly developed societies, affect the older worker far more than the younger. Older workers will have specialized skills or certain routines which if they become obsolescent are not easily discarded. Younger workers are more easily retrained—and are more readily accepted for retraining—than older men. They also tend to be more adaptable and mobile. Older people are likely to have built up strong ties within a community which act as a deterrent to moving to new developing areas. Unemployment statistics reveal that workers over forty have much longer durations of unemployment than younger men.

It is often argued that an ageing population will produce a conservative society: that economic, cultural, and political progress is retarded where the population is composed of a relatively large proportion of aged persons. This might be true if the aged had more power than other groups in industrial societies. In fact they seem to be one of the most powerless groups—unable, indeed, even to secure for themselves a reasonable standard of living. But quite apart from these considerations, the world's most conservative regions are those with a very young population, the non-industrial countries. In India, for example, the greatest justification for any practice has always been that it was always done that way in the past. The kind of society that can reduce its fertility to the point where there is a great proportion of old people in the population is necessarily a developing society. It must have cities, industrial technology, and science: it must be a constantly changing society.

The Royal Commission on Population (1949) argued that ageing of populations restricts social mobility:[4]

> In the nineteenth century the older and more experienced workers were relatively scarce. A high proportion of them obtained superior positions, and promotion tended to take place at relatively young ages. Nowadays the seniors are considerably thicker on the ground; other things being equal, there would not be the same pressure to promote young men, and a larger proportion would tend to miss promotion altogether. With still further ageing the competition for promotion must be expected to increase. . . . the tendency will be for only the most exceptional of the younger people to be promoted. The prospects for the younger may become so poor that a powerful sense of frustration may arise.

This paragraph contains a whole series of fallacious statements. It may well be true that if the top posts in a hierarchy were filled by persons chosen at random from the population, a society with a high proportion of old people would be more likely to have elderly leaders than a population with a low proportion of old people. But whether posts are filled by young persons or old persons depends upon the way in which office-holders are recruited. It also depends on whether the number of such posts is stationary, declining, or increasing. In an expanding economy where the demand for doctors, engineers, managers, teachers, and other high level people is increasing, the number of opportunities for promotion and social mobility will also increase. A highly industrial society is characterized by an increasing middle class and by a high rate of social mobility. In such a society the prospects for social mobility are far greater than in a non-industrial society with a young population. After all, the very process of ageing implies that the proportion of young people is declining: this should surely reduce competition among the young not increase frustration.

Another conceivable consequence of an ageing population is the economic drain of old-age dependency. In sheer numbers, however, the increased proportion of the aged has been counterbalanced by a decreased proportion of dependent children. Compared with 'under-developed' societies, industrial societies are in an advantageous position so far as the ratio of economically active (15–64 age group) to dependent age groups (0–14, and over 64) is concerned. Of course the weight of the dependency burden is determined not only by the ratio of dependants but also on the amount spent for the support of each dependant. Thus a reduction in the proportion of children in the society does not necessarily mean a proportionate decrease in the costs of childhood dependency. Children may be given better and longer education, improved medical care, better diet. The essential point to be remembered is that those societies which have a low proportion of children and a high proportion of old people are those with the highest productivity and the highest national income per capita. These societies can afford to carry a high burden of dependency, and they have, indeed, raised the standard of what is considered appropriate for children and for old people—higher levels of nutrition, education, housing, and medical care.

Notes

1 This section is based on Kingsley Davis, 'The world's population crisis' in Robert K. Merton and Robert Nisbet (eds), *Contemporary Social Problems* (3rd ed.), 1971, pp. 363–405.

2 This section is based on Kingsley Davis, 'Institutional patterns favoring high fertility in underdeveloped areas', *Eugenics Quarterly*, 2, 1 March 1955, pp. 33–9.

3 This section is based on Kingsley Davis and J. W. Combs, 'The sociology of an aging population', in *The Social and Biological Challenge of our Aging Population*, Proceedings of the Eastern States Health Education Conference, 1949. New York, 1950, pp. 146–70.

4 *Report of the Royal Commission on Population*, (Cmd 7695), London: HMSO, 1949, pp. 119–20.

Reading

Banks, J. A., *Prosperity and Parenthood*, London: Routledge & Kegan Paul, 1954. An excellent sociological study of family planning among the Victorian middle classes.

Cipolla, Carlo, *The Economic History of World Population*, Harmondsworth: Penguin, 1962. Brief, inexpensive, and valuable.

Davis, Kingsley and Blake, Judith, 'Social structure and fertility: an analytic framework' in *Sociology, The Progress of a Decade*, edited by S. M. Lipset and N. J. Smelser, pp. 356–77, Englewood Cliffs: Prentice-Hall, 1961 and the Bobbs-Merrill Reprint Series in the Social Sciences, S–371. Another of the many excellent articles by Kingsley Davis on the sociology of population.

Freedman, Ronald (ed.), *Population, The Vital Revolution*, New York: Doubleday Anchor, 1964. A well-chosen selection of short essays by leading American demographers.

Petersen, William, *Population*, London: Collier-Macmillan, 1969 (2nd ed.). In many ways the best textbook. Students will have no difficulty in recognizing those sections which are marred by Petersen's commitment to US capitalism.

Wrong, Dennis H., *Population and Society*, New York: Random House, 1967 (3rd ed.), The best short introduction to the sociology of population: includes a useful chapter on migration.

Further reading

Birmingham, W. B., Neustadt, I., and Omaboe, E. M. (eds), *A Study of Contemporary Ghana, Volume II: Some Aspects of Social Structure*, London: Allen & Unwin, 1967. The first four chapters on population, pp. 17–200 by Dr J. C. Caldwell are outstanding: one of the best studies of the population of a non-industrial society.

Davis, Kingsley, *The Population of India and Pakistan*, Princeton University Press, 1951. The other outstanding study of the population of an underdeveloped area.

Hawthorn, Geoffrey, *The Sociology of Fertility*, London: Collier-Macmillan, 1970. A stimulating critical review of the literature with an excellent annotated bibliography.

McKeown, Thomas, *Medicine in Modern Society*, London: Allen & Unwin, 1965. Part I, pp. 21–58, is the best discussion of the decline of mortality and population growth in England and Wales 1750–1900.

Susser, M. W. and Watson, W., *Sociology in Medicine*, London: Oxford University Press, 1971 (2nd ed.). The first chapter, pp. 1–54, contains much useful data.

The Department of Economic and Social Affairs (formerly the Department of Social Affairs) of the United Nations Organization, New York, has been responsible for the publication of many admirable studies of population. Students will find *Preliminary Report on the World Social Situation* (1952), and *Report on the World Social Situation* (1957, 1961, 1963, 1967, 1970) extremely useful. *The Determinants and Consequences of Population Trends* (1953) is a very thorough and lucid summary of all the important theories and facts about population up to 1952. *The Aging of Populations and its Economic and Social Implications* (1956) and *Recent Trends of Fertility in Industrialized Countries* (1957) are useful. *A Summary of the World Population Situation in 1970* (1971) is a very brief (36 page) survey of the field. *Demographic Yearbook* is the standard secondary source of world population statistics. It is indispensable for advanced study.

6 The family

The structure of the human family

For as far back into history as we have evidence human beings have lived in families of one sort or another. But family forms are not uniquely human; they can also be found in some other mammal species. The main difference is that the family forms of lower mammals are biologically conditioned whereas the human family has an immense variety of types and the particular form it takes is largely the outcome of social factors. The relationship between infants and other members of the species is especially important with human beings, partly because of the relative immaturity of the human infant at birth, and partly because human self-sufficiency is much more dependent upon learning processes than is that of most animals.

Perhaps the most important of these relationships is that between the infant and the mother. In birds and the lower mammals (for example, rats), the mother and the offspring are bound together by mechanisms which appear to be largely biological and 'instinctive'. The glandular processes of a pregnant rat drive her to build nests and, after the birth of her offspring, to perform the activities necessary for feeding and protecting them. These actions are performed in a highly standardized and stereotyped way which characterizes the whole species. At the level of monkeys, however, there is evidence to suggest that such maternal behaviour is no longer entirely biological and automatic, but dependent on complex learning processes. This is even more the case at the level of human beings, where the mechanisms binding the mother to the offspring are cultural and not biological. Rather than a universal 'maternal instinct' resulting in a standard form of maternal behaviour there is a wide variety of ways of treating children, ranging from neglect and selective infanticide in some societies, to the highly protective, child-centred household of modern Western society. Even the degree to which women want to have children (as well as how many they want) varies from society to society —a variation which itself can only be explained in terms of other aspects of the society: in some societies there are religious and economic rewards for having large numbers of children; in other societies there are religious and economic penalties. In short, although there is a physical relationship between a woman and her offspring, maternal behaviour is largely learned from the customs, values and beliefs of the society; as these differ so do the relations between mother and child.

Marriage

The biological link between the father and the offspring is less direct and less ostensible than that of the mother and child, but nevertheless in most societies there is a bond between a man and the woman-infants unit. In some societies the bond of marriage is a permanent one; in others it may be dissolved at will. In some societies one partner dominates the relationship; in others there is equality between the spouses. In some societies sexual relations are crucial to marriage; in others they are much less important. And so one could go on; marriage relationships are as variable as those between mother and child. In all societies, however, marriage (or some recognized form of man-woman union) has the support of law, custom and religion and in many societies it is highly valued. There are two factors which help us to understand why this is so and at the same time help to account for some of the variability of marriage relations from society to society. One is the economic division of labour between the sexes; and the other is the prohibition on incest.

Modern industrial society is historically unique in that a clear division of labour between the sexes does not prevail. Such a division of labour has been a feature of all previously existing societies and is also present in contemporary non-industrial societies. The nature of the tasks allocated to the two sexes, however, is variable. The allocation of domestic duties to women and 'bread-winning' tasks to men which characterized some sections of European society in the recent past, and is still held by many to be the ideal state, is only one of many variants. In most hunting and gathering societies the men are the hunters and the women are the food gatherers. In some other simple societies the division is between hunting and cultivation. In many West African societies women engage in trade and commerce, men in hunting and trapping, and agricultural tasks are systematically divided between the sexes. The consequences of such economic specialization for life in such societies are well illustrated by the following example related by the anthropologist Lévi-Strauss:[1]

> One of the strongest field recollections of this writer was his meeting, among the Bororo of central Brazil, of a man about thirty years old: unclean, ill-fed, sad, and lonesome. When asked if the man was seriously ill the natives' answer came as a shock: What was wrong with him?—nothing at all, he was just a bachelor, and true enough, in a society where labour is systematically shared between man and woman and where only the married status permits the man to benefit from the fruits of woman's work, including delousing, body painting, and hair-plucking as well as vegetable food and cooked food (since the Bororo woman tills the soil and makes pots), a bachelor is really only half a human being.

Clearly in such a society the benefits to be derived from having a complementary partner in social and economic tasks provide a very considerable incentive for men and women to get married and this helps us to understand the support given to marriage by law and custom.

The almost universal prohibition upon marriage or sexual relations with close relatives highlights another important function of marriage. As with the division of labour between the sexes, however, the precise form of marriage prohibition and of the incest taboo varies from society to society. In all known societies (with the exception of the royal houses of a few historical societies—the best known being ancient Egypt) sexual relations between parent-child and brother-sister are prohibited. Some societies have no further prohibitions; others prohibit sexual relations between different classes of cousins; yet others extend the ban to the whole lineage or clan. On the whole, marriage prohibitions follow similar patterns. There is some reason to believe that sexual unions between close kin may, in certain circumstances, have an undesirable genetic effect. But it is by no means unknown for human societies to adopt habits and to cling to them for centuries even though they are biologically harmful: witness the prohibition of beef to starving Indian peasants, or the ritual denial of meat, fish, eggs and milk to pregnant women and growing children in several East African tribes. Biological arguments are not a very satisfactory explanation of the universality of the taboo on incest; and they are no explanation at all of the variations from society to society of the relatives who shall be included in the prohibition.

Whatever the explanation of the incest taboo and the prohibitions on marriage that accompany it, its major function is to compel the young adult to participate in social groupings other than that of the parents. If the individual family is to be related to the wider society, if familial dependence and co-operation is to be incorporated into a wider social division of labour, then the offspring must form ties to families other than their own. This is particularly important because, in most societies, marriage is not the individual man-woman affair of Western industrial society, but essentially a bond between the families, lineages or clans providing the husband and wife. Thus 'marriage out' becomes a method of forging links of material obligations between groups. The importance of this is illustrated by a New Guinean view of marriage; to them the real purpose of getting married is not so much to obtain a wife, as to secure brothers-in-law. Which relatives are included in the marriage ban depends upon the structure of the wider society. In industrial societies, where family ties are not involved in wider societal organization, incest and marriage prohibitions only apply within the immediate family. On the other hand, in societies such as the Tonga of East Africa, where there are no specific laws or political institutions to settle disputes and govern, marriage with any member of the same clan is prohibited. Marriages must therefore be between clans and they form reciprocal obligations which give everyone an interest in other clans and so enhance economic co-operation. The result is that disputes are more likely to be settled without resort to open warfare and a measure of political stability is achieved.

These two factors give us a different perspective on marriage from that usually held. Whatever the motivations of the individuals involved, marriage provides a way of participating in the larger society; of forging bonds and reciprocal obligations between groups and individuals. It is also an avenue for engaging in the economic division of labour.

The focus of the family

It has already been suggested that family forms differ widely from society to society. One of the major variations is in the size and nature of the residential unit which is of crucial importance because it suggests where the major focus of the family lies. We can distinguish two major types of family unit along these lines: the 'conjugal', where the residential unit consists of husband, wife and children and is relatively independent of wider kinship connections; and the 'corporate', where several generations, their spouses and offspring, form a residential unit. The occurrence of one or other of these types in the societies of the world is not haphazard; on the contrary, it is systematically related to variations in other parts of the society.

Economic organization is particularly important and different types of economic pursuit are found in conjunction with characteristic types of family organization. The conjugal family type tends to occur at two widely separated levels of economic development. Advanced industrial economies and simple hunting and gathering economies both facilitate a relatively independent conjugal unit. In industrial societies people make their living outside the family, in specialized institutions—factories, offices and the like—where the pattern of organization rests on an impersonal, contractual basis. Kinship connections are, for the most part, relatively unimportant, both in getting a job and in carrying it out. Neither the laws and customs of property ownership and landholding, nor the organization of labour, are such as to hold one adult generation to the other. On the contrary, geographical mobility and social mobility are characteristic of industrial societies and both facilitate the emancipation of the child from the family in which he grew up. Similarly, hunting and gathering societies do not provide economic bonds for holding the generations together and are characterized by a conjugal family unit. Subsistence is usually too meagre and dispersed to support a large number of people in one economic unit. Further, the economic pursuits of hunting and gathering usually require constant seasonal mobility which prevents a residential concentration of kin. In the exceptional hunting and gathering societies where food is plentiful or where big-game hunting, necessitating organized co-operation, is a feature of the economy, a community of kin in a corporate family unit does tend to develop.

Large, corporate families tend to occur in societies where the generations are tied together by economic bonds. This is usually the case in agricultural economies with peasant cultivation where family land-holding and the need for organized co-operation hold the generations together around collective economic production and consumption. The limits to the expansion of such families are set by the size and productivity of the communal land and by the availability of alternative opportunities for making a living. Thus, in rural India, although the large corporate family is held to be the ideal form, the average family size seldom exceeds five or six people. This is because the peasant holdings are very small and, in addition, there is a demand for labour on larger estates. More recently there has been the additional possibility of migration to the towns which further hinders the achievement of the ideal. For these reasons it has only been among the prosperous peasants and the large landowners that the ideal of the large, corporate family has been realized.

Power and authority in the family

Another important way in which family structures differ is with regard to the distribution of authority. In some societies one member of the family (usually the father or the eldest male) may hold all property rights and may control the life of other members in the smallest detail. He can determine whom they shall meet, whom they should marry, what work they may do and how they shall behave in public. His permission may even be necessary before they can speak at table or leave the house. A family structure of this kind we call 'patriarchal'. A good example is the *paterfamilias* of ancient Rome, who derived his power and dominance from the ownership and complete control of land. In early republican Rome all other members of the family were dependent upon him for their subsistence and social standing. This dominance was embodied in the law of early Rome. For example, other members of the family had no property rights and the father had the power of life and death over them. However, with the development of Roman society, and particularly with the growth of occupational and career opportunities in its military and administrative ranks, this paternal monopoly of control over life chances broke down. This shift in the power situation is reflected in the development of the patrician family in the late Empire. Some laws relating to the family were changed; others were increasingly ignored. Considerable autonomy and freedom were enjoyed by wives and adult children.

Family relationships and sexual practices can often best be understood as manifestations of the distribution of power in the wider society. Thus, when there are wide disparities in wealth and power within a society, more powerful men can monopolize for themselves a large number of women. This can happen either through the practice of polygamy—or strictly speaking, polygyny—(as in Islamic societies) or through concubinage (as in Imperial China). In some societies, however (Christian societies for example), there are religious and/or legal pressures which make polygamy and formal concubinage impossible. In these cases powerful men resort to informal practices like that of 'taking mistresses' in the noble courts of Europe. Further, whenever older males have full control over the life chances of their women and juniors, they can impose sexual constraints which redound to their own advantage. If the dependants subsequently gain some degree of power, then this constraint is mitigated. In the noble Roman family already cited, for example, marriage became a way of establishing family alliances for political and financial ends. Increasingly the married woman became part of the power game and herself acquired power through the crucial position she occupied in alliances. She was able to defy the constraints imposed on her by the man-made laws and customs so that the relative sexual freedom of noble women during the later empire was partly due to this increased power. A similar process can be observed in the European (particularly French) aristocracies of the seventeenth and eighteenth centuries where again one finds a combination of marriage alliances and easy virtue. The increased sexual freedom of young people, particularly women, in contemporary industrial societies can be explained in terms of the increasing access of the young to sources of economic independence. The enforcement of the dual standards of Victorian middle-class morality in the nineteenth-century England was contingent upon the helplessness and dependence of women and young people and on the dominance of older men. Occupational opportunities for a woman were strictly limited and she had no legal right to hold property. Her legal personality, in so far as it existed at all, was incorporated in that of her husband. The young man, in order to assume a respectable middle-class position, had to undergo long periods of training and needed considerable financial help. In this he was largely dependent on his family. The recent expansion of occupations, particularly of tertiary occupations, created opportunities for women and younger people which had never previously existed. Because they were carried on in impersonal institutions which were independent of family power, such occupations afforded economic independence, or at least the possibility of such independence, from the family. Women and young men were able to rebel against the dual standards of morality which demanded from them standards of behaviour different from that demanded of the head of the household. More generally, the authoritarian relationship between the father and his family gave way to a more egalitarian relationship.

Conjugal stability

The distribution of power within the family is also relevant to the stability of marriage. The more a wife has sources of power and status independent of her husband, the greater is the likelihood of marital disputes or dissolution. Two very different examples demonstrate something of the range of marriage arrangements which make it possible for the wife to derive power and status from outside the conjugal household. In modern industrial societies the wife's power lies in her relative economic and social independence. The relatively open and impersonal labour market extends a wide range of employment opportunities to women and so gives them an autonomous social and economic base (see page 86). Moreover, with the relatively individualistic view of marriage common in such societies, there is a correspondingly great emphasis on romantic love and the mutual compatibility of husband and wife. Compared with most non-industrial societies, the marriage relationship is relatively independent of (and supported by) the wider structures of kinship and community. Because of this more fragile foundation, marital tensions and disputes are more likely to arise, and when they do arise, they are more likely to culminate in separation or divorce. As the social and economic autonomy of women has grown, and as marriage has become a more individual affair, there has been a progressive relaxation of divorce laws. This has put divorce within the reach of almost everyone by making it both easier and cheaper. In addition, the long-term trend is for more and more people to avail themselves of the opportunity offered by the new laws. The resultant increase in rates of divorce during the twentieth century is illustrated in Table 6.1.

Table 6.1 Divorce-rate per thousand marriages in selected industrial societies 1900–60

Country	*1900*	*1910*	*1920*	*1930*	*1940*	*1950*	*1960*
USA	75·3	87·4	133·3	173·9	165·3	231·7	259·0
Sweden	12·9	18·4	30·5	50·6	65·1	147·7	174·6
Australia	13·5	12·9	22·6	41·7	41·9	98·2	88·9
France	26·1	46·3	49·4	68·6	80·3	106·2	82·4
England and Wales		2·2	8·0	11·1	16·5	86·1	69·5

Source: William J. Goode, *World Revolution and Family Patterns*, New York: Free Press, 1963, p. 82.

Marital instability of a different nature characterizes some simple societies in which the lineage and clan organization conflict with the marriage relationship. In the traditional Ndembu society of Central Africa, for example, descent is traced through the mother's line; the kinship organization is matrilineal. When a man takes a wife he pays a bride-price to her brothers. The wife goes to live with the husband's family group, thus depriving her brothers of her labour and transferring this asset to her husband's group. Children of the marriage have divided allegiance between their mother's brothers, to whom they 'belong' and must eventually return, and their father's group with whom they are growing up. The mother, too, owes her primary allegiance to her brothers. They want her and her children back as their labour is of great economic value and their numbers add to the political power of the group. So there is a perpetual conflict between the woman-giving and the woman-receiving groups. In such a situation marital problems frequently culminate in the breakdown of the marriage. In the Ndembu situation, then, the wife can draw upon the power and status of her matrilineage, which is in conflict with her husband's kinship group precisely over the issue of her marriage.

Patriarchal families of all kinds provide a contrast to these two examples. As we have seen, in patriarchal families the eldest male controls the life chances and the status of the women and the young. A wife or a daughter in such a family has no opportunities outside her husband's or father's household; she is entirely dependent. A variety of cases, from the agricultural corporate families of India and China to the middle-class family of Victorian England illustrate the point. In such societies the severe consequences of divorce or separation for the woman lead to her acquiescence in the marital situation and her subjugation induces relative harmony. In addition marital stability is reinforced by the pressures and requirements of the wider kin or community to which both spouses are subjected. Exceptions to this general rule occur when the customary and legal powers of the husband over the wife are so great that he can divorce her at will. This has been the case in traditional Islamic societies and in Japan. In the latter case the legal protection of the rights of the wife, which came with industrialization, has led to a decline in the divorce rate.

To sum up: the structure of the human family is subject to considerable variations. The focal point of the whole family varies, and even within a single residential type—say the conjugal family—there are wide variations of structure according to the particular relationships between husband, wife and children. All of these variations are closely related to the structure of the wider society, and as the society changes so does the family structure.

The family in early stages of industrialization

Non-industrial societies, based as they are on an agricultural economy, are often characterized by a corporate family structure. As we have already seen, however, this is related to the *particular* form of economic production—namely peasant agriculture—which is dominant in most non-industrial societies. For peasant holding or tenancy tend to involve the wider kin in working on the land and sharing its products, thus holding them together as a unit. This system of cultivation was characteristic of most parts of pre-industrial Europe and is still typical of many parts of the world. But there are also non-industrial societies based on forms of agriculture other than peasant land-holding. The wage-labour systems characteristic of much of eighteenth- and nineteenth-century England, or of many parts of the West Indies today, concentrate production on large farms or estates and do not provide the kind of economic bonds between kinsmen which require common residence. In addition, such wage labour is a very insecure, often seasonal, form of employment which is poorly paid. The agricultural labourer also has to be prepared to travel in search of employment. Poverty, insecurity and mobility combine to make the upkeep of a corporate family group difficult or impossible. Sometimes, indeed, the labourer is not even able to support a conjugal group on his wages. Where this is the case (and it is a common situation among labourers in many parts of the West Indies), men are no more than occasional visitors to the household and the family unit is likely to be 'matrifocal'—that is the adult women are the heads of the family which they support as best they can.

The changes in family structure which are brought about by industrialization vary according to the nature of the family structure in the pre-industrial situation. Industrialization involves the transfer of the focus of economic production from agriculture to manufacture. The early stages of industrialization make little difference to the focal point of the agricultural wage-labourer's family; usually it merely transfers him from a rural situation of poverty, insecurity and mobility to a similar situation in the overcrowded slums of the town. When agriculture has previously been based upon peasant cultivation, however, the changes in family structure are more fundamental. The transfer of production from the domestic setting to specialized factories and workshops disrupts the cohesive productive function of the corporate family and heightens the importance of the conjugal type of family.

The disruption of the corporate family, however, does not lead to the total demise of wider kinship bonds. In England, Japan and the United States, for example, the wider kinship network has survived and continues to play an important part as a kind of mutual aid society for members. But the larger kinship group is no longer the dominant unit; it seldom has the economic production functions and the residential unity of such a group in most non-industrial societies. The conjugal group does become the principal form of family organization. An example of such a change in family structure can be seen below in the discussion of Japan.

As the first society to embark upon industrialization England is an important, although not necessarily typical, case. Pre-industrial England was *not* characterized by the large corporate family and, consequently, changes in family structure were perhaps less drastic than in some other industrializing societies. Developments in Britain since the Civil War had led to a transformation of agriculture from the traditional feudal system of small-holding tenant cultivation to a much larger scale of farming on farms and estates worked mainly by wage labour. This process must have weakened any larger kinship units which existed earlier and the individuation of labour involved in the transformation laid the foundation for the predominance of the conjugal family unit. At this time manufacturing crafts were carried out within the household, but in England these craft households were also characterized by the conjugal rather than the corporate family unit. The life of the pre-industrial rural worker has often been romanticized as one in which leisure and freedom to work at one's own pace provided conditions for the good life surrounded by loving kinsmen. Contemporary writers, however, painted a rather different picture. For example, a country parson wrote:[2]

> I could not but observe with concern their mean and distressed condition. I found them in general but indifferently fed; badly clothed; some children without shoes and stockings; very few put to school; and most families in debt to little shopkeepers. In short, there was scarcely any appearance of comfort about their dwellings, except that the children looked tolerably healthy. Yet I could not impute the wretchedness I saw either to sloth or wastefulness.

This shift of labour from agriculture and domestic industry to mining and manufacturing industry, from rural poverty to the emergent slums surrounding the new factories and mines, while not bringing about a change in the focus of the family, nevertheless had important consequences for family structure in other ways. In particular, women and children were more susceptible to the rigours of factory discipline and control than were men. They could also be paid lower wages, a possibility which predisposed some factory owners to employ women and children almost exclusively. The unemployment of men and the gross exploitation of women and children which followed from this provided a powerful motive for a variety of social and political agitations. Unlike rural misery, the new urban situation was geographically concentrated and readily visible to other social groups. This concentration of large numbers of workers in transparently exploitative conditions also facilitated the organization and growth of movements of discontent ranging from sporadic violence and destruction of factory machinery to the secret organization of rudimentary trade unions. These movements were among the forces which led to legislative reforms protecting women and children from the grossest forms of work exploitation. The reforms also had the indirect effect of excluding women from certain types of heavy work, thus ending the situation of exclusive male unemployment.

The precise effect on the family of these changes was variable and often depended on local conditions. One common feature, however, was the separation of family members from one another during working hours. Farm labour and domestic crafts had usually been carried out by members of the family working together; the long hours of factory work were spent apart. Economic survival was no longer dependent on family solidarity and stability. Such stability now depended much more on ties of affection; and such ties were not always present. A contemporary wrote of the situation in London:[3]

> Marriage as an institution is not fashionable in these districts. Ask if the men and women living together in these rookeries are married and your simplicity will cause a smile. Nobody knows. Nobody cares. Nobody expects that they are. Those who appear to be married are often separated by a mere quarrel and they do not hesitate to form similar companionships immediately.

The first stages of industrialization also transformed the middle classes and gave rise to new entrepreneurial strata. The pre-industrial middle classes carried out their trading and manufacturing activities largely within the domestic household. Women and children were often active in these business activities. But with the coming of factory production, and even with the earlier expansion and elaboration of trade and finance, business activities were increasingly carried out in specialized institutions. The middle-class household, and particularly the wife, were no longer involved in production and business. The family became merely the sphere in which the prosperous middle classes consolidated their financial gains in status display. The middle-class wife was relieved from domestic chores by the employment of servants; the numerous children she bore were taken off her hands in infancy by nursemaids and (after about 1850) in the later stages of childhood and youth by the public schools. Increasingly she became a powerless and almost functionless ornament. These changes in the location of economic activities lay behind the patriarchal pattern of the Victorian middle-class family: the active, dominant husband; the submissive, passive, virtuous wife; and the good children who were seen but never heard. The men controlled the economic life chances of their women and younger dependants (a control which was supported by the man-made laws of the land) and consequently could dominate and subordinate them socially.

The family in later stages of industrialization

The changes in the structure of the family that occur in the later stages of industrialization are primarily to do with the structure of the conjugal family, although there are also some changes in relationships with the wider kin. All these are related to the wider processes of social change; to continued individuation, bureaucratization, and urbanization, and to the persistence of geographical and social mobility. The later stages of industrialization invariably involve developments in all these spheres but the changes do not take place to the same degree in all industrializing societies. Variations in the wider processes of change are reflected in differences in the structure of the family from industrial society to industrial society.

In addition to the continuation of earlier changes which affect family life, the later stages of industrialization are characterized by three relatively new factors which have important implications for the family. (1) There are urban/industrial communities which have been established for several generations; the apparent transience of urban community and family life has in many places given way to stability. At the same time, however, in other parts of the society there is a re-ordering of city life—the drift to the suburbs—which provides a different environment for family life. (2) Bureaucratization and the associated growth of tertiary occupations leads to an unprecedented demand for administrative and clerical labour, which can usually only be satisfied by the employment of women in these jobs. 'Middle-class' occupations are increasingly available for women and a *career* (as distinct from a job) becomes a possibility for them. In turn this process is related to the political and social emancipation of women, a factor which continues to be crucial to changes in family relationships as it was in the earlier stages of industrialization. (3) Part of what we mean by bureaucratization is that a substantial proportion of the population is employed in jobs which have some sort of career prospects. The pursuit of a career frequently involves a high incidence of movement from job to job. This is especially the case in the USA where often the 'organization man' has to change his job several times in his life if he is to make the most of his career opportunities. This, too, has ramifications for family structure.

The highly industrial society is more complex than its predecessors, partly in that it encompasses a greater variety of social situations, including a greater variety of family situations. There is the family in the suburb; the family in the slum; and the family in the countryside. There is the family that spends all its days in one community; and the family that moves to a different town every two or three years. And there are (as there always have been) rich families and poor families; upper-class families and lower-class families. Some of the effects of industrialization are widely distributed throughout the society. The independent employment of women, for example, creates conditions throughout industrial societies in which social independence is a *possibility*; and yet some employed women remain subject to their husbands. The relationships within the conjugal family vary according to the nature of the relationships of husband and wife to their wider kin and to the wider community. These in turn are related to the degree of residential stability or mobility that exists. So finally, to put some order into the variety of family structures we must relate them to the question of mobility.

Changes in employment opportunities for women

We have seen how, in the early stages of industrialization, the position of women in the family was determined to a considerable extent by their economic position. In nineteenth-century England women of the lower classes had even worse pay and conditions than their menfolk. Property laws gave the husband the *right* to the earnings of his wife, even in cases where he had deserted wife and children. The wife's dependence, as well as her general physical dilapidation, was heightened by frequent pregnancies and births. Thus the economic activity of working-class women did not form a basis for a challenge to male dominance in the family. Among the middle classes the position was even more clear cut since most women did not work at all.

Changes in occupational distribution, particularly the growth of tertiary occupations, created a very different situation; the demand for white collar labour was such that it could only be met by employing women in these occupations and the exodus of large numbers of men for the battlefields of the first world war accentuated the process. The clerical, administrative and professional ranks which were gradually opened to women offered much greater power, prestige and independence than the occupations which had formerly been available and the employment situation was reflected in the gradual social and political emancipation of women. Closely related to these changes was the decline in size of middle-class families. Successful family limitation is dependent upon joint consultation between husband and wife and/or a position of considerable feminine power. In turn, relief from the drudgery of continual child-bearing enhances the woman's independence from her husband and provides opportunity for a more active life. These economic and social changes provided the possibility of a marriage relationship very different from the earlier one of male dominance and female subservience.

Individuation and marriage choice

The first stages of industrialization had involved a separation of economic production from the domestic setting. The dominance within the family of the father, however, normally preserved his influence over the marriage of his children. With improved employment opportunities for young people and the concomitant changes in the power structure of the family, young people gain more and more autonomy in this sphere. For the most part men and women choose their husbands and wives with little interference from wider kinship groups; marriage is more a matter between individuals and less one between two family groups than in non-industrial societies. Perhaps this statement is least true of the highest social classes where there is considerable family pressure upon young people to find 'suitable' marriage partners, thus maintaining status exclusiveness (and sometimes 'appropriate' patterns of inheritance). Take as an example, a recent statement by the Prince of Wales:[4]

> You've got to remember that when you marry, in my position, you are going to marry somebody who perhaps one day is going to become Queen. You've got to choose somebody very carefully, I think, who could perform this particular role; the one advantage about marrying a princess, or somebody from a royal family, is that they do know what happens.

In all social groups, however, people are more likely to marry members of the same locality, the same social class, the same ethnic group and the same religion. This is less due to any belief that this is right and proper (although such beliefs may still be very strong—for example, with regard to inter-racial marriages) than to the fact that people are more likely to meet marriageable members of their own groups than of other groups. Courting in Western industrial societies is usually carried on (or at least introductory meetings are effected) at dances, parties, schools and colleges, workplaces, coffee bars and the like. These situations have a tendency to be homogeneous in terms of locality, class and so on. So, in the language of demographers, one is exposed to a greater 'risk' of marriage to members of one's own group; in practical terms, the 'marriage market' is a very restricted one—although less so than in the homogeneous rural society.

Long-term residential stability

In some situations a residential pattern emerges in which the household is composed of the conjugal family but where wider kin are to be found in the immediate neighbourhood. This pattern is to be found where a family has lived in a neighbourhood for several generations and may occur in rural or urban areas. The conjugal family is the dominant unit but ties with more distant relations are far from unimportant. In urban areas the neighbourhoods characterized by this pattern are usually homogeneous in their class composition and are most likely to be working-class areas, partly because multi-generational residence in a neighbourhood is more characteristic of the working class than of other groups, and partly because these patterns are enhanced by poverty. The best known of them (best known because they have been studied by sociologists) are Bethnal Green in London, Ship Street in Liverpool, and 'Ashton' (a fictitious name for a small mining town) in Yorkshire, but many towns and cities have such an area.

The most important way residential stability influences the structure of the conjugal family is that there is no necessity for a couple to break off their pre-marital friendships. Marriage usually takes place between two people from the locality; it is consequently superimposed upon the existing friendship patterns of the couple. Each partner retains his or her group of friends and does not become exclusively dependent upon the conjugal relationship. Close and frequent relationships with parents remain possible after marriage and these communities are marked in particular by ties of co-operation between the mother and her married daughter. Because they live close to each other they are able to share the chores of daily life, particularly those to do with child care and child rearing. These two factors—the strength of the mother/daughter relationship and the retention of pre-marriage friendship patterns—form the basis for a close, co-operative community of women, who work together, gossip together and bring up their children together. Bringing up children is not restricted to the home but is shared with kinswomen in the locality and sometimes is carried out by the community as a whole. The child, like the whole family becomes 'neighbourhood centred' and grows up with the constant companionship of the other children of the neighbourhood. Children thus have considerable influence upon each other's beliefs, values and activities as they grow up; the peer group is an important agent of socialization and social control. Nevertheless, an important part of bringing up children is carried out by adults who are likely to use physical punishment to discourage undesirable behaviour that comes to their attention. But, because of the neighbourhood situation, no one adult is in constant contact with a child and so a lot of such behaviour goes unnoticed. The result is that punishment, while effectively controlling 'external' behaviour of children, has little effect on the formation of 'internal' guilt mechanisms.

The friendship groups of men, similarly, are single sex groups—a result, or sometimes a legacy, of poverty, poor housing conditions and long working hours, which alienated the man from his home and disposed him to seek the little leisure and pleasure he had in the company of his mates in the pub or club. In areas dominated by 'traditional' industries—mining, fishing, dock work—the physical and collective nature of the work in gangs or teams welded the men into loyal groups. Add to this fact that work-mates invariably lived close to each other and had grown up together and one is hardly surprised to find that the solidarity of the work group is carried over into the neighbourhood and reinforces the bonds of community. Hard times and poor facilities also enhanced the functions of the 'women's co-operative' in the neighbourhood, the women helping each other out in times of special need. With the improvement in standards of living and housing conditions which has recently come about in Europe and North America, the rigidity of these patterns of sexual separation is modified and there tends to be greater contact and co-operation between the conjugal pair. Men are likely to spend more time in the now more congenial home, a trend that has been accelerated by the advent of television. But these changes only modify the pattern; in spite of greater conjugal closeness and reciprocity, the main pattern of 'women's co-operative' and male comradeship persist as long as this kind of neighbourhood persists. It is only likely to change when, for one reason or another, young people no longer remain in the district to work and marry.

New towns, suburbs and estates

Many of these stable communities have been broken up by the movement of people from the city centres to suburbs and estates on the periphery of large towns or to newly created towns. This has been due, partly to rehousing schemes involving slum clearance in the city centres, and partly to government attempts to locate new industries away from the existing city centres. Families who move from a stable residential area to a new suburb, new estate or new town are in a very different family situation from that we have just described. The difference is especially acute for the first generation to move to the new area. There is likely to be very little mixing; little co-operation between neighbours; and in some cases there may be a covert, or even active, hostility between neighbours. The geographical distance separating the newly mobile family from their wider kin places a considerable strain on kinship relations. The change in the mother/married daughter relationship is particularly significant, for the older generation frequently remains in the old district. Although considerable efforts may be made to maintain frequent contact, the nature of the relationship necessarily changes fundamentally. With neither kin nor long established neighbours to rely on for day-to-day help, the wife becomes more dependent both materially and emotionally upon her husband.

The basis for the old patterns of male friendship groups are also undermined: the type of work available is less likely to be in one of the traditional industries than in a modern mass production industry, such as the motor industry. The work is mainly on the assembly line, each worker having his own task to perform. There is little of the solidaristic co-operation so characteristic of work gangs in mining or the docks. For the individual worker there is little emotional involvement in the work group. Added to this, workers are recruited from all over the country and have no common background and no common local culture. Studies of workers in the motor industry in England show that there is little sociability between work-mates outside work. Nor are work-mates normally neighbours; they live in different localities and neighbourhoods. This lack of congruence between work groups, neighbourhood groups and friendship groups contrasts strongly with the near identity of these groups in areas of residential stability. It coincides with and enhances the individualism of the work situation. So the man, too, relies more on his home and his wife for entertainment and companionship.

With this new situation new patterns of leisure activities emerge. Both men and women spend most of their leisure time in the home; there is little 'going out', little visiting and little entertaining. The home, rather than the neighbourhood or the pub, becomes the focus of people's lives; and the conjugal family, rather than the community or friendship groups, becomes the centre of people's activities. In short, people become more home-centred.

All this has important implications for the relationship between parents and children. The more home-centred the family becomes, the more child-centred it becomes as well; the child's welfare, behaviour and education become a focus for the parents' attention and concern. Furthermore, the child is brought up primarily within the conjugal family. Grandparents are usually too far away to exert day-to-day influence and the influence of the neighbourhood on the growing child is relatively unimportant. This is particularly the case in neighbourhoods of mixed or uncertain class composition, where children are often discouraged from playing with neighbours' children. The peer group consequently tends to be school-centred rather than neighbourhood-centred and does not become crucial in socialization until later in the child's life when, often enough, the parents of childhood friends do not know each other. In the early years the child, as well as the parents, is dependent upon the conjugal family and is in continual contact with his parents. There is, therefore, the possibility of non-physical means of controlling his behaviour. This requires, however, a level of verbal skill not always possessed by the parents. This is especially so with working-class parents with the result that the ways in which the child is disciplined are likely to be inconsistent and unpredictable.

We have suggested that this pattern is likely to be particularly noticeable among the first generation in a new area, but it is likely to be a semi-permanent form of family and social life. Certainly it is unlikely that the old type of communal life will ever be established in the new areas, for the housing estate poses problems different from those in the traditional communities and it affords new facilities. It consequently requires new adaptations. At the material level, the new house presents a challenge for the newcomers. They feel they must live up to it by furnishing it according to certain standards, tending the garden and acquiring domestic gadgets. In this respect the standards are already set by the neighbourhood; what the other houses have is an unspoken norm for the newcomers to keep. To quote from one study of such an area:[5]

> People struggle to raise their all-round standards to those of the home, and in the course of doing so, they must look to their present neighbours for guidance. To begin with, the first-comers had to make their own way, but the later arrivals have their model at hand. The neighbours have put up nice curtains. Have we? They have their garden planted with privet and grass seed. Have we? The new arrivals watch the first-comers and the first-comers watch the new arrivals.

To this end a substantial amount of family earnings is invested in hire purchase payments on furniture and appliances. The home becomes a comfortable place in which to spend leisure time, and one on which a good deal of maintenance work needs to be done. The television set facilitates this home-centredness.

In the new situation there are new expectations and new standards; different qualities and activities are highly esteemed. An action that would have been applauded in the old district may be derided in the new, and vice versa. Adjusting to these new values may be very difficult, for it may involve people in changing their self-image. Young and Willmott make this point well when they compare traditional Bethnal Green with a new housing estate they call Greenleigh:[6]

> In Bethnal Green, people belong to a close network of personal relations. They know intimately dozens of other local people living near. . . . In this situation, Bethnal Green is not, as we see it, concerned to any marked extent with what is normally thought of as status. It is true, of course, that people have different incomes, different kinds of jobs, different kinds of houses—in this respect there is much less uniformity than there is at Greenleigh—even different standards of education. But these attributes are not so important in evaluating others. It is personal characteristics which matter. The first thing they think of about Bert is not that he has a 'fridge' and a car. They see him as bad-tempered, or a real good sport, or the man with a way with women. . . . He is judged, if he is judged at all, more in the round, as a person with the usual mixture of all kinds of qualities, some good, some bad, many indefinable. He is more of a life-portrait than a figure on a scale.
>
> How different is Greenleigh . . . where nearly everyone is a stranger, there is no way of uncovering personality. People cannot be judged by their personal characteristics: a person can certainly see that his neighbour works in his shirt sleeves and his wife goes down to the shops in a blue coat, but that is not much of a guide to character. Judgement

> must, therefore, rest on the trappings of the man rather than on the man himself. If people have nothing else to go by, they judge from his appearance, his house, even his Minimotor. Once the accepted standards are few, and mostly to do with wealth, they become the standard by which status is judged.
>
> In the absence of small groups which join one family to another, in the absence of strong personal associations which extend from one household to another, people think that they are judged, and judge others, by the material standards which are the outward and visible marks of respectability.

These differing criteria of social evaluation, then, are the indices of a different kind of relationship to the neighbours; a more competitive and, to a certain extent, a hostile relationship. However, status competition does not necessarily rule out friendliness and sociability. Indeed, studies of American middle-class suburbs indicate that status competition is displayed within the context of intense neighbourhood sociability. The areas we are considering, however, are very largely working-class areas and we must take note of differences between the classes with regard to attitudes to friendship and with regard to certain technical skills that are necessary to sociability. To the working classes a friend is given, not 'made'. A friend is someone you grow up with, know at school, work with, and so on. He is someone with whom you share a common background and common assumptions about the world. To *make* friends who are not given in this way presupposes an ability to converse and to join in common activities with people where there is no common background. Linguistic and conceptual skills are necessary to elaborate common interests and recreations between people whose experience, assumptions and local cultures are not necessarily shared. Such skills are more characteristically middle-class. Moreover, activities which make for sociability—like mutual entertaining and joining recreational clubs and associations—are also more characteristic of the way of life of the middle classes.

The combination of all these factors—movement away from kin and long-established neighbours, work relationships which do not carry over into after-work hours, a competitive way of life in which some traditional working-class life styles and attitudes (especially those towards friendship) survive—produces a family structure with a distinctive combination of characteristics. There is a focus on the conjugal relationship and the parent/child relationship, a concentration of leisure activities in the home, and combined with this, a low level of sociability and neighbourliness.

Residential mobility

The way of life of modern industrial societies also produces a section of the population who frequently move their home, often from one part of the country to another and sometimes even from country to country. This is especially the case for those who undergo higher education; their education itself usually takes them away from their parents' home and they often enter the kind of occupations where moves are essential if they are to make the most of their opportunities. Consider the typical example of a young man in this situation. He spends his childhood and youth in the locality where his parents live and goes to school there. He goes to college in another area, and starts his first job in yet another. He is likely to move subsequently, following employment opportunities for career advancement. At some stage in his career, perhaps while at college, he meets his future wife; she is likely to have had a similar mobility pattern. Both of them make friends at every stage of their careers; and sometimes these are, from the start, joint friends. People undergoing this pattern of mobility have no firm psychological anchorage in a community, nor any stable network of informal social relationships, with the consequence that marriage and the conjugal relationship assume crucial importance. The conjugal family becomes the only relatively permanent point of reference and there is a great deal of emotional involvement and interdependence between husband and wife. Decisions are made jointly; household tasks are shared without rigid role allocation; finances are jointly administered.[7] Such couples tend to emphasize the importance of personal and sexual compatibility for the success of a marriage.

The career pattern of these groups is also important for the sociability pattern it entails. Friends are made by each spouse (or both) in their schools, colleges or jobs. But their friends are hardly ever neighbours; on the contrary they tend to be widely dispersed. Friendship is, therefore, distinguished by entertaining at home and, to a lesser extent, going out with friends. In this kind of sociability, the couple, and not the individual partner, is the friendship unit. Past friends of one partner who prove to be incompatible with the other are likely to be abandoned. Whether such a couple will also make friends with neighbours depends very much on the nature of the neighbourhood. If neighbours are of a similar occupational and social status level, then neighbourhood sociability is likely to develop. If, on the other hand, the neighbourhood is socially mixed, or if there is substantial ambiguity of social status in the district, then there will be very little neighbourhood sociability.

In these mobile families, too, the child is often the focus of parental attention and grows up largely within the confines of the conjugal family. The normally high educational level of the parents, however, ensures a high level of verbal skill which is invariably used in the disciplining and control of children. Physical punishment invariably takes a minor place and is sometimes not used at all. The parents have effective alternatives at their disposal and are in a position to make a choice.

The greater wealth of these families enables them to maintain contact with their more distant relatives if they want to. The motor car, the telephone, the postal service all facilitate regular contact in spite of distance; strong emotional ties can be maintained and are reinforced by family visits which are made possible by increased leisure time. Even in highly industrial societies kinship groups often serve as a kind of 'mutual benefit association' in which help and support is exchanged between the members. This is often particularly crucial for newly married couples who depend a great deal on their parents and older relatives for support and guidance and sometimes for financial help. In the poorer social groups, given the housing problems in most industrial societies, an initial roof over the heads of the newly married couple is often provided by the parental home. Nor is help to older family members entirely a thing of the past. While it is not extended to such a wide range of kinsmen as formerly, people normally feel some responsibility for the well-being of their aged parents.

In all family situations in highly industrial societies, then, the major changes of individuation and bureaucratization have left their mark on the structure of the family. The influence of geographical mobility is more variable. The greatest differences in family structure are between those families characterized by long-term residential stability and those (predominantly middle-class) families characterized by frequent moves. There are, however, significant differences between these latter families and those of the new estates and new towns, even though mobility has been characteristic of both. These differences are largely due to differences in the style of life between middle-class and working-class families and, in particular, to differences in sociability which derive from educational and occupational differences.

Modernization and the family

The diversity of family forms to be found in industrial societies is more than mirrored in the contemporary modernizing societies of Africa, Asia and Latin America. The variety of the traditional situation has been compounded by differential contact with the industrial world which has variously affected the structure of the family. In some of the more remote areas of Africa and Asia family relationships are little changed; in the mushrooming towns and cities they have changed drastically in the last half century. Two processes which have particularly important consequences for the family are urbanization and the growth of new occupations. And these are processes which not only affect the people who are themselves moving into the cities or changing their jobs, but which also have far-reaching consequences for the whole society. The fact that there are employment opportunities in government bureaucracies, commercial companies, mines and plantations—all areas which lie largely outside the sphere of family influence—affects the family relationships, attitudes, and behaviour even of those people who do not pursue such opportunities.

The single most important consequence of these processes is the individuation of labour and of economic opportunity. In traditional, predominantly agricultural, societies the family is the major unit of production. In such situations, as we have seen earlier, family power can be maintained partly through control over the economic opportunity of its members. Large-scale economic changes, resulting in the growth of new occupations located mainly in towns and cities, lessens the importance of the family as a productive force and consequently weakens the family's control over the life chances of its individual members. In addition these changes increase the incidence of geographical mobility. Where migration is a temporary phenomenon (as is the case with a good deal of mining and agricultural labour throughout tropical Africa) it invariably leads to a separation of the man from his wife, children and other family members. This may be a separation of a few weeks or of several years. Where the migration is more permanent (as with most forms of urbanization) the conjugal family usually moves together. In either case, however, while the *nature* of relationships between kinsmen and family members is transformed, economic dependence on the family may acquire new and more subtle forms.

The city provides a bewildering and hazardous experience for the rural migrant. He lacks the social skills and the contacts of the urbanite and therefore needs backing and 'sponsorship'. This is frequently provided by earlier migrants from his village to the city, some of whom are likely to be kinsmen. Former ties—including those of kinship—are thus by no means irrelevant. The economic insecurity of life in most modernizing societies also helps to sustain bonds of kinship. In the towns unemployment is often rife; in the rural areas there is frequent under-employment. The economies of these countries are often dependent upon world prices for one or two basic commodities and are consequently subject to wild fluctuations. Political instability sometimes contributes to the general economic insecurity. In this situation the maintenance of kinship obligations can provide at least some degree of security. If the worst comes to the worst the destitute urban dweller can go back to his kinsmen in the village and receive such support as they are able to give him. Conversely, when he is in employment he may remit some of his pay to his kinsmen.

It is, however, easy to overstate the mutual obligations of kinsmen in, say, contemporary West Africa. With continued economic and social development individual dependence on the family gradually weakens and the willingness to honour traditional obligations tends to decrease. This is especially so if a society is able to maintain high levels of employment, job stability and security—either through industrialization or through other forms of economic development.

Japan provides a good example of a society in which modernization has taken the form of successful industrialization. The traditional Japanese family ordered every aspect of the lives of its members and was supported in this by laws which upheld the authority of family heads. Laws of inheritance were also important. All household property, including the family's means of subsistence such as land or business, was passed on from the father to the eldest son. This led to a system that has become known as the 'stem family', the stem consisting of the line of eldest sons, who perpetuated the family name and property. Younger sons, on getting married, were expected to start a separate household and these, together with their descendants, are known as the 'branches'. Although they formed separate households these branch families were still dependent upon the stem families. The father or elder brother was expected to help the younger brothers to start their households. Typically, a propertied stem family would give a piece of land or a small part of a trading business to their 'branches' for this purpose. The decisions and dictates of the head of the stem household remained binding on the actions of other family members (although in the case of large and important families a council of household heads assumed this authority). In this stem and branch system the conjugal family of any given member was entirely subordinated to the larger family authority. Filial and fraternal bonds (especially to the eldest brother: note that the Japanese word for 'parents' means father, mother and elder brother) were much stronger and much more highly valued than marriage relationships.

In the early stages of industrialization in the last quarter of the nineteenth century, economic and political conditions were little more stable than in pre-industrial Japan and family dependence, particularly the dependence of the branch on the stem, continued. The newly urbanized worker needed the support and sustenance, however meagre, which his larger family could provide in difficult times. With the attainment of industrial maturity, however, the modern sector of the Japanese economy was increasingly able to offer subsequent generations of urban workers a considerable degree of security and stability, thus lessening their dependence upon traditional kinship connections. Indeed, the twentieth century has witnessed the gradual emancipation of the individual and the conjugal family from the hegemony of the corporate family. This emancipation has occurred both in law and in fact. There were legal and political struggles between the traditionalists and the reformers; the traditionalists claiming that the corporate family system lay at the very basis of society and as such must be protected by law; the reformers arguing that such a system is incompatible with a modern progressive society. Various compromises were reached in the legal reforms enacted in the post-second-world-war Japanese constitution and finally legal protection of traditional corporate ties was abandoned and the importance of conjugal family ties was emphasized.

However, even though the traditional family pattern as a mode of organization has largely disappeared, some of the affectional ties and the habits of thought associated with them still persist. This is particularly true of relations between men and women and the attitudes to female employment. Although women account for a substantial proportion of the labour force in Japan, most of the women at work are young and unmarried. Only a small, albeit increasing, proportion of married women are in paid employment. Moreover, there remains a strong current of opinion (especially, but not exclusively among men) which disapproves of married women working, particularly if they are mothers. In spite of this, however, the proportion of working married women is increasing. This suggests that the growth of employment opportunities, together with the influence of the wife's wage on the family's standard of living, are gradually changing the traditional patterns even in this area.

So far we have scarcely distinguished between the different groups in the societies under discussion. There are, of course, considerable differences in the life patterns and experiences of the different classes and groups whether in traditional societies, in modernizing societies or in industrial societies. For example, where the traditional family structures were patriarchal, there are indications that male domination was much greater and more firmly entrenched among the wealthier and more powerful strata. Among the poor, such domination was mitigated by the fact that the wife shared in the ardours of labour and shouldered much of the burden of poverty.

In modernizing societies there are, perhaps, greater differences to be observed than in any other societies. The development of modern occupations and of formal education and their co-existence with traditional patterns ensures a greater variation in social relationships and styles of life. In different parts of the same society there exist widely different family structures. And because of the peculiar recent history of many modernizing societies—with their recent independence from colonial rule and their recent and rapid development of a 'modern' sector—there are many persons who were themselves brought up in a corporate family or kinship group and find themselves parents in conjugal families of a very different structure. Since these changes are so recent, family relationships are often exposed to very considerable strain. Many young, educated West African men, for example, engage in a style of life quite different from that of previous generations. They are quite likely to be married to women who are themselves educated and who expect to have their own career and a considerable degree of independence. While it is by no means a new thing for women in West African societies to work, the modern, bureaucratic work situation lends support to their claims to an autonomy that the menfolk (because of the retention of a traditional orientation favourable to themselves) are often reluctant to concede. The relative rarity of educated women and the value placed upon having an educated wife for a go-ahead bureaucrat or businessman gives the educated woman an additional weapon in the battle of the sexes. For only such a wife is able to maintain the 'Western' style of life and engage in the patterns of sociability that are expected by the husband's working colleagues. Thus we have a contemporary example of the changing distribution of power between the sexes that we have earlier described in ancient Rome, eighteenth-century France, nineteenth-century England and twentieth-century Japan.

Conflicts may also arise between the educated man and his kinsmen in societies in which different sectors have very different expectations of mutual help. Those who occupy the positions of relative wealth and power that education can buy are frequently expected to honour their obligations to kinsmen by financial or other help to younger members of the kinship group. They are expected to use their influence to get them desirable jobs; to make substantial payments towards their education; and so on. Such traditional obligations may place a considerable burden on the relatively high, but not unlimited, income of educated men and women. Moreover, they conflict with the demands and requirements of the 'new' urban, conjugal family, and with the financial pressures of maintaining a 'modern' style of life.

Similarly, as in the industrializing societies of the Western world, the way in which marriage partners are chosen is changing. In some more extreme traditional cases, marriage had to be with a particular category of relative; thus in many African tribes some variant of marriage between cousins was the normal thing. Most traditional patterns, however, allow some individual choice, while restricting this choice to certain ethnic, tribal or village groups. Invariably the final authority for the choice lay with the parents or with the whole kin group. As we have already noted, however, there are now strong pressures encouraging the educated to marry among themselves and it is often difficult for a man to find a partner who is 'appropriate' in both the traditional and the modern sense. Increasingly, among this group, the choice is made in terms of the new rather than the old criteria of what constitutes a suitable partner.

These conflicts are characteristic of the rapidly changing situation of contemporary modernizing societies. They arise from the contradictory pressures and discordant expectations which result from the contact between industrial societies and relatively simple societies. In so far as economic and social development proceed in modernizing societies, we may expect the older patterns of family relationships to give way. However, as long as there remain substantial areas where the traditional agricultural sector is prominent the patterns of the corporate family and the wider kinship group will remain.

Notes

1 C. Lévi-Strauss, 'The family', in H. L. Shapiro (ed.), *Man, Culture and Society*, London: Oxford University Press, 1956, p. 269.
2 Rev. Davies, 'The case of labourers in husbandry', quoted in R. Fletcher, *The Family and Marriage*, Harmondsworth: Penguin, 1962, p. 74.
3 Rev. A. Mearns, *The Better Cry of Outcast London*, 1883, quoted in R. Fletcher, op. cit., p. 104. Note the similar situation in many Latin American and African towns of today. See, for example, O. Lewis, *Five Families*, New York: Mentor, 1959.
4 *Listener*, 82, 210, 3 July 1969.
5 M. Young and P. Willmott, *Family and Kinship in East London*, Harmondsworth: Penguin, 1962, pp. 159–60.
6 Ibid., from pp. 161–4.
7 This pattern has been elucidated by Elizabeth Bott in her book *Family and Social Network*, London: Tavistock, 1957.

Reading

Goode, W. J., *World Revolution and Family Patterns*, New York: Free Press, 1963. An account of changes in the structures of the family in the contemporary world. Includes chapters on the West, Japan, Africa, India, and China.

Harris, C. C., *The Family*, London: Allen & Unwin, 1969. A comprehensive textbook.

Klein, Josephine, *Samples from English Cultures*, London: Routledge & Kegan Paul, 1965. Contains summaries of a number of studies of family and community in England.

Lévi-Strauss, C., 'The family', in H. L. Shapiro (ed.), *Man, Culture and Society*, London, O.U.P., 1956. A good general essay on the nature of the family with particular reference to simple societies.

Lewis, Oscar, *Five Families*, New York: Mentor, 1959. Case studies of five Mexican families. Written by an anthropologist in the style of a novel.

McGregor, O. R., *Divorce in England*, London: Heinemann, 1957. In pursuing its main theme this very readable book also provides a good description of the Victorian family in England.

Queen, S. A., Habenstein, R. W., and Adams, J. B., *The Family in Various Cultures*, New York: Lippincott, 1961. Description of the family in a dozen different pre-industrial societies—European, African, Asian and American Indian.

Further reading

Ariès, Philippe, *Centuries of Childhood*, London: Cape, 1962. A perceptive and readable account of the development of the family in Europe since the middle ages.

Banks, J. A., *Prosperity and Parenthood*, London: Routledge & Kegan Paul, 1954. This study of Victorian family planning gives considerable insight into the Victorian middle-class family.

Edwards, J. N. (ed.), *The Family and Change*, New York: Knopf, 1969. A good collection of articles focusing upon the relationship between the family and the processes of industrialization and urbanization.

Goode, W. J. (ed.), *Readings on the Family and Society*, Englewood Cliffs: Prentice-Hall, 1968. Another useful collection of articles.

Laing, R. D. and Esterson, A., *Sanity, Madness and the Family*, Harmondsworth: Penguin, 1970. This collection of case studies of the families of schizophrenics has interesting implications for the social psychology of the family more generally.

Radcliffe-Brown, A. R. and Forde, D. (eds), *African Systems of Kinship and Marriage*, London: O.U.P., 1950. Anthropological studies of kinship in nine traditional African societies and an important introduction by the editors.

7 Socialization

The effects of isolation in childhood

At birth the human baby is completely helpless and absolutely dependent on others. Indeed, strictly speaking the infant is not a 'human' being in the fullest sense but rather a little 'animal' without speech or self-control, two of the most important attributes of the normal adult member of any human society. The term 'socialization' refers in a general way to the process of growing up into a human being, a process which necessitates contact with other people. It is through this process that the growing child acquires the language and standards of the social group into which it has been born.

Some indication of the necessity of human contact for the normal development of the child is furnished by the several cases of children who have been found living wild. One of the most striking of these cases was the so-called 'Wild Boy of Aveyron' who was found roaming in a French forest in the year 1799. He had apparently been eking out a precarious existence on what he could find to eat in the woods, although it was impossible to say how long he had existed in this way. Although he appeared to be about eleven he could not talk and simply grunted like an animal. This naked, dirty, scarred creature was taken to Paris where a young doctor named Itard devoted five years of his life to the boy's education. Considerable progress was made for, after a couple of years, the boy was clean, affectionate, able to read a few words and able to understand much that was said to him. Despite all Itard's efforts, however, the boy never learned to speak more than two words and in this respect the attempt to humanize him was a failure.

An even more dramatic case is that of the two Indian children who were reported to have been discovered in a wolf-den in Bengal in 1920. The den was excavated and the two children—girls about two and eight years old—were taken to an orphanage where they were cared for by a minister, the Rev. J. A. L. Singh, and his wife. The younger of the two, Amala, died soon after but the other girl, Kamala, lived in the orphanage until November 1929 when she also died. What Kamala's behaviour was like and the extent to which she had become humanized can be judged from a letter that the Rev. Singh wrote towards the end of 1926.[1]

> At the present time Kamala can utter about forty words. She is able to form a few sentences, each sentence containing two, or at the most, three words. She never talks unless spoken to, and when spoken to she may or may not reply. She is obedient to Mrs. Singh and myself only. Kamala is possessed of very acute hearing and evidences an exceedingly acute animal-like sense of smell. She can smell meat at a great distance. Never weeps or smiles, but has a 'smiling appearance'. Shed a single tear when Amala died and would not leave the place where she lay dead. She is learning very slowly to imitate. Does not now play at all and does not mingle with other children. Once, both Amala and Kamala somewhat liked the company of an infant by the name of Benjamin while he was crawling and learning to talk. But one day they gave him

> such a biting and scratching that the infant was frightened and would never approach the wolf-children again. Amala and Kamala liked the company of Mrs. Singh, and Kamala, the surviving one of the pair, is much attached to her. The eyes of the children possessed a peculiar glare, such as that observed in the eyes of dogs or cats in the dark. Up to the present time Kamala sees better at night than during the daytime and seldom sleeps after midnight. The children used to cry or howl in a peculiar voice, neither animal nor human. Kamala still makes these noises at times. She is averse to all cleanliness, and serves the calls of nature anywhere, wherever she may happen to be at the time. Used to tear her clothes off. Hence a loin-cloth was stitched to her in such a fashion that she could not open or tear it. Kamala used to eat and drink like a dog, lowering her mouth down to the plate, and never used her hands for the purpose of eating or drinking. She would gnaw a big bone on the ground and would rub it at times in order to separate the meat from the bone. At the present time she uses her hands for eating and walks straight on two legs, but cannot run at all.

Thus, after six years in the orphanage, Kamala showed some human characteristics. Although she apparently never talked spontaneously, she did have a limited command of language, and, what is particularly important, she had developed a definite emotional attachment to Mrs Singh and was obedient to her. In many other respects, however, Kamala was still relatively unsocialized and the Rev. Singh came to believe that the apparently animal-like features of her behaviour were due to her supposed contact with wolves. In this he was probably mistaken. It should be noted that the circumstances in which the children were found are not entirely clear; no one actually knew how they might have got into the wolf-den in the first place, nor how long they might have been there. Even if it were established beyond any doubt that the children had been found together with wolves, it does not follow that they had been *reared* by these animals. To suppose this without further evidence is sheer conjecture, however attractive it may be to the imagination. What one can say is that the two little girls were not human beings in their behaviour when they were found, and that Kamala would not have become even as humanized as she did without the efforts of the Rev. Singh and his wife. The same may be said about the 'Wild Boy of Aveyron' who would certainly not have made as much progress as he did without the unsparing efforts of Dr Itard. Of course, in these cases we do not know whether the children suffered from any inborn defects which might have limited their capacity to become fully human beings but, assuming they were not defective in this way, it seems reasonable to regard their lack of humanity as due to isolation from other human beings during critical periods of their lives.

Further insight into the effects of social isolation in childhood can be gained from a consideration of those cases where a child is deliberately isolated by the parents. For instance, in 1938 a girl of more than five years of age was found locked up in a room on a lonely farm in America. Apparently she had been incarcerated in this room from babyhood because she was illegitimate. When she was finally discovered and removed from the room she could not walk or talk and was in very poor physical shape altogether. After nearly two years in an institution 'Anna' could at least walk, feed herself and understand simple commands, but she still did not speak. In August 1939 she was taken to a private home for retarded children where she made much more progress. By July 1941 'Anna' had acquired firm habits of personal cleanliness and her feeding habits were normal, except that she still used a spoon as her sole implement. She could dress herself except for fastening her clothes. The most striking thing of all, however, was that she had finally begun to speak and could construct a few complete sentences. She made a little more progress during the following year but then died in August 1942. As in the cases previously considered, the absence of adequate social relationships in early life had resulted in a creature that was hardly recognizable as a human being. The human contact in the two institutions made some socialization possible, particularly in the areas of speech and self-control, but even so the final level reached was very low. Again it is impossible to say with any precision what 'Anna' would have been like if she had received a more normal upbringing from birth but she would almost certainly have reached a higher level of mental development than she did. Again there is the snag that the girl may have been feeble-minded and, in this particular case, there is some evidence that the girl's mother was mentally defective to some degree.

It is particularly instructive to compare the case of 'Anna' with that of another American girl, 'Isabelle', who had also been kept in seclusion because she was illegitimate. 'Isabelle' was discovered nine months after 'Anna' was found and at the time of discovery she was about six and a half years old. Her mother was a deaf-mute and apparently the two of them had spent most of their time together in a dark room shut off from the rest of the family. The girl did not speak and communicated with her mother only by means of gestures. Her behaviour towards strangers showed considerable fear and hostility and, like 'Anna', she was in poor physical shape. At first it was hard to tell whether she could even hear or not, and even when it was definitely established that she was not deaf the specialists thought that she was feeble-minded.[2]

> In spite of this interpretation, the individuals in charge of Isabelle launched a systematic and skilful programme of training. It seemed hopeless at first. The approach had to be through pantomime and dramatization, suitable to an infant. It required one week of intensive effort before she even made her first attempt at vocalization. Gradually she began to respond, however, and, after the first hurdles had at last been overcome, a curious thing happened. She went through the usual stages of learning characteristic of the years from one to six not only in proper succession but far more rapidly than normal. In a little over two months after her first vocalization she was putting sentences together. Nine months after that she could identify words and sentences on the printed page, could write well, could add to ten, and could retell a story after hearing it. Seven months beyond this point she had a vocabulary of 1,500 to 2,000 words and was asking complicated questions. . . . In short, she covered in two years the stages of learning that ordinarily requires six. . . . The speed with which she reached the normal level of mental development seems analogous to the recovery of body weight in a growing child after an illness, the recovery being achieved by an extra fast rate of growth for a period after the illness until normal weight for the given age is again attained.
>
> When the writer saw Isabelle a year and a a half after her discovery, she gave him the impression of being a very bright, cheerful, energetic little girl. She spoke well, walked and ran without trouble, and sang with gusto and accuracy. Today she is over fourteen years old . . . Her teachers say that she participates in all school activities as normally as other children.

Thus, compared with 'Anna', 'Isabelle' obviously made enormous progress, none of which, of course, could have been made without the stimulation of the adults who took such great pains over her training. 'Isabelle' probably had a greater inborn potential than 'Anna', although it must not be forgotten that she received a far more intensive and effective training as well. Moreover, the emotional relationship between 'Isabelle' and her mother seems to have been much more positive than that between 'Anna' and her mother, and this may well have resulted in a greater willingness to learn. The case of 'Isabelle' also suggests that, up to a certain age at least, deprivation of normal social contacts may be made good to quite a substantial degree by the provision of suitable contacts later on, although there is probably a limit to the degree of recovery. If 'Isabelle' had been ten or older when she was found it would have been even harder to teach her to speak and, above a certain age, it might have been impossible. It is significant that the 'Wild Boy of Aveyron', who was estimated to be about eleven when he was found, did not learn to speak although, as we have already noted, we cannot rule out the possibility that he was mentally defective at the outset.

Despite the numerous qualifications one has to make, all these cases show that deprivation of human contact in early life inhibits the development of normal social responses. All human beings, except those born with severe physical handicaps, have the inborn capacity to become fully mature members of society but, in order for this capacity to be realized, the child has to have adequate social relationships with others. *Social behaviour in humans is not inborn; in a very important sense we have to 'learn' to be human beings.*

Variations in patterns of socialization

In the normal course of events, every child grows up in a particular society in direct contact with particular people. He gradually takes on the characteristics of those people and becomes one of them. He learns to speak their language; he learns to think in terms of their concepts; he internalizes their standards of good and bad, right and wrong, and so on. There are, however, enormous variations in the patterns of socialization from one society to another; growing up in an African tribe is quite different from growing up in Britain. Even within a society there may be marked differences in the pattern of socialization. There is, for instance, a considerable difference between growing up in a large industrial city and growing up in a small village; and in the city, too, there is all the difference in the world between growing up in a rich and exclusive suburb and growing up in a poor neighbourhood.

The variations in patterns of socialization show us just how malleable so-called 'human nature' really is. Furthermore, knowing how people behave in societies different from our own enables us to take a fresh look at the way *we* behave, and to increase our understanding as a result. Many beliefs and forms of conduct which we take for granted and unconsciously assume to be universal are a part of the fabric of a particular society and may not be found in other societies. For example, all of us have certain ingrained ideas and opinions about the essential differences between 'masculine' and 'feminine' characteristics. We may believe that girls are 'naturally' submissive, intuitive, and unpractical, but even if most girls in a particular society are actually like this it does not follow that these traits are inborn and universal. Indeed, in other societies the definition of femininity and masculinity may be quite different. Thus, in a survey of the native inhabitants of what used to be British Central Africa it was found that spinning, weaving and sewing were very definitely regarded as men's work.[3]

> the men, in general, are neat-fingered and take to these things almost instinctively, while to their wives, who are gathered into sewing classes at the missions, by way of making them 'womanly', they are mostly pain and grief.

In some societies women do much of the manual labour, while in others cooking, housekeeping and looking after babies are regarded as proper male activities. Hunting is frequently regarded as an essentially masculine pursuit, but amongst the Aboriginal inhabitants of Tasmania seal-hunting was definitely women's work. They swam out to the seal rocks, stalked the animals and killed them with clubs. And finally, the idea that men are 'naturally' more aggressive than women is hardly born out by the practice of warfare, which is certainly not an exclusively male sphere. For instance, in some of the traditional societies of Africa regiments of women were occasionally formed. These women were specially trained to be warriors and enjoyed a considerable reputation for their proficiency and ferocity. And here one might also refer to the legendary Amazons who, whether legendary or not, have provided us with the word 'Amazonian' which means a strong, aggressive, or ironically enough, 'masculine' woman.

In any society there are widely shared conceptions as to how males and females should behave. These conceptions serve as models to which the growing child is expected to conform. Moreover, we generally come to accept the patterns of behaviour which are current in our own society as morally right. This makes it difficult for us to understand and appreciate people whose behaviour differs considerably from our own; there is the quite natural feeling that 'ours is the best way'. As we have just seen, however, there is likely to be considerable variation in what is regarded as 'the best way'. To the sociologist *all* varieties of human behaviour are worthy of study and it is no part of his task as a scientist to try to decide which pattern of conduct is the best.

Apart from the question of the behaviour of the different sexes, the comparative study of human societies indicates striking differences in many other aspects of social life, for instance in attitudes towards property. In some societies, our own for example, the emphasis tends to be on individual ownership, so much so that many people feel that common ownership is contrary to 'human nature'. On the other hand there are societies in which collective ownership is the norm, and people in these societies would in turn feel that individual ownership is 'unnatural'. These different attitudes are well illustrated in an essay by the anthropologist W. H. R. Rivers:[4]

> When I was travelling in 1908 on a vessel with four Polynesian natives of Niue or Savage Island, and took the opportunity of inquiring into their social organization, they retaliated in a manner I am always glad to encourage by asking me about the social customs of my own country . . . one of the first questions was directed to discover what I should do with a sovereign if I was fortunate enough to earn one. In response to my somewhat lame answers, they asked me the definitely leading question whether I should

share it with my parents, brothers and sisters. When I replied that I might do so if I liked, but that it was not the usual custom, they found my reply so ridiculous that it was long before they left off laughing. It was quite clear from their ejaculations that their amusement was altogether due to the incongruity with their own attitude of my conduct with regard to my earnings.

One can readily see that *sharing* would be completely taken for granted by these Polynesians, and their children would be taught to accept it as the right and proper thing to do. In fact, an ethic of sharing is quite common in many of those societies we would describe as 'primitive'. Among the Eskimo and similar peoples in Siberia any seal or whale killed by an individual is shared with the other members of the community. In such communities the successful hunter is morally bound to share his spoils with the unsuccessful. 'The hunter kills, other people have', say the Yukaghir of Siberia. In these societies food must always be made available to others on pain of ostracism and *giving away*, particularly at times of scarcity, is regarded as a moral duty. (Although the present tense is used here it should be noted that many of these communities are undergoing radical change as their members become increasingly involved in larger economic and political systems.)

It is clear that this behaviour does not conform to our stereotype of 'economic man' who is supposed to maximize his profit and minimize his loss, and it follows that we cannot understand the behaviour of primitive hunters and food gatherers in terms of our categories of economic analysis. This highlights the extremely important point that the socialization process in which we have participated and the consequent concepts and standards that we have internalized may act as a major obstacle to the understanding of a way of life which is radically different from our own. We are not normally aware of the relativity of our outlook and we unconsciously judge other peoples in the light of our own standards. Thus the missionaries in the example quoted earlier felt that sewing was *naturally* women's work and set about trying to teach the native women to do this, imposing their own values on people with different values. It may also happen that failure to appreciate the way in which our outlook has been shaped by growing up in a particular society may have rather surprising consequences in certain situations. For example, we tend to take it for granted that our desire for a higher standard of living and our acceptance of economic incentives are universally shared, and probably reflect some basic trait of 'human nature'. However, the importance we attach to these things is a fairly recent development:[5]

In earlier centuries wants were stable in the West and this led to widespread complaints, for example in England, that the result of giving workers higher wages was not a better but an inferior quality of industry, not more but less labour. As needs could be satisfied with a shorter period at work, many skilled labourers who were able to earn as much money as they required in less than the conventional work week spent only three or four days at their jobs and the rest in idleness. The generalized desire for more goods and therefore a higher income and the increasingly accepted demand for a disciplined labour force have lessened the frequency of this type of reaction in the West in the twentieth century.

In the poor countries, the desire for a higher standard of living developed at a later date, and indeed, is only now growing in many areas. In Burma at the turn of the century, rice fields were often left unharvested after the wants of the farmers had been satisfied, despite the existence of markets in which the grain could have been sold. The recruitment of a labour force for a textile factory in the middle of a poor agricultural district in Guatemala proceeded with great difficulty, although the wages offered by the factory were substantially higher than those in agriculture—it took fifty years to build a relatively stable labour force.

From the point of view of our standards, the above reaction to increased income and employment opportunities might seem to be 'irrational', but it must be remembered that from the different perspective of the people involved they would appear to be eminently 'rational'. Some evidence on the way in which these differing standards are already internalized in childhood is provided by a series of essays written by twenty-six children in Guatemala and twenty-six in Iowa, USA. The subject of the essays was 'My home, what I like about it, what I do not like, my ambitions for my home in the future'.[6]

> Twenty-two of the twenty-six children from Iowa mentioned the importance of material facilities and none of those from Guatemala; twenty-three out of twenty-six from Guatemala mentioned love and peace in the home as compared to thirteen in the USA, and eighteen from Guatemala mentioned the importance of space as compared to three in the USA.

It goes without saying that the children from Guatemala would consider their standards to be the best, and that the American children would consider their standards to be the best. From a sociological point of view the really important thing is that the standards and values are different. and then the problem becomes one of trying to explain why they are different.

The development of human behaviour

The examples we have discussed show that most of the differences in the patterns of behaviour of people in different countries, or between different classes and sections within a country, are not inborn in any biological sense; they are *acquired* patterns of behaviour. What is inborn in the biological sense is *the capacity to be different*, the capacity to respond in a different way if circumstances change. It is this that makes man such a flexible creature able to adapt to wide variations in environment. Apart from certain reflexes, human beings have very few fixed reactions at birth; human behaviour is something which *develops* in the context of social interaction. Of course there are inborn physical dispositions with respect, for instance, to temperament and intelligence, but the way in which these dispositions are woven into the texture of behaviour is largely patterned by social interaction. And even very basic 'biological needs' such as hunger and sex are everywhere overlaid by social influences. Thus, in every human society, sexual impulses are hedged around by a whole variety of customs and rules, and similarly, food habits vary enormously from one social group to another.

While granting that human behaviour patterns show remarkable flexibility, the question remains as to whether there are any *universal* features of the process of socialization. The results of socialization vary enormously but are there any common features which can be found in all societies? What are the underlying processes whereby the growing child learns to speak and think and take over the attitudes and values of the members of the group into which he has been born? We have seen that in the most general sense these processes are bound up with social interaction, and our earlier discussion of the effects of social isolation in childhood suggests that the crucial thing is the relationship that normally develops between the child and those that care for it (usually the biological parents, but not necessarily so). This relationship comes to have a strong emotional content; the child normally comes to need the love and affection of those that care for it as well as the satisfaction of its more physical needs for food, etc. In the world of the small child, emotional and physical needs are closely interwoven as can be seen by the fact that disturbances of feeding are often an indicator of emotional disturbance, and, indeed, the actual development of the need for love is very much bound up with experiences of feeding and handling.

Once the need for love and affection has begun to develop there exists a powerful lever for socialization; *in order to satisfy its emotional needs the growing child will come to accept the 'do's and don'ts' of those that care for it.* It is by no means self-evident to the small child that cleanliness is any better than being dirty; as a matter of fact small children evidently enjoy being dirty! Nevertheless, most children learn to accept the standards of cleanliness that the adult members of their society hold. Why is this if the child's spontaneous tendency is in an opposite direction? Putting it briefly, the answer is that being clean results in parental approval and being dirty results in parental disapproval; to the child who needs the continuing affection of those who care for it, learning to be clean is the required 'price' it has to pay. This goes for many other detailed forms of behaviour, for example the countless ways in which children normally imitate their parents. This vital process of imitation revolves around a basic emotional identification with the parents, as if the child were acting on the principle 'I want to be like my father and mother.' Of course, a child may want to be more like one parent than the other and this is directly encouraged by the different expectations parents have of boys and girls. It is through these reciprocal identifications and expectations that the patterns of behaviour appropriate to each sex are gradually exhibited.

The general truth of all this is born out in those cases where the child fails to behave according to parental requirements. Children are usually extremely ambivalent (i.e. have mixed feelings of love and hate) towards those that care for them. If the balance of the child's ambivalence is tilted towards hate it may well exhibit behavioural abnormalities and difficulties of various kinds. There may be regression in feeding and toilet habits, or the child may be generally difficult and intractable for a time. Even more drastic than this are those cases where there is something fundamentally abnormal in the relationship between the child and those who care for it. Consider the following case of an eight-year-old adopted girl who had got into trouble for telling lies and stealing:[7]

> After an illegitimate birth, the child was shifted about from one relative to another, finally brought to a child-placing agency, and then placed in a foster-home for two months before she came to the adoptive parents. . . . The parents described the child's reaction to the adoption as very casual. When they took her home and showed her the room she was to have all for herself, and took her on a tour of the house and grounds, she showed apparently no emotional response. Yet she appeared very vivacious and 'affectionate on the surface'. After a few weeks of experience with her, the adoptive mother complained to her husband that the child did not seem able to show any affection. The child, to use the mother's words 'would kiss you but it would mean nothing'. The husband told his wife that she was expecting too much, that she should give the child a a chance to get adapted to the situation. The mother was somewhat mollified by these remarks, but still insisted that something was wrong. The father said he saw nothing wrong with the child. In a few months, however, he made the same complaint. By this time, also it was noted that the child was deceitful and evasive. All methods of correction were of no avail.

In this case it appears that the instability of the child's early relationships with adults have prevented the formation of the normal emotional attachments of parents and children. Without these attachments the child has great difficulty in developing the generalized need for the approval of other people which is the basis for the acquisition of standards of right and wrong. There is, as it were, an inability to love or feel guilty, and one could say that the development of 'conscience' has been impaired. There are a number of situations which may have this result; apart from instability of relationships in early life, actual rejection of the child by the parents may have similar consequences. Socialization depends upon a reciprocity of affection between children and adults, and, without this, normal development does not occur. We might recall at this point our earlier discussion of the cases of 'Anna' and 'Isabelle'. 'Isabelle' did spend quite a lot of time with her mother and they did communicate, if only by means of gestures: 'Anna', by comparison, seemed to have been largely rejected by her mother. These differences in mother-child relationships may well have been part of the reason for the very difference responses of the two girls to subsequent training. In certain cases, like that of the eight-year-old girl quoted above, the inability to love or to feel guilt may lead the child to become delinquent, although it does not follow that *all* juvenile delinquency can be explained on this basis.

In considering the way in which socialization takes place, the important general point is that what are at first external standards imposed by the parents or other adults are gradually internalized by the child and become part of his own personal way of behaving. This process rests on the normal existence of a need to be accepted by others and ensures some degree of conformity to their expectations. The process can also be seen at work outside the immediate family, for instance among children and young people of the same age group, i.e. one's 'peer group'. The growing child learns some very important lessons in social conduct from his peers and, in this sense, socialization continues beyond and outside the family situation. Children's games, for example, provide an important context in which the concepts of 'fair play' and the 'rules of the game' can be acquired.

One famous study of Swiss boys traced the development of their grasp of the rules of the game of marbles.[8] At first the small child of two or three simply enjoys playing with the marbles without any conception of there being a 'game' with 'rules' which has 'winners' and 'losers'. At four or five, however, the child begins to understand the notion of 'rules'. Thus, you must draw a square of a certain size; you must stand outside this square; you must pitch one marble at a time, and if your marble goes outside instead of hitting that of your opponent, you have lost. At this stage the rules are usually regarded as fixed and unchangeable, but at seven or eight this begins to give way to a more flexible view in which the rules may be modified, providing everybody agrees. Finally, in the pre-adolescent period, considerations of equity may enter in to modify strict application of the rules; for instance, a boy with a physical handicap may be allowed certain advantages over the others by way of compensation.

If the growing child does not conform to the 'rules of the game' he may well be subjected to criticism or even ridicule by his peers. Conformity to the standards of one's peers is an extremely important process in societies like our own where peer groups play an important part in the social development of the child. In this connection it is important to note that what many people regard as the rebelliousness of teenagers in our society (in other words their frequent nonconformity to the standards of their parents) does not mean that they do not conform to *any* standards. On the contrary, they are probably just as conformist as their parents, possibly even more so, for in order to be accepted by the teenage peer group they must exhibit the characteristic attitudes, the likes and dislikes, and the modes of speech and dress which are current in that group.

Socialization, then, is not a process confined to the immediate family, although it is there that certain very basic social characteristics are acquired. The process continues beyond and outside the family into the peer group, and beyond that into adulthood. An extremely important part of this later socialization is the internalization of the standards and attitudes characteristic of one's occupational group, a process which is well described in the following passage:[9]

> Already at the age of twenty-five you see the professional mannerism settling down on the young commercial traveller, on the young doctor, on the young minister, on the young counsellor-at-law. You see the little lines of cleavage running through the character, the tricks of thought, the prejudices, the ways of the 'shop', in a word, from which the man can by-and-by no more escape than his coat-sleeve can suddenly fall into a new set of folds.

In a highly complex society like our own, socialization is indeed an intricate process. Apart from parents, peers and the members of one's occupational group, there are many other people who are directly and indirectly involved in shaping the outlook of the individual as he develops into a particular kind of person. There are the teachers at all levels of the educational system, and there are all those who are involved in the production of books, magazines, newspapers and television programmes. In less complex societies socialization is itself relatively less complicated. This is necessarily so, for to describe a society as less complex can be regarded as a shorthand way of saying that social life is less differentiated, that there are fewer distinct kinds of social groupings. In the simplest kinds of human society, activities like raising a family, getting a living, the maintenance of law and order, politics and religion are not sharply separated from each other as they are in more complex societies with the distinct social groupings of families, firms, political parties and churches. And, apart from these sorts of distinctions, more complex societies are frequently divided into different social classes which are differentiated from each other by inequalities of wealth and power. These class differences, in so far as they involve differences in outlook and standards, also entail diversification of patterns of socialization. The general point to note is that the more differentiated the society the greater the number of possible agencies and modes of socialization.

Socialization and social change

This picture of socialization as a continuous process extending into adulthood and involving interaction with different sets of people can help us to resolve a problem which has been implicit in much of what has been said so far. There is a temptation to over-emphasize the way in which socialization brings about *conformity*. If children were perfectly socialized to accept the standards of their parents, then how could *change* come about? There is a tendency to think of socialization as inherently conservative and orientated towards the past, with the individual as an essentially passive object being moulded to fit into society. From this point of view, deviance from current social norms is almost bound to be seen as undesirable. Yet, as we have seen, one must recognize that human beings have the capacity to be different, to innovate, to create something new. Innovation frequently involves some deviation from standard practice, and many great innovators have, as a matter of fact, found themselves in conflict with social traditions; for example, thinkers like Galileo, Darwin and Freud whose views brought them into sharp conflict with established ideas and values. So, deviance may be a positive, if painful thing without which new ideas and practices are impossible.

People frequently break with tradition because they are forced to in order to cope with changed circumstances, and herein lies part of the answer to our problem. If the world into which children grow up is changing, then many of the things they learn will lead them to have a different outlook from that of their parents. The consequent estrangement of the generations can be illustrated by what is happening today in those economically underdeveloped countries where large numbers of young people leave impoverished rural areas to seek work in towns and cities. These young migrants move into a new world where the standards and values are usually quite alien to those of parents and other kin in the tribe or village. In the process of adapting to the urban milieu, the migrant inevitably develops an outlook which is more or less foreign to that of the older generation rooted in rural ways of life. Even if the parents accompany or follow the young people to the urban area, the relationship between the generations is altered. The parents are usually strangers to urban ways of life and cannot effectively prepare their children for adulthood in the new environment. It is the children who are quicker to adapt to the new situation, and this can easily lead to loss of respect for the traditional wisdom and authority of the parents. However painful it may be for the people involved, conflict between generations is probably inevitable in periods of rapid social changes.

In industrial societies, too, there are many ways in which wider social changes bring about conflict between parents and children. Perhaps the most obvious of these is, as we previously noted, where the code of conduct of young people is at variance with parental conceptions of correct behaviour. More specifically one can readily see how the opportunities for personal advancement *via* higher education may lead to the estrangement of children from their parents. In a society with increasing equality of educational opportunity, an increasing number of boys and girls receive an education which enables them to 'climb the social ladder' and move a long way away from the world of their parents. This type of social mobility, however, is not usually achieved without some degree of personal conflict for the individuals involved. Thus, in order to become accepted in 'middle-class' society, the 'working-class' boy or girl is forced to acquire new standards of behaviour which often clash with old ones. In some cases this process is acutely painful. Here the process of socialization entails conflict between standards and values internalized in the context of home and neighbourhood and those embodied in the educational system.

These remarks on the way socialization may entail conflict between the generations lead us directly to the conclusion of this chapter. Socialization is a process which usually involves both continuity and discontinuity. Continuity is made possible by the internalization of traditional values which represent the past. Discontinuity occurs because the members of each new generation may have to reject some of the heritage of the past in order to cope with a changing present and an imagined future. The development of both individual and society depends upon the balance of these inherently opposed but inter-related tendencies.

Notes

1 Quoted in a note by P. C. Squires in *American Journal of Psychology*, vol. 38, 1927, pp. 314–15.
2 Kingsley Davis, 'Final note on a case of extreme isolation', *American Journal of Sociology*, vol. 52, 1947, pp. 436–7.
3 Alice Werner, *The Natives of British Central Africa*, London: Constable, 1906, pp. 196–7.
4 W. H. R. Rivers, *Psychology and Politics*, London: Kegan Paul, 1923, pp. 36–7.
5 R. Theobald, *The Rich and the Poor*, New York: Mentor, 1961, pp. 30–31.
6 Ibid., pp. 31–2.
7 Case quoted in J. Bowlby, *Child Care and the Growth of Love*, Harmondsworth: Penguin, 1953, pp. 33–4.
8 Jean Piaget, *The Moral Judgement of the Child*, London: Routledge & Kegan Paul, 1932.
9 Margaret Knight, *William James: A Selection from his Writings on Psychology*, Harmondsworth: Penguin, 1950, pp. 78–9.

Reading

Brim, Orville G. Jr and Wheeler, Stanton, *Socialization after Childhood: Two Essays*, New York: Wiley, 1966.
These essays are rather advanced, but the interested student might usefully tackle the first one which gives a comprehensive picture of 'Socialization through the Life Cycle' from a sociological point of view.

Elkin, F., *The Child and Society: The Process of Socialization*. New York: Random House, 1960. A short but fairly systematic introduction to the topic. Ideal for the beginner.

Lindesmith, A. R. and Strauss, A. L., *Social Psychology* (3rd ed.), New York: Holt, Rinehart & Winston, 1968. A good textbook for sociology students. Part 4, 'Socialization and Interaction', contains several excellent chapters in which socialization is consistently viewed in relation to the pattern of social relations of which it is part. This section includes a useful chapter on adult socialization.

Mead, Margaret, *Coming of Age in Samoa*, and, *Growing up in New Guinea*, Harmondsworth: Penguin, 1943 and 1942. Detailed accounts of growing up in societies very different from our own.

Piaget, Jean, *The Moral Judgement of the Child*, London: Routledge & Kegan Paul, 1932. A classic study of social relations among children as a factor in the development of moral judgment. Although Piaget possibly overstates his case, his approach is a useful reminder that socialization is not simply a matter of parent-child relations. The beginning student may well find Piaget a little difficult to follow but it is worth making the effort.

White, R. W., *Live in Progress* (2nd ed.), New York, Holt, Rinehart & Winston, 1966. A stimulating discussion of the development of personality based on detailed case histories of three very different people. The book brings out the real complexity of human growth and the many and varied factors involved in becoming a particular kind of person. The broader implications of the case histories are discussed in several very good theoretical chapters.

Further reading

Brown, Roger, *Social Psychology*, New York: Free Press, 1965 (see part 3, 'The Socialization of the Child'). A sophisticated textbook discussion which brings out the importance of symbolic processes in socialization; includes a good introduction to the work of Piaget and his colleagues on cognitive development.

Clausen, John A. (ed.), *Socialization and Society*, Boston: Little, Brown, 1968. This book is the outcome of the work of a special Committee on Socialization and Social Structure appointed in 1960 by the Social Science Research Council of America. It is concerned with the inter-relationships between social structure, socialization processes, and personality formation; particularly useful in so far as it brings together the psychological and sociological approaches to the study of socialization.

Goslin, David A. (ed.), *Handbook of Socialization Theory and Research*, Chicago: Rand McNally, 1969. A comprehensive collection of advanced essays on various aspects of socialization; particularly good on theoretical issues. The term 'handbook' is misleading; this is a very substantial volume of over 1,000 pages!

Isaacs, Susan, *Social Development in Young Children*, London: Routledge & Kegan Paul, 1933. A psycho-analytically oriented study of the emotional aspects of social relations in childhood, based on detailed observational records of the social and sexual development of children.

Parsons, Talcott, *Social Structure and Personality*, New York: Free Press, 1964. The first part of this collection of essays contains the author's various attempts to place Freudian theory in a sociological context. See particularly 'The superego and the theory of social systems' and 'The incest taboo in relation to social structure and the socialization of the child'. Several other essays in the book are also relevant to the topic of socialization, notably 'The school class as a social system'.

Zigler, Edward and Child, Irvin L., 'Socialization', in volume 3 of Gardner Lindsey and Elliot Aronson (eds), *The Handbook of Social Psychology* (2nd ed.), Reading, Mass.: Addison-Wesley, 1969. A useful review of the literature and the current state of research.

8 Education

The development of education

In simple societies education is synonymous with socialization. The homogeneity of the society and the relatively low level of technology enable the social skills necessary for adult life to be taught to the child informally, as part of his everyday contact with his elders. Consequently there are no special teachers entrusted specifically with the training of young people. Typically, boys learn the skills of hunting or farming from their fathers or other adult males; girls learn how to cook, sew, and perhaps farm from the women of the community. In this way the process of education (or socialization) is carried out through a loose form of apprenticeship and, as we have already seen, this informal learning process is present and important in all societies. In the more complex societies of the industrial world, however, where there is more division of labour and a large number of different adult roles, there are persons who specialize in educating the young. In intermediate stages of development this task is often given to the priests, and education becomes closely connected with religion, as in ancient Egypt, ancient India and medieval Europe. In the latter case, for example, the clergy held a monopoly of the skills of literacy and consequently were the only persons capable of carrying out educational tasks involving reading and writing. Gradually schools emerge as separate institutions specializing in education, and teachers emerge as a separate occupational group. Thus there grows up a new complex of institutions—an educational system—specially designed to perform an important part of the process of socialization. But in addition to the function of socialization an educational system has many other functions—some of them unintended and sometimes not even recognized. In other words the process of preparing young people for adult life has many side effects some of which may even be contrary to the stated aims of the educators.

The highly complicated systems of compulsory education that are to be found in industrial societies today did not emerge overnight. When the occupational roles demanding literacy are few, the specialized system of education remains the preserve of a minority, while for the majority 'education' is carried on as before. In England, it was not until the nineteenth century that it was thought necessary to provide formal education of any sort for the mass of the population. Prior to the eighteenth century 'young gentlemen' were tutored privately in the art of gentlemanly behaviour; a few of the sons of the rich attended the older of the public schools (the name by which they were later known); a few received education in one or other of the schools attached to the cathedrals; and a very few (including in this case the sons of 'commoners') were taught by the local parish priest. For the most part, however, all learning was in the hands of parents or others with whom the young people worked.

Such a system, with father teaching son, was geared to agricultural rather than industrial conditions and, although it could be adapted to the 'cottage' type of industry where parents and their children normally worked alongside each other, later changes made it unsuitable. With the changing nature of industry in the late eighteenth and early nineteenth centuries, and in particular with the accelerating growth of large towns, the drawbacks of this 'apprenticeship' type of system became more obvious. For some time the exploitation of children in the factories was so intense that there was not time for education of a more general sort. With the passing of the Factory Acts, however, education became a possibility. Indeed the Factory Acts themselves represent the earliest legislation directly related to education. The Factory Act of 1802, for example, required employers in the cotton industry to provide adequate instruction in reading, writing and arithmetic for at least four of the seven years of apprenticeship. The earliest schools of industry had been founded a hundred years before this legislation and such schools, although few in number, did provide the opportunity for some children to earn their keep while attending school part time.

In addition to this stimulation from the growth of industries there were in the late eighteenth and early nineteenth centuries important changes in the intellectual and political climate—changes which themselves were later to be encouraged by the spread of mass schooling. More egalitarian ideas were spreading to England from revolutionary France, and the gradual extension, throughout the nineteenth century, of political power at home gave increasing control to groups whose commercial interests made them more favourable to the spread of education than the landed gentry had been. There were, of course, counter-influences, often stemming from the same sources. For example, there was the fear of the ruling classes, most eloquently expressed in the writing of Edmund Burke, that education for the majority of the people would result in political unrest and perhaps even in a revolution similar to that experienced in France. For the most part, however, the idea of training the poor only to poverty was dying.

Even so, for the greater part of the nineteenth century education, in common with all activities not directly connected with law or defence, was not considered to be a realm appropriate for government action. Throughout the first part of the century educational development was exclusively in the hands of non-governmental agencies, and of these the most important were the churches. The breakdown of the moral and religious control by the churches which occurred when villagers moved to towns, combined with the religious enthusiasm of the middle classes during much of the nineteenth century, not to mention the rivalry between the Anglicans and the Nonconformists, provided a fertile ground for the initial growth of schools. In particular, the Nonconformist emphasis on the importance of being able to read the Bible for oneself led to a high evaluation of literacy. This religious interest in education was reflected in the Sunday School movement—a movement which frankly acknowledged the industrial conditions of the day by giving instruction on the only day of the week when the children were not labouring in the factories—and more systematically in the formation of the National Society for Promoting the Education of the Poor in the Principles of the Established Church, and the British and Foreign School Society (a Nonconformist run society whose schools were to contain no denominational teaching). But in the second half of the century, when enough growth had taken place to bring these groups into direct competition for the *same* pupils and when the possibility of substantial government grants arose, jealousy and suspicion between them hindered further growth and prevented the systematization of education. The 'religious question' exhibited a a regular pattern throughout the years of the struggle. Whenever there was a proposal before parliament to give financial support to denominational schools it was blocked by the Nonconformist group (as, for example, with the 1843 Education Bill), because such a measure would benefit the Anglicans with their greater number of schools. Whenever the plan was to assist 'non-denominational' schools from public funds there was Anglican opposition (as, for example, with the 1839 Education Bill). The consequent position of stalemate over the extension of state aid to education, which had begun in a small way in 1833, can thus only be understood in the light of the religious divisions in the country.

Christianity has also played a decisive role in the development of education in some other countries. In most European colonies and ex-colonies, for example, the agencies through which Western education was spread were initially the Christian missions. Indeed, the educational scene of much of English-speaking Africa bears a striking resemblance in this, as in other respects, to the English educational system a hundred years ago. In spite of a general upsurge of government activity in the years since independence many of the schools are still run either by local churches or foreign missions. But the emergence and continuance of these Western-style schools cannot be explained simply in terms of religious or humanitarian goodwill, any more than such an explanation is sufficient for the development of the English system. In the latter case the transformation from a situation where schooling was a luxury granted to very few to its establishment as a normal practice for all children was very closely connected with the whole complex of industrialization and urbanization. But the churches were the only non-governmental agencies capable of organizing on anything like the national scale required to meet the need for education although other bodies could and did provide a sprinkling of schools here and there.

In the same way, in many African societies before their contact with the West there was no need for a Western type of educational system. Literacy itself was a skill that had little relevance to traditional ways of life. Consequently when missionaries tried to start schools the response was one of apathy. On the west coast of Africa, for example, there were attempts of this kind over a period of more than three hundred years, but the only schools which met with even partial success were those catering for the children of the Europeans living in the coastal castles. It was not until the establishment of trading posts along the coast and a consequent re-orientation of the values of the indigenous peoples that any local interest was shown in the schools. Then it became increasingly evident that schooling provided a gateway to a new kind of job, as clerk or assistant to a European trader or missionary, and this occupational relevance of education began to popularize the schools.

From this example it is clear that religious zeal is not, of itself, sufficient to establish formal education. Only when the economic conditions are suitable for such development is pioneering action in education effective. Especially important in this respect is the emergence of occupations demanding a high level of literacy. The importance of religion in the development of the Western type of formal education was in the provision, through its denominations and its missionary societies, of a sponsoring organization for education at times when government action in the field of education was minimal.

Political considerations form a further element in the growth of educational systems. Reference has already been made to some of the political changes in nineteenth-century England which were especially relevant to education. The extension of political power to wider groups—or more accurately the passing of legislation which made such an extension a possibility even if not an actuality—gave the expansion of elementary education a boost in the expectation that it would in turn provide an educated, or at least a literate, electorate and perhaps also in the desire to exert some control over this newly influential group. The saying 'we must educate our masters' was a cynical formulation of this new attitude towards popular education. A rather more remarkable appreciation of the interaction of the economic, political and educational spheres was demonstrated by Mr W. E. Foster during the parliamentary debate on the 1870 Education Bill: 'Upon the speedy provision of elementary education depends our industrial prosperity ... upon this speedy provision depends also, I fully believe, the good, the safe working of our constitutional system. ... Upon this speedy provision of education depends also our national power.'[1]

Similarly, in modernizing societies political life has not been without relevance for the educational system. The rewards offered to educated people through the occupational structure of both industrial and modernizing countries provide what is perhaps the dominant motive of individuals when they seek education for themselves or their children. But once such motivation is present it becomes possible for other institutions to influence the extent to which it is satisfied. So it was impossible for the newly independent governments of Africa, dependent as they were in the early stages of independence upon popular support, to oppose the wishes of an education-seeking population by restricting education in the way that their colonial predecessors had done. The legislation of the first year after independence invariably includes measures to expand the educational system in one way or another. The governments of newly independent countries typically aim at compulsory, free primary education in the shortest possible time, partly from a genuine idealism and sense of social justice, and partly because they are pressed into such action by a pro-education electorate.

Thus it would appear that economic, political and religious factors are all important in determining the timing and pace of the emergence of education. But so far all our attention has been focused on primary education; what of the secondary schools? In England separate institutions for secondary and university education had existed even at the beginning of the nineteenth century albeit under the wing of the Church of England and, in a few cases, the

Nonconformist denominations. The universities of Oxford and Cambridge, however, were little more than places for rich young men to squander their wealth ostentatiously, and the schools—the endowed grammar schools and other independent foundations—attracted few pupils and had low physical and academic standards. Moreover, the Nonconformist academies which had, in the eighteenth century, been an important source of scientific innovation had subsequently declined into insignificance.

There was, however, a growing need for 'higher' education, so that when reforms occurred in some of the schools there was a rapidly growing clientele to make use of them. In spite of their wealth, the rising class of industrialists and businessmen were not accepted by the landed aristocracy on terms of equality. This helps to explain the eagerness with which they sought education for their children; for the reformed public schools, together with an increasing number of new foundations, provided an education which was at the same time a training for political and professional activities (the gentlemanly activities) and a means by which the sons of the *nouveaux riches* could learn the customs and habits of the upper classes and thus eventually attain the respectability denied their fathers. Furthermore, the improvements in transport—and especially the growth of the railways—which took place in the middle of the century enabled these schools to become national institutions, drawing their clientele from all over the country rather than from a single locality.

As was the case with the early primary schools, the first secondary schools were founded and controlled by non-governmental agencies, and the secondary school revival of the nineteenth century was also a revival of independent schools. This must be borne in mind when we look for an explanation of the *type* of secondary system of education which eventually grew up in England, for these schools attained a position of high prestige and a virtual monopoly over entry to powerful positions in the country. Consequently, when the state came to establish a system of secondary education at the beginning of the twentieth century it merely copied the established pattern of providing secondary education only for a minority. There were, however, forces other than imitation which influenced the establishment of secondary schools, and one of the most important of these has been the class structure.

Even a casual glance at English education in the nineteenth century makes it clear that it consisted of two *separate* streams rather than a unified system. There was elementary education—the education which was provided for the working classes, initially as an act of charity by voluntary organizations such as the churches, and after 1870 increasingly by the state. There was, second, the growth of the public schools and grammar schools for the sons (and in the latter part of the century the daughters as well) of the middle classes. It was this second sector that came to be known as 'secondary' education, and the division between elementary and secondary was in effect a division between two parallel systems, one being for the poor and one for the rich, with few links between them. This class basis of education was frankly recognized at the time and is implicit in the reports of all the major committees and commissions on education. A good example is the Taunton Commission which was set up in 1868 to investigate all secondary schools other than the nine chief public schools (which had been investigated separately). The Taunton Commissioners recommended that three types of school should be established, but the content of the report is perhaps of less interest than its phraseology. The first type of school, they said, should be for the sons of men of ample means or good education; the second for those whose means were 'straightened' but who wished to enter one of the professions; and the third for the 'sons of the smaller tenant farmers, the small tradesmen, the superior artisans'.

Towards the end of the century and for the first years of the twentieth century there was increased pressure for more secondary education, pressure which had its origin in industrial, political and other social changes. In particular the extension of the franchise in the last third of the nineteenth century had led to a more vocal condemnation of the economic and social inequality which showed itself in the class structure and which had previously always been taken for granted. The rise of the Labour party provided a national political party to voice this disquiet which eventually (after the first world war) took shape as the Labour party's campaign for 'secondary education for all'.

During the 1890s the demand for more 'higher' education was met largely by the growth of 'higher elementary' schools, created through the upward extension of some of the existing elementary schools. There was also some expansion of grammar schools. With the incorporation of secondary education into the state system after the 1902 Education Act, most of the higher elementary schools were converted into secondary schools and therefore they provided a similar education to the old grammar schools, although sometimes with more emphasis on science. But the entry of the state into the secondary field did not alter the basic pattern of an educational system split into separate elementary and secondary streams. Throughout the first half of the twentieth century social and economic conditions increasingly demanded that more and more children should stay longer at school. In response to this demand two things happened. First, the age of finishing compulsory school attendance was raised and attendance was more strictly enforced; second, greater provision was made for children to transfer from the elementary to the secondary stream by means of scholarships. But secondary education was still generally viewed as the education of a particular group rather than as a stage—the post-primary stage—in the education of all children.

The new view of secondary education as the education of an *age* group was developed by the various committees who were asked to report on post-primary education between the wars and during the second world war (the Hadow committee, 1927; the Spens committee, 1939; the Norwood committee, 1943). Each of these committees recommended the provision of separate types of secondary education for different groups of children. This pattern of secondary education, so important in later developments received a pseudo-theoretical justification in the report of the Norwood committee who submitted that there were three types of children: one type 'is interested in learning for its own sake'; the second type has abilities which 'lie markedly in the field of applied science or applied art'; and the third type 'deals more easily with concrete things than ideas'. This classification of the 'types' of children's mind was, claimed the committee, based upon 'common sense'. One might point out that it was also contrary to psychological evidence available to, but ignored by, the committee. As Professor Barnard has written:[2]

> the history of English education is full of examples of theoretical arguments advanced to justify an already existing state of affairs. The *a priori* classification outlined by the Norwood committee fitted in excellently with the scheme of post primary education laid down in the Spens report; and that in turn had been moulded largely on a system which had grown up in this country and had been determined mainly by historical, political and economic conditions.

In spite of its questionable foundations the Norwood report provided the initial justification for the practice of tripartitism (or dualism as it turned out in practice) which dominated English secondary education in the twenty-five years since the second world war. The dualism between grammar schools and secondary modern schools was, in effect, a continuation under new names of the old secondary-elementary dichotomy which itself originated in the class structure of the nineteenth century. Thus to a considerable extent the structure of the system of secondary education which emerged from the war reflected the class structure of a previous century.

The major change in the structure of secondary education since the war has been the movement towards 'comprehensive' secondary schooling. Even with the basic framework of the dual system, however, a number of significant changes have taken place. The most important of these has been the considerable increase in the average length of formal schooling. The minimum school leaving age was raised to fifteen in 1947, but since that time an ever-increasing number of young people have been continuing their full-time education beyond this minimum. In January 1947 there were 39,000 pupils over the age of seventeen in school; twenty years later the figure had risen to 164,000. Moreover, the tendency to stay on at school has been observable in all types of schools, although it has been most marked in those offering pupils an opportunity to sit for the General Certificate of Education. This represents an extension and an acceleration of changes which have been visible throughout the century. It is partly connected with the fact that the increasing complexity of industrial societies demands a longer period of learning, but in England much of this learning process has traditionally been carried on outside the schools and colleges through the institution of apprenticeship. (This is one of the reasons for the lower enrolment in English education after the age of compulsory school attendance when compared to the United States of America.) More closely related to the extension of education, and especially to the extension of the academic education which has characterized the grammar schools and higher education, have been the changes in the occupational structure represented by the growth of the professions and of white collar occupations such as clerks and typists.

The traditional association of secondary schools with occupations receiving high economic reward and prestige remained when these schools gradually opened their doors to the children of the lower classes. In addition, the increasingly bureaucratic nature of society made it more and more difficult for persons of working-class origin to achieve upward social mobility through success in business or industry; the best jobs went to those with the highest educational qualifications. The result was that the educational system—and particularly the grammar schools—became important as a channel through which young people of lowly origins could make their way to more respected, more highly remunerated and more prestigious occupations. In other words they became a major channel of social mobility. The secondary school, and the grammar school that replaced it, increasingly appeared as the only opportunity that working-class children had of rising to the ranks of the middle-class 'salariat' and it has been ambitious parents who have provided one of the driving forces behind the expansion of secondary education. In the years since the second world war the awareness shown by middle-class parents of the vocational relevance of grammar schooling spread to many working-class parents, and places at such schools come to be valued primarily for their occupational potential.

This also explains the strange history of the secondary modern schools. Designed for the children who 'deal more easily with concrete things than ideas', their early career was marked by curricular experiments, experiments in methods of teaching and a general emphasis on 'learning by doing'. Within a few years, however, many of them were training their children for GCE 'O' level examinations which involved a reversion to traditional curricula and teaching methods, and for those pupils who could not manage 'O' level another set of public examinations (the Certificate of Secondary Education) was introduced. Curiously enough it was the children and their parents who forced these changes, often against the opposition of teachers and educationalists, and curiously again, it is by the provision of such courses that secondary modern schools have increased their public appeal and been able to persuade pupils to stay at school beyond the statutory leaving age. It is the occupational relevance of these examinations, clearly seen in the demand of employers for paper qualifications, and the perception of this relevance by children and their parents that have been supremely important. Such occupational considerations dictated the direction of the development of secondary modern schools no less than they determined the expansion of the grammar schools.

There are, of course, other factors than the class structure and the occupational structure which help to determine the structure of education. In contemporary modernizing countries, as in the industrial countries in the past, the amount of money available for education is important in determining what type of educational system emerges. Where money is scarce it may be impossible to provide universal primary education and it will certainly be impossible to provide universal secondary education. In such a situation education can only be provided for a small proportion of school age children. Consequently immediate economic pressures are such as to encourage minority education. The growing educational systems of these countries are also open to influences from other countries, both through the examples offered by the existence of education elsewhere and more directly. Many of them had their first experiences of formal education while they were under colonial rule and frequently an educational system similar to that of the colonial power was grafted on to them irrespective of local conditions. Where this happened, the explanation of many facets of education lies outside the country altogether and can only be understood by an appreciation of conditions in the metropolitan country. Perhaps even more important than this, however, has been the world atmosphere of egalitarianism and democracy into which the newer countries have been born. The contemporary world is one in which widespread government action in the field of education is both expected and positively valued, so that most younger governments feel obliged to intervene to attempt to provide something akin to equality of educational opportunity. Partly because of this, there is government intervention at a much earlier stage in the development of the educational systems of the new countries than was the case in the now industrial countries.

One further difference between the 'new' and the 'old' countries needs mentioning. At the time when education was being grudgingly extended to the lower classes of the nations of Western Europe these countries had been in the process of industrializing for a hundred years or more. The contemporary modernizing countries, by contrast, have hardly started upon the road of industrialization. Thus, in the case of the 'old' countries, the growth of educational systems was a spontaneous response to the changing social conditions of industrializing societies, whereas in many modernizing societies there has been no such spontaneous development. Both the educational systems themselves and the factors giving rise to a local demand for education have been imported from other societies, and in this situation there has been a tendency for educational expansion to outrun other social changes. This in turn has important implications for further economic development, for unemployment, and even for political stability.

Socialization in schools

As we have already pointed out, socialization is only one of the functions of formal systems of education. It is nevertheless important and should not be ignored. In favourable circumstances the educational system provides an efficient processing machine, turning out its clients with particular skills, values and attitudes. One of the best examples of this was the work of the American schools, in the days of widespread immigration, in assimilating young people from diverse national origins into a single nation with a strong sense of their common nationhood. It was very largely through the educational system that the second and third generation of immigrants became fully American, a process which often necessitated a disruption of their ties with their parents. Socialization of the young generation into a new America could only be achieved by breaking down the values and customs of the immigrant community. Much the same was true in the USSR prior to the education reforms of 1958. Here the situation was more complex in that the problem of welding several nationalities into a single unit conflicted with the need to mollify the suspicion of Russian domination entertained by other ethnic groups. One of the concessions made was to give non-Russians the opportunity to receive their education in their native language, which in turn served to strengthen local sentiment. The consequent limitations on their ability in the Russian language limited the career prospects of many non-Russians but, on the other hand, this concession made the political aspect of some of the curriculum more palatable than it would otherwise have been and, in this way, smoothed the transition to a socialistic society tightly controlled from the centre. In other words, in the American case and to some extent in the case of the Soviet Union, the socializing influence of the school worked in the opposite direction to the socializing influence of the family. This illustrates a more general point that where a modern educational system is grafted on to a relatively simple society its socializing influence, and indeed its very existence, may be disruptive rather than supportive of the old society. The new educational system acts as an agent of socialization not into the existing society (i.e. the immigrant communities of America or the regions of the Soviet Union) but into the new *modern* society which sponsored the educational system in the first place.

The clearest examples of this are to be found in non-Western countries which have adopted a Western pattern of education. Throughout Africa and Asia the growth of educational systems and the gradual establishment of an occupational sector based upon educational qualifications has helped to destroy the traditional patterns of authority as well as the old customs and beliefs. Members of the new (educated) élite, who monopolized the important positions in the modern occupational sector and were invariably given such positions of responsibility as were delegated by the colonial powers, owed their position to their education not to tradition. Indeed, the pre-independence politics of many of these countries consisted of a struggle for power between the educated and the traditional rulers. This alienation from the traditional patterns of life was partly due to the nature of the socialization process within schools. But the most important thing about education was that it resulted in the introduction of a new element—an educational system—into the social structure. The very implications of formal education, especially the setting up of academic qualifications as a source of authority and a means of occupational selection, were incompatible with the assumptions of the traditional societies. It mattered little *what* was taught in the schools; the important thing was that they existed.

In colonial countries the establishment of schools also provided a training ground for those who were later to challenge the legitimacy of colonial rule. The leaders of the independence struggles of the middle decades of the twentieth century have invariably been the products of mission or government schools—often highly gifted persons who had received higher education in Western universities. Once again the important factor was not so much *what* they learnt at school or university, as the part played by educational institutions in the emergence of a new type of society; a society in which educated leaders had sufficient power successfully to challenge foreign supremacy.

Education and economic development

Contemporary modernizing societies also provide us with the opportunity of making contemporary observations of the part played by education in the early stages of economic development. Ever since social scientists first became interested in these problems in the 1950s it has generally been held that education plays a key part in determining economic growth; certainly this has been the expressed opinion of many practising politicians. The experience of industrial countries is often cited to suggest that educated personnel are needed to further the process of industrial development and that therefore expenditure on education can be a form of investment. Without such an investment, it is argued, industrial developments will prove unattainable. Those charged with planning educational policy have almost always advised vast expansion schemes which have, for political reasons, been attractive to governments. Our discussion of the growth of English education, however, has already cast some doubt over the dominance of education in economic change. Certainly the early stages of industrialization in England owed little to formal education for it was these very changes which created the major need for mass education. Closer observation of the economic problems of Africa, Latin America and Asia will lead us to further scepticism. Perhaps the major problem of economic growth in these continents is a shortage of capital for investment in power projects, factories, the modernization of agriculture and so on. Money spent on educational developments is money diverted from such directly productive investment. In the past it has been considered to be a praiseworthy diversion—an investment in manpower which while reducing the immediate benefit would pay ample dividends in the long run. It is now being realized, however, that excessive investment in education may actually retard economic development by using up a disproportionate amount of the available capital. In some countries, for example in Western and Eastern Nigeria prior to 1965, up to 40 per cent of all government expenditure has been on education. Many economists are now of the opinion that in purely economic terms direct investment in industry produces higher returns at this level of industrial development than a similar investment in education. Of course, it is necessary for the educational system of these countries to turn out enough educated persons to man the commercial and industrial sector of the economy: it is as inefficient to produce factories with nobody capable of running them as it is to produce managers, foremen and semi-skilled workers with nothing to run. But the size of the modern sector of the economy in such societies is very small—invariably less than 10 per cent of the total employed population and often very much less. In order to provide manpower for such a small sector it is not necessary to mount the huge compulsory education programmes that typify newly independent countries. A relatively small educational system would suffice for such a task. In purely economic terms growth beyond this minimum, far from stimulating industrial development, actually retards it.

In the contemporary modernizing countries, then, as in Western countries in their early stages of industrialization, education has little power over the economy and certainly much less than is commonly ascribed to it. At later stages of industrialization, however, education becomes a more powerful instrument of promoting or retarding further economic development. The modern industrial world is not short of capital, and massive investment in education need not prejudice the continued growth of industry or commerce. Indeed, the increasingly technological nature of society requires, for its very maintenance, a great increase in the type of training that can only be carried on within formal institutions of higher education. The educational systems and the economies of countries such as the USA, the USSR, and Great Britain are more highly *inter*-dependent that was the case a hundred years ago. A level of industrial development has been reached where the educational system has become an essential element in society, and further developments in the technology of such societies are dependent upon a continued supply of research scientists. Innovation thus becomes part of the very fabric of society.

Occupational selection

In industrial societies, then, the task of socialization through the educational system (the task of educating the young as it is called in everyday speech) involves, in particular, the preparation of young people for the jobs they are going to do in later life. In the early stages of industrialization in England the task of sorting out which people were best fitted for which jobs presented no problems; a person's first occupation, and consequently the education necessary to prepare him for it, was prescribed by his father's class position, while any social mobility took place through achievement *on the job*. Nowadays, however, social mobility takes place predominantly through achievement in education, since occupations are allocated largely according to educational merit. Thus the educational system performs the task of *occupational selection*; of selecting at a fairly early age which people are most likely to be suited to a given type of occupation and providing them with appropriate training.

This process of selection can be seen at work most clearly in the traditional English type of educational system, in which children are sent to different types of secondary schools to prepare for different types of jobs. But *all* educational systems of industrial societies (and those of societies industrializing or attempting to industrialize through the adoption of bureaucratic methods of appointment) are selective in this way; the difference lies in the point at which the selection is made. Where only a tiny minority receive any education at all (for example, throughout much of Africa in the first half of the twentieth century) it is possible for those with only three or four years of elementary schooling to monopolize clerical occupations. The important thing here is whether one has been to school or not. In Britain at the beginning of the century, however, or in tropical Africa today, the majority of children receive some elementary education and clerical posts are only open to those who have completed a more extensive schooling. What has happened in such situations is that the educational system has grown faster than the number of white collar jobs with the result that higher qualifications are now required for entry into a given occupation.

In England, the first major point of selection has until now been upon entry to secondary schools which have offered differential training for different types of occupations. Where comprehensive secondary schools predominate (as in the USA and elsewhere) a larger part of the selection process is carried out in the secondary school and a good deal of selection is delayed until the school leaving age or later. Entrance to college or university is another significant point of selection especially where a majority of children stay at school after the minimum school leaving age. In the USA further selection is made during the college course with the result that many students leave college without completing the course.

Education, social mobility, and the class structure

In societies where job allocation is made on grounds of educational qualifications (and this includes all societies with highly developed educational systems), this type of selection will always be an important function of education. In modern societies, however, it is usually considered important that the 'best' person should be selected for a given position irrespective of where he lives, what he looks like, what he believes and who his parents are. The selection processes are therefore designed to pick out the academically most able children to proceed to the next stage or to be trained for the top jobs. One of the main concerns of sociologists interested in education has been to measure how far the selection process is successful in selecting the most able children irrespective of their social background. Do educational systems in fact select the most able candidates for important and difficult jobs or do they function primarily to place the children of the élite in high occupational positions themselves? Do modern educational systems favour particular class, residential, religious or ethnic groups? The short answer is that in most countries the educational system *both* acts as an agent of social mobility *and* tends to reinforce inherited social positions, but to varying degrees in different countries and at different times. In many countries the position is complicated by the existence of an important private sector of secondary schools. The public schools in England have in the past performed the function of reinforcement—of passing on high status from father to son. The high fees charged have, for the most part, excluded the less wealthy members of society and even when, after the second world war as an outcome of the Fleming report on public schools, a few free places were made available to the working classes, these groups showed little inclination to send their children away to boarding schools to be educated. For the few working-class children who have taken up such scholarships, however, the very nature of education in a boarding school with an overwhelmingly middle-class clientele has facilitated the assimilation of middle-class values and behaviour patterns. At the other end of school life, the public schools have usually been able to place their pupils in prestigious and remunerative jobs, and, in addition, their close links with some of the Oxford and Cambridge colleges have given their pupils further advantages. A further important function of the minor public schools has been in the provision of an alternative line of 'academic' education for those sons of wealthy parents who have failed to gain entry to the grammar schools. This has been particularly important for the reinforcement function of the system since it has enabled such children to avoid *downward* social mobility through the educational system. This function of the public schools is likely to survive any schemes of reform designed to 'broaden' the public school entry. In the USA the private secondary schools play an essentially similar, if less extreme, part through their association with the Ivy League colleges. As with the English public schools, however, this link with higher education is now of decreasing importance.

Within the state sector of education, whether the selection process operates primarily as an agent of social mobility or primarily as a mechanism of status maintenance depends largely upon its accuracy in sorting out the most able from the rest. As has already been stated, the major point of selection in England in the past has been upon entry to secondary schools, and (public schools aside) the greatest opportunities to achieve positions of high income, status and power have been available to those who have gained entry to the grammar schools. How far has access to these schools been open to all classes? Formerly the grammar schools were very largely middle-class schools since their fees put them beyond the reach of the lower classes. In spite of the changes which have taken place since the entry of the state into the field of secondary education in 1902, many studies in the last decade or so have shown that children of the middle classes are still over-represented in the grammar schools and in the 'academic' streams of comprehensive schools. The earlier studies of this problem in the 1930s and early 1940s explained it simply in terms of poverty. Although it had become more possible for working-class children to gain entry to secondary schools, for many of them this never became a real possibility as their parents could not afford the extra expense involved even if they won a scholarship. The continued possibility of buying places in the secondary schools further explained the preponderance of middle-class children shown in these early studies. In 1944, however, fees were finally abolished and after that time it was only possible to attend the grammar schools by passing a test of ability of one kind or another. These tests were designed to select the most able children, and in order to do so various combinations of written examinations, intelligence tests and primary school teachers' reports have been used.

The abolition of fees and the introduction of selection tests of one kind or another did increase the representation in grammar schools of the sons of manual workers (compare Table 8.1, columns 1 and 2). Whatever the method of selection used, however, the grammar schools have invariably contained a higher proportion of children of professional workers and a lower proportion of the children of manual workers than has the population as a whole (compare Table 8.1, columns 2 and 3). Furthermore, the children of

Table 8.1 Occupational distribution of the fathers of boys entering grammar schools in England and Wales and of the male labour force (per cent)

Father's occupation	*GS entrants 1930–41*[1]		*GS entrants 1946–51*[2]		*Total male population aged 20–64, 1951*[2]
Professional and managerial	40	60	26	44	28
Clerical and non-manual	20		18		
Manual		40		56	72

Sources: (1) J. Floud, 'Social class factors in educational achievement', in A. H. Halsey (ed.), *Ability and Educational Opportunity*, OECD, 1961, p. 97, and (2) *1951 Population Census of England and Wales*, London: HMSO.

the working classes have shown a tendency to make less progress at school, and in particular tend to leave school at an earlier age than do their middle-class contemporaries. At the university level this social selection is even more acute. In the 1960–1 academic year only 25 per cent of the undergraduate population was the children of manual workers—a proportion which had hardly changed in thirty years despite dramatic university expansion. Table 8.2 shows in more detail the social background of undergraduates at university in 1961. A study of this table will show that occupational class I has about four times the representation among undergraduates in universities as it would have under a random distribution. At the other end of the scale class V would have about nine times *more* representa-

Table 8.2 Occupational distribution of undergraduates' fathers and of the male labour force, 1961 (per cent)

Father's occupation	*Undergraduates 1961/2*[1]	*Male labour Force 1961*[2]
I Higher professional	18	3·9
II Other professional and managerial	41	14·4
IIIa Clerical	12	11·0* } 49·8
IIIb Skilled manual	18	38·8* }
IV Semi-skilled manual	6	19·9
V Unskilled manual	1	8·6
Unclassified	4	3·4

*estimated from previous census

Sources: (1) *Higher Education*, Appendix 2(b) *Students and their education*, London: HMSO. Cmnd 2154, II–I, Table 5, p. 4, (2) *Population Census 1961*, London: HMSO.

tives in the universities were the distribution random. The position seems to have changed very little since that time. While the newer technological universities are not so exclusive in terms of social background as the others (especially Oxford and Cambridge where more than three-quarters of the students still come from professional and managerial backgrounds), the chief gains in this respect have been made by the children of 'white collar workers' rather than by those of manual workers. Moreover, in the university sector as a whole there has been, at most, a marginal change in the social background of students. Despite the post-Robbins expansion of universities, what we have called the reinforcement function of education still prospers at the expense of the mobility function.

How far is this a result of the division of English secondary education into secondary modern and grammar schools? This division has been the centre of the major politico-educational controversy of the second half of the century—the debate concerning the merits of the comprehensive system of secondary education against those of the dual system. The educational arguments in favour of a retention of grammar schools (only rarely have arguments been put forward to 'save our secondary modern schools') centre upon the need to safeguard the high academic standards for which the grammar schools have become noted and upon which the economic well-being of the country depends. The arguments in favour of comprehensive schools focus on the wastage of human talent through early and often inadequate selection; the unfortunate effects of selection upon the primary schools; the encouragement which comprehensive schools are thought to give to less able pupils; and upon the academic results which have been achieved in 'comprehensive' schools in some areas. Underlying the controversy, however, and accounting for much of the emotionalism and irrationality which often enter it, is the hope or fear that a new type of educational system would bring about radical changes in the nature of English society—particularly in the class structure.

As was pointed out earlier, the grammar school retained the old secondary school's function of preparing people for essentially middle-class positions in society. Changes during this century enabled some children of lowly origins to gain entry into the grammar schools, and thus climb the educational ladder to some of the highest positions in the land. The term 'meritocracy' has been given to this type of society where stratification is still important but positions are allocated not by birth or wealth, but by merit as measured by educational success. Many people see the existence of separate secondary schools for those destined for different positions in the occupational structure as a form of organization which will both reduce the amount of social mobility through education and intensify the differences between occupational groups and thereby perpetuate the existing differences.

Many who find the existence of social classes abhorrent have turned to comprehensive education as a way of overcoming these divisions. They argue that the education of all children in a common secondary school would allow children from different family backgrounds to mix socially. In this way the growth of separate sub-cultures would be minimized. Such a view, however, overstates the power of the educational system to alter the social structure and seems to stem from the popular confusion of class distinction with 'snobbery'. It is conceivable, although by no means certain, that the introduction of comprehensive schools might lessen status consciousness, but it is hardly likely that such educational changes would influence the distribution of economic and political power on which the class structure is equally dependent.

A sociological appreciation of the history of English education suggests that the class system has had a considerable influence on the type of education system which eventually emerged. The reciprocal influence of the educational system on the class structure has, however, been confined in the main to the partial preservation of the *status quo*. It is, then, highly doubtful that the extension of comprehensive education will initiate significant changes in the class structure. But the problem need not be left entirely at the level of conjecture for there are industrial societies with systems of comprehensive secondary education where we can see how such systems function.

A good example is the USA where there is both comprehensive schooling and a strong commitment to equality of educational opportunity. The early high schools in the USA were designed for the needs of the predominantly higher-class children who intended to enter professional or similar occupations. Their curriculum was consequently somewhat similar to that of their counterparts in England. As the numbers of children undergoing secondary education increased, and especially after the introduction of compulsory secondary education, it was felt that this highly academic curriculum was not suitable for the whole of the high school clientele, many of whom had no intention of entering professional occupations nor of going to college. The result was the establishment, alongside the academic or 'college preparatory' curriculum, of alternative courses variously called vocational, commercial or general courses. There is a considerable body of evidence to show that the children of parents with high occupational positions are very likely to take the college preparatory curriculum—the line that leads to higher education and/or high status employment, while the children of manual workers are much more likely to find themselves in one of the other streams. There is, in effect, a situation essentially similar to that in England whereby the type of schooling received by children tends to confirm them in the same class positions as those occupied by their parents. It is even possible that the comprehensive school in Britain may be less well suited to the task of promoting the social mobility of working-class children than the old grammar school. For one of the consequences of the élitist assumptions of the grammar schools was that they operated relatively efficiently as agencies of socialization into middle-class values. The comprehensive school may prove less well suited to persuading clever working-class children to raise their levels of aspirations.

Despite the comprehensive high school, the children of members of the American lower classes tend to finish their education and go out to work full time earlier in their lives than do the children of the upper classes. An American sociologist, Robert J. Havighurst, has demonstrated the way in which virtually all upper- and upper-middle-class children graduate from high school, while many lower-class children (more than one-half in some areas) fail to complete the high school course. He also shows that, in 1960, 85 per cent of upper- and upper-middle-class young men and 70 per cent of the young women entered college, while only 10 per cent of the males and 5 per cent of the females in what he calls the lower class did so. At the same time he points out that this represents a change from 1940 when virtually no lower-class children went to college, a change that is part of a vast absolute increase in college places between 1920 when 8 per cent of the appropriate age group were attending college and 1960 when more than one-third entered college.[3]

Again, in the USSR in 1958, nearly 70 per cent of the students in higher education in Moscow were the children of members of the intelligentsia or of the upper levels of the bureaucracy. In contrast with the West, however, this proportion had been rising for twenty years, a reaction against the extreme attempts to 'proletarianize' education during the 1930s. In a highly bureaucratic society like the Soviet Union, a person's future occupation depends almost entirely upon his education, with the result that here, too, education was operating largely to maintain the children of the present élite in positions of wealth and influence. This situation, which accorded so ill with the ideology of the government, was one of the important motivations behind the campaign begun in the late 1950s to establish boarding schools throughout the country. By 1964, 2,000 of these had been established and were attended by some 700,000 pupils drawn mainly from *lower*-class children. They thus represent an attempt to increase social mobility by providing better educational opportunities for lower-class children. The aim was that the boarding schools should eventually dominate Soviet education, thus removing the children from parental control and so shielding them from traditional values and influence, especially those reflecting status consciousness in any form. In this way it was hoped that the influence of the family in the eventual placement of the child would be minimized. This attempt to eliminate the influence of the family on a child's education and subsequent occupation was a more thorough attempt to provide equality of opportunity than any undertaken in the Western world, and if it had been carried through, might have been expected to yield more in the way of results. The magnitude of the task, however, was such that the scheme was never fully implemented, so the assumptions upon which it was based have still to be tested.

We may feel justified in concluding that whenever there are differential opportunities in education the most attractive types of schooling (in terms of the rewards offered) will be dominated by the children of the privileged sections of the society. Moreover, this appears to be the case at all levels of development where a formal educational system exists, irrespective of the *type* of educational system and irrespective of the political system. Indeed, it has been estimated that there is no country in which the working classes achieve more than one-half of parity, while in some of the less developed countries the lower occupational groups achieve considerably less than this.

Region, race and residence

But class is not the only important factor; there are also differences in educational opportunity between other groups. It has been shown that in a number of societies, both industrial and non-industrial, there are considerable differences in the chances that children have of reaching a given level of education according to where they live. Data from such diverse countries as the USA, France, Ghana, the USSR, and India show that *regions* of educational underprivilege are a worldwide problem. Within a given society the areas of greatest educational opportunity are the areas of highest economic development. Thus, for example, in the USA the southern states are both economically and educationally backward when compared with the northern states, while in West African coastal countries the coastal areas are both economically and educationally more advanced than the hinterland. Similarly, in all countries urban children have greater educational opportunities than rural children, for it is in the towns that a concentration of population makes both for pressure to provide schools and for ease in administering them. Contemporary modernizing societies clearly show how, in the early stages of educational development, school building tends to be concentrated in the large towns. But in highly industrial societies one finds similar, if less extreme, differences. In addition there are differences within the towns—suburban areas usually providing better opportunities than the city centres. These factors are closely related to the social-class composition of the various areas but also exercise some independent influence. In England, where the Local Education Authority has decided important matters of educational policy (including, for example, the number of grammar school places to be made available), the location of one's home one side or the other of a local government boundary, local government politics, or an accident of history have often been the deciding factors in a child's educational career. For example, in 1964 only 13·1 per cent of the eleven-year-old children in the south of England were offered places in grammar schools compared with 28·6 per cent of the same age group in Wales. In 1968 some local authorities had nearly 40 per cent of their children in grammar schools; others had more than 80 per cent in secondary modern schools. The same startling difference between local authority areas can be seen at the sixth-form level. In 1968 approximately 33 per cent of the seventeen year olds in Cardiganshire were still in school compared with only 8 per cent for the county borough of Middlesbrough.

In societies where there is a racially diverse population there are also differences in the educational chances of the different races. This can be seen most clearly in southern Africa where the educational system, and the positions of wealth, power and prestige in the society as a whole, are dominated by the white minority. In the Union of South Africa in 1962 only one-half of the Bantu population aged 6–16 was at school, compared to 77 per cent of the 'coloured' population and 100 per cent of the white population. In 1966, about one in 30,000 of the non-white population was attending university while for the white population the figure was one in eighty. Much of this differential opportunity derives from the policy of apartheid but racial differences, although less extreme than those in South Africa, can still be seen in countries with an ideology of equal educational opportunity between the races. Thus in the USA in 1962, for example, 13·1 per cent of the total 25–9 age group had completed four years of college education but only 4·2 per cent of the non-whites in the same age group had done so.

Perhaps the universality of findings referring to social selection is the more surprising in view of the fact that the various systems of education use quite different criteria of selection. In systems where fees are charged for secondary education, as was the case in the early stages of the educational development of industrial countries and is now the case in most modernizing countries, it is hardly surprising to find the channels to high occupational positions dominated by the children of the higher classes since they alone can afford the luxury of education. Where no such fees have been charged for many years, however, such dominance is harder to account for. In most parts of England since the second world war, intelligence tests have played a large part in the selection process and yet middle-class children have still been over-represented in the grammar schools. In America, on the other hand, there is considerable freedom of choice of curriculum in the junior high school but the results are similar to those in England. Are we to conclude that the children of the middle classes are inherently better suited to an academic type of education than are lower-class children? Certainly the English experience suggests that they do better at intelligence tests. But how far do such tests measure something which is inborn and how far do they measure something which has been developed by the process of socialization? It is now generally held that an important part of what we call intelligence is dependent upon the influence of the social environment, and the available evidence suggests that the same factors are likely to affect performance in the primary school, performance in written examinations, or even in the child's free choice of type of education. In any case, even at a given level of measured intelligence, selection still seems to operate in favour of some groups of children against others. Thus the Robbins report found that the proportion of middle-class children who enter grammar schools is higher than the proportion of working-class children *of the same measured ability* who do so. Consequently whether selection is based upon intelligence tests, teachers' reports, written examinations, or parental preferences the child's chances of selection are likely to be influenced by his social environment.

We must therefore ask what it is about working-class life, life in rural areas, life in economically depressed regions, and life in racially under-privileged communities that handicaps a child educationally. Where there are no legal barriers (such as those in South Africa or in the southern states of the USA before de-segregation) and no serious financial barriers (such as those which exist wherever education is not free), one important factor is the way in which education is viewed by the parents and by other members of the community. A number of community studies in working-class areas in English towns have suggested that such communities have viewed education as something 'not for the likes of us' and that a child attending a grammar school or college from such a community has been likely to be a lonely figure. Indeed, until recently there were frequent reports of children from such areas refusing grammar school places. After the statutory school leaving age there are further pressures to give up education, particularly the knowledge that one's contemporaries are earning wages and are now 'adults'. In this situation the encouragement of the parents is likely to be crucial in the decision to continue education, but parental commitment to education is not a notable characteristic of most such communities. That this situation has only recently begun to change is a reflection of the fifteen or twenty years that it has taken for these parental and community attitudes to adapt to the new situation initiated by the 1944 Education Act. Furthermore, the increased affluence of some sections of the working classes means that the attraction of an extra young wage earner in the house is of less importance and longer term considerations can be taken into account.

Another factor which may influence a child's educational chances is the size of the family into which he is born. Many studies, for example the Scottish Mental Health Survey, have shown that there is an inverse correlation between measured intelligence and family size, and on the whole working-class and rural families are larger than middle-class and urban ones. The larger the family, the less contact a child is likely to have with adults in his early years, and this tends to retard verbal development. This in turn handicaps the development of thinking which is dependent upon language. The American sociologist, A. Davis, has also found verbal retardation to be common among twins and suggested that this is because they tend to communicate with each other non-verbally and consequently have less need to develop verbal communication with adults. Moreover, some parents teach their children to verbalize their feelings and develop a pleasure in the use of words while other children acquire only a limited vocabulary and learn only a language of authority, not one of reason. Many classroom difficulties stem from this since the language of the teacher has no meaning for these latter children and there is a consequent breakdown of communication.

Thus family and community life appear to be the important factors which differentiate between the educationally privileged groups on the one hand and the educationally underprivileged on the other. Consequently attempts to eliminate inequality of educational opportunity by removing the child from the influence of the family (like the Russian attempt) are on the face of it likely to be more successful than changes in the structure of secondary education (such as the current English changes to comprehensive schools). It is equally clear, however, that such changes are unlikely to be implemented, or even seriously considered, in most industrial societies where they would offend other, deeply held, values.

Notes

1 Hansard, 3rd series, vol. cxxix, London, 1870, p. 466.
2 H. C. Barnard, *A History of English Education*, University of London Press, 1961, p. 264.
3 Robert J. Havighurst, 'Social class influences on American education', in Nelson Harvey (ed.), *Social Forces Influencing American Education*, University of Chicago Press, 1961.

Reading

Adams, D. and Bjork, R. M., *Education in Developing Areas*, New York: McKay, 1969. A useful survey of its field, combining wide coverage with brevity.

Banks, O., *The Sociology of Education*, London: Batsford, 1968. By far the best of many textbooks on the subject.

Bernbaum, G., *Social Change and the Schools 1918–1944*, London: Routledge & Kegan Paul, 1967. A sociological discussion of an important period in the development of English education.

Douglas, J. W. B., *The Home and the School*, London: Panther, 1967. A study of the relationship between family structure, and the ability and academic success of primary school children in England.

Eggleston, S. J., *The Social Context of the School*, London: Routledge & Kegan Paul, 1967. A clear survey of the literature relating the school to the local and national environment.

Grant, N., *Soviet Education*, Harmondsworth: Penguin, 1964. A very readable description of the Soviet educational system.

Sexton, P., *The American School*, Englewood Cliffs: Prentice-Hall, 1967. The relationships between the school, the educational system, the community, and the wider society are discussed in a clear general survey which includes an analysis of power in, and control over, education.

Further reading

Anderson, C. A. and Bowman, M. J. (eds), *Education and Economic Development*, London: Cass, 1965. A wide range of papers analysing the relationship between education and economic development, with evidence from American, English, Russian and Japanese history as well as from contemporary modernizing societies.

Banks, O., *Parity and Prestige in English Secondary Education*, London: Routledge & Kegan Paul, 1955. A sociological analysis of the development and major functions of English secondary education in the twentieth century.

Coleman, J. S. (ed.), *Education and Political Development*, Princeton University Press, 1965. Nine general papers relating to individual countries, and a number of more specific contributions on particular aspects of education. The whole is linked by a series of introductions by the editor.

Halsey, A. H., Floud, J. and Anderson, C. A. (eds), *Education, Economy and Society*, Chicago: Free Press, 1961. A useful and comprehensive collection of articles but limited in the main to Britain and the USA.

Hansen, D. A. and Gerstl, J. E., *On Education: Sociological Perspectives*, New York: Wiley, 1967. A variety of sociological essays on education. Includes essays on the relationship between education and social stratification and mobility, and an essay on education as a social institution.

Hargreaves, D. H., *Social Relations in a Secondary School*, London: Routledge & Kegan Paul, 1967. An analysis of the social structure of a school, including teacher-pupil relationships, relationships between pupils within a class, and relationships between streams.

Havighurst, R. J. (ed.), *Comparative Perspectives on Education*, Boston: Little, Brown, 1968. Sociological essays on aspects of education in France, the Soviet Union, Japan, Brazil, China, Ghana, Tudor England, South Africa, New Zealand, the Netherlands, the Sudan, and among the Hopi Indians.

Lawton, D., *Language, Social Class and Education*, London: Routledge & Kegan Paul, 1968. A critical survey of the literature on the relationship between language skills and the educational development of children.

Rosenthal, R. and Jacobsen, L., *Pygmalion in the Classroom: Teacher Expectations and Pupils' Intellectual Development*, New York: Holt, Rinehart & Winston, 1968. A study of how teachers' expectations affect school performance.

9 The professions

The word *profession* conjures up a wealth of images: of security, public service, respectability, independence, prestige and even wealth. Furthermore, the occupations we regard as professions—medicine, law, architecture, accountancy, science—are popularly accorded high prestige in comparison with other occupations. Today, both in industrial societies and in non-industrial societies, education for a career in one of the professions is increasingly regarded as the gateway to the good life. To the individual, it is worth the long and sometimes arduous years of training; and to many new occupational groups the lure of professional status is worth the self-discipline and expenditure of resources which may lead to eventual public recognition.

In recent decades large industrial corporations, both public and private, have become more and more dominant in the economic life of industrial societies. One important effect of this development has been the reduction of opportunities for individual success in business entrepreneurship. It has become increasingly difficult for the small businessman and the self-made man to compete with the industrial giants. One result of this is that a career in the professions is becoming a more important object of individual ambition. Such a career is equally attractive in contemporary modernizing countries where large-scale state dominance of business and industry has given high status to bureaucratic and professional occupations. The rapid expansion of professional occupations in industrial societies has been partly due to the expansion of existing professions, but the crystallization of new occupational tasks has also been important. These include many activities which are based upon the application of scientific and technical knowledge to new social needs. The emergence of new occupational tasks, such as those of the probation officer, the metallurgist, the radiographer and the atomic physicist, has diversified the field of professional practice and raises problems in the use of the term profession itself.

What is a profession?

Professional occupations are regarded as special in some way. They are said to have some unique characteristic which sets them apart from other types of occupation; to have highly important functions to perform in industrial societies which, to a large extent, explain the prestige, power and wealth they command. Interest in these 'unique characteristics' is by no means new, but it is only in industrial societies that a predominant social role has been claimed for professionals. In their capacity as experts they are sometimes feared to be taking over the leadership of societies to the exclusion of all others. On the other hand, they have also been counted among the 'bulwarks' of democracy by those who see the professional association as a model of collective control by members. It has also been claimed that, by virtue of their independent status, professions stand as a 'bastion' against state control of the individual; that, because of their corporate organization, they are a check upon the worst excesses of individualism; and that their ethic of public service enables them to cut across disruptive class ideologies.

These three features—their corporate organization, independence and ethic of public service—

are often said to characterize the professions. In recent years, however, the phenomenon of the salaried, dependent professional has increasingly dominated the professional scene; more and more professionals are employed within large organizations rather than working as independent or solo practitioners. An 'idealized' view of the professions, stressing the importance of independence and community service cannot account for this modern phenomenon of the 'bureaucratized' professional except as a pathological aberration resulting from the evils of big business and/or state intervention. Nor can such an idealized view account for the great disparities in power, prestige and income which exist between and even within professional groups. In all industrial societies teachers, for example, are significantly differentiated from doctors and lawyers, while great diversity exists within all three professions. What are the special characteristics which professional occupations share and why is it that some of them do not share the social and material benefits of others?

The crude distinction between 'brain' and 'brawn' is not a satisfactory criterion of a profession as against other occupations. Surgeons have remained essentially manual workers, yet they have grown steadily in prestige since their separation from the Barbers' Guild in seventeenth-century England. We have already pointed out that independent professionals relying upon fees from individual clients are a dwindling proportion of professionals as a whole. Thus, independence cannot be taken as a useful criterion. Nor can the professional be regarded in any way as unique in being organized within an association, for professional associations share many functions in common with trade unions. Professionals comprise a minority of those employed in occupations providing a service; more and more occupations today demand high-level, long-term periods of training and, in any case, craft apprenticeships have always been similar to professional training in this respect. And so we could go on: but any attempt to list the occupational characteristics which would enable us to recognize a profession is likely to prove unsatisfactory.

The sociologist, however, is interested in explaining a social phenomenon such as the professions in terms of social structure—that is to say, in terms of the patterned and persisting relationships which exist between professionals and their clients, between professionals and the wider society and among professionals themselves. Can we explain the importance of professional ethics, status and prestige in society in these terms? Certainly, it is true that all the so-called professions give a service, whether the client be an individual, a private corporation or a government department. It is also true that in giving such a service the professional is making use of his training; he is applying a body of knowledge in response to the needs of the client. But the crucial aspect of this relationship is that the client or layman finds it difficult to *judge the quality of the service* he is getting. The practice of a physician is not open to evaluation by the average layman; we have to take his diagnosis and treatment on trust. If we recover from an illness after seeking the advice of a doctor it is often difficult to know whether the treatment was successful or whether recovery would have been spontaneous. Similar problems exist when we consult an accountant, a solicitor or an architect; we remain dependent upon the judgment of the professional.

Thus the nature of the professional-client relationship is such that there is an inherent tension, resulting from the client's inability to judge the service provided. This problem does nor exist to the same extent with all services nor with most market transactions involving material goods. For example, if a corporation dustman inadequately performs the service of emptying our dustbins this is readily testable through our sense of smell; if a baker sells stale or inferior bread we can feel, taste, and perhaps see the inadequacy. In neither case are we dependent upon a guarantee of integrity. By contrast, conflict is built into the professional-client relationship because of the expertise of the professional and the ignorance of the client. As a result, various institutions have arisen to control this relationship.

One such form of control has been the professional association—such as the British Medical Association, the Law Society, or the Chartered Institute of Accountants. These bodies guarantee the integrity of their members (partly by enforcing a professional code of ethics) while in return their members gain control of the relationship with the client in such matters as fee-setting. This way of controlling the relationship between the client and the professional has frequently been regarded as the natural end-product of the dilemma created by the ignorance of the client. Carr-Saunders and Wilson, for example, claimed that no profession is a 'true' profession until it throws up an 'autonomous corporate association with the function of guaranteeing the competence, honour and security of its members'.[1] If, however, we were to apply the principle of autonomy to the professions in England today only barristers could be regarded as a 'true' profession. Moreover, many occupations which are in a position to exploit their ignorant clients are not, and never have been, organized in autonomous associations. This is because the tension which exists between a professional and his client can be resolved in a number of ways and through a variety of institutional forms.

A brief consideration of the way in which the professions have developed historically reveals, broadly speaking, three ways in which the tension has been resolved. In some cases, the members of an occupation have been able to determine who should receive their services—perhaps through the mechanism of a fee scale—and, by virtue of their recognized expertise, they have been able to set the standards of the service given. This is exemplified by the control over various services exerted by the autonomous professional associations which arose in the nineteenth century largely as a product of industrialization. Professional autonomy was linked to the increasing power of the urban middle class and was most nearly attained by the occupations of medicine and law. This professional domination of the relationship with the client is what we would normally refer to as *professionalism*, and involves various forms of colleague control which will be discussed later. A second way of resolving the tension between the client and the professional is where the client, because of his position in society, has the power to define his own needs, the way in which they are to be met, and the professional standards expected. This typically occurs in societies where a powerful group, such as an aristocracy, is the main consumer of professional services. This type of professional-client relationship we may call *client control*. Finally, both client and professional attempt to define the relationship which may be subordinated to external demands and definitions, such as those imposed by the church in medieval Europe, or the activities of modern states which regulate professional services in the process of extending various forms of welfare to all citizens or to special groups who are defined as being in need. The welfare state has, then, entailed the emergence of new forms of *third party control* over the professional-client relationship.

These alternative solutions to the problem of controlling the professional-client relationship provide a framework for the classification and analysis of professional occupations.

The professions in pre-industrial societies

In the simplest of societies the only forms of the social division of labour which exist are those between the sexes and between the young and old. Where there is division of labour between the sexes or between generations only, specialized occupations such as those we are calling 'professions' do not exist. Caring for the sick and infirm, for instance, is an activity which is incidental to other roles, such as a wife or mother. In societies where disease is attributed to 'bad magic' the care of the sick may devolve upon magical specialists but in many simple societies even this capacity to do harm or good by magical means is diffused through the whole community. Among the Dobuans, a Melanesian people who live on a small island north east of New Guinea, there is a belief that the only causes of disease are witchcraft and sorcery; that supernatural forces affect the health of individuals through the agency of other members of the Dobuan community. Ill-health is attributed to jealousy or a desire for revenge on the part of neighbours and is directly caused by ritual incantations. Healing is therefore possible only when the sorcerer recants and the cause is removed. In this manner all Dobuans have the potential capacity to cure as well as cause disease; there is no specialization involved.

The major limitation upon the development of specialized occupational tasks in simple societies is the subsistence economy; members who are not themselves food producers cannot be fed. Only when an economic surplus is produced can specialized occupations be supported by the community. In the evolution of human societies, among the first specialized activities to emerge were those of magical specialists and priests. Where people understood and explained their physical and social environment in terms of the intervention of supernatural beings or forces, knowledge and the rituals associated with it often came to be monopolized by a priesthood which was, in a number of senses, the archetypal profession. Like the modern medical profession it monopolized an area of knowledge vital to the health and general fortunes of the society as a whole: and, as is the case with many modern professions, it closely controlled entry into the occupation. Often the priesthood became an hereditary caste, entry being monopolized by a single family or a clan.

Even in the complex civilizations of Greece and Rome the practice of law and medicine did not give rise to specialized independent professional associations such as we know today. The physician in Greece was regarded as a craftsman who served an apprenticeship under a master and sought custom in the market place along with other craft specialists; in Rome he was typically a slave attached to a rich man's household. The Roman lawyer was not a specially trained advocate practising before a qualified judge, but more likely, the litigant's friend speaking to the litigant's equals, while in Greece, the practice of law was not differentiated from other more general forms of social control such as ethical custom, religious doctrine and public opinion. In such a situation the advocate in a dispute might be any man known for his oratory, and the business might be conducted by any literate man or scribe.

The development of professions in England

The church and the professions—third party control

For long periods in the history of many societies religious organizations have been so powerful that, as new specialized occupational tasks emerged, these organizations were able to maintain control over the relationship between the practitioner and his client. The power of the priesthood derived not only from its monopoly of knowledge but also from its control over a large slice of the economic surplus and sometimes from military power as well—as was the case with the warrior-priest kings of the ancient Mesopotamian city-states. In Europe the church enjoyed a monopoly of knowledge during the Middle Ages: a monopoly which was reinforced by its importance as a landholder in an agrarian society. The basis of all knowledge was contained in the 'revealed truth' of the Bible, and the Church's control of access to this truth enabled it to control man's interpretations of the universe, while attempting to exclude what it defined as heretical. The Church contained within its organization the specialists in thinking and in the application of knowledge. There were few specialist occupations in existence, but those which did exist were controlled and administered by the Church. Indeed the earliest meaning of the verb 'profess' noted by the *Shorter Oxford Dictionary* refers to taking the vows of a religious order. Until the twelfth century, medicine was the preserve of the monastic orders and later, when medical practice was forbidden to monks, it was taught only in the cathedral schools of Salerno in Italy and Montpellier in France. The activities carried out by physicians, lawyers, civil servants and educators were all performed under the aegis of the Church. The Church provided training and educational centres; the Church provided a system of rewards and statuses. Professionals typically took clerical orders and were rewarded with a canonry or rectory.

It was the Church which defined the manner in which professionals were to serve clients and, by virtue of its functions as a welfare agency, it also defined the needs of the clients themselves. Thus, the way the sick were treated was affected by the biblical injunction that clerics should not spill blood. As a consequence, surgery was excluded from the field of medicine for several centuries and was practised separately within the barber-surgeons' craft guild. Indeed, the surgeons craft was practised mainly on the battlefield.

Similarly, law was administered by the Church. Trials were not so much an investigation of the facts as a revelation of the judgment of God. Yet the emergence of the common lawyer in England provided an increasingly significant exception to the rule of Church control. One result of the growth of trade and commerce in the late medieval period and the processes of urbanization and centralization associated with them, was that the monarch gained power at the expense of the Church. The gradual secularization of law, whereby judgments proceeded from custom and precedent rather than from 'revealed' knowledge, and the emergence of the common lawyer to apply this secular knowledge, were related to these changes in the power structure. The services provided by the common lawyer were related to the administrative needs of an increasingly powerful monarch; they were related to the needs of the central administration itself; and they were related to the economic needs of an urban élite which was prospering under conditions of commercial expansion.

The period in which the relationship between the professional and his client was mediated and controlled by the Church was formally brought to a close by the Reformation. The Inns of Court, the university of the common lawyer, were already established in the fifteenth century. The victory of common lawyers over canon lawyers, which resulted in the exclusion of ecclesiastics from common law practice, was a process characteristic of the transition of any professional occupation from one form of institutional control to another.

A new occupational group providing a new service to meet new client needs came into conflict with entrenched professional groups who still exhibited the organization and values of the old order. By the sixteenth century medicine, too, had become a secular profession, although ecclesiastics remained as prominent members of the Royal College of Physicians until the end of that century. Church control of the relationship between the professional and his client was giving way to a new institutional form—that of patronage.

Patronage and the professions—client control

In England at the time of the Reformation a good deal of ecclesiastical wealth passed into private hands, a process which further diversified the sources of professional patronage. Those contemplating a professional career were no longer forced to take holy orders and, by the seventeenth and eighteenth centuries, secular professions were, by and large, servicing a small aristocratic élite and the landed gentry. In these new conditions the client came to dominate the relationship with the professional, defining his own needs and dictating the manner and content of the service. This dominance was clear cut in the case of the Royal College of Physicians whose limited membership serviced a small élite group, but it can also be seen in the case of lawyers where the patronage of the aristocracy was channelled through the political parties. The political control of medicine was also important as is shown by Charles II's exclusion of Papists and foreigners from Royal College Fellowships in 1676.

It was during this period in English history that the ideal of the professional gentleman arose. Membership of the Royal College of Physicians and a liberal education at an English university were the essential background of the cultured physician. Technical qualification was less important than social acceptability. The intimate relationship with a patron made it imperative that the medical doctor should be *socially* qualified to take his place in 'the ample life of the great houses'. A contemporary comment makes the point clearly:[2]

> The character of a physician ought to be that of a gentleman, which cannot be maintained with dignity but by a man of literature. If a gentleman engaged in the practice of physic, be destitute of that degree of a preliminary and ornamental learning, which is requisite; if he do so speak of any subject either in history or philosophy, is immediately out of his depth; (this) is a great discredit to the profession.

This particular injunction was directed against the claims of apothecaries who were, at the end of the eighteenth century, threatening the monopoly of the Royal College of Physicians. It illustrates one of the consequences of patron dominance—the way in which the professional's prestige was based not upon his professional knowledge or technique but upon the degree to which he conformed to the values and customs of a consumption-oriented leisure class. The great physicians of the eighteenth century—men like Garth and Arbuthnot—were known not so much for their medical skills as for their wit and elegance. The successful lawyer had to be politically sound as well as socially acceptable. Technical competence in law practice played only a minor part in entry to the profession; residence at the Inns of Court was no longer a necessity. Students were either the sons of gentlemen acquiring a vocation or party men in receipt of preferment and, by the eighteenth century, the Inns had become known for their 'masques and revels' rather than for law education.

Where the professional was in no position to control the relationship with his client on his own terms the type of knowledge accentuated by the profession was also affected. Medical knowledge of the day emphasized therapies (such as blood letting) which were guided by simple, single-factor explanations of disease. This type of knowledge reflected the physician's need for certainty and to do what was required of him without demur. Uncertainty is the prerogative of those who have power. Moreover, it was not possible for the physician to experiment upon a man of social position and it was only with the founding of hospitals for the poor that experimental medicine began to make headway.

Industrialization and professionalism—colleague control

Until the last quarter of the eighteenth century not more than half a dozen professional occupations existed in England. By the end of the century, however, nascent industrialization and the growth of commerce were bringing new forms of professional service into being. The growing complexity of trade and financial transactions made mercantile accounts and exchange procedures so intricate that they required the skilled services of a calculator or accountant. By the end of the eighteenth century an accountant of some kind, whether he was a lawyer specializing in financial affairs or the qualified apprentice of a 'writing master', was to be found on the staff of many large mercantile firms. It is estimated that, even by 1775, five hundred young men were studying accounting techniques in the City of Glasgow alone; and accountants were only one occupational group among many which were emerging. Industrialization opened the floodgates of professional growth. Developments in science and technology crystallized into techniques which provided the basis of new professional occupations such as civil engineering and, later, mechanical and electrical engineering. The new large-scale enterprises which were associated with changes in manufacturing technology, and the rapidly growing towns were the location of more new professional occupations. This development is most spectacularly demonstrated by the growth of civil service bureaucracies. The expansion of professionalism was so great that the period between 1841 and 1855 alone saw the foundation of six new professional associations.

This growth was only partly due to the creation of new scientific and organizational techniques; new social needs (and new definitions of 'need') were also important. Industrialization brought the rise to power of the urban middle class and it was members of this class who increasingly took up professional practice and who provided an expanding market for professional services. Demands which previously had been restricted to the upper stratum of society filtered down and outwards so that professional occupations such as medicine could no longer maintain themselves as small, socially prescribed cliques servicing a small group of patrons. They were in process of becoming large associations with a technically qualified membership servicing competing status groups of equals or near equals.

One example of transitional conflict which arose during the Industrial Revolution was that between the Royal College of Physicians and the apothecaries, which led to the Apothecaries Act of 1815 and later to the foundation of the British Medical Association in 1851. In this case the conflict between 'insiders' and 'outsiders' reached an intense form. The College of Physicians—entrenched, select and functioning in relation to the patronage system—was challenged by the growing power of the apothecaries, who had originally separated from the Grocers' Guild in 1617 to become dispensers and compounders of drugs. It has been claimed that general medical practice by apothecaries was established during the Great Plague of 1665 when the physicians fled London. In any case the physicians' charge that apothecaries were unlawfully treating patients was already familiar by the end of the seventeenth century. It was not until the eighteenth century, however, that large numbers of apothecaries were known to practise medicine. The expansion of medical practice by apothecaries was said by a contemporary to be the result of:[3]

> an increase of sickness among people, the 'middle orders' who were unable to produce medical aid by feeing Physicians as often as their situation required medical care, and the Members of the Royal College of Physicians having made no diminution in their accustomed fee, to meet the actual wants of persons in this class of society they were compelled to resort to others for advice.

Apothecaries, then, provided medical services for the rising middle class who were excluded by cost from the physician's consulting room. The middle classes were also the main source of recruits for apothecaries. The poet John Keats, for example, was one of the first to be licensed under the Apothecaries Act of 1815 which gave apothecaries the legal right to practise medicine.

So, once again, we see a new professional group coming into conflict with entrenched interests. In the case of the apothecaries the conflict was resolved by the new group taking on specialist tasks within the general field. This was to be a common pattern in the development of the medical profession. In the mid-nineteenth century, for example, such conflicts were resolved by the creation of the complementary groups of consultant physicians, surgeons and general practitioners. As we shall see, the twentieth-century development of several professions has followed similar lines.

During the nineteenth century the professional-client relationship took on a new form; one in which the professional himself increasingly dominated. It was in this historical period that *professionalism* emerged, with the creation of monopolistic and autonomous professional associations. Two factors were important in the development of this monopoly and autonomy. First, the professionals shared in the growing power of the middle class and were thus able to protect and enhance their interests, in particular through political pressure leading to state registration. At the same time the growth in size of the middle class provided a growing market for professional services, so reducing the professional's subservience to a patron. Second, the relationship between the professional and his new middle-class client was characterized by social distance deriving from the increasing technical authority of the professional; professional expertise became a more significant aspect of the relationship.

The competence and integrity of individual professionals came to be guaranteed by a self-disciplining, internally-regulated professional body. The autonomy of the professional association allowed the professionals themselves to determine who was to receive the service (by regulation of fees) and the manner in which clients' needs were catered for (by virtue of the establishment of an ethical code and the control of recruitment, training and entry into the profession). A by-product of professional control of this kind was a change in the character of professional knowledge. It was during this period of increasing professional control that knowledge began to be characterized by its scientific or systematic nature. In law, for example, the great systematization of common law and precedent was embarked upon and the lawyer gained prestige as a result of his forensic skill. More generally, the professional's prestige depended more upon his technical competence in a group of equals and less upon his social graces. The professions became the 'repositories of special knowledge', stressing research and rationality.

The professions in the contemporary world

The era of *professionalism* in England was short-lived. Even at its peak, at the end of the nineteenth century, the seeds of its decline were already present and gaining in force. Paradoxically, the creation of professional monopolies by Acts of Parliament in the nineteenth century was the precursor of state intervention which, in the twentieth century, has transformed the professional-client relationship once again. Industrialization has brought with it a new form of *third party control,* namely control by the state. And this is partly a result of increased working-class power. Second, industrialization has created new forms of *colleague control,* stemming largely from specialization within the professions, and differentiation of clientele. A third outcome of industrialization which has greatly affected professional services has been the growth of large-scale organization in both private business and public administration. As a result, the salaried career and employee status have become the normal expectation for large numbers of professionals, who are thereby subject to new forms of *client control.*

New forms of third party control

The professional occupations which exist in contemporary societies have emerged at different times and under varying social conditions. Because of this professional occupations not only vary in their organization from society to society but even in the same society they exhibit marked organizational differences which are a consequence of their historical development. A professional occupation which emerged in association with the rise of middle-class power in England brings with it into the twentieth century certain features which characterized the period of *professionalism,* even though increasing state control is characteristic of the present period. Today, in most industrial societies, the trappings of *professionalism* are present even though professional control in its purest form is, in most cases, a thing of the past.

Professionals who provide services for individual members of the public through a state agency are an increasing proportion of all professionals, but the degree to which they are dependent upon state regulation varies. In some cases the state defines not only who is in need of the service but also the manner in which these needs are to be met. This may be regarded as the nationalization of a profession and results in a minimum of autonomy for the profession. In many countries the teaching profession has been a familiar example. In England, the existence of school governors representing local interests and an agency such as the inspectorate of schools are symbolic of the teachers' lack of autonomy, although today the inspectorate is less an agency of central control than it was. A more recent addition to the 'nationalized' professions in industrial societies has been social work.

In some cases, however, the state merely defines who is to receive the service, leaving the profession to regulate the conditions and standards of the service. Such is the case with the British National Health Service. The creation of the National Health Service, which brought virtually all general practitioners into a state medical scheme, was not an abrupt loss of independence for the medical profession. Even in 1933 half the doctors had panel practices under the National Insurance Scheme. Nor has the National Health Service resulted in complete loss of autonomy for doctors. The profession itself still controls the manner of practice and, rather than receiving direct salaries from the state, members of the profession are paid from a pool which the profession itself administers. In some societies, however, the USSR for example, the medical profession is 'nationalized', in the sense referred to above, and this further loss of autonomy has led to a decline in the power and status of the occupation. At the other extreme is the United States of America where the medical profession, which has maintained a high degree of autonomy, has for many years successfully fought attempts by the federal government to introduce various forms of 'socialized medicine'.

The occupations we usually grouped together under the label 'social work'—for example, probation officers, psychiatric social workers, medical social workers, child care officers and so on—have grown directly out of the state's attempts, through legislation and the use of state funds, to rationalize and make more effective the 'philanthropic' response to social problems associated with industrialization. The state has also created new occupations in response to new social problems (the post of community relations officer is one recent example in Britain). As the task of aiding the 'deserving poor' was gradually taken over by statutory bodies, social workers found themselves the salaried agents of government. Social workers, like teachers, are therefore dependent professionals who have rarely been in a position to set up in independent practice. Furthermore, the fact that social workers are both members of a professional group and employees of a state agency may mean they are subject to conflicting expectations in carrying out their job, particularly where professional training stresses the need for a personal relationship with the client. Stressing the needs of the client may, for example, bring the probation officer into a head-on collision with the demands of the law courts of which he is legally an officer. His training and knowledge of his client may tell him that one course of action is necessary whilst the law may demand another.

All social work groups in Britain and the United States lay stress upon the importance of 'casework' in their jobs. In other words they emphasize the manipulation of their personal relationship with the client as a means of overcoming any social and/or emotional difficulties the client may be experiencing. Casework is considered to be the core of professional activity and any reform which threatens to weaken or reduce the possibility of this personal relationship is regarded as a threat to professional status. However, the areas of competence of the various social work groups in Britain and the lines of demarcation between them are not clearly defined. As a result conflict within the profession of social work centres upon attempts by the various sectors to define an area of competence and control within the casework relationship. Although the importance of 'liaison' between social workers is always stressed such co-operation is often fraught with hostility and 'demarcation disputes'.

New forms of colleague control

(a) The professional community The term colleague control is usually used to refer to the extent to which professionals are equal members of a homogeneous, self-disciplining professional group. It implies that the professions have many of the characteristics of a community. Professionals are bound by a sense of common identity, and a professional career involves a continuing status and permanent relationships with others. The professional career is a source of identity which has become increasingly important in modern society as other sources of identity (such as the family, village or locality) have become less important. The professional community controls its members in so far as it brings sanctions against those who deviate from the community rules and customs. These sanctions are enforced by the professional associations through their executive councils. Control over members also stems from the regulation of entry into the community. It is within the training period—characteristically long for professional occupations—that recruits are both taught the theory and techniques of practice and experience an intense period of adult socialization. They are inculcated into the values of the community and learn a common language which is only partially understood by 'outsiders'. One of the major concerns of emergent professional occupations is to agree upon a standardized terminology. This has, for example, been a continuing effort within the accountancy profession in both Britain and the United States. Standardized

terminology makes for easier communication with the professional group and, equally significantly, it excludes outsiders from participating in the group's activities.

There are, in all societies, common and sometimes extreme reactions to the 'community' aspects of professional organization. The high development of colleagueship leaves the layman with the feeling of a Kafkaesque hero; helpless in the face of professional silence, solidarity and ritual. George Bernard Shaw expressed this feeling well when he wrote in *The Doctor's Dilemma*: 'All professions are conspiracies against the laity.' In his later *Doctor's Delusions* he claimed that the success of this conspiracy depended upon 'dogmas of omniscience, omnipotence, and infallibility, and something very like the theory of the apostolic succession and kingship by anointment'.

There is, however, another face to professional solidarity—namely the guarantee it provides for the layman who cannot judge the quality of the service provided. Thus, within the professional community, the competence of all, from the newly qualified recruit to the practitioner who is about to draw his pension, is guaranteed. All are accorded equal competence. This fiction of equal competence (expressed, for example, in ethical rules with regard to advertising) maintains the service orientation of the professional man whilst protecting his interests. In this way the professional-client relationship is removed from the disruptive consequences of individualistic competition. The code of ethics of a profession prescribes the duties of members to each other and to the public. In addition, however, it usually reflects the interests of an historically powerful segment of the profession. Thus the codes express and reinforce a double fallacy: first, that there is always the possibility of an inclusive professional interest and, second, that this interest can at all times be harmonized with the public interest.

An over-concentration on the community aspects of professions minimizes the importance of a number of recent trends. As well as the proliferation of new professional occupations industrialization has also involved the diversification of single professional occupations. Many professions have become constellations of intensive and narrow specialisms and the various sub-groups do not necessarily share a common interest. The existing codes of ethics which formally control their behaviour may operate to the benefit of some sub-groups at the expense of others. Community identity and colleague equality is likely to be minimal in a heterogeneous group, as the case of the teaching profession illustrates.

Many modern professional occupations are loose amalgamations of specialists rather than close-knit communities of equals. Each specialist group pursues different objectives in different ways. Wherever such specialization occurs it results in cleavages in organization and differences of interest. Each speciality sees itself as having a 'unique mission' of supreme importance within the profession as a whole.[4] General medical practitioners and public health officers may be members of the same profession, but their 'missions' are quite different and often in conflict. They have different tasks and use different methods and techniques. There are physicians who continue to think of the surgeon as 'knife happy', and there are psychiatrists who differ from general practitioners about the importance of psychological as against physical causes of illness. Furthermore, different segments of a profession may service different ranges of clientele; the dock brief lawyer and the famous Queen's Counsel have different clients and in many cases differing interests result. The segments also have a different range of colleagues; psychiatric social workers and probation officers are fellow professionals, but the colleague network of the probation officer includes officers of the law courts while that of the psychiatric social worker also contains hospital staff. In many cases this gives these different professional workers differing views of the problems which need to be solved.

(*b*) *Professional hierarchies* As a result of this increasing heterogeneity new forms of colleague control have arisen in highly industrial societies. The growth in complexity of the organizational environment in which the professional finds himself and the expanding demand for professional services have led to new forms of professional organization—part of what the American sociologist, C. Wright Mills, has called 'the commercialization of the professions'. There are, for example, the 'law factories' in the United States of America and the accountancy partnerships which have developed into large-scale management consultancies. A comparable development in medicine is that of the private medical clinic of the USA and the state-run clinic of the USSR. In all such organizations the professional man is no longer 'free and independent'. Increasingly, he is fitted into new hierarchical organizations. Intensive and narrow specialization has replaced self-cultivation and wide knowledge; assistants and sub-professions perform routine, although often intricate, tasks while successful professional men become more and more the managerial type'.[5] In this situation new forms of colleague control arise in which some practitioners, by virtue of their position at the head of an organizational hierarchy, have authority over their professional colleagues.

By convention, English barristers cannot practise in partnership. Each barrister has an individual practice, although a group may share 'chambers', a clerk and a small secretarial staff. A solicitor, however, may practise in partnership or as an assistant to a principal. In England more than half the solicitors in private practice are in partnership, and nearly one-fifth work as salaried assistants to other solicitors. In the United States, by contrast, where the legal profession is not divided and the qualified lawyer performs all legal duties including that of barrister or counsellor, nearly 70 per cent are in solo practice while only 5 per cent are assistants. The remaining 25 per cent are in partnership which is a rapidly expanding form of organization among lawyers. There is no legal limit to the number who can enter a partnership and at least one New York law firm has more than a hundred partners.

The 'law factory' is still atypical of law practice but is securing a rapidly increasing proportion of the business. This shift in form of organization reflects a shift in the major functions of the lawyer. The lawyer who, as an officer of the courts, carries out a wide variety of tasks in response to an equally wide range of problems, is giving way to the specialist whose task is to shape the legal framework of public and private corporations. It is increasingly these specialist jobs in large enterprises that are the greatest attraction for the bright, young recruit. The large law firms of New York, for example, are able to be highly selective and draw 71 per cent of their recruits from the high-prestige law schools of Yale, Harvard and Columbia.[6] The firms' partners employ salaried lawyers who do the routine work in highly specialized departments. At times specialization is so intense that a team of lawyers, working under the supervision of a partner, is engaged continuously upon the solution of one type of legal problem or upon problems presented by a single client. The partners are essentially the 'business getters', providing work for the associates and assistants.

The form of colleague control which has developed in these firms illustrates a more general trend. The relationship between professionals is, in many areas, being transformed from one of colleagueship to one of hierarchical rankings. Increasingly, authority derives not from technical competence but from ownership of the firm and bureaucratic position within it.

In medicine, too, increased specialization (there are more than fifty listed medical specialisms in Britain) has given rise to new forms of professional organization; hierarchies of authority are imposed upon and modify the professional colleague system. The hospital in Britain, and the clinic in other countries, have superseded general practice as the foci of medical treatment, providing the technology and facilities without which modern practice could not be achieved. These developments have reduced the functions of the general practitioner, who is now the main agent in a formal referral system. In the United States even this function has declined drastically, with about 5 per cent of American physicians in general practice.

The development of the team of medical specialists has resulted in a situation where some doctors perform services dependent on diagnostic decisions made elsewhere. In large-scale organizations such as hospitals, the dependent position of these professionals is accompanied by relatively low status and pay and has, in recent years, led to the militancy of junior hospital doctors in England. In other words, increasing diversification of authority within a profession is likely to be related to diversification in status and reward.

Hierarchical forms of colleague control, such as are found in the modern hospital, have supplemented but not entirely replaced the older forms based upon social difference rather than technical competence. In one area of Canada, for example, the successful medical career has, in the recent past, been dependent upon gaining admittance to an 'inner-fraternity' whose members sponsored the careers of socially acceptable newcomers.[7] This inner-fraternity of Anglo-Saxon Protestants maintained itself as a stable, self-perpetuating group, controlling post-graduate training opportunities and the 'plums' of medical practice. No doctor was able to succeed as a specialist unless he gained entry to this inner-fraternity and accepted his subsequent obligations to other members and their protégés. Hospital appointments were crucial to the successful specialist career and the inner fraternity controlled these as well as the lucrative practices. In this way informal relationships, based upon non-medical criteria, were effective in controlling professional relationships and careers.

(*c*) *The marginal professions* Yet another form of colleague control gives rise to the phenomenon of the *marginal* profession. Many occupations—some of them old, such as nurse or midwife, and others new like probation officer or psychiatric social worker—are marginal in the sense that they share a number of characteristics with the classical professions yet fail to achieve similar status and rewards.

Some of these groups are marginal because they are auxiliary to, and are controlled by, another and more powerful professional body. Nurses, for example, are aides to the medical profession. Nursing care follows the doctor's diagnosis and his determination of the necessary treatment; the nurse may not act independently. Yet the relatively low status and rewards of nursing are not entirely a result of medical control. They also stem from a dependent status within the hospital administrative hierarchy and, in most societies, from the wider social disadvantage of being largely a woman's profession.

Other medical auxiliaries include almoners, health workers of various kinds and members of the 'professions supplementary to medicine'—physiotherapists, radiographers, dietitians, medical laboratory technicians, occupational therapists, remedial gymnasts and so on. In Britain the Medical Act of 1961 gave these practitioners formal recognition and a measure of control over internal discipline and training. In spite of this they remain subordinate to the medical establishment because they may only accept their patients from members of the medical profession and their treatment is subject to medical supervision. Other auxiliary professions include legal executives (formerly managing clerks) and book-keepers, who provide services for the solicitor and the accountant respectively, as well as pharmacists, who again are subordinate to the prescribing physician. The auxiliary status of the pharmacist may be further complicated by his involvement in business as a chemist. The ambiguity of his position is such that the American public is almost equally divided between those who think of pharmacists as professional workers and those who think of them as businessmen.

In the course of the historical development of professional occupations, auxiliary groups have often entered into direct competition with the established professions. We have already seen how the apothecaries (originally druggist-shopkeepers) successfully established themselves as medical practitioners in the face of fierce opposition from the Royal College of Physicians. Similar examples of successful competition with the established professions have been provided within the last hundred years by the development of accountancy. A number of accountants' associations originated in the attempts of book-keepers and clerks to provide accounting services (perhaps after working hours) for social groups who could not afford the fees of the established professionals. The process of fission in professional groups, where specialist and competing bodies hive off from the main body is the result of two concomitant processes. First, it results from changes in the social structure whereby new needs arise. For example, small-scale businessmen more and more demanded the services of lawyers and accountants to deal with the increasing complexities of business life—to guide them through the intricacies of taxation, of licensing law, and local government regulations. The great significance of international relationships has also led to the crystallization of specialist functions such as those of the international lawyer, the space lawyer and the United Nations diplomats. A second factor affecting this process of fission is the dynamic nature of a body of knowledge itself, the development of which creates a basis for the emergence of new occupational groups. Advances in the physical sciences lie behind the emergence of electronics engineering and computer programming; advances in the biological and social sciences lie behind the growth of psychiatry.

Other professional groups are marginal in the sense that their practice is of a limited nature. Again, there are examples of the limited professions in the medical field where pediatrists, chiropodists, audiologists and dispensing opticians have the area of their expertise defined by the medical body as a whole, although they retain control over the treatment given within their specialism. Dentists are the most fully established in their independence of all these groups, chiefly because the practice of dentistry has always been largely independent of medical control. This independence might be explained by the fact that until very recent times, that is until the development and application of anaesthetic and dental technology, the practice was regarded by physicians as a rather degrading manual occupation.

It is the goal of established professional associations to control, or where necessary eliminate, the competition of marginal groups, preferably by a legal restriction of practice to their own members. The greatest threat to the established professional is usually perceived as coming not from the creeping 'takeovers' of the auxiliary and limited professional groups, but from the frontal assaults of what are sometimes called the fringe or quasi-professions. This form of marginality stems from attempts to exclude groups whose practice is based on a body of knowledge which differs from that sustaining the established profession. Osteopaths, chiropractors, naturpaths, herbalists, homeopaths and hypnotherapists differ from auxiliaries in the medical field in that they lay claim to an explanatory system which they hold to be in some way superior to established medical knowledge. Thus the difference between the osteopath and the physiotherapist is that the osteopath claims to be able to diagnose and treat patients in his own right, whereas the physiotherapist remains subject to the physician's diagnosis and supervision. Attempts to bring bone manipulation within general medical practice in Britain have foundered on this difference; osteopaths refuse to enter the National Health Service on the terms accepted by physiotherapists. A recent study of 'fringe medicine' makes the point very clearly.[8]

> The physiotherapist is a medical auxiliary, the 1961 Act accorded (him) official recognition as a member of a Profession Supplementary to Medicine, but only so long as he agreed to treat only such patients who were referred to him by doctors and to treat them along the lines doctors suggested. The Osteopath rejects the implication that doctors are qualified to diagnose the right cases for, and supervise, manipulative treatment. On the contrary, he argues, they are disqualified by their lack of the appropriate training.

Osteopathy and chiropractice are far more widespread in the USA than in other industrial societies. American chiropractors treat about thirty million cases a year. This is partly a result of the high degree of specialization within the medical profession, which has left the field of general practice relatively open to the chiropractor and osteopath. Even so, the incorporation of osteopaths into the medical profession in the State of California in 1962 was only achieved in the face of bitter (and continuing) opposition from their colleagues in other States.

New forms of client control

(*a*) *Client choice* We have seen how, in eighteenth-century England, client control of professional activity was effective through a system of patronage. Client control as it exists in contemporary societies operates through other channels. The most obvious of these channels is client choice. The lawyer, the doctor and the accountant are all subject to the vagaries of client choice which often results from an informal system or referral in the community. The newcomer sooner or later gets round to asking friends, work-mates or colleagues: 'Do you know a good dentist?' or 'Which doctor do you go to?' Such judgments are necessarily based on non-technical criteria; a 'good' dentist may be defined in terms of social acceptability, good looks, religion and so on. To the degree that choices are extra-professional, some control over the professional man's activities passes to the client. Client choices are likely to work most effectively in relatively homogeneous village communities where few professionals would risk setting up in practice without strong local connections. The greater anonymity and the most specialized nature of social relationships in towns increases the importance of colleague referral systems. Even in towns, however, non-technical choices may be an important constraint on the professional. For example, a negro doctor in a white neighbourhood in the United States, or an Indian doctor in Britain may find successful general practice eludes them.

(*b*) *The employed professional* A more specific form of client control is found where professionals are directly employed by public or private organizations. Accountants, lawyers, architects, engineers and scientists are today employed in large numbers by business firms. Under this contemporary system of patronage the independent status of the professional is, in large part, a fiction, but it is a significant fiction. As a result of his socialization into the profession, the organization lawyer or accountant may identify more with the profession than with the firm. This ambivalence in the role of the employed professional involves tensions and conflicts. Such tensions, for example, are inherent in the position of the industrial scientist, who may be subject both to professional demands for publication and to commercial demands for secrecy. Similarly the government-employed architect may be subject both to professional aesthetic requirements and to utilitarian demands from his employer.

In all highly industrialized societies the proportion of professionals in independent practice is declining; in the underdeveloped world the professions have, to a much larger extent, been brought into being by state action, and their members are today employed by government agencies. In neither case is the typical professional an independent practitioner. In Britain in 1960, for example, only one-third of accountants were in private practice. In the case of surveyors the figure was 27 per cent; architects 25 per cent; actuaries 4 per cent; and engineers 2 per cent. Solicitors were unusual in that a majority (62 per cent for England and Wales) was engaged in private practice.[9] In the United States independent professionals make up about 1 per cent of the employed population. The proportion of salaried professionals, however, has risen to at least six times that number. This illustrates how the recent expansion of professional workers in industrial societies has taken place within bureaucratic employment. In other words, not only has bureaucracy invaded the professions—in the form of the law firms, the medical clinic, the management consultancy, and the mass university—but the professionals have infiltrated the bureaucracies. In Britain, the flow of accountants into business bureaucracies, and later into controlling positions on the boards of the corporations, was initiated by the Companies Act of 1867 (paralleled in the United States in 1896). This Act was a major step towards making audit by a qualified accountant compulsory for public companies. By the first world war accountants were joining the ranks of management in significant numbers. Later, in the great economic depression of the 1930s which resulted in the breakdown of *laissez-faire* economic policies, the services of accountants were at a premium. Their special talents as 'fixers', in working out the financial details of mergers, takeovers and price fixing, were in great demand as they have been ever since. Since the 1940s cost accountants have also become an important part of management as the techniques of budgetary control have been developed. Similarly, research and development needs of the large mass-production firm have increased the importance of the scientist and engineer who have, in their turn, begun to advance up the ladder of bureaucratic control to join the accountants on the boards. Latest in the line, but increasingly to be found in the higher ranks of management, are the men versed in the mystique of sales and market research—for the expensive, modern automated plant is built only when market research is complete and potential sales are known. This places the market expert at the heart of the decision-making process.

The professionalization of the business bureaucracy may occur not only as a result of the infiltration of the professional, but also through the growing claims to expertise and professional status of general managers. The authority of the general manager does not derive from technical competence but from the position he occupies in the managerial hierarchy. There is, however, an increasing tendency for such managers to call themselves professionals and to behave like professionals, instituting lengthy training schemes and creating professional bodies such as the British Institute of Managers, which was incorporated in 1947. This trend is partly the result of the growing size and complexity of business firms and the rapid rate of technological change. Under these conditions the skills needed to operate the organizational machine are difficult to acquire 'on the job' and cannot be passed from father to son. The claim to professional status, however, is usually limited to the managers of large firms in which corporate solidarity is conspicuous, where decision making has important consequences for the community at large, and the ethic of service has some relevance. Attempts to implement some kind of incomes policy in a number of industrial societies today appear to be founded on the belief that the manager (and the union official) has obligations to the public which should be recognized when wages, prices and profits are under consideration. Perhaps symbolic of these changes is the recent modification of the Rotary motto from 'He profits most who serves best' to 'Service above self'.

Another aspect of management's claim to professional status is that it now shares with established professions a dependence upon a complex body of knowledge. Aspects of psychology, economics, sociology and other disciplines are now incorporated into the syllabuses of business studies courses—a rapidly expanding sector of higher education. The extent of professional training for business managers in the United States is indicated by the fact that in 1958 there were 300,000 students enrolled on business administration courses at the undergraduate level alone. Formal management training of this kind is by no means as advanced in other countries but is expanding rapidly.

The professional society?

The great expansion in the numbers of professionals and the increased demand of many new occupational groups for a degree of self-control over their work activities are trends which are often thought to be transforming the nature of industrial societies. It is argued, for example, that as professionals make up a larger and larger proportion of the labour force so the peculiarities of professionalism will exert a more pervading influence leading ultimately to a society dominated by professionals. Our analysis of the character of the professions would lead us to challenge some of the more extreme claims associated with this line of argument.

Is industrial society increasingly dominated by professionalism? Certainly many occupations are developing some of the characteristics associated with professionalism. Some would argue that even manual workers are becoming professionals to the extent that manual occupations may involve a specialized technique and provide a career. There may also be an 'ethical code' in the form of conventions of fair practice—for example, rules of behaviour developed in management-union negotiations and in arbitration procedures. Similarly, business management is said to be becoming more professional, partly as a result of the inclusion of professionals in management but also through the development among managers of codes of ethics and specialisms which are based upon a theory of management practice. Our scepticism of the claim that we are witnessing 'the professionalization of everyone' is based on an appreciation of the variety of forms of control characterizing contemporary occupations that are called professions. Their practice may be controlled by a professional association, by the state, by their clients, or by a combination of these. Today control by the professional body alone is not a common means of regulating an occupational activity. This is most evident in the growth of large-scale organizations which employ experts of one kind or another. In a large hospital the task of co-ordination is carried out by specialist administrators. To do their job successfully they must have considerable authority and this reduces the independent authority of the salaried medical specialists. Consequently arguments to the effect that professional expansion will counter the bureaucratic impersonality and arbitrariness of large-scale organizations must be treated with caution. The work situation of the typical professional is no longer independent practice and the typical professional association is now as likely to be concerned with the pay and conditions of its members as with the maintenance of professional standards and conduct among solo practitioners. So the expansion of the professions need not necessarily result in the growth of professionalism.

These changes in the nature of professional organization must also be borne in mind when considering claims that a professional ethic increasingly permeates the institutions of modern industrial societies; that the humanistic and individualistic creeds of the professions provide a source of independent criticism in the face of 'monolithic, bureaucratic impersonality'. It has been suggested that the traditional 'personal service professions'—medicine, law and the clergy—allied with the new 'counselling' professions, such as social work, are influencing the moral ethos of our society.[10] The personal service ethic, it is said, will spread from the professions to society at large and will become the ideology by which many decisions of the ruling groups are justified. As planning and welfare become central to the modern industrial state so the personal service ethic, stressing collectivistic and altruistic considerations will become more relevant to the decision-making process. But the fact that most of the 'new' professionals and an increasing proportion of the 'old' are employed by public or private organizations should alert us to the possibility of changes in the functions and image of professionals. There is, for example, reason to doubt that professional codes and the service orientation will remain significant where the professional is subject to bureaucratic rules and authority. Moreover, the fastest growing professions are not those providing a service for an individual client but technologists, record keepers, and planners—engineers, auditors, accountants, town planners, computer programmers and so on.

This increasing application of specialized skills to all kinds of social and personal problems has been made possible by a massive growth in what has been called 'the knowledge industry' and has given rise to problems of control over new occupational groups. In addition the proliferation of sales techniques, the growth in house ownership, the development of mass tourism, all provide 'control' problems of the sort we have been discussing. The layman is equally incapable of judging the technical expertise of a television repair man or a garage maintenance mechanic; the advice of a tourist agent or house agent; and the work of a solicitor or physician. Who is going to provide the guarantee of integrity, competence and honour? The practitioner? The public? The state? The practitioners have an interest in maintaining a monopoly, but the state has the power to impose alternative forms of control and has done so in some cases. In recent years the public, too, has begun to play a more positive part in attempts to control a variety of services. Consumer bodies of various kinds are flourishing. Perhaps one consequence of the changes we have outlined will be the growing importance of 'consumer politics'. Whatever the outcome, it is certain that the development of these occupations, which enjoy high status and not a little power, will be of great significance in the future development of industrial societies.

Notes

1 A. M. Carr-Saunders, *Professions: Their Organisation and Place in Society*, Oxford: Clarendon Press, 1928, pp. 3–31.

2 From a pamphlet written in 1794 by the Medical Director of York County Hospital, quoted in Bernice Hamilton, 'The medical professions in the eighteenth century', *Economic History Review*, 4, 1951.

3 Robert Masters Kerrison, *Observations and Reflections on the Bill now in Progress through the House of Commons for Better Regulating the Medical Profession as far as regards Apothecaries*, 1815, pp. 18–19.

4 See R. Bucher and A. Strauss, 'Professions in process', *American Journal of Sociology*, 66, 1961, pp. 325–34, for a discussion of this point.

5 C. Wright Mills, *White Collar*, London: Oxford University Press, 1956, p. 112.

6 See O. Smigel, 'The impact of recruitment upon the organization of a large law firm', *American Sociological Review*, 25, 1960, pp. 56–66.

7 See O. Hall, 'The informal organisation of the medical profession', *Canadian Journal of Economics and Political Science*, 12, 1946, pp. 30–44.

8 Brian Inglis, *Fringe Medicine*, London: Faber, 1964, p. 109.

9 *Report of the Royal Commission on Doctors' and Dentists' Remuneration*, Cmnd 939, London: HMSO, February 1960, Table 14.

10 See Paul Halmos, *The Personal Service Society*, London: Constable, 1970.

Reading

Elliott, Philip, *The Sociology of the Professions*, London; Macmillan, 1972. An analysis of the development of professional occupations in terms of the move from traditional 'status professionalism' to 'occupational professionalism' associated with modern industry and commerce.

Lees, D. S., *Economic Consequences of the Professions*, London: Institute of Economic Affairs, 1966. A fifty-page pamphlet in which an economist looks at the monopoly position of professional associations and argues that it operates to the detriment of new entrants to the profession and 'consumer welfare'. Contains a brief case study of lawyers.

Lewis, R. and Maude, A., *Professional People*, Harmondsworth: Penguin, 1953. A great deal of useful information is presented in a value laden manner. The book is dominated by a spirit of nostalgia for the old independent professions as against the modern trends toward bureaucratization and state involvement.

Millerson, Geoffrey, *The Qualifying Associations*, London: Routledge & Kegan Paul. 1964. The significance of the qualifying associations in the development of professional occupations in England: their organization and functions in the provision of education and control over professional conduct.

Reader, W. J., *Professional Men*, London: Weidenfeld & Nicolson, 1966. A study of the changing structure of the traditional professions and the emergence of new professions associated with the development of the English middle classes in the nineteenth century.

Further reading

Carr-Saunders, A. M. and Wilson, P. A., *The Professions*, London: Cass, 1964. A thorough pioneering study first published in 1933.

Etzioni, A. (ed.), *The Semi-Professions and Their Organization*, New York: Free Press, 1969. Separate studies of elementary schoolteachers, nurses, and social workers in the USA and a commentary upon the dominance of women and the high levels of bureaucracy in these 'semi-professions'.

Halmos, Paul, *The Personal Service Society*, London:

Constable, 1970. An attempt to evaluate the social significance of the professions, arguing that the ideology of the 'personal service professions' has seeped into general belief systems and is in process of becoming the dominant ideology of industrial societies.

Jackson, J. A. (ed.), *Professions and Professionalization*, Cambridge University Press, 1970. A collection of essays presenting a variety of 'new' approaches to the study of the professions.

Johnson, Terence, *Professions and Power*, London: Macmillan, 1972. An evaluation of the present state of sociological theory relating to the professions and a theoretical discussion in elaboration of some of the approaches suggested in this chapter.

Prandy, K., *Professional Employees*, London: Faber, 1965. A study of engineers and technologists, and the effect of their situation as employees upon their status and power in society as a whole.

Vollmer, H. M. and Mills, D. L. (eds), *Professionalization*, Englewood Cliffs: Prentice-Hall, 1966. A wide selection of readings relating to such subjects as the concept of professionalization, the social context of professionalization, professional associates and colleague relations, professionals as employees, professionals and government, etc.

10 Social stratification

Wherever there is a systematic division of labour in economic and political life there are also differences in men's access to power. Where there are specialist occupations some specialists invariably manage to gain control over the lives of others, and to monopolize the surplus of production over consumption at the expense of others. The composition of this dominant group varies from society to society. In some societies the most powerful men are warriors led by a warrior king; in others they are priests; in others, landowners, merchants, or industrialists. In most industrial societies power is shared between two or more groups in such a way that it is difficult to locate it with any precision. In all complex societies, however, a minority of the population exercises power out of all proportion to its numbers.

How is it that some groups manage to control the distribution of the economic surplus and keep a major part of it for themselves? Why is the dominant group able to sustain a huge difference in life styles between themselves and the masses in some societies but not in others? What factors explain the differences from one society to another in the relationships between the powerful and the powerless? How can people pass on their privileged position to their children? The task of this chapter is to suggest some answers to these questions by looking at the development of social stratification in a variety of societies.

The emergence of social stratification

There are some human societies where there are no differences in power, where wealth is shared equally, and where high social standing is dependent entirely on ability and carries with it no economic or political 'perks'. In other words there are some societies where there is no social stratification. These are societies in which all persons of the same sex engage in the same tasks. It may be hunting; it may be the cultivation of small plots; it may be fighting. The differences in social standing and decision making which do exist are based upon age (which eventually comes to all and therefore provides no basis for semi-permanent differences in status position), or upon the universally recognized skills and abilities of an individual. A man who is especially skilled in a common activity—say, hunting—may be influential in directing the movements of the band, and his skills may win him a position of high honour. The nature of such a position of prestige may be gauged from the following description of the leader of a Bushman band.[1]

> Nobody ever contested Toma's position as leader, for it was not a position Toma held by force or pressure, but simply by his wisdom and ability, and people prospered under him. No Bushman wants prominence, but Toma went further than most in avoiding prominence; he had almost no possessions and gave away everything that came into his hands. He was diplomatic, for in exchange for his self-imposed poverty, he won the respect and following of all the people there.

There are very few material possessions in hunting societies, partly because the migrant nature of the band places severe restrictions on the accumulation of property. Consequently, ideas of ownership tend to focus very closely upon ownership of food, and there are invariably detailed rules concerning the obligations of ownership. It is generally obligatory to give food to all other members of the band when a kill has been made. In societies where the hold over life is so precarious, such customs 'spread the risk' of failing to make a kill. The members of hunting societies are well aware of this function of their sharing customs. As one anthropologist writes of the Eskimo: 'he knows that the best place for him to store his surplus is in someone else's stomach, because sooner or later he will want his gift repaid.'[2] The really important thing to note, however, is that 'ownership' does not mean the right to do what one likes with the game. There are deep-seated social obligations to give most of it away, and the man who fully honours his obligations is highly esteemed. The reward of the successful hunter is prestige, not meat. Wealth does not accumulate in the hands (or even in the stomachs) of the successful alone, so there are no significant differences in wealth. Moreover, the prestige accorded the successful and generous hunter relates primarily to his hunting prowess and generosity. In so far as it does become more general, it only gives him influence as long as the other members of the society willingly accord him a position of influence—as long, that is, as he is able to *persuade* them to follow him, and this is usually conditional upon his continued success as a hunter.

Some horticultural and pastoral societies are similar to hunting bands in that, despite a more complex technology and a more certain food supply, their economies produce only a very small surplus. Wherever there is little or no surplus of production over subsistence it is not possible for any person or group to secure a more than equal share of the products without pushing others below the line of subsistence. Since these are also societies which have not developed legal monopolies of force (i.e. a state form of organization) this is unlikely to occur. Moreover, everyone has to engage directly in the production process; none can be released from this labour. There is therefore little occupational specialization to provide a basis for the coalescence of dominant and subordinate groups.

Settled cultivation and pastoralism, however, do have potentialities for the creation of an economic surplus that are absent in all but the most fortunately placed hunting and gathering societies. The grains and roots produced by cultivators are suitable for storing and so can be accumulated, and the preservation of meat 'on the hoof' is simpler and more effective than the preservation of dead animals—especially in tropical areas. It is therefore in these societies that the phenomenon of accumulation first appears. The accumulation of a significant surplus over and above the small reserve required for security presents a society with the economic problem of what to do with it. One solution to this problem that is common among known simpler societies is the development, out of the egalitarian society, of the economic organization associated with chiefdoms. The major economic task of the chief is one of redistributing the surplus produce; of receiving, as gifts, produce of different sorts from the people, and redistributing it—often in 'wasteful' feasts. The chief possesses no power to coerce his fellow men into giving up their surplus, and his own position in the early stages of the development of a chiefdom would seem to be based entirely upon his ability to give more than others. This in turn is often based upon his greater capacity for hard work, so that the chief is not necessarily released from food production. There is rarely any accumulation of wealth by the chief so, although there is a strong tendency for the office of chief to be monopolized by a single lineage, there is no concomitant economic gain. Indeed, the chief's influence and prestige stem from his generosity; a man's 'wealth' only brings him prestige and influence if he fulfils his obligation to give it away.

As the size of the surplus increases, the chief and his close kin gradually become released from their obligations as food producers and increasingly become full-time distributors of produce and organizers of labour. Here we have social stratification in embryo. But this is not yet a stratified society. The chief has little power to organize people against their will. He lives in much the same way as his people, although he probably has a grander dwelling and the exclusive right to certain ornaments. Moreover, the whole population benefits from the redistribution process, although the chief and his kinsmen usually benefit somewhat more than others. All members of the society still have unrestricted access to the basic essentials of making a living. In some societies, Ashanti and other West African chiefdoms for example, land (the basic resource in a cultivating society) was held corporately by the lineage, and the chief's control over the use of land was a control exercised on behalf of the corporate group. As chiefdoms develop so the powers of the chief become more extreme. In many Polynesian societies, for example, the chief could re-allocate land on his accession. While chiefs rarely denied men access to the land they needed they could, and more frequently did, deny access to the equally crucial irrigation schemes which had been built, under chiefly direction, by communal labour. The higher level of technological development of these relatively complex chiefdoms thus gave greater powers to the chief, for he controlled the distribution of water which was vital for successful cultivation.

The greater gap between the chief (and his relatives) and the common man in highly developed chiefdoms is illustrated by the elaborateness of the taboos surrounding the paramount chief of Hawaii in the days before significant Western contact.[3]

> The following is only a partial list: it was prohibited for a man's shadow to fall on the paramount's house, back, robe, or any possession; it was prohibited to pass through his door, climb his stockade, to put out in a racing canoe before him, to put on his robe or his bark cloth; it was required that one kneel while he ate, not appear in his presence in a wet bark cloth, or with mud on one's head. . . . Even the ground the chief walked on became charged with mana and was avoided by others. In the presence of the paramount, all had to prostrate themselves on the ground in a posture of extreme humility and obeisance.

Early European travellers to Hawaii, reporting on these chiefly taboos, tell us that the usual punishment for a breach was death, but that the punishment would not be exacted if the wrongdoer had 'influential friends'. Similar inequality before the law occurred in Tonga, where there was no vengeance for the kinsman of a commoner killed by a chief, and in Tahiti. It is an inequality more typical of stratified societies, where a small group monopolizes the means of violence, and indeed, societies like Hawaii stand on the boundaries between 'rank' societies and stratified ones. Extreme exploitation, however, was lacking, largely because of the presence of the 'redistributive ethic'.

It is with the emergence of a state structure that social stratification in its full sense appears, for stratification involves the wielding of *power* by some groups at the expense of others. A small group uses its power over others to build a style of life more grand than the life styles of the mass of the population. In non-industrial societies there is a tendency for the very great bulk of the economic surplus to be used for the benefit of the rulers or those that serve them directly. As increases in food production allow a progressive division of labour, most of the specialists—goldsmiths, builders, domestic servants and the like—provide services only for a very limited section of the population. In other words, the surplus production, far from being equally divided, supports a few in lives of relative luxury. The larger the surplus, the greater the luxury and the greater the differences between the rich and powerful and the poor and powerless.

How does the ruling minority manage to keep such an unequal share of the society's wealth for its own use? Why does the majority continue to produce a surplus when it does not enjoy the benefits? Pre-industrial examples provide two broad answers: the rulers either gain their privileged position by physical coercion or by supernatural coercion. Either they establish their dominance by conquest and maintain it by the threat of physical violence, or they obtain it by controlling access to the gods and spirits whose goodwill is thought to be necessary for the well-being of the society. In the first case, the ruling stratum tends to be one of warriors; in the second, one of priests. In addition these two groups often combine in a ruling alliance.

Of the two oldest states one (Mesopotamia) developed an upper stratum of priests, and the other (Egypt) was based upon conquest. In Mesopotamia the surplus was drawn from the cultivators by priests, whose proximity to the deities gave them special knowledge of the requirements of the gods. The gifts of food and other goods to the gods were administered by the priests; the building of the temples to the glory and honour of the supernatural powers was directed by the priests. Their task of interpreting the divine will gave them an authority which placed them at the heart of the decision making process and made it right and proper that they should enjoy certain privileges not available to the ordinary man. Their privileged position was based upon a monopoly of knowledge which enabled them to control the thoughts and actions of men. For example, they alone recognized the regularity of climatic conditions. Their ability to predict such events as the annual floods consequently appeared to ordinary men to represent power over natural phenomena—a power which could not be ignored.

The early development of social stratification in middle America was also based upon religion (although later, military might became an equally important factor). About 900 BC the simple farming community gave way to a society of greater economic complexity, yielding a larger surplus on the basis of more diverse crops. At about the same time there is the first evidence of a social gulf between members of the society. Archaeological evidence from burial sites shows a priesthood set apart from ordinary men by differences in dress, deportment and skills. The organization of the society underwent a major change with the priest emerging as the dominant figure. The priests were specialists in organization as well as religious practitioners and could therefore exact tribute as well as worship from the rest of the population. The temples were also centres of political power and, since markets were attached to them, of economic activity. Priestly authority, however, ultimately derived from the task of mediation between human beings and the supernatural. Obedience was commanded in the name of the gods. The tight ideological control exercised by the priesthood seems to have rendered warfare largely unnecessary. Control over the population and the extraction of the greater part of the economic surplus from the majority was achieved through supernatural terror rather than physical terror.

The second type of domination—that based upon military might of one kind or another—is more common in pre-industrial societies. The stratification systems of Egypt, Mexico after AD 900, ancient Rome, and many of the African kingdoms of the eighteenth and nineteenth centuries, all seem to have arisen directly out of conquest or to have been substantially modified by conquest. In Egypt, for example, although religion played an important part, the first centralized accumulation and concentration of foodstuffs resulted from the conquest of the Nile delta by Menes, the king of Upper Egypt. The conquest placed Menes in control of comparatively vast resources, first as booty from the campaign and subsequently as a continuing revenue in the form of tribute. Much of the surplus was used to support labourers and craftsmen who worked on the construction of the royal tombs, and in obtaining the foreign material with which they were so lavishly constructed. A contemporary estimate suggested that 100,000 men were fully employed for ten years simply on quarrying stone for the great pyramid. The power of a ruler who could successfully organize such an enterprise is beyond dispute. Indeed, the pharaohs were considered divine. Other persons of high position in ancient Egypt merely absorbed some of the reflected glory of the king. They were, moreover, appointed by him and held office only as long as they continued to please him. One of the consequences of this absolutism was that persons from humble origins whose ability caught the eye of the pharaoh could be elevated to positions of very considerable power. Thus the Israelite Joseph, sold into slavery in Egypt as a boy, rose to become second only to the pharaoh in all the land. The chance of such a dramatic rise to power came most frequently (but still very infrequently) to those who were the household servants of the pharaoh, for it was they who came into most frequent contact with him and therefore had the opportunity to impress. It was a hazardous business, however, and there was a much higher chance of being condemned to death than of being promoted, as is shown by the fate of Joseph's fellow servants.

If we look at many of the traditional states of East Africa we find a distribution of power involving similar absolutism and also seemingly based upon conquest. These states also demonstrate the potentialities for clear-cut stratification even where the economic surplus is relatively small. Reconstructions of the history of the part of Africa lying between the great lakes suggests a southwards movement of tall, Nilotic, nomadic pastoralists who conquered the existing cultivators and set themselves up as a ruling group. A number of traditional kingdoms in this area—Rwanda; Ankole; Toro; Nyoro—have roughly similar structures, with the pastoralist and ethnically distinct minorities (usually about 10 per cent of the total population) ruling over agricultural serfs.

The kingdom of Ankole provides the least complicated example. The positions of the Bahima (pastoralists) and the Bairu (agriculturalists) were legally, politically, economically, and socially unequal. In economic terms, the domination of the Bahima was manifest in the compulsory tribute which had to be paid in food or labour by all Bairu. While only the king or the chiefs could levy this tax, all Bahima benefited from it since much of the produce was used by the king in feeding and provisioning his Bahima visitors. There is a significant difference here from the process of redistribution in a chiefdom which we observed earlier. In most chiefdoms the commoners could withhold their gifts to the chief if they were not satisfied with his behaviour, and even in the most highly developed chiefdoms like Hawaii, where this was not possible, everyone benefited to some extent from the redistribution through ceremonial feasts. In stratified societies, such redistribution as takes place is much more limited and benefits only a few. In the case of the Ankole, it was the Bahima who gained from this system of taxation.

A further economic difference between the two major groups lay in the prohibition of Bairu ownership of productive cattle, for cattle were the main form of wealth. Prohibitions of a non-economic kind furthered the difference. Bairu were not allowed to engage in military activities—a common prohibition placed upon conquered peoples, and one which clearly retains control of the means of force in the hands of the dominant stratum. They were also debarred from high official positions and were thus unable to bring any political influence to bear upon the king. The two groups stood in different legal positions in the sense that punishment depended upon which group one belonged to more than upon the nature of the offence. Bairu, for example, were not allowed to kill a Muhima under any circumstances. Without this right of blood revenge they were unprotected against any physical violence which the ruling group might direct against them.

As in many African states, the power of the Ankole king was very great and could be exercised arbitrarily. Part of the Bahima's high standing derived from their closeness to the king. The relationship between the king and his Bahima followers was one of clientship; that is to say, the king offered protection in return for certain services and homage payments (usually in cattle) from his clients. Such cattle were added to the royal herds which were used to replenish the stock of Bahima herdsmen in distress. In this, one can see the essential difference between the homage payment of the Bahima, which was freely paid in return for certain benefits, and which even in itself acted as an insurance against hard times, and the obligatory tribute exacted from the Bairu, who benefited hardly at all from the payment.

Social relations in traditional Ankole, then, were dominated by the distinction between Bahima and Bairu. Ultimately, the unequal relationship was maintained by a monopoly of the effective use of force and it probably had its origin in conquest. But naked power was overlaid with ideas about ethnicity and rights of cattle ownership. This is demonstrated by the ease with which conquered Bahima from neighbouring territories were assimilated into the dominant stratum. The Bairu of conquered areas fared less well, for some of them were taken as slaves to serve in the households of the king and chiefs. These slaves had no legal status whatsoever; they were the property of the master and he had the power of life and death over them. Their lowly position was summed up in the common practice of cutting off their ears so that they could be easily recognized as slaves if they escaped. For Ankole Bairu there were bounds to legitimate exploitation, and it was part of the task of the king to see that these were not exceeded. No such limitations were placed upon the treatment of slaves by their masters.

As societies grow more complex so their systems of stratification become more complex: new strata emerge and relationships between existing strata undergo subtle but important changes. Economic development creates an increasingly efficient economy and thus potentialities for greater differences between the strata. These changes may be observed in the social development of republican Rome, although access to political power remained crucial, as in all the societies we have considered so far, and the significance of military might and conquest grew more rather than less important. The unusual feature of the Roman republic is that it was not governed by an absolute ruler. Hence, the designation 'citizen' had considerable force and introduced a further complication into the relations between strata. This is not to say that all citizens were equal, and from the earliest records Roman society is divided into patricians and plebeians.

In the early days of the republic there was little difference of wealth between the two groups. The difference was essentially a legal and political one. As the military might of Rome grew and her frontiers expanded, the relations between the strata underwent a number of changes. The most important of these related to the increased prestige and wealth of senators; the growth of tribute from the provinces; the influx of slaves; the growth of trade; and ultimately, the development of a professional army under 'permanent' commanders who were increasingly an independent political force. It was a complex process and provides a good illustration of the fact that the gain of a state may not be equally shared by all its members (or even by all its citizens). Indeed, the growth of Rome as a world power was paralleled by a polarization of the upper stratum and the commoners.

One of the most decisive steps towards world

dominance—the conquest of Carthage—serves as an admirable illustration of one of the ways in which this happened. The Carthaginians were worthy military opponents and the Punic wars were long and costly. In the course of Hannibal's invasion of Italy enormous damage was done to the farming land around Rome. Added to years of neglect, brought about by the absence of the bulk of the male farmers on military service for lengthy periods, this made the problem of reconstruction after the war a colossal one. The peasant farmers who survived the war returned to find that their soldiers' pay was not sufficient to cover the necessary outlay in seed, stock and equipment, and they were forced into debt at ruinous terms. As a result, the small farms around Rome fell into the hands of those few who had the capital to re-stock them. The concentration of landownership was exacerbated by the state making over large tracts of public land in repayment of war loans, for it was the same wealthy people who had financed the costly war with Carthage. In this way the huge ranch-type farms of the Roman landed aristocracy developed, for pasture provided the landowner with a higher profit than agriculture. In addition, the wars had resulted in a huge influx of slaves, providing cheap labour which was especially suited to work on large estates.

The position of a substantial section of the farming citizenry was thus undermined by these twin processes resulting from the wars. They were forced to seek refuge in Rome itself where their position was little better. Here, too, the free labourer competed with slave labour. By the time the Republic came to an end there were some 200,000 slaves in Rome—one-fifth of the city's total population. The majority of these were domestic slaves, but there was a number of skilled craftsmen among them and this depressed the wages and living standards of the free artisans. That Julius Caesar found it expedient to pacify the citizens with a corn 'dole' is perhaps less significant as a sign of the value of citizenship than as a commentary upon the economic position of the townsman. The plight of the non-citizen freeman, who did not qualify for this state aid, was even worse.

The slaves themselves constituted the lowest stratum of Roman society. Although a few individual slaves exercised considerable influence (through their advisory position in the household of a great man) and one or two managed to become fairly wealthy, the general position of the slave must have been unenviable. His position in society is evidenced by the fact that in a Roman law court evidence from a slave was only admissible if it had been extracted under torture! Perhaps the best evidence of the deplorable life of slaves is the frequency of slave revolts—the actions of desperate men, with enormous odds against success.

There were also, of course, those who derived great benefit from Rome's wars. Tribute from subject peoples made taxation obsolete and, while this may have benefited the rich more than others, it also helped freemen who had achieved modest economic success, and perhaps it even provided some consolation for the unemployed who would otherwise have had taxation imposed upon their other burdens. The greatest direct beneficiaries from the wars, however, were those who conducted them and, to a lesser extent, those who subsequently ruled over the conquered peoples. It was loot, slaves, and tribute (as well as the effect of war upon landownership) that enabled the senatorial families to raise their standard of living so much above that of the common man. In the days before the Punic wars there had been a positive embargo on senatorial wealth, and any spoils of war had been faithfully paid into the Treasury. The ambition was not to be rich but to be powerful. In the days of world dominion, however, things were somewhat different. The sole compensation for a year's posting as governor to one of the provinces lay in the common expectation that this year's service of the state would put one in funds for life. The lower ranks of the army serving under such a governor made more modest, but still worthwhile, profits. When, as happened from time to time as with Cicero's appointment to Sicily, a governor was appointed whose sense of justice prevented him from operating this extortion, the provincials 'regarded him with speechless astonishment'.[4] We can imagine that the army under his command viewed him with similar astonishment but less gratitude. It is evident that great wealth was often associated with military success. In the latter days of the republic, especially, the great fortunes were made by military commanders like Pompey and Julius Caesar.

Another group to profit economically from Rome's military supremacy, however, was the rising stratum of *equites*. Part of their profit came from the flourishing business life of the Mediterranean and the favourable trading position they enjoyed under the sponsorship of Rome. By their very involvement in these profitable activities, however, they renounced all claim to the political life and thus to real power and prestige. For landownership alone of economic activities carried some *social* distinction, and business and trade was forbidden to men of senatorial rank. Such political influence as was exerted by individual men of this stratum (and it was sometimes considerable) was achieved through the financial backing they were able to provide for politicians. In spite of the 'dishonour' of their involvement in business, the most successful of them met senators socially on terms close to equality, and intermarriage was sought by both sides for their mutual advantage.

The emergence of the *equites* marks the development of a new stratum with an essentially economic base. Such a stratum is common in the more highly developed agrarian societies. Traditional Japan, Imperial China, Mughal India and medieval Europe all had a stratum of merchants whose wealth was often in excess of their social status and political power. Some of them became very wealthy (wealthy enough to underwrite the expenses of an aristocratic patron) although the majority were much less successful. In these traditional societies the merchants, to a large extent, stood apart from the dominant power relationship—that between landlord and tenant. Their own activities, especially in the economic sphere, were less easily controlled by landowners and rulers, and so they usually had a good deal more freedom of action than the peasants and tenant farmers.

There were also quite wide dissimilarities in the position of merchants from one agrarian society to another. In some societies, such as Mughal India, the merchants were unable to use their wealth to make even moderate political and social gains. Indeed, they often had the utmost difficulty in retaining their wealth. In some other societies they gradually managed, as a group, to exert political influence and to raise their social position. In the later Middle Ages in Western Europe, for example, the merchants were instrumental in securing the 'freedom of cities', sometimes through force, more often by purchasing privileges from the king. A number of English boroughs were established in this way and within them the wealthier and more powerful merchants to all intents and purposes constituted the government. This further stimulated trade and enhanced their position in the wider society, thereby paving the way for the great expansion of commerce in the fifteenth and sixteenth centuries. In turn, this 'commercial revolution' further enhanced the position of 'bourgeois' groups and helped to establish the springboard from which industrialization was later launched. Before the Industrial Revolution, however, the landed gentry were still socially and politically dominant. It was not until the rise of the industrial society that the rising economic stratum was able to capture political power, and ultimately social power as well.

Industrialization and the development of social classes in England

The process of industrialization had a crucial significance for social stratification. Relationships between existing strata—landowners, merchants, tenant farmers—underwent changes, but of far greater importance were the new strata thrown up by the fundamental processes of social change. The dominant economic position of the landowners, which had been challenged but not supplanted by the growth of commerce and trade, was substantially undermined by the economic success of a new breed of men—the industrial entrepreneurs. In many ways the interests of these men were fundamentally opposed to landed interests, and the creation, through industrialization, of this 'industrial middle class' paved the way for a gradual transfer of political power as well. Subsequently, as the scale of industrial enterprises increased, it became less easy for one man or one family to control the enterprise. Joint stock companies emerged in which managers were appointed to run the firm on behalf of shareholders. By the beginning of the twentieth century the typical industrial firm was no longer a family concern, but a bureaucratic institution operated by managers. The mode of earning a livelihood and the way of life of the mass of the population has also been completely changed by industrialization. The decline in the number engaged in agricultural labour has been balanced by an increase in industrial labour. And while the mid-nineteenth century was still characterized by a great deal of 'domestic' manufacture and craftsman production from small workshops as well as by factory production, it was the latter that was to become dominant. In addition there was, in the second half of the century, a growth in the number of miners as the industrial demand for coal rose, and an increase in dockers, stevedores and the like as the volume of international trade increased. The twentieth century has seen, in mass production, yet another change which has brought about the expansion of a previously relatively insignificant group—the semi-skilled factory workers.

It is these technological and social changes in the organization of work that lie behind the changes in stratification of the last two hundred years. Whatever the cause, however, it was so apparent to contemporaries in early industrial societies that the nature of the relationships between strata where changing, that a new terminology was evolved to describe the changed situation. Whereas writers in eighteenth-century England wrote of 'ranks' and 'orders', those of the nineteenth century increasingly spoke and wrote of 'classes'. By 1834 J. S. Mill could write that social commentators habitually distinguished three classes in society—landlords, capitalists and labourers. Yet, as we shall see, these three great classes were far from being homogeneous.

The rulers of pre-industrial and early industrial England were aristocrats and gentry. That is to say, they owed their position to their ownership of land (and, to some extent, to possession of a title). As landowners their economic fate was overwhelmingly linked to the prosperity of agriculture, although urban land rents were an important source of income for some. The ancestors of many of those with urban land had been merchants who, having achieved wealth from trade, bought estates and a title, retired from commerce, and, adopting the aristocratic style of life, lived off their land. This relative openness of the English aristocracy, the relative ease with which new groups were continually being assimilated, and the eagerness with which they married their sons and daughters to the hiers and hieresses of commercial fortunes, was one of its most important characteristics. It encouraged successful merchants to aspire to membership of the aristocracy and to identify with them. It did not necessarily, however, indicate a willingness to compromise with commercial or industrial interests for, unlike the later 'industrial peers', those adopted into the aristocracy before 1800 gave up their stakes in the world of commerce and trade and became part of 'the landed interest'. It is true that there were a number of landowners who made substantial profits from the mineral rights of their land, and whose economic and political interests did not coincide with those of their fellow landowners. They were joined after 1856 by industrialists, railway magnates and others who remained active in industry or commerce, and whose estates merely represented their surplus assets. By and large, however, in the early years of the century the economic interest of the rulers was wedded to agriculture. The political expression of this was the passing, in 1815, of the Corn Laws, imposing restrictions on the import of American corn and thus maintaining a high price for home farm produce. The close link between economic interest and political action has rarely been clearer. In a single action the ruling group demonstrated beyond all doubt their intention to govern in their own interest. The higher price of food which the Corn Laws entailed forced up the level of the subsistence wage and thus reduced industrial and commercial profits. The result was that the industrialists and merchants, who up to that time had shown little inclination to become permanently involved in politics, were driven to protest by political means. The experience drew the various industrial and trading elements closer together and gave them a common cause around which to unite. The campaign for the repeal of the Corn Laws and agitation for parliamentary reform, then, was the crucible in which the English middle class was formed. For campaign purposes a tactical alliance was made with some groups of manual workers, but this was abandoned in the settlement that led to the Reform Bill of 1832. Thereafter the political as well as the economic power of the middle class grew steadily and middle-class consciousness prospered.

The politics of compromise, by which the landowners extended political participation to the middle class but to them alone, enabled the aristocracy to continue to dominate political life. Furthermore, the mystique of the aristocracy retained some force long after the middle class could have assumed political as well as economic power. Industrialists, for example, often shared the view that the landed gentry were 'natural' rulers—that only they could maintain order and stability in the country. 'For we believe, we men of the middle class,' said one of them, 'that the conduct of national business calls for special men, men born and bred to the work for generations. . . .'[5] This is, perhaps, a peculiarly English form of social deference that is still far from dead and remains one of the more subtle aspects of the power relationships between classes. The relationship between gentlemanly behaviour and government and administration was to remain. Gradually, however, the belief spread that these attributes could be learned and, in particular, the public schools were viewed as the great training grounds for political leadership. Since the rich middle-class boy mixed with the sons of the landowners in the public schools, such an education gradually enabled non-gentry to play a fuller part in government. The purely social mystique of the aristocracy, however, survived their relative political decline.

In the course of the nineteenth century, then, the middle class gradually came to a larger share of power—first through pressure on a mainly aristocratic parliament, later by direct representation. It was this struggle to establish the political conditions within which industrial capitalism could thrive which, more than anything else, established them as a class. The solidarity thus formed was both demonstrated and strengthened by later struggles with their employees.

The power of employers over their employees had been apparent from the very beginning of factory employment. But, to begin with, it had been very much a local phenomenon—the power of a factory master over the factory hands. Very often the total subjection of the employees extended to all spheres of their lives. There is ample documentation of the miseries of factory conditions in the early nineteenth century, but this relationship between employer and employed is not necessarily symptomatic of the new 'class' society. Employers had exploited their workers long before industrialization. But there were differences in the new situation. Two stand out in their significance.

First, the newly dominant middle class had a philosophy of life which was different from that of the old aristocracy of the eighteenth century. Especially significant was the different view held of the poor and needy. The old view is well expressed by Bishop Butler in a sermon to the London Corporation in 1740:[6]

> He who had distributed men into these different ranks, and at the same time united them into one society . . . has by this constitution of things formally put the poor under the superintendency and patronage of the rich. The rich, then, are charged by natural providence, as much as by revealed appointment, with the care of the poor.

To the landed gentry, God has ordained the division into rich and poor *and* charged the rich with the care of the poor. Such a view was not accepted by the successful and often self-made industrialists. They held that the poor were poor because of a lack of self discipline, hard work and initiative. They saw their own success as a reward for these virtues. It followed that the poor must not be indulged in their indolence – a view which lay beneath that policy of the work-house which suggested that it should, as one Poor Law Commissioner put it, be as much like prison as possible. The middle-class view of poverty as indicative of *moral* inferiority was an important part of the changed relationship between the dominant stratum and the mass of the population. It provided a convenient justification for the neglect, or even the ill-treatment, of the poor.

The second significant difference in the new situation was that, after about 1815, it became increasingly an urban situation. In the towns the 'exploitation' of the workers was more transparent (if little worse) than that in rural industry and agriculture. And, as Karl Marx pointed out so clearly, the urban situation was one in which the workers became aware of their common situation. It took many decades, however, for the class consciousness of workers to develop fully—that is to say, for them to become aware of their position *and* to develop the organizations by which they could take economic and political action to change it. One reason for this was that it took a long time for solidarity to develop among the workers. The least privileged labourers are confronted as much with the relative prosperity of their more skilled (or more fully employed) fellows as with the riches of the landowners, rulers or factory owners. This is most striking to rural labourers who compare the factory workers' lot with their own. Agricultural labourers in nineteenth-century England might well have agreed with the views of the Sardinian soldiers brought to Turin to deal with strikes.[7]

> 'We have come to put down the gentlefolk who are on strike.'
> 'But these are not gentlefolk: they are workers and they are poor.'
> 'These chaps are all gentlefolk: they all wear a collar and tie and earn 30 lire a day. I know the poor folk and what they are dressed like. In Sassari they are poor; and we earn 1 lira 50 a day.'

For reasons such as these 'the working class' is generally held to be an urban-industrial phenomenon. Rural workers, even when they are wage earners but especially when they are peasants, are, at most, marginal in their membership. Their scattered situation does not easily lend itself to collective organization and action. Their chief significance to the developing class society of nineteenth-century England lay in the fact that they provided a constant stream of new recruits to the towns and thus acted as a depressant on urban wages.

Even in the towns and within industrial employment, however, there had always been very considerable differences in wealth, way of life, and social status. Henry Mayhew, writing in mid-century, describes some of the differences graphically:[8]

> In passing from the skilled operatives of the West End to the unskilled workers of the Eastern quarter of London the moral and intellectual change is so great that it seems as if we were in a new land, and among another race. The artisans are almost to a man red-hot politicians. They are sufficiently educated and thoughtful to have a sense of their importance to the State. The unskilled labourers are a difference class of people. As yet they are as unpolitical as footmen, and instead of entertaining violent democratic opinions, they appear to have no political opinion whatever.

Mayhew draws our attention to significant political differences between skilled and unskilled workers. Elsewhere in his volume he dwells upon the misery, hunger, and squalor of the casual (and often unemployed) worker which contrasts with the relative prosperity and security of the artisan. The social relationships between the groups, too, often read like those between strata. A writer of a decade earlier points out the status distinctions within the craft industry of carriage-making.[9]

> The body-makers are the wealthiest of all and compose among themselves a species of aristocracy to which the other workmen look up with feelings half of respect, half of jealousy. They feel their importance and treat the others with various consideration: carriage-makers are entitled to a species of condescending familiarity; trimmers are considered too good to be despised; a foreman of painters they may treat with respect, but working painters can at most be favoured with a nod.

The awareness of their difference from labourers was also expressed in the artisans' organization in unions. For these craft unions, even in factories, were more a protection for their members against competition from unskilled labour than against exploitation from employers. Yet it was union organization which first enabled manual workers to have some say in politics and, since they alone were unionized, the 'labour aristocracy' played an important part in the growth of the working class. It is the trade unions, gradually extending downwards through the hierarchy of labour, that are the mark of the nascent working class of the nineteenth century. They represent the disciplined organization through which the energies spent on sporadic and often desperate mob violence in the eighteenth and early nineteenth centuries were channelled into concerted action towards clearly defined political and economic goals. It was through the unions that the power latent in the large numbers of manual workers was partially realized through the Reform Bill of 1867. The result was a decade in which more industrial legislation favourable to workers was passed than in the whole of the previous hundred years. Such was the improvement that in 1895 Engels, writing a new preface to his *The Condition of the Working Class in England*, could include factory workers in the 'aristocracy of the working class':[10]

> A permanent improvement can be recognized for two 'protected' sections of the working class. Firstly, the factory hands. The fixing by Act of Parliament of their working day within relatively rational limits has restored their physical constitution and endowed them with a moral superiority, enhanced by their local concentration. They are undoubtedly better off than before 1848. . . . Secondly, the great Trades' Unions. . . . The engineers, the carpenters and joiners, the bricklayers, are each of them a power, to that extent that, as in the case of the bricklayers and bricklayers' labourers, they can even successfully resist the introduction of machinery. That their position has remarkably improved since 1848 there can be no doubt, and the best proof of this is in the fact that for more than fifteen years not only have their employers been with them, but they with their employers, upon exceedingly good terms. They form an aristocracy among the working class; they have succeeded in enforcing for themselves a relatively comfortable position, and they accept it as final.

For the great majority of non-union, unskilled labour, however, the position was very different. Engels continues his comments:[11]

> But as to the great mass of the working people, the state of misery and insecurity in which they live now is as low as ever, if not

> lower. The East end of London is an ever spreading pool of stagnant misery and desolation, of starvation when out of work and degradation, physical and moral, when in work.

Lest it should be thought that Engels was exaggerating the position for the sake of political advantage one might point out that he is supported from diverse sources. Religious leaders, such as Archbishop Tait of the Church of England and General William Booth of the Salvation Army reported on the London scene in almost identical terms to those used by Engels. The social scientists, Seebohm Rowntree in York and Charles Booth in London, concluded from their investigations that one-third of the population was living in poverty—that is, they simply did not have sufficient income to feed, clothe and house themselves.

For the 'great mass' of unorganized, unskilled labour there was little permanent gain until their own unionization—the 'New Unionism' as it was called—which was already well under way as Engels was writing in 1895. More significantly, the reaction of the middle class and the government to the New Unionism, and the gradual whittling away of trade-union rights granted in the legislation of the 1870s drew the skilled and unskilled workers together for the first time. Beginning with the dock strike of 1889 there is an increase in anti-union press comment; a growing tendency to employ the police and armed forces in strike-breaking; better organization in recruiting labour described variously as 'free' or 'blackleg' depending on the point of view of the writer; and, above all, a growing flood of judgments against the unions in the law courts. This culminated in the Taff Vale Judgment of 1901 which declared that a union could be held corporately liable for damages arising from the actions of its members. While it was the tactics of the New Unionism (in particular their use of the strike—the only effective weapon of men with no control over the abundant supply of labour) which provoked the reaction, the implications of the judgments were also critical for the older, more conservative skilled unions. Differences were therefore largely buried in the face of the common threat. The result was political action on behalf of *all* working groups—skilled and unskilled—and this led to the increase of direct representation of labour in parliament and to the Trade Disputes Act of 1906.

At the turn of the century, then, English society exhibited the characteristics of a 'class society' more clearly than at any earlier time. That is to say there were substantial differences in wealth and power which had some degree of inter-generational stability and, allied to an awareness of these differences, there were feelings of solidarity promoting economic and political action which reflected class interest and which encompassed the great majority of the population. Finally, the strata were in some real sense social entities, exhibiting different styles of life and feelings of group superiority and/or inferiority. Their members showed great selectivity in limiting significant social interaction on terms of equality to members of their own class. All this is not to say that all differences within the classes had disappeared. Rather that, as T. H. Marshall put it, class provides 'a force that unites into groups people who differ from one another, by over-riding the differences between them'.

Social classes in contemporary industrial societies

There have been a number of changes in the structure of social stratification in twentieth-century industrial societies. Two sets of changes have been especially significant. First, there have been important changes in occupational structure resulting from technological changes and the nature of economic developments. Second, in the years since the second world war, industrial societies have sustained marked increases in overall income which, together with changing patterns of residence, have had a marked effect upon ways of life—especially among manual workers. These economic changes have mingled with political and other social changes, part cause and part effect, so that the industrial world exhibits some marked differences in social stratification as well as some marked similarities.

One of the most substantial changes stemming from technological and economic developments has been a change in the distribution of occupations. One important aspect of this has been a steady expansion, since about the 1880s in Britain and America (a little later elsewhere), of what are usually called 'white collar occupations'. In Britain in 1851 clerks formed rather less than 1 per cent of the labour force; by 1966 they comprised some 13·5 per cent. In the USA the increase has been even more rapid; from 0·6 per cent in 1870 to more than 16·5 per cent in 1969. In twentieth-century Britain, the expansion has been from less than 5 per cent of the total occupied work force in 1911 to 13 per cent in 1961. On the face of it, this is just the type of change, creating a high rate of expansion of non-manual occupations relative to manual ones, which gives rise to upward social mobility. A closer look at the expansion of clerical jobs, however, shows that the proportion of the *male* labour force working at this level has expanded much more modestly—from 5·5 per cent in 1911 to 7 per cent in 1961. More than one-quarter of the *female* working population in 1961 was in the clerical grade. We must therefore be careful how we interpret such statistics. For, while the occupational position of single women has considerable bearing on their class position, the social class of *families* is much more closely related to the occupation of the father than of the mother. This has remained true in industrial societies despite the increase in the number of working wives. The type of work carried out by the wife/mother remains a minor determinant of class position and its main contribution is usually through the generation of additional family income. For this reason Table 10.1 is confined to the occupational distribution of the male population. The changes in percentage distribution between 1911 and 1951 are, on the whole, quite small, yet with the male labour force standing at 16 millions, a change of 1 per cent in a category signifies a changed occupational position for some 160,000 families. The changes shown in Table 10.1 which are of greatest relevance to social stratification are a decline in the relative numbers of semi-skilled workers (largely accountable in terms of movement out of agricultural activities which are included in this category) and a steady increase in professional and managerial occupations.

Table 10.1 Percentage distribution of the male occupied population of Great Britain 1911–51

	1911	*1921*	*1931*	*1951*
Higher professional	1·3	1·4	1·5	2·6
Lower professional	1·6	2·0	2·0	3·2
Employers and proprietors	7·7	7·7	7·7	5·7
Managers and administrators	3·9	4·3	4·5	6·8
Clerical workers	5·5	5·4	5·5	6·4
Foremen, supervisors and inspectors	1·8	1·9	2·0	3·3
Skilled manual workers	33·0	32·3	30·0	30·4
Semi-skilled manual workers	33·6	28·3	28·9	27·9
Unskilled manual workers	11·6	16·7	17·9	13·8

Source: Guy Routh, *Occupation and Pay in Great Britain, 1906–60*, Cambridge University Press, 1965, table 1, pp. 4–5.

The growth in managerial employment and the decline, since 1931, in the proportion of 'employers and proprietors' is generally indicative of a change in the organization of industry. 'The employers and proprietors' who made up 5·7 per cent of the working population in 1951 consisted almost entirely of small-scale proprietors. Most of them were engaged in trade or services—only one in twenty was concerned with manufacturing or mining. The enterprise owned and run by a single individual or a single family is no longer typical. There has been a proliferation of experts whose expertise is made necessary by the complexities of technological developments, and there has been a continuation of the growth, already well in evidence at the turn of the century, of the joint stock company and of relatively bureaucratic management.

Nearly three-quarters of both British and American companies are corporately owned—some of these with many thousands of shareholders. The growth of the joint stock company has resulted in what is usually called a separation of ownership and control—a process whereby the owners relinquish the day-to-day running of the enterprise which they place in the hands of professional managers. The significance of this change for the nature of the industrialist group lies not so much in the changed outlook of the new rulers of industry (which it is easy to exaggerate) as in the different patterns by which such industrial leaders are recruited. The self-made owner/manager of the early nineteenth century was often a man who had risen from the ranks of master craftsmen or small traders—a man who had, in his working life, significantly altered his social and economic position. He had engaged in a type of social mobility called 'intra-generational' mobility. This type of social mobility was able to continue during the growth of family firms and in the early days of the joint stock company. Frequently the man chosen as manager at whatever level was a man who had proved his abilities in the industrial situation—perhaps as a foreman, perhaps as an office supervisor. Even the giant corporations of the early decades of the twentieth century witnessed some careers of the 'office-boy to managing director' type. Gradually, however, with the increasing specialization of industry, the rise of 'the expert' and the growth of 'scientific management', it has become more difficult to learn the skills of management on the shop-floor and such meteoric careers have become less common. This is not to say, however, that there is necessarily less upward social mobility. New job requirements have produced new patterns of recruitment. Recruitment of 'management trainees' is increasingly recruitment of university graduates or of young people with other formal educational qualifications. Industry has thus undergone a bureaucratization of its recruitment activities. The expansion of education and the gradual opening of the educational system to members of all classes has consequently opened the way for a new type of upward social mobility—one which is achieved through the educational system rather than through promotion on-the-job, and one in which mobility is largely complete (or at least assured) by a relatively early age—say 25–30. The result of these industrial changes has been a decline in intra-generational mobility and an increase in inter-generational mobility. Whereas previously the process of upward mobility often occupied a large part of a man's working life, today, since the main channel of social mobility is the educational system, chances of mobility are very poor after the early twenties. Administrative occupations have an even greater tendency to recruit bureaucratically—that is, on the basis of paper qualifications. Since the great expansion of these positions has taken place this century, this has added to the trend from intra-generational upward mobility to inter-generational upward mobility.

The growth of the joint stock company has also increased the number of 'owners' of industry. Whereas in the heyday of the owner/manager there were few more owners than there were enterprises, there are now hundreds of thousands of persons with some stake in industry. In the USA in 1959, for example, 8 per cent of the population owned stock. In Britain in the middle of the 1960s, the figure was 5 per cent. The majority of such 'owners of industry', however, are small-scale stockholders. In the USA in 1953, the concentration of ownership within the stockholding group was such that a mere 1 per cent of the population owned three-quarters of the stock. In Britain the concentration was even more extreme—more than 80 per cent of the stocks and shares being held by 1 per cent of the population (1954).

In terms of their control over American industry, a very small group of men (estimated at about 2,500 in 1959) dominate the 200 leading corporations. These 200 in turn, dominate the rest of industry through their corporate ownership of 43 per cent of the assets of the smaller companies. There is considerable identity between this group and the very rich. In Britain, too, there is considerable evidence to suggest that a small group of men exercises disproportionate control over industry, and that this group is one of the wealthiest in the country. In the 1950s there were five companies where the average value of the directors' shares exceeded £100,000, and a company director is still more likely than a member of any other occupational group to hold a substantial number of industrial shares. (Interestingly, the landed aristocracy rank after company directors as the group most likely to hold industrial shares and in the middle 1960s owned some 15 per cent of such shares.)

The change to corporate ownership, then, does not signify any great change in the power-holding group in industry (except that in Britain it provides an illustration of the economic adaptability of the aristocracy) nor even any very significant alteration in the degree of concentration of ownership. Both in terms of ownership and in terms of the exercise of power, a small minority has remained in control. Yet the concentration of wealth is not quite so extreme as the figures relating to ownership of stocks and shares would suggest. While shareholding is perhaps the most significant form of wealth in industrial societies and is largely the prerogative of the wealthy few, other forms of wealth—cash and bank deposits, government securities, land, buildings, and the like—are not quite so unequally distributed. When all such forms of capital are taken into account for Britain in 1960 we find that 42 per cent was owned by 1 per cent of the population and 83 per cent was owned by 10 per cent of the population. (It should be noted, however, that since these figures are compiled from estate duty returns they exclude the smaller holdings and therefore overestimate the concentration of wealth —perhaps by as much as 35–40 per cent.) Table 10.2 shows the distribution of wealth liable for estate duty in Britain for selected years between 1911 and 1960, and indicates that the share of wealth held by the richest 1 per cent has been declining since 1911 when it stood at 69 per cent of the total. The share of the richest 10 per cent, however, has fallen much less sharply—a fall of

Table 10.2 Percentage distribution of wealth in Britain, 1911–60*

	1911–13	*1924–30*	*1936–8*	*1954*	*1960*
Wealthiest 1 per cent of adult population	69	62	56	43	42
Wealthiest 5 per cent of adult population	87	84	79	71	75
Wealthiest 10 per cent of adult population	92	91	88	79	83

* These figures represent something of an exaggeration of the degree of concentration of wealth since they are compiled from estate duty returns and therefore exclude smaller holdings.

Source: A. B. Atkinson, 'The reform of wealth taxes in Britain', *Political Quarterly*, 42, 1971, p. 46.

9 per cent in the fifty-year period. Indeed, if one excludes the wealthiest 1 per cent, the share of the remainder of the richest tenth has *risen* from 23 per cent of the total wealth to 41 per cent. This pattern of redistribution of wealth has continued along the same lines during the 1960s. It is a pattern which suggests that the bulk of the redistribution has been from the very rich to the moderately rich. As with the ownership of industrial stock, the concentration is rather less extreme in the USA where in the 1960s the wealthiest 1 per cent of the population owned 24 per cent of the personal capital.

The position between the two countries is very similar with regard to the distribution of income, even though the highest salaries in British industry bear no comparison with those in America. In both countries there has probably been some redistribution of income in the present century, but, as with the redistribution of wealth, this has taken place mainly between the upper and middle levels of the income range. Table 10.3 shows the changes in income distribution in the USA between 1910 and 1959. In his persuasive commentary upon these figures, Kolko argues that taxation makes little difference to the distribution (never more than a 3 per cent reduction in the highest tenth) and suggests that the decline in the share of the richest tenth since 1941 may well be due to an increase in the non-declaration of income (for purposes of tax avoidance) and that the real decline is much less. In addition the highest

Table 10.3 Percentage of United States national personal income (before tax) received by each income-tenth

	1910	*1921*	*1929*	*1934*	*1941*	*1945*	*1959*
Highest 10%	33·9	38·2	39·0	33·6	34·0	29·0	28·9
11–20%	12·3	12·8	12·3	13·1	16·0	16·0	15·8
21–30%	10·2	10·5	9·8	11·0	12·0	13·0	12·7
31–40%	8·8	8·9	9·0	9·4	10·0	11·0	10·7
41–50%	8·0	7·4	7·9	8·2	9·0	9·0	9·2
51–60%	7·0	6·5	6·5	7·3	7·0	7·0	7·8
61–70%	6·0	5·9	5·5	6·2	5·0	6·0	6·3
71–80%	5·5	4·6	4·6	5·3	4·0	5·0	4·6
81–90%	4·9	3·2	3·6	3·8	2·0	3·0	2·9
Lowest 10%	3·4	2·0	1·8	2·1	1·0	1·0	1·1

Source: G. Kolko, *Wealth and Power in America*, London: Thames & Hudson, 1962, table 1, p. 14.

income group has a variety of 'hidden' incomes. Take, for example, the view of the *Wall Street Journal*:[12]

> Hidden hunting lodges are one of the 'fringe benefits' awaiting officials who succeed in working their way up to the executive suite of a good many US corporations. Other impressive prizes: sharing use of yachts, private planes and railroad cars, jaunts to exotic watering places and spectacular soirees —all paid for by the corporation. . . . In this way, a good many executives whose fortune-building efforts are impaired by today's high taxes still are enjoying the frills enjoyed by the Mellors, Mongers and Baruchs.

Such perks are of particular significance to the study of social stratification because they enable a small group to maintain a style of life whose luxury cuts them off even from the well-to-do middle classes.

In Britain in the financial year 1968–9 there were some 7,000 pre-tax incomes in excess of £20,000 and a further 37,000 between £10,000 and £20,000. In the same year there were more than 10 million incomes below £1,000 and nearly 3 million below £500. The distribution of income in Britain for selected years between 1938 and 1963 is shown in Table 10.4. As in America, the highest income-tenth received about 29 per cent of the total income in 1959 and also in 1963 (the proportion was slightly lower in 1969). And as with the American figures there are doubtless distortions due to the non-declaration of income, and a variety of non-monetary benefits exist which make for further inequalities. The change in

Table 10.4 Percentage of personal income (before tax) in Great Britain received by various percentile groups

Percentile Group	*1938*	*1949*	*1957*	*1959*	*1963*
Highest 1%	16·2	11·2	8·2	8·4	7·9
	(11·7)	(6·4)	(5·0)	(5·2)	(5·2)
2–5%	12·8	12·6	10·9	11·5	11·2
	(12·5)	(11·3)	(9·9)	(10·6)	(10·5)
6–10%	9·0	9·4	9·0	9·5	9·6
	(9·5)	(9·4)	(9·1)	(9·4)	(9·5)
11–20%	12·0				
	(12·8)	34·9	37·5	38·4	39·0
20–40%		(37·0)	(38·5)	(39·8)	(39·5)
41–70%	50·0	19·2	23·1	22·5	22·6
	(53·5)	(21·3)	(24·1)	(23·8)	(23·5)
Lowest 30%		12·7	11·3	9·7	9·7
		(14·6)	(13·4)	(11·2)	(11·8)

Figures in brackets refer to incomes after tax.

Source: R. J. Nicholson, 'The distribution of personal income', *Lloyds Bank Reviews*, January 1967, pp. 14 and 16; and H. F. Lydall, 'The long term trend in the size distribution of income', *Journal of the Royal Statistical Society*, 122, 1959, tables 6 and 7, p. 14.

distribution of income observable between 1938 and 1963 is partly due to a number of wider social changes (for example, since in official figures incomes of husband and wife are treated as a single 'income unit', the trend towards earlier marriage and the growing practice whereby wives continue to work after their marriage has inflated the incomes of the lower placed 'income units'). Nevertheless, some redistribution—although rather more modest than that shown in Table 10.4—has taken place in the years since 1938. The major trends shown in Table 10.4 are for the richest 1 per cent *and the poorest 30 per cent* to receive a lower proportion of the personal income. The degree of redistribution of income through taxation can be assessed by comparison with the figures in brackets in Table 10.4 which refer to incomes after tax. For the highest income-tenth in 1963 taxation reduced their proportion of the total income from 28·7 per cent to 25·2 per cent. The lower income groups have a modestly higher proportion of the total income after tax than before tax but had a smaller share of the total post-tax income in 1963 than in 1949.

There is still a considerable concentration of income, wealth and economic power and it is evident that there remains, in both Britain and the USA, a small, powerful and highly privileged minority. In addition to this concentration of economic power the members of this 'new upper class', as it might well be called, are able, to a considerable extent, to pass not only their wealth but also their high occupational position on to their children. These élite groups recruit primarily from amongst their own number. For example, in Britain in 1958, 80 of the 149 directors of large insurance companies had been to the 'top' *five* public schools (46 had been to Eton alone), and 83 of the 166 directors of the Bank of England and the five other leading banks had been to these five schools (50 were Old Etonians).[13] None of the members of these powerful groups had working-class origins.

In terms of political power, however, the undoubtedly great influence of wealth and 'the industrial interest' has been tempered by the exercise of citizenship rights by substantial sections of the population. The gradual growth of the political participation of the working classes has brought Western industrial societies closer to political equality, in the sense that governments have to take some account of their wishes. In some countries, like Britain and Sweden, the development of 'the Welfare State' and the rise to power for substantial periods of Labour governments, which have been sympathetic to certain working-class grievances even if they have not governed in class interests, have significantly changed the condition of life of the majority of the population.

Rather more important in changing styles of life, however, has been the post-second-world-war prosperity enjoyed by industrial societies. In all Western industrial societies real incomes have risen steadily in a quarter of a century of relatively full employment. Thus, although the proportion of the national personal income of the USA received by the poorest tenth of the population has declined, this does not represent an absolute decline in living standards. The extent of poverty is no longer as great as at the time when Rowntree and Booth could conclude that one-third of the population of Britain was in a state of primary poverty. It is clear from Table 10.3 that there has been little change in the distribution of income in the USA in the post-war years of growing affluence. But if the cake is still divided in approximately the same proportions, nevertheless it is a larger cake. Moreover, there have, in these years, been some changes in the relative income of various occupational groups. In particular, the earlier income differential between the lower white collar jobs and the better paid of the manual occupations has been first eroded and then reversed. The emergence of the 'affluent workers' in an age of high mass consumption, allied to changes in industrial organization and patterns of residence, has lessened the sharpness of the differences between working-class life and middle-class life. The traditional pattern of working-class life in close-knit and densely populated communities is no longer typical (and was never universal). The relative political solidarity, forged in the discrimination of the nineteenth century and hardened in the continued poverty of the inter-war years, has given way in Britain to support for a Labour party which has become a moderate party. And the spread in industrial societies of something more nearly akin to equality of educational opportunity has brought about important changes in manual workers' attitudes and aspirations for their children. Such aspirations, even if they are frustrated more often than they are realized, are of considerable significance for relations between the strata. In these and other ways the 'affluent' section of the working class has inherited the mantle of the artisan rather than that of the labourer.

But there are some groups in modern industrial societies that have been by-passed by affluence. In Britain in 1970, two and three-quarter million persons were living below the standard of living at which Supplementary Benefit was given. In 1966, a Ministry of Social Security report concluded that 280,000 families with two or more children fell below the National Assistance standard. In the USA in 1953, 7 per cent of American families incurred medical debts of more than 20 per cent of their annual income. In 1964 the *Annual Report of the Council of Economic Advisers* informed President Johnson that there were 40 million Americans—'one-fifth of the nation'—living in poverty.

Of course, many of the causes of poverty are only indirectly related to social stratification. Old age is perhaps the commonest cause in societies where the basic pension is frequently inadequate and at times even falls below the current scales of Public Assistance. There is also, especially in America, an increasingly large number of families whose head is a woman, and women as a category are low earners. Even in these cases, however, it is old people and women in the working classes who are most likely to fall into poverty. But there are other reasons for poverty which are more directly related to class. Unemployment for instance, is almost entirely a working-class phenomenon, and large families (another factor in poverty) are more common among the working class. For these people in poverty—even if the poverty is, in absolute terms, less bad than in the nineteenth century—the affluence of the majority is a mockery which makes their position all the harder to bear. Moreover, the chance of them *or their children* escaping from their position is slight.

Social stratification and communism: the case of the USSR

The industrialization of the Western world brought about the rise of the class society and, despite significant changes, the stratification systems of the industrial West still have a basically class character. Political and social power, as well as economic power, continue to be based to a considerable extent upon wealth and economic position. Nor is economic position, in terms of occupation, in any way irrelevant in the stratification systems of communist countries. Here, too, different occupational groups have differential access to power and command different incomes and social esteem. The children of members of these groups have differential opportunities to make good in life. Yet a closer control is exercised by the political authorities over these economic forces than in the Western world. This, together with the fact that the political leadership is committed to a socialist ideology, has had an important effect upon the precise forms social stratification has taken and is taking. The other major factor which has influenced the development of social stratification, in the Soviet Union especially, has been the remarkably rapid industrialization during the half century since the revolution (particularly during the Stalin era).

Industrialization inevitably involves dramatic changes in the occupational structure, whatever the political regime under which it occurs. In the USSR the rapid growth (especially after 1928) in numbers of factory workers, engineers, scientists, administrators and white collar workers transformed a largely agrarian society, which was still in a relatively early stage of industrialization, into a highly differentiated industrial society (albeit one which still has a large rural sector). During the first two five-year plans (1928–37) the number working in industry multiplied by more than two and a half times. Yet the expansion was greatest in the most highly skilled occupations. For example, in the same period, the number of managers increased by four and a half times, the number of scientists by six times, and the number of engineers by nearly eight times. Such rapid occupational changes involved a substantial number of people in moving from one job to another and provided a wider spectrum of occupational opportunities. Peasants migrated to the towns and became industrial workers. Factory workers were promoted to the expanding ranks of supervisors and some, especially during the first five-year plan when political reliability was a major qualification for high office in industry, were promoted to the level of factory management. The nature of this social mobility, and perhaps also its degree, was somewhat similar to that which occurred in nineteenth-century England when a similar industrial expansion was taking place (although rather less rapidly), and may be viewed as an adjunct to such industrialization. The more than proportionate expansion of relatively high status occupations necessitates considerable upward mobility. Typically, mobility at this stage is intra-generational. Writing of the same phenomenon in the early (and rapid) stages of industrialization in Poland, a Polish sociologist states: 'The family no longer plays the traditional role as the elementary unit of social class: at the birthday table in a peasant's house an engineer and a miner, a junior or senior executive and an army officer, a peasant and a physician sit together.'[14] It is easy, however, to exaggerate the amount of social mobility in a society simply because those who are upwardly mobile are so noticeable. Doubtless the situation described is as rare in communist societies as in capitalist ones. In the Soviet case there were also exceptional factors which influenced social mobility and thus stratification. In the first place, the huge losses of the second world war created a chronic manpower shortage throughout industry which facilitated upward mobility during and after the war. Second, the frequent purges of the Stalin era created many vacancies in political circles, often at high levels. As a result, these circles were unusually open to members of the lower levels of the bureaucracy and army. This aspect of mobility in the Soviet Union at that time bears a closer resemblance to the non-industrial absolutist states discussed earlier in the chapter than to other industrial societies.

The close control of the political leaders over the distribution of economic and political power has resulted in a uniquely uneven development. Initially, after the revolution, there were attempts to establish the 'dictatorship of the proletariat' and to raise the position of the manual workers. Deliberate discrimination in favour of industrial workers, peasants and 'employees' in such crucial things as the allocation of ration cards and housing led to a sharply stratified society in which the old order of privilege was reversed. Those who had previously occupied positions of high status were made to suffer the indignities of the poor and the powerless. Furthermore, until 1930 only workers were admitted to membership of the party—the chief organ of political power. The political direction of revolutionary leaders is apparent in all these changes.

The subsequent periodic shifts in policy relating to income differences and party membership have emphasized the continued significance of central direction in these important spheres. Soviet history in this respect is remarkable chiefly for its oscillations. The period of 'war communism', with its drive towards economic equality and the political primacy of the workers, was followed in 1923 by the 'new economic policy' under which wage differentials were widened, private peasant agriculture was reinstated (allowing the reappearance of the Kulak or wealthy peasant), and the factories were largely managed by their former owners. The beginning of planned industrialization in 1928, however, brought a renewal of the revolutionary spirit. Many of those who had managed to retain or recover high position during the previous ten years were dismissed. A few lost their lives. The Kulaks were liquidated, and manual workers received preferential treatment in appointment to managerial positions and in selection for educational institutions. Stalin's speech of 1931 in which he condemned 'equality mongering' heralded another change with its contention that the workers' state needed its own intelligentsia. Income differentials were increased in favour of non-manual workers, party membership increasingly became dominated by the intelligentsia, and education became substantially the preserve of the wealthy through the re-introduction of tuition fees. Stalin defended the material aspects of these measures in the following terms:[15]

> The kind of Socialism under which everybody would get the same pay, an equal quantity of meat and an equal quantity of bread, would wear the same clothes and receive the same goods in the same quantities—such socialism is unknown to Marxism. . . . Equalitarianism has nothing in common with Marxist socialism.

The political and educational aspects of the policy, which ostensibly accord so ill with the objectives of the revolution, may be explained in terms of Stalin's need, in a time of rapid industrialization, for an industrial élite which was loyal, efficient, and well motivated. At the same time, the existence of this stratum provided the political leaders with some insulation from the mass of the industrial and agricultural workers upon whom the burdens of heavy investment in capital industries, with its consequent low consumption, fell most heavily. The political danger to the rulers of such a policy, however, lay in the increasing autonomy, and thus the potential opposition, of the élite group. The post-Stalin attempts at renewed social and economic levelling were in part a curb on a group that was beginning to acquire a basis for power independent of the party. Particularly important were Kruschev's attack on the high-handedness of managers and administrators, the drive to recruit workers and peasants to the party, the introduction of higher wages for the lowest paid groups (and a decrease in pay for some of the highly paid), and the abolition of tuition fees. In education, moreover, there was an attempt to give children from 'disadvantaged homes' preferential admission into some educational institutions. Total equality, however, was no more a part of Kruschev's policy than it was of Stalin's. As he told the Twenty First Party Congress: 'Under Socialism inequality of classes is excluded.[16] There remains only the inequality of the share one receives in the distribution of the products.[17]'

Table 10.5 Average (mean) monthly wages in roubles of three categories of occupations

	1940	*1950*	*1960*	*1966*
Manual workers	32·3	68·7	89·9	104·4
Engineering and technical workers	68·9	120·8	133·0	150·1
White collar workers	35·8	63·6	73·2	88·2

Source: David Lane, *Politics and Society in the USSR*, London: Weidenfeld & Nicolson, 1970, p. 402.

Table 10.5 shows the average monthly wages for various occupational categories in selected years between 1940 and 1966. Rather than any radical equalization of incomes, the *relative* incomes of the main occupational categories have remained more or less constant. The only significant change has been some gain by manual workers relative to white collar workers. It should be noted, however, that a similar change has occurred in the industrial West where there is no ideology of the superiority of manual work. Income figures, however, have a rather different significance than in the Western world and do not give an entirely satisfactory picture of inequality in the USSR. Because of the shortage of consumption goods, scarce resources are more likely to be allocated by the party than sold on the open market. In such cases the political control over the distribution of consumption goods is clearly apparent.

The frequency of these changes in policy, and the resultant variations in group incomes further illustrate the relative ease with which economic factors can, in the Soviet Union, be manipulated by those in political power. The variations in the access of different occupational groups to the party—the main channel for the exercise of political power—are therefore crucial and they, too, illustrate the political dominance of the ruling élite. The members of the élite have been able to maintain their own power, and, at the same time, through their control over party membership and party offices, they have determined who shall occupy the middle and lower levels of political power.

This highlights the main difference in the stratification systems of East and West. Yet there are also striking similarities. In the USSR, as in the West, industrialization has been associated with bureaucratization. One important aspect of this is the close link between occupational placement and possession of educational qualifications. Where this is the case, and where income, status and, to a large extent, political power depend upon occupation, educational opportunity becomes crucial in determining the degree of rigidity of the stratification system. Herein lies the significance of the educational policies discussed earlier. Such meagre evidence as is available suggests that access to higher education (and thus to desirable occupations) is perhaps slightly more open to the children of manual workers in the USSR than in Western industrial countries (with the possible exception of the USA). One of the reasons for this is the greater and more systematic provision in the Soviet Union of facilities for part-time higher education. On the other hand, the serious and universal underprivilege of rural workers in this respect is more significant in the USSR since they make up a much larger proportion of the working population.

The success of the political leadership in shaping ideas on social status, however, appears to be more limited. The ideology of communism concerning the value of industrial manual work has had some effect, at least to the extent that, in all communist countries for which we have information, such occupations are more highly regarded than in the Western world. But this is also partly due to the ready comparison with the much larger agricultural sector which is characterized by largely unskilled and unmechanized work for relatively poor economic rewards. There is some indirect evidence to suggest that a good deal of the old prestige order of occupations has remained. For example, the frequent exhortations from party officials concerning the value of manual work and the mobility of physical labour, not to mention the castigations of those who 'desert' the ranks of the workers for the pleasures of life in the intelligentsia, testify at least as much to the popular retention of the old 'bourgeois' scale of values as to the determination of the political leadership to wipe them out. It is clear too that there is considerable motivation to undertake higher education and it is reasonable to assume that this is not unconnected with the desirability of the non-manual occupations to which such education leads. There is also some evidence of a non-scientific kind (especially in the writings of recent Soviet novelists) of the existence of fairly widespread status distinctions. Take, for example, a passage in Solzhenitsyn's *Cancer Ward* on the question of 'suitable' marriage partners.[18]

> He was such a naive boy, he might be led up the garden path by some ordinary weaver girl from the textile factory. Well, perhaps not a weaver, there'd be nowhere for them to meet, they wouldn't frequent the same places. . . . Look at Shendyapin's daughter, how she'd very nearly married a student in her year at teachers' training college. He was only a boy from the country and his mother was an ordinary collective farmer. Just imagine the Shendyapin's flat, their furniture and the influential people they had as guests and suddenly there's this old woman in a white headscarf sitting at their table, their daughter's mother-in-law. . . . Thank goodness they'd managed to discredit the family politically and save their daughter.

The probability is that such feelings of social superiority (and reciprocal inferiority?) cannot be discounted, even after more than fifty years of communist party rule. The order of precedence of occupational groups may vary in detail from those of other industrial societies, but this cannot be determined as long as social scientists work only within an official ideology which ignores all such status distinctions.

In Soviety society, then, social stratification does not rest primarily on an economic basis. Rather, as in pre-industrial societies, it rests upon a monopoly of political power and the legitimate use of force—on control of the state apparatus. While the political leaders have not been entirely successful in controlling the status dimension of stratification, they have been able to control access to major and minor positions of economic and political power. Changing patterns of privilege during the Soviet era represent the manipulations of the political leaders in their (successful) attempt to prevent any other group from achieving a position of independence, cohesion and self-consciousness.

Notes

1 Elizabeth Marshall Thomas, *The Harmless People*, Harmondsworth: Penguin, pp. 179–80.
2 Peter Farb, *Man's Rise to Civilization*, London: Secker & Warburg, 1969, p. 43.
3 M. Sahlins, *Social Stratification in Polynesia*, Seattle: University of Washington Press, 1958, pp. 20–1.
4 See F. R. Cowell, *Cicero and the Roman Republic*, Harmondsworth: Penguin, 1956, p. 293.
5 Quoted in S. G. Checkland, *The Rise of Industrial Society in England, 1815–1885*, London: Longmans, 1964, p. 284.
6 Quoted in Asa Briggs, 'Middle class consciousness in English politics, 1780–1846', *Past and Present*, 9, 1956.
7 Quoted in E. J. Hobsbawm, *Labouring Men*, London: Weidenfeld & Nicolson, 1964, p. 302.
8 Henry Mayhew, *London Labour and the London Poor*, London: Griffin, Bohn, 1861–2, vol. III, p. 243.
9 W. B. Adams, *English Pleasure Carriages* (1837), quoted in E. J. Hobsbawm, 'Custom, wages and work-load in nineteenth century industry', in A. Briggs and J. Saville (eds), *Essays in Labour History*, London: Macmillan, 1960, p. 116.
10 F. Engels, *The Condition of the Working Class in England*, London: Panther, 1969, p. 31.
11 Ibid., p. 31.
12 *Wall Street Journal*, 18 March 1958, quoted in G. Kolko, *Wealth and Power in America*, London: Thames & Hudson, 1962, p. 18.

13 See W. L. Guttsman, *The British Political Elite*, London: MacGibbon & Kee, 1963, table III, p. 336.
14 Z. Bauman, 'Economic growth, social structure, élite formation: the case of Poland', in R. Bendix and S. M. Lipset (eds), *Class Status & Power*, London: Routledge & Kegan Paul, 1967, p. 537.
15 J. V. Stalin, Talk with Emil Ludwig, *Collected Works*, London: Lawrence & Wishart, 1952, vol. 13, pp. 120–21.
16 To Soviet politicans and officials (and social scientists) classes are defined in strict Marxist terms—that is, in terms of ownership. According to the Soviet view, therefore, there are only two classes in the USSR: the workers and the collective farmers. Collective farmers are conceptualized as a separate class because they own their seed and the produce of their labour. Included in the official category of workers are the 9 million agricultural workers on State farms, the 7 million forestry workers and the 'intelligentsia' (comprising white collar workers, scientists, politicians, and other 'mental' workers). This categorization bears little relationship to the ways of life, standards of living, or life chances of the Soviet people, but it is necessary to understand it if one is to make any sense out of Soviet statistics or official pronouncements.
17 N. Kruschev, speech to Twenty First Party Congress, quoted in A. Brodersen, *The Soviet Worker*, New York: Random House, 1966, p. 171.
18 A. Solzhenitsyn, *Cancer Ward*, quoted in David Lane, *Politics and Society in the USSR*, London: Weidenfeld & Nicolson, 1970, p. 410.

Reading

Beteille, A. (ed.), *Social Inequality*, Harmondsworth: Penguin, 1969. Extracts from eighteen sources on social stratification in simple societies, agrarian societies and industrial societies.

Bottomore, T., *Social Classes*, London: Allen & Unwin, 1965. A brief and clearly written introduction.

Domhoff, G. W., *Who Rules America?*, Englewood Cliffs: Prentice-Hall, 1967. An analysis of the distribution of economic and political power in the modern USA.

Lockwood, D., *The Blackcoated Worker*, London: Allen & Unwin, 1958. An excellent study of the social position of clerks in Britain, with special reference to problems of class consciousness.

Macquet, J. J., *Power and Society in Africa*, London: Weidenfeld & Nicolson, 1971. The middle chapters deal with social stratification in traditional Africa, with special (but not exclusive) reference to Rwanda. There is also some discussion of modern Africa.

Perkin, H., *The Origins of English Society, 1780–1880*, London: Routledge & Kegan Paul, 1969. A book by a social historian on industrialization in England, paying particular attention to the development and growing importance of social classes.

Zinkin, T., *Caste Today*, London: Oxford University Press, 1962. A brief discussion of the nature of caste as it was in traditional India and of some recent changes. Clearly and simply written.

Further reading

Bendix, R. and Lipset, S. M. (eds), *Class Status & Power*, New York: Free Press, 1966 and London: Routledge & Kegan Paul, 1967. This edition is the largest and most comprehensive collection of both theoretical and empirical articles.

Cowell, F. R., *Cicero and the Roman Republic*, Harmondsworth: Penguin, 1956. A general discussion of the Roman republic by an historian which contains a good deal of material relevant to questions of stratification.

Goldthorpe, J. *et al.*, *The Affluent Worker in the Class Structure*, Cambridge University Press, 1969. An analysis of changes in the patterns of life among wealthier sections of the working classes in Britain in the 1960s, including a demolition of the thesis that such workers are 'becoming middle class'.

Lane, David, *The End of Inequality? Stratification Under State Socialism*, Harmondsworth: Penguin, 1971. A brief and useful discussion of the 'official' communist views on stratification and of the evidence relating to stratification in Soviet Russia and Eastern Europe.

Lenski, G., *Power and Privilege*, New York: McGraw-Hill, 1966. A mammoth comparative study of the distribution of wealth and power in different types of societies. Full of examples.

Miller, S. M., 'Comparative social mobility', *Current Sociology*, 9, 1960. A 'trend report' and bibliography which provides not only invaluable comparative information on social mobility but also a sophisticated conceptual discussion of social mobility.

Tuden, A. and Plotnicov, L. (eds), *Social Stratification in Africa*, New York: Free Press, 1970. Fourteen articles on social stratification in traditional societies of Africa.

11 Race relations

Relations between 'racial' groups pose some of the most urgent and intractable problems in the world today. The United States, South Africa, Rhodesia, Uganda, and many other countries are currently facing serious, often mounting, racial tension. Brazil appears to be one of the few racially heterogeneous societies which *may* be avoiding severe problems of this sort. Not so long ago, it was widely thought that Britain was immune to them. Now, with the relatively large-scale influx of West Indians, Indians, Pakistanis, and East African Asians, problems of racial tension have become one of the central political issues in British society.

A constitutive feature of 'race relations situations' is the fact that members of the groups involved tend to adhere strongly to exaggerated, often erroneous, beliefs about the biological, behavioural and social differences between the groups. They also tend to perceive such differences as inherited genetically. The findings of modern science, however, suggest strongly that behavioural and social differences between human groups—for example, in intelligence, temperament and customs—are *learned*. The only differences which are *known* to be transmitted genetically are differences in physical characteristics such as skin colour, eye colour, hair form, lip and nose shape. It follows that 'racist' beliefs and the patterns of social relations to which they correspond have to be explained in sociological terms.

In many ways, racial groups are types of social strata, that is, groups with differing access to wealth, status and political power. There are, however, two main differences between racial and other forms of social stratification: first, beliefs about the genetic inheritance of group characteristics tend to be stronger and more deeply entrenched in the racial forms of stratification, though, of course, they are not entirely absent in the 'non-racial' forms; second, physical traits such as skin colour, lip and nose shape, because they are transmitted genetically and unalterable by the individual, can serve as marks of more or less permanent inequality and give a 'caste-like' rigidity to a society in which they are stressed. Movement out of a racial group is much more difficult because the marks of membership are so much clearer.

The emergence of 'white domination'

The most serious problems of race relations in the modern world have arisen in relations between 'white' and 'coloured' peoples, not because of any biologically inherited qualities of these groups, but simply because it was members of 'white' European countries who achieved world dominance and the possibility of subordinating other races. The social development of Western Europe, even as early as the Renaissance, made available means of transport (especially efficient sailing ships), scientific knowledge (for example, the knowledge that the world is round), and technical inventions (such as the lodestone and the sextant), which facilitated the exploration and circumnavigation of the earth. Growing economic surpluses enabled voyages of exploration to be financed and military developments, such as the invention of firearms, enabled Europeans to control and dominate newly discovered territories and peoples. In its turn, colonial expansion increased the wealth and power of European societies and, in some, proved to be a key factor in their further development. In the case of Britain, the first country to industrialize, there is reason to believe that the gradual development of the modern urban-industrial-nation-state was heavily dependent on extensive colonization. Subsequently, industrialization made possible further colonization and a more effective domination of colonial peoples. Contemporary problems of relations between white and coloured peoples have developed from the relations between racial groups established through colonization and industrialization. These processes, therefore, form an essential starting point for an understanding of modern race relations.

Some of the territories over which Europeans gained control were already heavily populated and many of these provided markets which were crucial to England's early industrialization. Others, for example in the West Indies and the Americas, were only sparsely populated. In these territories, Europeans who wished to extract minerals, or produce and sell tropical crops such as sugar, tobacco and cotton, were faced with an acute labour shortage. At first they forcibly recruited natives. Before long, however, the native inhabitants of the West Indies had been practically wiped out—partly as a result of the conditions under which they were forced to work, partly through the ravages of diseases brought by the Europeans. The Amerindian populations of Central and South America fared little better. The difficulties faced by the Spanish and Portuguese, the first to establish colonies in the 'New World', were further increased by Jesuit opposition to the enslavement of the people they had come to convert to Christianity. In this, the Jesuits were supported by the Spanish and Portuguese kings. Similar objections, however, were not raised, at least on a significant scale, to the importation of Africans as slaves. As is well known, it was these negro slaves who came to provide the bulk of the labour force, not only for the Spanish and Portuguese, but also for the other European colonies in the New World. At first, slave labour was supplemented by convict labour and by the labour of poor, white, indentured servants (often working out a service contract in return for their passage to the New World). Such men, however, often had aspirations to independence that made them bad plantation workers. Negro slaves were more amenable to the discipline and rigid control of the plantations, partly because their capture and transportation had disrupted their lives and social organization to such an extent that they found it difficult to organize effective resistance. Above all, negro slaves provided a cheaper labour force. A planter could buy a negro for life with the money that would secure a white man's services for only ten years. As a Governor of Barbados put it, the planters on that island soon discovered that 'three blacks work better and cheaper than one white man'.

For three and a half centuries, beginning in the middle of the sixteenth century, the Atlantic slave trade supplied the labour force for the plantations of the West Indies and the Americas. Some 15 million Africans arrived at their destination. Many more died or committed suicide on the march to the sea and during the 'middle passage'. In the eighteenth century, Britain emerged as the dominant colonial power and the slave trade came to form part of the extremely lucrative 'triangular trade'. This involved the purchase of negroes in Africa with British manufactures, their transportation and sale to the colonial plantations where they produced sugar, tobacco and cotton for shipment to Britain where, in turn, new industries grew up to process the raw materials. The slave trade played an important part in the development of several British ports (between 1783 and 1793 Liverpool alone put 878 ships into the slave trade and Liverpool merchants received a net income of more than £2,300,000 solely from this trade). 'The profits obtained', wrote Eric Williams, 'provided one of the mainstreams of that accumulation of capital in England which financed the Industrial revolution.'[1] However, the importance of slavery for the beginnings of industrialization lay more in the fact that it was the slave plantations which furnished the raw material on which the Lancashire cotton industry was built. It is significant that this industry became established in the hinterlands of Liverpool—the greatest of the slave trading ports. At first, its raw material was principally provided by the slave plantations of the West Indies but after 1790 a virtually unlimited source of supply was provided by the slave plantations of the Southern United States which became, in part, an economic dependency of Lancashire. In this manner, the most advanced centre of production in the world at that time helped to preserve and extend plantation slavery in the American South.

White domination and planter society in the American South

Some of the harshest and most exploitative forms of dominance over a subject group even known developed on the slave plantations of the American South and in the 'planter society' that emerged with them. American negroes have still not fully succeeded in overcoming the effects of plantation slavery on their culture, personality and institutions. To understand contemporary race relations in the USA it is therefore necessary to look first of all at social relations in the Old South.

Most of the slaves in the South at the height of the 'Cotton Kingdom'—there were nearly four million in 1860—were owned by a rich 'planter aristocracy'. This class dominated Southern society through their ownership of property (land and slaves), through their control of politics and state governments, and by serving as a 'model' for small owners and poor whites (non-slaveowners who constituted three-quarters of the one and a half million free families in the *ante-bellum* South). The large plantations were usually characterized by a simple division of labour between household slaves and field slaves, the latter subject to control by a white overseer. Since the slaves had little or no incentive to work, force often had to be employed. Frequent whippings, use of the stocks, and imprisonment in the plantation jail were common. Runaways were hunted with dogs and, when caught, they were clapped in irons, branded with their master's mark and even castrated. As an Arkansas planter expressed it in 1860:[2]

> Now, I speak what I know, when I say it is like casting pearls before swine to try to *persuade* a negro to work. He must be *made* to work, and should always be given to understand that if he fails to perform his duty he will be punished for it.

The master had virtually absolute power over his slaves and this power was supported by law. Writing in 1856, George M. Stroud, an abolitionist, condensed the legal nature of the master–slave relationship into the following twelve propositions:[3]

1. The master may determine the kind and degree, and time of labour to which the slave shall be subjected.
2. The master may supply the slave with such food and clothing only, both as to quantity and quality, as he may think proper or find convenient.
3. The master may, at his discretion, inflict any punishment on the person of his slave.
4. All the power of the master over his slave may be exercised not only by himself in person, but by anyone whom he may depute as his agent.
5. Slaves have no legal rights of property in things, real or personal; but whatever they may acquire belongs, in point of law, to their masters.
6. The slave, being a *personal chattel*, is at all times liable to be sold absolutely, or mortgaged or leased, at the will of his master.
7. He may also be sold by process of law for the satisfaction of the debts of a living, or the debts and bequests of a deceased master, at the suit of creditors or legatees.
8. A slave cannot be a party before a judicial tribunal, in any species of action against his master, no matter how atrocious may have been the injury received from him.
9. Slaves cannot redeem themselves, nor obtain a change of masters, though cruel treatment may have rendered such change necessary for their personal safety.
10. Slaves being objects of *property*, if injured by third persons, their owners may bring suit, and recover damages for the injury
11. Slaves can make no contract.
12. Slavery is hereditary and perpetual.

The slave stood at the mercy of the master's whims. The only effective restraint lay in the economic interests of the master. It is recorded that on one occasion, on a plantation in Mississippi, a slave attacked an overseer and almost killed him, yet went unpunished. Had the master executed the slave for this 'crime' he would have lost a valuable 'piece of property' in which he had invested a considerable sum of money.

According to a Georgia slaveowner writing in 1854, punishment did not make the negro revengeful but tended 'to win his attachment and promote his happiness and well-being'.[4] Although this sounds rather far-fetched, it may have contained a grain of truth. It is not uncommon for people under conditions of harsh oppression to identify with their oppressors and even, in a way, to 'love' as well as to hate them. If, from birth, their independence is systematically crushed, they have no models to identify with other than that of the masters. In this way, many slaves tended to see white culture as superior, to regard the (white) law as right and to believe in the legitimacy of their masters' rule and power to punish.

A central corollary of the near absolute power of the master was the almost total and permanent dependence of the slave. 'The negro', wrote John Pendleton Kennedy in 1832, is 'a dependent on the white race; dependent for guidance and direction even to the procurement of his most indispensable necessaries. Apart from this protection he has the helplessness of a child—without foresight, without faculty of contrivance, without thrift of any kind.'[5] 'I love the simple and unadulterated slave', wrote Edward Pollard in 1859, 'with his geniality, his mirth, his swagger and his nonsense. . . . The Negro, in his true nature, is always a boy, let him be ever so old.'[6] The stereotype of negroes expressed in these statements was, no doubt, an ideology which facilitated their exploitation. Such statements were written, at a time when the system was under severe attack, in order to justify slavery and to 'prove' that negroes could not be awarded independence. But they probably had some basis in reality as well. The slave had few opportunities to develop the personality traits and modes of behaviour thought appropriate by adult Southern whites. Like a child, he had only limited possibilities for initiating independent action. Unlike a child, his dependence was total, permanent and maintained by powerful sanctions. From the slave's point of view, moreover, the plantation was a closed system, a kind of 'total institution' in which virtually the whole of his life was encapsulated. He was hardly able to broaden his experience by contact with the outside world and by exposure to models different from those of his master.

Statements of the kind made by Kennedy and Pollard also suggest that identification between masters and slaves was a two-way process, that masters often grew fond of their slaves—provided, of course, that they kept to their 'proper' place. But just as the slaves' feelings for their masters tended towards ambivalence so, reciprocally, did those of the masters for their slaves. Affection probably mingled with guilt over treating human beings as property and the whole relationship was overlaid with a more or less constant fear of slave uprisings. That there were so few of these may well have had something to do with the ambivalent nature of the master–slave relationship, comprising, as it did on both sides, elements of affection as well as hate, identification as well as rejection.

The abolition of slavery and the emergence of 'colour caste'

Just as England's industrialization was crucial in the development of American slavery, so the development of industrial capitalism in the United States was instrumental in changing the pattern of relations between black and white. For the increasingly powerful industrial capitalists of the North East, and the dependent, increasingly market-oriented farmers of the Middle West, had interests which conflicted strongly with those of the 'planter-aristocrats' who were dominant in the Southern states. The differences were rooted in the two differing socio-economic systems and at first took the form of a struggle to control the federal government. Later the conflict led to the attempted secession of the South and so, in 1861, to the civil war which resulted in the abolition of slavery. Slavery formed a focus of the conflict largely because it marked a crucial difference in the *economic* structures of North and South. The South wanted to expand the plantation system into the new Western states, partly because of the profitable ventures that those regions promised and partly because their methods of agriculture tended to impoverish the soil. The North wanted to encourage the growth of independent farming in the West, partly because this would expand the market for Northern products. Moral revulsion against slavery, and sympathy for negroes, also played a part in the growing movement for abolition, but *anti*-negro prejudice was a more decisive factor. As early as 1835, Alexis de Tocqueville noticed that 'the prejudice of race appears to be stronger in the states that have abolished slavery than in those where it still exists; and nowhere is it so intolerant as in those states where servitude has never been known.'[7] In 1856, in a referendum conducted in Kansas—it was boycotted by those in favour of slavery and therefore confined to anti-slavery groups—1,287 voted to exclude negroes from the territory and only 453 voted against the proposition. One of the chief arguments used against slavery, there as elsewhere, was that it would eventually produce a free negro population.

The North was more interested in preserving the union than in abolishing slavery and tried, to the last—although unsuccessfully—to effect a compromise with the South. Civil war broke out and, two years later, abolition was declared by federal decree. Even though they lost the war, the Southern states continued to regard negroes as a form of property—a fact attested by the 'Black Codes' in which most of the restrictions on the behaviour of slaves, and the punishments for breaches of these restrictions, were re-enacted with reference to free negroes. Even the First Reconstruction Act (1867), which placed the South under military rule in an attempt to guarantee negroes the right to vote, was ineffective. This was partly because of the vehemence of Southern opposition, and partly because of the unwillingness of the federal government and the Northern industrialists to spend the considerable sums of money needed to make the Act effective.

Moreover, the majority of negroes at that time were, by themselves, incapable of solving the problems which they faced. They were very poor and had to devote most of their energies simply to keeping alive. Slavery had kept them dependent upon whites and emancipation led to widespread demoralization and aimlessness among them. Such a condition was not conducive to the formation of the well-organized, politically conscious groups which alone could effectively have challenged the dominance of the whites. So slavery was replaced by a system of domination in which negroes, although nominally free, continued to be controlled and exploited by whites. On the economic level this took the form of 'sharecropping' and similar forms of 'debt peonage' whereby the propertyless negro was given a tract of land for growing cotton in return for a fixed proportion—usually a half and sometimes as much as three-quarters—of the crop. The landlord, however, marketed even the tenant's share and the latter had no means of ensuring that he received a fair price. The poverty of the tenants continually placed them in debt to the landlords for seed, tools, clothing and food, and for most of the year they were forced to live on credit at a high rate of interest. In these and other ways the landlords were guaranteed a more or less permanent supply of cheap labour.

Yet it was not only negroes who were placed in this position. The concentration of the best land in the hands of the wealthy few also forced more and more poor whites to become sharecroppers, and for a time, during the 1880s and 1890s, a united movement of the poor of both races seemed a possibility. A political movement known as 'Populism' arose and appealed for such a united front. In the words of Tom Watson, who was one of its leaders, speaking in Georgia in 1892:[8]

> ... the People's Party says to these two men, 'You are kept apart that you may be separately fleeced of your earnings. You are made to hate each other because upon that hatred is rested the keystone of the arch of financial despotism which enslaves you both. You are deceived and blinded that you may not see how this racial antagonism perpetuates a monetary system which beggars you both'.

But the legacy of dependence on the planter-aristocracy made negroes poor political partners. They were prey to political manipulation by the dominant planter class and the Populists turned against them. The majority of poor whites retained the racism from which they derived considerable social satisfaction. For, even though they were poor and stood at the bottom of the *white* social hierarchy, they were not at the bottom of the *Southern* social order. It was to protect this position from 'negro domination'—about which they developed unrealistic, exaggerated fears—and from the economic competition of negroes, that they formed a number of secret societies such as the Ku Klux Klan which terrorized negroes into acceptance of their subordinate position. In their campaign against negroes, the poor whites received support from most sections of the white population. A variety of devices were used to circumvent the fifteenth amendment to the Constitution (which, in 1870, had established that 'The rights of citizens of the United States to vote shall not be denied or abridged by the United States or any State on account of race, colour or previous condition of servitude') and these virtually disenfranchised the negro once again. In Louisiana, for example, there were in 1896, 130,334 registered negro voters; by 1904 there were only 1,342.

In 1890, an act was passed, also in Louisiana, legalizing the segregation of railway carriages. It was declared constitutional by the Federal Supreme Court in 1896 in the case of *Plessy* v. *Ferguson*. This was a crucial decision upholding the provisions of the Southern constitutions whereby transport, residential areas, schools and shops were increasingly segregated. Such segregation secured important gains for whites. For the white upper classes, it helped to remove the threat of a racially united working class. For the poor whites, it buttressed their feelings of superiority and secured important gains in fields such as education, for state funds were systematically diverted to 'white' schools with a resultant improvement in the education, and thus the life chances, of white children.

'Segregation', however, never meant a cessation of all contact between the races—this would have made economic and other forms of exploitation impossible—but rather that contact should take place within a context of ritual which emphasized the subordinate position of the negro. As under the old slave regime, negroes were expected to address a white person as 'Mr', 'Mrs', or 'Miss' or by a title such as 'Cap'n' or 'Judge'. In return, he would be addressed as 'boy' or 'uncle' or by his first name. A negro was not allowed to contradict a white and was expected to give way to him on the street. If he addressed a white man in 'proper' English, this was regarded as an insult, as tantamount to a claim to equality. Breaches in such rules of inter-racial etiquette were swiftly and severely punished and negroes as a group were insufficiently powerful and too insecure and dependent to resist the pressures of white domination. They continued, by and large, to accept the white man's notion of negro inferiority. In these and other ways, the abolition of slavery resulted in a rigid, caste-like system of white domination and not in the emergence of racial equality.

The urbanization of American negroes

As the nineteenth century drew to a close, the position of the United States as the world's chief producer of cotton began to be challenged, particularly by Egypt and China. Prices started to fall, a trend which was reinforced as artificial fibres came increasingly into use in textile manufacture. The response of the Southern states was twofold; they attempted firstly to diversify their economy by embarking on a process of industrialization and secondly to cut labour costs by mechanizing the growing of cotton. Negroes began to be pushed into towns (in the North and West as well as in the South) as a result of declining employment opportunities in rural areas and were simultaneously attracted to them by the growing demand for factory labour. In the course of this process of urbanization, negroes began to be transformed from a regional peasant group into a segment of the national urban working class.

The pattern of negro migration to the towns between 1900 and 1950 is shown in Table 11.1. As this table shows, in 1900, 90 per cent of the American negro population lived in the South. By 1950, this figure had fallen to 68 per cent. Ten years later, just over 50 per cent remained within that region. The table also shows the northward and westward movement which corresponded to the growing demand for factory labour in the cities of the North and West.

Table 11.1 Distribution of the US negro population by region and urban-rural residence, 1900–50 (per cent)

	1900	*1920*	*1940*	*1950*[1]
South[2]	90	85	77	68
Rural	74	64	49	35
Urban	16	21	28	33
Other regions	10	15	23	32
Rural	3	2	2	2
Urban	7	13	21	30
Total rural	77	66	51	37
Total urban	23	34	49	63

[1]Because of a change in the census definition of 'urban' between 1940 and 1950, these figures are not exactly comparable with earlier data.

[2]Alabama, Arkansas, Delaware, Florida, Georgia, Kentucky, Louisiana, Maryland, Mississippi, North Carolina, Oklahoma, South Carolina, Tennessee, Texas, Virginia, Washington D.C., West Virginia.

Source: Eli Ginzberg, *The Negro Potential*, New York: Columbia University Press, 1956, p. 15.

During the second half of the nineteenth century, the demand for unskilled and semi-skilled factory labour in the rapidly industrializing Northern states had been satisfied mainly through migration from Europe. The first world war and the strict immigration controls established after the war reduced this flow to a trickle. Northern industrialists were forced to draw on the large reservoirs of surplus labour that had been building up for some time in rural areas, particularly in the South. Negroes were especially valuable to employers: they were willing to work for low wages, ready to submit to the employers' authority and could be used as strike breakers. They showed little inclination to join trade unions and when they tried to do so they were usually prevented. But employers were not the only group to benefit from the addition of negroes to the urban work force. Landlords were able to charge high rents for overcrowded accommodation, the white middle classes were supplied with cheap domestic servants, and the white working classes benefited from the distinction which grew up between 'white' and 'negro' jobs – the latter being poorly paid and/or unpleasant.

The majority of negro migrants settled in the city centres, partly because these areas were cheaper, partly because negroes were usually excluded from more desirable residential areas by discriminatory practices. The result, hastened by the movement of the more affluent whites to the suburbs, was the growth of 'black belts' in most American cities. By 1960, New York had over a million negroes in the Harlem, Bedford Stuyvesant and Bronx ghettos; Chicago had 890,000 in its 'black belt' on the South Side; Los Angeles had 334,000 primarily in crowded suburbs such as Watts. By 1960, too, negroes constituted 14 per cent of the population of New York, 23 per cent of Chicago, 26 per cent of Philadelphia, 29 per cent of Detroit, 34 per cent of Newark (it has since risen to over 50 per cent), 35 per cent of Baltimore, 37 per cent of New Orleans and Memphis, 38 per cent of Atlanta and 54 per cent of Washington D.C.

This urban concentration enabled negroes to organize themselves more effectively for collective action and so had important consequences for the balance of power between black and white. Under these conditions peaceful protest and riot were effective weapons and, gradually, negroes began to 'slough off' the sense of inferiority (and its corollary, the belief in white superiority) which they had inherited from slavery. They began to be able, as a group, to stand up to whites and to reject their own subordinate status.

An important part of this process was the emergence and expansion of the negro middle class—the 'black bourgeoisie'. The emergence of this class was centrally connected with the ghetto mode of living which most negroes were forced to adopt. Residential segregation and the rising income of the urban negro (in absolute terms although not relative to whites) gave rise to an increasing demand for the services of teachers, ministers of religion, doctors, lawyers, owners of hairdressing and beauty salons, undertakers and newspaper proprietors, all catering to the special needs of the segregated community. Businessmen and professionals such as these have come to stand at the apex of economic, political and other forms of social power within the negro community, yet they are in a marginal and ambiguous position. On the one hand, they are distinguished from the majority of negroes—with whom they have little in common other than race—by their income, education and style of life. On the other, they have been systematically rebuffed by whites of comparable income, wealth and occupation (although this may be decreasing somewhat at the present time), and forced to live a segregated life. This ambiguity has led to an ambivalent identification with both the white middle classes and the negro masses. In spite of their relatively high occupational positions, their awareness of themselves as negroes makes them a more radical group politically than is usually the case with persons in similar positions in the white social hierarchy. Historically, members of the black bourgeoisie have been prominent in forming and supporting protest organizations such as the National Association for the Advancement of Coloured People (founded in 1909), and in providing leaders for the struggle for civil rights. Their education has given them the ability to articulate, publicize and explain their objectives. Their comparative affluence has enabled them both to finance such organizations and to focus upon long-term objectives rather than short-term gains. Thus, although the NAACP and similar bodies have substantial white membership and get some of their funds from white philanthropists, they owe their existence, their permanence and their policies primarily to the 'black bourgeoisie'.

The political and legal pressures of the NAACP have met with some success, most notably in 1954 when they secured the reversal, by the Federal Supreme Court, of the 'separate but equal' doctrine in public education. This success spurred negroes to a new militancy in their struggle for civil rights but also stimulated white opposition, especially in the South where federal troops had to be sent to Little Rock, Arkansas and Oxford, Mississippi to secure implementation of the Supreme Court decision. It was in the South, too, that the early militant negro protests occurred. Sit-ins at segregated establishments, marches and 'freedom rides' were organized by the Southern Christian Leadership Conference which was led, after his role in the highly successful bus boycott in Montgomery, Alabama in the winter of 1955 and 1956, by Martin Luther King. The relative stability and integration of the negro community in Southern (as opposed to Northern and Western) towns, and the organizational basis provided by the negro churches, enabled such movements to keep tight control over their members. This control enabled a non-violent campaign to be sustained which was influenced equally by New Testament ethics, the philosophy and political methods of Mahatma

Gandhi, and a realistic appreciation of the tactical hopelessness of the use of violence on a large scale by a small and relatively powerless minority group. Demonstrations were planned in detail and carefully organized. Potential demonstrators were thoroughly screened and trained not to retaliate, even in the face of severe white provocation.

This non-violent protest movement was fed by the growing affluence of the better-off part of the negro population and by their (partly consequential) improved chances of obtaining higher education. In 1930, there were only 27,141 negroes in college in the whole of the USA; by 1960, the number had risen to more than 200,000. In the colleges, especially in the segregated ones, large numbers of young people were gathered together in a situation relatively free from parental restraint. This facilitated the discussion of grievances and the organization of collective protest, and helps to explain why negro college students were so prominent in the demonstrations of this period. The success of the non-violent protest movement began to raise the confidence and self-respect of negroes as a group (which was one of its primary aims). It was aided in this by the emergence, in the late 1950s and the 1960s, of independent black African states and the appearance in Washington and New York of black diplomats and politicians.

The Civil Rights Acts of 1957, 1960 and 1964 mark the success of protest in that period in securing better employment opportunities for negroes, in realizing their voting rights on a local level (which was especially important in the South) and in forcing the desegregation of public facilities. But the mass of poorer negroes were too involved in the business of making a living to be over-concerned with niceties such as the desegregation of restaurants and art galleries. Moreover, the changing employment policies of the white establishment, which increased the number of white collar and managerial jobs available to negroes, only benefited the educated. For the vast mass of poorer, less well-educated negroes, the successes of the civil rights movement served only to raise vain hopes that they, too, would share the affluence of the post-war USA. Martin Luther King recognized this and saw why some negroes were turning against non-violent protest. Commenting on an incident in 1966, in which he was booed by 'black power' activists, he wrote:[9]

> For twelve years I, and others like me, had held out radiant promises of progress. I had preached to them about my dream. I had lectured to them about the not too distant day when they would have freedom, 'all here and now'. I had urged them to have faith in America and in white society. Their hopes had soared. They were now booing because they felt that we were unable to deliver on our promises. They were booing because we had urged them to have faith in people who had too often proved to be unfaithful. They were now hostile because they were watching the dream that they had so readily accepted turn into a frustrating nightmare.

This rising disillusionment was connected with the worsening employment situation of poorer negroes. Automation made it difficult for those who were ill-educated, many of them only recent migrants to the northern cities, to obtain jobs. The same problem was faced by school-leavers entering the labour market for the first time, especially by high school 'drop-outs'. In employment, as elsewhere, negroes came off worse than whites. In nine large cities surveyed in 1966 by the US Department of Labour, 7·3 per cent of negroes were unemployed (the figure was 9·3 per cent in the poorest negro districts) compared with only 3·3 per cent of whites.

Moreover, despite the long-term improvement in educational opportunities for negroes, wide discrepancies between the races continued to exist. White males continue, on average, to receive considerably longer schooling than do non-white males although the difference is less than it was. Much the same pattern is apparent in income distribution. In spite of a decline in the proportion of negro families with incomes of less than $3,000 per annum and an increase in the proportion of negro families in the higher income groups, substantial income differences between the racial groups are evident. The median income of gainfully employed negro males increased threefold (in real terms) between 1939 and 1962. In spite of this increase, however, the median income of negro families in 1966 was only 58 per cent of that of white families. In the same year, 28 per cent of negro families and 55 per cent of white families had an income in excess of $7,000. At the other end of the income scale, 32 per cent of negro families and 13 per cent of white families had an income of less than $3,000.

With the exception of the numerically small (but expanding) black bourgeoisie, the lot of negro Americans, however much it had improved in absolute terms, had not been improving *relative to whites*—at least not in the fields of employment, income and education. This continued deprivation among the mass of negroes led to a growing despair in the inability of the non-violent civil rights movement to effect any significant short-term gains for them. The race riots in the ghettos of most major American cities, starting in the summer of 1963, grew out of negro resentment against this continued inequality and the hopelessness of the situation. Most of these riots have been violent. In the Los Angeles suburb of Watts in August 1965, for example, the rioting lasted for more than two days and nights. Both police and rioters made heavy use of firearms. Thirty-four persons were killed and hundreds severely wounded. The number of arrests totalled almost 4,000 and the damage done by arson and bomb throwing was estimated at $35 million.

These riots marked the end of unqualified support for moderate leaders committed to a strategy of non-violent demonstrations. Younger negro leaders began to reject integration into white society as a possible or desirable goal. 'We feel that integration is irrelevant; it is just a substitute for white supremacy', argued Stokeley Carmichael in 1966. Yet militant 'black power' leaders, such as Carmichael, the late Malcolm X and Eldridge Cleaver, appear—so far at least—not to have gained widespread support among negroes (in spite of the lavish reporting—and misreporting—of their speeches and activities in the press). They have, nevertheless, had an important effect upon patterns of negro protest in that they have acted as a 'ginger group', helping to sustain and even to increase the militancy of more moderate civil rights leaders. They have drawn attention to the plight of the mass of urban negroes and away from the outward trappings of white supremacy such as segregated theatres and bowling alleys. There is now a greater awareness among moderate leaders in the protest movement that they are engaged in a struggle for power, a struggle for a share in the control of the political and economic institutions of American society. Take, for example, the following passage from the last book written by Martin Luther King. In it he argues against the separatism urged by many black power groups:[10]

> Just as the Negro cannot achieve political power in isolation, neither can he gain economic power through separatism. While there must be a continued emphasis on the need for blacks to pool their economic resources and withdraw consumer support from discriminating firms, we must not be oblivious to the fact that the larger economic problems confronting the Negro community will only be solved by federal programmes involving billions of dollars. One unfortunate thing about Black Power is that it gives priority to race precisely at a time when the impact of automation and other forces have made the economic question fundamental for blacks and whites alike. In this context a slogan Power for Poor People would be much more appropriate than the slogan Black Power.
>
> However much we pool our resources and 'buy black', this cannot create the multiplicity of new jobs and provide the number of low-cost houses that will lift the Negro out of the economic depression caused by centuries of deprivation. Neither can our resources supply quality integrated education. All of this requires billions of dollars which only an alliance of liberal – labour – civil rights forces can stimulate. In short, the Negro's problem cannot be solved unless the whole of American society takes a new turn toward greater economic justice.

Clearly, King was coming to see the struggle for civil rights as a class struggle shared by poor whites, even though they tend to be the most intransigently prejudiced of all white groups.

From its inception, the negro protest movement in the USA produced a counter-movement on the part of whites anxious to maintain the *status quo*. Poor whites, in particular, have not moved beyond their dependence on negro subordination as a source of self-esteem. Newly affluent whites, insecure in their new-found affluence, feel threatened by the increasingly urgent negro demands for *their* share of the cake. It is here that the 'white backlash' has erupted with its greatest fury. The open advocacy of armed insurrection by some 'black power' sects has only served to increase the scope and intensity of the reaction, and armed 'vigilante' groups have been formed by whites in many cities. In this manner, the violence of the confrontation has tended to escalate. There has also been a tendency towards racial polarization. Negroes have come increasingly to distrust and reject the help of sympathetic whites, and whites who formerly supported the negro cause have become alienated by the increasing advocacy and use of violence.

The escalation since 1954 of negro protest towards greater militancy, the trend since 1963 towards greater organized and unorganized violence, and the corresponding escalation of the white reaction, have presented a serious shock to the American social fabric. It remains to be seen whether rapid advance can be made towards the solution of the 'American dilemma' without significant changes in American society, or whether frustration at the slowness of advance towards their goals will lead more negroes to support the advocates of armed insurrection. If the advocacy and use of violence increases, the white response is likely to be massive. White control over industry, government, the armed forces and the police would enable any such insurrection to be crushed. In the process, power in the white community would probably shift even further towards anti-negro groups, and the emergence nationally of a virulently racist regime would be a distinct possibility.

Brazil: development towards racial integration?

A comparison of negro–white relations in the USA with their counterpart in Brazil provides another indication of how a society's course of development affects its patterns of race relations. While the degree of racial integration and equality in Brazil has often been exaggerated, there is little doubt that the barriers there against negroes are less clearly defined than those in the USA. Most Brazilian negroes are poor and ill-educated. Most of them work in less prestigious, less well-paid, mainly manual occupations. But those who manage to acquire wealth and education, particularly if they are light-skinned, are not consistently rejected by whites of comparable social standing (except with regard to marriage). There is, thus, some basis to the popular Brazilian sayings that 'money bleaches' and 'a rich negro is a white man'. (Of course, the emphasis on 'whiteness' in these sayings is also indicative of the general dominance of whites.) In Brazil, moreover, black and white members of the working classes are not so segregated residentially as they are in the United States. Trades unions are more racially integrated and negroes sometimes hold positions of authority over whites (though not as frequently as their proportion in the population as a whole would lead one to expect). In short, in Brazil, distinctions between the races are not so sharply drawn and the different social classes are more integrated racially than is the case in the USA.

The emergence in Brazil of this specific pattern of negro–white relations forms one strand in the overall social development of that country. It can only be understood in relation to this wider social process. In many ways, the peculiar pattern of Brazilian social development stems from the level of development of Portugal, the colonizing power, at the time of colonization. Although nationally unified at an early stage (which helps to explain why they were the first European societies to embark on colonization), Portugal and Spain were, in other respects, characterized by a 'medieval' social order. Church, king, and the landed, military aristocracy remained the principal social 'powers'. There was a small commercial bourgeoisie, but it was weak and was accorded low social status. By and large, this social configuration was transferred to the Brazilian colony. A consequence was that most colonists strove to recreate on their plantations the patriarchal form of social relations that had characterized their estates at home. Production for the market in order to make a profit was not their primary orientation. Most of them held to the chivalric concept of *hidalgo*, an ethic which celebrated the man who did no work with his hands and to whom business was contemptible. By contrast, the planter aristocracy in the Southern USA modelled itself more on the English concept of the 'gentleman' and this did not impose such a strong taboo on engaging in trade and making a profit.

In the course of the nineteenth century, market-oriented plantations did spring up in parts of Brazil. These were comparable in many respects to the type which arose in the USA, but their sugar and coffee were produced mainly for the Brazilian and Portuguese markets. Unlike the plantations in the American South, production never became geared, during the period of slavery, to an expanding industrial market. Within the Brazilian colony, moreover, transport and communications remained poor. This imposed further restrictions on production for a wider market. The growth of 'capitalist' plantations was, therefore, limited. They did not become the dominant institutional setting of slavery in Brazil.

In such a social situation, the laws and customs relating to domestic slavery which had grown up in Portugal and Spain—they were codified as early as 1263–5 in *Las Siete Partidas del Roy Alfonso*—could be transferred, more or less effectively, to the colony. The colonists did not have to create a slave code *de novo*. A student has summarized *Las Siete Partidas* as follows:[11]

> The slave might marry a free person if the slave status was known to the other party. Slaves could marry against the will of their master if they continued serving him as before. Once married, they could not be sold apart, except under conditions permitting them to live as man and wife. If the slave married a free person with the knowledge of his master, and the master did not announce the fact of the existing slave status, then the slave by that mere fact became free. If married slaves owned by separate masters could not live together because of distance, the church should persuade one or the other to sell his slave. If neither of the masters could be persuaded, the church was to buy one of them so that the married slaves could live together. The children followed the status of their mother, and the child of a free mother remained free even if she later became a slave. In spite of his full powers over his slave, the master might neither kill him nor injure him unless authorized by the judge, nor abuse him against reason or nature, nor starve him to death. But if the master did any of these things, the slave could complain to the judge, and if the complaint were verified, the judge must sell him, giving the price to the owner, and the slave might never be returned to the original owner.

In practice there may have been divergence from this code. Nevertheless, it reflects a general type of slavery which could only have grown up in a non-capitalist context. In Brazil, as in Portugal and Spain, slave marriages and slave families enjoyed some protection in law, and the laws relating to slavery were, to some extent upheld by the church. Slaves had access to the courts and their legal status was that of unfree *persons*, not that of a commodity that could be treated arbitrarily by the owner in order to maximize his short-term advantage. *Las Siete Partidas*, moreover, defined the conditions under which slaves could be manumitted—and manumission was a not infrequent occurrence. Since slaves were allowed to earn money and own property, it was possible for some to buy their freedom. The children of slave women and white fathers were often freed. Sometimes they were fully acknowledged and brought up as part of the white family, a fact which helps to explain the comparative tolerance shown towards light-skinned negroes in Brazil. Slaves who were not needed on the master's estate could go to the towns where, although they usually had to remit a fixed monthly sum to their owners, they were often able to earn enough to buy their freedom as well. The whites, therefore, became accustomed to the existence of free negroes as a social category long before the final abolition of slavery in 1888. A corollary was the fact that substantial numbers of negroes became accustomed to a degree of independence prior to this date. Even those who remained slaves were better able to maintain—at least to some degree—a sense of self-esteem and personal autonomy. This maintenance of a separate identity was aided by the fact that African tribal and linguistic groups were not systematically dispersed as they were in the USA. Some slave groups even maintained their religious identity as Moslems. Given such conditions, the Brazilian slave was better able to conceive of himself as a rebel than his northern counterpart. During the seventeenth century, for example, escaped slaves established the Palmares Republic and successfully defended it for more than fifty years. In general, slave uprisings were more frequent and more successful than they were in the USA.

In Brazil, emancipation came peacefully over a period of several years. The final decree was issued in 1888 in a situation where continued pressure by the British navy on the slave trade had led to a shortage of slaves and rising costs. Further, economic developments in the late nineteenth century—particularly the beginnings of Brazil's emergence as a major producer of coffee for the world market—made it increasingly apparent that it was cheaper and more efficient to run plantations using wage labourers who were formally free.

Large numbers of negroes moved into the towns immediately after emancipation. Their lack of familiarity with urban life and a free status led many to lapse into vagabondage and drunkenness. At first, they formed a kind of sub-proletariat within the towns. As a result, the economic position of the established white manual workers was not seriously threatened—a factor which may go some way towards explaining the relative lack of anti-negro prejudice. When, in the early 1900s, large-scale immigration from Europe began, many negroes were already second-generation town dwellers. Although, for the most part, they were uneducated and unskilled, they were able to compete, more or less effectively, with the newcomers (many of whom were also uneducated and unskilled). Rather than developing a view of themselves as an underprivileged *racial* group, negroes who had established themselves in the towns began to see themselves as part of an emerging *working class*. Their acceptance into the trades union movement at all levels has enhanced this tendency.

Race relations in Britain

Britain has been centrally involved in the development of white dominance all over the world through her slave trading activities, her colonialism and her industrialization. Yet until the immigration of coloured people began to assume significant proportions in the 1950s, the comparative absence of a coloured population meant that there were no *domestic* problems of race relations in this country. Of course, there had been previous foreign immigration. The arrival of linguistically and culturally distinct groups, such as Jews, Italians or Poles, frequently aroused hostility and prejudice. But the fact that they were not racially distinct (although the British often *viewed* them as being so) made it relatively easy for them to integrate with the host society. The more recent coloured immigrants, because of their racial distinctiveness, find such assimilation much more difficult. There is therefore a greater possibility that, if it is in the interests of powerful groups (in the working class as well as in the upper and middle classes) and if the immigrants themselves remain powerless and unable to resist, they may become a more or less permanent and easily exploitable 'sub-proletariat'.

Commonwealth immigration into Britain in the 1950s and 1960s was part of a more general movement. Between 1945 and 1957, for example, there was a net migration of more than 350,000 Europeans into the United Kingdom. This, and immigration from the Commonwealth until the Commonwealth Immigration Act of 1962, corresponded to the chronic labour shortage of the post-war period. At first, the majority of Commonwealth immigrants came to Britain from the West Indies. Since 1961 the numbers of Indians and Pakistanis have also been growing. Thus, of the estimated 1,113,000 coloured people in England and Wales in 1968, 49 per cent were from the West Indies and 39 per cent were from India and Pakistan. Table 11.2 gives a more detailed breakdown of Britain's coloured population.

Table 11.2 Total estimated coloured population resident in England and Wales, 1966 census, by area of origin

Area of Origin	*Born overseas*	*Born in the United Kingdom*	*Total*
India[1]	180,400	43,200	223,600
Pakistan[2]	109,600	10,100	119,700
Ceylon	12,900	3,200	16,100
Jamaica	188,100	85,700	273,800
Other Caribbean	129,800	50,500	180,300
West Africa	43,100	7,600	50,700
Far East	47,000	13,000	60,000
Total	710,900	213,300	924,200

[1]Excluding white Indians
[2]Excluding white Pakistanis

Source: E. J. B. Rose *et al.*, *Colour and Citizenship*, London: Oxford University Press, 1969.

Whatever their country of origin coloured immigrants to Britain have tended to be employed in jobs that are losing ground in terms of pay and status (such as those in public transport) or in jobs that are generally considered unpleasant (such as refuse collection or foundry work). With the relatively full employment of the post-war years and the increasing demand for skilled and/or highly paid labour, the locally born labour force has tended to move out of the less desirable (but nevertheless essential) jobs, thereby creating vacancies which coloured immigrants have been willing and able to fill. Such jobs require few skills and even the lowest British wage rates have allowed a higher standard of living than is normally possible in the Indian sub-continent and the West Indies. The nature of economic change in post-war Britain, then, has encouraged and facilitated immigration, and has concentrated the immigrants in the lowest paid and lowest status jobs in the country.

In addition to these economic forces, coloured immigrants also had to contend with colour prejudice. This is nothing new in Britain (despite the small numbers of coloured inhabitants before 1950). As long ago as 1602 an order was issued commanding certain 'blackamoors' to be transported from the country; in the late eighteenth and early nineteenth centuries the St Giles 'blackbirds' were concentrated in a kind of ghetto; and in 1919 the sudden increase in the numbers of negro immigrants following the first world war sparked off serious disturbances in a number of towns. Such incidents, however, since they were infrequent and relatively minor, did little to disturb the complacent view that racial disturbances were foreign to British society. The myth of a racially tolerant Britain remained unchallenged until the racial disturbances of 1958. Thereafter the 'problem' of race relations grew. In riots in the Notting Hill district of London in 1958 126 white and 51 coloured people were arrested, mainly on charges of causing grievous bodily harm, possessing offensive weapons, or using threatening words and behaviour. In Nottingham, also in that year, a 'pub brawl' in which four Englishmen were stabbed by West Indians led large crowds to gather and fight every evening for a week. By 1962, fear of coloured immigration, especially among certain sectors of the working classes who saw immigrants as a threat to their employment and their housing, prompted the government to pass an act restricting immigration from the Commonwealth. In 1964, race became, for the first time, a major issue in a British election when a Conservative candidate, standing on an anti-immigrant platform, was returned in Smethwick—generally reckoned to be a 'safe' Labour seat.

The anti-immigration movement found a leader in Enoch Powell, a former Minister of Health who, in a speech in Birmingham in April 1968, argued that the 'flood' of coloured immigrants was likely, in the near future, to dislodge native-born Englishmen from several British towns. He therefore proposed that, in order to prevent the repetition in Great Britain of what he later called 'the haunting tragedy of the United States', immigration be stopped totally and that measures be adopted to 'promote the maximum outflow'. Mr Powell's speeches became the focus for the immigration issue. Condemned by the majority of leading politicians, clergymen, television and radio commentators, and by most national newspapers, his views nevertheless commanded considerable popular support. More than a thousand dockers marched from the West India docks to Westminster to demonstrate in his favour. Later, the leader of a group of Smithfield meat porters proclaimed:[12]

> At last the Englishman has had some guts. This is as important as Dunkirk. We are becoming second class citizens in our own country. Immigrants have been brought here to undercut our wages in times of crisis. When there is vast unemployment in this country, immigrants will compete with you for your jobs.

It is clear from this comment that, in periods of crisis, 'national' and 'racial' sentiments can easily outweigh any identification with the coloured population as fellow workers who share certain interests with members of the white working class. It is significant that the main expressions of support for 'Powellism' come from men employed in work which is unskilled and notoriously insecure. Such men tend to be poorly educated. They are likely, in consequence, to come into *direct* competition with immigrants for jobs, especially in periods of high unemployment.

However, antagonism towards coloured immigrants does not always stem from factors so apparently rational as competition in the labour and housing markets. Such evidence as is available suggests that approximately 10 per cent of the total population is generally prejudiced against them. In a study (carried out in 1966–7) of five English boroughs with relatively high proportions of coloured residents, one-third of all the white adults interviewed expressed views with virtually no trace of hostility towards coloured people. A further two-fifths were strongly disposed in the direction of tolerance whilst the remainder, although strongly inclined towards prejudice, were not unconditionally hostile and were prepared to make exceptions. The highest incidence of extreme prejudice was found among skilled manual workers and their wives and among the lower-middle classes. Such prejudice may stem in part from their status marginality and their consequent insecurity. That is, they may perceive immigrant competition as a threat to their relative affluence—recently gained and all too uncertainly held.

But prejudice is not the only factor of significance—nor perhaps the most important one. Unprejudiced people can (and do) also engage in racial discrimination if they perceive it to be in their interests. Thus, in spite of some evidence suggesting a relative lack of prejudice, there is also considerable evidence of racial discrimination in the fields of employment and housing and in the provision of goods, facilities and services.

The seriousness of the situation and the prevalence of discrimination were recognized by Parliament in the passing, in 1968, of a Race Relations Act whereby racial discrimination in these fields was made illegal. If, in spite of the Race Relations Act, such discrimination continues, the coloured immigrants—and more importantly their children—will probably develop into a more or less permanent and easily exploitable 'sub-proletariat'. The outcome will depend partly on whether they can organize themselves successfully to protect their own interests and here they face several problems. Most coloured immigrants are strangers both to the English way of life and to the urban-industrial environment in which it takes place. Many of them are consequently too fully occupied in finding and keeping jobs and houses to devote time and energy to the development of organizations with the long-term aim of securing integration into British society (or even to raising the standard of living of immigrants as a group). In addition, the linguistic and cultural differences between West Indians, Pakistanis and Indians form a formidable barrier to a comprehensive immigrants' organization. Even the West Indians come from a variety of different islands many of which have long-standing traditions of hostility towards each other. West Indian society is, moreover, based upon a form of social stratification in which dark brown skins tend to be associated with low status and light brown skins tend to be associated with high status. The tensions and conflicts arising from these differences are often transferred to the British context where they undermine the common experiences of immigrant status.

Pakistani immigrants are also divided among themselves—principally between those from East Pakistan (or Bangladesh as it is now called) and those from West Pakistan. In spite of their capacity to organize successful commercial enterprises, they have so far failed to create effective political organizations. A striking exception is their activity in local elections, most notably in Bradford where a Pakistani councillor was elected as early as 1964. A more recent form of 'political' organization has taken the form of defensive vigilante groups against the 'Paki-bashing' activities of 'skinheads'.

By far the most successful of immigrant groups in terms of political organization have been the Indians. Their relative success has its origins in the India League and the Indian Workers' Association. These were formed before the second world war by Indians in this country in order to help the Indian struggle for independence. The Indian Workers' Association was revived in 1953 when large-scale migration from the Punjab began. The Punjabi origin of the majority gives the Indian migrants a homogeneity in experience, beliefs and values which helps to explain their organizational success relative to other immigrant groups. In addition, the nature of their communities, with their strong emphasis on mutual obligations between groups of kinsmen, has helped to draw individuals into the activities of the IWA. The organization was strong enough in 1966 to engage in a six-week strike in a Southall rubber factory over the dismissal of one of its members. Such organization is perhaps a precondition of achieving a measure of equality with the host population in key areas of social life. Yet successful organization, too, has its problems in that it may produce a counter-reaction—a 'white backlash'. Indeed, Mr Powell has already identified the halting development of immigrant organizations as a move towards 'black domination' (domination, that is by 2 per cent of the population over the 98 per cent who include the incumbents of all the major and minor power positions in the land)! Such are the dangers of political organization. Without it, however, immigrant groups are likely to remain outsiders. With hard work and sacrifice some of them may become comparatively affluent, but affluence, as the experience of the Jews shows so clearly, is no guarantee that they will not become a target of hostility, especially in times of national stress.

Notes

1 Eric Williams, *Capitalism and Slavery*, London: Deutsch, 1964, p. 19.
2 Quoted in Kenneth M. Stampp, *The Peculiar Institution. Slavery in the Ante-Bellum South*, New York: Knopf, 1956, p. 171.
3 George M. Stroud, *A Sketch of the Laws relating to Slavery in the several States of the United States of America*, Philadelphia, 1856, quoted in Michael Banton, *Race Relations*, London: Tavistock, 1967, p. 121.
4 Quoted in Stampp, op. cit., p. 172.
5 John Pendleton Kennedy, *Swallow Barn*, quoted in S. M. Elkins, *Slavery: A Problem in American Institutional and Intellectual Life*, University of Chicago Press, 1959, p. 132.
6 Edward A. Pollard, *Black Diamonds Gathered in the Darkey Homes of the South*, quoted in Elkins, op. cit., p. 132.
7 Alexis de Tocqueville, *Democracy in America*, Vol. I, New York: Vintage, 1945, p. 373.
8 Quoted in C. Vann Woodward, *The Strange Career of Jim Crow*, New York: Oxford University Press, 1960, pp. 44–5.

9 Martin Luther King, *Chaos or Community*, Harmondsworth: Penguin, 1969, p. 50.
10 Ibid., pp. 53–4.
11 Frank Tannenbaum, *Slave and Citizen*, New York: Vintage, 1946, p. 49.
12 Speech by Dennis Herbert Harmston, quoted in Bill Smithers and Peter Fiddick, *Enoch Powell on Immigration*, London: Sphere, 1969, pp. 12–13.

Reading

Banton, M., *Race Relations*, London: Tavistock, 1967. A useful introduction to the study of race and race relations.

Franklin-Frazier, E., *Black Bourgeoisie*, New York: Collier, 1962. This study by a negro sociologist remains the best so far carried out on middle-class negroes in the United States.

Killian, L., *The Impossible Revolution*, New York: Random House, 1968. A thorough, thought-provoking study of negro protest in the USA.

Mason, P., *Race Relations*, London: Oxford University Press, 1970. A short introduction which reviews biological, psychological and anthropological approaches to the subject and sets current racial problems in the perspective of world history.

Rex, J. and Moore, R., *Race, Community and Conflict*, London: Oxford University Press, 1967. By far the best sociological study so far carried out of race relations in Britain.

Rose, E. J. B. *et al.*, *Colour and Citizenship*, London: Oxford University Press, 1969. Not sociological but none the less a useful and instructive compendium of information on race and immigration in the United Kingdom.

Further reading

Genovese, Eugene D., *The Political Economy of Slavery*, New York: Pantheon, 1965. A stimulating study by a Marxist historian of the consequences of slavery for the social structure of the American South.

Genovese, Eugene D., *The World the Slaveholders Made*, London: Allen Lane, 1970. Contains two important essays: a comparative study of colonialism, slavery, and social structure in various parts of the 'New World', and an essay on the ideology of slaveholders in the Southern USA.

Hunter, G. (ed.), *Industrialization and Race Relations*, London: Oxford University Press, 1965. A useful symposium on industrialization and race relations in world perspective.

Mason, P., *Patterns of Dominance*, London: Oxford University Press, 1970. A useful, highly readable comparative and historical analysis of patterns of racial dominance.

Schermerhorn, R. A., *Comparative Ethnic Relations*, New York: Random House, 1970. Compares the usefulness of different approaches to the comparative study of ethnic and race relations. Lucid, readable and brings together a wealth of information in a systematic way.

12 Industrial relations

In industrial societies almost everyone is, has been or will be an employee at some time during their life. Indeed, for most of us this particular status will dominate much of our adult life. This situation is in marked contrast to that in non-industrial societies where three-quarters or more of the occupied population are employers, self-employed or family workers. Thus, the focus of this chapter—the social relations of employers and employees—is one which directly concerns all of us who live in industrial societies. This state of affairs is relatively recent and has been associated with the emergence of the factory system of production, a system which only became dominant during the nineteenth century, first in Britain and then elsewhere.

The factory system

The factory system of production developed in Britain alongside the craftsman and the domestic system and only over a period of several decades did it come to predominate. Even now self-employed craftsmen remain important in several occupations, such as shoe repairing and picture framing, where the demand for capital is not great; and 'putting out' is also still to be found, for instance in the hosiery industry in the East Midlands. In industrial societies today, however, factories are dominant in manufacturing industry and, even in other spheres, work is characterized by a similar pattern of social relations.

The organization of production in factories was the outcome of several distinct changes from earlier modes of production. It resulted, moreover, in marked changes in the social situation of the worker. In the first place, it meant the concentration of labour in one workshop or factory, and the consequent separation of home and work. Second, it involved the discipline and control of the workers by the manufacturer, and this made possible a much more elaborate and far-reaching division of labour than had existed among craftsmen or under the domestic system. Third, it was associated with the use of power machinery and the mechanization of tasks wherever possible and thus with the employment of very much greater amounts of fixed capital than even the merchant employer had required. Whilst isolated examples of the concentration of workers into workshops, and even of their working under the discipline of the employer, can be found much earlier than the eighteenth century, the use of water- or steam-powered machinery, which developed from the middle of that century onwards, was only possible within a factory system.

In contrast to the situation of the factory worker, the independent craftsman owned his tools and place of work, purchased his raw materials and sold the finished product direct to the consumer. The worker under the domestic system was more dependent on the merchant employer, but might still own his own tools and place of work. Within the limits set by the need to do enough work to support themselves and their dependants these workers could work in their own way and at their own pace. It was common experience in the domestic system for work to be concentrated into the latter half of the week. For example, the Children's Employment Commission provided the following description of the West Midland's lock and key industry in 1843:[1]

> The majority of the working classes do no work at all on Monday. Half of them do not work much on Tuesday. Wednesday is the market day, and this is an excuse for many of them to do only half a day's work; and in consequence of attending the market they are often very unfit for work on Thursday morning. Lights are seen in the shops of many of the small masters as late as ten and eleven o'clock at night on Thursday. During the whole of Friday the town is silent in all the main streets and thoroughfares, and seems to have been depopulated of all its manufacturers. Lights appear in the workshops to a late hour in the night—sometimes till morning. All Saturday morning the streets present the same comparatively barren and silent appearance. Everybody is working for his life. Among the small masters, their wives, children and apprentices are being almost worked to death. Kicks, cuffs, curses and blows are abundantly administered to the children at this crisis of the work . . . . About two o'clock . . . some of those who did some work on Tuesday begin to appear in the streets; and large masses issue forth between 4 and 5 o'clock. The wives and elder girls go to market; the husbands and other adults to the beer shops. By 7 or 8 o'clock the market is full; the streets are all alive; the beer-shops and gin-shops are full; and all the other shops are full. The manufacturers are stretching their limbs, expanding their souls to the utmost, and spending their money as fast as they possibly can. No one ever thinks of saving a shilling.

By contrast, although he was legally free, the factory worker was subordinate and dependent, economically and socially. He was subject to the discipline of the employer, who demanded that he started and stopped work at fixed times and that he worked with regular intensity. The factory system also made possible much greater division of labour and specialization developed further as machine power was introduced. Thus much factory work (though not all) involved, and indeed still involves, performing semi-skilled or unskilled tasks which are only a fragment of the total process. The intrinsic satisfactions which might be derived from the task itself and from the completion of a finished product were diminished. Work life involving inherent deprivations became sharply separated from home life and leisure in which satisfactions might be hoped for.

These marked differences in the formal social relations of production between the craftsman, domestic and factory systems represent changes in the individual's socially defined rights of access to means of making a living. However much the autonomy and independence of the craftsman depended on guild regulation of an occupation, it stands in marked contrast to the economic dependence of the factory worker who has no rights over materials, tools or product, and is related to his employer by impersonal market forces and subject to factory discipline. Social relations at work under the factory system vary considerably depending on a variety of other factors, but they must be considered within this initial framework.

Some of the contrasts and changes outlined above may be made more meaningful by considering a detailed account of such changes and resistance to them. Two American social scientists, Lloyd Warner and J. O. Low, have outlined the changes which took place in the organization of the shoe industry in 'Yankee City' (Newburyport) in New England.[2] In the seventeenth century, shoe production was carried out in the family using a few simple hand tools and producing primarily for domestic needs. Gradually certain people specialized in shoe-making and made shoes to order for local customers. This system was changed with the emergence of entrepreneurs who got workers at home to make shoes for them to sell in a wider market. On the basis of this domestic system it was also possible to introduce a measure of specialization; materials were sorted in a central shop and each workman performed only some of the operations necessary for making a complete boot or shoe. The market was local and only when it began to expand with improved transport facilities did the 'merchant-master' come to dominate the journeyman and their interests begin to conflict seriously.

The introduction of machinery from the middle of the nineteenth century onwards was associated with the growth of a factory system; the process of manufacture was transformed from a single skilled trade carried on by craftsmen from start to finish, to one of several thousand operations carried out by semi-skilled operatives on specialized machines. A trade union, the Knights of St Crispin, was unable to prevent this process of increasing mechanization and the consequent substitution of 'green hands' for old-time craftsmen, and was short lived (1868–72). The workers remained subordinate to the factory owners (mostly local men) and subject to the effects of cyclical and seasonal trade fluctuations and to the pressure for lower costs and greater productivity. However, because the owners were prominent members of the local community, the conflict of interests between them and their employees was mitigated somewhat by the fact that they were thought to be guided in their actions by community as well as commercial considerations and by the personal relationships between the two groups.

The final stage came with the transfer of ownership and control from local families to businessmen in distant New York for whom the 'Yankee City' factories were only one unimportant producing unit among many others. With this change were associated further mechanization and the use of assembly-line methods so that nearly all jobs were low skilled and many were highly routinized. The market became even wider but retail outlets were controlled by the big manufacturers. A large industrial union organized the workers (who took part in a successful strike) and it made possible some protection of workers' interests in the face of a large, impersonal, bureaucratic management organization.

Attempts to resist the spread of the factory system were not confined to the New England shoe industry, but were widespread in Europe and North America. Some of this resistance can be attributed to the harsh and unpleasant conditions of work in many establishments during the early stages of industrialization, but often another important factor was the loss of autonomy and the imposition of disciplined work habits which factory employment involved. Thus employers can be found complaining that because they valued their independence workmen would not 'walk across the street' to work in a factory even though their earnings under the domestic system were markedly less. One of the most interesting examples of an attempt to preserve this independence and yet to gain the advantages of steam power was the building of 'cottage factories' for the Coventry ribbon weavers during the 1850s. In these cases rows of weavers' houses, each with a workshop on the second floor, were built with a steam engine at one end and shafting running along the row to supply power for the looms in each cottage. Each weaver could thus work in his own home for whatever time he chose and could employ members of his family as ancillary workers, but could also use a power loom.

Employer–employee relations are often concerned with this 'frontier of control' in the workplace, with the employee attempting—partly through collective action and partly by less formal and less organized means—to gain a measure of control over his work situation.

The development of the factory system

Industrialization in Britain and North America took place entirely within a capitalist framework. The initiative in establishing factories, employing workers and exploiting new markets came from the entrepreneur who, using his own or borrowed capital, was oriented to the rational pursuit of economic gain, and attempted to achieve this through the rational organization of free labour. The growth of the factory system and the consequent changes in the social relations of production were significantly affected by this; there was an emphasis on free markets, and on the primacy of commercial considerations. In other societies, however, the process of industrialization has taken different forms. In some parts of Western Europe (such as Germany) and in Tsarist Russia the central government played a more active part, though within a basically capitalist framework. In Soviet Russia, Eastern Europe and some of the modernizing societies of the present time the initiative has come from the government and ownership of the means of production has been in the hands of the state. In other modernizing societies colonial administrations or overseas companies have been the prime initiators of such changes and in others a mixed economy has been developed. Thus, whilst relations between employers and employees may have certain elements in common in all industrial societies, there are also important differences and the full significance of these has still to be explored. There are certain common technological and organizational features of large-scale industrial organizations which set limits to the form social relations may take but they do not determine them in all respects.

In order to understand contemporary relations between employers and employees in the industrial West it is necessary to examine the specific developments in these societies. The most important of these are the growth of industrial bureaucracy, the divorce of ownership and control, the changing role of the government and the rise of trade unions.

(1) The early factories had no very elaborate management organization. Managerial tasks were performed by members of the owning family or by the partners in the business, assisted by relatively few foremen and clerks. One common procedure was the use of sub-contractors to perform many of the necessary tasks. These men were autonomous and they recruited, trained, instructed, disciplined, paid and dismissed the workers they needed. In such cases the worker often had a personal relationship with his employer, though this did not eliminate harshness and exploitation. As firms and plants grew in size and as technical methods became increasingly complex, such administrative methods were inadequate; management became increasingly bureaucratic with the adoption of rational formal procedures in place of traditional practices. These changes were reflected in the increased proportion of administrative personnel of all kinds in industry; so that, for example, administrative personnel increased as a percentage of production workers. In Britain in 1907 administrative personnel were 8·6 per cent of production workers; in 1948 they were 20 per cent; in 1966 they were 24·3 per cent. In the USA they were 7·7 per cent in 1899 and 21·6 per cent in 1947. These trends have continued. The employer–employee relationship was affected by the change from relatively small family firms to large corporations and it inevitably became more impersonal. It was increasingly governed by rules and procedures which were intended to apply to all employees without favouritism or malice.

(2) Parallel with the development of industrial bureaucracy there occurred marked changes in the patterns of ownership so that the predominant form of enterprise became the limited liability joint stock company. In smaller companies a small group of important shareholders, sometimes members of the same family, have often continued to exercise control, and this is occasionally the case even in larger companies. In the majority of large firms, however, the dispersal of shareholding means that effective control rests in the hands of full-time directors and top executives who are themselves employees and have no share, or only a nominal one, in the ownership of the company.

The interests of these executives may diverge from that of their subordinates but are nevertheless not always identical with that of the shareholders. They may, for example, place greater emphasis on the long-term growth of their businesses than on the maximizing of profits. Furthermore, in Britain and some Western European societies a substantial part of industry is publicly owned. Top management's responsibility is to the relevant Minister and to Parliament rather than to shareholders and considerations of social policy have influenced industrial relations at least at certain times. In many other respects, however, there appears to be little difference between nationalized concerns and large privately owned companies.

(3) Although the influence of the government on industry and industrial relations is most obvious in societies where the means of production are publicly controlled, nevertheless governments play an important part in industry in all highly industrialized societies. This is in marked contrast to the position in Britain during the early stages of industrialization when *laissez-faire* prevailed very much in fact as well as in theory. Increasingly, however, the government intervened to regulate conditions in factories and mines, to prohibit or regulate the employment of women and children, and to influence industrial relations. This increasing intervention, which can be observed in many industrial societies, is not due primarily to changing ideas about the role of government, though the ideas and interests of various parties and pressure groups have materially influenced the form of the intervention at different times. Rather it is a necessary course of action for any industrial society that is to avoid the widespread social disorganization which would result from an unregulated power struggle between employers and employees.

(4) Employer–employee relations have been even more significantly affected by the growth of trade unions. Collective action by workers in the same trade can be traced back to well before the Industrial Revolution but the development of trade unions in their modern form is very much a phenomenon of industrial societies. Though by no means all employees, even in highly industrialized societies like Britain, are members of trade unions (or for that matter employees' associations of any sort) the terms and conditions of employment for the great majority are influenced directly or indirectly by trade-union action. The growth of trade unions appears to be a universal feature of industrial societies. Their independence, the extent of union organization and the nature of union activities, however, vary widely depending largely on the particular course of development and the political structure in each society. In the

industrial West trade unions now play such an important part in industrial relations that we must look at them in more detail.

Trade unions

Trade unions are primarily interest groups formed to protect and further the interests of a particular occupational group against the interests of their employers, or sometimes those of other occupational groups. In any industrial society where there is in any sense a free labour market the individual employee is in a very weak bargaining position; the employer normally acts from a position of much greater strength. Only if the employee combines with others in his negotiations with employers and takes collective action to improve the terms of the employment contract is some sort of parity possible. Thus trade unionism can be seen as a product of what is sometimes called the *market situation* of the worker in a society in which his livelihood depends on the bargain he can make in selling his labour to an employer. Not all workers share precisely the same market situation, though they may have common interests in some general issues (and this is reflected in the existence of organizations, such as the Trades Union Congress in Great Britain, which aim to represent the interests of all trade unionists). The distinctive interests of workers with particular skills, or associated with particular industries or occupations, are reflected in the existence of different trade unions or other employees' associations to protect their interests.

In addition, however, the individual employee usually shares a common *work situation* with his fellow employees. The extent to which this is so may be important in determining the extent to which employees become aware of their common position in the labour market. In addition the employee is in a relationship of subordination to his employer and has to accept the discipline and loss of autonomy that this entails. Particularly in large bureaucratic organizations manual workers and routine clerical workers are physically and socially separated from management. By taking collective action employees can affect, sometimes very considerably, the way in which the authority of the employer is exercised. Trade unionism can thus also be seen as a defence against arbitrary action by the employer and as an expression of the solidarity which is brought about by the work situation.

The growth of trade unions can therefore be seen as a result of the divisions and conflicts which are a feature of modern economic organization. The activities of the different groups which arise from this division of labour, however, are differentially evaluated by others; people who do similar jobs are usually accorded a common social status. In terms of the dominant value system in most industrial societies this means that manual workers have an inferior social status; non-manual workers, even though also employees, may claim and be accorded higher social status. (There are, of course, important differences within each broad grouping.) Trade unionism may be partly a reaction to just such a shared and inferior status situation. It may be seen as offering hope of an improvement in social status by asserting the value of the activities in question, by securing improved economic circumstances which make possible a more desirable style of life, and by increasing the power of such groups *vis-à-vis* other status groups in the society.

This way of looking at trade unions provides a coherent explanation of the patterns of unionism —perhaps best exemplified by David Lockwood's study of clerical workers.[3] Clerical trade unionism presents two problems. First, why clerical workers, who like manual workers are property-less and dependent on their labour for their livelihood, do not form trade unions to the same extent as manual workers. Second, why in more recent years trade unionism has developed among clerical workers but has become much stronger among some categories of clerical workers than among others.

Although both manual and clerical workers are property-less their market situations are by no means identical. Traditionally, clerks had significantly higher incomes, especially if these are calculated on the basis of a lifetime's earnings. In addition, they had greater job security because of the value of their services to the organization, their superior chances of promotion, and very often the possession of a number of fringe benefits and non-pecuniary advantages not received by manual workers. Their work situation was characterized by personal relations with the employer and not by uniformity of work or conditions, so that the basis for consciousness of common interests with other clerks, or of collective action with them, did not exist. Furthermore, black-coated workers claimed and were granted distinctively higher social status than even skilled manual workers. Thus traditionally neither the market, work nor status situations of clerical workers were really similar to those of manual workers, and the individual clerk could probably best hope to improve his situation by being loyal to his employer and thus maximizing the possibility of promotion within the enterprise.

Increasingly, however, this situation has changed, and with the change has come a growth of 'white collar' trade unionism. In particular, with increasing literacy and with the routinization of many clerical tasks the market situation of clerical workers has worsened relative to other groups, a change which has been reflected in decreased pay differentials and in the spread of fringe benefits of various sorts to manual workers. More or less full employment and certain statutory measures have increased the security of employment of all workers, but especially of manual workers. Even more important, the growth of large-scale bureaucratic organizations of all sorts, employing large numbers of clerks, has radically altered the black-coated worker's work situation. Large numbers of clerks now perform similar tasks under standardized conditions of employment so that personal relationships with employers are no longer possible. Furthermore, the increased number of clerks desiring promotion and the increased demand for formal qualifications, rather than just experience, for entry to higher-level positions in the bureaucratic hierarchy means that chances of promotion are much reduced or even blocked altogether. Finally, the status situation of clerical workers has become ambiguous as they have become a more numerous and more diverse group less clearly distinguished from manual workers in social origins, education and style of life.

Within the general category of clerical worker, however, there are important differences which are reflected both in membership statistics and in the nature of the unions—for example in their militancy. In the 1960s a very high proportion of clerks in national and local government and in the railways were members of their respective unions. A considerably smaller proportion of bank clerks were members of the National Union of Bank Employees, although many others were members of the less militant staff associations. An extremely small but increasing proportion of clerical workers in most other industrial and commercial establishments were members of the Clerical and Administrative Workers' Union or of any other union. Differences in pay, conditions and social status are less helpful in explaining these differences than are the differences in the degree of bureaucratization of the work situation. Uniformity of conditions and blocked chances for upward mobility characterized those industries with strong and militant white collar unions. The banks by contrast did not act together as employers in the provision of uniform conditions and they provided rather better chances of promotion. Under these conditions membership of the less militant staff associations was higher than that of the NUBE. The low membership rates of clerical unions in industry generally reflect the diversity of employment conditions for these clerks.

Differences in the market situation and social status of different groups of clerical workers do not correlate with union membership; thus the high status Civil Service Clerical Association and the low status Transport Salaried Staff Association both have a high level of membership. Such differences do, however, help explain the differences in militancy of different unions and the varying extent to which white collar unions have been prepared to associate with the Labour movement as a whole. The Civil Service Clerical Association is not affiliated to the Labour Party; the Transport Salaried Staff Association is affiliated but has, nevertheless, maintained its separateness from other railway workers' unions. Similarly the increased militancy which has been observable in recent years among bank clerks and teachers stems in part from changes in their economic and social position relative to other groups.

Industrial conflict

Conflict between employers and employees is a normal and permanent feature of industrial society. In most industrial societies, however, there are organizations and procedures for dealing with industrial disputes. Relations between employers and employees are conducted within a framework of rules and for the most part their conflicting interests do not disrupt the industrial enterprise. In other words, industrial conflict has been institutionalized.

The conflict between employers and employees may remain submerged; there are potentially conflicting interests, but for lack of awareness or lack of opportunity they do not break out openly. Conflict may, however, be open, visible and yet unorganized; employees may act individually in ways which are contrary to the employer's interests, for example by going absent without permission, leaving employment or withholding effort. On the other hand, it may be organized, involving collective action whether or not this be through a formal organization. Such action might take the form of a strike, a collective go-slow, or grievances presented by representatives of a group of employees.

The organization of the parties to the conflict is a necessary step in the institutionalization of industrial conflict. It is perhaps obvious that one cannot hope to establish negotiating procedures with an aggregate of individual employees who don't act collectively; it is, however, equally important that employers be permanent and organized parties to agreements, thus obviating any possibility of disowning agreements reached by representatives or escaping their obligations by legal technicalities.

By no means all employees are trade-union members but trade unions dominate the employees' side of industrial relations procedures in Britain and in most other Western industrial societies. At least partly in reaction to this, employers in different industries have organized themselves in federations so as to present a united front. The organization of the parties to the conflict in this way gives rise to further problems in that in such large organizations maintaining adequate communications between union or federation officials and the rank-and-file members becomes difficult. Yet if unorganized manifestations of conflict are to be minimized, the interests of members must somehow be adequately represented. It is also necessary for the parties to the conflict to recognize each others' interests as legitimate. If employers refuse to recognize unions or attempt to eliminate them, or if unions act to produce changes in property ownership by revolutionary means, the institutionalization of industrial conflict cannot take place.

A further necessary stage in the institutionalization of industrial conflict is the establishment of negotiating procedures through which substantive agreements can be arrived at. These are rules governing the relations of the parties to each other at various levels—'rules of the game' as it were. In Britain there is a wide variety of such procedures in different industries and this reflects the relative autonomy of the system of industrial relations in this country; an autonomy which has, however, been restricted by recent attempts to secure an incomes policy and by changes in the law. In some other societies, such as Sweden, collective bargaining procedures are more highly centralized; in others, for example the United States, they are decentralized but much more uniform because of statutory regulation. All, however, have the same function of making it possible for conflicts of interest to be worked out within a framework of rules and, except in a minority of cases, without resort to force (for example, strikes and lock-outs).

In many societies the institutionalization of industrial conflict has included a further stage, the establishment of procedures for conciliation and arbitration; and in some cases, such as in Australia for over half a century, compulsory arbitration has been statutorily enforced. This means that disputes not previously resolved must be submitted to arbitration and the decision of the arbitrator must be accepted by both parties. In Britain until very recently this has only been the case exceptionally (for example, during and immediately after the two world wars), partly because of the difficulty of enforcing such decisions. However, largely because of government initiative, machinery for conciliation and voluntary arbitration has existed for many years and is of considerable importance.

The institutionalization of industrial conflict does not necessarily mean that there is less conflict (though this may be so), but it does mean that conflict tends to change its outward manifestations. In particular, the strike, which can be regarded as the most important sanction in the hands of employees, may be used less often. The changing pattern of industrial conflict between 1900 and 1956 in fifteen selected countries is summarized in Table 12.1.[4] The figures suggest that strikes are less significant than they were at the beginning of the century. The table also shows that in the most recent period (up to 1956) there were important differences between the fifteen societies. In Britain, Denmark, West Germany, the Netherlands, Norway and Sweden very few union members went on strike in any one year (Britain had the highest rate, averaging 5·9 per cent per year); strikes tended to be short, except in Norway and Sweden; and relatively few working days were lost per union member (Britain was again highest with an average of 22·5 days per 100 union members). In comparison with this group, the USA and Canada exhibited a rather higher propensity to strike; they had somewhat longer strikes, and ten times as many working days lost per union member. In France, Italy, Japan and India an even higher percentage of union members struck each year, but strikes were of short duration, so that the average

Table 12.1 Changing patterns of industrial conflict

Country	*Membership involvement ratio* *Workers involved in strikes as a % of union membership (per year)* 1900–29	1930–47	1948–56	*Duration of strikes* *Working days lost per striker (per year)* 1900–29	1930–47	1948–56	*Membership loss ratio* *Working days lost per 100 union members (per year)* 1900–29	1930–47	1948–56
Denmark	6·3	2·4	1·4	28·7	24·3	4·3	203·7	64·9	17·1
Netherlands	7·0	2·6	1·3	32·7	21·3	7·5	212·6	51·7	10·4
United Kingdom	16·1	6·4	5·9	23·0	6·6	4·3	434·4	45·2	22·5
Germany	14·2	3·7	2·6	15·6	12·5	9·9	221·3	—	15·1
Norway	27·0	6·8	1·2	33·6	43·0	15·2	941·8	542·2	16·2
Sweden	22·7	3·0	0·3	37·1	51·0	22·6	893·9	183·0	13·3
France	27·1	29·0	62·4	14·4	14·9	2·9	415·7	175·5	171·2
Italy	—	—	35·2	—	—	2·7	—	—	85·5
Japan	30·3	39·0	21·5	—	9·1	4·9	—	170·8	110·1
India	—	102·2	37·2	26·6	11·8	8·8	—	1,192·8	315·2
United States	33·2	20·3	15·4	—	14·6	14·6	—	296·4	235·6
Canada	14·7	13·3	6·3	27·1	11·0	19·3	445·4	138·9	129·7
Australia	18·2	14·8	25·2	14·2	7·0	3·2	261·9	86·7	86·4
Finland	24·5	9·0	13·9	36·0	14·5	15·8	810·4	125·7	579·8
South Africa	24·4	3·9	1·4	15·8	9·4	2·6	315·2	38·1	5·0

Source: A. M. Ross and P. T. Hartman, *Changing Patterns of Industrial Conflict*, New York: Wiley, 1960.

number of working days lost per union member was much the same as in the USA and Canada. Australia, Finland, and South Africa did not fit neatly into any of these patterns. That considerable differences between countries have continued to exist is illustrated by the figures in Table 12.2.

These trends and differences have been explained by two sets of factors: by changes in the social structure of industrial and industrializing societies—changes which include a decline in class antagonism and the growth of more heterogeneous communities; and by the growth of effective industrial relations procedures—so that strikes decline and become means of protest rather than an inevitable stage in long drawn out disputes. The fifteen societies differed in the extent to which these changes in social structure had taken place, and perhaps more obviously, in the degree of 'success' with which conflict had been institutionalized. In the first group of societies there were firm and stable trade-union movements, stable and relatively centralized collective bargaining machinery, and apparently realistic political alternatives to industrial action (in the form of powerful Labour or Social Democratic parties). Moreover, except in Norway and Sweden, the government had intervened to settle industrial disputes and done so largely successfully. In France, Italy, India and Japan, which presented the most marked contrast, unions were unstable, negotiating machinery was not strongly established, left-wing political parties did not offer a realistic alternative to industrial action, and government intervention, when it occurred, was resented.

Table 12.2 Working days lost due to industrial disputes: selected countries 1964–6

Country	*Average number of working days lost per 1,000 employees, 1964–6*
Republic of Ireland	1,620
Italy	1,170
Canada	970
USA	870
Australia	400
Japan	240
France	200
United Kingdom	190
Denmark	160
Finland	80
Sweden	40
Netherlands	20
Federal Republic of Germany, Norway	less than 10

Source: H. A. Turner, *Is Britain Really Strike-Prone?*, Cambridge University Press, 1969, p. 7.

The tendency for strikes to decline in frequency and severity, however, has not continued. In many, though not all, of the societies listed in Table 12.1 there was an increase in strike activity in the 1960s, so that the thesis that we have been observing, 'the withering away of the strike' would, at best, appear premature. In Britain, for example, there were more working days lost through strikes (though not more strikes) in 1971 than at any time since 1926, the year of the General Strike.

Explanations of this change in the strike pattern vary. It may appear to be a temporary break in the long-term decline in strike activity in highly industrial countries. Alternatively, it may be seen as an indication that there are limits in the extent to which industrial conflict can be institutionalized. The organization of workers in trade unions gives rise to problems of intra-union conflict between its officials and rank-and-file members, and so to the likelihood of more unofficial strikes which are contrary to the official union policy as well as to the employers' interests. Moreover, the pursuit of the goal of 'industrial peace' may only be possible at the cost of apparently inflationary wage settlements, and government policies to secure wage restraint may be resisted through strike action. Third, an increase in the rate of technical change, or rising expectations on the part of employees, may lead to new demands and new forms of conflict (for example, the 'work-in') which cannot be contained within existing institutions. More radically, the change in the strike pattern may be seen as a reflection of the inherent instabilities of capitalist societies, characterized as they are by marked inequalities of income and wealth, and of their persistent economic problems. From such a perspective, overt industrial conflict is normal, and the problem is to explain the absence, rather than the presence, of strike activity. Thus, even a brief examination of international strike patterns involves a consideration of some of the central problems in the analysis of the structure of industrial societies as a whole.

Conflict in particular industries

Within industrial societies there are differences in the level and intensity of conflict from industry to industry and from firm to firm; differences in the degree to which there is awareness of conflicting interests; and differences in the way in which conflict manifests itself. Thus, while in some enterprises stoppages of work appear to be endemic, in others they are unknown and employees identify with the firm and regard its interests as their interests. The explanation of these differences is complex. Some firms, for example, emphasize a traditional, paternalist relationship with their employees, which plays down the market transaction of buying and selling labour and stresses the employer's responsibility for his 'family' and his 'fatherly' authority over them. Yet such an alternative is not really open to large enterprises or to those with fluctuating demands for labour, and in any case it involves disadvantages as well as advantages.

Nor is this type of explanation, concentrating as it does on managerial policies, entirely adequate to explain the regularities in strike rates in different industries. For differences in propensity to strike are not only to be found between firms but also between industries. Working days lost as a proportion of those employed are consistently high for some industries and consistently low for others (see Table 12.3).[5] Any adequate explanation of such differences must be applicable very

Table 12.3 General pattern of strike propensities

Propensity to strike	*Industry*
High	Mining
	Maritime and longshore
Medium high	Lumber
	Textile
Medium	Chemical
	Printing
	Leather
	Manufacturing (general)
	Construction
	Food and kindred products
Medium low	Clothing
	Gas, water, and electricity
	Services (hotels, restaurants, etc.)
Low	Railroad
	Agriculture
	Trade

Note: This table is based on data from eleven countries for varying periods between 1915 and 1949. Strike propensity is in terms of man days lost related to the employment size of the industry. The countries are Australia, Czechoslovakia, Germany, Italy, the Netherlands, New Zealand, Norway, Sweden, Switzerland, the United Kingdom, and the United States.

Source: C. Kerr and A. Siegal, 'The inter-industry propensity to strike—an international comparison', in A. Kornhauser, R. Dubin and A. M. Ross (eds), *Industrial Conflict*, New York: McGraw-Hill, 1954.

generally and therefore some popular explanations of high strike rates, such as militant union leadership or bad human relations practices, are unlikely to be true of all cases. Rather, one must look for characteristics which are common to industries with a high propensity to strike but which at the same time distinguish them from industries with low strike rates. The most conspicuous of these is the location of the worker in society.

Industrial workers like miners and dockers tend to be members of relatively homogeneous communities which are socially and/or geographically isolated from the rest of the society. Whilst all workers have grievances, these workers have the same grievances against the same employers, at the same time and in the same place. Because of the absence of other forms of employment in the area they cannot respond to a conflict situation by changing jobs; and because there is little differentiation within the occupation such workers cannot improve their situation by gaining promotion to a more highly paid job. In such circumstances conflict tends to be intensified and it tends more often to take the form of strike action. In contrast workers in industries with low strike rates are typically members of occupationally heterogeneous communities. This means that they have the possibility of occupational choice, of changes in employment, and in addition very frequently the possibility of improving their situation by upward mobility within an occupation or industry. They belong to associations with heterogeneous membership and mix with others who have different grievances against different employers. In cases of industrial conflict there are strong pressures on both sides from neutrals to settle quickly and peaceably.

It is also noticeable that the industries with a high propensity to strike tend to be characterized by jobs which are physically difficult and unpleasant, relatively unskilled, and casual or seasonal. In contrast, the 'peaceful' industries tend to be characterized by jobs which are physically easier, skilled, responsible and steady. Strikes can therefore be expected to occur most frequently where there are large numbers of workers who are socially segregated and doing relatively unpleasant jobs.

These explanations cannot be regarded as accounting for all variations in inter-industry strike patterns. Some industries, steel for example, are much more strike prone in some countries than in others. They can, however, be related to the earlier discussion of trade unionism. It is especially in industries such as mining and dock work that the market and work situations of the employee, and indeed his status situation, lead to awareness of common interests over and against those of the employer. In addition, the structure of the industry and the community provide few, if any, alternatives to direct conflict with the employer if the worker is to improve his situation.

Industrial conflict, then, can and must be explained in terms of social structures. It is latent in all relations between employers and employees because they have conflicting interests in the price of labour and in the exercise of power in the enterprise, if for no other reasons. Differences in the degree and incidence of industrial conflict are to be explained in terms of the social situations of the parties (in particular in the market, work and status situations of the employee), and in terms of the nature and effectiveness of the institutionalized means for resolving such conflicts.

Social relations at the workplace

The pattern of relations between workers and managers at the workplace can to some extent be explained in the same terms as the pattern of industrial relations in a whole industry. The nature of the relevant industrial relations procedures, for example, is obviously reflected in social relations at this level but in order to explain differences between firms or between groups of workers within a firm a more detailed examination is necessary. In addition to such factors as the pattern of industrial relations in an industry or society as a whole one must consider factors which are characteristic of *particular* situations.

One of the most important of these differences between industries or firms is the type of production system. This may vary even within an industry, and can change quite radically over time. In industries without a standardized product, such as shipbuilding or printing, there is less possibility of extreme rationalization and production depends on the skills of the craftsman, who has considerable autonomy and can derive considerable intrinsic satisfaction from his work. On the motor car assembly line, in contrast, there is extreme fragmentation of tasks and the worker's job is characterized by a mechanically controlled work pace, extreme repetitiveness, a minimum of skill, predetermination of tools and techniques, and only surface demands on the worker's mental attention. In a process production industry, for example certain chemical plants, production is entirely mechanized but the worker may again have the possibility of deriving satisfaction from the responsibility of controlling the largely automated system.

'Craft' industries, mass production and process production differ not only in the extent to which the work offers intrinsic satisfaction, but also in the nature of social relations between workers. In craft industries workers of necessity interact on the job and share a common identity as high-status, skilled craftsmen. Process production operatives tend to be organized in work groups which are hierarchically structured internally and which make for a highly cohesive work organization. In marked contrast, workers on the assembly line tend to be tied to one place on the line and lack membership of a clearly defined work group.

Within a single plant the position of a group of workers in the production process is often relevant to its relations with other groups of workers and with management. In general, highly paid high-status groups tend to be 'conservative' in terms of industrial relations behaviour, only rarely using restrained pressure to redress a specific grievance. Those groups which are in the middle ranges of a factory status hierarchy tend to be more active in attempts to improve their relative status position. If such work groups are internally united their attempts are likely to be pursued as part of a consistent and well-organized 'strategy'; if the work groups are less cohesive their attempts to improve their position are likely to be more 'erratic' and less rational. Low-status groups, which generally lack cohesion or have a transient membership tend to be 'apathetic' in their relations with management.[6]

Among British coalminers it has also been shown that the high-status face workers were likely to take concerted action to secure their aims *vis-à-vis* management, while the lower-status haulage and surface workers expressed their dissatisfaction in high levels of absence.[7] The hierarchically structured work groups in the steel industry provide a further example of the importance of the occupational structure of the plant. Production workers in this industry can work up to more responsible and highly paid positions on the basis of seniority, and this is often considered to be an important reason for the relative stability of management–worker relations in the industry.

Thus the nature of the division of labour within a plant has important consequences for relations within and between groups of workers and between workers and management. It is closely related to technology but can vary independently of it. Indeed, several studies have shown how a different allocation of tasks within the same production system can lead to important differences in social relations and behaviour.

In any particular situation other factors may be more decisive than the technology and division of labour at the workplace. One such factor is the economic situation of the firm or industry. The stability of the demand for labour, the extent to which wages are a high proportion of total costs, and the degree to which competition makes for pressure to reduce labour costs are also important considerations for management–worker relations. Certain industries, for example shipbuilding, have been characterized by considerable instability of employment. The relatively high levels of conflict between different occupational groups (demarcation disputes) and between workers and management in this 'craft' industry must be seen in the light of this instability and the continuing preoccupation with the supply of work. By contrast, in an oil refinery, where labour costs are a relatively small proportion of total costs and employment is very stable, there is a good basis for 'productivity bargaining'. In such cases the already relatively peaceful management–worker relations can be improved by an offer of considerably higher rates of pay in exchange for alterations in working practices.

Equally important are the expectations of the workers themselves. These expectations are partly a result of socialization into the workplace (most notably in apprenticeship) and of membership in work groups. To a significant extent, however, they are also a consequence of the situation of the worker outside the workplace and the roles he plays in the family, the community and the class structure. The traditional working-class communities of coalminers, dockworkers and others have been characterized by norms of solidarity with fellow workers and by antagonism towards 'them'—employers, managers and others in authority. This orientation, as well as being a part of the explanation of higher strike rates in these industries, was reflected in workplace relationships.

A rather different example of the importance of the workers' expectations and orientation to work comes from a study of assembly-line workers in a motor car factory in Luton.[8] It might have been expected that these workers would be dissatisfied with their situation and hostile to management because of the nature of their tasks and the difficulty of establishing any stable personal relations with others at work. Such findings have been reported in American studies of assembly-line workers. In the Luton case, however, although there was dissatisfaction with the actual *tasks* to be done, the workers were satisfied with their *jobs* and relatively favourably disposed towards management. Because of their desire to maintain a particular style of life, and in the absence of any contrary pressures in the relatively recently established communities in which they lived, these workers had sought the highest paid jobs available to anyone with their particular abilities and qualifications. Their demands from their work were financial and they did not seek either intrinsically interesting tasks or the satisfactions of having close personal relations with fellow workers. Because their employment by and large met the demands they made of it, they felt no particular antagonism towards management (nor any particular loyalty to the firm). In a situation of full employment they were, to a marked extent, a self-selected labour force. This selection had been made, to their general satisfaction, in terms of a prior orientation to work, and only in terms of this could their attitudes and behaviour at work be understood.

Any study of management–worker relations, even at the face-to-face level in a particular factory or workshop, has to take into account not only the characteristics of the situation itself, but also the 'external' influences upon it. More generally, the pattern of industrial relations at any level—plant, industry or society—can only be understood and explained if it is related to the structure of the wider society.

Industrial relations in modernizing societies

This chapter has so far been confined to industrial societies since it is in these societies that relationships between employers and employees become significant. With the increasing importance of employment in modernizing societies, however, relations of production bearing some similarity to those we have been discussing begin to emerge. In many modernizing societies—most of Africa for example—industrial employment is still relatively rare and employer–employee relations are to be found principally in mining, on the railways and in plantation agriculture. Large-scale mining and plantation agriculture have invariably been developed in the first instance by white settlers or overseas companies; in other words the entrepreneurial activity came from persons and companies with a background of an industrial society. Skilled manual labour, too, has in the past been mainly immigrant labour, especially in South and Central Africa where skilled occupations were, and in South Africa still are, open only to whites. Much of the semi-skilled and unskilled labour of African mines and plantations has been provided by African migrants of varying degrees of permanence. Sometimes they travel annually to spend part of the year in the towns; sometimes they stay for several years, returning to their rural home and their families only when they have earned enough money to pay required taxes or to buy desired consumer goods. Such migrant labour is cheaper and easier for the employer to control than a more stable labour force; its lack of permanence and, in colonial and southern Africa its political subordination, provide no basis for the emergence of powerful trade unions. The relative inefficiency of migrant labour, however, has encouraged some mining companies to introduce elaborate selection and training schemes in an attempt to raise levels of productivity.

Throughout Africa, the northern half of Latin America and, with few exceptions, Asia the proportion of the population engaged in industrial activities is very small. To the extent that industrialization spreads, an increasing number of workers will become permanently dependent upon employment for their livelihood. There is no reason to suppose, however, that the particular course of development which we have surveyed in the industrial West will necessarily be followed elsewhere. Indeed, in the most important example to date of industrialization in a non-Western society—Japan—the growth of the factory system of production has led to a very different pattern of social relations.[9] In spite of a general expectation of permanent employer–employee relations, traditional norms and values have a continuing influence. Employees are recruited at the end of their full-time education. Many employers recruit from a limited number of sources and look especially for workers who have the 'right' personal qualities, who will be 'stable', and who will fit easily into the traditional employer–employee relationship. *Personal* contacts between firms and the schools, colleges and universities are important in this process. The level of education attained determines the level at which the employee enters the firm and the range of positions open to him. Subsequent promotion to such positions depends partly on ability but also on age and length of service (which are closely related). The pattern of payment is similar and a considerable proportion of the total pay packet is determined by factors like age, status and family responsibilities. In addition, larger employers customarily provide a wide range of non-pecuniary benefits, such as subsidized housing, company medical services, and so on. Thus paternalism, kinship and hierarchy, all of which were very important in traditional Japanese society, are reflected in the social relations even of modern Japanese factories. Even large firms, where face-to-face contact between the employer and all employees is impossible, are in many respects 'family-like'.

Important aspects of traditional social relations have survived Japan's rapid industrialization; the factory system of production has been moulded to conform with them. In some respects such a system may appear 'inefficient'. It is not possible for a firm to dismiss employees (with the exception of the small proportion of temporaries) just because they are incompetent or because trade is slack; the payment system too, emphasizes loyalty and commitment to the firm rather than rewarding individual effort and efficiency. The expectations of employers and employees, however, are very different from those common in a society like Britain and, because of the mutual obligation to maintain their relationship for the whole of the employee's working life, some of the grounds for conflict which we have discussed may be less strongly felt. Certainly Japan's comparative industrial performance during the last two decades does not suggest that such a pattern is necessarily less effective in terms of production than that of the West. In Japanese industry trade unions have rather different functions from those described for Britain. With such a close family-like relationship between employer and employee there is little room for a third party. So, although unions are formally quite strong, they tend to be unimportant at the plant and shop-floor level, having as their main function bargaining with the employer about the level of the twice yearly bonus.

The example of Japan should make us aware of the possibility of alternative paths of industrial development from that followed by the Western world. The Soviet Union, with its heavy involvement of the state in the industrialization process is a clear example of yet another course. So even if the contemporary modernizing societies undergo a process of industrialization—and in the short run at least this is by no means inevitable—there is no reason to expect the actual course of events to approximate to earlier industrialization experiences.

Such developments in industrial relations as have taken place already show some very clear differences. The way in which trade unionism has developed in Africa, for example, can only be understood in the light of the total structure and development of African societies. Under colonial administrations any form of union activity tended to be seen by the government as subversive, especially if it was action by government employees. Inevitably, therefore, unions became involved to a greater or lesser extent in opposition to the government and so in the struggle for independence. In some colonies, such as Kenya, the trade-union movement acted as a substitute for the banned nationalist party although it had to pursue non-militant industrial policies in order to avoid being banned itself. In others, like the Gold Coast and Tanganyika, the nationalist party secured dominance over the union movement (though not without some resistance from established union leaders) and the two were seen as part of the same campaign for independence. In either case the wider problems of colonialism provided a context for union growth which encouraged direct political action on the part of the unions. Very often the unions of the newly independent countries were more political bodies than economic.

In Latin America, too, despite the absence of widespread formal colonialism this century, developments have been far from identical with those of the West. Here many of the 'feudal' personal relationships which had been developed between patron and peasant in the rural areas were carried over into the urban industrial situation. The employer was often seen as the provider of protection and services in return for which the employee gave his political loyalty. These personal loyalties cut across class lines so that the unions were more mechanisms for the mobilization of political support and for the provision of medical, legal and other services for their members than agencies of conflict. (Perhaps one should point out that there has also been a group of unions, made up mostly of immigrants from Europe, which has not had this personalist orientation and which has functioned more as an agency of conflict between classes.)

In both Africa and Latin America the contemporary economic situation is one of very considerable unemployment and/or underemployment. One of the consequences of this is that the bargaining power of the industrial workers is very weak (except where their skills are scarce or where they are protected by discriminatory legislation). This, combined with the usually slow growth of industrial occupations, has two correlates. First, the employed workers who form the trade unions are among the economically privileged, and the unions are concerned with protecting their members against new migrants to the towns rather than with protecting them against the employers (and often the state is the main employer anyway). Second, there is a widespread recognition that economic action by the unions is unlikely to prove an effective way of improving their position; political action may be a much quicker road to success. So there are contemporary reasons as well as historical ones why many union movements—especially but not only those in Latin America—are deeply and *directly* involved in the political process. They may even provide the main source of support for the government and in Latin America some unions have even been formed by politicians seeking to create a basis for power.

Enough has been said to show that the nature and development of industrial relations can vary widely. The differences in the development of industrial relations so far are at least as significant as the similarities, and future developments are likely to be different again. Any further industrialization of the modernizing world will add to the already vast variety of human social situations. For the sociologist, this variety provides an opportunity to use comparative methods to increase our understanding of the nature and causes of the different social relations between employers and employees.

Notes

1 Children's Employment Commission, quoted in H. D. Fong, *The Triumph of the Factory System in England*, Tientsin: Chihli Press, 1930.
2 See Lloyd Warner and J. O. Low, *Yankee City*, New Haven: Yale University Press, 1963.
3 D. Lockwood, *The Blackcoated Worker*, London: Allen & Unwin, 1958. The following discussion summarizes Lockwood's argument on trade unionism.
4 The figures in this table and the discussion of them are based on A. M. Ross and P. T. Hartman, *Changing Patterns of Industrial Conflict*, New York: Wiley, 1960.
5 C. Kerr and A. J. Siegel, 'The inter-industry propensity to strike—an international comparison', in A. Kornhauser, R. Dubin and A. M. Ross (eds), *Industrial Conflict*, New York: McGraw-Hill, 1954. The following discussion is based largely on this source.
6 L. R. Sayles, *Behaviour of Industrial Work Groups*, New York: Wiley, 1958.
7 W. H. Scott *et al.*, *Coal and Conflict*, Liverpool University Press, 1963.
8 F. Bechoffer, J. H. Goldthorpe, D. Lockwood and Jennifer Platt, *The Affluent Worker: Industrial Attitudes and Behaviour*, Cambridge University Press, 1968.
9 J. C. Abegglen, *The Japanese Factory*, Chicago: Free Press, 1960.

Reading

Bendix, R., *Work and Authority in Industry*, New York: Harper, 1963. A study of industrialization in eighteenth- and nineteenth-century Britain and Russia and twentieth-century America and East Germany which contrasts the ideologies through which managers have sought to justify their authority over their employees.

Davies, I., *African Trade Unions*, Harmondsworth: Penguin, 1966. A survey of the development and functions of trade unions in Africa.

Flanders, A. (ed.), *Collective Bargaining*, Harmondsworth: Penguin, 1969. This wide-ranging collection of papers on industrial relations covers a number of societies and gives a good idea of current approaches to the subject.

Gouldner, A. W., *Patterns of Industrial Bureaucracy*, London: Routledge & Kegan Paul, 1955, and *Wild Cat Strike*, London: Routledge & Kegan Paul, 1955. Gouldner studied a gypsum plant during a period in which the management attempted to introduce more bureaucratic means of control and traced the consequences for manager-worker relations. Each book is self-contained, though they describe different aspects of the same situation.

Hyman, R., *Strikes*, London: Fontana/Collins, 1972. An account of industrial conflict in Britain and an incisive critique of explanations of it.

Lockwood, D., *The Blackcoated Worker*, London: Allen & Unwin, 1958. A study of class consciousness which includes an important chapter on trade unionism among clerical workers. Already a 'classic'.

Parker, S. R. *et al.*, *The Sociology of Industry*, London: Allen & Unwin, 1972. An introduction to the whole field of industrial sociology which indicates the scope of the subject and includes suggestions for more detailed reading.

Further reading

Baldamus, W., *Efficiency and Effort*, London: Tavistock, 1961. An important theoretical analysis of the nature and consequences of industrial conflict.

Blauner, R., *Alienation and Freedom*, Chicago University Press, 1964. The author compares the worker's situation in four industries (printing, textiles, motor car assembly, chemicals) which have contrasting technologies.

Burns, T. (ed.), *Industrial Man*, Harmondsworth: Penguin, 1969. This excellent collection of articles and extracts is designed to indicate the range of influences of industrialization on societies.

Eldridge, J. E. T., *Industrial Disputes*, London: Routledge & Kegan Paul, 1968. This volume contains some general essays on industrial conflict and detailed studies of disputes in shipbuilding, the steel industry and the constructional engineering industry.

Goldthorpe, J. H. *et al.*, *The Affluent Worker: Industrial Attitudes and Behaviour*, Cambridge University Press, 1968. A study of workers in three different industries which is of interest in itself and for its critical comments on previous analyses of workers' attitudes and behaviour.

Lupton, T., *On the Shop Floor*, London: Pergamon, 1963. A detailed comparison of two workshop situations. Lupton suggests a range of internal and external factors which need to be taken into account to explain the workers' different responses to incentive payment systems.

Sayles, L. R., *Behaviour of Industrial Work Groups*, New York: Wiley, 1958. An extensive comparison of 'work groups' in which grievance behaviour is related to the workers' varied positions in the production process.

13 Religion

In all societies there are rules of behaviour, ideals of perfection, explanations of disasters and illnesses, and theories concerning the origin of man and the world. Frequently these rules and explanations are related to what we would call supernatural forces. Religion consists of belief in such forces and of the activities which result, directly or indirectly, from this belief. In some societies the belief is the most important thing; in others ritualistic actions are dominant. But different societies have different rules and explanations; phenomena explained by religion in one society may have a non-religious explanation in another; activities which have profound religious implications in one society may have none in another. Whilst this has always been the case, the very rapid social change which has occurred in the world in the last three hundred or so years shows the differences particularly clearly.

The history of mankind may be viewed as the gradual extension of human control over the physical environment. This process has become less and less gradual and the extensions of this control which have occurred even within our own lifetime are enormous. Through the activities of science we can, for example, understand (and therefore prevent or cure) many diseases which in the past were (and in some societies are still) explained in supernatural terms. One of the results of this is that in many spheres scientific explanations have superseded religious ones and, in many ways, modern industrial societies are less religious than were pre-industrial societies. One should however, beware of presenting scientific or 'natural' explanations and religious explanations as alternatives since they have existed side by side in all known societies.

We are chiefly interested, however, in the social conditions under which different types of religious organization flourish and for this purpose we must look at religion in different types of societies and, in complex societies, among different sections of the population. And we must expect to find considerable differences; for although religious activities and beliefs are to be found in, say, industrial societies, they are rarely of the kind that suggest that one's wife will be barren unless an ox is sacrificed at the wedding.

Religion in simple societies

In simple societies people as a rule believe that all activities are under the control of 'supernatural' forces which may intervene to alter the course of events. These forces may take the form of supreme gods, fetishes (material objects, for example statues, believed to have inherent powers), personal spirits, or totems (usually a species of animal with which the members of a clan or descent group are linked). But in addition to such beliefs all simple societies exhibit religious rituals which may be much more important than the beliefs, although the two are usually related. Rituals and beliefs involve the whole community and permeate the whole of life so that, in a very real sense, one can describe these societies as religious societies.

In simple societies a good deal of time and energy is taken up with attempting to influence the gods, spirits or whatever, and there are invariably prescribed ways of doing this. It is convenient to distinguish two main aspects of religious ritual. The first is in the nature of ceremonial which marks important occasions in the life of an individual or a group. Such occasions often mark changes in legal or social position and can best be summed up by the French term *rites de passage* which has been adopted untranslated into English usage to refer to just such occasions. The second aspect of religious ritual is concerned primarily with the well-being of individual members of the society but may also be related to the well-being of society as a whole.

A good example of the first aspect of ritual can be found in the description by the anthropologist Peter Farb of the ceremonies surrounding the initiation into manhood of boys among the Indian bands of southern California.[1]

> Several youths of puberty age were gathered at night into a special enclosure where they drank a concoction prepared from the roots of Jimsonweed. The effects of the drug lasted from two to four days. During that time the initiates experienced visions of spirits, which they believed gave them supernatural powers. Later the initiates had to descend into a pit dug in the ground, symbolic of death, and then climb out again, supposedly indicating rebirth. Inside the pit they had to jump from one flat stone to another, and if a boy stumbled, that clearly indicated a short life for him. They were put through several physical ordeals; the severest one was to lie motionless while being bitten repeatedly by hordes of angry ants. As ordeal passed to new ordeal throughout the ceremony, the candidate received long lectures on proper conduct, on how to become a man of value, and on the religious practices of his band.

In addition to initiation rites, the ceremonies surrounding marriage, childbirth, and death are invariably marked in simple societies (as in modern societies) by solemn ritual. Similarly with the great occasions of the whole community. In agricultural societies the most important events are those connected with the crops and one finds seedtime, the coming of the rains, and especially harvest are usually times of great religious festivals. Thus among the Akan people of Ghana and the Trobriand islanders of the Pacific the yam festival is the great annual gathering.

But these rites and ceremonies not only mark the passing from one period of the farming year to the next, or from one status in an individual's life to the next (for example, childhood to adulthood). They are also believed to be necessary in ensuring success in the next stage. Thus agricultural rites ensure the fertility of the soil; marriage rites ensure the fertility of the women. One can see here the second aspect of rites—that of securing the assistance of supernatural forces in the ordinary events of daily life. We find ritual behaviour particularly intense, however, in situations of danger, at times of illness, or when the normally benevolent gods turn nasty—for example in time of famine: in short, when the well-being of an individual or a community is threatened. In societies with a high level of belief in the supernatural, illness or a great calamity such as famine or defeat in battle is often thought to be brought about by some fault in the individual or community concerned. The gods or spirits have been wronged and matters cannot be set right until the wrong has in some way been atoned. This may involve the performance of a specific ritual or it may involve the whole society in the adoption of a more moral way of life. The story of the people of Israel as told in the Old Testament is full of such incidents. For example:[2]

> And the Lord sent fiery serpents among the people and they bit the people; and much people of Israel died. Therefore the people came to Moses and said, We have sinned for we have spoken against the Lord and against thee; pray unto the Lord that he take away the serpents from us. And Moses prayed for the people. And the Lord said unto Moses, Make thee a fiery serpent and set it upon a pole: and it shall come to pass that every one that is bitten, when he looketh upon it, shall live. And Moses made a serpent of brass, and put it upon a pole, and it came to pass, that if a serpent had bitten any man, when he beheld the serpent of brass, he lived.

Indeed, the reader of the Old Testament is struck by the way in which the whole history of Israel seems to be a cycle of disobedience to God; a crisis of some sort, interpreted as a punishment; atonement either by sacrifice or by the reinstitution a moral way of life; followed by success in battle or in some other material field.

It is at such times of crisis that the power of the religious specialist is at its height. His knowledge of what it is the gods require—moral behaviour, sacrifices, performance of ritual, etc.—gives him power to command obedience. Once again the Old Testament provides us with many illustrations of the efficacy of religion in obtaining adherence to the rule of law. An example of a threatening God will perhaps suffice:[3]

> Behold I set before you this day a blessing and a curse; A blessing if ye obey the commandments of the Lord your God, which I command you this day: And a curse, if ye will not obey the commandments of the Lord your God.

In a society where there is belief in divine retribution the religious specialist therefore has considerable power and is often, as was the case with Moses, the political leader as well.

This second aspect of ritual is not, in essentials, different for a community in trouble through famine or war than for a sick individual. The problem is to find out in what way one's behaviour has been lacking and to correct the fault. Such is the propensity of man not to live up to his ideals that the resultant searchings of conscience invariably reveal such inadequacies. Nevertheless, it is not always possible to locate personal or communal behaviour which has angered the gods or spirits. An alternative supernatural explanation is that evil influences are seeking to do the sick man or the community harm. Frequently these evil influences are conceived of in human terms or as spirits who take possession of human beings thus giving rise to the phenomena of witches and witchcraft.

If it is not recognized that misfortune can occur by chance, witchcraft provides an acceptable explanation for undeserved misfortune. One of the earliest and best studies of witchcraft—that of witchcraft among the Azande (a tribe of the Sudan-Congo border) carried out by the anthropologist Evans-Pritchard—also showed that belief in witchcraft is by no means incompatible with what we should call natural explanations. There are obvious 'natural' explanations of death caused when a charging elephant treads upon a human being. What is not so obvious is why the paths of the elephant and that particular man should have coincided. Once chance is eliminated as an explanation the man might well ask, 'what have I done to deserve this?' If the answer is 'nothing' the only other explanation provided by the belief system of societies such as the Azande is that the man concerned was the victim of witchcraft. In cases of death of this kind or in cases of illness, attempts may be made to identify the witch through whom the evil was passed and those who had recently quarrelled with the victim were the first to be accused. So along with witchcraft one invariably finds counter-witchcraft which may take the form of trials followed by the execution of the guilty.

Witchcraft beliefs and activities, then, relate to a personification of forces of evil (and/or good) in human beings. But in some societies such forces are also believed to inhere in inanimate substances and can therefore be used to force confession by the guilty or to judge the innocence or guilt of a suspect. This is another of the ways in which the supernatural is invoked in support of the rule of law in simpler societies. An eye-witness account of such a trial may help to convey something of the nature of such societies. The description is of a trial by ordeal (of boiling oil) of a young man in Liberia accused of theft.[4]

> Keke (the diviner) would allow no one to assist him in the smallest detail of preparing for the trial. He had a skin pouch slung over his shoulder, his *baka* which contained his medicine and magic. This was the tangible source of his power, his link with the supernatural, and it must not be contaminated by anyone's touch.
>
> Finally, he had everything just the way he wanted it, the fire properly hot, a three legged iron ring over it to support an enormous clay pot, the supply of rich red palm oil to be heated, the polished brass belled anklet which Comma was to pluck from the bottom of the pot, and a kettle full of leaves which he had bruised in a mortar until they were an arsenic green paste.
>
> Keke now placed the ordeal pot in the iron stand over the fire and poured the palm oil into it. [He] made a long oration while the oil was heating. Keke then talked to the pot, and told it that, if Comma had not stolen, it must not hurt him in the least, but that if he had spoiled the Loma name along with his own, it must bite him deep. Keke next addressed Comma, telling him that he could refuse the trial, confess without the ordeal if he wished and take the punishment the Old Ones would decide. Comma shook his head, indicated that the trial should go on. Keke next took the paste of leaves and smeared it in a thick coating over Comma's right hand and arm, being careful to get it between all the fingers. Then he held up

> the three-knobbed brass ring and spoke at length about it. The paste of leaves was meanwhile drying into a crust over Comma's hand. It had turned a shade of sage-green where it was thinnest. There was less smoke coming off the oil now and it was less blue in colour. After another coating of the paste was rubbed on Comma, the brass anklet was dropped into the pot. Quick as a flash, Comma dived his hand in after it and brought it up, dripping oil as red as blood. A great collective sigh swept like a wind through the crowd and then the roar of approval and triumph. They carried him off to the waterside on their shoulders.

The main context for the discussion so far has been tribal societies, but there is much that has been said that is equally relevant to a consideration of religion in more complex societies. Trial by ordeal, for example, was a common feature of medieval Europe and beliefs in witchcraft and the persecution of those suspected of being witches persisted well into the eighteenth century. In Scotland the last known burning for witchcraft took place in 1722 and the widespread belief in witches certainly lasted until much later. Similarly it is not difficult to find examples from contemporary Europe of a belief in the efficacy of ritual and magical actions to avert calamities or to influence deities in the distribution of their favours. The following newspaper report is of an incident which took place in May 1967.[5]

> Several thousand Neapolitans prayed throughout the day in the Church of St. Clare that the blood of St. Janarius should liquefy and thus save Naples from what the praying crowds think will be a great disaster. By sunset the small flask of the saint's congealed blood had failed to bubble. St. Janarius was a bishop who was beheaded in 305, somewhere near Naples. In the fifteenth century it was observed that a four inch glass flask, said to contain his blood, would liquefy if there were fervent prayers said to it and, at the same time, its failure to liquefy could only mean disaster. When the dark substance failed to liquefy in 1527 Naples was ravaged by plague; in 1569 there was famine; in 1835 the miracle did not occur and there was cholera. In 1941, the blood remained solid and Allied war planes bombed Naples. In 1943 the blood liquefied ahead of programme—also a bad omen—and Vesuvius erupted the following year.
>
> When the miracle had not taken place late last night, Archbishop Corrado Ursi ordered the reliquary containing the blood to be carried through the streets so that motorists and other Neapolitans could add their prayers to the city's patron saint that Naples be spared the threatened and still unknown calamity.

Despite such evidence of belief and ritual concerning supernatural intervention in daily life which shows a marked similarity with the religious life of simple societies, there have been numerous and important changes in the religion of European societies especially over the last four hundred years. One of these changes has been the marked decline of such beliefs and rituals both in the society as a whole and within the churches. But in order to understand such changes we must first look briefly at the changes which have occurred in the organization of religion, and we shall draw our illustrations from the Christian religion.

The social sources of religious differences

The most striking change in the organization of religion in Western Europe in the last four hundred years has been the break-up of the monolithic Christian Church into a diversity of sects and denominations. This proliferation of Christian groups can be better understood by looking at differences in the relations between religious institutions and the wider society and also at certain differences in the internal organization of religion. It is convenient and helpful to distinguish between three main types of religious organization: sect, denomination and church. These distinctions allow us to see more clearly the different functions performed by religious institutions in different social situations. The basic distinction, made more than fifty years ago by the German theologian Ernst Troeltsch between church-type institutions and sect-type institutions has subsequently proved to be one of the most useful tools with which to analyse the forms which Western Christianity has taken. The difference between the two, says Troeltsch, is quite clear:[6]

> The church is that type of organization which is overwhelmingly conservative, which to a certain extent accepts the secular order and dominates the masses; in principle, therefore, it is universal, that is it desires to cover the whole life of humanity. The sects, on the

> other hand, are comparatively small groups; they aspire after inward personal perfection and they aim at a direct personal fellowship between the members of each group. From the very beginning, therefore, they are forced to organize themselves in small groups, and to renounce the idea of dominating the world. Their attitude towards the world, the State, and society may be indifferent, tolerant, or hostile, since they have no desire to control and incorporate these forms of social life; on the contrary they tend to avoid them.

Because of these different relationships with the wider society the two types tend to attract different types of people. The fully developed church utilizes, or even dominates, the state and becomes an integral and supportive part of the social order. Because of this the church tends to become identified with the upper classes (although its membership is made up of all classes). The sects, on the other hand, are connected with those elements in society which are opposed to the state or at least indifferent to it, in most cases the lower classes or peasantry.

To this basic distinction between sect and church it is useful to add a third type of religious organization—the denomination. The denomination combines some of the characteristics of the sect with others of the church and also has characteristics possessed by neither of the other two. Thus the denomination compromises with the secular world (for example with regard to ethical standards) but does not seek to dominate it; it seeks neither the domination of the world nor the domination of its members; it has voluntary membership but at the same time it is an educative institution, laying less stress on particular (usually experiential) characteristics of its members than does the sect. Finally, the denomination differs from both sect and church in its tolerance of other beliefs, even to the extent of allowing that they may possess some part of the truth. The major characteristics of these three types of religious institution are summarized in Figure 13.1.

A scheme such as this allows us not only to observe differences between religious organizations but also provides a framework whereby we can observe the changes and/or schisms which particular institutions can undergo. It helps us to describe such differences and changes. Christianity itself, for example, began in a sectarian form, evolving a church-type organization only with its

Figure 13.1 The sect; the church; the denomination

	SECT	DENOMINATION	CHURCH
Attitude to wider society	Rejects values and way of life	Compromise: no attempt to dominate society	Compromise: seeks to dominate the whole society
Attitude of wider society	Ostracized	Either fashionable or neglected	Fashionable
Attitude to other religious groups	Intolerant	Tolerant	Intolerant
Attitude to members	Ideological and social domination of members	Ideological and social influence over members	Concentrates on domination of world not of members
Type of membership	Voluntary	Voluntary	Obligatory therefore large
Basis of membership	Experiential (exclusive)	Loose formal membership requirements	No membership requirements other than ritualistic
Social background of members	Typically the deprived	Middle classes	All inclusive; but leaders are wealthy and powerful
Scope	Local	National (or international)	National (or international)
Internal organization	Often charismatic	Bureaucratic	Bureaucratic

adoption as the official religion of the Roman Empire. But the church-sect-denomination typology does not in itself explain why such differences exist between one Christian body and another; still less why an organization should change from, say, a sect-type institution to a denomination. The typology merely draws our attention to certain characteristics which may be important in explanation.

The changes within Christianity in the last four hundred years provide rich material for investigating these phenomena. The Reformation and subsequent changes reflect the religious expression of newly emerging power groups and the religious protest of economically and politically deprived sections of the population. By and large the former, for example the nationalistic rulers of the German states, adopted a churchly form of organization and doctrine (such as Lutheranism), whereas the deprived adopted a sectarian form (such as the Anabaptist movement). Thus the emergence of Lutheranism or Calvinism is best understood from the sociological point of view as being the religious expression respectively of the German princes and the rising middle classes of Geneva. The German princes had a political need to be independent of the religious (and political) influence of the Pope. Consequently they championed Luther and made his cause their own. In doing so they entrenched Lutheranism as an established church predominantly serving the aristocracy and wealthy members of society. Not that Luther himself was especially notable for his love of the poor, particularly if they showed signs of attempting to alter their position. 'Remember', he wrote in his pamphlet *Against the Thieving and Murderous Hordes of Peasants*, 'that nothing can be more poisonous, harmful and devilish than a revolutionary.' Thus the peasants of Germany soon made the discovery that the new Protestantism was a protest not against their masters but against their masters' enemies.

With this disillusionment there arose the first sect of Protestantism—the Anabaptists. It was a movement made up from the peasants and poorer craftsmen; from those who were both economically and politically powerless. As has so often been the case when a depressed group has no chance of political or economic protest open to them, their activities were turned into religious channels. The Anabaptists were poorly organized and lacking in adequate leadership and they failed to survive the extreme persecution to which they were subjected. But the pattern of open religious rebellion of the poor and powerless was to be repeated again and again throughout the next two hundred years in Europe and North America. In seventeenth-century England the Quakers emerged as a form of religious expression of the radical poor; in the eighteenth century the Methodists drew their support largely from the new urban working classes (although their leaders were from a very different social background). Both groups had in common a rapid accommodation to the wider society, swift compromise with some of their original principles and a rapid retreat into respectability. A revolutionary fervour is difficult to maintain for long, and the Quakers soon abandoned their revolutionary ideals of a new social order and instead attempted to ameliorate the effects of the old order by providing mutual aid to their members and later by engaging in social reform. The Methodists, in common with many other new religious formations of the poor (a good later example is the Salvation Army), found that the religious discipline they imposed upon their members resulted, over decades, in a betterment in the social position of those members so that the social composition of Methodism became increasingly middle-class and the nature of their religious requirements changed accordingly. In short, the tendency of many sectarian institutions like early Methodism is to become more and more denominational. Less emphasis is laid upon the peculiar characteristics of members whether in the sphere of doctrine (such as the demand for a conversion experience) or in the field of morality (such as the requirement of total abstinence). They become increasingly respectable, middle-class and tolerant, a tolerance which in the case of Methodism has led to a serious consideration of the prospects of union with other denominations, particularly with the Church of England. Indeed, in all of the features referred to in Figure 13.1, many (but not all) sects lose their original characteristics and become denominations.

The fervour, spontaneity and political violence of the earlier European sects are sometimes repeated when Christianity is exported to modernizing societies. Once again one can see the relationship between the deprivation of sections of the population and the emergence of millennial movements of a sectarian nature. In these societies, however, there are usually additional factors in that those in positions of secular power have often been aliens, and the societies have been undergoing very rapid social change.

In southern Africa many of the 'Ethiopian'

churches broke away from their parent bodies in more or less open protest against the colour bar in the existing churches. Moreover, in most of the modernizing world in the first half of the twentieth century, colonialism resulted in a distribution of power which effectively excluded the possibility of political action by the mass of the population. In this situation, as in Europe earlier, protest frequently took a religious form; the religious breakaway was often symptomatic of a more deep-seated desire for political freedom. A millennial remedy was offered for the political and economic evils under which the Africans were suffering and, depending upon the situation, this could function either to divert attention from material problems on to transcendental ends or to bring these same material problems into sharper focus.

The Messianic movements of Africa have, by and large, functioned in the latter manner. They have been closely bound up with ideas of independent rule and are often inseparable from the early nationalist movements. The Zulu uprising of 1906 found the Ethiopian preachers a ready channel of communication and their pulpits were used to incite the people to rebellion; the Shire Highlands uprising against British rule in Nyasaland in 1915 derived directly from the religious ferment of the Watchtower movement; and it was a Messianic movement among the Kikuyu which sparked off the Mau Mau uprisings in Kenya in the 1950s.

One of the most interesting, and certainly one of the best documented, of these movements that broke away from the orthodox Christianity of the the missions was that founded in the region of the lower Congo by Simon Kimbangu. It serves well as an illustration.[7] Kimbangu had been brought up in a Protestant mission and worked for some time as a catechist. He first became widely known as a prophet with gifts of healing in the year 1921. He upheld many of the principles of the Christian missions by requiring the destruction of fetishes and by forbidding polygamy and 'obscene' dancing. His fame and following spread rapidly, to the initial delight of the Protestant missions who regarded him as an ally. The interpretation put upon the Biblical (usually Old Testament) passages which were so central to his teaching, however, was primarily anti-European and especially anti-colonial, so that his followers were soon proclaiming him to be the God of the Black Man in contrast to the Christ of the Missionaries. In keeping with the Biblical imagery, the village he came from was renamed Jerusalem; Kimbangu himself was referred to as a 'saviour'; and he appointed twelve apostles to follow him.

The anti-European element in his preaching soon led him into trouble with the government authorities. He encouraged his followers to defy the government and to refuse to work for Europeans, telling them that this would force the Belgians to leave the country which in turn would bring the millennium. In the end he was arrested and deported by a government which saw no political implications in their actions and he died behind bars in 1950. But, as is often the case, the martyrdom of the leader merely added to the success of the movement. Kimbangu's identification of himself with the sufferings of Moses and Jesus became more real and his successors were able to continue his call for emancipation from white domination.

After his initial deportation the movement was driven underground under the leadership of André Matswa, a Congolese who had fought in France in the first world war and had also been involved in French trade union politics. Like Kimbangu, Matswa was arrested and deported and his death in 1942 raised expectations among his followers of a triumphant, liberating return. The persons of Kimbangu and Matswa thus provided a focus which made the messages of Christianity relevant to the situation of the Congolese. Kimbanguism drew on the Judaeo-Christian tradition of an oppressed people liberated by a Messiah who, in spite of martyrdom, triumphed over his enemies and promised a kingdom in which the injustices of this world would be set right. At the same time, however, it provided its own martyrs with their message of special relevance to the African colonial situation. Orthodox Christianity was seen as a religion which served to keep wealth and power in the hands of the white man and was thus in direct contrast to the message of Kimbangu.

The vitality of the Kimbangu movement and its offshoots can be seen by the reaction to two very different events. The first of them was the arrival in the Congo in 1935 of the Salvation Army. With its interest in humanitarian matters and its lack of connection with the government, the Salvation Army quickly became popular at the expense of the older missions. Moreover, the similarity of some of its emphases to the teaching of Kimbangu —especially the opposition to 'magic' and fetishism —and the appeal of uniforms, flags, drums and bands attracted many Kimbanguists to the Army. Among some of them there formed the belief that these European men and women were the reincarnation of the spirit of Simon Kimbangu and that the letter S worn on the uniform was the insignia of their prophet. Later the Kimbanguist element separated under a new leader, Simon Pierre Mpadi, to form the *Mission des Noirs*, organized on Salvation Army lines and often known as the 'khaki movement' from their khaki uniforms. Here the Kimbangu element became explicit: 'God gave us Simon Kimbangu who is for us what Moses is to the Jews, Christ to white men, and Mahommed to Arabs.'

The second wave of reaction that is of particular interest was to the German invasion and occupation of Belgium in the second world war. Pro-German factions resulted in a new sect proclaiming that the defeat of Belgium heralded the final withdrawal of the Belgian colonial government and the arrival of the millennium preached by Kimbangu. More recently the movement has become more respectable and the local groups have gathered together in a single organization, the *Église de Jésus Christ sur la Terre par le Prophète Simon Kimbangu.* The *Église* now claims to be a non-political religious sect although the favourite texts remained those which denounce the oppressive practices of the white man. During the nationalistic uprisings which preceded independence the *Église* was active in organizing boycotts of the missions, illustrating once again the close relationship between religion and politics in colonial Africa.

The story of Kimbanguism illustrates the two possible functions of religious movements with regard to anti-European, anti-colonial feeling. One possibility is that they may act as a safety valve, diverting protest into religious rather than political channels. As such they provide an alternative to total submission to the ruling (and in this case alien) power. The other is that the protest against the government may be expressed directly through the religious organizations in which case the sects themselves become the organizing agents of political protest.

Some of the most spectacular religious reactions to a situation combining economic and political deprivation with sweeping social changes are to be found in the island regions of the Southern Pacific. Cargo cults (the name derives from the importance placed upon the acquisition by the indigenous people of the 'cargo' or material goods of the white man) have sprung up all over Melanesia and Polynesia with remarkable regularity, at least since the 1870s. With the arrival of the white man and his cargo boats, the coastal inhabitants of New Guinea and the smaller islands were faced with a totally new situation: large numbers of white men accompanied by crates of extraordinary objects. The cargo cults were the immediate reaction of the coastal peoples, but further inland change was much longer delayed and only with the coming of aeroplanes in the 1930s did the arrival of European goods create the conditions for this type of religious reaction. The details differ from cult to cult but they have in common a belief in a millennium which will occur with the return of the ancestors who will bring with them European goods and plentiful supplies of food so that there will be no need for further work. The consequent abandoning of the fields by the workers was one among several factors which made the cults unpopular with the colonial governments and particularly with the European employers. The only thing holding up the return of the ancestors is believed to be the presence of Europeans, so the first necessity is that the Europeans should be driven out.

The origins of these movements lie in a complex of factors. The establishment of alien rule through colonization; the introduction of a new religion through Christian proselytizing; the destruction of many of the indigenous institutions by the missionaries and administrators; the adoption of a cash crop economy invariably based upon a single product which was highly vulnerable to changes in the world market; and in addition to all this, a failure to provide either an understanding of these changes or the possibility of fully participating in them.

Although the cults have occurred throughout the twentieth century there have been some times when social conditions have been especially suitable to them. Thus the second world war and the years following it provided changes in the domination and administration of many of these societies from English or Australian to Japanese; from Japanese to American; and from American back to Australian. Such changes, especially if the ruling group was driven out by violence, were seen as clear indications of the ending of an era and as heralding the millennium.

As an example of one of these cargo cults let us look at the John Frum movement in the New Hebridean island of Tanna.[8] Tanna was an island which came under formal British administration in 1912. The greater part of European influence, however, had come from Christian missionaries of whom the Presbyterians were the first to arrive.

In 1921 80 per cent of the inhabitants were Presbyterian but their monopoly was broken by the arrival of Seventh Day Adventist missionaries in 1931 and Roman Catholics in 1933. In spite of formal adherence to the missions there was apparently considerable dissatisfaction with mission teaching. In particular, there was widespread disappointment that embracing the new religion did not appear to lead immediately to material gain. It did not enable the islanders to live, as did the white missionaries, without 'working'. To this situation was added, at the beginning of the second world war, a severe economic depression brought by the world slump in copra prices. The first signs of disturbance appeared in early 1940 with the emergence of a prophet by the name of John Frum. John Frum prophesied a volcanic cataclysm after which the reign of bliss would commence when all the material benefits of the Europeans would be rightfully diverted to the local people.

The immediate attainment of utopia was prevented by the presence of white men on the island so the expulsion of all white men was necessary. The use of European money was also to cease and a return to selected traditional customs (polygamy, dancing etc. which had been banned by the missionaries) was encouraged. Any money required in the future paradise would be supplied by John Frum himself. The result was a huge spending spree, a 'bluing' of the soon-to-be-useless European money—a factor which gave the cult a temporary popularity with the white trading community. Huge feasts were also held to use up food. The followers of John Frum deserted the missions and joined the pagan groups in the interior of the island.

A further, and more significant, outbreak occurred a year later and the leaders were arrested. John Frum himself—a young man named Manehivi—was imprisoned and later exiled; other leaders were imprisoned and chiefs who had followed them were heavily fined. But the movement flourished in spite of this repression. Myths built up about John Frum in his absence that would have been difficult to sustain had he been present. One such myth was that he was king of America and that he and the ancestors would return from America. The arrival of American troops in response to the threat of Japanese invasion, therefore, was a clear indication of the imminence of the millennium, particularly as many of the American soldiers were black. The movement consequently prospered all the more; the missions remained deserted; and more and more arrests and deportations were made.

From time to time during the next five years new leaders arose calling themselves John Frum. One organized Tannese labour to build an airstrip for the arrival, by American Liberator planes, of the 'cargo'. Another instructed his followers to raid the stores and tear price labels off the goods. Both were arrested and imprisoned along with their leading followers. Such continued suppression had a weakening effect on the movement, but probably more important was the revival of the price of copra in 1948 with its attendant general improvement in the economic well-being of the island. Indeed, when the price again fell four years later it became apparent that there was still considerable unrest in Tanna and that the movement still had considerable popular appeal in times of economic and political stress.

The John Frum movement shows how alien rule, the activities of missionaries, a single crop economy highly vulnerable to shifts in world prices and the highly visible but not accessible material goods of the Europeans are all bound up in the cargo cults. It shows quite clearly that in order to *understand* such movements one must look not only at the religious setting but also at the total social situation.

Religion in industrial societies

Even the most casual comparison between life in the non-industrial societies we have been considering until now and life in industrial societies reveals a considerable difference in the place of religion. A comparison of contemporary England with medieval England highlights these differences. Then, the Church was one of the main foundations of the society on both the national and the community level; now it is an organization which deals largely with one small area of men's affairs. Then, leading Churchmen, by virtue of their religious office, exercised great power in the governing of the nation; now they are one among many claimants for the ear of professional politicians. Then, the Church directly influenced the lives of everyone and the overwhelming majority owed allegiance to it; now its active members are a small minority of the total population. The term secularization has come into use as a shorthand term for these processes, but secularization is far from being a simple process. Indeed, the term is widely used to describe two processes which are better distinguished. First there is the way in which the *society* has become more secular; secondly there is the way in which *religion* itself has become more secular.

The secularization of society

It is commonplace nowadays for discussions about religion, from Lambeth conferences to televised discussions, to centre upon the decline in religiosity in England over the last hundred years. Basically there are three main ways in which religion in England may be said to have declined. First, there has been a change in the pattern of thinking common to Englishmen so that everyday patterns of thought are now less 'religious' than once they were. Secondly, religious institutions have declined in the power and influence they wield in the society as a whole. Thirdly, a declining proportion of the population either attend or claim membership of religious bodies.

The first of these will be dealt with very briefly, partly because it is so often exaggerated. There is considerable evidence to suggest that although sociologists and (some) theologians may exhibit a scientific view of the world, this is demonstrably not so of the majority of the population. One would be surprised if this were the case. As a British sociologist has pointed out, 'it would be absurd to suppose that a population widely nurtured on the *Daily Express* and *Old Moore's Almanack* finds the New Testament an intellectual insult or Thomism not compatible with modern logic.'[9] Most people still think in terms of the supernatural (even if not in terms of a traditional Christian God) but such considerations no longer have any influence on the daily life of the majority. The secularization of thought has taken place among ordinary laymen more in the decreased significance of religious questions than in any decline in belief in the supernatural. Similarly, although it might be possible to trace a decline in belief among those who hold powerful or influential positions in the society, there are still religious men to be found in politics, industrial management, journalism and so on. But again the significance of their religion for their day-to-day activities is not always evident.

This brings us to the second aspect of the decline in religion, one which is much more important. Just as religion today plays a smaller part in the lives even of some of those who engage in it, so religious institutions play a smaller part in the life of the nation as a whole. Medieval Europe was dominated by the Church. Throughout the nineteenth century, religious bodies in England were highly instrumental both in promoting and in hindering social reform. In England, of course, one must be careful not to overstate the loss of position of religious institutions—a process which has gone much further in most other European countries. There are still formal ties of establishment between the Church of England and the state; one still finds, as part of that establishment, bishops with *ex officio* seats in the House of Lords (a very different thing from life peerages conferred upon prominent churchmen in that it represents the influence of an institution—the Church of England—rather than the influence of an individual); the major denominations still have the ear of the press on all sorts of issues, both religious in the narrow sense and secular. The difference, however, is that nowadays they have no real power. They no longer make major political, economic and social decisions. They are one interest group, albeit an influential one, among many.

Some examples may serve to make this trend clear. The field of education has been especially noticeable for the decline of religious control. In the early nineteenth century primary education was dominated by religious bodies. Such secondary schools as existed were equally under religious patronage. Now, the last vestiges of institutional control of education by the churches are to be found in the Roman Catholic schools, a few Anglican state schools and in church control of some important public schools. By and large the influence of religion is confined to 'religious instruction' and to the influence of individual teachers. Indeed, the very concept of religious instruction is interesting evidence of one aspect of secularization, separating as it does religious education from education as a whole. In the past all education was considered to be religious education; now religion is allocated a named place on the timetable and usually confined to it.

Equally in the field of politics the place of institutional religion has declined considerably. Until the sixteenth century the highest offices of church and state were often combined and even in the nineteenth century denominational differences were often the very stuff of politics. But religion is no longer a political issue. It is indicative of the decline of religious institutions, in relation to other institutions, that politics is now an issue for the churches rather than the reverse. This decline in the general position of religious organizations in our society is part of the more general process of specialization which can be observed in societies. The process of development consists of precisely

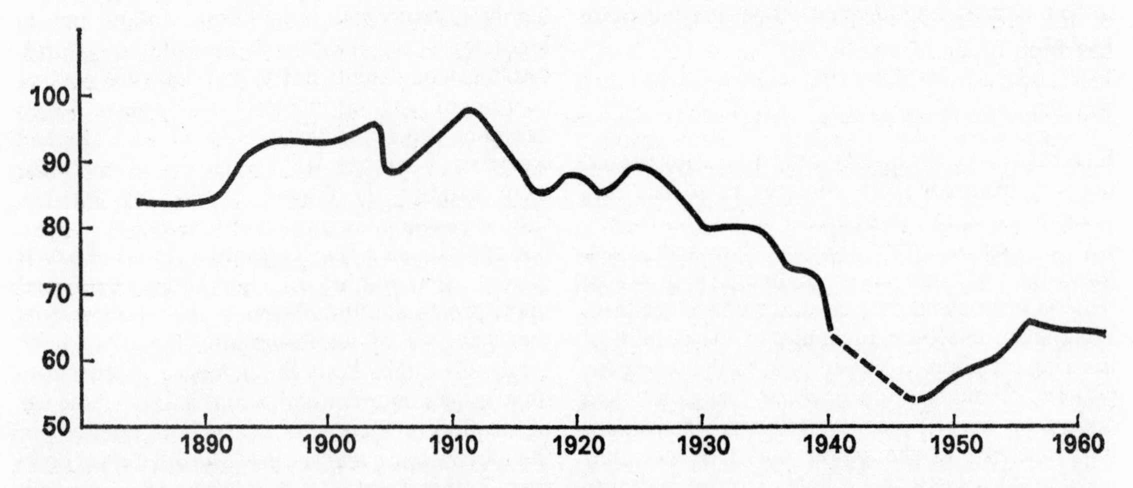

Figure 13.2 Easter communicants in the Church of England per 1,000 persons aged 15 and over, 1885–1962

Source: *Facts and Figures About the Church of England,* Numbers 2 & 3, London: Church Information Office, 1959, 1965.

this sort of change; functions previously performed by a single agency come to be performed by a variety of different ones. In this case there has been a separation of educational, political and religious activities into different institutions.

The third aspect of the decline in religion concerns the question of the size of church attendance and membership. Whatever criteria one takes into account, such a decline is apparent. Membership of the Free Churches has decreased; numbers of Easter communicants in the Church of England have declined; and attendance at Roman Catholic mass, while showing some small absolute increase has declined in proportion to the total population. Figure 13.2 shows the trend in one index of church-going, namely attendance at Easter Communion in the Church of England. Given the importance attached to Easter Communion by Anglicans one may view this as a fair indication of minimum commitment to the Anglican church. For the period concerned, it is generally reckoned that non-Anglicans and Anglicans were about equal in numbers, so we can suggest that between approximately 12 and 14 per cent of the adult population were church-goers in the middle of the twentieth century, compared to 18 or 20 per cent at the beginning of the century. In popular thought the comparison usually made is between the 'religious' Victorians and the 'irreligious' Elizabethans. But if some decline in religious observance since the end of the nineteenth century can be seen from Figure 13.2, a much more striking factor would seem to be the modest proportion of the population involved in church-going *during* the nineteenth century. The lack of support for religious bodies during this supposedly 'religious' period is confirmed by contemporary comments on the situation. Writing of the City of Sheffield in 1817 the Reverend Mark Docker claimed:[10]

> Sheffield is not the most irreligious town in the Kingdom, and here are great numbers, I trust, who pay a becoming respect to Divine worship, both in the Establishment and out of it . . . yet when compared with the bulk of the population, how small. I believe all the various places of worship in the town will not be found to contain accommodation for above one third of its inhabitants, and are they filled by regular attendants? Not by far. Look at the families surrounding your dwellings, and you perhaps see a solitary instance where a whole household of several persons are regular attendants.

There is no reason to doubt Rev. Docker's statement that Sheffield was not exceptional in its lack of religious observance, and this at the beginning of the nineteenth century. It would appear that church attendance in England as a whole had become a minority phenomenon by the second half of the century. Consequently, rather than the normal view of a religious England that has suddenly turned secular in the twentieth century a more accurate assessment reveals a long-term decline in church attendance, punctuated by shorter periods (such as the second half of the nineteenth century) when the decline was slowed but scarcely ever stopped.

An appreciation of the fact that the proportion of the population attending places of worship has been declining for at least a century and a half, and the probability that it has been declining for nearer three centuries, is necessary if we are to reach some understanding of these changes. Perhaps the basic clue is to be found by diligent readers of the Church of England report on the deployment and payment of the clergy which shows a grave concern about the disparity between the geographical distribution of parishes and the distribution of the population. The Anglican church in particular never came to terms with the processes of urbanization and industrialization and even the Nonconformist denominations, whose later birth gave them some advantage in this respect, had little more success in providing accommodation for the growing urban population of the last two centuries. In particular, the churches failed to attract to themselves a significant number of the urban working classes. From their emergence, the working classes have, as a class, been estranged from organized religion, and indeed many sections of the churches have been totally indifferent to this situation. It was this urban working class which was the first sizeable group among whom *non*-attendance and *non*-membership became the normal pattern. In terms of their institutional attachments they were *from the start* a secular group.

Nor does the relative success of the churches in the second half of the nineteenth century signify any great change in this situation. Archbishop Tait, then Bishop of London, was one of the few churchmen of the day to see the situation at all clearly.[11]

> It is the upper and middle classes who form the churchgoers throughout this country (he wrote), and a vast mass of the population are estranged not only from the Church of England, but from the Gospel itself . . . in our crowded cities and in our remote country districts there is a very numerous body of the poor who cannot, and another who will not enter the churches.

That the religious bodies managed to hold their own in the second half of the century in terms of the proportion of the total population in membership or attending, was not due to any changes in the allegiance of the working classes but rather to changes in the distribution of persons between occupations and classes. The occupational groups which were expanding were the very groups among which church attendance *was* the normal pattern of behaviour. Conversely, the failure of the churches to maintain their proportional membership in the twentieth century has reflected the increasing alienation even of these groups. Looking at church-goers in terms of their occupations in this way shows that the decline in church-going in English society requires a multiple explanation. It is not enough to argue that the process of alienation stemmed from the increasing rationality of man in a world where scientific solutions were increasingly applied to what had previously been considered 'religious' problems. This is not to deny that such a process may have alienated some individuals from religious activities, but the *groups* which first absented themselves in large numbers were the very groups among which such intellectual factors were likely to have the least effect, that is the working classes.

Far more important was the fact that Christianity, born as were the other world religions in a rural (though relatively sophisticated) society, was in England organized to serve the needs of a rural, pre-industrial society. This organization is most clearly shown in the parish system which has survived the many and rapid social changes of the last three hundred years. Whatever the effect of some forms of Christianity upon the transformation of that society into an industrial one, the organization of the religious bodies was not adapted to the ever increasing urbanization process. True enough the emerging middle classes of the new towns embraced religion eagerly—especially the Nonconformist denominations which also served as a rallying point for the political expression of this class—but the mass of the inhabitants of the urban areas, the artisans and the labourers, were, with very few exceptions, estranged from organized religion. Even at the end of the nineteenth century, in a period marked by some revival of religious fortune, the appearance of the Salvation Army and working men's missions is of interest more as a commentary upon the irreligion of the poor than as movements that made any significant statistical difference to the situation. The relative success of Nonconformity in the urban areas of the late nineteenth century can be attributed partly to its political role *vis à vis* the urban middle classes and partly to the nature of its internal organization, especially in the newer branches. Methodism, for example, drew its members into local communities in a way that had more in common with the old rural Anglican parishes than with most of their urban successors.

The twentieth-century decline in religious observance can be traced to a change in the pattern of behaviour of the middle classes. Figures for the period since the first world war suggest a continued drift away from religious membership and worship—a drift that is commonly supposed to be due to changes in fashions. It is now a much smaller group among whom going to church is the 'done thing' and the accepted habit of church attendance has had to contend with new competitors. More fundamentally, however, people have increasingly ceased to support an institution that no longer appears to have relevance to their lives. The churches are no longer political, economic or social units of consequence and are therefore, in general, attended regularly only by those who feel a strong *religious* commitment to them.

The importance of this social setting to religious behaviour can be seen more clearly when we compare this English situation with the strongly contrasting situation in the United States of America. (Other interesting comparisons can be made—for example with Scotland.) In America allegiance to the churches and denominations (and synagogues) as reflected by statistics of membership and attendance has grown since the second world war and, many would argue, throughout the century. And yet America is undeniably largely an urban society and is, by most measures, the most highly industrialized society in the world. In terms of our analysis of English society, then, we are faced with the apparently contradictory position of an urban, industrial society where nearly two-thirds of the population is in membership of a religious body and nearly one half takes part in religious worship every Sunday. In other words, to a very considerable extent, organized religion in America *has* come to terms with the urban situation.

This paradox has been resolved by the theologian-cum-sociologist Will Herberg[12] who has argued that, in post-immigrant America, being religious is one of the most acceptable ways of expressing American-ness. Membership of and attendance at church or synagogue is a national value; commitment to a religion provides evidence of being a complete American. Sufficient religious tolerance has been developed, however, for it to matter little which of the major religious faiths are followed since all reinforce the American way of life. Furthermore, in a society that has moved further than any other towards the pole of bureaucracy and impersonality, religion largely through its establishment of a community, provides one of the few institutions capable of giving meaning to life. The local churches of America seem to have had considerable success in reinstating religion as an expression of the local community and in this they are singularly different from their counterparts in Europe. More surprisingly this has been the case in spite of the higher incidence of geographical mobility in America.

The secularization of religion

But Herberg and other observers of the American religious scene have also pointed to certain changes in the activities of the churches. They have maintained and increased their membership and attendance, but at the same time some of them have lost their sole emphasis on 'religion' in its narrow sense. In our terms religion itself has become more secular; or in terms of our earlier typology there has been an increasing compromise with worldly values. Perhaps this is most graphically pictured in Peter de Vries's amusing caricature of American liberal Christianity.[13]

> Our church is, I believe, the first split-level church in America. It has five rooms and two baths downstairs—dining area, kitchen and three parlours for committee and group meetings—with a crawl space behind the furnace ending in the hillside into which the structure is built. Upstairs is one huge all-purpose interior, divisible into different sized components by means of sliding walls and convertible into an auditorium for putting on plays, a gymnasium for athletics, and a ballroom for dances. There is a small worship area at one end. This has a platform cantilevered on both sides, with a free form pulpit designed by Noguchi. It consists of a slab of marble set on four legs of four delicately differing fruit-woods, to symbolize the four gospels and their failure to harmonize. Behind it dangles a large multi-coloured mobile, its interdenominational parts swaying, as one might fancy, in perpetual reminder of the Pauline stricture against those 'blown by every wind of doctrine'. Its proximity to the pulpit inspires a steady flow of more familiar congregational whim, at which we shall not long demur, going on with our tour to say that in back of this building is a newly erected clinic, with medical and neuropsychiatric wings, both indefinitely expandable. Thus People's

> Liberal is a church designed to meet the needs of today, and to serve the whole man. This includes worship of a God free of outmoded theological definitions and palatable to a mind come of age in the era of Relativity. 'It is the final proof of God's omnipotence that he need not exist in order to save us,' Mackerel had preached. . . . This aphorism seemed to his hearers so much better than anything Voltaire had said on the subject that he was given an immediate hike in pay and invited out to more dinners than he could possibly eat.

This is a particularly perceptive piece of satire in that it clearly locates two aspects of the secularization of the religion. First, it points to the secularization of the church's activities—the gymnasium, the ballroom, the clinic; secondly it points to the secularization of theology—the decline in transcendental belief. Clearly we may expect these twin processes (which may, however, occur independently of each other) to be related to the secularization of the wider society but they are far from being a simple reaction to the wider process. In the first place, many of the origins of the secularization of patterns of thought can be traced to the theology and organization of the Reformation—itself ostensibly a religious phenomenon. The decline in ritual, the changing patterns of authority and the relative freedom of thought consequent upon the Reformation broke the monolithic pattern of the Middle Ages and made it more possible for scientists and philosophers to challenge religious statements or beliefs if they so wished. The significance of the name 'Methodists' has often been remarked upon. The methodical approach to life that they advocated exemplifies one aspect of the process of rationalization which the sociologist Max Weber emphasized as the crucial transformation of the Christian ethic under Protestantism in general and Calvinism in particular. Changes within Christianity in the general direction of a more 'secular' theology were thus partly responsible for the development of the wide processes of social change associated with industrialization in Western Europe; and the process of industrialization in turn led to the situation of a largely secular Europe.

The churches, faced with this process of the secularization of the society, have two possible courses of action. Either they can adopt a defensive attitude, that is they can retain their traditional beliefs and practices in an alien milieu. Or alternatively they can accommodate to the new situation; they can re-interpret their message to suit the new age. Thus the 'Rediscovery of the Church'—a theological movement led by the Swiss theologian Karl Barth—may be seen as the ideological reaction of the churches to the perceived need in a modern urban society for more tightly integrated community structures. Or more recently, the 'New Theology' in England and the 'God is Dead' school in America are self-confessed attempts to re-interpret Christianity to a new age—to generations who find the transcendentalism of the past difficult to swallow. Interestingly enough, the choice of alternatives does not seem materially to affect the success of religious bodies in holding their members or gaining new ones. If, once more, we take England and America as our examples, we find that in England fundamentalist and liberal groups both have small memberships. In America, on the the other hand, both are expanding. American life is, however, sufficiently compartmentalized for there to be little or no conflict between fundamentalist denominations such as the Southern Baptists and the basic values of the secular society. It is no longer necessary to construct sectarian barriers to protect members from the wicked world, because the world is not concerned with things religious and fundamentalist Christianity is not concerned with things secular. Their religious focus is upon a transcendental God and an after life. De Vries's fictional Rev. Mackerel provides an extreme case of the adherents of the more liberal beliefs. In real life the Congregationalists provide the best denominational example, but liberal (and radical) beliefs tend to cut across the lines of the major denominations. While expanding in terms of absolute numbers the liberals are, as near as one can judge, merely holding their own in proportion to the total population. This suggests that theological 'compromise' —the re-interpretation of belief and doctrine to suit the new age—does not necessarily produce success in terms of statistical expansion. This may, however, well be because, in America especially, the greatest scope for expansion of membership lies among the lower classes who are not much interested in theological (or any intellectual) speculation.

All strands which we have distinguished in the process of secularization can be related to the earlier typology of Christian groups. The process of the secularization of society corresponds to a movement away from the church-type, characterized by its domination of society, to a society whose religious life is characterized by sects or denominations. As such a secularization of society proceeds, religion retreats into one corner of society where it may become sectarian in its rejection of the values of the world or (more usually in societies which have developed a value of tolerance) denominational in its accommodation to worldly standards and values. In this latter case, the theological position of the denominations may be either traditional or liberal, and in the latter case especially the theological or doctrinal element tends to decline in importance in relation to social beliefs and practices.

This leads us directly to the last section of this chapter, namely to an analysis of the ecumenical movement which has become important in the Christian church during the last half century. The ecumenical movement is closely tied to the process of secularization not so much because it is, in part, an attempted consolidation of their declining position by religious bodies that have become relatively weak, but for two other reasons which may at first seem contradictory. In so far as it is largely (although not entirely) a movement of religious professionals, it reflects the retreat of religion into one part of society by its concentration upon the internal relations of the denominations. But this is to place too much emphasis upon the church unity element of the ecumenical movement which, while it may be the most important and most visible element, is not the only one. Secondly, and paradoxically, it is those denominations who have abandoned (or who never held) a fundamentalist position that are most deeply involved in the ecumenical movement. The aspects of ecumenism not directly related to unity concern the extension of Christian influence into other spheres of society. It is concerned with the influence of the church rather than with its numerical expansion and its evangelism is aimed at the salvation of the world rather than the salvation of individuals *from* the world. Thus the ideology of the movement represents the secularization of religion while its personnel suggest that it is part of the secularization of society. There is consequently much more concern with the secular institutions of society—with politics, race relations, industrial relations and so on. In other words the ecumenical movement is made up largely of the more secular wing of organized Christianity so that its relationship with the whole complex process of secularization is far more complicated than it at first seems to be. It is as much a part of the secularization of religion as of the secularization of society.

What has the sociological perspective to contribute to an understanding of the narrower question of church unity? One explanation relates the growing unity to the secularization of society by pointing out that movements towards unity tend to take place when religious bodies are weak and becoming weaker.[14] At times when the expansion of the European churches must seem like little more than a pipe-dream, the transference of the focus from the church-world relationship to inter-denominational relationships must be reassuring to clergymen. Nevertheless such an explanation, although contributing fuel to the fire of unity in some circumstances, is far from being a satisfactory explanation. The movement towards unity is also strong in the USA where, as we have seen, the denominations are thriving. Moreover, the movement in England started in earnest at the *beginning* of the twentieth century (the Edinburgh conference of the International Missionary Council in 1912 was particularly important) at a time when the denominations in Britain had enjoyed their most successful half century since the beginning of industrialization.

Much more significant is the fact that the denominational divisions themselves were originally primarily social divisions not theological ones. We need not here repeat the evidence on this point but simply remark that, by the twentieth century, the social divisions that gave rise to denominationalism no longer existed. More accurately perhaps one should say that the social divisions have lost their sharpness, and those which still exist find their expression not in new religious movements but in political activities. While the separate religious institutions have long survived the particular social protest which gave rise to them, these changed social conditions mean that there is much less resistance to union schemes than would otherwise be the case. The major objections that are offered are now theological (partly because of the prominence of theologians in the consultations) and these are less intractable than social differences. The increasing homogeneity of society, or at the very least a softening of the original lines of division, is therefore a basic pre-requisite of any movement towards unity. In any situation where religious organizations still reflect meaningful social divisions which cannot be expressed in political action (for example, the racial division in South Africa) there are no substantial movements towards unity.

Thus, while there are relationships between the three processes—the secularization of society; the secularization of religion; and the movement towards unity—it would appear to be unwise to postulate direct causal relationships between them. Rather, all three seem to be connected with the broad processes of social change broadly subsumed under the headings industrialization and urbanization.

Notes

1 Peter Farb, *Man's Rise to Civilization*, London: Secker & Warburg, 1969, pp. 71–2.
2 Numbers 21: 6–9.
3 Deuteronomy 11: 26–8.
4 Esther Warner, *Trial by Sasswood*, Harmondsworth: Penguin, 1965, taken from pp. 208–14.
5 *Guardian*, 8 May 1967.
6 E. Troeltsch, *The Social Teaching of the Christian Church*, London: Allen & Unwin, 1931.
7 This account is based chiefly on E. Anderson, *Messianic Popular Movements in the Lower Congo*, Uppsala: Almqvist & Wiksell, 1958.
8 This account is based chiefly on P. Worsley, *The Trumpet Shall Sound*, London: MacGibbon & Kee, 1957.
9 D. A. Martin, *The Sociology of English Religion*, London: S.C.M., 1967, p. 114.
10 Quoted in E. R. Wickham, *Church and People in an Industrial City*, London: Lutterworth, 1957, pp. 84–5.
11 Quoted in ibid., p. 113.
12 See W. Herberg, *Protestant, Catholic, Jew*, New York: Doubleday, 1960.
13 P. de Vries, *The Mackerel Plaza*, Harmondsworth: Penguin, 1963, pp. 10–11.
14 See B. R. Wilson, *Religion in a Secular Society*, London: Watts, 1966.

Reading

Howells, W., *The Heathens*, New York: Doubleday, 1962. Despite a somewhat unfortunate title, this is an attractively written and informative introduction to religion in simple societies. It includes a discussion of magic, witchcraft, totemism, and ancestor worship and draws examples from a large number of societies.

Lanternari, V., *Religions of the Oppressed*, New York: Mentor, 1963. A study of millennial movements throughout the world. Excellent in its description: less satisfying in its explanations.

Niebuhr, H. R., *The Social Sources of Denominationalism*, Connecticut: Shoe string, 1954. Highly readable discussion of the social roots of the Reformation, Methodism, and a variety of other religious groups.

Robertson, R. (ed.), *Sociology of Religion*, Harmondsworth: Penguin, 1969. A useful collection of articles and extracts relating to societies at various levels of development.

Scharf, Betty R., *The Sociological Study of Religion*, London: Hutchinson, 1970. A clearly written introduction along textbook lines.

Wilson, B. R., *Religion in a Secular Society*, Harmondsworth: Penguin, 1969. An analysis of the process of secularization in England and America, and of the religious response to this process.

Wilson, B. R., *Religious Sects*, London: Weidenfeld & Nicolson, 1970. A brief but comprehensive study of different types of Christian sects. Full of excellent descriptions.

Further Reading

Glock, G. Y. and Stark, R., *Religion and Society in Tension*, Chicago: Rand MacNally, 1965. One of the most perceptive and sophisticated discussions of religion in modern America.

Lessa, W. A. and Vogt, E. Z., *Reader in Comparative Religion*, New York: Harper & Row, 1965. A collection of anthropological writings which is impressive in its quality and its breadth. Contains sections on myth, totemism, Shamans, ancestor worship, and magic, as well as on theoretical and methodological problems.

Troeltsch, E., *The Social Teaching of the Christian Churches*, London: Allen & Unwin, 1931. First published in 1911, but still one of the most useful sources for those interested in the social history of Christianity.

Weber, M., *The Protestant Ethic and the Spirit of Capitalism*, London: Allen & Unwin, 1968. Weber's classic work in which he traces the relationship between Protestant asceticism and the capitalist ethos.

Wilson, B. R. (ed.), *Patterns of English Sectarianism*, London: Heinemann, 1967. Studies of nine English sects prefaced by Wilson's important article 'An analysis of sect development'.

Worsley, P., *The Trumpet Shall Sound*, London: MacGibbon & Kee, 1957 and Paladin, 1970. An analysis of Melanesian cargo cults.

14 Crime

Law and lawbreaking

In all societies there are shared ideas about how people ought to behave. These ideas form the morality and the customs of the society—sometimes called norms. Each generation passes these ideas on to the next; they are preached in pulpits and 'problem pages' of women's magazines and are implicit in most of our everyday conversation, in our literature, in our art and even in the very language we speak. They vary considerably in the extent to which they are held to be important, from the most deeply felt and central ones—like the norms forbidding incest, high treason and the taking of life—to the more trivial customs of the society—ideas about etiquette, proper dress, eating habits and so on. It is often difficult, especially in complex or rapidly changing societies, to assess the importance of any particular norm. How important, for example, is the norm condemning adultery in Britain? In the past those sections of society that condemned adultery (the churches are the most obvious example) dominated the moral scene, whereas today their influence is waning and many people do not think adultery matters very much. There is ambiguity and disagreement about the whole question. To some degree, however, the norms of society are internalized in the course of the socializing process, so that in adulthood they are experienced as conscience—the inner sense of what is right or what is 'done'.

But internalization alone is not enough to make people conform to the norms of their society. Some people fail to internalize them properly and we are all tempted to rebel at one time or another. 'For, after all, there is no need to prohibit something that no one desires to do,' as Freud put it.[1] Furthermore, the norms themselves sometimes conflict and do not give adequate guidance for action in some situations. For instance: 'a man should do all he can to support his wife and family'; 'a man should not steal'. Poor people may often have to choose between these two maxims. Internalization of the customs and moral ideas of the society is supplemented by external methods of social control. These vary from one pound fines, gossip, smiles of encouragement and 'tuts' of disapproval, to imprisonments, a place in the Birthday Honours List and the angry father's 'never darken my doors again'. Some of these sanctions are informal in the sense that they are not applied according to any set of rules, but are a spontaneous reaction of others to a person's conformity to, or deviation from, the norms. The unmarried mother may be 'dropped' by her friends; the long-haired boy finds it hard to get an office job; the honest businessman has the respect of the local community. Other sanctions are formal in that there are rules according to which some kinds of behaviour are positively or negatively sanctioned and these sanctions are administered impersonally. Saving money is rewarded with interest; saving lives with a medal (though in war, taking lives is rewarded with a medal too). But unprofessional behaviour by a doctor is sanctioned by removal from the Register and 'professional' behaviour by a prostitute by a fine or imprisonment.

At the level of society as a whole the criminal law is the most conspicuous formal mechanism of social control. (Civil law, too, is a means of controlling social relations in a wide variety of spheres. It will not be discussed here since the behaviour it deals with is not defined as crime.) In industrial societies, however, the administration of justice and the treatment of offenders is becoming less and less formal. In the case of children, this is true, not simply in the sense that the procedure in juvenile courts is becoming less ritualistic and more intimate and everyday, but also in that the treatment of the delinquent is decided increasingly according to the particular needs of the individual child. Formal justice has traditionally operated without respect to persons, making the punishment fit the crime; the modern juvenile court is moving in the direction of making the treatment fit the delinquent. The police now have juvenile bureaux which deal informally with young first offenders rather than taking them to court at all. There is thus a tendency for the penal system to merge with social work in the control of unwanted behaviour among young people. There is developing a new kind of social control agency, centrally organized yet relatively flexible and informal. The reason for this change is that as people become more sophisticated in their understanding of human behaviour, they become less willing to assign deviants absolute responsibility for their actions. There is an inclination to see them as 'sick' rather than 'sinful' and to give them 'help' rather than 'punishment'. One result is that the distinction between delinquent and disturbed children has become blurred, and in Britain, for example, children who are 'in need of care and control' are on probation and in community homes along with delinquents, and delinquents are in children's homes along with orphans and those from disrupted homes.

The treatment accorded to adult criminals, too, is becoming less formal. There is an increasing use of systems of probation, of psychiatric treatment and other forms of counselling in prison, and of after-care for ex-prisoners. The indeterminate sentence, whose length is not decided by the court but depends in the end on how likely the prisoner is to stay out of trouble, is another example of less formal treatment, and one that was recently introduced for adults in Britain in the form of parole. The distinctive feature of these kinds of treatment is not so much that they lack the harsh, punitive character of much treatment of criminals from the seventeenth century onwards, but that they are adapted to the particular offender and rely on the establishment of a personal relationship between him and the rehabilitative agent.

The criminal law, however, is only one among many mechanisms of social control. It covers only a narrow range of behaviour and would be quite ineffective even there, were it not that norms are internalized and supported by strong informal sanctions. Although the law with its attendant penal sanctions represents the power of the state in the control of behaviour, it is not always the most potent form of social control. In many situations the fear of exposure to informal sanctions is probably more of a deterrent than the fear of actual legal sanctions. This would be true, for instance, of sharp practice by a businessman or perjury by a public figure. Neither does the law necessarily deal with the most important norms of the society. There are no laws against adultery, fornication or, in general, against telling lies, yet there are laws against failing to license a dog and parking a car in the wrong place. In many cases laws have been introduced to regulate behaviour precisely because the relevant norms were not well enough established to ensure conformity without the threat of formal penal sanctions.

In many ways it is misleading to think of laws as the embodiment of norms of the *society* at all. The creation and enforcement of laws are social activities in which some groups play a greater part than others—parties, pressure groups, parliament, civil servants, judges, police and so on; laws are made by some people within society in order to control the behaviour of other people. The laws relating to the hours at which shops may be open, for instance, are made in the interests of the larger shops who employ assistants, to reduce competition from smaller family shops. Even the laws against stealing, while they are clearly in almost everybody's interest to some extent, nevertheless are much more important to the interests of the people who own more property; they are primarily laws which protect the property of rich people.

The actual content of the law varies considerably from society to society and the more complex societies generally have by far the most complex bodies of law, while some simpler societies have no written law at all. The laws of each society are closely related to the structure of that society. Seventeenth-century Puritan Massachusetts[2] provides a good example, though a rather unusual one since the law there did not evolve gradually as in so many countries, but was created in a brief period by the early colonists. The Puritans believed there should be a very close connection between church and state; everyone was a member of the church and subject to its control. Yet those who left England for Massachusetts believed also that the church should have a membership comprising only 'visible saints', men who could be seen to be among the elect of God. The laws of the new colony were therefore closely based on the Bible—so much so that in cases of doubt, ministers of religion were often asked to 'set a rule' which they would justify with Biblical quotations. Everyday life was governed with great severity and in the minutest detail. Court records contain the following revealing examples:[3]

(1) Francis Usselton fined for cursing a swine of Henry Hogget, 'A pox o' God upon her and the Devil take her.'
(2) Joseph Swett's wife fined ten shillings for wearing a silk hood.
(3) It is further ordered, that no person, householder or other, shall spend his time idly or unprofitably, under pain of such punishment as the Court shall think meet to inflict . . . especially . . . common costers, unprofitable fowlers and tobacco takers.

We have seen that law varies from society to society, both in content and in its importance as a means of social control. By and large urbanization and industrialization enhance the importance of legal means of social control as compared with less formal means with the result that 'breaking the law' is more common. There are three aspects of the complexity of urban industrial society which help to explain why this is so.

1. Informal forms of social control, which operate well in the kind of community where everyone knows everyone else's business, are made ineffective by urbanization. In the city it is easier to deviate without others noticing, and even when they do notice it is easier to be unaffected by informal social pressure. So legal mechanisms are more frequently used to govern behaviour that was previously controlled informally. The police are more likely to be called in to deal with street fights and even family quarrels.

2. In industrial societies people engage in many new activities which bring them into new and complicated relationships with others. The co-ordination of these relationships requires formal—often bureaucratic—rules, opening up new opportunities for infringement of the law. The advent of the motor car provides a good example for it has created a whole new class of laws for people to fall foul of and today a large proportion of 'crime' is against these laws. (Incidentally, *some* of the modifications to laws arising from new activities of this kind are in the direction of more lax rather than more stringent control. As fatal road accidents have become more common, a new offence of 'causing death by dangerous driving' has developed, which is treated more leniently than the general offence of manslaughter.)

3. The greater complexity of society also creates new opportunities for the infringement of old laws. The fact that our city streets are lined with empty cars for much of the day creates endless opportunities for larceny, so we need not be surprised to find that the increase in the number of cars on the roads is accompanied by an increase in the common juvenile offence of larceny from motor cars. The complexity of financial and business life has created an intricate web of paper transactions, record-keeping, delegated authority and trust which is full of new opportunities for embezzlement, tax evasion, false description of goods, as well as for newer offences against monopoly acts and so on.

Some laws, of course have disappeared with industrialization. With the separation of church and state, for instance the church gradually gave up its control over secular behaviour, and the state its control over religious behaviour. The church has no monopoly over marriage in contemporary Britain, while heresy, blasphemy, having commission with the devil, suicide and failing to attend church are no longer civil crimes (though the crime of sacrilege and laws relating to Sunday observance still exist). But on balance we have gained far more laws than we have lost: the law has become more important as a means of social control. Wider ranges of behaviour are defined as criminal than formerly.

Crime and changing social structures

Changes in the organization of crime

On the whole, with urbanization and industrialization people become less, rather than more, law abiding. While this is partly due to the greater number of laws, some of the increase in crime can be attributed to the greater complexity and efficiency of criminal organization. The earliest full-time thieves were crude brigands and robbers living often in the forests or the hills and making a livelihood by waylaying travellers or attacking farms. Medieval outlaws, such as Robin Hood, are typical of this kind of criminal. Their followers were able-bodied men with no particular skills and they relied mainly on violence to gain their ends. Sometimes this kind of brigandage has developed into a more sophisticated form: some of the criminal tribes of India—and in particular the notorious Thugs who were suppressed in the early decades of the nineteenth century—used elaborate techniques of strangling or poisoning to overcome their victims.

The kind of crime that relies mainly on simple violence declines in importance as societies become urban and industrial. Highway robbery and street robbery in towns were the last to survive; they flourished in England as late as the eighteenth century, but disappeared, except as amateur activities, once the country through which the highways passed became more densely populated and the city streets became better lit and better policed. Today, the professional criminal normally eschews violence and in doing so keeps himself relatively safe from the worst sanctions of the law. It is true that violence plays a minor part in the carefully planned bank robbery and the like, but the plan basically relies on timing, co-ordination and expertise for its success. It is also used in some rackets, such as the 'protection racket', where the victim himself is on the wrong side of the law and cannot seek its protection. But otherwise, violent robbery is the province of the amateur and the juvenile.

The kind of crime that dominated the scene from the end of the Middle Ages right through the early industrial period was highly specialized, skilled theft and trickery. The techniques of picking pockets and cutting purses, of 'lifting' goods from stalls, of inveigling out-of-town victims into trying to cheat at cards or at bowls and then cheating them in turn—all these were well worked out in Elizabethan London and have been used with very little variation ever since. Each technique is practised by groups of two or three people, who go through the same routine time and time again with one victim after another. Skilled thieves can make a steady, but not very spectacular, income if they work regularly using these methods. Thieves of this kind form an underworld, a distinctive subculture within urban society, with its own haunts, its own slang, its own standards of behaviour. The underworld probably first emerged in the sanctuaries of fifteenth-century London, the areas where, in medieval times, men had been safe from the execution of justice. By the nineteenth century there was a distinct 'criminal class' living in areas known as 'rookeries' in the larger cities—London, Liverpool, Bristol, Manchester, Birmingham, Leeds. They frequented 'flash houses'—pubs, lodging houses, coffee shops and cook houses—where they could expect to meet other criminals, to gossip and make business arrangements. Children who lived in these areas were early recruited into the ranks of professional crime, often assisted, as Dickens shows in *Oliver Twist*, by a man who made a business of receiving stolen goods, for every thief needed a Fagin if he was to make a living from his operations. The 'criminal class' living in a predominantly criminal neighbourhood has virtually disappeared, but the criminal of the traditional type still exists and still practises his 'craft' developing new tricks to meet new situations.

In the more advanced industrial societies, however, there are more tempting prizes than the contents of a man's wallet or even his bank account, and more attractive booty than can be found even in the fur and jewellery departments of the most elegant shops. For wages and bullion in transit and the contents of bank vaults are now of such value that they offer a worthwhile reward for months of planning by a team of men. So new forms of criminal organization have emerged to exploit these new opportunities. As well as the permanent team of two or three equals doing a series of small repetitive 'jobs' together, there are now also *ad hoc* groups of specialists gathered together by a leader to carry out a particular big 'job'. A typical robbery of this kind will be based on initial information bought for a percentage from one man; another man will get in touch with a team of men, some of them previously unknown to him or known only by reputation, through an underworld runner or 'spiv'; he may need a 'peter' man or safe expert, a lock man, an alarm system specialist, a 'wheel' man or driver, a gun man and a strong-arm man. After careful observation of the target, lasting days or weeks, a detailed plan will be formulated and a date chosen. The plan specifies the timing and allocation of tasks and the arrangements for leaving the scene of the crime in such a way that as few people as possible know that the robbery is taking place until the thieves are well away; thus the need for violence, intimidation and restraint are minimized. The plan also covers the disposal of the booty—even banknotes can be traced—and the division of the proceeds; and the thieves must be careful not to alter their spending habits or make themselves conspicuous in any way.

The greatest examples of this kind of robbery have been the 'Great Brink's Holdup' in Boston, Massachusetts in 1950 when the stronghold of an armoured-car company was robbed of $2¾ million, and the Great Train Robbery in England in 1963, when a train carrying £2½ million in used banknotes was waylaid. Each of them took over a year to plan and in each case the *ad hoc* gang carried out other robberies during the planning stage to provide working capital or needed information. The organization of this new kind of crime is more complex than that of routinized 'craft' crime; it is more hierarchical and at the same time more flexible. But the profits are immensely greater and as the participants gain experience they learn to reduce the risks. The two 'Great' robberies were failures, for most of the men got caught; but similar principles are regularly used with success on smaller but none the less lucrative jobs.

Another form of criminal activity that required complex organization is racketeering. The racket does not involve stealing money but getting it from a more or less willing person (with his knowledge) by one of two ways: by extorting it under the threat of force or by providing illegal goods and services to people who are ostensibly law-abiding citizens. Extortion has a long history but only flourishes where state power is weak. The Mafia in Sicily provides a good example of a racket of this kind in a non-industrial society. For centuries Sicily has been governed ineptly but exploitatively from outside. Within the country unofficial organizations, which have become known as Mafias, grew up, taking over many of the functions nominally belonging to the government. One Mafia, for instance, controlled an area including eleven villages from about 1895 to 1924. It had a private police force of over a hundred armed men; it eliminated freelance banditry and thieving; it collected unofficial taxes from all the landowners and supervised all agricultural and economic activities in the area. But the members of such a Mafia benefit at the expense of the rest of the population. Their 'private government' enables them to engage in robbery, blackmail and murder with impunity. The 'protection racket' of the Kray brothers and the American 'labor racket' are versions of this kind of crime which have flourished in an urban-industrial setting.

The scope of the second kind of racket, the evasion of regulations, depends on how much people are willing to pay for things that are illegal in any particular state. In England a black market flourished under wartime rationing and controls, but now there are relatively few controls that full-time criminals can take advantage of. The Prohibition period in the United States opened up an enormous illegal market for liquor, and since then, gambling, drugs and prostitution have provided ample opportunities for racketeers. In America the opportunities have been so great and state control so ineffective that professional criminals have moved into all sorts of activities that can be turned into rackets and have created a vast network that has been described as 'the government of crime'.

Rackets of both kinds—extortion and illegal provision—share three features which distinguish them from other kinds of criminal activity. 1. To be effective both require a permanent organization to keep up the pressure on victims in the one case, to keep the market open in the other. 2. To make a profit the organization tries to maintain a monopoly in its field of activity; extortionists to preserve the credibility of their threat of force; the providers of illegal goods and services to prevent the undercutting of their prices. 3. Racketeers must try to evade the enforcement of the law but the fact that they get their income from a large number of 'respectable' citizens means that they cannot keep their activities a complete secret. These conditions account for many of the characteristics of rackets: their hierarchical organization with a boss; the constant struggle for dominance between rival groups of racketeers, often resulting in 'gangland murders'; and the fact that the most successful racketeers—those in the United States—influence agencies of law enforcement as well as controlling the racket organization itself. This kind of development, one that occurs as society becomes more complex with industrialization, has led to an enormous increase in the amount of crime committed. It has increased it more than the crime figures reveal, for one aspect of the greater efficiency of organized crime is the greater effectiveness in avoiding detection and conviction.

The effects of rapid social change

The disruption of social relationships produced by rapid industrialization or urbanization typically results in a sharp increase in crime. With urbanization, in particular, the old institutions based on kinship become less effective as agencies of social control. Yet the new institutions and organizations of urban society take some time to form and they have to absorb a constant flood of migrants to the town.

In Ghana, for example, the rural kinship system used to provide for the upbringing of any orphans of the lineage. In the subsistence economy such children were useful extra hands on the farm. Nowadays, however, children are more or less obliged to attend school and are less of an economic asset. One result is that orphaned children are more likely to be neglected by their kinsmen and sometimes even drift to the towns on their own. In this situation they may easily take to crime to support themselves. The kinship group no longer looks after orphans as a matter of course but charity orphanages and local authority children's departments have not yet filled the gap. Furthermore, in modernizing societies towns often grow faster than industry and commerce, with the result that many townsmen are unemployed or under-employed. In addition the provision of housing fails to keep pace with the inflow of migrants, so that people live in grossly overcrowded conditions. In such conditions people are more likely to turn to crime.

Another factor contributing to the upsurge in crime rates is the difference between the norms and laws of industrial societies and those of the traditional societies. In traditional Algeria, for instance, when a woman committed adultery her family of origin was disgraced and her father or her brother was expected to kill her; when French law was introduced, such killing became illegal. Similarly, in Sicily a man whose daughter was seduced was expected to kill the seducer; one Sicilian immigrant to the United States was surprised to find that when he did this in defence of the family honour it was considered illegal. Individuals who find themselves at the confluence of two sets of ideals are placed in a situation of conflict by such variations. In following the dictates of one culture, they must defy those of the other. Such was the tragic case of Siberian women when a new Soviet law forbade the wearing of veils; so important were veils to traditional Siberian society that women who abandoned them were killed by their relatives for obeying the law. Obviously, crimes are likely to be common when the new laws thus contradict traditional customs.

The conflict of cultures also has an indirect effect on the crime rate. For when people move from a traditional rural area into the world of the city, their old codes of conduct and standards suddenly become inappropriate. The things they were trained to strive for—a subsistence living, the respect of the village, the good of the family—are either much easier to achieve or else irrelevant. Things become possible that had once seemed impossible. When such a change is abrupt, socially approved norms and standards break down and man's conduct is less strictly controlled. This situation was described by the French sociologist Emile Durkheim at the turn of the century as anomie (or normlessness). He used the concept to explain why suicide rates sometimes rise at times of crisis or rapid change, but anomie and the loss of faith in established norms can procure other forms of deviant behaviour, among them crime and delinquency. When people find themselves in an anomic situation, many of the constraints upon their behaviour lose their force.

Culture conflict and anomie, then, typically accompany rapid social change and also arise whenever individuals move between widely divergent societies. Immigrants to Israel provide a typical example.[4] Many of them had a high level of education and a respected status in the countries they came from, but found that these counted for nothing in the new country. Others had unrealistically high hopes of a new and successful life in a new land, and they too were often disappointed. Many of them found that their ideas of patriarchal authority were very different from the ideas of modern Israel, so that their children, accepting the new ideas, appeared defiant and ungovernable. One immigrant from North Africa expressed this feeling when he said:[5]

> I cannot really understand what happens here with parents and children. . . . At home we knew our place with our father, and he would not allow any disobedience. He knew what was right for us. But here the children are becoming wild and unruly. They think they should not obey the parents, that they are much wiser than the father and mother. . . . It is the school, their teachers and their 'groups' that teach them all this. Whoever heard that children should have groups of their own and not obey the elders?

These are words that may well soon be on the lips of Pakistani and Cypriot immigrants in Britain.

When the first generation are at loggerheads with the society to which they have come, their children are torn between two opposing ways of life. They commonly turn away from their parents and find companionship among their own age groups, frequently in groups which are oriented towards delinquency and often, in adulthood, towards crime.

The distribution of crime in industrial societies

Age, sex and social class

Barbara Wootton once wrote, 'the crude criminal statistics suggest (that) crime is the product of youth and masculinity',[6] a statement that is vividly illustrated by the figures for England and Wales published in the annual *Criminal Statistics* (see Table 14.1). They show that the age distribution of offences is similar for both sexes. The frequency of convictions rises steeply from the age of ten—the age at which criminal responsibility formally begins—to a peak at fourteen to seventeen and declines fairly steadily after that, more rapidly for females than for males.

Table 14.1 Crime rates in England and Wales

Age or age group	*Number of persons found guilty of indictable offences per 100,000 of population of the age group*			
	Males		*Females*	
	1950	*1971*	*1950*	*1971*
10*	1,399	330	90	19
11*	1,667	715	117	53
12*	1,872	1,434	148	139
13	2,101	2,302	173	272
14	2,303	3,606	206	453
15	1,540	4,285	188	538
16	1,415	4,694	184	547
17	1,292	6,027	171	723
18	933	5,705	158	664
19	958	4,987	149	570
20	823	4,181	137	511
21–4	856	2,827	114	376
25–9	699	1,937	95	318
30–9	449	1,280	85	260
40–9	279	634	67	174
50–9	157	318	47	138
60 and over	64	101	19	37
All ages	553	1,414	76	210

*Declining rates in these age groups are largely due to an increased reluctance to prosecute youngsters formally.

Source: Adapted from *Criminal Statistics for England and Wales, 1968*, London: HMSO, 1969, Cmnd 4098, p. lix and *Criminal Statistics for England and Wales, 1971*, London: HMSO, 1972, Cmnd 5020, p. liv.

The figures in Table 14.1 refer to 'indictable' offences, that is offences (often thought of as the most serious ones) which can usually be tried by a jury instead of being dealt with summarily in a Magistrates' Court. About half of the people convicted of indictable offences are under twenty-one, although in the country as a whole only about 20 per cent of people over ten are under twenty-one. So the conviction-rate for young people is about double that for older people. The picture is rather different for non-indictable offences. Here young people are under-represented among those found guilty—largely because motoring offences predominate in this category. In other words the offences that juveniles tend to commit are treated more seriously than those which adults go in for.

The fact that the delinquency-rate declines after the middle teens suggests that youngsters tend to grow out of delinquency. Most of those who appear before a court only appear there once and even among those who appear more than once, most of them are not arrested once they are adult. On the other hand delinquency can sometimes be an apprenticeship for crime; for although most delinquents do not become criminal, they are more likely to do so than non-delinquents. Similarly, although many criminals begin their careers in adulthood, a large number of them begin as juveniles.

This discussion of the age-distribution of crime points to the need to distinguish between two broad categories of criminal. For while it is true to say that adolescence is the peak period for crime, it would be ridiculous to say that adolescents are a prominent group among criminals—if by criminals we mean professional and systematic rather than casual offenders. A large proportion of crimes are committed by people who do not earn all, or even a significant part, of their income by crime. Indeed many crimes—like murder, many sex offences and crimes of violence—are rarely money-making at all. We must separate, therefore, the casual from the professional criminal. Juvenile delinquents are generally casual criminals and account for a large proportion of crime of this type.

The other striking thing shown by the figures in Table 14.1 is that women and girls are brought before the courts far less often than men and boys. Perhaps this is partly due to the fact that there are alternative ways in which girls can protest against conformity and against the adult world; ways that are not usually defined as delinquent. For example, the stronger condemnation of early sexual behaviour for girls means that sex can serve as a protest in a way that it cannot for boys. In any case girls engage less in ordinary delinquent behaviour and the offences they do commit tend to be simple larceny rather than 'breaking and entering' (which accounts for a third of boys' convictions), violence or robbery. Among adults, too, women's crimes are typically less sophisticated in technique and organization and frequently tend to be interpreted as expressions of unhappiness or resentment, rather than as instrumental to financial gain.

The published statistics do not reveal the occupational class background of offenders, but other evidence shows that, both in Britain and in the United States of America, a larger proportion of the lower classes than of the middle classes are convicted of crimes. A number of surveys of London boys in remand homes and in borstal institutions show that very few of them have fathers who are businessmen or professionals, while a large proportion have fathers who are unskilled manual workers. This distribution of delinquents can be compared with that of the total population and it can be calculated that manual workers' boys are four times as likely to be found delinquent as the sons of businessmen and professionals.

The limitations of criminal statistics

Does this really mean that working-class boys are four times as likely to engage in stealing, vandalism and so on? We have already pointed out that crime statistics are not a good measure of actual criminal behaviour, because many criminals do not get caught and never get into the statistics. Roughly 40 per cent of all crimes that are 'known to the police' are cleared up. So 60 per cent of *recorded* crimes never get into the court statistics and we can never know much about the kind of person who committed them. With a large number of property offences the culprit is never caught, whereas some crimes, such as sexual offences and embezzlement, are seldom known to have happened unless the author of the crime is known. In addition, of course, there are many crimes that nobody bothers to record. 'No Parking' areas are often lined with cars, but the police and traffic wardens do not have time even to record most of them. Big department stores suffer enormous losses—some American shops lose as much as 5 per cent of the value of their turnover—which they euphemistically call 'inventory shrinkage' but which are mainly due to shoplifting and thefts by shop employees. There must be a great deal of minor fiddling of records and accounts by shop and office employees that never comes to light.

Probably the most serious source of bias in adult criminal statistics is the fact that those who live by crime, the professional criminals, are extremely skilled at evading detection and conviction. They know the safest times and places to work; they plan each 'job' carefully; they arrange a method of leaving the scene of the crime; they have trustworthy channels for disposing of stolen goods or money; they know when and how to bribe the police and others to act in their interests. The amateur, on the other hand, frequently acts impulsively and does not have the experience and contacts to protect him from detection and conviction. This is not to say that professional criminals never get caught: few go through a career of crime without one or more convictions. But the likelihood of a professional being brought to justice for any one crime is much lower than that for an amateur. So the court's records, the probation officer's case-load and the prison population all have a gross over-representation of amateurs.

In the case of juveniles, the most important reason why the court figures are inaccurate measures of delinquency is probably that the police, when they catch a delinquent, do not always think it wise to take him to court. Particularly if it is the first time a boy has come to their notice, they may think that the best thing to do is to warn him sternly or to talk to his parents or his school teacher rather than give him the stigma of being officially labelled as a delinquent. We have already mentioned the juvenile bureaux in the British police which have institutionalized this practice. They also keep in touch with boys who are potentially delinquent, and try to ensure that they do not get into serious trouble. All police also have power to take the official action of 'cautioning' an offender without taking him to court. Private people, too, when they catch a delinquent, have the option of reporting him to the police or using more informal methods of control.

Both the police and other people are likely to use the most severe methods in the cases they think of as being the most intractable. If they think parental discipline will have the desired effect, they will tell the boy's father rather than use the more formal approach. The result of this is that some delinquents are less likely to come before a court than others. If it is his first offence, if he seems to have been led astray by his friends, if his behaviour can be seen as a 'boyish prank', if his home seems to be a 'good' one, if it is felt that a court record would be damaging to his future life—then the less severe, informal sanctions will be used. On the other hand, if his appearance, clothes and family make him seem a potential delinquent and there are no influences in his neighbourhood or at home that would tend to keep him in check, then the formal legal sanctions will be brought into play. Justice is thus rather unequal in its treatment of different people. It seems to aim at a punishment just sufficient to correct each particular offender, rather than at one proportionate to the heinousness of the offence.

For similar reasons boys are more likely to be dealt with in court than girls. The police 'caution' 46 per cent of the girls they deal with officially for indictable offences but only 28 per cent of the boys (1971 figures): they are more willing to use the less formal sanction for girls. So police decisions are part of the reason why there are fewer girls than boys among the officially recorded delinquents. Similarly, police decisions account in part for the fact that there are more working-class than middle-class boys. It is the working-class (and especially the rougher working-class) boys who will seem to the police to be tougher nuts to crack, to come from rougher neighbourhoods and broken or undisciplined homes, and to have less to lose by going to court in the sense that they have less hope of growing up to a 'respectable' position where a court record would matter. Also the police tend to see their behaviour as serious and the middle-class boys' as pranks.

All of this makes the criminal statistics rather meaningless as indicators of how much criminal behaviour goes on and who engages in it. Is there any other measure? Some investigators have conducted surveys in which they asked people to report their past illegal actions. It is difficult, of course, to be sure how honest people are even under the cloak of anonymity, but the results are rather surprising in the extent of illegal behaviour revealed. In various countries between 50 per cent and 90 per cent of the people questioned admit to having engaged in some kind of illegal behaviour. Perhaps even more surprising, some studies found the percentages were much the same in each of the different social classes. The evidence on this important matter is still not very adequate, but it does seem that the self-reported delinquency of working-class boys is more persistent and more often of a serious nature than that of middle-class boys; and in spite of the considerable element of chance in getting caught, the self-confessed delinquency of officially labelled delinquents is more extensive than that of others. While sporadic delinquency and delinquent fads are a part of almost all teenage life, systematic and persistent delinquency and gangs oriented towards delinquent behaviour are characteristic primarily of lower-working-class neighbourhoods.

Recent trends in delinquency

Since the young feature most prominently in crime statistics it is of some interest to look briefly at some of the trends in juvenile crime. During the years since the second world war the delinquency figures as recorded in the annual *Criminal Statistics*, have risen considerably. These increases are due in part to the increase in the number of boys in the juvenile age group. But, even when we take the changes in population into account, the juvenile delinquency *rates* can be seen to have increased as well (see Table 14.2).

The rates for some crimes have increased more than others. In particular, in recent years the rates for crimes of violence have increased more than those for other offences. This sometimes causes considerable concern, but three things should be remembered. First, crimes of violence are a very minor proportion of all crimes and have been ever since the eighteenth century (they now represent about 6 per cent of indictable crimes for the under-21's). Second, the typical form of 'violence against the person' is not the coshing of a defenceless old shopkeeper but a fight among friends, neighbours, or relatives, or a public brawl; weapons are rarely used. Third, the increase in convictions is likely to be due to a greater intolerance of violence and a greater willingness to call in the police as well as to an upsurge in the amount of violence actually going on. Vandalism—especially mischievous damage to such things as schools, railway carriages, public telephones and vending machines—has been growing, though not in the under-17 group. Again vandalism is not a very large proportion of crime, representing only about 1 per cent of all crime. Among juveniles the offence of 'taking a motor without consent'—often for a joy-ride—has been increasing in the United States and in other European countries as well as in Britain.

One particularly interesting development is the occurrence in various countries of a new phenomenon: waves of teenage rioting. West Germany experienced such a wave in 1956–8 when showings of the film *Rock Around the Clock* and appear-

Table 14.2 Recent trends in juvenile delinquency in England and Wales

Year	*Number of persons found guilty of indictable offences per 100,000 of the population of the age group*			
	Males		*Females*	
	Age 14–16	*Age 17–20*	*Age 14–16*	*Age 17–20*
1950	1,758	1,022	193	153
1951	2,044	1,192	195	160
1952	1,981	1,229	210	172
1953	1,663	1,066	192	168
1954	1,548	1,021	188	165
1955	1,603	1,099	172	161
1956	1,783	1,285	177	155
1957	2,058	1,555	198	182
1958	2,274	1,974	227	221
1959	2,313	2,033	240	201
1960	2,436	2,189	275	236
1961	2,535	2,275	310	265
1962	2,606	2,457	336	276
1963	2,764	2,525	340	272
1964	2,907	2,459	420	277
1965	3,076	2,667	491	295
1966	3,199	2,944	516	318
1967	3,242	3,024	479	346
1968	3,489	3,496	488	381
1969*	4,252	4,721	516	469
1970*	4,484	5,102	557	544
1971*	4,184	5,231	512	617

*The figures for 1969 and later years are affected by the Theft Act 1968, under which all theft became indictable. Many of these offences (particularly 'taking and driving away a motor vehicle', which is a common juvenile offence) were previously non-indictable.

Source: Adapted from *Criminal Statistics for England and Wales, 1958*, London: HMSO, 1959, Cmnd 803, pp. xlvi–xlvii, *Criminal Statistics for England and Wales, 1968*, London: HMSO, 1969, Cmnd 4098, pp. lvii–lviii and *Criminal Statistics for England and Wales, 1971*, London: HMSO, 1972, Cmnd 5020, p. liii.

ances of 'Rock'n Roll' groups were greeted not only with screams and fainting but with uncontrolled dancing in the aisles and damage to the auditorium. The running battles of 'mods' and 'rockers' in English seaside resorts during 1964 and 1965 were somewhat similar in the sense that for a short while they were a 'craze'. People went to certain places at certain times expecting that there would be trouble because there had been in similar situations previously and police and others expected trouble and were ready with a dramatic reaction. Both were also examples of crowd behaviour in that quite ordinary people found themselves behaving in extraordinary ways because they got involved in the unthinking contagious excitement of the mob. Crazes of this kind are made possible by the rapid transmission of news through the mass media. These occasional waves of rioting are very different from the 'rumbles' of rival fighting gangs in the slum areas of the big cities; for fighting gangs are permanent semi-organized groups and their hostilities are chronic and along clear-cut lines.

The explanation of crime and its distribution

The sociologist is interested in explaining various aspects of crime. Why is there crime at all? Why does it take certain forms? Why is it committed by certain groups of people? The answer to the first two questions is largely implicit in the earlier discussion. There is crime because there is law; there is theft because there is property; there is fraud because there is trust; there is illegal diamond traffic because there is a legalized diamond monopoly. The kinds of crimes that predominate and the way that crime is organized change with other changes in society. So at any given time the individual who turns to professional crime adopts the techniques and operates within forms of organization that are currently in use in the criminal world. Let us examine the third question, in the context of industrial societies. Why is 'amateur' crime so heavily concentrated among working-class teenage boys, rather than among some other groups?

The youth culture

To understand why 13–20 is the peak age for crime we need to look at the situation of the teenager in industrial society. The word teenager is a new one, coined to designate the member of a new social group. In non-industrial societies, the terms child and adult are adequate for referring to two distinct age roles; the transition from a dependent, incompetent and subordinate childhood to full adulthood is usually clear cut and may even be marked by an initiation ceremony. In industrial societies, on the other hand, the transition takes many years; in Britain there is a series of formal stages from the age of criminal responsibility at ten to the age of majority at eighteen. The main reason for this lies in the complexity of the adult roles that have to be learned. There is some compulsory schooling in all industrial societies and for many people formal education continues far beyond the school leaving age. Yet full adult status is still not granted to students—even those in their early twenties. Similarly the unmarried are often not thought of as fully adult; yet, because of the responsibility entailed in marriage and the establishment of a separate household, the age of marriage is much higher than in most non-industrial societies.

Paradoxically although the transition to full adulthood is so long delayed, the period of complete subordination to parental or other adult authority is relatively short. English teenagers, as contrasted with say, young Indians, are very free to manage their own lives. They can spend their evenings out, choose their own friends, spend their pocket money how they will, and go away for holidays on their own. Children in school and students in colleges and universities expect to have some part in the running of the organization. All of this freedom is a preparation for the eventual assumption of adult responsibility in a society where *individual* responsibility is important.

So there has emerged a new, distinct period of life which is neither adulthood nor childhood; and teenagers have little in common with either adults or children. They form a social group whose distinctness is enhanced by the development of a separate 'youth culture', centring round taste in entertainment—particularly music—and in clothes. This in turn has been fostered by the commercial exploitation of the new teenage purchasing power, which changes in the labour market and relatively high wages for young people have made possible. In addition, the wide and changing variety of adult occupations means that very few sons follow in their father's footsteps, and even those who do often find the job has changed greatly since their father's day. Teenagers tend to identify with others of their own age and to feel somewhat isolated from older people. This accounts for the importance of gangs and friendship groups in teenage life. These peer groups often have more control over teenage behaviour than do older people.

The emergence of a youth culture, however, is only half the picture. The teenager is also in an ambiguous position. There are a number of aspects to this. First there is a good deal of disagreement about how teenagers should be treated: How much pocket-money? How late should they come home? Should their parents know where they have been and with whom? Second, some of the demands made of the teenager are contradictory: he is expected to be responsible, yet is not given responsibility; he is sexually mature—indeed at his most potent—yet is apparently expected to be chaste; and so on. Third, the teenager's social status is not always clear: a child has the status of his father; an adult's status is determined mainly by his job, in a society where social mobility is possible and is encouraged; but a teenager's status is still indeterminate—yet he is told that his future depends on what he does now, whether he gets a dead-end job or goes to evening classes. It is during the teenage years, the last years of school and the first years of work, that the optimistic aspirations of childhood must be converted into the realistic plans and resignation of later life. The frustration involved is blamed either on those who encouraged the aspirations, or on the system which makes their fulfilment impossible. This goes far towards explaining the teenager's hostility to the grown-up: but the grown-up is also hostile to the teenager. Because the teenager's situation is ambiguous, parents and other adults often find that he does not come up to expectations. He is neither obedient nor responsible; he has too much money and carries too few burdens; he lives with his parents but refuses to participate in their family life.

Conflict is not the whole story of adult-youth relations but it is an important element of them. Delinquent behaviour among teenagers and the adult reaction to it are one of the forms that this conflict takes. Also, many children who are not themselves in direct conflict with their parents are involved in a youth sub-culture and so come to participate in delinquency and hooliganism.

Social class

It used to be thought that the very poor were so lacking in the necessities of life that they stole in order to supply their needs. While in Victorian times this may have seemed a plausible explanation, it is hardly adequate today when the poor are, in absolute terms, much better off. Real poverty does still exist, but it tends to occur in isolated pockets—among the long-term unemployed, especially in depressed areas, among old people and among families with no father or with no adequate wage-earner. Yet delinquency is not much more frequent among these groups than among other lower-class people.

Why, then, are working-class boys more delinquent than others? At the beginning of this chapter, we saw that conformity to the norms of a society is ensured partly by socialization and partly by the distribution of rewards, which is structured in such a way that people are *motivated* to conform. These two mechanisms reinforce one another. There are, however, many regional and class variations in the beliefs and behaviour patterns considered appropriate. Some of them may differ markedly from those enshrined in the law and there may even be a few parents who encourage directly criminal attitudes in their children. Lower-class culture differs from middle-class culture in the things that it stresses and the goals that it encourages people to pursue. It tends to stress 'staying out of trouble' rather than being 'good' or 'bad'; to encourage a tougher approach to life and to reject dependency and gullibility. This culture helps to account for the orientation towards delinquency of many lower-class groups. If people brought up in this culture become delinquent, it is not because they have been 'inadequately' socialized but because they have been socialized into a different culture from the dominant one.

If we look at the way in which the second mechanism of social control, the reward structure, operates for the lower-class teenager, as compared with the middle-class boy, we see that it is less in his interest to be law-abiding.[7] In a society which has an ideology of equal opportunity for all whatever their class origins, everyone is likely to have aspirations to 'succeed'. Indeed, it is considered weak to be satisfied with a low position in society. Yet in fact, equal opportunity is a myth; many able people cannot achieve upward social mobility and, even if they work hard at school and in their jobs, they see little hope of 'getting on'. The goals that are socially prescribed cannot be achieved by the legal means. In this situation some people continue to pursue the goal of economic success but make use of illegitimate means, such as stealing. Other forms of 'deviant' behaviour, such as becoming a down-and-out or a drug-taker, or the more constructive one of joining a revolutionary party, are alternative ways of dealing with the situation. And many people, of course, just struggle on and end up feeling that they must be failures.

The nature of class in our society, then, explains a number of things about the distribution of crime. It explains why more of the poor than of the rich become criminal: because it is they rather than the rich who have severely limited opportunities for (legitimate) success. It explains why the young in this group are more criminal than the old: for it is around the time of leaving school and embarking on work that people gain a depressingly realistic picture of how limited legitimate opportunities are. It explains why boys are more delinquent than girls: for class position and economic success or failure are primarily male characteristics, women deriving their status first from their father, and later from their husband. And finally it explains why delinquency is higher in the United States than in European countries, and possibly why it is rising in Britain: for the class system affects crime not through absolute or even relative poverty, but through the disjunction between aspirations and opportunity. Opportunity, as measured by the amount of social mobility, is much the same in all highly industrial societies, but aspirations vary. In the United States there is a deep-dyed egalitarian ideology; in some European countries, where the present class system has only slowly emerged out of a feudal society, there is still strong support for social distinctions based on birth rather than achievement and many people do not expect or hope to 'better themselves'.

Delinquent subcultures

Delinquency is a social activity: not only are more than one half of delinquent acts committed in groups, usually of two or three boys, but even the solitary delinquent is very much affected by his friends and associates. Edwin H. Sutherland, the American criminologist, put the matter succinctly when he said, 'Criminal behaviour is learned in interaction with other persons.'[8] In this respect it differs little from most other kinds of human behaviour. If we think of crime as 'deviant' behaviour, we tend to assume that none of the ordinary rules apply to it, whereas in fact criminal behaviour patterns are acquired in much the same way as other behaviour patterns.

If we trace the career of someone who becomes an amateur golfer we find that other people enter into it in a number of ways. He probably meets a few people who play golf, or comes from a golf-playing family or neighbourhood. The closer and more enduring his contacts with other golfers the more likely he is to take it up and stick to it. Then he needs others, and books written by others, to teach him the skill of golfing; he needs to become a member of a club and he needs merchants who supply golfing equipment and, later, he needs organizations which hold tournaments. Through his contact with other golfers and with friends and family members who favour golfing, he develops an appropriate frame of mind so that, unlike most of us, he comes to see a fine Saturday or Sunday as 'a good day for golf' rather than a good day for the zoo or a nap in the garden. Furthermore, non-golfers think of him as a golfer and expect him to behave like one. All of these forms of learning from other people find their parallels in the career of the criminal. If a boy becomes a delinquent he is likelv to be aided in various ways by other people. Because of this some boys—those who are more likely to meet these other people—have a greater chance of becoming delinquent than others. In other words *illegitimate* opportunities are as unevenly distributed as legitimate ones. One boy grows up in the kind of neighbourhood where delinquency is very common, so there is a very high probability that he will pick up delinquent habits. Another grows up where delinquency is rare, so that even if he were suffering from a gross blockage of legitimate opportunities, he finds that the illegitimate opportunities are almost equally unavailable and he is unlikely to get involved in any systematic or regular form of delinquency.

What kind of neighbourhood is likely to provide plentiful opportunities for delinquency? In many cities there are small areas that have exceptionally high delinquency rates. These are often the 'zones in transition' or 'twilight areas', the areas of rented property in poor condition, inhabited by a variety of lower-class people, many of them unmarried, and many newcomers to the city. It is in this sort of population that one finds individuals in the frustrating situation of blocked opportunities. Indeed, the very fact of living in such a 'bad' area tends to close some of the doors of opportunity, for the schools are poor, the accent and clothing fashions are 'rough', there is little stimulus to ambition and few people around to help. So, to one degree or another, all the boys in such an area are prone to delinquency. Being thrown together in one neighbourhood they develop a 'subculture' of their own, different from the dominant culture of the society and favourable to delinquency. There are neighbourhoods in all our major cities where a boy can say, 'Three quarters of the boys in this school swipe things. Nearly everyone in our class (4B) has except X. He's too posh, him.'[9]

In addition to the influence of other young delinquents, the twilight areas also contain an undue proportion of adult criminals. For these are areas at once heterogeneous and anonymous, where deviations from respectability are too common to be conspicuous. The presence of these adults opens up opportunities for more systematic delinquency. If there are adult criminals in contact with juveniles, they encourage more purposeful thieving and deprecate delinquent activity that is merely spiteful or 'for kicks'. They can also make it easier for the young thieves to sell their booty and can help them when they get into trouble with the law. In the absence of such adult aid, delinquency is more likely to be sporadic and disorganized and to take the form of violence or vandalism, rather than of stealing for profit.

So delinquency, which to the naïve observer may appear to be an individual act against society, turns out on closer inspection, to be very much a social activity, intimately linked with important aspects of the wider social structure and in particular with the age structure, with social class and with the neighbourhood structure of cities.

Notes

1 Sigmund Freud, *Totem and Taboo*, London: Routledge & Kegan Paul, 1960, p. 69.
2 See Kai Erikson, *Wayward Puritans: A Study in the Sociology of Deviance*, New York: Wiley, 1966.
3 Ibid., p. 169.
4 See S. N. Eisenstadt, 'Delinquent group formation among immigrant youth', *British Journal of Delinquency*, II, 1, 1951, pp. 34–45.
5 Ibid., p. 43.
6 Barbara Wootton, *Crime and the Criminal Law*, London: Stevens, 1963, p. 5.
7 The discussion that follows is based on Robert K. Merton, *Social Theory and Social Structure*, Chicago: Free Press, 1957, chapters 4 and 5.
8 E. H. Sutherland and Donald R. Cressey, *Principles of Criminology* (5th ed.), New York: Lippincott, 1955, p. 75.
9 David H. Hargreaves, *Social Relations in a Secondary School*, London: Routledge & Kegan Paul, 1967, p. 114.

Reading

Chambliss, William J. (ed.), *Crime and the Legal Process*, New York: McGraw-Hill, 1969. A collection of twenty-five articles dealing with the emergence of legal norms and the way in which they are implemented through systems of policing, justice and punishment. Together with the valuable introductions to each section, the collection provides a good basis for relating the sociology of law to the sociology of crime.

Cloward, R. A. and Ohlin, L., *Delinquency and Opportunity*, New York: Free Press, 1966. A study of the way in which different kinds of urban neighbourhood provide different opportunities for becoming delinquent. Already a classic.

Downes, David, *The Delinquent Solution: A Study in Subcultural Theory*, London: Routledge & Kegan Paul, 1966. A sophisticated analysis of delinquent sub-cultures and the way in which they embody a delinquent solution to typical problems of adjustment experienced by lower-class boys in towns. Backed by a study of delinquency in two East London boroughs, Stepney and Poplar.

Gibbons, Don C., *Society, Crime and Criminal Careers*, Englewood Cliffs: Prentice-Hall, 1968. An introductory textbook in sociological criminology. Focuses on the nature of the deviant career for various types of crime in contemporary America.

Hibbert, Christopher, *The Root of Evil: A Social History of Crime and Punishment*, Harmondsworth: Penguin, 1966. A lively and balanced history, concentrating mainly on law, detection and punishment.

Hood, Roger and Sparks, Richard, *Key Issues in Criminology*, London: Weidenfeld & Nicolson, 1970. A straightforward introduction to some of the disputes in criminology and presentation of evidence relating to them.

Taylor, Laurie, *Deviance and Society*, London: Michael Joseph, 1972. A valuable introduction to recent thinking and research in the study of deviance.

Further reading

Cressey, Donald R. and Ward, David A. (eds), *Delinquency, Crime and Social Process*, New York: Harper & Row, 1969. A collection of sixty-three 'readings', both theoretical and descriptive. The best selection in the field.

Hobsbawm, E. J., *Bandits*, London: Weidenfeld & Nicolson, 1969. A fascinating analysis of the 'social bandit' (a type of hero-robber like Robin Hood) found in many peasant societies. Illustrates the problem of distinguishing between the social reformer and the criminal.

McIntosh, Mary, 'Changes in the organization of thieving' in Stanley Cohen (ed.), *Deviants and Others*, Harmondsworth: Penguin, 1971. Discusses the effects of urbanization and industrialization on professional thieving in England since the Middle Ages.

Mannheim, Herman, *Comparative Criminology: a text book*, 2 vols, London: Routledge & Kegan Paul, 1965. A comprehensive and eclectic survey of research and theorizing on 'factors and causes related to crime'.

Tobias, J. J., *Crime and Industrial Society in the Nineteenth Century*, London: Batsford, 1967. A useful historical survey of crime in England at an important stage of development.

Index

Colaiste Oideachais Mhuire Gan Smal
Luimneach

Coinage in Ninth-Century Northumbria

The Tenth Oxford Symposium on Coinage and Monetary History

edited by
D. M. Metcalf

BAR British Series 180
1987

B.A.R.

5, Centremead, Osney Mead, Oxford OX2 0DQ, England.

BAR British Series 180, 1987: 'Coinage in Ninth-Century Northumbria'

Price £24.00 post free throughout the world. Payments made in dollars must be calculated at the current rate of exchange and $8.00 added to cover exchange charges. Cheques should be made payable to B.A.R. and sent to the above address.
Typeset by Lasercomp at Oxford University Computing Service

ISBN 0 86054 494 X

For details of all new B.A.R. publications in print please write to the above address. Information on new titles is sent regularly on request, with no obligation to purchase.

Volumes are distributed from the publisher. All B.A.R. prices are inclusive of postage by surface mail anywhere in the world.

Printed in Great Britain

CONTENTS

Introduction

NINTH-CENTURY Northumbrians used two kinds of coinage that were very different in their outward appearance, namely the small, dumpy, debased pennies that numismatists have since the eighteenth century called stycas, and (right at the end of the ninth century) the broad, thin, heavier coins of good silver minted by the Vikings of York. The difference in intrinsic value, and presumably in purchasing power, between the Viking pennies and the Anglian coins they replaced was, we may imagine, at least ten- or twelve-fold. More modest needs were not neglected: silver halfpennies were struck from numerous dies. There are also a few cut halfpennies. Even so, the scope for using coins in small transactions will have been seriously curtailed. The monetary reform was no doubt guided by wider considerations of the needs of international and inter-regional trade.

In meeting to share our ideas on the coinage of ninth-century Northumbria in its historical context we have chosen, then, to look at parts of two chapters of monetary history which have much in common, in their shared regional background, but which also offer contrasts that may be instructive. If our concern were purely numismatic, it would be tidier to look either at the whole of the Anglian series, from the reign of Eadberht to the fall of York, or the whole of the Viking series, running into the tenth century. But if our primary objective is to elucidate the monetary evidence, there may be some advantage in a strategy which allows us to make comparisons, and to use one series to strike ideas off the other.

Thus, seeing the heavier, good-silver Viking coins out of the corner of our eye should make us ask more insistently why the stycas became so debased during the reign of Eanred and beyond. Northumbria presumably suffered from a progressive short-fall of silver, while at the same time the demand for coin continued or even grew. Debasement, one would have thought, was liable to be damaging to commercial confidence and to open the door to malpractice. It was an expedient that prudent kings would not willingly adopt. How was it managed, and who benefitted from it? Was it a slippery slope?

There were precedents: the sceatta coinages of southern England had plunged into debasement beginning in the 720s. Their increasing unreliability may well have been one of the factors that decided Eadberht to introduce his own, Northumbrian coinage. The sceattas were eventually swept away and replaced by the good silver pennies of King Offa, but Northumbria was unable to follow suit. The drain on the region's silver stocks could not be halted, perhaps because of a persistent tendency towards a regional balance-of-payments deficit. Yet at the same time the production of coin was buoyant, and in the second quarter of the ninth century the complement of moneyers rose from half a dozen to a dozen or more.

We now have the benefit of a growing body of analytical information on the metal contents of the coins. From very early in the sequence of Eanred's issues, the silver was alloyed with brass. This marks an important departure. Hwætræd and Cynewulf struck zinc-free coins for Eanred, with about 40% silver and 7% tin, that is, silver alloyed with bronze. But very soon an alloy containing only 15–20% silver was in use, alloyed with good-quality brass in which zinc made up 20–25%. As debasement proceeded, the coins came to consist of 80% brass, then 90–92% brass, and eventually in Æthelred's reign 97 or 98% brass, always with the addition of 2 or 3% tin. When the coins were new, they were presumably of a quite attractive golden colour. The issue in the second half of the ninth century of what were virtually brass coins is something extremely unusual in the numismatic history of medieval Europe, and it forms a very early and isolated chapter in the known history of medieval brass technology. It seems very probable that the zinc ores were mined in Northumbria, perhaps in the district around Alston. The suggestion by a nineteenth-century numismatist that the brass in the stycas was obtained by reminting Roman coins found by chance in the vicinity of Hadrian's Wall is quite unrealistic, for the ninth-century coins were struck from more than 2,000 dies, and would have needed something in the order of 20 tonnes of Roman orichalcum coins. Metal analyses contribute both to the history of minting and to the history of the currency. Alone, or—better still—in conjunction with die-studies, they create a network of new facts, allowing us to date and quantify the stages of debasement, and thus to understand the differences in intrinsic value which would have made the withdrawal of old coins from circulation worth-while.

The Northumbrian experience was shared in southern England. At Canterbury there was severe debasement in the second quarter of the ninth century, when Archbishop Ceolnoth's coins fall to as little as 55% silver contents. An attempt to restore the situation in the 850s quickly ended in failure, with silver contents as low as 25% by *c.* 862. Under Burgred another attempt to produce coins of better quality again lasted only for a short time, and by the early 870s the coins were again a quarter fine or less. In southern England, too, debasement was accompanied by accelerating production of coins. The Low Countries and north-eastern Francia seem largely to have escaped debasement, perhaps because they were beneficiaries in the imbalance of payments. Even there, however, there were monetary problems, as revealed by a sharp drop after 845 in the money charges payable by *mansi*. The story seems to be that Dorestad sneezed, and people all round the North Sea caught a cold. Why the stycas were debased falls well within the category of idiot questions. The reasons are not to be sought only within Northumbria, even if Northumbria suffered more severely than other regions; and the continued requirement for large quantities of coin, in the face of such difficulties, is all the clearer as evidence. If we ask, 'As evidence of what?', the answers will depend on whether we suppose that calls on the moneyers' services came simply from private individuals, and in particular merchants with foreign money to change, or whether the king was somehow able to promote the flow of bullion through the mints, in order to derive a larger cash income from the re-issue of the coinage. The latter is improbable, as there are only three occasions in the ninth century when debasement could have brought substantial profits to the king from reminting, namely the moment when Eanred's coins were reduced to about 20% silver, likewise when they were reduced to about 10% or less, and the abandonment of silver on Æthelred's restoration.

There is a total absence of official documentary information about the coinage or about the work of the moneyers. It is reasonable to assume that many of the practices were similar to those of later centuries, which are better understood. The lack of documentary information about prices is, however, irremediable.

By contrast the coins have survived very plentifully. They were scarce until the nineteenth century, but then two famous hoards brought many thousands of specimens to light. At Hexham in October 1832 the sexton and his assistant, in digging an unusually deep grave, came upon a bronze bucket containing some seven or eight thousand stycas, and at Cuerdale near Preston in May 1840, close to the former bank of the River Ribble, workmen found the vestiges of a lead-lined chest with some 7,000 coins and nearly 40 kg of *hacksilber*. The treasure included over 3,000 Viking coins of York, which should be enough to provide us with several specimens from virtually every die that was ever used. The Cuerdale hoard remains without parallel, except for a tiny hoard from Dysart in Ireland, but several other large hoards of stycas have since come to light, in York itself and at Bolton Percy, so that potentially our information about the later part of that series is also remarkably complete, in the sense that there are several specimens in existence from virtually every die. Both the Hexham and Cuerdale hoards met with responsible rescuers. Adamson quickly published what was, by the numismatic standards of the day, a full and exemplary record of the Hexham coins, with accurate engravings by James Basire (the engraver to the Society of Antiquaries) of over 900 different varieties. Edward Hawkins similarly wrote a long and careful account of the Cuerdale find, accompanied by ten plates of line drawings by F. W. Fairholt. The hoards were inevitably dispersed, and numismatists ever since have been attempting to re-assemble the evidence—gleaning where Adamson and Hawkins reaped.

It is a hard truth, and perhaps unpalatable, that this wealth of numismatic information has not yielded a matching wealth of ideas or conclusions about the monetary economy of Northumbria. If we seek to relate the evidence of the coinage to the needs and purposes it served, we quickly learn that the answers are not going to fall out of the numismatic detail just by shaking it. We need to approach it equipped with hypotheses to test. What were the stycas used for? What were the Viking silver pennies used for? Was it predominantly for long-distance trade, or for local exchanges, or for taxation, or as a store of wealth? Did monetary exchanges enter into the internal economy of the great monastic estates? Was the currency concentrated within the trading city of York? It is really very difficult to find ways of using the evidence to answer simple questions such as these.

Jean-Paul Devroey in a recent article, 'Reflexions sur l'économie des premiers temps carolingiens (768–877): grands domaines et action politique entre Seine et Rhin',[1] has sketched the characteristics of the ninth-century political economy, as revealed by written surveys of *villae*, the *polyptiques*. He points to traditional and very conservative agricultural strategies as the background to ideals of peaceful stability, regular production, foresight in the storage of surpluses, and political paternalism. The estate economy had few outlets: revenues derived from agricultural surpluses were often not applied to any economic purpose, but were used up in almsgiving, in the building of churches, or in the purchase of precious objects such as books or vestments. Alongside this rather static survival-economy, there are signs, which we do not understand at all clearly, of a money economy, which, in tension with demographic trends, held out the possibilities of progressive social change and a spiral of economic development. The relationship between the estate economy and the money economy in Northumbria is if possible even more obscure than it is in southern England in the ninth century. To speak about the two being 'alongside' each other merely affirms the obvious, namely that they could co-exist, and leaves open the question of their relationship. That question, indeed, comes close to the nub of our enquiries. York might in principle have had the character of a trading emporium which was socially very different from the broad

[1] In *Francia* 13 (1985), 475–88.

acres over which the Northumbrian kings ruled, an island where money was in daily use, in a sea of subsistence and barter. Such a view is challenged, however, by stray finds of coins which, if not particularly plentiful, are certainly widespread through much of Northumbria, including the southern uplands of Scotland, and regions to the west of the Pennines. This scatter of finds may be taken to suggest either that the commercial influence of York was felt in its hinterland, or perhaps merely that the monetary system which York dominated spilled over into the hinterland. We can press this conclusion a little harder by pointing out that there are a surprising number of finds of foreign, particularly Carolingian, coins among the stray losses and the hoard material. These are coins that managed to escape the net of compulsory reminting, which certainly applied. They come not only from York itself, in some abundance, but also from the hinterland. Finds of stycas in the hinterland might be judged to be to some extent ambiguous for the purposes of this argument (namely whether York's commercial influence was felt or whether merely its monetary system spilled over) because stycas could be construed in terms of taxation. But finds of Carolingian coins, minted mostly in the lower Rhinelands, are unlikely to reflect anything but commercial contacts. Their evidence should thus be particularly precious to the monetary historian.

Our approaches to the coin evidence can be seen as falling into two categories. We can ask, quite directly, how the coins were used, or we can ask how they were made, as indirect evidence of need or intention. In the virtual absence of documents our knowledge of how coins were used comes exclusively from finds, the distribution patterns of which are our only direct evidence for the area over which the currency circulated. For this particular purpose a stray find, of a single coin accidentally lost, may be just as valuable as a large hoard, or even more so. Of the Viking coinages so richly represented in the Cuerdale hoard, there is otherwise, from Northumbria, one coin found in York (Skeldergate) in 1879, one excavation coin published from York, an *Alvvaldus* from York (said to be from Walmgate, but it is not certain that it is from the hoard), and another *Alvvaldus* from North Ferriby. Where would we be without Cuerdale? Although a hoard can be counted at best as one find for a distribution map, hoards do offer invaluable direct evidence of the age-structure of the currency, and of the degree to which different issues became mingled in circulation. The styca hoards seem on the whole to be free from long runs of coins all from the same die, and one could devise statistical ways of assessing the clustering of die-duplicates, as a measure of the intensity with which the currency was used, or the frequency of transactions. But the hoards other than Hexham are all from the very end of the styca period, and their evidence for the state of the currency can illuminate only those closing years.

Our other category is how the coins were made—the history of minting, rather than the history of the currency. This is a topic of which it should in principle be possible to give a straightforward, if fact-laden, account. In practice the correct marshalling of the facts presents us with unwieldy and perplexing problems of interpretation, while holding out the hope of unexpected insights. There are various specialist lines of approach to the history of minting, including the study of the moneyers' names, and the measurement of the alloy of the coins. Die-studies, however, hold a commanding position, because when the interpretation of the coinage is in dispute, it is usually the case that die-links are trumps.

It is a familiar idea that medieval rulers were not necessarily considerate of popular requirements for coinage, and it follows that changes in the work of the mints are not necessarily sensitive indicators of changed monetary circumstances. They should be interpreted with caution. Nevertheless, we have to recognize that very little progress can be made until the coins have been correctly attributed and dated.

The styca series was within living memory a happy hunting-ground for numismatists of somewhat narrow vision and limited scholarly experience eager to attribute coins in their collections to new kings, or to make dramatic discoveries. The collectors of fifty to a hundred years ago can now be seen to have made little impact on the subject, and their contributions were sometimes of negative value. Some bizarre ideas were washed up on the wilder shores of emulation. A coin from the Hexham hoard, for example, (concealed as you will recall in the middle of the ninth century) was cheerfully attributed to Æthelbald, who became archbishop some fifty years later. Jonathan Rashleigh convinced himself that stycas reading Ethelred and Ethilred belonged to different kings, and went on, 'There are a few names of moneyers which appear on coins of both Ethelred and Ethilred, such as e.g. "Leofthegn", "Monne", and "Fordred", and it may be urged against my argument, that this fact points to an absence of any fixed rule of spelling the name, even by the same moneyer. But I deny that they are the same moneyers . . . It is manifest, for example, that there must have been two, or three, Leofthegns'. There is all the difference in the world between this wild and implausible assertion unsupported by a shred of evidence, and the cautious hypotheses in Miss Pirie's discussion paper that die-linking seems to indicate that there were several different regal workshops, that the spellings AEDILRED, EDELRED, EDILRED, and so on are a basis for classifying the coinage, and that the irregular coins of classes R I, R II, and R III 'are each made up of a number of tight-knit balls of coins, closely die-linked, with one ball knotted to another by no more than one or two cross-links'. The sheer quantity of organized information with which any theories must conform is now formidable. The cautious common sense and clear-headedness of the general historian are as hard of attainment as ever, perhaps harder. They are still needed to arrive at a view of the administrative and practical arrangements of which the die-links are the archaeological record. We need to remember that Æthelred's first reign is unlikely to have been more than about four years long, and that the number of dies used was probably fewer than under Eanred. But if the coins do in fact demonstrate elaborate administrative arrangements, then they may well eventually throw unexpected light on Northumbrian history, just as the die-cutting centres of the period 973–1066 bring valuable new evidence to the study of provincial centres and regionalism in southern England in that period.

It all seems a far cry from the intellectually rather isolated antiquarianism of the nineteenth century. Historians and others should understand how deeply poor judgement in the past has scarred the British numismatic soul. We still feel embarrassed about it, and need to tell the rest of the world that we are reformed characters.

In 1956, Stewart Lyon's paper, 'A reappraisal of the sceatta and styca coinages of Northumbria' was published, and one saw that a Prince Merlin had appeared to confound mere conjurers. His paper is still the foundation document of styca research, a testimony to the superior merits of breadth and thoroughness, and of course to the unanswerable force of arguments properly based on die-studies. This was followed in 1961 by a joint paper by Stewart Lyon and Ian Stewart, 'The Northumbrian Viking coins in the Cuerdale hoard'. This paper was comprehensive, definitive, a classic of technical numismatic research, based on die-linkage, die-estimation, and survival rates applied to an extremely puzzling set of coin-types, from a decade about which the historical sources tell us little. The numismatic results, which have rightly been seen as conclusive, are related to the historical problems with, on the whole, abstemious precision. This does not mean that there is nothing left for us to discuss. Alfred Smyth in 1975 gave us an historian's response in his chapter, 'Early kings and the coinage of Danish York', solving the conundrum by the acceptance of an otherwise almost unknown King Knútr who was the successor of King Sigfrid,—and by equating the *Adalbrigt* of the Norse sagas with Æthelwold, the atheling of the *Anglo-Saxon Chronicle*. Smyth will hear nothing of Guthfrith, and rebukes numismatists who assume that they are entitled to force an equation between the coins and the first 'historical' contemporary king who comes to hand, whatever his name,—whether CNVT with Guthfrith, or CNVT with Sigfrid. Alternative interpretations of the Cuerdale hoard involve shifting its postulated *terminus post quem* by only a year or two—902 or 903, 905 or 906. What is beyond dispute is that within a very few years a large volume of coinage of good silver was suddenly initiated, where before there had been no minting. It is clear that about 700 to 750 reverse dies were used, and, if one can accept an average output per die of 10,000, therefore some 9 to 10 tonnes of coinage silver were to hand. The equivalent of about £30,000 may be compared with the Danegelds of which the Annals of Saint Bertin speak in the 850s and 860s—sums of the order of £5,000. What the numismatist can usefully add is that the Cuerdale hoard appears to reflect two phases of mint output, an earlier one during which a one-to-one reverse-to-obverse die ratio seems to have been the norm, and a later phase during which it seems to have been as high as three to one or even possibly four to one, evidently reflecting an increased tempo of production, as the numbers of dies are very unevenly distributed between the two phases. Halfpennies are a feature of the earlier phase. Perhaps there was a large accession of bullion part-way through the series, and one wonders whether the expulsion of the Vikings from Dublin brought new faces to York. If the deposition of the hoard post-dates the expulsion, incidentally, it becomes more difficult to argue that the money was in transit in either direction. Much may hinge, therefore, on the shifting of dates by only a year or two, but the commercial and social changes in York itself were presumably considerable whatever their exact date. They may not have been as sudden as the Viking coinage considered in isolation would imply, for there may have been significant amounts of southern English and Carolingian money in York in the 870s and 880s. When we try to assess the historical context of the beginnings of Viking coinage in York—the small beginnings, if Cuerdale is to be believed—we should take care to deprive ourselves of the benefit of hindsight, and should see York as lying at the northern limit of the rapidly expanding Alfredian and southern Danelaw currency. The Chester mint at this moment was already in the flood of expansion. Alfred had succeeded in the politically difficult enterprise of sweeping away the debased currency of the early 870s, and had replaced it with new and heavier coins of the highest purity of silver, weighing about 1.5g. The Cuerdale coinages at York should be seen in general terms as following suit, with grouped legends in Alfredian style (+EB IAI CEC IVI), but on the lower (Danelaw) standard of *c.* 1.35g. The earliest minting of broad silver pennies at York, albeit on an extremely small scale, may have been the imitations of the East Anglian 'St Edmund Memorial' coinage reading ERIAICE CIV (*BMC* 650–1). A specimen which may well be a very blundered version of the same was found at York, in the Walmgate hoard, (*SCBI*

Yorks 983) along with an *Alvvaldus*. Both would seem to be stray survivors in the hoard, from the phase before the main block of 'Cuerdale' issues. *Alvvaldus* seems to stand near the beginnings of the new coinage (although the critical evidence of a die-link to tie any of the five known specimens into the main series is lacking), and it may be thought that a coinage which asserts that the Lord God is king, is making an implied statement that no-one else is king.

Most of the Cuerdale varieties bear a king's name in the normal way, but the prominence given to the legend EBRAICE CIVITAS (something which is not borrowed from the Alfredian models) should make us ponder on the balance of political power between the city of York and the Northumbrian rulers. We may suspect that the citizens (like those of London in the eleventh and twelfth centuries) perceived their common interests as being distinct, and bound up with the city's maritime trade. In uncertain times their political instinct would presumably be to lay claim to as much liberty as they could. The legends of the coins may to some extent reflect these sentiments. In any case the commercial context of the Cuerdale coins is that they were the currency of a city that lived by its trading contacts.

Controversy has blown up on another topic, namely whether the stycas were all minted at York. The coins do not name their mint-place, but it has hitherto seemed self-evident that the great bulk of them were likely to have been produced at York. Again, the Alfredian strategy of moneyers in every town lay in the future, and the contemporary southern pattern was to have one mint-place in each kingdom. If it could be demonstrated that there was more than one Northumbrian mint-place, we should be presented with the opportunity of analysing, from the numerical evidence of hoards, how coins emanating from different centres mingled in circulation. This would be potentially a very informative approach to the question how coins were used. If it could be combined with an analysis of age-structure it might serve to demonstrate, what is at present unknown, the general velocity of monetary circulation in Northumbria. One's instinct would be to look for differences between the city of York itself, the East Riding and the Vale of York, Bernicia, the southern districts of Deira, and the trans-Pennine territories. The East Riding is an archaeologically rich area, conspicuous in the distribution-maps of artefacts of many periods. But if there were another mint one would be looking for it I suppose in Bernicia, more for political than for commercial reasons. Lyon in 1956 divided Eanred's moneyers into Groups A and B and pointed out that the relatively much higher representation of Group A coins at Hexham than in hoards from York must be either because they contained more silver and were melted down during the later stages of the coinage, or because they were struck at a mint other than York. He also pointed out that three of the Group A moneyers worked also for Archbishop Eanbald. In 1967 in his presidential address to the British Numismatic Society he said (of Hugh Pagan, who was then working on the first half of the ninth century), 'I hope he will not close his mind to the possibility of more than one mint having been in operation at the time, for this might explain the rarity of the coins of Eanred and Æthelred by certain moneyers, notably Cuthheard, Tidwine and Tidwulf, who do not fit into the general pattern of die-linking, and the lack of any such linking between Osberht's moneyer Winiberht and the other moneyers of that reign'. In 1968 I was able, with Mrs Julia Merrick and Miss Lynette Hamblin, to analyse three specimens by Cuthheard and Tidwulf for Æthelred from Lyon's collection, and to show that their high silver contents marked them out as being very much earlier in date. Hugh Pagan argued in detail in 1969 that they are in fact coins of a different

King Æthelred. It is accordingly not surprising that they do not die-link into Æthelred II's issues, and historians should understand that as evidence for a second mint they are a *canard*. We also analysed a good number of coins of Eanred, and Gordon Gilmore and I have analysed another large batch since, and have shown that Group A coins are indeed of much better silver than Group B coins, with little overlap between the two groups. Only Eanred's coin by Tidwine, *BMC* 230, remains problematic. Pagan in 1974 was content to leave the door ajar, when he wrote in the Hexham volume edited by David Kirby, 'There is certainly a dramatic difference between the 151:161 ratio for coins of Eanred of Series A and Series B in Hexham and the 5:207 ratio that obtained for the same classes of coin in the 1967 Bolton Percy hoard and *that difference need not be solely due to the Bolton Percy hoard's later date of deposit*' [my italics]. This was an open-minded, not to say a generous verdict, for Pagan had made a die-study of some 1,250 of Eanred's coins in 1967 which revealed *inter alia* that the Group A moneyers originally used around 500 reverse dies whereas the Group B moneyers used around 350. Any suggestion that we should remove the larger part of Eanred's coinage to a mint other than York seems very unrealistic. Unless some positive evidence comes to light it is a dead duck. The statistics also show that in Group A a reverse-to-obverse die ratio close to one-in-one was the norm, whereas in Group B it was either two-to-one or three-to-one. This probably implies that Group B should be compressed into a short period in the closing years of Eanred's reign, and seen as a recoinage.

Miss Pirie's re-opening of the two-mint hypothesis in 1982, without new evidence, seeks to keep alive what can be only a glimmer of hope. Ideally, of course, we would all like to be arguing the case from figures based on several hoards concealed during Eanred's reign, in various parts of Northumbria. Alas, no hoards from Eanred's reign are known. If the idea of a second, more northerly mint were to stand up, it would I think have to work for the Bamburgh evidence, where, so far, only four coins out of 67 are of Eanred, and all four are of Group B.

One would be much less unhappy with the theory that some or all of the Hexham irregulars—that is, a tiny proportion of the hoard, often combining two moneyers' names—are from a second mint. Here as everywhere else, however, one must bow to the evidence of die-linkage.

In 1969 Hugh Pagan dropped a large stone into the pool with his paper, 'Northumbrian numismatic chronology in the ninth century'. This sought to move the traditional chronology forward by some twelve or fourteen years, and thus to bring the styca coinage to an end in 867 rather than the early 850s. The implications of the traditional chronology were either that Osberht soon ceased to exercise effective political control over a kingdom that was in a chronic state of civil war, or that confidence in the silver-less coinage so declined that it became impossible to issue any more. The new chronology allows the volume of Osberht's coinage to be related to a much shorter reign, it makes better sense of the **Talnotry** hoard, which is dated by coins of Burgred, and it comes closer to solving the problem of the silver penny of Eanred which was found in the Trewhiddle hoard, from Cornwall. The hoards from York can more easily be seen as dating from 866–7. Many other adjustments become possible, including a redating of Eanred's issues. The task of refining on the new chronology depends on historical rather than numismatic arguments, and a large measure of agreement seems now to be within our grasp. There are still, perhaps, numismatic contributions to be made, in the fuller interpretation of the 'blundered or derivative' coins. The very large number of dies in this category is newly apparent from the 1967 Bolton Percy hoard, and their alloy has been studied in relation to that of Osberht's reformed coins, some of which were, for the first time, of a pure, high-tin bronze, with no zinc in their composition. In the blundered series, even more than elsewhere, die-links are unanswerable, and there are other shots in the numismatists' locker, in particular the study of die-adjustment. Lyon's 1956 paper made it clear that the derivative coins were die-linked into Æthelred's second-reign issues and to coins of Osberht and Archbishop Wulfhere, and that the chain of die-links is very extensive. Modification of dies during their period in use allows the sequences to be determined, and tends to show that part at least of the series post-dates Osberht's coinage. The general historical interpretation of the derivative coins remains very far from clear. It depends, I suppose, on whether we think that most of them were made in York, and in what political circumstances. The sharp contrast between the moneyers' coins, which are usually accomplished in their design, well struck up on neat flans, and die-adjusted, and the derivative coins which are illiterate, clumsy, often deficient in weight, often metallurgically distinctive—and yet die-linked into the regular series—is mainly an aesthetic contrast which might not in itself imply any loss of political control. But the lack of accountability, when die-linkage shows that the so-called moneyers' names on the derivative coins are meaningless—*that* surely shows a loss of political control. When, on the new chronology, did it occur? If the demand for coin was so insistent that it could be satisfied with such makeshift, no-questions-asked substitutes for the real thing, and if the substitutes were produced on a great scale (like tradesmen's tokens in the seventeenth century, perhaps?) what does that tell us about the uses of coinage in the closing years of the Anglian kingdom? It is probably heretical to ask whether the issue of stycas may not have continued at York after 867. This might account for the evident loss of control over their minting, but it would have awkward consequences in requiring later dates for most of the York hoards. (We need not doubt that stycas continued in *use* for some time after 867, even if their *issue* ceased: the **Talnotry** hoard is post-867, for example; and various grave-finds are also likely to be Viking rather than Anglian.)

There is a lot of work still to be tackled in creating a detailed picture of the minting of the irregular coins and in then making, in terms of that picture, a numerical analysis of various hoards and site-finds. In so far as the irregular coins were of recent issue at the dates when they were hoarded, the patterns they reveal should be reasonably clear, because the coins had not had very long to be become mingled in circulation. The potential of the Bamburgh finds, among which there is a far higher proportion of irregular coins than at Whitby or Sancton, is tantalizing. But what will emerge from this numismatic research is at present completely hidden from our view.

Finally, there are still clarifications to be made in the series of moneyers' coins in the names of King Ælfwald and Æthelred I, in the late eighth or early ninth centuries. With them, we leave behind the hot-house atmosphere generated by an abnormally high survival-rate, and have to make what we can out of a mere handful of surviving coins. But statistical estimation of the numbers of dies suggests that the scale of the currency was already large, and the stray finds show that it was already widespread in its use. Perhaps another hoard is still hidden under seven feet of churchyard mould or in some river's bank, which will one day be as rich a source of information about the beginning of the ninth century as Hexham and Cuerdale are about its middle and end. More probably, the advances in our understanding in the next decade or so will derive from single finds and from carefully recorded contexts in archaeological excavations.

D. M. M.

Northumbria in the ninth century

D. P. KIRBY

TWENTY years ago Stewart Lyon commented that 'For the study of the ninth-century Northumbrian coinage there is an embarrassing wealth of numismatic material but a dearth of documentary evidence against which to appraise it!'[1] In this period, in the words of Sir Frank Stenton, Northumbria 'lies almost outside recorded history',[2] and P. H. Sawyer has contrasted the 'documentary poverty' of ninth- and tenth-century Northumbria with the 'rich literary remains of the age of Bede',[3] this contrast being at its most acute for the period of the ninth century. The fine series of eighth-century Northumbrian Latin annals preserved in part in the early twelfth-century *Historia Regum*[4] and in part in the *Anglo-Saxon Chronicle* D,[5] terminates in 801 with only a brief continuation to 806 in *Chronicle* D.[6] From this point onwards for the period to the capture of York by the Vikings in 866 only the most sparse of historical information is preserved in, for example, Symeon of Durham's early twelfth-century *Historia Dunelmensis Ecclesiae*[7] or in the early thirteenth-century *Flores Historiarum* of Roger of Wendover.[8] The resultant difficulties are further compounded by disagreements between Symeon and Roger on the details of Northumbrian royal chronology. Moreover, Symeon of Durham's short account of the archbishops of York[9] apart, the absence of information concerning the metropolitan centre of the Northumbrian Church creates an historical vacuum in the very heart of the

1 S. Lyon, 'Historical problems of Anglo-Saxon coinage (1)', *BNJ* 36 (1967), 215–21 (p.217).

2 F. M. Stenton, *Anglo-Saxon England* (3rd ed., Oxford, 1971), 243.

3 P. H. Sawyer, 'Some sources for the history of Viking Northumbria', *Viking Age York and the North*, ed. R. A. Hall (CBA Research Report no.27: 1978), 3–7 (p.3).

4 *Symeonis Monachi Opera Omnia* (henceforth cited as *S*), ed. T. Arnold, II (Rolls series: London, 1885), 30 ff. For a translation see *Church Historians of England* III (pt.2), trans. J. Stevenson (London, 1855).

5 *An Anglo-Saxon Chronicle from British Museum Cotton MS., Tiberius B. iv*, ed. E. Classen and F. E. Harmer (Manchester, 1926).

6 For translations of this material, see *EHD* I, nos.1 and 3, and for discussion see also P. Hunter Blair, 'Some observations on the "*Historia Regum*" attributed to Symeon of Durham', *Celt and Saxon: Studies in the Early British Border*, ed. N. K. Chadwick (Cambridge, 1963), 63–118 (pp.86–99) (reprinted *Anglo-Saxon Northumbria*, ed. M. Lapidge and P. Hunter Blair (London, 1984), 63–118); M. Lapidge, 'Byrhtferth and the early sections of the "*Historia Regum*"', *ASE* 10 (1982), 97–122; and C. Hart, 'Byrhtferth's Northumbrian chronicle', *EHR* 97 (1982), 558–82.

7 *Symeonis Monachi Opera Omnia* (henceforth cited as *S*), ed. T. Arnold, I (Rolls series: London, 1882), 3 ff. For a translation see *Church Historians of England* III (pt. 2), and for discussion, B. Meehan, 'Outsiders, insiders, and property in Durham around 1100', *Studies in Church History*, ed. D. Baker, 12 (1975), 45–58. Forthcoming is *St. Cuthbert, His Cult and Community to AD 1200*, ed. D. Rollason, G. Bonner and C. Stancliffe (Woodbridge, 1988).

8 *Roger de Wendover Chronica sive Flores Historiarum*, ed. H. O. Coxe, I (London, 1841), and for a translation of this material see *EHD* I, no.4.

9 *S* I, 222–8. For a translation see *Church Historians of England* II (pt.2).

Northumbrian realm. Even the account in the Northumbrian sources of the capture of York by the Vikings in 866 and the subsequent siege of the city by the Northumbrians in 867[10] is largely dependent on the Alfredian version of events in the *Anglo-Saxon Chronicle* A[11] as expanded by Asser in his *Life of Alfred*.[12] This Alfredian account shows that information concerning the Northumbrian kingdom was reaching Wessex but it was certainly compiled with the primary didactic purpose of warning against the dangers of civil war, whether in Northumbria or elsewhere. As such it may shed more light on the Alfredian dread of civil war in Wessex in the 890s than on the Northumbrian situation of the mid-860s.[13] By stressing the discord between the Northumbrian leaders, Ælle and Osberht, and reporting that both 'kings' were slain, the West Saxon account communicates the impression that Northumbria was torn by a struggle between two kings right up to the eve of the battle for York. The Irish annals, however, record simply that 'the dark foreigners won a battle over the northern Saxons at York, in which fell Ælle, king of the northern Saxons'.[14] In 867, therefore, so far as the Irish annalist was concerned, the Northumbrians had one king, not two. For Dr Alfred Smyth, the Irish annals 'stress the role of King Ælle as sole ruler of the Northumbrians'.[15]

It is possible, moreover, to take too pessimistic a view of the historical evidence for Northumbria in the ninth century. Students of Anglo-Saxon history have to come to terms with slender evidence for other areas in this period. Our knowledge of East Anglian history in the first half of the ninth century is largely dependent on numismatic evidence and for East Anglia across much of the second half of the eighth century even numismatic evidence was until recently lacking. The situation, so far as ninth-century Northumbria is concerned, therefore, could be worse. In the first place, a set of what may be tenth-century Northumbrian annals in origin (though in their extant form of eleventh-century date) reaches back into the ninth century and extends from 888 to 957.[16] Secondly, it is really quite remarkable that Roger of Wendover in the early thirteenth century should still have had access to previously untapped evidence for Northumbria in the ninth century, including details of a king, Redwulf, who seized power only to perish within the year in a battle with pagans.[17] This episode is otherwise unrecorded but Redwulf's existence is corroborated by coins struck in his name across a period of probably no more than six months.[18] Though the ways in which historical information about Northumbria at this time was preserved remain to be identified, there can be no doubt that in his reference to King

[10] *S* I, 54–5: II, 74–5.

[11] *The Anglo-Saxon Chronicle* 3: MS A, ed. J. M. Bately (Cambridge, 1986), s.a. 867.

[12] *Asser's Life of King Alfred*, ed. W. H. Stevenson (reprinted Oxford, 1959), 22–3. For a translation see M. Lapidge and S. Keynes, *Alfred the Great, Asser's Life of King Alfred and Other Contemporary Sources* (Penguin Classics, 1983). The account in *S* II, 105–6 is derived from the *Chronicon ex Chronicis*, ed. B. Thorpe (English Historical Society, 1848 I, 80), which is in turn derived from Asser (cf. P. Hunter Blair, *art. cit.*, 107f).

[13] Cf. D. P. Kirby, 'Asser's Life of Alfred', *Studia Celtica* 6 (1971), 12–35 (pp.29–30).

[14] *The Annals of Ulster*, ed. S. Mac Airt and G. Mac Niocaill, Part I (Dublin Institute for Advanced Studies, 1983), 322–3 (*s.a.* 867).

[15] A. P. Smyth, *Scandinavian Kings in the British Isles 850–880* (Oxford, 1977), 187.

[16] *S* II, 91–5: P. Hunter Blair, *art. cit.*, 104–6.

[17] *Flores Historiarum* I, 282–3.

[18] C. S. S. Lyon, 'A reappraisal of the sceatta and styca coinage of Northumbria', *BNJ* 28 (1957), 227–43 (p.233).

Redwulf and his short reign Roger was drawing on genuine ninth-century material. In particular, the historian of Northumbria in the ninth century benefits from the range of materials which emanate from the community of St Cuthbert, established at Durham in 995 after over a hundred years at Chester-le-Street. Symeon's *Historia Dunelmensis Ecclesiae* used earlier sources, some of which still survive. The *Historia de Sancto Cuthberto* in its present form is a mid-eleventh-century record,[19] described by P. H. Sawyer, who emphasises a tenth-century nucleus, as an 'important if neglected source',[20] and the Durham chronicle, which Sir Edmund Craster reconstructed, was completed between 1072 and 1083.[21] Both these works were used by Symeon of Durham and together they contribute significantly to the materials which illustrate the history of the community of St Cuthbert in the pre- and post-Viking periods. Much of their content concerns the landed endowments of the church and the *Historia de Sancto Cuthberto*, for example, has been described as 'rather an ancient estate roll than a history'.[22] This means that it does not tell us as much about the political history of Northumbria as might have been wished but it does shed valuable light on the history of the estates of an ecclesiastical community in the far north of the Anglo-Saxon realm and not least on the fortunes of some of these estates in the aftermath of the Viking capture of York.

Northern Britain as a whole in the ninth century was a changing world. Scandinavian settlement had been occurring in the northern and western isles since *c*.850.[23] The Pictish kingdom was overthrown when the Dalriadic Cenél Loairn attacked the northern Picts[24] and the Cenél nGabráin, under the leadership of Cinaedh (Kenneth), son of Alpin, perhaps in alliance, it has been suggested, with Vikings,[25] attacked the southern,[26] and new Scottish principalities emerged north of the Forth by 848. Later Scottish tradition maintained that the last kings of the Picts were given military assistance by the Northumbrians, though to no avail,[27] and Cinaedh is said to have invaded Northumbria as many

[19] *S* I, 196–214, but see also the edition in *Simeon of Durham*, ed. J. Hodgson Hinde (Surtees Society 51: 1868), 138–52.

[20] P. H. Sawyer, '*Sources*', 4.

[21] E. Craster, 'The Red Book of Durham', *EHR* 40 (1925), 504–32.

[22] *S* I, xxv. For a handlist of early Northumbrian monastic endowments, see C. Hart, *The Early Charters of Northern England and the North Midlands* (Leicester, 1975), 131ff.

[23] F. T. Wainwright, 'The Scandinavian settlement', *The Northern Isles*, ed. F. T. Wainwright (Edinburgh, 1962), 117–62 (cf. A. Crawford, 'Viking colonization in the Northern and Western Isles of Scotland', *Proc. of the Eighth Viking Congress: Århus, 1977*, ed. H. Bekker-Nielsen *et al.* (Odense, 1981), 259–69); W. H. F. Nicolaisen, 'The Viking settlement of Scotland: the evidence of place-names', *The Vikings*, ed. R. T. Farrell (London, 1982), 95–115; *The Northern and Western Isles in the Viking World*, ed. A. Fenton and H. Pálsson (Edinburgh, 1984); and now B. E. Crawford, *Scotland in the Early Middle Ages. 2: Scandinavian Scotland* (Leicester, 1987), 108.

[24] D. P. Kirby, 'Moray prior to *c*.1100', *An Historical Atlas of Scotland c.400–c.1600*, ed. P. McNeill and R. Nicholson (St Andrews, 1975), 20–1; M. Miller, 'The last century of Pictish succession', *Scottish Studies* 23 (1979), 39–67 (p.62, n.14); A. P. Smyth, *Warlords and Holy Men: Scotland A.D. 80–1000* (London, 1984), 220.

[25] A. P. Smyth, *Warlords and Holy Men*, 190–2.

[26] M. O. Anderson, 'Dalriada and the creation of the kingdom of the Scots', *Ireland in Early Medieval Europe*, ed. D. Whitelock *et al.* (Cambridge, 1982), 106–32.

[27] *John of Fordun's Chronicle of the Scottish Nation*, Historians of Scotland I, ed. W. F. Skene (Edinburgh, 1861), 147, 157, and Historians of Scotland IV, trans. F. J. H. Skene (Edinburgh, 1872), 138, 147.

as six times, burning Dunbar and Melrose.[28] In the later ninth century, a Scottish attack on Lindisfarne is alleged to have brought the Danish king of York, Guthred, north to inflict defeat upon them,[29] but Giric, king of the Scots (878–89), was remembered as having subjected the Northumbrians to his authority[30] and Bernicia, certainly, can be seen as very much within a Scottish sphere of influence by the early tenth.[31] Simultaneously, Scottish influence was being extended into Strathclyde. By 945 when Edmund, king of Wessex, ceded Strathclyde or Cumbria to Malcolm, king of the Scots, on condition that Malcolm became his helper by land and sea,[32] this British territory was clearly falling under Scottish control, but there is some evidence that from much earlier, from *c.*900 if not from *c.*899, Strathclyde was a sub-kingdom of the Scots with Scottish princes established as kings over the Britons.[33]

Substantial alterations of the political map were taking place in the ninth century, therefore, beyond the frontiers of Northumbria. What of Northumbria itself? Historians have generally not been impressed. R. H. Hodgkin saw Northumbria in the ninth century as 'the most backward part of England',[34] and for Alfred Smyth, 'Both the native Anglian kingship and the Church were in a very degenerate state in the last years of Northumbrian independence'.[35] Perhaps the surest indicator of a crisis of some significance in Northumbria is the abandonment of a silver coinage at the end of the eighth century and its eventual replacement by what Dr R. H. M. Dolley called 'wretched' stycas[36] in the course of the first half of the ninth. In Dolley's opinion, when the Vikings took York 'they overthrew a kingdom that had long been bankrupt, economically if not spiritually as well'.[37] On the other hand, it would be possible to exaggerate the disarray of the Northumbrian kingdom at this time. The best land was probably already quite intensively settled and farmed.[38] The archaeological evidence of the pollen record reveals the countryside around York, for example, as 'extensively deforested and largely agricultural, a mixture of arable and pastureland',[39] and if not yet the emporium it was to become in the late Old English period, York was already emerging as a commercial centre.[40] There was 'a competent sculptural

[28] M. O. Anderson, *Kings and Kingship in Early Scotland* (Edinburgh, 1973), 250.

[29] *S* I, 213–4.

[30] M. O. Anderson, *Kings and Kingship*, 267, 274, 288, 290 (see also 283, n.107).

[31] A. P. Smyth, *Warlords and Holy Men*, 198, 232.

[32] *Anglo-Saxon Chronicle* A, *s.a.* 945; *Annales Cambriae*, ed. E. Phillimore. *Y Cymmrodor* 9 (1888), 169. On Strathclyde and Cumbria, see D. P. Kirby, 'Strathclyde and Cumbria: A survey of historical development to 1092', *Trans. of the Cumberland and Westmorland Antiquarian and Archaeological Society* 62 (1962), 77–94, but also P. A. Wilson, 'On the use of the terms "Strathclyde" and "Cumbria"', *loc. cit.* 66 (1966), 57–92.

[33] A. P. Smyth, *Warlords and Holy Men*, 215ff.

[34] R. H. Hodgkin, *A History of the Anglo-Saxons* (3rd ed., Oxford, 1952), II, 405.

[35] A. P. Smyth, *Scandinavian York and Dublin: The History and Archaeology of Two Related Viking Kingdoms* I (Dublin, 1965), 54.

[36] R. H. M. Dolley, 'The post-Brunanburh Viking coinage of York', *Nordisk Num. Arsskr.* (1957–8), 13–85 (p.38).

[37] R. H. M. Dolley, *art. cit.*, 16.

[38] P. H. Sawyer, *From Roman Britain to Norman England* (London, 1978), 132–67 (pp. 161–2).

[39] H. Kenward *et al.*, 'The environment of Anglo-Scandinavian York', *Viking Age York and the North*, 58–70 (p.61).

[40] A. MacGregor, 'Industry and commerce in Anglo-Scandinavian York', *Viking Age York and the North*, 35–57 (p.37); cf. the comments of I. Jansson in *Medieval Archaeology* 24 (1980), 275.

tradition' in the city[41] and the cathedral school of the church of St Peter, York, though on the periphery of Carolingian Europe, remained in touch with continental centres of learning.[42] Northumbrian ecclesiastical organization was rationalized on the four bishoprics of York, Lindisfarne, Hexham, and Whithorn, York possessing metropolitan authority since 735 over the northern province of the English Church,[43] and the greater Northumbrian monasteries of the age of Bede continued to flourish. If the lively monastic cell of Æthelwulf, author of *De Abbatibus*, was not untypical of Northumbrian houses, monasticism north of the Humber retained considerable vitality, at least in the early part of the ninth century.[44] Though there appears to have been no major tradition of manuscript production in ninth-century Northumbria, very few manuscripts were produced anywhere in England in the ninth century outside the court circle of King Alfred:[45] moreover, the *Liber Vitae* of the community of St Cuthbert on Lindisfarne, dating in its earliest section to *c*.840,[46] a fragment containing part of the eighth chapter of the Book of Daniel and written in a hand similar to that of the *Liber Vitae*,[47] and a Northumbrian liturgical and computistical text dating to 867–92[48] should warn against the idea that nothing was produced or that Northumbria was isolated from Carolingian artistic influences. The Northumbrian monasteries were primarily responsible for the Anglian sculpture which is so distinctive a feature of the cultural life of the kingdom,[49] and the period down to *c*.865–75 continued to be characterized in Northumbrian cross sculpture by what have been described as 'swift and lively developments'.[50] Moreover,

[41] J. Lang, 'Continuity and innovation in Anglo-Scandinavian sculpture', *Anglo-Saxon and Viking Age Sculpture and Its Context: Papers from the Collingwood Symposium on Insular Sculpture from 800 to 1066*, ed. J. Lang (BAR 49: 1978), 145–72 (p.146).

[42] As evidenced by the letter of Lupus, abbot of Ferrières, to Ealdsige, abbot of York, in 852: *Councils and Ecclesiastical Documents Relating to Great Britain and Ireland*, ed. A. W. Hadden and W. Stubbs, III (Oxford, 1871), 635–6 (trans. *EHD* I, no.216).

[43] N. Brooks, *The Early History of the Church of Canterbury* (Leicester, 1984), 83.

[44] *Æthelwulf De Abbatibus*, ed. A. Campbell (Oxford, 1967): cf. D. R. Howlett, 'The provenance, date and structure of *De Abbatibus*', *Archaeologia Aeliana* 3 (1975), 121–30.

[45] H. Gneuss, 'King Alfred and the history of Anglo-Saxon libraries', *Modes of Interpretation in Old English Literature: Essays in Honour of Stanley B. Greenfield*, ed. P. R. Brown, G. R. Gampton and F. C. Robinson (Toronto, 1987), 29–49. I am grateful to Professor Gneuss for allowing me to see a copy of this paper prior to publication.

[46] A. H. Thompson, *Liber Vitae Ecclesiae Dunelmensis* (Surtees Society 136: 1923): cf. *Catalogue of Ancient Manuscripts in the British Museum* II (London, 1884), 81–4.

[47] R. McKitterick, J. Stevens, S. Tyacke and J. Whalley, *Catalogue of the Pepys Library at Magdalene College, Cambridge*, iv: *Music, Maps and Calligraphy* (Woodbridge, 1987). I am grateful to Professor Gneuss who called this manuscript (MS. Cambridge, Magdalene College Pepys 2981(4)) to my attention and to Dr McKitterick who provided me with details in advance of publication.

[48] N. R. Ker, *Catalogue of Manuscripts Containing Anglo-Saxon* (Oxford, 1957), no. 319; F. Wormald, *English Kalendars before A.D. 1100* (Henry Bradshaw Society 72: 1934), 1–13; cf. P. H. Sawyer, 'Some sources for the history of Viking Northumbria', 5–6, and J. Morrish, 'King Alfred's letter as a source on learning in England in the ninth century', *Studies in Earlier Old English Prose*, ed. P. E. Szarmach (New York, 1986), 87–107 (p.99).

[49] R. N. Bailey, *Viking Age Sculpture in Northern England* (London, 1980), 76, 81ff.

[50] R. Cramp, 'The Anglian tradition in the ninth century', *Anglo-Saxon and Viking Age Sculpture and its Context*, 1–32 (p.9). See, for specific details in individual cases, the British Academy *Corpus of Anglo-Saxon Stone Sculpture in England* I, i, *County Durham and Northumberland*, ed. R. Cramp (Oxford, 1984).

monastic patronage of the sculpture created, as a consequence of a network of monastic contacts, 'a certain pan-Northumbrian unity' of style and decoration, which, it has been suggested 'presumably reflects the political unity of the north at this time'.[51] By contrast, the proliferation of local styles in the tenth century seems to represent a cultural fragmentation which mirrors the political dismemberment of the Northumbrian kingdom after the fall of York,[52] the more conservative Bernician area contrasting with the new Scandinavian art world of Deira.[53]

The impression that Northumbria in the ninth century was in disarray derives essentially from the fragmentary political record, on the one hand, and the collapse of the kingdom in the face of Viking attack, on the other.

A crucial aspect of the fragmentary political record is chronological. Here, the contribution of H. E. Pagan to the study of Northumbrian history in the ninth century[54] has been of fundamental importance. Pagan argued that the chronology of ninth-century Northumbrian sceattas and stycas in the period down to the capture of York in 866–7 is quite at variance with the chronology of the written sources and proposed the substitution for the traditional chronology of a new and entirely different time-scale. For example, he argued that the pre-Viking Northumbrian coinage ended (apart from imitative issues) *c.*865, so that King Osberht, who may have minted coins for no more than two or three years, could only have succeeded as king on the assassination of his predecessor, Æthelred, *c.*862, rather than many years before this (*c.*848/9) as the written sources indicate; so that the years immediately preceding the capture of York were years of extreme political crisis in the Northumbrian kingdom. To what extent Pagan's revised chronology can be sustained is part of the concern of this symposium and will be the subject of subsequent papers. Without prejudging the outcome, it will be useful at this stage to review the literary evidence to establish any possible degree of inexactitude. The matter is also particularly relevant to the study of Northumbrian political history.

Discrepancies in the literary sources mean that a number of reconstructions of ninth-century Northumbrian royal chronology, displaying minor variations, can be proposed, but the broad outlines of received Northumbrian chronological tradition by the early twelfth century are clear. King Ælle was regarded as in his fifth year on 1 November, 866,[55] and this may explain why his predecessor, Osberht, is given a reign of thirteen years in Northumbrian regnal tradition[56] but eighteen in the *Flores Historiarum*,[57] Wendover or his source presumably including Ælle's five years in Osberht's regnal length and not regarding Osberht's reign as interrupted by Ælle. Eighteen years from 867, the year in which Osberht

[51] R. N. Bailey, 'The chronology of Viking Age sculpture in Northumbria', *Anglo-Saxon and Viking Age Sculpture and its Context*, 173–203 (p.175).

[52] R. N. Bailey, *Viking Age Sculpture in Northern England*, 84.

[53] *Corpus* I, i, *County Durham and Northumberland*, 4, 29.

[54] H. E. Pagan, 'Northumbrian numismatic chronology in the ninth century', *BNJ* 38 (1969), 1–15. For a recent discussion of Pagan's views, see P. Grierson and M. Blackburn, *Medieval European Coinage* I, *The Early Middle Ages* (Cambridge, 1986), 301–3.

[55] *S* I, 54; cf. his reign of four years in the twelfth-century annals of Lindisfarne: *MGH, SS* 19, ed. G. H. Perz (Hanover, 1866), 506.

[56] *S* II, 377, 391.

[57] *Flores Historiarum* I, 284.

and Ælle perished, indicates 849 for Osberht's accession. Osberht's predecessor, Æthelred, is given a reign of nine years in Northumbrian regnal tradition,[58] and, though Wendover only allows him seven,[59] he places his accession in 840 and his death in 848. Symeon regarded 845 as Æthelred's fifth year[60] and also, therefore, in all probability, will have reckoned 840 as the year of his accession. Æthelred's father and predecessor, Eanred, enjoys a long reign in the record, variously given as thirty-three years[61] or thirty-two.[62] The chronological framework of Wendover's annals only allows for a reign of thirty years,[63] which seems to be as aberrant as Roger's arrangement of Æthelred's reign. If Eanred succeeded thirty-two years before 840, he would have become king in 808. In this case, the figure of thirty-two or thirty-three years would have to embrace a second reign of his predecessor, the Northumbrian king, Eardwulf, in the same way as Osberht's eighteen years in the *Flores Historiarum* embraced Ælle's alleged five-year reign. This is because, although Eardwulf was expelled from his kingdom in 806,[64] he was restored in 808 through the good offices of Charlemagne and the pope,[65] and it must be assumed that he reigned for a little while after his restoration. It might be conjectured that Eardwulf reigned for another two years and Eanred only for the thirty which Wendover's annalistic framework allows. But there is another possible solution. There was a variant tradition about the chronology of Osberht's overthrow by Ælle which could be important. According to the *Historia de Sancto Cuthberto*, Osberht lost his life and kingdom within the space of one year from his seizure of certain estates of the church of Lindisfarne:[66] in other words, Osberht was deposed only months before he was slain, i.e. in 866 probably. If this were so, Osberht, overthrown in 866, will have become king in 853. Æthelred will have succeeded in 844 and Eanred's reign will have begun in 811 or 812, depending on whether he reigned thirty-two or thirty-three years. This leaves a perfectly adequate period of time for the second reign of Eardwulf. Perhaps it was a failure to integrate into the record a second reign of three or four years for Eardwulf which occasioned subsequent Northumbrian historians so much difficulty, leaving a period of time in the 860s which could only be accounted for on the assumption that Ælle reigned four or five years or Osberht eighteen. The resulting regnal chronology is as follows: Eardwulf's second reign (808–811/12), Eanred (811/12–844), Æthelred (844–853), Osberht (853–866), Ælle (866–7). There would be a minor variation if Æthelred were thought of as ruling only seven or eight years but there is no obvious reason to prefer Roger of Wendover on this point. The date of Redwulf, king of Northumbria, of course, will be affected by this revised chronology. Wendover places Redwulf's usurpation, his expulsion of Æthelred and subsequent battle against pagans in 844,[67] and indeed in that year a continental source records that the Northmen were victorious in a three-day battle in the territory of

[58] *S* II, 377, 391.
[59] *Flores Historiarum* I, 281.
[60] *S* I, 53.
[61] *S* I, 52: II, 391.
[62] *S* II, 377: *Flores Historiarum* I, 271.
[63] *Flores Historiarum* I, 271, 281.
[64] *Anglo-Saxon Chronicle* D, *s.a.* 806.
[65] *Annales Regni Francorum*, ed. F. Kurze, *Scriptores Regum Germanicarum in Usum Scholarum ex Monumentis Germaniae Historicis* (Hanover, 1895), 126.
[66] *S* I, 201.
[67] *Flores Historiarum* I, 282–3.

the Anglo-Saxons,[68] but if Æthelred only succeeded in 844, his expulsion by Redwulf cannot have taken place until *c*.848. There is no record of a battle against Vikings in the *Anglo-Saxon Chronicle* for 848 but neither is the conflict of 844 recorded in the *Chronicle*. It is difficult to see how Northumbrian regnal chronology can be adjusted further on the literary evidence available. A reign of thirteen years for Osberht seems to be deeply imbedded in the record. Whether the literary evidence needs to be abandoned altogether if it does not accord with numismatic evidence is for this symposium to consider.

The political record, fragmentary though it is, bears witness to the deposition of three kings—Eardwulf, Æthelred, and Osberht—and the assassination of one, Æthelred again. Three depositions and one assassination across sixty years (805–66) compare favourably with the five depositions and three royal assassinations of the sixty years in the eighth century in Northumbria from 736 to 796. It is certainly possible that Eanred's long reign constituted a watershed between two phases of Northumbrian history. Moreover, the description of Ælle by the Alfredian chronicler as of non-royal lineage,[69] no doubt meant to imply an ultimate and total degeneracy of Northumbrian royalty, is best seen as a device by the chronicler to heighten the didactic content of his account. In the *Historia de Sancto Cuthberto* Ælle is described as Osberht's brother,[70] and there is no suggestion that he was a non-royal upstart. The West Saxon representation of Ælle may be compared with the description in the *Chronicle* of Ceolwulf II, king of Mercia, as 'a foolish king's thegn',[71] whereas documentary evidence reveals Ceolwulf reigning in Mercia with every appearance of legitimacy.[72]

Certainly, however, the Northumbrian kingdom collapsed in the face of the Viking attack of 866. Does this suggest a significant degree of military and political weakness? Professor Nicholas Brooks has stressed that the consistent evidence from contemporary sources from widely separated parts of Europe is that Viking armies 'remained in the field for long campaigns often over several years, comprised between fifty and 250 ships, and that fleets of 100–200 ships were by no means rare'.[73] The army which arrived in East Anglia in 865 is described by the *Chronicle* as 'a large heathen army', that which arrived in 871 as 'a large summer force', and that which arrived in 892 as 'the large army'. The large heathen army of 865 was particularly significant because it overwhelmed in quite rapid succession not only Northumbria but also the kingdoms of East Anglia and Mercia during the years 865–873/4, and threatened Wessex in 871. The fact that Alfred never again after 871 encountered the undivided great army of 865 was undoubtedly a factor in his survival.[74] Professor Brooks concludes that it was the

[68] *Annales de Saint-Bertin*, ed. F. Grat, J. Vielliard and S. Clémencet (Paris, 1964), 48.

[69] *Anglo-Saxon Chronicle* A, *s.a.* 867.

[70] *S* I, 202.

[71] *Anglo-Saxon Chronicle* A, *s.a.* 874.

[72] *Cartularium Saxonicum*, ed. W. de Gray Birch, I (London, 1885), no.540; trans. *EHD* I, no.95. The validity of Ceolwulf's grants was accepted by Æthelred and Æthelflaed of Mercia: *Cartularium Saxonicum* II, no.607 (P. H. Sawyer, *Anglo-Saxon Charters: An Annotated List and Bibliography* (Royal Historical Society Guides and Handbooks 8, 1968), no.361), and cf. M. Gelling, *The Early Charters of the Thames Valley* (Leicester, 1979), no.267.

[73] N. Brooks, 'England in the ninth century: the crucible of defeat', *TRHS* 29 (1979), 1–20 (pp.6ff.); cf. P. Wormald, 'Viking studies: whence and whither?', *The Vikings*, ed. R. T. Farrell, 128–53 (pp.134–7).

[74] D. P. Kirby, *The Making of Early England* (London, 1967), 80.

large size of this great heathen army which 'made possible the conquest and initial settlement of three English kingdoms'.[75] The annal for 876 in the *Anglo-Saxon Chronicle* A states that the Danish leader, Hálfdan, shared out the land of the Northumbrians and that the Danes in the army proceeded to plough and to support themselves,[76] or, as Roger of Wendover puts it in what may be a variant of this annal, 'Hálfdan occupied Northumbria and divided it among himself and his thegns and had it cultivated by his army'.[77] These passages suggest that the principal agent of Scandinavian colonization was the army.[78] If this is so, and if, as seems likely, 'political control was followed by economic takeover of estates'[79] by those who remained in England, the impact of the large heathen army will have been considerable and immediate. The military collapse of Northumbria in 866–7, therefore, need not mean that Northumbria was significantly more vulnerable militarily or less stable politically than any of the other English kingdoms in the mid-ninth century. As Sawyer observed, we should not be misled 'into thinking that Northumbrian society was unstable or that the kingdom was on the verge of collapse'.[80]

Under the Viking impact, however, the kingdom fractured. For Patrick Wormald the effects of the Viking attack were 'very serious indeed; as serious, locally, as those of the Anglo-Saxon invasions',[81] and it is the Northumbrian sources which illustrate many of their effects. The Vikings are thought to have secured themselves in possession of York, perhaps establishing a headquarters by the south-east gatehouse of the Roman fortress,[82] and assumed direct control of Deira, appointing a puppet ruler, Ecgberht, beyond the Tyne, who reigned for five or six years.[83] In 872, while the Danish army was campaigning in southern England, the Northumbrians expelled King Ecgberht and Wulfhere, archbishop of York, both of whom took refuge with Burgred, king of Mercia,[84] and a certain Ricsige became king in 873 for three years,[85] clearly in opposition to the Danes. It was against Ricsige that the Danish leader, Hálfdan, led his army across

[75] N. Brooks, 'England in the ninth century', 11.

[76] *Anglo-Saxon Chronicle* A, *s.a.* 876.

[77] *Flores Historiarum* I, 327. P. H. Sawyer, 'Conquest and colonization: Scandinavians in the Danelaw and Normandy', 128, draws attention to this passage.

[78] Cf. N. Lund, 'The settlers: where do we get them from—and do we need them?', *Proc. of the English Viking Congress*, 147–71. Cf. P. H. Sawyer, 'Anglo-Saxon settlement: the documentary evidence', *Anglo-Saxon Settlement and Landscape*, ed. T. Rowley (BAR 6, 1974), 109–19; P. H. Sawyer, 'Some sources for the history of Viking Northumbria', *Viking Age York and the North*, 7; and 'Conquest and colonization: Scandinavians in the Danelaw and Normandy', *Proc. of the Eighth Viking Congress* 123–31 (pp.125–6); G. F. Jensen, 'Scandinavian settlement in England: the place-name evidence', *Nordboer i Danelagen*, ed. H. Bekker-Nielsen and H. F. Nielsen (Odense, 1982), 9–31 (p.31).

[79] C. D. Morris, 'The Vikings in the British Isles: some aspects of their settlement and economy', *The Vikings*, ed. R. T. Farrell, 70–94 (p.86).

[80] P. H. Sawyer, *Roman Britain to Norman England* (London, 1978), 107.

[81] P. Wormald, 'Viking studies: whence and whither?', 139.

[82] *An Inventory of the Historical Monuments of the City of York* II: *The Defences* (RCHM, 1972), 8; R. A. Hall, 'The topography of Anglo-Scandinavian York', *Viking Age York and the North*, 31–7.

[83] *S* I, 55, 225: II, 106, 377, 391.

[84] *S* I, 55–6, 225: II, 110; *Flores Historiarum* I, 323–4.

[85] *S* I, 56, 225: II, 110, 377, 397; *Flores Historiarum* I, 325.

the Tyne in 875, before ravaging across north Britain.[86] In the following year, 876, Hálfdan settled his army in Northumbria but without necessarily having secured control of Bernicia. Indeed, the evidence of place-names and of the distribution of Viking sculpture suggests that the whole area north of the Tees remained culturally distinct from Scandinavian Deira throughout the Viking period.[87] Ricsige died in 876 but was succeeded by Ecgberht II, not known to have been a Danish puppet, who reigned certainly for two years and possibly for twelve.[88] That the Danes of York exercised little influence beyond the Tyne is confirmed perhaps by the absence of any record of grants of land involving Danes north of the Tyne in the estate records of the community of St Cuthbert. The Danish king of York, Guthred, was in a position to grant land as far north as the Tyne to the community of St Cuthbert,[89] but beyond the Tyne independent princes ruled and in the early tenth century Ragnald made Ealdred and Uhtred, sons of Eadwulf of Bamburgh, his primary target of attack.[90] The connection between these lords or reeves of Bamburgh and the late ninth-century kings of Bernicia is unknown, but Eadwulf, who died in 913,[91] was remembered as having been 'dear to Alfred'[92] and it seems likely that he was the political heir of Ecgberht II.

Political dismemberment, therefore, was a consequence of the Viking capture of York with the Danes securely established in Deira though with no continuing influence north of the Tyne. Simultaneously, monastic life and ecclesiastical organization was disrupted. Many of the greater monastic houses of Northumbria —Wearmouth and Jarrow, Whitby, Coldingham—simply vanish from the records and probably ceased to exist as monastic institutions in the course of the late ninth century. The Church in Deira must have been immediately affected by the flight of Wulfhere, archbishop of York, from York to Addingham in Wharfedale in 866, from whence he was expelled in 872 with Ecgberht I, returning in 873 to York.[93] Wulfhere's long archiepiscopate, however, probably conferred continuity of direction on the Church in Deira across these troubled years. He died either in 892 in his thirty-ninth year as archbishop[94] or in 900 in his forty-seventh:[95] either way, he became archbishop in 854, which is the date given in the *Historia Regum*.[96] The history of the church of York is so obscure in the ninth century that even the dates of Wulfhere's immediate predecessors are unclear, though Wigmund, who died in his sixteenth year,[97] must have become

[86] *Anglo-Saxon Chronicle* A *s.a.* 875; *S* I, 56, 202–3; *Flores Historiarum* I, 327.

[87] R. N. Bailey, *Viking Age Sculpture in Northern England*, 29, 34, 73, 91; cf. *Corpus* I, i, 29.

[88] *S* I, 225: II, 111, 377, 391; *Flores Historiarum* I, 327. The *Historia Regum* implies that Ecgberht II was still alive in 883 (*S* II, 114), so perhaps ii is an error for xii.

[89] *S* I, 68–71, 203: II, 114–5. See also C. D. Morris, 'Northumbria and the Viking settlement: the evidence for land-holding', *Archaeologia Aeliana* 5 (1977), 81–103; and 'Viking and native in northern England: a case-study', *Proc. of the Eighth Viking Congress*, 223–44.

[90] *S* I, 209. See A. P. Smyth, *Scandinavian York and Dublin* I, 60ff.

[91] *The Chronicle of Æthelweard*, ed. A. Campbell (Edinburgh and London, 1962), 53.

[92] *S* I, 209.

[93] *S* I, 225, according to which source (*Epistola de Archiepiscopis Eboraci*) Wulfhere remained seven years at Addingham, which would indicate 865–72, but probably the solution is that Wulfhere was away from York for seven years, 866–73.

[94] *S* II, 119.

[95] *S* I, 225.

[96] *S* II, 71, 101.

[97] *S* I, 224.

archbishop *c.*838, and Wigmund's predecessor, Wulfsige, was certainly archbishop *c.*835, though when he succeeded Eanbald II is unknown.[98] There appear, however, to be no irregularities or breaks in the archiepiscopal succession. The letter of Ecgred, bishop of Lindisfarne, to Archbishop Wulfsige shows the archbishop actively combatting heretical notions,[99] and that of Lupus, abbot of Ferrières, to Archbishop Wigmund, perhaps *c.*851, something of the church of York's contacts with the wider Carolingian world.[100]

With Wulfhere's return to York in 873, the Church in Deira resumed its traditional administrative pattern. The Church in Bernicia was thrown into far greater confusion for far longer by the Danish attack and here the traditional administrative pattern was totally disrupted. The last known bishop of Hexham, Tidfrith, died on his way to Rome *c.*821. After his death the diocese is said to have been administered by the bishops of Lindisfarne,[101] but, certainly, across the ninth century, the see of Hexham 'disappeared for good'.[102] So too, in the west, did Whithorn.[103] The community of St Cuthbert, fleeing before the attack of Hálfdan in 875, is said to have contemplated crossing to Ireland and was at one time in the vicinity of Whithorn,[104] and it may be that the leaders of the church of Whithorn had already departed for Ireland by this date. The flight of such communities in the face of Viking attack must have been a critical blow to organized Church life. Symeon of Durham preserves a detailed account, based on earlier tradition, of the departure of the community from Lindisfarne, with the body of St Cuthbert and the treasures (including manuscripts) of the church, under the direction of Bishop Eardwulf and Abbot Ealdred, to wander, perhaps from place to place where the community possessed estates, for a period of seven (or nine)[105] years across north Britain.[106] While Symeon's account no doubt illustrates one of the features of the period, the displacement of religious communities, and Symeon was following older narratives,[107] the details of his story may not be wholly historical. The body of St Cuthbert, with that of King Ceolwulf, had been translated to Norham on the Tweed by Bishop Ecgred (830–46),[108] and the claim that the body was taken from Lindisfarne in 875 could be 'due to the importance of the island in the life of Cuthbert, reinforced by the natural desire on the part of later members of the community to minimise the

[98] R. Kay, 'Wulfsige and ninth-century Northumbrian chronology', *Northern History* 19 (1983), 8–14.

[99] *Councils and Ecclesiastical Documents* III, 615ff. (trans. *EHD* I, no.214); cf. D. Whitelock, 'Bishop Egred, Pehtred and Niall', *Ireland in Early Medieval Europe*, 47–68.

[100] *Councils and Ecclesiastical Documents* III, 634–5 (trans. *EHD* I, no.215).

[101] *Priory of Hexham*, ed. J. Raine, I (Surtees Society 44, 1864), 44–5 (cf. H. E. Craster, 'The Red Book of Durham', 524); H. S. Offler, 'A note on the last medieval bishop of Hexham', *Archaeologia Aeliana* 40 (1962), 163–9.

[102] P. Wormald, 'Viking studies: whence and whither?', 139.

[103] On a possible successor to Badwulf, bishop of Whithorn, consecrated in 791, see K. Sisam, 'Cynewulf and his poetry', *PBA* 18 (1932), 303–31 (p.326).

[104] *S* I, 63–8 (p.67), 207.

[105] *S* II, 92.

[106] *S* I, 56ff. Cf. D. W. Rollason, 'The Wanderings of St Cuthbert', *Cuthbert, Saint and Patron*, ed. D. W. Rollason (Durham, 1987), 45–59 (p.50).

[107] *S* I, 207.

[108] *S* I, 201. Symeon ignored this translation of St Cuthbert: *S* I, 52. The ninth-century section of the *List of Saints' Resting-Places in England* locates Cuthbert's body at Norham: D. Rollason, 'Lists of saints' resting-places in Anglo-Saxon England', *ASE* 7 (1978), 61–93 (pp.63–4, 84).

importance of Norham'.[109] Nor was the connection with Norham lost. In the early tenth century, Tilred, abbot of Heversham in Westmorland gave land to the community of St Cuthbert, so that he might become a brother in the community, and land at Norham, so that he might be abbot there:[110] and in 915 he became bishop of St Cuthbert at Chester-le-Street.[111]

The community of St Cuthbert eventually came to the monastery of Crayke, near York, an event dated to 883 in a late twelfth-century interpolation in the *Historia Regum*,[112] and, according to the later tradition of the church of Durham, took the leading part in raising to the kingship of the Danes at York Guthred, son of Harthacnut, allegedly before this a slave at Whittingham, where the community of St Cuthbert possessed estates; the community then established itself at Chester-le-Street and received from King Guthred an extensive endowment of land between the rivers Wear and Tyne.[113] C. D. Morris has suggested that what Guthred gave were originally estates belonging to the monastery of Wearmouth and Jarrow which had now ceased to function as a monastic community.[114] It certainly looks as if the accession of Guthred was an event of some considerable significance for the restoration of more ordered conditions in northern England, and that the community of St Cuthbert was among those who did well under the new regime. The emphasis in the northern tradition about these events on the visionary, however, the total exclusion from the account of Guthred's accession of any role of the York clergy, the absence of an explanation as to why a Danish slave from Bernicia should have been raised as king of York, and the traditional character of the story make it difficult to ascertain what was really taking place.[115] The history of the kingdom of York immediately preceding these events is also unclear. The community of St Cuthbert is said to have returned into eastern Northumbria on the death of Hálfdan,[116] which, by implication, took place at the end of seven (or nine) years, that is *c.*882 (or *c.*884), but, if Hálfdan is to be identified with the Albann of Irish annals,[117] he perished at Strangford Lough in 877[118] and there was an interval of five to seven years from 877 to *c.*882/4 when the history of Viking York is unknown. It is quite possible that the community of St Cuthbert had established itself at Chester-le-Street earlier than *c.*882/4, for Bishop Eardwulf, who died in 899, is said to have died nineteen years after the founding of Chester-le-Street.[119] These details suggest 880 as the year the community settled there, though if Eardwulf died in his nineteenth year the

[109] P. H. Sawyer, 'Sources for the history of Viking Northumbria', 5.

[110] *S* I, 208 (cf. *EHD* I, no.6).

[111] *S* I, 74. The identification of Abbot Tilred with Bishop Tilred is not made in the sources but seems probable.

[112] *S* II, 114. D. N. Dumville pointed out in discussion the late character of the annal for 883.

[113] *S* I, 68ff., 203; E. Craster, 'The Red Book of Durham', 524.

[114] C. D. Morris, 'Northumbria and the Viking settlement: the evidence for land-holding', 92.

[115] A. Mawer, 'The Scandinavian kingdom of Northumbria', *Saga Book of the Viking Society* 7 (1911–12), 38–64 (pp.44–8).

[116] *S* I, 68, 203.

[117] *Annals of Ulster* I, 332–3 (*s.a.* 876).

[118] A. P. Smyth, *Scandinavian Kings in the British Isles 850–880* (Oxford, 1977), argues that Hálfdan and Albann were identical, which R. McTurk, 'Ragnarr Loðbrók in the Irish annals?', *Proc. of the Seventh Viking Congress: Dublin 1973*, ed. B. Almqvist and D. Greene (Dundalk, 1976), 93–123, is prepared to accept as possible but not certain (p.121); cf. D. Ó Corráin, 'High-kings, Vikings and other kings', *Irish Historical Studies* 21 (1979), 283–323 (pp.320–2).

[119] *S* I, 72.

date of the founding of the new bishopric could have been 881. This would reduce the period during which the community wandered across north Britain. It would also bring the community to Chester-le-Street before the accession of Guthred, if that event continues to be placed in 883. It could be, however, that Guthred was established as king of York before 883. Guthred is given a reign of fourteen years in the Northumbrian regnal lists,[120] and his death is placed in 894.[121] A Guthfrith, king of the Northumbrians, died in August 895.[122] It is usually thought that Guthred and Guthfrith were one and the same, in which case Guthred/Guthfrith will have reigned 881–95. If they were not identical, however, and there is no reason to assume that they were, Guthred will have reigned from 880–94. In this case, his elevation to the kingship could still have preceded, as it does in Durham tradition, the re-settling of the community of St Cuthbert at Chester-le-Street. Even so, the years from 877 to 880 will remain a blank in the history of Viking York. Guthred's accession could only be pushed nearer 877 by abandoning 894 as the year of his death. Not that this is necessary. Hálfdan's departure for Ireland may have left the Northumbrian Danes temporarily leaderless. The attention of part at least of the original great heathen army was focussed on Wessex in 878–9 and it was not until 880 that Danish forces settled down to cultivate the land in East Anglia. Perhaps, similarly, it was only *c.*880 that a new political order crystallized in Northumbria. Scandinavian genealogical tradition regarded Guthred's father, Harthacnut, as the grandson of King Ælle's daughter, Blaeja.[123] If this tradition recalls a genuine relationship of some kind, Guthred could have been a compromise choice in the north, a descendant of the old Northumbrian line who had been brought up in Anglian territory and whose existence and whereabouts might be known to Bernician churchmen. The election of Guthred, possibly an Anglo-Danish prince, therefore, by Danes and English at *Oswiesdune*, when the whole army swore peace and fidelity over the body of St Cuthbert,[124] may represent an attempt to create a new Northumbrian kingship to which both peoples could respond.

Not that the Northumbrian Danes were rendered passive. They continued to support other Danish armies in their attacks on English territories and allied with the king of Gwynedd against Alfred.[125] Even so, after Sigeferth, a Viking pirate from Northumbria, had ravaged the English coast in 893, the West Saxon ealdorman, Æthelnoth, went to York and campaigned against him,[126] presumably without hindrance from King Guthred. According to the Northumbrian sources, on the death of Guthred, the Northumbrians established peace with Alfred who had the disposal of the entire Northumbrian kingdom,[127] but this is more likely to have been the situation on the death and burial in the cathedral church of York of King Guthfrith in 895[128] (unless Guthred and Guthfrith were the same person). This evidence suggests that the Northumbrian Danes reached a

[120] *S* II, 377, 391.
[121] *S* I, 71: II, 92.
[122] *Chronicle of Æthelweard*, 51.
[123] A. Mawer, *art. cit.*, 48; cf. A. P. Smyth, *Scandinavian Kings in the British Isles*, 13.
[124] *S* I, 69, 203.
[125] On these events, see D. P. Kirby, 'Northumbria in the reign of Alfred the Great', *Trans. of the Architectural and Archaeological Society of Durham and Northumberland* 11 (1965), 335–46; and 'Asser's Life of Alfred', *Studia Celtica* 6 (1971), 12–35.
[126] *Chronicle of Æthelweard*, 50–1.
[127] *S* I, 71: II, 119.
[128] *Chronicle of Æthelweard*, 51.

new understanding with the Church within Northumbria, on the one hand, and entered into a new relationship with Alfred and the West Saxons, on the other. Coins in imitation of King Alfred's were circulated in the Danelaw in the late 880s and 890s, including one which has the name GVNDEF, possibly Guthfrith, on the obverse and which seems to have been struck in the territory of the Five Boroughs in the east midlands.[129] Moreover, when Guthfrith died, he appears to have been succeeded at York by a king, Sigfrid, perhaps but not certainly the Sigeferth of 893, who was responsible for the first Danish coinage at York—'the coinage of a highly civilised and largely Christianized society'.[130] Sigfrid's later coins show him sharing royal power *c.*897 with another king, Cnut, who subsequently issued coins on his own and is presumed to have succeeded Sigfrid.[131] The coins of Sigfrid and Cnut were minted at York bearing Christian Latin inscriptions and the Christian symbol of the cross, and from *c.*905 for a period of perhaps fourteen years a coinage in the name of St Peter replaced these royal issues.[132] What this sequence seems to show is the increasing importance of the part played by the clergy of York minster in the Northumbrian mint at the end of the ninth century and the beginning of the tenth. As Alfred Smyth comments, 'it looked for a while as if the new Anglo-Danish realm would be little different from its pre-Viking counterpart'.[133]

Finally, the acceptance as king in York of Æthelwold, nephew of Alfred and West Saxon royal rival to Alfred's son and successor, Edward, in Wessex, in 899–900 may seem to presuppose a remarkable identification of common interests when a West Saxon prince and the Northumbrian Danes could make common cause: but in west Europe generally discontented or disadvantaged princes were prepared to ally with the Vikings to further their own interests, and earlier in England Ceolwulf II and Ecgberht I may have been in a similar position—discontented athelings who could advance themselves through an alliance with the Danes. The ascendancy in York of Æthelwold, perhaps the *Alvaldus* who appears on a few Northumbrian coins of *c.*900, may be connected with a great disturbance among the Northumbrians in 900 to which Æthelweard refers.[134] Certainly the outcome here for the Northumbrians was disastrous. Edward's forces not only slew Æthelwold in 903, they went on to invade the territory of the Northumbrian Danes in 909 and to inflict a crushing defeat on the Northumbrian army at Wednesfield in 910. This exposed Northumbria to exploitation by new Viking armies somewhat less inclined to seek the same

[129] Grierson and Blackburn, *Medieval European Coinage* I, 318–9.

[130] R. H. M. Dolley, 'The Viking coinage of York', 38.

[131] C. S. S. Lyon and B. H. I. H. Stewart, 'The Northumbrian Viking coins in the Cuerdale hoard', *Anglo-Saxon Coins: Studies Presented to F. M. Stenton*, ed. R. H. M. Dolley (London, 1961), 96–121; cf. I. Stewart, 'The early Viking mint of York', *Seaby's Coin and Medal Bulletin* (1967), 454–61. For a possible identification of Cnut with a Knútr of later saga literature, see A. P. Smyth, *Scandinavian York and Dublin* I, 47ff.

[132] M. Dolley, 'The Anglo-Danish and Anglo-Norse coinages of York', *Viking Age York and the North*, 26–31 (pp.26–7): see also now Grierson and Blackburn, *Medieval European Coinage* I, 322–3.

[133] A. P. Smyth, *Warlords and Holy Men*, 196.

[134] *Chronicle of Æthelweard*, 50–1: see A. P. Smyth, *Scandinavian York and Dublin* I, 48ff. On the identity of *Alvaldus*, see Grierson and Blackburn, *Medieval European Coinage* I, 321.

degree of accommodation with the native communities in the north or with the West Saxon dynasty in the south.[135]

[135] Cf. A. P. Smyth, *Warlords and Holy Men*, 196–7.

Ninth-century Northumbrian chronology

STEWART LYON

1. THIS note builds on ideas for a revised chronology for the ninth-century kings of Northumbria and archbishops of York contained in H. E. Pagan's article 'Northumbrian numismatic chronology in the ninth century', *BNJ* 38 (1969), pp.1–15. Mr. Pagan put forward his chronology primarily on numismatic grounds and supported it by pointing to deficiencies in the accounts of this period given in surviving chronicles. The purpose of this note is to demonstrate that a mechanistic resolution of the inconsistencies between the various sources could satisfy in large measure the revisions demanded by the numismatic evidence. Textual criticism to evaluate such a resolution is, however, beyond the scope of the note (and the competence of its author).

2. The main sources for mid-ninth century Northumbrian chronology are Roger of Wendover's *Flores Historiarum,*[1] the various works associated with Symeon of Durham,[2] and the *Annales Lindisfarnenses et Dunelmenses.*[3] The compilers must have had access to northern records, now lost, which listed the kings of Northumbria, archbishops of York, and bishops of Lindisfarne in the decades preceding the overthrow of the Northumbrian kingdom in 867 and for a few years afterwards. For the beginning of the century they could draw on the northern source which was embodied in MSS. D and E of the *Anglo-Saxon Chronicle*[4] and for the end of the century they could make use of some sketchy information recorded by Æthelweard,[5] but otherwise, except for the comparatively well documented campaign of 867, they must have had to fill the gap as best they could using the lost northern listings.[6] In addition Roger had to incorporate some descriptive information which was apparently not available to the other compilers.

3. Six of the works associated with Symeon are relevant. There are two tracts—*De Primo Saxonum Adventu Libellus* (*DPSAL*)[7] and *Series Regum Northanhymbrorum* (*SRN*)[8] which quantify, with slight variations, the reigns of seven ninth-century kings of Northumbria ending a decade or so after the fall of York:

[1] I have used the extracts in *EHD* I, ed. D. Whitelock (1955) pp.255–8.

[2] *Symeonis Monachi Opera*, ed. T. Arnold (Rolls Series, 2 vols., 1882 and 1885) (cited below as Arnold I and II).

[3] W. Levison, 'Die Annales Lindisfarnenses et Dunelmenses, kritisch untersucht und neu herausgegeben', *Deutsches Archiv* 22 (1961), 447–506 at pp.483–5. I am grateful to the late Professor Whitelock for drawing my attention to this source.

[4] See *EHD* I pp.168–70.

[5] *The Chronicle of Æthelweard*, ed. A. Campbell (1962), at pp.51–2.

[6] See *EHD* I pp.118–9 and 251.

[7] Arnold II at pp.376–7.

[8] Arnold II at p.391.

however, no dates are attached to them. In *De Archiepiscopis Eboraci* (*DAE*)[9] the episcopates of two ninth-century archbishops are measured out of four mentioned, and a single date is given (900) for which Symeon could have drawn on Æthelweard. The episcopates of four ninth-century bishops of Lindisfarne are recorded in the *Historia Dunelmensis Ecclesiae* (*HDE*)[10] which also restates the reigns of several of the kings and provides some cross-references between the two series to link their chronology. One of these has a specific date (854) which, as we shall see, provides something of a landmark but is not without its difficulties. Finally there are two accounts in the *Historia Regum* (*HR*), a work that dates each annal. Unfortunately, the first account (*HR*1) after recording events up to 801, is silent about Northumbrian affairs until 854, when it refers to episcopal changes at York and Durham consistently with *DAE* and *HDE*. The second account (*HR*2) starts in 848, giving much the same information for 854 but also specifying the reigning Northumbrian king. Both accounts subsequently record the campaign of 867 and events during the following decade, together with the episcopal successions at York and Durham at the end of the century.[11]

Roger, writing a century later than Symeon, provides us with a dated chronicle in which he refers to all the ninth-century Northumbrian dignitaries mentioned in Symeon's work with the exception of one bishop of Lindisfarne. He also adds a king (Redwulf) not recorded by Symeon, but known from coins. On the other hand the lengths of the reigns of kings and archbishops differ in several instances from those given by Symeon, and in the case of the bishops of Lindisfarne Roger is clearly confused.

The compiler of *ALD* gives us little more than an annalistic version of the undated *SRN*, with corresponding information for the bishops of Lindisfarne. The only archbishop mentioned is Wulfhere.

4. The northern recension of the *Anglo-Saxon Chronicle*, in its last entry about Northumbria before the disaster of 867, states that in 806 Eardwulf, king of the Northumbrians, was driven from his kingdom (and Eanberht, bishop of Hexham, died). The two undated Symeon tracts then record a two-year reign of a certain Ælfwald, as does *ALD*; both Roger and *ALD* date his accession to the year 808. *HDE* additionally says that Eardwulf had fled in the tenth year of his reign and Roger informs us that it was Ælfwald who had put him to flight. All five documents say or imply that Ælfwald was succeeded by Eanred, with *ALD* dating this 809 and Roger 810. It appears to be incorrect, however. The *Annals of the Frankish Kingdom* record under the year 808 that Eardwulf (who is said by *ALD*, in its only gloss on a ninth-century king before the débâcle of 867, to have married Charlemagne's daughter) came to the emperor at Nijmegen on his way to Rome. After returning from Rome he was escorted back to his kingdom by envoys of the pope and the emperor. The return of these envoys to the continent

[9] Arnold I at pp.224–5.

[10] Arnold I at pp.52–5.

[11] Dr. Michael Lapidge has recently shown that the first five sections of the *Historia Regum*, including a list of early Northumbrian kings (Arnold II, pp.13–15), a chronicle from 732 to 802 (pp.30–68), and another from 849 to 887, based mainly on Asser (pp.69–91), were in all probability written by Byrhtferth of Ramsey early in the eleventh century (see *ASE* 10, pp.97–122). Pages 92 and 101–21 of Arnold II are also relevant for this note.

is mentioned under the year 809, which seems to indicate that Eardwulf had successfully ended Ælfwald's revolt.[12] The year of Eardwulf's death is not recorded, but whenever it was it did not lead to a change of dynasty if *HDE* is correct in its statement that Eanred was Eardwulf's son.

5. Taking as their starting point that Eanred succeeded Ælfwald, the chroniclers span the period up to the fall of York in 867 by assigning to Eanred a reign of 33 (*HDE, SRN, ALD*) or 32 years (*DPSAL* and Roger); to his son Æthelred 9 (*SRN, DPSAL, ALD*) or 7 years (Roger); then after Æthelred was killed (*SRN, HDE*, Roger), to Osberht 13 (*SRN, DPSAL, ALD*) or 18 years (Roger), and, finally, to Ælle, after Osberht was deposed (*SRN, DPSAL, HDE, DAE, HR*, Roger), a reign of 5 (*HDE*) or 4 years (*ALD*). In addition Roger interpolates a brief usurpation in the middle of Æthelred's reign by Redwulf, whom he says was killed by *pagani* and Æthelred then restored. Roger's dates for the various events do not always agree with his regnal lengths, and the same is true of *ALD*. A comparison of their dates with those that can be deduced from *DPSAL, SRN*, and *HDE*, starting from the *Anglo-Saxon Chronicle*'s date of 806 for Eardwulf's expulsion, is as follows:

Roger	*ALD*		*DPSAL (implied)*	*SRN (implied)*	*HDE (implied)*
808	808	Accession of Ælfwald	(806)	(806)	(806)
810	809	Accession of Eanred	(808)	(808)	(808)
840	841	Accession of Æthelred	(840)	(841)	(841)
844	—	Usurpation of Redwulf	—	—	—
848	850	Accession of Osberht	(849)	(850)	(849)
(866)	863	Accession of Ælle	(862)	(863)	(862)

However, it seems clear from both Roger and the *Anglo-Saxon Chronicle*, and even more so from Æthelweard, that the civil strife leading to Osberht's deposition was taking place at the time the Danish army crossed the Humber, namely in the autumn of 866, and that the invasion caused Osberht and his rival Ælle to be reconciled. It is therefore unlikely that the latter could actually have reigned for the four or five years that the sources other than Roger suggest. If *SRN, DPSAL*, and *ALD* are right in limiting Osberht's reign to 13 years the possibility exists that Eanred's succession and all subsequent royal events are dated several years too early, presumably because of the chroniclers' lack of knowledge of the restoration of Eardwulf.

6. Their lack of direct information about who occupied the Northumbrian throne in the years following 808 seems to be paralleled for the archiepiscopal see of York. It is known from the *Anglo-Saxon Chronicle* that Eanbald II succeeded another archbishop of the same name in 796, but none of the sources gives either the date of his death or the duration of his episcopate. *DAE* simply states that he died during Eanred's reign, and this is supported by the nature of his coinage. Interestingly, a forged charter of Wiglaf (Sawyer 189) would have him still alive

12 *EHD* I p.313.

in 833. His successor Wulfsige (of whom no coins are known) also died in Eanred's reign and was followed by Wigmund (*DAE*); according to Roger this happened in 831. We are given to believe that Wigmund was dead by 854, when Wulfhere is said to have succeeded to the archbishopric (Roger) or, alternatively, to have received the pallium (*HR*1, *HR*2). The latter is not inconsistent with *ALD*'s date of 852 for Wulfhere's ordination as archbishop. However, *DAE* says that Wigmund having died in the sixteenth year of his episcopate (which on Roger's dating of his succession would be 847), Wulfhere succeeded to the archbishopric. A five-year interval between Wigmund's death and Wulfhere's ordination could scarcely be accepted without question. In any case there is evidence that Wigmund was still alive in 850; a letter to him from Lupus of Ferrières has survived and is unlikely to have been written before that year.[13]

7. The year 854 is one of the few dates in the middle of the century that is explicitly mentioned in several documents, so it cannot be lightly rejected. It is not found in *DAE* or *ALD*, nor of course in *SRN* or *DPSAL* but *HDE* gives it as the year of appointment of Bishop Eardwulf of Lindisfarne and describes it as the fifth year of Osberht's reign. *HR*1 and *HR*2 date Eardwulf's appointment and also Wulfhere's receipt of the pallium to 854, whilst *HR*2 adds that it was the sixth year since the birth of King Alfred and in the reign of King Osberht over the Northumbrians.

Roger, however, states that in 854 both Wulfhere and Eardwulf succeeded to their respective sees. But the numismatic evidence (see 8(e) below) suggests that, even if the ecclesiastical events are correctly dated, Æthelred may still have been reigning when Wulfhere was appointed to the archbishopric of York.

8. Some attempt needs to be made to rationalize the inconsistencies in the chronology of ninth-century Northumbria in an endeavour to overcome the problems presented by the numismatic evidence.[14] Briefly, this evidence is:

(a) A silver penny in the name of a King Eanred exists. Its dies were apparently of southern manufacture and the style of portraiture resembles that on some early pence of Æthelwulf's last issue. The Eanred penny is more likely to have been produced after than before 850 and no southern Eanred is known to whom it can be attributed. Lacking a moneyer's name (it reads ÐES MONETA, presumably for 'that person's coin', i.e. Eanred's) it may have been part of a ceremonial issue. It was found at Trewhiddle, near St. Austell, Cornwall, in 1774.[15]

(b) Apart from this silver penny and a gold solidus in the name of Archbishop Wigmund, the surviving Northumbrian coinage is entirely of so-called stycas struck on a small module. These do not bear a portrait; their

[13] *EHD* I pp.807–8.

[14] For general studies of the numismatic evidence see C.S.S. Lyon, 'A reappraisal of the sceatta and styca coinage of Northumbria', *BNJ* 28 (1957) pp.227–42, and H.E. Pagan, 'Northumbrian numismatic chronology in the ninth century', *BNJ* 38 (1969) pp.1–15.

[15] D.M. Wilson and C.E. Blunt, 'The Trewhiddle hoard', *Archaeologia* 98 (1961) pp. 75–122 at pp.113–16, where it is concluded by C.E. Blunt on the basis of conventional dating that the coin cannot be of Eanred of Northumbria but must have been issued 'by a historically unknown king, who was ruling, possibly in the Midlands, about 850'.

silver content, which gave them a recognizably silvery appearance under Archbishop Eanbald and the parallel royal issues, progressively declined to a minimal level.

(c) No coins are known of Archbishop Wulfsige. His episcopate must have been fairly brief, though if minting rights were associated with the receipt of the pallium (about which we have no evidence—but see (e) below) the absence of coins might reflect a delay in that occurrence: thus Æthelbald only received his in his fourth year (see 13 below). Another possibility is of a gap in the Northumbrian coinage which happened to coincide with Wulfsige's episcopacy. It is true that one of Eanbald's moneyers survived to mint for Wigmund but this does not of itself preclude a gap of some years between them, whatever its cause.

(d) Die links indicate that Wigmund was minting at the time of Æthelred II's accession but it is not yet apparent how early in his coinage that event took place. There are issues of Wigmund's that appear to be contemporary with Redwulf's brief coinage. On the other hand it is clear that Wigmund was not minting during the last years of Æthelred's reign—a period when the royal issues were largely in the hands of a single but highly productive moneyer.

(e) Archbishop Wulfhere took as his sole moneyer a man who also worked for Æthelred late in his reign. One of this moneyer's dies was vicariously coupled with obverses of Æthelred, Osberht, and the archbishop, suggesting that Wulfhere was already minting at the time of Æthelred's death. However, there is no continuity between Wigmund's and Wulfhere's coinage so it may well be that the archiepiscopal issues were suspended for a time during the second part of Æthelred's reign, either towards the end of Wigmund's episcopate (if, for example, he was held to have condoned Redwulf's usurpation) or following his death (perhaps because Wulfhere had not yet had his appointment confirmed from Rome).

(f) Although more extensive than Archbishop Wulfhere's, Osberht's coinage is on a much smaller scale than would be expected had he reigned for thirteen years, still less for eighteen.

(g) There is a substantial group of derivative, blundered coins which comes late in the series, perhaps mainly during Osberht's reign though it may have begun earlier. It points to a loss of royal control over minting.

(h) No coins are known of King Eardwulf. Those that used to be attributed to him are nowadays regarded as referring in some cases to Eanred's moneyer Wulfheard and in others to Æthelred II's moneyer Eardwulf. However, a small group of coins of relatively good silver, in the name of a king Æthelred and bearing a moneyer's name, is puzzling. All the indications are that it antedates Eanred and, since one of the moneyers (Cuthheard) is known, in a variant spelling, for a King Ælfwald it would seem natural to assign these coins to the period ± 790. The difficulty is that a moneyer of the same name is also found in Eanred's early coinage, which has led to the suggestion that the Ælfwald is Ælfwald II and the Æthelred an unknown king who came between Ælfwald II and Eanred.[16]

[16] See James Booth, 'Sceattas in Northumbria', in *Sceattas in England and on the Continent*, ed. D. Hill and D.M. Metcalf (BAR British Series 128) (Oxford, 1984) pp.71–97.

9. It is possible to build a new chronology for the middle of the century by making the simple assumptions that Roger, while wrong in his absolute dating for reasons already explained, has placed Wulfsige's death correctly in relation to Eanred's, Redwulf's and Æthelred's; and that the regnal lengths given by Roger and several Symeon sources for Eanred, and by *DAE* for Wigmund, are correct. Putting Y as the true date of Eanred's accession we then obtain the following approximate scheme:

Accession of Eanred	Y
Death of Wulfsige	Y + 23
Death of Eanred	Y + 32
Revolt of Redwulf	Y + 36
Death of Wigmund	Y + 39
Death of Æthelred	Y + 40

Apart from opening up the question of the absolute value of Y this does no violence to the documentary sources for events dated prior to 854 but it goes a long way to meet numismatic objections to the accepted relative chronology. However, it remains to be considered whether such a scheme could be reconciled with the annals relating to Wulfhere, Osberht, and Ælle and whether any reasonable interpretation of Y would enable Eanred's death to be placed late enough to take care of the silver penny.

10. Now if *SRN, DPSAL*, and *ALD* are right in assigning a thirteen-year reign to Osberht but *HDE* and *ALD* are mistaken in believing that Ælle ruled for four or five years—in other words if we interpret the annals for 867 in the *Anglo-Saxon Chronicle*, Æthelweard, and Roger as meaning that the revolt in Northumbria took place not long before the autumn of 866, when the Danish army captured York—we could try equating Y + 53 with the year 866. This would produce the following series of dates:

Accession of Eanred	813
Death of Wulfsige	836
Death of Eanred	845
Revolt of Redwulf	849
Death of Wigmund	852
Death of Æthelred	853
Revolt of Ælle	866
Deaths of Osberht and Ælle	867

11. Such an arrangement would not be at variance with the statement in *HR*1 and *HR*2 that Wulfhere received the pallium in 854. A further point in its favour is that a date as early as 831 for Wulfsige's death seems inconsistent with the

See also J. Booth and I. Blowers, 'Finds of sceattas and stycas from Sancton', *NC* 143 (1983), pp.139–45.

better-recorded chronology of the bishops of Lindisfarne. Bishop Ecgred, who held the see from 830 (*ALD*) for 16 years (*ALD, HDE*) and died eight years before 854 (*HDE*), was the author of a letter to Wulfsige which has survived;[17] if Wulfsige died as early as 831 this letter would have to be dated to the months following Ecgred's appointment, but its tone is hardly that of a newly consecrated bishop addressing his superior and it refers to considerable past correspondence between the two men. However, the arrangement discards *HDE*'s five-year and *ALD*'s four-year reign for Ælle, *HDE*'s statement that the ecclesiastical events of 854 took place in the fifth year of the reign of King Osberht, and Roger's assertion that Wulfhere received the archbishopric (as distinct from the pallium) in 854; for this we find ourselves accepting *ALD*'s date of 852. The arrangement rejects the opinion of several sources that Eanred succeeded to the Northumbrian kingdom two years after Eardwulf's expulsion by Ælfwald, an opinion that seems to be in direct conflict with the Frankish annals. Instead, a five-year gap in our knowledge is created, between 808 and 813, which could have been filled by Eardwulf himself, restored through Charlemagne's intervention.

12. But is this enough? Eanred still does not survive as late as seems necessary to associate the unique silver penny with him, and if it was not his, whose was it? Also, thirteen years for Osberht's reign still seems too long having regard to the limited scale of his coinage. Ideally one would wish, from a numismatic viewpoint, to retard the whole chronology prior to 866 by several further years, with the royal dates slightly more retarded than the ecclesiastical.

13. We have not so far discussed the confusion in the sources over the date of Wulfhere's death and the length of his archiepiscopate. According to *HR*1/2 he died in 892 in the 39th year; Roger says it was in 895; *ALD*, in 898; and *DAE*, 900 in the 47th year. All except *ALD*, which fails to mention it, agree that Wulfhere was succeeded by Æthelbald. Roger and *DAE* imply that the succession was immediate, but *HR*1/2 leave a gap of eight years by giving 900 as the year of Æthelbald's consecration. This date is supported by the chronicler Æthelweard, who says the consecration took place in London. *DAE* informs us that Æthelbald did not receive the pallium until the fourth year after he received the primacy.

14. There appears to be supporting evidence for *HR*'s dating of 892 in the Latin entries in MSS E and F of the *Anglo-Saxon Chronicle*. But are the sources independent? And did Wulfhere hold the see for 38/9 years or 46/7? Roger might seem to be inclining to the latter opinion when he separates the annals recording the deaths of Wulfsige and Wulfhere by 64 years; on the other hand he records Wulfhere's succession to Wigmund in his annal for 854, which cannot be reconciled with his other dates and the supposed archiepiscopal reigns.

If we accept *ALD*'s date of 852 for Wulfhere's succession and *HR*'s of 854 for his receipt of the pallium, then *ALD*'s date of 898 for his death is consistent with *DAE*'s statement that he died in the 47th year of his episcopate. This is not so long before the consecration of Æthelbald in 900 as to be implausible, but is long enough to explain why the two events seem not to have been linked in the

[17] *EHD* I pp.806–7.

sources drawn upon by Æthelweard, *ALD*, and *HR*. But suppose Wulfhere did not hold the see for 46/7 years, and that *HR* is right in giving 38/9 years as the length of his episcopate? The author of *HR* might have arrived at 892 for the date of Wulfhere's death by adding 38 to an assumed succession in 854. Some support for this view is to be found in Dr. A.P. Smyth's observation that *HR* dates a number of events in the period in question six years too early.[18] If Wulfhere received the pallium in 860 rather than 854 and died in 898 rather than 892, he could well have been appointed in 859. Depending on the immediacy of his succession to Wigmund, the latter's appointment would then need to be dated to ±843.

15. Taking the death of Wigmund as Y + 39 (see paragraph 10) and that of Wulfhere as 898, we can produce alternative chronologies based on episcopal reigns of 46 and 39 years for Wulfhere—in other words equating 898 with Y + 85 and Y + 78 respectively. The other dates emerge as follows:

	Chronology (A)		*Chronology (B)*	
Accession of Eanred	Y	813	Y	820
Death of Wulfsige	Y + 23	836	Y + 23	843
Death of Eanred	Y + 32	845	Y + 32	852
Revolt of Redwulf	Y + 36	849	Y + 36	856
Death of Wigmund	Y + 39	852	Y + 39	859
Death of Æthelred	Y + 40	853	Y + 40	860
Revolt of Ælle	Y + 53	866	(Y + 46)	866
Deaths of Osberht and Ælle	Y + 54	867	(Y + 47)	867
Death of Wulfhere	Y + 85	898	Y + 78	898

Chronology (A) is an extension of the arrangement in paragraph 10. Chronology (B) represents a retardation by seven years of all the events before 866. Minor variations of either are, of course, quite possible.

16. A chronology such as (B) would accommodate the Eanred penny, which might perhaps be interpreted as the minting, at a southern mint, of silver bequeathed in his will, much as in the next century King Eadred left gold to be minted into mancuses and distributed. More difficult is whether a date circa 856 is consistent with Roger's statement that Redwulf was killed in a battle with *pagani*. The accepted date of 844 was a year in which, according to the Annals of St. Bertin's, 'the Northmen attacked with war the island of Britain, especially in the part which is inhabited by the Anglo-Saxons, and fighting for three days were victorious, committed plunder, rapine, and slaughter everywhere, and possessed the land at their pleasure'.[19] But there is no necessary association between two events, and the chronicler at St. Bertin's otherwise displays no obvious knowledge of events in England outside Wessex. More relevant, perhaps, is a charter of Burgred, given in 855 'when the pagans were in the province of the Wrekin-dwellers'.[20] It is evident from this that southern chroniclers were not

[18] A.P. Smyth, *Scandinavian York and Dublin* I (Dublin, 1975), at pp.56–7 n.22.

[19] *EHD* I p.314 no.23.

[20] *EHD* I p.486 no.90.

sufficiently aware of Viking raids on Mercia, still less Northumbria, to record them for posterity.

17. However, unlike Chronology (A), Chronology (B) unhinges us from the date of 854 specifically given in both *HR*1 and *HR*2 for Wulfhere's receipt of the pallium. Less seriously, given the numismatic evidence, it also destroys the regnal length of 13 years assigned to Osberht by *SRN, DPSAL* and *ALD*. But what seems fatal for it is the circumstantial evidence of episcopal lists contained in two southern manuscripts.[21]

17.1 *MS Cotton Vespasian B VI* was first compiled, probably in Mercia, between 805 and 814 when Eanbald was the latest name listed at York. It was updated by a second scribe after Ceolnoth became archbishop of Canterbury (833) but before this scribe knew of the succession to Wigthegn and Hereferth at Winchester (they both died in 836). However, he did add 'Wulfsig' at York, which suggests that Wulfsige must have acceded in or before 836 and could even have died by then, for the numismatic evidence is that his reign is likely to have been quite short. (Scribe II was apparently unaware that Ecgred had succeeded Heathured at Lindisfarne in 830 (*ALD*) so his general knowledge of Northumbria must have been limited.)

17.2 The episcopal lists in the related *MS Corpus Christi College Cambridge 183*, a West Saxon manuscript dated between 934 and 942, seem not to have been updated after the early 840s except for Canterbury and the West Saxon sees of Ramsbury, Sherborne, Wells, and Crediton. Elsewhere south of the Humber, all changes known to have taken place before 841 are incorporated, but none of those known to have occurred after 844; moreover the latest Mercian king in the regnal lists is Berhtwulf. Once again the Northumbrian sees are out of date, except for the archiepiscopal see where the list ends with Wigmund. This appears to give us a firm *terminus ante quem* of 841 x 844 for Wigmund's accession.

By itself, CCCC 183 is not inconsistent with Chronology (B), or something close to it. However, taken in conjunction with Vespasian B VI and the apparent brevity of Wulfsige's episcopate, it is more likely that Wigmund succeeded him in the middle or late 830s—in other words at a date broadly consistent with Chronology (A)—than in the 840s. Interestingly, Eanbald II may well have lived as late as 833, the purported date of the forged charter that lists him.

18. Is there scope for reconciling Chronology (A) for the archbishops with Chronology (B) for the kings? So far we have assumed that Roger, whilst he dated Wulfsige's death several years too early, placed it correctly in relation to Eanred's. There is no certainty that this is correct, however. Numismatically it seems to leave too short a gap between Wigmund's death and Æthelred's unless the archbishop was deprived of minting rights after Redwulf's usurpation (see 8(d) and (e) above). If we postulate that Wigmund was succeeded by Wulfhere in

[21] R.I. Page, 'Anglo-Saxon episcopal lists', *Nottingham Mediaeval Studies* 9 (1965), 71–95, and 10 (1966), 2–24; see also David Dumville, 'The Anglian collection of royal genealogies and regnal lists', *ASE* 5 (1976), pp.23–50, and R. Kay, 'Wulfsige and ninth-century Northumbrian chronology', *Northern History* 19 (1983), 8–14.

854 (rather than 852) and that this was the year following Redwulf's usurpation, we produce a compromise Chronology (C) which is probably as late as is consistent with historical credibility, viz.

	Chronology (C)
Accession of Eanred	818
Death of Wulfsige	838
Death of Eanred	850
Revolt of Redwulf	853
Death of Wigmund	854
Death of Æthelred	858
Revolt of Ælle	866
Deaths of Osberht and Ælle	867
Death of Wulfhere	900

In the process we retard the traditional royal chronology by nine or ten years, leaving Osberht with a reign of only eight years compared with the thirteen or eighteen given him by the chroniclers.

19. Chronology (C) would just about enable us to regard the Eanred silver penny as a memorial issue. Also, like Chronology (A), it would open up a gap of several years between Eardwulf's restoration and his son Eanred's accession. Do the silvery coins of an Æthelred have any relevance to that gap? If so, where do the comparable coins of Ælfwald fit in, given the absence of any coins of Eardwulf? If not, and if Æthelred and Ælfwald are the late-eighth century kings of those names, why do they share a moneyer with Eanred and why was Eardwulf's reign coinless?

DISCUSSION

Dr Dumville's contribution to the discussion of Mr Lyon's paper is printed, in a fuller version, as a separate paper below.

THE EANRED PENNY

[PLATE 1]

The unique silver penny reading EANRED REX, if it is attributed to King Eanred of Northumbria, raises acute problems of interpretation which have never been completely satisfactorily solved. It is inconceivable that it was intended to circulate alongside Eanred's stycas.

It could, in principle, be the only surviving specimen of an abortive reform of the coinage by which Eanred planned to bring Northumbria into line with southern England. It is quite possible that there was a gap in the minting of coinage at the beginning of Eanred's reign, and certainly his stycas, when their issue began, are a reformed coinage, as their metrology (and silver contents) show. Eanred could, as another possibility, have attempted a reform later in his reign; but by then the pressure on the availability of bullion should have made it obvious in advance that a good-silver penny coinage was likely to encounter problems.

Alternatively, the coin could perhaps have been struck at a mint which normally struck pennies, e.g. a Mercian mint, in some way as a courtesy to Eanred or for his benefit—although it would, I think, be the only known example where such a facility was extended, for some special occasion, to the ruler of another kingdom.

A way of escaping from the above difficulties would be to suggest that the King Eanred whom the coin names is not Eanred of Northumbria, but an otherwise unknown king from the middle of the ninth-century, ruling south of the Humber, e.g. a short-lived successor to King Berhtwulf of Mercia.

All three of the solutions just sketched verge on special pleading; and the details of the coin itself add a further prickly crop of difficulties.

First, its stylistic affinities seem to be with coins that are later in date than the death of Eanred. Desperate responses to this have been to try to move forward the date of Eanred's death (Mr Pagan's position of 1969, restated by Mr Lyon); or to question the authenticity of the coin, which however has a long pedigree, so that it could only be a question of substitution before the first photograph was published.

Secondly, the reverse inscription, which has always been read as *Thes moneta*, again seems to be quite without parallel. *Thes* is not the name of a moneyer (which is what one would certainly expect to find on the reverse of a ninth-century penny), and this is the major obstacle to attributing the coin to an unknown southern king: had the solution been along these lines, one would have expected not just *a* moneyer's name, but a *known* moneyer's name. It is an obstacle likewise to seeing the coin as the sole survivor of an abortive reform; and it is the positive encouragement behind the idea of a small issue struck specially to carry out Eanred's testamentary dispositions among persons in the south mentioned in his will. This latter idea, it must be said, seems far-fetched. If on the other hand *thes* is an Anglo-Saxon word, its general sense in context is still by no means obvious. The pedigree of the coin and the word *thes* are discussed below by Mr Pagan and Dr Smart respectively.

Without being able to offer any way out of the difficulties which abound, I add a few details about the coin's stylistic affinities and its design. The obverse seems closest to Æthelred's Open Cross type (minted from the early 850s onwards): this would point to Canterbury as the mint. The hairstyle, diadem, features of the face, and drapery of the bust are not however so close as to rule out coincidence and make the hand of the die-cutter certain. The reverse type, a cross with crosslets and letters (cursive M or omega) added, is more unusual, but can be matched, quite closely, on coins of Berhtwulf and, less closely, on Kentish and West Saxon coins (where the letter cannot refer to Mercia). A comparable coin of Berhtwulf (*BMC*) is shown on Plate 1, where it will be noticed that the drapery of the bust is very different, and that the orientation of the coin is 90° different.

One detail of the coin which has not received comment and which needs to be taken into account in any completely satisfactory explanation is the last letter or symbol of the reverse inscription. From the enlarged direct photograph (the coin has a dark patina and is difficult to reproduce except from a cast) it can just be seen as an omega with a titulus joined to the central bar, as in the sketch below. I have no idea how to explain it. A word beginning with a long O?—Othes?

The surface appearance of the coin is extremely convincing, its weight is as stated by Ruding (1.07g/16.54gr), and its pedigree impeccable, but I would still like to see it submitted to a thorough investigation by electron-microscopy and EPMA.

D. M. M.

MR PAGAN: The earliest reliable evidence for the coins represented in the 1774 discovery of ninth-century coins and ornamental metalwork at Trewhiddle, near St Austell, Cornwall, is the information contained in a run of five leaves from a notebook kept by Philip Rashleigh (1739-1811), the Cornish landowner into whose possession fifty-seven coins from the hoard passed soon after its discovery.[1]

The presence in the hoard of a coin of a King Eanred is established by an entry in a summary list of 'Coins found in Trewhiddle about half a mile south of St Austell ... in 1774', which appears on the recto of the third leaf concerned. The entry is itself not wholly straightforward, for it reads 'Eanred 2:do:', beneath an entry reading 'Aethelred 2:do:', which in its turn is beneath an entry reading 'Ethelulf - 2:no face - 3 nearly the same'. A close study of the list as a whole suggests however that the figure 2 which appears in these entries, and in nine other entries, does not indicate the number of coins to which the entry relates, but rather their dimensions, on a scale in which the figure 1 relates to coins of less than penny dimension and larger figures relate to coins of increasing dimensions. Similarly, the 'do' in the entry for Eanred is intended in the context of the list as a whole to indicate that the obverse of the coin carried a 'side face looking to the right', rather than 'no face' as its position two below the Æthelwulf entry might at first suggest.

The presence in the hoard of one, and only one, coin of Eanred is rather more straightforwardly evidenced by the entry 'EANRED.1' in a rough tabulation on the verso of the fourth leaf of the notebook. Here Rashleigh is listing the coins that he had acquired from the hoard according to the spelling of the issuers' names on their obverses and the entry for Eanred comes between entries for a coin of 'Ludovicus' (a

[1] These leaves are in a bound volume of Rashleigh MSS in the Department of Coins and Medals, British Museum (the volume was presented to the Department by the late Prof. Michael Dolley, M.R.I.A., F.S.A.). It should be noted that the hoard was actually found on land belonging to Philip Rashleigh's younger brother John Rashleigh (1742–1813), and that this accounts for the fact that the objects of metalwork and a few of the coins bypassed Philip Rashleigh and devolved, via John Rashleigh's son Sir Colman Rashleigh, Bart., on the neighbouring Rogers family of Penrose.

temple-type denier in the name of an emperor Louis) and entries for coins of Archbishop Ceolnoth of Canterbury with the archbishop's name spelled in three different ways.

Neither of these entries is in itself sufficient to demonstrate that the coin of Eanred in question was the well-known Eanred penny, but a volume of Ruding's papers in the Department of Manuscripts in the British Library contains a list of sixty-seven Anglo-Saxon coins demonstrably in Philip Rashleigh's possession sometime before the death of the Rev. Richard Southgate on 25 Jan 1795.[2] The first fifty-five of these appear all to derive from Trewhiddle, and the Eanred penny occupies forty-fifth place among them, the entry for it reading 'Eanred. Thes - 16½ [sc.grains]'.

It figures once more, this time fully described, in a list of eighty-four coins from Philip Rashleigh's collection drawn up by Taylor Combe shortly after 23 July 1802, the date at which he wrote Philip Rashleigh a letter acknowledging their receipt on loan.[3]

There is no sign either on the list in Ruding's papers or on Taylor Combe's list that Philip Rashleigh by then possessed a styca of Eanred, and there can be no serious doubt that the Eanred penny was the coin of Eanred which he had obtained from the Trewhiddle hoard.

The coin passed eventually with the rest of Philip Rashleigh's collection into the possession of his great-nephew Jonathan Rashleigh (1820–1905), a keen collector and student of coins, and was offered for sale as lot 151 at the sale of the family collection by Jonathan's son Evelyn William Rashleigh at Sotheby's 21 June 1909 following. It subsequently passed through the collections of George Jonathan Bascom and Richard Cyril Lockett, and was purchased for the British Museum at the sale of the first portion of Lockett's English collection in 1955.

DR SMART: Amongst the other anomalous features of the Eanred penny, the reverse legend ÐES MONETA is no less puzzling. The formula is unique to this coin and is half in Latin and half in the vernacular, *moneta* being the Latin word for mint, money, or coin.

OE *ðes* in the literary (WS) language is the nominative singular masculine of the demonstrative pronoun and adjective (*ðes* m., *ðios* f., *ðis* n.) 'this'. Such a parsing would seem incorrect here, however, since *moneta* is feminine in Latin and if the writer had in his mind the OE equivalent, OE *mynet* is neuter. *Moneta* might still be compatible with a masculine adjective if it were an abbreviation of *monetarius* 'moneyer' but the translation 'this moneyer' makes poor sense.

In the Anglian dialects (Mercian and Northumbrian) *ðes* may be a form of *ðæs*, which is the genitive singular masculine and neuter of the demonstrative (*se* m., *seo* f., *ðæt* n.) 'that, the'. If we take *moneta* to be the whole word in the nominative case the rendering would be 'the coin of that (man)'. There are few parallels in OE usage where this demonstrative in an oblique case stands alone without the noun

[2] British Library, Add MS 18093 f.112. The list carries an annotation by Ruding 'from Mr Southgate's MSS'. The list has its limitations, for it only very occasionally gives any indication of the types of the coins concerned, but it gives a weight for nearly every coin.

[3] This list by Taylor Combe is also in the Department of Coins and Medals, British Museum.

which it qualifies but the closest given by Bosworth and Toller's *Anglo-Saxon Dictionary* are: *he ðæs dyde hreowsunga* 'he did penance for that (crime)' and *he ðæs hæfde mede* 'he received a reward for that (good action)'. Even here, the demonstrative immediately follows on the sentence where the thing to which it refers has occurred. On this analogy, we should perhaps refer to the obverse and read the reverse as its complement: 'the coin of that (king)'. The idea that *ðæs* refers to the moneyer, either alone 'the coin of that (moneyer)' or in agreement with a truncated *monetarii* 'of that moneyer' is less attractive on stylistic grounds, but all possible interpretations need to be aired, and the reverse is traditionally the moneyer's place.

PLATE 1

1a

1b

2

Textual archaeology and Northumbrian history subsequent to Bede

DAVID N. DUMVILLE

ABOUT fifteen years ago I first encountered a classic piece of archaeological literature which made a deep impression and has remained in my mind ever since. In it the writer described a visit to see ancient earthworks at Dunragit in Wigtownshire.[1] He reported that Mr Ralegh Radford, on observing the site, pronounced it to be without doubt a British (Celtic) fortification of the fifth or sixth century. I doubt that archaeologists today would be so enthusiastic about giving datings to monuments merely on the basis of such morphological features as are visible on site before excavation. In just the same way the historian must exercise skills of textual criticism on the literary and documentary sources which constitute so much of his stock-in-trade. He must excavate his texts, not in the spirit of a treasure-hunter seeking little more than the thrill of whatever finds may come to hand, but in as measured and scientific a fashion as possible. In the academic discipline of history, as in archaeology, the time for treasure-hunting has now passed. In spite of occasional lapses, methods and standards of criticism are rigorous and well advertized.

The sources for Northumbrian history in the period from the completion and 'publication' in 731 of St Bede's *Historia ecclesiastica gentis Anglorum* to the seizure of York by Scandinavian forces in 867 fall into two groups. On the one hand there are those which are obviously contemporary or proceed from contemporary testimony by a reasonably clearly established line of transmission. On the other hand there is a mass of non-contemporary literature, largely twelfth-century in date, whose constituents have either not been examined in depth or, having been analysed, have proved to be antiquarian exercises of no value for eighth- and ninth-century history. Into the very last category fall, for example, the twelfth-century *Annales Lindisfarnenses et Dunelmenses*, studied in

This paper originated in remarks made as part of the discussion of Stewart Lyon's paper, printed above. I am indebted to Michael Metcalf both for the original invitation to the symposium (from participating in which gathering I learned much) and for his vigorous encouragement to write up these observations. I am also obliged to Mark Blackburn and Simon Keynes for kindly reading and commenting on the galley-proofs.

[1] R. C. Reid, 'Dunragit', *Transactions of the Dumfriesshire and Galloway Natural History and Antiquarian Society*, 3rd S., 29 (1950/1) 155–64, especially pp. 155–6.

detail by Wilhelm Levison who showed them to be of no independent merit.[2]

In general, it is the deficiencies rather than the strengths of the literary sources for this period of Northumbrian history which are the more apparent. Especially for the second half of the period 731–867, most of our information is mediated through, or originates in, twelfth- or thirteenth-century texts. Such a situation naturally creates conditions in which the historically minded investigator may choose speculation or resort to different classes of evidence in order to attempt to create a useful picture of the period in question. So it was that in 1969 Hugh Pagan, in a characteristically impressive and stimulating paper, sought to brush aside much of the chronology of the Northumbrian ninth century provided by post-Conquest literary sources in favour of one deduced from its royal and archiepiscopal coinage.[3] This approach was attempted in no haughty spirit but with due attention to the textual prehistory of certain post-Conquest histories as well as to the numismatic evidence. If his case fails to convince, it does so (I think) not because of any inaccuracies in his argument but for the reason that his examination of the literary sources did not go nearly far enough; but I am not sure that he does fail to convince—for me, his interdisciplinary attempt to solve the troublesome problems of ninth-century Northumbrian chronology remains the most intelligent and persuasive articulation of the difficulties.

In his paper, 'Ninth-century Northumbrian chronology',[4] Stewart Lyon has sought broadly to support Pagan's conclusions by manipulating into various hypothetical patterns the chronological evidence provided by a substantial number of apparent witnesses to ninth-century Northumbrian history. The principal difficulty which the historian must feel in face of this exercise is that there is insufficient indication of discrimination between the several texts pressed into service.

It may therefore be helpful to offer a rapid survey of the textual evidence in question, pointing out our areas of ignorance where new work is greatly to be desired, and drawing attention to the broad preferences which the generality of historians is likely to share when faced with the task of discrimination between the information presented by the several sources. For the sake of brevity, I confine myself to the sources mentioned by Lyon and Pagan.[5]

I begin with the latest texts used. The massive *Flores historiarum* of Roger Wendover, written from a great variety of sources at St Albans Abbey in the early thirteenth century, has not been edited since the 1840s and awaits a thorough modern investigation, for which the essential precondition has been met by an examination of the historical works of his St Albans successor, Matthew Paris.[6]

[2] 'Die "Annales Lindisfarnenses et Dunelmenses" kritisch untersucht und neu herausgegeben', *Deutsches Archiv für Erforschung des Mittelalters* 17 (1961) 447–506.

[3] H. E. Pagan, 'Northumbrian numismatic chronology in the ninth century', *British Numismatic Journal* 38 (1969) 1–15.

[4] above, pp. 27–36.

[5] Many others do exist: one may refer, for example, to the works of Alcuin, the *uitae* of English missionary saints, medieval Irish and Welsh chronicles, papal documentation, the York metrical martyrology, and the *Historia de Sancto Cuthberto*. All these, and more, have their part to play in building a picture of Northumbrian history between 731 and 867.

[6] *Rogeri de Wendover Chronica, sive Flores Historiarum*, ed. Henry O. Coxe (5 vols, London 1841–4): for the pre-Conquest period see volume 1; even so, the whole of the *Flores*

Hugh Pagan performed a signal service by demonstrating the relationship between one of Roger's sources for ninth-century history, 'a register of events in Northumbria' from 806 to 876 which 'apparently referred only to the succession of kings, archbishops, and bishops of Lindisfarne', and a similar text used by the author of the *Historia Dunelmensis ecclesie.*[7] However, the implication is that the ultimate source was a collection (or collections) of regnal and episcopal lists—presumably of the sort which is found in the ultimately eighth-century 'Anglian collection' (now surviving in ninth-century and later copies), but updated to take account of ninth-century successions in Northumbria.[8] The similarity between the treatment of this material in the named St Albans and Durham sources suggests also the existence of an intermediate source used in both: the date and quality of that witness is the crucial issue for the historian seeking to evaluate the evidential value of the extant sources of information. The presence of unique information about Redwulf's usurpation, so easily assimilable to the numismatic testimony, has seemed to many to validate Roger's source for ninth-century Northumbrian history and therefore to permit use, without further concern, of his annals for that period. The incorporation of a selection of these in Dorothy Whitelock's *English Historical Documents c. 500–1042* has further encouraged such casual employment.[9]

In the twelfth century, and particularly during its first half, Durham cathedral priory was a hotbed of historiographic activity. As the texts created or revised then spilled out from Durham they encouraged, or were assimilated into, historiographic activity elsewhere in the Northern province. In some cases, we now know the Durham literature only from its later Northern derivatives. The standard modern account of this process remains the inaugural lecture (1958) of Professor H. S. Offler—in its wit, elegance, clarity, and learning a classic of the genre.[10]

I have already mentioned, in passing, *Annales Lindisfarnenses et Dunelmenses*, a twelfth-century Durham series of retrospective paschal annals. Published for the first time only a quarter-century ago, this chronicle, surviving in two manuscripts, is much less well known than those published in successive editions from the mid-seventeenth century to the late nineteenth. However, the quality of its testimony, all necessarily non-contemporary, was denounced by its editor, Wilhelm Levison.[11] Its sources and their employment must nonetheless be

was not printed by Coxe. For criticism see V. H. Galbraith, *Roger Wendover and Matthew Paris* (Glasgow 1944); Richard Vaughan, *Matthew Paris* (Cambridge 1958; rev. imp., 1979).

7 'Northumbrian numismatic chronology', p. 4.

8 For such collections see R. I. Page, 'Anglo-Saxon episcopal lists', *Nottingham Mediaeval Studies* 9 (1965) 71–95 *and* 10 (1966) 2–24; D. N. Dumville, 'The Anglian collection of royal genealogies and regnal lists', *Anglo-Saxon England* 5 (1976) 23–50. I return to these sources below.

9 (2nd edn., London 1979), pp. 281–4 (no. 4).

10 *Medieval Historians of Durham* (Durham 1958). See further J. M. Todd & H. S. Offler, 'A medieval chronicle from Scotland', *Scottish Historical Review* 36 (1957) 151–9, and H. S. Offler, 'Hexham and the *Historia Regum*', *Transactions of the Architectural and Archaeological Society of Durham and Northumberland*, N.S., 2 (1970) 51–62.

11 See n. 2 above; Offler, *Medieval Historians*, pp. 10–11 and 21, n. 21, entered a plea for the further consideration of their annals 793, 797, 808, and 820, *inter alia*.

considered when twelfth-century Durham historiography receives a comprehensive re-evaluation.

Since the later twelfth century an increasing number of works has been attributed to Symeon of Durham. Some of these attributions are the responsibility of sixteenth-century or other modern writers, often made with remarkable casualness. Others derive from rubrics in medieval manuscripts but must, for various reasons, be viewed with the utmost suspicion until a comprehensive examination of the texts in question provides evidence allowing definition of authorship. Only one text, the letter *De archiepiscopis Eboracensibus*, written in 1090 × 1109 or 1130 × 1132 to Hugh, dean of York, is self-evidently Symeon's work.[12] A significant weakness, therefore, of published work on the twelfth-century texts' information about ninth-century Northumbrian history derives from the assumption that the methods and resources of a single author may be seen in a number of the crucial texts.

The most widely used, but also one of the most difficult, of these texts is that known as the *Historia regum*.[13] Its very complex history as a text, stretching back to the late tenth-century Fenland monastery of Ramsey, has been the subject of a number of illuminating publications during the last quarter-century.[14] The whole work, as published in the editions of 1652 to 1885, was probably created at Durham in or soon after 1129, the date of its last annal. However, that text of *c.* 1130 is at present irrecoverable in detail for it survives only in a series of subsequent twelfth-century recensions which have suffered considerable interference. Broadly speaking, the *Historia regum* divides into two parts: a somewhat eccentric and discontinuous history from the death of Bede (albeit with a variety of prefatory matter concerning the seventh and earlier eighth centuries and including a Northumbrian king-list from Ida to Ceolwulf) to the mid-tenth century,[15] followed by a continuous annalistic history from AD 848 to 1129. Down to the year 887 Part One was written by Byrhtferth of Ramsey *c.* AD 1000, some further annals for 888–951 (which incorporate a Chester-le-Street element) being appended subsequently. Part Two draws largely on the *Chronicarum chronica* of John of Worcester, apparently first published in 1131 but circulating among interested scholars for a number of years previously:[16] the text begins with the birth of King

[12] *Symeonis Monachi Opera Omnia*, ed. Thomas Arnold (2 vols, London 1882/5), I. 222–8; see also the introduction to that volume.

[13] Best, but still poorly, edited by Hodgson Hinde, *Symeonis Dunelmensis Opera et Collectanea* (Durham 1868); see also Arnold, *Symeonis Monachi Opera Omnia*, II.

[14] P. Hunter Blair, 'Some observations on the *Historia Regum* attributed to Symeon of Durham', in *Celt and Saxon. Studies in the Early British Border*, ed. N. K. Chadwick (Cambridge 1963; rev. imp., 1964), pp. 63–118; M. Lapidge, 'Byrhtferth of Ramsey and the early sections of the *Historia Regum* attributed to Symeon of Durham', *Anglo-Saxon England* 10 (1982) 97–122; C. Hart, 'Byrhtferth's Northumbrian chronicle', *English Historical Review* 97 (1982) 558–82; M. Lapidge, 'A tenth-century metrical calendar from Ramsey', *Revue bénédictine* 94 (1984) 326–69; M. Brett, 'John of Worcester and his contemporaries', in *The Writing of History in the Middle Ages. Essays presented to Richard William Southern*, edd. R. H. C. Davis *et al.* (Oxford 1981), pp. 101–26.

[15] A new edition, *The Historia Regum* Part 1, edd. D. Dumville and M. Lapidge, is at press as volume 16 of *The Anglo-Saxon Chronicle. A Collaborative Edition*, gen. edd. D. Dumville and S. Keynes (23 vols, Cambridge 1982–).

[16] On John of Worcester see the paper by M. Brett (n. 14 above); a new edition of his Chronicle, by R. R. Darlington and P. McGurk,

Alfred, but only its last decade incorporates a substantially original and Northern element. It is this latter part of the *Historia regum*, and perhaps also its combination with Part One, which has been thought to be the work of Symeon. However, the attribution of the *Historia regum* to him depends on the testimony of a single twelfth-century mauscript from Sawley Abbey:[17] attributions of authorship are known to have been rather freely accorded to anonymous texts read and copied there.

The *Historia Dunelmensis ecclesie* (or, better, the *Libellus de exordio atque procursu... Dunelmensis ecclesie*) was written in the first decade of the twelfth century, perhaps in 1104 × 1107.[18] It is a work in four books, carrying its story down to 1096. The attribution to Symeon occurs principally in another Sawley manuscript, but is found also in two later manuscripts: but the implications of this distribution remain unclear.[19] The text is preserved in its earliest and anonymous form in a hypothetically authorial manuscript in Durham University Library.[20]

Interpolated into *Historia Dunelmensis ecclesie* in the Sawley manuscript only, between *capitula* and text, is a regnal list from Ida of Bernicia to Henry I which has been printed under the heading *Series regum Northymbrensium*.[21] This is a version of notably poor quality when compared with other, earlier texts of the Northumbrian regnal list, including that embedded in the *Historia regum*, Part One. Its sole apparent merit is that, unlike earlier witnesses, it continues beyond 796. Given the low quality of its textually testable section, however, one must not be over-enthusiastic for its information about the ninth and tenth centuries.

Finally, in this group, we come to the *Libellus de primo Saxonum aduentu*, one of the earliest of that genre of post-Conquest histories of the 'heptarchic' period of Anglo-Saxon England. The *Libellus* survives in more than one recension and has never been fully published. It concludes with lists of the archbishops of Canterbury, the archbishops of York, and the bishops of Durham. Apparently first written in the reign of Henry I, it has been freely quoted; but it seems to be a scholar's reconstruction of a distant Anglo-Saxon past, using inadequate materials; as we know from many examples, a medieval scholarly history is much less likely to contain readily usable information than is a mere compilation.[22]

---

will appear in the series 'Oxford Medieval Texts'.

[17] Cambridge, Corpus Christi College, MS. 139, on which see the papers collected in David N. Dumville, *Histories and Pseudo-histories of the Insular Middle Ages* (Variorum Reprints, London 1988), and D. Baker, 'Scissors and paste: Corpus Christi, Cambridge, MS 139 again', *Studies in Church History* 11 (1975) 83–123.

[18] *Symeonis Monachi Opera Omnia*, ed. Arnold, I.17–135: on the authorship, p. xxiii; on the date, pp. xix and 111, n. a; cf. Offler, *Medieval Historians*, pp. 6–8.

[19] Cambridge, Corpus Christi College, MS. 66, and University Library Ff.I.27 (1160), probably written at Sawley *c*. 1200: *Historia* in Ff.I.27, pp. 122–186. The other manuscripts bearing an attribution have been discussed by Offler, *Medieval Historians*, p. 20, n. 8.

[20] Durham, University Library, MS. Cosin V.ii.6.

[21] Ff.I.27, pp. 128–30: published by Arnold, *Symeonis Monachi Opera Omnia*, II.389–93.

[22] The text was last, but still incompletely, published by Arnold, *ibid.*, II.365–84, from the earliest known recension; for another witness see S. R. T. O. d'Ardenne, 'A neglected manuscript of British history', in *English and Medieval Studies presented to J. R. R. Tolkien on the Occasion of his Seventieth Birthday*, edd. Norman Davis and C. L. Wrenn (London 1962), pp. 84–93. Generally on this text see Offler, *Medieval Historians*, pp. 11–12 and 22, nn. 23–24.

All these twelfth-century Durham 'histories' require to be re-edited and thoroughly studied before we can hope to understand how their statements about earlier Northumbrian history may be interpreted and used. For the moment, however, it must be said that, with one exception, they fail the historian's first basic test. They are non-contemporary sources whose information has no identified pedigree(s). As such, they are not available for use by students of ninth-century Northumbria. The exception is Part One of the *Historia regum*, most sections of whose record have had their sources identified and examined. This does not mean that use of their information will be uncomplicated, but interpretation of it may now proceed beyond the phase of purely internal criticism. For our immediate purposes, the unfortunate fact is that the early annals of Northumbrian (and perhaps York) origin cease to be employed in it after AD 802, leaving a half-century's hiatus in the text's chronological structure and cutting off our simple and reasonably reliable access to Northern history.

Two other types of chronicle-text have been brought to bear in the debate about ninth-century Northumbrian chronology. The first, and perhaps less complicated, is Frankish, providing apparently contemporary witness to British events of 808, 809, 813 (?), 839, 844, 850, 855, 856, 858, 860, 861, 862, and 864; but few of these entries bear on Northumbrian history. The works in question are the *Annales regni Francorum* (AD 741–813, revised and continued to 829) and an apparent continuation, the so-called 'Annals of Saint-Bertin' (covering 830–882).[23]

From the English side of the Channel, various versions and relatives of the Anglo-Saxon Chronicle contribute relevant information. The annals proper to the 'common stock' of the Chronicle, as written (or completed) and 'published' in 892, are of West Saxon origin. The extent of their contribution to Northumbrian history, however, is represented by the very controversial annal for 829, and then the series of annals for 867 and subsequent years (these latter finding their way also into Asser's biography of King Alfred) which chronicle Scandinavian activity in Northumbria. On the other hand, three eleventh- and twelfth-century manuscripts of the Anglo-Saxon Chronicle (viz DEF) attest a version revised by an author with a marked Northumbrian bias and Northumbrian sources of information which he interpolated into his inherited Chronicle-text. This so-called 'Northern recension' of the Chronicle is written in the West Saxon literary dialect: it probably emanates from York in the period after 956 when Southern clerics held the Northern archbishopric.[24] Among its sources was a version, extending to AD 806, of the

[23] *Annales Regni Francorum inde ab A. 741 usque ad A. 829 qui dicuntur Annales Laurissenses Maiores et Einhardi*, ed. Friedrich Kurze (Hannover 1895); the whole text has been translated by Bernhard Walter Scholz and B. Rogers, *Carolingian Chronicles.* Royal Frankish Annals *and Nithard's* Histories (Ann Arbor, Michigan 1970). *Annales de Saint-Bertin*, edd. Félix Grat *et al.* (Paris 1964); a translation has been prepared by Dr Janet L. Nelson. For translated excerpts from these two texts, see Whitelock, *English Historical Documents*, pp. 341–2 (no. 21) and 342–4 (no. 23).

[24] For a brief introductory survey of the problems posed by the textual history of the Anglo-Saxon Chronicle see Whitelock, *ibid.*, pp. 109–25; on Asser see first Simon Keynes and M. Lapidge, *Alfred the Great. Asser's* Life of King Alfred *and Other Contemporary Sources* (Harmondsworth 1983). On AD 892 and the Chronicle see P. H. Sawyer, *The Age of the Vikings* (2nd edn., London 1971), chapter 2, and David N. Dumville, *Wessex and England from Alfred to Edgar* (Woodbridge 1987), chapter 3.

Northern (and perhaps York) annals also underlying the *Continuatio Baedae* (to 766)[25] and the *Historia regum*, Part One (to 801); but its version of these annals often differs materially from the Latin tradition. Unfortunately the detailed work of comparison and criticism which might enable these discrepancies to be explained and the information to be satisfactorily interpreted has not yet been completed and published. Likewise we still lack a sufficiently detailed analysis of the Chronicle's 'Northern recension' as a whole to enable us to define the precise circumstances of the transmission of its information.[26]

The *Chronicon* of Ealdorman Æthelweard, written in 978 x 988 and apparently in southwestern England, represents in part a translation of the common stock of the Anglo-Saxon Chronicle. From the 890s the *Chronicon* shows access to an independent source of information about Northern affairs. This difficult text was edited and translated by Alistair Campbell in 1962, but his pioneering work is already showing severe signs of wear: it needs to be revised or replaced and Æthelweard's work reassessed.[27]

Two texts which lie on the boundary between the literary and the documentary must be mentioned briefly. The undoubtedly genuine letter of Ecgred, bishop of 'Lindisfarne' ('bishop of St Cuthbert' might be better), to Wulfsige, archbishop of York, concerning heterodoxy and sabbatarianism, is undated but at least demonstrates that these prelates were at some point contemporary in office.[28] The episcopal lists already mentioned do not, in Anglo-Saxon manuscripts, carry Northumbrian information beyond *c.* 840 (while the associated regnal list does not extend beyond the conclusion, in 796, of Æthelred Æthelwalding's second reign).[29] It may be worth tabulating the Northumbrian lists' information here.[30]

25 See *Bede's Ecclesiastical History of the English People*, edd. and transl. Bertram Colgrave and R. A. B. Mynors (Oxford 1969), pp. lxvii–lxix and 572–7: Mynors on p. lxix and Colgrave on p. 575, n. 9 (cf. Whitelock *English Historical Documents*, p. 286, n. 2), are in unacknowledged but direct conflict on the date and nature of the *Continuatio*; there is no possibility that *Continuatio Baedae* is a tenth- rather than an eighth-century text.

26 This work is being undertaken by P. A. Bibire and D. N. Dumville for volume 2 of the edition mentioned in n. 15 above.

27 *The Chronicle of Æthelweard*, ed. and transl. Alistair Campbell (Edinburgh 1962). Cf. M. Winterbottom, 'The style of Æthelweard', *Medium Ævum* 36 (1967) 109–18, and M. Lapidge, 'The hermeneutic style in tent h-century Anglo-Latin literature', *Anglo-Saxon England* 4 (1975) 67–111, at pp. 97–8. See also Keynes and Lapidge, *Alfred the Great*, pp. 189–91, 334–8. On his Chronicle-source see further E. E. Barker, 'The Anglo-Saxon Chronicle used by Æthelweard', *Bulletin of the Institute of Historical Research* 40 (1967) 74–91; Whitelock, *English Historical Documents*, p. 118; Janet M. Bately, in the edition mentioned in n. 15 above, III.lxxix–lxxxviii. For reviews of Campbell's edition, see F. Blatt, *Notes and Queries* 208 [N.S., 10] (1963) 386–8; R. R. Darlington, *History*, N.S., 48 (1963) 354–5; E. P. M. Dronke and U. Dronke, *Modern Language Review* 59 (1964) 94–5; G. N. Garmonsway, *Medium Ævum* 33 (1964) 209–12; F. E. Harmer, *Journal of Ecclesiastical History* 15 (1964) 126–7; P. H. Sawyer, *English Historical Review* 79 (1964) 819–20; B. W. Scholz, *Speculum* 40 (1965) 334–6.

28 Edited by D. Whitelock, 'Bishop Ecgred, Pehtred and Niall', in *Ireland in Early Mediaeval Europe. Studies in Memory of Kathleen Hughes*, edd. Dorothy Whitelock *et al.* (Cambridge 1982), pp. 47–68.

29 See the papers cited above, n. 8, which contain editions of the texts in British Library MSS. Cotton Vespasian B.vi and Cotton Tiberius B.v, vol. 1, and in Cambridge, Corpus Christi College, MSS. 140 and 183. For those in Rochester, Cathedral Library, MS. A.3.5, one must consult the facsimile-edition: *Textus Roffensis*, vol. 1, ed. P. H. Sawyer (Copenhagen 1957).

After the opening piece of prose, which is here faithful to the manuscripts, my lists give the bishops' name-forms in a standardized orthography.[31]

Nomina episcoporum gentis Norðanhymbrorum

Primus Paulinus a Iusto archiepiscopo ordinatus.

.ii.	Aeðan
.iii.	Fine
.iiii.	Colman
.v.	Tuda.

Postea in duas parrochias diuiditur:
Cedda Eboracensi ecclesiae ordinatu⟨s⟩,
Uilfrið Hagstaldensiae ordinatus.
Depositoque Uilfriðo a rege Ecgfrido,
Eota pro eo ordinatus episcopus Hagstaldensiae.
Pro Ceddan Bosa Eburaici (Eboracensi),
defuncto Eatan Iohann⟨e⟩s pro eo ordinatus.
Post longum uero exilium Uilfrið iterum in episcopatum Hagstaldensem receptus est.
Et idem Iohann⟨e⟩s, defuncto Bosan, Eburaici (Eboraci) substitutus est.

Eboracensis ecclesiae	*Hagstaldensis ecclesiae*	*Lindisfarnensis insulae*	*ecclesiae quae dicitur Candida Casa*
Wilfrið	Acca	Æðan	Pehthelm
Ecgberht	Frioðoberht	Fine	Frioðowald
Coena	Alhmund	Colman	Pehtwine
Eanbald [I]	Tilberht	Eata	Æðelberht
Eanbald [II]	Æðelberht	Cuðberht	Beadwulf
//Wulfsige//	Heardred	Eadberht	//Heaðored//
///Wigmund///	Eanberht	Eatferð/Eadfrið	
	/Tidferð/	Oeðelwald	
		Cyn(e)wulf	
		Hyg(e)bald	
		/Ecgberht/	
		//Eadmund//	

It has been suspected that such a collection of lists was already in existence in Bede's lifetime.[32] From the four manuscripts which preserve the information presented above we see evidence for periodic (but not necessarily successful) updating of the lists in 805 × 814,[33] again not later than 814,[34] in 833 × 836,[35] and in 840 × 845,[36]

[30] The texts in Page's edition (n. 8 above) are given diplomatically. What follows here is therefore an attempt to bring their information together. It is worth remembering that we possess no ancient list of the succession to the Northumbrian bishopric at Mayo in Ireland: on that church see Kathleen Hughes, *Church and Society in Ireland* AD *400–1200* (Variorum Reprints, London 1987), essay XVI, pp. 51–2.

[31] Wherever possible I follow MS. Cotton Vespasian B.vi (henceforth V), an early ninth-century Mercian manuscript, but it is occasionally too damaged to be read. Forms in angle-brackets are emendations against manuscript-authority. Forms in round brackets are variants from CCCC MS. 183. The first scribe's own additions to V are indicated by /.../, the second scribe's additions by //...//, and the last layer of Mercian additions (represented by CCCC 183, BL Cotton Tiberius B.v, and *Textus Roffensis*) by ///...///.

[32] Page, 'Anglo-Saxon episcopal lists', pp. 84–5.

[33] This date-range is achieved by excluding the evidence of the Northumbrian lists which were evidently not up to date (see further below, n. 37). For the calculation the key-figures are on the one hand Archbishop Wulfred (Canterbury) who succeeded in 805,

all these phases taking place in Mercia and not necessarily succeeding in bringing the Northumbrian lists wholly up to date each time. In 805 × 814 they were current only to 800 × 803;[37] they were probably successfully updated by 814, and possibly but less certainly so in 833 × 836 and 840 × 845. So little has the process been understood, that these dates are partly established here for the first time, and it is strange to have to point out that Eadmund, bishop of 'Lindisfarne', presumably flourishing in 833 × 836 at the time of the second updating of the list-collection in BL MS. Cotton Vespasian B.vi, is missing from our standard reference-books.[38] His accession can therefore be dated 803 × 836 (but allowing for his predecessor, Ecgberht, who held office after Hygbald's death in 803 and who had probably not died before the last of the old Northumbrian annals, for 806 × 808, was written). Eadmund's death cannot be dated: he presumably preceded that Ecgred who was Archbishop Wulfsige's correspondent (Wulfsige had been succeeded in office by 845 at the very latest).[39] The Bishop Heathured who stands in Eadmund's place in the twelfth-century Durham sources was presumably the same who was the bishop of Whithorn after Bishop Beadwulf (who was still alive in 803): he may have been translated either in fact or, perhaps more likely, by a few strokes of the pen.[40]

---

and on the other Alhheard, bishop of Elmham, and Alhmund, bishop of Winchester, whose successors were in office in 814.

[34] The three additions made by the first scribe were Wigthegn of Winchester (bishop 805 × 814–836) and the bishops of Hexham and Lindisfarne. This indicates that the collection was updated after 806 (the earliest date for the accession of Tidferth of Hexham) but still before or in 814. It seems also from this that Alhmund of Winchester left office before Alhheard of Elmham. In addition to keeping his Southumbrian records current, the scribe had evidently made some further enquiries to enable him to bring his Northumbrian lists up to date.

[35] The second scribe added to all the lists except those for Rochester (Beornmod: 804–842 × 844), Lindsey (Eadwulf: 796–836 × 839), and Hexham (Tidferth: 806 × 808–?), the implication being that the last bishops recorded by scribe 1 were still in office. As we see, that was plainly so at Rochester and in Lindsey: for Hexham, we have no acceptable evidence as to the end of Tidferth's episcopate. For dating scribe 2's activity the significant figures are Ceolnoth, archbishop of Canterbury, who took office in 833, and Hunberht, bishop of Lichfield, whose successor was in office in 836.

[36] For the date 840 × 845, see Dumville, 'The Anglian collection', pp. 41–2 and 46 (the date, 837, given there on p. 41 for Wigmund's accession should now be abandoned). For our Northumbrian purposes the relevant fact is that another Mercian compiler, quite independent of those who had three times brought up to date the lists now presented to us by V, had updated from AD 796 to 840 × 845 the collection inherited from V's ultimate exemplar. In principle, therefore, the ninth-century information presented by MSS. CCCC 183, Cotton Tiberius B.v, and *Textus Roffensis* is independent of that in V and partly confirms (and supplements)it; it shows that Archbishop Wigmund was alive within 840 × 845, but it does not know bishops of Hexham after Eanberht, of Lindisfarne after Ecgberht, or of Whithorn after Beadwulf.

[37] Eanberht of Hexham took office in 800; Hygbald of Lindisfarne died in 803. The York and Whithorn information is consistent with this date-range.

[38] The standard modern list of Anglo-Saxon bishops has recently been well revised by Simon Keynes: see *Handbook of British Chronology*, edd. E. B. Fryde *et al.* (3rd edn., London 1986), pp. 209–24, but—as he has pointed out (p. 209)—the tables there remain 'no more than an interim statement, pending the systematic analysis of all the available evidence'.

[39] See above, n. 36, for the episcopal lists' evidence about Wigmund's succession to Wulfsige. Lupus of Ferrières wrote to Archbishop Wigmund in 851/2: Whitelock, *English Historical Documents*, pp. 876–7 (no. 215).

[40] One must note also the difficulties created by the errors and apparent historical ignorance of V's scribe 2: see D. Whitelock, 'The pre-Viking Age Church in East Anglia', *Anglo-Saxon England* 1 (1972) 1–22, at pp.

It was the implication of Pagan's discussion of the *Flores historiarum* and *Historia Dunelmensis ecclesie* that such lists were maintained in ninth-century Northumbria. However, this view must be qualified by the knowledge that the unanimity of the twelfth-century Durham texts is sometimes in shared error or doubtful deduction. Continuity of accurate record is not therefore to be assumed, and any information with such an uncertain pedigree cannot sustain very confident use.

Finally we come to the thoroughly documentary. It is not known how the forger worked who created the extraordinary series of mind-bogglingly unlikely Anglo-Saxon charters found in the late medieval archive of Crowland Abbey (Lincs.). Stewart Lyon has cited one of these, dated 833 (S.189), as bearing an attestation of Eanbald II, archbishop of York.[41] The date is not impossible, if a little unlikely: Wulfsige had succeeded by 833 × 836, on the evidence of the later stratum of additions to the lists in Cotton Vespasian B.vi. But the point is that the Crowland forgeries are a source which no Anglo-Saxon historian would at present care to use for any purpose. Lyon has implied that this pseudo-charter and Symeon of Durham's *De archiepiscopis Eboracensibus* are mutually supportive, and that Symeon's observation that Archbishop Eanbald II's death (and Wulfsige's) occurred in the reign of King Eanred is therefore to be credited.[42] Such synchronisms, universal in the twelfth-century Durham(/York?) material which we have been studying, as also in Roger Wendover's work, were much beloved of medieval chroniclers and computists: on the whole, they are a secondary, not a primary, feature of historical record.

Lyon has laid some stress on the date 854 in Northumbrian historical record, observing that it 'is explicitly mentioned in several documents, so it cannot be lightly rejected'.[43] The first essential point is that it is not mentioned in any *document* at all, for we have none surviving from early Anglo-Saxon Northumbria. That very absence speaks volumes for the nature of institutional discontinuity in the Anglo-Scandinavian period. The date 854 is mentioned in a number of twelfth- and thirteenth-century *literary* texts. In discussing a historical subject, we must not lapse into the loose language of the archaeologist who is unaccustomed to written sources: not all written texts are documents; documentary and literary texts have a different status and require somewhat different handling. The date 854 is mentioned in both parts of the *Historia regum*, in *Historia Dunelmensis ecclesie* (II.5), and by Roger Wendover: they attribute to it the appointment of Archbishop Wulfhere and Eardwulf, bishop of Lindisfarne. *Historia regum*, Part Two, and *Historia Dunelmensis ecclesie* both explicitly place that year in the reign of King Osberht. Unfortunately, the annal is a late interpolation in the unique manuscript of *Historia regum*, Part One, and was probably drawn mediately or immediately

19–22. It is not impossible that, equally, Eadmund and Heaðored have mistakenly been put in each other's column.

[41] See above, pp. 29f. The charter is calendared by P. H. Sawyer, *Anglo-Saxon Charters. An Annotated List and Bibliography* (London 1968), p. 119, no. 189. On Crowland forgery see the remarks by Marjorie Chibnall (ed. and transl.), *The Ecclesiastical History of Orderic Vitalis* (6 vols, Oxford 1969–80), II, introduction; cf. C. R. Hart, *The Early Charters of Eastern England* (Leicester 1966), p. 11, n. 2.

[42] Symeon of Durham, *De archiepiscopis Eboracensibus*, §2: see *Symeonis Monachi Opera Omnia*, ed. Arnold, I.224.

[43] See above, p. 30.

from Part Two. Both the remaining texts are Durham sources of much the same period, and many scholars have hypothesized a single author for them, thus causing them to be taken as a single witness, unable to give one another support. And until we know what knowledge Roger had of twelfth-century Northumbrian historiography—St Albans, with its dependency at Tynemouth, was well placed to be in contact[44]—we cannot treat him as independent. For all practical purposes, therefore, we have a single twelfth-century witness to this date's association with the events and the synchronism. The stepping-stone methods by which such dates and synchronisms could be constructed are all too visible in the *Historia Dunelmensis ecclesie*. The nature and quality of the transmitted information remain at issue.

The instinct displayed by Hugh Pagan in 1969—for the numismatist to dispense with the apparent information of the written sources for much of ninth-century Northumbrian history and rely on evidence derivable directly from coinage[45]—must, I think, command the assent of the historian. Hopeful manipulation of the twelfth-century literature serves little purpose. The historian can offer only the broadest dates and incomplete lists for ninth-century Northumbrian successions. The numismatist should not feel embarrassed or apologetic for trying to do better by the sole use of his proper source-materials.

From Pagan's consideration of the numismatic evidence, two problems of procedure are apparent to this historian, at least. Anglo-Saxon numismatists often comment on the difficulties apparent in trying to reconcile observed or hypothesized numbers or volumes of coin-issues with chronological structures largely imposed by literary and/or documentary sources. If the historians have worked accurately but flexibly, all will normally concede evidential priority to their chronologies. But in a situation where a historical chronology is largely wanting, any hope of progress will rest on whether agreement can be reached about how to calculate 'numismatic time'. Where the historian must feel uneasy with Pagan's alternative, numismatic chronology is in his failure to set out the assumptions and calculations by which numismatic time is reckoned. One needs to know not that the coinages of Æthelred II and Redwulf 'covered a period of eight years',[46] for that information is derived from Roger Wendover:[47] rather one needs to be shown a historically secure measure of comparison and a method which then provides an absolute, if approximate, quantification of time appropriate to the observed numismatic facts. Some indication of the margins of error in such calculations would also be welcome. Numismatists seem frequently to make such calculations; the historian would like to be able to probe the logic underlying them, thus satisfying himself that he is not the hapless victim of a numismatic determinism.

The other problem of procedure concerns the now famous silver penny—from

[44] On Tynemouth see David Knowles *et al.*, *The Heads of Religious Houses, England and Wales 940–1216* (Cambridge 1972), pp. 96–7; for its medieval books see N. R. Ker, *Medieval Libraries of Great Britain* (2nd edn., London 1964), p. 191.

[45] See above, n. 3.

[46] Pagan, 'Northumbrian numismatic chronology', p. 7.

[47] *Flores historiarum, sub annis* 840, 844, 848: ed. Coxe, I.281–4.

the Trewhiddle hoard, buried in Cornwall *c.* 875 × *c.* 895—bearing the name of a King Eanred.[48] Careful study of this coin has allowed the seemingly secure conclusion that it is to be compared with the coinage issued by Æthelwulf of Wessex in the 850s and Berhtwulf of Mercia in the 840s.[49] The only known king of the name is the ruler of Northumbria to whom our twelfth- and thirteenth-century sources attribute a lengthy reign within the period 806–42.[50] This king is well represented by an appropriate coinage. Neither the form nor the style of the Eanred silver penny seems to suit an equation with a Northumbrian king of the first half of the ninth century. Furthermore, G. C. Brooke gave it as his opinion that 'the style of the coin seems...to prove it to be an issue of the Canterbury mint.[51]

To meet this difficulty, extraordinary hypotheses have been advanced. It may not be wholly unfair to suspect that it provided much of the fuel powering Pagan's radical reassessment of Northumbrian chronology. Alternatively we have been invited to allow the existence of 'a historically unknown king, who was ruling, possibly in the Midlands, about 850'.[52]

The starting point for further enquiry must be the hoard itself. The earliest coin attributed to it is one of Offa of Mercia (757–96). But the bulk of its numismatic contents consists of coins of the Mercian kings Berhtwulf (840–52) and especially Burgred (852–74), Æthelwulf of Wessex (839–58) and Archbishop Ceolnoth (833–70): together these account for some eighty of the ninety-five coins of which precise record survives. No overtly Northumbrian coins were in the hoard, whose major numismatic content was approximately 52 coins of King Burgred.

In attributing this penny to an otherwise unknown ruler, scholars have tacitly admitted that our knowledge of Southumbrian ninth-century history has lacunae of the sort to which the Northumbrian problems discussed here have accustomed us. Kings of East Anglia in this period are known only from numismatic evidence. The historian must admit that the Mercian succession of Burgred to Berhtwulf is not well documented:[53] in principle, another ruler might have intervened, but one would have expected him to have been recorded in the regnal list preserved at

[48] See D. M. Wilson and C. E. Blunt, 'The Trewhiddle hoard', *Archaeologia* 98 [2nd S., 48] (1961) 75–122, especially pp. 109–20 and plate XXXI.

[49] *Ibid.*, pp. 113–16. Mark Blackburn has kindly pointed out to me that the obverse is to be compared with Æthelwulf's and the reverse with Berhtwulf's coins.

[50] He succeeded after perhaps two (brief?) reigns which had begun with a deposition in 806 × 808: for the deposition of King Eardwulf see Anglo-Saxon Chronicle *s.a.* 806 DE and *Annales regni Francorum*, *s.a.* 808. The latest date for Eanred's death is implied by *Historia Dunelmensis ecclesie*, II.5 (ed. Arnold, I.50–3), viz AD 840 × 842, years calculated by stepping-stone dating. The *Historia* implies that he reigned for thirty-three years; *Series regum Northymbrensium* (*ibid.*, II.391) states this directly, while the *Libellus de primo Saxonum aduentu* gives thirty-two (*ibid.*, II. 377).

[51] *English Coins from the Seventh Century to the Present Day* (3rd edn., London 1950), p. 44. Mark Blackburn supports the Kentish ascription, but has suggested that Rochester may provide a more satisfactory point of origin: see P. Grierson and M. Blackburn, *Medieval European Coinage*, I (Cambridge 1986), pp. 300–1. Cf. also S. Keynes and M. Blackburn, *Anglo-Saxon Coins: An Exhibition* (Fitzwilliam Museum, Cambridge 1985), pp. 7–8.

[52] Wilson and Blunt, 'The Trewhiddle hoard', p. 116.

[53] Cf. Anglo-Saxon Chronicle, *s.aa.* 851 and 853. No genuine Mercian royal diploma can be attributed to the years 850–854: see Sawyer, *Anglo-Saxon Charters*, pp. 121–3.

Worcester and datable 907 × 911.[54] On the other hand, another (and more recent) radical suggestion by Hugh Pagan might be brought into play. In 851 Canterbury was stormed by a Scandinavian army. Noting that 'in the immediate aftermath... the production of coinage seems' almost completely to have stopped and that the small series of archiepiscopal issues continued in almost splendid isolation and independence, Pagan found it 'tempting to see the explanation as a loss of political control in Kent by the West Saxon royal house'. Such 'would certainly explain the complete cessation of coinage from Rochester'.[55] This is an attractive hypothesis. If we have to find space for an otherwise unknown Southumbrian king *c.* AD 850, then an 'independent' Kent in the few years from 851 might prove to be a very convenient location. Certainly there is a hiatus in the charter-series of West Saxon royal diplomas concerning land in Kent: AD 851, 852, 853, and 854 all lack such records.[56] Such a location would also meet the demands of, and suggestions arising from, the numismatic evidence. Without a sufficient number of provenanced coins of Eanred to allow a distribution-map to be created, all this is speculation. But such a solution may seem more economical than the carving out of new kingdoms from Mercian territory or the wholesale reorganization of Northumbrian royal and episcopal chronology.

A plea for the archaeology of texts has brought us a long way from our starting point. Let us return there. The most basic laws of historical evidence are very straightforward. History must be written from contemporary sources or with the aid of testimony carried to a later era by an identifiable and acceptable line of transmission. Many texts which present themselves for our consideration as testimony to Anglo-Saxon history are creations remote from that age. Historical writing may be entertaining if an author chooses to cut corners or ignore the rules of evidence when assessing such works—but it will not be worth the paper it is printed on.

[54] London, British Library, MS. Cotton Tiberius A.xiii, fo 114v, a copy of *c.* AD 1000: see further D. N. Dumville, 'Kingship, genealogies and regnal lists', in *Early Medieval Kingship*, edd. P. H. Sawyer and I. N. Wood (Leeds 1977), pp. 72–104, at 99–100; cf. Frank Merry Stenton, *Preparatory to 'Anglo-Saxon England'* (Oxford 1970), p. 372.

[55] H. Pagan, 'Coinage in southern England, 796–874', in *Anglo-Saxon Monetary History. Essays in Memory of Michael Dolley, ed. M. A. S. Blackburn (Leicester 1986), pp. 45–65, at 57.*

[56] Cf. Sawyer, *Anglo-Saxon Charters*, pp. 145–9. I take S.316 (*ibid.*, p. 149) as belonging to AD 855; the last previous Kentish charter of even approximate plausibility is S.300, dated 850 (*ibid.*, p. 145). One may compare this situation with that in Mercia (above, n. 53). There is also an absence of West Saxon royal diplomas for AD 851, 852, and 853 (*ibid.*, p. 145).

Coinage and Northumbrian history: *c.*790–*c.*810

JAMES BOOTH

[PLATES 2–3]

AT SOME time towards the end of the eighth century the silver so-called 'sceatta' coinage of Northumbria underwent a change of reverse type. The obverse continued, as before, to show a cross surrounded by the king's name. But the 'fantastic animal' which had appeared on the reverses of Northumbrian regal coins since the reign of Eadberht (737–58) was now replaced by a cross surrounded by the name of a moneyer. As far as has been ascertained the metal quality of the first coins of the new type, struck in the names of Æthelred[1] and Ælfwald, remained unchanged, so the new typology seems to have been of administrative rather than economic significance. In broad terms the historical context of these silver moneyer's-name coins is clear enough, though there remain one or two ambiguities. Hugh Pagan has now abandoned his hypothesis, evolved at an earlier stage of research into the series, that the larger group, in the name of Æthelred, could belong to an otherwise unrecorded king reigning in the 820s.[2]

Acknowledgements. Without the advice and the unstinting help of Miss E. J. E. Pirie of Leeds City Museum, in providing access to her extensive records and photographs of coins in this series, the corpus of specimens would have been extremely difficult to compile, and would have been very incomplete. I am indebted to Dr D. M. Metcalf of the Ashmolean, to Miss M. M. Archibald of the British Museum, and to Hugh Pagan, for their help and advice at various stages in writing. Other direct and indirect debts are mentioned in the notes. The understanding of so sparse and widely scattered a body of historical evidence can only be, of necessity, a co-operative venture. Any mistakes in the present paper, however, are the responsibility of the author alone.

Permission to publish particular coins was kindly given by the British Museum, the Ashmolean Museum, the Museum of Antiquities, University of Newcastle-upon-Tyne, the Thetford Museum, the Glasgow Museum and Art Gallery, Kelvingrove, the Ryedale Folk Museum, Hutton-le-Hole, and by several private collectors. Thanks for photographs and photocopies are due to Miss E. J. E. Pirie (nos.2–4, 9–10, 14, 19–20, 24, 27, 32, 36, 38, 41, 43, 49–50, 55, 60, 64–5), the British Museum (nos.8, 13, 15, 17–18, 21, 23, 25, 29–30, 33, 39–40, 42, 44, 52, 56, 58, 61–2), the Ashmolean Museum (nos.12, 28, 31, 34, 45–6, 54, 59, 68, 70), Tony Meech (nos.1, 7 and 63), Hull University Photographic Service (no.37), Glasgow Museum and Art Gallery, Kelvingrove (no.26), David Wicks of the Norfolk Archaeological Unit (no.57), and Mr A. Gunstone (no.69).

[1] The correct identification of the coins which belong to this silver moneyer's-name group began with the work of Ian Stewart and C. S. S. Lyon (Lyon 1955–7), pp.228–9. Before this time many blundered brass coins of the mid-ninth century were incorrectly attributed to Ælfwald I, Æthelred I, Eardwulf, and Ælfwald II. This is the case for example with all the coins illustrated by H. A. Parsons in 'The coins of Æthelred I of Northumbria', *BNJ* 10 (1913), 1–8.

[2] Pagan, 1969, pp.3 and 13. Booth, 1984, pp.86–8.

There now seems little doubt that most, if not all, of these coins belong to the second reign of Æthelred I (790–6).[3] They thus provide important primary evidence for the period half a century and more after the death of Bede, a time when the northern kingdom begins to slip from the historian's view, eclipsed by the paucity of written records. In the south Mercian hegemony had been established under Æthelbald and Offa, and on the continent Charles the Great was well embarked on the series of conquests which would shortly lead to his coronation as 'Emperor of the Romans'. It is indeed in the court of Charles that we find the only Northumbrian of this period whose name is now generally remembered: Alcuin.

The most striking feature of this coinage is the evidence it gives of an abrupt cessation (or drastic reduction) of minting at some point during Æthelred I's second reign. The coinage of relatively good silver, which had been issued from the 740s onwards, in fluctuating volume but probably without a significant break, either failed completely at some time in the early 790s, or was reduced to such small quantities that no specimens have survived in the name of Æthelred's successor, Eardwulf (796–808). When the coinage again appears in view, after a hiatus of more than a decade, it preserves the same typology but aims, as metal analyses of the coins of Eanred (810–41) show, at a significantly lowered silver standard. Our knowledge of relative metal quality is imperfect, and the earlier analytical results are now considered to be generally unreliable. Nevertheless it seems probable that Æthelred's coins aimed at a standard of 60 per cent silver or more, whereas Eanred's earliest coins barely exceeded 40 per cent silver. The standard degenerated further during Eanred's reign, and the majority of his surviving coins are, like those of his successors, struck in a brass alloy containing only 8 or 10 per cent silver.[4] Numismatists have long been accustomed to call these new debased coins of the ninth century 'stycas', although, as is well known, this word has, like 'sceattas', no real historical justification, all the coins most probably having been called 'pennies' by their users. The distinction of nomenclature does however serve to highlight the dramatic break in the continuity of economic activity which occurred in Northumbria at this time.[5]

Unfortunately the other, much smaller group of coins, struck in the name of Ælfwald, cannot be conclusively attributed, since it fits into the historical sequence with equal plausibility at two different points. It is possible that the transition from animal to moneyer's-name reverse occurred during the reign of Æthelred's predecessor, Ælfwald I (779–88). The coins may thus belong to him, and Æthelred's coins may be a development from them. The discovery of a specimen in the name of Osred, the intervening king (788–90) would perhaps go some way towards substantiating this attribution. It is however also possible that

[3] For discussion of the possibility that some of the coins belong to Æthelred's first reign (774–9) see below.

[4] D. M. Metcalf, J. M. Merrick, and L. K. Hamblin, *Studies in the Composition of Early Medieval Coins*, Newcastle-upon-Tyne, 1968, pp.52–4. Gilmore and Metcalf, 1980, p.94.

[5] Miss Pirie's usage, which terms all moneyer's-name and named archiepiscopal coins 'stycas' (Pirie, 1986, p.67), though typologically exact, has the disadvantage of giving prominence to the change of design at the expense of the more historically important change of metal-quality. See J. Booth, 'History *vs.* numismatics: "sceattas and stycas"', *Spink Numismatic Circular* 95 (1987), 6.

it was Ælfwald II (808–10), who revived the coinage after the break in minting, rather than his successor Eanred (810–41), and these coins may therefore belong instead at the beginning of the ninth-century series. Reliable metal analysis which showed the Ælfwald coins to be of low silver content would be reasonably conclusive proof of this interpretation. But if the coins prove to have a higher silver content, they may nevertheless still belong to this second Ælfwald, representing perhaps an abortive attempt by him to restore the coinage on the standard of the previous century. Unfortunately no specimen of the issue has yet been analysed for metal quality.

But the problem of whether the Ælfwald coins are to be assigned to the period before or after the break in minting is a relatively minor one compared with that of the break in minting itself. Why, it must be asked, did the coinage collapse during the reign of Æthelred I, as it apparently did? Furthermore, why do no coins survive from the twelve-year reign of the dynamic and enterprising king Eardwulf? It is in the posing and answering of these questions that the numismatist has perhaps his most significant contribution to make to the understanding of the history of Northumbria in the late eighth and early ninth centuries.

THE DOCUMENTS

Before considering the surviving numismatic material it will be useful to summarize the history of these two decades, as it has been preserved in the surviving documents. Apart from the annals, which give the dates of the kings and bishops, and of one or two public events, we are fortunate in the case of the 790s in possessing another substantial source, in the form of letters written by Alcuin from the court of Charles the Great, to three Northumbrian kings, to the archbishop of York, to the bishop of Lindisfarne, and to others. These help, at least to some extent, in fleshing out events and personages and show in some detail what one important Northumbrian felt about them. Thus although we do not exactly have a wealth of documentation from this decade, we have significantly more than from any other period in the history of the kingdom between the death of Bede in 734 and the Danish conquest of 867.

Our information about dates in the period *c*.790–*c*.810 is derived substantially from a single set of northern annals which seem to have been intended as a continuation of Bede's chronological epitome.[6] These do not survive in their original form, but only as copied by later writers, who select and omit material according to their own particular preoccupations. The *History of the Kings*, which survives in a late twelfth-century manuscript,[7] seems to preserve this original faithfully enough, but suddenly abandons its northern source after the annal for 801. MSS D and E of the Ælfredian Chronicle also preserve the Northumbrian original, with some slight variations, and take the record up to 806. Fortunately the northern material was added late and is thus unaffected by the copyist's

[6] See J. Earle and C. Plummer, *Two of the Saxon Chronicles Parallel, with Supplementary Extracts from the Others*, 1899, reissued 1952, vol.2, p.lxix.

[7] The attribution to Simeon of Durham, which appears in the manuscript, is questionable. My remarks in this section are largely indebted to Pagan, 1969.

confusion by which most events between 754 and 845 are usually dated two or three years too early.[8] There are nevertheless two occasions, as we shall see, where the *Chronicle*'s northern dates do still need to be corrected by reference to the *History of the Kings*. The third significant source for this period is the *Flowers of the Histories* by Roger of Wendover, written in the early thirteenth century, which includes entries for 808 and 810 not present in either of the other sources. The other less detailed English chronicles which refer to this period, namely *The Annals of Lindisfarne and Durham*, and two pieces attributed to Simeon of Durham (*The Series of Northumbrian Kings* and *The History of the Church of Durham*) add few details and seem to have no independent authority. Corroboration of events and dates is however offered by the occasional reference to Northumbria in independent Frankish sources.

From these surviving annals a framework of dates emerges, for the most part apparently secure. In 788 (MSS D and E of the *Chronicle* have 789) the 'excellent king' Ælfwald I was killed as the result of a conspiracy, and was succeeded by Osred, his nephew and son of King Alchred (765–74).[9] Osred thus belonged to the legitimate royal family, the house of Ida. The legitimacy of his claim to the throne however did him little good. In 790, as the *History of the Kings* relates, he was ousted by Æthelred I, a representative of the rival royal house of Northumbria, which had first come to the fore under Æthelred's father, king Æthelwald Moll (759–65). Osred, 'deceived by the guile of his nobles', was taken prisoner and forcibly tonsured, before fleeing into exile. Under the annal for this same year, 790, the future king Eardwulf makes his first appearance. King Osred had attempted unsuccessfully to have him executed:

> In his second year, Ealdorman Eardwulf was captured and brought to Ripon, and orders were given by the aforesaid king for him to be killed there outside the gate of the monastery. And the brethren carried his body to the church with Gregorian chants, and placed it outside in a tent, and after midnight he was found in the church, alive.[10]

Æthelred I's second reign shows him resorting to the traditional means of murder and marriage to secure his position. He prevented internal threats by murdering rival claimants to the throne: first the two sons of Ælfwald in 791, then the former king Osred on his return from exile in the following year. Also in 792 Æthelred attempted to defuse the military threat from the south by marrying Ælfflæd, daughter of Offa, king of the Mercians. It was however in the next year, 793, that the event occurred for which his reign will always be most vividly remembered. As MS D of the *Chronicle* relates:

> In this year dire portents appeared over Northumbria and sorely frightened the people. They consisted of immense whirlwinds and flashes of lightning, and fiery dragons were seen flying

[8] *EHD*, no.1, p.162. See Earle and Plummer, vol.2, pp.cii–civ.

[9] *History of the Kings, EHD*, no.3, p.246.

[10] *EHD*, no.3, p.246. The Latin wording of the annal makes it clear that Osred is the king in question, rather than Æthelred, as the translation in *EHD* ambiguously suggests. See Symeonis Dunelmensis, *Opera et Collectanea*, vol.I, Surtees Society (1868), p.30.

in the air, and a little after that in the same year, on 8 June, the ravages of heathen men miserably destroyed God's church on Lindisfarne, with plunder and slaughter.[11]

In the following year the monastery at Jarrow was also attacked. As we shall see the amount of disruption and damage caused by these raids has been the subject of some doubt. The coins of the period may be seen as crucial evidence in the argument.

Certainly Alcuin viewed the Viking attack in the most serious light as a manifestation of the wrath of God against the kingdom. A letter to King Æthelred points the finger, with the barest show of deference, at the vices and extravagance of the aristocracy and the court as the cause of this divine anger. Since the days of King Ælfwald, he says, 'fornications, adulteries, and incest have poured over the land, so that these sins have been committed without any shame and even against handmaids dedicated to God.' Alcuin goes on to mention 'avarice, robbery, violent judgements', in a clear warning to the king and his men.

Whoever reads holy scriptures and ponders ancient histories and considers the fortune of the world will find that for sins of this kind kings lost kingdoms and peoples their country; and while the strong unjustly seized the goods of others, they justly lost their own. The princes' superfluity is poverty for the people... Some labour under an enormity of clothes, others perish with cold; some are inundated with delicacies and feastings like Dives clothed in purple, and Lazarus dies of hunger at the gate. Where is brotherly love? Where the pity which we are admonished to have for the wretched? The satiety of the rich is the hunger of the poor.

And he concludes 'Be rulers of the people, not robbers; shepherds, not plunderers'.[12] For all its superstition, its hectic gusto and cluttered biblical citations, this letter is a rhetorical *tour de force* which still has the power to move the reader. From the historian's point of view however its evidence concerning actual events and conditions is difficult to assess. It may be felt, as we shall see, that the coin evidence from Æthelred's reign offers a qualification to the picture of unrest and discontent which Alcuin's lurid moralizing seems to imply.

In 796 (MSS D and E of the *Chronicle* have 794 by mistake)[13] Æthelred was killed by his own men, an act of treachery which so incensed Charles that it was only Alcuin's intercession on behalf of his fellow Northumbrians (as he told Offa in a letter) that stopped the Frankish king putting into effect 'whatever evil he could have contrived' against them.[14] An ealdorman named Osbald succeeded to the throne, but after only 27 days he 'was deserted by the whole company of the royal household and the nobles, put to flight and banished from the kingdom.' A letter written to this Osbald by Alcuin later in 796, at a time when he was exiled among the Picts, indicates that he belonged to the legitimate royal family:

[11] *Anglo-Saxon Chronicle, EHD*, no.1, p.167. The account of the raid in the *History of the Kings* has been overlaid with lurid rhetorical ornament and lacks the grim immediacy of the Chronicle's version.

[12] *EHD*, no.193, pp.776–7.

[13] *EHD*, no.3, p.248. See Earle and Plummer, vol.2, p.63.

[14] *EHD*, no.198, p.783.

> Consider how much blood of kings, princes, and people has been shed through you or through your kinsfolk. An unhappy line through which such great evils have befallen the country! Free yourself, I implore you by God, lest your soul perish in eternity.[15]

Alcuin chides Osbald for not having followed the advice given in earlier letters to eschew political power and 'serve God according to your vow'. The speculation seems inevitable that Osbald had been forced to take the tonsure in order to prevent him from laying claim to the throne, and Alcuin seems to have been recruited, probably by Æthelred himself, to persuade Osbald to reconcile himself to his religious life. Osbald, it seems, ignoring this advice, had plotted against Æthelred, or at least had taken advantage of the plotting of others.

The king who ascended the throne upon Osbald's banishment was the Eardwulf who had earlier survived execution. It is not mentioned that he was related to either of the competing royal clans and this probably means that he was not. It seems evident however that the coming to the throne of a man whom God had earlier miraculously preserved from death was an event which was viewed as propitious by many of his subjects. The annals put explicit stress on the religious element of his coronation: 'Eardwulf... was recalled from exile and raised to the crown of the kingdom, and was consecrated on 26 May in York in the church of St Peter at the altar of the blessed Apostle Paul, where the nation first received the grace of baptism.'[16] Alcuin took the opportunity to write the new king a letter of sage advice, exhorting him to 'Consider most intently, for what sins your predecessors lost life and kingdom, and watch most carefully that you do not the like; lest a similar judgement befall you.' And he went on to hope that Eardwulf's escape from death was a sign that he had been 'preserved for better times and reserved for the correction of your country, with the help of God's grace'.[17] Shortly afterwards the new archbishop of York, Eanbald II, received the *pallium* from Rome, and many Northumbrians may well have hoped for a similar period of stable government to that which the kingdom had experienced half a century before under King Eadberht and his brother, Archbishop Ecgberht.

The crowded events of Eardwulf's reign certainly show him to have been a confident, energetic ruler, though it was not long before he offended the church. As early as 797 Alcuin was expressing the fear that his immorality in divorcing his wife and remarrying might incur divine displeasure and cost him the kingdom.[18] In 798 a more practical threat arose when the murderers of Æthelred raised an army against the king, only to be defeated, after 'many had been killed on both sides'.[19] Nevertheless the calling of a synod in the same year, presided over by the archbishop (the king is not mentioned), seems to indicate a measure of stability. But Eardwulf's troubles continued and in 799 an ealdorman named Moll is recorded as having been killed by his 'urgent order'.[20] In the same year, however, Osbald died, and was buried 'in the church in the city of York', having apparently been allowed to return from banishment as an abbot, a move which

[15] *EHD*, no.200, p.785.

[16] *History of the Kings, EHD*, no.3, p.248.

[17] *EHD*, no.199, pp.784–5.

[18] F. M. Stenton, *Anglo-Saxon England*, Oxford, 3rd edn. (1971), pp.94–5.

[19] *History of the Kings, EHD*, no.3, p.249.

[20] *EHD*, no.3, p.250. This may have been a member of the same family as Æthelwald Moll and Æthelred I.

suggests confidence on Eardwulf's part. But other contenders for the throne were still perceived as a threat, and in 800 'certain fugitives, including Alhmund, the son, as some say, of King Alhred', were seized and killed on Eardwulf's orders.[21] Eardwulf, it seems, prosecuted the familiar policy of preemptive murder with an enthusiasm at least equal to that of his predecessor. Eardwulf's marriage also, to the daughter of the emperor Charles, exceeded in ambition that of Æthelred, to the daughter of Offa.

Two letters of Alcuin of 801 give a glimpse into the tone of church life at the time. Archbishop Eanbald had it seems offended the king and had appealed to Alcuin for support. Alcuin's reply is a scarcely veiled rebuke. 'I think that part of your trouble arises from your own fault. You perhaps receive the king's enemies or protect the possessions of his enemies.'[22] Eanbald it seems was trying to hedge his bets in the insecure climate of the times. In a companion letter to two of his Northumbrian pupils Alcuin is free to speak more openly, giving in the process an insight into the secular and political activities of a worldly and ambitious prelate more than a century before the Benedictine reform movement established itself in England.

> I am afraid he is suffering, to some extent for his landed possessions or for harbouring the king's enemies. Let his own possessions suffice him; let him not strive after those of others, which often result in peril for their possessors. While he may think he is benefiting a few, he is injuring many for whom he ought daily to intercede, and he may harm the flock which he ought to govern.
>
> And what does he want with such a number of thegns in his retinue?[23]

It is scarcely surprising that later, during the reign of Eanred, this powerful man should have been able to claim the right to strike coins in his own name. What is surprising is that no coins should apparently have been struck during the reign of Eardwulf, either by king or archbishop.

In 801 the familiar problem of plotting 'fugitives' became the occasion (or perhaps the pretext) for Eardwulf's invasion of Cenwulf's Mercia. After a long campaign the two kings made peace, without mention being made of any specific advantage for either side. At this point the *History of the Kings* ceases to use its northern source. Roger of Wendover (still presumably using the same source as the *History of the Kings*) records in the briefest terms Eardwulf's flight from the kingdom and the accession of Ælfwald II under the year 808, a date independently corroborated by the Frankish *Annals of St Bertin's*.[24] (MSS D and E of the chronicle date Eardwulf's deposition to 806, presumably as a result of a similar mistake to that which had led them to misplace Æthelred I's murder, also by two years.) Roger of Wendover goes on to record the death of Ælfwald II in 810 and the succession of Eanred, who is said to have reigned for 32 years. These events are absent from the *Chronicle*, which is silent about Northumbria from this time until the Danish invasion of 866–7. At this point however an additional source offers itself, which merits careful attention. In the *Annals of the Frankish Kingdom* it is related that in 808 the fugitive Eardwulf came to the court of his father-in-law

21 *loc. cit.*

22 *EHD*, no.207, p.796.

23 *EHD*, no.207, p.797.

24 See *EHD*, no.4, p.255.

Charles the Great at Nijmegen, on his way to Rome in search of support from the Pope for his claim to the Northumbrian throne. The annals continue: 'on his return from Rome he was escorted by envoys of the Roman pontiff and of the Lord Emperor back into his kingdom'.[25] The evidence of the strength of the international, 'European', dimension in Anglo-Saxon affairs given by this account of Eardwulf's choice of strategy in asserting his rights, is striking, and of great historical importance.

Some caution is perhaps necessary, however, in using this Frankish source as evidence for events within Northumbria. How much of this apparently successful exertion of papal and imperial authority was reality, and how much propaganda? Modern commentators have perhaps been too ready to deduce a second reign for Eardwulf from these foreign annals. Stenton is characteristically cautious, following his account of Eardwulf's restoration with the hesitant inference: 'He died in power, in *or before* 810' (my emphasis). J. M. Wallace-Hadrill fleshes out the story with more freedom, asserting that Eardwulf 'returned to his throne as the *fidelis* of an emperor who had exercised the power of *imperialis defensio*', and that Cenwulf 'accepted the restoration at least to the extent of not intervening.'[26] Hugh Pagan uses the Frankish account in his redistribution of the regnal dates of ninth-century Northumbria, accepting the *Chronicle*'s dubious date of 806 for Ælfwald II's accession, and seeing Eardwulf reigning for a second time from 808–10, at which time he was succeeded by his son Eanred.[27] These large inferences of Wallace-Hadrill and Pagan are by no means inevitable. The Frankish court historian is primarily concerned to show the western emperor and the pope acting together in an impressive way in a distant province of the old Empire, and when he reports that Eardwulf was 'conducted back into his kingdom' he gives the impression that the Northumbrian church and people readily bent to this exertion of papal and 'imperial' authority. But did they? We have no real evidence that they did. Certainly the papal envoys would have carried great weight with the Northumbrian clergy and king. But the quarrels of both Offa and Cenwulf with the pope and his bishops show that his authority did not always carry the day. And it can be confidently assumed that the authority of the western 'Emperor of the Romans' carried no weight whatsoever in the internal affairs of Northumbria, unsupported by the realistic threat of military action.

The Frankish chronicler tells us nothing about the ultimate fate of Eardwulf. Perhaps the king died almost at once, like Swein or Eadmund Ironside in a later period. He may well have been uneasily restored to power with the support of a favourable faction, only to be deposed again as soon as the Roman and Frankish envoys had left. Possibly he was killed in battle, leaving his son Eanred to accede to the throne after two years of further exile or a civil war with Ælfwald. This would explain why the English annals make no mention of his phantom second

[25] *EHD*, no.21, p.313. The entry for 809 concludes the account of this most interesting episode by relating how one of the Pope's envoys, 'a Saxon by race' named Ealdwulf, was captured by pirates on his return journey and had to be ransomed before he could return to Rome.

[26] Stenton, p.95. J. M. Wallace-Hadrill, 'Charlemagne and England', *Karl der Grosse, Band I: Persönlichkeit und Geschichte*, Helmut Beumann (ed.), Düsseldorf (1965), pp.683–98, at p.696.

[27] Pagan, 1969, p.11.

reign. The English record may be scanty at this point, but the Frankish annal does not give us any real sanction to doubt its version, as it is recorded by Roger of Wendover. Apart from a minor mistake in the *Chronicle*, the English record gives a clear sequence: Eardwulf's deposition, 808; Ælfwald's reign, 808–10; Eanred's accession, 810. The reality and duration of Eardwulf's 'second reign' must, it seems, for ever remain conjectural.

THE COINS

The evidence of the documents suffers from certain limitations. From the annals we gather a chronology of political events, and can trace the alternation of kingship between the competing royal houses, a pattern familiar in Northumbria before and after this period. We can also observe in Eardwulf's remarkable actions of 808 an attempt to assert over the primitive teutonic pattern of personal loyalty and rivalries a more sophisticated conception of international law. In addition the letters of Alcuin provide some insight into the texture of current religious and moral attitudes. What the documents cannot provide are such objective facts as the 'standard of living' in Northumbria at the time, or whether the kingdom was in a flourishing state, or in decline. Nor do they always give an unambiguous idea of the significance of particular personages and events. Both Alcuin and the annalists write from within a context very different from our own. It is often difficult or impossible to disentangle objective facts and conditions from subjective impressions. When Alcuin inveighs against luxurious living and excessive clothing at Æthelred's court we gain no precise idea about the wealth of the kingdom, or its distribution. When both the annals and Alcuin lament the devastating effect of the Viking incursions of 793–4 it is not clear whether they are speaking of mere coastal raids, the demoralising effect of which was exaggerated by the destruction of national religious centres, or rather of serious invasions which caused widespread destruction of life and property. It is in the consideration of such questions as these that the relatively objective evidence of the coins may help, to some modest extent, in filling out the historical picture.

It will be convenient to deal first with the coins in the name of Ælfwald (Appendix 1, and Pl.2). The issue is very rare, no specimen being present in the British Museum collection nor in any of the *SCBI* volumes so far published. The obverse reads ᚫΓEVAΓDVƧ , or a slight variant of this, always round a seriffed cross. The reverse reads CVDhEART, with slight variations, also around a cross. The seven specimens located were struck from as many as six obverse and five reverse dies, so it seems likely that accumulating finds will show this to have been a larger issue than the number at present known might suggest. No other moneyer is recorded in the type though it is not impossible that others may yet come to light. The attribution of the group, as has been said, remains stubbornly ambiguous, and there are as yet no metal analyses which might help. Some inconclusive factors point towards Ælfwald I (779–88). The obverse reading of the coins, with its runic Æ (ᚫ) and L (Γ) is identical with that on the largest group of the known 'fantastic animal' coins of Ælfwald I. The lower case form of h is a feature shared by the legends of Ælfwald I's earlier animal coins and of this group, as is hypercorrection of V to ∀ or A, or *vice versa*. Both features are rare on the later coins of Æthelred I and of Eanred. Moreover there is the negative consideration that the first Ælfwald is already known to have struck coins, whereas nothing whatsoever is recorded of the brief two-year reign of Ælfwald II, which seems likely to have been disrupted by dissension and civil war. The fact that the moneyer's name, CVDhEART, occurs, in the form CVDHEARD, on the coinage of Æthelred I would seem also to favour Ælfwald I; but the recurrence of the name, in the form CVDHARD, on coins of Ælfwald II's successor, Eanred, makes the later attribution equally possible. Also favouring the attribution to Ælfwald II (808–10) is the apparent confinement of the type to a single moneyer, which contrasts, as we shall see, with the five or more varieties of Ælfwald I's animal type and the six moneyers of Æthelred I's coinage. A small-scale single-moneyer issue looks more likely to be a failed coinage of the later king than an intermediate coinage between the animal coins of Ælfwald I and the moneyer's-name coins of Æthelred I. But whichever of the two Ælfwalds these coins belong to, all three Cuthheards, striking under Ælfwald I, Æthelred, and Eanred (or Æthelred I, Ælfwald II, and Eanred) *could*, as Elizabeth Pirie has pointed out, be the same man—whose career would thus stretch from the late 780s or the early 790s to some time after 810.

If these coins were issued by Ælfwald I they must belong late in his reign, his earlier coinage having been a continuation of the 'fantastic animal' type. The survival rate of Ælfwald's animal coins has been low, but the extant specimens are sufficient to show a system of differencing marks, which have led to the tentative identification of at least five distinct groups.[28] One possible interpretation of these marks is that they represent the productions of individual moneyers, in which case Ælfwald in introducing the new type can be seen as simply continuing the previous system in a way more in line with the contemporary southern practice. Beonna of East Anglia and Offa of Mercia had already by this time adopted the moneyer's-name reverse (together with a broader flan) in imitation of the reform pence of Pepin II of Francia. Whether the moneyer's-name type was indeed introduced by Ælfwald I or rather by his successor Æthelred I, the change of design indicates a less isolated position for the northern kingdom than the retention of the small 'sceatta' module might seem to suggest. The weight of the new penny was of course at first the same as that of the old 'sceatta'.

Turning to the coins of Æthelred (Appendix 1, Pls.2–3) some broad conclusions immediately suggest themselves. In the first place the number of moneyers is apparently six: Ceolbald, Cuthgils, Cuthheard, Eanbald, Hnifula and Tidwulf.[29] This compares with the five differenced groups so far identified in the animal coinage of Ælfwald, lending weight to the hypothesis that the differencing ornaments on the earlier coins may in fact represent moneyers. It also tends to suggest that there was a smooth transition between the two types, implying that

[28] Booth, 1984, pp.85–7, and fig.2.

[29] Hugh Pagan previously assigned a coin of the moneyer Eadwine to this issue, citing an example in Adamson, 1834, from Hexham. 'Anglo-Saxon coins found at Hexham', in *Saint Wilfrid at Hexham*, D. P. Kirby (ed.), Newcastle-upon-Tyne (1974), pp.185–90, at pp.185–6. This specimen is now in the British Museum (*BMC* Æthelred II 295, reverse reading EADVIN) and is, like similar examples in the Lockett Collection (lot 290) and *SCBI* Copenhagen 184, a blundered brass coin of the mid-ninth century.

the monetary system was robust enough at this time to survive intact the disruption of Ælfwald's murder, the brief interlude of Osred's (coinless?) reign (788–90) and the subsequent regaining of the kingdom by a member of the rival royal house.

Secondly the number of dies represented in the located coins is high, indicating a low rate of survival. Almost all the coins are single finds, and the only hoard represented, Hexham, was deposited too long after the currency of the coins to show any clusters of die-duplication. The find situation is thus similar to that of the earlier animal coins, and comparisons are unlikely to be misleading. The 57 obverses and 56 reverses of this group which were in good enough condition to allow comparison, prove to have been struck from 44 obverse dies (77.2%) and 45 reverses (80.4%). This compares with a total of 99 obverse dies (87.6%) and 92 reverses (81.5%) yielded by 113 coins of the reign of Eadberht (both regal and archiepiscopal). The numbers of coins surviving of Eadberht's immediate successors is too small for reliable deductions to be made concerning the size of their issues. Twenty-one coins of Alchred (regal and archiepiscopal) yielded 20 obverse (95.2%) and 18 reverse dies (85.7%), while 12 animal coins of Ælfwald I revealed 12 obverse dies (100%) and 10 reverses (83.3%). What does seem certain enough from these comparisons, however, is that the survival rate of Æthelred's second-reign coins has not been dramatically higher than that of the earlier issues. And since relatively far more of these coins survive than those of Æthelwald, Alchred, and Ælfwald, it seems very probable that Æthelred's coinage was much larger in volume than any since that of Eadberht in the 740s and 750s. It suggests a prosperous and flourishing economy in Northumbria at the time, and one in which the medium of coined money played a significant part (though presumably coined money was at this stage only one element in an economy based to an extent on more primitive mechanisms).

The third initial point is that the coins of each moneyer display a distinct identity of type, both of reverse and of obverse. The reverse type, which bears witness to the moneyer's identity is—not surprisingly—carefully standardized within each moneyer's productions. There is no variation in the spelling of each moneyer's name from die to die, and other design elements are similarly invariable. Ceolbald's name always surrounds a boss within a beaded circle; Cuthgils' name always appears in two segments on each side of a triangle surmounted by a cross; Cuthheard always has a plain cross; Tidwulf a cross within a beaded circle. Only Eanbald and Hnifula show alternation between cross and boss as the central ornament, and Eanbald's name sometimes appears retrograde. Obverse types show greater variation, though significantly each distinct type, with only one exception, is confined to a particular moneyer. Ceolbald is unusual in the variety of his obverse types, he alone employing obverses with cross-and-pellets, cross-and-wedges, boss within beaded square, cross-crosslet and R within beaded circle. Only one of his surviving obverse types (var. v, boss-within-beaded circle) corresponds exactly with a type used by a different moneyer (Eanbald). Cuthgils' obverse always has a plain cross in the centre, and misplaces the initial cross in the legend (ED+ΓRED, or—on one die—ED 7+RED); Cuthheard's obverse is similarly invariable, distinguished by its inclusion of the king's title (+AEDILREDR̄); all but one (or two) of Eanbald's obverse dies have a boss within a beaded circle as their central ornament; Hnifula's two known obverse dies both show the same form (+EDILRED round plain cross); and Tidwulf's obverses, though showing differences in spelling, always have a plain cross as their central ornament. It seems then that the practised official at the time would have had no difficulty whatsoever in recognizing each moneyer's productions. Indeed a mere glance at the obverse of a coin would in most cases have been sufficient for identification. The system of 'privy marks' familiar in late medieval coinage—slight misspellings, added pellets, misplaced or reversed letters, etc.—seems to have reached quite an advanced stage in Northumbria even at this early period.

The clear distinction between obverse types is perhaps significant also in suggesting that each moneyer or die cutter (presumably the same person at this stage), though working within a strictly administered system, was independent in his manner, and perhaps also in his place, of working. No obverse die-duplication linking different moneyers—such as is widespread in the ninth-century series—is yet evident. If the moneyers were working together in the same workshop it seems that their obverse dies were strictly separated from each other. This pattern is similar to that which is evident in the coinage of Offa, where the productions of each moneyer (or small group of moneyers) also show distinctive stylistic features with little or no sharing of dies.[30] The double obverse coin (no.8) presents a possible exception to this separation of moneyers, but its evidence is very inconclusive. One die certainly belongs to Ceolbald's var. viii, with R in the centre. The other (+AEDILRED round a plain cross) is presumably another obverse rather than evidence of a seventh moneyer. But though similar in type to obverses used by Cuthheard, Eanbald, and Tidwulf, it differs from the relevant dies of the last two in spelling, and from those of all three in lacking the indication of the king's title (R or ℞). It seems most probable then that no muling between moneyers is involved here, and that this second die belongs also to Ceolbald, representing a variety from which no regular coin has survived.

Whether the differences between the moneyers' productions should be taken to imply that they were working in different centres is impossible to establish, the scatter of find-provenances showing no geographical concentration of the coins of any single moneyer. It may be that all the moneyers were working at York—perhaps at their own separate establishments, rather than in a centralized mint. But it must seem equally likely that coins were also produced elsewhere, perhaps in Bamburgh or Hexham. It cannot be assumed that Northumbria, with its vast area and its two distinct provinces, would necessarily at this time have concentrated minting only in the south. It was only after the relegation of the northern kingdom to a mere region, following the simplifications brought by the Vikings and by Ælfred's successors that the southern centre of York gained such overwhelming pre-eminence as the Northumbrian capital. Equally, the six moneyers may not all have been striking at the same time, though in the absence of substantial hoard evidence any chronological sequence of issues will be very difficult to establish.

[30] D. M. Metcalf, 'Offa's pence reconsidered', *Cunobelin* 9 (1963), 37–52.

Turning to more specific points we meet with a number of possibilities and hypotheses to which no satisfactory solution is at present possible. The coins of the Cuthgils group, for instance, have been assigned to the church by previous commentators,[31] partly because of their distinctive reverse ornament, which mounts the customary cross upon a beaded triangle. In earlier days of numismatic speculation Lord Grantley imaginatively identified this design as representing 'The shrine of St Cuthbert sideways?', and saw in the legend, ƐVD ƐLS, a possible reference to this: 'I would suggest for this reverse S[epulchrum] S[an]C[t]I CVD[berhti].'[32] Even if we reject Grantley's reading as forced, the possibility remains that the coins are an ecclesiastical issue, and that the anomalously disposed letters do not represent the name of a moneyer. If this is the case the group *could* belong, not with the moneyer's name coins of the 790s, but with the animal-type coins of Æthelred's first reign (774–9), though the fact that a specimen of the group was present in the Hexham hoard, deposited as late as 845, tells against this idea. The whole religious interpretation of the central motif has however seemed considerably less certain since the legend was persuasively reread by C. S. S. Lyon and Hugh Pagan as the name of a moneyer, Cuthgils.[33] On this interpretation it could well be that the central motif is no more than an ornamental elaboration with no specific religious connotation, a variant of the familiar cross-on-steps design of some Merovingian and earlier English coins. And even if we do read a particular significance into the central design, we still cannot be certain that the coins are an ecclesiastical rather than a regal issue, since, unlike the earlier and later archiepiscopal coins, they do not bear an archbishop's name. It remains most likely then that Cuthgils is after all, as Pagan suggested, one of Æthelred's second-reign moneyers.

The case of Eanbald is more ambiguous, and from the time of Grantley, Parsons, and Creeke it has frequently been assumed that the coins bearing this name were issued by Eanbald I, archbishop from 778 to 796. If we allow this possibility then there must be an even stronger case than with the Cuthgils group for assigning the coins to Æthelred's first reign. Such an issue, which would be precisely datable to 778–9, would be a natural successor to that of the same type struck jointly by Archbishop Ecgberht and Kings Eadberht, Æthelwald, and Alchred between the 740s and 766. Only the discovery of a hoard which associated these coins with Æthelred's animal-type could offer proof of this hypothesis. Otherwise it must seem just as likely that the coins belong to Æthelred's second reign, during which Eanbald I was still archbishop. It must be stressed however that we cannot be at all certain that this man is in fact the archbishop. The coins bear no indication of the archiepiscopal title, as do the earlier coins of Archbishop Ecgberht, and those struck later in the name of Archbishop Eanbald II during the reign of Eanred. This is of course not conclusive, since the king's name on the obverse of the coins usually also lacks an indication of title. But on the present evidence it must seem a very distinct possibility that this Eanbald is simply a moneyer of the same name as the

[31] Lord Grantley, 'Saint Cuthbert's pennies', *BNJ* 8 (1911), 49–53. Lyon, 1955–7, p.229. Pagan, 1969, pp.12–13.

[32] Grantley, p.51.

[33] Pagan, 1969, p.13.

archbishop, in which case the coins would almost certainly belong to Æthelred's second reign.

Of Æthelred's remaining moneyers the most interesting is Ceolbald. His coins have survived in greater numbers than those of the others, and since no significant hoard element distorts the corpus, they were probably originally more numerous in circulation. Their style, as has been said, is sometimes more impressive and elaborate than that of the other moneyers, and while his reverse design is invariable (boss within beaded circle) his obverses divide into eight probable subgroups, to all appearances intentionally differenced from each other, though it is difficult to be certain of the significance of these design variations. Like Leofthegn in the next century, Ceolbald seems to have been far more prolific and inventive than his colleagues, and it possible that he possessed a superior status—or perhaps he merely had a longer career. Ceolbald is also important in a larger context, in that there seems a distinct possibility that he is the same man as the Ceolbald who struck pennies for Cenwulf and Ceolwulf I of Mercia in the early 820s. The cross-crosslet design on his var. vii obverses is identical, as Pagan has pointed out, with that on some Mercian pennies bearing the same moneyer's name.[34] This would suggest that this particularly dynamic and professional craftsman had moved south at some time after the collapse of the coinage in the northern kingdom. Ceolbald's later, Mercian issues would thus seem a natural development in design from his more rudimentary sceattas. Such a move would be important both in indicating the probable degree of economic disruption in the north at this period, and in showing a connection between the northern and southern coinages. Unfortunately this identity between the Northumbrian and the Mercian Ceolbald will forever remain conjectural.

At this point we must consider the questions of weight-standard and metal quality. The available weights suggest some intriguing possibilities, though their small number barely constitutes a statistically significant sample. One point is certain enough however. Taken as a whole this coinage is, like the earlier animal issues, significantly lighter than the coins of Eanred, including his first 'silver' issues. The coins of Eanred from the Hexham hoard, as Dr Metcalf shows elsewhere in this volume, yield a neat and regular histogram with its peak at 1.22 g. Only one of the coins of Æthelred I so far weighed (no. 21, of Ceolbald) reaches this level. Moreover a histogram based on the 40 Æthelred I weights (excluding the fragmentary nos. 28, 33, and 62) could be taken to suggest that two different standards were in operation during the reign, presumably successively (see Fig. 1). Given the smallness of the sample however, and bearing in mind the diverse effects of corrosion and cleaning, this remains as yet only a possible hypothesis.

Any more detailed conclusions are highly speculative. It is tempting to note the lightness of the three Ælfwald/Cuthheard coins which have been weighed (0.69g, 0.78g, 0.86g) and to contrast this with the 5 heavier Æthelred/Cuthheard readings (0.97g–1.05g). This evidence might be taken as supporting the attribution of the former group to Ælfwald I, since Ælfwald II would be expected to

[34] *loc. cit.* See also C. E. Blunt, C. S. S. Lyon and B. H. I. H. Stewart, 'The coinage of southern England', *BNJ* 32 (1963), 33, pl.7, Cl.23 and Cl.24.

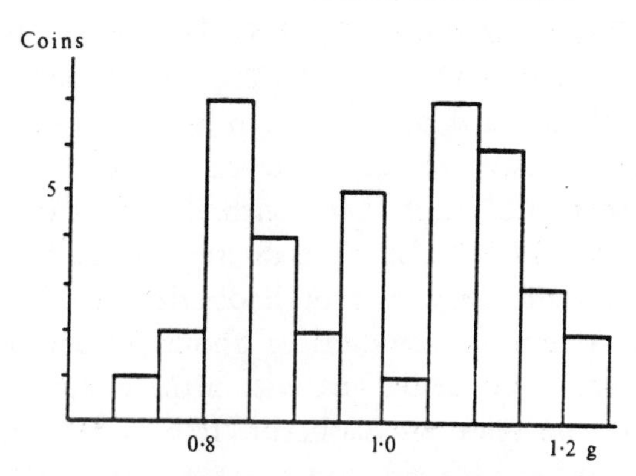

FIG.1. Weights of coins of Æthelred I

have adopted a relatively heavy standard (as Eanred later did) in his attempt to re-establish the coinage. But one of the Ælfwald coins in question is cracked and chipped and the other two are badly corroded, so their weights may well be quite misleading. Similar problems apply to other specific interpretations of the weight evidence. All four Cuthheard coins which have been weighed, both of the Hnifulas, and three of the four Eanbalds (the exception being the only specimen of var. iii) fall into a 'heavy' band, from just under 1.0g to just over 1.2g; whereas the coins of Ceolbald, Cuthgils and Tidwulf give a wider spread from 0.7g or 0.8g up to about 1.2g. We might conclude that the first three moneyers produced all their coins in an early phase of the coinage, while the others continued striking into a second, lighter phase. But again the data are too few and unreliable to support anything but inconclusive speculation.

In order to place the metal-quality of the coins of Æthelred I in its proper context it will be useful to review the entire eighth-century series of which these coins are the last representatives. A list of the three sets of analytical results so far available for the series is given in Appendix 2. Unfortunately the two earlier sets of results are now considered to be generally too high, and when they contradict the results in the last column they should probably be disregarded. Even ignoring the earlier results however it is not easy to detect a detailed coherence in them. Marion Archibald argues that 'Mr Cowell's analyses have shown that Eadberht's issues begin at about 70 per cent silver... but they thereafter declined to around the 50 per cent mark'.[35] As their typology suggests, Classes A and B emerge in the analyses as earlier and purer than C, D, E, and G, and it is satisfying in this context that the lowest of Mr Cowell's precious metal readings for a Class B coin (50.6%) is yielded by a possibly irregular specimen of anomalous style. We can then feel secure in detecting two phases in Eadberht's coinage.

The analytical results from the later eighth century however are too few and too diverse to give an unambiguous picture. Miss Archibald continues: 'the coins of Alchred, 765–74, analysed by Mr Cowell are on the band of 50 per cent or less, and never achieved a 70 per cent standard.'[36] Certainly none of the coins of Alchred analysed by Mr Cowell gives a result approaching 70 per cent, but the 9 analyses (regal and archiepiscopal) do show an uncomfortably wide spectrum of

[35] M. M. Archibald, 'The coinage of Beonna', *BNJ* 55 (1985), pp.31–2.

[36] *loc. cit.*

results, from 62% to 32.4%. Only three fall below 50 per cent however, while two rise above 60 per cent. If the readings are to be trusted they would seem to suggest an initial standard of more than 60 per cent. Moneyers would not put more silver than officially required into their coins, though they might put less if they thought they could get away with it. The two recent analyses of animal coins of Ælfwald (779–88) also gave discrepant results. One (66.7%) seems to be as pure as all but the very best of Eadberht's coins, but the other (46.3%) is consistent with a reduced standard of about 50 per cent. On this evidence we might hypothesize a similar decline within the coinage of Ælfwald to that which occurred during the reign of Eadberht. It may possibly be that the purer coin (with no ornaments in the field) comes early in the reign, and the baser coin (with two ornaments in the field) comes later. But at the present stage this hypothesis remains untestable.

When we reach the moneyer's-name coins of Æthelred I we find the same pattern. One of the three recent readings (59.8%) seems to suggest the maintenance of the 60 per cent official standard; another (51.9%) suggests a reduced standard somewhat over 50 per cent; while the third (35%) is almost as base as the worst of the Alchred coins. The matter is complicated by the fact that the highest and lowest of the three Æthelred readings are both yielded by coins of the same moneyer: Cuthgils. Perhaps of relevance here is the fact that the baser of the two Cuthgils coins differs slightly in obverse design from the other surviving examples of the group. It is not impossible that it belongs to an irregular or imitative issue—even one of later date. It comes from the Hexham hoard, deposited fifty or more years after the currency of the coins. But these are merely speculative guesses, and only with the accumulating evidence of further analyses will it become possible to gain a clear picture of this coinage. The evidence so far however, such as it is, certainly does not point to any overall difference in metal quality between the moneyer's-name coins of Æthelred and the earlier animal coins. It seems that, after the initial decline of metal under Eadberht, a standard of over 60 per cent silver became the rule. Probably the standard was reasserted at the beginning of each new issue or reign, only to slip back to 50 per cent, or below, as time went on. And this variable, but nevertheless relatively stable, standard was maintained unaltered through the change of type into the moneyer's-name issues of (Ælfwald I? and) Æthelred I.

THE COLLAPSE OF THE COINAGE

As has been said, the single most striking fact about the surviving coins is the complete absence of any specimens in the name of Eardwulf. This fact of course does not in itself prove that none were struck. It must be remembered that the coinages of several of the earlier kings have survived only in tiny numbers, so one should not perhaps presume too much on this lack of evidence. Æthelwald Moll's six-year reign (which coincided with the complete collapse of the sceatta coinage in the south of the country) is represented by one (or two) surviving coins only, and the five-year first reign of Æthelred I by a similar number.[37] But it must still

[37] Booth, 1984, p.96.

be certain enough that any issue of Eardwulf's reign, if there was one, will have been very small compared with those of his predecessors. Twelve obverse and 10 reverse dies are represented in 12 located specimens of Ælfwald I's animal type; 6 obverse and 5 reverse dies in the 7 moneyer's-name coins of Ælfwald, which may belong to the same nine-year reign. And, as we have seen, at least 44 obverse and 45 reverse dies occur in the 63 coins of Æthelred I's six-year second reign. In the light of these comparisons the absence of coins from Eardwulf's reign must be of real significance.

But why should the coinage suddenly have failed at this particular moment? Eardwulf reigned for twelve years. The events of his reign show him to have been as energetic a ruler as his predecessor, and as the developments of 808 show, he was a man of wide political perspectives. His reign follows almost immediately on that of Æthelred, whose coinage was extensive. On this evidence it seems that if any king in this period *ought* to have struck coins it is Eardwulf. This fact needs to be stressed since numismatists have been perhaps too ready in the past to see the eighth-century coinage as endemically 'intermittent', and to view the hiatus during Eardwulf's reign as merely an unremarkable episode in a series of discontinuities. The importance of this hiatus has also been further obscured by the absence, until very recently, of metal analyses, an absence which fostered the erroneous impression that the metal quality of late-eighth century coins had already embarked on the drastic debasement which overtook the coinage in the ninth century. Thus Æthelred I's *c*.50–60% silver coins of the 790s have frequently been grouped together with Eanred's *c*.40% silver coins of the 810s or 820s, in a supposed homogeneous phase of 'base-silver and silver-alloy' coins.

In the light of the accumulating evidence and closer study of the coins, this version must be abandoned. In the first place it is now clear that the eighth-century series was not nearly as intermittent as has been thought. With the recent reattribution of one (perhaps two) coins to the reign of Æthelwald Moll[38] it emerges that from the time of Eadberht to that of Æthelred I each of the five kings who reigned for longer than two years certainly issued coins, and in some cases these issues were undoubtedly very large. Though fluctuations no doubt occurred, hundreds of thousands, if not millions, of these coins were probably in circulation at any given time throughout the period *c*.740–*c*.796. The picture of the eighth-century Northumbrian money economy which is emerging is of a well administered system, showing signs of strain now and then, but no radical weakness. It is to this economic climate that the moneyer's-name coins of Æthelred I belong. And it is not until after an apparently complete failure in the issue of the coinage and a gap of at least twelve years, that a new, more modest coinage was attempted, in an economic climate which resulted in a series of debasements and the effective disappearance of silver from the coinage altogether. The eighth- and ninth-century coinages should then be seen as quite distinct, and separated from each other by a drastic economic collapse.

[38] The flaked surface of Alchred/Ecgberht 6 (Booth, 1984, pl.6) led the present writer (working from a photograph) to misread the D of +EDILVALD as an inverted A, and so to reattribute the coin to Alchred. Ian Stewart has now shown the previous attribution to Æthelwald to be, almost certainly, correct. This makes it probable also that the coin illustrated in *The Gentleman's Magazine* 1832 (Booth, 1984, p.81) is a coin of the same issue.

In general terms the failure of the coinage is perhaps not totally unexpected. It seems very likely that Northumbria was in a state of slow if undramatic decline throughout the eighth century. Eric John has persuasively suggested that the root of this decline lay in the lavish granting of tax-exempt 'bookland' by earlier kings to the monasteries which were springing up in all quarters.[39] In his letter of 734 to Archbishop Ecgberht, Bede was already advocating a reduction in the number of foundations and forecasting dire consequences from the self-indulgence of many young men, who instead of making ready for the defence of the nation, were idling their time away in monastic tax-havens. The concentration of so much of the productive capacity of the economy in the hands of religious houses perpetually exempt from secular taxes and civic obligations, was clearly dysfunctional. In John's view Offa's more robust stance in relation to church rights and exemptions (including the abolition of privileges previously granted by the 'sub-kings' whose territories he conquered) gave Mercia a distinct economic advantage over its northern neighbour. Unfortunately, although the robust policy of Offa is clear enough from the extant charters of his reign, no similar charters from Northumbria remain in existence, so it is difficult to be certain as to the exact economic relationship between church and state in the north at this time. Nevertheless Bede's anxieties are perhaps sufficient indication of the situation. It is in this context that we should perhaps see the apparent reduction of metal standard in the coinage during the reign of Eadberht and the repeated failure later in the eighth century to maintain this lower standard consistently. The ultimate collapse of the coinage is not then an unexpected development. But we still have no explanation as to why it should have failed so suddenly and unexpectedly when it did, immediately after an apparent revival under Æthelred I.

The catalyst which transformed this instability into a collapse seems to have been, as Michael Dolley once suggested, the Viking onslaught of 793–4.[40] It is difficult not to interpret the coin evidence now available as demonstrating, quite dramatically, that these raids were not mere incursions of essentially symbolic significance, but that they disrupted the ailing Northumbrian economy quite radically. Even if coined money did not yet play a central part in the economy at this time, the complete disappearance of this complex, centrally administered system after fifty years of relative success and stability is still a dramatic historical event, requiring a dramatic explanation. Such an argument will perhaps not satisfy those who wish to minimize the destructive effect of the Vikings. Peter Sawyer has sternly warned: 'If the Viking menace is to be measured by its consequences it is important that only those which can be proved should be taken into account.'[41] We can prove that the raids brought the issue of coinage to an end. We may indeed be dealing with an event which has more complex precipitating causes than the one stridently advertised by contemporary clerical observers, eager as always to exaggerate the impact of the heathen men. But against Sawyer's minimalist view of historical evidence and its permitted uses, we may oppose the maximalism of Eric John: 'It must be remembered that this is a

[39] Eric John, *Orbis Britanniae*, Leicester (1966), pp.21–7.

[40] M. Dolley, 'The coins', in *The Archaeology of Anglo-Saxon England*, D. M. Wilson (ed.), pp.349–72, at p.355.

[41] P. H. Sawyer, *The Age of the Vikings*, London (1962), p.142.

period in which very little evidence of anything at all survives. We must always beware of minimizing evidence merely because it is exiguous.'[42] In this case, although the evidence is indeed exiguous, it is both clear and compelling: 63 or more recorded coins of Æthelred; no coins of Eardwulf whatsoever. If there *were* other precipitating causes for the sudden collapse of the coinage at this point they are no longer visible to us. The connection of the advent of the Vikings in Northumbria with the cessation of its well-established coinage is surely too plausible to be dismissed out of hand.

In any case we do not in fact need to reject Sawyer's wider scepticism about the size and destructiveness of the Viking raids in order to impute to these particular attacks a uniquely momentous effect. It must be remembered that these were the first significant raids of their kind to have occurred in England. They were quite unexpected. As Alcuin remarks, over the 350 years during which 'we and our fathers have inhabited this most lovely land' no-one had ever imagined 'that such an inroad from the sea could be made.'[43] The disruptive effect of these first attacks, repeated over successive years, may have been much greater than that of later raids. Moreover Northumbrian monasteries were perhaps particularly important institutions in the local and national economy at this time. Like religious houses elsewhere they would probably have been used as safe repositories for secular wealth, so the material plunder carried off from Lindisfarne and Jarrow may have been very considerable indeed, notwithstanding their distance from the commercial centre of York. But also the skills and expertise of monks was a valuable commodity in itself at this time, perhaps particularly so in Northumbria whose established preeminence in scholarship and art was only just beginning to fade. The surviving *Lindisfarne Gospels, Codex Amiatinus*, and other manuscripts show how great and widely respected the achievement had been. Though the evidence is lacking it could be that the supply of less prestigious texts of the Gospels and of Benedict's *Rule* to the southern and continental monasteries which were springing up throughout the century, was in itself a source—if in a haphazard and unsystematic way—of the economic prosperity of the kingdom as a whole. When the 'pagans' arrived, as *The History of the Kings* rhetorically laments, they

> laid everything waste with grievous plundering, trampled the holy places with polluted steps, dug up the altars, and seized all the treasures of the holy church. They killed some of the brothers, took some away with them in fetters, many they drove out, naked and loaded with insults, some they drowned in the sea.[44]

The craftsmanship of scribes and illuminators was thus lost, and irreplaceable libraries were presumably also destroyed or scattered.

But it seems most likely that these raids did not stop at the monasteries themselves. As the history of the succeeding century or so confirms, before Ælfred and his successors had been stimulated to organize the defensive system of the *burhs*, all the Anglo-Saxon kingdoms were virtually defenceless against a seaborne attack from even a small number of men. A few dozen warriors

[42] John, p.10.
[43] *EHD*, no.193, p.776.
[44] *EHD*, no.3, p.247.

descending unannounced on the Northumbrian coast could have pillaged at will over an extensive area for some time before the local people or the king would have been able to raise any organized opposition. We may then imagine the raids on Lindisfarne in 793 and on Jarrow in 794 as more than a mere plundering of churches. They were quite probably extensive pillaging operations, disrupting agriculture and trade over a wider area. Most important of all, the new Viking threat must have created a commercial insecurity on a larger scale, striking at east-coast shipping and thereby reducing the flow of foreign trade and foreign money into York. And the economic decline which inevitably ensued is evidenced by the sudden and surprising termination of the well-established silver coinage of the kingdom, and its subsequent replacement, after a lengthy period, by a coinage of inferior metal quality.

APPENDIX 1
LIST OF COINS CONSULTED

Because of the small number of surviving specimens, the ordering, and sometimes even the definition of different varieties within the coinage of Æthelred is inevitably arbitrary, and implies no necessary chronological or other relationship. Die-linked coins are grouped together and, in the case of the numerous varieties of Ceolbald, simpler designs are placed before more elaborate ones.

Coins from the Whitby Abbey excavations of the 1920s, sketchily summarized by J. Allan in 'The Coins from Whitby', *Archaeologia* 89 (1943), 85–6, are cited with their original inventory numbers.

Dies

The variable quality of both coins and photographs renders die-comparison very difficult. Some mistakes will inevitablt have been made.

xx indicates dies different from those of any other known specimen. ?? indicates dies which could not be compared.

Plates

The numbering of specimens on the plates corresponds with that in the List. Scale approximately 3:2. All of the coins, except nos.48 and 53, are illustrated either in the plates or by line drawings in the List.

ÆLFWALD I (779–788) or ÆLFWALD II (808–810)

Cuthheard

Obv. +ᚨΓEVAΓDVϨ, +ᚨΓEVAΓ·D∀Ϩ or ᚨΓEVAΓD∀Ϩ round cross.
Rev. CVDhEART, CVDhEVRT or C∀DhEART round cross.

		Die identities	*Weight (g)*	*Where found*
1	Private possession. Booth and Blowers 1983, 24	Dies as 2	0.86	Sancton, 1980
2	Sewerby Hall, Bridlington	Dies as 1	—	Thwing, Paddock Hill, 1985
3	Leeds City Museum. Booth and Blowers 1983, 26	Rev as 4	0.78	Sancton, 1979

4	York Archaeological Trust 32	Rev as 3	—	York, Old County Hospital
5	Lord Grantley, *NC* (1897) p.138–9, pl.VII, 5	xx	—	—
6	Formerly Yorkshire Museum. Lyon, 1955–7, pl.XVIII 7. Now lost	xx	—	—
7	Private possession. Booth and Blowers 1983, 25	xx	0.69	Sancton, before 1982

ÆTHELRED I (Second Reign 790–796)

Ceolbald

The reverse reads +CEOLBALD on nos.9–14; +[EOLBALD, +[EOLBAED or +[EOLBΛLD on nos.15–32. In each case the name surrounds a boss within a beaded circle. (No.9 has pellets within the angles of the initial cross, and on nos.25 and 26 the beaded circle is doubled.)

Var. i: *Obv*.: +AEDILRED round plain cross.

Double obverse: combined with a die of var. viii.

8	Private possession. Booth and Blowers 1983, 28	xx	0.86	Sancton, before 1982

Var. ii: *Obv*.: +AEDILRED round cross within beaded circle.

9	British Museum. Whitby 914	Obv as 10 Rev as 10?	1.19	Whitby Abbey, 1920s
10	Whitby, Pannet Park Museum. Pirie 1986, 69	Obv as 9 Rev as 9?	—	Whitby, Spa Ladder, E. Cliff, 1931

Var. iii: *Obv*.: As var. ii but pellets added in the angles of the central cross.

11	Museum of Antiquities, University of Newcastle upon Tyne. Pirie 1986, 84	Obv as 12?	—	Newcastle-upon-Tyne, Black Gate, 1977
12	Oxford, Ashmolean	Obv as 11?	0.90	—

Var. iv: *Obv*.: +AEDILRED (on no.15 +AEDILREDR) round cross and wedges within beaded circle.

13	*BMC* (Æthelred II) 284	Dies as 14	1.08	—
14	Yorkshire Museum	Dies as 13	0.80	—
15	British Museum. Whitby 24	Rev as 16–17	0.70	Whitby Abbey, 1920s

Var. v: *Obv*.: +AEDILRED round boss within beaded circle (nos.16 and 17 have wedges in the angles of the initial cross).

16	*SCBI* Mack 368. Adamson 1836, 11	Obv as 17 Rev as 15 and 17	1.13	Hexham hoard, 1832

17	British Museum. Whitby 22	Obv as 16 Rev as 15–16	0.98	Whitby Abbey, 1920s
18	British Museum. Whitby 23	Dies as 19	0.83	Whitby Abbey, 1920s
19	Private possession. Booth and Blowers 1983, 29	Dies as 18	0.88	Sancton, 1979
20	Yorkshire Museum. Pirie 1986, 78	xx	0.91	?Hexham, Abbey Churchyard, 1932

Var. vi: *Obv*.: + ·A·EDILRED or + ·A·ED·I·LR·ED round boss within beaded square.

21	*BMC* (Æthelred II) 285	xx	1.24	—

22	Adamson 1834, Ethelred 31 (This is clearly not the same coin as no.21. It could be a specimen of var. v. See ill.)	xx	—	Hexham hoard, 1832

Var. vii: *Obv*.: + AEDILRED round cross-crosslet or cross within lined square.

23	*SCBI* Mack 368a	xx	1.20	—
24	Jarrow Hall, Jarrow, Tyne and Wear. Pirie 1986, 81	xx	—	Jarrow, Anglo-Saxon Minster
25	British Museum. Whitby 748	xx	0.80	Whitby Abbey, 1920s
26	Glasgow Art Gallery and Museum, Kelvingrove, '55–96. Pirie 1986, 108	xx	0.79	Luce Sands, Wigtownshire

Var. viii: *Obv*.: + AEDILRED (starting at 6 o'clock) round R or ℞ within beaded circle. The A on both obv. and rev. is barred at the top, and may lack the cross-piece.

27	*SCBI* Yorks. xl 25. Pirie 1986, 51	Dies as 28	0.83	York Minster, 1970–71
28	Oxford, Ashmolean. Metcalf *et al* 1968, 085	Dies as 27	0.73	—
29	British Museum. Whitby 744	Dies as 30	0.78	Whitby Abbey, 1920s
30	*BMC* (Æthelred II) 283	Dies as 29	1.13	—
31	Oxford, Ashmolean. Metcalf *et al* 1968, 085*bis*	xx	1.15	—

32	Yorkshire Museum	xx	—	York: Tanner Row, General Accident site
33	British Museum. Whitby 961b	??	0.35	Whitby Abbey, 1920s

Cuthgils

Obv.: ED+ΓRED (on no.6 ED˥+RED) round cross.
Rev.: ꞆVD ꞆLS in two segments each side of a beaded triangle surmounted by a cross.

34	Oxford, Ashmolean, ex Firth, ex Grantley	xx	0.88	—
35	*SCBI* Copenhagen 273, ex Bruun 44, ex Rashleigh 141, ex Loscombe 1046, ex Rich	xx	1.06	—
36	Private possession. Booth and Blowers 1983, 27	xx	0.85	Sancton, 1982
37	Ryedale Folk Museum. *YAJ* 41, 1966, 566–7	xx	—	Kirkbymoorside, All Saints' Churchyard, 1965
38	Yorkshire Museum. This is undoubtedly the same specimen as Adamson 1836, Uncertain 1	xx	1.16	Hexham hoard, 1832

Cuthheard

Obv.: +AEDILREDR (with a bar over the final R) round cross. (On no.46 the legend is retrograde).
Rev.: +ꞆVDHEARD round cross.

39	British Museum. Whitby 742	Obv as 40	0.97	Whitby Abbey, 1920s
40	British Museum. Whitby 886	Obv as 39 Rev as 41	1.00	Whitby Abbey, 1920s
41	Spink Auction 32, 1.12.83, lot 385 (part)	Rev as 40	—	—
42	*BMC* (Æthelred II) 293	Obv as 43	—	—
43	York Archaeological Trust	Obv as 42 Rev ?	—	York: Fishergate, Refearn's Glassworks site, 1986
44	British Museum, E4203. In collection before 1838 but not in *BMC*	xx	0.97	—
45	Oxford, Ashmolean. Metcalf *et al.* 1968, 086	xx	0.99	—
46	C. S. S. Lyon collection. Metcalf *et al.* 1968, Ly3	xx	1.05	—

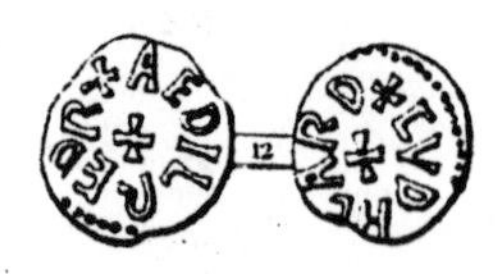

47	Adamson 1836, Ethelred 12 (See ill.)	xx	—	Hexham hoard, 1832
48	Private possession. *YAJ* 45 (1973) 203	??	—	Settle, Attemire Cave, 1970

Eanbald

Var. i: *Obv*.: + AEDILRED (no.51 without initial cross) round boss within beaded circle.
Rev.: EAИBALD (nos.50–1 retrograde) round cross.

49	Private possession	xx	—	Barmby Moor, 1986
50	Sewerby Hall, Bridlington. Pirie, *British Archaeological Reports*, British Series 128 (1984), pp.211–12, pl.11, 20	xx	1.08	Thwing, Paddock Hill, 1983
51	*SCBI* Glasgow 178	xx	1.09	—

Var. ii: *Obv*.: AEDILRED round boss within beaded circle.
Rev.: + EAИBALD round cross within beaded circle.

52	British Museum. Whitby 972	xx	1.10	Whitby Abbey, 1920s

53 Joseph Fairless (*NC* 1845, p.36) records a coin apparently of this variety together with some later ninth-century pieces, found 'for the most part' at Hexham, in the 'precinct of the church'. He states that it was 'inscribed EΛNBALD with a pelletted circle, and a cross in the centre. On the other side ΛEDILRED, without the cross'. The coin cannot now be located.

Var. iii: *Obv*.: As var. ii.
Rev.: EAИBALD retrograde round boss within beaded circle.

54	Private possession. Booth and Blowers 1983, 30	xx	0.83	Sancton, before 1982

Var. iv: *Obv*.: EDILR + EDR round cross.
Rev.: + EAИBALD retrograde round boss within beaded circle.

55	Jarrow Hall, Jarrow, Tyne and Wear. Pirie 1986, no.24	xx	—	Jarrow, Anglo-Saxon Minster, 1976

Hnifula

Var. i: *Obv*.: + EDILRED round cross.
Rev.: + HNIFVLA round cross within beaded circle.

56	*BMC* (Æthelred II) 429. Adamson 1834, 136	Dies as 57	1.11	Hexham hoard, 1832
57	Norwich Castle Museum, Norfolk. *East Anglian Archaeology Report* No.22, 1984, 68	Dies as 56	—	Thetford, Norfolk, 1977

Var. ii: *Obv*.: As var. i.
Rev.: As var. i but boss instead of cross in centre.

58	*BMC* (Æthelred II) 430	xx	1.09	—

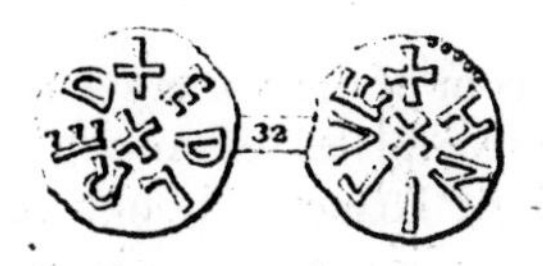

Note: Adamson 1834, Uncertain 26, and Adamson 1836, Ethelred 32 (both from the Hexham hoard) could be coins of this reign and moneyer, though they are more probably blundered coins of Æthelred II (see ills.).

Tidwulf

All reverse dies read +TIDVVLF or +TIDVV[F round cross within beaded circle.

Var. i: *Obv*.: +AED RIEDR round cross.

59	C. S. S. Lyon collection. Metcalf *et al.* 1968, Ly4	Obv as 60	1.06	—
60	Yorkshire Museum	Obv as 59	1.12	?Hexham hoard, 1832

Var. ii: *Obv*.: +EDLREDRE round cross.

61	British Museum. Whitby 1027	xx	1.10	Whitby Abbey, 1920s
62	*BMC* (Æthelred II) 580	xx	0.93	—
63	Private possession. Booth and Blowers 1983, 31	xx	—	Sancton, 1981
64	Humberside Archaeological Unit	??	—	Beverley, Lurk Lane, 1980

Var. iii: *Obv*.: +EDƎ⅃DRE round cross.

65	Pannet Park Museum, Whitby. Pirie 1986, 68	Obv as 66–8 Rev as 66	—	Whitby?
66	*SCBI Glasgow* 225	Obv as 65 and 67–8 Rev as 65	0.98	—
67	*SCBI Glasgow* 224	Obv as 65–6 and 68 Rev as 68	0.81	—
68	Oxford, Ashmolean	Obv as 65–7 and 68 Rev as 67	0.81	—

69 A coin of this variety was illustrated by John White in 1756, along with other 'sceattas', in two plates 'of Ancient and Singular Coins which were lately found near and in the Isle of Thanet.' Though very similar to no.68, and probably from the same dies, it seems not to be the same coin (see ill.)

70	C. S. S. Lyon collection. Metcalf *et al.* 1968, Ly5	xx	0.97	—

APPENDIX 2
ANALYSES OF EIGHTH-CENTURY NORTHUMBRIAN COINS

Animal-type coins are identified by their numbering in Booth, 1984; moneyer's-name coins by their numbering in Appendix 1 of the present paper. All figures are percentages of precious metal. The small percentage of gold (usually less than 2%) detectable in most coins has been aggregated into the 'silver' total, assuming it to have found its way into them as an impurity in the silver bullion used.

M: Metcalf, Merrick and Hamblin, *Studies in the Composition of Early Medieval Coins*, Newcastle-upon-Tyne, 1968.
B: Analyses performed in the Department of Archaeological Sciences, University of Bradford, 1976–9; in Booth, 1984.
C: Analyses performed by M. R. Cowell, some published in M. M. Archibald, 'The Coinage of Beonna', *BNJ* 55, 1985, Appendix 4; others to be published in the forthcoming *Metallurgy and Numsimatics 2* (reproduced with permission).

Aldfrith (685–704)

	M	B	C
4			93.3

Eadberht (738–757) Animal Type

	M	B	C
A3	83.5–84.5	73	
A5			63.6
A6		60	
A7		60	
A9			70.5
A16		97	
A18		67	
B/A			85.6 (inc. 9.5% gold)
B1			59.1
B2	58.5–82.5	61	64.7
B4		81	
B11	46.5–54.5		
B17			75.1
B18			60.6
B19			57.8
B21			68.9
B23			50.6
C2			55.7
C4		50	
C5		70	
C8			47.2
D2	82.5–85.5		
D5	92.5–93.5		
D/E	62.5–66.5	63	
E1	37.5		
E4			43.7
E6			50.8
E7		48	
F3			61.8
G1			41.5
G2			50.7
G10			50.9

Eadberht (738–757) with Ecgberht (734–766)

	M	B	C
1			53.2
2	70–87		47.3

	M	B	C
12			55.8
13			63.6
16	67–72		
20			46.6
21			58.6
Alchred (765–774) Animal Type			
1			62.0
4			32.4
5			55.8
6			46.6
7			51.4
8			61.7
Alchred (765–774) with Ecgberht (734–766)			
1			49.1
2			53.1
4			51.7

	M	B	C
Æthelred I (first reign, 774–779)			
1			58.2
Ælfwald (779–788) Animal Type			
A2			66.7
E1			46.3
E2	48.5–52.5		
Æthelred I (second reign 790–796)			
22			51.9
26	67–74		
28	91.75		
34			59.8
38		6.2	35.0
44	62.5		
46	67.75–81.75		
59	77–84		
70	66–72		

DISCUSSION

Dr Metcalf: Mr Booth handles the intriguing metrological evidence from Æthelred's second reign with his customary sound judgement, and rightly points out that it may be misleading for two reasons, namely that we have a record of weight for only two-thirds of the specimens, and that chipped or corroded coins may now be significantly lighter than when they were made. This should make us cautious of the idea, suggested by the two peaks of the histogram, that there was a lighter and a heavier weight-standard, belonging respectively to an earlier and later phase of Æthelred's coinage,—or *vice versa.* If this were so, if there were such an administrative change during the years 790–6, it would offer an important new insight into the coinage and monetary history of the late eighth century. Also, it would very probably clinch the attribution of Ælfwald's coins. But the evidence all seems, as Mr Booth says, to be ambiguous: it is just not clear whether we should deduce that heavier coins were followed by lighter, or the other way round.

The difficulties appear to be even greater than Mr Booth warns us, for not only do the coins of the moneyers Ceolbeald, Cuthgils, and Tidwulf vary widely in weight, sometimes between die-linked specimens, but also the varieties into which they have now been classified are not internally consistent in their weights.

Is it fortuitous and deceptive that some moneyers seem to be controlling the weights of their flans much more accurately than others? Could most of the variation in fact be put down to loss of weight through wear, corrosion, and leaching? The specimens with Hexham hoard provenances, nos. 16, 38, 56, and (?)60 weigh 1.13, 1.16, 1.11, and 1.12g, and we can probably add no. 21 (*BMC* 285), 1.24g. The average weight of these specimens from a hoard with a t.p.q. half a century after their issue, is well above the average for the corpus. These are coins in good condition, which may be presumed to have lost very little of their original weight. They may have spent most of those fifty years out of circulation. They give us an idea of a weight-standard of, at best, around 1.15g—against which we can assess the rest of the evidence. The Whitby excavation coins, for example, range quite widely in weight, averaging about 0.95g. Does this difference(of about 17 per cent) reflect loss of weight by wear, or harsh soil conditions, or a genuine difference in original weights of the coins? Perhaps it would be useful to compare the later stycas from Whitby, since they were certainly struck on a single weight-standard, about which exact information is available. The specimens weighing around 0.8 to 0.85g, which produce the lower peak of the histogram, are 25 to 30 per cent lighter than the histogram average. That is a substantial difference, and unless such a coin looks obviously worn or defective, experience with other series suggests that if numerous specimens are like that, many of them were originally lighter than 1.15g. This does not add up to evidence of two deliberate weight standards, much less two phases: one might account for the facts more economically by saying that some moneyers produced rather a high proportion of sub-standard coins. Further, one cannot altogether rule out the possibility that in the earlier stages of setting aside the coins hoarded at Hexham, heavier specimens were preferred. After all, the time-scale of Æthelred's reign, of at most seven years, does not allow long for Hexham to include, through natural wastage, only the later, hypothetically heavier, issues. So the question does seem regrettably inconclusive. The one point that is relatively free from second thoughts is that the moneyer's-name coins of Ælfwald are likely to be early, otherwise there would probably have been more of them in Hexham. A more complete set of weights for Ælfwald might be a big help.

We have no evidence that coinage had ceased to *circulate* in Northumbria in the time of Eardwulf; what ceased dramatically was minting. This might be taken to imply that 'foreign' silver (southern English or continental), requiring to be reminted, ceased to reach York. It is not obvious that sporadic raids striking directly across the North Sea at Bernicia would disrupt the east-coast shipping route to York, nor that they would reduce the economy of the entire kingdom to a standstill. Perhaps we should be looking for a collection of causes further to the south. Æthelred's reign coincided closely with the breach in commercial relations between Offa and Charlemagne. The reopening of the southern English ports in 796 may have diverted some merchants to more lucrative routes. More important, piracy in the southern North Sea may have deterred merchants from making the longer voyage. Peter Sawyer, in his book *Kings and Vikings*, has reminded us that our knowledge of the early Viking attacks is very defective, and that the attack on Lindisfarne in 793 was by no means an isolated event. Alcuin's indignation was perhaps aroused specifically because such a holy place had been violated; and he was astonished that an attack without warning, from the open sea, was possible. But already by 792 Offa was organizing defences in Kent against 'pagan seamen'; and by 800 Charlemagne had had to build defences along the coasts of Francia as far west as the Seine.

If the explanation for the end of minting was along these lines, we might look for a falling-off during Æthelred's reign, with the raids of 793–4 as an additional factor, and one possible outline would include a re-coinage of the earlier 'animal' types at some date in Æthelred's reign, when several new moneyers were recruited to assist Cuthheard, and a better weight-standard was aimed at. The erratic alloy of

Æthelred's coins can hardly derive, in the 790s, from reminting only southern or continental coins, but it could perhaps derive from taking the earlier 'animal' coins at face value. Perhaps only Ceolbeald remained active once the reform was accomplished; and as York felt the effects of piracy, the weights of the coins quickly became erratic. This is not a particularly complicated sequence of events to envisage, but the available numismatic evidence falls far short of what would be necessary to prove it. The eight varieties of Ceolbeald's coins ought to be a way into the problem, but it is not obvious what one can make of them.

PLATE 2

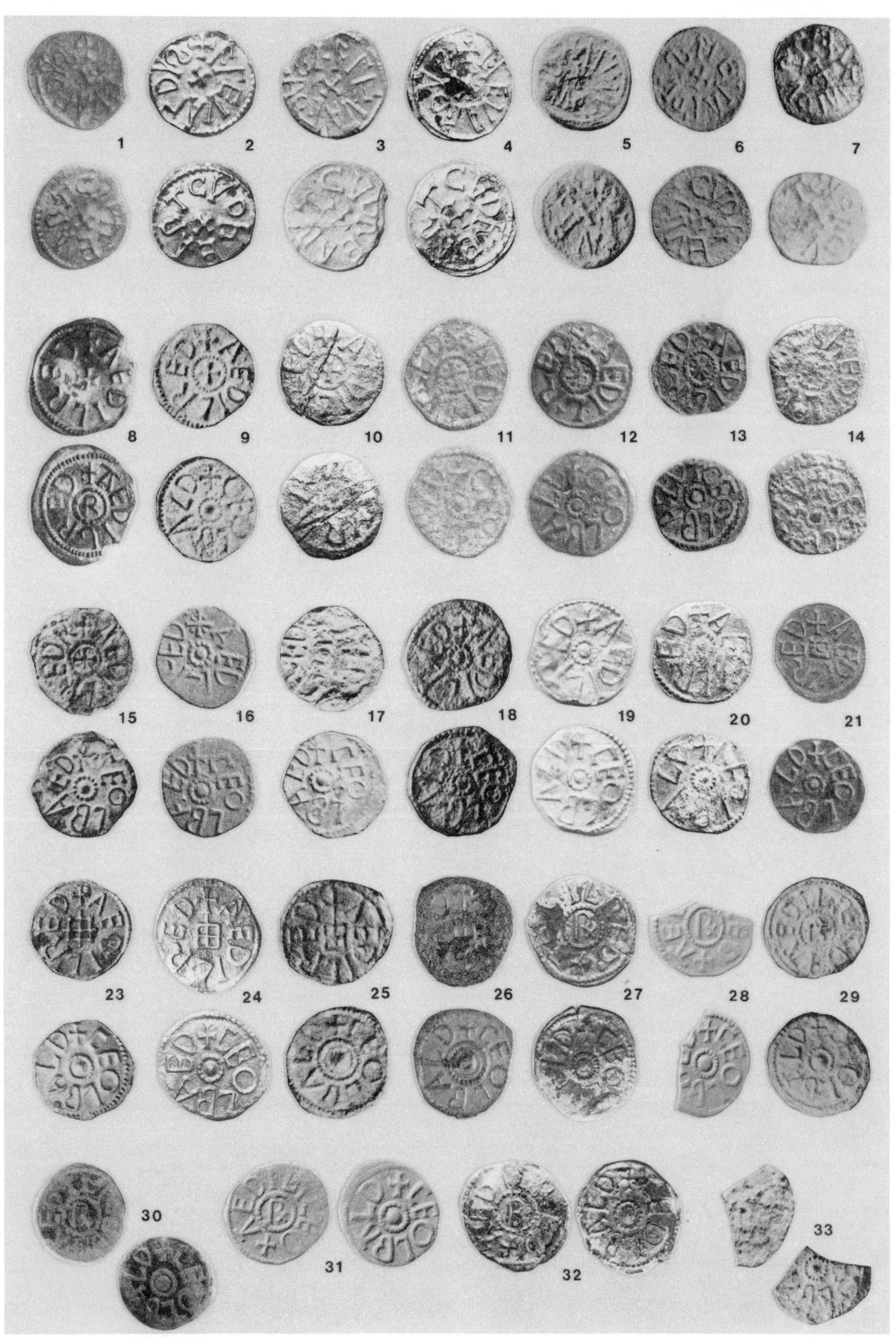

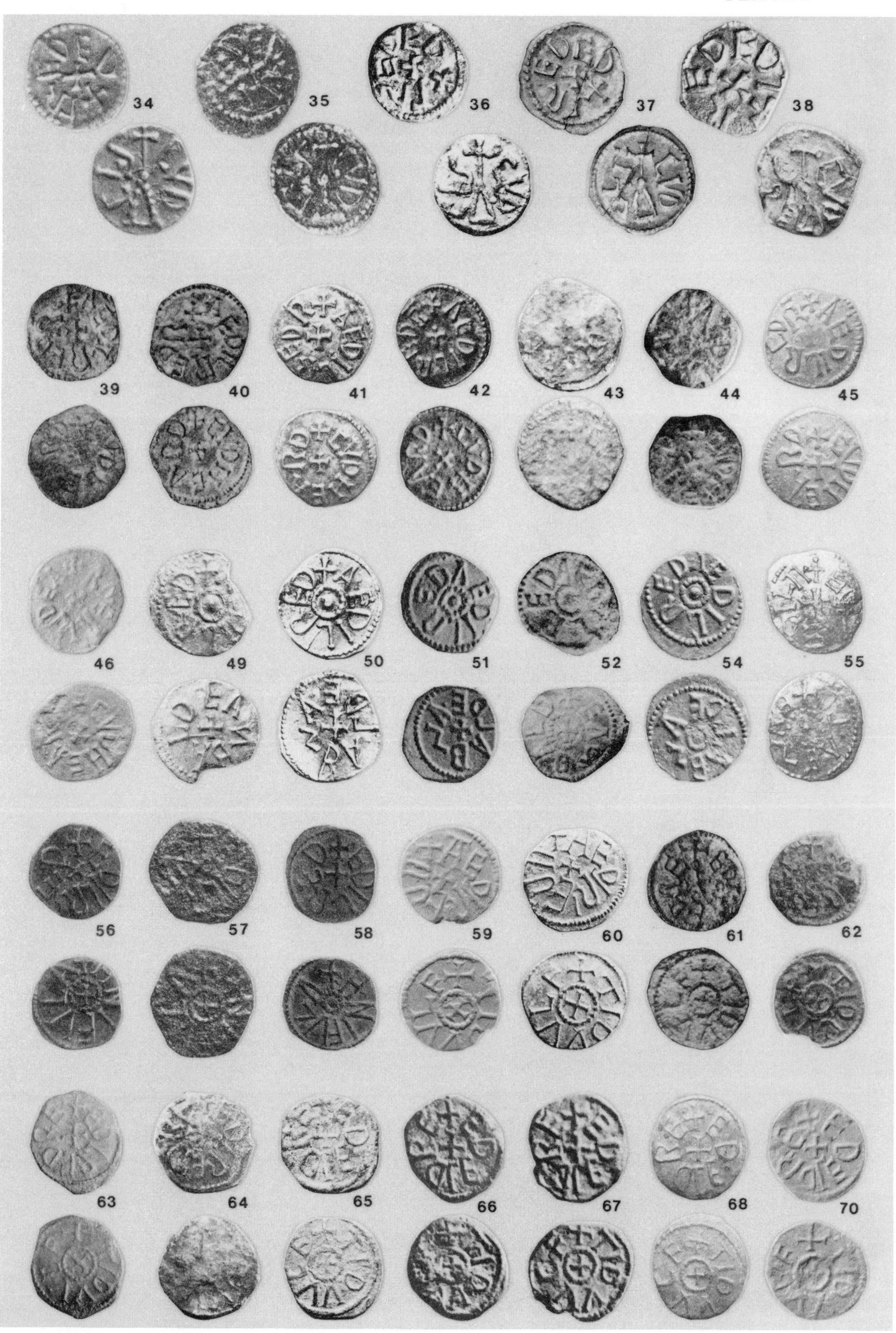
34
35
36
37
38
39
40
41
42
43
44
45
46
49
50
51
52
54
55
56
57
58
59
60
61
62
63
64
65
66
67
68
70

Herreth

D. M. METCALF and J. P. NORTHOVER

[PLATES 4–5]

HERERÆD, who was a Group A moneyer for King Eanred, struck coins on which his name was spelt *Herred*. There exist other coins on which the moneyer's name is spelt almost identically, but with an edh—*Herreth*. It is usually assumed that this is a corruption of 'Herred', by hypercorrection, since no obvious reading comes to mind for -reth. The reading HEAREÐI, which occurs on the earliest of the *Herreth* series, may suggest however that a different name underlay the coruption, viz. Hea(h)ræd. Be that as it may, there are other, and more compelling reasons to look suspiciously at the coins of 'Herreth'. Some of them are ostensibly struck from two reverse dies. They read either *Herreth/Herreth* or *Herreth/Alfheard* (for Wulfheard).The two dies used to strike a coin in the middle ages were normally quite diferent in shape. The obverse or lower die ended in a spike, so that it could be driven into a heavy block of timber to hold it firm, while the reverse or upper die was shaped more like a cold chisel, to be held in the hand or with tongs while the free end was struck with a hammer. If the reverse die was spiked, it is difficult to envisage how two reverse dies could be used in combination, and almost as difficult to imagine two obverse dies being used together, except as a very makeshift and unsatisfactory arrangement. One might almost as well try to use two plugs, or two sockets, to make an electrical connection.

Admittedly, the lower die was not necessarily spiked: it could have a flat base and simply stand loosely on an anvil. But one can see that at every hammer blow it would bounce about and tend to slide off.

The two dies were often located in reference to each other by a collar, which ensured that the two faces of the coin coincided on the flan. If the collar was square, it would result in the sort of regular die-adjustment which is familiar in the Anglo-Saxon series, and which was normal in much of the styca series.

One of each pair of the *Herreth* or *Herreth/Alfheard* dies was of necessity, then, the lower die, and whatever its shape, it was technically the obverse, even if by the content of its design it was formally a reverse.

An Anglo-Saxon coin—any coin—which is of exactly the same pattern on both sides draws attention to itself as an unnatural artefact, a monstrosity, which contravenes the aesthetic laws of coin design, whatever the technicalities of its manufacture. The first step in exploring the circumstances in which it was made and issued is to determine its date. The double-reverse coins of Herreth (and also those of *Herreth/Alfheard* or *vice versa*) are known almost exclusively from the Hexham hoard. This provenance confirms that they are of an earlier date than the t.p.q. of the hoard, that is, early in Æthelred's second reign, and is probably sufficient to separate them from the large and varied series of derivative or imitative coins that was then beginning. Because of their careful style, their use of the names of two of Eanred's moneyers, and their relative scarcity or absence in hoards of the 860s, they have been identified as an earlier phase of 'derivative' coinage, beginning in Eanred's reign or very soon after it.

They should not, however, be considered in isolation. There are related coins reading XEANREd on the obverse and XHERREĐ on the reverse, which appear to stand at the head of the little sequence of dies, of which the *Herreth/Herreth* dies form a later part. They will be discussed in detail below, but we make the general point now, that the omission of the title REX (only occasionally reduced to R) is highly unusual among Eanred's coins. For that reason Miss Pirie has interpreted XEANREd as a moneyer, on a specimen (Newcastle 118) which she therefore sees as another 'double-reverse' variety, and which she suggests may have been struck early in Æthelred's reign (because Eanræd is a moneyer for Æthelred, but not for King Eanred). We shall give reasons which incline us to the view that XEANREd represents the king's name, and for us, therefore, the coin raises a somewhat different problem of numismatic interpretation, although more or less the same problem of political interpretation. Eanred's coinage is otherwise very regular in its legends, and obviously under royal control. There is no equivalent during his reign to the copious 'irregular' stycas of Æthelred's second reign, whose legends are often meaningless or mendacious. There are one or two other, but only one or two, apparently early coins that fall into the same category as the 'Herreth' varieties: double reverses with the name of Æthelweard, and double obverses reading +EANRED REX on both sides. These will be examined below. But of all Eanred's moneyers, Hereræd and Wulfheard seem to be the only ones whose names are, so to speak, taken in vain. (Miss Pirie's tentative reading of Newcastle 116 as Herreth/?Hwætræd, on a corroded coin, is unconfirmed. We wonder whether the correct reading could be EANRED retrograde.) Were these various coins officially sanctioned, or were they in the nature of contemporary counterfeits? If the latter, what was the particular attraction of Herreth's name? (Might he, possibly, have been known to be deceased, and therefore no longer liable to be called to account by the king for sub-standard coins bearing his name?)—Were the double-reverse coins minted in York, or at some other mint place? If they originated in Eanred's reign, what were the circumstances in which perfectly competent workmen could prudently produce them?

Our only way of exploring these and similar questions is through the coins themselves, and the patterns of their relationship. The first and obvious question to ask is what their silver contents were. (As it helps considerably to focus the historical problem, we will say straight away that some specimens contain as much as 26 per cent 'silver' (silver plus gold plus lead) and that this makes it in our view certain that the little series originated during a very early phase of Eanred's issues. It also suggests that they are in some sense regular issues rather than fradulent counterfeits.) Secondly one can ask whether their pattern of weights is, so far as can be judged from only a few specimens, the same as that observed among Eanred's Group A. Thirdly, one will feel more confident that one has taken the measure of the problem when the known dies and die-links have been listed, and (if possible) the survival-rate assessed against Group A in general.

The basic contribution which this paper seeks to make is to put on record analyses of eight coins reading *Herreth/Herreth*, *Herreth/Alfheard*, *Ethilveard/Ethilveard*, or *Eanred Rex/Eanred Rex* or a blundered version of the same. The results are summarized below:

	Weight	'Silver'	Zinc in brass	Tin	Gold: silver
1. XHERREÐ/ ΛLFHEARD	1.19	26.2	20.6	-	0.16
2. XHERREÐ/ ΛLFHEARD	1.23	17.5	17.9	4.6	2.02
[3. XHERREÐ/XHERREÐ	1.23	22.3	9.6	2.6	1.39
4.] XHERREÐ/XHERREÐ	1.29	17.4	12.0	1.7	3.52
[5. +EDILVEARD/+EDILVEVRD	1.25	10.6	16.0	3.1	0.56
6.] +EDILVEARD/+EDILVEVRD	1.11	6.6	21.4	2.4	0.64
7. +EANRED REX/+EANRED REX	1.06	9.7	12.7	8.0	2.24
8. +ENVEX/+ENDREX	1.36	5.6	19.1	3.1	0.55

The eight coins seem from their silver content not to belong closely together, and it is only those associated with Herreth that are clearly as early as the reign of Eanred. The quality of the brass in nos. 3–4, which are die-duplicates (along with *BMC* 815), is inferior to that in any other coins of Eanred with which they could be compared (although Hereræd's coins have not yet been analysed). This may perhaps be seen as a pointer to Herreth's coins having been produced away from the main centre of minting.

Nos. 5–6 are double-reverse coins of Æthelweard, who was a moneyer for Archbishop Wigmund. Close inspection confirms that the two coins are die-duplicates. Their 'silver' contents of 10.6 and 6.6% respectively lie comfortably within the range of values that has previously been found for Wigmund's coins. This suggests that they are contemporary with Phase B of King Eanred's coins, or (less probably) with the first reign of Æthelred.

The coin reading *Eanred rex* on both sides (no. 7) is of a brass-bronze mixture, heavily leaded (Pb = 5.6%) with only 4.0% Ag. It does not, so far as we can see, fit convincingly anywhere in the official series, and should perhaps be considered to be unofficial—although to say that about stycas is liable to be merely a confession of ignorance, always liable to be shown up by a pattern of die-links.

No. 8, with badly blundered legends attempting *Eanred Rex*, is perhaps related to the coins of 'Teveh', which were analysed on a previous occasion (*NC* 1984) and found to contain negligible amounts of silver, even though die-linked to an Eanred die. The alloy of no. 8 would pass muster in the last phase of Eanred's coinage.

These analytical results, although they represent only a first approach to an intriguing problem, suggest that Herreth, whether alone or with Wulfheard, is an isolated phenomenon at an early stage of the styca series. The four relevant analyses all show high silver contents.

A stylistic examination of the coins reading *Herred* and *Herreth* reveals that there is a clear division, among specimens with Eanred's name on the obverse, between the two forms of moneyer's name, and suggests that 'Herred' consistently uses the formula *Eanred rex*, whereas 'Herreth' omits the *rex*. We have not assembled an exhaustive corpus of specimens, and realise that it would only take one die-link, or one pair of similar dies, to link the two types into a single sequence, but even then, we should certainly still be considering two essentially separate phases. Herreth's coins characteristically have an initial cross in the form of an X, and the two letters R are placed at an awkward angle to each other. One specimen with a retrograde obverse (*BMC* 196 = **Pl. 4, F**) is from a reverse die pretty clearly by the same hand as nos. 3–4. Others write *Eanred* with a diminutive cursive D not used by 'Herred'.

The coin which on grounds of style looks to stand at the head of the sequence is *BMC* 193, with *rev*., cross in inner circle, and the moneyer's name in the form *Hearethi* (**Pl. 4, A**). Two other reverse dies are used with the same obverse, both reading *Herreth*, one with a normal initial cross and the other with the characteristic X (**Pl. 4, B, C**). The next obverse is almost a mirror image of the first, although the cursive D is not as tiny. Again it is used with three reverses (*BMC* 194–6 = **Pl. 4, D-F**). Another obverse, similarly retrograde, (Ashm. 1.13g, **Pl. 4, G**) provides a die-link to the 'double-reverse' coins, nos. 3–4 above (and shows which reverse is the reverse!) This die-link, together with the 'silver' contents of the double-reverse coins in question, more or less refutes Miss Pirie's suggestion that the *Eanred* coins are double-moneyer coins dating from Æthelred's reign. The use of reverse and obverse dies in a ratio of three to one (or more?) is a pointer to the official character of Herreth's work. As Eanred's Group A moneyers seem, in general, to have employed a one-to-one ratio, it also suggests that Herreth was operating independently, and perhaps therefore elsewhere than in the main centre of minting. This argument would be overturned, however, if it were to be shown that a higher ratio was characteristic of the very earliest stage of the work of other moneyers, who then changed to one-to-one.

The weights of these same coins also offer some small measure of support for the same interpretation. The weight-standard is, as might be expected, nominally the same as that of all other stycas, but in practice it is higher. Ten specimens have a mean weight of 1.252g, which may be compared with 1.218g for Eanred's Group A moneyers in the Hexham hoard.

If Herreth was out of touch because he was based elsewhere than York, it would of course make it much easier to understand how an irregular form of the royal name was used, and how its omission altogether could pass muster, in officially sanctioned issues.

The survival rate of the *Eanred/Herreth* and *Herreth/Herreth* coins is higher (on the evidence of a small sample) than for the Group A coinage in general. This offers some encouragement to the view that it is perhaps over-represented in the Hexham hoard because it is from a northerly mint-place.

The connexion between Wulfheard and Herreth is not at all clear. The double-reverse coins with both names are stylistically closely related to the *Herreth/Herreth* coins, but do not fit into a matrix of other dies naming Wulfheard. His work does not obviously fall into two separate parts, like that of 'Herred' and 'Herreth'. It is, however, characterized by blundered obverse dies reading +EANHEDHEX, XEAHREDRE (**Pl. 4, H**, Ashm. ex Hexham; same die as *BMC* 180 ex Hexham) or XEAREDR (**Pl. 4; I and J**, from the same obverse die, *BMC* 183 ex Hexham; and Ashm.) The reading ALFHEARD, with or without an initial cross, is found on a minority of dies, but we have not come across a die-link between these and the *Herreth/Alfheard* specimens, nos. 1 and 2 above. The Herreth dies of the two coins should probably be seen as the obverses, although it is difficult to tell. The initial cross in the form of an X may, incidentally, be an echo of, or even be intended to suggest at a glance, the X of REX. On grounds of style one would guess that the

Herreth/Alfheard coins are not quite so early in the sequence as specimens such as *BMC* 193–4. On the other hand no.1 lacks any measurable amount of tin in its alloy. This is unusual, although there are coins for Eanred by the moneyer Eadwine which contain only 0.5% tin or less. The variability, from zero to 4.6%, in two very similar coins is perhaps a pointer to the workman not having settled into a steady routine. But in any case, we are probably talking about a very short interval of time between the cutting of the dies, given that nos. 1–2 have very similar silver contents to nos.3–4.

Miss Pirie has suggested that, because on other coins the initial cross is sometimes mistakenly inserted in the middle of the legend instead of at the beginning, one should not immediately rule out the reading *Heardwulf*. *Heard-* as a first element is relatively uncommon; and it is perhaps just worth saying that there seems to be no possibility of an attribution to Eardwulf. *Wulfheard* must be the correct reading of the die on which the D is transferred to the centre of the flan, as the motif. An interesting coin found at Segontium, north Wales, in the standing ruins of the guard-chamber at the south-west gate, has both obverse and reverse legends awkwardly spaced, with a gap left at what is (certainly on the obverse and presumably on the reverse) the end of the legend: XEAHREDRE, HEARDVVLF. This coin faces us with the choice of suggesting that two moneyers are involved, namely Wulfheard and Heardwulf; or (more plausibly) that the die-cutter of the Segontium coin (which is quite silvery in appearance) was confused or uninformed—and that he was taking his 'copy' from a coin.

To sum up, this summary of the evidence at a detailed level has, we hope, placed Herreth in context even if few of the conclusions are hard and fast. The high silver contents of the first four specimens analysed are, in our judgement, crucial evidence. Our general impression is that a) the silver contents imply that the Herreth 'series' began at a very early stage in Eanred's Group A issues; b) the Herreth/*Alfheard* coins are equally early; c) the use of dies in a three-to-one ratio is distinctive and probably implies an official recoinage; d) if Group A was launched as a recoinage, the Herreth and related issues may have been intended to implement the change promptly at a centre too far from York for people to make the journey easily; e) if d is correct it is a matter of speculation where that centre might have been. An obvious guess, we think, is Carlisle. At the date in question, finds are becoming plentiful at, for example, Whithorn; and if monetary requirements west of the Pennines failed to develop much thereafter, that would be unknown when a decision was taken to open a second mint. We must emphasize that this suggestion is very speculative.

To prove a case, one would need the clear evidence of localization. As the Herreth group forms only a tiny proportion of Eanred's Group A, negative evidence from a site which has yielded only(!) a dozen coins of Group A would be inconclusive. Thus, if the place of origin was Bamburgh, the site finds even there would be numerous enough to afford proof only if the Herreth series were well represented among them. The only provenance on record so far for the double-reverse coins is Monkwearmouth.

There remain aspects of *Herred/Herreth* that have not been explored in this discussion. *BMC* includes, for example, four coins with a Hexham provenance (*BMC* 813-815, 818) in much rougher style than the specimens that have been analysed. Our first reactions to them are that they quite possibly extend the Herreth series into a severely blundered phase, in which the distinction between D and edh was lost. *BMC* 815 appears to be by the same hand as 197, with the following readings:

197 XEHNREd (retrograde)/XHEIIII EÐ (**Pl. 5, O**) 1.084g
815 +EA⊣DI VH/+HERRD (**Pl. 5, P**) 1.420g

BMC 813-14 and 818 are in sketchier style, with the central crosses more or less pommee instead of being neatly seriffed. They are even more blundered

813 (?) +ƎИVREX (retrograde)/+HENRED (**Pl. 5, Q**) 1.111g
814 +ƎИVREX (retrograde)/+HERREÐ (**Pl. 5, R**) 1.200g
818 +HΓVXREV (retrograde)/+HERREΓα . (**Pl. 5, S**) 1.178g

Nos. 813–14 are related by their obverse, but 814 has a cross of pellets as the central motif. Compare no.7 above. No. 818 has a pellet in annulet as the central motif of the reverse. If these coins were not from Hexham, one would be inclined to throw them in with the late blundered series. It will be interesting, one day, to see what their metal contents look like.

We return now to the two coins of Æthelweard, the archbishop's moneyer, which are from the same dies. Their reverse is linked to another obverse (**Pl. 5, K**), on which the archbishop's name and title are retrograde. This obverse in turn is also used with a regular reverse die (**Pl. 5, L**) that is found in another combination (**Pl. 5, M**). So the 'double-reverses' are in this case anchored very firmly into the main series. They are as unusual among Wigmund's coins as Herreth's are among the coins of Eadred. They cannot be nearly as early in date.

Anchored though they are, they show technical features somewhat out of the ordinary. Their obverse has a soft and soapy look to it, as though it was highly polished (and worn)—probably because it was of a different metal from the usual run of dies. No. 5 in particular (the coin with the higher silver contents, but doubtless the later of the two) shows the dies in a battered state. No. 6 is on a noticeably square flan. On the reverse die-link, the raised surfaces of the letters look rusty, whereas the field is smooth and flat (**Pl. 5, K**). On no. 6, by contrast, one can see the flow-bulges (e.g. around the cross) where the metal of the die has risen up in reaction to the hammering in of the punches. The die is deeply cut. It looks very much as if what has happened is that the whole die rusted, and was then cleaned up by rubbing its face flat and clean—thus lowering the relief and, of course, leaving the rust in the recesses which the letters formed on the die. If that rests on correct observation, the regular die comes *after* rather than *before* the irregular one. There is, however, another reverse (**Pl. 5, N**) on which the cross lacks one arm, which is clearly the same die as **Pl. 5, 6-K**. The question is whether it is an earlier or later state. Was the lower limb accidentally omitted, and added as an afterthought, or did the die become clogged at a later stage? Close examination of the coin shows no trace of the missing limb; and several of the letters appeared to be thinner, as if they were subsequently punched or gouged in more deeply when the limb was added. If that is correct, the flow- bulges around the cross will have been caused during re-working of the die; and the double reverses are sandwiched into the middle of the sequence.

TABLE OF ANALYSES

The analyses were undertaken as part of the same programme, and in exactly the same way, as those of Æthelred II and Osberht published below.

	Fe	Co	Ni	Cu	Zn	Bi	Sb	Sn	Ag	Pb	Au	
1	0.05	–	–	58.51	15.20	–	0.13	–	25.17	0.88	0.04	1
2	0.09	tr	0.01	63.82	13.87	–	0.09	4.63	15.31	1.87	0.31	2
3	0.28	0.01	0.03	67.53	7.17	0.01	0.04	2.63	20.19	1.81	0.28	3
4	0.12	0.01	0.03	70.59	9.62	–	0.58	1.66	14.20	2.68	0.50	4
5	0.09	tr	0.10	74.63	14.20	tr	0.05	3.09	7.10	3.49	0.09	5
6	0.06	–	0.01	71.38	19.49	tr	0.06	2.43	6.29	0.24	0.04	6
7	0.10	tr	0.10	71.58	10.40	0.01	0.07	8.04	4.01	5.60	0.09	7
8	0.09	tr	tr	73.70	17.37	0.03	0.10	3.09	5.43	0.13	0.03	8

DISCUSSION

MISS PIRIE: Let me begin by agreeing that my attributions (made in 1980) for the Newcastle specimens must now be subject to revision. Further work on the York collection has made it clear that the *Eanred* dies associated with those of *Herreth* are for the king rather than for the later moneyer. There is, incidentally, in the Birmingham collection, a further example with the obverse reading EANRED, retrograde.

Nevertheless, the ramifications of the coinage of which the *Herreth* dies are the focus are such that one can hardly accept its output as normal, all from an official workshop—even a minor one sited away from York.

Mack (*SCBI* 20, no. 388) gives us a double-obverse with the legends EANREDREX/EAHREÐ (the latter, retrograde). The first die is similar in style to others with HERRED reverses; the second appears to be that (or similar to that) of Adamson's 1836 Eanred 83, *Eahreth/Herreth.* Apart from the double-reverse specimens for *Herreth* himself, the York collection has a double-reverse for *Eadvini*: in the same cabinet is a specimen on which one of those *Eadvini* dies is combined with one for *Herreth* (see also Adamson 1834, Eanred Uncertain 223). Apart, too, from the *Herreth/Alfheard* specimens, Mr Blunt's collection has an example of the *Herreth/Daegberct* combination. The little purse-hoard from Beverley, 1981 (Pirie, 1986, no. 39) affords evidence of a coin which, though partly worn, shows legends reading HERRE[D]I/HVAETR[ED].

Such combinations of reverses, and the range of moneyers they reflect, must surely emanate from somewhere other than an official centre.

PLATE 4

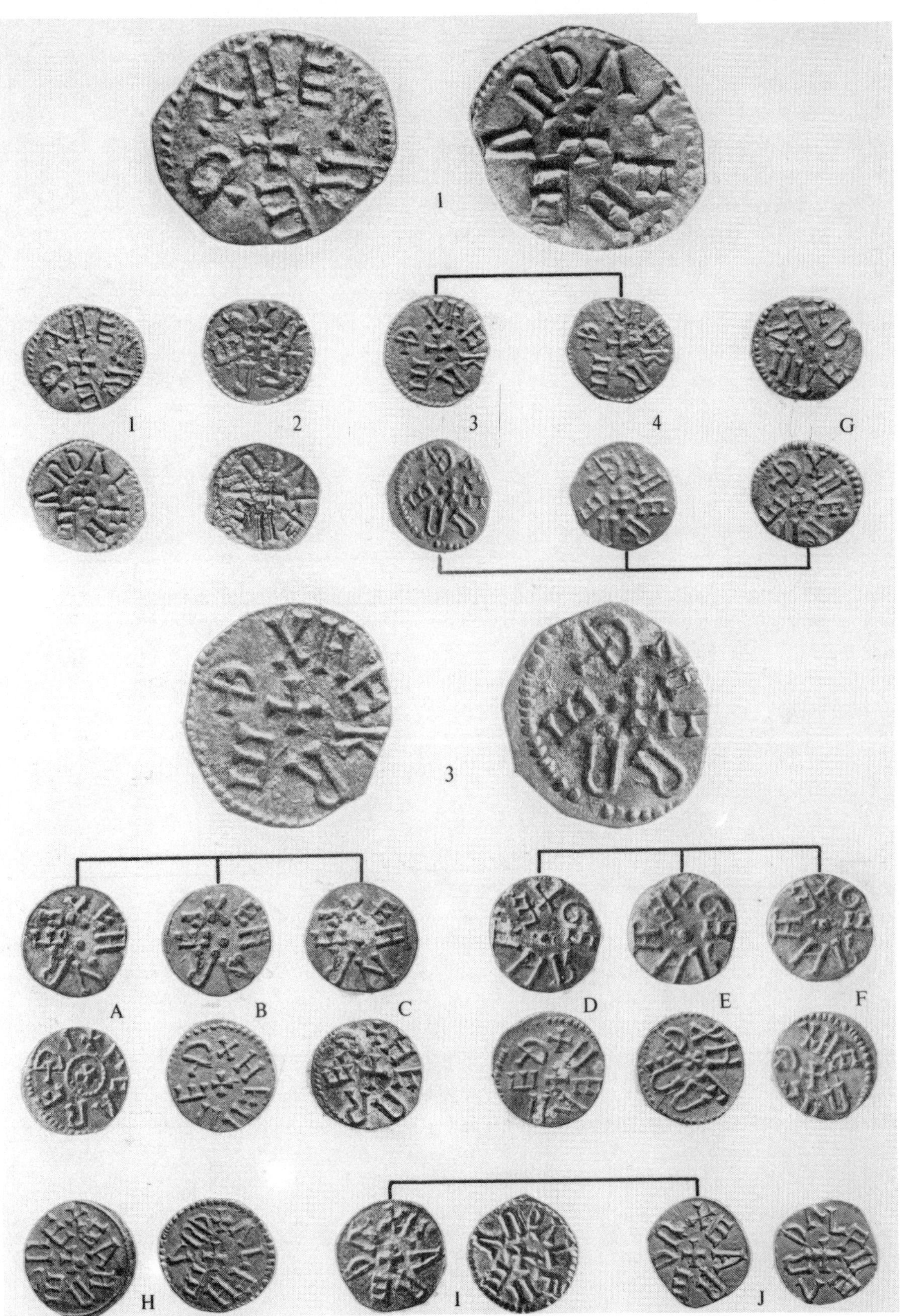

PLATE 5

Phases and groups within the styca coinage of Northumbria

E. J. E. PIRIE

[PLATES 6–11]

THERE is no doubt that the main coinage of ninth-century Northumbria is very different from that produced in the kingdoms of Mercia, East Anglia, Kent, and Wessex. The adoption of brass alloys for some of the northern money has done more to set it apart from the silver pence issued elsewhere than has the retention of the small flan which was common to all the earlier sceattas. Dolley[1] has suggested that the change from silver to base metal occurred because the Northumbrians had become poverty-stricken victims of Viking raids.

Yet it may be a grave mistake to compare monetary developments in the north with the relative sophistication of work in the south, to the former's detriment. One would rather have the styca coinage of Northumbria seen to be a natural successor to the previous coinages in the area and itself subject, during the course of its lifetime, to a certain amount of change and development.

The purpose of this paper is to review the development of the late eighth- and ninth-century coinage of Northumbria and to consider evidence that in its later stage, at least, the production of coins was closely related to the existence of a number of different die-cutting workshops. These working-places must have varied in size and efficiency, from major official establishments (which might themselves encompass the work of several craftsmen) to smaller, more informal *ateliers* operated by artisans more concerned, perhaps, with the quantity rather than the quality of die-cutting work required for unauthorized issues of coin.

The first concern, in studying the material, must be with analysis of the official coinage. It becomes clear that, during the second phase, most if not all of the regular moneyers must have acquired their dies from more than one official die-cutting organization.

The situation which obtained in mid-ninth-century Northumbria might seem to be analogous to one which will be more familiar to students of the Anglo-Saxon coinage after the reform of *c.*973. During that later period, dies were supplied to moneyers in many different towns from a restricted number of die-cutting centres, the location of which can often be conjectured (London, Winchester, Canterbury, and so on). A moneyer in any particular town might obtain dies, for each new type to be issued, from more than one centre and use

[1] Dolley (1976), 355.

them more or less concurrently. The *coins* name the moneyer for whom their dies were prepared, and the town where he was working; the place of origin of the *dies*, on the other hand, has to be decided by a careful stylistic analysis. The operation of this system can be demonstrated conclusively for southern England, essentially because every coin names its mint-place.

For Northumbria, it might seem that something comparable was happening but the stycas do not, of course, name their place of origin, and there is no clear differentiation of types.

All that one can hope to achieve by a study of their style is, in theory, an attribution of the *dies* to the workshops at which they were made. Work on styca dies is, however, not completed without tracing their use and re-use in various combinations (normally of obverse with reverse, exceptionally of obverse with obverse or reverse with reverse). Instances occur of what one might term hybrid combinations, in which an obverse die whose style relates it to one particular school of production is paired with a reverse which originated elsewhere. The use of such combinations of dies should be attributed to the group in which the dominant die, the obverse, is native. It must be made quite clear, at this point, that the divisions which will shortly be defined are based on the use of certain dies, in combination one with another, rather than on mere production of the dies themselves. Certainly, the obverse dies concerned, if attributed correctly in each case, should be seen as native to the group; the majority of reverses can also be related to the parent die-cutting source. Yet the existence of hybrids, which themselves provide the links between one group of material and another, precludes our identifying the groups as those of dies only. The groups are of *coins* produced with the use of particular dies in combination.

As to *where* the dies were used, that is another question. In theory, evidence pertinent to the resolution of this problem could be derived from analysis of the composition of styca-finds, and comparison of the range of issues common in each area of discovery. Until recent years, hoards have been the major source of material for such study. Within the last two decades or so, site-finds from excavations throughout the north of England (and beyond) have already extended the geographical distribution patterns which steadily become more detailed as more such recoveries are recorded.

Die-linking, which has already been remarked in noting the re-use of dies, is prodigious in both the official and the unofficial issues. On that count, too, the early Northumbrian coinage stands apart from all other series. Certainly, wide-spread die-linking between the official styca-moneyers offers a marked contrast with the later situation in southern England. That such ties occurred at all could most easily and obviously be explained by accepting that most of the men worked in the same place, which should no doubt be identified as York. Apart from the regal officials, there were also moneyers for the archbishops and there is die-link evidence of occasional association between the royal and the episcopal officers. A coinage so profusely die-linked affords no overt sign that work by any group of moneyers is separate and therefore possibly from another place. With so much evidence of *how* the dies were used, the question of where they were used, apart from at York, may appear to be irrelevant.

The question of *when*, within a long reign, particular dies were used is yet another matter which requires investigation, even if resolution is beset with difficulty by the very complexity of die-linking. Although analysis of the pattern of linking must begin with studying the coins of a single moneyer, the complete picture may emerge only when such output is related to the work of others. There is a wealth of evidence which implies that many dies were in service concurrently: a tangled web of cross-links takes reverse dies from obverse to obverse; the use of eight or more reverses with one obverse occurs in the work of several of Æthelred II's moneyers. Such features may be significant in determining the history of minting and sequence of issue. Correlation of the die-linking detail with the choice of motif in the design of the dies may enable one to explore the hypothesis that different motifs were to some extent used successively. (There could, of course, be no possible analogy with the type-changes and validity-periods characteristic of the eleventh-century coinage, for the styca hoards afford no evidence of the brass coins having been systematically withdrawn.) Die-chains may be too tangled and cross-linked to serve effectively in establishing the chronology of the coinage, although links between reigns could be critical in showing the directions of development. One must always be aware that some dies could have had primary use over an extended period or even been put into service again (for secondary use) after a considerable passage of time: one cannot confidently assume that die-linked coins are in every case close to each other in date.

Charting of extensive die-linkage is an essential part of documenting stycas, and supplements the identification and illustration of many hundreds of dies which form over two thousand die-combinations. These are in a major collection of early Northumbrian coins which can be cross-referenced to many further specimens elsewhere. It is to be hoped that such a record of the material will provide the impetus for further research. Many pertinent questions will arise as systematic study of correlations becomes possible. What are the survival rates for coins from particular dies? Have coins from the reverse dies that were used in large clusters, for example, had a higher or lower survival rate than the average; are they heavier or lighter, of better or of poorer alloy than other issues? Does the composition of a particular hoard show any unusual bias or unexpected selectivity in the range of dies included?

A stylistic study of the dies for the later stycas, then, is directed towards gaining an understanding of work from different die-cutting workshops, while a study of die-links has a bearing on the dies in use; die-links between moneyers, particularly, are relevant to the question of where the coins were struck.

The present study has its roots in the preparation for publication of the massive collection of these coins in the Yorkshire Museum at York which, by its very size, has demanded investigation of arrangement otherwise than by complete distinction of regal from episcopal and within each term of ruler or archbishop, the alphabetical separation of moneyer from moneyer. At best, this form, introduced by Adamson in 1834, gives the impression that coin-production was little more than private enterprise on the part of a number of officials, each going his own way. With lip-service only to the occurrence of links between moneyers, little attention has so far been paid to what die-links may have meant in practice. It

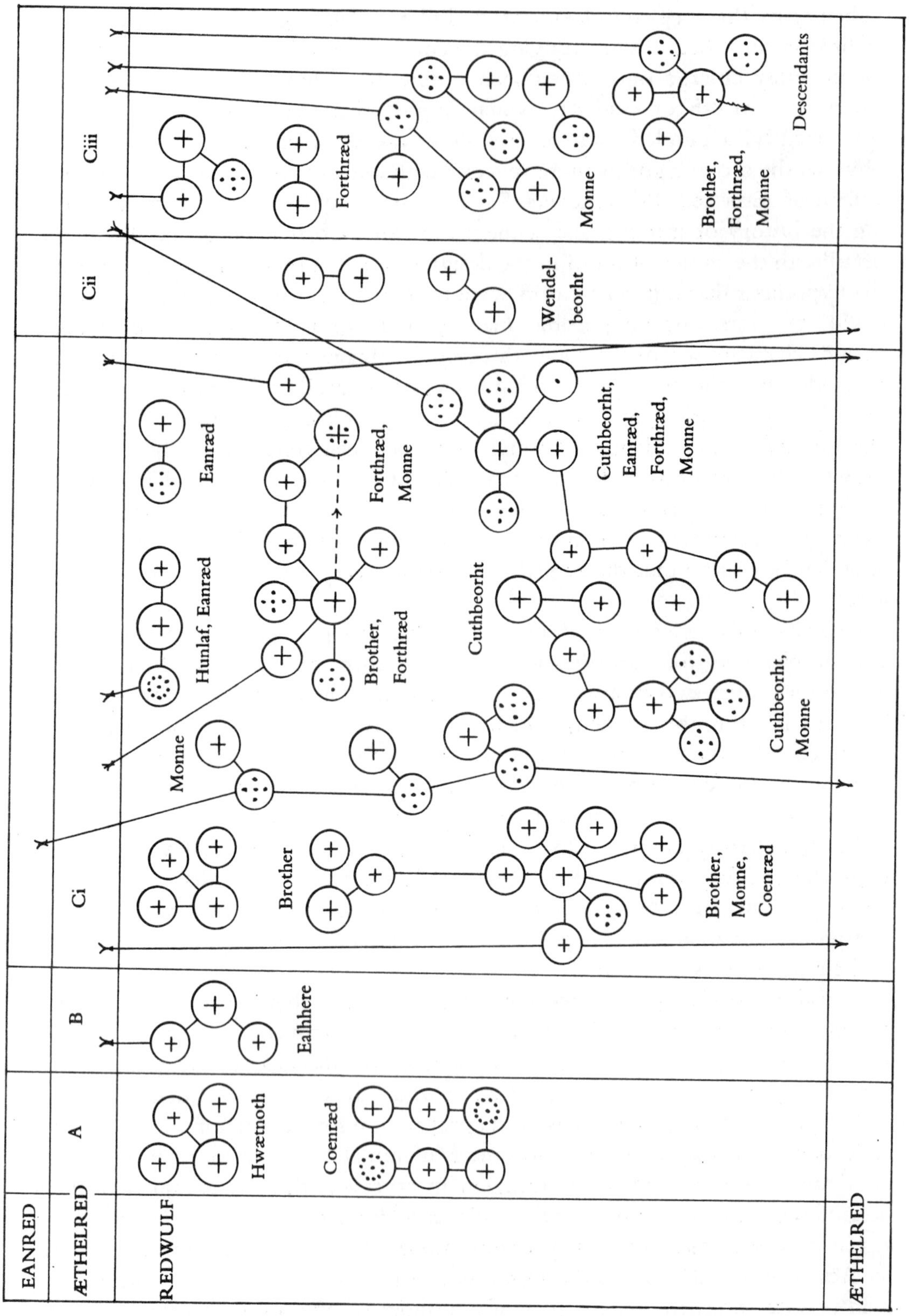

FIG.1. The coinage of Redwulf.

would surely be foolish to waste the resources of the York collection by registration in conventional format if they could be used to introduce a more adequate arrangement which would reflect the work of moneyers in relation to each other. Initial efforts were directed towards the establishment of a typology based on the use of motif and observed by the various moneyers in concert. That exercise led to an appreciation that there are blocks of dies which, though not entirely independent of each other, were in use concurrently rather than consecutively. One could also appreciate that, since it is made up of material recovered in or near the city, the York collection and the range of issues it represents would have considerable evidential value when the time came to debate the question of whether or not all the dies were made and used in York alone.

It must be understood that many details of orthography and epigraphy, metrology and actual sequence within the broad outline mentioned in this present context must await discussion in a fuller commentary which cannot convincingly be divorced from publication of the York evidence in pictorial form.

In the interim, two samples of the evidence will perhaps convey its character and flavour. Fig.1 shows the pattern of die-linking in the principal issues for King Redwulf. The larger circles represent obverse dies, of which twenty-eight are recorded (there is one instance of a die probably having had its motif altered before re-use); what cannot be denoted at this scale is the fact that six dies (for Forthræd and Monne in Ciii) have retrograde legends. The smaller circles are reverse dies which come from fifty-one *tools*; mixed use of these reverses accounts for there being sixty-three die-combinations. The motifs which appear on the dies are indicated. The moneyers responsible for the work are designated. The links with their work for Æthelred are shown by lines joining the other reign: at the top, to express ties with Æthelred's coins with various cross motifs; at the bottom, to relate to issues with other designs.

TABLE 1. *Reverse dies used by a selection of Æthelred's moneyers (Calculations allow for the re-use of dies from other divisions)*

Moneyer				*Section*			*sum*	*minus*	*total*
	Ai	*Aii*	*B*	*Ci*	*Cii*	*Ciii*			
Brother	6	10	—	14	8(-1)	—	38	1	37
Eanræd	5	18	31(-4)	37(-3)	64(-17)	2	157	24	133
Forthræd	—	32	—	8	43(-1)	35(-3)	118	4	114
Leofthegn	61	—	8(-3)	20(-1)	12(-2)	—	101	6	95
Monne	49	5(-2)	—	75(-6)	16(-3)	16(-6)	161	17	144
Wulfræd	1	—	—	27	6(-2)	2(-1)	36	3	33
Wihtræd	7	16(-2)	—	5(-2)	—	—	28	4	24
Totals	129	77	32	174	123	45	—	—	580

Secondly, Table 1 shows the numbers of reverse dies used by a selection of Æthelred's moneyers, and their division between different stylistic groups which reflect different batches of die-cutting, and, presumably, the work of separate die-cutters. The Table summarizes the use of some 580 dies.

The purpose of the following pages, then, is two-fold. One must attempt, on the one hand, to describe in broad outline the course of the early styca issues, at a time from which comparatively few specimens have survived, and to identify the nature of those emissions. One must attempt, on the other hand, to discuss at greater length the great mass of surviving coins struck in brass alloys about which one's primary concern is to present elsewhere the results of die-analysis and of the incidence of die-links. The first exercise may not be entirely free of thoughts on interpretation. The second should be considered as identification and ordering of a number of different elements which, once recognized, may later form a suitable basis for further discussion. Such can be focussed especially on organization of the coinage and on its evidence in an archaeological and an historical context.

REVIEW OF EARLIER WORK

Stycas have been the subject of appraisal since at least the end of the seventeenth century. It was Archdeacon Nicholson of Carlisle who first applied the name styca to the small Northumbrian coin[2] at the time when Ralph Thoresby of Leeds was working on specimens from the Ripon hoard recovered in 1695. Thoresby's published comments[3] on items in his own Ripon parcel noted the different central ornaments on some, and the different styles of die-cutting which he took to be indicative of different mints. In May 1833, Adamson of Newcastle presented a paper to the Society of Antiquaries of London on the coins found at Hexham in October of the previous year. His publication[4] listed most of the varieties which he had been able to identify among the coins which reached him before dispersal; a supplement[5] recorded further details. In both cases, the material was arranged reign by reign for Eanred, Æthelred II, and Redwulf and for the archbishops Eanbald and Wigmund separately. Within each block, the coins were presented as the work of the individual moneyers, registered in the alphabetical sequence of their names. Illustrations included those for a number of irregular pieces whose nonsense legends defied attribution.

The discovery of further hoards occurred in and near York in 1831 near St Mary's Abbey, then at St Leonard's Place in the city in 1842, and at Bolton Percy in 1847. Unlike the Hexham hoard, all these finds included coins of Osberht and Archbishop Wulfhere. The growing number of recoveries gave rise to a number of other papers in the *Numismatic Chronicle* and the *Archaeological Journal*. Fairless of Hexham[6] noted briefly the extent of die-linking which he had observed within the series.

In 1957, Lyon published a short paper in which both the sceattas and stycas of Northumbria were reviewed. He identified the need to separate Eanred's moneyers who struck stycas in a silvery alloy from those whose coins contained very little silver; on the basis of the relative numbers of known dies, he attributed the former to the period 830–5 and the latter to *c*.837–40.[7] For Eanred's money to

2 Pirie (1982), 84.
3 *Ducatus* (1715), 343.
4 Adamson (1834), 279–310.
5 Idem (1836), 346–8.
6 Fairless (1845), 35.
7 Lyon (1957), 233–4.

have begun as late as 830, one must recognize a break in continuity of issue from the silver coins attributable to Æthelred I, *c*.790–6. The two-year restraint in striking, between 835 and 837, can be seen to coincide with the time of Wulfsige, Eanbald's successor as archbishop: no coins are known for Wulfsige. Lyon noted that the Hexham hoard alone contained the silvery issues as an appreciable element of its composition. In order to establish some sequence for the later issues in copper he again contrasted Hexham with York, 1842 and Bolton Percy, 1847. The first of these had a remarkably small proportion of issues by Eardwulf, reputedly the most prolific moneyer for Æthelred II. Lyon therefore identified Eardwulf as virtually the sole moneyer of Æthelred's second reign and placed the deposition of the *cache* at Hexham in 845 at the latest, shortly after the king's restoration. Further, he identified two series of irregular issues: an early one represented in Hexham and another which is well represented in the other finds and is, in the main, absent from Hexham.[8] The later coins were considered to be derived from the orthodox coins of Eardwulf, and to be very late—even anomalous in that, attempting as they did to record the name of Æthelred, die-links could show the coins to belong to the time of Osberht. It was considered that the official coinage for Osberht himself was too limited in quantity to have occupied more than a short period at the beginning of his reign. There arose the difficulty of relating to the regal work issues for Wulfhere, who received the *pallium* in 854, since the archbishop's coins, in style, were more akin to Æthelred's later coins than to those of Osberht.

In 1969, Pagan published a re-appraisal of the conventional chronology and proposed that the reigns of Eanred, Æthelred II, Redwulf, and Osberht should each be recognized as having begun a good twelve or fifteen years later than historians had previously thought. Apart from thus allowing Eanred to have been alive, *c*.850, at the time to which Blunt[9] has attributed the penny in that name found at Trewhiddle, Pagan went further. He proposed an additional Æthelred[10] as Eanred's immediate predecessor to whom could be attributed silver coins issued in the name of Æthelred. His argument for this rested on his identification of Æthelred's moneyer Ceolbeald as the official who worked in Mercia from *c*.796 to *c*.823: Pagan thought the man ended his career in Northumbria by striking there in the mid-820s.

It is a pity that too little attention was paid, by both Lyon and Pagan, to the real identity of the moneyer assigned by North[11] to Ælfwald I under the name of Cuthbeorht.

THE BACKGROUND OF THE EARLIEST COINAGES

From the start of coinage in Northumbria—at least from the silver issues for Aldfrith, *c*.685–705,[12] if not from the gold of the so-called York thrymsas[13]—the

[8] Lyon, *op.cit.*, 232, mentioned coins which had in the past been attributed to the kings Æthelred I, Eardwulf, 'Hoaud', Ælfwald II and Beonna; rightly, he noted that none of these have been recorded in the composition of the Hexham find. Nevertheless, a few specimens which *can* be attributed to the later series have been recognized in the hoard (see the Hexham paper, above).

[9] Wilson and Blunt (1961), 113–16.

[10] Pagan (1969), 13.

[11] North (1963), no.183.

[12] Pirie (1984), 209–11.

[13] Grierson (1962), 8–10.

content of the dies is highly individual. Authority in the united kingdom north of the Humber must have catered for its monetary needs without reference to what was going on elsewhere. The acknowledged authority in the middle and later eighth century for the late series of sceattas was not only that of the king but of the king and the archbishop of York, for whom there were several joint issues. This duality of control continued to be observed in the new styca coinage for which the moneyers responsible were no longer anonymous: at this stage, however, the archbishops had, for the most part, their own officials and their own coins. Yet, although the episcopal coinage seems to have been struck on a much smaller scale than were the regal issues, the two strands cannot well be divorced from each other for, as each started in silver, each ended in copper. If we are to understand the coinage as a whole, we would do well to consider the issues of each archbishop in conjunction with the contemporary regal money.

THE EARLY STYCAS: ÆTHELRED I, ÆLFWALD, AND EANRED (PHASES IA AND IB)

Among the silver coins found at Sancton between 1979 and 1982 were three specimens[14] for the king Ælfwald by a moneyer whose name can be clearly read as Cuthheard. The opportunity to correct the earlier error must lead to re-examination of the early sequence and, indeed, to identification of the nature of the coinage represented by the silvery stycas.

We now know of Cuthheard as a moneyer striking in silver for three kings: Æthelred, Ælfwald and Eanred. Had he still been known only for the first and last, one could perhaps have attempted to make a case for the silvery and coppery coins representing two different denominations, in the reigns of Eanred and Æthelred II. As it is, one must see Cuthheard ending his career early in the reign of Eanred after working for that king's predecessors. Eanred's coinage, therefore, need no longer be considered to have started a good while after he came to the throne: his silver issues, at least, seem to have been spread out over a number of years. If one can accept them as the outcome of producing an intermittent coinage, one can look back to earlier reigns, not just for the genesis of the new coinage on which moneyers were to be named but for the adoption of the policy of issuing money as and when official projects required funds.

The new styca coinage was presumably introduced during the second reign of Æthelred I, *c.*790–6. Of the moneyers then meeting regal needs—Tidwulf, Hnifula, Ceolbeald and Cuthheard—only the last worked later in Northumbria. No coins are known for Æthelred's immediate successor, King Eardwulf, and it is to be supposed that the moneyers faced the reality of redundancy. Ceolbeald, one assumes, got on his bike and went south to work in Mercia. Cuthheard alone struck for Ælfwald II, *c.*806–8; he worked finally for Eanred. In just what order Eanred's other moneyers followed Cuthheard is still not clear. The evidence of

[14] Booth and Blowers (1983), nos.24–6. Booth's work (1984) on the sceattas of Northumbria included coins of relatively good silver, with moneyers' names, as the last of the sceatta series. They were, he argued, the results of experiments with an alternative to the usual animal reverse, in the reigns of Ælfwald I (or II) and in the second reign of Æthelred I. Since Booth accepted Lyon's identification of Eanred's coinage having begun only as late as 830, he saw no connection between issues of the late eighth century and of the ninth. Nevertheless, such a connection should be recognized, in the continuing work of Cuthheard.

analysis which has identified coins of reasonably good silver[15] suggests that the officials Hwætræd and Cynewulf may have worked soon after him. Little or no die-linking between moneyers has been observed apart from an isolated instance of Cynewulf and (?) Æthelheah (EDILECH)[16] sharing an obverse. (The latter moneyer seems to be known only from one coin in the Yorkshire Museum; the related coin of Cynewulf is in Leeds City Museum.) Wilheah, Eadwine (EADVINI), even Æthelweard (EDILVARD) and Tidwine (TIDVINI) may have come next. Eadwine seems to have had a longer span of issues than the others. Tidwine is known[17] to have used an obverse cut in the same style as one for Hereræd who, with Eadwine, Dægbeorht (DAEGBERCT) and Wulfheard, may be accounted the last to strike in an alloy containing much silver.

Coins which are now attributed to Wulfheard are struck from reverses which all seem to be aberrant in some particular. The majority of the dies omit the initial cross, which causes confusion in identifying the name as Wulfheard or as Heardwulf. Dies *with* the cross read +ALFHEARD which seems to point to Wulfheard as the individual concerned. One should remember, however, that a more common aberration (in both the early and the later issues) is the placing of the cross *within* the name (cf. Pl.6, 3 and 20); recognition of HEARD+ALF for Heardwulf remains a possibility. One makes this comment, not to imply that two moneyers might be involved but rather to suggest that the one moneyer's identity is uncertain. It is worth drawing attention to this little group of coins as it may well have been the prototype for some later unofficial copying.

During the course of the coinage in silver, the needs of the church were not overlooked. Among the moneyers working in the time of Æthelred I, there was Cuthgils whose distinctive reverse motif, identified by Lord Grantley[18] as a shrine, may be indicative of the king having authorized money for some ecclesiastical purpose. By the time of Eanred, his archbishop Eanbald had coins in his own name but which for some while, apparently, were not struck by moneyers of his own. It would seem that Eanbald's first coins were the work of the regal moneyers Cynewulf, Eadwine, and Æthelweard before Æthelweard himself and Eadwulf worked only for the archbishop.

At some point before the last of the early moneyers, with one exception, stopped working, something seems to have happened which deprived them of their normal supply of silver for the stycas. Eadwine, Dægbeorht, Wulfheard and Hereræd, together with Eadwulf and Æthelweard (whose dies now read EDILVEARD rather than EDILVARD) struck instead in a coppery alloy for what must have proved to be the last lap in an intermittent coinage. The adoption of the baser alloy seems to have opened the door to contemporary imitation on a small scale. Pieces exist which appear to be copies in very base metal of the work of early 'silver' moneyers: Eanred's Cynewulf[19] and Eanbald's Eadwulf (unpublished). Dies in the name of Hereræd (spelt HERREÐ, not HERRED) are

[15] Metcalf *et al.* (1968), 34–5.

[16] *Edilech* may be an aberrant form of *Edilhech* which is recorded in the *Liber Vitae* (Sweet, 1885, 155). Dr Smart (personal communication) comments on the use of the *ch* being very un-English. It may therefore be incorrect to relate the form, as it appears on the coin, to the name Æthelheah.

[17] *AY* 18/1 (1986), no.16.

[18] Grantley (1912), at p.3.

[19] Pirie (1981), no.325.

combined with a number of others in the names of Hwætræd, Eadwine, and Wulfheard.

The first phase of Northumbria's styca coinage must therefore be seen to encompass two stages: Ia, the work in a brass alloy containing visible amounts of silver; Ib, the first work in a more coppery-looking alloy. The first should be recognized as having lasted from *c*.790 to *c*.830 and the second for the short time, *c*.830–5. It is this phase which Dolley[20] identified as one in which the coinage was fiscal in intent. Its own developments must be recognized as quite separate from those which occurred a year or two later when minting was resumed under the aegis of a new team of regal moneyers.

Comparatively little material survives from Phase I and it has been beyond the scope of the current work on the Yorkshire collections to present a detailed analysis of dies.[21]

PHASE II OF THE COINAGE, UNDER EANRED, ÆTHELRED II, REDWULF, OSBERHT, WIGMUND, AND WULFHERE

Phase II of the coinage is that which sees a new team of moneyers striking in brass mixed with very little silver. There is no evidence that personnel from Phase I continued in office, except that Æthelweard worked for Wigmund who became archbishop *c*.837 at the time when the debased regal coinage must have started to become both more intensive and more constant in output. From the last years of Eanred's reign to the first of Osberht we have surviving a tremendous number of specimens, of both official and unauthorized origin. It should be possible soon to present the first results of an analysis of their dies. Most of the material which has formed the basis of the study is in the unrivalled collection held by the Yorkshire Museum, which may fairly be described as a somewhat moth-eaten representation of the known production from Phase II; some parts are more moth-eaten than others. Scraps for patching the recognizable holes can be found in the bit-bags of collections elsewhere.

At this stage, it is imperative to record some of the multitude of questions which have had to be asked throughout the work.

It must surely be a matter of common sense when dealing with a large mass of material to identify within the whole a number of individual units and to examine the detail of each and the relationships of one to another.

For the regular coinage of Phase II, we have the regal issues for Eanred, Æthelred II, Redwulf, and Osberht together with the work for the archbishops Wigmund and Wulfhere. Within each of these six units there have been the sub-divisions formed by the work of individual moneyers. Yet when one comes to consider the massive output of one such as Monne for Æthelred, almost the first questions to spring up are: how can we determine when within the period a particular coin was struck; which coin should be listed first in the register of a man's work? Is there any rhyme or reason in the use of motifs which might determine the progression of any one man's issues? Hard on the heels of these come further questions. Is one really justified in maintaining the separation of

20 Dolley (1976), 355.

21 For such an analysis, see James Booth's paper, above.

moneyers to the extent which has prevailed for so long? If most moneyers use the same range of motifs, can one establish a typology observed by moneyers working in concert? If one can identify types and their varieties, in what order do they occur?

The range of standard motifs on the official coinage is effectively small; six seem to represent two traditions of iconography. Three may be recognized to have religious connotations. There is the simple small cross. There are also the cross with a pellet in each angle and the cross formed of five pellets: both are to be found in other artistic contexts. The first occurs on a much larger scale in a fresco which formed part of the ninth-century restoration of one of the early churches of Rome; this now underlies the church of San Martino ai Monti. The somewhat exiguous remains of the painting (considerably less now than when seen by Wilpert[22]) allow one to determine that the circles lying in each angle of the cross enclose the representation of a volume. The motif as a whole has been seen to represent the Cross and the Four Gospels; it is still used with such symbolism. The five pellets on some of the coins are miniatures of the five bosses which occur also on some of the stone crosses such as the *Crux Guriat*[23] on the Isle of Man. Finlay[24] identifies them as symbols used in place of the figure of Christ crucified. If names for types were required one could suggest that these be called *Evangelistic Cross* and *Passion Cross* respectively. Three motifs, in contrast, seem to have secular significance. Apart from the simple pellet, there are the rosette of pellets and the pellet-in-annulet. Again, the last two are to be found in other media. The shoulder-brooch worn by Charlemagne on his statue in Grisons, Switzerland[25] is in the form of a rosette: this may perhaps be seen as a badge of royalty. The pellet-in-annulet and its variation—where the basic motif is itself surrounded by pellets—may be traced back to the ancient Celtic world and can be found there, too, on coins.[26] The selection of emblems such as these for the coins by the Northumbrian moneyers will surely have been accompanied by appreciation of their symbolism and perhaps of their appropriateness for particular issues.

In the use of motifs, particular *types* may be identified when both obverse and reverse bear the same device. A *variety* may be identified when an obverse with one motif is combined with a reverse bearing another design. Recognition of types and varieties may seem to be easy and it is straightforward enough to sort the material of a reign into blocks comprising the coins of all moneyers which have the same motif-combinations. To determine the order in which the issues occurred is yet another matter and other questions arise, primarily that of how the evidence of die-linking contributes to clarification of the sequence. How many die-links occur in the types, both within the work of individual moneyers and between that of two or more? How many such links occur in the varieties? How many links connect the varieties to specific types? Which reverses form links between one reign and the next? Where, too, might there be evidence of altered dies, changed at least by emendation of motif?

In the coinage produced during the last years of Eanred's reign there is clearly a very marked preponderance of specimens whose dies both bear the small cross.

22 Wilpert (1917), I, 322.
23 Chadwick (1963), 38.
24 Finlay (1979), 225.
25 Simons (1971), 100.
26 See Allen (1978), nos.115, 118.

Motifs in the rosette and annulet tradition *are* present but are certainly in the minority. Questions of style creep in to help identify a sequence depending on separation of *First, Intermediate*, and *Last Small Cross* (and their varieties) interspersed with the types which have secular motifs, and followed by a short-lived issue of *Evangelistic Cross* which might be the first instalment of a type continued at the beginning of Æthelred's reign. Among the specimens to be allocated to *Last Small Cross* are coins of Brother (BRODR) whose obverse is altered from one having the pellet motif; the linked reverses include those with the name rendered in runes, a trait shared with reverses for Wihtræd. These last are combined with an obverse used in common with Monne. Reverses for both Wihtræd and Monne, known first with the one obverse for Eanred, can be seen to be re-used in the reign of Æthelred.

Hopes of seeing Æthelred's coinage as introduced with an *Evangelistic Cross* issue in continuation of that with which Eanred's seemed to end have fallen by the wayside. The inter-reign links formed by Wihtræd's reverses lead into further *small cross* combinations. Monne's dies from the same early group are used in conjunction with an obverse having a *cross potent* motif; indeed, there is another instance of an early pellet motif being altered to form a matching *cross potent* on one of the re-used reverses. The new motif, in this form, is used by Monne alone but a variation is used by Leofthegn, one of the reign's new moneyers, who has long been noted for the number of different motifs which he alone employs. Among the questions arising at this stage are, inevitably: where do these individual designs, several of which have recognizable religious connotations, find their place in relation to the standard ones; and how does the sole pictorial design of this period, Leofthegn's 'hound' reverse (known from only one die) relate to his other work? One may notice also that Monne and Leofthegn are not the only men who depart from the norm. Wigmund's moneyer Coenræd seems to emulate Leofthegn in representing, somewhat crudely, one of the same religious symbols.

Æthelred's coins struck by Wihtræd and Monne with reverses used in Eanred's time are demonstrably early in the reign's sequence. There is further work by Monne and others which links with the coinage of Redwulf. It is when one looks for the issues which fill the gap between these early and later coins that difficulties arise.

Forthræd has an inter-reign link from Eanred to Æthelred; the use of the reverse for Æthelred forms part of a very short chain involving the use of two obverses by him, the moneyer Eanræd, Wulfræd, and Monne; one of those reverses for Monne links with his coins for Redwulf.

Furthermore, Monne has four other inter-reign links from Eanred to Æthelred besides those two which are associated with work by Wihtræd. One of the relevant reverses is used with five different obverses: one for the reign of Eanred, one for Æthelred and three for Redwulf. [See Appendix I.]

Where can one fit in Monne's *cross potent* issues? The continuity of die-linking between the three reigns, demonstrable in the work of Monne alone, together with that in the Forthræd–Eanræd–Wulfræd–Monne complex, leaves no room for insertion in the coinage of Æthelred of any additional types such as Monne's *cross potent* and others by Leofthegn, Wihtræd and Forthræd. Is one right in assuming that there is only one stream of coinage in which one could expect to identify a single sequence of types? Might there not be two or, possibly, even more separate blocks of coinage (each with its own pattern of work) which were issued concurrently?

The evidence of die-linking at least seems to indicate that there are, in the output of Phase II, the products of several different regal workshops and that connections can be found between these centres and the work of the archbishop's moneyers.

THE IDENTIFICATION OF SEPARATE REGAL WORKSHOPS IN PHASE II

There is, in the coinage of Æthelred, a marked dichotomy of issue which may be identified, quite apart from the use of motif, by the spelling of the king's name. In most cases, the middle syllable is spelt with an I as *Edilred*, but the form with the middle syllable having E as its vowel also appears on a considerable number of dies. It is the *Edilred* coinage which is enclosed between the issues of Eanred's reign and those of Redwulf; it is the *Edelred* coinage which, although linked in the work of Monne and Wihtræd from some coins of Eanred, stands apart. It seems that each group should be considered separately even though some of the king's moneyers work in both. All appear to work in the so-called *Edilred* group, which is by far the larger.

a) THE *EDILRED* GROUP

The issues here comprise work of different extent by Brother, Cynemund, Ealhhere (ALGHERE), Eanræd, Eanwulf, Eardwulf, Forthræd, Leofthegn, Monne, Odilo, Wendelbeorht, Wihtræd, Wulfræd, and Wulfsige, together with some coins for the king struck by Wigmund's moneyer, Hunlaf. In this instance, too, we are faced with a mass of material difficult to handle as a whole. It could be ordered in types and varieties, among which Leofthegn's 'hound' coins would stand alone. Coins linking to the issues of Eanred would be early as those linking to Redwulf would be later and those linking to Osberht, perhaps later still. It would still be difficult, however, to demonstrate effectively the associations which occur between each moneyer and one or more of his colleagues. To leave the *Edilred* group in its entirety would be to overlook further peculiarities of spelling and other epigraphic features which seem to identify sub-divisions within the whole.

Within the entire group there are at least four variations of the rendering of Æthelred's name: EDILRED, EDIΓRED, EDLIRED, apart from AEDILRED. Each form is used by more than one moneyer. Each may be taken as an indication of a possible division of the material. The first includes work by Monne which depends on four links from the previous reign; it encompasses the whole of Eardwulf's regular output. Within the division, one can note some variation in style. The second has a major part of Forthræd's work for the reign and includes the re-use of his reverse which was first cut in Eanred's time; Wendelbeorht has the L of his own name inverted. The third division (*Edlired*), with work by the moneyers Eanræd, Forthræd (shown as EORDRED), Monne, Wulfræd and Wulfsige, has the obvious peculiarity of spelling the king's name. Pagan[27] refers

[27] Pagan (1973), 26.

to Monne having an old *Edilred* die re-cut in this form. There is indeed one instance where this can be seen to have happened, yet it cannot be said that all these obverses have been so refurbished: no others (several of them are retrograde) can be traced back to *Edilred* originals. One must accept that they were from the first intended to represent the I and L transposed from their normal order; if there can be any argument, it should concern the possibility that the letters *are* in their right order but that the L is reversed. On some of his personal dies, Monne has the final E of his name reversed. The *Aedilred* form is used principally by Ealhhere, and, to a small extent, by Eanræd and Leofthegn. It can be noticed that Ealhhere, who uses on his reverse dies the round L, virtually confines his work to coins bearing the *small cross* or the *evangelistic cross*; there is one die with the *passion cross*.

Once one begins to appreciate such divisions, and their difference in size, further questions arise. Are they, during the reign, each only part of longer divisions, beginning in the time of Eanred and continuing throughout the duration of the coinage? Should one abandon the potential typology devised for the last years of Eanred's reign and examine that material again for the antecedents of each section? Is the material of Redwulf's short usurpation also capable of separation? And that of Osberht? How does the episcopal coinage relate to the regal?

It is possible to pick out from the issues of the early reign many of the coins by Forthræd for Eanred, struck from dies of an individual style, and to see them as the forerunners of those whose obverse legend has the inverted L. It is also possible to identify coins by Monne, Forthræd, and others which have the obverse peculiarity of Eanred's initial in the reverse position, even when the legend is retrograde; these coins may be seen as the antecedents of the *Edlired* issues. The predecessor of Ealhhere may be Aldates who, like Ealhhere, works virtually independently of the other moneyers and, with a round L in his own name, uses only the *small cross* and *evangelistic cross* motifs. Among Eanred's remaining coins are issues for Monne, Wulfræd, and others which, apart from Monne's actual die-links, demonstrate stylistic affinities with the *Edilred* coinage.

Many moneyers working in the *Edilred* division have die-links drawing them into a section of coinage for Redwulf which is itself heavily die-linked. Wendelbeorht alone uses his distinctive 'inverted L' reverses for the usurper with obverses spelling the name as REDVVLF rather than REDVLF. Forthræd and Monne, with retrograde obverses on which the letters of Redwulf's name are themselves reversed, may be seen to continue from the *Edlired* division; Monne's reverses again have the reversed E. Ealhhere, working alone like Wendelbeorht, strikes for Redwulf and re-uses a reverse from the *Aedilred* division. It is clear that there is a strong measure of continuity through the various reigns for each strand of the coinage.

Examination of this group-identity cannot fail to draw attention to the position within the whole of the official work of Æthelred's moneyer Eardwulf. He invariably uses the basic *Edilred* form but does he really only strike during the king's second reign as Lyon has postulated? If that is so, his association with Wulfræd must occur in the later period. But Wulfræd, who is known for the reign of Eanred, is obviously on the scene fairly early and has been thought to have ended his career as a regal moneyer during Æthelred's first reign. He does not strike for Redwulf any more than Eardwulf does. Does the evidence afford any explanation for some moneyers failing to work for the usurper? Is the association between Eardwulf and Wulfræd more apparent than real? Is the evidence of their sharing, on more than one occasion, the same obverses to be explained by recognizing that Eardwulf could have been using, at a late stage, left-over dies which were originally employed by Wulfræd? Does the very puzzle of this matter not raise doubts about the validity of the generally accepted theory that most moneyers ended their careers, suddenly, at the time of Redwulf? Could the end of work by several officials have occurred more gradually during the course of Æthelred's second reign?

As one begins to consider the arrangement of the material within each division, one can also note relationships with the episcopal coinage.

Although recognition that there are several concurrent sections of coinage has cut short the early attempt to determine a typology for a single stream of regal and episcopal issues, the use of motifs must still be taken into account.

Within the four principal divisions already outlined, work for Eanred portrays, in the main, the *small cross* with some examples of the other cross forms; the secular motifs are clearly in a subsidiary position. Work for Redwulf is essentially the same (see Fig.1). Within the whole of this coinage for Æthelred, both strains of symbolism are employed with almost equal emphasis; nevertheless, some moneyers use only the cross forms while others, including Eardwulf, use them as well as the secular *pellet, rosette of pellets* and the *pellet-in-annulet*. May Redwulf's coinage be taken as evidence of the cross motifs continuing to dominate until that time, so that the secular symbols on Æthelred's coins indicate the attribution of these issues to his second reign? The sheer volume of material is such that one feels justified in affirming that such a pattern of issue could be accepted, even if it implies that some moneyers, such as Eanræd, Forthræd and Monne, worked on for a while after the usurpation was over and Æthelred was restored to power.

Within each division, therefore, one can begin to sort the material for each reign, and within each reign for each moneyer. It is here, in the divisional context, that one is content at this stage to see an unbroken instalment of a moneyer's work. The first proviso one would make is that, for each man, his coins should be arranged in a specific order according to motif, so that, for instance, those with the *evangelistic cross* or *passion cross* should follow the *small cross*. Again, one would argue in favour of distinguishing moneyers whose output at the time is prolific from those whose work there is on a smaller scale and recording coins of the major officials separately.

The first division's work for Eanred is that of Monne, Brother, and Forthræd as major moneyers and of 'Gadutes', Badigils, Fulcnoth and Odilo as minor moneyers. The succeeding work for Æthelred (as *Edilred*) includes that of some new men: Eanræd, Eardwulf and Leofthegn together with Monne and Wendelbeorht are the major officials; Ealhhere, Brother, Forthræd, Wulfræd and Wihtræd are here the minor ones. The standard range of motifs is limited to the cross forms but the rendering of Æthelred's name establishes the attribution to this division of Leofthegn's coins with the 'hound' reverse. Hunlaf's single reverse with the *rosette* motif may well be considered in this context, too, in spite of the general limitation of motifs at this period if it is accepted that the secular rosette did have regal connotations; the moneyer may have deliberately selected this symbol on the occasion of his working exceptionally with the regal team, in association with the moneyer Eanræd. In this instance, attribution to the first reign may be seen to depend on the small cross of the obverse. Associations which occur between Eanræd paired with Leofthegn, Wendelbeorht, and Wihtræd and between Forthræd paired with Leofthegn, Monne, and Wendelbeorht can be clearly seen in various other instances of shared obverses. Ealhhere can also be seen working in conjunction with Brother; Wulfræd shares with both Eardwulf and Monne. Somewhat more enigmatic are the instances of obverses, regularly used by Brother on the one hand and by Eardwulf and Wulfræd on the other, which are employed also in combination with a number of inferior dies purporting to be for other moneyers: Leofthegn and the episcopal official, Æthelweard, are two of those for whom Brother's obverse is re-used. Such sub-standard coins should, one suggests, be registered at the end of this part of Æthelred's coinage.

Forthræd and Monne, with Hunlaf, are those who establish definite links on to the coinage for Redwulf, where their coins are closely associated with work by Brother, Eanræd, and a new official, Cuthbeorht.

Use of the secular motifs assigns some work by Eanræd, Leofthegn, Wulfræd, and Wihtræd to Æthelred's second reign as minor moneyers, and by Eardwulf and Monne each in a major capacity. A link from Redwulf back to Æthelred may be seen to occur in Monne's work. Associations can be seen between Monne and Wulfræd and between Wulfræd and Eardwulf. There is no doubt that at this point Eardwulf is not just prolific but is also systematic. His work can be arranged as principal issues, with *rosette* or *pellet-in-annulet*, together with primary varieties where such obverses are combined with reverses in the *cross* tradition and secondary varieties where *cross* obverses appear in conjunction with the so-called secular reverses. There is also a small but tightly die-linked group of coins for Eardwulf, in another style, which should be separated from the rest; it cannot be identified as wholly irregular, but may well be late in emission.

There are no recorded links with the coinage of Osberht.

This division of the regal work is by far the largest in Phase II and may perhaps be deemed to represent the products of several workshops. It may be possible at some later stage to analyse further the various stylistic strains and to establish some sub-divisions. Developing in parallel with this principal part of the king's coinage is a portion of the archbishop's coinage. Æthelweard is the only one of all the moneyers who started his career before the beginning of Phase II; he is likely to have been working for Wigmund during the last years of Eanred's reign. This moneyer invariably has the *small cross* motif on his dies but he spells Wigmund's title in two ways, either as AREP (which continues the rendering used for Eanbald) or as IREP. It seems reasonable to identify the former as indicative of Wigmund's early issues and to assign the relevant coins to the period *c*.837–41. The issues with IREP must surely follow at the time of Æthelred's first reign. At that stage, Hunlaf, who also shows the title as IREP (or IR), must begin, with his *small cross* coins; his *rosette* issues may be later, in accordance with general practice.

One must admit that there is no overt evidence of Æthelweard having any direct association with this part of the group and the attribution is based primarily on matching seniority with major production. The situation is different in respect of Hunlaf who has been seen to tie in here with the regal coinage. For the sake of completeness, one should record that two specimens (one in the Merseyside collection[28] and the other in the Lyon collection) purporting to be for Æthelred in this group and struck by another episcopal moneyer, Æthelhelm (EDELHELM), have both been shown to be nineteenth-century forgeries cast in lead and bismuth.[29] There is now no authentic evidence of Æthelhelm having any connection with this section of the work.

One can perhaps enlarge more swiftly on the early scope of the smaller second and third divisions.

In the second section, for Eanred's reign Forthræd and Brother produce major work; there are lesser contributions by 'Gadutes', Odilo, Monne, and Wulfræd. For Æthelred, Forthræd and the moneyer Eanræd are pre-eminent during his first reign; on a lesser scale is the work of Brother, Cynemund, Ealhhere, Leofthegn, Monne, Wendelbeorht, and Wulfræd. Associations can be seen between Eanræd and Wendelbeorht, Forthræd and Leofthegn and—in a triple liaison—between Forthræd, Brother, and Monne. Both Forthræd and Wulfræd use for normal coins obverses which are then paired with other reverses of inferior workmanship cut in the names of other moneyers, including Leofthegn; a die with Odilo's name forms a crucial link with Redwulf in the third division. Wendelbeorht alone strikes for Redwulf. The use of secular motifs identifies issues made for Æthelred by Leofthegn, Monne, and Wulfræd as minor moneyers while Forthræd and Eanræd are again prolific. There are then two further examples of three moneyers sharing one obverse: in work by Eanræd, Forthræd, and Wulfræd on the one hand and by Eanræd, Monne, and Wulfræd on the other. Again, there are no recorded links with work for Osberht. It must be suggested that Æthelhelm's work for Wigmund during Æthelred's reign should be included in this division. The man stands apart from his episcopal colleagues in that he never accords the archbishop any form of title: his obverses record only the name. In the rendering of his own name, Æthelhelm invariably has both Ls inverted. Moreover, with his *rosette* issues (*small cross/rosette* varieties) a parallel may be observed with practice in the regal work: Leofthegn has an instance of one *rosette* reverse combined with four *small cross* obverses; so does Æthelhelm.

There is no evidence of episcopal coinage in the third division. Monne is the major moneyer at the end of Eanred's reign and there are minor contributions by Wulfræd, Forthræd, Fulcnoth, and Badigils, all of whose coins have the peculiarity of the reversed E for Eanred's initial. For Æthelred's first reign, Forthræd is prolific; Monne, Eanræd, and Cynemund work in a minor capacity. Forthræd shares obverses with Monne and with Eanræd; in the latter instance, the common die is also used with one of inferior quality whose legend may attempt the king's name. Both Forthræd and Monne have reverses which are re-used for Redwulf.

Cynemund's dies are aberrant and, on the obverse, have a scatter of pellets in the field; this quirk is seen again on an obverse for Redwulf which, like those of Æthelred which have already been remarked, is used in combination with reverses of inferior quality; in this instance, one of the names involved is

[28] *SCBI* 29, no.113.

[29] See Pirie and Warren (1983).

NERRED, which can only be an echo of HERRED from Phase I. These coins cannot be accepted as wholly regular. The link through one of two Odilo dies to the comparable issues for Æthelred identifies the point at which all such coins, derived from all three divisions, must have been struck. In the course of recent work on the series the normal, official coins produced with the relevant obverses have earned the nickname of 'ancestors' and those with the inferior reverses have been dubbed the 'descendants'.

INWARD-POINTING LETTERS

In this third division, Æthelred's coins with the secular motifs are very few, struck by Eanræd, Forthræd, Wulfræd and Monne. Pagan[30] has implied that there was a break in the second-reign coinage, before the occurrence of issues which link through to the reign of Osberht. In this division, if nowhere else, there is some evidence of an interval in the course of production. Judging by the use of motif, most of the coins struck by Wulfsige might have been assigned to Æthelred's first reign, especially as he twice uses obverses used also by Forthræd. Yet there is another factor to be taken into account. The reverse dies with the moneyer's name are cut so that the letters point inward to the centre: the name, though going clock-wise round the flan, has, in effect, to be read as though it were retrograde. This feature of the reverse occurs also on the coins of Monne and Eanwulf (in association) on all of which the *small cross* is depicted. These issues are certainly late in Æthelred's reign for they form a connection with the same moneyers' coinage for Osberht. Two stages of production during the second reign should therefore be recognized here, and work by Wulfsige, Monne, and Eanwulf attributed to the second.

Monne and Eanwulf are the only two of Osberht's few moneyers who work together during his reign. By this time, both their reverses and their obverses are cut with the inward-pointing letters: they are of comparatively poor style with several aberrations of spelling. The relatively new practice in die-cutting is observed also for all the dies used by Osberht's official, Æthelhelm. It would seem that the erstwhile episcopal moneyer continued to work in the second division but obtained his dies in the regal workshop. His work there is more than a little crude. Winebeorht's coins for Osberht also show the new direction in the lettering: it seems that his coins, of better quality than the rest, may have come from the principal regal workshops of the first division.

By this time—if not earlier—the episcopal issues for Wulfhere by his sole moneyer Wulfræd may have been struck quite independently of the main regal centre. One is reminded that the relative dates for Osberht and Wulfhere still have to be determined, for if the paucity of the regal coinage suggests that issues for Osberht ceased within two or three years of his accession (*c.*850), one must still debate the likelihood of Wulfhere having been in a position to authorize coinage much before he received the *pallium* in 854. One would imagine that he would not continue to make issues once the regal coinage had collapsed. At the risk of implying that the archbishops's reception of the *pallium* was unduly delayed (perhaps because of the political situation in Northumbria?) one would go as far as to suggest that Wulfhere's coins started in—if they do not all belong to—the last

[30] Pagan (1973), 9.

year or so of Æthelred's reign. In effect, Wulfræd was working for the archbishop while Eardwulf was still working for Æthelred. The evidence on which this idea may be based is the remarkable lack of inversion in the lettering of Wulfhere's coins. If one is looking for parallels between the regal and episcopal coinage there is, on Wulfræd's dies for Wulfhere, no sign of the inward-pointing legends which appear on Osberht's coins. There are aberrations of spelling on the archbishop's dies: the title is rendered as ABED: at the most, there are two instances of a triangular A which one could identify in an inverted position. The work must have at least started before there was any question of changing the appearance of the legends and, in as much as some of it was probably contemporary with Osberht's coinage, the archbishop conservatively maintained the old form.

During the very few years that Osberht's coinage can have lasted, the regal work of these three divisions was quite distinct, with different moneyers in each. It was not entirely so in the time of Æthelred when several moneyers worked in more than one of the divisions. The transfer of a few reverses from one section to another creates a number of links between the workshops—a number which is small in comparison with the extent of die-linking within the individual division.

But one must notice that there are no links at all between these three parts, already detailed, and the coinage identified by the spelling of the king's name as *Aedilred*. This small section of the regal coinage must be regarded as separate, in spite of the middle I. It has already been proposed that Ealhhere, for Æthelred, here succeeded Eanred's moneyer Aldates. The moneyers Eanræd and Leofthegn also contribute to Æthelred's *cross* issues. Ealhhere alone works for Redwulf, then Eanræd and Leofthegn appear again for Æthelred with *pellet* and *rosette* issues. It is at this point that some of the obverses, used principally by Eanræd, but shared with Leofthegn, render the name as *Aeilred*. The links which Eanræd and Leofthegn form between this group and another are with the coinage which uses the *Edelred* version for the royal name.

b) THE *EDELRED* GROUP

The section of Æthelred's official coinage which remains to be discussed in more detail is that which does not use the letter I in the king's name. The relevant coins form part of a small but distinct group of issues which start in the last years of Eanred's reign. At that time, Monne and Wihtræd, associated in the use of a common obverse die, produce coins whose reverses provide direct links with the subsequent issues. It is here that some of Wihtræd's personal dies have his name rendered in runes; so, too, do some of Brother's dies for Eanred. Brother is here briefly associated with Forthræd; some of their dies have two further peculiarities: the king's name is rendered as EAHRED and the lettering, particularly on reverses, is adorned with knobs.

The limited range of the early material in this group makes it difficult to determine sub-divisions which may each be the antecedents of one of the sections more clearly seen in work for Æthelred. In this instance, the few examples of the formal spelling AEDELRED may be amalgamated with the more usual EDELRED; there is, however, a not inconsiderable body of work on which the name appears as EÐFLRED: some twenty-six obverses are known, used by Brother, Eanræd, Forthræd, Monne, and Wihtræd in conjunction with over eighty reverses. This peculiar form must have been cut deliberately and not, as one might at first imagine, as the result of a careless die-cutter omitting the lowest bar from a central E on only one or two dies. One should, therefore, separate the relevant coins from the others, even as one notes that Monne's early dies appear again on the *Edelred* work while Wihtræd's occur with both *Edelred* and *Ethflred*.

The standard range of motifs is, in each section, supplemented by others, both religious and secular. It is in the *Ethflred* section that there appears most often the motif made up of pellet-in-annulet surrounded by pellets; it is used as a type-motif by Wihtræd and on varieties by Eanræd, Monne, and Forthræd. Forthræd is the major moneyer in this block. It is in the *[A]Edelred* section that Leofthegn employs all the special designs for which he has been given credit, with the exception of the hound. Leofthegn and Monne are here the principal moneyers: in one instance they are associated with a third man, Odilo, who makes only a brief appearance. Leofthegn is also associated with Eanræd and it is from here that their reverses link to the *Ae[d]ilred* work.

Leofthegn is also associated with Coenræd who normally works for Wigmund but who also uses one of Leofthegn's obverses to strike for Æthelred. In this instance, Coenræd's reverse links back to a block of his episcopal work. It has already been noted that, alone among Wigmund's moneyers, Coenræd uses not only the standard motifs but one or two others as well in an attempt to emulate Leofthegn. In attributing *all* Coenræd's episcopal issues to this group, at this stage of the research, one must make the proviso that it may subsequently be possible to separate some which should be more correctly assigned elsewhere.

There are no direct reverse-links between Æthelred's coinage here and that for Redwulf, but Coenræd strikes for the usurper: his dies spell the name REDVVLF. Hwætnoth's single obverse has the same spelling and is of the same style of die-cutting, as are his three reverses. A variation on the theme of 'ancestors and descendants'—in the background at the time of Redwulf—may be seen in work which appears to emanate from Wihtræd. A reverse in the name of 'Erwinne', which has as motif a cross composed exceptionally of eight pellets, is known in conjunction with four obverses: one for Eanred and two for Æthelred have been used here normally by Wihtræd; a fourth is borrowed (presumably) from Æthelweard's work for Wigmund.

Although one is prepared to recognize the inclusion of a small part of Redwulf's work, the total material for Æthelred is still too limited for one to be sure that the work produced in this group follows the same pattern that has been identified for the *Edilred* divisions. No distinction has as yet been made between the issues of Æthelred's first reign and those of the second. One can note, however, that Monne alone moves two reverse dies between the *[A]Edelred* and *Ethflred* sections. He transfers more between the *Edelred* and *Edilred* sections; Leofthegn and Wihtræd both have one such move. Wihtræd alone moves a die between *Ethflred* and *Edilred* but Brother and Eanræd both move between *Ethflred* and *Edilred* (with L inverted).

If one is to attempt to complete the regal sequence, it seems possible to do so by assigning to this group (and perhaps, by way of cross-reference, also to the *Aedilred* group) coins for Osberht by the moneyer Wulfsige (VVLFSIgT). The name may be a variation of VVLFSIC and the man the same as he whose coins for Æthelred have already been assigned to a late stage in the principal group. But the single reverse die of Wulfsige's official coins stands apart from the other work for Osberht because it is cut without inversion of the letters. The one reverse, moreover, is used in conjunction with eight obverses. Of these, only two can be seen (from the R and the T) to have inverted legends. In this pattern of work, one must suggest, may be seen movement of the common die from one workshop to another: from one where the die-cutter did not observe the usual practice of the time to one where the new custom *was* followed.

TABLE 2. *Obverses used in each section, together with percentages: for the shared dies within a section and for section-totals as portions of the whole*

Group	*Sole use*	*Shared use*	*Total*	
Ai	32	10 = 23.8%	of 42;	42 = 17.87% of 235
Aii	23	4 = 15.3%	of 27;	27 = 11.48% of 235
B	10	2 = 16.6%	of 12;	12 = 5.10% of 235
Ci	61	19 = 23.75%	of 80;	80 = 34.04% of 235
Cii	51	7 = 12.07%	of 58;	58 = 24.68% of 235
Ciii	12	4 = 25.0%	of 16;	16 = 6.80% of 235
Totals	189	46	235	

The foregoing discussion of the content of the official coinage issued during Phase II has been more than a little involved, but deliberately so, even at the risk of seeming to echo the terminology of sport, with repeated references to first, second, and third divisions. The various groups need simple labels. It may now be appreciated, however, that there is a sense of anticlimax in turning to the smaller groups after considering the detail of the main work. It is therefore easier to have the material arranged thus:

[A]Edelred–Ethflred	:	Group A
Aedilred–Aeilred	:	Group B
Edilred (all)	:	Group C
Edilred	:	Ci
Edilred (Γ)	:	Cii
Edlired	:	Ciii

As a sample of the occurrence of obverses of the different groups, and of the linkage between them, Table 2 shows the distribution for 235 obverse dies used by the moneyers whose reverse dies are analysed in Table 1 above.

THE UNOFFICIAL COINAGE

Besides the regular issues, there are the irregulars for which the coinage as a whole may be deemed notorious. Most such coins reflect the official work of Group C, in that they essay the name *Edilred*. There are so many of these that it is

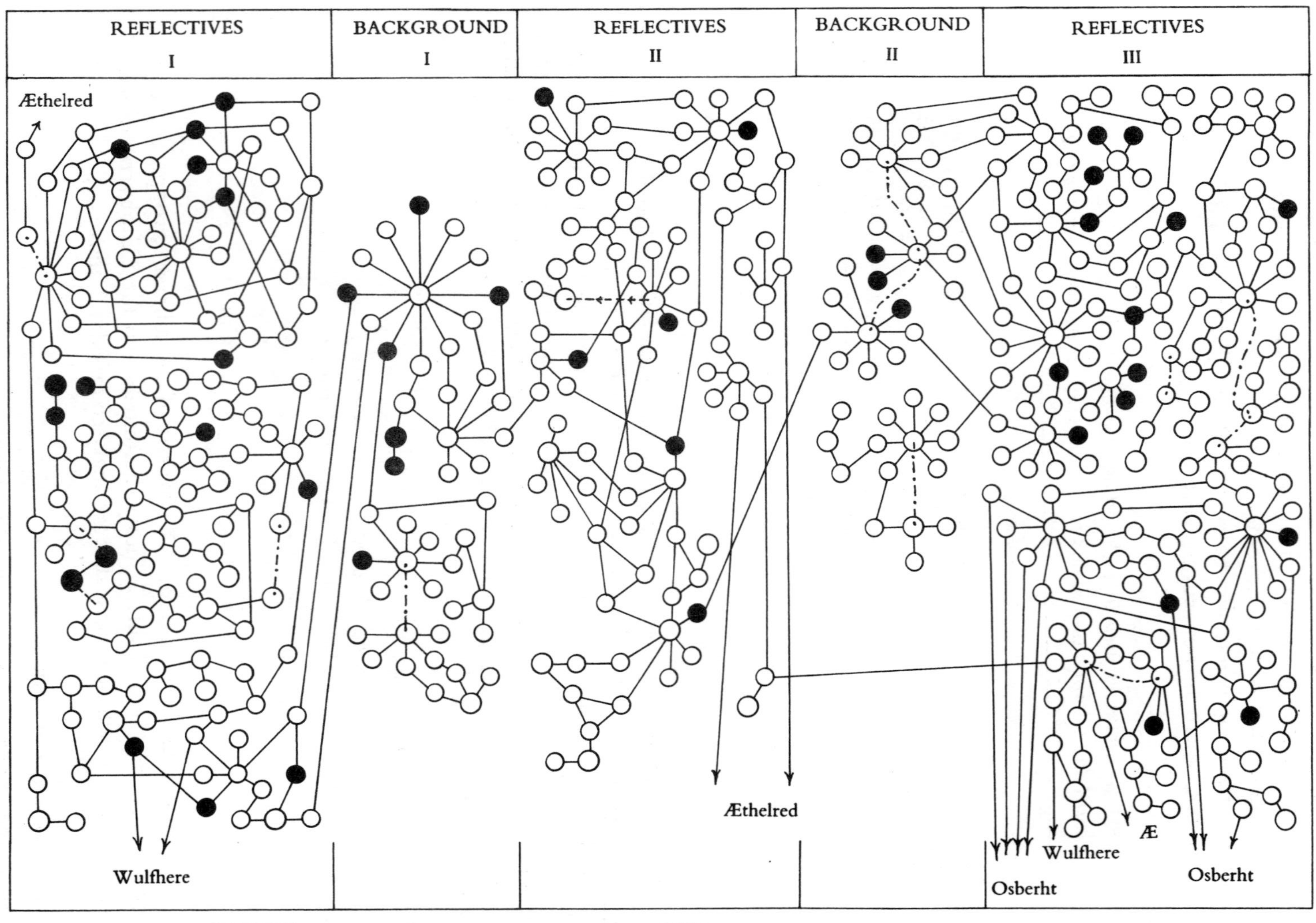

FIG.2. Die-links in Group D (the irregular issues). The diagram is based on material in the Yorkshire Collections (at York and Leeds); represented in black are specimens known in other cabinets. A broken line (arrowed) relates a die to its use after alteration; similar dies are related by other broken lines, thus: – · – · –. Ties with the regular issues are shown.

TABLE 3. *Phase II: Æthelred's moneyers [MAJOR and minor], group by group, with sub-divisions for their use of motif*

[A]Edelred	*Ethflred*	*Aedilred/Aeilred*	*Edilred*	*Edilred* (Γ)	*Edlired*
all motifs	*all motifs*	*cross motifs*	*cross motifs*	*cross motifs*	*cross motifs*
LEOFTHEGN	FORTHRÆD	EALHERE	EANRÆD	EANRÆD	FORTHRÆD
MONNE	Brother	Eanræd	EARDWULF	FORTHRÆD	Monne
Brother	Eanræd	Leofthegn	LEOFTHEGN	Ealhhere	Eanræd
Eanræd	Monne		MONNE	Brother	Cynemund
Odilo	Wihtræd		WENDELBEORHT	Cynemund	
Wulfræd			Ealhhere	Leofthegn	
Wihtræd			Brother	Monne	
Coenræd (epis.)			Forthræd	Wendelbeorht	
			Wulfræd	Wulfræd	
			Wihtræd		
			Hunlaf (epis.)		
		other motifs	*other motifs*	*other motifs*	*other motifs*
		Eanræd	Eanræd	Leofthegn	1. Eanræd
		Leofthegn	Leofthegn	Monne	Forthræd
			Wulfræd	Wulfræd	Wulfræd
			Wihtræd	EANRÆD	Monne
			EARDWULF	FORTHRÆD	2. Wulfsige
			MONNE		Monne
					Eanwulf

convenient to establish for them another Group, D. Fewer in number are those that relate to Group A.

To Group A can be added several small clusters of die-linked coins. Among the earliest may be those which relate to the official work of Monne and Wihtræd for Eanred: *their* common die is used with two others whose legends may be nonsense. That on the first may be read as Teveh or as Teven (cf. the aberration EAHRED); both it and the second, ΛHIXИEF, are used with another of equal incomprehensibility. Also with legends incapable of recognition as Anglo-Saxon names is at least one other group. A variety of styles is known for such pieces. Slightly later, is a short chain starting with Ethflred/Monne and running into double-reverses of Monne, Brother, Forthræd, and nonsense: the style of lettering is knobby. Also knobby are the legends in the chain giving us the names ƿERNVĐ (Wernuth?), Wilheah and ANTEDI: in the first two instances, the names are spelt with the initial *wen* rather than with V. Another early 'silver' moneyer besides Wilheah is echoed in the name Hwætr[æ]d which is on a die used in conjunction with that reading HOAVD and with others: again, the lettering is in the distinctive knobby style.

Quite different is the work to be assigned to Group D. Apart from one or two small and separate clusters in which the names Hwætræd, Wilheah (VILHEAH) and Wulfræd can be discerned, besides Æthelred, there is the main chain composed of some four hundred linking die-combinations most of which bear the king's name; the archbishop's name does not appear although the identifiable moneyers are both regal and episcopal. This mesh of reflectives may be handled in concurrent instalments: three main ones (Reflectives I, II, and III) and two subsidiary. It is possible that these principal divisions all echo some part of the Group C coinage: it can be demonstrated that Reflectives I links to Ci and Reflectives III to Ciii. RI, II, and III are each made up of a number of tight-knit balls of coins, closely die-linked, with one ball knotted to another by no more than one or two cross-links (see Fig.2). On several occasions, the obverses seem to have been cut in sets of three, tantalizingly similar yet each with identifiable differences. Most of the obverses are used in conjunction with several dies purporting to be for a variety of moneyers; there is an element of nonsense represented by some of the reverses. The 'obverses' in the two subsidiary, background, groups are also unintelligible nonsense, although many of their reverses bear recognizable names.

Different opinions have already been expressed concerning the date of these pieces now assigned to Group D. Lyon[31] saw them as late, even after the cessation of the official issues in Osberht's reign. Pagan[32] regarded them as having started in the last years of Æthelred's life. It is possible to identify the inception of the main chain at about the time of Redwulf's usurpation, not only because the majority of the motifs are in the *cross* tradition but because the nature of the irregular work, with its multiplicity of moneyers dependent on the same obverse, echoes that of the semi-official 'descendants'. The circumstances which led to the break in the pattern of Æthelred's coinage, and which gave rise to the 'descendants' could have also provided the flash-point which started the spate of reflectives. For those who favour a very late date for their production there is perhaps a loop-hole, in the coinage of Wulfhere (and of the moneyer Wulfsige), to show that the outward-pointing legends did not disappear altogether in the time of Osberht. Yet, so few of the irregulars have inward-pointing lettering that this evidence of epigraphy must surely support the view that these coins were being put into circulation earlier than hitherto supposed. Most of the few links with the official coinage occur towards the end rather than at the beginning of the imitations. At the start of Osberht's reign the dividing line between what was official and what irregular may have been very thin indeed.

CONCLUSION

This brief preliminary survey of the various elements identifiable within Phase II of the styca coinage has concentrated on orthographic and epigraphic differences as well as on the use of motif (see Appendix II). Little has been said of other physical attributes of the coins, such as weight and metallurgical analysis. During recent work on the York collection, it has been observed that the coins of Groups A and B show a larger proportion of specimens weighing over 1.30 grammes than do those of Group C as a whole, although within C itself the tendency towards heavy weights may be more marked in Cii than in i and iii. So far, all too little analysis of the baser issues has been effected. One would like to see analysed a considerable number of specimens by different moneyers from each and every group, so that the range within each may be determined before it is compared or contrasted with that of another. If the relatively large body of material at present

[31] Lyon (1957), 232.

[32] Pagan (1973), 11.

assigned to Group Ci *is* capable of further division, one might hope that metallurgical analysis would there complement the analysis of die-detail.

Concern with assessment of the later coinage in the styca series has concentrated at this stage on exploration of group-relationships which may govern the format in which such material may be recorded. The matter of sequence within the main groups needs much further consideration; it is still very far from being established. One is aware of opinion which considers that the work so far encompasses a large measure of interpretation, itself leading to attributions which seem to be unacceptable.

Recognition of groups within the coinage is itself only part of a study of this material; as the result of die-analysis, it is not an end in itself but only a means to further research. Many more pertinent questions relate to topics which require exploration and interpretation in quite separate ways.

Some factors relating to chronology *have* been touched on, but not as yet that which may be crucial: the relationship of Redwulf's reign to that of Eanred. When, within the total reign of Æthelred II, did the usurpation of Redwulf occur? Was it really at the half-way point or was it closer in time to the death of Eanred than has been supposed? Detailed discussion of the chronology of the reigns, for which the inter-reign die-link evidence of Group C may be critical, should, however, be the subject of a separate paper. So, too, should be any attempt to interpret the coinage of Phase II which, with its official issues, 'descendants' and irregular emissions, may possibly illuminate the contemporary political scene. There is a sense in which consideration of such matters as time and politics must await resolution of where the coinage came from. Lyon has said that the extent of die-linking is such that most if not all the official coinage must have been struck at one place and that, York. The possibility of one or two moneyers working independently elsewhere was mooted ten years later;[33] although moneyers mentioned then—Cuthheard, Tidwine and Tidwulf—did not work in the later period now under review, Lyon's citation of Osberht's official Winebeorht working apart from his colleagues allows his suggestion to apply to Phase II as well. One is aware that in reciting the movement by moneyers of some reverse dies from division to division, from group to group, the impression may have been given, inadvertently, that the workshops are bound to have been located in different areas. A great deal more evidence would have to be adduced before one could propose that they represent a network of official production centres throughout the kingdom and that they are mirrored by a rash of illicit *ateliers* uttering imitations on a regional basis. This whole matter involves more than discussion of the composition of hoards and the range of site-finds in the light of group-representation. It requires, also, consideration of the problematic question of the physical movement of the senior regal moneyers round the kingdom and that of episcopal moneyers operating outside the main ecclesiastical centre at York.

One is more concerned at this stage with the reality of the groups as they have been defined. It must be urged that they be recognized as manageable instalments in the arrangement of specimens from the second phase of development. Further

[33] Lyon (1967), 218.

consideration of detail within each group will almost certainly lead to refinements of identification and modification of presentation.

Nevertheless, groups of work in which the moneyers are related to each other surely provide firmer ground on which to base discussion of the coinage and its problems than does the work of each moneyer in isolation.

Appendix I
EANRED–EDILRED-REDWULF

Some doubt has been and may still be expressed about the validity of the three-reign link in the coinage of Monne. Lyon himself vouched for the authenticity of the relevant three coins in his collection,[34] but he argued that the first was struck when the obverse for Eanred was so old, flawed, and rusty that its use in conjunction with that reverse may well have occurred during the confusion of Redwulf's reign. One could discount that theory by pointing to the existence of other dies on which flaws can be seen to develop and grow, and by asserting that such small dies may well have had an inherent tendency to flaw. It is, indeed, noticeable that obverse dies became less than perfect during use; they were, if necessary, available to more than one moneyer. By contrast, the large number of reverse dies may indicate the individual's care in replacing without delay those personal implements that showed the slightest sign of damage.

The Eanred obverse is known to have been used with five other reverses so its worn condition on Lyon's coin need not indicate long-delayed, posthumous striking. Yet, if the coin's attribution continues to be in dispute, we may have to admit only the evidence of the repeated use of the common reverse linking Monne's output for Æthelred with his work for Redwulf. It might then seem that the central argument for separation of the *Edelred* coinage, because of the closure of the *Edilred* material between Eanred and Redwulf, should fall to the ground. This is not so. The matter may still stand for, apart from the links noted for the moneyer Forthræd, Monne's other die-links remain significant. The very *Edilred* obverse whose reverse link with Redwulf's issues can be accepted is tied to the coinage of Eanred by the use of other reverses. Two of the three definite Eanred/*Edilred* connections are involved. In the first, the link is direct; with the second, the *Edilred* die initially related to Eanred's coinage by one reverse is related by another to the *Edilred*/Redwulf connection.

Were there no question at all of a single reverse linking the coinage of three kings, the surviving evidence would still be strong enough to speak for continuity in issues of which the *Edelred* dies form no part.

Appendix II
ORTHOGRAPHY AND CONVENTION

There is a marked conflict of interest between historians who expect Anglo-Saxon personal names to be rendered in a conventional manner, however far removed from actual usage the acceptable form may be, and the numismatist who attempts to be sensitive to the normal and its variations in the legends of a specific series of coins. Attention to orthography is particularly crucial when the subject of discussion is the money of early Northumbria for, alone among all Anglo-Saxon coinages, the styca issues include a remarkable amount of unauthorized work. Responsible consideration of the official output (and its different parts), together with that of elements in the irregular

[34] Lyon (1957), p.234; Pl.18, 27–9.

issues, is very seriously hampered when conventional name-forms for the moneyers are required to predominate.

The matter must be examined in a separate paper, for one has great misgivings about the unchallenged continuation of the current practice.

NOTES ON THE PLATES

(All specimens are shown one and a half times their actual size.)

PLATE 6

PHASE Ia. *Æthelred I*: 1, Ceolbeald; 2, Tidwulf; 3, Cuthc[i]ls (aberrant obv.: shrine on rev.); 4, Cuthheard. *Ælfwald II*: 5, Cuthheard. *Eanred*: 6, Cuthheard; 7, Hwætræd; 8, Cynewulf; 9, 'Edilech' (same obv. as 8); 10, Wilheah; 11, Tidwine; 12, Eadwine. *Abp. Eanbald II*: 13, Cynewulf; 14, Eadwine; 15, Æthelweard.

PHASE Ib. *Regular*: *Eanred*: 16, Dægbeorht; 17, Heardwulf [aberrant: Hrrdvvlfe); 18, Hereræd. *Irregular*: 19, 'Herreth' (double-rev.); 20, Eanbald (Ean + bad, retrograde)/ Eadwulf.

PLATE 7

PHASE II, Group A. *Eanred*: 21, Brother—Eahred/*Brodr*; 22, Brother—Eanhred (obv. that of 21 with altered motif)/*Brodr*, in runes; 23, Eahred/Forthræd (same obv. as 22); 24, Monne; 25, Monne; 26, Wihtræd (same obv. as 25: rev. with runes); 27, Wihtræd. *Æthelred II* ([A]Edelred, Ethfired): 28, Monne (rev. altered from 24); 29, Monne (same rev. as 25); 30, Eanræd (same obv. as 35: same rev. as 61 [Gr.B]); 31, Wihtræd (same rev. as 27); 32, Leofthegn (same rev. as 62 [Gr.B]); 33, Leofthegn (*Alpha* obv.—note position of initial cross: same rev. as 34); 34, Leofthegn (?*Omega* obv.—note position of initial cross, also the wire-line border); 35, Leofthegn (same obv. as 30, same rev. as 36); 36, Leofthegn (aberrant obv., retrograde with wire-line border); 37, Coenræd [episcopal] (same obv. as 36); 38, Wihtræd (aberrant rev.); 39, Forthræd. *Abp. Wigmund*: 40, Coenræd (same rev. as 37); 41, Coenræd (?crude *Omega* on rev.).

PLATE 8

PHASE IIA, continued. ?'**Descendant**', *temp. Redwulf*: 42, 'Erwinne' (same obv. as 38). *Redwulf*: 43, Hwætnoth; 44, Coenræd. *Osberht*: 45, Wulfsige; 46, Wulfsige (aberrant obv.: same rev. as 45—note wire-line border). **Irregular**: 47, Eanred/Nonsense (same obv. as 25–6); 48, Nonsense (obv. worn)/Nonsense (same rev. as 47); 49, Nonsense. 50, Ethfired/Monne (both dies retrograde—the beginning of a chain including Brother, Forthræd and nonsense); 51, Wernuth/[An]tedi (retrograde); 52, Hwætr[æ]d (retrograde)/Houad.

PHASE IIB. *Eanred*: 53, Aldates; 54, 'Gadutes' (?'Ladutes'; same obv. as 53); 55, Aldates (same obv. as 53–4). *Æthelred* (1st reign: Aedilred): 56, Ealhhere; 57, Ealhhere; 58, Eanræd; 59, Leofthegn. *Redwulf*: 60, Ealhhere. *Æthelred* (2nd reign: Aeilred): 61, Eanræd (same rev. as 30 [Gr.A]); 62, Leofthegn (same rev. as 32 [Gr.A]).

PLATE 9

PHASE IICi. *Eanred*: 63, Fulcnoth; 64, Monne; 65, Monne; 66, Monne (same obv. as 65). *Abp. Wigmund*: 67, Æthelweard (obv. title as ARE). *Æthelred* (1st reign: Edilred): 68, Monne (same rev. as 65); 69, Monne (same rev. as 64); 70, Eanræd; 71, Hunlaf [episcopal] (same obv. as 70); 72, Leofthegn ('hound' rev.); 73, Eardwulf; 74, '**Descendant**' [?*temp.* Redwulf] (double obv.—1st, that of 73; 2nd. Aeilred). *Abp. Wigmund*: 75, Æthelweard (title as IREP). *Redwulf*: 76, Cuthbeorht; 77, Hunlaf [episcopal] (same rev. as 71); 78, Monne. *Æthelred* (2nd reign): 79, Monne (same rev. as 66); 80, Monne (same rev. as 78—also known with obv. of 65–6); 81, Eardwulf; 82, Wulfræd (same obv. as 73–4).

Abp. Wigmund: 83, Hunlaf. *Osberht*: 84, Winebeorht. *Abp. Wulfhere*: 85, Wulfræd (both dies retrograde).

PLATE 10

PHASE IICii. *Eanred*: 86, Forthræd; 87, Forthræd. *Æthelred* (1st reign: Edilred[Γ]): 88, Eanræd; 89, Forthræd; 90, Leofthegn (same obv. as 89); 91, Wulfræd; 92, **'Descendant'** [*temp.* Redwulf] (same obv. as 91: Odilo); 93, 'Descendant' [*temp.* Redwulf] (same obv. as 91: [F]orthræd, retrograde). *Abp. Wigmund*: 94, Æthelhelm. *Redwulf*: 95, Wendelbeorht. *Æthelred* (2nd reign): 96, Forthræd (same rev. as 87). *Osberht*: 97, Æthe[lhel]m.

PHASE IICiii. *Eanred*: 98, Monne; 99, Fulcnoth (*Folcnod*, retrograde—same obv. as 98). *Æthelred* (1st reign: Edlired): 100, Forthræd (*Eordred*); 101, Monne (rev. retrograde). *Redwulf*: 102, Monne (both dies retrograde); 103, 'Nerred' (retrograde—?unofficial). *Æthelred* (2nd reign): first phase: 104, Eanræd; second phase: 105, Wulfsige (same obv. as 100); 106, Monne (both legends anti-clockwise); 107, Eanwulf (same obv. as 106). *Osberht*: 108, Monne (same rev. as 106); 109, Eanwulf (same obv. as 108, same rev. as 107).

PLATE 11

PHASE IID Irregulars—*most dies retrograde.* **Reflectives I**: 110, Eadwine; 111, Eadwine (same rev. as 110); 112, Hereræd (same obv. as 111); 113, Hereræd (same rev. as 112); 114, Eardwulf; 115, Eardwulf (same rev. as 114); 116, Nonsense. **Background I**: 117, Nonsense (same 'rev.' as 116); 118, Nonsense (same 'obv.' as 117); 119, Eardwulf (worn); 120, Nonsense. **RII**: 121, Eardwulf (rev. similar to that of 119); 122, Eardwulf (same rev. as 121); 123, Eodwulf [episcopal] (same obv. as 122); 124, Wihtræd. **BII**: 125, 'Roen'; 126, Wulfræd; 127 'Delo' (125–7 are from similar 'obv.' dies): **RIII** (Æthelred—Osberht): 128, Wulfræd (same rev. as 126); 129, double-obv.; 130, Monne; 131, Monne; 132, Monne (same rev. as 131); 133, Æthelhelm.

ABBREVIATIONS AND BIBLIOGRAPHY

Adamson, 1834: J. Adamson, 'An account of the discovery at Hexham, in the county of Northumberland, of a brass vessel containing a number of Anglo-Saxon coins called stycas', *Archaeologia* 25 (1834), 279–310 and 23 plates.

Adamson, 1836: Idem, 'Further account of the Anglo-Saxon coins, called stycas, recently discovered at Hexham in the county of Northumberland', *Archaeologia* 26 (1836), 346–8 and 7 plates.

Allen, 1978: D.F. Allen, *An Introduction to Celtic Coins* [edited by J.P.C. Kent], 1978.

AY: *Archaeology of York. 18/1: Post-Roman Coins from York Excavations, 1971–81*, E.J.E. Pirie with M.M. Archibald and R.A. Hall, 1986.

BNJ: *British Numismatic Journal.*

Booth, 1984: J. Booth, 'Sceattas in Northumbria', *Sceattas in England and on the Continent*, D. Hill and D.M. Metcalf, eds. (1984), 71–111.

Booth and Blowers, 1983: J. Booth and I. Blowers, 'Finds of sceattas and stycas from Sancton', *Numismatic Chronicle* 143 (1983), 139–45.

Chadwick, 1963: N. Chadwick, *Celtic Britain*, 1963.

Dolley, 1976: M. Dolley, 'The coins', *The Archaeology of Anglo-Saxon England*, D. M. Wilson, ed. (1976), 349–72.

Ducatus: R. Thoresby, *Ducatus Leodiensis*, 1715.

Fairless, 1845: J. Fairless, 'Stycas found at York', *Numismatic Chronicle* 7 (1845), 34–36.

Finlay, 1979: I. Finlay, *Columba*, 1979.

Grantley, 1912: Lord Grantley, 'St Cuthbert's Pennies', *BNJ* 8 (1912), 1–5.

Grierson, 1962: P. Grierson, 'The authenticity of the York thrymsas', *BNJ* 31 (1962), 8–10.

Lyon, 1957: C.S.S. Lyon, 'A re-appraisal of

the sceatta and styca coinage of Northumbria', *BNJ* 28 (1957), 227–42.

Lyon, 1967: Idem, 'Historical problems of Anglo-Saxon coinage (1)', *BNJ* 36 (1967), 215–24.

Metcalf *et al.*, 1968: D.M. Metcalf, J.M. Merrick and L.K. Hamblin, *Studies in the Composition of Early Medieval Coins*, 1968.

North, 1963: J.J. North, *English Hammered Coinage I*, 1963 [2nd ed., 1980].

Pagan, 1969: H.E. Pagan, 'Northumbrian numismatic chronology in the ninth century', *BNJ* 38 (1969), 1–15.

Pagan, 1973: Idem, 'The Bolton Percy hoard of 1967', *BNJ* 43 (1973), 1–44.

Pirie, 1981: E.J.E. Pirie, 'Early Northumbrian coins at auction, 1981', *BNJ* 51 (1981), 32–51.

Pirie, 1982: Eadem, 'The Ripon hoard, 1695: contemporary and current interest', *BNJ* 52 (1982), 84–103.

Pirie, 1984: Eadem, 'Some Northumbrian finds of sceattas', *Sceattas in England and on the Continent*, D. Hill and D.M. Metcalf, eds. (1984), 207–13.

Pirie and Warren, 1983: E.J.E Pirie and S.E. Warren, 'Bismuth alloy forgeries of early Northumbrian coins', *Proceedings of the 22nd Symposium on Archaeometry [1982]*, 1983, 254–60.

SCBI: *Sylloge of Coins of the British Isles*: 11. University Collection, Reading, C.E. Blunt and M. Dolley; 29. Merseyside County Museums, M. Warhurst.

Simons, 1971: G. Simons, *The Birth of Europe*, 1971.

Sweet, 1885: H. Sweet, 'Liber Vitae (Northumbrian)', *The Oldest English Texts* (1885), 153–66 [Early English Text Society, Original Series: 83].

Wilpert, 1917: J. Wilpert, *Die Römischen Mosaiken und Malereien der kirchlichen Bauten vom IV.–XIII. Jahrhundert* [Freiburg], 1917.

Wilson and Blunt, 1961: D.M. Wilson and C.E. Blunt, 'The Trewhiddle hoard', *Archaeologia* 98 (1961), 75–122.

DISCUSSION

DR METCALF: It has been a labour of love, and a labour of many years, to undertake the sort of die analysis that Miss Pirie has made of Æthelred's coins, indeed of much more than this—of two complex phases of coinage, the first stretching from Eanred's Group B through to the reign of Redwulf, and the second her ragged army of *sans-culottes*, the imitatives and reflectives and descendants and so on. This is back-room numismatics at its most professional, and (when it is all published) an achievement to crown an academic career. When so many thousands of coins have survived, when the survival-rate has been so high that there are several specimens from almost every die, and when the dies are so heavily linked together into patterns of intriguing complexity, the styca series is obviously destined, as a result of her work, to become a fertile field of research, where all sorts of technical ideas can be tested, in a way that is rarely possible in medieval numismatics. A complete list of the dies, together with the charts which illustrate their linkage, is the 'open sesame' to a cavern of numismatic wealth; and Miss Pirie is, make no mistake, in possession of the magic key. In any matter of interpretation which hinges upon numismatic detail, her ready access to *all* the facts places her in a very superior position, as our discussions have shown time after time. With luck one may be able to make an essentially correct judgement from an incomplete random selection of the facts, but how much more exactly, and confidently, one should be able to weigh matters when one knows that all the existing information is to hand. Miss Pirie and I both witnessed that golden age of late Anglo-Saxon numismatics which began in the early 1950s and in which Michael Dolley was a leading figure. A stream of articles based on a very detailed acquaintance with the coins gradually restructured the subject and greatly increased its historical usefulness. It would be an exaggeration to suggest that the stycas hold as great a potential, but the prospects of similarly arriving at novel generalizations through research based on the minutiae of the coins are very tempting.

We may be standing in the entrance of the cavern, but we have not yet got our hands on the treasure. What is implied by all these complex patterns of die-links is still ambiguous, because there are some crucial questions of general principle that must first be answered. Miss Pirie has until recently perhaps tended to assume too readily that the patterns of die-cutting matched, or at least found a clear reflection in the pattern of issue of the coins that were struck from the dies. It would be reasonable for some sort of correspondence to exist, if only to account for the exceptional complexity of the die-cutting arrangements. But where the question is so crucial, assumptions are hazardous. Experience in the well-studied field of late Anglo-Saxon numismatics may guide us here. We can imagine, by analogy with the supply of dies to a single mint from different regional die-cutting centres in the late Anglo-Saxon coinage in the south (as is demonstrable), how far astray one could be led in determining the mint-place of coins solely by the style of their dies. Because the stycas do not tell us where they were struck (even if the common-sense assumption is that they were virtually all struck in York), there is really no way around the need for evidence of where the coins were used. What this means in practice is that we need to be able to compare at least three or four large samples of coins from widely separated regions within the Northumbrian kingdom, in order to see whether any of Miss Pirie's groups show signs of being localized in their occurrence, or different from each other in their behaviour. She has, after all, made the question a pointed one, by describing the groups. If they are not localized (and most of us will need persuading), what are they? What administrative arrangements do they reflect? The basic point that needs to be given prominence is that individual moneyers drew their dies from more than one group. This is, frankly, fatal to the localization hypothesis; one would need to resort to the wildly implausible theory of peripatetic moneyers visiting fixed, but scattered, die-cutting centres. So what are the groups?

Clear-headed statistical comparisons will be needed, and the numbers of finds will have to be large enough for the margins of statistical uncertainty to be acceptable. Hoards will serve, if handled cautiously. Stray finds from a site or from a restricted region would be statistically preferable, if there were enough of them. Obviously we are all pinning our hopes and our curiosity on Bamburgh, where the excavations have yielded a rich series of coin finds. It should be possible one day to make statistically useful comparisons between the Bamburgh site-finds and the York hoards, and that should tell us whether minting was, after all, divided between different centres or whether it was all or virtually all concentrated at York. If York was the mint-place of upwards of 80 or 90 per cent of stycas, the die-groupings will perhaps prove to be of only limited interest for monetary history. If, however, minting was decentralized, some very enticing opportunities for the analysis of monetary circulation will arise. We need to know for sure, one way or another.

Perhaps I may be allowed to refer briefly to the division of Æthelred's coins between his first and second reigns. One can imagine circumstances in which the evidence of die-linkage might override the hoard-evidence, but I do not for a moment believe that such could prove to be the case in the years before and after Redwulf. The contrast between the Hexham hoard and the later hoards, and the withdrawal of all silver from the alloy, by a reform undertaken by the moneyer Eardwulf, together seem to me to be rock-solid evidence against any scheme which seeks to divide the 'first-reign' coins (as hitherto attributed) between the first and second reigns on the evidence of typology, die-links, or whatever. I would be very, very surprised if any future discoveries were to substantiate such an arrangement.

MR BOOTH: My remarks are confined to the supposed 'group' of coins which Miss Pirie classifies as 'The Early Stycas: Æthelred I, Ælfwald, and Eanred (Phases IA and IB)'. Two criticisms arise: one a general matter of methodology, and one of specific terminology.

Miss Pirie offends on occasion against an important methodological principle, in presenting possibilities and hypotheses as though they were established facts, sometimes even failing to mention the alternatives. The most important example of this is her ascription of the coins in the name of Ælfwald to Ælfwald II, whose dates she gives as *c.*806–8. She may prove to be correct in her assumptions here. But at this stage of our knowledge mention should have been made of the possibility that the coins may belong to Ælfwald I (779–88), and also of the evidence from Roger of Wendover and the Frankish Annals which point to 808–10 as more probable dates for the reign of Ælfwald II.

Elsewhere Miss Pirie asserts: 'We now know of Cuthheard as a moneyer striking in silver for three kings', and traces his career from its beginning in the reign of Æthelred I (790–6), through that of Ælfwald II and into that of Eanred (810–41). She shows no hesitation in ascribing all three groups of coins to a single man. Again she *may* be correct, but surely it remains possible that the CVDhEART of the Ælfwald coins is not the same man as the CVDHEARD who struck coins for Æthelred, and that the CVDHARD of Eanred's reign is a different person from one or both of the others. Miss Pirie is right to use the Cuthheard evidence in her attack on the tenuous assumption that 'Eanred's coinage . . . started a good while after he came to the throne'. But she should make clear that the force of this evidence (and it does have force) relies heavily on unproven assumptions about the identities of the Ælfwald and Cuthheards of the series.

The comment that Cuthheard strikes '*in silver*' for three kings, brings up a second issue: this time of interpretation and terminology. Miss Pirie's perspective here seems to show insufficient regard to the (admittedly scanty) analytical evidence, which points to a clear difference between the 'silver' of Æthelred I and that of Eanred. What metal analyses there are show a similar spread of silver values in Æthelred's moneyer's-name coins to those of the animal coins of the latter part of Eadberht's reign (738–57) and of the reigns of Alchred (765–74) and Ælfwald I (779–88). They suggest a probable official standard through most of the eighth century of more than 60 per cent silver, slipping on occasions to 50 per cent or below. Analyses of the coins of Eanred, however, *never* give a result higher than *c.*43

per cent silver, implying an initial, official standard significantly lower than that of the previous century.

Thus towards the end of the century the moneyer's-name issues of Æthelred could have circulated freely alongside the earlier animal coins. But even Eanred's earliest 'silver' coins of the 810s or 820s, are unlikely to have impressed their users as of the same metal as the coins of two or more decades earlier. It seems likely that the greater intrinsic value of the eighth-century coins ensured that they were soon hoarded out of circulation, as happened recently in the case of pre-1947 silver coins. The eighth-century and ninth-century series should thus be seen as separate. The earlier series achieved a moderately high and relatively stable metal-quality until the sudden collapse in the 790s; the later series began on a lower metal standard and thereafter moved into a drastic decline.

With these considerations in view it seems unfortunate that Miss Pirie should continue to insist so emphatically on a terminology which distinguishes 'stycas' from 'sceattas' on the grounds of their reverse design. The distinction is set out in Pirie, 1984: 'All the authorized "stycas" depict on their reverse the name of one or other of the officials responsible to the king or to the archbishop for their coinage . . . The "sceattas" themselves have the die with the king's name combined either with one portraying a prancing animal or with one recording the archbishop's name' (67–8). It is this distinction which leads Miss Pirie to list coins of Æthelred I's moneyer Eanbald separately from Æthelred's other coins, along with the earlier animal-type issues. Eanbald is assumed (without argument) to be the Archbishop, and so the coins become 'sceattas' rather than 'stycas'—a distinction which would certainly have baffled the people who made and used them.

Much more significantly, however, the issues of Æthelred's second reign, which historically and economically belong at the end of the eighth century series, are by this taxonomy tacked on to the beginning of the baser ninth-century coinage of Eanred, in a supposed 'group' of 'silver and early brass alloy' coins, or 'early stycas'. This can only confuse the historical picture. Although the adoption of the moneyer's-name reverse by Ælfwald I or Æthelred I certainly had some administrative significance, the collapse of the coinage and the change of metal-quality were undoubtedly changes of far greater historical and economic importance. To impose an artificial modern terminology upon the coins, which gives prominence to the earlier change of design at the expense of the later change of metal quality, is to risk replacing the actual processes of history with a purely abstract numismatic structuralism.

A simple answer to this whole problem would be to abandon the modern mystificatory jargon of 'sceattas' and 'stycas' altogether, and to speak only about different kinds of 'early pennies', or simply 'coins'.

PLATE 6

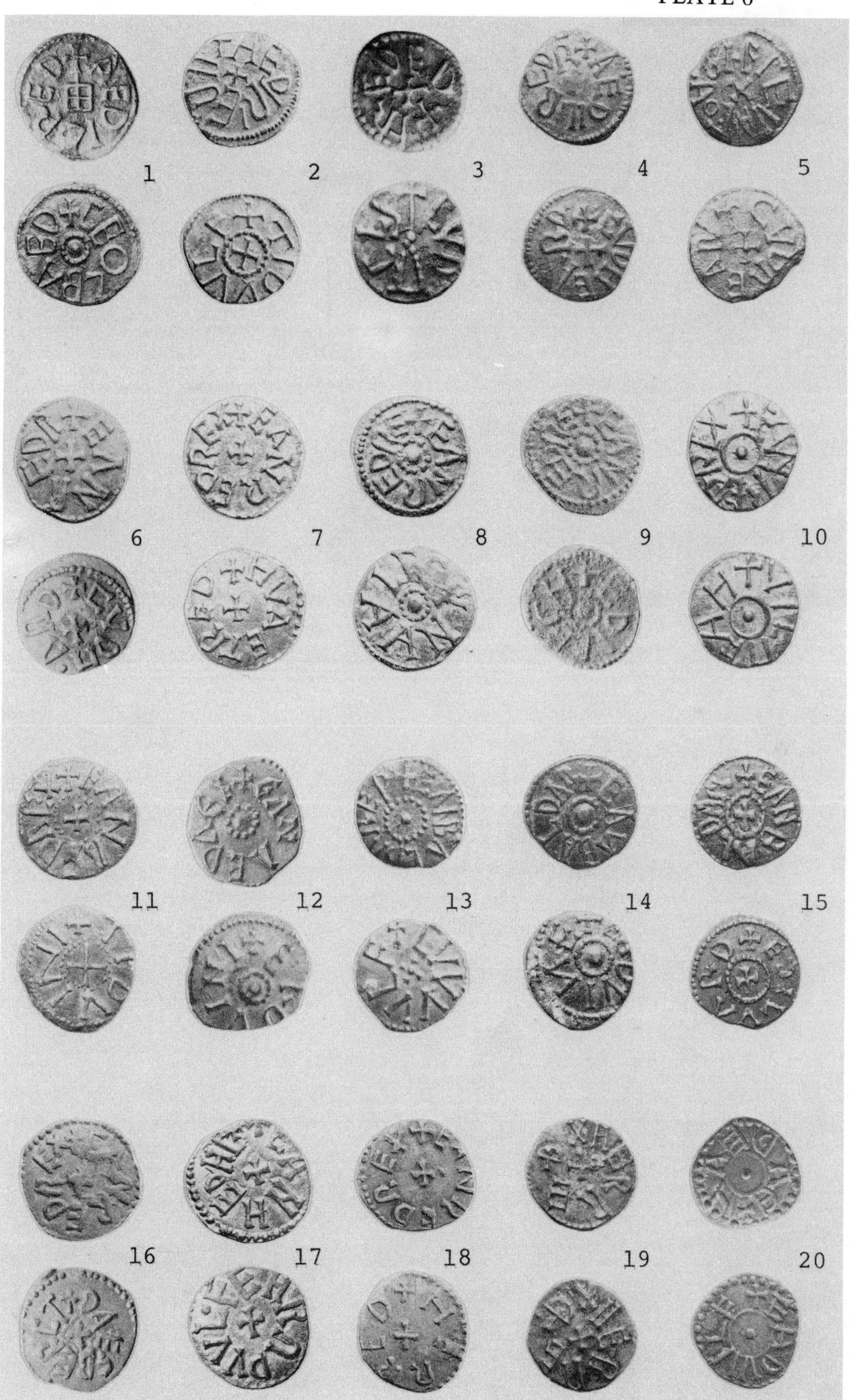

PLATE 7

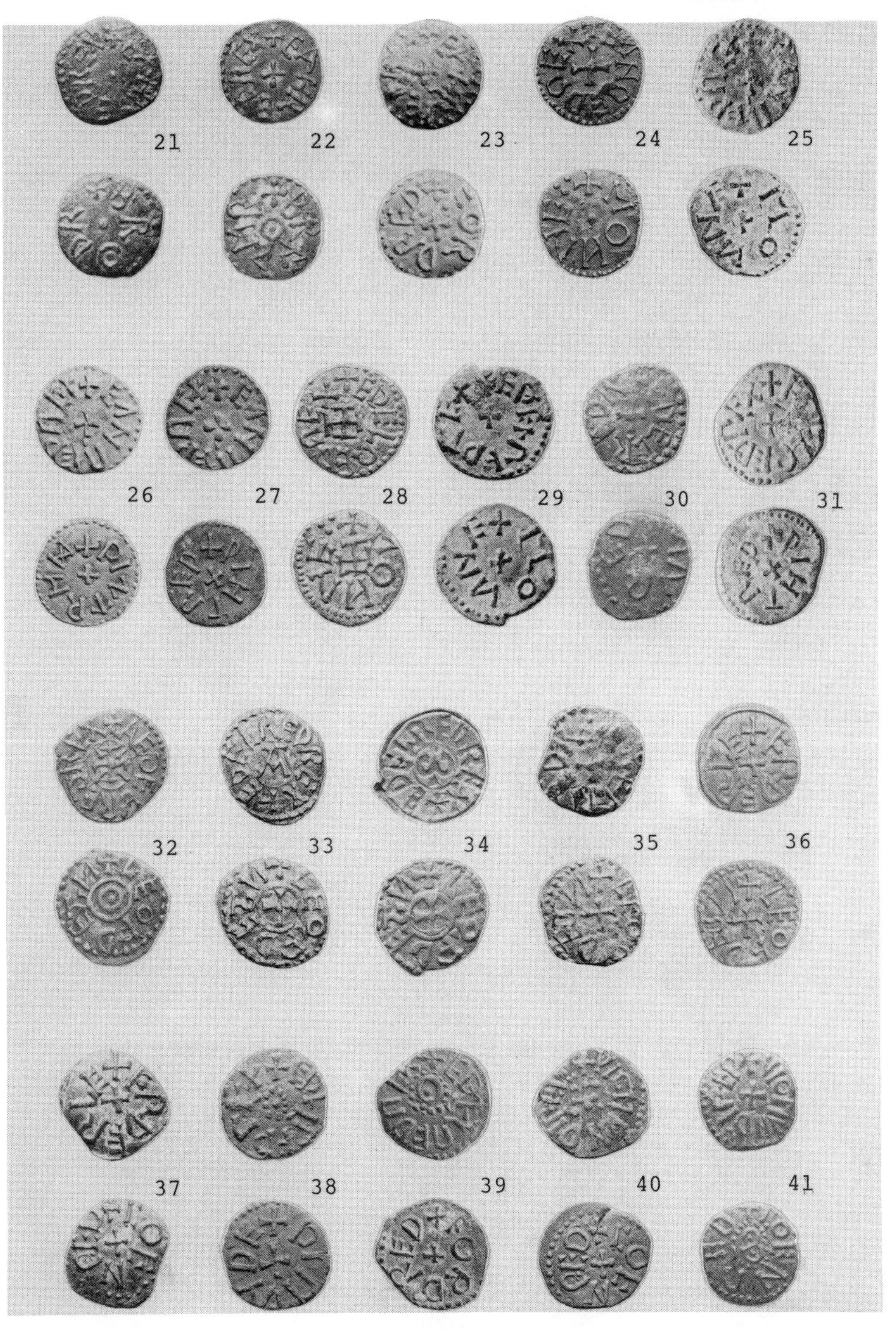

PLATE 8

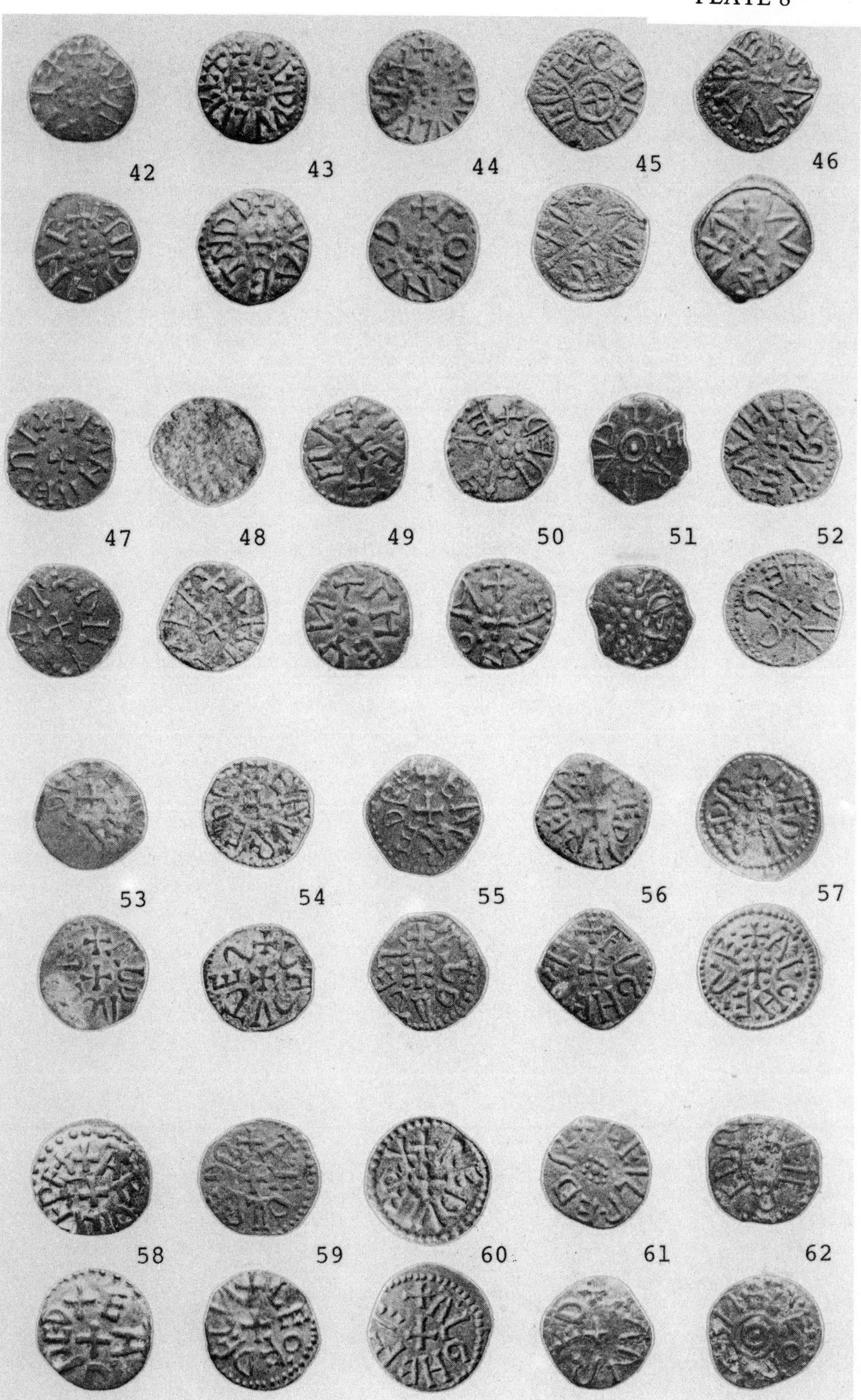

PLATE 9

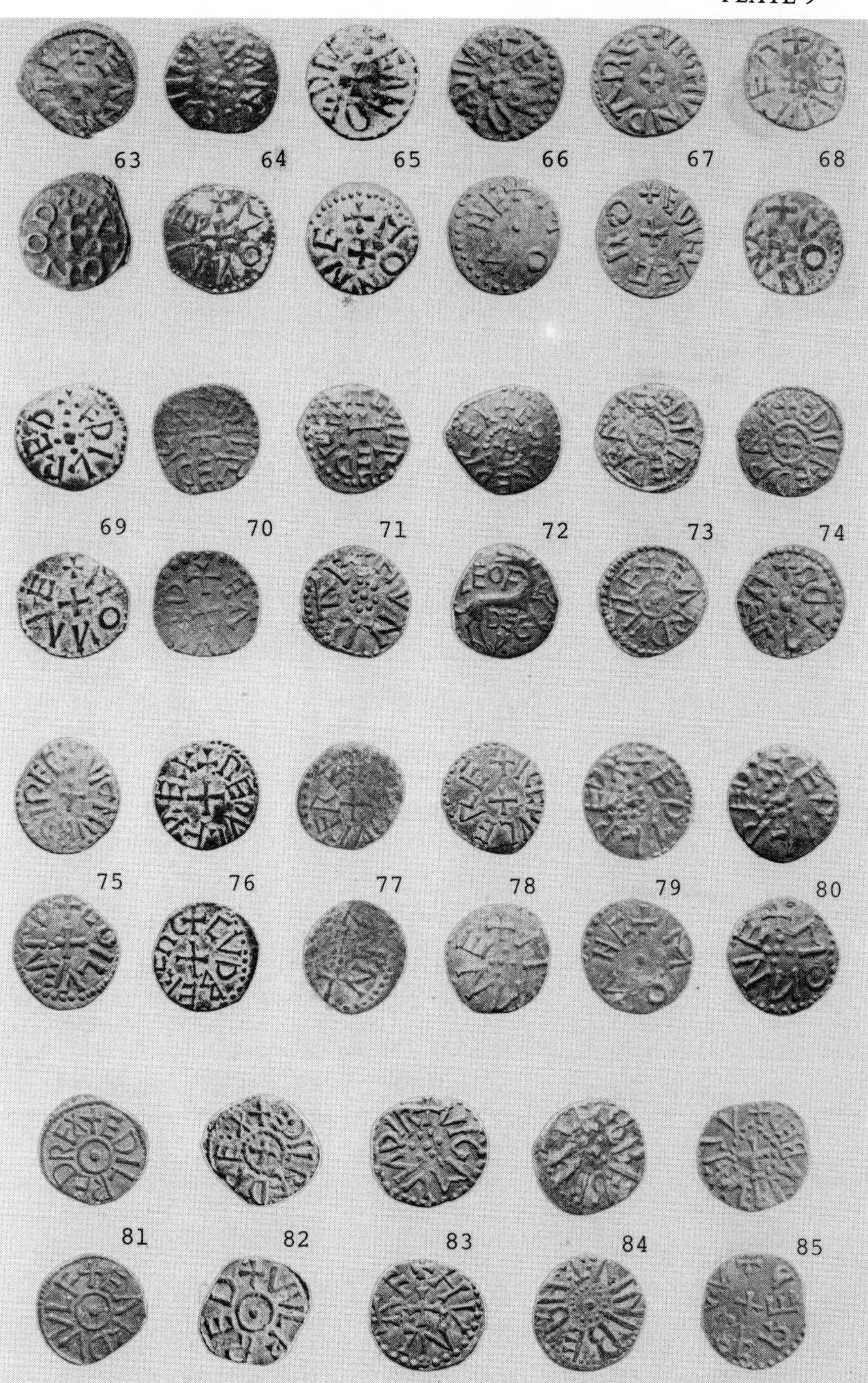

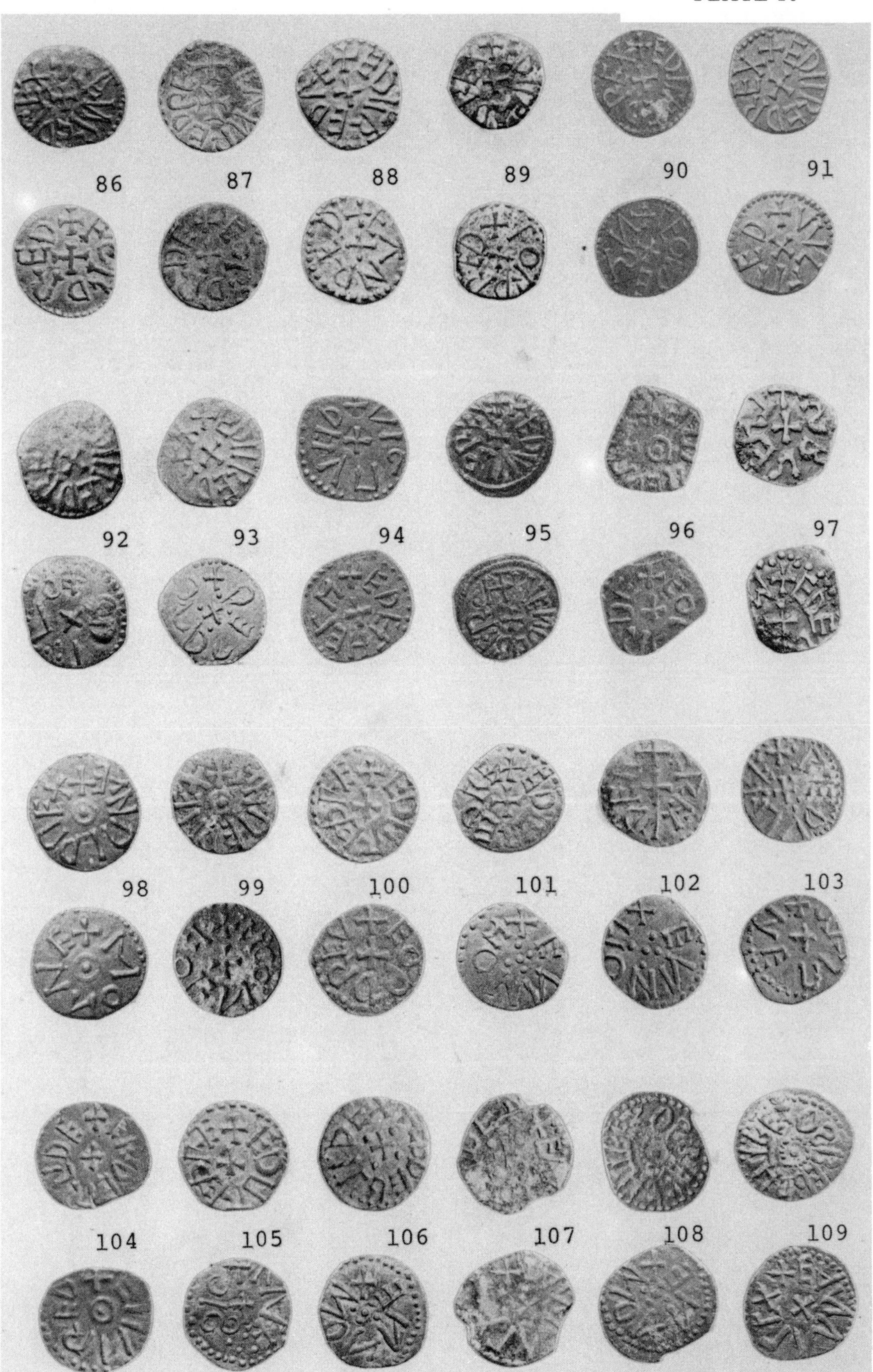
86
87
88
89
90
91
92
93
94
95
96
97
98
99
100
101
102
103
104
105
106
107
108
109

PLATE 11

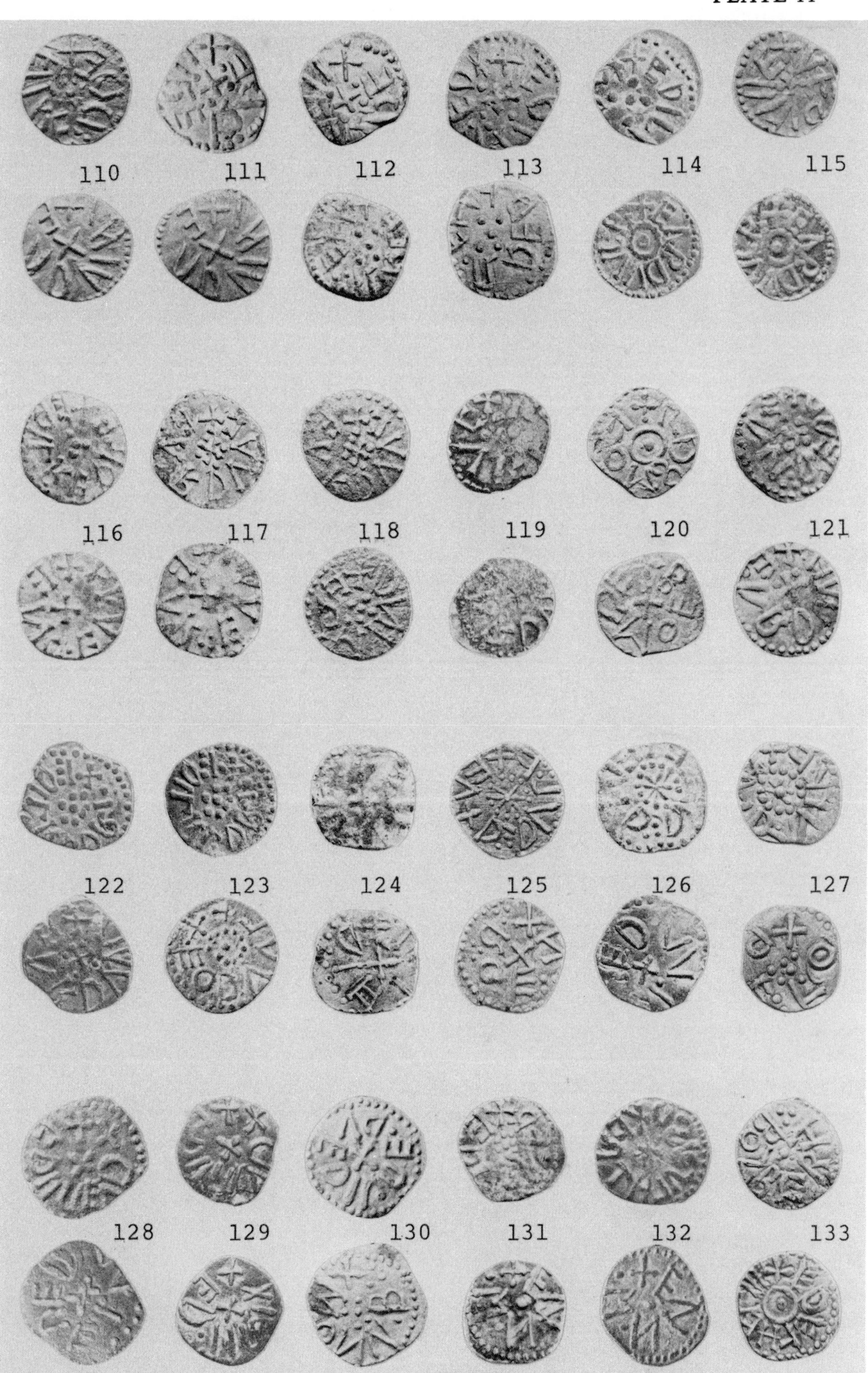
110
111
112
113
114
115
116
117
118
119
120
121
122
123
124
125
126
127
128
129
130
131
132
133

Some thoughts on the hoard evidence for the Northumbrian styca coinage

H. E. PAGAN

IT WAS the discovery of a hoard of ninth-century Northumbrian coins at Ripon some time in the early summer of 1695 that first drew the attention of scholars to the Northumbrian series as such. The hoard contained coins spanning the reigns of Northumbrian kings from Eanred to Osberht, and it was the first of a series of such hoards that have come to light over the last three centuries. Its composition cannot now be reconstructed in exact detail, but Elizabeth Pirie has been able to bring together evidence to show that it resembled other hoards in ending more or less at the point when the Northumbrian styca coinage itself ends:[1] that is to say, it included a sufficient spread of coins in the names of Osberht and of contemporary or near-contemporary coins with derivative or blundered inscriptions to suggest that although it may not have contained every last variety of these late issues, the coins that it did contain were a fair cross-section of them. If it did differ in any substantial respect from other comparative hoards, it was in being somewhat more heavily weighted towards these late issues, for among some 112 relevant coins in the collections of Archbishop Sharp and Ralph Thoresby only six were of Eanred,[2] and the preponderance of later and less intelligible coins in it was such that it left the scholars into whose hands the coins came in considerable doubt as to their identification. Sir Andrew Fountaine, writing a decade later and relying almost entirely on coins from the the Ripon hoard for his knowledge of the series, was not indeed able to isolate the separate issues of individual Northumbrian rulers, and had to group all under the general heading of coins struck by kings or—his word—'satraps' of Northumbria.[3] It was no doubt also the preponderance of late issues that caused Thoresby and Archdeacon Nicolson to speak of the styca coinage as a brass coinage rather than as a copper coinage as they might have, had the hoard contained more of the superficially copper coins of Eanred and of Æthelred II's first reign.[4] One can thus not unreasonably see the Ripon hoard as one deposited at or near the close of the period during which the

[1] Elizabeth J. E. Pirie, 'The Ripon hoard, 1695: contemporary and current interest', *BNJ* 52 (1982), 84–103.

[2] Pirie, loc.cit., 87, 91. It is not necessarily the case that all these 112 coins derived from the Ripon hoard, but the great majority doubtless did.

[3] A. Fountaine, *Numismata Anglo-Saxonica & Anglo-Danica breviter illustrata*, Oxford, 1705, p.182.

[4] Nicolson writes of 'your late discovered brass coins' in a letter to Thoresby of 1 August 1696 (Pirie, op.cit., 85), and entries relating to coins from the Ripon hoard in Thoresby's museum accession book refer to 'small brass Saxon stycas' and 'Saxon brass coins' (Pirie, op.cit., n.13 on pp.98–9).

Northumbrians used stycas and as containing a higher proportion than usual of recently struck coin.[5]

Most of the hoards that have come to light since have likewise ended with coins of Osberht, and their evidential value is rather collective than individual, for our state of knowledge about the coinage is not profound enough to draw useful distinctions between hoards of such broadly similar composition, and our knowledge of the hoards is in any case patchy. The most significant of the hoards are one from Kirkoswald, in Cumbria, found in 1808;[6] one found on a site near St Mary's Abbey, York, in 1831;[7] a very large hoard found in St Leonard's Place, York, in 1842;[8] and two large hoards from Bolton Percy, on the River Wharfe between York and Tadcaster, found respectively in 1847 and 1967 but perhaps originally parts of one and the same concealed sum of money.[9]

Of these hoards, we have a full publication of the only recent one, the 1967 Bolton Percy hoard. Various lists were made of parcels from the York 1842 hoard and the Bolton Percy hoard of 1847 at the time of their discovery, and although these give only a general idea of the hoards' contents, one of the parcels from the 1847 hoard turned up in its entirety at a Christie's sale in April 1981 and Elizabeth Pirie has published the 469 coins involved.[10] Beyond that, 322 of the original 360 coins from the York 1831 hoard survive at Stonyhurst and a parcel of 39 coins still remains together from the Kirkoswald hoard. We are thus potentially not too badly placed in assessing the range of varieties present in each hoard. Statistical comparison of the hoards is much more difficult, for the Christie's parcel from the 1847 Bolton Percy hoard is a parcel specially picked out by a contemporary collector and consequently not a random selection from the hoard, and selectivity may have had its impact also on the surviving parcels at Stonyhurst and

[5] In her reconstruction of the hoard Miss Pirie identifies all but one of the stycas illustrated by Fountaine which had not previously been illustrated in other publications with specimens belonging either to Thoresby or to Sharp. This is probably not altogether correct, for Fountaine states that Nicolson supplied him with 'nummos haud paucos, cum ex aere tum ex argento conflatos' for illustration on his plates, and a proportion of these must have been stycas (Fountaine, op.cit., 166). It serves however rather to confirm the general picture of the hoard given by Miss Pirie than to impair it, for it is an indication that there must have been close correspondence between the coins from the hoard possessed by Nicolson and those possessed by Thoresby and Sharp. For evidence that Nicolson's stycas came from the Ripon hoard see his letter to Thoresby of 25 Nov. 1695, in whcih he thanks Thoresby for giving him 'half a score coins of our old Northumbrian kings' (*Letters of Eminent Men, Addressed to Ralph Thoresby, F.R.S.*, 1832, vol. i, 220); his letter to Edward Lloyd of 25 Jan. 1696/7, in which he states that he has 'a score of the latter metal [sc. brass], found in Yorkshire' (*Letters ... to and from William Nicolson, D.D.*, ed. J. Nichols, 1809, vol. i, 54); and a passage in his *English Historical Library* in which he records that parcels of coins from the Ripon hoard had been distributed to various interested persons by the local landowner Sir Edward Blackett Bt., a fact which Nicolson would presumably only have bothered to record if he had been (via Thoresby) the ultimate gainer from such benevolence.

[6] E. J. E. Pirie, 'Finds of sceattas and stycas of Northumbria', in M. A. S. Blackburn, ed., *Anglo-Saxon Monetary History, Essays in Memory of Michael Dolley*, 1986, pp.67–90 (find no.96 at pp.81–2).

[7] Pirie, loc.cit., 1986, find no.33 at p.75.

[8] Pirie, loc.cit., 1986, find no.36 at p.76.

[9] Pirie, loc.cit., 1986, finds nos.40, 41 at p.76. For the 1967 Bolton Percy hoard see H. E. Pagan, 'The Bolton Percy hoard of 1967', *BNJ* 43 (1973), 1–44.

[10] E. J. E. Pirie, 'Early Northumbrian coins at auction, 1981', *BNJ* 51 (1981), 32–51.

Kirkoswald.[11] Nor is it as yet possible to describe the content of each hoard in an uniform manner, for we have not quite arrived at a consensus about which of the coins in the later part of the series are official regal issues and which are not, and we have not devised an effective numismatic shorthand with which to describe imitative and irregular pieces. All therefore that one can do at the moment is to tabulate the relative proportions of coins of each broad category in the 1967 Bolton Percy hoard, in the Christie's parcel from the 1847 Bolton Percy hoard, and in the Stonyhurst coins that survive from the 1831 York hoard, and see how the figures look.[12]

	Bolton Percy 1967 (%)	*Bolton Percy 1847 (%)*	*York 1831 (%)*
Eanred	12.0	13.4	10.7
Æthelred (1st reign)	33.7	35.2	39.2
Redwulf	2.1	1.3	2.5
Æthelred (2nd reign)	9.2	6.8	7.8
Osberht	4.2	3.8	2.8
Derivative regal	22.4	26.6	21.2
Abp Eanbald	0.2	—	—
Abp Wigmund	12.0	10.2	14.0
Abp Wulfhere	0.8	1.1	2.2
Not classified	3.2	1.6	—

It is not sensible to build too much on individual figures, or on the variations between them, but the picture that all three columns present is that some 60% of the content of these hoards was made up by regular regal and archiepiscopal coins struck in the reign of Eanred, the first reign of Æthelred and the reign of Redwulf, while the balance was made up by later regal and archiepiscopal coins in the names of Æthelred, Osberht, and Archbishop Wulfhere, accounting for some 13 or 14% of the total, and by a large group of late issues with derivative types and inscriptions, accounting for somewhere around a fifth or a quarter of the total depending on the hoard.

These figures look rather different from the admittedly much less reliable figures that can be calculated on the same basis for the Ripon hoard, where only some 22% of the coins belonging to Sharp and Thoresby were of the Eanred to Redwulf period and the rest were of the later period of coinage. The most likely cause of this is not that the Ripon hoard was deposited later than the other hoards,

[11] The Kirkoswald parcel is evidently a residue left after the remainder of the hoard had been dispersed. As for the coins at Stonyhurst, Miss Pirie believes that the hoard came to Stonyhurst in its entirety, and the only point at issue is whether the coins that have gone missing since included a disproportionate number of coins of scarcer varieties.

[12] The figures given for the 1967 Bolton Percy hoard are those that can be extracted from Table 1 on pp.3–4 of Pagan, 1973, loc.cit. Those for the 1847 hoard have been calculated from the data given by Pirie, 1981, loc.cit., with some adjustment to bring her arrangement of the coins into line with that adopted for the 1967 hoard. The figures for the York hoard are taken without much adjustment from the summary given by Pirie, 1986, loc.cit.

for it does not seem to have contained anything that is not in the other hoards, but that, as suggested earlier, it was a sum of relatively recently struck coin and had less of a savings or accumulated treasure element than the hoards from York and Bolton Percy.

This leaves for discussion the one remaining substantial hoard of stycas, namely the Hexham hoard. On 15 October 1832 a hoard of some 8,000 Northumbrian coins of the ninth century, preserved in a bronze bucket of the same period, came to light while a grave was being dug outside the north transept of Hexham Abbey. About 5,000 of these were seen by the Newcastle solicitor and antiquary John Adamson, and it is on his published account of the hoard in *Archaeologia*[13] that one must chiefly depend. What he says in the text of his article is not in fact of much use, but the plates which illustrate it carry accurate representations of 944 of the coins found and these are sufficiently numerous and selected with such apparent care that scholars have felt able to rely on them as evidence for the range of coins contained in the hoard as a whole. It may be that Adamson failed to illustrate the occasional coin of significance for the hoard's dating or for the chronology of the styca series, but if one wishes to argue that any particular interesting variety of coin was present in the hoard although not illustrated by Adamson, the case for this must be made out properly.[14]

The Hexham hoard is of central importance for the styca series, for it is the only styca hoard of any size to have been deposited in the reign of a king other than Osberht. We can work out that its date of deposit was some time in the second reign of Æthelred, for it contained no coins of Osberht or of Archbishop Wulfhere or of a late grouping of coins in the name of Æthelred by the moneyers Eanwulf and Monne which die-link with coins of Osberht; and we do in fact know what the latest coins of Æthelred present in the hoard were. Adamson's plates, as well as illustrating no fewer than 384 coins of the main phase of Æthelred's coinage, during which responsibility for its manufacture was shared between several moneyers, illustrate just 11 coins belonging to a new phase of coinage in which responsibility essentially rested with the moneyer Eardwulf only.

I speak of a new phase of coinage because one can demonstrate that these 11 coins belong to a new phase of coinage by arguments quite independent of those tending to show that they belong to a new reign. The main evidence that a new phase of the coinage is involved is the fact that whereas Adamson's plates illustrate a full range of coins of all Æthelred's other moneyers (leaving aside the coins of Eanwulf and Monne just referred to), they illustrate only a portion of the known varieties of coins struck by this particular moneyer Eardwulf, and that portion is in no sense a random selection from his output, for it has at its core coins struck from a well-defined grouping of dies of neat style, usually with small, carefully executed lettering and with beaded inner circles. This group accounts for five of the nine coins of Eardwulf that Adamson illustrates (nos.85–7, 89–90 on his plates). He illustrates two other coins which are struck from a similar obverse die

[13] J. Adamson, 'An account of the discovery at Hexham... of a brass vessel containing a number of the Anglo-Saxon coins called stycas', *Archaeologia* 25 (1834), 279–310.

[14] See the remarks by the present writer, *BNJ* 52 (1982), 253–4.

but are from crudely cut reverse dies with retrograde legends reading respectively 'Fordred' and 'Aeilred R' (nos.124, 314). The four remaining illustrated coins of Eardwulf divide into two of not dissimilar character but which have plain inner circles on each side (no.84 and Supplement no.22), and two with less carefully executed obverse dies (nos.88, 91). These last two coins belong to a grouping of dies well represented in all the later hoards, and it is clear that the reason why Adamson was able to illustrate only two dies of this grouping was that the Hexham hoard was deposited at an early date within the new phase of coinage when only the first few of these less carefully executed dies had come into use. Just to underline this, the 1967 Bolton Percy hoard contained, alongside 598 main-phase coins of Æthelred, as many as 149 coins of Eardwulf; these were struck from 41 obverse dies of which only some 4 or 5 are dies that had been used to strike coins present in the Hexham hoard.

One ground for supposing that all these coins belong to a new phase of Æthelred's coinage is thus that whereas Hexham contains a complete range of the coins of the coinage's main phase, it contains only a chronologically early instalment of those carrying the name of the moneyer Eardwulf.

It is not the only ground for supposing that these coins belong to a new phase of coinage. First, the grouping of coins is essentially a grouping of coins struck by this one moneyer Eardwulf only. It is true that an obverse die used by Eardwulf is found, as already noted, with crude reverse dies reading 'Fordred' and 'Aeilred R', and obverse dies used by Eardwulf are also found with a crude reverse die reading 'Odilo' and one or two reverse dies of good style reading 'Wulfred'; but there are other instances of styca die-cutters cutting reverse dies in the names of moneyers who were not in fact working at the time that the dies were cut,[15] and I attach no importance to the 'Fordred', 'Odilo' and 'Aeilred R' reverse dies, which have no matching obverse dies and were obviously intended for use with an obverse die or dies cut for Eardwulf. Wulfræd is a little more puzzling, and it may be that for a brief moment he worked alongside Eardwulf.[16] It is however quite certain that Eardwulf is the only substantive moneyer in this grouping, and this is in sharp contrast with the manner in which responsibility for the regal coinage can be seen to have been divided among some nine or ten moneyers only just beforehand; Redwulf's coinage had been struck by as many as ten moneyers, and a similar number of Æthelred's earlier moneyers seem to have worked concurrently. The obvious deduction is that the striking of these coins of Eardwulf coincided with a reform in the manner in which the striking of the coinage was organized, and that from this point onwards we are in a new phase of coinage.

This deduction is supported by the appearance of the Eardwulf coins themselves. The important ingredient in their design is not their typology, for

[15] On an occasion in Æthelred's reign a die-cutter cut more or less simultaneously reverse dies in the names of seven different moneyers, of whom one, Coenræd, was not a regal moneyer at the time (Pagan, 1973, loc. cit., 7).

[16] Wulfræd's career presents problems, for although coins of a moneyer Wulfræd exist for Eanred, for the main phase of Æthelred's coinage, for its Eardwulf phase (the coins discussed here), and for Archbishop Wulfhere, there is no continuity from any of these groups to the next one chronologically.

they carry a variety of central features on obverse and reverse, but the fact that on every single Eardwulf coin illustrated by Adamson—and indeed on the majority of Eardwulf's coins viewed as a whole—the central feature on obverse or reverse, be it cross, pellet, or star, is separated from the surrounding inscription by an inner circle. One might well imagine that this was standard practice on stycas generally, but one has to go back to the coinage struck for Archbishop Eanbald II in Eanred's reign to find a series where inner circles on both sides of the coin are customary, and it seems apparent, coupling the use of inner circles on Eardwulf's dies with the very neat style of those dies that are earliest, that the organizational reform that gave Eardwulf his dominant role as a moneyer was joined with a new approach to the way in which the dies were designed. Design standards can be seen to fall away as this phase of coinage progresses, but that should not obscure what does seem to have been a moment of uplift on the design front.[17]

So much for the arguments for treating these coins as belonging to a separate phase of the coinage. When Stewart Lyon and I worked on the styca series, respectively in the mid 1950s and at the end of the 1960s, we both took the view that the main phase of Æthelred's coinage should be identified as the coinage of his first reign and that one should attribute to the second reign what can be called the Eardwulf phase of coinage. It is not however strictly necessary that the administrative reorganization that gave rise to the Eardwulf phase should have coincided with the start of Æthelred's second-reign coinage, and it is theoretically feasible that instead of attributing the whole of the main phase of Æthelred's coinage to his first reign, one could attribute part of it to his first reign and part of it to the first year or two of his second reign, leaving the Eardwulf phase of coinage to occupy only the later years of the second reign. To do this, a way would have to be found of distinguishing those coins of the main phase of Æthelred's coinage that precede the coinage of Redwulf from those which follow it. One should not dismiss the possibility of being able to achieve this, for some of the numerous Æthelred–Redwulf die-links that exist may turn out on closer examination to be Redwulf–Æthelred die-links, i.e. die-links where a shared reverse die was used with a Redwulf obverse die before it was used with an Æthelred obverse die.

What speaks a little against the probability of Æthelred's main-phase coinage falling into separate pre- and post-Redwulf portions is that Redwulf's moneyers include two, Cuthbeorht and Hwætnoth, who do not coin for Æthelred at all, while they exclude Æthelred's most prolific main phase moneyer, Leofthegn. This is readily explicable if all Æthelred's main-phase coins precede Redwulf's, in which case Cuthbeorht and Hwætnoth may be seen as replacements in Redwulf's reign for Leofthegn or for any other moneyer of Æthelred no longer active at the time Redwulf became king, but is not so easy to account for if Redwulf's coinage is to be sandwiched between two groups of Æthelred's main-phase coins. Redwulf's coinage is indeed tightly die-linked internally by the sharing of obverse dies between moneyers and tightly die-linked to Æthelred's coinage by

[17] Additionally, Michael Metcalf and Peter Northover show elsewhere in this volume that at this stage in the coinage there was a reform of its alloy: the new coins by Eardwulf mark the deliberate abandonment of any attempt to include silver in the coinage metal.

shared reverse dies, and if there was in fact a further period of Æthelred's main-phase coinage after Æthelred's recovery of power it is a little puzzling that the new moneyers Cuthbeorht and Hwætnoth do not participate in it.[18]

What certainly seems unlikely is that the main-phase coinage can be divided into a first-reign group and a second-reign group on the basis of obverse and reverse type. In the immediately preceding period, at the end of the reign of Eanred, it is apparent that one moneyer, Brother, uses a majority of dies carrying pellet and pellet-in-circle designs at the same time as other moneyers are employing dies with cross designs; while another Eanred moneyer, Monne, most of whose dies carry cross designs, mixes with them a substantial minority of dies carrying pellet-in-circle designs. From this point in Eanred's reign onwards there is a continuous flow of coinage right down to the time when the coinage is reorganized and its design rethought at the beginning of the Eardwulf phase of coinage, and there is no point at which one can prove any conscious attempt at getting all the moneyers to strike coins with the same design.

It is of course the case that most of Redwulf's coins are struck from dies carrying small crosses or crosses of pellets, but to my mind this is no more than an incidental consequence of the dies having been cut by the same hand at roughly the same point in time, and there was certainly no intention to restrict Redwulf's coinage to cross designs, for there exist Redwulf obverse dies for the moneyer Coenræd carrying the design of a single pellet within a beaded circle, and the moneyer Monne uses reverses with pellet designs in conjunction with cross-design Redwulf obverses.

I have argued in the past in connection with the later coins of Eanred that the small variations in obverse inscription that occur between dies used by one moneyer and dies used by a colleague reflect a wish to distinguish which dies should be used by which moneyer, and thus that variations of this nature are not evidence that particular dies were cut by different die-cutters but rather evidence that they all derived from a common source.[19] With Æthelred's main-phase coinage the position is much more complex, and the dies used by one moneyer, Leofthegn, certainly include a proportion supplied by a die-cutter who at that time was cutting dies for Leofthegn only; but I think notwithstanding that during the main-phase coinage much of the diversity in obverse inscription and type that occurs is, as under Eanred, not evidence that the dies involved were cut in different workshops or at different periods of time, but evidence of a single die-cutting workshop veering between variety and uniformity in design as it cut groups of dies in rapid succession for distribution between up to ten different moneyers.

Variety and uniformity in coin design are in a sense, if I may put a metaphor to more pointed use than usual, different sides of the same coin; for, while uniformity can only really be achieved if one die-cutting workshop is responsible for an entire issue, so also really effective variation in design is most readily

[18] Cuthbeorht and Hwætnoth may appear and then disappear because they were appointees of Redwulf and were ousted on Æthelred's restoration, but it remains to be established that outside political events would have had this sort of effect on the personnel of the Northumbrian mint.

[19] Pagan, 1973, loc.cit., 6.

feasible where the varying is being done by one workshop and care can be taken that dies cut at one time are differentiated from dies cut at another time.

The Hexham hoard also tells us more than the other hoards do about the coinage that had circulated in Northumbria in the reign of Eanred. Eanred's coinage divides fairly neatly into an early series struck from an alloy containing a reasonably good proportion of silver; an intermediate group of coins struck by a few of the same moneyers but in a more debased alloy; and a late series struck in a brass alloy containing much less silver by a new team of moneyers. On Adamson's plates illustrations of coins of the early series and of the intermediate group reckoned together number 156 against 161 illustrations of coins of the late series. These figures contrast very sharply with the figures from the 1967 Bolton Percy hoard, which contained just one early and four intermediate coins against 208 of the late series. As we have seen, the Bolton Percy hoard seems to have contained more of a savings or accumulated element than the Ripon hoard, and it is clear from it that by Osberht's reign no meaningful amount of Eanred's silver coinage survived even in a hoard with a savings element.

This disappearance of Eanred's silver coins has had the effect of making them seem a smaller and less significant ingredient in the ninth-century coinage of Northumbria than was in fact the case, and it now seems to me more likely than it did fifteen years ago that Eanred's silver coinage could have extended over a substantial period of time. If it did, there is a much stronger case for supposing that the silver coins struck by a small number of moneyers for a king Æthelred are coins of the late-eighth century king of that name rather than coins of a historically unrecorded king filling a gap between Eardwulf and Eanred.[20] A detailed scholarly study of Eanred's coinage is necessary—I began such a study in the 1960s but was distracted from it by the discovery of the 1967 Bolton Percy hoard—and this is not the place to discuss it in detail, but in the context of the Hexham hoard one may legitimately note the oddity of the fact that although Eanred's silver coinage had been replaced by a more debased coinage some measurable time before the end of Eanred's reign, and further time had elapsed between the end of Eanred's reign and the date of the hoard's deposit, Eanred's silver coins were still relatively well represented among the coins found at Hexham.

One can indulge in speculation about Bernician coin users having a positive attachment to silver coin, just as Maria Theresa thalers have long been the preferred currency in parts of East Africa, but the probability is rather that Bernicia was backward economically and that the circulation of coinage in it was really rather slow, so that the religious community at Hexham might well in Æthelred's second reign still have been keeping coins in their money box which had disappeared from circulation further south.[21]

It is here where may lie part of the solution to a remaining problem presented by the Hexham hoard. The 944 coins illustrated on Adamson's plates divide into

[20] This suggestion can be found e.g. in the present writer's contribution to D. P. Kirby, ed., *Saint Wilfrid at Hexham*, 1974, at p.188.

[21] For the hint that the Hexham bucket should be regarded as a money box rather than anything more sophisticated see the remarks by Mr R. N. Bailey in Kirby, ed., op.cit., 1974, at p.150.

755 coins of Northumbrian kings, 139 coins of archbishops of York, and 50 which it is easiest to describe as 'imitative'. Some of these fifty coins carry inscriptions directly echoing those on silver coins of Eanred by such moneyers as 'Herred' (Hereræd), but the majority carry inscriptions which are meaningless and appear indeed to be deliberately meaningless. Imitative coins of this particular nature are scarcely found in other hoards, and Miss Pirie has quite rightly raised the possibility that this is because these particular imitations are of Bernician origin; others of this nature have turned up in the excavations at Bamburgh, and that might serve as supporting evidence. It may be that this is correct, and I have no hard evidence to set against it. At the same time these imitations evidently belong in the main to Eanred's reign, both on grounds of fabric and because their inscriptions, meaningless though they are, mirror a short king's name such as Eanred rather than the slightly longer name of Æthelred. If so, many were already some years old when the Hexham hoard was deposited, and their survival in numbers in Hexham and virtual absence from the later hoards can be ascribed not just to the fact that the Hexham hoard was deposited before the other hoards but also to the slower circulation of currency in Bernicia, and may have nothing whatever to do with where they were struck.

One complicating factor, as I understand it, is that a die or dies used in the manufacture of the Hexham group of imitative coins was also used in a die-chain belonging to a quite different phase of imitative coinage struck during the second reign of Æthelred or later.[22] We must await publication of the die-link involved, but it seems in principle not inconceivable that it stems from the reuse of a die or dies that had lain idle for a number of years.

It will be apparent from the general drift of my remarks that I do not think that the arrangement of the styca coinage is in essence a matter of difficulty. There are areas within it that are of very considerable complexity—the late imitative series dating from the second reign of Æthelred and the reign of Osberht especially so—and the discovery of a hoard of any sort deposited during the early part of Eanred's reign would cast a flood of light on how we are to arrange his silver coinage. But bafflement about the obscurest areas of the coinage should not distract us from the fact that from the commencement of Eanred's brass coinage to the point in Osberht's reign where the coinages of Osberht and Archbishop Wulfhere stop we have a relatively straightforward sequence of official regal and archiepiscopal issues.

The absolute chronology of the ninth-century Northumbrian series falls outside the boundaries of the present paper, but if for the sake of argument we accept the division of Æthelred's reign into two periods of roughly four years each separated by a brief reign for Redwulf, and attribute the main-phase coinage to the first period and the remaining coins to the second period, we are hypothesizing that a very great volume of coin was produced within a relatively short period of time. In such a scenario it seems perfectly understandable, especially where the main-phase coinage is concerned, that in meeting production

[22] See Pirie, 1981, loc.cit., at p.41, where she refers to "York style specimens—nonsense legends; die-linked examples from the group represented by these specimens are among the irregulars known from the Hexham hoard".

requirements dies were cut and distributed, and coins struck, in a speedier and less well organized fashion than had been the case in Eanred's reign. In the circumstances it would not seem of enormous consequence whether one group of dies within each of these periods was cut earlier than a comparable group, and any current uncertainty on such points should not be unduly disturbing.

The hoard evidence does not at present assist us with the coinage of Osberht, but one may properly conclude this review of the material by saying just a little on that subject. When Stewart Lyon studied the styca series in the mid 1950s, he did not do more in connection with the coinage of Osberht than to note how relatively small the coinage was and to argue from the pattern of external and internal die-linkage that its duration must have been short.[23] In the mid 1980s nothing has changed so far as the evidence for the coinage is concerned, for no meaningful new varieties of it have turned up, and the number of dies employed to strike it remains small. What is however now more apparent is that the coinage does not form one single unit, but falls into four distinct groupings: coins by the moneyers Eanwulf and Monne which can be seen to belong to the start of Osberht's reign because they die-link with coins of Æthelred by the same moneyers; coins by the moneyer Æthelhelm; coins by the moneyer Winebeorht; and coins by the moneyer 'Wulfsixt' (Wulfsige). This allows a number of choices as to how coinage production in Osberht's reign was organized. It is clear that initially coin production was shared between Eanwulf and Monne and that they then ceased production. My own current view is that the remaining moneyers then operated in succession to each other rather than as a college of moneyers sharing production between them. If so, they probably succeeded each other quite quickly, for none of them produced any substantial amount of coin, but the coinage might none the less have extended a little further into Osberht's reign than recent scholarship has suggested, and that would make it more possible that Archbishop Wulfhere became archbishop and had his coinage struck at a point some five years into Osberht's reign, as the traditional chronology for ninth-century Northumbria requires. It does not seem to me that the extant coins of the archbishop need date, either on grounds of style or on the evidence of die-linkage, to the same point in the series as the latest coins of Æthelred and the earliest coins of Osberht; and we need not be over-influenced in this context by the die-link which Lyon published connecting coins of Osberht and Archbishop Wulfhere with a coin of Æthelred, for although the Æthelred coin is of relatively accomplished workmanship it does not belong to any regular grouping of coins in Æthelred's name and might reasonably be classed with the late imitative series.

DISCUSSION

Miss Pirie: Mr Pagan has argued that the tendency under Redwulf for the cross motif to dominate is the result of the die-cutting having been the work of one hand

[23] C. S. S. Lyon, 'A reappraisal of the sceatta and styca coinage of Northumbria', *BNJ* 28 (1955–8), 227–42, at 234–5.

during a short period. This can hardly be so: there are indications that more than one die-cutter *was* involved. If there had been a single craftsman at work, one would not expect to find the difference in spelling which gives the king's name as REDVLF and as REDVVLF; the latter form is used only for the totally independent moneyers, Wendelbeorht and Hwætnoth, and for Coenræd on the occasion when he worked alone. One would not find, either, six instances of retrograde obverses, (two for Forthræd and four for Monne—see 'Phases and groups', Fig.1, Ciii). There were clearly several hands at work on the dies. Cross motifs, in one form or another, dominate the coinage. Of seventy-nine dies recorded for Redwulf's principal issues (28 obverses and 51 reverses), only four show *other* designs: three dies have a central rosette of four pellets and one has no more than a single pellet. The rosette motifs are used only by those moneyers who normally work for Wigmund, namely Coenræd and Hunlaf. For the time when he works alone, Coenræd's two obverses bear this cluster of pellets; the dies' legends use REDVVLF as the spelling of the king's name, rather than the more usual REDVLF. Although each obverse is used with a pair of reverses, there is no link from this work to any other. Hunlaf, by contrast, has a rosette-reverse which is known also in combination with a pellet-obverse for Æthelred. The circumstances of his using the die for Redwulf may be exceptional, for the relevant obverse is shared with three other moneyers—Cuthbeorht, Eanræd and Forthræd.

DR. METCALF: Some bare statistics have been preserved about the Kirkoswald hoard of 1808, and it is perhaps worth looking at them in the light of Mr Pagan's tabular analysis. Adamson lists a parcel of 542 coins, as follows (with percentages added):

Eanred	99	18.3%
Æthelred II	350	64.6%
Redwulf	14	2.6%
Osberht	15	2.8%
Eanbald (with title)	1	0.2%
Wigmund	58	10.7%
Wulfhere	5	0.9%

The interesting figure here is the 18.3 per cent for Eanred. As the other percentage figures correspond quite well with the table, it seems clear that the Æthelreds include the derivatives, etc.

The Revd. Walker Featherstonhaugh in 1892 (i.e. about three generations after the discovery) reported that the hoard had originally contained 800–1,000 coins, 'much decayed'. He spoke of 'my namesake . . . to whom I am indebted for specimens of the find now in my possession'. The Timothy Fetherstonhaugh referred to was almost certainly of the branch of the family who were landowners at Kirkoswald at the time of the discovery; and one may conjecture that the hoard remained in the possession of the family, at least in part, until the late ninteenth century. The question arises whether the 542 coins listed by Adamson were a random sample as regards the proportions of the different kings and archbishops. There seems to be no way to test the question, nor any reason to doubt that the figures are acceptable.

The further question arises whether the Kirkoswald hoard was put together from coinage available in the Eden valley, or whether it was a traveller's hoard. There is no reason to postulate a non-local origin (except the doctrinaire belief that coinage was not available west of the Pennines–now challenged by the recent Carlisle, Whithorn, and Dacre finds.) More positively, the hoard was concealed in an earthenware vessel, which perhaps suggests a local owner rather than someone fleeing from the east. The unusually high proportion of coins of Eanred (18 per cent, cf 11, 12, or 13 per cent at Bolton Percy and York) invites comparison with Hexham, and lends added interest to Mr Pagan's speculations about sluggish circulation in Bernicia, and/or the savings character of the Hexham hoard.

The place-name, although not attested until 1167, shows Irish-Scandinavian influence. It should make us wonder whether a church or minster stood on the spot already in Anglian times, and if so whether (in view of the dedication) it had any royal connections or origins. In other words, is the Kirkoswald hoard yet another find from the vicinity of an ecclesiastical site? (The best evidence is that the hoard was found 'near Kirkoswald'.) The fine-quality silver and garnet tribrach ornament found with the coins, possibly a brooch, which was apparently old when it was concealed, and which would certainly have served to identify the owner of the treasure, is unique in shape among English finds. There are tribrachs on coins of Coenwulf and, of course, Eadberht of Northumbria, and the symbol is not necessarily ecclesiastical even if it is trinitarian. The church itself does not figure in the Taylors' great work. There is a fragment of a cross-head built into one windowsill. Apart from this, there seems to be no archaeological evidence amounting to anything.

Metal analysis of the Northumbrian stycas: review and suggestions

G. R. GILMORE

[PLATE 12]

THERE is little need to remind anybody acquainted with the Northumbrian stycas that almost every aspect of their study is subject to doubt and, in some cases, controversy. Their chronology and the accompanying standards of fineness are matters of debate not helped by the uncertainties in the regnal dates. It has long been hoped that chemical analysis of the stycas would help to resolve some of these problems.

Although a handful of analyses were published in 1834 and 1962[1] the first major study of the composition of the stycas in their own right was undertaken by X-ray fluorescence analysis (XRF) using the 'milliprobe' in 1968.[2] The numismatic information obtained was restricted by the limitations of the technique which only provided a concentration range for the major elements and gave scant information on the minor elements. No other analytical work was undertaken until the late 1970s when neutron activation analysis (NAA) of minute drillings was applied to the problem.[3] Drilling allowed the bulk of the coin, rather than the surface, to be sampled and more accurate data were obtained. It was hoped this might clear up some of the difficulties surrounding the relationships between composition and date. In fact, the new data served only to confirm that there was more to the styca than meets the eye.

Forty-five stycas from the Ashmolean collection were sampled including five previously examined by the milliprobe and one coin suspected of being a modern forgery. Samples were collected using a hand-held model maker's electric drill with a 0.5 mm bit, and holding the styca between the fingers of the other hand. In this first NAA study the coins were analysed for eight elements: copper, silver, and zinc (the major components of the alloy), tin (a common 'addition'), gold (which presumably entered the alloy with the silver), arsenic, antimony, and

[1] J. S. Forbes and D. B. Dalladay, 'Composition of English silver coins 870–1300', *BNJ* 30 (1960–1), 82–7; E.J. Harris, 'Debasement of the coinage', *Seaby's Coin and Medal Bulletin* 1962, 5–7.

[2] D. M. Metcalf, J. M. Merrick, and L. K. Hamblin, *Studies in the Composition of Early Medieval Coins*, Newcastle-upon-Tyne, 1968.

[3] G. R. Gilmore and D. M. Metcalf, 'The alloy of Northumbrian coinage in the mid-ninth century', in *Metallurgy in Numismatics* 1 (Eds. D. M. Metcalf and W. A. Oddy), 1980, 83–98; G. R. Gilmore and D. M. Metcalf, 'Consistency in the alloy of the Northumbrian stycas: evidence from die-linked specimens', *NC* 146 (1986), 192–8.

indium. In later studies five additional trace elements were included in the analysis. In principle, the major element concentrations can be expected to indicate the metallurgical intentions of the moneyer and the minor and trace elements may provide some indication of smelting technology or, less likely, the source of the copper used.

The suspect modern forgery was found to be made of silver with a very low proportion of gold (0.01%) and this, together with the complete absence of impurities such as arsenic and antimony, confirmed it as a modern rather than an ancient forgery. One other coin was also identified as a forgery and, although not recognized as such at the time, is almost certainly one of the nineteenth-century bismuth/lead/tin alloy forgeries described by Elizabeth Pirie.[4] The composition of these forgeries is similar to that of the low melting point fusible alloys such as Rose's metal and Newton's fusible alloy. The particular example analysed here has a composition very similar to a fusible plug alloy (8 parts bismuth, 8 parts lead and 3 parts tin) with a melting point of 128°C. Such alloys also have the useful property of expanding on cooling which would make them ideal for the fabrication of counterfeits.

The analysis of the remaining forty-three true stycas confirmed the general composition pattern deduced from the earlier analyses: early stycas made of a silver/copper alloy with a substantial addition of tin and later coins a silver-containing brass with a generally lower level of tin. The changeover in alloy type occurred at some time during the reign of Eanred and is generally supposed to be a consequence of a silver shortage. The NAA analysis of the five coins previously analysed by milliprobe demonstrated inaccuracies in the XRF results attributable to surface corrosion and showed up inadequacies in the previous gold and tin values. However, in spite of the better quality of the new results, the picture was no less confusing. Although there may be scope for identifying a silver standard in the pre-zinc coinage no clear silver standards were evident in the zinc-containing coinage. Splitting the coinage into groups according to moneyer also fails to reveal any convincing structure in the data. Comparison of the king's and archbishop's issues is similarly fruitless. No matter how the data are grouped the most consistent feature of the zinc-containing coinage is the zinc-in-brass ratio of 18–20%.

Little of significance could be deduced from the minor and trace element results. Gold-to-silver ratios show no clear within-sample variation. A correlation between antimony and arsenic concentrations was found and, moreover, coins minted for Archbishop Wigmund and those minted by Aldates and Eadwine for King Eanred fell in different regions along this correlation line, each being successively lower in impurity concentration. The general view is that all the stycas were probably minted at York and it is unlikely that at one point in time different moneyers would be using different sources of raw materials. As the impurity levels in these materials could change with time it is conceivable that the differences in arsenic and antimony levels of these groups of coins do represent a

[4] E. J. E. Pirie and S. E. Warren, 'Bismuth alloy forgeries of early Northumbrian coins', *Proc. 22nd Symposium on Archaeometry*, Bradford, 1982, pp.254–61.

chronological difference. Unfortunately the differences could also be a consequence of other factors such as changes in smelting practice.

We assume that brass would have been made by cementation in the ninth century. Because zinc has such a low boiling point (906°C) relative to the melting point of the alloys (820°C to 980°C[5]), the production of a brass of consistent quality must have been difficult. It is possible, then, that the technological difficulties associated with making the coinage obscures the real (and possibly simple) monetary intention. Alternatively the variability of composition might be due to a very complicated scheme of monetary intention which is obscured by our selection of items for analysis.

In order to decide between the two possibilities the next step was to examine a group of die-linked coins when, during the short lifetime of a die, we might reasonably expect the monetary intention to be constant. This should then allow us to assess the ability of the moneyers to achieve this intention. A further batch of 20 coins was therefore selected containing some die-duplicates of coins already analysed and other linked and similar coins. The results are listed in Table 1 and were, by and large, disappointing with few cases where consistent silver compositions could be found. In Table 1 (and other tables) the columns 'Brass' and 'Bronze' indicate the quality of the brass or bronze to which silver might have been added to produce the observed composition on the assumption that all the copper in the coin entered its alloy in that form. The silver values should, perhaps, be quoted as silver-plus-gold but since the gold concentrations are in most cases less than 1% of the silver values their inclusion would not materially alter the picture or conclusions drawn from it.

The two cases where consistency in silver was found were set 1, a pair of similar, but not die-linked, coins by Hwætræd, and set 2 by Cynewulf, linked by their obverse. In the first case the overall composition, including minor and trace elements, is so similar as to suggest that both coins could have been made from the same batch of alloy. Both pairs are early coins and we seem to be dealing with a bronze with silver added quite precisely.

The three coins in set 3, by Eadwine, are similar and appear to span the changeover from bronze plus silver to brass plus silver. The accepted explanation of the differences in silver between coin 48, which is not unlike the silver in set 1, and coins 8 and 49 is that the coinage has suffered debasement. I shall eventually suggest that this is not necessarily the case. Each of the other pairs of coins is die-linked and none shows any great consistency in silver concentrations. Considering the short time-span over which we would expect the coins within

[5] D. M. K. de Grinberg, 'A quaternary equilibrium diagram applied to the study of Anglo-Saxon coins', presented at the Symposium on Archaeometry and Archaeological Prospection, Brookhaven, 1981.

Dr. de Grinberg estimated the melting-points of the styca alloys to be:

Issuer	*Moneyer*	*N*	*Ag %*	*Zn %*	*Sn %*	*m.p.*
Eanred	Hwætræd	2	40.5	0.8	6.6	821
Eanred	Eadwine	2	27.4	14.2	1.5	930
Eanbald	Æthelweard	3	25.2	13.4	1.3	901
Eanred	Cynewulf	4	24.7	8.1	4.4	886
Eanred	Eadwine	4	23.0	16.3	0.4	896
Eanbald	Eadwulf	3	14.0	16.8	1.8	927
Wigmund	Æthelweard	6	11.4	17.0	2.3	935
Eanred	Aldates	5	9.8	16.4	3.2	952
Æthelred	Leofthegn	9	7.1	19.1	2.7	954
Wigmund	Coenræd	4	6.8	18.8	2.7	951
Wulfhere	Wulfræd	2	0.3	10.4	6.7	982

The groups are arranged in decreasing order of silver concentration. The quoted concentrations are the mean values for the group of N coins considered.

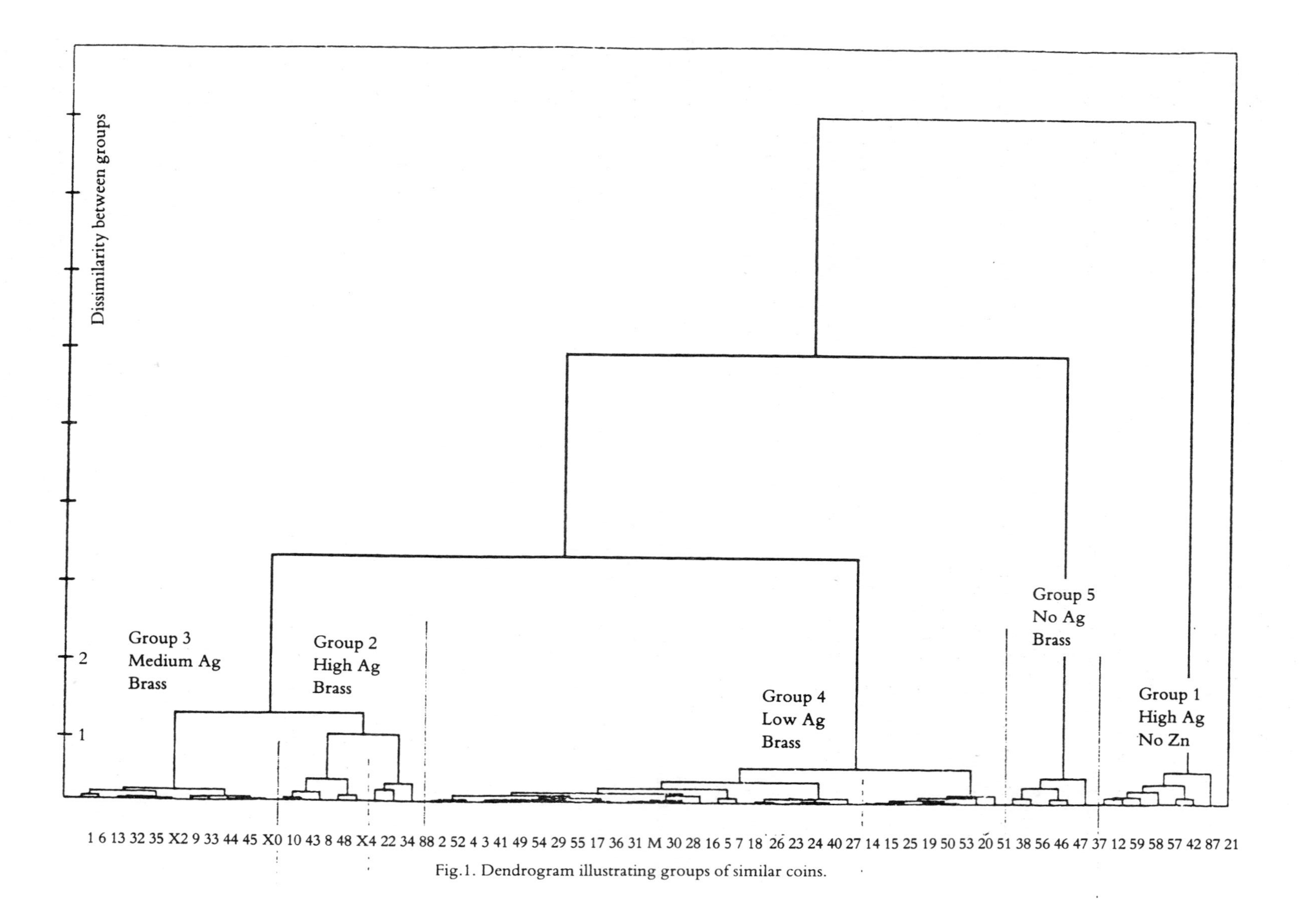

Fig.1. Dendrogram illustrating groups of similar coins.

TABLE 1. *Composition of die-linked stycas*

Coin	Silver %	Zinc %	Tin %	Brass	Bronze
1. Eanred–Hwætræd (Similar but not linked)					
1	40.1	ND	7.1	—	11.6
52	40.9	ND	6.0	—	11.5
2. Eanred–Cynewulf (Same obverse)					
46	24.2	1.6	6.8	—	9.2
47	24.7	0.3	7.4	—	9.9
3. Eanred–Eadwine (Similar coins not linked)					
48	38.1	0.2	4.9	—	7.8
8	23.6	15.8	0.5	20.6	—
49	29.6	12.1	0.3	17.3	—
4. Eanred–Aldates (all four obverse-linked. Pairs are duplicates)					
14	8.7	17.9	3.1	20.1	—
45	7.0	17.3	3.3	19.5	—
13	10.2	19.8	2.6	22.2	—
44	17.6	15.5	1.8	19.4	—
5. Wigmund–Æthelweard (all have same obverse)					
26	15.3	16.5	1.9	20.2	—
61	11.9	14.1	3.0	16.8	—
62	10.9	17.7	2.0	20.6	—
6. Wulfhere–Wulfræd (Same obverse)					
43	0.1	11.7	5.4	12.2	—
63	0.5	9.1	8.1	11.2	—
7. 'Teveh' (duplicates)					
59	1.2	21.2	3.8	22.6	—
60	0.5	21.7	2.3	22.6	—
8. Æthelred–Leofthegn (each group is obverse-linked)					
37	12.6	18.3	2.3	20.9	—
54	4.6	20.7	1.1	22.3	—
55	7.8	17.5	4.6	20.3	—
56	8.6	21.0	2.4	23.8	—
57	5.5	20.1	3.6	22.4	—
40	5.9	20.6	1.3	21.1	—
58	4.2	21.4	3.2	23.4	—

Coin numbers refer to the published results, coins 1–43 Ref. 3a, coins 44–63 Ref. 3b. 'Brass' is Zn/(Cu + Zn) and 'Bronze' is Sn/(Cu + Sn) both expressed as percentages.

these groups to have been minted this is somewhat surprising. Again we note the relative stability of the quality of the brass.

Set 7 is a duplicate pair of coins of uncertain attribution with a well-known obverse of Eanred. The composition is so different from other coins of Eanred that these coins should be regarded as irregular or unofficial issues, perhaps of a later date. We will return to this problem later.

After much puzzling over the results, looking for order within different groups of coins, I decided to submit the complete batch of data to the PODS multivariate analysis program on the Salford University computer.[6] This approach has been used most successfully in deducing structure in the large amount of trace-element data produced while provenancing pottery. Although the styca data are not ideal a trial did not seem unreasonable. Basically the computer seeks to find order in the data by plotting the n variables (i.e. element concentrations—in this case $n=8$) in n-dimensional space and looking for items which cluster together within that space. The advantages of such a computer program are that it can include all the element concentrations in the data analysis and, in some respects more importantly, it allows an analysis without the hindrance of preconceptions. One hopes that the inclusion of the trace-elements in the data set will reveal some feature of the composition which, while not intended by the moneyer, will serve to distinguish between coins. To be valid all the elements in the data set must have equal statistical variances. Like all multivariate analysis programs, PODS provides facilities to normalize and transform the element concentrations to achieve this.

In its simplest form the output from the program is a list of items which are most alike. More visually appealing presentations can be produced in various manners of which the dendrogram (Fig.1) is one. In this diagram related items (where 'related' indicates a statistical relationship and not necessarily a real or numismatic relationship) are joined by a horizontal line, the height of which represents the dissimilarity of the items. Groups of items can be selected by eye, somewhat arbitrarily, by choosing a threshold level of dissimilarity ('dissimilarity' is a numerical convenience and has no absolute quantitative significance). For example, in the dendrogram shown a line drawn at a dissimilarity level of 1.2 splits the data set into five groups. The general characteristics of these groups are shown in Table 2. These groups do make some numismatic sense but, apart from the comforting fact that the computer-selected grouping is similar to the general pattern deduced manually the only conclusion which could be reached was that the coins in the largest group (group 4) were statistically indistinguishable. Further examination of the zinc-containing groups alone revealed an antimony-containing sub-group of group 2 and a split of group 4 into two sub-groups with different mean silver concentrations. Unfortunately there was no obvious numismatic significance in these sub-groups, the same moneyers and some die-linked pairs being represented in both. With the exception of one coin which

[6] G. R. Gilmore, 'The use of mathematical clustering techniques for the analysis of coin composition data', *Revue d'Archéometrie* 2, part 5 (1981), 97–107. The program used was PODS (Program for Ordinations and Dendrograms) written by Richard Baker and implemented on the Salford University Computer.

tended to wander from group to group, the groups were stable to changes in the size of the data set. This gives some confidence in their statistical validity but there may be some scope for further treatment with the inclusion of newer data and taking more account of possible correlations between elements.

TABLE 2. *Conclusions of the multivariate analysis.*

Group 1	7 coins	High silver 25–43%	High tin 4–8%	No zinc
Group 2	8 coins	High silver 17–35%	No tin <1.5%	High zinc 15.3% mean
Group 3	11 coins	Medium silver 10–24%	Slight tin 1–2.5%	High zinc 15.5% mean
Group 4	32 coins	Low silver 3–15%	Low tin 1–5%	High zinc 18.5% mean
Group 5	5 coins	No silver <1.5%	High tin 2.5–8%	High zinc 14.9% mean

The designations 'high', 'low' etc. are arbitrary, being based on the group mean concentrations.

The data on which this multivariate analysis was based have also been analysed by Dr. de Grinberg, a metallurgist from the National University of Mexico.[7] She examined the data in relation to quaternary copper-silver-zinc-tin diagrams plotted in three dimensions. Dr. de Grinberg presented her results in the form of a 16mm film showing the coins plotted within the tetrahedron of the quaternary diagram. In spite of the very different visualization of the data her analysis is no different in principle from the computer program, the only difference being the number of elements included—four instead of eight. It is not clear whether taking only the major elements rather than the combination of major elements (whose concentrations are determined by the moneyer) together with elements which are purely adventitious provides a better data set for multivariate analysis. If a decision is made to include only the alloy elements, one then has to decide whether gold, coming with the silver, is adventitious or not.

Dr. de Grinberg came to the conclusion that the groups derived by my multivariate analysis were not valid and instead suggested that the coins of individual moneyers should be grouped together. It should be emphasized that her decision to treat the data moneyer by moneyer was not based on perceived groups within the equilibrium diagram but was a choice based on the wish to find differences between the king/moneyer groups. On the basis of a concentration 'consistency' factor within each group of coins she claimed to show that the alloys were produced in some cases by the addition of a silver/tin alloy to a brass (of a variable composition depending on moneyer) and in others by adding zinc, tin, and silver to copper. Leaving aside the fact that metallic zinc would not be available to the ninth-century moneyer and while I do not regard the groups in Table 2 as sacrosanct, I must take issue with her conclusions because the groups of

[7] D. M. K. de Grinberg, *op.cit.*

coins which she selects contain in many cases as few as two and three coins and have no statistical validity whatsoever.

It now appeared reasonable to limit the scope of the investigation even further by examining sets of die-linked coins produced within a short period of time. Since King Redwulf reigned for less than a year, one might expect the pattern of his monetary policy to be reasonably simple. Miss Elizabeth Pirie made available for sampling 20 coins of Redwulf from the York collection providing *inter alia* a chain of seven die-links and four pairs of duplicate coins. The analysis of Redwulf's coins is described fully elsewhere in this volume.[8]

Leaving aside the (presumably) early pre-zinc issues and the very late silver-free issues, the overall pattern of styca compositions is of scattered silver concentrations falling with time, fairly constant zinc concentrations, plus some tin and a smattering of arsenic, antimony, and gold impurities. In the Redwulf analyses we find exactly the same pattern. Looking at the composition of the 'grand chain' of linked coins (Y4–9 and Y13 in Table 3) it is difficult to believe that they could have been made to the same silver standard. One could, perhaps, argue that Redwulf, as a usurper, would have been in a particularly unstable economic situation. His supplies of silver might have been irregular and uncertain and this might be reflected in variability in his coinage. On the other hand, looking at these results in the wider context of all the zinc-containing stycas there is nothing to distinguish Redwulf's coinage as in any way different from the other issues which went before.

TABLE 3. *Composition of die-linked stycas of Redwulf.*

Coin	Silver %	Zinc %	Tin %	Brass	Moneyer
Set 1—all linked by their obverse, each pair are duplicates.					
Y4	4.4	21.2	2.6	22.6	Cuthbeorht
Y5	6.1	18.2	2.8	20.7	Cuthbeorht
Y6	2.9	20.8	2.8	22.2	Eanræd
Y7	2.4	19.7	3.0	22.1	Eanræd
Y8	3.0	22.0	3.2	24.1	Forthræd
Y9	2.1	21.6	3.0	23.6	Forthræd
Y13	5.2	18.2	3.1	20.3	Monne
Set 2—Similar obverse.					
Y12	0.1	17.7	6.1	19.3	Monne
Y2	2.9	22.0	3.3	23.8	Brother
Set 3—Same obverse.					
Y14	4.7	20.5	2.8	22.9	Fordræd
Y15	1.4	21.1	4.2	23.0	Hereræd
Y16	1.5	20.6	3.6	21.4	Odilo

Coin numbers Y1–20 refer to the published results in Ref. 7.

[8] G. R. Gilmore and E. J. E. Pirie, 'Consistency in the alloy of the Northumbrian stycas: evidence from a short reign', in this volume.

Faced with this consistent inconsistency it seemed prudent to confirm the quality of the analytical results. I was satisfied that the sampling successfully avoided the enriched surface layer and I had always assumed, on the basis of one or two repeat drillings, that the sample of a few milligrammes was representative of the whole coin composition. However, before continuing with further sampling I decided the time had come to lay the ghost of analytical uncertainty. Michael Metcalf and Elizabeth Pirie both donated coins from which I was invited to take several samples. In the event I chose the coin from Dr. Metcalf's own collection, minted by Coenræd for Wigmund and containing 7.2% of silver, simply because it had already been sampled. (In fact it bore the first hole drilled in any styca, to demonstrate that it could be done without disastrous damage to a coin.) Alongside analytical uncertainty there was also the possibility that the coin itself might not be of uniform composition and Dr. Metcalf suggested that, since this particular coin would inevitably end up like an Emmenthal cheese, it should at the same time be sectioned and metallographs obtained to lay another ghost, that of coin heterogeneity.

Rubbings of the coin were made and then it was cut in half across the face with a fine saw. The sawings were collected and, after separating the flakes of patina, split into fine and coarse samples. The patina was also analysed for interest. One half of the coin was then drilled five times in the normal manner. Altogether eleven analyses were made: five new drilled samples, two of which were analysed twice; a re-analysis of the original sample; coarse and fine sawings; and the patina.

The other half of the coin was embedded in perspex and photomicrographs of the polished and etched surface obtained. I was also fortunate enough to be able to have the polished section examined on the scanning electron microscope (SEM) with EDAX (X-ray analysis) facilities and obtain semi-quantitative analysis of small regions of the microstructure of the coin.

I had arranged that the saw cut should intersect the original hole made in the coin and, as hoped, this allowed the microstructure of the coin to be assessed in relation to the size of the sample (**Pl.12a**). This work is being published in full[9] but since this will be in an archaeological rather than a numismatic journal it may be helpful to repeat the general conclusions here:

a) Semi-quantitative analyses of areas about 0.5 mm × 0.6 mm along the length of the coin section gave consistent values for silver, copper, zinc, and tin. Leaving aside the clearly altered surface layer, the coin is homogeneous throughout its bulk.

b) The grain structure of the alloy is much smaller than the size of the sample and consequently one would expect even a sample as small as 1–2 mg to be representative of the bulk as long as the surface layers are avoided.

c) The microstructure (**Pl.12b**) consists of grains of about 40 μm diameter with a composition similar to the overall composition but somewhat depleted in silver (Table 4). The missing silver appears in the interstices between the grains with small proportions of the other components.

[9] G. R. Gilmore, 'A chemical and metallurgical examination of a Northumbrian styca', presented at the Symposium on Archaeometry, Athens, 1986 (proceedings in press).

d) The surface is much depleted in zinc and correspondingly enhanced in silver and tin.

e) The replicate neutron activation analyses indicated that the analytical uncertainties were much smaller than the variability of composition of the stycas. To put the matter in perspective the analytical plus sampling uncertainty on the measurement of silver was 5.1% compared with 41.0% for the Redwulf 'grand chain' discussed above. This may be compared with uncertainties of 3.5% and 7.8% respectively for zinc.

f) The short time available on the SEM precluded proper calibration for the silver/zinc/tin/copper alloy and consequently the results obtained by NAA and SEM differed slightly. The general conclusions using both sets of analyses are the same.

g) There was no significant difference between composition of the fine sawings and that of the coarse sawings. This eliminated the slight possibility that the silver from between the grains might be preferentially lost as very fine dust when the drilled samples were manipulated.

TABLE 4. *EDAX and NAA analysis of a styca.*

	N	Ag %	Zn %	Sn %	Cu %
EDAX					
Overall	4	10.9	19.2	3.7	66.0
Grains	5	8.3	19.9	3.3	68.5
Interstices	4	84.6	5.2	4.5	5.7
Surface	1	16.3	1.3	4.9	75.8
NAA					
Overall	10	7.2	17.3	2.6	71.9
Patina	1	11.3	4.2	4.2	67.1

'N' is the number of points analysed. The quoted concentrations are the mean of N values.

If we accept that this particular coin of Wigmund is representative of the stycas in general there can be no doubt that the inconsistency in the silver concentrations and the relative constancy of the zinc concentrations, as measured by NAA, are real.

As one examines the styca compositions one is again and again struck by the fact that while the silver concentrations are so variable the zinc concentration is much more consistent. It has been suggested that this peculiar copper-silver-zinc-tin alloy posed particular problems in production. Even after manufacture of the brass, when it was remelted in order to add the silver and tin, difficulties would arise because of the low boiling point of zinc. The silver and tin could, perhaps, have been added at the cementation stage[10] but in either case

[10] It is not clear whether cementation would be effective in the presence of substantial proportions of silver and tin. The addition of these elements to copper produces an alloy with a lower melting-point than that of copper. Since the cementation process depends upon intimate

special competence would be needed. Even so, it is difficult to see how the 'difficult' element, zinc, can be so consistent relative to the copper when the 'easy' element, silver ('easy' because one presumably only had to weigh it out and tip it in) is so variable especially when this 'easy' element gives the coin its value. By way of example, if a coin were to be made by the addition of silver to a brass with 25% of zinc and sufficient zinc were lost to reduce its concentration to 15% this would result in a maximum variation of silver of about 11% and on average much less than this. In fact, the variation of silver concentrations, even in cases where we might reasonably expect consistency, is much greater than this.

It is easy to dismiss the variation as small and well within acceptable mint tolerance. For example, one could argue that the duplicate pair of coins in Table 3, minted by Fordræd with silver concentrations of 3.0% and 2.1% silver are similar. But the difference represents a 50% difference in value if the silver is indeed the important element. Would this be regarded as an acceptable tolerance in a period when, it is suggested, silver was scarce?

Perhaps it is time to leave silver aside and consider the implications if we suppose that it is the zinc, or rather brass, which is the important component of the alloy. We tend to view brass in twentieth-century terms as a base alloy. Was this so in the ninth century? Consider its preparation—we take copper, a zinc ore such as calamine, cover with charcoal and heat for a long time and 'Hey presto!' we have increased the amount of metal and it now has a desirable golden colour. Was brass indeed regarded as base? The medieval alchemists thought of it as a half-way stage in turning base metal into gold. In the context of a shortage of silver might brass not have been an acceptable coinage substitute?

We have, of course, to explain the presence of tin and, more immediately, of silver in the coinage. I would like to suggest that incorporation of old silver-rich coinage into the new issues is a valid explanation. Over a period of time this would, of course, lead to a gradual reduction in silver levels as the original silver became more and more dilute in the brass stock. The hypothesis needs to be tested against the numismatic evidence, in so far as it is possible to arrange the coins into their exact chronological order. Initially this would also explain the presence of the tin since the pre-zinc coinage was essentially bronze plus silver. This cannot be the full story for many coins, such as the Redwulf coins in Table 3, contain too much tin for it to be there solely by progressive dilution of the original silver/bronze stock. In later coinage the regularity of the tin contents suggests that the concentration of tin in the alloys may have been subject to some degree of control. There are also examples of coins which contain too little tin.

If silver had been abandoned there would be little point in having a mint-prescription or recipe of so many old coins plus so much brass. The actual composition would depend upon what was available for melting down at that particular moment. We can imagine the moneyer receiving orders to produce a certain weight of coinage. For his metal he takes copper and zinc ore (or perhaps ready-made brass), any coinage returned to the mint for recycling, and a little extra tin, perhaps to improve the workability of the final product. If on a

contact of copper and zinc at the moment of reduction of zinc ore to zinc the loss of copper by draining to the bottom of the crucible might make it difficult to produce a high-zinc brass in the presence of silver and tin.

particular day there was no coinage for recycling we can envisage a 'pure' brass issue. Returning to the enigmatic coins of Teveh, need we assume that they are 'rogues'? If they have an obverse of Eanred might they not, in fact, be an official issue in the new-fangled brass? Arguments based upon the fact that the 'moneyer's' name is apparently meaningless are more valid reasons to suspect the origin of the Teveh coins than is reliance on composition alone.

Table 5 lists the possible compositions of stycas minted from various proportions of coins similar to the coin of Hwætræd in Table 1 (No.52) mixed with a very good brass of 28% zinc. It is easy to find in the published lists of analyses coins to fit almost every example and slight changes in the brass or recycled coin composition will fit the rest. I do not suggest that the numbers in Table 5 should be taken seriously. The actual mix would vary from day to day and would presumably, from time to time, include coins already containing brass. Nevertheless, the important point is that the mixture of old coinage with brass could produce the correct general composition and, of course, the day-to-day variation in the resources available to the moneyer[11] could amply explain the observed variation in the silver concentrations. Once brass itself began to be recycled this would tend to stabilize the copper/zinc ratio. Although one might expect a downward trend in the zinc-in-brass ratio due to evaporative losses of zinc during remelting this may be limited by the vapour pressure of zinc in solution at temperatures not greatly above its normal boiling point.

TABLE 5. *Composition of mixtures of old silver/bronze coins with new brass.*

Component compositions						
		Ag %	Zn %	Sn %	Cu %	
	Coins	43.0	—	5.0	52.0	
	Brass	—	28.0	—	72.0	
Composition of mixtures						
% Coins used	% Brass used	Ag %	Zn %	Sn %	Cu %	Brass quality
20	80	8.6	22.4	1.0	68.0	24.8
25	75	10.7	21.0	1.2	67.0	23.9
30	70	12.9	19.6	1.5	66.0	22.9
35	65	15.1	18.2	1.7	65.0	21.9
40	60	17.2	16.8	2.0	64.0	20.8
45	55	19.4	15.4	2.2	63.0	19.6
50	50	21.5	14.0	2.5	62.0	18.4
55	45	23.6	12.6	2.7	61.0	17.1
60	40	25.8	11.2	3.0	60.0	15.7
65	35	28.0	9.8	3.2	59.0	14.2
70	30	30.1	8.4	3.5	58.0	12.7
75	25	32.2	7.0	3.7	57.0	10.9

[11] In *Anglo-Saxon Monetary History* (Ed. M.A.S. Blackburn), Leicester, 1986, p.5, Henry Loyn suggests that, at some time, the moneyers themselves might have been actively involved in the collection of taxes. One can speculate that if this were so during the currency of the stycas differences in composition between moneyers might reflect different degrees of involvement in the collection process.

It may be, of course, that silver was not abandoned at the same time as zinc was introduced. There may have been silver/brass issues produced to a defined silver standard which might be revealed by further study. If so, then there may be additional numismatic problems since the silver concentrations of the silver/bronze and silver/brass issues overlap. The former fall to about 25% silver and there are several examples of the latter containing as much as 33% of silver.

If we accept that the later stycas, at least, were produced by remelting of old coinage we must also suppose that there were good reasons for not recovering the silver from the old coinage. Metcalf and Northover[12] have suggested several possibilities (although, it must be said, they do not support the idea of an abandoning of the silver standard). If we accept that the brass itself was of some intrinsic value then clearly the brass lost during cupellation might well be of greater value than the silver recovered.

When we look at the later stycas, those of Wulfhere and Osberht, we find levels of silver so low and tin levels so high as to suggest that the mint procedure had changed drastically once again. Indeed, some coins of Osberht are unashamed bronze containing no zinc at all. The composition of the brasses is so poor (Table 6) that we may well be justified in describing the alloy as a debased brass although it is unlikely that the observed zinc levels defined a monetary standard but rather defined the best contemporary brass-making capability. The very low concentration of silver in these late coins excludes the possibility that preceding issues were merely diluted with copper or bronze unless the degree of dilution was very large (perhaps a factor of 30 or 40). Although the number of analyses is small there does appear to be a break from the fairly constant 20% brass and whether one should reject these very debased issues as being stycas at all, or regard them as a natural progression from the brass styca is still a debatable matter.

TABLE 6. *Composition of late brass stycas.*

Coin	Issuer	Moneyer	Ag %	Zn %	Brass %
43	Wulfhere	Wulfræd	0.1	11.7	12.2
63	Wulfhere	Wulfræd	0.5	9.1	10.1
38	Osberht	Monne	0.1	10.9	11.9

In summary I envisage the sequence of events following Eardwulf's reign thus:

a) High-silver bronze coinage. The information available at present indicates possible standards of around 40% and 25% silver.

b) A possible brief phase of high-silver brass coinage made to a definite standard prepared by adding silver to a brass.

c) The control of silver is abandoned and the coinage becomes brass with silver present only because old coinage is recycled by adding to new brass. Later, small amounts of tin are added. This phase continues through the reigns of Æthelred and Redwulf.

[12] 'The Northumbrian royal coinage in the time of Æthelred II and Osberht', below.

d) Wulfhere and Osberht produce some brass coinage of poor quality.

e) Osberht turns to bronze coinage.

Although there is less analytical information available there is every reason to believe that the episcopal coinage followed the same sequence throughout the currency of the stycas.

Looking at the data without the benefit, or possibly hindrance, of long-standing numismatic experience I can see no compelling reason to accept the idea of a complicated series of issues when the much simpler hypothesis of a 'brass standard' seems to answer so many questions. While the acceptance of this idea, and the rejection of successive silver standards, seems to take away something numismatically I would imagine that calculations based upon the 'decay rate' of the silver might produce useful information to correlate with other estimates of rates of issue and the like.

In any case, it would seem wise at the present time to stand back from the problem and consider future analytical strategy. In order to avoid unnecessary sampling I would suggest that it may be more effective to attempt to demolish the 'brass standard hypothesis' rather than chase phantom silver standards.

Acknowledgments

I would like to record my sincere thanks to the following: Dr. Michael Metcalf, for his considerable help and advice, for permission to sample coins in the Ashmolean collection, and not least for the sacrifice of one of his own coins; Elizabeth Pirie, for encouragement and access to the coins of Redwulf in the York collection; the Department of Metallurgy and Materials Science of the University of Manchester Institute of Science and Technology for access to facilities, and expertise of Dr. Norman Ridley and Mr. Ivan Easden for the metallographic preparation, Mr. Frank Knowles for the optical micrographs, and Mr. Ian Brough for the electron microscope examination.

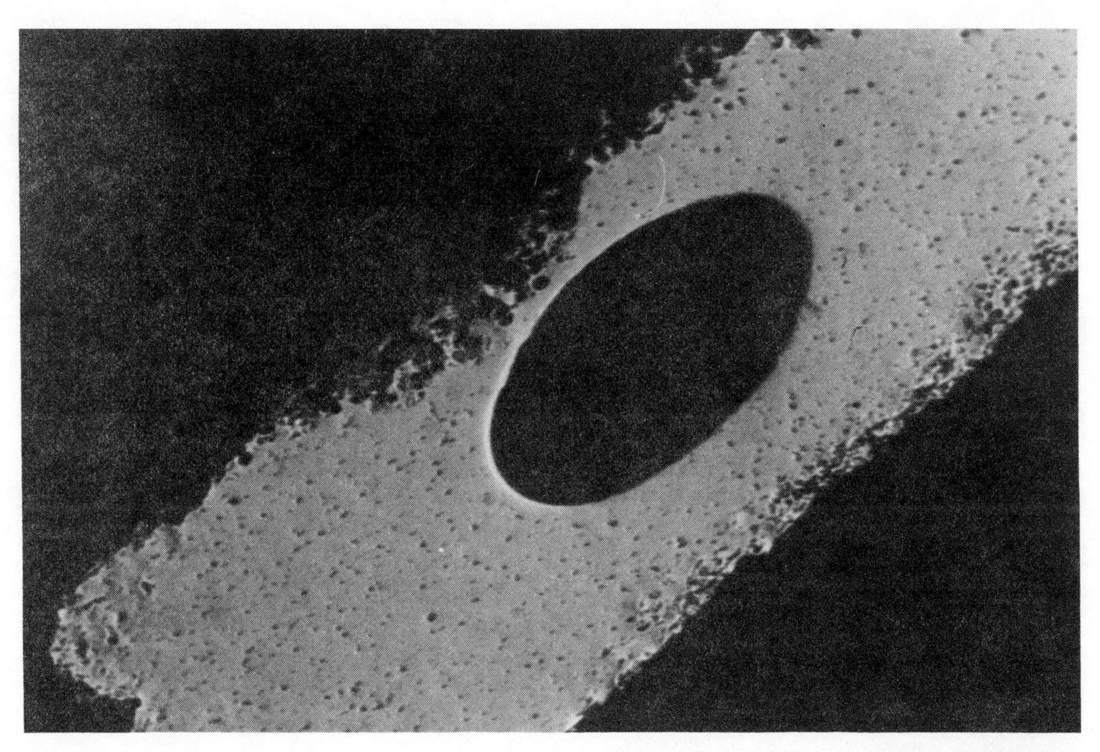

a) Photomicrograph of the sectioned styca. The width of the hole is 0.5 mm.

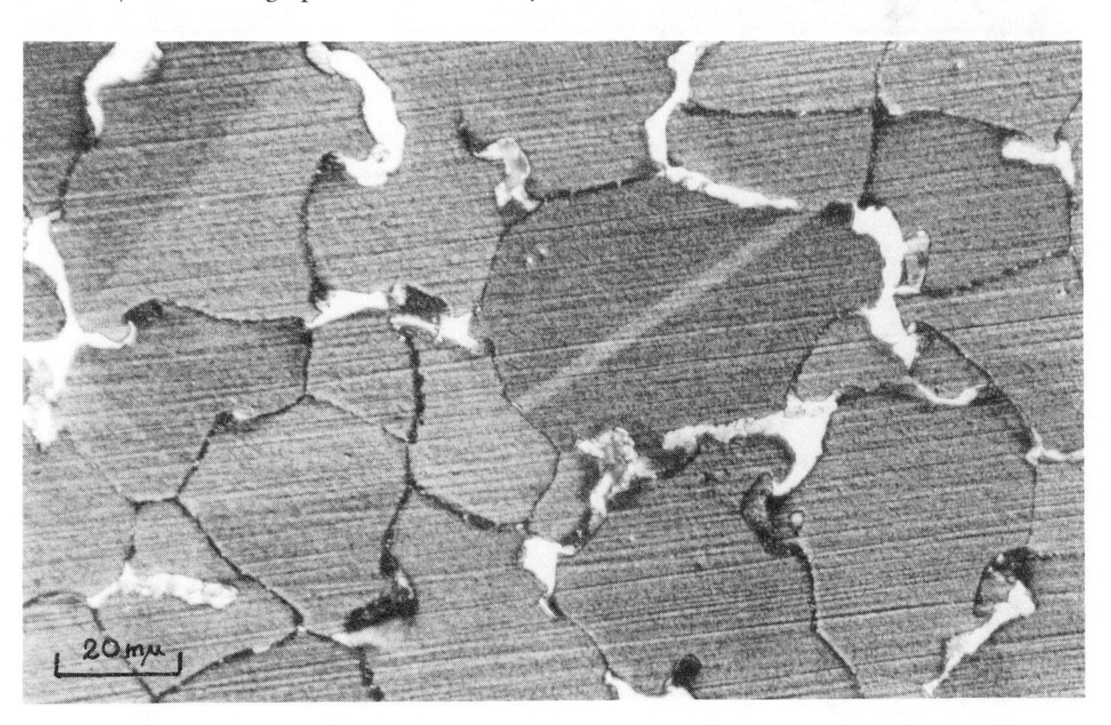

b) Photomicrograph of the microstructure of the styca. Lines across individual grains (excluding polishing scratches) indicate twinning of the grains suggesting that the alloy has been annealed.

Consistency in the alloy of the Northumbrian stycas: evidence from Redwulf's short reign

G. R. GILMORE and E. J. E. PIRIE

[PLATE 13]

THE series of Northumbrian stycas has long been recognized as one which underwent marked debasement during the course of its career in the ninth century. Several studies have already been concerned in part or in whole with the analysis of selected specimens. The present paper records results for the latest stage in a reasoned programme of research.

Three papers, which are the immediate forerunners of this one, must be summarized briefly. The first, *Studies in the Composition of Early Medieval Coins*, was published in 1968.[1] The project was designed as a preliminary inspection of the various coinages within the monetary *bloc* of north-western Europe during the seventh, eighth, and ninth centuries; the currencies which underwent debasement were acknowledged to have particular interest and to need a greater degree of examination before the pattern of debasement could be traced in detail either geographically or chronologically: further analyses were anticipated. As far as Northumbrian coins were then concerned, results of analysis by X-ray fluorescence were quoted for thirty-eight specimens (including ten sceattas which, for now, may be set aside); in addition, data were given for further stycas examined by other researchers. Of the issues by moneyers identified in 1957 by Lyon[2] as having been struck in the first stage of coinage for King Eanred some had a relatively high proportion of silver, while others had an alloy of silver and zinc. It was seen that the zinc continued to form a part of the composition as the quantity of silver was reduced in favour of an increase in the amount of copper. Various questions were posed: where did the mint obtain appropriate quantities of zinc; why was it added to the fabric of the coinage, and how did the mint personnel manage to achieve the necessary proportions.

This concern with the remarkable use of zinc led in due course to the second group of styca analyses, published in 1980.[3] The process of examination adopted

[1] D. M. Metcalf, J. M. Merrick, and L. K. Hamblin, *Studies in the Composition of Early Medieval Coins* (Minerva Numismatic Handbooks, no. 3), Newcastle-upon-Tyne, 1968.

[2] C. S. S. Lyon, 'A reappraisal of the sceatta and styca coinage of Northumbria', *BNJ* 28 (1957), 227–42, at p. 233.

[3] G. R. Gilmore and D. M. Metcalf, 'The alloy of Northumbrian coinage in the mid-ninth century', *Metallurgy in Numismatics* 1 (1980), 83–98.

then (and since continued) was neutron activation followed by gamma-spectrometry analysis. Some of the items investigated by X-ray fluorescence in 1968 were re-analysed, together with others selected from both the regal and the episcopal issues—if not from the beginning of the official coinage in the reign of Eadberht, at least to the end in the time of Osberht. It was admitted that the earlier results showed silver contents with disappointingly little signs of grouping. Whereas the Northumbrian sceattas of the eighth century had shown a fairly clear diminution of silver from around 75 per cent first to 66⅔ per cent then to 50 per cent, no such correlation with conjectural alloy standards below 50 per cent could be obtained for the stycas. Explanation for this state of affairs was seen to be provided by one of three factors: the coinage followed a very complex pattern, the intended proportions of the metals in the alloy were inaccurately achieved by the mint, or the quantities responding to analysis had been inaccurately measured. It was not yet clear which of these should be seen to prevail.

In 1980, the new series of results was acknowledged to have confirmed those obtained earlier: namely, that the silver contents showed no obvious signs of grouping. It could be seen that there was an apparent lack of consistency, in that some coins of Æthelred and Archbishop Wigmund had marginally more silver than did some of the slightly earlier issues of Eanred and Eanbald. If, indeed, the alloy was so variable, analysis could be no real guide to the chronological arrangement of issues within a reign. A further project was identified as that concerned with the analytical evidence of die-linked coins, which might prove or disprove such lack of consistency.

That part of the work was published in 1986.[4] Although no more than twenty coins were studied—some of them to be related to specimens already analysed—the results were seen to support recognition of varying quality in closely-connected coins. The idea was mooted, in explanation, that moneyers might have followed different technological practices.

Variations already noted have been considered for determining chronological sequence within reigns lasting for several years. Nevertheless, apart from the possibility of marking an intermediate stage in the early coinage (when copper content was still relatively low) at which the silver was alloyed with zinc, the work so far offers no real guide to the arrangement of issues of which large numbers of coins survive, struck on metal which is essentially a copper-zinc-silver alloy.

So, as a further test of variability and particularly of its extent within a limited period, material selected from the coinage of Redwulf was analysed in 1984. In this instance, the specimens come from the classic collection of stycas belonging to the Yorkshire Museum in York; the contents of the cabinet are derived mainly from the hoards of York and district. Although it has 4,525 coins, of which only seventy are of Redwulf, representation of the series as a whole is not complete.

Redwulf's coins are relatively few in number, even at York, because his reign was short: as a usurper, he ruled for only a few months between the deposition and restoration of Æthelred II. Just when that short period occurred may be a matter of dispute. According to the chronology proposed by Pagan,[5] it was as late as 858. The

[4] G. R. Gilmore and D. M. Metcalf, 'Consistency in the alloy of the Northumbrian stycas: evidence from die-linked specimens', *NC* 144 (1984), 192–98.

[5] H. E. Pagan, 'Northumbrian numismatic chronology in the ninth century', *BNJ* 38 (1969), 1–15.

date traditionally accepted is 844 although there are, perhaps, grounds for recognizing the emendation of that to 843.[6] The question can really be debated properly only in the context of relationships between the coinage of this reign and those of Æthelred II whose issues must be attributed either to his first rule or to his second.

There is considerable variation in the coinage of Redwulf's short reign. Moneyers who had already worked for Æthelred are Brother, Eanræd, Wendelbeorht, Ealhhere (ALGHERE), Forthræd and Monne; the last three, with the re-use of reverses, provide inter-reign links. Cuthbeorht and Hwætnoth are new for the reign (their work is confined to this limited period). Two episcopal moneyers, Coenræd and Hunlaf, are also included in the regal scene; Hunlaf, the only man whose coins have not been examined in this analysis, uses a reverse which he also employed for Æthelred. Ealhhere, Wendelbeorht, Hwætnoth, and (in the main) Coenræd work alone throughout, for the regular coinage; the others work both alone and in partnership with one or more of their colleagues, sharing obverse dies.

Apart from the coins which are undoubtedly official, there is a small group of issues which cannot be wholly regular. An obverse which is of less than perfect style (see nos 14–16) is used normally by Brother and Monne—and possibly also by Forthræd—presumably before being combined with poor-quality dies in the names of Eanræd, Odilo, Coenræd, and Hereræd (NERRED): the last provides an echo of a moneyer who can be shown to belong to the middle of Eanred's reign. This subsidiary section links, through another Odilo die,[7] to a much larger cluster of reverses which are more obviously of cartoon style: they are combined with an obverse normally used by the moneyer Wulfræd, for Æthelred. In the present context—when it is not possible to discuss Æthelred's coinage more fully—it must suffice to suggest that the existence of these odd groups hints at (or, rather, confirms) the political climate of the time as having been less than normal.

One must take the opportunity of saying that the coinage of Redwulf's short reign exhibits, on a smaller scale, the same range of permutations and combinations in the work of moneyers alone, and in co-operation with others, which is to be seen throughout the massive output of base coins which began in the last years of Eanred's reign.

The selection of material which has been analysed affords a reasonable coverage of the various elements in Redwulf's coinage, as may be seen from the diagram (Fig. 1) which shows the coins analysed in their context of the pattern of die-linkage for Redwulf's reign. Of the moneyers who are connected with each other, Brother is represented by two coins (1–2) from different dies and Monne, in the first instance, by three (10–12); the style of Brother's second obverse can be compared with that of Monne's third. One of Cuthbeorht's (3) is a die-duplicate of Oxford 41, published in 1980. Coins of Monne, Cuthbeorht, Eanræd, and Forthræd are shown in a chain

[6] See *English Historical Documents,* vol. 1, *c. 600–1042,* edited by D. Whitelock, 1955: at p. 256. Roger of Wendover's annal for 844 (from *Flores Historiarum*) records Æthelred's expulsion and Redwulf's succession in the same year [at the battle of Carhampton]. The editorial footnote comments of Wendover's dating of Carhampton being a year late: it is conceded that the dating of Northumbrian events may be correct yet, if they *were* contemporary with Carhampton, they too may be assigned to 843.

[7] *SCBI Copenhagen* 368 (Redwulf, Odilo).

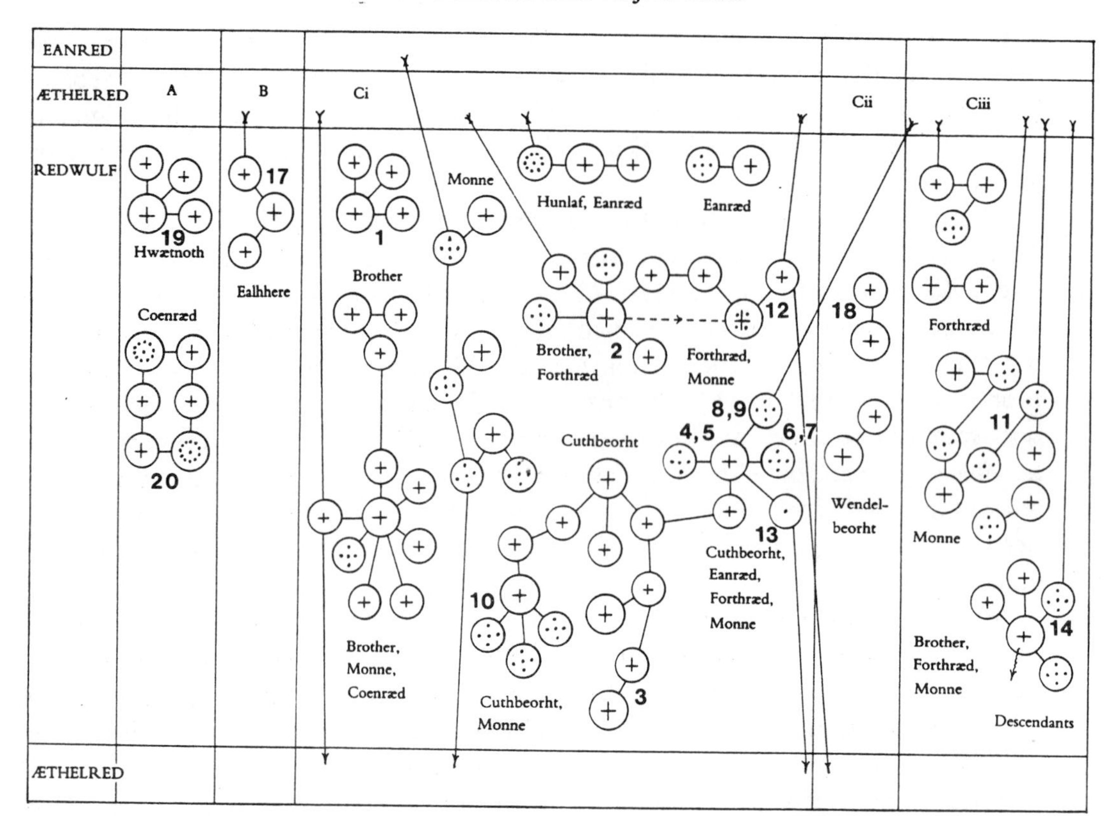

FIG. 1. The analysed coins in the context of the die-links.

formed by the common use of one obverse (4–9,13); the specimens include die-duplicates for each but Monne. The reverses for both Forthræd and Monne are also used in the reign of Æthelred; all three coins, it can be noticed, are of weights slightly above average. The subsidiary group, to which reference has been made, is illustrated by the coins naming Forthræd, 'NERRED', and Odilo (14–16). Last, but not least, come the coins of the independent moneyers Ealhhere, Wendelbeorht, Hwætnoth, and Coenræd (17–20). Ealhhere's reverse is one of two used with this particular obverse, and it has been carried forward from the reign of Æthelred; in this instance, the coin is abnormally heavy (1.52 g) compared with the other specimens in this collection.

The same method of chemical analysis used in previous work[8] was used here. Samples of between 1 and 6 mg were taken by drilling into the edge of each coin. These samples were analysed by neutron activation analysis using a short epithermal irradiation and subsequent long mixed neutron irradiation followed in each case by gamma-spectrometry. Thirteen chemical elements were measured, in particular the major components copper, silver, zinc, and tin. For completeness the minor and trace elements arsenic, antimony, gold, cobalt, chromium, iron, nickel, selenium, and indium were also measured although (with the possible exception of gold which is an impurity of the silver) these appear to have no significance. The full results are tabulated in the Appendix to this paper and the silver concentrations are also set out in the Table in a rearranged order to allow comparison of related coins.

The results exhibit a degree of variability comparable to that noticed in the previous studies. While there are instances of close correspondence between die-

[8] See notes 3 and 4 above.

duplicate coins (e.g. 6 and 7, 3 and 21) what are we to make of coins 8 and 9 with a 50 per cent difference in silver content? There is no evidence of any consistency within the set of obverse-linked coins, nor even within the output of a single moneyer. Because the differences occur even between die-duplicates there may be, in this, confirmation that whatever recipes the mint personnel were using in preparation of the metal, the proportions they required were inaccurately achieved.

TABLE 1. *Silver contents of Redwulf's coins*

Coin	*Moneyer*	*Silver %*	*Comments*
Associated moneyers			
1	Brother	3.29	
2	Brother	2.92	Similar style to 12
12	Monne	0.10	
10	Monne	3.97	
11	Monne	4.34	
13	Monne	5.18	
6	Eanræd	2.85	Die-duplicate of 7
7	Eanræd	2.41	Die-duplicate of 6
8	Forthræd	3.03	Die-duplicate of 9
9	Forthræd	2.09	Die-duplicate of 8
4	Cuthbeorht	4.37	Die-duplicate of 5
5	Cuthbeorht	6.10	Die-duplicate of 4
		(4–9 and 13 are all obverse die-linked)	
3	Cuthbeorht	6.10	Die-duplicate of 21
21	Cuthbeorht	5.60	Coin 41 in ref. 3
Subsidiary issues			
14	Forthræd	4.70	Same obverse as 15, 16
15	NERRED	1.36	Same obverse as 14, 16
16	Odilo	1.51	Same obverse as 14, 15
Independent moneyers			
17	ALGHERE	5.73	
18	Wendelbeorht	5.5	
19	Hwætnoth	3.6	
20	Coenræd (episc.)	2.22	

Yet one cannot afford to ignore another of the factors mentioned in 1980: that the inconsistency reflects in some measure a complex pattern of workshop practice and procedure. Before we come to dismiss analysis as useless in the identification of different standards of fineness occurring over a period of time, let us first question why the coinage was so complex in the use and re-use of dies (both obverses and reverses) by moneyers working alone and together. The orthodox view of Northumbrian coinage seems to stress debasement as a major factor in the fairly swift development of a single-stream, compact currency. An alternative view, based on the continuing study of the York collection but as yet highly unorthodox, dares to suggest that the evidence of the dies and their use points to there having been

Table of Analyses

Northumbrian stycas issued by Redwulf

The quoted experimental uncertainties are based only on counting statistics and represent one standard deviation. The '<' symbol indicates an element sought but not found, followed by a value which is the calculated limit of measurement. nm = not measured. Included at the end of the table are the results of the analyses of two standard reference materials to allow the quality of the analyses to be assessed.

Coin, YM No.	*Moneyer*	*Coin Wt (g)*	*Sample Wt (g)*	*Ag %*	*Cu %*	*Zn %*	*Sn %*	*Au %*	*As %*	*Sb %*	*Fe %*	*Ni %*	*In ppm*	*Co ppm*	*Se ppm*	*Cr ppm*	*Coin*
1 2042	Brother	1.217	0.98	3.29±0.03	66.4±0.7	17.4±0.2	2.54±0.03	0.031±0.001	1.11±0.01	0.073±0.002	< 1	< 0.2	2.3±0.2	40±10	< 100	< 200	1
2 2047	Brother	1.044	1.72	2.92±0.02	70.3±0.7	22.0±0.3	3.3±0.2	0.0312±0.0004	1.00±0.02	0.076±0.002	< 1	< 0.2	7.1±0.2	112±8	< 100	< 200	2
3 2055	Cuthbeorht	1.165	3.333	6.1±0.2	67.7±1.0	18.0±0.3	3.50±0.10	0.0553±0.0008	1.09±0.02	0.0857±0.0008	< 1	< 0.5	4.4±0.1	20±9	< 70	< 100	3
4 2072	Cuthbeorht	1.381	3.29	4.37±0.03	72.5±0.8	21.2±0.4	2.63±0.05	0.0442±0.0007	1.08±0.03	0.0782±0.0010	< 1	< 0.6	4.3±0.2	68±6	< 60	< 100	4
5 2074	Cuthbeorht	1.241	5.02	6.1±0.2	69.7±0.7	18.2±0.6	2.8±0.1	0.059±0.002	1.02±0.02	0.0791±0.0007	< 0.9	< 0.6	7.3±0.2	18±8	< 60	< 100	5
6 2075	Eanræd	1.175	3.047	2.85±0.03	73.0±0.7	20.8±0.6	2.81±0.09	0.0337±0.0006	1.31±0.02	0.129±0.002	< 0.8	< 0.5	3.6±0.2	57±6	< 70	< 200	6
7 2076	Eanræd	1.15	3.689	2.41±0.02	69.5±0.7	19.7±0.4	3.01±0.04	0.0204±0.0008	1.87±0.02	0.098±0.002	< 0.7	< 0.5	2.2±0.1	16±6	< 50	< 90	7
8 2079	Fordræd	1.323	3.604	3.03±0.05	69.3±0.7	22.0±0.8	3.16±0.07	0.0359±0.0006	1.07±0.02	0.091±0.002	< 0.8	< 0.4	3.6±0.1	135±8	< 50	< 200	8
9 2080	Fordræd	1.469	2.759	2.09±0.02	70±2	21.6±0.2	3.00±0.03	0.0117±0.0004	1.03±0.02	0.063±0.002	< 1	< 0.5	5.5±0.2	89±7	< 50	< 200	9
10 2089	Monne	1.259	1.214	3.97±0.03	70.7±0.7	21.3±0.2	3.01±0.03	0.0347±0.0004	1.06±0.01	0.077±0.003	< 2	< 0.3	4.8±0.2	50±10	< 100	< 300	10
11 2091	Monne	1.249	6.126	4.34±0.03	71±2	20.6±0.5	2.48±0.05	0.039±0.002	1.40±0.03	0.086±0.002	< 0.7	< 0.4	3.5±0.1	60±6	< 50	< 100	11
12 2093	Monne	1.087	4.518	0.102±0.002	74±2	17.7±0.3	6.12±0.06	0.0013±0.00005	0.138±0.006	0.173±0.003	0.8±0.3	0.28±0.05	3.00±0.07	44±3	110±30	< 50	12
13 2103	Monne	1.382	5.651	5.18±0.05	71.5±0.7	18.2±0.5	3.12±0.09	0.053±0.002	1.15±0.02	0.097±0.004	< 0.8	< 0.1	5.0±0.1	18±7	< 50	< 200	13
14 2082	Fordræd	1.095	2.745	4.7±0.1	69.1±0.7	20.5±0.2	2.79±0.05	0.0394±0.0008	0.490±0.007	0.0322±0.0007	< 1	< 0.4	3.8±0.2	20±8	< 70	< 300	14
15 2060	NERRED	1.042	3.996	1.36±0.02	70.8±0.7	21.1±0.3	4.15±0.09	0.0115±0.0002	1.11±0.02	0.046±0.002	< 0.6	< 0.3	4.8±0.2	8±3	< 40	< 80	15
16 2067	Odilo	1.104	3.172	1.51±0.02	75.7±1.0	20.6±0.5	3.62±0.03	0.0224±0.0003	0.79±0.02	0.0411±0.0006	<0.6	< 0.2	5.4±0.2	107±6	< 40	< 100	16
17 2035	Ealhhere	1.509	3.589	5.73±0.04	70±2	18.2±0.5	3.16±0.05	0.064±0.002	0.95±0.03	0.077±0.004	< 1	< 0.7	4.8±0.2	45±9	< 80	< 200	17
18 2069	Wendelbeorht	1.261	2.316	5.5±0.2	67.0±0.7	23.5±0.3	2.63±0.03	0.0397±0.0007	0.906±0.010	0.067±0.001	< 1	< 0.6	5.2±0.2	< 30	< 80	< 200	18
19 2064	Hwætnoth	1.222	2.964	3.6±0.1	73.2±0.9	20.0±0.2	3.39±0.06	0.0351±0.0006	1.16±0.01	0.096±0.001	< 0.9	< 0.5	5.4±0.2	72±9	< 60	< 100	19
20 2100	Coenræd	1.193	2.686	2.22±0.03	70±1	19.6±0.5	4.49±0.05	0.0389±0.0008	1.21±0.03	0.086±0.001	< 0.8	< 0.4	4.7±0.2	31±7	< 40	< 100	20
21 Oxf 41	Cuthbeorht		1.928	5.6±0.6	72±2	21.0±0.3	1.8±0.1	0.0490±0.0010	1.05±0.04	0.063±0.008	nm	nm	2.8±0.2	nm	nm	nm	21
NBS 124d	Bronze metal		9.98	0.0192±0.0008	81±2	4.84±0.05	4.27±0.08	0.0001±0.00005	0.016±0.004	0.146±0.004	< 0.2	1.04±0.05	3.14±0.09	46±3	< 20	< 40	
NBS 88E	Sheet brass		11.24	< 0.003	69.6±0.7	27.9±0.3	1.03±0.03	nm	< 0.006	< 0.0005	< 0.2	0.57±0.05	0.19±0.05	6.1±0.6	< 20	< 40	

several workshops in operation to produce different, although concurrent, sections of the coinage. So far, however, too few specimens have been analysed from each of the relevant parts for one to be able to compare like with like within each and, in that context, perhaps to discover a measure of consistency in the metallurgical data.

DISCUSSION

Dr. Metcalf: The analyses published in 1980 showed a positive correlation between antimony and arsenic (*MIN* 1, p. 93). A diagram drawn to the same scale for the new analyses for the reign of Redwulf which Dr Gilmore and Miss Pirie have presented shows (Fig. 1) a much tighter distribution of values, clustering around As = 1.1–1.2%, Sb = 0.07–0.09%. This tight distribution is an interesting and useful result even if its interpretation is uncertain. It lies at the upper end of the ranges previously observed. The symbols in Fig. 1 (open circle, cross, triangle) distinguish the different categories of moneyers identified by Gilmore and Pirie, namely 'associated', 'subsidiary', and 'independent'. It is fairly clear from the diagram that

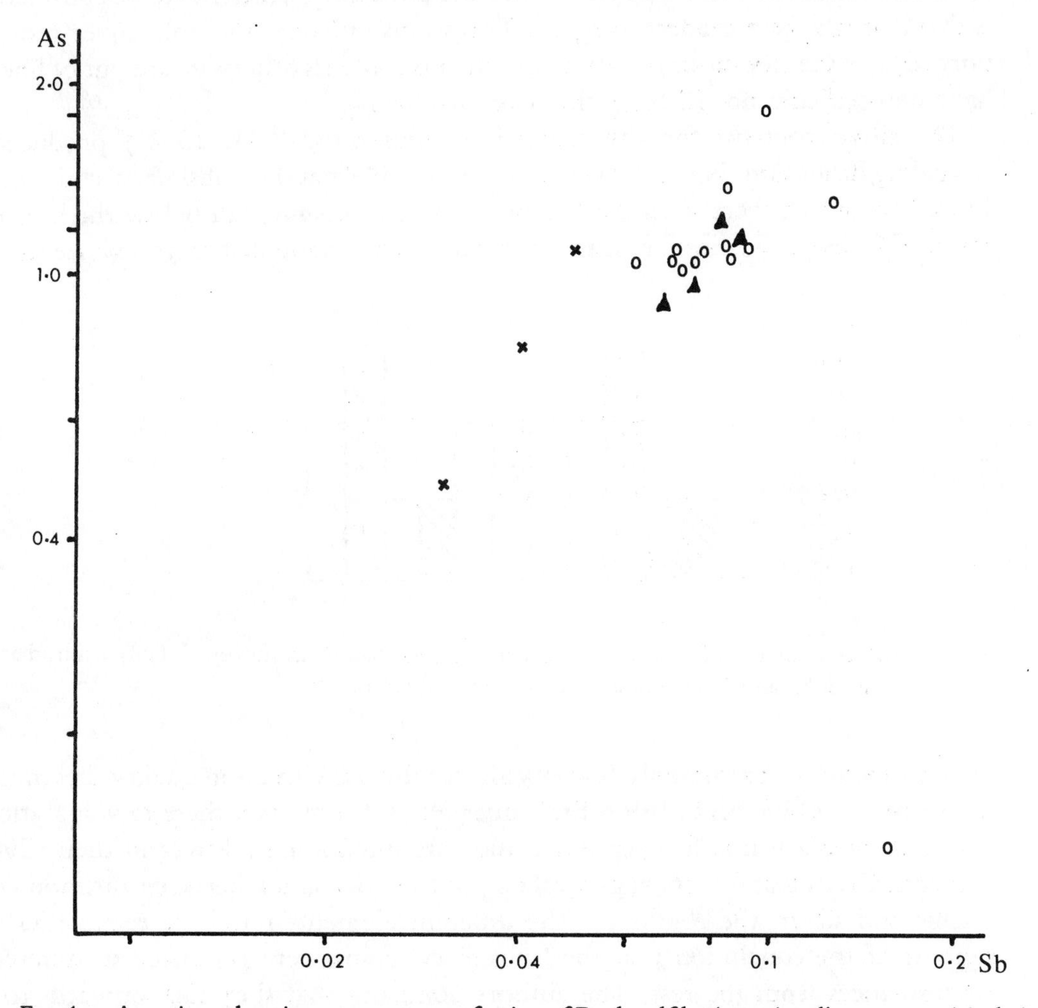

Fig. 1. Arsenic and antimony contents of coins of Redwulf by 'associated' moneyers (circles), 'subsidiary' moneyers (crosses), and 'independent' moneyers (triangles). Cf. the diagram in *MIN* 1, p. 93.

the 'subsidiary' moneyers, whose issues (it is suggested) 'cannot be wholly regular', are using an alloy in which the antimony and particularly the arsenic levels are identifiably different from those in the coins of the 'associated' and 'independent' moneyers (between which there is no significant difference). It would be prudent to look for at least three or four more analyses of 'subsidiary' coins to make sure that the pattern is confirmed, but even with only three results to go on, one would be surprised if it were not. What the contrast means in terms of the attribution of the coins to their date and place of manufacture, and how it arose in terms of the fabrication of the coins are still completely open questions, but the data are surely grist to Miss Pirie's mill.

Coin no. 12 is conspicuously the 'odd man out' in the lower part of the diagram, with only about one-eighth as much arsenic as the average. When one notices that this coin contains virtually no silver, and has exceptionally high levels of tin—double the usual amount—and is moreover the only coin in the sample to contain measurable amounts of iron and nickel, one is bound to view it with suspicion. Can it be a regular coin from Redwulf's reign? One possibility is that it might be an unusually literate 'irregular', presumably post-dating Eardwulf's reform by which silver was abandoned from the alloy. Another possibility which has to be considered is that it might be a modern forgery. This seems unlikely: the gold-silver ratio is normal, as is the zinc-in-brass ratio; only the tin contents otherwise are out of line. I have omitted coin no. 12 from the diagrams below.

The silver contents for the remaining coins (nos. 1–11, 13–21) produce a straggling histogram (Fig. 2), in which it is noticeable that the 'subsidiary' coins, nos. 15 and 16 (which were irregular for antimony and arsenic) fall below the normal range. Of these two coins Dr Gilmore and Miss Pirie write that their obverse die 'is

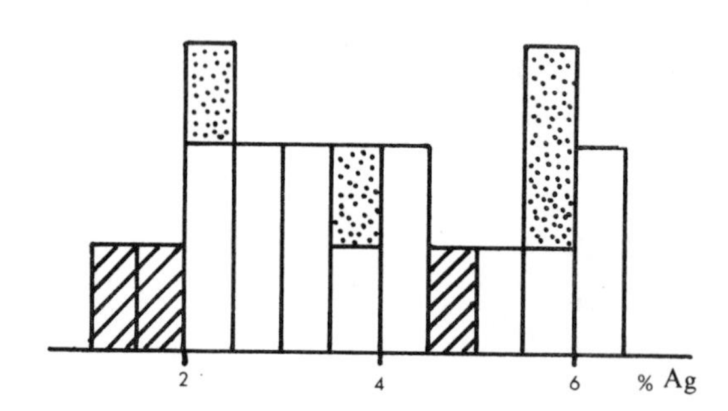

FIG. 2. Silver contents of coins of Redwulf by 'associated' moneyers (plain), 'subsidiary' moneyers (shaded), and 'independent' moneyers (stippled).

used normally . . . presumably *before* being combined with poor-quality dies in the names of . . . Odilo and NERRED' (my italics). From even these few analytical results there is a prima-facie case that they are intentionally lower in their silver contents. Given that there is in general no positive correlation between antimony or arsenic and silver, the results for the different elements reinforce each other in support of the conclusion that the 'subsidiary' coins were produced in different circumstances from the rest. The authors point out that they link onwards to a 'much larger cluster of reverses which are more obviously of cartoon style'. Are we to envisage the 'subsidiary' coins being struck during Redwulf's reign, or after it?—at the mint in York (if there was a single place where the moneyers worked), or elsewhere in Northumbria,—or elsewhere in York?—Back-door moneyers? Bucket-shop stycas? It seems a very difficult concept, and the onward linking to even sketchier coins favours a chronological explanation. One ought, probably, to go to the trouble of checking the provenances, in the unlikely event that they might reveal a different distribution pattern for the 'subsidiary' coins.

There is also a prima-facie case that Cuthbeorht's coins have higher average silver contents than those of Redwulf's coins in general, even though they share an obverse die used by Eanræd and Forthræd.

The zinc-in-brass ratios for Redwulf's coins (Fig. 3) give a somewhat more compact distribution than Æthelred's, around a very similar mean (22.3%, omitting no. 12). Because of the difficulties of sampling and of calibration one should hesitate

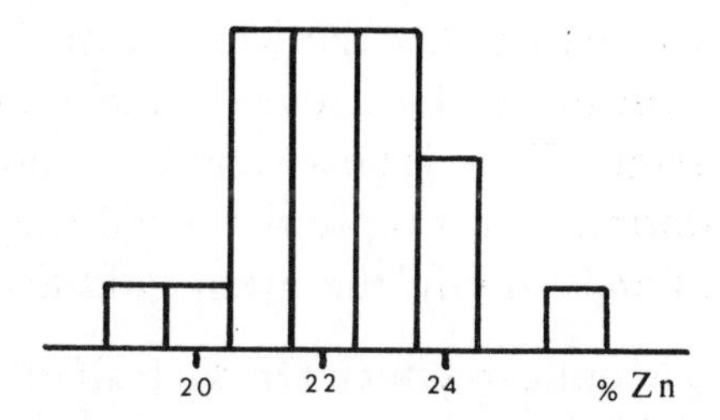

FIG. 3. Zinc-in-brass ratios of coins of Redwulf.

to press the comparison further. The 'subsidiary' coins are no different from the others. No. 12, at 19.3%, falls below the bottom of the range, but well within that for Æthelred.

Tin contents show exactly the same pattern for Redwulf (Fig 4) as for Æthelred.

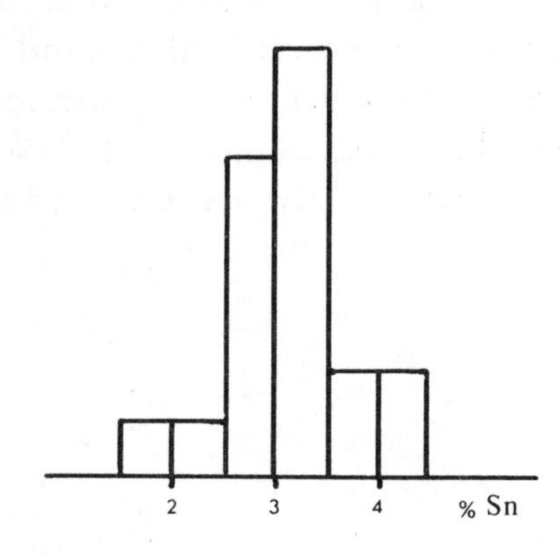

FIG. 4. Tin contents of coins of Redwulf.

The gold-to-100 parts silver ratios provide valuable evidence, which the EPMA analyses cannot pretend to match. They yield a reasonably compact distribution (Fig. 5) with a couple of outlying higher values and only one value below 0.7%. This offers an interesting contrast with the results published in *MIN* 1, in which one can now detect a difference between the figures for Eanred and Eanbald and those for Æthelred and Wigmund. For the earlier pair, the mean gold level was 1.05%, varying very considerably however, with a group of values in the range 0.2–0.3%, and others as high as 2.0% or even 3.0%. The high values can perhaps be discounted as resulting from the inclusion of silver-gilt scrap, but the cluster of low values is

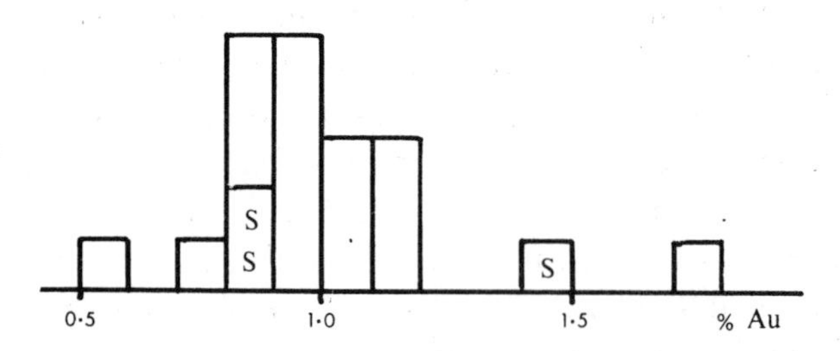

Fig. 5. Gold-to-silver ratios of coins of Redwulf, with 'subsidiary' moneyers shaded.

more likely to reflect a particular silver source. For Æthelred and Wigmund there is much less variation, with a mean gold level of 0.84%. Allowing for sampling variation, one might conjecture that the later set of figures could arise from the homogenizing of the existing stock of silver in the course of the recoinage which began late in Eanred's reign. There is however no reason to think that the recycling of pre-reform coins continued to supply the metal for the new coins throughout Æthelred's first reign. For Redwulf the mean gold level is 1.00%.

Miss Pirie: The coin by Monne to which Dr. Metcalf draws attention (no. 12) is one of two in the Yorkshire Museum; the other is even more worn than this one. The obverse, with the only cross-and-pellets of the time, looks as if it might have been altered from another die, used by Brother and Forthræd: Forthræd uses one reverse with both obverses. (The Yorkshire Museum has no specimen of Forthræd with the cross-and-pellets obv.) Among Redwulf's coins, this is one of two reverses for Monne which are used twice for Æthelred; the metal of no. 12 may be odd, but the die does not seem exceptional. For Æthelred, the rev. of no. 12 is used in combination with a cross-obverse shared with Wulfræd; and again with a pellet-in-annulet obverse which is shared with both Wulfræd and Eanræd. I have wondered whether any of the triple-sharings denote irregular issues in Æthelred's reign. Perhaps we should, some time, test examples of these other coins of Monne, Wulfræd, and Eanræd, so that we can see the Redwulf/Monne coin in that perspective.

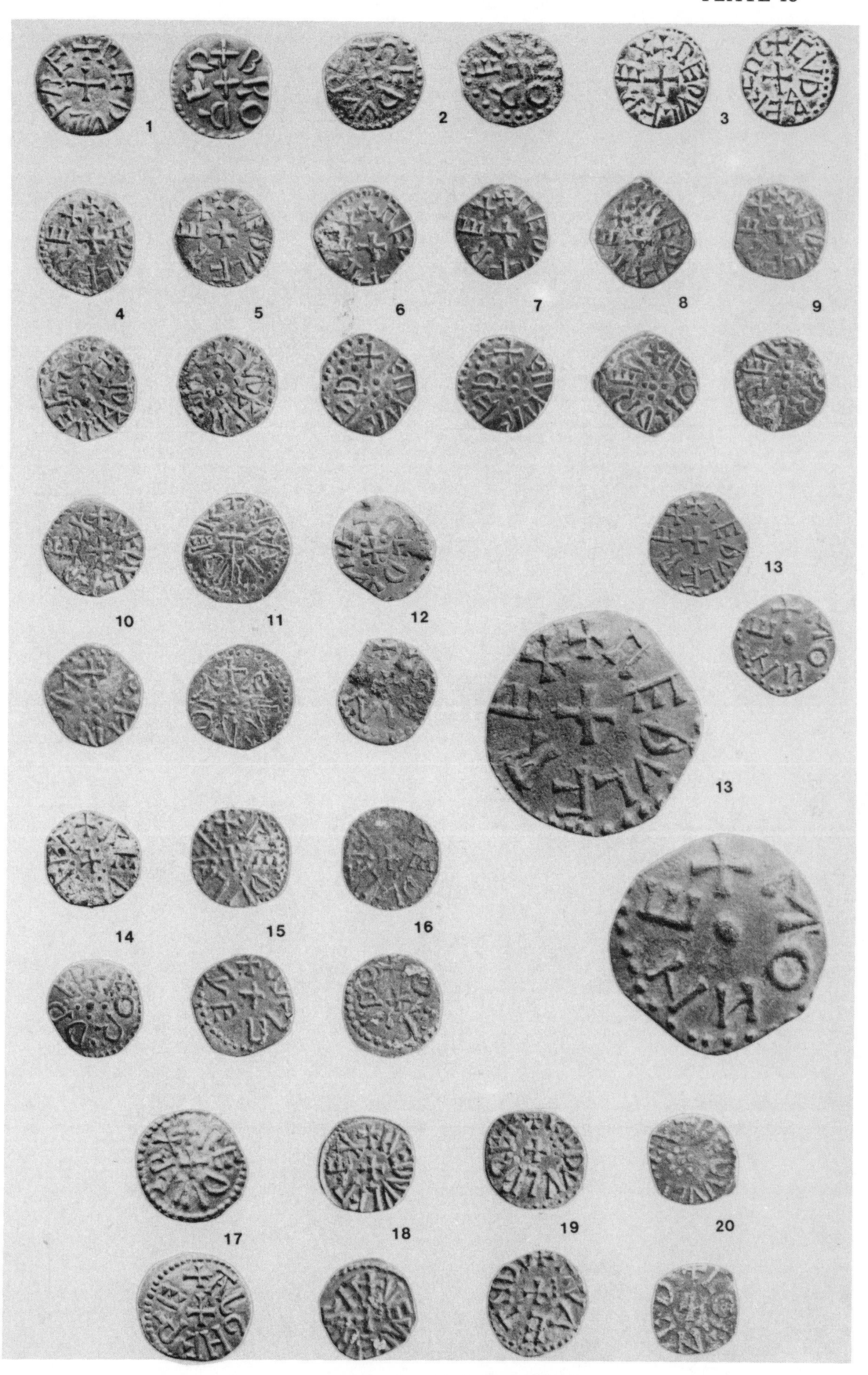

STYCAS OF REDWULF

The Northumbrian royal coinage in the time of Æthelred II and Osberht

D. M. METCALF and J. P. NORTHOVER

[PLATES 14–21]

ÆTHELRED's reign was interrupted for a matter of months, at an uncertain date in the 840s or possibly the early 850s, by the reign of Redwulf.[1] The coins in Æthelred's name can be divided between the first and second parts of his reign on the basis of the following considerations. The Hexham hoard, which included coins of Redwulf but very few if any of Æthelred's successor Osberht,[2] apparently contained few of Æthelred's coins by the moneyer Eardwulf,[3] whereas various other hoards which reflect the composition of the currency after Osberht's accession have certainly contained a large number of Eardwulf's issues. The Hexham hoard is essentially an earlier hoard, even if we cannot be quite sure that a few extra coins were not added to it three or four years after it was otherwise complete. There is a clear contrast in composition between Hexham and the later hoards, and we can safely assert that the great bulk of the Hexham hoard terminates early in Æthelred's second reign. Eardwulf, who is involved in die-links between Æthelred and Osberht, would seem to have worked as a moneyer up to the very end of the reign. It appears, therefore, that Eardwulf's prolific issues may have been more or less the sole official coinage of the second reign, and that all the other varieties, by many moneyers, can be assigned to the first reign.

This general argument, which was expounded by Stewart Lyon thirty years ago,[4] has since been confirmed and to some extent quantified from a more detailed

Acknowledgements. We are grateful to Miss E.J.E. Pirie for detailed expert advice, particularly on the imitative coins.

[1] For the chronology, see the papers by David Kirby and Stewart Lyon above.

[2] The uncertainties attaching to the coins of Osberht said to have come from the Hexham hoard are well discussed in Pirie, 1982, p.3. She inclines to the opinion that they are likely to have come from the second Hexham churchyard find, in 1841; but it is virtually certain that the 1841 coins, found when the same grave was reopened for another burial, were part of the 1833 hoard. Any answers to the conundrum, it seems, will have to remain conjectural, but that does not affect any of the arguments from the Hexham hoard advanced in this paper.

[3] One must say apparently, because our evidence for the proportions of different varieties in the hoard is imprecise. Adamson (1834, 1836) was concerned to record all the different varieties, but does not report how many of each variety he saw. Eardwulf's coins are rather uniform.

[4] This basic analysis of the division of Æthelred's coins between his first and second reigns was clearly set out in Lyon, 1955–7.

comparison of the dies of Eardwulf's coins in the Hexham and Bolton Percy 1967 hoards. Out of 149 second-reign coins in Bolton Percy, only 21 were struck from dies included in Hexham.[5] For that argument to be watertight, one needs to know how many dies altogether are likely to have been used by Eardwulf, in order to be able to judge what degree of overlap might be expected between two random samples of the sizes in question. But we may safely accept that much of the range of second-reign coinage is unrepresented in Hexham. If it were not for the awkward reference to coins of Osberht, one would say that much of the range post-dates Hexham, i.e. that Hexham was concealed early in the second reign. That is almost certainly the truth of the matter, whether or not the Osberhts are an honest mistake on the part of a nineteenth-century collector.

The broad picture, therefore, is that Æthelred's first and second reigns were numismatically quite different in character from each other. In the first reign, some 13 to 15 moneyers worked for the king, of whom about half had already worked for Eanred, and about half (with some overlap) went on to work for Redwulf. In the second reign, by contrast, the great bulk of the coinage bore the name of a single moneyer (Eardwulf), although two or three (or more?) of the first-reign moneyers apparently struck a very few coins late in the second reign. Eardwulf may have been a master-moneyer, taking responsibility for all the coins produced by a team of under-moneyers; or there may have been such a sudden and dramatic reduction in the demand for coinage that only one moneyer was needed.

In order to grasp the full measure of the contrast, it is necessary to add some numbers. The Bolton Percy hoard of 1967, concealed after Æthelred's reign, allows us to give totals (which may or may not be typical) for the various moneyers, as shown in Table 1. Eardwulf, we can now see, was a very productive moneyer, even if he struck only about a quarter as many coins as all the first-reign moneyers in aggregate. There is a wide range in the levels of activity of the first-reign moneyers as represented at Bolton Percy. Four or five are very active; another four are moderately active; and the rest are proportionately insignificant. This carries over a very similar arrangement from the reigns of Eanred, in which Forthræd and Monne were (again) very active, Brother, Wihtræd, and Wulfræd were moderately active, and Erwinne and Odilo were insignificant. There seem, in other words, to be permanent differences in status or function between individual moneyers: some struck far more coinage than others. The reasons are hidden from us, but we should bear the disparities in mind. The total shown for Redwulf is incomplete, because the table omits two of his moneyers who did not work for Æthelred, namely Cuthbeorht and Hwætnoth (5 and 2 specimens), but in any case the volume of Redwulf's coinage was far smaller than Æthelred's, either because it was produced over only a very short time, or because the rate of production had by then dwindled. It is to some extent die-linked into Æthelred's coinage.

The idea was expressed by Lyon in 1956 and has since been repeated, that there was a 'complement' of ten royal and two archiepiscopal moneyers. As we have just seen, there certainly were not ten equally active moneyers. In so far as at least 13 moneyers worked for the king during the first reign, one would have to assume that three or more were replacements who took up office when another moneyer relinquished it. In the context of Table 1 below, and of the somewhat lower range of

[5] Pagan 1974.

silver contents found in Redwulf's coins, the analyses that have been made (and which have been limited to six moneyers) can offer no help in identifying moneyers who may have worked for only part of the reign. In order to solve the problem, one needs a hoard concealed not more than twelve months into Æthelred's reign.

On the evidence that has been summarized so far, it would be reasonable to ask how sure we can be that the change in character in Æthelred's coinage came precisely at the end of his first reign and not, for example, at an intermediate date in the second reign. On the latter scheme, the evidence of the Hexham hoard for relative chronology would retain exactly the same force, i.e. Hexham was concealed shortly into the 'second reign' coinage, which might not have begun, however, until a year or so after the restoration. Against that, it might be argued that the new moneyers who worked for Redwulf (namely Cuthbeorht and Hwætnoth) would then be likely to have gone on working for Æthelred (restored). That is a matter of probability, in a situation where moneyers could have been going out of commission *seriatim.* Their tenure of office may perhaps have been influenced by wider client relationships; and we should remember that the numbers of specimens are very small. Nevertheless, it is a good *prima facie* argument.

TABLE 1. *Æthelred's moneyers, together with their activity in the preceding and following reigns (numbers of coins in the Bolton Percy 1967 hoard)*

	Eanred	Æthelred 1st reign	Redwulf	Æthelred 2nd reign	Osberht
Very active moneyers					
Eanræd		128	x		
Forthræd	x	88	8	1	
Leofthegn		75			
Monne	x	154	11	8	x
Eardwulf				149	
Less active moneyers					
Brother	x	16	3		
Coenræd		1	6		
Cynemund		3			
Ealhhere (ALGHERE)		43	1		
'EDELHER'		1			
'ERPINNE'	x	1			
Hunlaf		1			
Odilo	x	3		1	
Wendelbeorht		26	1		
Wihtræd	x	20			
Wulfræd	x	19			
Wulfsige (VVLFSIG)		6			
Eanwulf				5	x

One might hope that metal analysis would throw some light on the date at which the large establishment of moneyers was disbanded, through a comparison of the range of 'silver' contents of the 'first-reign' and 'second-reign' coins with those of Redwulf, although the overriding evidence might still have to come from the complex die-linkage which is a feature of the later stycas. ('Silver' has been calculated by adding together the measured values for silver, lead, and gold, on the grounds that that is the best approximation to what the ninth-century moneyers would have perceived as 'pure silver'.) It will be shown below that the 'first-reign' coins vary widely in their silver contents from around 8–9% down to 2–3% or occasionally even less, while the 'second-reign' coins generally have less than 0.1% silver: thus, a very clear difference. Redwulf's coins fall in between, ranging from 5–6% down to 2–3%. As his reign was so brief, this looks like a measure of the tolerance that was permitted at one and the same moment, and because there were also quite wide tolerances in Æthelred's first reign, it will obviously be difficult to extract any precise conclusions, even from a large number of analyses.

Another major topic in the styca series concerns the many severely blundered 'imitative' or 'derivative' coins which occur in the hoards. The Hexham hoard already includes some, notably coins with King Eanred's name on both sides, and others with the names of the moneyers Hereræd (HERRED) and Wulfheard in combination, or with Hereræd's name on both sides. We have written about the earlier series of imitations in a separate note, elsewhere in the volume. The later hoards include more numerous specimens, which are die-linked into Osberht's coins by the moneyers Æthelhelm, Eanwulf, Eardwulf, Monne, and Wulfræd. The blundered coins form a series, often with the name of Æthelred and/or one of his moneyers, which on the evidence of die-links are at least in part later than Osberht's coins. We analysed a number of the wilder imitations, and also a few more coins of Osberht, in order to see how their alloys compared. The results throw up a difficult problem. Osberht's coins show a radical change in alloy. In some of them zinc disappears completely, to be replaced by 13–15% tin, with no silver. The coins are thus simply of a high-tin bronze. Silver had already disappeared from the alloy of the stycas with Eardwulf's reformed issues in Æthelred's second reign. The problem arises because there are some coins, including apparently official coins of Osberht and of Archbishop Wulfhere, which are intermediate in character: they are of a mixed brass/bronze. A good proportion of the 'blundered or derivative' series are mixed, but with no clear pattern. Die-linked pairs of coins can be of good-quality brass and brass-bronze respectively. If the blundered coins post-date Osberht's bronze issues, what happened? Did the authorities throw up their hands and stop trying; or were the derivative coins from purloined dies, or by moneyers no longer working for the king? Could they even have been minted in York after the Danish occupation? Should this affect one's judgement of the dating of the derivative coins, i.e. ought one to consider whether the late hoards are post-conquest? In the longer perspective, it is a very reasonable supposition that the sudden appearance of a clutch of hoards in York itself in the 860s or thereabouts reflects the events of 866–7. But could some of them not equally well have been lost in troubled times as late as 869 or even 872–3? There are arguments based on die-linkage against extending the derivative series too far beyond the reign of Osberht, and in any case a later dating even of *all* of the hoards would not prove that any of the derivative coins were struck after 866: it would merely make room for that hypothesis.

Our judgements about the derivative coins and indeed about several other aspects of the styca series will be affected by information about the scale of output. The recording of die-duplication in the Bolton Percy hoard allows us to make at least rough estimates, moneyer by moneyer, of output, measured in terms of the numbers of obverse and reverse dies employed. The figures set out in Table 2 include a couple of what look like erratic estimates, in which no great confidence should be placed. The general run of the ratios for specimens from each estimated reverse die (a measure of the survival-rate) clusters consistently, however, around 1.2. It is no greater for Æthelred's second reign, and this may be taken as a reasonably clear indication that the first-reign coins were not systematically withdrawn when the silver contents of the new issues were cut almost to zero. (The hoard could, in principle, be selective in favour of the better of the available coins, but there is no obvious reason to think that that is so.)

TABLE 2. *Estimates of the numbers of dies employed under Æthelred II, Redwulf, and Osberht. (Source: the Bolton Percy hoard of 1967)*

	Specimens	Known dies		Estimated dies		Specimens	Rev. dies
		obv.	rev.	obv.	rev.	per rev. die	per obv. die
Æthelred II, first reign							
Eanræd	128	31	71	33	100	1.3	3.0
Forthræd	88	33	47	40	65	1.4	1.6
Leofthegn	75	29	48	33	80	0.9	2.4
Monne	154	39	81	43	124	1.2	2.9
Brother	16	8	15	10	120?	0.1?	12.0?
Coenræd	1	1	1	1	2	2.0	2.0
Cynemund	3	2	2	2	3	1.0	1.5
Ealhhere (ALGHERE)	43	9	17	10	20	2.2	2.0
'EDELHER'	1	1	1	1	1	1.0	1.0
'ERPINNE'	1	1	1	1	1	1.0	1.0
Hunlaf	1	1	1	1	1	1.0	1.0
Odilo	3	3	2	5	5	0.6	1.0
Wendelbeorht	26	8	14	10	20	1.3	2.0
Wihtræd	20	7	7	8	8	2.5	1.0
Wulfræd	19	8	11	10	16	1.2	1.6
Wulfsige	5	2	4	2	10?	0.5?	5.0?
Sub-total (adjusted)	*584*	*183*	*323*	*210*	*c.500*	*c.1.2*	*c.2.4*
Redwulf	38	17	24	22	40	1.0	2.0
Æthelred II, second reign							
Group (a)	147	41	80	50	120	1.2	2.4
Group (b)	17	6	15	7	64	0.3??	9.0??
Osberht	75	31	48	46	106	0.7	2.3
Derivative							
Early series	16	12	13	28	45	0.4	1.6
Later series	381	127	199	145	293	1.3	2.0

The Bolton Percy hoard may yield figures which are to some extent underestimates. A single hoard often does so. The figure of 40 reverse dies for Redwulf can be judged by comparison with Lyon's die-analysis based on about 200 specimens, which indicated a total of about 49 reverse dies (15 of which were also used in Æthelred's reign.)

If coins of appreciably different intrinsic value could circulate alongside each other, doubtless at the same face value, what historical conclusions should we draw? A range of different conclusions would be possible, e.g.

a) The currency in the time of Osberht, and by extension during Æthelred's second reign, still commanded general acceptance within Northumbria at its face value. Even though the more recent coins were very inferior in silver contents, the earlier ones were not driven out by the operation of Gresham's Law.

b) Depending on the market price of brass, about which we know nothing, perhaps the intrinsic value of the later stycas derived mostly from the 'base metal' constituents in their alloy—at 6% silver, they were made of 15 parts of brass to one of silver, so that even if the value of brass was only one-fifteenth that of silver, the intrinsic value of the coin would have been evenly balanced between the two metals. Less optimistically, one might conjecture that

c) The charge levied for reminting old coins was so high that in spite of the difference in silver contents it was not profitable to sort through one's money and withdraw the older coins; or

d) The moneyers (who no longer needed silver to put into the coinage) declined to accept old coins for reminting on the basis of their higher silver contents; or

e) The costs of recovering the silver in the 6% coins by cupellation (fuel, crucibles, etc.) were too high for culling to be undertaken by private enterprise. Cupellation would have wasted the brass, and that prompts the thought that the economical way to remint older coins, e.g. those of Eanred containing 10–20% silver, would have been to melt them together with extra brass and tin, thereby diluting the silver. If this were done with batches of Eanred's coins, the alloy of which was not precisely known, the variability of the resulting alloy would depend on the batch size and on the extent to which Eanred's coins had become mingled in circulation before withdrawal. There is some reason to think that the work of Eanred's Group B moneyers reflects a recoinage, and that the systematic withdrawal of the Group A coinage may have taken place essentially in the closing years of that reign. The Group B coinage has not yet been analysed in depth. We do not in any case think that it is mathematically plausible that the variability in silver contents of Æthelred's coins can be explained in this way. Similarly we doubt whether southern English or continental coins, which could have been compulsorily reminted on the assumption that they were of good silver, were debased or variable enough during Æthelred's first reign to provide an explanation. It might be just about possible, on a 'late' chronology, but the phenomenon of variability is one that originates in Eanred's reign.

The total number of estimated reverse dies for the first reign in Table 2 has been arbitrarily adjusted downwards to take account of a couple of results which look erratic. Allowing for the margins of uncertainty and statistical error, it is nevertheless reasonably clear that the official 'second reign' issues were only a quarter to a third as plentiful as those from the first reign, but that the 'blundered' or 'derivative' coins were produced from large numbers of dies—far larger, for example, than the total for Osberht's official dies. Our historical assessment of these numbers will depend a good deal on our view of the chronology of the 'derivative' coins. On a broad view, lumping all the post-Redwulf, debased coins together, the appropriate comment seems to be that the disappearance of silver from the alloy was accompanied, in the last fourteen or so years before the fall of York, by a decline in the average annual output, but not by a drastic decline. It appears that there was a continuing demand for the moneyers' services, even if the shortage of silver was so acute that the decision had to be taken to make the coins entirely out of brass or bronze. That demand must, we think, have been a public demand: it would be very difficult to sustain the thesis that the silver-less coins were made directly for the king and the archbishop, and given forced currency by being put into circulation by them in their capacities as heads of church and state.

THE COINAGE ALLOY DURING ÆTHELRED'S FIRST REIGN

Earlier research. A considerable analytical effort has been devoted to Eanred's Group A coins, but very little to those of Æthelred. The few available figures showed a variation from 13% to 2% 'silver', together with substantial amounts of zinc and minor amounts of tin. The poorest of Eanred's Group B coins went down to 4% 'silver', thus creating an apparent problem of overlap between the two reigns, coins with 4% being certainly earlier in date than others with 13%. The extreme results are, admittedly, uncharacteristic: Eanred's coins rarely fall below about 8%, and Æthelred's coins are rarely much better than 8% silver.

Harris analysed two coins by the moneyer Eanræd (6% and 3% silver), and Metcalf, Merrick, and Hamblin (1968) analysed one coin of Leofthegn by XRF (2% silver). Four more coins of Leofthegn were analysed by Gilmore and Metcalf using NAA (1980), showing silver contents of 13, 9, 8, and 6%, with 17–21% zinc and 1–2% tin. Leofthegn's unique pictorial type (beast right, with triquetra) proved rather surprisingly to have the lowest silver contents. In 1982 Miss Pirie published analyses of four coins in the Newcastle collection (by Eanræd, 3.5, 2, and 15% 'silver'; Leofthegn, 2.8% 'silver'. The coin with 15.3% 'silver' has 10.5% Ag, 4.8% Pb, and 18.8% Sn, and doubt must rest on its authenticity.) In 1984 Gilmore and Metcalf published analyses of 5 more coins of Leofthegn as part of a small project to explore the variation between die-linked specimens, and found that they might vary as widely as from 13 to 5%.

Altogether, then, eleven coins by the moneyer Leofthegn have been analysed by modern methods, and five coins by Eanræd. Some 13 to 15 moneyers worked for Æthelred and, as we shall see, there are systematic differences in the silver contents of their coins. A sketchy analysis of the work of only two moneyers may thus be said to leave the topic 90 per cent unexplored.

Strategy and preliminary results. Bearing in mind the possibility that different moneyers may have used slightly different alloys concurrently, if the smelting and alloying processes were not centralized, and bearing in mind also that in the face of variability between die-linked coins the moneyers' intentions could only be recovered through the study of a statistically adequate sample, we thought it would be most profitable to concentrate our efforts at this stage on a few moneyers. The

Oxford collection contains nearly 400 coins from the first reign, and we were therefore able to make two useful choices, namely to build on the existing analyses of Leofthegn's coins in order to make a relatively full study of them, and secondly to concentrate on some of the moneyers whose level of activity was modest. Leofthegn seemed a promising choice because his *œuvre* is distinctive in employing a wide range of designs, which are often more artistically elaborate than the simple crosses, annulets, and pellets used by other moneyers. We planned to look at the correlation between design and alloy, on the hypothesis that particular designs might have been struck for a limited period (of two or three months) at some particular time during the first reign. The opportunity to arrange the coins into a sequence is an extension of the strategy of comparing die-linked coins, and should permit more precise statistical conclusions than an analysis which treats specimens merely as members of a group. We deliberately left on one side the issues of the very active moneyers Eanræd, Forthræd, and Monne, which are plentiful in all collections, in order to examine and compare, secondly, the coins of Brother, Cynemund, Ealhhere, Wendelbeorht, and Wihtræd. By taking account of die-linkage and also general similarities of style we arranged the coins of each moneyer into some sort of order, and were better able in that way both to discount the tolerated variations of alloy, and to identify here and there coins which were superior in both design and alloy, and others which were from inferior dies and debased. More intriguingly, we found significant differences in silver contents (but not in the quality of the brass, nor in the small additions of tin) between moneyers.

The sample of coins chosen for analysis deliberately included numerous die-linked specimens. Through our study both of Leofthegn and of the less active moneyers we were thus able to establish a much more solid base of evidence relating to variability between die-linked coins, than that published in 1984. The presumption is that die-linked coins were in most cases struck at very much the same time and that they should therefore show what consistency of alloy was achieved at any one moment, or what variation was tolerated. This evidence is liable to be occasionally misleading, because of the quite frequent sharing of obverse dies between moneyers, and the continued use or re-use of reverse dies, e.g. from Æthelred's reign into that of Redwulf. We wondered whether there might be any statistical difference in variability between duplicates and reverse links on the one hand (reverse dies normally have a shorter life) and obverse links on the other, given that the obverse to reverse die ratio was generally 1 to 2 or more. Obviously the best starting-point for approaching the topic of variability of alloy through die-linkage was to look at a group of coins certainly from a very short period. King Redwulf's coins seemed to be the perfect choice, and we were grateful to Miss Pirie and Dr Gilmore for allowing us an advance sight of the results from their project on that reign. The results give a strong hint that, as under Æthelred, different moneyers were producing coins of different average silver contents, and indeed we suspect that some individual moneyers will eventually be seen to be 'high-silver' or 'low-silver' men in both reigns.

At the same time as looking for clues to the pattern of the first-reign coinage in these ways, we were interested to accumulate reliable data for other constituents of the alloys, as a source of evidence for possible changes in metallurgical practice or for variation in the sources of the copper or brass and of the silver. We have thought about the zinc contents in terms of the Zn : (Cu + Zn) ratio, where 28% has been found to be the upper limit of what can be achieved unless the copper is very finely granulated for the cementation process. Virtually all the first-reign coins are in fact of a good-quality brass (19–24%) and also have moderate tin contents (2–4.5%). This approach makes the assumption that all the copper entered the alloy of the coins as brass, and therefore that the tin was added as tin, and not in bronze. If it had been added in the form of a high-tin bronze, with a composition of say 15% tin, then the measured tin contents in the coins would account in most cases for 11–25% of copper, leaving so little to have entered the alloy in combination with the zinc as to imply zinc-in-brass figures often well over 30%. Furthermore, if bronze had been used in the cementation process, its significantly lower melting-point would have led to very poor results in the absorption of the zinc.

Systematic information about the brass and tin in the stycas should serve as a corrective to thinking exclusively about their silver contents. The important point is that there is no positive correlation with silver contents. Moneyers who are making coins with average silver contents varying from one moneyer to another are all maintaining very similar standards in their additions of brass and tin. As we have just seen, it looks as if it would be technically almost impossible to achieve such high zinc ratios unless the brass was made separately, and the silver and tin added to it. The alloys of the 'lower silver' moneyers cannot therefore be explained in terms of the dilution with extra brass of metal obtained by melting down better coins, unless one postulates that extra tin was added as well. Here and there, there is a slight inverse correlation, suggesting that a decline in the silver contents was compensated by an improvement in the brass or by an increase in tin contents.

The traces of gold in the coins can be satisfactorily interpreted as being in association with the silver. Our EPMA results for gold are however often close to or below the theoretical limit of detection for the standard length of counting time we used, and may well therefore be subject to systematic error (the weight % limit for Au, measuring the Mα line, was calculated as 0.04%). When one calculates the ratio of gold to 100 parts silver, any inaccuracies are magnified, and the errors are likely to become worse as the silver contents fall. Comparison of the gold ratio in Æthelred's first and second reigns, for example, therefore becomes impossible. The results obtained by NAA for the gold contents of the stycas were much more precise, and Dr Gilmore's analyses for Eanred, Redwulf, Osberht, and Archbishop Wulfhere may safely be compared. They show convincingly that the gold traces correlate with silver. The ratio for coins of Redwulf is distributed very compactly around a mode of *c.* 0.9–1.0 parts per hundred. The looser distribution of the EPMA results is probably a reflection of their short counting time, and notice should be taken only of those individual results where the gold measurement is clearly above the limit of detection.

The same reservation applies to the EPMA results for other trace elements and minor constituents, the limits of detection being calculated as follows:

Fe	Kα	0.01%	Bi	Mα	0.02%	Pb	Mα	0.04%
Co	Kα	0.01%	Sb	Lα	0.02%	Au	Mα	0.04%
Ni	Kα	0.01%						

The measurement of bismuth using the Mα instead of the Lα line represents an improvement in the limit of detection over our earlier Anglo-Saxon analyses published in *NC* and *BNJ*.

General assessment of the results. We analysed 83 first-reign coins of selected moneyers, plus three or four others of individual interest. Over-all, the 'silver' contents ranged from 10% to 2%, with a few specimens outside that range. The bar-graph (Fig. 1) bears some resemblance to a normal distribution, in so far as there is a

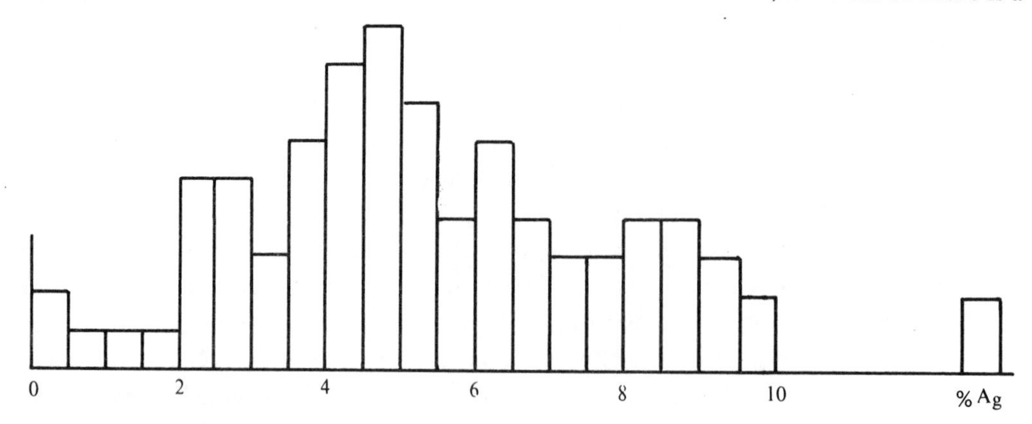

FIG. 1. Æthelred's first reign: silver contents (Ag + Pb + Au) of 83 selected specimens.

peak of sorts at 4–5.5%. It is flanked, however, by what might be other peaks at 2–3%, 6–6.5%, and 8–9%. This is frankly a very untidy result. The pattern may be multi-modal, but more evidence would be required to show that that was so, in particular the corroboration of negative evidence from die-linked coins. A comparison with the corresponding bar-graph for Redwulf's coins (Fig. 9 below), which cuts off at about 6.5%, hints at the possibility of a decline during even so short a period as the first reign.

The variation in silver contents between die-duplicate or die-linked specimens is not as great, over-all, as might at first sight appear. A few figures as high as 8% create an appearance of great variability, but almost two-thirds of the differences are less than 2.5% (see Fig. 2). Obverse links show, on average, a greater difference than reverse links or duplicate coins, but not markedly so (2.9% as against 2.1%). In relation to silver contents of only around 4 to 6%, the variations are, of course, large,

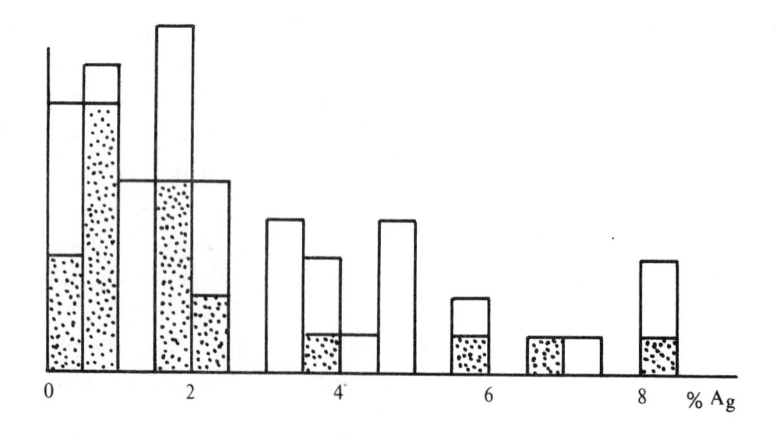

FIG. 2. Æthelred's first reign: differences between the 'silver' contents of die-linked or die-duplicate specimens (including earlier analytical results by neutron activation). Stippled squares = reverse die-links or duplicate coins. Plain squares = obverse die-links. Where three coins (a, b, and c) are linked, three values have been entered in the diagram (a–b, b–c, c–a). Total, 53 differences.

and they seem often to be much larger than could be put down to any technical incompetence.

While the 'silver' contents are variable, the quality of the brass is notably uniform, showing a compact distribution mostly between 19 and 24% Zn : (Cu + Zn), with only a few lower proportions (Fig. 3). There is no correlation, positive or negative, between 'silver' and the quality of the brass (Fig. 4). Nor is there any correlation between the silver contents and the weights of the coins (Fig. 5). We

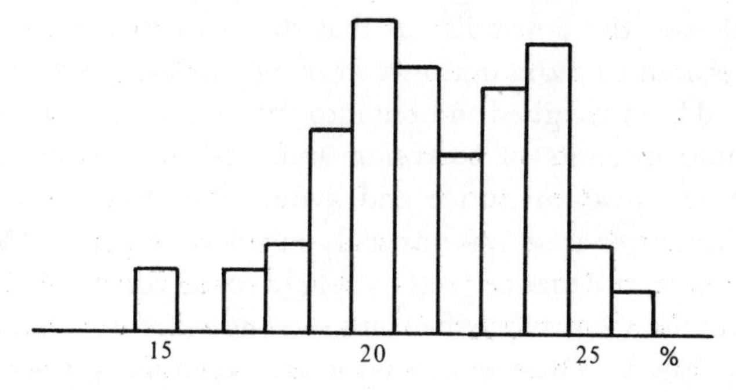

FIG. 3. Æthelred's first reign: the quality of the brass (Zn: Cu + Zn) on the asumption that all the copper in the coins entered their alloy as brass. Total, 83 values.

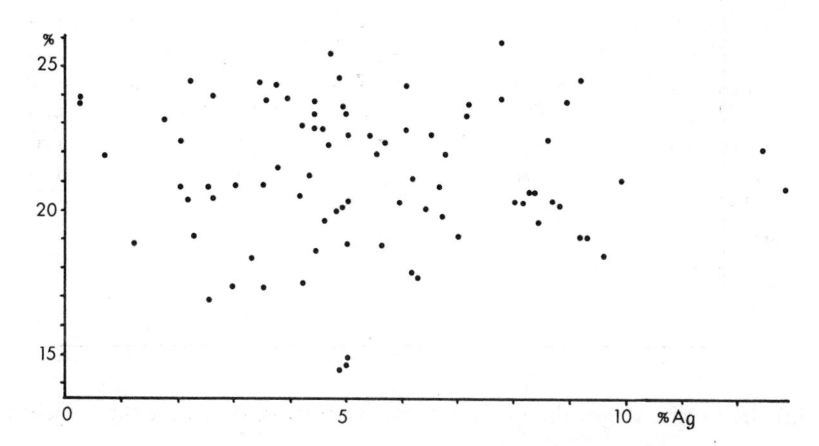

FIG. 4. Æthelred's first reign: 'silver' contents plotted against the quality of the brass.

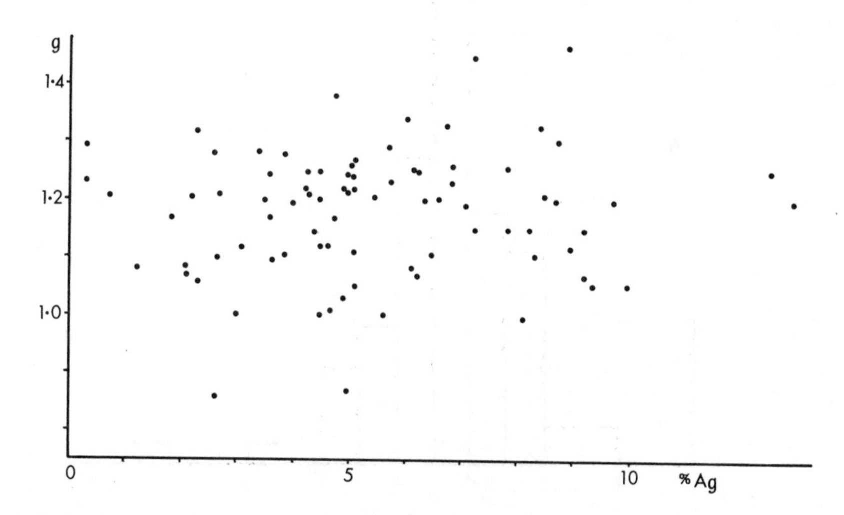

FIG. 5. Æthelred's first reign: 'silver' contents plotted against the weights of the coins.

looked at this correlation very carefully in view of the finding by Dumas and Barrandon that billon coins of the Arras mint in the Gisors hoard showed a strong negative correlation between weight and silver contents. If one plots the absolute 'silver' contents of Æthelred's stycas, however, the resulting bar-graph (with a step interval related to the average weight of the coins) retains exactly the same characteristics as seen in Fig. 1. We looked finally for any correlation between the quality of the brass and the weight of the coins, but found none (Fig. 6). Figs 4–6 effectively rule out the possibility a) that the workmen were frustrated in their intentions to produce a more uniform alloy by working losses e.g. of zinc after the constituents had been weighed and put into the coinage-metal, and b) that the coins suffered variable amounts of corrosion and leaching, which microscopy of the polished sections failed to notice and avoid. We think that the grinding and polishing of the sample areas was normally sufficient to get well below any layers of surface enrichment, and that our results should correspond sufficiently well with the compositions of the alloys when the coins were new, for our assessment of the results to be validly based. These conclusions are strongly supported by a detailed

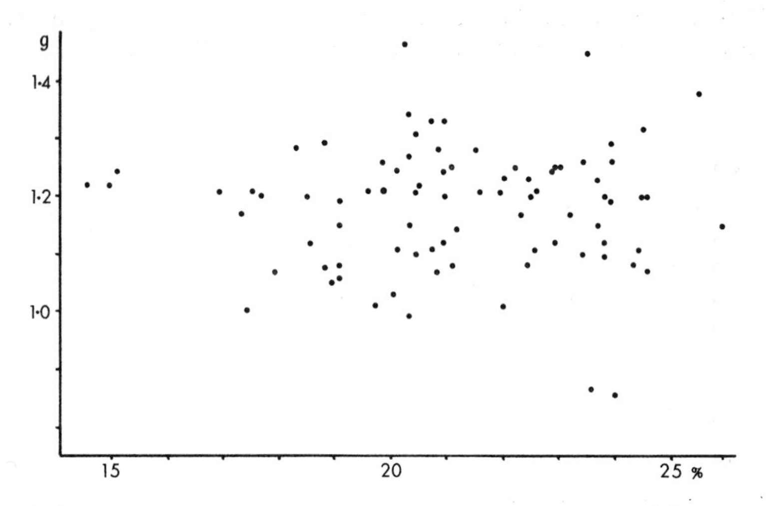

FIG. 6. Æthelred's first reign: the quality of the brass plotted against the weight of the coins.

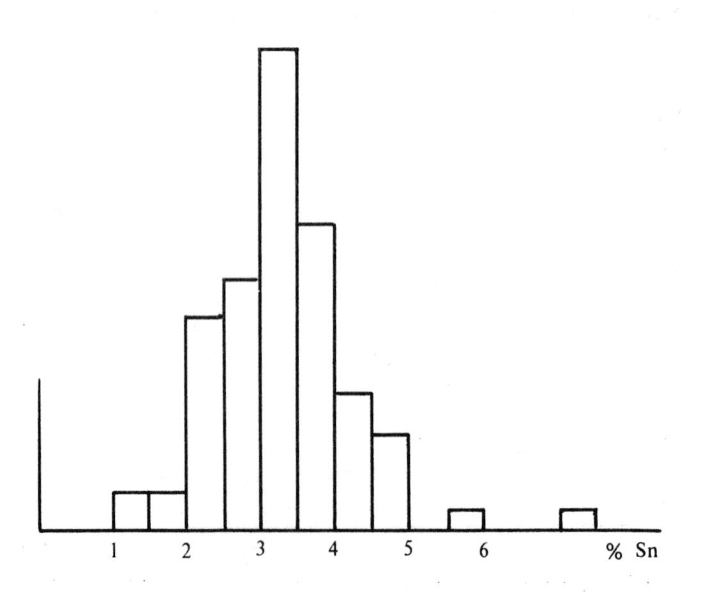

FIG. 7. Æthelred's first reign: tin contents of 83 selected specimens.

examination of results for die-linked specimens and (more generally) by a consideration of the results in their proper numismatic sequence of related legends, designs, and so on. All this adds, we think, to the force of our findings as regards the presence of tin in the stycas.

The tin contents are remarkably consistent, showing a normal distribution with a pronounced modal value at 3–3.5% (Fig. 7). This seems to us to offer important evidence for intention and success in controlling the composition of the coinage metal. All the moneyers conformed closely to the average. It is intriguing to speculate where the tin came from. (One remembers that the Eanred silver penny was found in Cornwall, of all places.)

There appears to be a slight negative correlation between tin contents and the quality of the brass (Fig. 8), but it is difficult to interpret this sensibly in terms of the

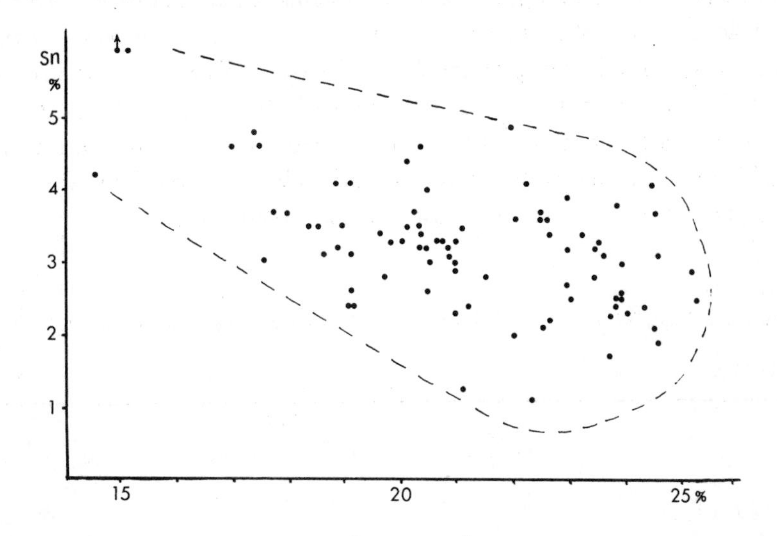

FIG. 8. Æthelred's first reign: the quality of the brass plotted against the tin contents.

fabrication of the coinage metal. It may be no more than an occasional effect of leaching or enrichment.

In the tabulations in the text below, gold : silver ratios based on measured gold contents of 0.06% or more are marked 'a'. The unmarked results are based on measurements close to or below the limit of detection and should not be relied upon.

In view of the positive correlation between antimony and arsenic, and the differences between moneyers in these two elements, noted by Gilmore and Metcalf, we looked at the range of antimony values (arsenic was not measured) but found no clear evidence of differences between Æthelred's moneyers, except that Wendelbeorht's coins were marginally lower in antimony than the others, which were quite uniform at the higher end of the previously observed range.

Die-linkage is shown diagrammatically in the tabulations by means of lines beside the running numbers of the specimens. A linking line to the left of the numbers indicates a shared obverse die, and one to the right a shared reverse die.

Leofthegn. Analyses of 36 specimens (including those already published) should constitute an adequate sample, as they include 26 varied obverse dies, out of about 33 estimated above to have been used by Leofthegn. (But Adamson's plates suggest that this is an underestimate.) Most of the 36 specimens can be grouped in accordance with distinctive designs, such as the letters M or A, a quadruped, etc. An exhaustive check for die-links found 6 shared obverses (involving 16 specimens) and 3 shared reverses (8 specimens, partly overlapping with the obverse linkage). The links were within rather than between groups of coins of similar style.

The coins were arranged into groups according to their designs on the assumption that, whatever their alloy, coins of the same distinctive design or of designs of similar style are likely to be close to one another in date whether or not they are die-linked. This assumption is not logically inevitable: Leofthegn could have returned to the same design from time to time. Where coins of similar design are die-linked, however, (as is often the case) the presumption is much stronger.

Die-linked coins can vary widely in their silver contents, e.g. from 12 to 4 per cent (see nos 1 and 3, and also nos 6 and 10). The strategy of grouping the coins allows mean averages for the sub-groups to be calculated, which should reflect more fairly than single analyses the average composition of Leofthegn's output over short periods. The grouped averages are shown below as Table 3. It will be noticed that 23 out of the 36 analyses have grouped averages in the range 5.0% to 8.0% 'silver', and inspection suggests that the upper and lower ends of this range might well be curtailed if extra results were incorporated. The individual results are spread fairly evenly between 5 and 8%, with no obvious clustering.

TABLE 3. *Leofthegn's coins. Grouped average results, arranged by obverse legend.*

	Weight	'Silver'	Zinc in brass	Tin	Gold: silver
AEDELRED					
1–3	1.17	8.6	21.2	2.7	0.48
4	1.03	4.9	20.0	3.3	0.66
EDELRED					
5	1.47	8.9	20.2	3.7	0.62
6–7	1.32	8.6	23.9	3.5	1.00
8–11	1.17	6.0	21.9	3.7	1.05
12–17	1.23	6.8	23.1	3.3	1.47
18–19	1.14	5.9	17.5	4.6	0.79
20–2	1.18	5.1	21.7	3.0	0.51
EDILRED					
23–7	1.15	7.6	20.1	2.9	1.70
28–30	1.14	5.6	20.8	2.7	0.83
31–5	1.19	3.4	20.4	3.9	0.69
36	1.23	0.3	23.7	1.7	–

On the available evidence, one should hesitate to suppose that the groups can be placed into any chronological order.

Nos. 31–5, however, are significantly worse than the average with 3.4% silver, and no. 36 (one of Miss Pirie's 'descendants') has only 0.3% 'silver' (Ag, 0.05%, cf. the coins of Eardwulf, below.)

It is reasonably clear that the highest values, of 12–13%, are atypical, and that the highest silver 'standard' (if one can speak of a standard) is 8–9%. The assessment reached by Gilmore and Metcalf in 1980, that Æthelred's first-reign coinage showed a decline from 13% down to 6% or less, can now be modified accordingly. Indeed, it is by no means obvious that there was a decline, except with nos. 31–6. Although the coins have been arranged in descending order of the average silver contents of the groups, there is no evidence from style that the order corresponds with the sequence of issues.

The numismatist's instinct should be to attempt a classification of Leofthegn's coins on the basis of their legends. There is an obvious correlation between the groups (based on the designs) and the spelling of the king's name AEDELRED, EDELRED, or EDILRED. If we arrange the summary tables accordingly we obtain the results already shown in Table 3. All three varieties of the king's name include groups with over 7.5% 'silver' contents. The values below 4% are confined to the groups reading EDILRED. The Table reveals no general correlation, whether positive or negative, between weight and type or silver contents, but two or three specimens are of individual interest. No. 23 is the only coin in the sample with a runic *n* in Leofthegn, and its high silver content encourages one to interpret it as an experimental die and an early issue. No. 13, the only example with the elaborate legend LEOFTHEGN MONET, is unusually heavy and of better silver than the average for its group. No. 22 is of low weight and low silver contents for its group. No. 36, with virtually no silver, is one of the only two specimens on which the moneyer's name is retrograde (the other being no. 19).

	Weight	'Silver'	Zinc in brass	Tin	Gold: silver	
1. *Obverse legend AEDELRED*						
Double annulet						
1	1.20	12.9	20.9	2.3	0.36 n	*MIN* 37
2	1.15	8.2	20.3	4.6	0.85 n	
3	1.17	4.7	22.3	1.1	0.22 n	
Swastika design						
4	1.03	4.9	20.0	3.3	0.66	
2. *Obverse legend EDELRED*						
Cross/cross						
5	1.47	8.9	20.2	3.7	0.62	Rev = 9, 11
Letter ᛏ *(or omega?)*						
6	1.25	12.6	22.2	4.1	1.09 a	Rev = 10
7	1.38	4.7	25.5	2.9	0.91	
Letter Ѫ*/celtic cross*						
8	1.15	9.2	19.1	4.1	0.95 a	
Letter Ѫ*/cross*						
9	0.99	8.1	20.3	3.2	0.77 a	Rev = 5, 11
10	1.20	4.4	23.8	3.8	1.53 a	Rev = 6
11	1.32	2.2	24.5	3.7	0.96	Rev = 5, 9
Four annulets crosswise/celtic cross						
12	1.21	6.5	22.6	3.6	0.47	
*Chrismon/celtic cross (*ᛏ*ONET)*						
13	1.45	7.2	23.5	3.3	tr	
Chrismon/cross and pellets						
14	1.24	4.9	20.1	4.4	5.49 a	
15	1.15	7.8	25.9	2.5	0.52	
16	1.12	8.9	23.8	2.4	0.34 n	

Chrismon/cross pommee						
17	1.23	5.7	22.4	3.6	0.55 n	
Cross of wedges						
18	1.26	6.8	19.8	3.3	1.58 a	
19	1.01	5.6	22.0	3.6	0.74	
Double annulet						
┌20	1.33	6.7	20.9	3.3	0.46	
├21	1.34	6.0	20.3	3.5	1.08 a	
└22	0.86	2.7	24.0	2.3	—	
3. *Obverse legend EDILRED*						
Cross with pellets in angles/group of 7 or 8 dots						
23	1.08	9.9	21.1	3.5	3.54 n	
24	1.22	4.9	14.5	4.2	1.38 a	
Cross with pellets/cross with pellets						
25	1.08	9.3	19.1	2.2	1.14 n	*MIN* 38
Cross with pellets/cross, circle of pellets						
26	1.15	7.2	23.7	2.3	0.86 a	
Cross, circle of pellets/cross						
27	1.23	6.8	22.0	2.0	1.59 a	
Cross with pellets/Northumbrian beast, triquetra						
28┐	1.07	6.2*	17.9*	3.7*	0.93*	
Cross/Northumbrian beast, triquetra						
┌29┤	1.25	6.2	21.1	1.3	1.15 n	*MIN* 40
└30┘	1.10	4.4	23.4	3.2	0.40 n	
Cross/group of 7 dots						
31	1.25	4.4	22.9	3.9	0.47	
Group of 7 dots/cross						
32	1.08	2.02	22.4	3.7	1.61	
Cross/cross						
33	1.12	3.1	20.9	2.9	—	
34	1.28	2.6	20.8	3.2	1.37	
35	1.24	5.1	15.1	5.9	—	
Cross/cross (different style)						
36	1.23	0.3	23.7	1.7	—	

a Measured gold contents of 0.06% or more
n Gold contents measured by neutron activation analysis

There are no visible trends or correlations between 'silver' contents and the quality of the brass, or the tin contents, or the gold-in-silver ratios. One or two coins have abnormally low zinc contents (nos. 24, 35, and perhaps 28, with 14.5, 15.1, and 17.9*%),perhaps due merely to a poor batch of brass.

In summary, then, half or more of Leofthegn's coins can be interpreted as having intended silver contents of 5–8% 'silver'. The few groups that exceed that figure, averaging 8–9%, are very erratic. A few coins fall below 4%. The correlation of 'silver' contents with the detailed classification of the coins thus offers very little encouragement to detect a downward trend, until we come to nos. 31–6.

Less active moneyers. Eight coins by Brother, 7 by Cynemund, 9 by Ealhhere (ALGHERE), 12 by Wendelbeorht and 11 by Wihtræd were analysed, with the averaged results for each moneyer as set out in Table 4. The mean 'silver' contents (Ag + Au + Pb) are so different from one moneyer to another as to make it difficult to believe that they were working to the same standard. Only Wihtræd shows a good correlation between varieties of design and silver contents. There is no very satisfactory way of harmonizing the evidence from Leofthegn and Wihtræd, except perhaps to suggest that most of Leofthegn's output was concentrated early in the first reign. We are not obliged to assume that minting was spread evenly through the reign, or that each moneyer's activity was equally spread.

Although silver contents vary between moneyers, and sometimes, apparently, within the *œuvre* of a single moneyer, the quality of the brass and also the tin contents are generally very consistent. The exceptions are a couple of sub-groups where a slightly lower quality of brass may be a real difference. The break-down of some moneyers' coins into two sub-groups is explained below.

TABLE 4. *Averaged results for selected moneyers.*

	Weight	'Silver' contents mean	mode	Brass quality	Tin	Gold: silver
Brother (2)	1.20	9.2	–	20.5	2.8	2.1
" (6)	1.17	4.0	4.2	22.1	2.7	2.0
Cynemund (7)	1.12	2.5	2.2	20.8	3.3	0.7
Ealhhere (7)	1.22	7.2	7.8	22.1	3.0	0.9
" (2)	1.25	0.5	–	22.9	3.7	(high)
Leofthegn (36)	1.19	6.2	6.2	21.5	3.2	1.0
Wendelbeorht (10)	1.18	4.5	(4.7)	20.3	3.5	0.9
" (2)	1.14	2.5	–	19.3	3.9	2.0
Wihtræd (7)	1.20	6.7	6.4	20.3	3.3	0.7
" (4)	1.08	4.4	(4.4)	21.0	3.3	1.0

Brother. Eight coins of Brother include two with silver contents of 8–9%, four with 4–5%, and two with lower silver contents. There are no obvious clues to the sequence of the coins, except perhaps that the coin with 9.7% silver is of a different obverse design.

		Weight	'Silver'	Zinc in brass	Tin	Gold: silver
37	Obv. ⁘	1.20	9.7	18.5	3.5	1.4 a
38 ⌉	Obv. hooked X in REX	1.20	8.7	22.5	2.1	2.7 a
39 ⌋	Obv. ✱ hooked X in REX	1.22	4.9	24.6	1.9	4.1 a
40	Obv. ✱	1.01	4.7	19.7	2.8	0.9
41		1.22	4.2	20.5	3.0	0.8
42		1.25	4.2	23.0	2.5	2.7 a
43		1.20	3.5	24.5	2.1	2.2 a
44		1.10	2.6	20.4	4.0	1.3

The quality of the brass is variable, but shows no trend in relation to silver contents. The tin contents in Brother's coins are slightly lower than for other moneyers investigated, and would be more so if the first and/or last coins in the above list were atypical.

An attempt to group the coins according to their silver contents may well be made fallacious by the vagaries of the sample. As things stand, there is a big gap between the coins with over 8% silver and those with under 5%, and in the summary (above), the averages have been calculated accordingly,—but the two groups are die-linked.

Cynemund. The only clear difference in metal contents among the seven coins of Cynemund analysed is that two of them, which are die-linked, have unusually low zinc contents. Should one place them at the beginning or the end of the sequence? The best solution seems to be to interpret them as early, taking account of the use of a runic *x* (ᛉ) in REX, and in spite of the low silver contents of no. 50. A runic *n* (ᚾ) in CVNEMV*n*D is normal. Nos. 49–50 are severely blundered, while the coin placed last in the sequence, no. 51, has retrograde legends on both dies, and a (reversed) N in CVNEMVND.

	Weight	'Silver'	Zinc in brass	Tin	Gold: silver
45	1.08	1.2	18.8	4.1	1.9
46	1.00	3.0	17.4	4.6	–
47	1.09	3.6	23.8	2.5	0.9
48	1.21	2.2	20.4	2.6	2.3
49	1.24	3.5	20.9	3.0	(tr)
50	1.17	1.8	23.2	3.4	–
51	1.07	2.1	20.8	3.1	–

Although none of the individual results should be relied upon, the gold traces in Cynemund's coins appear to be consistently low.

Ealhhere. Nine coins by Ealhhere (ALGHERE) are heavily die-linked, and can be arranged into a sequence in which the most elaborate dies (rev., cross with pellets in angles) have the highest silver contents. No. 58 reads ALDHERE. The obverses read +AEDILRED℞ or eventually +AEDILRE℞.

Two of the nine coins (nos 59–60) are entirely different in style and contain virtually no silver. They read +EDILREDREX. They are obvious candidates for reattribution to Æthelred's second reign.

Two further coins, which are apparently modern (cast) forgeries are discussed below.

	Weight	'Silver'	Zinc in brass	Tin	Gold: silver
52	1.26	7.8	23.9	3.0	0.7
53	1.31	8.7	20.4	3.2	0.6
54	1.07	9.1	24.6	3.1	0.8 a
55	1.19	7.1	19.1	2.6	0.4
56	1.26	5.0	23.4	2.8	0.8
57	1.12	4.6	22.9	3.2	1.2
58	1.33	8.4	20.7	3.3	1.6 a
59	1.29	0.3	23.9	2.5	40.0 !
60	1.21	0.7	21.9	4.9	6.8

Wendelbeorht. Of 12 coins analysed, ten were noticeably consistent in their silver contents, while the remaining two were inferior and were from the only retrograde obverse die. The coins have been arranged in sequence in which reverse dies beginning with a V of normal size are grouped first. (But it is one of these dies, nos. 63–4, which is used also by Redwulf, for a coin containing *c.* 5.8% 'silver'!) The coin placed at the head of the sequence has significantly low zinc and high tin contents. The last five coins all have rather low zinc contents.

	Weight	'Silver'	Zinc in brass	Tin	Gold:silver
61	1.22	5.1	14.9	7.3	–
62	1.27	5.1	20.3	3.4	0.6
[63	1.11	5.1	22.6	2.2	1.1
64]	1.14	4.4	21.2	2.4	–
[65	1.08	6.0	24.3	2.4	0.6 a
66]	1.28	3.8	21.5	2.8	0.9
67	1.19	3.9	23.9	2.6	1.1
[68	1.05	5.1	18.9	3.5	1.5 a
69] [69	1.17	3.5	17.3	4.8	2.3 a
70]	1.28	3.3	18.3	3.5	1.1
[71	1.21	2.6	16.9	4.6	2.5 a
72]	1.06	2.3	19.1	3.1	1.5

Wihtræd. The eleven coins analysed include a range of designs and legends, with a good correlation between design, legend, and silver contents, confirmed by die-links and identities. The reverse die of nos. 74–5 had been used for coins of Eanred.

		Weight	'Silver'	Zinc in brass	Tin	Gold: silver
Coins reading EÐFL ..., PIHTRED						
73	Elaborate central crosses	1.21	8.5	19.6	3.4	0.9 a
[74]		1.11	8.3	20.7	3.3	1.2 a
75]		1.20	6.3	17.7	3.7	0.9
76	(Pihtred retrograde)	1.11	6.4	20.1	3.5	0.5
77	℞ Annulet with dots	1.25	6.1	22.9	2.7	0.5
[78	O + ℞ Annulet with dots	1.29	5.7	18.8	3.2	0.7
79]		1.21	5.4	22.6	3.4	0.4
Coins reading EDIL..., PIHTRED						
[80	Obv.	0.87	4.9	23.6	3.1	1.1
81]		1.11	3.8	24.4	4.1	–
Coins reading EDIL..., VIHTRED						
[82		1.21	4.2	17.5	3.0	0.7
83]		1.12	4.5	18.6	3.1	2.0 a

It is tempting to interpret this evidence in terms of a progressive series of reductions in silver contents, but there is insufficient evidence to demonstrate separate standards of 8–9% and around 6%. The difference in the types perhaps entitles us to calculate averages separately for the first seven and the last four coins.

The use of a runic *t* in Vih*t*red is apparently not an early feature—at least, it is not associated with high silver contents.

Neither the zinc nor the tin contents show any obvious correlations or trends.

Additional analyses

Coenræd (and Wulfræd). Coenræd was an archbishop's moneyer, but dies with his name are very occasionally used with royal obverses. A die-linked group of three shows 'Coenræd' re-using an obverse die previously used by Wulfræd. Another pair, from a single reverse die of Coenræd, have obverses respectively of Wigmund and (retrograde) ELREDRF. The silver contents suggest that the explanation in the first case might be the re-use by Coenræd of an inappropriate royal obverse die at a date some years later, whereas in the second case the blundered coin is of good metal and may well be contemporary.

		Weight	'Silver'	Zinc in brass	Tin	Gold: silver
84	Wulfræd	1.13	5.1	13.2	3.0	1.5 a
85	Coenræd	1.01	0.6	22.9	4.5	tr
86	Coenræd	1.09	1.9	20.0	2.1	2.5
87	Wigmund/ Coenræd	1.03	7.2	17.2	2.5	1.3 a
88	ELRED/ Coenræd	1.17	6.7	15.5	2.9	1.4 a

Odilo. Only two coins were available for analysis, and the results for one of them are possibly affected by corrosion, but they have been included because they are die-duplicates and as contributory evidence that individual moneyers may have employed similar alloys under Æthelred and Redwulf.

	Weight	'Silver'	Zinc in brass	Tin	Gold: silver
89	1.29	5.3*	14.3*	3.8*	0.8*
90	1.12	3.2	21.4	1.8	-

THE REIGN OF REDWULF

Nine more coins of Redwulf were analysed, of which one proved to be a modern forgery, and one in very poor style to be probably an ancient forgery. The seven remaining analyses when set against the one previously published, and twenty newly analysed by Gilmore and Pirie, create a strong suspicion that different moneyers were achieving different average silver contents, as seems to have been the case under Æthelred. The overlap of moneyers between the two reigns, as represented among the results, is hardly enough to allow us to suggest, further, that individual moneyers were ranked similarly in the two reigns, but we note the high figure for Ealhhere and the low figures for Eanræd (Table 5). The approximate 'silver' contents (Fig. 9) may be compared with those for Æthelred's first reign: for Redwulf there are no values above 6.5%, and there seems to be a modal value at little more than 3%.

TABLE 5. *Approximate 'silver' contents for Redwulf's moneyers*

Æthelred		*Redwulf*	*Average*
6 coins average 4.0	Brother	3.6^{n},3.2^{n}, 2.6	3.1
	Coenræd	3.0, 2.5^{n}	2.8
	Cuthbeorht	6.4^{n},6.4^{n},5.9,4.7^{n}	5.9
(7.23)	Ealhhere	6.1^{n}, 5.3	5.7
3.5, 2.3	Eanræd	3.1^{n}, 2.6^{n}	2.9
	Forthræd	5.0^{n}, 3.6, 3.3^{n}, 2.3^{n}	3.6
	'Herreth'	1.6^{n}	1.6
	Hwætnoth	3.9^{n}, 3.9, 3.0	3.6
	Monne	5.5^{n}, 4.6^{n}, 4.6, 4.2^{n}, 0.2^{n}	4.7 (4)
5.3*, 3.2	Odilo	1.7^{n}	1.7
(4.53)	Wendelbeorht	5.8^{n}	5.8

The silver values of NA analyses have been increased arbitrarily by 0.2–0.3% to make some minimum allowance for lead, which could not be measured by this method.

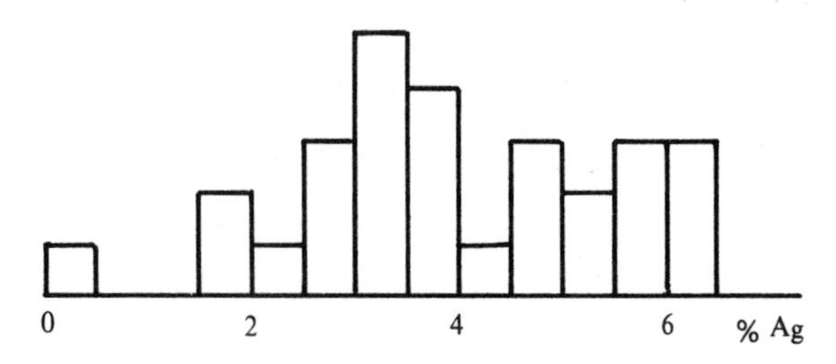

FIG. 9. Redwulf: approximate 'silver' contents of 28 selected specimens. (Source: Table 5).

The high figure for Wendelbeorht under Redwulf (5.8%) suggest that his worst two results under Æthelred should be interpreted as defective rather than as a deliberate reduction in standard late in Æthelred's first reign.

		Weight	'Silver'	Zinc in brass	Tin	Gold: silver
[91	Brother	1.21	2.6	26.0	2.7	0.9
92	Coenræd	1.17	3.0	21.9	1.9	(tr)
93	Ealhhere	1.28	5.3	22.9	3.1	1.1
94	Forthræd	1.20	3.6	18.7	3.3	1.8 a
95]	Hwætnoth	1.21	3.0	22.2	2.8	2.6
96	Hwætnoth	1.07	3.9	19.4	2.6	(tr)
97	Monne	1.14	4.6	21.5	2.7	1.1
98	Monne (forgery?)	1.46	0.7	26.0	0.3	(tr)
99–100	Vacant					

Alternatively, it might be possible to argue that the two low values (2.6%, 2.3%) belong to the beginning of Æthelred's second reign. Similarly, the case for interpreting the two low-value coins by Ealhhere as second-reign coins is strengthened by the similarity of style of Redwulf's coins to Æthelred's better coins.

The zinc contents of Redwulf's coins are much the same as Æthelred's. The tin contents are marginally lower, with an average (omitting the forgery, which has hardly any tin) of 2.8%.

ÆTHELRED'S SECOND REIGN: EARDWULF

Eardwulf's coins, which mostly contain only residual traces of silver, create an impression of neatness and regularity. Closer inspection reveals an interesting range of minor variations in design and in the quality of the lettering. Carefully seriffed lettering appears to be an early feature, as do dotted inner circles. The specimen that has been placed at the head of the series analysed has unusually high tin contents, as has no. 102 with three pellets in the legend. The series as a whole maintains a high quality of brass (median value, 22.7% zinc in brass) and a generous amount of tin (median, 3.9%). No. 105, with an unusual reverse type, has lower zinc contents, and raises the question whether more than one production line may have operated under Eardwulf's control and responsibility. No. 120, with a retrograde inscription, seems likely to be an unofficial product, as it contains hardly any tin.

The silver contents of Eardwulf's coins (Ag only, not Ag + Pb + Au) fall into two categories. Most specimens show very low values of around 0.04%–0.08%, but a few are as high as 1% or even 2%, that is, fifteen or twenty times as much. The separation between the categories is so clear-cut (Fig. 10) that one must suppose two

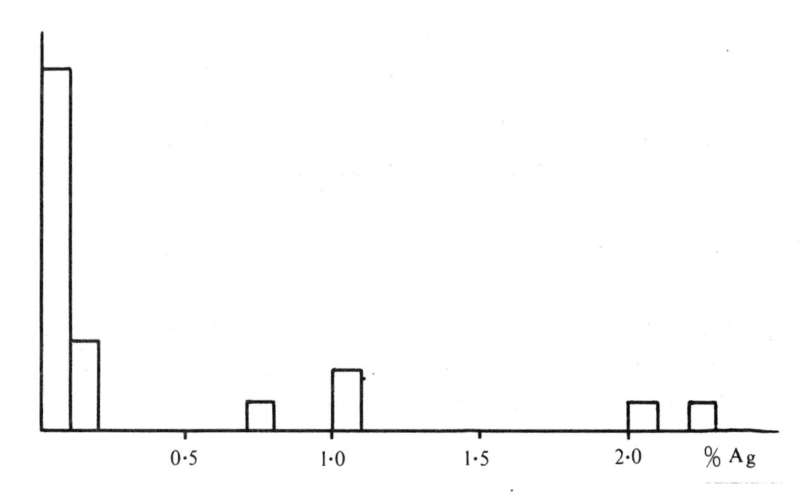

FIG. 10. Æthelred's second reign: silver (Ag only) contents of Eardwulf's coins.

very different procedures for the preparation of the alloy. One would guess that in the majority of the coins the silver is adventitious, having entered the alloy probably with the copper, and that this coinage metal was newly prepared, and not derived from the recycling of old coins. In the specimens with higher silver contents, a certain proportion of old coins may have been thrown into the crucible. The coins with higher silver contents are nos. 102, 103, 106, 112, and 120, of which the last has been noted as possibly unofficial. The other specimens tend to fall in the earlier part of Eardwulf's issues (coins with a dotted rather than a linear inner circle). Die-links (nos. 103–4 and 106–7) show that very low-silver and higher-silver coins belong closely together. As a die would strike far more coinage than could be produced from one crucible of metal, one should probably envisage that occasional batches of metal, more or less at random, but especially in the early stages of the reform, included some old coins.

		Weight	'Silver'	Brass	Tin
101	Cross/5 pellets	1.20	1.25	15.6	7.5
102	Cross/star (in legend)	1.06	2.94	18.3	6.1
[103	Cross/star	1.28	1.17	20.3	4.1
104]	Cross/star	1.08	0.56	22.4	3.3
105	Cross/cinquefoil	1.19	0.80	18.8	4.2
[106]	Cross/cross and pellets	1.11	0.72	27.6	3.2
[107]	Cross/cross and pellets	1.31	0.79	23.1	4.3
[108	Cross/star	1.12	0.71	23.3	3.9
109	Cross/star	1.16	0.57	21.6	3.1
110]	Cross/star	1.06	0.33	24.7	3.9
111	Cross/star	1.20	0.24	21.6	3.3
[112	Cross/pellet	1.07	0.08	20.0	4.5
113]	Cross/pellet	1.07	0.35	24.6	4.4
114	Cross/pellet	0.95	0.14	22.2	3.2
115	Cross/pellet	1.06	1.30	16.7	8.2
116	Pellet/pellet	1.39	3.66	23.9	2.8
117	Cross/5 pellets	0.96	1.26	22.5	3.5
118	Cross/cross	1.21	0.28	24.0	2.7
119	Pellet/cross	0.94	0.66	17.9	3.9
120	Pellet/pellet (retrograde)	1.23	2.37	24.2	0.7

ÆTHELRED'S SECOND REIGN AND LATER: OTHER MONEYERS AND DERIVATIVE COINS

Most of the coins recorded in this section are from heavily blundered, derivative dies, usually with an echo of the name of Æthelred, but not necessarily struck during his reign. There are also blundered copies of the names of earlier moneyers: Odilo, Monne, Brother, even Hereræd. The alloy of these coins is deplorable. The silver contents are again mostly negligible, the main constituent of the total listed below as 'silver' being lead. This is commonly in excess of 2%, and in one coin 8.9% lead was measured. The bulk of the coins is sometimes brass (of the usual quality), sometimes a brass-bronze mixture, with 6–9% tin and 10–15% zinc. In many of the brass-based coins the previously usual 3% tin is much reduced or virtually absent. No rhyme or reason is apparent in the variations of alloy, and the coins have been roughly grouped on the basis of die-links and of style. The distinction between 'regular' second-reign coins by moneyers other than Eardwulf, and 'derivative' coins is in no way reinforced by these analyses. Coins naming Æthelhelm and Wulfræd, for example (nos. 123–5 and 127–8) fall into the same pattern of alloys as the other, more severely blundered examples.

The silver contents of the 'derivative' coins (Ag only) offer a distinct contrast with those by the moneyer Eardwulf. The very low silver values, of under 0.1%, are repeated, but a somewhat larger number of values lies in the range 0.1–0.3% (Fig. 11). Moreover, an attempt to correlate the style of the coins with their silver contents suggests that values of under 0.1% tend to occur with particular styles of die-cutting, e.g. nos. 130–4. The sample of coins analysed included only one higher silver value, of 2.23% (no. 139).

There is an even more pronounced contrast between Eardwulf's coins and the 'derivative' series in their lead and antimony contents (Fig. 12). Antimony correlates very closely with lead. We cannot explain why this should be so. But the 'derivative' coins contain several times as much antimony as those of Eardwulf or indeed as almost all earlier stycas. Osberht's coins (below) are exceptionally free from antimony, but there is no correlation between antimony and zinc.

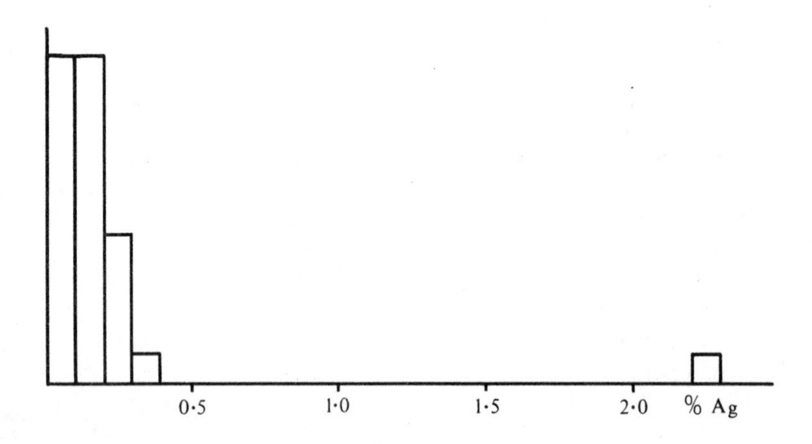

FIG. 11. Æthelred's second reign or later: silver (Ag only) contents of the derivative coins.

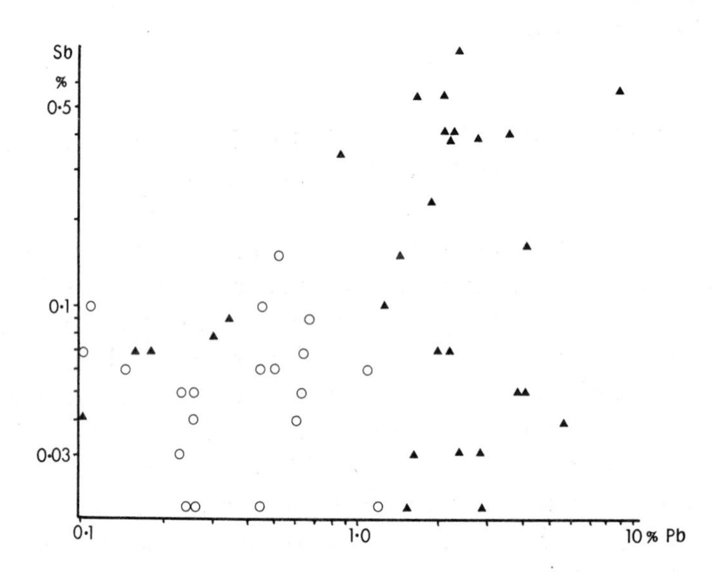

FIG. 12. Æthelred's second reign or later: lead contents plotted against antimony contents. Open circles = coins by the moneyer Eardwulf. Triangles = 'derivative' coins.

		Weight	'Silver'	Brass	Tin
121	EDIL RED RE/ ODILO	0.90	4.2	23.4	1.2
122	EDILREDRI/ ...EDELI	0.81	4.2	28.0	1.0
123	EDILRED.X/ EDELHFI	0.96	2.0	14.5	8.2
124	VVΓ.../ EDILHLIH	0.92	2.4	20.2	3.5
125	EDELHELM/ EDELHELM	1.02	1.1	25.5	3.2
126	EDILBED/ MONNE	1.11	0.8	10.8	8.9

127	EIIREDFE/ VVLRED	1.05	1.6	10.9	7.5
128	EIIREDFE/ VVLRED	0.83	1.9	16.7	3.3
129	EDIIRE/ EDIREDRE	1.04	1.0	12.5	7.3
130	ERDER∵VE/ HE∵RRED	0.94	3.0	9.1	9.1
131	ERDER VE/ HVVDRV	1.16	0.2	23.3	2.1
132	ERDER VE/ FVRVVLF	1.02	1.8	9.9	9.5
133	EDILRED/ HEVDDVVL	1.12	4.2	21.1	1.8
134	EDIL..EX/ EARDVVLF	1.19	2.4	11.6	8.8
135	EAENDEX/ EDLVEAIID	1.07	1.4	26.2	2.7
136	EDILREDREX/ EDILREDEX	1.14	0.2	15.1	7.2
137	EDILREDRX/ IEDVLFD	1.03	2.6	21.5	0.4
138	EDILRED/ IEDVLFD	0.88	2.5	20.5	tr
139	EDILRED/ IEDVLFD	1.02	4.6	25.5	0.1
140	EVXDIREX/ HIINEVI	1.09	0.4	21.5	2.7
141	EVXDIREX/ VEDHEN	1.28	0.4	24.0	3.0
142	EVXDIREX/ VEDHEN	0.95	0.2	24.2	2.1
143	FORODR/ BEOMRE	1.13	1.7	5.5	8.9
144	DRT...VH/OID∵T	0.96	9.2	19.1	4.3
145	RODER/MONNE	1.09	2.3	22.3	2.6
146	DFVIHX/RDOVHE	0.98	2.4	11.9	6.6
147	MADBVE/ HEHLDVE	1.15	2.9	13.3	7.8
148	EVDDVIE/EDILVD	0.97	2.3	23.2	1.1
149	FLIVDVI/ FIDVVID	0.91	5.5	25.1	tr
150	FLIVDVI/ RIFNRD	0.84	2.1	24.5	2.4
151	ENGA/VI..VT	0.96	3.6	2.4	6.3

OSBERHT

Three more coins of Osberht were analysed, and were found to be uniformly of high-tin bronze with no or virtually no zinc. Tin concentrations of 14–15% are higher than in any other stycas. Traces of silver are minimal, the figure for 'silver' consisting mostly of lead. This new alloy seems best understood as a planned reform of the coinage.

Two coins of Osberht and one of Wulfhere had previously been analysed. All were, unlike the newly analysed specimens, of brass-bronze still with some zinc, but with no silver. They are:

Osberht, moneyer Monne. *MIN* 42. 10.9% Zn, 7.4% Sn
Osberht, moneyer Eanwulf. Pirie 419. 2.4% Zn, 6.5% Sn
Wulfhere, moneyer Wulfræd. *MIN* 43. 11.7% Zn, 5.4% Sn

The much higher tin contents of the new analyses clearly reflect a deliberate change in the alloy.

The apparent absence of antimony (the limit of detection being calculated as 0.02%) in nos. 152–4 is most unusual for the styca series, and makes one wonder whether the bronze was from a non-Northumbrian source. But the levels of silver (Ag = *c.* 0.15%) match those in the 'derivatives'.

It will be desirable to analyse a larger sample of Osberht's coins, preferably in the context of a die-chain.

		Weight	'Silver'	Brass	Tin
152	Æthelhelm	1.23	1.2	-	15.2
153	Eanberht	1.27	1.7	-	15.1
154	Eanwulf	1.23	2.2	-	13.8

SUMMARY AND GENERAL INTERPRETATION

Analysis contributes the following points to an understanding of the Northumbrian coinage in the third quarter of the ninth century.

1. There is the clearest possible difference between the coinage of the two halves of Æthelred's reign. In the first period, a dozen or more moneyers produce coins of essentially good-quality brass, with rather variable silver contents between 2% and 10%, with some sort of modal value around 5% (Fig. 1). The alloy contains very regular additions of around 3–3.5% tin. In the second period, we see only one moneyer, Eardwulf, and he produces extremely neat coins in a very regular style, containing virtually no silver, but still made of brass of as good a quality as before, and still with the same addition of tin. In a word, there was a reform of the coinage. Clearly, a political decision was taken by Æthelred, soon after his restoration to power, to abandon the failing effort to keep up any silver content in the coinage, and instead to strike coins that were made simply of brass.

2. This was not accompanied by, nor did it result in, the withdrawal of the earlier coins which still had some silver content. The two categories circulated alongside each other, and in a largely illiterate society, they must have had the same face value. We should eschew the value judgement that Æthelred's later stycas were 'of wretched quality' and that they reflected a society in the terminal stages of civil strife and collapse. Maybe the opposite conclusion would be more appropriate, namely that political control and public confidence were in sufficiently good shape during Æthelred's second reign for a token coinage to be accepted as equal in face value to coins containing some silver, without Gresham's Law taking effect.

3. Redwulf's coins are like those of Æthelred's first reign, except that their silver contents fall within a smaller range, cutting off at approximately 6–7%. In quantity they amount to something like one-twelfth of the issues of Æthelred's first reign. We simply do not know how long Redwulf held power. If Æthelred's first reign lasted for four years, and the same level of mint output was maintained under Redwulf, his coins would suggest a period of four months. If output was disrupted at all, the coins would indicate a rather longer period. The patterns of die-linkage within Redwulf's coins and between them and Æthelred's (together with the continuity of moneyers' careers) strongly imply that most if not all of Redwulf's coins were in fact produced in the main centre of minting. There is nothing to suggest, for example, that he minted many of his coins elsewhere in Northumbria, concurrently and in rivalry with Æthelred.

4. A detailed study of Æthelred's first-reign coins to see whether there was any evidence of a downward trend in silver values during the four years or so of the reign offers very little encouragement to detect such a trend.

5. If that is so, the lower average silver contents under Redwulf should perhaps be seen as reflecting a sudden decline. A political rather than an economic explanation should be sought. It is not at all clear what may lie behind the observed difference in the coinage. Perhaps Redwulf, on taking power, ordered a devaluation whereby customers bringing foreign silver coins to the moneyers received more stycas in exchange than they had under Æthelred.

6. Some individual moneyers seem to have struck coins with different average silver contents, in Æthelred's first reign. On very limited evidence, it seems that the same moneyers may have produced coins with similarly discrepant average silver contents in Redwulf's reign, and perhaps also in phase B of Eanred's coinage. This evidence is difficult to understand and may perhaps be misleading. If it is valid it suggests that the moneyers in question worked independently, supervising the whole process from the preparation of the alloy onwards.

7. Osberht's coins reflect further changes in the coinage alloy which can hardly have been made other than as a matter of policy, and under royal control. Brass was no longer used. It was replaced either by a roughly half-and-half mixture of brass and bronze, or more intriguingly, by pure bronze (with tin contents of 14–15%). Many more analyses of Osberht's coins are needed, before any clear conclusions can be drawn.

8. The 'derivative' or 'reflective' issues again contain virtually no silver, but various features of their alloys distinguish them from Eardwulf's coins. On the one hand they evidently represent some sort of breakdown in political control over the coinage, for the reverse legends which should give the moneyers' names are severely blundered and, as die-linkage shows, in many cases are meaningless (see, for example, nos. 130–2). On the other hand the tight networks of die-links into which virtually all the derivatives fit, and the very large numbers of dies involved, both encourage the view that their production was in some sense organized or centralized, i.e. they are certainly not to be seen as small-scale counterfeiting by private individuals. When were they made? Lyon published a number of die-chains which indicate that the 'derivatives' post-date Osberht's coinage. They do not prove conclusively that *all* the 'derivatives' are post-Osberht. The variety of die-links do, however, make it difficult to envisage an intermittent coinage continuing over

many years, and they make it even more difficult on any acceptable chronology, to see the 'derivatives' post-dating the capture of York. If that is correct, then the coins may indeed point to the collapse of effective royal government before 866. One should not lose sight, however, of the coins signed by moneyers with new names, particularly Æthelhelm and Wulfræd, of whom the former worked for Osberht and the latter for Archbishop Wulfhere. It is easy to imagine that experienced moneyers might have continued to function. The ideas that are much more difficult to absorb are that the facility of skilled, literate die-cutting should have suddenly ceased to be available; and that in a political context in which the accountability of moneyers appears to have gone by the board, there should still have been a strong demand for new coins. Illiteracy in the dies does not in itself amount to clear proof that all political control of moneying had disappeared: it is rather the inappropriate combinations of names that cast grave doubts on the working of the system.

9. Most of the 'derivative' coins are of the usual good-quality brass, and nearly always with the regular small amounts of tin (but note three coins of 'Iædwulf', nos. 137–9). Some, however, are roughly half-and-half brass-bronze (like some of the coins of Osberht and Wulfhere), with no obvious pattern of occurrence of brass or brass-bronze emerging from our analyses. If they are post-Osberht in date, it must appear that Osberht's reform of the coinage-metal was subsequently abandoned.

10. The silver, lead, and antimony contents of the 'derivative' coins are so different from those of Eardwulf as to suggest that different procedures were being followed in the preparation of the coinage-metal. This makes the problem of understanding how the final phase of minting was related to what had gone before even more acute.

11. A further programme of analysis of carefully selected 'derivative' coins, and of coins of the second-reign moneyers Æthelhelm, Eanwulf, Monne, and Wulfræd needs to be planned in such a way as to give balanced coverage of Miss Pirie's various 'reflective' and 'background' groups, RI, RII, RIII, etc., as well as her 'descendants'. One can only hope that this would narrow our options in the general interpretation of the final phases of the styca issues.

APPENDIX: MODERN FORGERIES

Among the coins selected for analysis, three turned out to be modern forgeries. One, which should have been identifiable by eye, is a coin of Redwulf (no. 155). Its composition is

Fe	-	Sb	-
Co	tr	Sn	20.98
Ni	0.02	Ag	0.17
Cu	1.52	Pb	27.72
Zn	0.61	Au	–
Bi	48.62		

It belongs to a well-known group of forgeries made, apparently, from Wood's metal or one of a variety of similar fusible alloys. Other specimens which have been analysed (Pirie, 1982, pp. 2 and 18–19) show lead contents ranging from 25 to 40% tin from 5 to 13%, and bismuth from 44 to 62%. The coin of Cuthbeorht is from the same 'dies' as Pirie 460–1. The weight is much too high at 1.54g.

Two 'die-duplicate' coins of Æthelred's first reign by the moneyer Ealhhere are also clearly modern forgeries, although much more deceptive until they are compared, when it can be seen that the exact outline of the flan is in each case the same. One of them has been distressed quite skilfully to give the appearance of a greenish clay incrustation. The metal compositions differ widely and both are far outside the range found among genuine coins. In particular, the zinc contents are negligible, and the tin contents are much too high. The silver contents are either too low or much too high.

The analyses showed:

	156	157		156	157
Fe	tr	tr	Sb	tr	–
Co	tr	–	Sn	14.54	12.87
Ni	0.03	0.03	Ag	0.03	57.40
Cu	84.82	29.56	Pb	0.10	0.17
Zn	0.06	0.06	Au	–	0.06
Bi	0.09	0.04			

The weights are 1.14 and 1.30g. The die-axis is irregular (135°). Pirie (1982), no. 185 falls under suspicion of being a forgery of the same kind.

TABLE OF ANALYSES

For each coin, the results are the mean averages of readings taken at three points on a polished section of the edge, adjusted to a sum of 100%. The numbering of the Table corresponds with the sectional summaries in the text and with the numbering of the plates. nd = not determined; – = below limit of detection; tr = trace; * = result probably misleading because of e.g. corrosion and leaching, or inhomogeneity.

	Fe	Co	Ni	Cu	Zn	Bi	Sb	Sn	Ag	Pb	Au	
Leofthegn												
1	nd	nd	nd	69.3	18.3	nd	0.09	2.3	12.6	nd	0.05	1
2	nd	nd	nd	68.9	17.5	nd	0.06	4.64	7.8	nd	0.07	2
3	nd	nd	nd	72.2	20.7	nd	0.13	1.11	4.56	nd	0.01	3
4	0.83	–	0.05	72.74	18.18	tr	0.06	3.28	4.56	0.26	0.03	4
5	0.04	–	tr	69.66	17.63	0.01	0.09	3.69	8.01	0.79	0.05	5
6	0.08	0.01	0.02	64.68	18.50	0.04	0.08	4.05	11.92	0.50	0.13	6
7	0.05	–	0.06	68.76	23.54	–	0.06	2.85	4.38	0.30	0.04	7
8	0.12	–	0.01	69.91	16.48	0.03	0.12	4.12	8.41	0.66	0.08	8
9	0.08	–	0.01	70.62	17.99	–	0.04	3.17	7.76	0.23	0.06	9
10	0.05	–	0.01	69.80	21.83	0.01	0.09	3.78	3.92	0.44	0.06	10
11	0.07	–	0.04	70.86	22.96	0.01	0.06	3.73	2.08	0.14	0.02	11
12	0.03	tr	–	69.46	20.23	–	0.03	3.61	6.39	0.10	0.03	12
13	0.13	0.01	0.02	68.25	21.00	–	0.07	3.30	6.89	0.26	tr	13
14	0.05	–	0.03	72.37	18.23	–	0.05	4.40	4.37	0.31	0.24	14
15	0.07	–	0.01	66.39	23.20	0.02	0.05	2.45	7.62	0.12	0.04	15
16	nd	nd	nd	67.1	21.0	nd	0.07	2.40	8.6	nd	0.03	16
17	nd	nd	nd	69.7	20.1	nd	0.06	3.6	5.48	nd	0.03	17
18	0.03	0.01	0.02	72.10	17.76	tr	0.04	3.28	6.32	0.34	0.10	18
18	nd	nd	nd	73.5	17.4	nd	0.07	2.4	7.7	nd	0.09	18
19	0.20	–	0.03	70.56	19.93	tr	0.04	3.60	5.39	0.18	0.04	19
20	0.09	0.01	0.01	71.04	18.79	–	0.06	3.29	6.47	0.21	0.03	20
21	0.11	–	0.02	71.96	18.35	–	0.05	3.53	5.57	0.35	0.06	21
22	0.06	–	0.03	72.06	22.74	0.04	0.12	2.29	2.47	0.19	–	22
23	0.06	–	0.01	68.19	18.20	–	0.09	3.52	9.32	0.27	0.33	23
24	0.67	tr	0.04	77.29	13.06	tr	0.07	4.19	4.36	0.47	0.06	24
25	nd	nd	nd	74.5	19.0	nd	0.09	2.2	9.0	nd	0.10	25
26	0.18	–	0.01	68.84	21.36	–	0.06	2.27	6.94	0.23	0.06	26

	Fe	Co	Ni	Cu	Zn	Bi	Sb	Sn	Ag	Pb	Au	
27	0.31	0.01	0.04	70.80	19.97	*0.02	0.06	1.98	6.30	0.38	0.10	27
28	*0.12	*–	*0.02	*73.57	*16.09	*–	*0.12	*3.72	*5.36	*0.79	*0.05	28
29	nd	nd	nd	76.8	20.6	nd	0.11	1.3	5.9	nd	0.07	29
30	nd	nd	nd	70.1	21.4	nd	0.05	3.20	4.20	nd	0.02	30
31	0.10	0.01	0.02	70.10	20.78	–	0.10	3.87	4.29	0.08	0.02	31
32	0.44	–	0.06	72.78	20.96	–	0.07	3.65	1.86	0.13	0.03	32
33	0.45	tr	0.05	73.76	19.51	–	0.08	2.86	2.12	0.93	–	33
34	0.18	tr	0.02	74.33	19.56	tr	0.10	3.22	2.19	0.34	0.03	34
35	0.10	–	0.04	78.21	13.86	0.03	0.04	5.94	4.92	0.13	–	35
36	0.35	–	0.02	74.36	23.16	0.03	0.06	1.74	0.05	0.22	–	36
Brother												
37	0.17	–	0.04	70.60	15.98	–	0.09	3.48	9.13	0.40	0.13	37
38	0.32	tr	0.03	68.80	19.94	0.01	0.06	2.12	*8.04	0.40	0.22	38
39	0.05	–	0.03	70.15	22.92	tr	0.08	1.87	4.59	0.11	0.19	39
40	0.07	tr	tr	74.15	18.21	0.01	0.05	2.84	4.40	0.21	0.04	40
41	0.14	0.01	0.02	73.56	18.98	0.03	0.10	2.99	3.96	0.20	0.03	41
42	0.38	0.01	0.03	71.45	21.30	–	0.08	2.54	3.65	0.47	0.10	42
43	0.21	–	0.03	71.05	23.07	–	0.07	2.13	3.13	0.26	0.07	43
44	0.18	–	0.03	74.10	18.99	–	0.08	4.04	2.23	0.38	0.03	44
Cynemund												
45	0.33	0.01	0.03	76.52	17.67	tr	0.09	4.11	1.03	0.18	0.02	45
46	0.38	–	0.03	75.91	15.94	0.03	0.10	4.61	1.92	1.07	–	46
47	0.27	0.01	0.08	71.02	22.19	tr	0.32	2.50	3.33	0.24	0.03	47
48	0.19	0.01	0.02	75.78	19.41	–	0.06	2.56	1.77	0.37	0.04	48
49	0.15	–	0.04	73.72	19.43	0.01	0.08	3.00	3.31	0.23	tr	49
50	0.62	–	0.02	72.24	21.85	–	0.09	3.38	1.48	0.29	–	50
51	0.12	0.01	0.03	74.94	19.64	0.03	0.09	3.09	1.87	0.19	–	51
Ealhhere												
52	0.05	–	0.03	67.80	21.34	–	0.06	2.97	7.56	0.15	0.05	52
53	0.05	tr	0.02	70.10	18.01	tr	0.08	3.16	8.36	0.29	0.05	53
54	0.05	–	0.02	66.00	21.52	tr	0.09	3.10	8.94	0.13	0.07	54
55	0.26	tr	0.03	72.73	17.17	–	0.06	2.61	6.84	0.21	0.03	55
56	0.19	–	0.03	70.39	21.49	0.05	0.07	2.77	4.79	0.17	0.04	56
57	0.12	–	0.03	71.07	21.05	–	0.06	3.20	4.24	0.30	0.05	57
58	0.05	–	0.02	69.96	18.28	–	0.03	3.29	7.64	0.61	0.12	58
59	0.18	tr	0.02	73.81	23.23	0.02	0.07	2.53	0.10	0.13	0.04	59
60	0.36	–	0.01	73.35	20.57	*0.03	0.07	4.87	0.59	0.09	0.04	60
Wendelbeorht												
61	0.13	–	0.08	74.32	13.01	–	0.04	7.30	3.75	1.32	–	61
62	0.13	–	0.05	72.81	18.55	–	0.04	3.37	4.71	0.35	0.03	62
63	0.10	–	0.05	71.46	20.85	0.05	0.07	2.18	4.55	0.47	0.05	63
64	0.12	–	0.03	73.47	19.76	0.03	0.04	2.44	4.20	0.16	–	64
65	0.06	–	0.02	70.00	22.45	–	0.06	2.35	4.97	1.01	0.06	65
66	0.17	–	0.02	73.16	20.03	–	0.08	2.75	3.53	0.24	0.03	66
67	0.13	–	0.02	70.91	22.22	–	0.14	2.61	3.53	0.37	0.04	67
68	0.25	–	0.03	73.94	17.18	0.02	0.09	3.47	4.70	0.28	0.07	68
69	0.26	tr	0.04	75.44	15.81	–	0.06	4.84	3.08	0.38	0.07	69
70	0.39	–	0.03	75.68	17.00	–	0.06	3.49	2.86	0.44	0.03	70
71	0.10	0.02	0.05	75.62	16.87	0.02	0.04	4.63	2.43	0.14	0.06	71
72	0.27	–	0.04	74.81	19.12	tr	0.04	3.11	1.95	0.29	0.03	72
Wihtræd												
73	0.07	tr	–	70.67	17.22	0.03	0.07	3.43	8.25	0.14	0.07	73
74	0.06	–	0.01	69.95	18.28	tr	0.06	3.29	8.05	0.13	0.10	74
75	0.09	–	0.03	73.67	15.80	–	0.30	3.68	4.34	1.95	0.04	75
76	0.02	–	0.02	71.82	18.11	tr	0.07	3.51	6.13	0.24	0.03	76
77	0.04	0.01	0.04	70.13	20.88	0.01	0.08	2.69	5.99	0.10	0.03	77
78	0.04	tr	0.03	73.88	17.10	–	0.05	3.21	5.63	0.02	0.04	78
79	0.06	0.01	0.02	70.40	20.61	–	0.07	3.37	5.23	0.18	0.02	79

	Fe	Co	Ni	Cu	Zn	Bi	Sb	Sn	Ag	Pb	Au	
80	0.23	0.01	0.05	70.09	21.62	tr	0.08	3.14	4.37	0.48	0.05	80
81	0.09	tr	0.03	69.45	22.43	–	0.06	4.11	3.64	0.16	–	81
82	0.19	–	0.05	76.27	16.20	0.01	0.10	2.96	4.04	0.17	0.03	82
83	0.23	–	0.02	74.98	17.15	0.02	0.08	3.09	3.90	0.49	0.08	83
Wulfræd, Coenræd												
84	0.14	0.01	0.01	79.42	12.13	0.02	0.12	3.00	4.58	0.44	0.07	84
85	0.22	tr	0.01	72.97	21.63	–	0.03	4.47	0.39	0.22	tr	85
86	0.07	0.01	0.01	76.73	19.13	0.02	0.03	2.11	1.18	0.67	0.03	86
87	0.04	tr	0.01	73.67	15.35	tr	0.08	2.53	6.95	0.14	0.09	87
88	0.15	tr	0.03	76.11	15.92	–	0.07	2.94	6.28	0.36	0.09	88
Odilo												
89	*0.12	*–	*0.02	*77.20	*12.90	*–	*0.13	*3.83	*4.93	*0.32	*0.04	89
90	0.12	tr	0.02	74.02	20.19	–	0.08	1.75	3.24	0.50	–	90
Redwulf												
91	0.20	tr	tr	69.86	24.49	0.01	0.08	2.73	2.20	0.41	0.02	91
92	0.15	tr	0.02	74.08	20.74	0.01	0.09	1.94	2.69	0.26	tr	92
93	0.11	tr	0.02	70.41	20.94	0.04	0.09	3.10	4.56	0.67	0.05	93
94	0.41	tr	0.05	75.13	17.29	0.05	0.09	3.34	3.30	0.28	0.06	94
95	0.24	tr	0.04	73.08	20.84	0.03	0.10	2.78	2.67	0.21	0.07	95
96	0.75	–	0.03	74.77	17.96	–	0.03	2.60	3.29	0.64	tr	96
97	0.06	tr	0.01	72.38	19.77	0.04	0.07	2.72	4.43	0.13	0.05	97
98	0.57	–	0.06	72.66	25.58	–	0.06	0.34	0.09	0.64	tr	98
99	Vacat											
100	Vacat											
Eardwulf												
101	0.06	–	0.02	76.35	19.06	tr	0.07	4.47	0.04	0.04	–	101
102	0.17	–	0.01	74.03	16.62	tr	0.05	6.10	2.28	0.62	0.04	102
103	0.35	–	0.02	75.12	19.18	0.01	0.02	4.07	0.73	0.44	tr	103
104	0.18	–	0.01	74.39	21.47	–	0.06	3.33	0.12	0.44	–	104
105	0.04	tr	0.03	76.90	17.79	–	0.07	4.17	0.06	0.67	0.07	105
106	0.10	–	0.02	75.22	15.10	–	0.01	8.17	1.01	0.25	0.04	106
107	0.45	tr	0.03	72.59	21.86	0.01	0.06	4.31	0.10	0.51	*0.18	107
108	0.61	–	0.03	71.22	23.26	–	0.04	4.41	0.08	0.27	–	108
109	0.11	–	0.02	75.13	20.73	*0.04	0.10	3.10	0.08	0.45	0.04	109
110	0.57	–	0.06	71.66	23.47	–	0.05	3.88	0.06	0.27	tr	110
111	0.04	0.01	0.01	75.44	20.81	0.02	0.06	3.33	0.08	0.14	0.02	111
112	0.19	–	0.02	73.66	21.39	0.03	0.02	3.53	1.02	0.24	tr	112
113	0.19	–	0.02	76.78	14.17	tr	0.02	7.54	0.06	1.19	–	113
114	0.05	–	–	75.05	21.42	0.02	0.10	3.16	0.03	0.11	tr	114
115	0.71	tr	0.03	72.59	22.03	–	0.04	3.90	0,07	0.61	0.03	115
116	0.16	–	0.01	71.15	24.32	0.02	0.06	3.17	0.04	1.07	–	116
117	0.10	–	0.01	71.74	27.35	–	0.09	3.22	0.04	0.68	–	117
118	0.12	–	0.04	73.56	23.28	0.02	0.05	2.66	0.05	0.23	–	118
119	0.08	–	0.02	77.42	16.85	–	0.15	3.92	0.14	0.52	–	119
120	0.14	–	0.02	71.86	22.91	–	0.03	0.67	2.09	0.23	0.05	120
Blundered												
121	0.57	–	0.03	71.89	21.94	tr	0.16	1.19	0.15	4.05	tr	121
122	0.13	–	0.01	67.64	26.51	0.02	0.49	1.02	0.21	3.97	–	122
123	*0.50	tr	0.03	75.81	12.87	0.02	0.23	8.24	0.10	1.87	–	123
124	0.18	–	0.03	74.49	18.83	tr	0.42	3.46	0.25	2.10	–	124
125	0.29	–	0.02	70.58	22.21	–	0.42	2.79	0.18	3.48	tr	125
126	0.10	tr	0.07	80.46	9.76	–	0.07	8.88	0.09	0.65	0.02	126
127	0.06	0.01	0.05	80.59	9.90	tr	0.15	7.47	0.17	1.43	0.02	127
128	0.07	–	0.01	78.42	15.69	–	0.54	3.34	0.19	1.69	–	128
129	0.05	tr	0.03	79.91	11.38	0.02	0.34	7.30	0.11	0.88	tr	129
130	0.08	tr	0.05	83.14	8.34	0.02	0.01	9.14	0.06	2.95	–	130
131	0.07	–	0.02	77.57	10.16	tr	0.03	8.76	0.08	2.35	tr	131
132	0.09	–	0.03	79.74	8.77	–	0.03	9.53	0.06	1.66	0.06	132

	Fe	Co	Ni	Cu	Zn	Bi	Sb	Sn	Ag	Pb	Au	
133	0.28	0.01	0.05	73.67	19.68	tr	0.05	1.83	0.19	3.96	0.04	133
134	0.05	tr	0.03	75.07	22.84	–	0.07	2.07	0.04	0.16	–	134
135	0.94	tr	0.07	69.98	24.79	0.04	0.10	2.68	0.05	1.24	0.08	135
136	0.04	–	0.03	78.55	13.98	0.04	0.04	7.16	0.06	0.09	tr	136
137	0.37	tr	0.06	74.78	20.51	0.03	0.84	0.39	0.22	2.39	–	137
138	0.26	–	0.06	76.59	19.80	0.01	0.41	tr	0.25	2.23	0.04	138
139	0.14	–	0.01	72.10	24.67	0.04	0.39	0.08	2.23	2.34	–	139
140	0.13	tr	0.02	75.76	20.81	0.04	0.09	2.68	0.05	0.33	tr	140
141	0.18	tr	0.04	73.22	23.10	–	0.08	2.99	0.04	0.30	0.03	141
142	0.35	tr	0.03	73.67	23.56	0.01	0.07	2.07	0.03	0.18	–	142
143	0.04	tr	0.02	84.46	4.47	tr	tr	8.85	0.17	1.57	–	143
144	0.05	tr	tr	69.48	16.36	tr	0.58	4.29	0.09	2.18	0.02	144
145	0.04	tr	0.01	73.36	21.09	0.01	0.55	2.60	0.20	2.06	0.02	145
146	0.12	–	0.05	79.98	10.78	0.02	0.07	6.60	0.17	2.17	0.03	146
147	0.10	tr	0.03	76.98	11.84	tr	0.39	7.74	0.13	2.79	tr	147
148	0.50	tr	0.01	73.41	22.19	0.08	0.38	1.14	0.09	2.18	0.02	148
149	0.28	0.03	0.07	70.42	23.61	–	0.04	tr	0.04	5.49	–	149
150	0.12	tr	0.02	71.09	24.20	–	0.07	2.43	0.13	1.94	–	151
151	0.17	tr	0.03	87.71	2.12	–	0.03	6.33	0.37	2.82	0.41	151
Osberht												
152	0.04	0.01	0.02	83.45	tr	0.01	–	15.20	0.16	1.07	tr	152
153	0.05	0.01	*0.01	83.08	–	tr	–	15.08	0.16	1.57	tr	153
154	0.06	tr	0.02	83.88	–	–	–	13.83	0.15	2.05	tr	154
Forgeries												
155	–	tr	0.02	1.52	0.61	48.62	–	20.98	0.17	27.72	–	155
156	tr	tr	0.03	84.82	0.06	0.09	tr	14.54	0.33	0.10	–	156
157	tr	–	0.03	29.56	0.06	0.04	–	12.87	57.40	0.17	0.06	157

DISCUSSION

MISS PIRIE: The bronze alloy of the three newly-analysed coins of Osberht is so unusual and its implications are so puzzling that it seems worth while to establish as clearly as possible that the coins are authentic. Fortunately, this is not difficult. Of no. 152 there are two further specimens in the Yorkshire Museum, and they share an obverse with another coin, from the Bolton Percy hoard of 1847 (Pirie, 1981, no. 319). The same combination of dies as no. 153 is registered in the Yorkshire Museum, and there are other specimens there from the same obverse. The reverse is also known in another combination. No. 154 is matched by three specimens in the Yorkshire Museum, but (surprisingly) there are no associated die-links.

PLATE 14

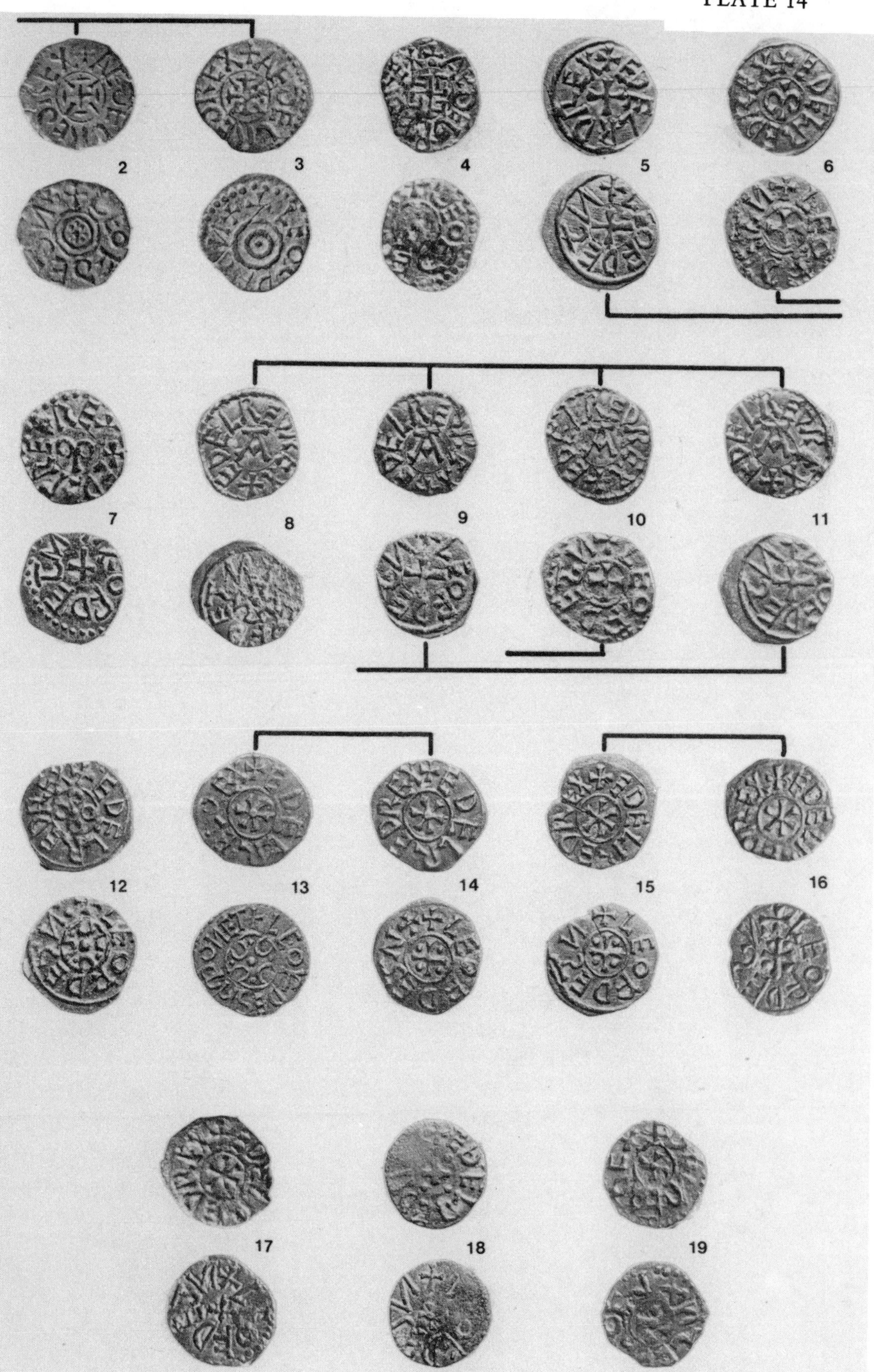

PLATE 15

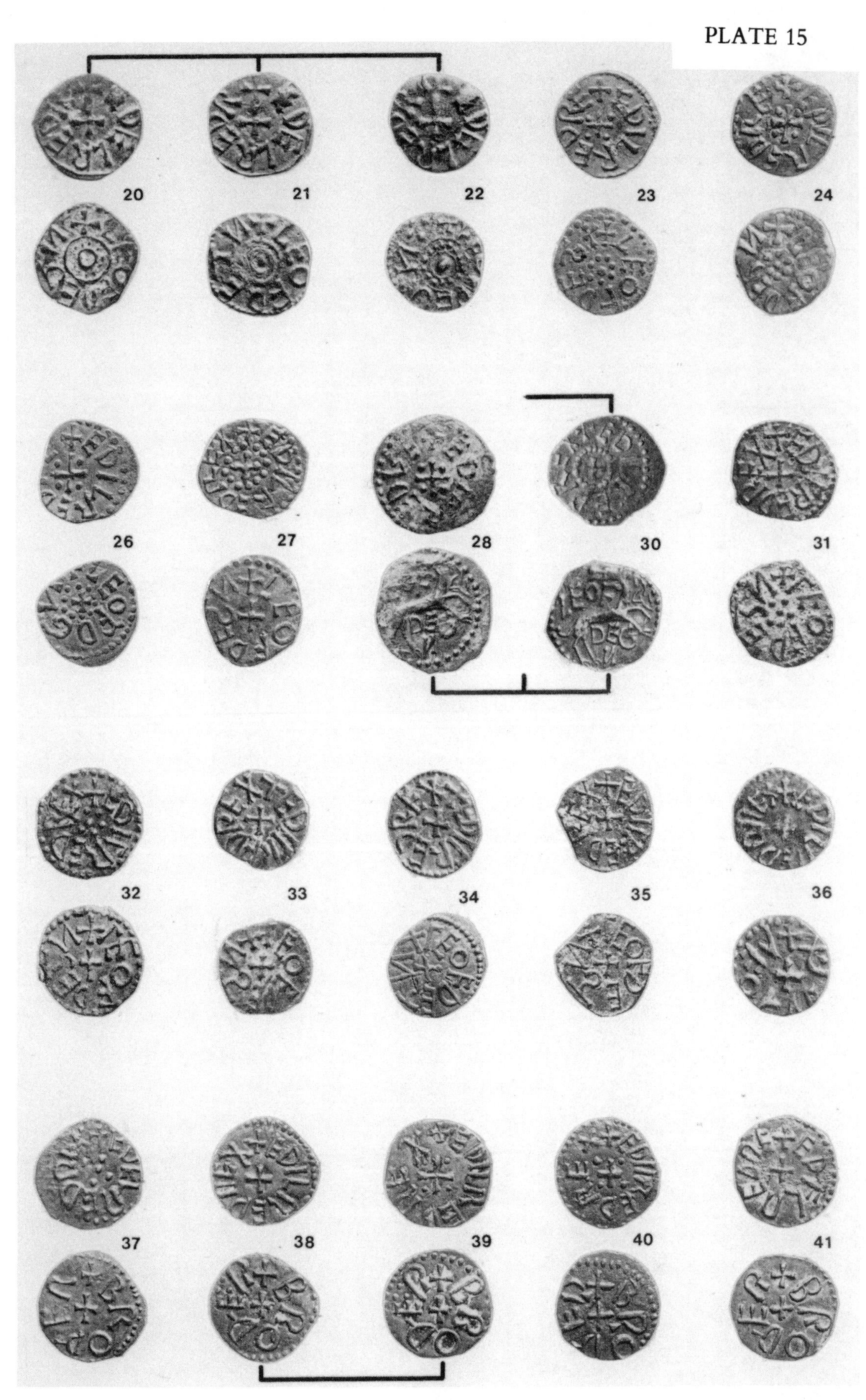

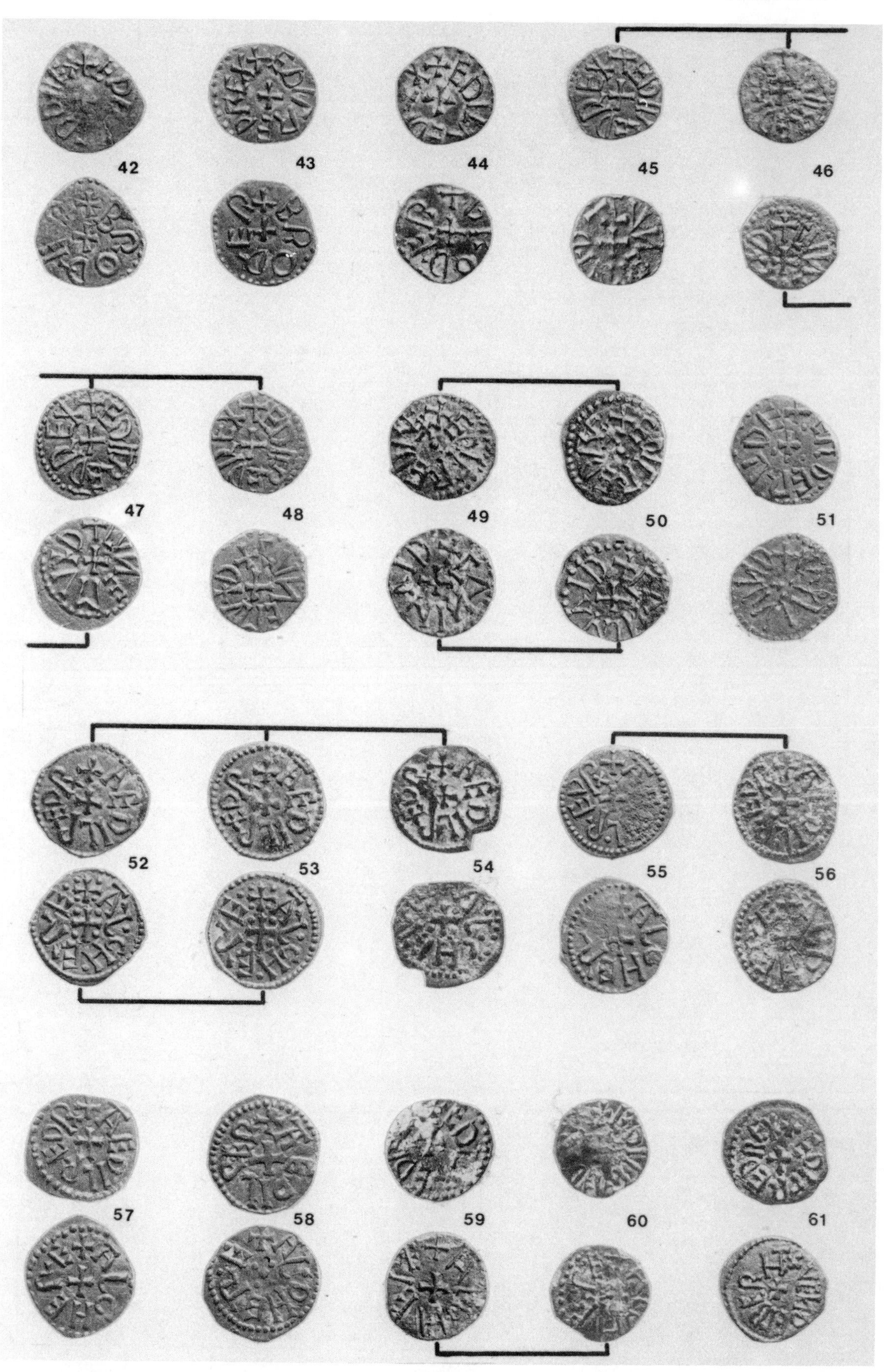

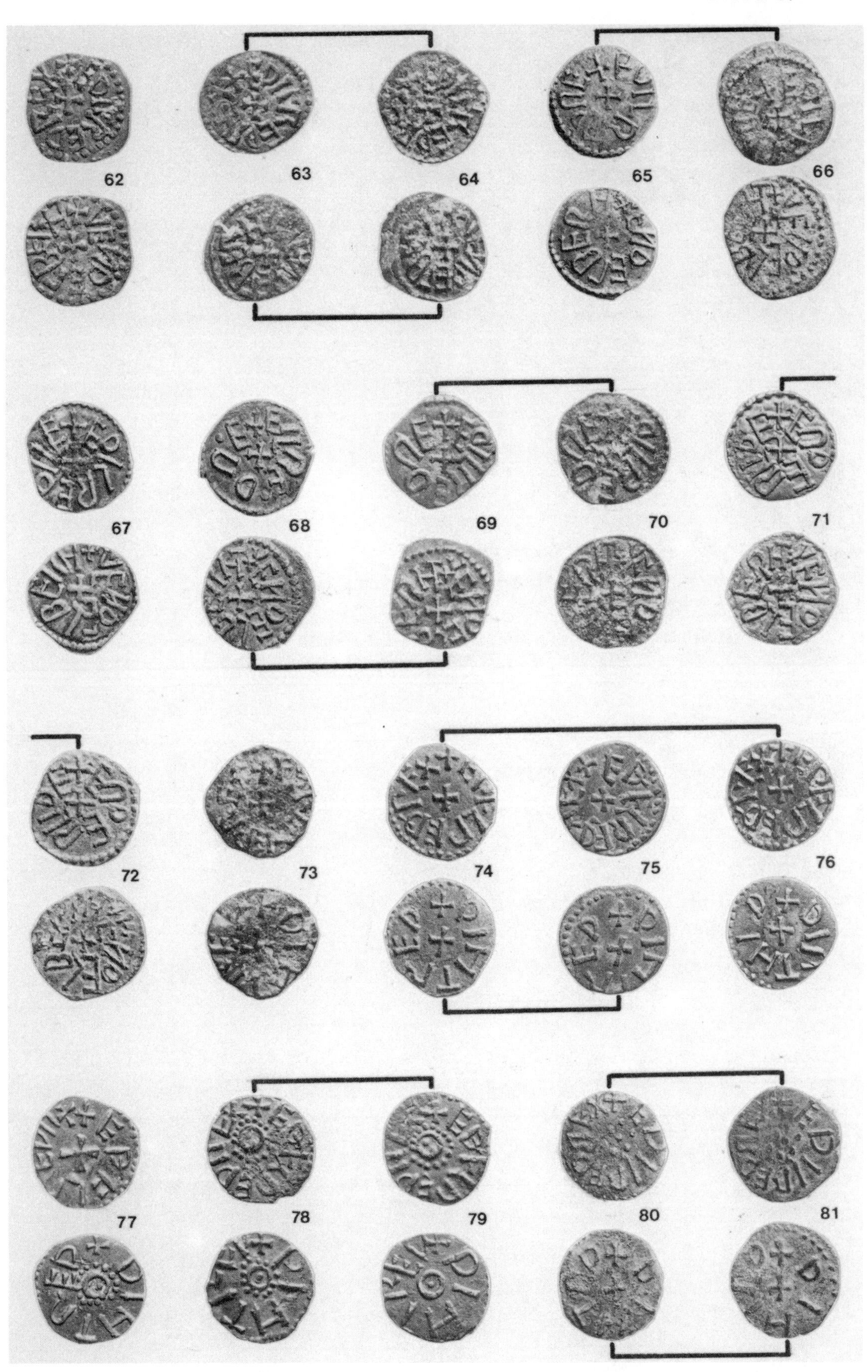
62
63
64
65
66
67
68
69
70
71
72
73
74
75
76
77
78
79
80
81

PLATE 18

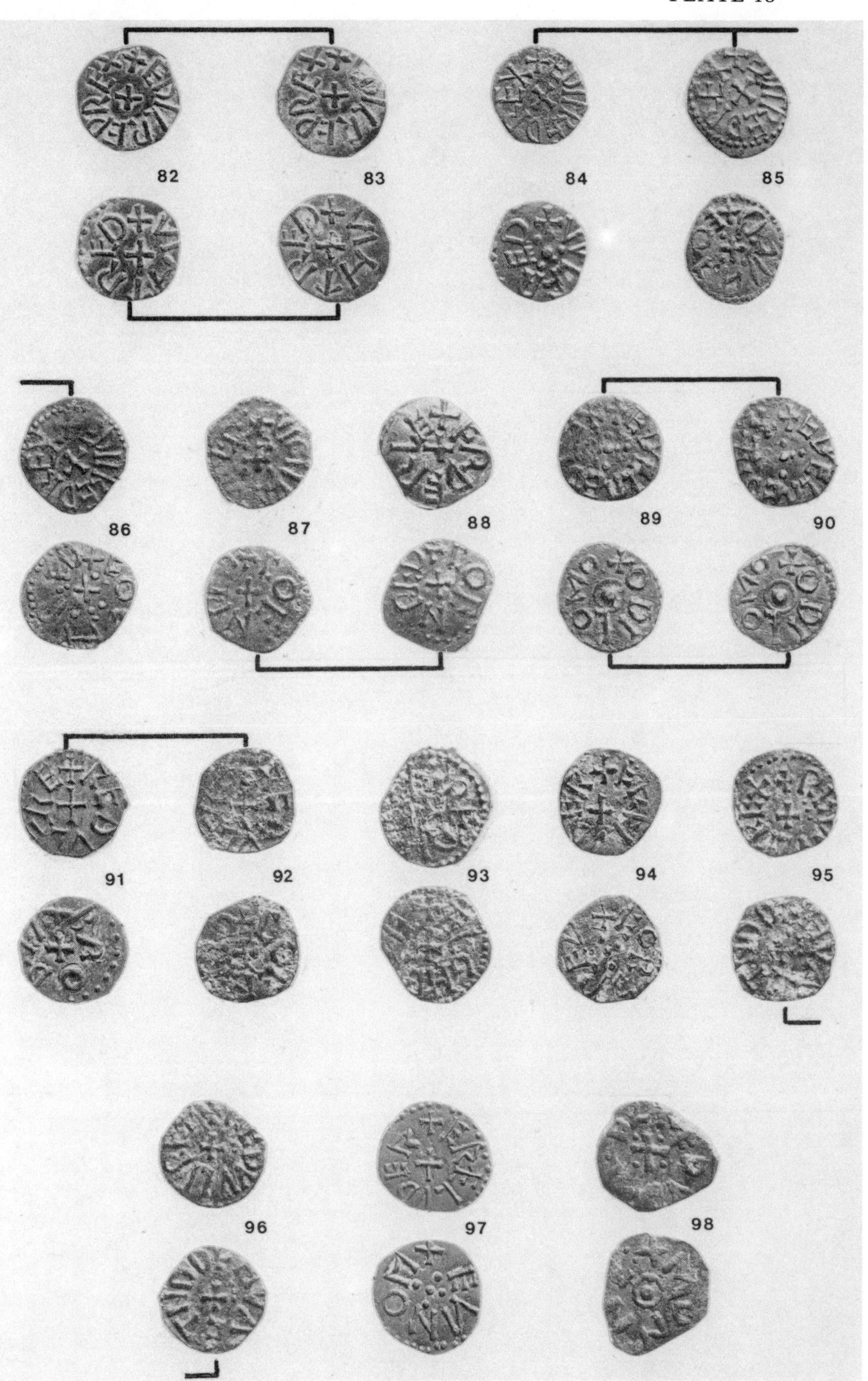

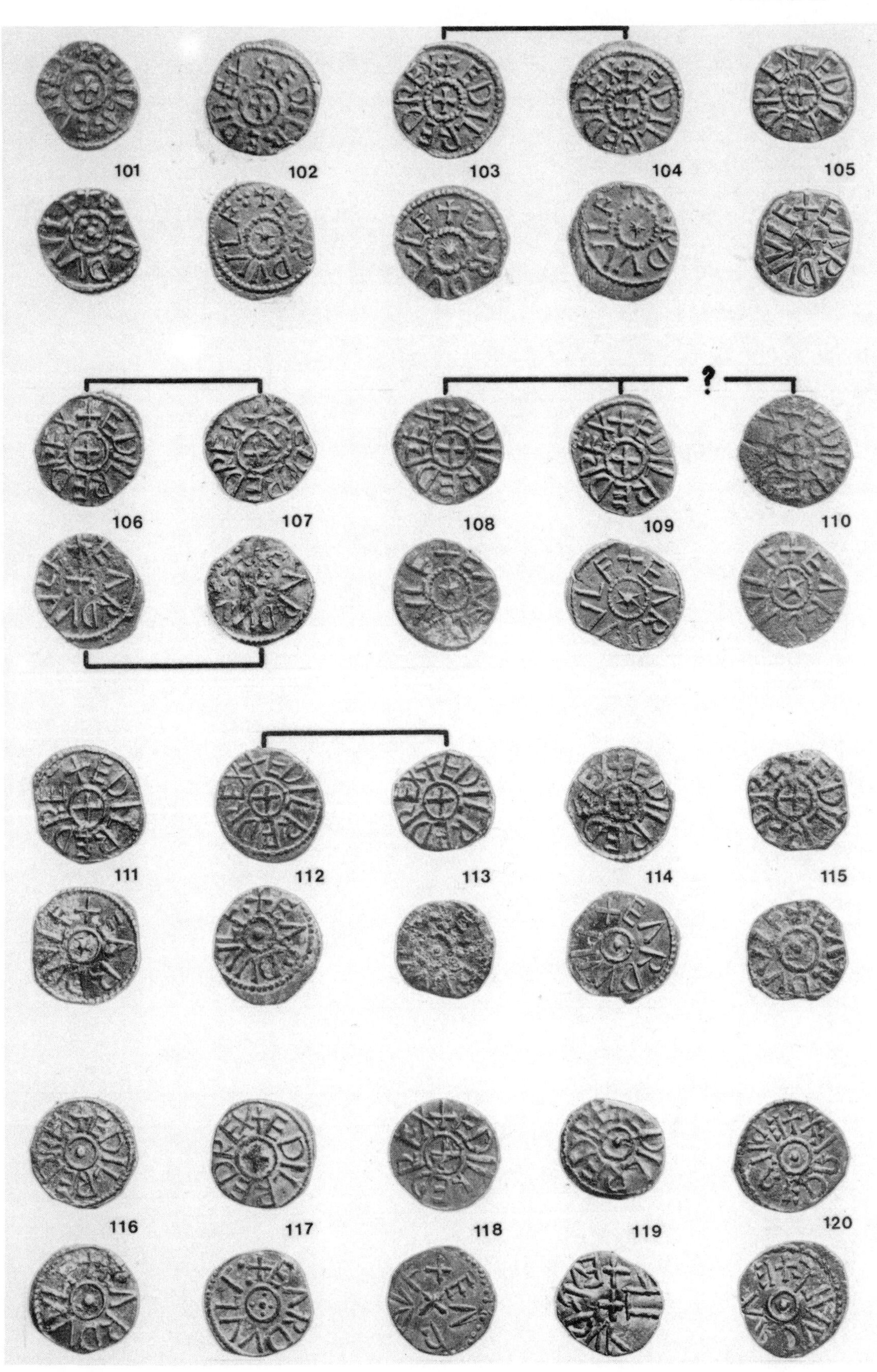
101
102
103
104
105
106
107
108
109
?
110
111
112
113
114
115
116
117
118
119
120

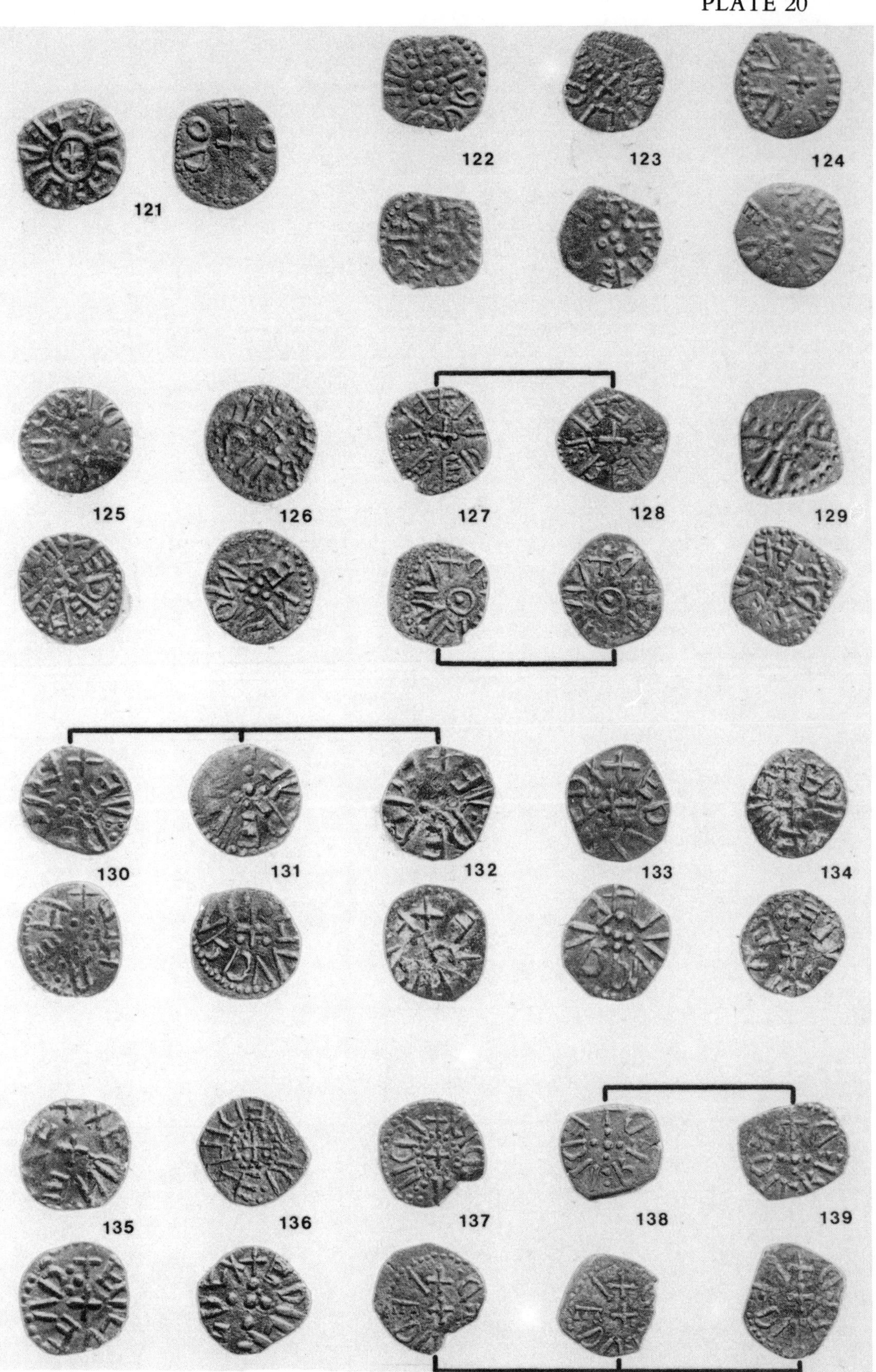

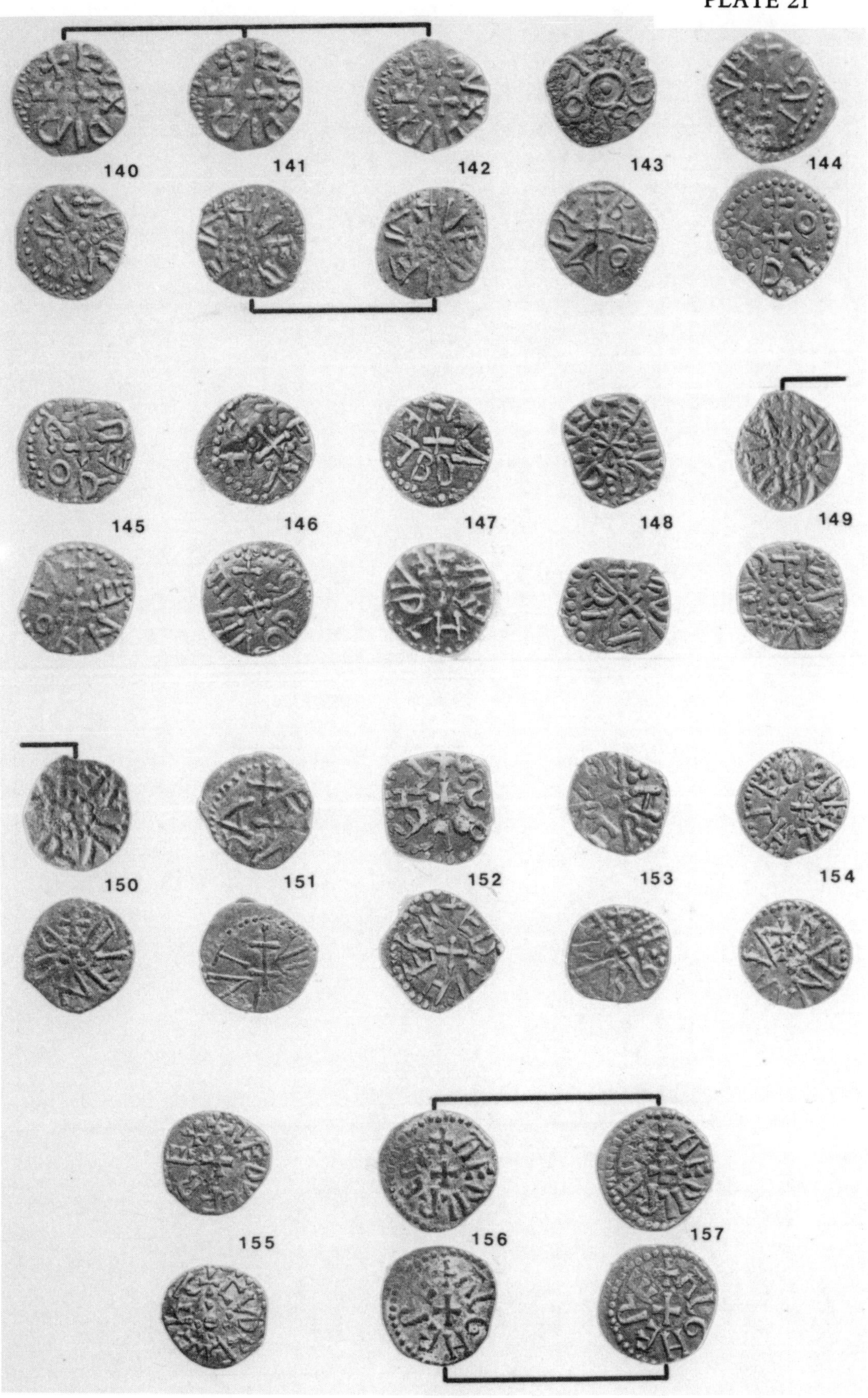
140
141
142
143
144
145
146
147
148
149
150
151
152
153
154
155
156
157

Dating the so-called King Hoaud stycas

D.C. AXE

[PLATE 22]

ONE of the persistent questions in Northumbrian numismatics is the status of the Hoavdre/Hvaetrd styca.[1] The material to be presented here will not prove or disprove the existence of a so-called King Hoaud or Hoauth, but it can help locate these coins within the chronology of the styca series. The data support the placement of these Hoaud stycas towards the end of Æthelred's second reign or at the beginning of Osberht's reign.

Two Hoaud stycas were included in an EPMA analysis recently carried out by the author on the metallic content of sixty sycas. These two stycas are illustrated as **Pl. 22, 1 and 2**. They appear to be from the same dies, reading HOAVDRE or retrograde ERDVAOH on the obverse and DRTEAVH or HVAETRD with an incomplete letter 'A', on the reverse.

There are reportedly other dies for Hoaud stycas, but the author has been unable to locate and examine specimens with any obverse other than those illustrated. Some additional examples of Hoaud stycas found in the mid 19th century were described by Heywood in several articles published in the 1890s.[2]

A brief review of the general characteristics of styca composition may be helpful in understanding the relative placement of the two Hoaud stycas in the series as a whole.

For many years it has been generally accepted that during Eanred's reign, presumably early, at least early in terms of styca production by his moneyers, there began a significant drop in silver content with a concurrent increase in the zinc content.[3]

[1] See for example: I. H. Stewart, 'Ex-King Hoaud', *Seaby Coin and Medal Bulletin* 1956, 138–40.

[2] N. Heywood, 'Notes on Northumbrian stycas inscribed HOAVĐ RE+', *NC* 3 10 (1890), 335 and 'The stycas of North Humbria', *Transactions of the Lancashire and Cheshire Antiquarian Society* 15 (1897), 81-99, at p.90. In 1897 Heywood knew of only four specimens, apparently from three different pairs of dies. During the symposium Miss Pirie confirmed that she had also seen other Hoaud die examples.

[3] While it is clear that Eanred's stycas in general contain a higher percentage of silver than those of Æthelred, the EPMA analyses supporting this paper do not reinforce nor do they detract from the assumption that the silver content within each reign progresses from a higher to a lower percentage. The author wishes to acknowledge that he is simply following in the footsteps of others in this respect. It rests with die-link analysis and hoard evidence to detect intra-regnal trends.

This process continued throughout the reigns of Æthelred and Redwulf with zinc approaching a concentration limited by the cementation process assumed to be the source of the brass used in ninth-century Northumbria. This development is well documented in Gilmore and Metcalf.[4] By the end of Æthelred's second reign, silver content had dropped to or very close to zero with zinc content typically between 16.5 and 23 to 24 per cent.

By Osberht's time, the available evidence indicates that the zinc concentration began to drop, being replaced by tin and higher amounts of copper. Silver remained at or near zero. It should be noted that the archiepiscopal series follows the same general trend as the royal series. The decline in zinc content in Osberht's time is reinforced by the analysis of a single styca of Wulfhere by Gilmore and Metcalf[5] (silver 0.08%, zinc 11.7%) and another single Wulfhere styca analysed by the author (silver 0%, zinc 13.8%).

Returning to the royal series, if one were to plot the measured results of the analysis of many stycas it should be possible to assign regions of silver/zinc concentration to each king (Fig. 1). Eanred starts with silver concentrations of 40 to 50 per cent and very little zinc and ends with approximately 20 per cent zinc and only 6 per cent silver. Æthelred overlaps Eanred a bit. Æthelred starts at silver levels of 10 to 12 per cent and ends with silver at zero. Redwulf's stycas typically occupy a region between about 1.5 and 6 per cent silver and a relatively narrow range of 20.5 to 22.5 per cent zinc. Finally, Osberht's stycas lie towards zero per cent silver with zinc varying from about 20 to 21 per cent downwards to 1 to 2 per cent.

The data used in making this chart came from Gilmore and Metcalf's 1980 paper[6] which concentrated on the earlier years of the styca series, and the author's own work which concentrated more on the later styca period. By excluding the more widely scattered points in Figure 1, constituting perhaps 10 per cent of the total data, generalized regions of silver/zinc concentration can be rather easily constructed for each king. There would be one or two exceptions having zinc/silver ratios outside each ruler's generalized region. But the trend would be clear and these exceptions should then be examined more closely in their own right. Obviously, as more data become available, the regions can be better defined.

If one notes the silver/zinc concentration of the two Hoaud stycas on the generalized silver/zinc chart, one can see where they lie relative to other stycas. For clarity, the left hand area of Fig. 1 has been expanded in Fig. 2. It can be seen from this expanded graph that the two Hoaud stycas, in terms of their silver and zinc concentrations, fit either at the end of Æthelred's or at the beginning of Osberht's reign.

Let us now turn to a more detailed analysis of the metallic content of these two stycas. Each styca was analysed for the ten elements listed in Table 1. The last column on the right in Table 1 labelled 'Brass' shows the zinc content expressed as a percentage of the zinc-plus-copper content of each styca.

The two Hoaud stycas are quite similar to each other in their composition. Were it not for the trace bismuth content measured in one of them, it would be tempting to state that they came from the same melting pot.

For comparison, four other stycas (**Pl. 22, 3–6**) most closely resembling the composition of the two Hoaud stycas were chosen from the 60 stycas analysed. It is

[4] Gilmore and Metcalf, 1980, 83-98.   [5] Ibid., 94.   [6] Ibid.

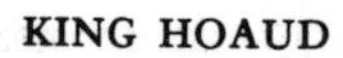

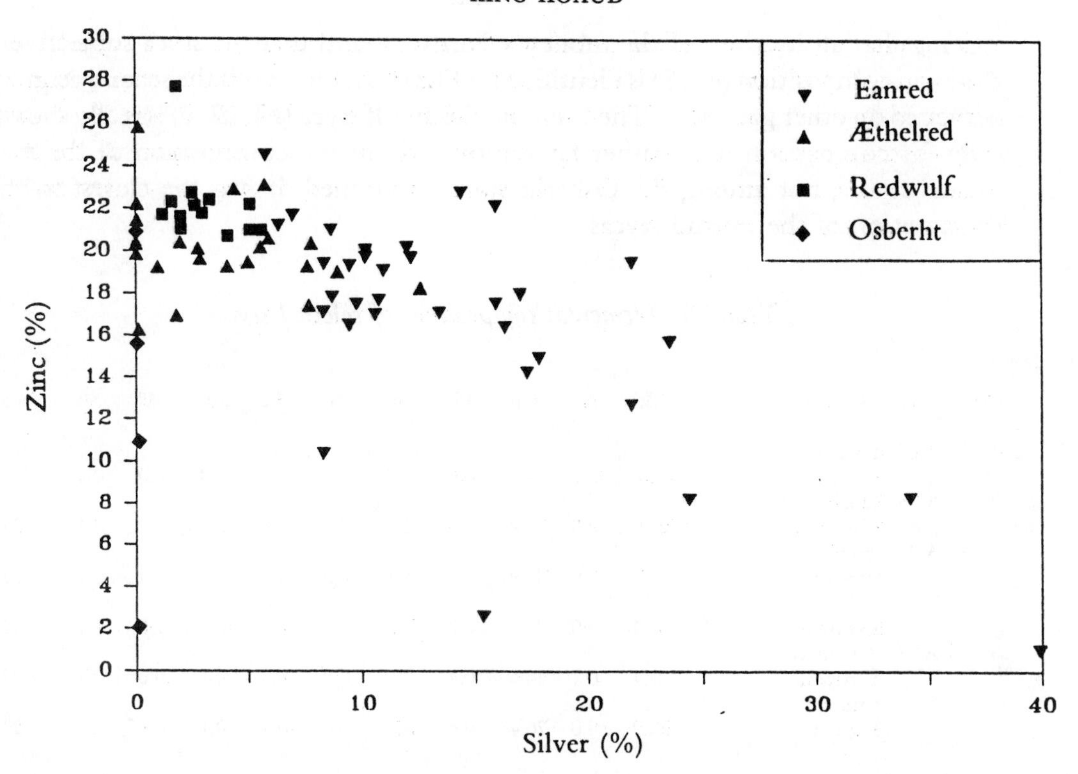

FIG. 1. Zinc and silver concentrations of royal stycas, from Eanred to Osberht.

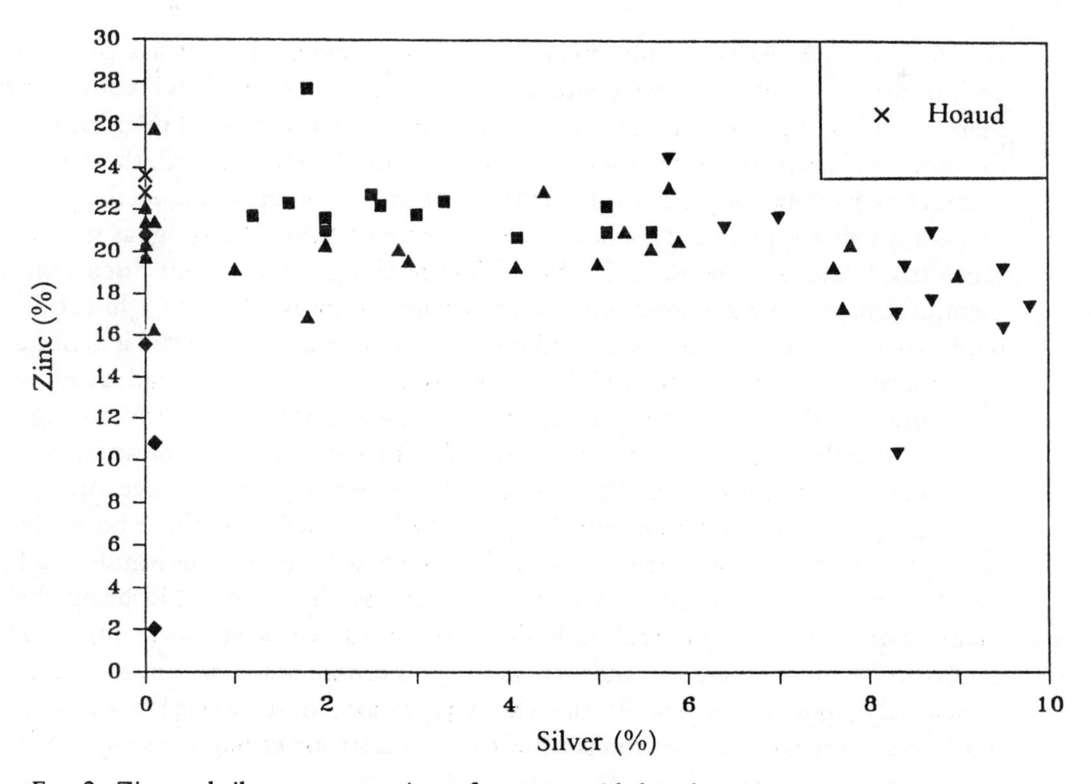

FIG. 2. Zinc and silver concentrations, for stycas with less than 10 per cent silver (expanded version of part of Fig. 1).

striking that all four are of the moneyer Eardwulf and that the styca subjectively closest in composition (no. 3) is identified by Elizabeth Pirie with the second reign of Æthelred on other grounds.[7] The Osberht/Eardwulf styca (**Pl. 22, 6**) is really shown only for comparison. It is rather far removed from the composition of the two Hoaud stycas; but among the Osberht stycas examined, it was the closest to the composition of the Hoaud stycas.

TABLE 1. *Elemental composition of selected stycas*

No.	*Code*	*Obv./Rev.*	Zn	Ag	Cu	Pb	Sn	Bi	Fe	Au	As	Sb	Brass
1.	A.34	Hoaud-Hwætræd	22.8	0.0	74.1	0.0	2.2	0.4	0.0	0.0	0.0	0.4	23.5
2.	A.35	Hoaud-Hwætræd	23.6	0.0	73.2	0.0	2.8	0.0	0.0	0.0	0.0	0.4	24.4
3.	A.22	Æthelred-Eardwulf	22.2	0.0	72.9	0.2	4.1	0.0	0.0	0.0	0.4	0.1	23.3
4.	A.50	Æthelred-Eardwulf	21.4	0.0	74.1	0.2	2.2	0.2	0.0	0.0	1.9	0.1	22.4
5.	A.23	Æthelred-Eardwulf	21.4	0.1	74.5	0.4	2.9	0.0	0.5	0.1	0.0	0.1	22.3
6.	A.33	Osberht-Eardwulf	20.9	0.0	76.4	0.6	1.2	0.0	0.4	0.1	0.0	0.5	21.5

DISCUSSION

DR METCALF: Mr Axe has ably demonstrated, what no numismatist would now wish to dispute, that the metal contents of the so-called HOAVDRE coins locate them in the latest phase of the styca series, post-dating the reform implemented by the moneyer Eardwulf. Given their absence from the Hexham hoard, their date of manufacture is to be sought in the late 850s or thereabouts (depending on the general chronology that is preferred). There is no question of their belonging, as was once suggested, to the time of King Eardwulf. The sticking point, in our discussion of them, is whether we can assert that their interpretation in terms of a historically unrecorded person with a name something like Huth, Huath, or Hoaud is definitely nonsensical, or whether we should be prepared to leave the door ajar and say merely that, although there is no prospect of ever associating the coins with any figure mentioned in the written sources, their legend may have had some meaning at the time, which now eludes us. This would not necessarily be to leave open the possibility of an otherwise unknown king, for the letters RE might have been added simply to make the coins resemble the official product—to add verisimilitude for semi-literate or illiterate users. And yet, the date of the coins could bring them within a period when political authority seems to have been crumbling. Tight control over the coinage certainly crumbled.—Perhaps some would-be usurper, some local magnate? The non-Anglo-Saxon appearance of the name is a stumbling-block; but in the end the question is whether we feel strong enough to say positively

[7] E. J. E. Pirie to D. C. Axe, private communication, 4 Sept. 1985. Miss Pirie, however, places Pl. 22, 5 in Æthelred's first reign.

that the attribution is nonsensical. Some ambivalence was expressed by Mr Lyon in his 1956 survey,[1] when he cautiously observed that the HOAVDRE coins were not connected into the extensive chain of die-links among Osberht's coins. This observation has gained in force with the progress of research, as it has become clear how tightly linked together almost all the imitative coins are. Any little group of them which was, so far as known, not linked into the skein ought now to attract our suspicious attention whatever their legends. The implication of their being separate might be that their dies were cut at a different time or place from the great majority of the imitative coins—which, one supposes, can only be from York. Current research has also established the size of the problem more clearly. It was always appreciated that the HOAVDRE coins were very scarce, but we now have a much better idea of the survival-rate of the imitative series, and can predict that the known die-varieties reflect a very high proportion of the original output. So few dies of Hoaud were ever made that the claim that they reflect an individual with that name lacks historical plausibility. Had there been such a person who issued coins in the 850s, he would surely have issued more. Rather, one's comment would be that die-cutters were persons of habit, even when they were cutting nonsense legends, and that plenty of examples could be offered of a little run of three or four closely similar dies which may be assumed to have been produced at the same time. All the 'Hoaud' dies could have been the whimsy of a single day's work on the part of the die-cutter.

One could perhaps point to the little group of coins reading EVXDIREX as analogous in many respects to those reading HOAVDRE. Recognizing analogies, and locating the HOAVDRE coins within wider patterns among the imitative dies, is in any case one obvious way in which we might hope to advance our understanding (since we have decided there is no way of relating them to the written sources). If provenances showed that the HOAVDRE coins had a different geographical distribution from the bulk of the imitatives, that would of course be another way forward, again essentially a matter of locating them within a wider pattern—but it remains only a theoretical possibility.

Lyon's passing comment on the coins, namely that they were unconnected with the main block of Osberht's coins, was quickly followed by a response from Dr Stewart, who produced an important new piece of evidence, and offered a radical revision.[2] He said that he had found another coin from the same *reverse* die as the Hoauds, reading HVVETRD retrograde (i.e. attempting the name of the moneyer Hwætræd). The linked obverse read EARDVVRE retrograde (i.e.echoing the name of the moneyer Eardwulf). Stewart went on to point out that the letters DRE on the one HOAVDRE die known to him were in fact retrograde, and that the remaining letters HOAV were ambiguous, being reversible from left to right. Thus of the three linked dies two were retrograde and the third was, when one came to look at it attentively, retrograde. It would be perverse to construe it in any other way than as ERDVAOH retrograde. That was, or should have been, the end of Hoaud's long run for his money. And that is where the matter has stood since 1956.

The rest is of antiquarian interest only, and does very little credit to the numismatic fraternity. The king who never was began his career in 1837, announced by no less a figure than Sir Henry Ellis, the indefatigable Secretary of the Society of Antiquaries, and one of the founding fathers of the Numismatic Society of London

[1] Lyon, 1956.

[2] I. H. Stewart, 'Ex-King Hoaud', *Seaby's Coin and Medal Bulletin* 1956, 138–40.

(later to become the Royal Numismatic Society). He published in the *Numismatic Journal* a styca which he read as HVAD.REX and, citing Bromton, proposed to attribute to Huth, son of Harald, who allegedly succeeded Anlaf as king of Northumberland (sic) in about 952.[3] This was, of course, at least two generations after the minting of stycas ceased. Ellis's note prompted another, in the next issue of the *Numismatic Journal*, from the eminent numismatist John Lindsay, of Cork, seeking to add to the canon of Huath's coins the sceattas of Series B, because he found the lettters HVAT among their blundered legends.[4] We now know that these coins were minted around 700, and that they are found chiefly in Kent and Essex.

Nathan Heywood, realizing that a tenth-century date was impossible, embroidered matters further by postulating another, historically unnoticed, king of the same name.[5] He described three die-varieties, in four specimens.[6]

B. Buckley suggested (tentatively), in 1956, that HOAVD was a phonetic rendering of Eochaid, 'a Gaelic name that was borne by several of the Dalriadic kings of Scotland, notably by Eochad III who commenced to reign in 781 and who was the paternal grandfather of Kenneth MacAlpin'.[7] This prompted the article by Dr Stewart already quoted, which dealt thoroughly and very sensibly with the errors that abounded. Its only lapse appears to be the assertion that all the 'Hoaud' coins come from the same die.

Miss Pirie: There are perhaps three elements of the total discussion on which one would like to comment, for more could be said about the identification of Hoaud as a personal name, as well as about the place in the scheme of things of the coins whose metallic composition Mr Axe has demonstrated. Nevertheless, at this juncture, it is more relevant to review the evidence of the dies in the little group to which that reading HOAV*DRE*[8] belongs.

So much attention is paid to Hoaud himself that too little has been given to the ostensible moneyer recorded on the companion die as HVAETRD. This in itself is almost enough to identify the issue as irregular for it is yet another instance of the recall of early moneyers from the first part of Eanred's reign; it is comparable to other such dies for *Vilheah*, *Eadvini*, and *Herred*. Further, this *Hvaetred* die is one of two; the other reads HV∴ETRD.[9] Pairs of similar dies are known in the main complex of irregulars, but have so far been noted in the smaller clusters only here. Both these dies are dominant reverses in that they are each common to a number of combinations. In this respect they are comparable to another, 'free-standing' cluster

[3] H. Ellis, 'Styca of Huth', *Numismatic Journal* 2 (1837–8), 99–100. On Ellis see *DNB* and R. A. G. Carson and H. Pagan, *A History of the Royal Numismatic Society*, 1986, p.3. Ellis's note was perhaps prompted in some sense by the publication in *Archaeologia* of the Hexham hoard.

[4] J. Lindsay, 'Coins of the Huath king of Northumberland', *Numismatic Journal* 2 (1837–8), 234–6.

[5] N. Heywood, loc. cit., 1890 (Axe, n.2 above)

[6] id., 1897 (ibid.).

[7] B.Buckley, 'Hoaud, king of Northumbria', *Seaby's Coin and Medal Bulletin* 1956, 54.

[8] The italicizing of capitals indicates that the letters are reversed.

[9] Both dies are retrograde, as indeed are all but the three primary ones for Hoaud. Pagan has read another die as HVTR+ED (1973, no. 1373). Although sets of three very similar dies are known among the main irregulars, this last cannot be set besides the other *Hvaetreds*. In the first place, it is not yet known as a dominant die (as are the others); in the second, the reading is almost certainly HVΓR+ED or +EDHVΓR (see Pirie, 1981, no. 326).

which depends on a single *Vilheah* die combined with each of eight nonsense dies. (May one suggest that in such cases, the die-cap element, bearing on its face the name of the ostensible moneyer, was welded onto a tanged shaft so that, in striking, it took the lower position normally meant for a proper obverse?). The first of these *Hvaetred* dies is combined not only with the Hoaud die already cited but with two others, reading +EARDVVRE and +HVOLHEA (or VOLHEA+H, for *Vilheah*?), respectively. The second is known paired with each of five dies: the first *Hoaud* die, a second reading +OAV*DRE*, and a possible third, +OVH[.]*ER*;[10] the fourth has a nonsense legend, T∴DIO;[11] the fifth shows DVIR*E*.[12]

The last die is used also in one of four combinations which have the common die DEV*RE*; two more of the dies involved have legends which are nonsense; the fourth pair has as its second die a possible fourth version of the name of Hoaud, if one reads the legend as HVODR+E.[13]

This whole complex is teetering on the brink of nonsense: as a personal name, Hoaud is balanced between those that are recognizable, such as *Hvaetred*, [*H*]*Eardvvlf* and, possibly, also *Vilheah*, and those that seem completely unintelligible. Nevertheless, as there are the four dies which reflect the name with varying degrees of precision, they seem to stand at the core of the cluster of coins which may have been prompted by an individual of as yet undetermined ethnic origin.

Pace Dr Metcalf, it may not be entirely apposite to relate this work, which includes *Hoavdre*, *Eardvvre* and *Devre*, directly to the *Euxdire* line. The common element, RE, may indeed be significant, but the single *Euxdire* die (which is not retrograde) and its combination with eight nonsense 'reverses' still stand unconnected to any other work. The general styles of die-cutting, too, are different. For the whole of the *Hvaetred*/*Hoaud* complex, with the exception of the first *Hvaetred* die, the lettering is that which is profusely adorned with knobs; in contrast, the *Euxdire* work is comparatively plain.

Addendum. Heywood's list of dies. Heywood[14] claimed three *Hoaud* dies and cited the relevant combination of legends. In almost each case there is inaccuracy, even in the first which adds the X to HOAVD REX. The second misreads the detail of the *Hvaetred* reverse and fails to indicate that the legend is retrograde.

The third pair of legends presents a real puzzle for correct attribution since the second die is recorded as ERDVLFON. Heywood's cryptic comment on the attempts of others to construe it as Eardwulf if read backwards would seem to imply that he himself was reading it from right to left. But if he thought the legend was retrograde in the first place, it is the right-to-left reading which he would have considered backwards! Eardwulf does not really come into the picture since there is no independent evidence of the *Hoaudre* die and the *Eardvvre* one having been combined. It is not altogether outside the bounds of possibility to realise that, in dealing with a particularly worn specimen, Heywood mis-read HVAETRED as HOAV*DRE* and HOAV*DRE* as ERDVLFON, retrograde! The last of his three is surely another example of his first.

[10] Pagan (1973), nos. 1359–61; all three coins are now in the Yorkshire Museum.

[11] An example is known in the Ashmolean Museum.

[12] The coin in question is in Stonyhurst College, *ex* York, 1831.

[13] Pagan, (1973), no. 1364: now in the Yorkshire Museum.

[14] N. Heywood, *The Stycas of North Humbria*, 1899 [reprint], 11.

Dr Metcalf: The full pattern of the die evidence for Hoaud, of which Miss Pirie has given us a résumé, has never previously been stated. One can see very well from this miniature example just how superior her knowledge of the dies and die-chains is, and what major advances it will make possible. Ironically, at the end of the consideration, she and I reach almost diametrically opposite opinions about Hoaud as a person—even though his coins are, one would have thought, a very small, mangeable problem. What should perhaps intrigue general historians is to work out where we diverge. It isn't, I think, over dies or die-links, but it is when we come to the more tentative deductions for which the pattern of dies provides the groundwork. It seems that these deductions are, after all, not open-and-shut, and that the case bears more resemblance to advocacy than to mathematical proof. Perhaps, in retrospect, that may be seen to be a characteristic mode of argument from numismatics to monetary history.

PLATE 22

The personal names on the pre-Viking Northumbrian coinages

VERONICA SMART

WHOEVER the scribes were who wrote down the patterns for the die-cutters of the stycas and the inscribed Northumbrian sceattas, it seems clear that they were working within an orderly established convention which closely parallels what we know of Northumbrian usage from manuscript sources. The recording of the names on the coins is in most respects identical with what we find in the Durham *Liber Vitae*, a volume brought to and continued at Durham but written for the main part in the Lindisfarne community in the first half of the ninth century, probably *c.* 840, listing over three thousand names of benefactors and others worthy of commemoration. There are also strong similarities to an earlier record of OE names in the MSS of Bede's *Historia Ecclesiastica* which preserve Northumbrian features.

I ORTHOGRAPHY

1. LVD and HE represent *w* by a single **u**, very occasionally by **uu**. The adoption of the runic symbol *wyn* into the Roman alphabet to distinguish the consonant is totally lacking from LVD and HE. The coins follow this usage, employing V as the epigraphic form of **u**. The presence of the ƿ rune in the moneyer's name *Wihtræd* is clearly in a runic capacity since this name habitually exhibits runic characters; this is not evidence for the adoption of this symbol into normal Roman orthography at this time. The evaluation of ƿ with the initial V in this name is a further indication that V on the coins represents *w*.

Since the representation of *w* by **uu** is exceptional in Northumbrian MSS of this period the probability is that VVLF- on the coins is a representation of *Wulf-* rather than *Wlf-* with the vowel omitted.

2. HE represents th [ð, θ] where it occurs medially or finally by **d** (*Cudbercto*, Cudualdi, Fordheri). LVD has no regular system but uses the symbols, **th**, **ð**, **d** and occasionally **t** to represent the sounds (*Cuðheard*, *Cutheard*; *Fordheri*, *Forðred*; *Leofðegn*, *Cynidegn*, *Tilthegn*), but **d** is less frequent than **ð** and **th**. The innovation of the diacritic mark on D and **d** to distinguish *th*, like the introduction of ƿ for *w*, seems to have arisen in Mercia, but seemingly reached Northumbria by the time the LVD lists were written. The coin-spellings would then appear to be somewhat

archaic in their preference for undifferentiated D as found in Bede (LEOFDEGN, FORDRED; LVD *leofðegn*, *forðred*). The D may have been substituted by the die-cutters for a written Đ, since hypercorrection in HERREĐ (-red) may indicate unfamiliarity with the function of the diacritic.

3. Both HE and LVD represent the fricative [χ] before *t* by **c** (*-berct*), and as **ch** finally in the element (LVD *edilhech*, *alchfrith*). The coin-legends follow this spelling on the dies reading DÆGBERCT and EDILECH, but in CUDBEREHT there is an **h** spelling unusual in Northumbrian texts but paralleled by EOTBEREHTUS on the dies of the eighth-century king (the parasitic vowel occurs in HE with **c** spellings *Ecgberecti*, *Sigberecto* but not in LVD). EOTBEREHTUS like Bede's *-berectus* forms may be consequent on latinisation, in that some Germanic consonant-clusters may have been thought diseuphonious in that language. CUDBEREHT and VILHEAH on the coins would appear to reflect a non-Northumbrian—though one cannot say a non-OE—orthographic usage.

In *Ealhhere* G appears to be used for the sound under notice: ALGHERE. This may merely be an alternative letter-form for C, but if VILHEOX on a coin with blundered obverse is to be accepted, the final symbol can be interpreted as the g rune (*-heah*) and would provide an additional example of **g** for [χ]. In LVD the form *Regenhaeg* is classified by Sweet as a *-heah* name and this would appear to be the only MS parallel.

4. As mentioned in I1. above the legends in this series use a number of runic characters. In the Name-List I have distinguished those which are of distinctive form, but some others which differ only in small detail from their Roman form cannot always be so distinguished on the coins. Runic l is ᛚ, and since inverted letters are not infrequent ᚴ may be interpreted either way. Runic h is ᚻ or ᚺ, similar to Roman H or N; since the angle of the cross-bar is frequently ambiguous, wherever the context demands H I have so transcribed it.

In the archbishop's name Ecgberht the form EYBERHT is found; Y may be an inversion of the c rune ᚳ.

In *Cynewulf* the form of the letter y presents a problem. I take the form ᛘ to be an inversion of the normal y of the English runic alphabet ᚣ but ᛉ is difficult to explain. In no scheme of runes compatible with ninth-century England does this symbol represent a vowel. Originally in PrG it stood for z, and represented the nominative-case ending r in Norwegian inscriptions. In late Scandinavian inscriptions it is sometimes used as an equivalent to y but in English runes it stood for x. Although it does not appear in non-runic epigraphic scripts I would regard it probably as an idiosyncratic rendering of Roman Y, or possibly of the rune. In the Name-List I have rendered ᛘ as y for the rune and ᛉ as Y.

II PHONOLOGY

1. WG *ă* was unbroken in the Anglian dialects before *l*, *r*, + consonant, hence ALCHRED (WS *Ealh-*), CVDHARD (WS *-heard*), CEOLBALD (WS *-beald*), EDILVARD (WS *-weard*).

2. In BADIGILS the unbroken vowel is due to a dialectal variation in fronting and

subsequent back-mutation of WG *a*. The *ea* forms (*Beadu-*) are properly Mercian but occur more widely, according to Campbell as a result of poetic texts which were copied in Mercia.

3. In Anglian dialects the diphthong *ēa* became *ē* before (*c*)*h*, thus EDILECH (WS *-heah*)

4. PrG *x* which became *ǣ* regularly in WS became *ē* in all other dialects, hence ALCHRED, TIDRED, HERRED (WS *-rǣd*)

5. WG *au* passed through several stages to become the OE diphthong *ēa*; at one stage this was *eo* and this is presumably what is reflected by EOTBEREHTVS, EODVLF and perhaps VILHEOG, though this spelling was already archaic in Bede's time, since it is less usual than *ea* even in HE.

6. The variant forms of the element *Æthel* require some explanation. These are: EDIL-, AEDIL-, EDEL-, AEDEL-. The element is associated with the OE adjective *aethele* 'noble' from WG *athali* but is not identical with it. The presence of *-il* forms suggests an early variant **athili* must have existed to produce OE *æthil* and hence *ethil* by the mutating influence of the following i, alongside *æthel* from *athali*. Hybrid forms *æthil*, *ethel* would rise through conflation of the two variants once their separate origins had been forgotten. Some influence from *Œthil-*, *Ethil-* 'native land' cannot be discounted.

BMC (p. 151) suggests that on king Æthelred's coins which read EÐFRED, F may there be a confusion with the rune ᚠ . In OE runes ᚫ stands for *æ*, and the resulting *Ethælred* would be anomalous and archaic.

The spellings AEILRED, EILRED appear to be deliberate and would support Coleman's suggestion that the sound-change whereby [ð] is lost between two front vowels where the second is followed by *l* is of greater antiquity than the eleventh century *Ægel-*, *Æl-* forms found on the coins of Æthelred II of England.

7. The early OE (from WG) endings of elements in the composition-joint or finally in the name are frequently retained in LVD and on the coins, but some have been modified or lost already.

-wini invariably retains its ending on the coins of Tidwine, an Eanred moneyer, and on the Eanred coins of Eadwine, but an Æthelred II coin of Eadwine reads EADVIN.

Cyni- has lost its ending in CYNVVLF and is weakened to *e* in CYNEMVND. In LVD *cyni-* is the more usual form but *cyneh*, *cynheard*, *cynhelm* also occur.

-sigi in LVD is always *-sig* without the vowel ending, paralleled by VVLFSIC on the coins.

-heri: both *-heri* and *-here* are found in LVD.

Badi in BADIGILS is irregular since the element is properly *Badu-*, but the *i* spelling is paralleled in LVD. This presumably reflects uncertainty about the value of the unstressed vowel in traditional spelling at a time when the old endings were becoming lost or weakened in speech; *i* has been supplied by analogy with *-sigi*, *-heri*.

III THE NON-OE ELEMENT IN THE NAMES

1. As one would expect from the context, almost all the names on the stycas and the earlier Northumbrian sceattas are of OE origin. Only one name is at all likely to derive from another source and that is ODILO, which must be the CG name *Odilo* (Förstemann 1183), an uncompounded suffixed derivative of *Othal-*, *Odal-*, related to *othal-* 'native land'. OE names are not found suffixed in *-o*. The name is very common in CG sources; see also Morlet 276.

2. BRODER (with its variants) is rather more problematical, but is most probably OE. As a vocabulary-word *brothor* is found in OE also in the earlier forms *brother*, *brothur*, although the form omitting the second vowel *brothr*, which could be an early variant of the period when the vowel was changing, is peculiar to the personal name on the coins. *Brother* does not occur amongst the names in LVD, and its otherwise late appearance only in 11th century charters led von Feilitzen to assign to the Domesday Book instances a Scandinavian origin, East Scandinavian *Brother*, whilst conceding an OE origin for the ninth-century moneyer's name. We have a parallel use of OE *sweoster* 'sister' as a personal name in OE from a tenth century will (Redin 41). There does not seem to me to be any necessity to regard the personal name *Brother* as a Scandinavian introduction, with its implication of Scandinavian settlement in Northumbria at such an early date.

3. In a paper in *BNJ* in 1967 Michael Dolley argued that the element *-thegn* in OE personal names was introduced as a translation of OIr *Gilla-*. Of *Leofthegn* he wrote that it was 'confined to Northumbria, an area where Irish influences from the 7th century onwards were introduced, and even there to the copper coins of one ninth century king'. This is misleading. In LVD *-thegn* names are extremely common; we find *Beaduthegn*, *Cynethegn*, *Cuththegn*, *Eadthegn*, *Ealdthegn*, *Ealuthegn*, *Leofthegn*, *Tilthegn*, *Wigthegn*, *Wilthegn*. In all of these names *-thegn* behaves exactly as any OE second element, in combination with conventional first elements, quite unlike the Celtic *Gilla* names which have as a second element the name of a saint or ecclesiastical functionary. Secondly, the element is not confined to Northumbria. Reliable instances can be found for Worcester, Peterborough, Winchester and Shropshire (Searle s.n. *Cynethegn*, *Cuththegn*, *Wigthegn*, *Tilthegn*: PNDB s.n. *Ertein*). Thirdly, *-thegn* in personal names is common to all branches of the Germanic languages and no other origin need be looked for.

IV THE NAME-LIST

The names are listed under their normalized dictionary forms, followed by the forms found in LVD as representative of contemporary Northumbrian language and usage. The comparative frequency of the name in LVD is shown by the number of occurrences (× n) following, or if only one occurrence, the line number preceding, the given form. The elements from which the name is constructed are then explained.

Forms of names are listed under reigns, all kings before all archbishops. Abbreviations are as in *SCBI Index* except that [Enr], [Enb] have been emended to [Eanr], [Eanb] for Eanred, Eanbald, and 'Northumbria' and 'styca' omitted as unnecessary in this context.

Individual instances in *SCBI* may be traced through the *SCBI Index*.

Æthelhēah

LVD 68 *edilhech*, 165 *eðilhech*

OE *æthele* 'noble' + *hēah* 'high' (I, 2,3; II 3,6)

[Eanr] EDILECH Yorkshire Museum

Æthelhelm

LVD 387 *eðilhelm*

OE *æthele*: see *Æthelhēah* + *helm* 'helmet' (runic 1 I 4)

([Æthr II] *BMC* p. 159 list only)
[Osb] EDELHELM *SCBI*
[Abp Wi] EDELHELM *SCBI*, *BMC* 739–48

(**Æthelnōth** *BMC* p. 144 list only)

Æthelrǣd

LVD *eðilred* × 2 but cf. HE where *Aedilred* is more common.

OE *æthele*: see *Æthelhēah* + *rǣd* 'counsel' (II 4)

King's name: Æthelred I AEDILRED *BMC* 283–5, 293
Æthelred II EDILRED most commonly, and the sole form on the late coins (moneyer Eardwulf) of the second reign. Otherwise AEDELRED, AEDILRED, AEÐILRED, EÐILRED, EÐELRED, EDELRED, AEILRED, EILRED, AEðEL-REð, EDILDRED, EDLIRED, EDFLRED

Æthelweard

LVD –

OE *æthele*: see *Æthelhēah* + *weard* 'guardian' (I 1, II 1)

[Eanr] EDILVARD *BMC* 127, EDILVEVD *BMC* 128 (retro., blundered obv., perhaps not Eanred), EDELVAR? *BMC* 129
([Æthr II] *BMC* p. 159 list only)
[Abp Eanb] EDILVARD *SCBI*, *BMC* 711–17, EDILVEARD *SCBI*, *BMC* 709
[Abp Wi] EDILVEARD *SCBI*, *BMC* 749–60, 764–70 (752, 760, 765 retro.); EDIVEARD *SCBI*; EDILVENID *BMC* 761, 763 retro.; EDILVEIIED *BMC* 762 retro.; EILVEVAD *BMC* 771
[double reverse] EDILVEARD *BMC* 811

Aldates

obscure; the first element may be OE *eald* 'old'. Lettering similar to *Gadutels* q.v.

[Eanr] ALDATES *SCBI*, *BMC* 24–7
([Æthr II] *BMC* p. 159 list only)

Beadugils

LVD 328 *badigils*, 446 *beadugils*

OE *beadu* 'battle' + *gisl* 'hostage', always -*gils* by metathesis in personal names (II 2,7)

[Eanr] BADIGILS *BMC* 255–8 (256–7 retro.)

Brother

LVD –

OE *brother* 'brother' (III 2)

[Eanr] BRODER *SCBI*,*BMC* 32–4; BROER *SCBI*, *BMC* 45; BRODR *SCBI*, *BMC* 35–44, 46–8 (37–8 retro.); BRother (partly runic)

SCBI, *BMC* 28–31; BROÐER *SCBI*
[Æthr II] BROÐER *BMC* 631–3; VBRODER *BMC* 281–2
[Rdw] BRODER *BMC* 273, 280 retro.; BROÐER *BMC* 272, 274–7 (277 retro.)

Cēolbeald

LVD 6 *ceolbald*

OE *cēol* 'keel' + *beald* 'bold' (II 1)

[Æthr I] CEOLBALD *SCBI*, *BMC* 283–5; CEOLBAED *SCBI*

Coenrǣd

LVD *coenred* × 3

OE *coen* 'keen' + *rǣd*: see *Æthelrǣd*

([Eanr] *BMC* p. 144 list only)
[Rdw] COENRED *BMC* 634; COENED *SCBI*, *BMC* 636
[Abp Wi] COENRED *SCBI*, *BMC* 719–26, 728–34; CONERED *SCBI*, *BMC* 727, 736; EOENRED *BMC* 735 retro.

Cūthbeorht

LVD *cuthbercht* × 2, *cuthberct* × 6, 418 *cuðberct*

OE *cūth* 'known, famous' + *beorht* 'bright' (I 2,3)

[Rdw] CVDBEREHT *SCBI*, *BMC* 636–9 (638 retro.)
([Osb] *BMC* p. 187 list only)

Cūthgils

LVD *cuthgils* × 4

OE *cūth*: see *Cūthbeorht* + *gisl*: see *Beadugils*

[Æthr I] CVDGILS *SCBI*

Cūthheard

LVD 228 *cutheard*, *cuðheard* × 2

OE *cūth*: see *Cūthbeorht* + *heard* 'hardy' (I, 2; II 1)

[Æthr I] CVDHEARD *BMC* 293
[Ælfwald] CVDHEART Sancton find
[Eanr] CVDHARD *BMC* 72–4

Cynemund

LVD *cynimund* × 3

OE *cyn* 'family, kin' + *mund* 'power' (II 7)

[Æthr II] CVNEMVND *SCBI*, *BMC* 290; CVNEMVnD (runic n) *SCBI*, *BMC* 287–9; CVNIMVID *BMC* 291; CVNIVIIND *BMC* 292.

Cynewulf

LVD *cyniuulf* × 21

OE *cyn*: see *Cynemund* + *wulf* 'wolf' (I 1,4)

[Eanr] CyNVVLF *SCBI*, *BMC* 50–1, 56, 58, 64–6 retro., 68–9; CYNVVLF *SCBI*, *BMC* 53–5, 57, 63; CyVVNLF *SCBI*, *BMC* 59–60, 70–1; CYVVNLF *BMC* 52; CyVNNLF? *BMC* 61–2
[Abp Eanb] CyNVVLF *SCBI*, *BMC* 679–80 (680 retro.); CyVNVLF *BMC* 681; CyNVLF *BMC* 678

Dirinde

obscure; perhaps for *Wihtred*?

[Æthr II] DIRINDE *BMC* 294

Dægbeorht

LVD *daegberct* × 5

OE *dæg* 'day' + *beorht*: see *Cūthbeorht*

[Eanr] DAEGBERCT *SCBI*, *BMC* 75–82, 84–5; DAEgBERCT (runic g) *BMC* 86; DAEgBERC (runic g) *BMC* 83, 87.

Of the two coins catalogued in *SCBI* as *Daegberht* one (6.4) is certainly -BERCT; the other (2.142) is indistinct

Ēadbeorht

LVD *eadberct* × 45, *eadbercht* × 4

OE *ēad* 'property, riches' + *beorht*: see *Cūthbeorht* (II 5)

King's name: EOTBEREHTVS *SCBI*, *BMC* 4–7, 9; EOTBERHTVS *SCBI*, *BMC* 8; EOTBERETVS (anti-clockwise but letters not reversed) *BMC* 11; EOTBERERTS (as last) *BMC* 12; EOTBREHTVS *SCBI*; EADBEREHTVS *SCBI*; EADBERHTVS *SCBI*, *BMC* 10

Ēadwine

LVD *eaduini* × 18

OE *ēad*: see *Eadbeorht* + *wine* 'friend' (II 7)

('Eardwulf' *BMC* p. 143 list only—

probably a blundered 9th century coin)
[Eanr] EADVINI *SCBI*, *BMC* 88–96, 98–116; IEADVINE (anti-clockwise but letters not reversed) *BMC* 97
[Æthr II] EADVIN *BMC* 295
[blundered mid 9th century] EADVINI (retro.) 1 obv. EILRED, 1 obv. ECEVALDE *SCBI*

Ēadwulf

LVD *eaduulf* × 54, 324 *eoduulf*

OE *ēad*: see *Eadbeorht* + *wulf*: see *Cynewulf* (II 5)

[Abp Eanb] EADVVLF *SCBI*, *BMC* 682–95; AEDVVLF *BMC* 696; EADVVOLF *BMC* 697–8; EADLVVF *BMC* 699; EODVVLF *SCBI*, *BMC* 700–6 (705–6 retro.), 708, EVVLAFD *BMC* 707.
[blundered mid 9th century] EAOVVLF *BMC* 807.

Ealhhere

LVD 372 *alcheri*

OE *ealh* 'temple' + *here* 'army' (I 3; II 1,7)

[Æthr II] ALGHERE *SCBI*, *BMC* 260–4, 267–8 (268 retro.); ALCHERE *BMC* 265–6; ALDHERE *BMC* 269–71
[Rdw] ALGHERE *SCBI*, *BMC* 629–30

ALDHERE might alternatively be identified with OE *Ealdhere*.

Ealhrǣd

LVD –

OE *ealh*: see *Ealhhere* + *ræd*: see *Æthelrǣd*

King's name: ALCHRED *SCBI*, *BMC* 13–15

Ēanbeald

LVD *eanbald* × 13

OE *Ēan-*, a common OE name-element of obscure origin, + *beald*: see *Cēolbeald*

Archbishop's name: EANBALD *SCBI*, *BMC* 678, 680–705, 707, 709–10, 712–17; EANGALD *BMC* 706; EANBAID *BMC* 711; ANBALD *SCBI*; ANALD *BMC* 697; EANBAD *SCBI*, *BMC* 708; ENDALD *SCBI*.

Ēanræd

LVD *eanred* × 24

OE *Ēan-*: see *Ēanbeald* + *rǣd*: see *Æthelrǣd*

King's name: almost all examples read EANRED. There are some omissions and transpositions of letters e.g. EANRD, EANAED, ERANRED, but no significant variations.

[Eanr] EANRED *BMC* 117–8 (118 retro.); EANREÐ *BMC* 119 retro.
[Æthr II] EANRED *SCBI*, *BMC* 296–323 (315 retro.), 328–42, 346–8, 350; EANREDE *BMC* 324; ANRED *SCBI*, *BMC* 325–7, 351; INRED *BMC* 352; IEAARE? *BMC* 353; EANREDR *BMC* 343–5, 349 (moneyer, or double obv.?).

Eardwulf

LVD *earduulf* × 18

OE *eard* 'earth' + *wulf*: see *Cynewulf*

[Æthr II] EARDVVLF *SCBI*, *BMC* 354–76 (355, 366, 374–5 retro., 368 anti-clockwise but letters not reversed); EARDVVLI *BMC* 377; EARDVVF *SCBI*
[blundered mid 9th century] EARDVVC (retro.) *BMC* 808.

Ecgbeorht

LVD *ecgberct* × 7, 15 *ecgbercht*

OE *ecg* 'edge, blade' + *beorht*: see *Cūthbeorht* (I 4)

Archbishop's name: ECGBERHT *SCBI*, *BMC* 677: EYBERHT *SCBI*

Folcnōth

LVD –

OE *folc* 'people, nation' + *nōth* 'temerity' (I 2)

[Eanr] FOLCNOD *BMC* 130–6 (131, 133–6 retro.); FVLCNOD *BMC* 137, 140–1; FVLNOD *BMC* 139; FVLHIOD? *BMC* 138.

Forthrǣd

LVD *forðred* × 4

OE *forth* 'forwards' + *rǣd*: see *Æthelrǣd* (I 2)

[Eanr] FORDRED *SCBI*, *BMC* 142–50, 153 (anti-clockwise but letters not reversed), 155–7, 161–5; EORDRDE *BMC* 152; EORDRED (anti-clockwise but letters not reversed) *BMC* 158; EORDRE (do.) *BMC*
[Æthr II] FORDRED *SCBI*, *BMC* 386, 389–91, 394–405, 412–14, 417–27; EORDRED *BMC* 385, 387–8 retro., 406–11 (407 retro.), 415–16; EOFRED *BMC* 392; EORIRDED (this moneyer?)
[Rdw] FORDRED *SCBI*, *BMC* 649; EORDRED *SCBI*, *BMC* 644–5, 648; EORDRER *BMC* 643; EORDRE *BMC* 646.

Gadutels

obscure. Lettering similar to *Aldates*, q.v.

Heardwulf see *Wulfheard*

Hererǣd

LVD *herred* × 3

OE *here* 'army' + *rǣd*: see *Æthelrǣd* (II 7)

[Eanr] HERRED *SCBI*, *BMC* 184–9, 191; HERREÐ *BMC* 192, 194–6; HRRED *BMC* 190; HEAREÐI *BMC* 193; HEIIIIED *BMC* 197; EHHRED (anti-clockwise but letters not reversed) *SCBI*.

HEAREÐI may alternatively be identified with OE *Hēahrǣd*.

Hwætnōth

LVD –

OE *hwæt* 'brisk, brave' + *nōth*: see *Folcnōth* (I 2)

[Rdw] HVAETNDD *SCBI*, *BMC* 650–2 (652 retro.)

Hwætrǣd

LVD *huaetred* × 5

OE *hwæt*: *Hwætnōth* + *rǣd*: see *Æthelrǣd*

[Eanr] HVAETRED *SCBI*, *BMC* 198–201;
[blundered mid 9th century] HVAETRD *SCBI* obv. HOAVD RE, (retro.) *BMC* 22 obv. EARDVV REX; HVAETREI *SCBI* obv. doubtful.

Hūnlāf

LVD –

OE *Hūn-* is probably to be associated with a Gc root *hun-* which appears in Scand. *húnn* 'young bear' but which has not given rise to a cognate vocabulary word in OE. The earlier association with the folk-name of the Huns is not now accepted. + *lāf* 'relict, something left', which though a fem. noun in common use, is a masc. personal name element.

[Æthr II] HVNLAF *SCBI*, *BMC* 431
[Rdw] HVNL[ ] *BMC* 653
[Abp Wi] HVNLAF *SCBI*, *BMC* 773–94 (790–2 retro.); HNALAF *SCBI*

Hnifula

LVD –

Perhaps no more than a blundering of *Hunlaf*, but the coins of this moneyer belong to an earlier Æthelred than those of the moneyer Hunlaf. Cf. OE *hnifol*, *hneofula* 'forehead'; personal names formed from parts of the body are rare in OE, but bynames are found which could become personal names. See also the small class of personal names in *-ula* (Redin 148), the existence of which may have helped to assimilate *hnifula* as a name.

[Æthr I] HNIFVLA *BMC* 429–30 (attributed to Æthr II).

Lēofthegn

LVD 156 *leofðegn*

OE *lēof* 'beloved' + *thegn* 'servant' (I 2,4; III 3)

[Æthr II] LEOFDEGN *SCBI*, *BMC* 432–96 (440, 443, 469, 481 retro.; 443, 449, 450, 460, 470 have runic n, 486–8, 492 have N followed by n rune); LE[ ]DEGN *SCBI* L+XFDEGN *BMC* 478; LEOFDDN *BMC* 481

[blundered mid 9th century] LAFEDEHN *SCBI* obv. EDREDOME

Monne

LVD –

The form is consistently in final *-e* which

suggests a different suffix from that found in the name *Manna, Monna. Monne* may be explained as reflecting an older diminutive *Monni* as suggested by von Feilitzen in *SCBI* 11a (pp. 11–12).

[Eanr] MONNE *SCBI, BMC* 202–24 (224 retro.)
[Æthr II] MONNE *SCBI, BMC* 497–56 (509, 517, 525, 531, 553 retro.)

[Rdw] MONNE *SCBI, BMC* 654–59 (657–9 retro.)

Odilo

LVD –

CG *Odilo* (Föfstemann 1183), *othal* 'native land' + *-o* suffix (III 1)

[Eanr] ODILO *SCBI, BMC* 226–8 (227 reads ODILO MO 228 ODILO MON)
[Æthr II] ODILO *SCBI, BMC* 577–8 (ODILO MON)
[Rdw] ODILO *SCBI*
[blundered mid 9th century] ODILO *SCBI, BMC* 23 (obv. EARDVVL)

Ōsbeorht

LVD *osberct* × 2, 92 *osbercht*, 326 *osberht*

OE *ōs* 'god' + *beorht*: see *Cūthbeorht*

King's name: OSBERCHT *SCBI, BMC* 663, 665–6; OSBRCHT *SCBI, BMC* 664; OSBERCH *BMC* 667; OSBBERCHT *BMC* 670; OSBEREHT *BMC* 671–2; OSBERTHT *BMC* 673–4; OSBERH *SCBI*; OSBEHBEB *BMC* 675; OSBEBLHT, OSBTLHT *SCBI*

Rǣdwulf

LVD *reduulf* × 7

OE *rǣd*: see *Æthelrǣd* + *wulf*: see *Cynewulf*

King's name: REDVVLF *SCBI, BMC* 635, 650–2; REDVLF *SCBI, BMC* 629–32, 634, 636–44, 647–9, 653–6 (647–9 retro.); REDVL *SCBI, BMC* 633, 645–6; REDVLE 657–9 (anti-clockwise but letters not reversed); HEDVVLF *BMC* 660–2

Teveh

obscure: ? for *Tiw* 'the god Tiw' + *hēah*: see *Æthelhēah*; cf. *tiuuald* LVD.

[Eanr] TEVEH *BMC* 229

Tīdwine

LVD *tiduini* × 12

OE *tīd* 'time' + *wine*: see *Eadwine*

[Eanr] TIDVINI *BMC* 230; TIDVNI *SCBI, BMC* 231; TIDIVNI *SCBI*

Tīdwulf

LVD *tiduulf* × 7

OE *tīd*: see *Tidwine* + *wulf*: see *Cynewulf*

[Æthr II] TIDVVLF *SCBI, BMC* 580, 581 (retro.)

Wendelbeorht

LVD 97 *uendilbercht*

OE *wendlas*, a folk-name, probably 'Vandals' but the alternative suggestion is made in B-T that it refers to the people of Vendsyssel in Jutland. The folk-name appears in *Beowulf* and *Widsith*. + *beorht*: see *Cūthbeorht*. (I 1)

[Æthr II] VENDELBERHT *SCBI, BMC* 582–92
[Rdw] VENDELBERHT *BMC* 660–2

Wīgmund

LVD *uigmund* × 5

OE *wīg* 'war' + *mund*: see *Cynemund* (I 1)

Archbishop's name: VIGMVND *SCBI, BMC* 718–37, 739–46, 749–67, 772–98 (763–7, 790–2 retro.); VIMUND *SCBI*; VGMVND *BMC* 771; IGMVND *BMC* 768–70; FGMVND *BMC* 738 (retro.); EIGMVND *BMC* 747–8.

Wihtræd

LVD 67 *uichtred*

OE *wiht* 'creature' + *ræd*: see *Æthelrǣd* (I 1)

[Eanr] wihtred (all runic) *SCBI, BMC* 239; wIHTRED (runic w) *BMC* 240–3; wIHTRR (runic w) *SCBI, BMC* 244–5 (245 retro.)
[Æthr II] VIHtRED (runic t) *SCBI, BMC* 593–4; VIHTRED *BMC* 595; wIHTRD (runic w) *SCBI, BMC* 596–7, 600, 604–5; wIHTRED (runic w) *SCBI, BMC* 598–600, 607–8; wIHTRR (runic w) *BMC* 602 retro.;

WIHTRID (runic w) *BMC* 603 (anti-clockwise but letters not reversed); WIRT-NDE (runic w) *BMC* 606

Wilhēah

LVD –

OE *Wil-* related to *willa* 'will' + *hēah*: see *Æthelhēah* (I 1; II 5)

[Eanr] VILHEAH *SCBI*, *BMC* 232–8
([Abp Wi] *BMC* p. 193 list only)
[blundered mid 9th century] VILHEOX (X = runic g?) *SCBI*(retro.) obv. EARDVVL?

Wulfheard

LVD *uulfheard* × 25, *uulfhard* × 2, *uulfheord* × 2

OE *wulf*: see *Cynewulf* + *heard*: see *Cūthheard*

[Eanr] VVLFEHRRD *SCBI*, *BMC* 246; VVLFHEARD *BMC* 247–9 (249 retro. with final D in centre); VLFHEARD *SCBI* (ALFHEARD *SCBI* = VLFHEARD with inverted V).

BMC 177–8 are catalogued as HEARDVVLF, 179–83 as HEARDVLF, but the only one of these legends to incorporate a cross is that on 180–1 HEARD+VLF, which would suggest VLF as the first element.

Wulfhere

LVD *uulfheri* × 3

OE *wulf*: see *Cynewulf* + *here*: see *Hererǣd*

Archbishop's name: VLFHERE *SCBI*, *BMC* 799 retro.; VVLFHERE *SCBI*, *BMC* 800 retro.

Wulfrǣd

LVD *uulfred* × 3

OE *wulf*: see *Cynewulf* + *rǣd*: see *Æthelrǣd*

[Eanr] VVLFRED *SCBI*, *BMC* 250–4
[Æthr II] VVLFRED *SCBI*, *BMC* 609–22, 624; VVLERED *SCBI*, *BMC* 623.
[Abp Wfh] VVLFRED *SCBI* (some retro.; in 4.444 cross breaks legend), *BMC* 799 (retro.); VVLFREĐ *BMC* 800 (retro., cross breaks legend).

Wulfsige

LVD *uulfsig* × 20, 96 *uulsig*

OE *wulf*: see *Cynewulf* + *sige* 'victory'

[Æthr II] VVLFSIC *SCBI*,*BMC* 625–8 (retro)
[Osb] VVLFSIXT *BMC* 675; VVLFSXIT *SCBI* (X, the rune for the spirant may here stand for G; T, unless an error for E or I, is difficult to explain.)

Bibliography, References, and Abbreviations

—	*An Anglo-Saxon Dictionary based on the MS collections of J. Bosworth*, edited by T. N. Toller, Oxford (1898), supplement and addenda by A. Campbell (1972)
Bede	see HE
BMC	H. A. Grueber and C. F. Keary, *A Catalogue of English Coins in the British Museum, Anglo-Saxon Series* I, London (1887).
Campbell	A. Campbell, *Old English Grammar*, Oxford (1959).
CG	Continental Germanic
Colman	F. Colman, 'The name-element Æðel- and related problems' *Notes and Queries* NS 28 (1981) pp. 295–301.
Dolley	R. H. M. Dolley, 'Christ-thegn—an unsuspected instance of Early Middle Irish influence on OE namegiving', *BNJ* 36 (1967) pp. 40–5.
Förstemann	*Altdeutsches Namenbuch*, Bonn (1900).
HE	Bede, *Historia Ecclesiastica Gentis Anglorum*; see also Ström, H.
LVD	*Liber Vitæ* (*Ecclesiæ Dunelmensis*) ed. H. Sweet in *The Oldest English Texts* (Early English Text Society 83) Oxford (1885).

—	Köhler, T., *Die altenglischen Namen in Bædas Historia Ecclesiastica und auf den altnordhumbrischen Münzen* Part 1, Part 2i[1] Berlin (1908).
Morlet	M.-T. Morlet, *Les Noms de Personne sur le Territoire de l'Ancienne Gaule du VI–XII siècle*, Paris (1968)
—	Müller, R., *Über die Namen des Northumbrisches Liber Vitæ* (*Palæstra* 9) Berlin (1901)
OE	Old English
OIr	Old Irish
—	Okasha, E., 'The Non-Runic Scripts of Anglo-Saxon Inscriptions', *Transactions of the Cambridge Bibliographical Society* 4, pp. 321–8
—	Page, R. I., *An Introduction to English Runes*, London (1973).
—	Pirie, E. J. E., 'Finds of "sceattas" and "stycas" of Northumbria', *Anglo-Saxon Monetary History* ed. M. A. S. Blackburn, Leicester (1986)
PNDB	Olof von Feilitzen, *The Pre-Conquest Personal Names of Domesday Book*, Uppsala (1937).
PrG	Primitive Germanic
Redin	M. Redin, *Uncompounded Personal Names in Old English*, Uppsala (1919).
Sancton Find	see Pirie, E. J. E.
Searle	W. G. Searle, *Onomasticon Anglosaxonicum*, Cambridge (1894).
—	Ström, H., *Old English Personal Names in Bede's History*, (Lund Studies in English 8), Lund (1939).
Sweet	see LVD
von Feilitzen	see PNDB
WG	West Germanic
WS	West Saxon

[1] This part gives only a list for the moneyers' names. Part 2ii in which all the personal names were to be discussed was, according to the title-page, to be published as *Palæstra* 80 but did not appear in this series. Despite the help of Dr David Dumville, Cambridge, and Dr John Insley in Berlin I have been unable to discover where, if at all, it was published.

Adamson's Hexham plates

E. J. E. PIRIE

THE greater part of a hoard of several thousand Northumbrian coins, contained in a bronze pail, was unearthed when a grave was dug in the churchyard of Hexham Abbey on October 15th, 1832. Further specimens were recovered when the grave was opened again in 1841 though even then, one understands, a fall of soil prevented the sexton removing all which still remained in the ground (Hodges and Gibson, 1919, 87).

In 1832, the Revd William Airey of Hexham managed to secure a great part of the find so that the coins could be recorded, but many were dispersed. John Adamson, of the Newcastle Society of Antiquaries, undertook their study in preparation for an address to the Society of Antiquaries of London in May 1833. Publication of his paper in 1834 included twenty-three plates; a further seven were printed two years later, by which time Adamson had had the opportunity of inspecting additional specimens. Altogether, 945 coins are illustrated on these plates; the 1834 text is interspersed with drawings of six more. The total may perhaps be deemed to represent about one in eight or nine of all the coins recovered.

Adamson's main purpose in providing so many illustrations seems to have been to record for each moneyer every minor variety of work of which he was aware. The resulting totals for the individual moneyers, in the later coinage at least, reflect very well the extent to which they used dies cut with differences of legend or use of motif.

There is no unequivocal evidence of the hoard having contained coins of Osberht and Archbishop Wulfhere from the end of the series. We have no usable record of the specimens recovered in 1841 and, in publication of the Newcastle collection (Pirie, 1982, 3) one was prepared to accept a nineteenth-century reference to coins of Osberht and Wulfhere having been in the find. One can realize now that the original misconception probably arose from Adamson's identification of two coins as those of Ælla (1834, p.303) and of Archbishop Æthelbald (1834, p.310) which, if correct, would have meant that the hoard encompassed material of the time of Osberht and later. Since Lyon's reappraisal of the Northumbrian coinage in 1957, it has been appreciated that these two specimens and a third (1834, p.310), which Adamson suggested might be attributed to Æthelwulf, represent irregulars struck during the middle of the ninth century. So, too, do the coins (1834, p.292) which Adamson used to support the view that the coinage in the hoard began in the reign of Eardwulf. The coins in question are double-reverses of Hereræd and Heardwulf (see p. 260) from the reign of Eanred. None of these illustrations can yet be matched certainly with actual specimens. One would suggest, however, that the one (1834, p.310) which shows, inverted, a die reading EANREd should also be assigned to the early phase of issue; obverses like this are known to have been used by Tidwine and Hereræd and its combination with an abnormal reverse may afford another instance of behaviour represented on the main plates by an Eanred obverse joined with a runic reverse (see p. 260). Adamson can hardly have been fully aware of the great extent of such irregular issues in the coinage as a whole.

One should no longer entertain the idea that any coins later than those of Æthelred II and even of Archbishop Wulfhere are involved in the find. The plates appear to cover a substantial range of coinage for the reigns of Eanred, Æthelred (II) and Redwulf, and for the archbishops Eanbald II and Wigmund. It is apposite, perhaps, to comment at this point, that Adamson used the spelling of names which appears on the coins without any attempt to normalize what may be deliberate Northumbrian (if not only early) forms into conventional renderings of Anglo-Saxon names. Isolating from one another coins which have variations in spelling of the same name has led Adamson to identify more moneyers than are now recognized. He has not, however, distinguished those whose work was in silver; the illustrations lack annotation of metal content for the originals.

Since 1836, there have been many more discoveries of stycas and, with growing understanding of the coinage, there have already been two re-assessments of the Hexham material which Adamson recorded. Lyon (1957) and Pagan (1974) have each offered textual re-attributions and summaries of the hoard's range of material. One welcomes this new publication of the plates as an opportunity for further consideration of the find's composition. The quality of the drawings makes it impossible to identify most of the dies exactly so one hesitates to compile a new catalogue of every individual piece. Nevertheless, some dies are distinctive enough to be related to actual coins or, indeed, for the accuracy of their illustration to be queried. It must be remembered that the condition of many of the Hexham coins is far from perfect: several still have a considerable degree of corrosion products on them. Although no doubt the best available examples were chosen for illustration, one wonders just how many of them had detail obscured by wear as, for example, on Eanred 10 (Pl.XXXV) or distorted by residual accretion. Many of the specimens from which the drawings were made are now in London, for the nucleus of the British Museum's collection of early Northumbrian coins is the principal parcel from the Hexham hoard. In several instances, one can refer to the originals, when appraising the detail which Adamson published. In the analysis which follows, the bare list of names and illustration numbers is interspersed with a number of comments on identification and attribution.

The first concern now is to distinguish within the coins of Æthelred those which can be assigned to the second reign of Æthelred I, and within the coins of Eanred those of the earlier moneyers who worked in Phase I. Such coins, together with issues for Eanbald II and certain irregular pieces, number at least 231 (almost 25% of all the illustrations); there are five more whose attribution to the phase must be queried. This body of material seems to form a larger element of the whole than is normally the case in the southern hoards where, so far, comparatively few coins struck before *c.*830 have been recorded. Nevertheless, the bulk of the hoard must belong to the period when the coins were produced in brass alloys, after *c*.837. The ramifications of this phase of coinage are prodigious. It can here be remarked that Adamson did not illustrate all varieties of official or unofficial work that *are* known in various parcels from the hoard (for example: Pirie, 1982, no.163—a coin of Æthelred II by the moneyer Eanræd). Among these later coins, it would seem that those of the prolific moneyer Eardwulf are conspicuous by their virtual absence from the find; this factor led Lyon (1957, 231) to identify the man as having worked alone during Æthelred's second reign. Yet there are coins of Redwulf as well as those of Æthelred which have come to be nicknamed the 'descendants'. Dr Metcalf has commented (pers. comm.) that the time-lag implied by the fact of Redwulf's money reaching Hexham in the course of circulation may counter Lyon's theory that the coins were deposited *early* in Æthelred's second reign, soon after Eardwulf started work.

The small number of illustrations (only nine) for coins of Eardwulf may be misleading, if it represents only the comparative absence of variety in his official work rather than the extent to which his issues were present in the hoard. The number of his coins might well have been greater than supposed. The text which accompanies Adamson's plates gives little or no definite evidence of the comparative rarity or frequency of each of the wide range of issues, even in relation to that part of the find which came to his notice. It is the lack of this information which tantalizes, when evaluating both the composition and the date of deposition of the hoard.

If too much emphasis has hitherto been placed on the absence of coinage by Eardwulf as a factor crucial for dating, and attention is shifted instead to the presence of Redwulf's issues, other considerations must surely follow. If deposition occurred some considerable time after Æthelred was restored, one must begin to realize that coins by other moneyers besides Eardwulf may be attributed to the post-Redwulf period. Were the later material shown on Adamson's Hexham plates to be arranged according to the groups defined in another paper (pp. 103–31), it could be seen, perhaps, that the issues extend almost to the last months of Æthelred's total reign.

One must note that, on the plates, the coins for kings, and archbishops as well as for those of uncertain attribution, are numbered separately for each section. In the lists which follow, the main numbers cited are those from the 1834 plates. Of the twenty-three plates then published, one (LVI) is a supplement with its own numbers; these are distinguished as, for example, 2s. References to Adamson's main supplement, the 1836 illustrations, are quoted as S10 and so on.

It is pleasant to record thanks to Dr V. J. Smart of St Andrews and to Professor R. I. Page of Cambridge, with whom I have had correspondence during the course of my work on stycas in the Yorkshire Collections; it has been relevant to cite their opinions on some matters raised in my comments on various Hexham coins. I would also thank Dr D. M. Metcalf most warmly, for his decision to reprint the Hexham plates in the Symposium volume has prompted this paper.

ANALYSIS OF THE PLATES

PHASE I
ISSUES IN SILVER AND EARLY BRASS ALLOYS (231 [?236] coins)

ÆTHELRED I, second reign: *c*.790–6 (5 [?7] coins)

Ex Ethelred and Uncertain illustrations:

Ceolbeald:	31 and S11	(2)
Hnifula:	136 and (?) S32	(1 [?2])
Cuthgils:	Uncertain S1	(1)
Cuthheard:	S12	(1)
Irregular:	Uncertain 26 (?)	(?1)

The reverse seems to attempt the name of Hnifula; whether the piece was produced as early as this, or later, it appears to imitate an early coin.

EANRED, *c*.810–35 (163 [?165] coins)

Cuthheard:	15–17	(3)
Hwætræd:	155–7	(3)
Cynewulf:	18–37, S14–19 and S44	(27)
Tidwine:	192–3, S76–8	(5)
Wilheah:	194–201, S79	(9)
Dægbeorht:	40–53, S20–25	(20)
Eadwine:	54–75 and 158; 15–16s; S27–38	(37)
Heardwulf (?)—with Alfheard, Eardwulf and Wulfheard:	5, 78–84, 129–36, 202–5, 2s, S50, S80–82	(25)
Hereræd:	137–54, S51–3	(21)
Æthelweard [episcopal]:	85–6, S40	(3)
Irregular:	77 and S39; 222–3 (Eanred, uncertain); Uncertain 5, 8, 19 (?), 28; 14s; S9, S83, S84	(11 [?12])

Of these irregular coins, six or seven must belong to the group dominated by 'Herreth' dies of Hereræd which produce double-reverses such as 222–3. No.77 and S39 may be taken as double-obverses, with the second die reading *Eanreth*. One suspects that the 'Eanreth' die is the same as that used for S83.

The coin of Cynewulf (14s) would appear to be struck in brass alloy; another specimen of what is probably an early imitation is known at York.

The coin (S84), whose obverse (without title) is known to have been used by both Eadwine and Dægbeorht, is here used with a reverse which is partially runic in character. Transcription of the name is uncertain. Professor Page of Cambridge has suggested (pers. comm.) that the legend could be understood to represent the name Dægbeorht—which is plausible in this context—or be seen as an aberrant form of Wihtræd. Although the latter moneyer is also known to use runes for his name (see 217–18) he is normally associated with Eanred's later issues which follow through to the coinage of Æthelred II. His appearance at this early stage, even with—or especially with—an abnormal die, may be judged unlikely.

ARCHBISHOP EANBALD II, *temp*. Eanred, *c*.810–35 (63 [?64] coins)

Cynewulf: Eanred/Cynewulf 38–39 (the obverse is inverted in each case); Eanbald 15–18, 28s, S1–3 (10)

Eadwulf [with Eodwulf and variants]: 1–14, 19–26, 29s, S4–11, S17–23 (the reverse of S23 is inverted); ? and Eanred/Eodwulf, S41 (38 [?39])

Æthelw(e)ard: 27–32, S12–16 (11)

Irregular: Eanred S26 (the obverse inverted); Uncertain 6–7 and 29 (4)

The first has an obverse which can be read as EAN+BAD, retrograde; Eadwulf's name is clear on the reverse. The other three illustrations each have an obverse reading AENAD. That of no.6 is transposed with its reverse which also clearly records Eadwulf; the last two reverses are blundered versions of the name. If these three are not first-degree imitations, they may be copies of copies?

PHASE II

LATER ISSUES IN BRASS ALLOYS (707 [?709] coins)

EANRED, *c*.837–41 (165 coins)

Aldates: 1–4, 1s (5)

'Gadutes' [and variants]: 118–28, S48–49; also, Ethelred 135 ('Gadutes' is *not* a moneyer for Æthelred II) (14)

The obverse of this last coin should read EANRED: the sideways R points to the use of a very distinctive die for Eanred's reign (see Eanred 126).

'Gadutes' cannot be accepted as a name in its own right (V. J. Smart, pers. comm.); it can plausibly be recognized as an aberrant form of Aldates, especially since obverse die-links are known between coins with these legends on the reverses. It is worth questioning, however, if 'Gadutes' should be the correct reading of the form: the initial is rounded, as is the L of Aldates, so one wonders if the aberration first occurred by transposition of the first two letters of the proper name. Should the form 'Ladutes' now be used?

Brother [Brodr and variants]: 6–11, 13–14, 3–13s, S2–13 (31)

The obverse of 12, retrograde and with a distinctive .AN..., is not one known for Brother; the correct identity of the worn reverse is surely Fulcnoth (as *Folcnod*—see 110).

Badigils [and variants]: 188–90 (3)

Forthræd [with variants Eordred, Ordred, etc.]: 87–105, Ethelred 26s; S45–47; also, Ethelred 102 (re-attribution noted by Adamson: the obverse is retrograde) (24)

Fulcnoth [and variants]: 106–17, and 12 (see above) (13)

Folcnoth is usually accepted as the normal form of the name, but this must be questioned, since it occurs only on coins whose obverses are retrograde; *Fulcnod* is the form which appears with a wholly orthodox obverse (see 113).

Monne: 159–82, S54–72 (43)

Odilo: 183–6, S73–4 (6)

Wulfræd: 206–12 (7)

Wihtræd [and variants]: 213–21 (9)

Irregular: 'Erwinne': S43; 'Teveh': 187; Nonsense: Uncertain 30, 17s; 'Euxdire': Uncertain 1–3 and S8, S10; double-Eanred: 76 (10)

The sole 'Erwinne' die, used here with an obverse normally employed by Wihtræd, is known also with two of that moneyer's obverses for Æthelred II (see Ethelred 103 and S21) and with one from Wigmund's moneyer, Æthelweard. 'Erwinne' itself may be an aberrant form of Wihtræd.

'Teveh' is not a recognizable Anglo-Saxon name. The obverse of this coin is one normally shared by Monne and Wihtræd (cf. 218—Wihtræd): the same obverse is used for the specimen illustrated in the 1834 supplementary plate as Uncertain 17. In that case, the worn reverse has a nonsense legend, xAHIxNEF (an unprovenanced specimen in Leeds confirms the reading) which appears again on Uncertain 30, where it is combined with another nonsense die. The latter is also known to be used with the 'Teveh' die. Attribution of the five coins (Uncertain 1–3 and S8, 10) is not clear. Their reverses are nonsense; one may suggest that the common obverse, which reads EVXDIRE, may be understood as EANDIRE—the X a runic N—that is, as Eanred Rex.

Attribution of the specimen illustrated as 76, which has the name *Eanred* on both dies, is also uncertain. The exact detail of both dies is known from a specimen in York and only one can be matched on a coin apparently of Æthelred's moneyer, Eanræd. That (Ethelred 83) must be discussed in a later context. On the other hand, also known at York is another coin, naming E[a]nred Rex and the moneyer Odilo, which is of much the same style and quality as the double-Eanred piece. It seems possible to identify both as imitative coins stemming from the last years of Eanred's reign or, at the latest, to the first years of Æthelred's reign—when use of the cross motifs was still normal.

ÆTHELRED II: both reigns, *c*.841–4 and 844–9 (392 [?393] coins)

Principal issues (381 [?382] coins)

Brother: 22–30, S7–10 and Eanred, 13s (14)

The reverse reading, Brother, must be taken as decisive in attributing the coin, 13s, to this reign. The obverse reading should be *Edilred*.

Cynemund: 33–39, 21s (8)

Ealhhere [Alghere and variant Aldhere]: 4–15, S5–6 (14)

Eanræd [and variant Anred]: 1–3, 16–20, 41–83, 18–19s and 23s; S1–4, S13–16 (62)

Adamson identified some of these coins (1–3, 18–19s and S1–4) as being possible joint issues by the kings Eanred and Æthelred, for the Eanred dies as well as those of Æthelred end with the letter R after the name. Nevertheless, the issues can now be accepted as those for Æthelred by the moneyer Eanræd. They all belong to the group on which the king's name is rendered as *Aeilred* (see 76–81); some of the relevant reverses link into the group which shows the king's name as *Edelred*.

Eardwulf: 84–91, 22s (9)

Forthræd [and variants]: 93–101, 105–23, 125–34; ? 27s; S18–20, S22–31 (51 [?52])

Hunlaf [episcopal]: 137 (1)

Hunlaf uses only the one reverse in the regal series; for Æthelred, he shares an obverse used by Eanred (cf. 50).

Leofthegn: 138–175, 177–213, S33–51 (98)

This magnificent run of material for the one moneyer highlights the fact that the Hexham hoard included what appears to be a full run of the coins on which Leofthegn depicts motifs outside the standard range used by most of his colleagues: the *cross potent* (153–6) which is more ornate than that favoured by Monne (256–8 and 260), the *swastika* (157–8), the *quatrefoil* (160) and others. In this, Hexham must be the envy of the southern hoards, in which the range of such issues is not nearly so complete.

It is worth noting that the convention of having the legend's initial cross almost invariably [see Redwulf 4!] at the top of the illustration has resulted in the A motif of 193–4 being inverted. Once the flans of these two—and of 195 (whose motif appears as an ω)—are turned so that the A, at least, is the right way up, the motifs may be identified as *Alpha* and *Omega*, respectively. As such, they are not out of place among devices whose symbolism often has religious connotations. The obverse motif of 190 is, as drawn, unique in the series. The coin itself has been recognized among the British Museum duplicates. Inspection of its worn obverse confirms that the motif is, in fact, the same as that which appears on 187–9. One wonders if the obverse of 196 has suffered from similar misunderstanding of detail. In this case, the original has not been traced and checked. Coins with a very similar obverse *are* known, but there is no independent evidence of that die being used in combination with the reverse which Adamson illustrates. *That* reverse appears to be the one known on a crude piece which is now in the York collection; its companion obverse has the same motif. It seems just possible that a worn example could be subject to misinterpretation by an artist.

Monne: 214–72, S52–63 (71)

Odilo: 273–5 (3)

Inspection of actual coins leads one to identify the reverse as the same die in all three instances; indeed, 273 and 275 should be die-duplicates whose obverse, with cross-of-pellets motif, is shared with Monne. (There is no clear example, on the plates, of Monne's use of the die.) The obverse of 274 is known to be shared with both Leofthegn and Monne; the illustration for Leofthegn (201) is a better representation of the die in question.

Wendelbeorht: 291–301 (11)

Wulfræd: 276–86, S72–76 (16)

Wulfsige: 287–90 (4)

Wihtræd [and variants]: 302–13, S65–71 (19)

Subsidiary issues (11 coins)

The 'descendants': 314, 124, 32, 176, S64, 315, 92 (7)

The character of these pieces and their attribution to the time of Redwulf is outlined in the 'Phases and Groups' paper (pp.000–000). Obverses which are used in normal circumstances by Wulfræd, Eardwulf, Brother and Forthræd, in the main block of coinage, are known as well in combination with dies which, by comparison with the usual official work, can be described as cartoons. In most cases, such dies (retrograde) reflect the names of moneyers. It is because of the undoubted links with the fully authorized issues that these odd coins have been nickname the descendants.

a) Ethelred 314: this is, in effect, a double-obverse. The first die is used normally by both Eardwulf (86) and Wulfræd; the cartoon represents the name of Æthelred as *Aeilred*, retrograde.

b) Ethelred 124: Forthræd; the obverse is again that used by Eardwulf and Wulfræd; it is the same as for (a).

c) Ethelred 32: Coenræd; in this case, the obverse is one used first by Wulfræd (see 281–2).

d) Ethelred 176: Leofthegn; the obverse is the same as that used for (c) and (e–f).

e) Ethelred S64: Forthræd; the obverse is the same as that used for (c–d) and (f).

f) Ethelred 315: Wulfræd (?); the obverse is the same as that used for (c–e).

g) Ethelred 92: the obverse is first used by Brother (see S7); the reverse may be interpreted as the name of *Alghere*, which is usual on the normal coins for Ealhhere.

Others identified as semi-official: 'Eudrteda', 104; Eanræd, 83; 'Erwinne', 103 and S21 (4)

Most of the 'descendants' may be recognized relatively easily because of the poor quality of the reverse dies. Other coins must be attributed to the same category of issue with far less certainty because the calibre of their dies and the nature of their combination are less obviously abnormal. Among the 'descendants' themselves one might include Ethelred 104, which has the unusual reverse reading EVDRTEDA, were it not that—for a specimen at York—one has been unable to match the obverse with any normal work. It is possible, however, that that die was new and as yet unused when circumstances gave rise to production of the main 'descendants' and other coins which may be related in purpose. For Ethelred 104, the reverse legend, which defies recognition as the name of any known moneyer, may signal that we are justified in thinking that there was more than one instance of unusual, semi-official, production at the time.

Although most of the names essayed on 'descendant' reverses *are* recognizable as those of moneyers, there can be no guarantee that *all* the individuals so named were actively engaged in the manufacture of these coins. We may, perhaps, suppose that Wulfræd had a finger in the pie: four of the obverses which he used normally are involved in the work. Two of these (of which one is Adamson's Ethelred 281–2) belong to the section of the regular coinage which records the king's name with the L inverted. In the same division, another obverse is certainly tied to other examples of his normal work and, through a link with Monne, to the reign of Redwulf. The die in question is apparently shared with both Forthræd and Eanræd. In the first instance, Forthræd's reverse is carried through from the reign of Eanred; in the second (see Ethelred 83), the reverse is one of those from the double-Eanred (Eanred 76) on which comment has already been made. Attribution to the normal issue cannot be unequivocal.

Although the re-use of Forthræd's die for Eanred, at or near the time of Redwulf, may itself prompt a query concerning the chronological relationship of Eanred's reign and Redwulf's usurpation, there is another factor to be considered. Both the Forthræd die and the Eanræd one are virtually conspicuous by their lack of links into the rest of the moneyers' work for Æthelred which, in each case, is tightly knit by re-use of dies. Within the apparent triple-liaison of Wulfræd, Forthræd and Eanræd, the second and third elements may well be deemed as semi-official in much the same way as may be the 'descendants'. Instead of being used with poor-quality dies, especially cut, the normal obverse for Æthelred was combined with dies left over from an earlier period.

The examples so far considered all relate to the main block of coinage within the official regal series. The coins of 'Erwinne' (103 and S21) have obverses which relate them to the smaller group of material where the royal name is recorded as *Edelred* or *Ethflred*. There, the obverse of S21 is shared in normal work by Wihtræd and Eanræd; the obverse of 103 is used by Wihtræd. From a different source, therefore, and with a different pattern of combinations, unofficial work was produced at some point during the reign of Æthelred. The sole 'Erwinne' die is that seen already with an obverse of Wihtræd's for Eanred (Eanred, S43) and it is known, too, with an obverse cut for the coinage of Wigmund. This complete little complex may be Wihtræd's version of the 'descendants', about the time of Redwulf.

REDWULF, *c*.844 (37 coins)

Brother: 3–6, S2 (5)

Coenræd [episcopal]: 7–8 (2)

As far as one is aware, only the reverse combined with a rosette obverse (7)—of which there are two—has the spelling COENED; the reverse of 8 *should* read COENRED.

Cuthbeorht: 9–12 (4)

The illustration of 11 shows the reverse motif as a trefoil of pellets but this must be an error caused, perhaps, by detail having been obscured by the remains of accretion. For this moneyer, only one die is known which has the cross-of-pellets motif; the present writer knows of its having been used with only one obverse. In effect, 11 and 12 should be considered as die-duplicates:

Ealhhere [Alghere]: 1–2, S1 (3)

Eanræd: 13–14 (2)

Forthræd [and Eordred]: 15–21, S3 (8)

Hunlaf [episcopal]: 24 (1)

The obverse is shared with Eanræd; the reverse is that used also for Ethelred 137.

Hwætnoth: 22–4, S4 (4)

Only one obverse die is known for this moneyer, and three reverses. Only the small cross is used as the motif but the obverse and one reverse have a trail of three pellets in the field. Although 24 is clearly a worn specimen, its identification of the moneyer is correct; the surviving detail for the centre of each die has been mis-interpreted. 22 (with the pellet trail on both obverse and reverse), 24 and S4 should be die-duplicates.

Monne: 26–30 (5)

Wendelbeorht: 31–32, S5 (3)

The first two are likely to be die-duplicates; S5 has the second obverse which reads as HEDVVLF.

ARCHBISHOP WIGMUND, *c*.837–54 (80 coins)

Æthelweard: 24–44, 61–4, S9–12 (29)

The moneyer is known to have worked in Phase I, for Eanbald II; some of his coins—? those with the archbishop's title reading AREP—are likely to have been the earliest struck for Wigmund. The double-obverses, 61 and 62, can be identified as those used by Æthelweard with reverses in the normal way. The dies of the double-reverse (63) are also known in normal use. The specimen which is shown as 64 is clearly mis-struck.

Hunlaf: 45–60, S13–16 (20)

Æthelhelm: 17–23, S7–8 (9)

Coenræd [and variants]: 1–16, S1–6 (22)

It can be remarked that the motifs shown on 5, 6 and S6 are outside the range normally used by the episcopal moneyers. In this departure from the standard practice, Coenræd seems to emulate the regal moneyer Leofthegn. One must suggest that these motifs are all attempts to represent an *Omega*.

IRREGULAR ISSUES (33 coins)

Æthelred II: Eadwine: 40 (1)

Identification of no.40 as a coin of Æthelred I must account for Pagan (1974, 186) having included the moneyer, Eadwine, among the register of officials at that early period. The attribution cannot stand unchallenged. There is no independent evidence of Eadwine having worked before the early part of Eanred's reign; further, the coin (now *BMC* Northumbria 295) is not of silver, such as one would expect for the time of Æthelred I, but of brass alloy. In the context of Æthelred II's reign it cannot be accepted as official work, for Eadwine's real output was long since over. The coin must be unofficial; both the obverse, EDLRED, and the reverse, EADVIN, are at least aberrant. The main complex of the irregulars includes several dies with the name EADVINI, ostensibly as a moneyer for Æthelred, for one of the features of this work is the remembrance of past officials among whom Hwætræd and Hereræd (Herred) are included. The Hexham coin cannot be die-linked to any known cluster of irregulars. Although it stands apart, it can perhaps be compared to a coin from the Bolton Percy hoard of 1967 (Pagan, 1973, no.1468) which, with an obverse for Æthelred, carries the name of yet another early moneyer, Wilheah. The latter specimen is also so far unrelated to others.

Nonsense legends: Eanred, uncertain 224–7 [note the error in numbering as 215–17]; Uncertain 4–22, 25, 27, 31, 32; S2–7; see also Uncertain 23–24 (32)

Most of these pieces are clearly of the same style as that which characterises the 'Teveh' complex (see above, p. 262); it depends on each die showing what appears to be a random selection of letters and crosses round the central motif. Since the Hexham find is the only one which has produced such specimens in any numbers, one seems justified in referring to their appearance as the Hexham style. There is, as yet, only limited evidence of die-linking within these coins; Adamson himself noted one such example (Eanred 226–27). The 'Teveh' example (Eanred 187) relates specimens to the last years of Eanred's reign, at least; there is, however, nothing to show that their production did not last until the time of the hoard's deposition.

Two specimens (Uncertain 23–24) are clearly of a different style, at least as far as the second (right-hand side) drawing of each is concerned. At this stage, one cannot identify them with certainty and attribute them to any particular *atelier*.

One of the items which Adamson did *not* illustrate is now Newcastle 439 (Pirie, 1982); this is a specimen which fits into part (Background II) of the massive chain of irregulars which are common in the hoards of York and Bolton Percy. Most of the Hexham irregulars in the British Museum have not yet been catalogued or, indeed, numbered individually (see *BMC* Northumbria 819–68). They include another specimen from the same background section of the chain, and two others which belong to shorter runs of die-linked coins not as yet tied to the main block of imitations. These pieces occur in the Hexham find as rarely as do specimens of Hexham style in the southern hoards. One cannot avoid the conclusion that production of irregular coins was a local affair and that their circulation was very largely confined to their home area. Certainly, the inclusion of southern irregulars in the Hexham hoard indicates that coins in this category were in course of production during the time of Æthelred and were not necessarily all as late as Lyon has suggested (1957, 231–2).

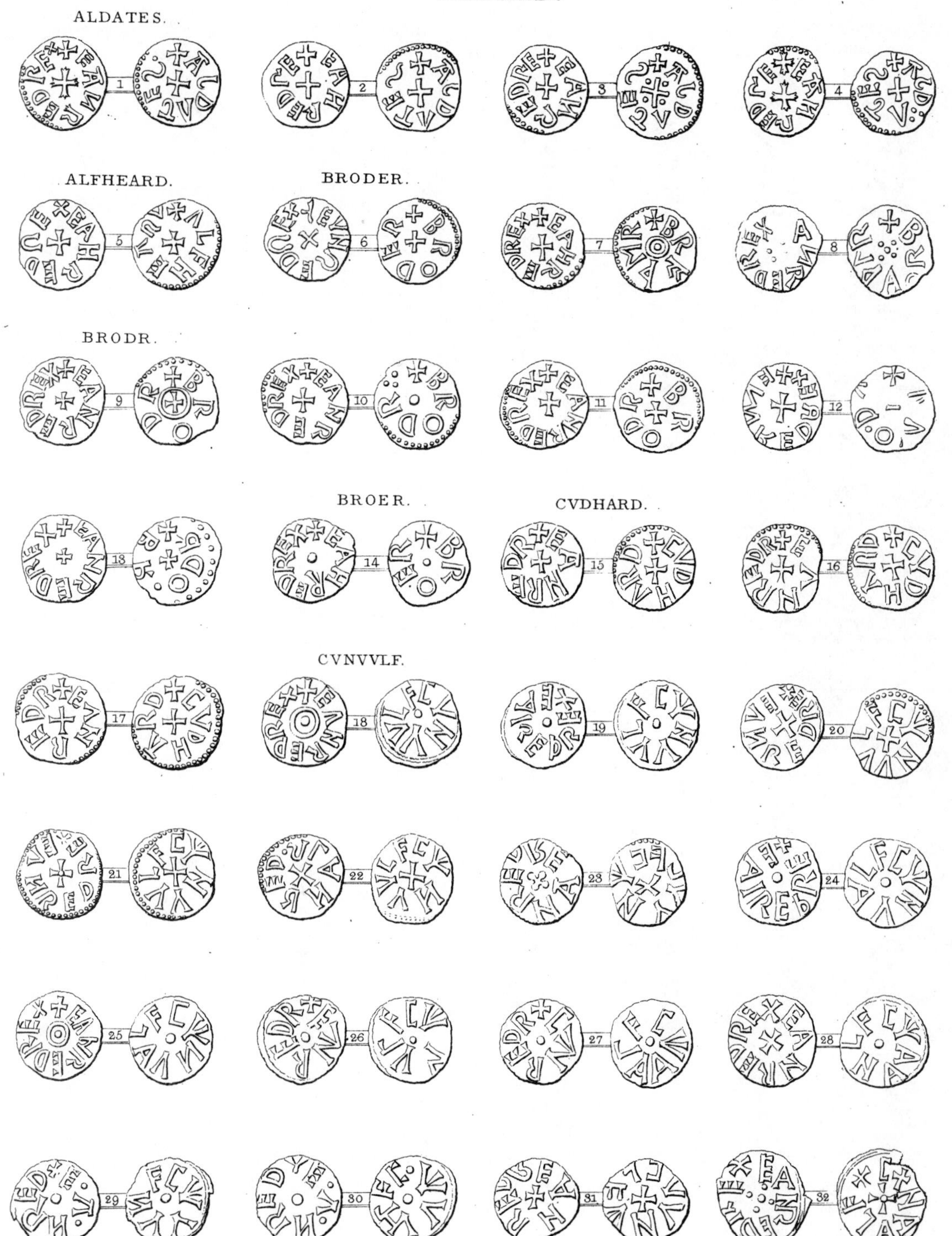
EANRED.
ALDATES.
ALFHEARD.
BRODER.
BRODR.
BROER.
CVDHARD.
CVNVVLF.

J. Basire. sc.

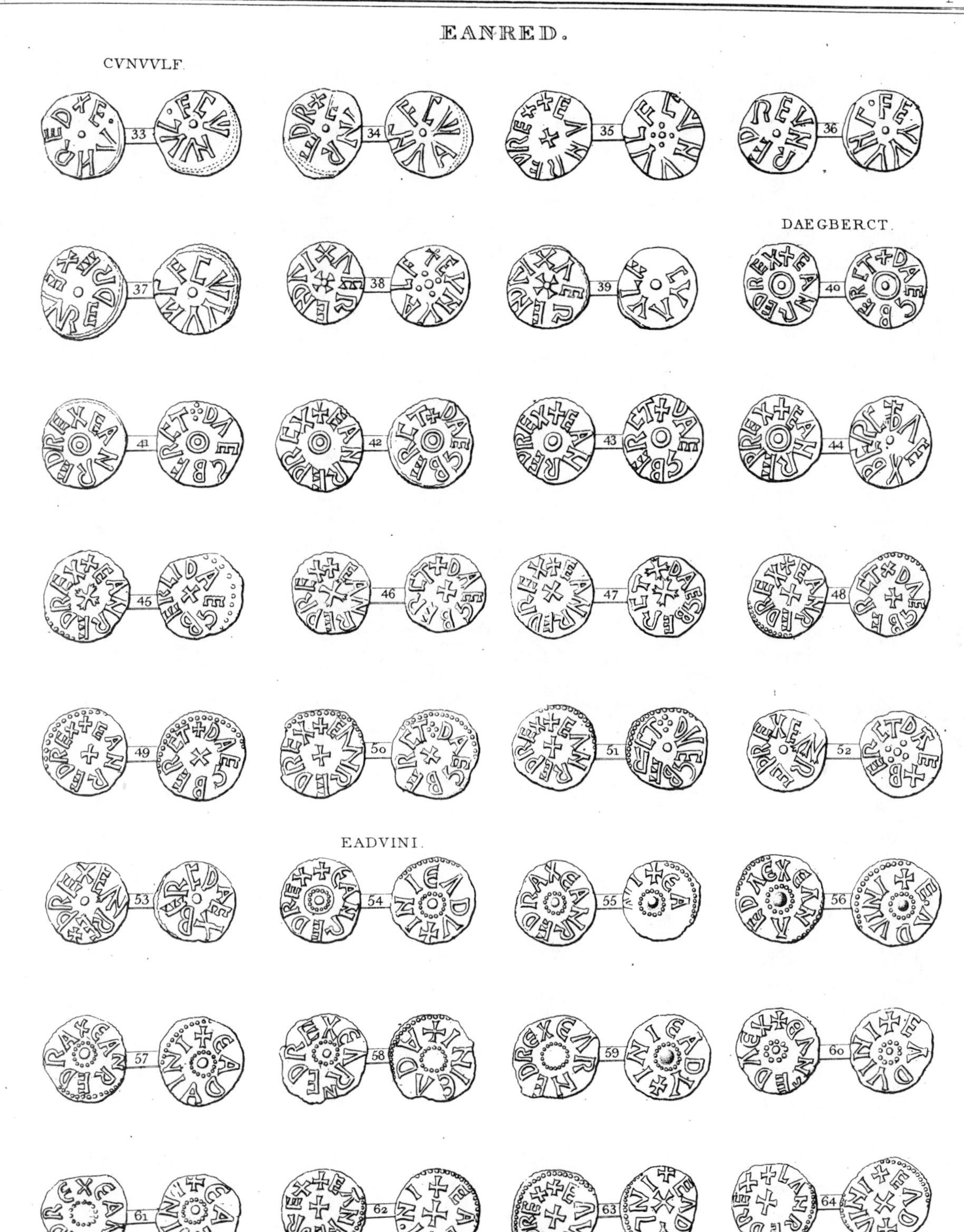

J. Basire sc.

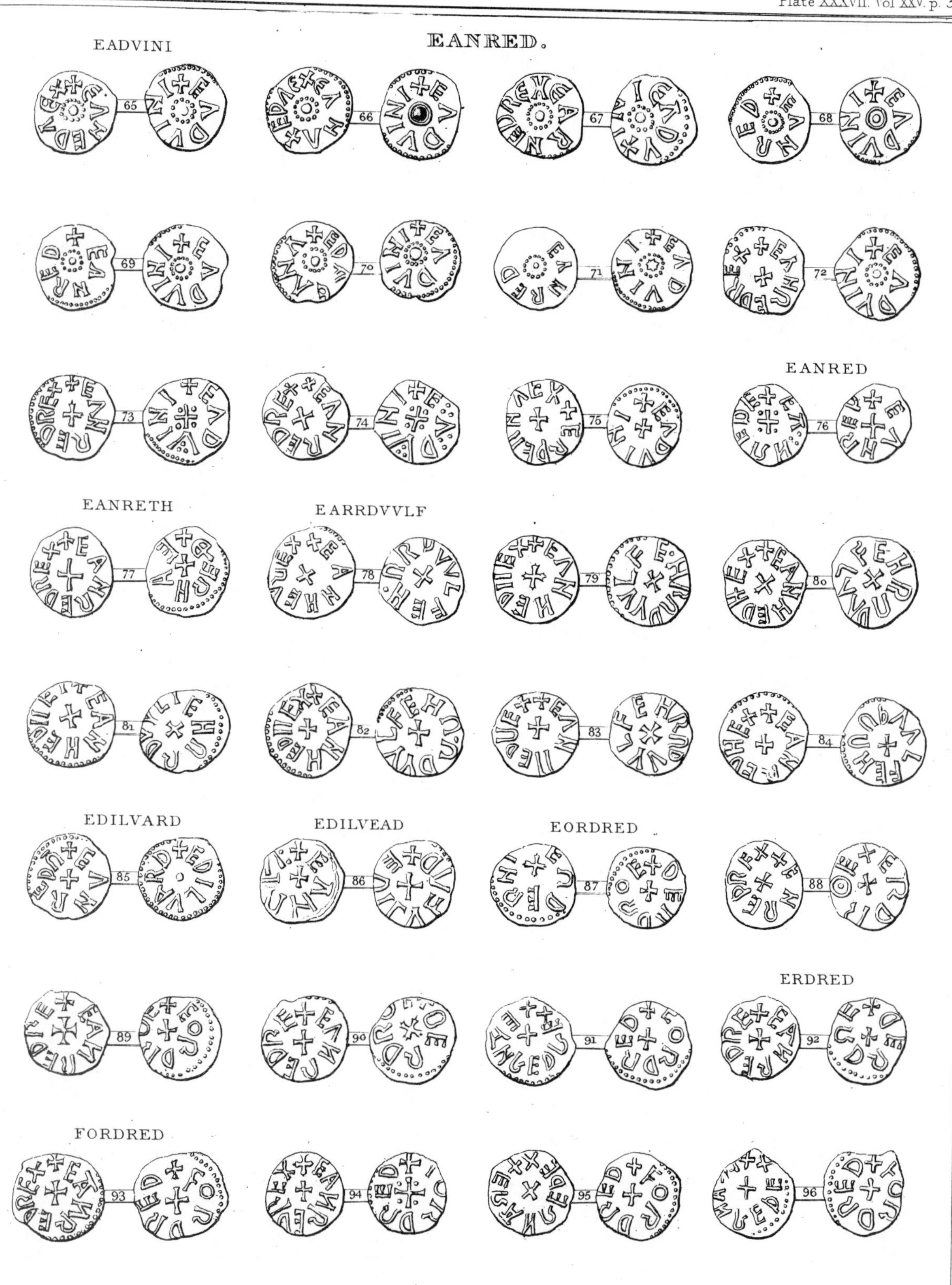
EANRED.
EADVINI
EANRED
EANRETH
EARRDVVLF
EDILVARD
EDILVEAD
EORDRED
ERDRED
FORDRED
65
66
67
68
69
70
71
72
73
74
75
76
77
78
79
80
81
82
83
84
85
86
87
88
89
90
91
92
93
94
95
96

J.s Basire sc.

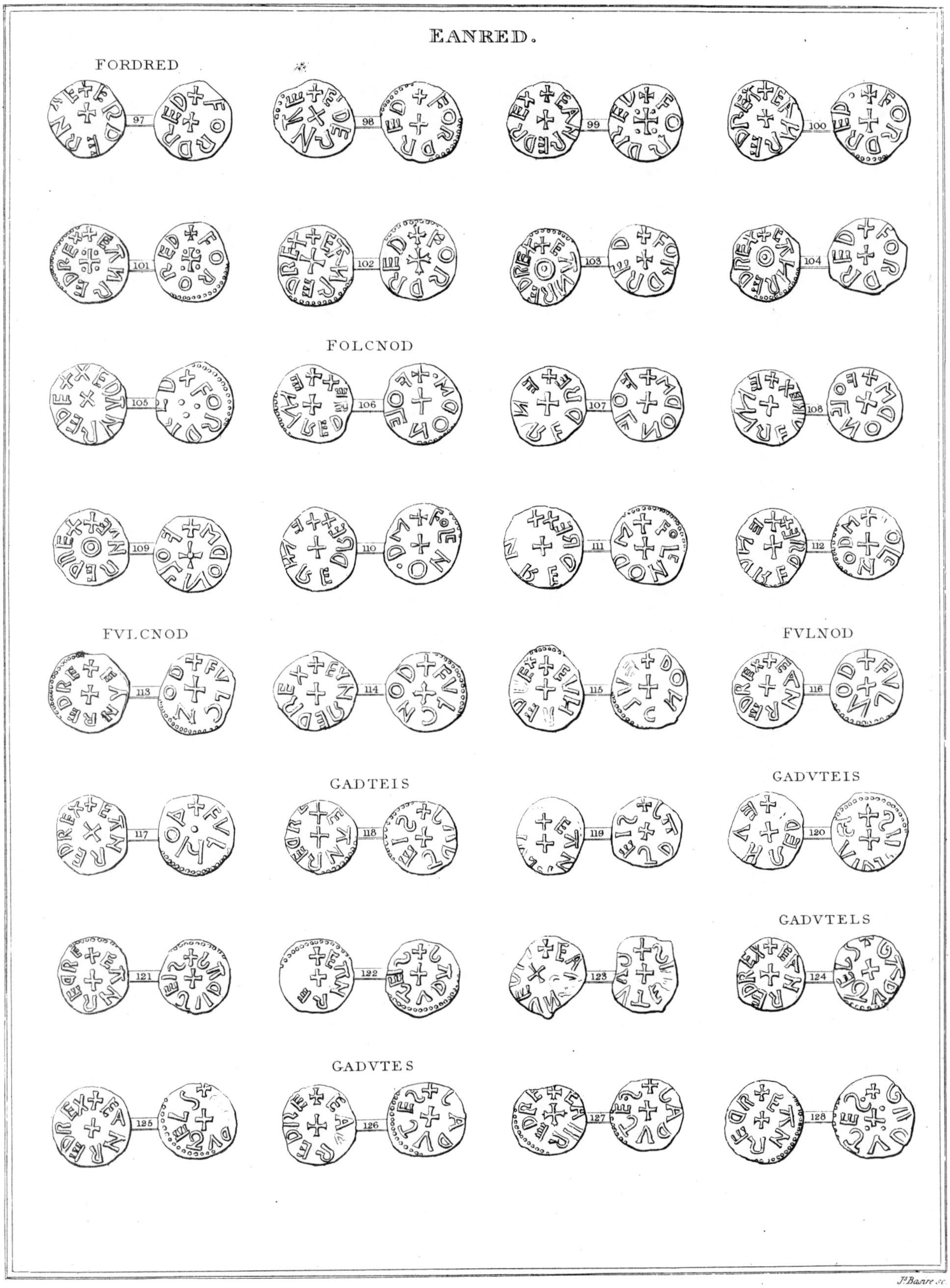

EANRED.

FORDRED

97 98 99 100

101 102 103 104

FOLCNOD

105 106 107 108

109 110 111 112

FVLCNOD

113 114 115

FVLNOD

116

117

GADTEIS

118 119

GADVTEIS

120

121 122 123

GADVTELS

124

125

GADVTES

126 127 128

J. Basire sc.

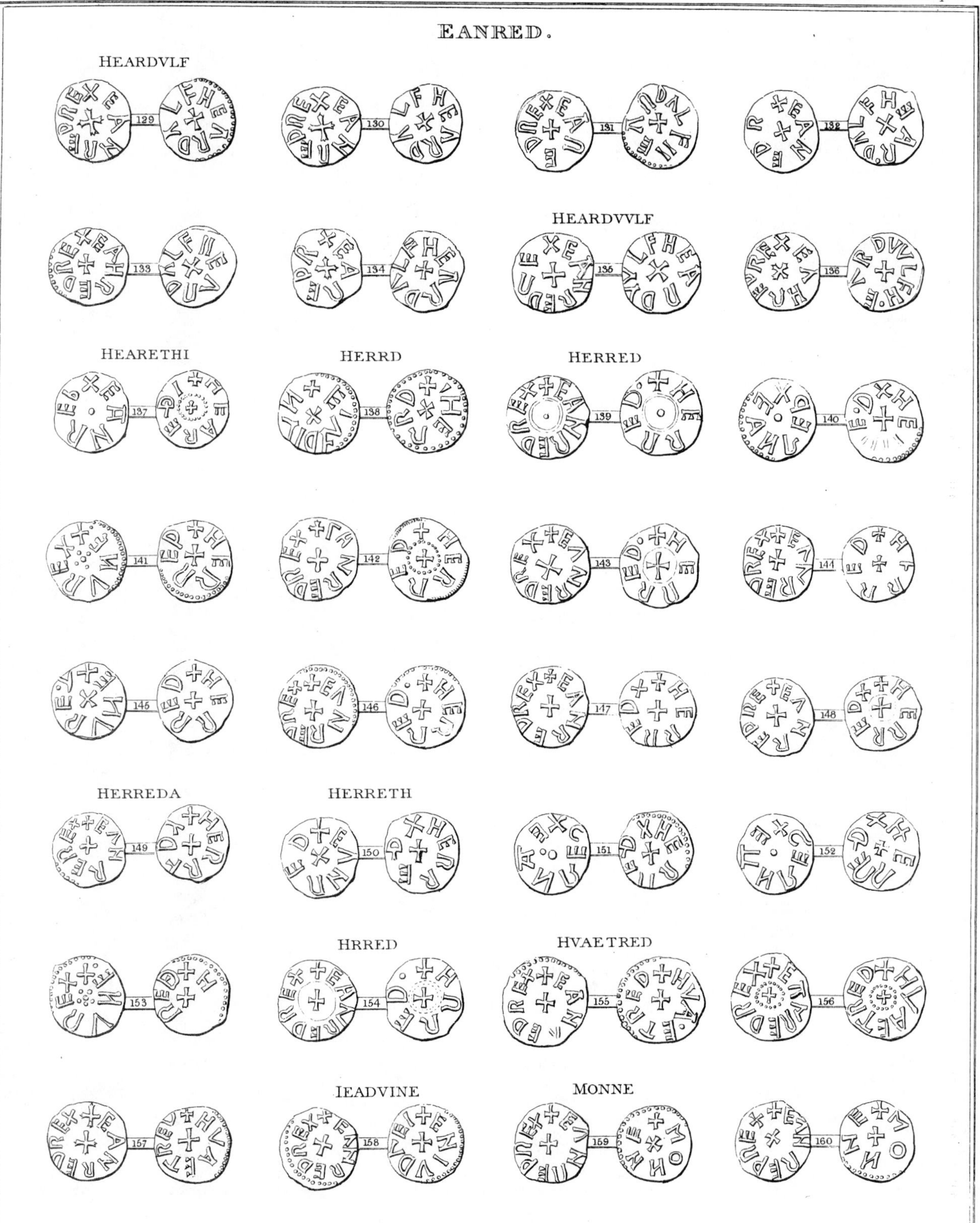
EANRED.
HEARDVLF
129
130
131
132
133
134
HEARDVVLF
135
136
HEARETHI
137
HERRD
138
HERRED
139
140
141
142
143
144
145
146
147
148
HERREDA
149
HERRETH
150
151
152
153
HRRED
154
HVAETRED
155
156
157
IEADVINE
158
MONNE
159
160
Jª Basire sc.

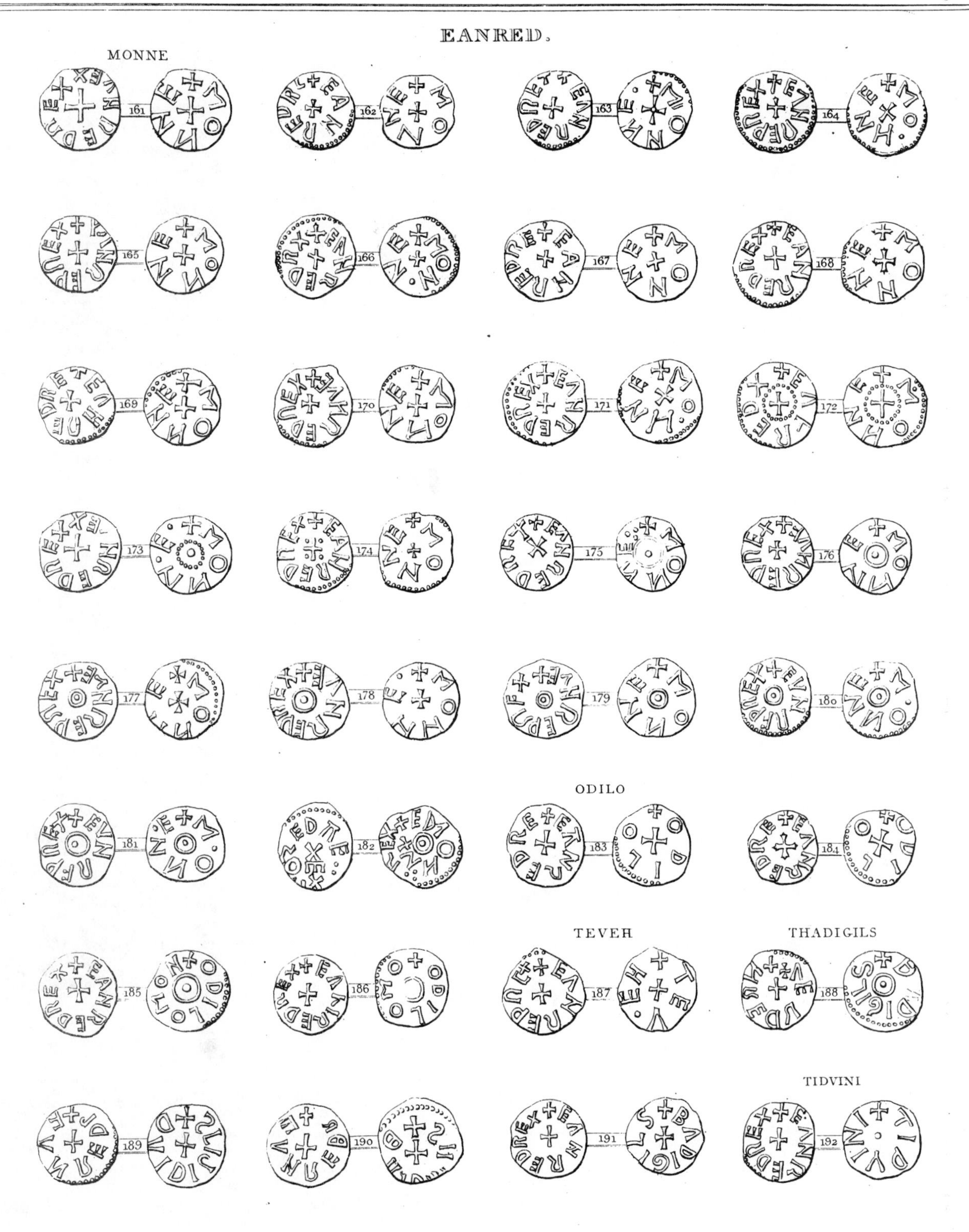
EANRED.
MONNE
161
162
163
164
165
166
167
168
169
170
171
172
173
174
175
176
177
178
179
180
ODILO
181
182
183
184
TEVEH
THADIGILS
185
186
187
188
TIDVINI
189
190
191
192

J^s Basire sc.

EANRED.

TIDVNI

193

VILHEAH

194 195 196

197 198 199 200

201

VVLFHEARD

202 203 204

205

VVLFRED

206 207 208

209 210 211 212

WINTRD

213

WINTRED

214 215 216

WINTRHM

217 218

WINTRR

219 220

221

UNCERTAIN

222 223 224

Jas Basire sc.

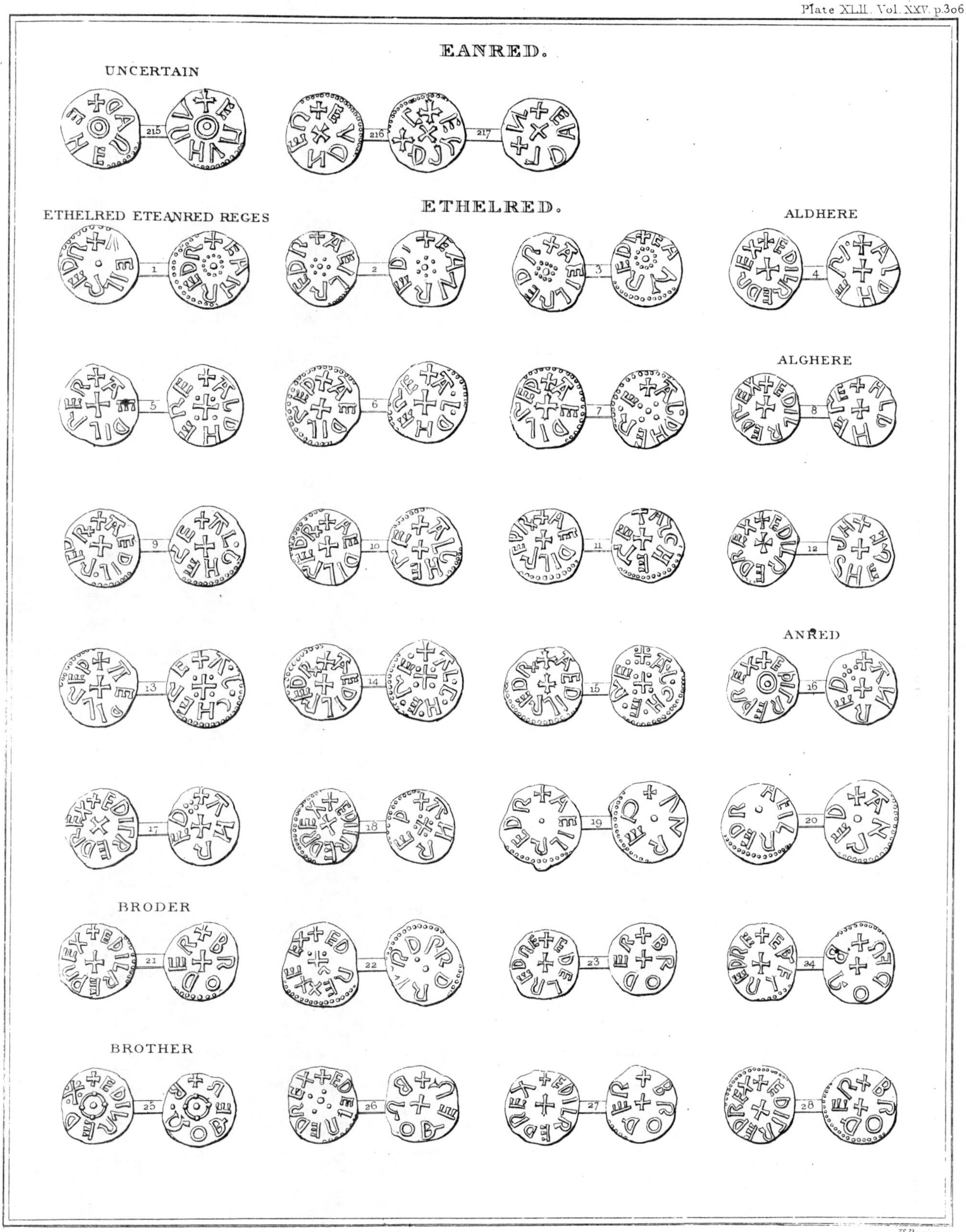

EANRED.

UNCERTAIN

215 216 217

ETHELRED ETEANRED REGES

ETHELRED.

ALDHERE

1 2 3 4

5 6 7

ALGHERE

8

9 10 11 12

13 14 15

ANRED

16

17 18 19 20

BRODER

21 22 23 24

BROTHER

25 26 27 28

J^s. Basire sc.

ETHELRED.

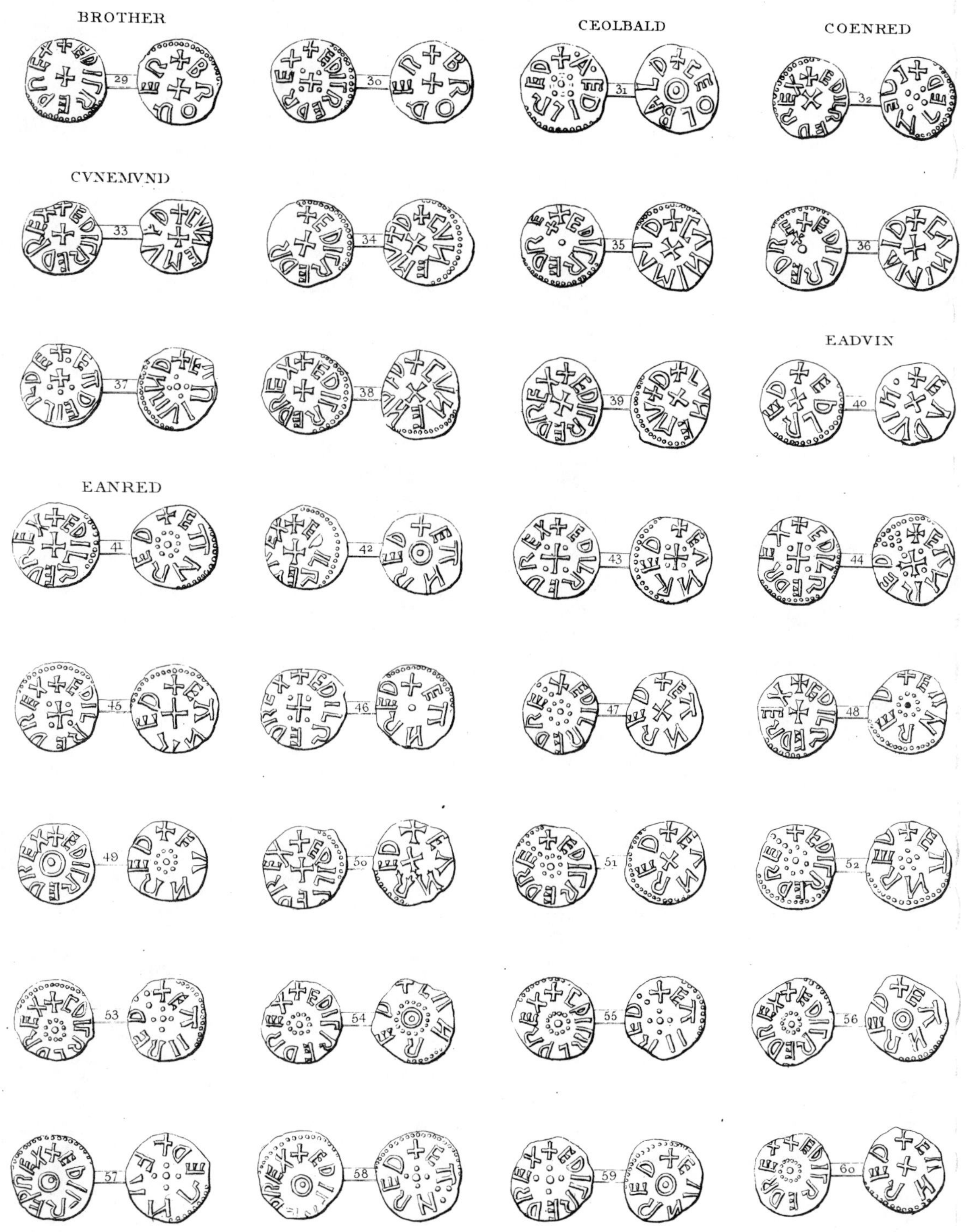

J. Basire sc.

ETHELRED.

EANRED

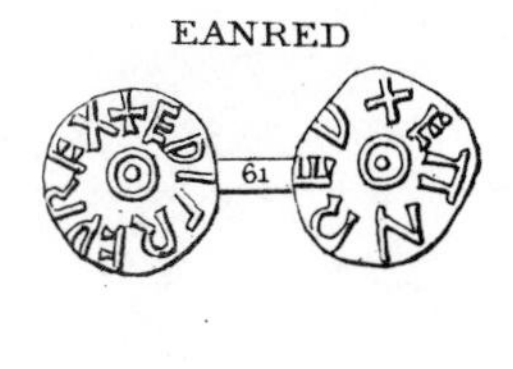

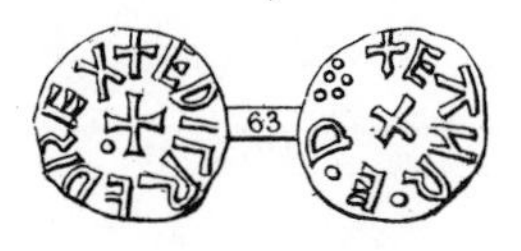

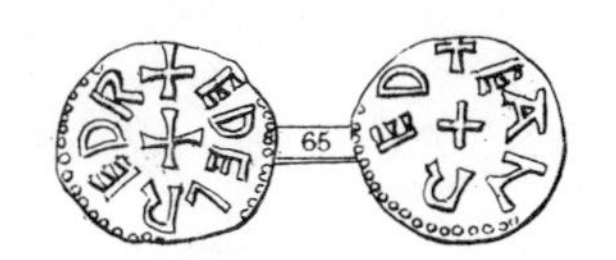

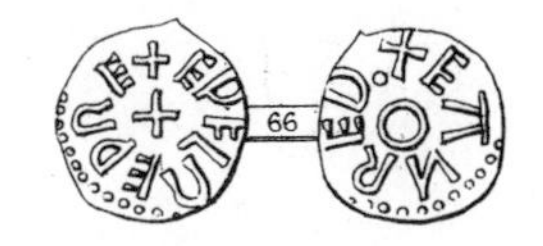

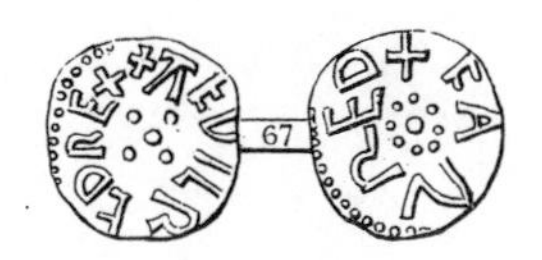

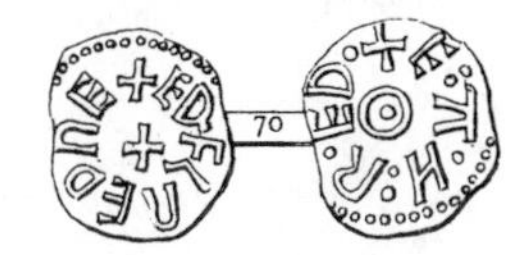

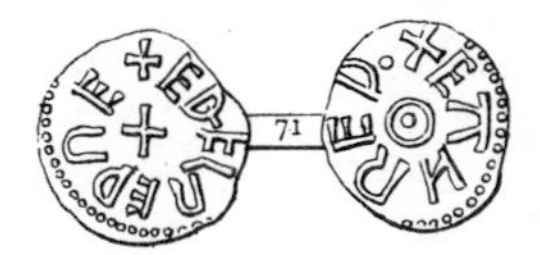

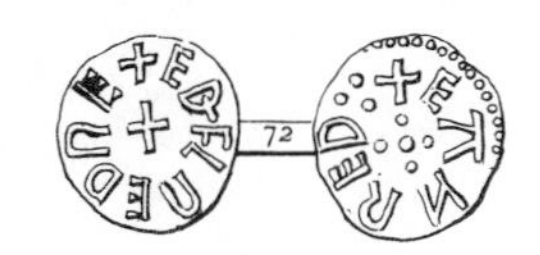

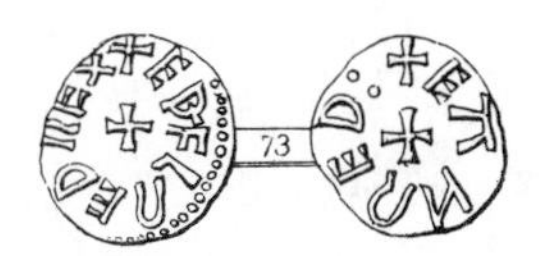

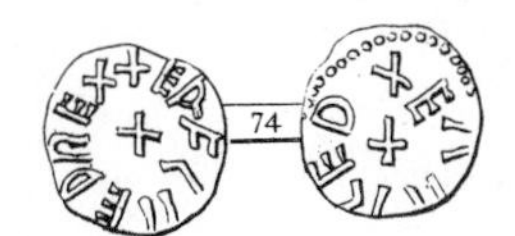

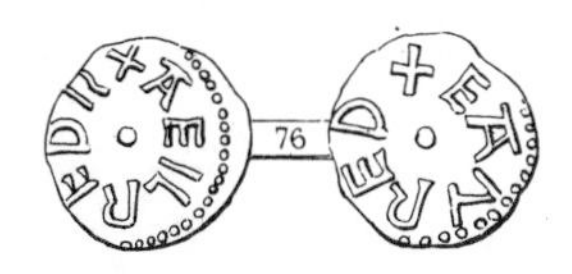

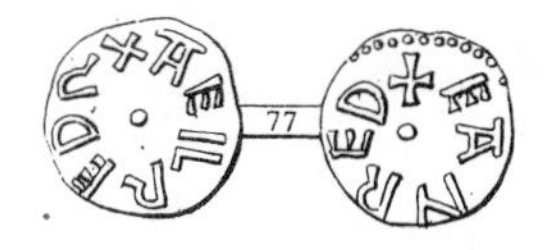

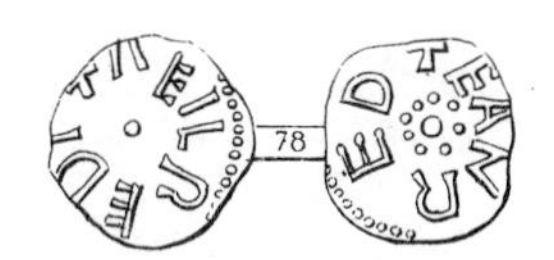

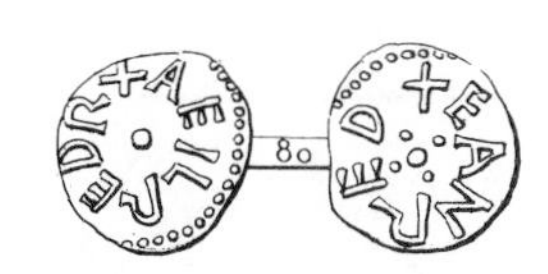

EANREDE

EARDVVLF

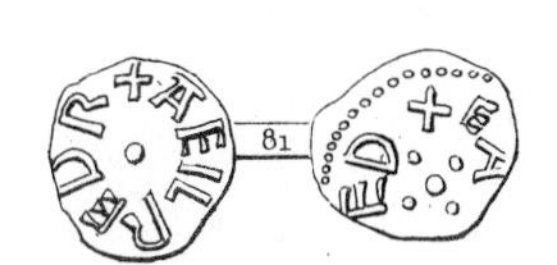

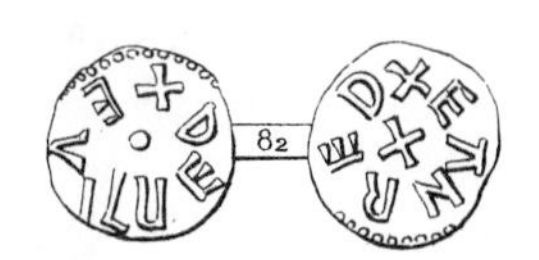

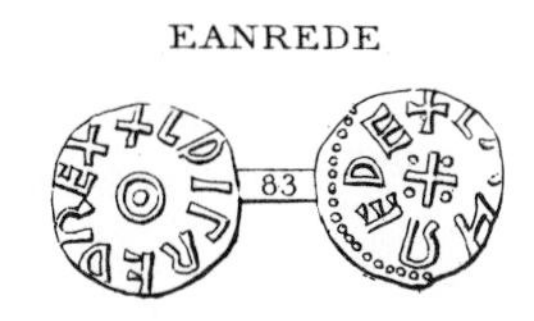

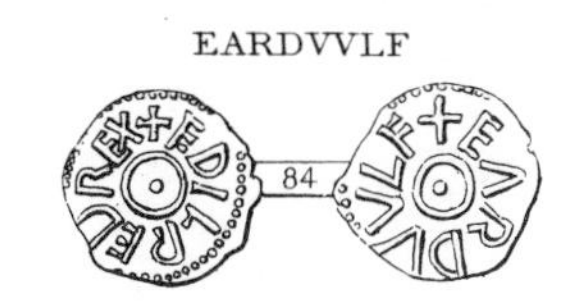

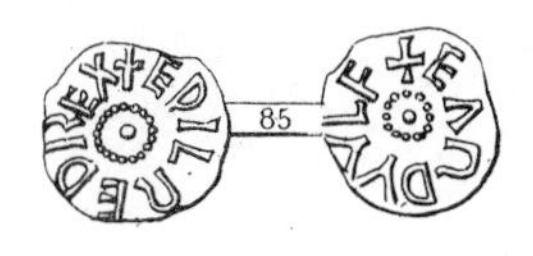

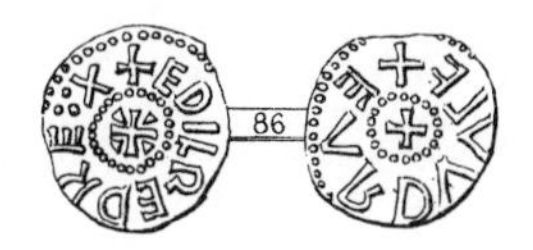

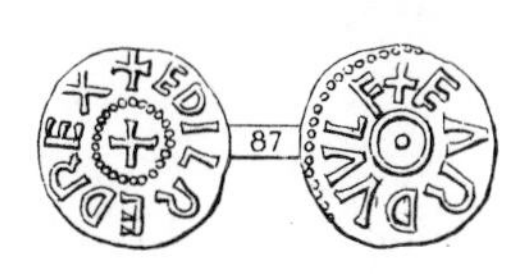

ELEHOJH

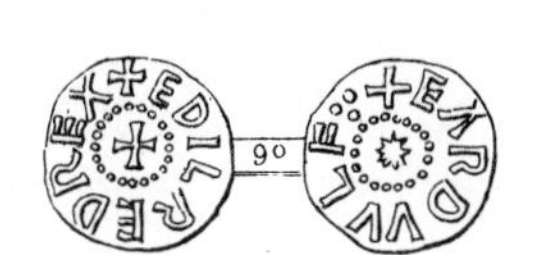

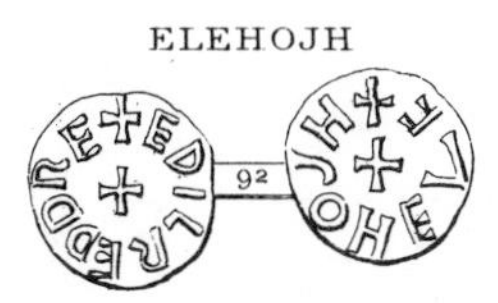

Jas Basire sc.

ETHELRED.

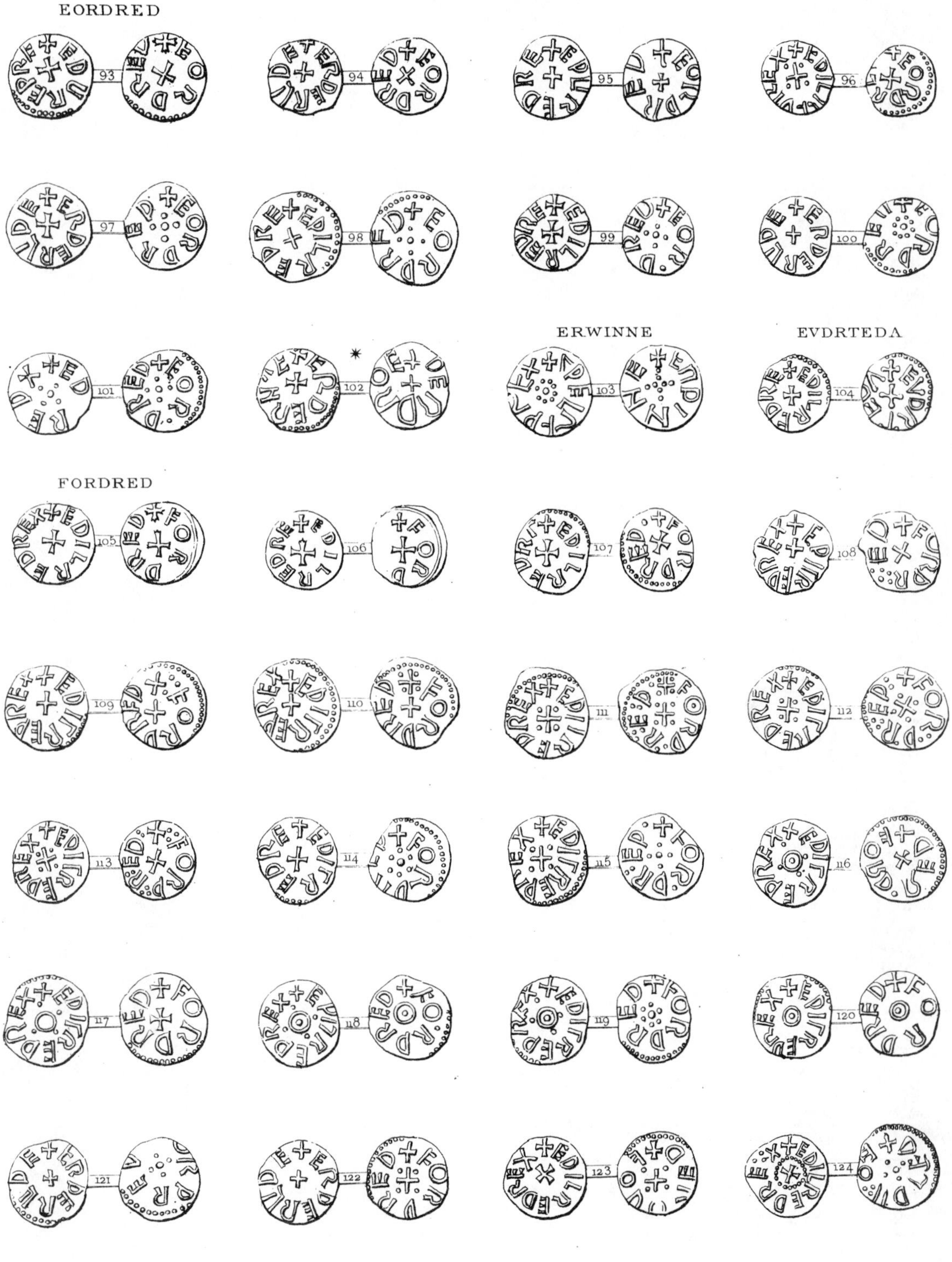

EORDRED

93 94 95 96

97 98 99 100

ERWINNE EVDRTEDA

101 102 * 103 104

FORDRED

105 106 107 108

109 110 111 112

113 114 115 116

117 118 119 120

121 122 123 124

* *This Coin belongs to Eanred, and should have been amongst the Coins of that King.* — J.A.

F. Basire sc.

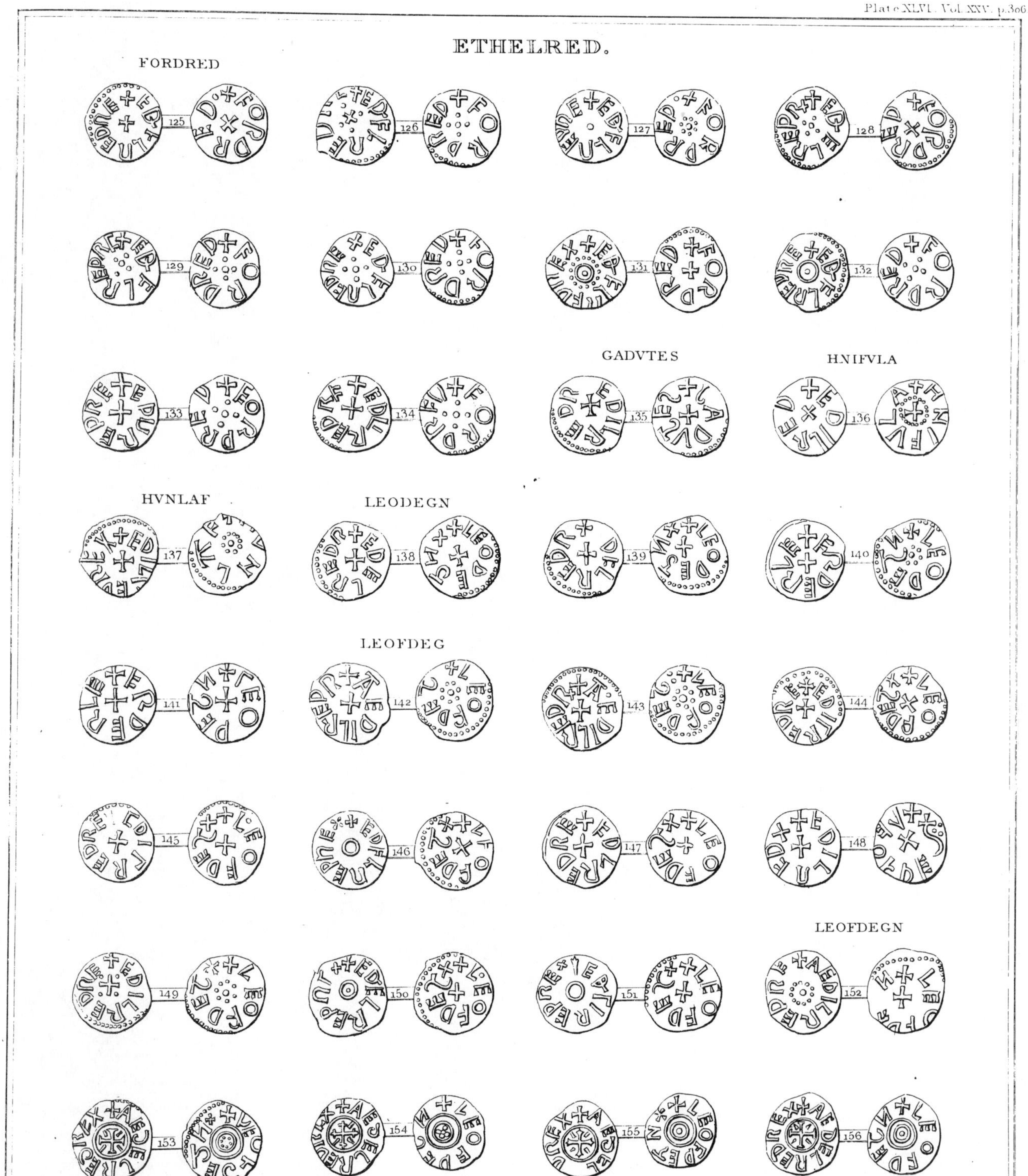

ETHELRED.

FORDRED

125 126 127 128

129 130 131 132

133 134

GADVTES

135

HNIFVLA

136

HVNLAF

137

LEODEGN

138 139 140

141

LEOFDEG

142 143 144

145 146 147 148

149 150 151

LEOFDEGN

152

153 154 155 156

J^s. Basire sc.

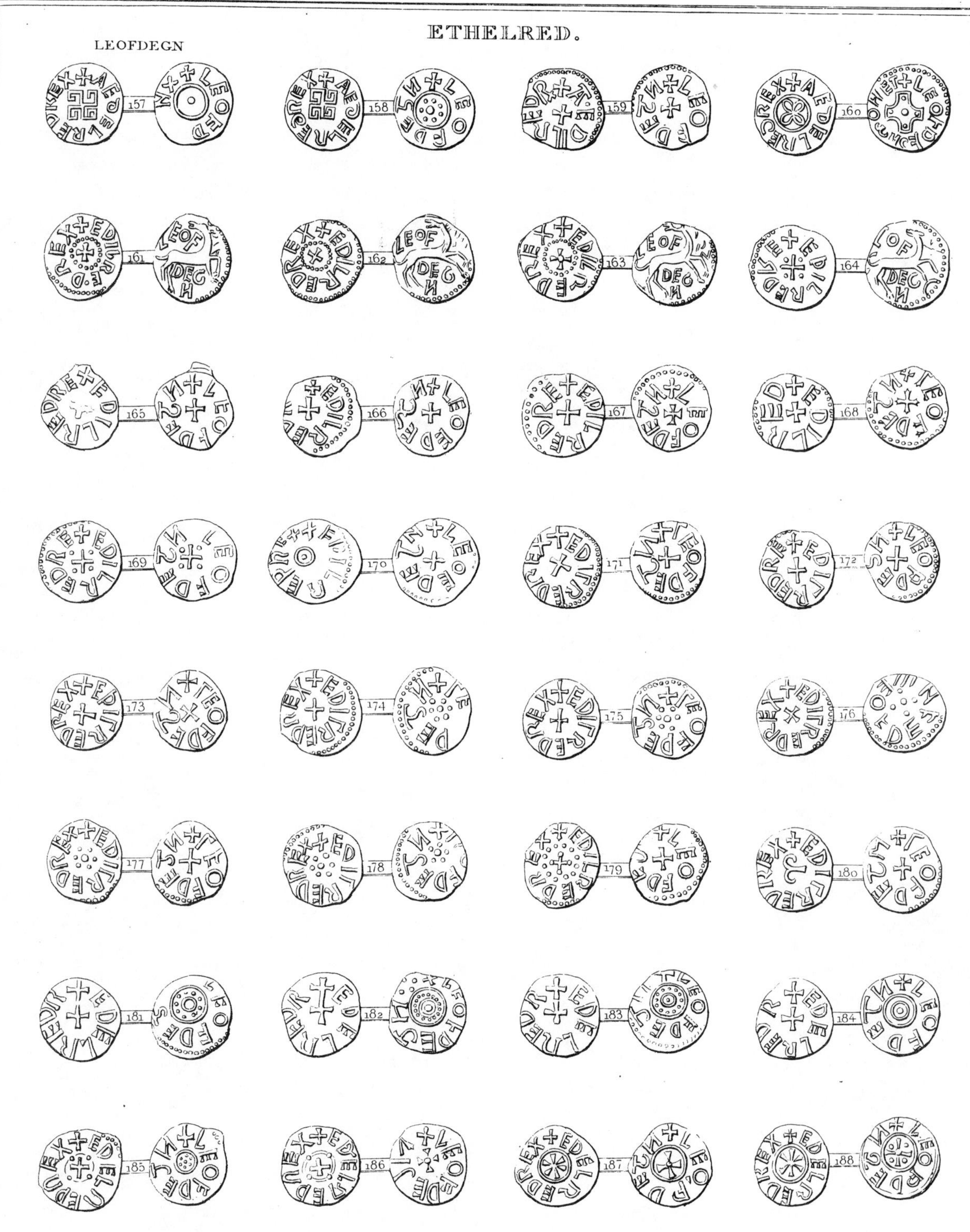
ETHELRED.
LEOFDEGN
157
158
159
160
161
162
163
164
165
166
167
168
169
170
171
172
173
174
175
176
177
178
179
180
181
182
183
184
185
186
187
188

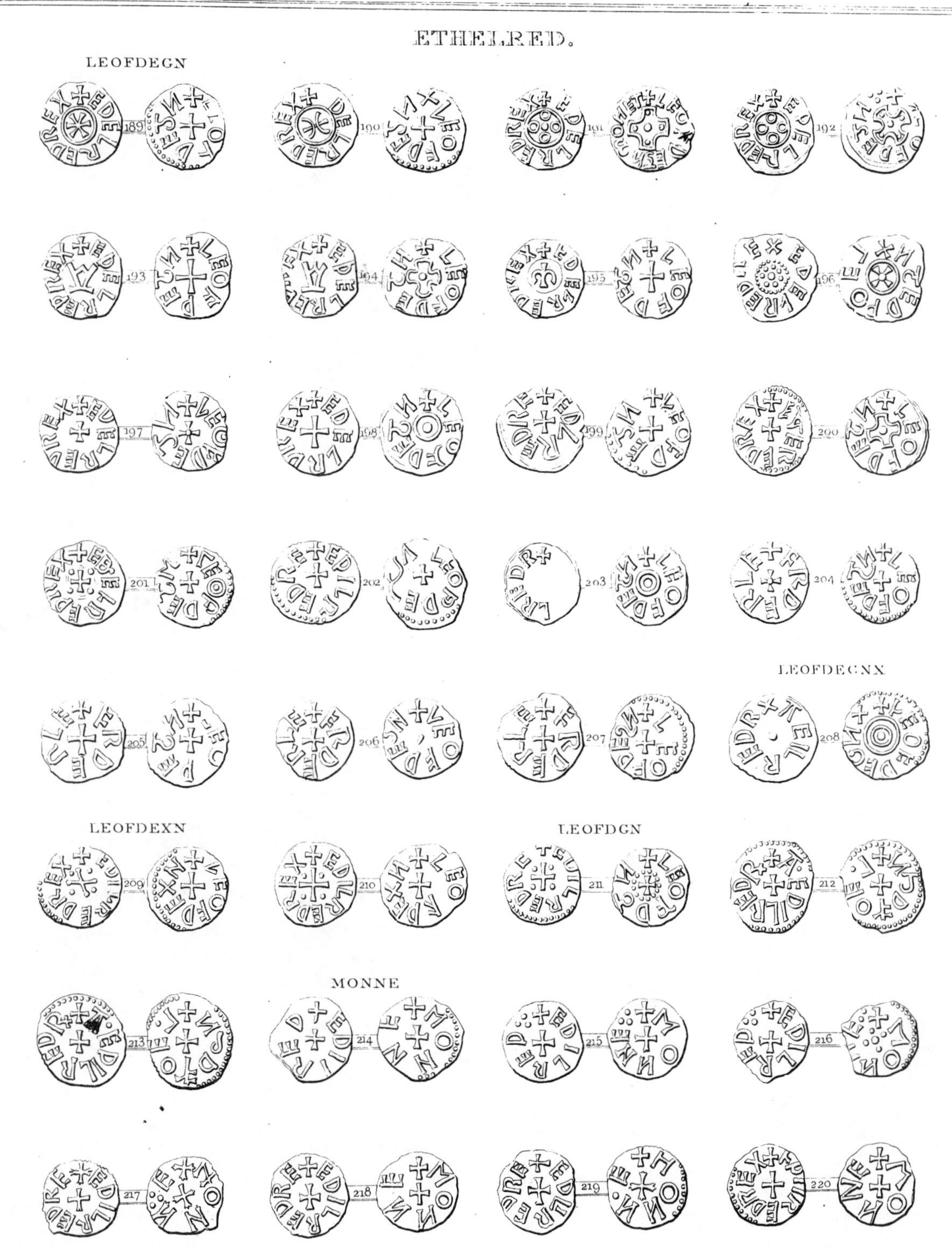

J. Basire sc.

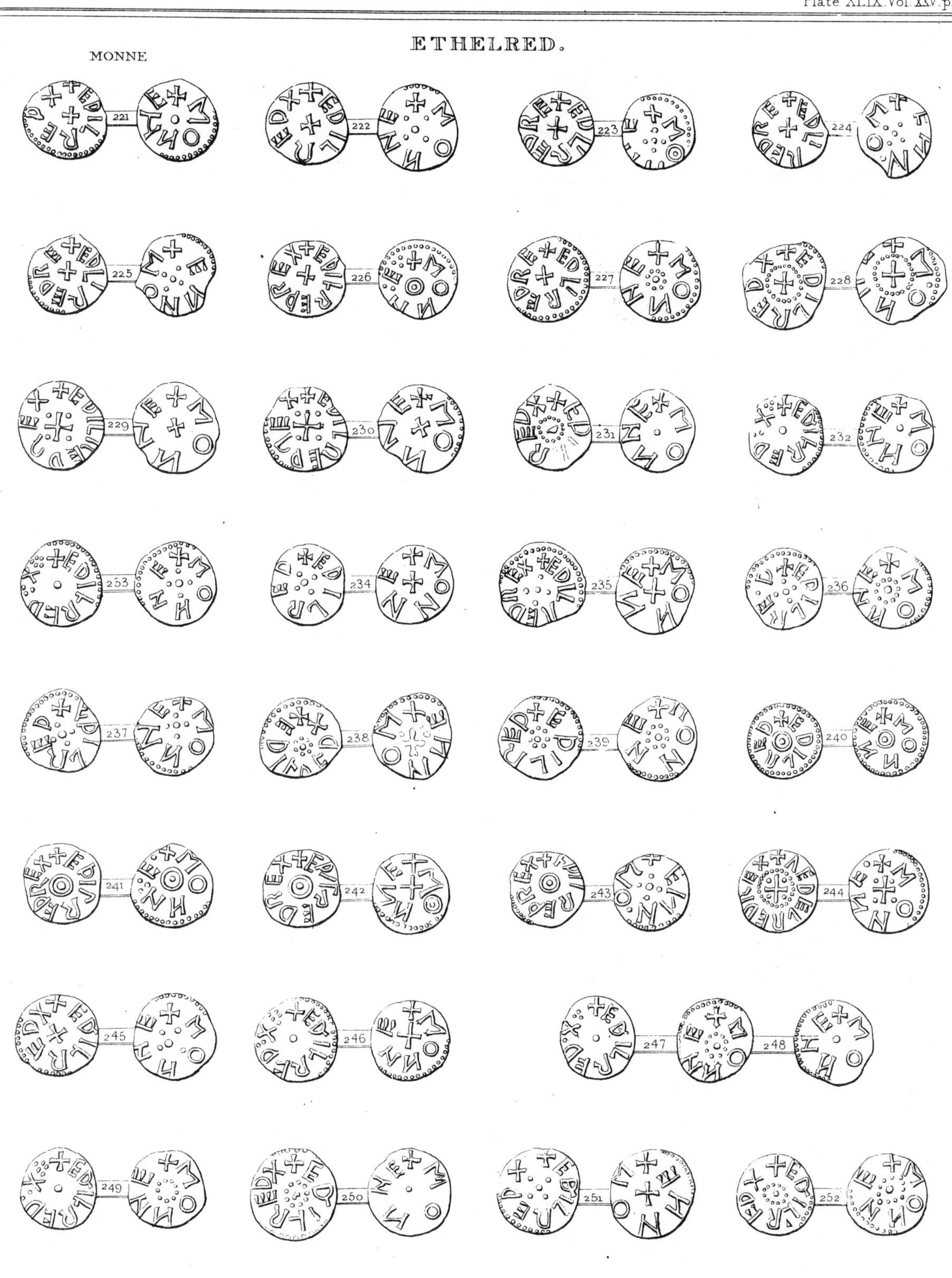

J.s Basire sc.

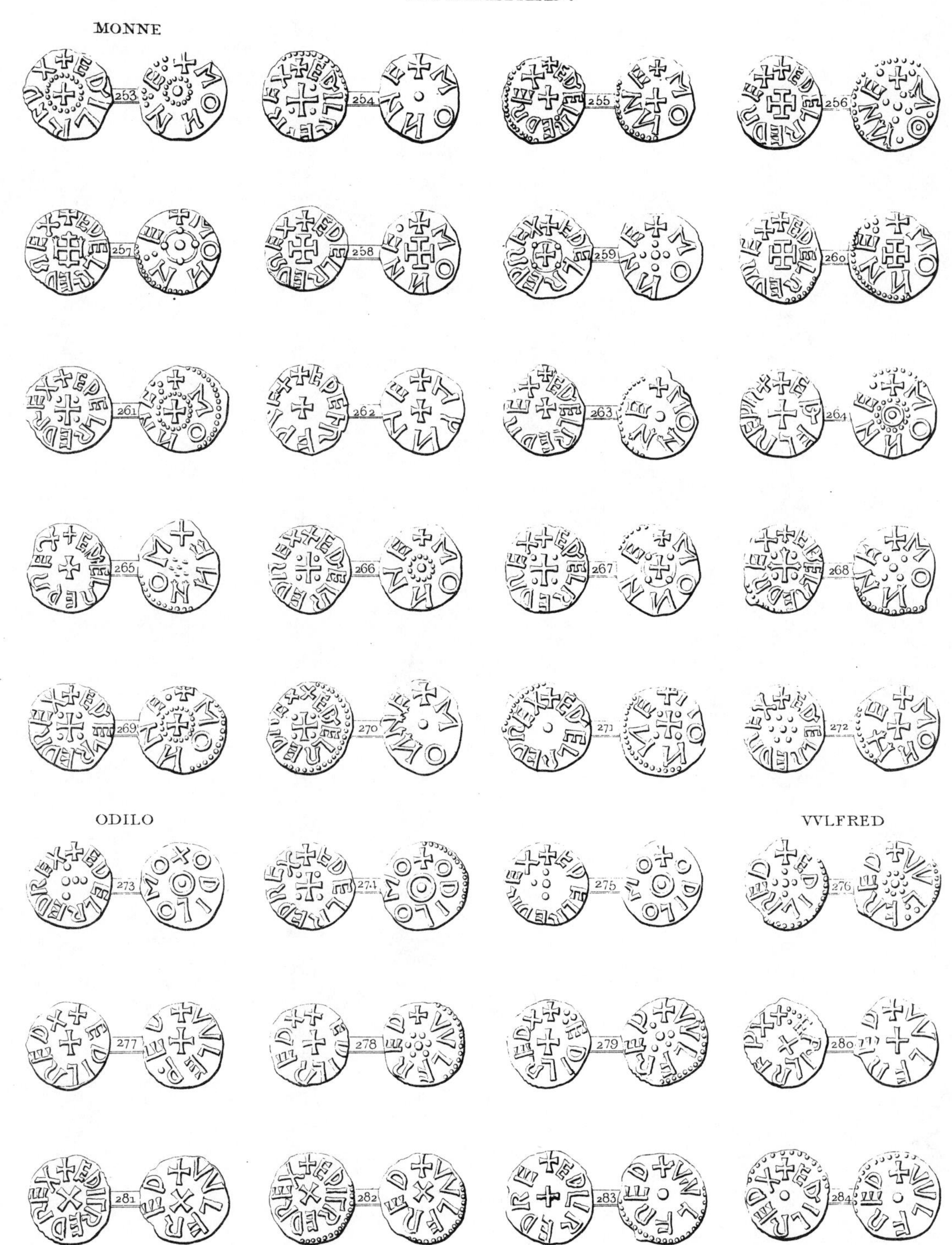

J. Basire sculp.

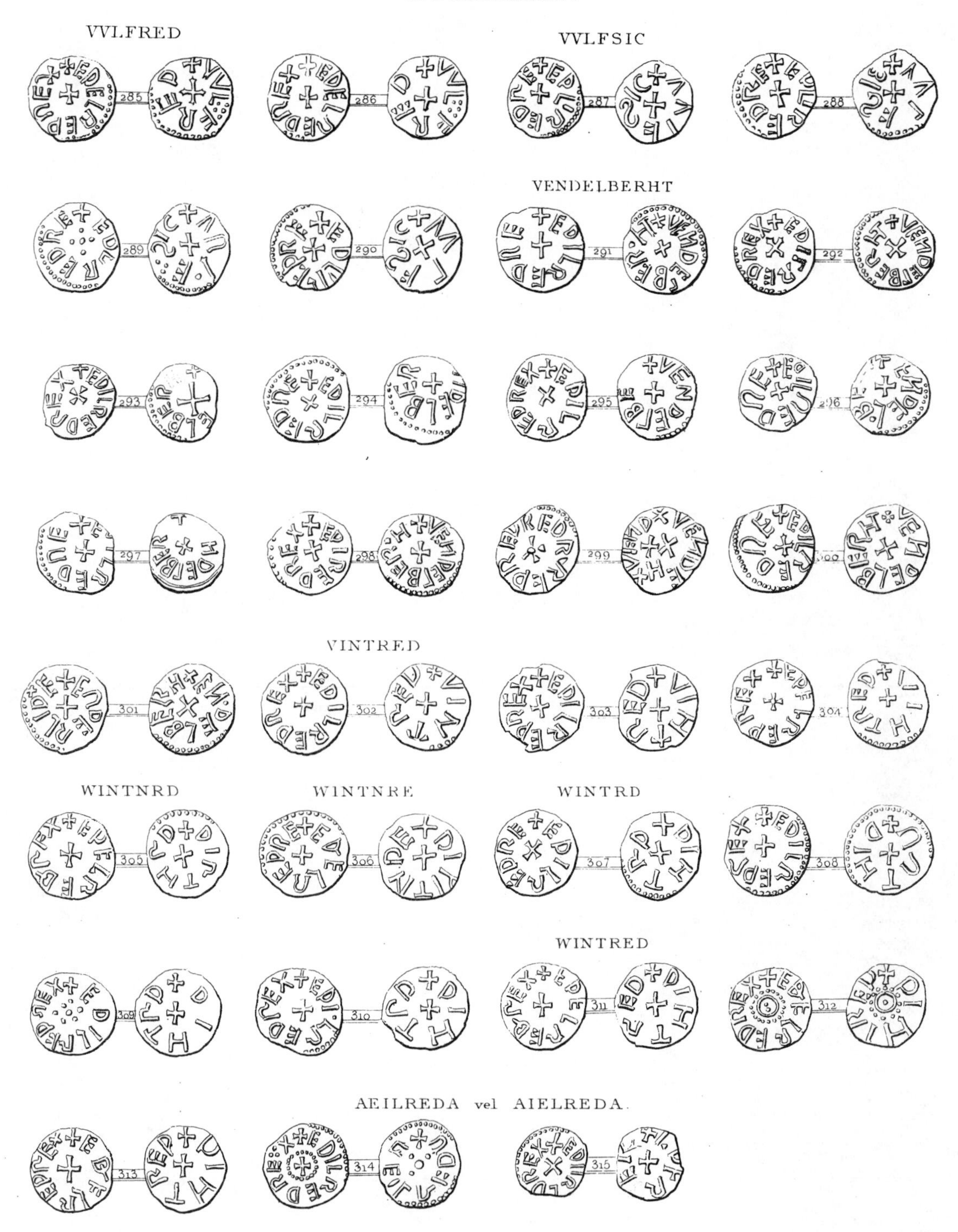

J. Basire sculp.

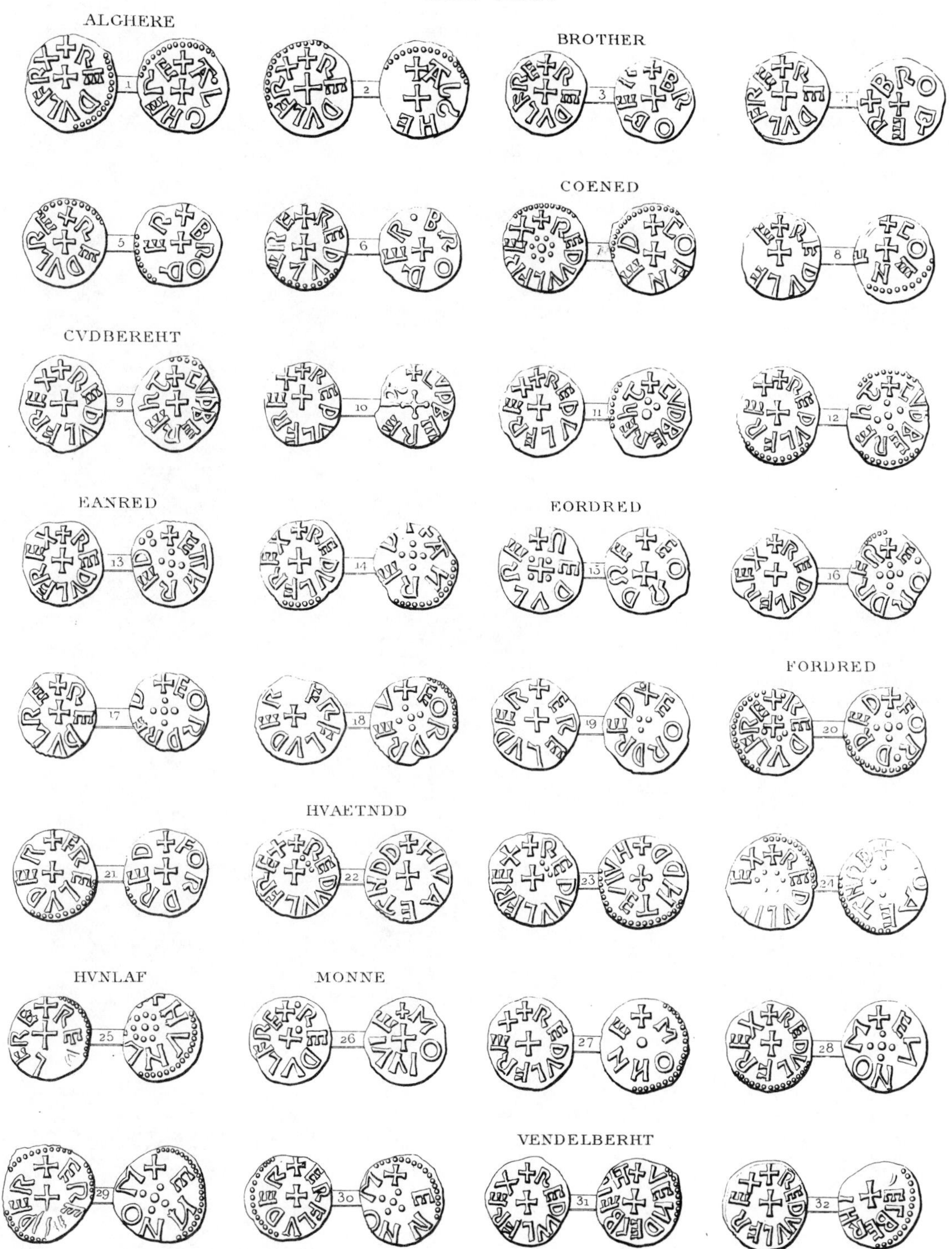

Js Basire sculp.

EANBALD.

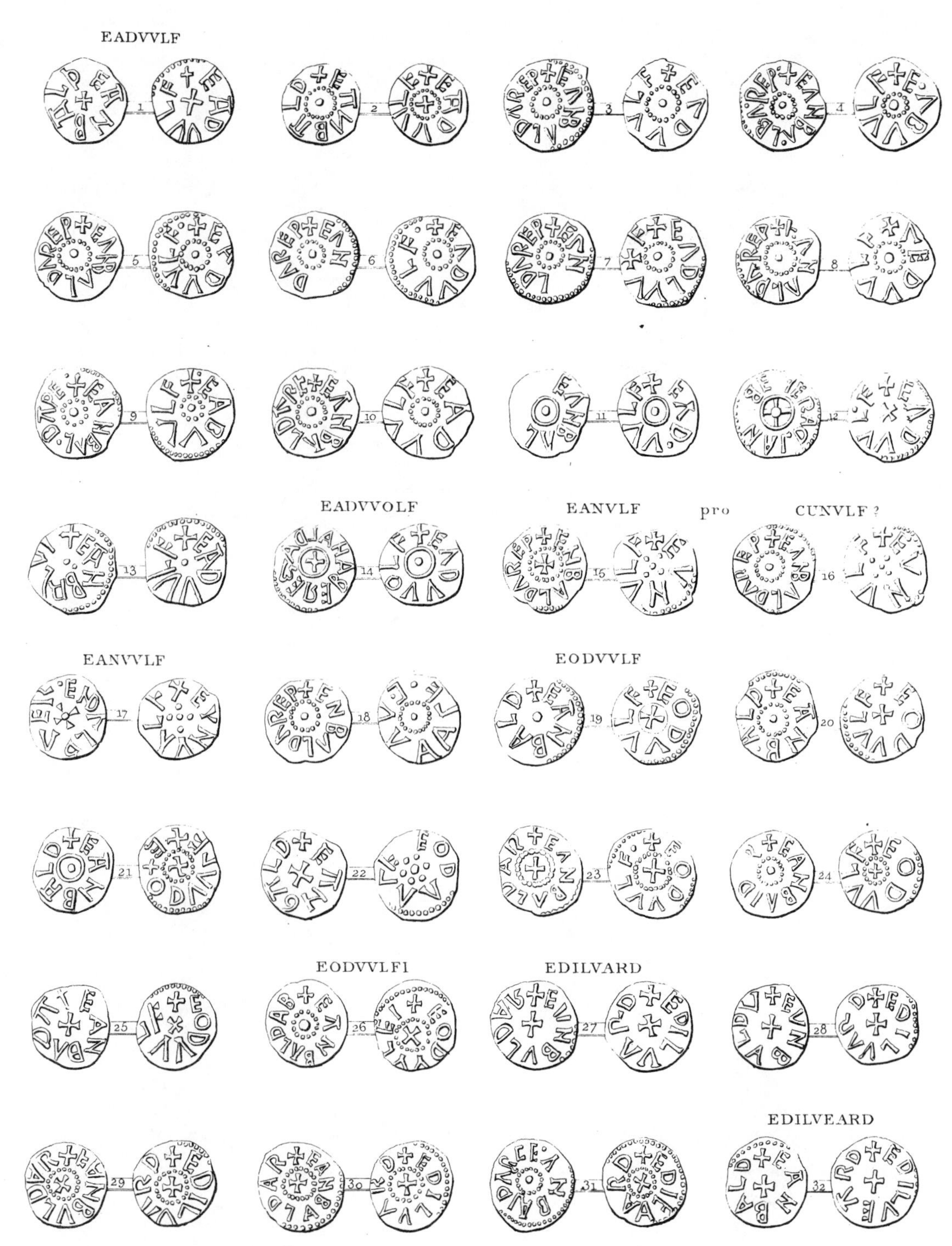

J^s Basire sculp

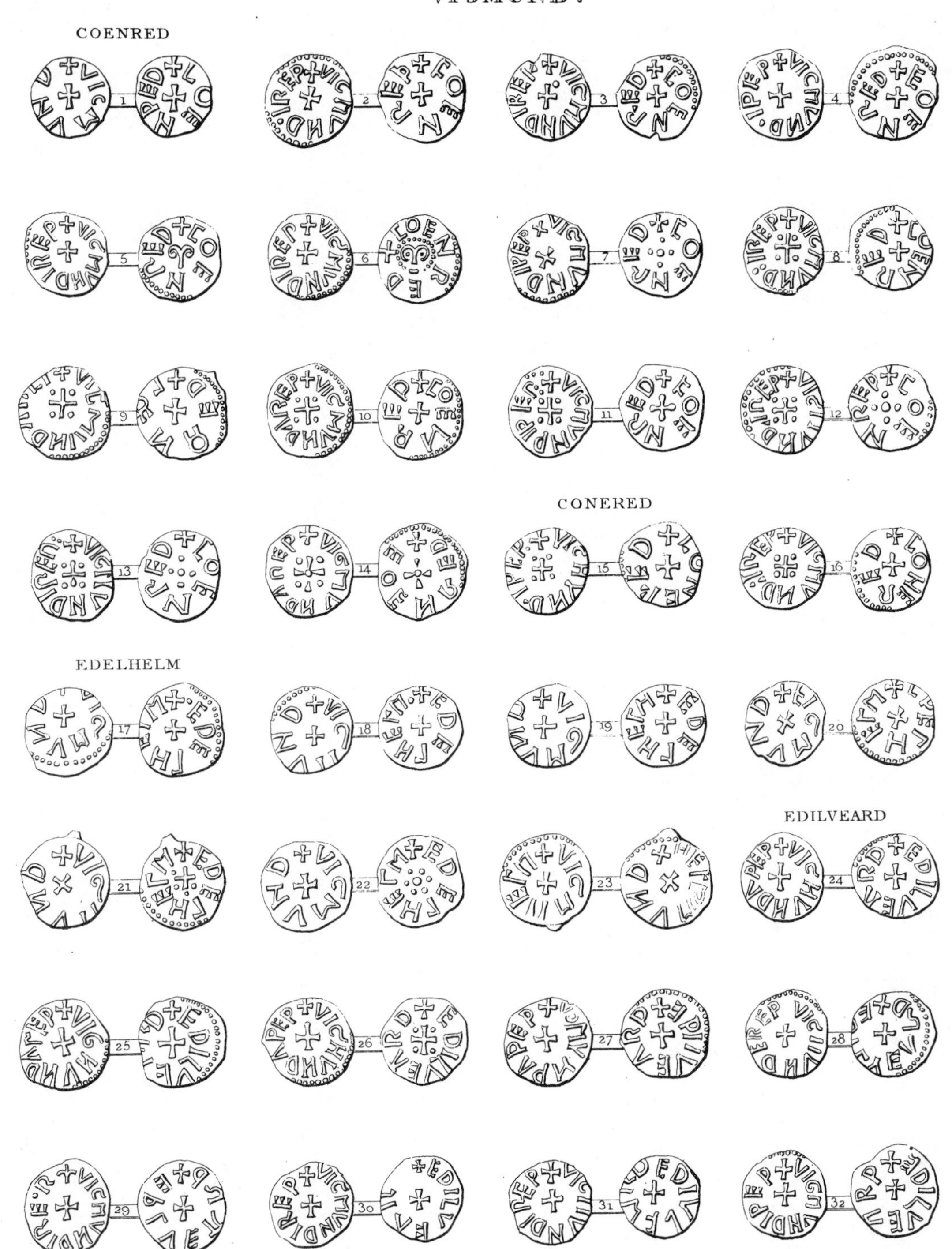

J^s Basire sculp.

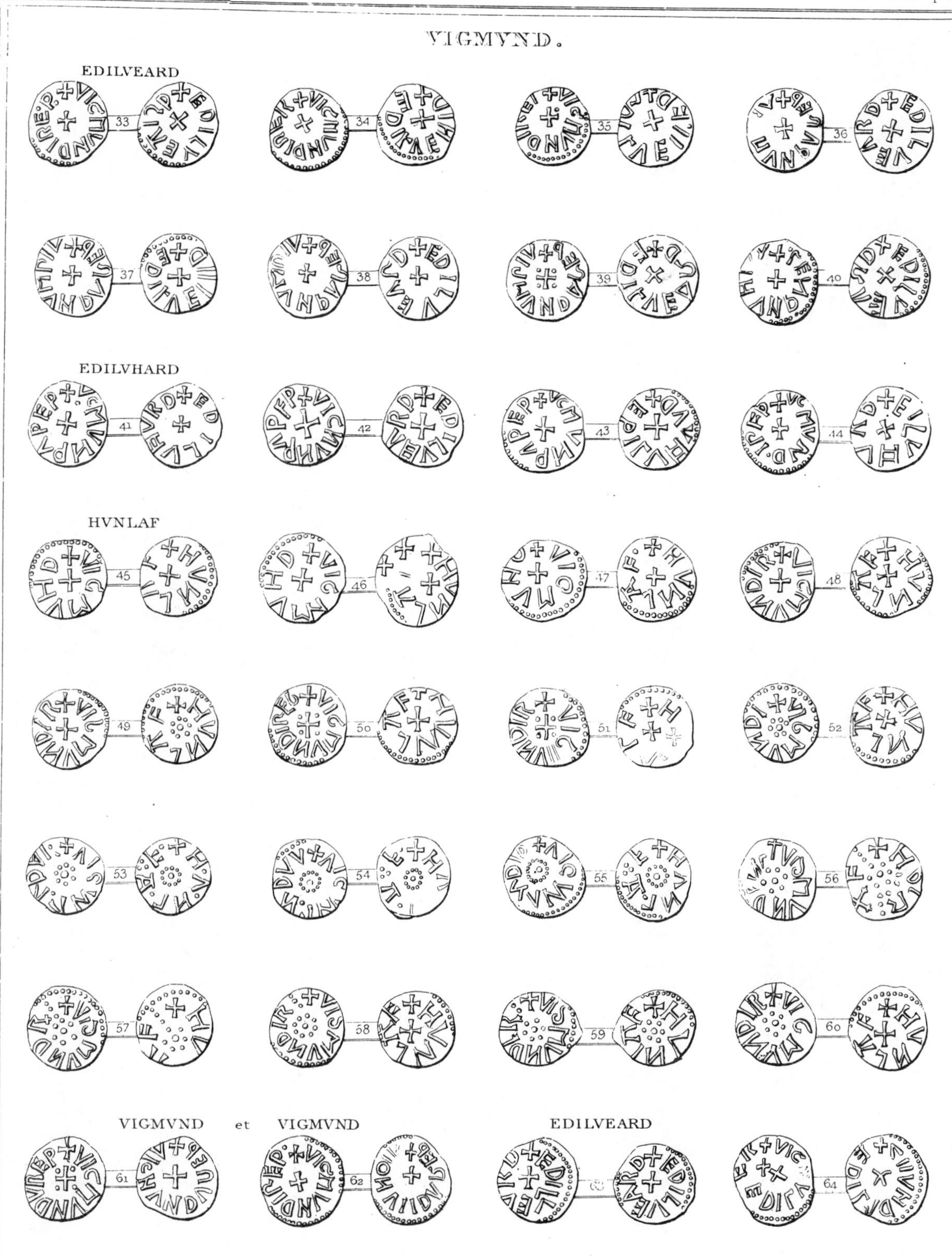

J. Basire sculp.

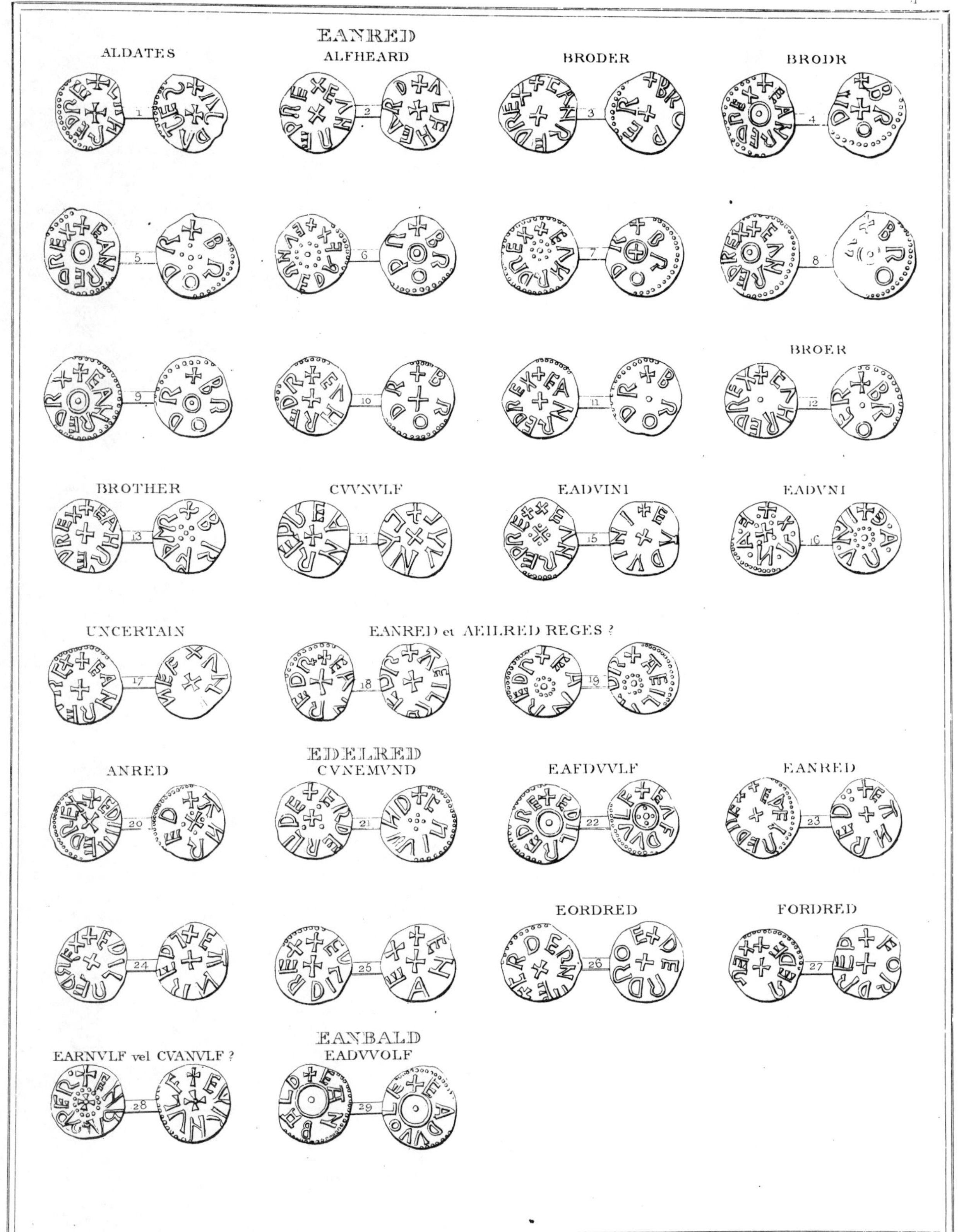
EANRED
ALDATES
ALFHEARD
BRODER
BRODR
BROER
BROTHER
CVVNVLF
EADVINI
EADVNI
UNCERTAIN
EANRED et AEILRED REGES ?
EDELRED
ANRED
CVNEMVND
EAFDVVLF
EANRED
EORDRED
FORDRED
EANBALD
EARNVLF vel CVANVLF ?
EADVVOLF
Jas Basire sculp.

UNCERTAIN.

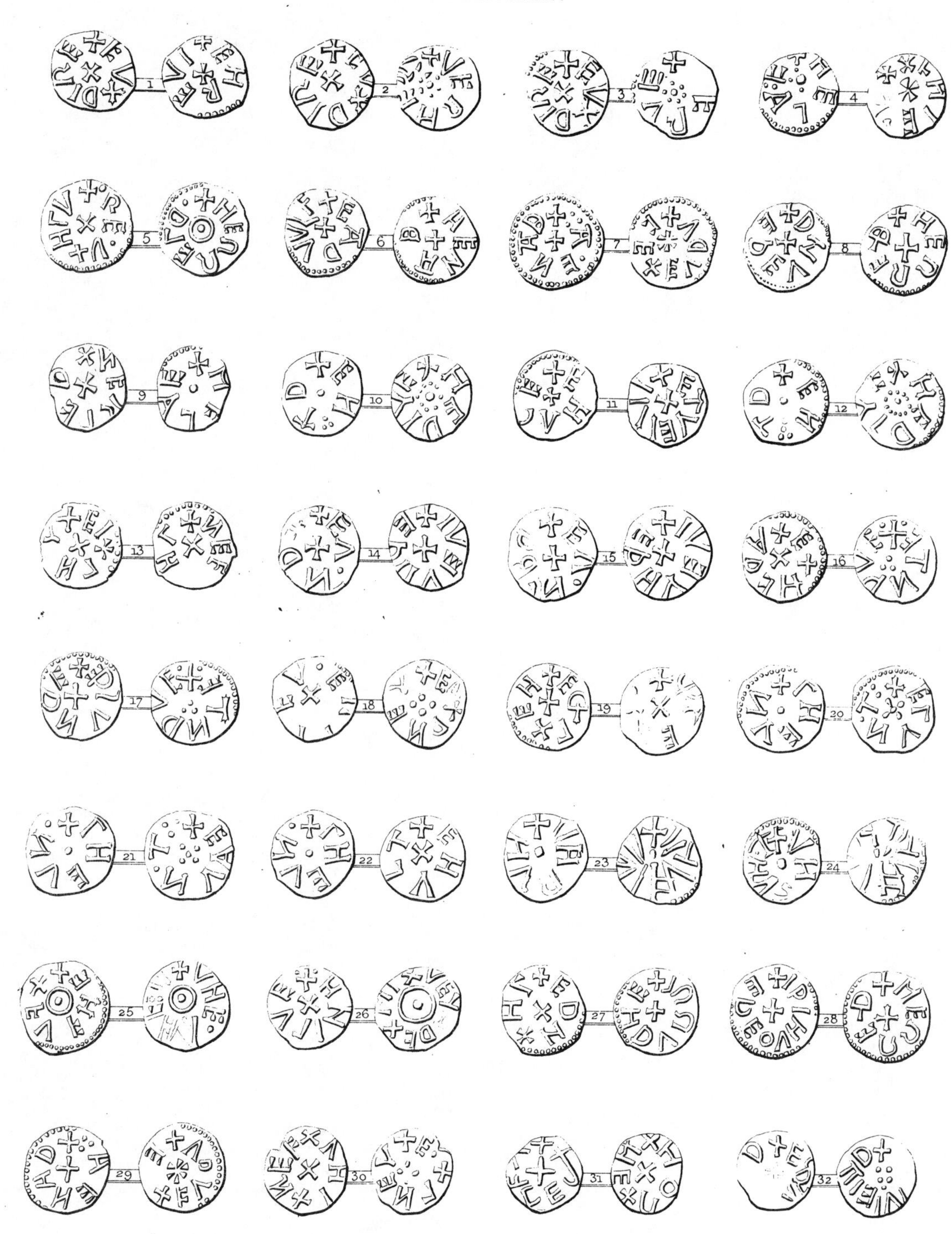

J^s Basire sculp.

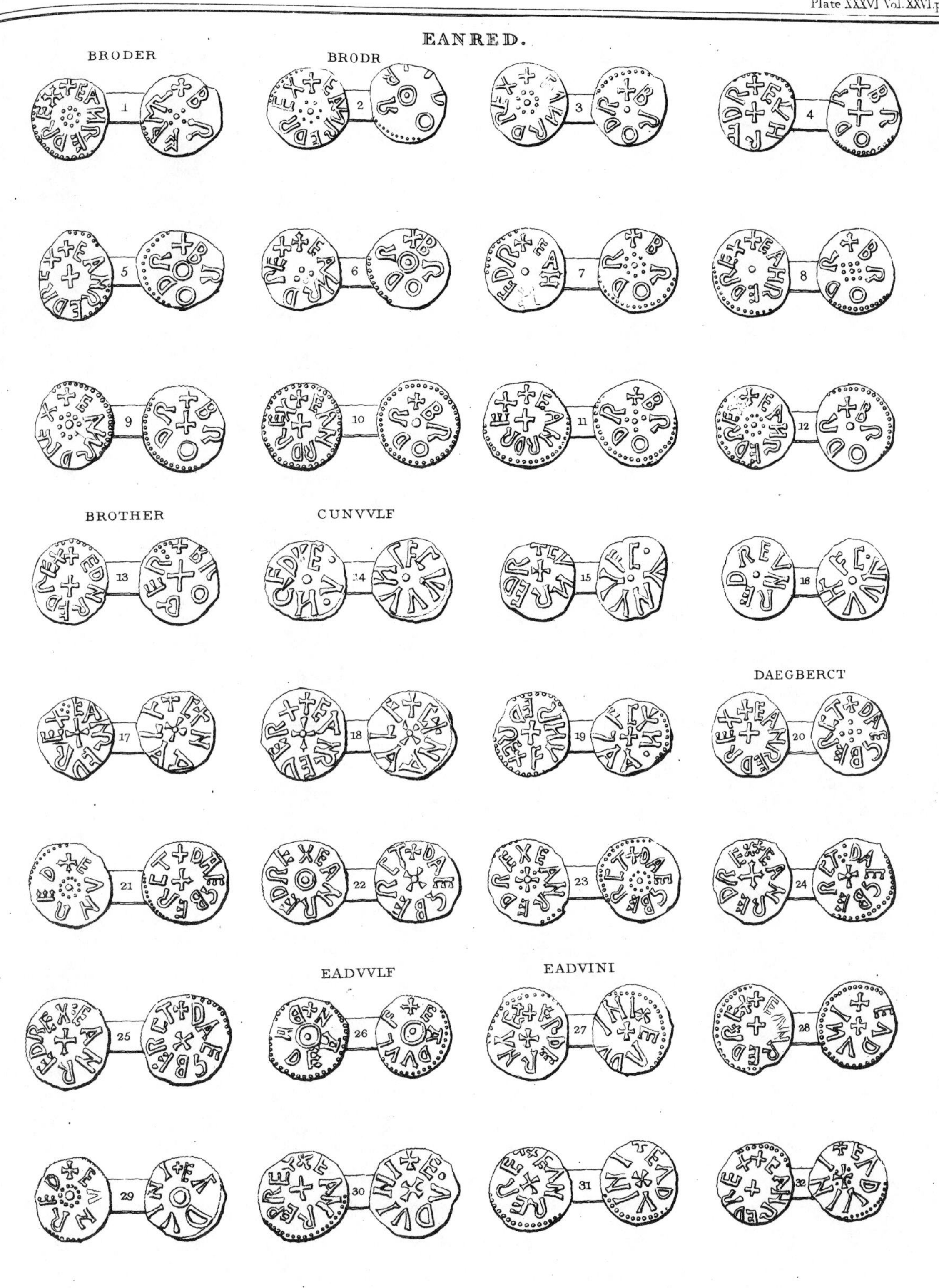
EANRED.
BRODER
BRODR
BROTHER
CUNVVLF
DAEGBERCT
EADVVLF
EADVINI

J. Basire, sc.

EANRED.

EADVINI

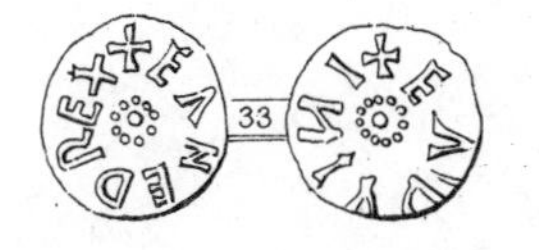
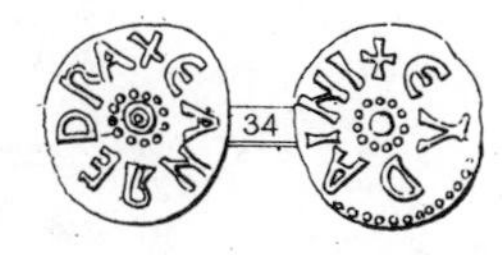
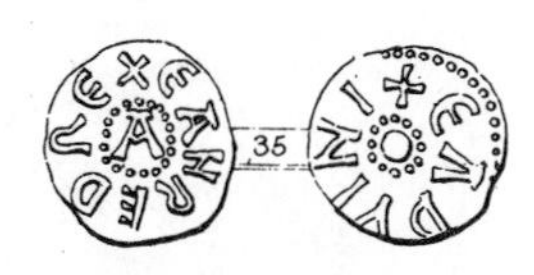
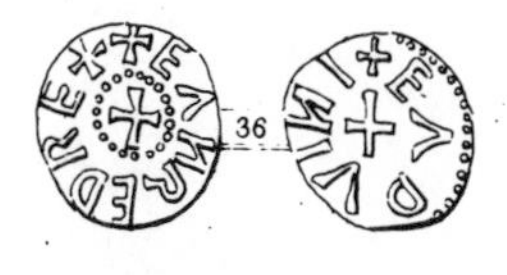

EANRETH

EDILVEAD

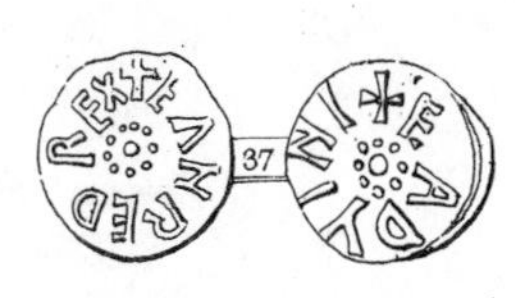
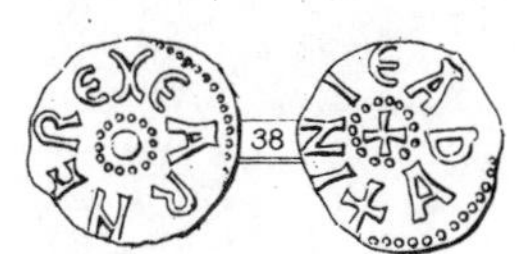
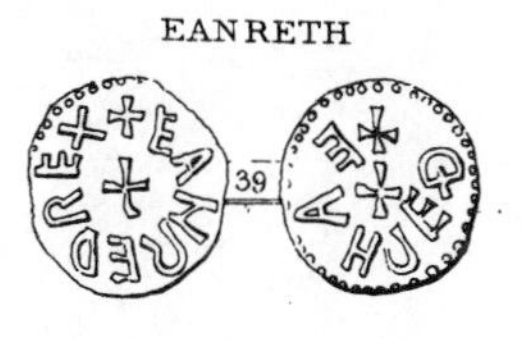
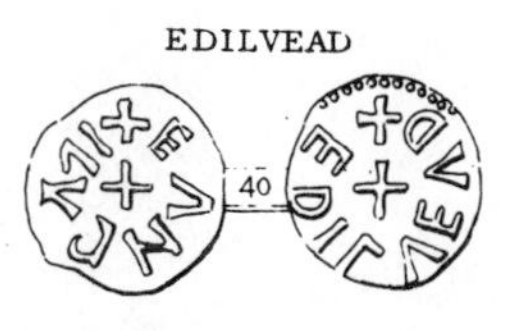

EODVVLF

EORDRED

ERWINNE

EYNVVLF

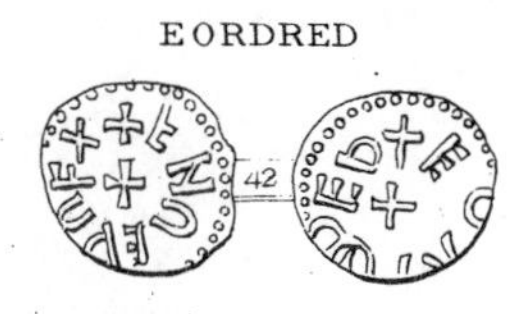
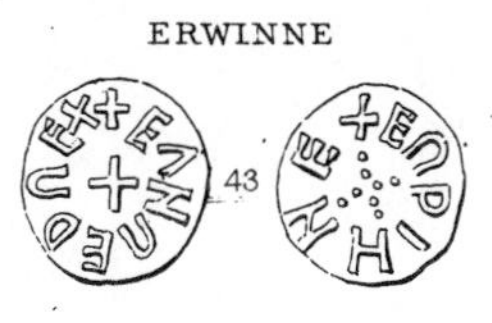
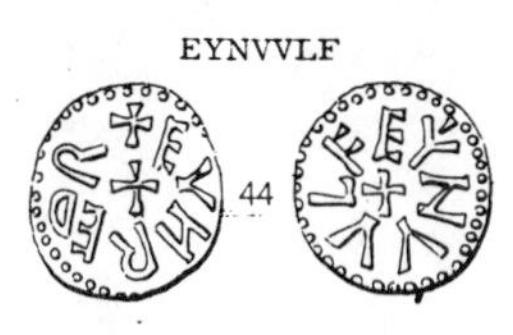

FORDRED

GADUTEIS

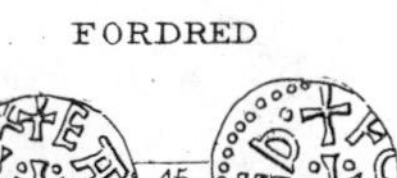
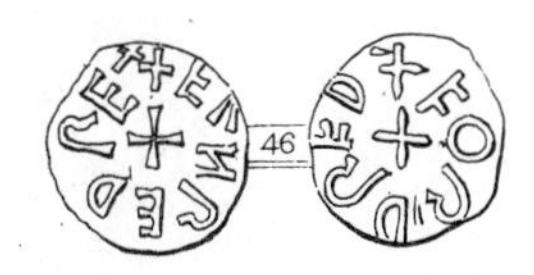
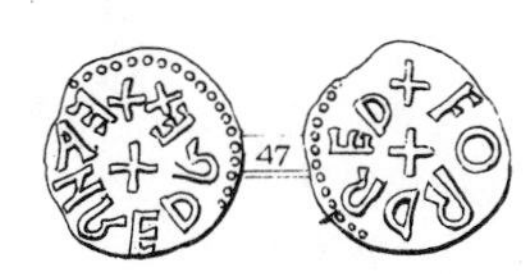
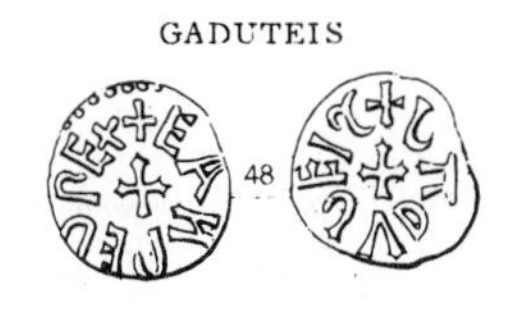

HEARDVLF

HERRED

HERRETH

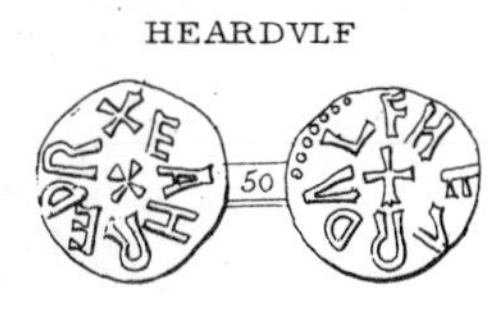

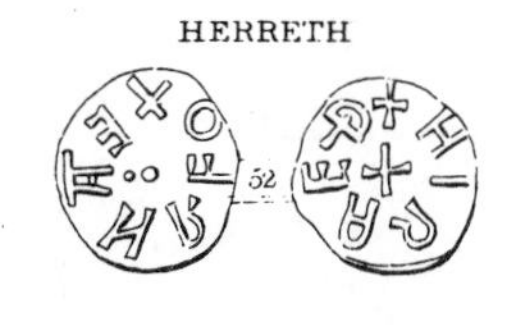

MONNE

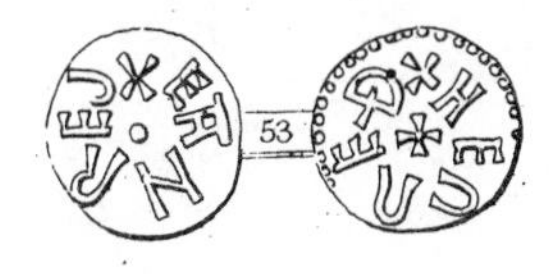

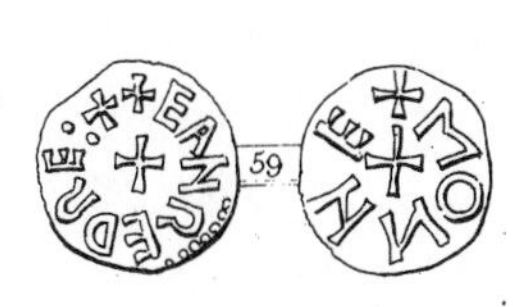
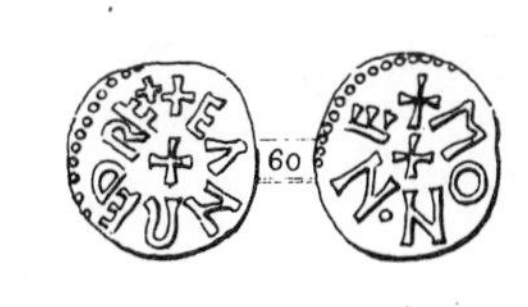

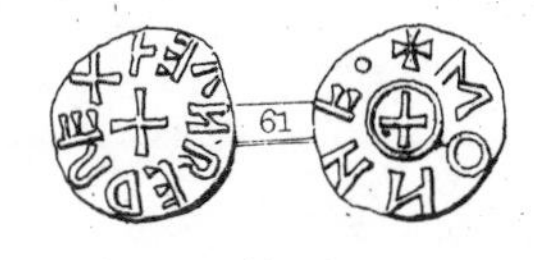
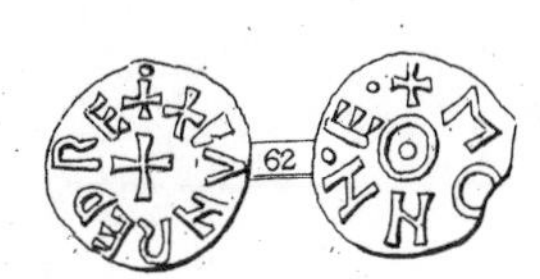
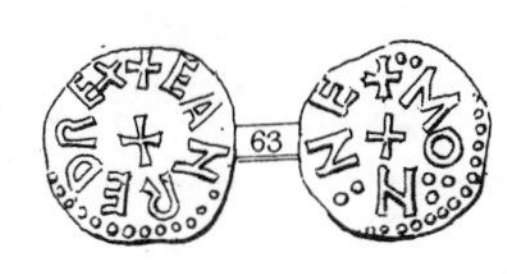

J^s Basire, sc.

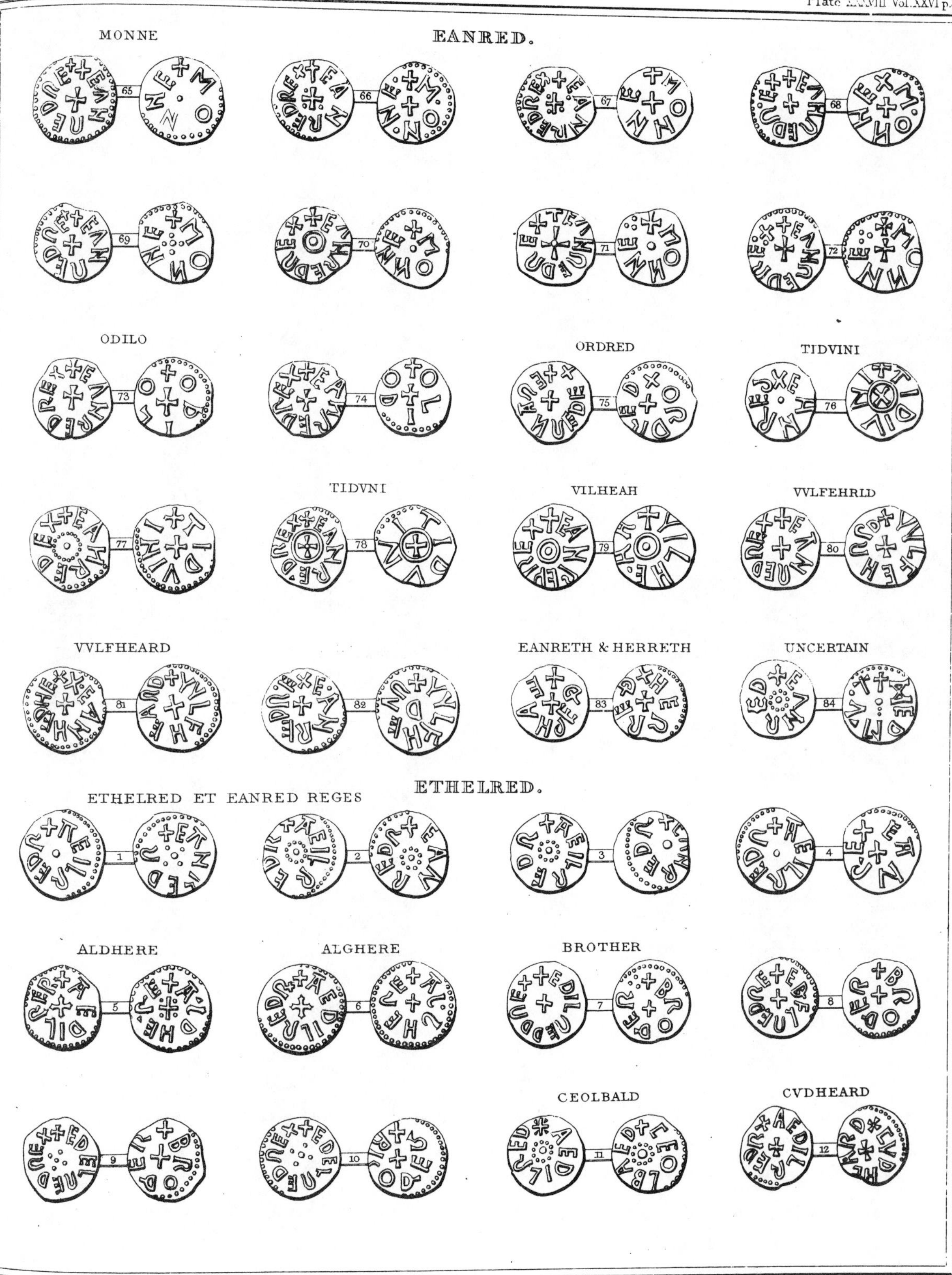
Plate XXVIII Vol. XXVI p.318.
EANRED.
MONNE
ODILO
ORDRED
TIDVINI
TIDVNI
VILHEAH
VVLFEHRID
VVLFHEARD
EANRETH & HERRETH
UNCERTAIN
ETHELRED.
ETHELRED ET EANRED REGES
ALDHERE
ALGHERE
BROTHER
CEOLBALD
CVDHEARD
Js Basire. sc.

ETHELRED.

EANRED

13 14 15 16

ELEOFDEGN

17

EORDRED

18 19 20

ERWINNE

21

FORDRED

22 23 24

25 26 27 28

29 30 31

HVNLAF

32

LEOFDEG

33

LEOFDEGN

34 35 36

37 38 39 40

41 42 43 44

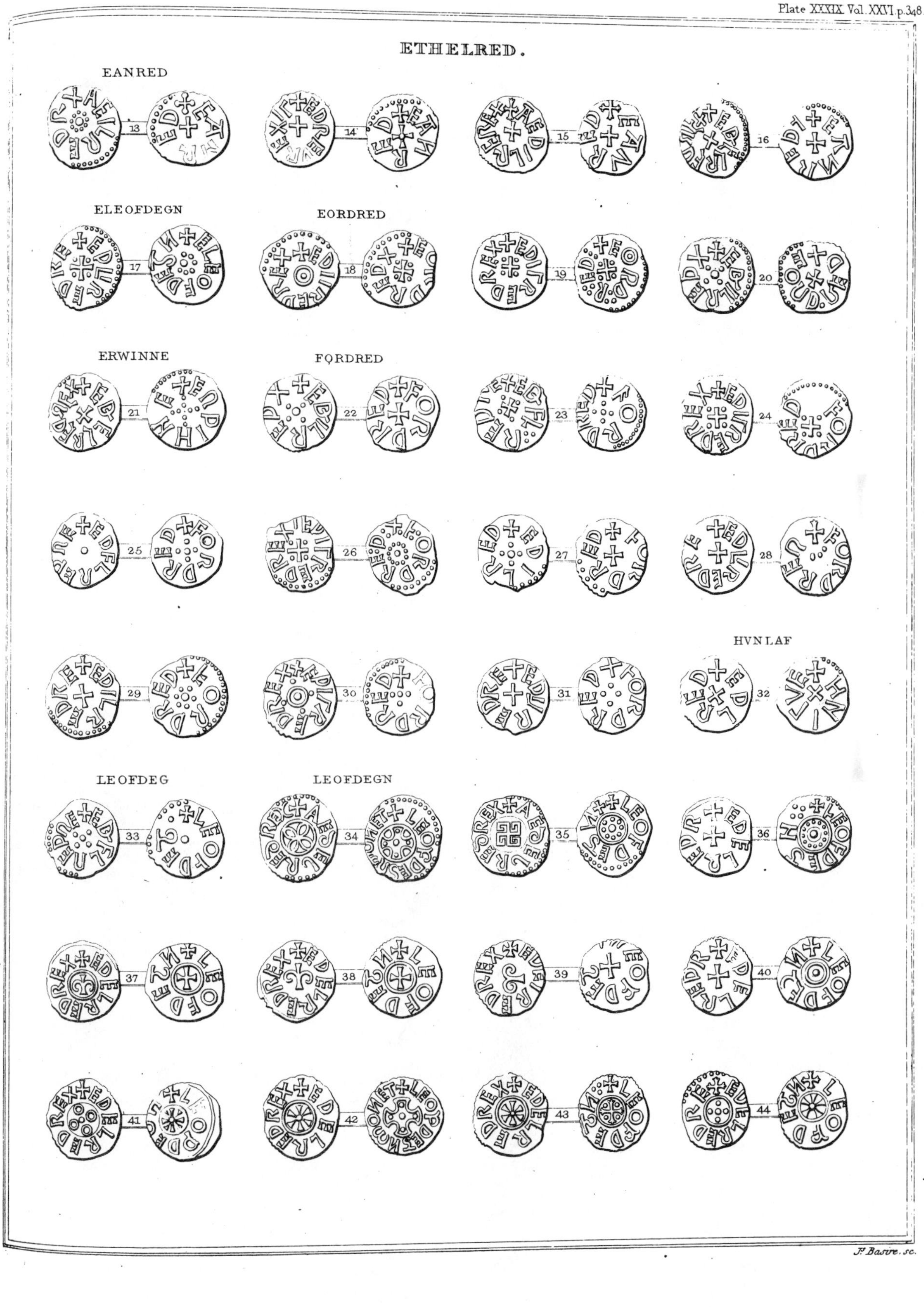

J. Basire. sc.

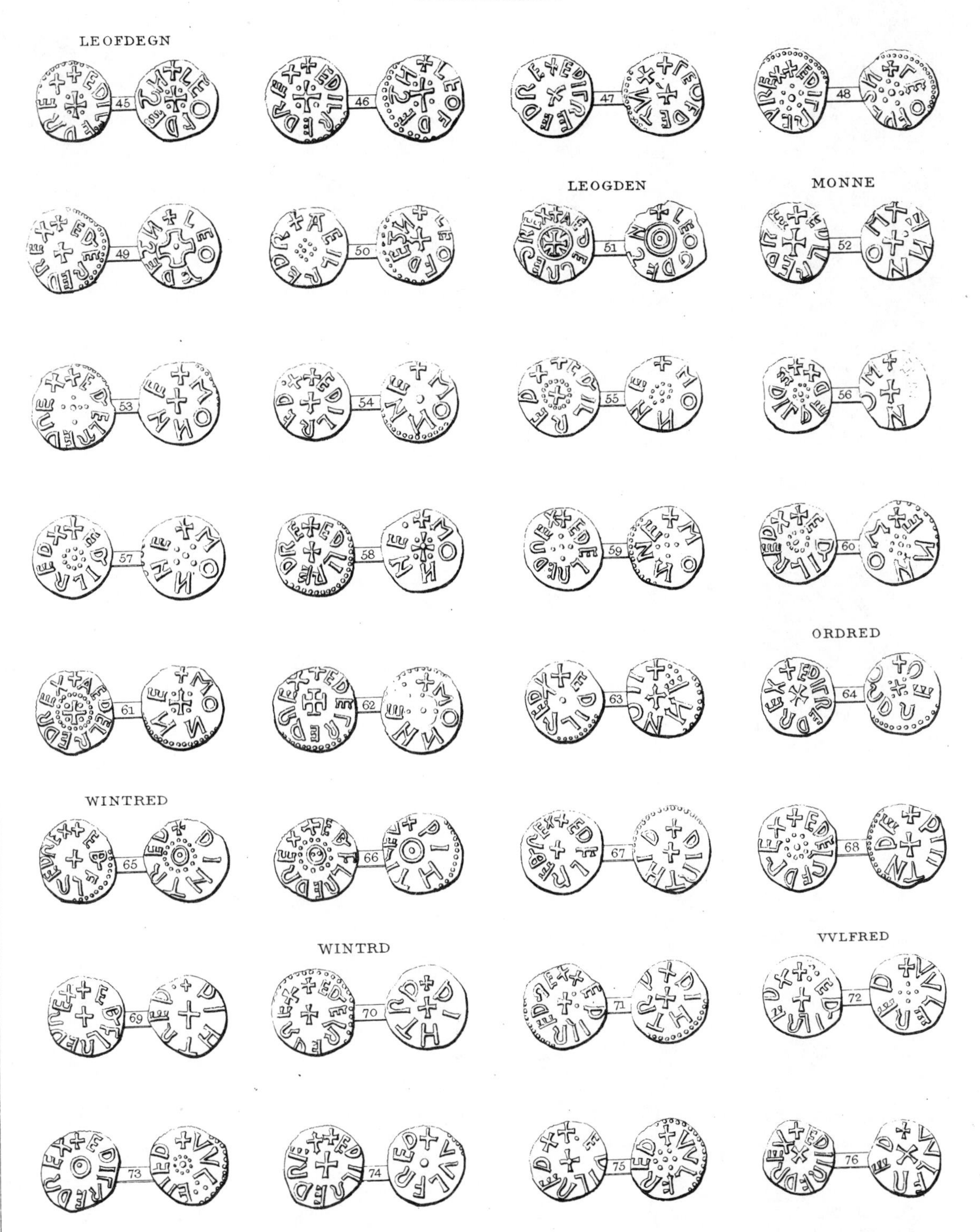
ETHELRED.
LEOFDEGN
LEOGDEN
MONNE
ORDRED
WINTRED
WINTRD
VVLFRED

J^s Basire, sc.

Plate XLI. Vol. XXVI. p. 348.

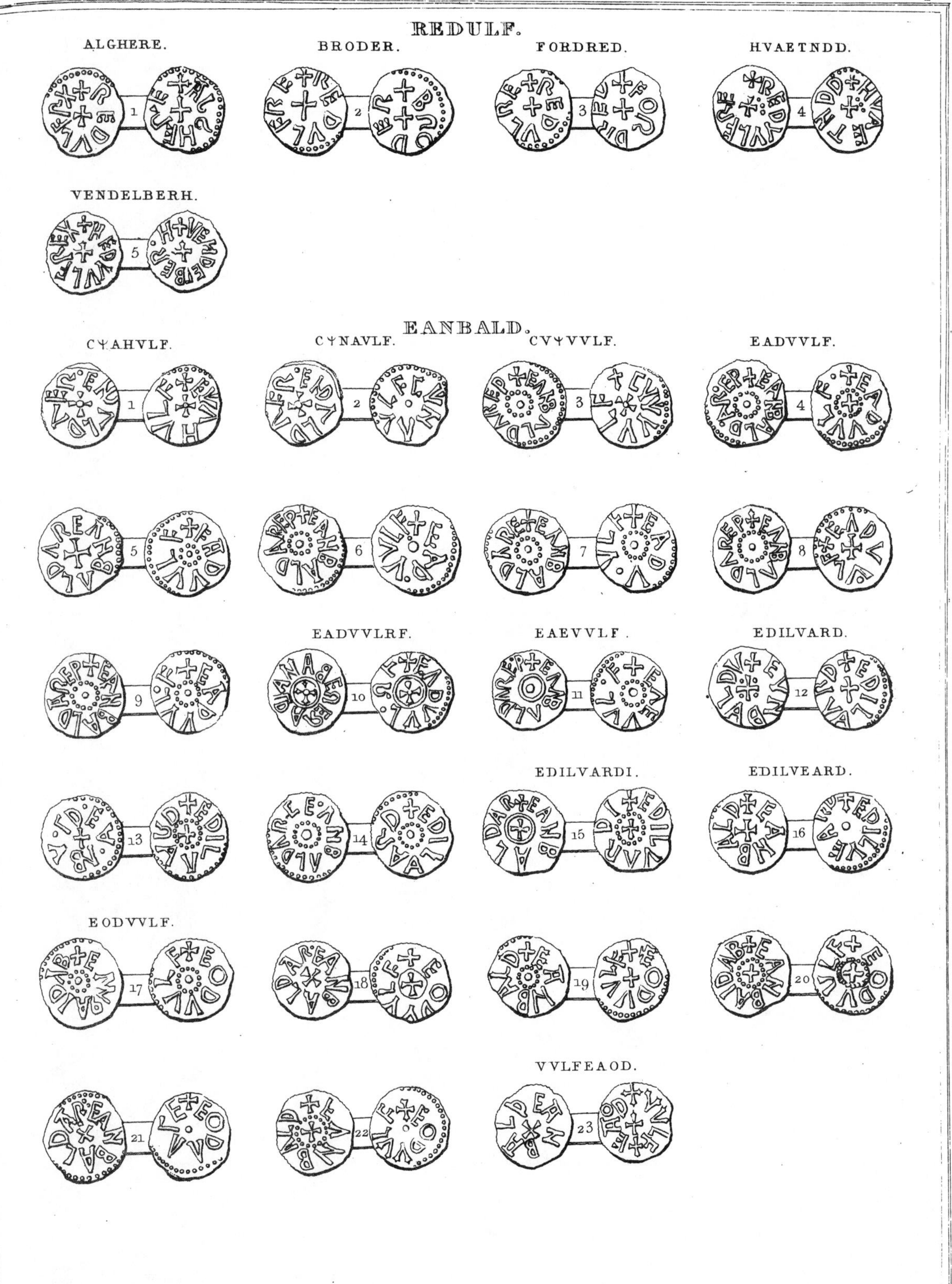

J.s Basire sc.

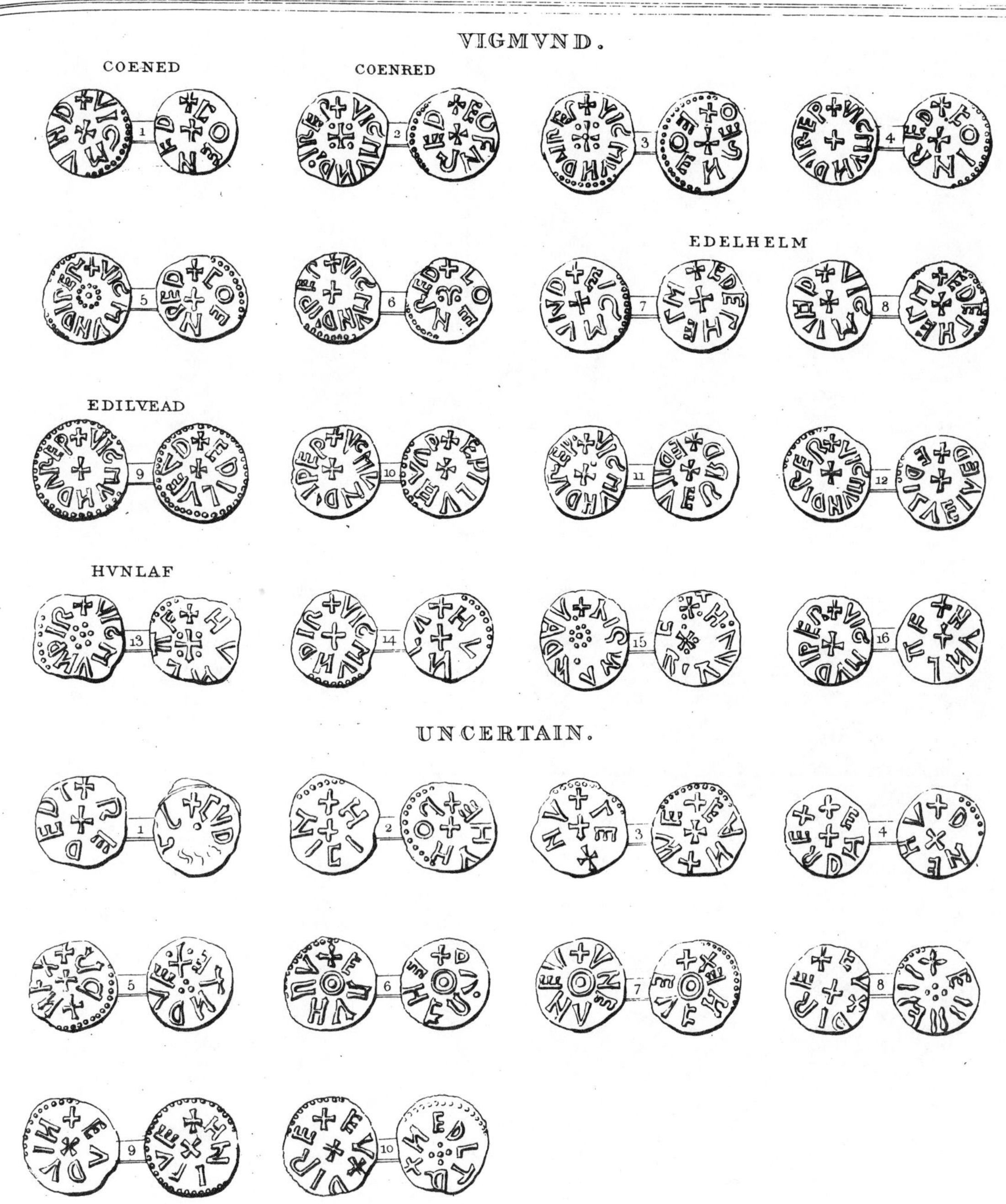
VIGMVND.
COENED
COENRED
EDELHELM
EDILVEAD
HVNLAF
UNCERTAIN.

J. Basire sc.

Some archaeological reflections on the Cuerdale hoard

JAMES GRAHAM-CAMPBELL

THE 150th anniversary of the discovery in 1840 of the Cuerdale hoard, near Preston in Lancashire, will see the first full publication of its surviving non-numismatic or bullion material, by which is meant the ingots and ornaments, and their 'hack-silver' fragments. The catalogue and discussion, supported by a numismatic overview to be contributed by Mr Christopher Blunt, will also be accompanied by a reconstruction of the events surrounding the actual discovery, the subsequent Inquest, and the dispersal of the treasure trove material, based largely on unpublished sources in the Duchy of Lancaster Office. The volume is to be entitled *The Cuerdale Hoard and Related Viking Age Silver from Britain and Ireland in the British Museum* (British Museum Publications), although the Cuerdale section will embrace the holdings of the Ashmolean Museum (formerly the Evans collection), the Liverpool Museum (formerly the Nelson collection) and the Fitzwilliam Museum, through their kind co-operation, as well as material in other public and private collections, most notably that of the Assheton family (now on loan to the British Museum).

The paper presented at the Tenth Oxford Symposium on Coinage and Monetary History (1987) was coupled with one by Blunt to provoke discussion on the nature and value of the Cuerdale hoard, on the method and whereabouts of its assembly, and on possible reasons for its deposition in *c*.905. It thus contained much that was speculative, whilst the data presented were (and remain) in a provisional state, arising out of the work in progress towards the main publication. It is printed here in partially revised form, but without full documentation, in order to stimulate further comment which it is hoped may be sent directly to the author. It is, in every sense, an interim report to be used with caution.[1]

ON SIZE AND WEIGHT

The Cuerdale silver artefacts to be catalogued will total just over 1,000 items. Allowing for missing ingots (for example, the whereabouts of only twelve of the largest, so-called 'mark', ingots are now known, whereas sixteen were recorded at the Inquest), and allowing for 'abstractions' or 'escapes' (material which, for various reasons already outlined in print by Blunt,[2] was never surrendered to the

[1] I am most grateful to Christopher Blunt for his help with the numismatic aspects of this paper and with my Cuerdale researches in general, as also to Marion Archibald, Mark Blackburn, Hugh Pagan, Michael Metcalf, and Ian Stewart for further numismatic advice and assistance before, during, and after the Symposium.

[2] C. E. Blunt, 'The composition of the Cuerdale hoard', *BNJ* 53 (1983), 1–6.

authorities), a reasonable estimate for the original total of non-numismatic silver is around 1,100 pieces.

'Escapes' include an untraced arm-ring exhibited by the Rev. Thomas Hugo in 1853 (Fig.1);[3] other pieces survive. For instance, the Assheton collection at one time or another has included thirteen items of bullion over and above the 159 allocated by the Duchy, amongst which were an extra four 'marks'; some, at least, of this additional material can now be shown to have been purchased at auction in Preston.

This revised estimate of *c*.1,100 items is somewhat lower than my previously published total of 'over 1,300',[4] but this figure was based on a preliminary inspection of the Duchy's distribution records when it was unclear to me whether various entries concerning 'Sundries' referred to hack-silver or (as has become clear from more detailed study) to miscellaneous coins. Incidentally, the Duchy records reveal that the number of official recipients of the hoard, chiefly of coins, amounted to a total of over 170 institutions and individuals.

Blunt argued in his Symposium paper that the number of coins in the Cuerdale hoard is likely to have been between 7,250 and 7,500. We are thus left with a best total estimate of *c*.8,500 individual items of silver, found together with the remains of a lead chest, or the lead lining of a wooden chest (as was the Bossall/Flaxton (Yorks.) hoard deposited some twenty years later), and five bone pins—or so it is believed, for no mention is made of the latter items (discussed further below) in any of the proceedings connected with the Inquest or other documentary sources from 1840/1. It has been suggested that the pins were used to fasten cloth money bags, although this practice does not appear to be one paralleled in other Viking-Age hoards from either Scandinavia or Britain and Ireland. Any information on this matter relating to insular and continental medieval hoards would be particularly welcome.

The figures for the total weight of the silver presented at the Inquest (and subsequently forwarded to the British Museum for study) show that the hoard weighed a minimum of 105 lbs troy, divided into approximately 25 lbs of coins and 80 lbs of bullion. The number of coins included in this figure was, however, only some 6,800 and the total weight of *c*.7,500 coins would have been somewhere between 10 and 10.5 kg. To the *c*.30 kg of recorded bullion must be added an allowance for the 'escapes' (an additional four 'marks' would represent another 1 kg) and thus we arrive at a minimum total of not less than 40 kg of silver for the entire hoard.

The Cuerdale hoard is thus five time heavier than its nearest Viking-Age equivalent from Britain—the Skaill (Orkney) hoard, deposited *c*.950, weighing *c*.8 kg.[5] From Ireland there is now known the remarkable hoard of sixty massive ingots from Carrick, on the eastern shore of Lough Ennell, weighing almost 32 kg in total, but these are not of Scandinavian type—even if they are most probably

[3] T. Hugo, 'On the field of Cuerdale', *J. Brit. Archaeol. Assoc.* 8 (1852–3), 330–5.

[4] J. Graham-Campbell, 'An Anglo-Saxon ornamented silver strip from the Cuerdale hoard', *Med. Archaeol.* 14 (1970), 152–3, at 152; also J. Graham-Campbell, *Viking Artefacts: A Select Catalogue* (London, 1980), 87 (no.301).

[5] J. Graham-Campbell, 'Two Viking-age silver brooch fragments believed to be from the Skaill (Orkney) hoard', *Proc. Soc. Antiq. Scot.* 114 (1984), 289–301, at 293–5, and note 9.

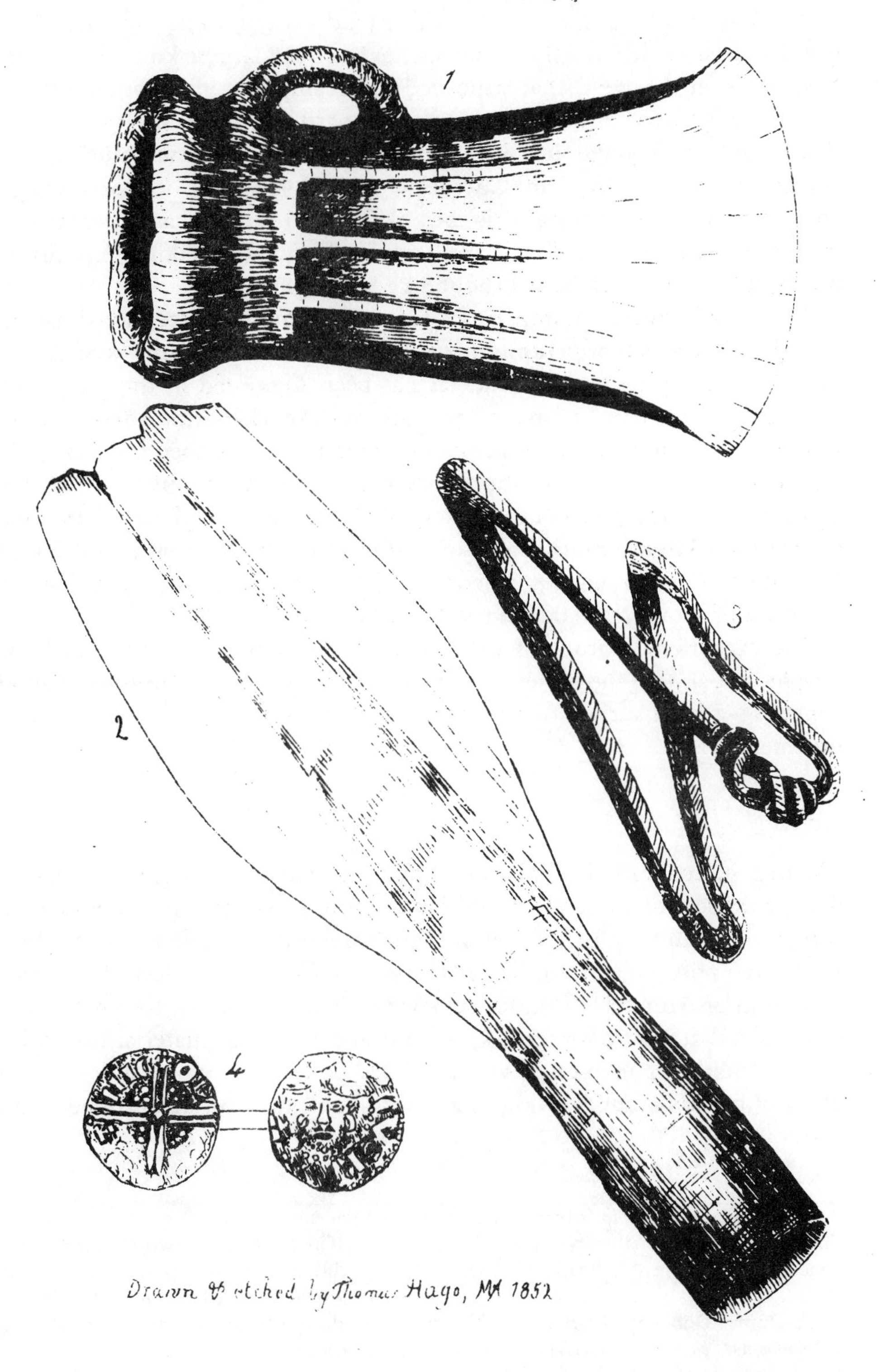

FIG.1. A lost arm-ring from the Cuerdale hoard (no.3).

of Viking-Age date. The Lough Ennell (Co. Westmeath) hoard most similar to Cuerdale, deposited *c*.910, weighs less than one kilogram (Dysart Island no.4).[6]

There is thus no doubt that Cuerdale is exceptional in an Insular context in terms of its weight, as also in the number (and variety) of its contents. The same is true for western and northern Europe, even if the largest known early medieval coin-hoard in the west, that deposited at Fécamp in *c*.980, contained perhaps as many as 9,000 coins.[7] The largest known hoard from Viking-Age Scandinavia is that found at Äspinge in Skåne (deposited even later in *c*.1047).[8] This also contained more coins than Cuerdale—over 8,400—but its total weight only amounted to some 8.75 kg. It is thus Skaill-sized rather than Cuerdale-sized and the same holds true even for Gotland where the greatest Viking-Age silver hoards do not seem to have exceeded about 8 kg in weight.[9]

These are important comparisons for establishing the exceptional nature of the Cuerdale hoard as representing more than individual or family wealth, consistent indeed with pay for a war-band (as has been suggested in the past), even if its Viking-Age value in terms of pounds sterling does not sound immediately impressive. With 7,700 silver pennies representing £30, then the rest of Cuerdale might have amounted to the equivalent of £96, giving a total monetary equivalent of some £125 in round terms. However, a rough calculation suggested at the Oxford Symposium, based on a 10th-century valuation of a sheep as worth 5p, with a 20th-century equivalent of £50, gives a notional equivalent value for Cuerdale of about £300,000 in modern terms.

The exceptional nature of the Cuerdale hoard rests not only on its size and weight, but also on the variety (and often the rarity) of its numismatic and bullion contents—a brief survey of aspects of the latter follows, divided into ingots and ornaments.

INGOTS

The largest recognizable component (other than assorted ring fragments) amongst the Cuerdale bullion consists of ingots and ingot fragments which together comprise a minimum of 350 out of the 1,000 items available for study. Miss Susan Kruse, as a postgraduate student at University College London,[10] has examined a total of approximately 10 kg of surviving Cuerdale ingots, to which there needs to be added at least another 2 kg of lost and 'escaped' material (including eight missing 'marks' at an average weight of 256 g). In other words at least 12 of about 31 kg of bullion consists of ingots and fragments thereof, or in round figures they

[6] M. Ryan *et al.*, 'Six silver finds of the Viking period from the vicinity of Lough Ennell, Co. Westmeath', *Peritia* 3 (1984), 334–81.

[7] F. Dumas-Dubourg, *Le trésor de Fécamp et le monnayage en France occidentale pendant la seconde moitié du Xe siècle* (Paris, 1971).

[8] B. Hårdh, *Wikingerzeitliche Depotfunde aus Südschweden: Katalog und Tafeln* (Acta Archaeologica Lundensia, Series in 4°, No.9), 52–4, at 53.

[9] The heaviest known Gotlandic silver hoard (weighing 10.369 kg) was not deposited until *c*.1140, at Burge, Lummelunda: see P. Berghaus *et al.*, 'Gotlands största silverskatt', *Gotländskt Arkiv* 41 (1969), 7–60.

[10] I am most grateful for the assistance of Susan Kruse with this section; aspects of her ingot researches are forthcoming in *World Archaeology* 20:2 (1988).

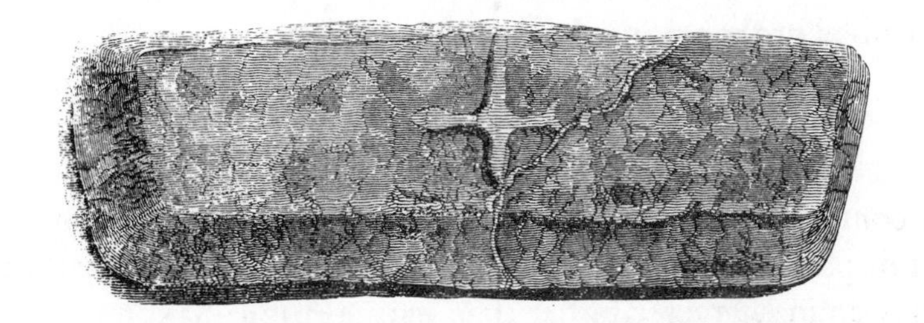

FIG.2. A 'mark' ingot from Cuerdale.

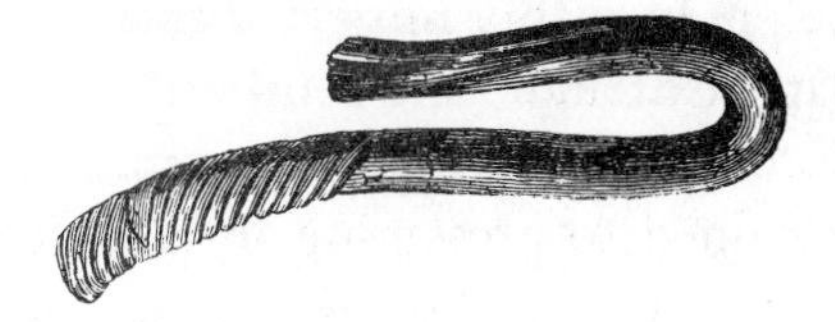

FIG.3. Spiral-ring fragments from Cuerdale.

FIG.4. A twisted rod arm-ring from Cuerdale.

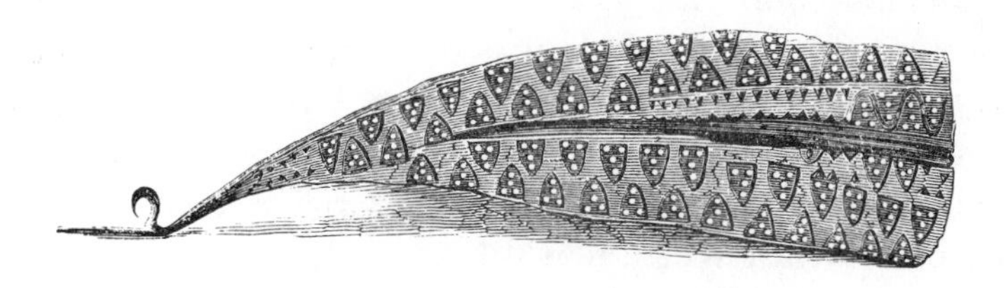

FIG.5. A 'ribbon bracelet' fragment from Cuerdale.

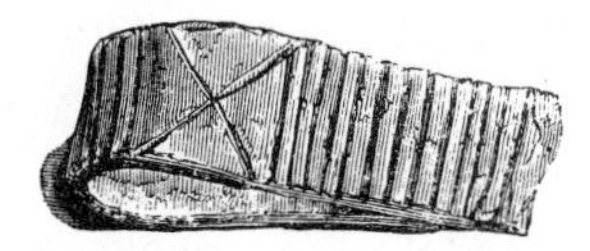

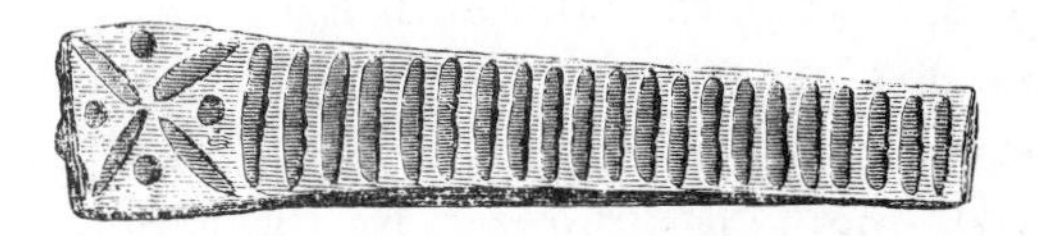

FIGS.6–7. Danish prototype and Hiberno-Viking arm-ring fragments from Cuerdale.

represent perhaps 40 per cent of the bullion by weight. Looked at another way, the hoard can be broken down by weight as follows:

25% coins and fragments
29% ingots and fragments
46% ornaments and misc. hack-silver

Hoards containing ingots (alongside hack-silver and coins) from both England and Wales display a markedly northern distribution and have all been interpreted as Scandinavian in character rather than native Anglo-Saxon or Welsh. However, the simplest cast bar ingots are not in themselves culturally or regionally diagnostic, although Cuerdale does contain one ingot fragment unique in an Insular context: part of a large flattish circular ingot of the so-called '*Gusskuchen* type', presumably imported from Scandinavia where they become more common in later Gotlandic and southern Swedish hoards.[11]

Kruse's study of the ingot material is not yet completed and so comment here is confined to presenting in advance of her own publication, and with her kind permission, some of her conclusions concerning the 'mark' ingots (Fig.2) in relation to Mrs Jennifer Lewis's earlier study of this category,[12] because of their wider implications for the interpretation of the hoard as a whole.

Lewis suggested that the average 'mark' ingot weight of 256 g (discounting one underweight example in the Nelson collection, now shown by Kruse to be of base metal) represented two-thirds of an account pound of 384 g, given the relationship of 160 to 240 pence. This she related to the Carolingian account pound, calculated from late ninth-century coins in the name of an Emperor Charles (Charles the Bald in West Francia, Charles the Fat in Lotharingia)—an attribution regarded as reasonable given the Frankish influence on the Northumbrian Viking coin issues. However, the standard of these issues was lower than those of Frankia and another complication is that the contemporary coins of Edward the Elder would also probably have produced an account pound not that different from 384 g. A further problem in interpretation is presented by the existence of both an account pound and a commercial (or bullion) pound. Suffice it to say, at present, that Kruse feels that the Cuerdale 'mark' ingots are more likely to relate to a commercial pound, perhaps of eight öre of twenty pence, than two-thirds of the Carolingian account pound. It is in any case clear that both authorities are convinced that this unique ingot series was not meant for a purely Scandinavian economy, for which it was heavier than necessary. It is most likely to have originated in an Anglo-Saxon or Anglo-Scandinavian milieu.

Two other important points to note about the 'marks' are that they are all complete and that some amongst them have no nicking (indeed there is little nicking to be observed amongst the group as a whole). On the other hand, complete ornaments form a very small element in the hoard and nicking is widespread on the bullion. It is a reasonable presumption with a hack-silver hoard such as Cuerdale that the heaviest objects, when intact, are likely to have been amongst the latest items to have been incorporated. This interpretation of the 'mark' ingots is supported by the general trend in Cuerdale coin-pecking, noted

[11] E.g. *op.cit.* in note 8, Taf.5.

[12] J. Lewis, 'Silver ingots from the Cuerdale hoard in two northern collections', *Lancs. Archaeol. J.* 2 (1982), 47–80.

FIG.8. Carolingian belt-fittings from Cuerdale.

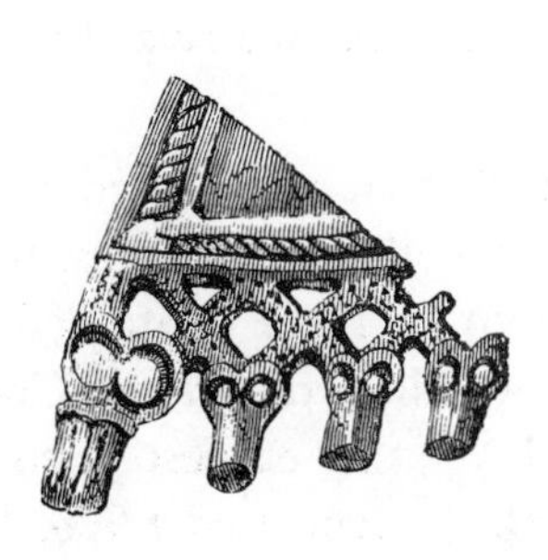
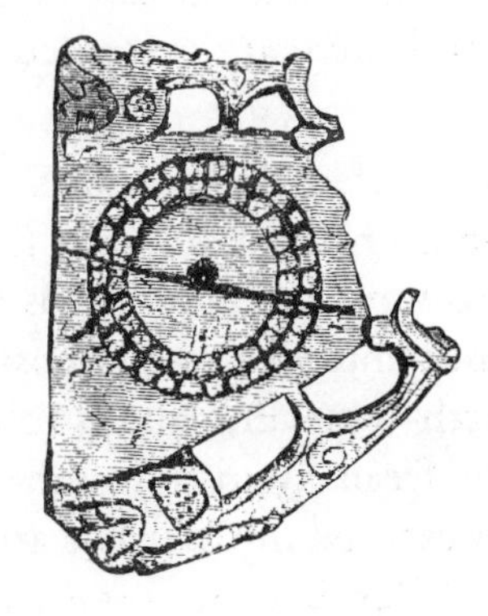

FIGS.9–11. Hiberno-Viking and Irish brooch fragments from Cuerdale.

FIG.12. Plain rod arm-ring (of lozenge-shaped cross-section) from Cuerdale.

by Miss Marion Archibald, in which over 90 per cent of the *Cunnetti* are unpecked, as are most of the coins of Edward the Elder.[13]

If we accept that the Cuerdale 'mark' ingots cannot be tied down to a Northumbrian Viking-Age weight-system, then their region of origin cannot yet be precisely established. However, they do not represent Scandinavian or other continental imports, nor do they appear to be of Scottish or Irish origin—'made in England' must suffice for now (along with *c*.6,000 of the coins).

THE ORNAMENTS

It is not possible with much of the Cuerdale hack-silver to suggest regional attributions for its manufacture, but the purpose of this paper will concentrate on that which is diagnostic. Such material can be conveniently divided for present purposes into six groups and these are presented here moving westward from the Baltic to the Irish Sea.

(i) *Baltic*. It was demonstrated by Nicholas Lowick that the Cuerdale Kufic coins (which may now be numbered at about fifty) travelled to the west by way of the Baltic.[14] There are now twenty hoards known to have contained Kufic coins in Britain and Ireland and all those deposited within a decade of Cuerdale are from Ireland or north-west England (Table 1);[15] the earliest such from north-east England is that from Goldsborough (Yorks.), deposited *c*.920, but its Kufic mints and those represented in Cuerdale are mutually exclusive.

Fragments of so-called 'Permian' or spiral-rings will have joined these Kufic coins as they passed through the Baltic, and some forty pieces are present in the Cuerdale hoard (Fig.3)—their only findspot in England other than the unique early hoard from Croydon in the south-east.[16] Also present in Cuerdale are a few fragments of arm-rings and penannular brooches of types paralleled in the Baltic (as on Gotland)—some unique in an Insular context and others found only in Ireland.

It is suggested therefore that the Kufic coins and Baltic material arrived in north-west England by means of a westerly (Irish Sea) route rather than through the north-east—initially by way of Denmark and Ireland, but also perhaps of Norway and Scotland. However, although Kufic coins were imported into Norway during the early Viking Age,[17] spiral-rings are a rarity there, being present in only two hoards. In contrast, there are nineteen individual finds from Denmark, where Permian rings appear to have been sufficiently popular to have been copied.

[13] M. Archibald in *Viking Artefacts*, 120, and in British Museum '9th-Century Symposium' paper (January 1987).

[14] N. M. Lowick, 'The Kufic coins from Cuerdale', *BNJ* 46 (1976), 19–28.

[15] All coin-hoard dates throughout this paper are from M. Blackburn and H. Pagan, 'A revised check-list of coin hoards from the British Isles, *c*.500–1100' in M. A. S. Blackburn (ed.), *Anglo-Saxon Monetary History: Essays in Memory of R. H. M. Dolley* (Leicester, 1986), 291–313, where references for individual hoards may also be found.

[16] N. P. Brooks and J. A. Graham-Campbell, 'Reflections on the Viking-Age silver hoard from Croydon, Surrey' in *Anglo-Saxon Monetary History*, 91–110, with a discussion of spiral-rings on pp.95–6.

[17] K. Skaare, *Coins and Coinage in Viking-Age Norway* (Oslo, 1976), 47–53.

TABLE 1. *Hoards from Britain and Ireland containing Kufic coins (total: 20)*

Location	*Area*	*Deposition*
Croydon	SEE	*c.*872
Talnotrie	SWS	*c.*875?
Cuerdale	NWE	*c.*905
Drogheda	I	*c.*905
Harkirk	NWE	*c.*910
Dysart (no.4)	I	*c.*910
Co. Londonderry	I	*c.*910
Magheralagan	I	*c.*910?
Dean	NWE	*c.*910
Leggagh	I	*c.*915
Goldsborough	NEE	*c.*920
Bangor	NW	*c.*925
Bossall/Flaxton	NEE	*c.*925
Glasnevin	I	*c.*927
Dunmore Cave	I	*c.*928
Co. Kildare	I	*c.*935
Storr Rock (Skye)	WS	*c.*935
Skaill (Orkney)	NS	*c.*950
Co. Meath	I	*c.*970
Machrie (Islay)	WS	*c.*970

(ii) *Scandinavian.* The small number of standard Scandinavian neck-rings and arm-rings of plaited and twisted rods (Fig.4), together with a multitude of small fragments, might have had any origin and have travelled any route to become incorporated in the Cuerdale hoard. On the other hand, the rare 'ribbon bracelets' of very thin sheet metal with distinctive stamped ornament (Fig.5) are more common in Ireland than in Britain (Table 2), although one such represents the only surviving non-numismatic item from the kilogram of silver that constituted the Bossall/Flaxton (Yorks.) hoard, deposited *c.*925. Their origins have yet to be determined.

The four Hedeby coins represent the most obviously Danish material in Cuerdale,[18] but there is also a single fragment (Fig.6) of the Danish arm-ring type recognised by Mr John Sheehan as the prototype for the well-known Hiberno-Viking arm-ring series (Fig.7: to be mentioned below). One complete prototype ring is known from Ireland, suggestive of a western route into England; so too are a few fragments of Norwegian trefoil-headed pins for which Cuerdale again provides the unique British findspot, whilst a fragment may also now be recognized in Ireland, in the Dysart Island (no.4) hoard.[19]

(iii) *Pictish.* It is suggested that two objects might be the work of Pictish silversmiths and thus be derived from Viking activity in the north of Britain; both are fragments. One is an interlace ornamented strip with decorative parallels in

[18] See M. Dolley and T. Talvio in *NC*[7] 14 (1974), 190–2; and M. Archibald in *Hikuin* 11 (1985), 79–82. The fourth coin is adduced by Christopher Blunt from William Hardy's ms. list of the coins in the Duchy Office.

[19] J. Petersen, *Vikingetidens smykker* (Stavanger, 1928), 190–2, fig.236.

TABLE 2. *Hoards from Britain and Ireland containing 'ribbon bracelets'* (f = fragments; c = complete)

Location	*Deposition*	
Cuerdale	*c*.905	f
Dysart (no.4)	*c*.910	f
Bossall/Flaxton	*c*.925	c
Athlone	—	c
Hare Island	—	c
Liffeyside	—	c

the St Ninian's Isle (Shetland) hoard and the other is a unique comb fragment, with possible parallels in lost silver combs recorded in the Broch of Burgar (Orkney) hoard.[20]

(iv) *Anglo-Saxon.* Given that there are over 1,000 Anglo-Saxon coins in Cuerdale, it is striking that there are only two small pieces of 9th-century Trewhiddle-style metalwork from the hoard: one is a tiny fragment of a strip,[21] and the other a worn and thoroughly nicked strap-end.[22] It is probable that a fragmentary beaded circular mount is also of Anglo-Saxon workmanship;[23] its centrepiece, probably a coin (or imitation), has not been recognised in the hoard. These three items would seem likely to have been in circulation as bullion (Viking loot?) and so could well have become incorporated into the Cuerdale hoard independently of the Anglo-Saxon coins; they would certainly seem to have nothing to do with the fresh issues of Edward the Elder.

(v) *Carolingian.* There were also over 1,000 continental (Frankish and Italian) coins in Cuerdale, mainly from Melle, Limoges, and Le Mans of late 9th-century date, representing loot from the Loire valley in the mid-890s, with additions from slightly later raiding (*c*.902) in the Rhine-Maas delta; the former have been quite heavily pecked and thus in circulation. The same is certainly true of the three of four pieces of Carolingian ornamented metalwork in the hoard, comprising one or two fragments of filigree decorated equal-armed brooches, with a gilt belt-mount and buckle-loop (Fig.8)—the former has a broken suspension-loop and will have seen service as a pendant before being treated simply as a lump of bullion.[24] It is thus most unlikely that these few pieces derive from such an early 10th-century continental raid and they will have reached north-west England along with other bullion by an unknown route (which might even have included Scandinavia).

[20] J. A. Graham-Campbell, 'A lost Pictish treasure (and two Viking-age gold arm-rings) from the Broch of Burgar, Orkney', *Proc. Soc. Antiq. Scot.* 115 (1985), 241–61, at 251–2 and 253, illus. 3 and 5.

[21] *Op. cit.* in note 4.

[22] D. M. Wilson, *Anglo-Saxon Ornamental Metalwork, 700–1100, in the British Museum* (London, 1964), no.13.

[23] E.g. *ibid.*, no.64.

[24] The Carolingian silver fragments are to be discussed by Dr Egon Wamers of the Museum für Vor- u. Frühgeschichte, Frankfurt.

(vi) *Hiberno-Viking and Irish.* In contrast to the small number of the bits and pieces so far discussed, the major diagnostic component of the Cuerdale bullion consists of complete and fragmentary examples of broad band arm-rings (both plain and decorated) of the type that I suggested a decade ago were best described as 'Hiberno-Viking' (Fig.7).[25] Hiberno-Viking arm-rings have now been the subject of detailed analysis by Mr John Sheehan developing and refining my preliminary suggestions.[26]

A preliminary (guess) estimate is that some 25 per cent of the bullion comprises such Hiberno-Viking arm-ring material and some of the rings are complete, in fresh condition and without nicks, once again suggesting that they are amongst the most recent additions to the bullion stock. It should also be pointed out that they were made by hammering out standard cast bar ingots which might indicate a source in Ireland for many of these as well.

Sheehan has isolated a second type of 'Hiberno-Viking' ring, called by him the 'double armlet' of characteristically oval-sectioned rods. There are a minimum of seventeen on record from Ireland, including examples in five hoards (Table 3), in an overlapping distribution with the true Hiberno-Viking type; a few fragments have now been recognised in Cuerdale, again representing a unique British findspot.

TABLE 3. *Hoards from Britain and Ireland containing 'double armlets'*
(f = fragments; c = complete; H/V = Hiberno-Viking type also present)

Location	*Deposition*		
Cuerdale	*c*.905	f	H/V
Dysart (no.4)	*c*.910	f	H/V
N.W. Inishowen	—	c	H/V
Nr. Galway	—	c	—
Nr. Raphoe	—	c	H/V
Lough Derravaragh	—	c	H/V

Alongside the arm-ring material, there are three or four brooch fragments that represent Hiberno-Viking workmanship (Fig.9), but many more (perhaps forty in all) belong to the native Irish tradition, consisting also of fragments and representing for the most part the sequence of bossed (Fig.10) and early ball-type pennanulars (the latter being the solid 'thistle-brooch' variety: Fig.11).[27]

[25] J. A. Graham-Campbell, 'The Viking-Age silver hoards of Ireland', in B. Almqvist and D. Greene (eds.), *Proceedings of the Seventh Viking Congress* (Dublin, 1976), 39–74, at 51–3.

[26] I am most grateful to John Sheehan for providing me with a copy of his M.A. thesis, 'Viking Age silver arm-rings from Ireland' (University College Galway, 1985), which he is in process of revising for publication.

[27] J. A. Graham-Campbell, 'Bossed penannular brooches: a review of recent research', *Med. Archaeol.* 19 (1975), 33–47; and 'Some Viking-age penannular brooches from Scotland and the origins of the "thistle-brooch"', in A. O'Connor and D. V. Clarke (eds.), *From the Stone Age to the 'Forty-Five* (Edinburgh, 1983), 310–23.

Finally, much of the rest of the bullion is made up of complete and fragmentary examples of simple single rod arm-rings, of both circular and lozenge-shaped sections (Fig.12),[28] as are well-known in both Scandinavian and Insular Viking-Age contexts. Similar uncertainty must surround the origins of even such a diagnostically Scandinavian-type artefact as the intact Thor's hammer pendant which might as easily be a product of a Scandinavian settlement in the west as of the homelands.[29] This—and other such pieces of considerable interest in their own right—must await discussion in the main publication.

The conclusion is therefore that not less than 30 per cent of the Cuerdale bullion must have originated in Ireland, and probably also a considerable proportion of the 35 per cent ingot material (not forgetting, however, that the run of 'marks' is more likely to be from an Anglo-Saxon or Anglo-Scandinavian source). Much, if not all, of the remaining 35 per cent of ornaments and derived hack-silver may well have entered northern England at this period by way of Ireland. Such material is (so far at any rate) known only in north-east England from contexts 15–20 years later in date than Cuerdale, that is in the Goldsborough and Bossall/Flaxton hoards (Table 4).

TABLE 4. *Coin-dated hack-silver hoards (900–30) from Britain and Ireland*

Location	*Coins*	*Deposition*
Cuerdale, Lancs.	A/S,V,C,K,B	*c.*905
Harkirk, Lancs.	A/S,V,C,K	*c.*910
Dysart Island (no.4), Co. Westmeath	A/S,V,C,K	*c.*910
Magheralagan, Co. Down	K(+?)	*c.*910?
Goldsborough, Yorks.	A/S,V,K	*c.*920
Bossall/Flaxton, Yorks.	A/S,V,K	*c.*925
Bangor, Caer.	A/S,V,K	*c.*925
Dunmore Cave, Co. Kilkenny	A/S,V,K	*c.*928

It is self-evident that as there was no Irish, Scottish, or Manx coinage at the period this movement of silver into northern England from the west cannot be represented directly in the numismatic evidence, although it was suggested above that the Kufic coins might reflect this, at least in part. If the Cuerdale hoard as a whole was travelling westwards when deposited (see below), having perhaps been assembled in the north-east at York, as the large parcel of freshly-minted Northumbrian Viking coins might seem to indicate, then much of the bullion would have had to have been on a return journey. The fact is, however, that 75 per cent of the Cuerdale hoard by weight consists of bullion rather than coins and the problem remains, if this bullion had indeed reached York, why it had not been minted when York was so clearly operating a large-scale monetary economy at this very period (*c.*900/5).

[28] E.g. figs. 48–9 and 53–4 in E. Hawkins, 'An account of coins and treasure found in Cuerdale', *Archaeol. J.* 4 (1847), 111–130, 189–99.

[29] *Ibid.*, fig.85.

THE BONE PINS

The five bone pins were kept together in a local family until 1940 with a 19th-century label associating them with the Cuerdale hoard. Even if the contemporary sources are silent concerning this attribution, as noted above, the likelihood of their having derived from the hoard is increased by the apparent non-local origin of some at least of them.

Mr Ben Edwards has suggested that nos.1, 3, and 4 are Roman (Fig.13) and no.2 might be likewise.[30] He concluded that 'nowhere to the west of York' would have provided a source for them and thus, if they had been used to close

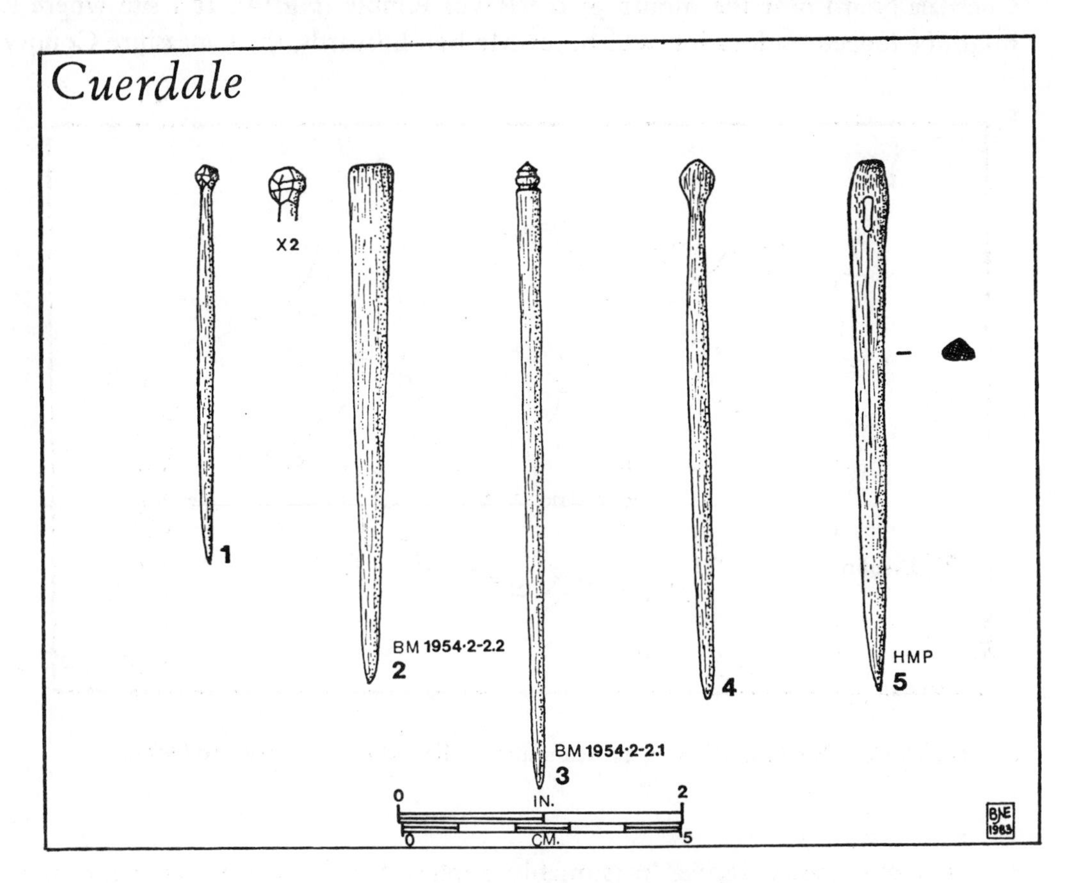

FIG.13. Bone pins from Cuerdale (¾).

moneybags, they provided evidence that the hoard was headed west. This conclusion need not of course apply to the entire hoard, but it was obviously necessary in the light of this important comment to seek the opinion of the Finds Research specialists of the York Archaeological Trust.[31] I am grateful for their view that no.3 is 'certainly Roman' and nos.1, 4, and 5 are 'probably Roman', with the additional information that 'Roman pins are commonly found as residual objects in Anglo-Scandinavian levels at York—they are tediously

[30] B. J. N. Edwards, 'Roman bone pins from the Cuerdale hoard', *Antiq. J.* 64 (1984), 365–6.

[31] I am most grateful to Dr Dominic Tweddle for his assistance in this matter (6.1.86).

durable'. 'No.2 is too simple to say anything—such things turn up both in Roman and Anglo-Scandinavian contexts.' It is in fact, from my own observations, very much lighter in colour than the others and might well therefore be attributed a younger age (i.e. freshly made, rather than a residual artefact, at the time of deposition).

LOCATION

There are several possible explanations to account for the general location of the Cuerdale hoard near the mouth of the River Ribble (Fig.14), at a site where it might be forded—a location which, for Mr Ben Edwards, the Lancashire County

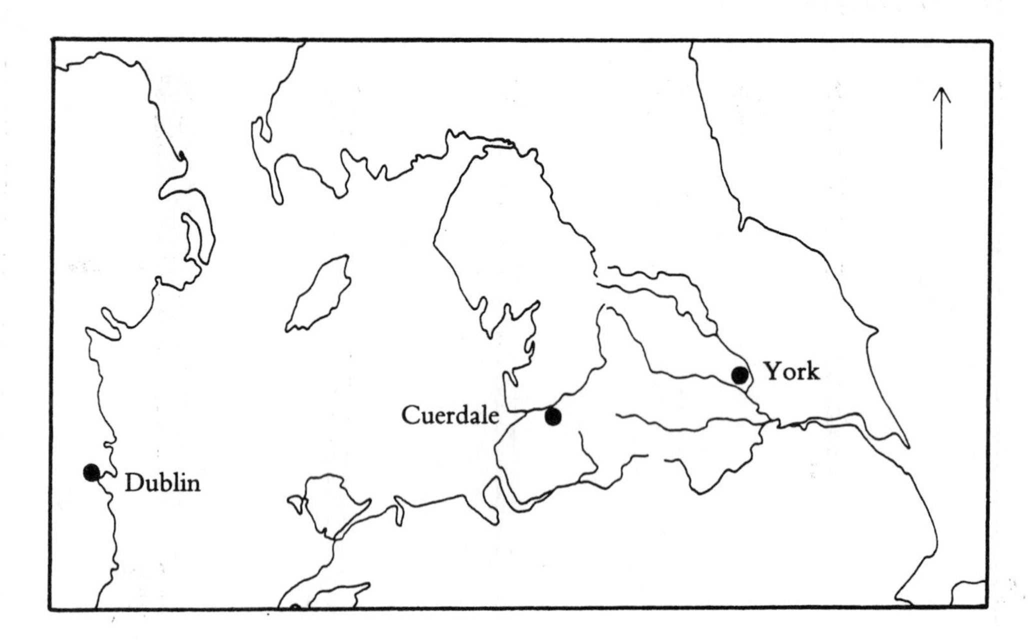

FIG.14. Cuerdale in relation to the Scandinavian Kingdoms of York and Dublin.

Archaeologist quoted above, 'presumably implies that the hoard was in transit at the time of deposition'.[32] Indeed, the first possibility—that this was the buried treasure of a local resident—would seem to be ruled out both by its exceptional size and by its specific place of concealment, at a river crossing.

The second possibility is in some ways related, in that it postulates the hoard's having been deposited not far from the place of its final assembly—that, in other words, it is a local hoard in the sense that its accumulation (as well as its burial) was concerned directly with local events, whatever the source(s) of its components.

Thirdly, the hoard may (in its entirety) have been travelling from west to east; or fourthly, from east to west (on the Dublin/York axis). The west/east

[32] *Op.cit.* in note 30, at 366.

explanation has been argued by myself in the past and found favour with Professor Michael Dolley; it appeared particularly attractive (given the nature of the bullion) whilst the deposition date was being suggested as '903 ± 2', given the expulsion of the Norse from Dublin in 902.[33] However, I now fully accept the strength of the numismatic arguments that such is highly improbable, at any rate for the whole hoard. Mr Christopher Blunt argued at the Symposium for the east/west theory, suggesting that the treasure was accumulated over a relatively short period and finally closed in York.

The fifth and sixth possibilities are that the hoard was travelling north/south or south/north. At a local level, the likelihood is that it was heading north for it was concealed in the south bank of the river presumably before crossing. As the Duchy of Lancaster's surveyor reported to the Inquest, 'there is a great extent of Rocks in the bed of the River opposite to the Hall & lower down great part of which are generally bare in the ordinary state of the River'. In fact the Roman crossing-point was a mile down-river at Walton-le-Dale, where the Ribble was still tidal at ordinary tides—the tide only occasionally reaching 'near the commencement of the Rocks & opposite to the stake where the Coins were found', according to the Duchy's surveyor again. However, a W/E or E/W direction (or combination) attracts more obvious attention than the N/S or S/N one, for the simple reason that, as Edwards has observed, 'the find-spot is precisely on the only probable route between the two Viking kingdoms of early tenth-century Britain, York and Dublin' (Fig.14).[34]

CONTEXT

The Ribble valley leads to the Aire Gap, dividing the Pennine dales to the north from the Pennine Moors to the south, through which one passes to descend to the Vale of York. It is the natural communication route through the Pennines and was the line followed by the Roman road. But in or about the year 905 we should not be talking of it literally as a route between the two Viking kingdoms of York and Dublin, for the Dublin Norse were temporarily dislodged in the period from 902 to about 917; the Cuerdale hoard cannot therefore have been in transit between the two.

'Viking' Dublin was, as it were, in abeyance and that there was a major interruption in its development is perhaps indicated by the fact that 10th-century Dublin flourished on a different site to that of the original *longphort* which had been established in 841. In fact Dr Patrick Wallace is of the recently expressed opinion that the resurgence or re-creation of Dublin 'may not have happened immediately after 917 but could have followed the 927 expulsion of the Irish-Norse from York, after which there was a flurry of Viking activity in Ireland'.[35]

It is therefore the events of the very beginning of the tenth century which

33 *Op.cit.* in note 25, at 54.

34 *Op.cit.* in note 30, at 366.

35 P. F. Wallace, 'The English presence in Viking Dublin', in *Anglo-Saxon Monetary History*, 201–21, at 203.

must provide us with an explanation for the particular nature of the Cuerdale hoard and the reasons for its deposition. There are three main factors to bear in mind:

(i) a background of Irish-Norse dynastic interest in York/Northumbria;
(ii) the expulsion by the Irish of the Norse from Dublin in 902;
(iii) the commencement of Irish-Norse settlement in the Wirral/Chester area and in the adjoining coastlands of Lancashire.

Following on from these factors, there might be added the determination to re-establish Norse power in Ireland (ultimately successful) which might provide the context for the deposition of two hoards in Ireland, both *c*.910, with some obvious similarities to Cuerdale (Table 4): the largely unknown coastal hoard from Magheralagan, near Downpatrick;[36] and, more clearly, the Dysart Island (no.4) hoard which in so many ways reflects Cuerdale in miniature.[37] To understand Dysart more fully may yet help to interpret Cuerdale.

CONCLUSION

My own hypothesis to account for the nature, location, and context of the Cuerdale hoard is that it was linked with some attempt to use the Ribble estuary, in an area of Scandinavian settlement, as a powerbase from which to reassert Norse control across the Irish Sea—its contents representing Irish-Norse exiled wealth, newly topped up with coins and ingots from supporters in the Kingdom of York. At the Symposium, this suggestion received particular support from Mr Nick Higham who will be arguing elsewhere that the Ribble estuary did indeed form a base for the more belligerent of the exiled Dublin Norse, with their probable headquarters at Preston.

This suggestion may at any rate serve to provide a new focus for discussion, but ultimately of course who buried the Cuerdale hoard, and why, will remain a mystery.

[36] C. S. Briggs and J. A. Graham-Campbell, 'A lost hoard of Viking-age silver from Magheralagan, County Down', *Ulster J. Archaeol.* 39 (1976), 20–4; and C. S. Briggs, 'The Magheralagan hoard: an additional note', *ibid.* 41 (1978), 102.

[37] *Op.cit.* in note 6, at 339ff.

Acknowledgement: Fig.1 is reproduced from *J. Brit. Archaeol. Assoc.* 8 (1852–3), pl.37. Fig.13 is reproduced from *Antiq. J.* 64 (1984), 366, with permission of the Society of Antiquaries of London and of B. J. N. Edwards. Fig.14 is by J. Lewis in *Lancs. Archaeol. J.* 2 (1982), 73. Figs.2–12 are from E. Hawkins in *Archaeol. J.* 4 (1847).

CVNNETTI reconsidered

IAN STEWART

IN 1957 Stewart Lyon and I read a paper to the Royal Numismatic Society on the *Cunnetti* and other Northumbrian coins from the Cuerdale hoard, which was subsequently published (1961) in the volume presented to Sir Frank Stenton for his eightieth birthday.[1] It astonishes me to find that thirty years have now elapsed since we did our basic work on the series and, although the analysis and the main conclusions have generally been found acceptable, it would indeed be surprising if there were nothing to correct, adjust, or add after such an interval. I therefore thought it might be opportune to take advantage of this symposium and its publication to record some of the points that have since emerged which would I think have caused us to express matters differently if we had been writing the paper today. In the first place, there is some new material, very little in fact, but not without its significance. Then there are the implications for the Cuerdale Northumbrian series of advances in our knowledge and understanding of certain related coinages. Finally, there are contributions by other writers which need to be taken into account.

Since 1961 many more specimens have been illustrated through the medium of the *Sylloge*, the Copenhagen, Yorkshire, and Merseyside volumes being particularly important. Two new hoards have contained examples of the coinage. The Norfolk hoard from Morley St. Peter[2] contained one *Cunnetti* and the Irish hoard from Dysart (Lough Ennell) had two *Cunnetti* coins, one Cnut coin of York, and two unidentified fragments of Northumbrian coinage.[3] By way of single finds, we can add one of *Alvaldus* from North Ferriby, Yorkshire,[4] a *Mirabilia Fecit* from Derby,[5] two *Cunnetti* coins from York[6] and another *Cunnetti* from Southoe in Huntingdonshire.[7]

So far as the origin of the coinage is concerned, some new but to my mind fanciful suggestions were put forward by the late Mr. F. (Monty) Banks and by Mr. Peter Seaby. I do not think that the attribution to York is now seriously

[1] *NC* 1958, proc., p.4; 'The Northumbrian Viking coins in the Cuerdale hoard', *Anglo-Saxon Coins*, ed. Dolley, 1961, pp.96–121. I am grateful to Mr. Lyon for comments on the present note, and for expressing his general approval of it.

[2] *SCBI* East Anglia 24.

[3] Ryan, M., *et al.*, 'Six silver finds of the Viking period from the vicinity of Lough Ennell, Co. Westmeath', *Peritia* 3 (1984), 334–81 (p.354).

[4] Blunt, C. E., 'Northumbrian coins in the name of Alwaldus', *BNJ* 55 (1985), 192–4. In addition to the examples of early loss of -th- (or -g-) from Aethel- (or Aegel-) cited by Mr. Blunt, ÆELRIC (Edmund, HTI; BMS 278) may be relevant.

[5] *SCBI* Midlands 116.

[6] *SCBI* Yorkshire 25 (Skeldergate); and Pirie, E. J. E., *Post-Roman Coins from York Excavations*, no.40 (Coppergate).

[7] *BNJ* 55, p.71, no.63.

contested.[8] In 1961 we suggested that the coins in the name of Cnut with the inscription QVENTOVICI emanated from the Frankish port of Quentovic, but this may not be right. Michael Dolley noticed that there were die-links involving the Cnut dies, suggesting that, unlike the circular inscription dies in the York series, the dies with the Quentovic inscription were the upper or reverse dies. In the light of this, and the fact that the *Qventovici* coins of Cnut are on the lower English weight standard, and not the heavier French one, there are grounds for thinking that they are in fact Danelaw imitations, as recently noted by Mr. Blackburn.[9]

The date we previously adopted for the burial of the hoard was *c*.903. During the last ten years Mr. Lyon and I have been doing detailed work on the coinage of Edward the Elder and on the contemporary Viking coinages respectively. For the purposes of classification of the coins of Edward, Mr. Lyon has identified three periods, Early, Middle, and Late, each divided into two phases. On the grounds that the latest English coins of the West Saxon and West Mercian series in the hoard are of the second phase of the Early period, Mr. Lyon now suggests that *c*.905 may be a better date for the hoard than *c*.903. Oddly enough, in the first section of the Morley St. Peter hoard the English coins run only to the first phase of the Early period of Edward, but in addition to the one *Cunnetti* coin there were some very early examples of the next York coinage which was in the name of St. Peter. We used to think that the use of the *Karolus* monogram on some of the coins of Cnut and in the St. Peter series constituted a link between the two. I now believe that the St. Peter coins with the monogram come at the very end of the swordless series, *c*.918, just before the arrival of Regnald at York, who also used the monogram on two his three types.[10]

We do not know whether the Northumbrian coinage of the Cuerdale types was complete by the time the hoard was put together. It is possible that it continued for a limited period thereafter. The only clues we have in this direction are the coins from other sources, which are remarkably few. But it may be significant that the single *Cunnetti* coin from Morley St. Peter reads CVII NET instead of the usual CVN NET TI. This blundering could suggest lateness, and it is noteworthy that the die does not appear to have been represented in the Cuerdale hoard (it is not in the British Museum Cuerdale series, which was carefully selected according to dies, nor does it seem to be recorded elsewhere). The Southoe *Cunnetti* also appears to be from non-Cuerdale dies. These coins could thus perhaps be survivors from a limited post-Cuerdale extension of the *Cunnetti* series, if there was one. A comparable consideration could apply to the single *Mirabilia Fecit* find from the excavation of St. Alkmund's church in Derby. The reverse die is slightly blundered (with reversed S) and again it was not represented in Cuerdale.

The personal names on this Northumbrian series have excited vigorous debate for a century and a half since the hoard was discovered. The one identification

[8] Banks, F., *The Problem of Cuerdale*; Seaby, P., 'Some Cuerdale queries', *Seaby's Coin & Medal Bulletin*, 1967, July, Aug., Sept.; disputed by Stewart, I., 'The early Viking coinage at York', *ibid.*, 1967, Dec.

[9] *MEC* I, p.322.

[10] Blunt, C. E., and Stewart, B. H. I. H., 'The coinage of Regnald I of York and the Bossall hoard', *NC* 1983, 146–63.

which has been universally accepted is that of *Siefredus*, or *Sievert*, on the coins with the Sigeferth who attacked the Devonshire coast *c*.894 and was described by Æthelweard as a 'pirate from the land of the Northumbrians'. He may have succeeded Guthfrith as king of the Northumbrian Danes *c*.895, and his coinage comes early in the Cuerdale series. It is difficult to recall these days that until the 1950s the Cuerdale coins in the name of Cnut were generally associated with Guthfrith on the entirely unfounded assumption that Cnut might have been an alternative or baptismal name for the historical Viking leader of whom no coins were known. Although Mr. Lyon and I were in no doubt that this association was untenable, if for no other reason because the Cnut coins were generally later than those of Siefred, it is none the less satisfactory to be able to point now to a coin from the recent Ashdon find with an inscription beginning GVDEF-, which appears to represent an issue, albeit from further south than Northumbria, in the name of Guthfrith.[11]

One of the problems considered in our 1961 paper was the relationship between Cnut and Siefred. Their coinage appears to have overlapped, and the extensive pattern of die-linking includes coins reading CNVT REX on one side and SIEFREDVS on the other. Without enthusiasm, we even considered the possibility that Cnut and Siefred might have been the same person. This hypothesis, never more than highly speculative, can now be definitively abandoned in the light of new evidence for the identification of Cnut himself. Dr. Smyth[12] has found references in later Norse literature to a Danish Knútr who fought battles north of Cleveland and near Scarborough *c*.900 and was killed at Dublin a few years later; and in this connection the late Dr. Georg Galster[13] noted that in 1085 Knud Svendson described himself as Cnuto Quartus which would imply another Danish king of this name, earlier than Cnut the Great and Harthacnut. It is unlikely that the coins combining the names of Cnut and Siefred are the result of an accidental mixture of dies, since of the four Siefred dies involved only one is known with the alternative pairing REX. Given that in the rest of the series the pairing of incompatible dies was carefully avoided, and in view of the number of dies involved, it is worth consideration whether these coins may have been issued jointly by the two rulers.

In working during recent years on the Anglo-Viking coinages of the 940s (which will be fully discussed in *Coinage in Tenth-Century England*[14]), I have been struck by the impossibility of arranging the coins of York of the two or three years up to the expulsion of the Viking rulers by Edmund in 944 without making the assumption that coins were being issued in the name of two or even three kings, Anlaf, Regnald, and Sitric, more or less concurrently. Kingship in the Viking world was based on the leadership of people rather than the control of specific territory, and even in an important centre such as York it does not seem to have been monarchical. At times there seems to have been more than one king

11 *MEC* I, p.319.

12 Smyth, A., *Scandinavian York and Dublin*, I (1975).

13 Galster, G., '"Cnut Rex" is Gorm the Old's Father', *Num. Circ.* 1978, 581–2.

14 Blunt, C. E., Stewart, B. H. I. H., and Lyon, C. S. S., in the press. See chapter 3 of this work for a reference, which we owe to Mr. Pagan, to a *Cunnetti* in a small find from Anglesey in the 1690s.

on the scene, and at other times perhaps none at all. The implications of this for the inscriptions on the coins were not fully taken into account in our 1961 paper.

Like other writers before us, Mr. Lyon and I devoted considerable space to the question of the meaning of the word *Cunnetti*, without coming up with a satisfactory solution. We noted that this inscription is only found with obverses in the name of Cnut, and suggested that since these coins are die-linked closely into types bearing the name of the city of York, it was most unlikely that *Cunnetti* could be the name of another mint. We also rejected the idea that it could be a moneyer's name, and wondered whether it was in some way connected with the name or title of the ruler. Having made no progress on that front after many years of reflection, I think it might be worth considering (although I suggest this with some hesitation) whether the word *Cunnetti* could be the name of another Viking leader, occurring on the other side of Cnut's coins in the way that Siefred's had sometimes done. In our 1961 paper Mr. Lyon and I speculated whether the name Cnut could have been Latinized as Hundeus, the Viking *dux* who sailed down the Seine in 896 and was baptized by Charles the Simple in the following year. However, one of the readings of this leader's name is *Hunedeus* and this opens up another possibility. Leaving off the Latin termination and taking D and E as the equivalent of T and I, which they so frequently are, we find a remarkable correlation between Hunede and *Cunnetti* (or Cuneti, since the duplication of the consonant can be ignored). The guttural sound represented by CH was sometimes in the Dark Ages indicated by the letter C or the letter H, but I must leave it to philologists to judge whether C and H could be regarded as interchangeable in this context. If so it would be possible to see

CVNETI
and HVNEDE

as different phonetic spellings of the same name. Hunedeus was presumably leader of the band of Norsemen who, after wintering by the Loire, harried parts of Aquitaine and Neustria in the spring of 898 and, although intercepted by the king's army, managed to get through to their fleet. It is certainly possible that substantial sums of silver found their way up the North Sea through his agency.

Alvaldus presents rather more problems. We pointed out that he is not styled *Rex* on his coins, and wondered whether he might be a moneyer. We thought his coins came too early in the series for him to be identified with the atheling Æthelwald, Alfred's nephew, who was received by the Danes at York after failing to obtain the West Saxon crown on Alfred's death in 899. At that time, we had not taken account of a mule coin with its obverse of the *Mirabilia Fecit* type and its reverse of the type used by *Alvaldus*.[15] Not only does this coin attach the *Alvaldus* coinage more closely to the rest of the Northumbrian series, but it also casts doubt on our argument that the *Alvaldus* coins are too early in date to be associated with Æthelwald. Mr. Blunt has recently argued that they should be attributed to this prince, and both Mr. Lyon and I are in agreement with him. Here again the attribution is easier to reconcile with the evidence if we are not constrained by supposing that the Viking leadership could only be held singly and consecutively by different rulers. The slightly later dating of the Cuerdale hoard

[15] *SCBI* Oxford 200.

also provides more flexibility in the relative chronology of the coins. Associating the *Alvaldus* coins with Æthelwald does not, however, explain the unresolved question about this issue, namely why only one coin is known from each of the dies involved, and how it came about that two of the five known specimens are from non-Cuerdale sources. Even the earliest of the Cuerdale groups include extensive die duplication, and no non-Cuerdale specimens at all appear to be recorded of most of the Cuerdale types (except the commonest). But whether they come early, mid-way or late in the Cuerdale series, the statistics of the *Alvaldus* coins are conspicuously different from those of all the other types, and in consequence difficult to explain.

From time to time it has been suggested that the Northumbrian coins in Cuerdale which carry the name of no personal ruler at all, but some combination of dies with DNS DS (O) REX, MIRABILIA FECIT, or a York mint signature, were to be seen as issued by the church, or for the archbishop. This idea was based partly on the fact that the archbishops of York had enjoyed minting rights under the old English kings of Northumbria, but partly also on the assumption that the York coinage in the name of St. Peter, which followed soon after the Cuerdale period, was an ecclesiastical issue. In my view that is not so. After the beginning of the tenth century there is a lack of references to individual rulers at York before Regnald and I would prefer to see the St. Peter coinage as a kind of municipal issue of the leaders of the Viking community at York, without any more religious connotation than many continental coinages of cities such as Tours (St. Martin) whose civic issues carried the name of the local patron saint. I do not therefore think that the St. Peter coinage is in this sense directly relevant to the question of the Cuerdale coins without a king's name. They are closely die-linked to the rest of the Northumbrian series, and I should prefer to look for other explanations for them. The less clear-cut a view we take of the nature of kingship at this time, the less it would seem to matter if some of the coins did not carry a ruler's name at all.[16]

Finally, there are one or two more general observations to make. In estimating the number of dies involved in the Northumbrian coinage from Cuerdale and multiplying this by a possible figure for average die-output, we were conscious of using a technique which apparently had not been applied before to estimation of the size of an issue of early medieval coinage. It is a technique which has been used extensively since, and I am glad that it has been, but I do not think it can be emphasized too often how fragile the assumptions may be on which the calculations are made. An average figure for die-output can conceal a very wide range of actual outputs, thus affecting the likelihood of individual dies being represented in a sample of surviving coins. Furthermore, there are few cases such as Cuerdale where we can be so sure that the circumstances of survival over the whole of the coinage concerned were similar, and we cannot assume that survival patterns, the physical capacity of dies, or the extent to which they were actually used, were consistent from one period or region to another. Nonetheless, our estimate that the Northumbrian coinage in Cuerdale may have been minted from

[16] Stewart, I., 'The Nelson Collection at Liverpool and some York questions', *BNJ* 52 (1982), pp.247–51.

between three and four tons of silver into between two and three million coins, still seems to me to be a useful and probably valid indicator of the scale of it. We do not know why the coinage was undertaken at all, but what made it possible after many years without a regular coinage at York must surely have been the booty obtained by Viking leaders such as Hunedeus. It seems to me likely that one of the purposes of the coinage may have been to distribute shares among the participants in such expeditions. How such a large portion of it ended up as part of the great treasure hidden near the bank of the River Ribble we shall never know. One can only imagine that those who brought it found themselves unable to carry it across the river, but were in some need of continuing their journey without delay. There must have been several of them to travel with such a heavy and valuable treasure, and it is a melancholy thought that none of them can have survived to repossess it or even to have passed on word of it to heirs or comrades who might have done so. Such enormous riches would hardly have been abandoned without exceptional efforts at recovery unless it became impossible for their owners to return to the location, because it was occupied by their enemies, or because they all perished soon after the treasure had been buried.

DISCUSSION

DR METCALF: The original calculations of the scale of the Northumbrian Viking coinage, published as long ago as 1961, were made on the basis of obverse dies, and a multiplier of 10,000 as the average output of a die. It is worth studying a parallel set of figures for reverse dies, for two reasons. First, the reverse die is the one that wears out, whereas the life of an obverse die is fairly elastic. Estimates of the scale of other Anglo-Saxon issues since 1961 have regularly been based on reverse dies, as the more reliable indicator, and on the conventional (and perhaps conservative) multiplier of 10,000. For comparability, therefore, it might be helpful to do the same for Northumbria. Secondly, comparing both sets of figures draws attention to the ratio in which dies were used. For the earlier Anglo-Viking varieties struck at York, this was close to one-to-one, but for the later varieties it was higher. It is, I think, clear that there was a distinct change in mint-practice at an intermediate date.

Where the numbers of obverse and reverse dies recorded for a variety are approximately equal, as they are for many of the (scarce) early varieties, the die-ratio will also, within the limit of accuracy set by the sample size, obviously also be approximately one-to-one. One has to say approximately, because the numbers are small. In variety Ia, for example, 7 coins were examined by Lyon and Stewart, and found to be from 5 obverse and 5 reverse dies. When the numbers are consistently close to parity for a succession of varieties, however, there will be a presumption that one-to-one was the normal practice of the mint.

Where there are twice as many reverse as obverse dies recorded, it does not follow, statistically, that the ratio was two-to-one. If the sample were a random sample, it would be very much higher than two-to-one. It is far from random, as Stewart and Lyon made clear. They included in their survey the coins in the British Museum, the Merseyside County Museums, the Fitzwilliam Museum, the Assheton cabinet (over 150 specimens), and at least three other collections. 'As our study progressed', they wrote, 'it became apparent that the British Museum had chosen its selection of coins from the hoard with great care, so as to include every possible variety. This has meant that relatively few new dies have been recorded from other collections, except in the case of the "Cunnetti" series . . . We therefore have considerable confidence in the survival rates of obverse dies which are shown in the table . . .'

Let us consider the 52 specimens of varieties Ip and Is (EC–1/CR–G), among which 25 obverse dies and about 50 reverse dies were noted. What sort of original totals of dies does this imply? Even in a random sample, 25 obverses among 52 specimens would point to a fairly complete coverage; but 50 reverses among 52 would imply a huge original total. The sample is, however, only partly random as regards reverse dies. *BMC* includes 22 specimens which were no doubt carefully chosen, but the other 30 probably approximate to a random sample from what was left over. One could make calculations on the assumption that the whole sample was random, and then end by suggesting that the truth lay somewhere in between the conflicting results. A better method, available since 1982, is to draw on the Liverpool *Sylloge*, which includes the large collection formed by Dr Philip Nelson. He bought Cuerdale material avidly, and certainly did not reject duplicates. Where *BMC* has 22 specimens, Nelson had 26, which are from 15 obverse and 23 reverse dies. One may reasonably assume that they, at any rate, are more or less a random sample. If one applies the formula (made familiar by Stewart Lyon) which states that

$$\frac{\text{non-singletons}}{\text{sample}} \doteqdot \frac{\text{output of known dies}}{\text{total output}}$$

the result would be

$$\frac{16}{26} \doteqdot \frac{15}{c.25 \text{ obverse dies}}$$

but

$$\frac{8}{26} \doteqdot \frac{22}{c.70 \text{ reverse dies}}$$

This is distinctly higher than the number of reverse dies actually noted by Lyon and Stewart and suggests a die-ratio approaching three-to-one.

If we look at the even more plentiful varieties IIb and IIe (C–1/CR–G), of which Lyon and Stewart examined 220 specimens and recorded 111 obverse and *c*.200 reverse dies, the Nelson collection contains 100 specimens, from 66 obverse and 88 reverse dies. There are 59 obverse non-singletons and 20 reverse non-singletons, implying original totals (if the Nelson sample is random) of 111 obverse dies (by a coincidence, again exactly the figure reached by Lyon and Stewart) and 440 reverse dies—a ratio of four-to-one.

Lyon and Stewart's total of 250 obverse dies for the Northumbrian series as represented in Cuerdale may be accepted with considerable confidence. Their suggestion that 'the number of reverse dies may be half as much again' seems to lack statistical support. A total of 700 to 750 would be a better guess. Using the conventional multiplier of 10,000, this yields a coinage of 7–7.5 million coins, or nine to ten tonnes of coinage silver.

Survival-rates calculated from estimated numbers of obverse dies are obviously a false guide to the chronology of the series, which would seem to have had a fairly uniform survival-rate for early and late varieties.

An independent approach to the chronology of the varieites is seemingly afforded by the study of pecking—a topic which Miss Archibald has explored in a lecture to the Royal Numismatic Society in May 1986. She showed clearly that the older coins in the Cuerdale hoard were much more heavily pecked (thus matching the findings of Brita Malmer in her study of the Swedish Viking-age hoards); but she entered the caveat that one could not be sure, in the case of East Anglian, southern English, or Carolingian coins, of the region in which the pecking had taken place.It is very unlikely that more than a handful of the Northumbrian coins in Cuerdale had ever been in circulation in a zone outside Northumbria where pecking was practised. If they are pecked, it is to be presumed that they were pecked while in use in Northumbria. This sounds as though it might provide interesting evidence that the new Viking pennies had actually passed from hand to hand, in York or elsewhere, before being hoarded, and lost at Cuerdale.

Although there is evidence which can be read as a 'gradient' in the degree of pecking according to age, in the Cuerdale hoard as a whole, the evidence for a 'gradient' within the Northumbrian series is debateable. From the sample of specimens in the British Museum and the Ashmolean Museum one can see a sharp contrast in the proportions of coins that are pecked, from one variety to another. Some varieties are heavily pecked, others are hardly at all; and the heavily pecked varieties are the older varieties. Half or more of the specimens with two-line reverses are pecked (notably MF/DDOR), and this proportion extends to reverse design B (cross on steps—somewhat resembling a two-line type). Designs C and D are occasionally pecked, G very rarely. This is, numerically, not so much a gradient as a discontinuity, and although it can be interpreted in terms of chronology, another interpretation is preferable, namely that users were suspicious of two-line types. Whether the pecking took place north of the Humber, or elsewhere in the northern Danelaw, is by no means certain. The evidence proves, I think, that some people looked carefully at the coins they were offered in payments, and tested varieties of unfamiliar or suspect design. So although no-one will doubt that the reverse designs A-D are the earlier part of the Northumbrian series, pecking does not after all provide unambiguous evidence in support of the detailed chronology.

The main point is, however, made quite convincingly by the changeover to a higher die-ratio. The number of reverse dies used in the earlier phase would seem to have been very roughly 120, and in the later phase, equally approximately, 600. This could be because the later phase was of much longer duration, but in the light of the increased die-ratio the correct interpretation is almost certainly that the rate of production of coinage accelerated greatly. A sudden accession of wealth in York is, from the numismatic evidence, a distinct possibility. Why, in these circumstances, several different obverse designs should have been used in parallel with each other remains puzzling. All one can say is that the parallelism seems to antedate the moment when production accelerated,—and that it survived in the new circumstances.

MR LYON: When I did the die-analysis for our paper in *Anglo-Saxon Coins* I was, of course, not then thinking of statistical estimators, and so the information that Ian and I published about numbers of dies was not as complete as it could have been. My analysis covered the British Museum, Nelson, Assheton, Fitzwilliam, and a parcel of coins held at that time by Baldwin's. There is a good case now for extending it to cover the other SCBI volumes, not to mention completing it for the named collections so far as the common types are concerned.

Dr Metcalf suggests that the Nelson collection can be treated as a more or less random sample, but I think this could be a dangerous assumption. Here, for example, is how the number of coins, known dies and singleton dies develops as one adds further collections, one by one, to the BM collection for two groups of the less numerous types, one an obverse group and the other a reverse group. Halfpence have been excluded.

Collection	*Coins*	*New dies*	*Singleton dies*
A. Obverses S, DDR, and MF			
British Mus.	62	35	23
Nelson	51	3	+ 3 -12
Assheton	37	2	+ 2 - 2
Fitzwilliam	7	0	0
Baldwin	27	0	- 2
Total	184	40	12
B. Reverses other than CR			
British Mus.	61	55	50
Nelson	45	13	+11 -19
Assheton	36	6	+ 6 -10
Fitzwilliam	5	0	- 5
Baldwin	18	0	- 5
Total	165	75	34

N.B. The Baldwin analysis in Table B is incomplete, because for some reason that I cannot now remember I did not record their coins with EC obverses. They might have had another half dozen specimens, but I doubt whether they would significantly have altered the total number of dies. Perhaps the number of singleton dies would have fallen by two, say.

Given that virtually all other coins of this series came from the Cuerdale hoard and that the British Museum, as is apparent from these tables, chose die varieties with great care, the addition of other sylloge material would be unlikely to add greatly to the total number of dies, but it would doubtless reduce the total of singletons. Thus the ratios of singletons to sample size in Tables A and B are 7% and 20% respectively; with the inclusion of Oxford and Copenhagen another 68 coins would be added to Table A and 70 to Table B; even with no reduction in singletons the ratios would fall to 5% and 15%. I therefore suspect that the application of my formula to the enhanced material, assuming equal output, would result in an estimate of about 45 for the total of S, DDR, and MF obverse dies and 90-95 for the total of reverse dies other than CR. Although the two groups of material do not precisely correspond (because about 25% of the coins in Table B have EC obverses), nevertheless it would seem reasonable to conclude that the normal ratio of reverse to obverse dies was two to one. Without detailed analysis I would be reluctant to accept a higher ratio for the more common issues, and I therefore think that an estimate of 700-750 reverse dies for the total coinage is too high in relation to an estimate of 250 obverses.

One must not forget, of course, that the coinage may have continued for a time after the hoard was assembled. There is no way in which such continuation can be quantified, but one suspects that it is small in relation to the issues we know.

Two curious coins of Alfred

C. E. BLUNT

[PLATE 23]

I AM diffident about writing on the two coins that form the subject of this note because I can, in one case, offer only a very tentative solution to the problems it presents, and in the other none at all. My reason for doing so, however, is to bring to notice two interesting pieces that have been neglected, in the hope that a reader of this note may be able to help in their explanation.

Both are pennies of Alfred's two-line type bearing his name; both are in the British Museum, and both were found in the Cuerdale hoard. The first is of *BMC* type xiv:

Obv. +EL FR ED RE legend divided into four segments; cross in centre.

Rev. EDELS̄R.| · | GELDA in two lines with a single pellet between them.

BMC 309, directly from the Cuerdale hoard. Wt 1·39 g/21·4 gr., pecked **(pl. 23, 1)**

This is the only specimen known.

Though listed by Hawkins in his report on the Cuerdale hoard,[1] this is done without comment. It is left to Daniel Haigh, publishing in 1870, to look at the problem. He writes: 'The reverse legend is remarkable. The hyphen over the S, and the dot after the R, seem to be marks of abbreviation of the name and title of Ethelstan. *Gelda* may be the name of a mint, Geldestone in Norfolk, or it may be a Latinized form of the English word *geld*, "payment"; as in *Edelstani regis gelda*, "payment" or "tribute of King Ethelstan"'. Can this, he ends, 'be a part of the treasure bestowed upon him on the occasion of his baptism?'[2] Subsequent writers appear to have ignored the coin. In the British Museum *Catalogue* the reverse is recorded as reading 'Edelstan and Gelda' without comment, implying that they are regarded as the names of two moneyers.

Professor Whitelock, with whom I had correspondence about this coin in 1957, wrote: 'The trouble about Gelda, as it strikes me, is that if Old English, it could only be a genitive plural, in the sense of payment, compensation. Whereas it is the nominative singular of the agent noun 'one who pays', 'one who worships', and (later on) a 'Guildsman'. I should think it more likely to be a personal name, perhaps a short form from names like Geldwine, than a word meaning compensation. I don't think a Latinized *Geldum* occurs until much later in England & one wouldn't expect to have a plural. If it were a personal name, could it be a moneyer on the same side as Ethels(tani) R(egis), which seems a probable reading seeing that the obverse is occupied by King Alfred?'[3]

[1] *NC* 5 (1843), 16.

[2] *NC*[2] 10 (1870), 33–4.

[3] D. Whitelock in personal correspondence.

I have been fortunate enough more recently to have been in touch with Professor H. R. Loyn, Dr S. D. Keynes, and Mr M. Blackburn all of whom have given me advice on some of the problems posed by this peculiar coin. This is reflected in what I am now writing, but they must not be held responsible for any of the conclusions that I have drawn.

Three possible explanations have been offered in the past:

1 That *Gelda* is a mint-name
2 That it is a personal name or by-name
3 That it is in some way indicating a payment

To take these points in that order. A mint-name on a two-line coin of Alfred would, save for some of the coins of Canterbury, be sufficiently improbable as to enable it to be ruled out. In any case Geldestone is unlikely to have had a mint. It is not, apparently, mentioned in Domesday Book.

It could be a personal name such as Geldwine. By-names and double names are occasionally found on coins in the Anglo-Saxon period, but only later. It would be unique in Alfred's time; and Geldwine is a rare name. This possible explanation, particularly in view of Professor Whitelock's instinct that it is likely to be a personal name, must mean that it is one that should certainly not be ignored.

This leave the third option and it appears that this is the one that holds the best possibility of success. Professor Whitelock has pointed out that *gelda* is a genitive plural of a word meaning payment of tribute. If the first part of the reverse legend is expanded to *Ethelstani Regis* (as both Haigh and Whitelock suggest) could the whole be interpreted 'of the payments of King Athelstan'? An alternative suggested to me by Professor Loyn, is to interpret *gelda* simply as 'one who pays' on analogy with 'gafolgelda' one who pays *gafol* on tribute or rent. In either case, who would Athelstan be? The strongest possibility is Guthrum, the Viking ruler who, after his defeat at the battle of Edington in 878, was baptized and adopted the name of Athelstan at a ceremony at which Alfred stood sponsor. He struck coins in his own name of Alfredian type, presumably in East Anglia. There is a die-link between a coin in his name and one in the name of Alfred[4] which must mean that they come from a mint that produced coin in the name of both kings. Guthrum-Athelstan died in 890. Mr Blackburn, who has made a special study of this two-line issue in connection with the report he is making on the Ashdon hoard, has identified the *gelda* coin as the product of an East Anglian mint.

So far we go along with Haigh, but we must part company with him when he suggests that this might be a payment connected with Guthrum's baptism. This took place in 878 and it was not until some years later, perhaps not till 886, that Alfred introduced his two-line type. We have no record of any payment by Athelstan to Alfred, but we could easily imagine circumstances in which one might be made.

This then is, I would tentatively suggest on the evidence available, the most acceptable of the three alternative explanations that have been offered. And it is perhaps worth remembering, when considering the question, those curious eleemosynary pieces of Alfred, *BMC* 158–9.

[4] *BNJ* 27 (1952–4), 56–7.

Of the second coin, of which four specimens are known, Hawkins lists three from Cuerdale. The fourth also claims this provenance which may well be correct. They may be described as follows:

1 *Obv*. +ÆL FRE DRE legend divided into three segments, cross in centre.

Rev. two lines of mysterious writing, a cross at top and bottom, three crosses between.

(a) *BMC* 453 direct from the Cuerdale hoard. Wt 1·45 g/22·3 gr.

(b) Fitzwilliam Museum, Cambridge ex Ryan (1952) 723 there said to be from Cuerdale but no intervening collections mentioned. Wt 1·48 g/22·9 gr. Ill. *MEC* vol. 1, p. 60, 1382.

(c) Blunt, ex Lockett (1955) 498, ex Bliss (1916) 85, ex Rashleigh (1909) 226, ex Bergne (1873) 165, ex Cuerdale. Wt *c*. 1·52 g/23½ gr. **(pl. 23, 2)**

These three are from the same dies.

2 *Obv*. +EL+ FRE DRE type as last but die differs.

Rev. similar to the last but the die differs.

(a) Merseyside Museum *SCBI* 145, ex Nelson (1953), ex Seaby (1946), ex Grantley (1944) 1024, ex Murdoch (1903) 91, ex Montagu (1895) 571, ex Shepherd (1885) 78, ex Murchison (1866) 201, ex Cuff (1854) 466, ex Cuerdale. Wt 1·14 g/17·6 gr. **(pl. 23, 3)**

In this case again it is the reverse that presents problems. Even Haigh is defeated. In his paper published in 1870 he writes: 'The reverse legend is in characters which have hitherto eluded all attempts to explain them'.[5] Only two writers have, as far as I have been able to trace, attempted an explanation. One is Lord Grantley who, writing in 1911, read the legend as A Omega R and on the second line SSC. This he 'diffidently' suggested might be expanded to AUR[UM] S[EPULCHRI] S[ANCTI] C[UDBERTI] and he adds 'that these coins may have been struck by the episcopal authorities either at York or Chester-le-Street'. He supports this by reference to the enquiry under Edward I which confirmed that the bishops of Durham 'had enjoyed all royal privileges from the time of the conquest of England and before'.[6] This suggestion has not found favour.

The other writer was a parson in the neighbourhood of Cuerdale, the Revd Dr Whitaker of Blackburn who read a paper to the Numismatic Society on Jan 23, 1845, 'in which he endeavoured to prove that they [the Cunnetti coins] were minted by a Spanish Jew, named Cortena, whose name Dr Whitaker considered to be given on the obverse of the Cunnetti coins...and in Hebrew characters on the reverse of a penny of Alfred'.[7] The editors of the *Numismatic Chronicle* appear to have decided, no doubt wisely, not to publish this paper.

The engraving of the characters on the reverse is well executed and looks deliberate. The weights of three specimens are normal; the fourth though light is not unacceptably so.

5 *NC*[2] 10 (1870), 34.

6 *BNJ* 8, (1911), 52–3.

7 *Proc. Num. Soc.* 1844–5, p. 5.

The fact that there are two reverse dies suggests that the 'writing' is intentional and therefore should be susceptible to interpretation. But I fear that I have no explanation to offer; there is even doubt as to which way up it should be. The writer would welcome suggestions.

DISCUSSION

Dr Metcalf: Nos. 2 and 3 couple perfectly literate obverses with reverses in which it is momentarily tempting to see an example of some outlandish or unknown script. One thinks of the very curious letters on coins of Charlemagne from Melle, which write METOLO with an ampersand supplemented, apparently, by Tironian notes. The shape of the O on these coins is a little like the fifth letter on these reverses. But another possibility is that the die-cutter is so illiterate that he is not even schooled in the basic shapes of the letters of the Roman alphabet. One could imagine A[ ]R/S[ ]C. An A in which the limbs cross, and an R which shares a curved member (for the main down-stroke) with the very curious second letter is the work of a very unlettered hand indeed. Perhaps it is worth distinguishing between ignorance and rough workmanship,—which do not have to go hand in hand. The range of punches with which the dies are sunk is very limited, much use being made of a simple cresecent-shaped punch. On coin no. 2, one suspects that the same punch has been used eight or nine times. Yet the letter C is carefully seriffed on both 2 and 3, and the crosses and (particularly on no. 3) the grained border are of quite acceptable workmanship. The reliance on a crescent-shaped punch offers some encouragement to read the first letter as an A. One could point to a somewhat similar crescent-barred A in lieu of a chevron-barred A on a few erratic St Edmund Memorial pennies. Similarly if the three crescents of the second letter could be reinterpreted as straight strokes, one might see an E. The inscription as a whole ought to represent a moneyer's name; but whichever way round one looks at it, it is not possible to detect the abbreviation MO. Nor can the second line be construed as any obvious second element of an OE name. The extreme similarity of the two reverse dies is among our best clues. It certainly implies very careful copying—almost, one might say, an atttempt at facsimile, and this in itself is perhaps an argument that the die-cutter was illiterate: if he had thought he knew what the signs stood for, he would have had much less reason to reproduce them so exactly. But it is difficult to say whether both dies were copied from the same (manuscript?) model, or whether one was simply copied from the other.

PLATE 23

A topographical commentary on the coin finds from ninth-century Northumbria (*c.* 780–*c.* 870)

D. M. METCALF

TOPOGRAPHICAL patterns and details among the coin finds from ninth-century Northumbria[1] suggest various ideas about monetary circulation within the kingdom. It is worthwhile to formulate those ideas as explicitly as possible, if only to assess how far they are beset by the pitfalls of negative evidence and lack of evidence. The last decade has seen an explosion of information south of the Humber in relation to single finds of eighth and ninth-century coins, in particular the little eighth-century sceattas, which match the Northumbrian ninth-century stycas in size. This explosion results partly from an increased interest among archaeologists in the excavation of middle Saxon sites, but even more from the activity of metal-detector enthusiasts and—equally important—the cooperation and good will of dealers and museum staff in encouraging the proper recording of their finds. Metal detectors have become a major means of recovery of stray losses of stycas within the Northumbrian kingdom. The coins are if anything even more difficult to find by eye than sceattas, because their debased alloy ensures that they are dull in colour. The number of sites from which single finds of stycas have been recorded remains very much smaller than the number of sites yielding sceattas south of the Humber, and one is left wondering whether this situation could be transformed dramatically in the next ten years as the picture south of the Humber has been changed in the last ten years, or whether it reflects a genuine difference in the circumstances of monetary circulation. Carlisle, for example, was virtually a blank on the map of styca finds until 1977, there being only two coins, of Eanred and of Æthelred's first reign, found in a tumulus 'near Carlisle' in September 1876 and donated to Trinity College Cambridge in that same year.[2] Since 1977 single

Acknowledgements. I am grateful to Martin Biddle, James Booth, Marilyn Brown, Stewart Lyon, and Liz Pirie, who read an earlier draft of this article and kindly pointed out a number of corrections and improvements.

[1] This commentary relies heavily on the inventory in Pirie, 1986b and on supplementary material which Miss Pirie has collected and has generously placed at my disposal prior to publication. For the avoidance of confusion, one may mention that the résumé of the Sancton finds in Pirie 1986b omits one coin of Eanbald published by Booth and Blowers, 1983, and referred to below. Information about finds for which no authority is offered in the text below will be found in Miss Pirie's inventories.

[2] *SCBI Cambridge* 282 and 310 = P. Grierson and M. A. S. Blackburn, *Medieval European Coinage*, vol. 1, Cambridge, 1986, nos. 1202 and 1223.

finds of stycas have been recovered from four different sites in the modern city—yielding 3, 2, 4, and 6 coins respectively. This is much weightier evidence for a monetary economy in Carlisle than if 15 coins had been found on one site—and, obviously, far weightier than if a hoard of 15 coins had been discovered, for that would have ranked as one find, with attendant uncertainty whether it had been concealed by a traveller arriving in Carlisle. These finds of the last ten years are entirely new evidence for monetary history, and must cause us to think carefully not only about Carlisle in the ninth century, but about other finds which we may now wish to reconsider in the light of the stycas, for example the late-eighth century Beneventan gold tremissis found 'near Carlisle', and the hitherto improbable-seeming discovery of a unique sceat of *c.* 720–30 at or near Carlisle.[3]

Carlisle is not the only place where what might have been read as negative evidence has suddenly become, or is about to become, very positive. Whithorn, even further to the west, began to yield stycas from excavations in 1984, and the 1986 campaign produced a large crop.[4] We now have a sceat of Eadberht, an East Anglian penny of Beonna, and 15 stycas, of which 13 are of Eanred. This is a chronologically most unusual pattern in comparison with major sites in the east, where the coins of Æthelred II and later are heavily predominant, and one wonders whether the availability of coin at Whithorn dwindled dramatically in the decades immediately following the disappearance of the see. The Whithorn finds are from midden material, which makes it rather more difficult to suppose that the finds are atypical for the site. Bamburgh yielded 67 stycas from the season of excavations of the castle in 1971. It is only recently that a summary listing of them has appeared, to supplement the one coin recorded in 1894 that was hitherto our only clue to the use of coinage at the Bernician royal residence. Further substantial quantities of stycas from the excavations at Bamburgh since 1971 await the numismatist's eye. It should need no pointing out that, provided they can be fully published, they will stand as a major source of evidence for monetary circulation in ninth-century Northumbria, complementing in certain respects what the hoards can tell us.

Forty or more stycas have been found, one by one, on a prolific site about half-way between York and Hull, again since 1979. They were placed on record by Booth and Blowers in 1983, and the site identified as Sancton. The finders have been much less than candid, and the careful rescuing of so much information is something of a triumph. Another batch of coins has come, more recently, from Barmby Moor, not far away. It plants some seeds of doubt whether the earlier series of finds may not also have come from there, or whether (as is of course quite possible) there are two rich sites quite close to each other.[5] In any case we now have from the Vale of York, for the first time, a series of stray finds large enough to give a reliable impression of the pattern of losses, and of the monetary circulation that lay behind it.

[3] D. M. Metcalf, 'Some finds of medieval coins from Scotland and the north of England', *BNJ* 30 (1960–1), 80–123, nos. 81–2.

[4] I am indebted to Marilyn Brown for preliminary information about the finds from the 1986 season at Whithorn.

[5] On the reliability of the Barmby Moor find-spot, I am indebted to advice from Mr David Feather. For the finds, see M. A. S. Blackburn and M. J. Bonser, 'Single finds of Anglo-Saxon and Norman coins—3', *BNJ* 56 (1986), forthcoming.

Here and there, excavations of middle Saxon habitation sites seem to be producing stycas, at least in ones and twos, and it is necessary to understand (with the benefit of southern experience at sites like Barham in Suffolk or Royston, Herts.[6]) that the total number of finds from a site may depend very much on the effort put into searching for them, and that disparities between one site and another are not necessarily a reflection of genuine differences in the intensity of monetary activity. One is on much safer ground in making comparisons within the finds from a single site, e.g. between numbers of early and late losses, but even there, there is a serious difficulty in that coins with a lower purchasing power may be expected to have a much higher loss rate, and we do not know whether debasement was accompanied by inflation.

Because numerical comparisons between sites are almost worthless as evidence, keener interest will attach to finding reliable clues, in the topographical patterns and details, to the character and intensity of monetary circulation. If stycas turn up in remote and unexpected places, the argument will be, 'by how much the more are they not likely to have been in use in busy places from which, by chance, we have no information'. One may cite as examples Malham Moor, Gateshead Moor, 'a haugh of the River Jed' near Jedburgh, or—most strikingly—the excavation of the high moorland farmstead of Ribblehead, in North Yorkshire. Here, two coins were found in the wall core of the end wall of the farmhouse, another lying on an end wall kerb stone (these three within 1·2 m of each other), and a fourth on the paving immediately outside. They provoked thorough discussion among the excavators, who were satisfied that they were not a disturbed hoard. They may date the building of the farmhouse (possibly post-867).[7]

This argument *Quo magis* applies to stray losses but not to hoards, for which an out-of-the-way place of concealment may well have been deliberately chosen.

Should we not assume that our knowledge of stray losses is likely to be still very incomplete, and possibly misleading? And if that is so, ought we not to proceed with great caution in drawing conclusions from the finds that are known to us? In particular, when we look at the distribution pattern, we ought frequently to remind ourselves that each dot on the map is not necessarily of the same evidential value; and blank spaces could be very misleading indeed.

Even if the distribution pattern were fair, representative, and free from pitfalls, it would still be a mistake to equate the absence of stray finds with the absence of a circulating medium. One would be correct, in those very theoretical conditions, to deduce that monetary exchanges were much less frequent: a relative difference. But the ratio of losses to transactions may well have been extremely small, and the ratio of coins found to coins still in the ground may be equally small. When Benedict Biscop was setting off on a book-buying spree, with what did he fill his purse?

[6] For the rich series of finds from Royston, see Blackburn and Bonser, loc. cit.

[7] A. King, 'Gauber high pasture, Ribblehead —an interim report', in *Viking Age York and the North*, ed. R. A. Hall, 1978, 21–6; *Medieval Archaeology* 19 (1975), 230 (a coin naming Odilo). The location is SD 771785, on the north-east flank of Ingleborough.

THE FINDS AS EVIDENCE FOR THE SCALE OF THE LOCAL CURRENCY

With that caveat, the main outlines of a distribution map appear to be something like a ladder of which the legs are the coastal plains to the east and west of the Pennines, and the rungs are the trans-Pennine routes. Thus, there is a concentration of finds (and especially of hoards) in York itself, and to a lesser extent in the Vale of York; finds suggestive of coast-wise access up the east coast, from Whitby to Bamburgh and beyond; to the west of the Pennines, finds from a variety of coastal sites in the Irish Sea coastlands, from Meols and Otterspool northwards, as far as Whithorn and Luce Bay, and beyond, shading off into grave-finds in Viking burials in Arran and Colonsay; and then there are finds which hint at the routes by which traffic crossed the Pennines to reach the newer Anglian territories—by the Tyne valley to Hexham and from there, perhaps, towards the mining areas from where, almost certainly, the zinc came for the coinage,[8] and so across to Carlisle—or by Airedale to Malham and Settle, and thence to Lancaster and Heysham, Grange-over-Sands and Cartmel. To see a pattern resembling a ladder in the finds is of course only a way of imposing order on isolated fragments of information as an aid to thinking about them. It must have more contact with reality than ploughs or bears in the sky, but it is merely a construction, not a fact. To sketch such a geographical framework already implies, one may say, quite a positive answer to the question, how widespread the circulation of coinage was in ninth-century Northumbria. But, as we have seen, even the framework is beset by comparative uncertainties and the problems of negative evidence. Was the currency to the west of the Pennines, and in the Irish Sea coastlands, to any degree comparable with that in the plain of York? Similarly, was coinage used in other than minor quantities in Bernicia north of the Tyne—always excluding one or two coastal localities, specifically Bamburgh, where the excavations reveal a concentrated use? In other words, were the regional economies of Strathclyde, Bernicia, and Deira radically different from each other—with whatever political repercussions such differences might have had? These questions, which are the sort of questions we need to be asking if we are to make the step from numismatics to monetary history, are inescapably quantitative. We cannot manage without speculating about comparisons between the *numbers* of coins in use in different parts of Northumbria.

Our attempts to frame answers to such questions, or more exactly to find evidence which would have a bearing on them, can usefully begin with the observation that the Northumbrian coinage was struck on a large scale and that it has had a very uneven survival-rate. From the reign of Alchred through to an intermediate date in Eanred's reign the survival-rate has been extremely low. Something of the order of 500 dies were used, for example, for the 'animal' coins of Alchred, Æthelred, and Ælfwald, implying the possibility of something like 5 million coins, of which only the merest handful are known today: one coin in

[8] Estimates of the total amount of zinc used can be obtained through estimates of the original numbers of dies, taken in combination with analytical results.

perhaps 150,000 has survived.[9] In complete contrast the coins of Æthelred II and his successors have had an exceptionally high survival-rate because so many large hoards of them were concealed probably in the face of the Viking threat in the 860s. The survival-rate is probably one coin in about five hundred, out of a total currency which, until the time of Redwulf, may have been of a similar size to that of the later eighth century.[10] In answer to the question, how widespread was the currency, then, we are entitled to make the preliminary point that there was a great deal of coinage in existence, and that while much of it may have been concentrated in the coffers of a few, it changed hands freely enough to become quite thoroughly mingled in circulation, at least by the mid-ninth century.

One very useful technique for studying the ways in which coin moved about is unfortunately not available to us for Northumbria. South of the Humber in the pre-Viking age one can identify the products of several mints and, by plotting the distances that stray finds had travelled from their mint of origin before they were lost, one can attempt a regional analysis of the overall mingling of the currency from different sources. In Northumbria it seems that no similar exercise will be possible, because all or virtually all the coins emanated from the one mint-town of York. (Or, if this view should one day be superseded, surely they all emanated from east of the Pennines. Intensive die-linking, which is such a well-known feature of the styca series, puts severe obstacles in the way of any theory that there was more than one important mint.) Thus, the detailed composition of the find-assemblages from west of the Pennines is unlikely to offer any clues to the relative scale of the currencies in the eastern and western regions. Of course, one's prior expectation, based on a wider perspective of British medieval monetary history, will be that until the dramatic rise to importance of the mint of Chester, beginning very early in the tenth century,[11] the north-west was the back of beyond in terms of commercial and monetary matters.

THE HUMBER ESTUARY AS THE MAIN GATEWAY FOR INTER-REGIONAL TRADE

Basing our judgement again on the wider perspective, we can point with some confidence to the main route of entry of the eighth-century monetary economy north of the Humber: it was the estuary of the Humber itself. The contrast between the coin finds from North Ferriby and from York gives a clue. North Ferriby is unusual in that it is a site which has yielded predominantly primary- and intermediate-phase sceattas (from *c.* 700 onwards).[12]

There are southern sceattas from York, of intermediate and secondary date, but until very recently there were not many, whereas there were numerous finds of

[9] D. M. Metcalf, 'Estimation of the volume of the Northumbrian coinage, *c.* 738–88', in *Sceattas in England and on the Continent*, ed. D. Hill and D. M. Metcalf, Oxford, 1984, pp. 113–16.

[10] Estimates can be derived from the catalogue in Pagan, 1973.

[11] Or perhaps even the late ninth century. See D. M. Metcalf, 'The monetary history of England in the tenth century viewed in the perspective of the eleventh century', in *Anglo-Saxon Monetary History*, ed. M. A. S. Blackburn, Leicester, 1986, pp. 133–57, at pp. 142 f.

[12] E. J. E. Pirie, 'Some Northumbrian finds of sceattas', in *Sceattas in England and on the Continent*, ed. D. Hill and D. M. Metcalf, Oxford, 1984, pp. 207–15, at pp. 208 f.

Northumbrian sceattas, distributed widely through York, from the reign of Eadberht or later.[13] Thus the contrast between North Ferriby and York suggested that trade was reaching the Humber estuary already in the first quarter of the eighth century, and that monetary exchanges were conducted at a market at or near the coast (as they were at coastal *wics* in southern England), but that the market-place was soon moved up the Ouse to York itself—possibly first at Fishergate—and a little later received a decisive impetus through some royal initiative, with which was linked the minting of coins locally from *c.* 740.[14] Recent excavations in Fishergate have brought to light rubbish pits which have so far yielded five or six 'porcupine' sceattas,[15] and it looks as if the site will in due course impose as substantial a reassessment of Northumbrian monetary history as the recent finds from Carlisle. 'Porcupines' are arguably from the area of the Rhine mouths, and if it turns out that they are plentiful among the coins from the site between Blue Bridge Lane, the River Foss, and Fishergate, one will be strongly tempted to conclude that here, rather than in Skeldergate, lay the *vicus Frisonum*. The close dating of the 'porcupines' from Fishergate will have to be judged when it is known exactly which varieties they were, but in any case they almost certainly antedate Eadberht's coinage. It seems that trade and the use of coinage may have gained a first foothold at York in the southern *suburbium*, where maritime shipping would approach the city. This offers an apparent contrast with Hamwic where so far there is no reason to believe that the early finds or the Frisian finds of coins are in any way topographically restricted.

The first stirrings of the Scottish medieval monetary economy, stimulated by maritime trade with England, offer such intriguing parallels with the situation of Northumbria four hundred years previously as to excuse another digression. King David began to strike a national coinage to take the place of incoming English money, and at more or less the same date, in the foundation charter which he granted to Holyrood Abbey, we see him providing the canons with, among other things, a cash income derived from the receipts of the east-coast trade. In the first instance he gives them income in kind from lands and rents and rights and tithes, and the free taking of timber, and oil from stranded whales, and so forth; and then he goes on to give them, apparently, also a cash income: 'forty shillings from my burgh of Edinburgh yearly; and a rent of a hundred shillings yearly for the clothing of the canons, from my cain of Perth, and this from the first ships that come to Perth for the sake of trade; and if it happens that they do not come, I grant to the aforesaid Church, from my seat of Edinburgh forty shillings, and from Stirling twenty shillings, and from Perth forty shillings'. Further, the canons are freed from

[13] S. E. Rigold and D. M. Metcalf, 'A revised check-list of English finds of sceattas', ibid., pp. 245–68, at p. 267, listing 23 single finds, of which 16 are of Eadberht or later.

[14] D. M. Metcalf, 'Monetary circulation in southern England in the first half of the eighth century', ibid., pp. 27–69, at p. 68. One should mention two problematic harbingers, namely the 'York' thrymsas and the early sceattas of King Aldfrith of Northumbria. Two of the latter were among the Whitby finds—which of course included a range of pre-Eadberhtian sceattas; but Whitby is on the coast.

[15] R. Kemp, 'Pit your "wics", or how to excavate Anglian York', *Interim* 11/3 (autumn 1986), 8–16.

tolls and customs 'on all things that they buy and sell.'[16]

In the early monetary history of Northumbria, it is tempting to see some similar ingredients, particularly trade with the south as the first motor of the monetary economy, and a notable concentration of monetary exchanges at a few royally-supported monastic sites, including cathedral communities. Can one doubt that the rich series of coin finds from Whitby, 'the mausoleum of the Deiran kings', are in some sense the result of maritime trade with south-eastern England and the lower Rhinelands? (There is even a pair of die-linked sceattas, one found in Whitby and the other in Canterbury.[17])

The virtual absence of 'foreign' coins in Northumbria after the decline of the southern sceattas in the mid-eighth century is not to be taken as a sign of isolation, but rather as evidence that from the time of Eadberht onwards the currency was strictly controlled, and that foreign money was required to be reminted. This became the normal practice south of the Humber at about the same date, and makes it quite surprising that stycas should occur as stray losses in Lincolnshire and East Anglia. Until the late 1970s hardly any such finds from south of the Humber were known, and it was not unreasonable to treat the authenticity (as finds) of the few that were with some reserve. Dolley could write in 1966 '...they do not overlap the silver hoards... The currency of the *styca* must have been purely domestic and confined to the kingdom of Northumbria'. This assessment has been placed in doubt by a surprising number of metal-detector finds in the last ten years, the authenticity of which cannot in general be doubted. There are also a few coins from controlled excavations. At Brandon, the odd styca can hardly be other than an early loss; and if one of the Thetford finds is from an eleventh-century rubbish-pit, it is nevertheless almost certainly the redeposition of a coin lost in the ninth century. The intrinsic value of the stycas was low in relation to southern pennies: even the best of Eanred's coins are rarely better than 20 per cent silver. When they were, moreover, so different in size and thickness from silver pennies, it is difficult to envisage that they could gain monetary acceptance when there was no royal guarantee to back them. Whether or not such coins were in use as money when they were lost is therefore a puzzling question, but they certainly occur as stray losses. Nor are they confined to the coastal ports, although one notes recent metal-detector finds from the hinterlands of Grimsby, Lowestoft, Ipswich, and even Chichester, Sussex. Perhaps they were well enough known in Lincolnshire and East Anglia to be used as, for example, farthings. Stycas occur, of course, in Deira south of the line of the Humber, having been found at sites near Pontefract,[18] Doncaster, and Sheffield, and also at Castleton in the Peak District.

In spite of the known presence of Frisian merchants in York, stycas are absent from the prolific site of Domburg. At Dorestad one coin of Eadberht and either two or three stycas are recorded: these are by no means insignificant among the smaller total of coins found there. Their evidence is reinforced by a find from

[16] G. Donaldson, *Scottish Historical Documents*, 1970, pp. 20–3.

[17] Rigold and Metcalf, loc. cit. (note 13 above), at pp. 249 (Canterbury VIII) and 265 (Whitby XIII).

[18] Wentbridge. See M. A. S. Blackburn and M. J. Bonser, 'Single finds of Anglo-Saxon and Norman coins—2', *BNJ* 55 (1985), 55–78, at 72f. (two coins, nos. 68 and 69).

Schouwen, and another from as far down the Rhine as Mainz. The Dorestad stycas in particular, from a foreign commercial site, again raise the question of the acceptability of debased coins outside their official circulation-area. It also makes one wonder whether Northumbria may not have exported brass to the Low Countries. It is unthinkable that brass was produced in Northumbria solely for use as coinage, and the industry may well have had a longer history than the coins reveal. (One would like to know what metal Edwin's public drinking cups were made of.[19])

In the other direction there are eight or nine separate finds of 'foreign' coins which had escaped the melting-pot in Northumbria—an unexpectedly high proportion of the finds, particularly in York itself. Several of them may have been lost after 867, when English royal control of the currency was no longer effective, and they may exaggerate the impression that foreign coins were plentiful. Of only one of the coins can we assert that it was very probably a pre-867 loss, although several others also could well be. The earliest is a pre-reform coin of Charlemagne, found at Sancton, probably from a Rhinelands mint.[20] The excavations at York Minster in 1970–1 yielded a West Saxon penny of King Ecgbeorht (802–39), very probably an early loss, and also a denier of Charles the Bald (840–77) minted at Quentovic. From elsewhere in York there are a penny of Æthelwulf (839–58) of a type antedating the reform of *c.* 855, and therefore again quite probably a pre-867 loss, a penny of Æthelberht (858–65) from Fishergate, and pennies of Burgred of Mercia from Aldwark and from Skeldergate.[21] An obole of Charles the Bald of the Palace mint, from Coppergate, was minted after 864, and the chances must be, therefore, that it reached York after 867. This merely tends to show, however, (as some of the other finds may also show, if they are in fact post-867) that the lower Rhinelands link survived the Viking occupation of York. Of the two hoards from Coney Street, York in 1760, one consisted of about a hundred silver coins, described only very vaguely as English, but among which were said to be a few *Christiana Religio* (temple-type Carolingian) deniers of Lothaire.

On the grounds that they read LOTHARIVS REX (or HLOTHARIVS REX?) rather than LOTHARIVS IMP, they must be assumed to have been coins of Lothaire II (855–69), and therefore candidates for loss at the time of the capture of York or later. They may well be from the lower Rhinelands, and are more likely to be from the beginning than the end of Lothaire's reign. The name Lothaire was of interest to the eighteenth-century antiquary who noted it because he thought the coins might be attributed to a king of Kent.[22]

[19] Bede, II, xvi, 'aereos'.

[20] Booth and Blowers, 1983, no. 1. Conventionally attributed to Mainz, but in *Hamburger Beiträge zur Numismatik* 18/19 (1964/65), 13–20 I argued for a Rhine-mouths location, possibly Domburg.

[21] E. J. E. Pirie, *Post-Roman Coins from York Excavations 1971–81* (The Archaeology of York, vol. 18/1), 1986, nos. 37–9.

[22] D. M. Metcalf, 'Find-records of medieval coins from Gough's Camden's *Britannia*', *NC*[6] 17 (1957), 181–207, at pp. 199ff. Cf. K. F. Morrison and H. Grunthal, *Carolingian Coinage*, New York, 1967, no. 1190. One should consider carefully the advocacy in M. Dolley, 'New light on the pre-1760 Coney Street (York) find of coins of the Duurstede mint', *Jaarboek voor Munt- en Penningkunde* 52/53 (1965/6), 1–7, suggesting that the whole hoard was Carolingian, on the (persuasive) grounds that an eighteenth-century antiquary could not have failed to recognize the names of con-

All these finds from York, of both Carolingian and southern English silver, are of course a reflection of the intensity of archaeological excavation there, and are not necessarily good evidence that York was dramatically different from the rest of Northumbria in this respect. It is the ratio of 'foreign' coins to stycas among the single finds *from York* that offers valid evidence.

Perhaps the most intriguing Carolingian find from Northumbria, just because it is not from York, is a coin in the name of Lothaire I (840–55, but possibly later?) naming Dorestad as its mint. It was found in Attermire Cave, Settle—the source also of a sceat and five stycas. The cave is about 2 km east of Settle, high above Ribblesdale and remote from any settlement.

Another foreign find which is likely to have entered Northumbria by way of the Humber estuary is the penny of Beonna from Whithorn.[23]

A fragment of a XPISTIANA RELIGIO denier in the Talnotry hoard, from near Newton Stewart in Galloway, may on the other hand have travelled from the Carolingian Empire to Northumbria via Scandinavia, for it was found together with fragmentary dirhams.[24]

Lebecq, in his two-volume monograph *Marchands et navigateurs frisons du haut moyen âge*, generalizes the archaeological and historical evidence for Frisian links with Northumbria so far as to suggest that Yorkshire was the main sphere of Frisian activity in England. He analyses the story of the Frisian student Liudger who had to flee from York in 773 with all the Frisian merchants, in order to escape a vendetta after a young Northumbrian of noble family was killed in a brawl; he mentions Alcuin's reference in *c.* 800 to 'the boats of the Frisians' plying between Yorkshire and the Rhine mouths; and he draws attention to Alcuin's sending 100 pounds of (?) tin (*stagnum*) to Archbishop Eanbald II '*ut domuncula cloccarum stagno tegatur*'. He refers also to the finds of Carolingian coins and of Tating and Pingsdorf ware, and sums up: 'c'est surtout sur les rivages de la Humber et dans le Northumberland [*scilicet* Northumbria] que, grâce à l'archéologie, on a le plus sûrement reconnu la trace des Frisons... c'est avec ces contrées—actuel Yorkshire—que les marchands/navigateurs frisons du haut moyen âge paraissent avoir entretenu les rapports les plus constants, en Angleterre du moins; et que trouverait du même coup expliquée l'extraordinaire réussite des missions northumbriennes en Frise.'[25]

---

temporary English kings such as Ceolwulf, Beornwulf, Ludica, Wiglaf, or Berhtwulf with a shout of triumph. His argument rests to some extent on his prior identification of Carolingian candidates for the hoard-provenance in the Eyre and Banks collections. As the record is totally silent about the attribution of the alleged English coins, it may be that the writer had not set eyes on any of them and I am inclined to think that, on balance, it is speculative to disregard our sources. If all the hoard *had* been Carolingian, we might have looked for more specimens to have survived from eighteenth-century collections. Also, Dolley minimized the significance of REX versus IMP.

[23] It is close in date to the denier of Charlemagne from Sancton. Both could have entered Northumbria at moments when the mint was inactive.

[24] *SCBI Edinburgh* 695 and, for the scrappy character of the hoard, ibid., pp. xii f.

[25] S. Lebecq, *Marchands et navigateurs frisons du haut moyen âge*, Lille, 1983, p. 109.

MINSTER SITES, CHURCHYARD SITES, AND GRAVE-FINDS

To return to the comparison with the charter of Holyrood Abbey: as regards finds in Northumbria on monastic and other church sites, such a high proportion of the known find-spots fall into the category that one needs to consider carefully, and in detail, what the significance of such a pattern might be. Whithorn (monastic buildings, west of the medieval church) and Dacre (excavations of the monastic site)[26] are the most remote examples, and therefore the most cogent. The Coldingham find is also geographically so isolated that its association in some sense with the monastery will seem probable, even if it was found more than a mile to the south of its site. Hartlepool (Church Close) has produced sceattas of Eadberht from a monastic site. For the styca series, the most obvious localities to mention are Whitby, Lindisfarne, Jarrow, Monkwearmouth, and Tynemouth. Single finds are alleged to have come from Hexham churchyard, but there is only the slenderest evidence to support this assertion, made after the discovery of the large hoard there. One might add to the list finds from the York Minster excavations, from Beverley (minster collegiate buildings), and from Ripon ('Scots monastery'). R. B. K. Stevenson suggested that Paisley and Jedburgh may likewise have had an ecclesiastical background, although the evidence is tenuous.[27] Should one add Carlisle?—do the coins found there reflect its location close to the Solway Firth, or the power of the church in the city?

Although our knowledge of ninth-century minsters is probably very incomplete, some coin finds from the proximity of churches seem hardly to fall into the minster category. Kirkbymoorside (churchyard) and Wharram Priory (chancel area of church) may be examples. The Lancaster parish church find hints at a building of more substantial scale than a domestic habitation site: 'to the north side of the nave, the remains of a wall about three feet wide running north. A few feet to the east of it a fireplace was found, with a flue or drain below, running north and south. Close to the wall about twenty stycas were picked up, also a copper coin of Diocletian'.[28] The wall, etc., might of course be later in date by several centuries than the coins. The Hexham hoard is a somewhat uncertain addition: it was concealed after the see was transferred, and was found very close to what was, apparently, the north-west corner of a pre-Norman north transept or linking structure, buried just below the then ground level (but seven or eight feet deep in 1832). The find barm was made while digging a grave for William Errington. When the grave was re-opened in 1841 for the burial of his nephew, some 50 more coins were recovered, undoubtedly from the same original concealment.[29]

Slightly later hoards of the debased silver of Burgred and Alfred continue the churchyard theme (e.g. Gainford, co. Durham, from an excavation 'outside the

[26] R. H. Leech, 'Excavations at Dacre, 1982–4: an interim report', *Trans. of the Cumberland and Westmorland Antiq. and Archaeol. Soc.* 85 (1985), 87–93.

[27] In *SCBI Edinburgh*, p. xii.

[28] *Historic Society of Lancs. and Cheshire* 1914, 271 and cf. Pirie, 1986, inv. no. 99.

[29] R. N. Bailey, 'The Anglo-Saxon metalwork from Hexham', in *Saint Wilfred at Hexham*, ed. D. P. Kirby, 1974, pp. 141–67, at 141–3 gives a thorough account of the discovery and the site, and clarifies the 1841 find. In modern terms, the area was known as Campey Hill, in reference to a mound, since levelled. It was a modern extension, and not previously part, of the churchyard.

church').[30] The Heworth churchyard find is *not* to be added to the above list, as it is a case of nineteenth-century fraud.

Churchyard finds are not necessarily grave-finds. The latter, of which there are a few supposed instances, raise problems in the context of Christian burial. In southern England there is a well-documented series of tenth-century grave-finds in which sums of money were placed beneath the skull. They can best be interpreted on the conjecture that they are burials of Danish settlers, among whom pagan religious beliefs persisted. Similarly in Northumbria there should be a presumption that grave-finds of stycas are post-867 deposits until proved otherwise. Unless such coins have been meticulously excavated, there will often be a degree of uncertainty as to whether they were genuinely grave-goods, or merely residual, e.g. from the back-filling of a grave. There are finds from Wharram Percy, Monkwearmouth, and Whitby ('site two', a burial-ground south-east of the Abbey). At Rudston, a styca of Eanred was found in a rabbit-scrape in a sand-pit which had previously produced Anglo-Saxon inhumations.

Several of the York, Coppergate finds which were later in date than a burned surface dated archaeomagnetically to 860 ± 20 and tentatively associated with the events of 867, include one coin from above a burial. Whether or not it was residual, these finds again raise the question whether stycas may not have continued to be used in York until *c.* 895.[31]

The Ripon finds are a good illustration of the difficulties of disentangling the categories of minster finds, churchyard finds, and grave finds. They are associated more or less closely with Ailcy Hill, which lies about 200 m east of Ripon Minster. It is a mound some 25 m high, and is essentially a natural feature, the sides and summit of which were used as a cemetery in the Anglo-Saxon period.[32] (It may, however, have been so used because it was believed to be an ancient burial mound. The same may be true of the tumulus find near Carlisle, mentioned above.) The Ailcy Hill find of 1695, which has been shown to contain upwards of 137 stycas terminating with Osberht,[33] was evidently a hoard of some size, and may have been concealed in hallowed ground for extra security. Other finds from the centre of Ripon have been described (perhaps with the earlier hoard in mind) as from 'near Ailcy Hill' or 'in the Minster Yard'. A small hoard was described in 1846, and there were apparently some stray finds later in the nineteenth century to the north of Ailcy Hill, possibly from the site of the ninth-century 'Scots Monastery'. Recent archaeological excavations of Ailcy Hill have revealed a number of burials, not all of the same date, but they have not added to the numismatic material.

The lack of proper contextual evidence fortunately detracts very little from the general argument of a correlation between styca finds and minster sites: it is enough, for example, that coins were found in the centre of Ripon on several different occasions.

[30] *NC* NS 4 (1864), 225.

[31] R. A. Hall, 'Numismatic finds from 16–22 Coppergate. Archaeological aspects', in Pirie 1986a, pp. 16 f.

[32] R. Hall and M. Whyman, 'Ripon yarns… getting to the root of the problem', *Interim* 11/4 (winter 1986/7, 29–37); id., 'Ailcy Hill, Ripon', *Bulletin of the CBA Churches Committee* 24 (1986), 17–20.

[33] E. J. E. Pirie, 'The Ripon hoard, 1695; contemporary and current interest', *BNJ* 52 (1982), 84–103.

There is a double reason for thinking that the 'monastic' distribution to which the finds point is a real one, and not merely a misleading effect of patchy evidence. If we compare the pattern of sceatta finds south of the Humber, at a time when the list of finds was much shorter than it is now—say, by reference to C. H. V. Sutherland's list of 1942[34] (before metal detectors were in use)—there is no comparable emphasis on ecclesiastical sites. In his list, there are relatively far more finds from the open countryside. The flow of finds of the last ten years or so in the south has made the contrast even sharper. Although it is virtually impossible to guess at all the factors which lie behind coin losses, we can perhaps discount many of them by making this comparison between north and south. Secondly, and encouragingly, one can detect some sort of transition between north and south. As sceatta finds thin out northwards into the north midlands, there seems to be a growing concentration on ecclesiastical sites, e.g. Repton, Breedon-on-the-Hill, and Southwell,[35] which adumbrates the Northumbrian pattern.

Another worth-while comparison is with the prevalence of finds of Roman coins in Northumbria. On extensively excavated Roman sites, one might have expected to encounter the occasional ninth-century coin as a stray loss. This seems not to happen, and it probably amounts to useful negative evidence for Bernicia. In Deira there has been more random prospecting, again with mainly negative results as regards stycas.

Can we, then, take the find-assemblage more or less at its face value, and draw from it the conclusion that in ninth-century Northumbria the use of coinage was significantly concentrated at ecclesiastical sites? Is this the way that a money economy was 'seeded' at the outer limits of a rather marginal circulation-area—like tufts of marram-grass advancing against the sand? If so, what sort of a system would be implied? Would coinage have been used mainly for a specialized range of commodities of interest to religious communities, a money economy restricted to a long-distance 'luxury' trade, coexisting with a non-monetized economy for the ordinary rural population? Is there a parallel with the canons of Holyrood, freed from tolls and customs on all the things that they bought and sold? Have we at last found a real-life situation to which the 'model' that sees the early middle ages sunk in a barter economy—so often defended in the teeth of numismatic evidence—actually applies? It is difficult, as always, to envisage how in Northumbria such payments for 'luxuries' could be balanced, for cash had to accrue to the monastic communities before they could spend it. Charitable giving by the local population is presumably ruled out by the model. Even if we were to postulate an annual income by royal deed as at Holyrood, and thus a transfer from one part of the kingdom to another (a practice for which there is no supporting evidence) it would still be necessary to suppose that the king was able to collect cash through tolls and taxes, imposed on a 'normal' monetary economy somewhere within Northumbria.

Could we, alternatively, think of monasteries serving as safe meeting-places or markets, where ordinary people met to trade with each other? The practice of

[34] *NC*[6] 2 (1942), 42–70.

[35] Metcalf, loc. cit. (note 14 above), Figs. 1–3 and ibid., pp. 245 ff.

hospitality, and the lack of any other suitable places for merchants to stay, may have led monastic communities into fulfilling a social function not particularly of their choosing—in the same way that social pressures lay behind a secular style of monastic life that Bede disliked. The major houses, and in particular the community of St. Cuthbert, held wide estates, which must have given rise to some administrative arrangements for their management.

If trade is the explanation we should prefer, the number of coins recovered from a minster site might then be expected, pitfalls apart, to be a measure more of the regional or locational importance of the market, than of the size or wealth of the religious community. (But a connexion between these two may not be fortuitous. One recalls Rosemary Cramp's detailed exposition of the way in which the monasteries 'preside over the major river mouths and the natural anchorages and harbours, and also along the lengths of the more open river valleys'.[36]) Whitby is the prime example for the monetary historian, and it is deeply disappointing that the archaeological opportunity to gather secure information on the topography of coin losses within the site was squandered and indeed destroyed for ever, when the contexts of the 127 stycas from the excavations of the 1920s were so inadequately recorded.

We ought, finally, to make allowance for the degree to which archaeological effort has been concentrated on the more famous monastic sites. Again, Rosemary Cramp's survey of settlement[37] offers a reminder of how much remains unexplored.

FINDS FROM REMOTE PLACES AND FROM HABITATION SITES

If accidental losses were in proportion to the number of transactions (as one would expect them to be), the concentration of stray finds at minster markets might well give a false impression of the spread of ownership of cash, and particular interest would attach to even very limited evidence of finds from remote places (this argument has already been touched on) or from settlement sites. One recalls the find of an eighth-century sceat in the hinterland of Whitby, on Westerdale Moor, 'remote from any known track'.[38]

In southern England many sceatta finds, it is clear, come from what were in the eighth century ploughed fields on which domestic rubbish was spread as manure. Coins accidentally lost in a domestic setting were carted out with the rubbish, to be found, we must suppose, some distance away. Herein lies the distinctive archaeological value of finds by metal-detector enthusiasts, many or even most of whose eighth-century finds are not from 'sites' at all. There is as yet little or no evidence in this category from Northumbria. In assessing the very small number of stycas from habitation sites, we should remember that in southern England sceattas are not plentiful on habitation sites either, but that this is not because coinage was not in use in villages.

[36] R. Cramp, 'Anglo-Saxon settlement', in *Settlement in North Britain 1000 BC–AD 1000. Papers Presented to George Jobey*, ed. J. C. Chapman and H. C. Mytam (B.A.R. 118), Oxford, 1983, pp. 263–97, at pp. 278–9.

[37] ibid.

[38] *Yorks.Arch.Jl.* 41 (1966), 566–7.

FINDS FROM MOUNDS AND HILL-TOP SITES

The use of Ailcy Hill as a cemetery perhaps because it was believed to be an ancient burial mound has been mentioned, along with the finds from a tumulus near Carlisle. A penchant for hill-top sites is further illustrated by the stycas from Castle Head, Grange, and Castle Hill, Castleton. Two more examples from South Yorkshire have been tentatively interpreted by Dolby, in a careful study of their topography, as being in the context of a defensive system overlooking the Don and Dearne valleys, in the borders between Northumbria and Mercia. Moses Seat, North and South Anston, (SK 5425 8205) is a prominent hill-top on Lindrick Common; and Pot Ridings Wood, where three stycas were found scattered over a distance of about 25 m, was possibly the site of a defensive enclosure which gave rise to the nearby field-name of Castle Hill.

THE PATTERN OF EARLY LOSSES

Because the wider geographical distribution-patterns may be misleading, because the total number of sites that have yielded stycas is still small, and because there are so few losses that can be associated with habitation sites, the most secure procedure to follow, in attempting to reach conclusions about monetary circulation and the uses of coinage, would seem to be one that relies, essentially, on comparisons and contrasts within individual sites.

By taking a combined view of all these within-site comparisons, one can perhaps arrive at an impression of how the losses of early stycas compare topographically with losses of the later, very debased issues. The method is at best impressionistic, and relies on having at least a few sites, such as Sancton, from which there are a good number of single finds, to serve as a yardstick. (This is part of the potential of the Bamburgh finds.) The Northumbrian coinage can be conveniently divided into six phases, namely

I	Incoming Frisian and southern English sceattas
II	Northumbrian 'animal' sceattas, *c.* 738–*c.* 785
III	Moneyers'-name stycas of relatively good silver, of Ælfwald and of Æthelred I (and Archbishop Eanbald?)
IV	Issues of Eanred (Series A moneyers) and Eanbald mostly containing *c.* 20% silver
V	a) Debased issues of the Series A moneyers, and b) similar coins of Eanred (Series B moneyers) and of Æthelred's first reign, of Redwulf, and of Archbishop Wigmund.
VI	The silverless coins of Æthelred's second reign and of Osberht and Archbishop Wulfhere, and their derivatives.

The late hoards, which it would be most natural to associate with the events of the 860s, contain coins of phases V and VI, but very few of phases III or IV. The York (St. Leonards Place) hoard of 1842, for example, included 41 coins of phases III and IV out of about 3,000 listed, that is, only a residual 1·4 per cent. By contrast, there were ten times as many of Eanred's Series B coins, namely 416. The disappearance of the Series A coins is even more pronounced in the Bolton Percy hoard of 1967 (which was more completely recorded), with only 5 specimens, or 0·3 per cent, of

Series A, but 208 specimens of Series B.[39] Series A, then, had effectively disappeared from the currency by *c.* 867, but we do not know (because the evidence could only come from a series of earlier hoards) whether they were systematically withdrawn or disappeared gradually. The Hexham hoard still contained a surprisingly wide range of Series A coins, at a date when the current issues were of only *c.* 6% silver,[40] but it could, perhaps, be a savings hoard that had been put together over a period of time, and therefore not exactly typical of the currency at the time of its t.p.q.

The main point is that any stray find of a phase-V or phase-VI coin could, as the hoards show, have been lost as late as the 860s, but that a phase-III or IV coin is very unlikely to have been such a late loss. Not only should a list of all the finds of phase-III and IV coins include information about a period on which the hoards are virtually silent, but it should also be reasonably free from any hidden distortions introduced into the later topographical pattern by the fighting and insecurity of the last years of the Northumbrian kingdom. The list is surprisingly long, if we include the moneyers'-name coins of Ælfwald, Æthelred I, and Archbishop Eanbald, as well as Eanred's Series A (Table 1). The total number of provenanced specimens are:

Ælfwald	6
Æthelred I	25
Eanred	41+
Eanbald	6

This gratifyingly large body of material will include losses from the whole of phases III and IV and perhaps also much of phase V (if we accept the evidence of the Hexham hoard), but the proportion of earlier coins to those of Eanred, of about 30 to 40 (the date of the Eanbald coins being ambiguous) shows quite clearly that it reflects at least some early losses, for the proportion among the Hexham illustrations is 6 to 156 (plus 59 for Eanbald, which strongly suggests that most of his coins in Hexham were contemporary with Eanred's, but does not tell us when his issues began). The map of finds of phase-III and IV coins (Fig. 1) may thus be thought to provide evidence about a period of Northumbrian monetary history, at the beginning of the ninth century, about which we otherwise know remarkably little. The map of finds of phase-II coins already shows a wide distribution in the east, but with much less in the west. There is one coin from Attermire Cave, Settle, and one from Whithorn. In phases III and IV, there are westerly finds from Carlisle (from two separate sites[41]), from Whithorn, and from Glenluce Sands (at least two well-attested finds, of which one is of Æthelred I). Beneath the sand-dunes, which stretch for miles, there lies a dark, sandy humus layer representing a grassy heath; finds of all kinds have been made for many decades. The wider locational

[39] Pagan, 1973.

[40] Pagan, 1974.

[41] For the general background see P. F. Gosling, 'Carlisle—an archaeological survey of the historic town', in P. A. G. Clack and P. F. Gosling, *Archaeology in the North. Report of the Northern Archaeological Survey*, Durham, 1976, pp. 165–85.

significance of the Glenluce Bay site is, however, unclear.[42] One may add, finally a phase-IV find from Segontium (Caernarfon).[43]

TABLE 1

Finds of coins of Ælfwald, Æthelred I, Eanred (Series A), and Eanbald

	Ælfwald	*Æthelred I*	*Eanred*	*Eanbald*
York (various sites)	2	2	8	–
Sancton	3	4	6	1
Beverley	–	1	–	–
Thwing	1	–	1	–
Kirkbymoorside	–	1	–	–
Whitby	–	12	12	2
Ripon	–	–	2	–
Settle	–	1	–	–
Hexham	–	–	–	1?
Monkwearmouth	–	–	2	–
Jarrow	–	1	¼	¼
Newcastle	–	1	–	–
Coldingham	–	–	–	1
Carlisle (different sites)	–	–	2	–
Whithorn	–	–	2+	–
Luce Sands	–	1 (2?)	1 (2?)	–
Dacre	–	–	1	–
Winteringham	–	–	1	–
Kirmington	–	–	1	–
Thetford	–	1	–	–
Caernarfon	–	–	1	–
Total	6	25	41+	6
cf. Hexham illustrations	–	6	156	59

[42] See J. Williams, 'Some "medieval" objects from Luce Bay Sands in the Mann collection', *Trans. Dumf. and Galloway Nat. Hist. and Antiquarian Soc.*[3] 52 (1976–7), 77–87, and E. M. Jope and H. M. Jope, 'A hoard of fifteenth -century coins from Glenluce sand-dunes and their context', *Medieval Archaeology* 3 (1959), 259–79. Of the coins listed in Miss Pirie's inventory, the Glenluce provenance of the four in *SCBI Glasgow*, including two of phase II, is somewhat conjectural, and I have not relied on them here, even though there is a presumption that the Neilson collection was of local origin. There is admirably detailed evidence that other stycas were widely scattered finds: one of Eanred (Forthræd) 150 m S of Mid Torrs, another of Eanred (Monne) in 1962, 200 m SW of the above, and two in the Kelvingrove Museum, of Æthelred I (Ceolbeald) and Æthelred II (Eardwulf) half a mile further SW. See *Trans DGNHAAS* 39 (1960–1), 159–60 and 42 (1964–5), 149–50).

[43] *Archaeologia Cambrensis* 1922, 266; D. W. Dykes, *Anglo-Saxon Coins in the National Museum of Wales*, [1976] (=an expanded reprint from *Amgueddfa, Bulletin of the National Museum of Wales* 24 (winter 1976)), p. 27. (The moneyer is Wulfheard.)

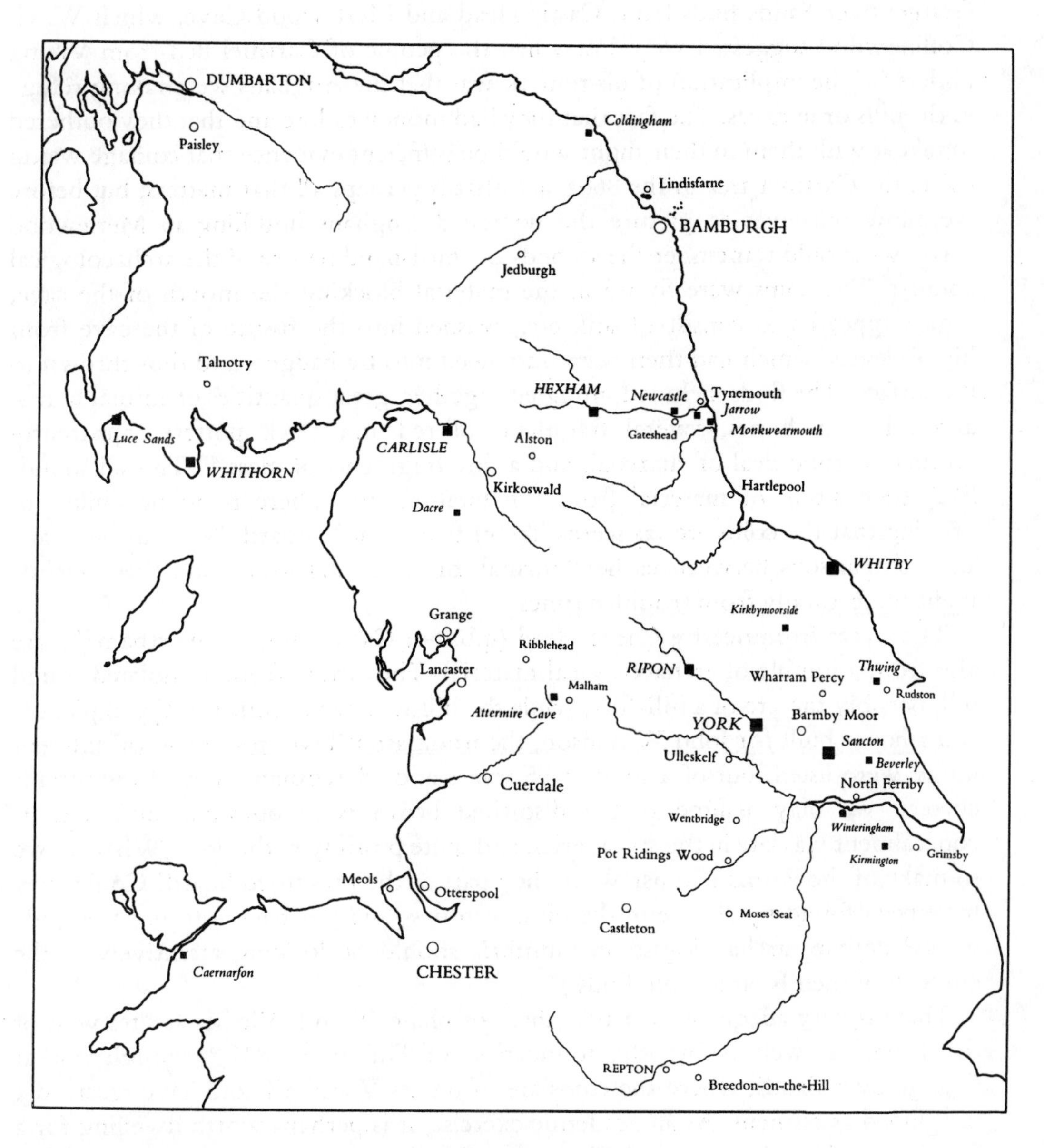

FIG. 1. Finds of stycas from Northumbria and the adjoining regions. Place-names in italics, and solid black squares, indicate sites from which early finds have been reported (as listed in Table 1).

All this adds up to evidence of a different complexion from, for example, the Grange-over-Sands finds from Castle Head and Merlewood Cave, which W. G. Collingwood suggested were lost when the people of Cartmel fled from Viking raiders.[44] The implication of his remark was that the Anglians were taking refuge in the hills or in caves. The fact that they had money to lose and that they bothered to take it with them in their flight would be sufficient evidence that coinage was in use in the Cartmel area in the 860s, and that is perhaps all that matters; but before we allow ourselves to picture the wretched Anglians huddling in Merlewood Cave, we should remember the second- or third-hand nature of the archaeological context. The coins were found in the material blocking the mouth of the cave, which appeared to consist of soil, etc., washed into the fissure of the cave from higher levels, which had then been burrowed into by badgers and thus thrown to the surface. The finds included, mingled together, great quantities of animal bones, a few human bones, several fragments of red and black pottery, apparently Roman, a good deal of charcoal, and a few fragments of glass.[45] This all sounds like redeposition of material from a habitation site. There is no possibility of proving that the coins are (as seems likely) from a little hoard. Nor can we make any comparisons between earlier 'normal' or accidental losses, and this concealment conjecturally from troubled times.

The stycas from nearby Castle Head (n.b. not Castle Hill, Penwortham[46]), are also from a jumble of archaeological material. They came from an isolated round hill, possibly the site of a hill-fort, while the hill was being 'improved' and planted and a house built for John Wilkinson, the ironmaster. Five specimens 'of different kings' were listed, out of a total of 95 stycas and 75 Roman coins. If the total is correct, we may assume that a disturbed hoard is in question, and that its concealment was late in the styca series, and quite possibly in the 860s (What are we to make of the Roman coins? Were they part of the presumed hoard? Could they have been found by chance in the ninth century, and put back into use alongside stycas? Perhaps archaeologists in Cumbria should be looking attentively at the contexts of their Roman coin finds.)

There is very adequate evidence, then, of phase-III and IVlosses at sites west of the Pennines, well before the foundation of Dublin in 841,—though not at Grange-over-Sands, where the coins are of phases V and VI, and have received a misguided assessment. As an academic exercise, it is perhaps worth dwelling for a few moments on the errors of judgement of earlier commentaries. Michael Dolley in 1963 wrote, 'From west of the Pennines and areas where we may suspect that the *styca* was not normally current, there is [list of finds]. There is much to be said for the suggestion that this group of finds, three at least of which also contained silver ornaments, may reflect the plight of those fleeing from the Danish assault upon Northumbria only to find themselves caught up in the Norwegian attacks upon

44 W. G. Collingwood, 'The Angles in Furness and Cartmel', *Trans.Cumb.Westm. AAS* NS 24 (1924), 288–94.

45 H. S. Cooper, 'Bone cave at Grange'. *Proc.Soc.Antiq.*² 14 (1891–3), 227–30.

46 Higher Penwortham is near Preston: the Castle Head finds are mentioned by way of comparison in the interesting account in W. Thornber, 'The castle hill of Penwortham', *Historic Soc. of Lancs. and Cheshire* 9 (1856–7), 61–76.

Cumbria, but it is just possible that the southern group may indicate a trade-route between York and Ireland, though again it must be stressed that the copper *styca* was not a trade-coin and has not been found in Ireland.'[47] The main error here was to allow oneself to be distracted from the early-ninth century evidence by the welter of evidence from the third quarter of the century,—although Michael Dolley would surely have been quick to seize on the interest of the new finds from Carlisle, had they been available at the time. One more example, taken from a distinguished recent historical analysis of English Northumbria, will be enough. Nick Higham (1986) writes, 'A series of hoards consisting of Northumbrian *stycas* were deposited in the period AD 865–70, and this may also reflect local reaction to Norse raiding. However, these hoards contrast with the apparent coinlessness of Cumbria during the earlier ninth century, and may therefore have been deposited by fugitives from the Danish conquest east of the Pennines (Dolley 1966), and need not be linked directly to Irish-Norse raids', and on another page, 'At Carlisle, isolated coin finds from recent excavations include the only *sceattas*[48] so far found west of the northern Pennines, and may imply a coin-using community within and around the monastery. Three coin hoards with varying claims to authenticity have been found in the Cartmel peninsula... Both Cartmel and Carlisle are peculiar for their known ecclesiastical associations'.[49] If one were being critical, one might ask for the evidence by which any of the 'series of hoards' other than Kirkoswald can be shown to be a hoard and can be dated so narrowly as to 865–70. As to coinlessness, this is no doubt a matter of perspective: the early-ninth century finds from the west are thin on the ground, and they are thinner on the ground than the finds of corresponding date in the east (although that particular numerical comparison is somewhat difficult). No doubt the balance between a subsistence economy and a money economy was tilted more towards subsistence in the west. But the numismatic evidence deserves to be properly analysed in itself before an attempt is made to put it into its historical context. The greater numbers of late losses in the west are very unlikely to be an index of a dramatic increase in monetary circulation, any more than they are in the east. The numismatic evidence offers no warrant to speak of coinlessness. On the contrary, the ratio of coins of Æthelred I to those of Eanred points to coin use from an early date and therefore over a period of decades. It appears to be on a very limited scale, but it is not a flash in the pan. The need for special explanations for the finds from the third quarter of the century arises from the hypothesis of 'coinlessness', an hypothesis which should now be seen as being at variance with the numismatic evidence, and which in any case should not be used in support of uncritical readings of the finds from the third quarter of the century. Refugees from east of the Pennines really are a flight of fancy.

If one counts up the totals of single finds from east and west of the Pennines respectively, there is an enormous disparity—in very much the same way as there is among the southern English sceatta finds east and west of a line through, say,

[47] R. H. M. Dolley, *The Hiberno-Norse Coins in the British Museum*, 1966, p. 23.

[48] From Blackfriars Street, originally misreported as sceattas, but in fact stycas.

[49] N. Higham, *The Northern Counties to AD 1000*, 1986, p. 322, 303.

Sheffield and Coventry. The totals may well give an adequately true indication of the numbers of transactions, and thus of the degree of monetization of the economy.

In light of our consideration of the finds from Cartmel, we may be able to see more clearly how to view the Paisley hoard of 1782. Our only detailed evidence for its composition lies in a gift of 15 specimens to the Society of Antiquaries of Scotland in September 1782. The presumption that these are from the Paisley hoard is a little uncertain, although the coincidence of date is encouraging. No major hoard is known between Ripon 1695 and Paisley 1782, but we should note that Hunter had a well-chosen selection of 76 stycas. It is just possible that he acquired them from the Paisley hoard before his death in March 1783, and one is reluctant to believe that a major hoard other than Paisley escaped any record. Charles Combe refers to the Hunterian stycas at a date soon after Hunter's death.

Ten more stycas 'in good preservation' were donated to the Society in December 1783 by Mr Selkirk Stewart. It seems, then, that a styca hoard was being dispersed among Scottish collectors in 1782–3, and there is no other known hoard from so early a date which could be the source of these specimens. There is in any case no reason to question the reliability of Lindsay's record of a find at Paisley.[50] The topographical significance of the find-spot, which lay only a few miles from Dumbarton and well beyond Anglian-controlled territory, lies presumably in its proximity to the Firth of Clyde, Dublin's 'back door' into northern Britain. A major shift in the balance of power in the region occurred in 870–2, when the four-month siege of the British stronghold of Al Cluith (on Dumbarton Rock) by a coalition of Vikings from York and from Ireland and Scotland destroyed the kingdom of Strathclyde. The flower of the northern British aristocracy was cut down or led away in slavery from the Clyde to Dublin in 200 longships.[51] These events introduced a period of half a century when Strathclyde's strategic significance can be perceived in the historical record. From the decades before 870 there is virtually no historical evidence, but British influence was presumably strong. The context of the Paisley hoard depends very much, therefore, on its date of deposit, before or after 870, and this is something which we are in no position to determine. At the risk of falling into the same sort of error as Collingwood and his commentators, one is tempted to suggest that the Paisley hoard may have been concealed in connexion with the events of 870–2. Certainly, there is as yet no supporting evidence for the 'normal' circulation of stycas on Clydeside.

The phase-III and IV finds from Bernicia are marginally more plentiful than those from the west, but offer fewer points for discussion. One coin, particularly precious for its context, was excavated at Jarrow, on the upper terrace. There, the gravel floor of a hut yielded evidence for glass-working in the shape of a millefiori rod and glass slag, as well as a blundered but apparently quite early coin

[50] For details of the Paisley find see Metcalf, loc. cit. (note 3 above), no 39 (p. 98), and critical comments by R. B. K. Stevenson in *SCBI Edinburgh*, pp. viii and xxii. For the reasons here set out, I think Stevenson's 'what is at best a possibility' a little too sceptical. On Hunter's stycas, which seem to be a good selection of varieties, in good condition, i.e. the pick of a larger number, see *SCBI Glasgow* pp. viii–xi and the preliminary note to Plate 4.

[51] See A. P. Smyth, *Warlords and Holy Men*, 1984, 1984, pp. 215 f.

(*c.* 720–30?) naming the moneyer Eadwulf.[52] This sets the coin usefully in an industrial context (there were also bone combs on the gravel surface not far away), within a monastic site. The chance find from the churchyard at Coldingham is of Archbishop Eanbald, again by Eadwulf (EODVVLF). This was not, however, the site of the royal monastic foundation of *Coludesburh*, which was on St. Abb's Head high above the sea.[53] At Monkwearmouth, two out of the six excavation coins are of Eanred, Series A. At Jarrow, including the coin just mentioned, one out of the eight is of phase III, and two are of phase IV. At Newcastle, there is one phase-IV coin out of eight. At Bamburgh, on the other hand, among the 67 coins from the 1971 excavations, not one is of phase III or IV, which is perhaps surprising. There is no charter evidence such as would prove that Æthelred I and Eanred were frequently resident in the Bernician centre, but its occupation by either the king or a powerful liege is unlikely to have been interrupted. One awaits a report on the coin finds from later seasons with impatience.

From Whitby, which was of course a major phase-I and phase-II site, there are no fewer than 25 phase-III and IV finds, of which 24 are from the Abbey excavations and one is from Spa Ladder. This one, and eleven from the Abbey, are of Æthelred I. Seven of the eleven and also the one from Spa Ladder, are by the moneyer Ceolbeald; it would have been a comfort to know that they were all found separately. At Sancton, the best-published site, coins of phases III and IV were relatively even more plentiful—15 out of a total of 49 styca finds (this includes an Eanbald omitted by oversight from Elizabeth Pirie's inventory, and an Eanred among the Barmby Moor finds). The 15 included 3 of Ælfwald, 4 of Æthelred, and one of Eanbald/Æthelred, against 7 of Eanred. With 3 of Ælfwald's 'animal' type also among the Sancton finds, this offers the clearest evidence of a steady rate of losses from the currency from the late eighth century onwards.

From York itself, there are 9 phase-III or IV finds from six sites, out of a total of about 40 finds. The 9 include two of Ælfwald and one of Æthelred.

The finds already spread into Lincolnshire and East Anglia in phase IV.

This is about as far as an internal analysis of the list of early finds should be pressed. One might note that all six Ælfwalds are from York or the East Riding; but as they amount to only about 20 per cent of the finds from that region, their absence elsewhere, e.g. west of the Pennines, could well be statistically fortuitous. Only at Whitby is the total number of finds large enough for the absence of Ælfwalds to attract attention, and there is of course no lack of coins from earlier than Ælfwald's reign at Whitby. As regards the difficult questions of the

[52] R. Cramp, 'Anglo-Saxon monasteries of the north', *Scottish Archaeological Forum* 5 (1973), 104–24, at 122; *Medieval Archaeology* 13 (1969), 52. The coin is illustrated in Pirie, 1986, p. 89, no. 10, and is attributed by her to Eanbald II (796–*c.* 830). Fortunately the variety is recorded from the Hexham hoard (Adamson 1836, pl. 36, 26) and so cannot belong to the late derivative series. Eadwulf is an Eanbald moneyer, and the linear annular type with pellet at centre, obv. and rev. is uncommon after the time of Eanred. The silver contents of the Jarrow coin would be the best guide to its date, which may be *c.* 720–30. Cf. also Adamson, 1834, pl. 53, 11 and pl. 42, 215. There is a coin related to the Jarrow find, i.e. probably by the same hand in the Ashmolean, reading ÐAÐENA, cf Adamson pl. 36, 26

[53] I am grateful to Marilyn Brown, of the Royal Commission on the Ancient and Historical Monuments of Scotland, for her helpful comments on the Scottish evidence.

attribution to Ælfwald I or II and the dating of Æthelred I's coins, Booth has pointed to the continuity of runic letter forms on the 'animal' and moneyer's name types of Cuthheard's coins for Ælfwald. The facts that Ælfwald employs only one moneyer, against Æthelred's six, and that the finds of his coins are so many fewer than Æthelred's can be explained most easily if Ælfwald was the earlier; but one then has to add that Ceolbeald's neat and distinctive work for Æthelred (790–6, after Osred was exiled?) looks like some sort of new beginning. If one searches for other geographical concentrations among the finds, it is precisely Ceolbeald's coins that are the most interesting. They seem to show a northerly emphasis: Newcastle, Jarrow, Luce Sands, and 8 from Whitby—compared with one from York and one or two from Sancton.

I have drawn attention to a phase of Northumbrian monetary history—or rather, two phases (for the silver contents of the coins are quite different before and after Eadwulf's reign)—running from the 780s until late in Eanred's reign, and have suggested that the topography of the earlier coin finds provides more reliable evidence of the normal patterns of monetary circulation than the finds from the last decades of the kingdom. The hoards are heavily concentrated in those closing years, doubtless because of widespread insecurity. Several of them come from York itself, and if it were not for them, the dominant position of York in the record of finds would be less evident. The large size of several of the hoards may hint at patterns in the social ownership of wealth, and also perhaps at the dwindling purchasing power of the styca. If the coin's value fell during Æthelred's second reign, one would expect a sharply increased loss-rate. One's reading of the evidence on that point depends a good deal on how long the very debased issues remained in use, and on the assumption that their eventual value as scrap brass was sufficient to prevent their being thrown away. The evidence from the major sites of Whitby, Bamburgh, and Sancton points to continuity with only a moderate increase in the loss-rate.

Hexham and Cuerdale: two notes on metrology

D.M. METCALF

I

How much do stycas weigh? Were they all struck to the same weight standard? Were their flans carefully controlled? Did all moneyers work to the same standard and with the same degree of care? Do histograms reveal a 'tail' of defective or sub-standard flans? Is there any evidence that heavier coins were culled while in circulation? To questions such as these, no careful answers have ever been attempted. The *British Museum Catalogue* judged the matter of so little interest that no weights were printed unless the stycas were silvery in appearance.

Most collections yield a rather bumpy, irregular histogram, and the reason is not far to seek: coins coming from different hoards are liable to be appreciably different in their average weight. An exploratory examination of two parcels of coins in the Ashmolean Museum showed that Hexham coins mostly fell between 1.12 and 1.32g, whereas the same varieties from the Bateman collection fell between 0.96 and 1.16—hardly overlapping. The Bateman coins are from the first Bolton Percy hoard. If one calculated an average weight from a mixture of Hexham and Bolton Percy coins, the result would depend on the proportions of specimens from the two sources; and comparisons of averages e.g. for different reigns would be vitiated unless the proportions were the same. Even more misleading, histograms drawn from a mixture of coins would be the wrong shape, with the peak or modal value obscured or duplicated. The difference in weight between coins from the two hoards could be caused by wear and tear during circulation, by culling, by the effects of corrosion and leaching during the centuries when the coins lay buried in the soil, or by modern chemical cleaning. All four may be factors, and it is neither practicable nor necessary to try to disentangle them. What one needs to do is discount the difficulties by conducting a metrological study of the stycas using coins from only one hoard at a time. The Hexham hoard is an obvious choice, as there are three substantial groups of coins easily accessible, which are known to come from Hexham. (The Newcastle collection, among others, undoubtedly contains a great many coins from Hexham, but their provenance is to some extent conjectural.) The British Museum has a fine run of Hexham coins, and the Ashmolean has a smaller selection. These two together provide a very adequate sample from which to study the metrology of the stycas. The Manchester parcel[1] could also have been used, but

[1] K.F. Sugden and M. Warhurst, 'An unrecorded parcel from the Hexham hoard', *NC* 139 (1979), 212–17.

it would have been desirable to re-weigh the coins to three decimal places. The results should provide a basis for comparisons in the future, if any new large hoards are brought to light. A future hoard may yield a somewhat different average weight, because of the soil conditions in which it was buried, but the parameters and the within-sample variations (e.g. between coins of one reign and another) will deserve comparison.

The method followed was to construct histograms with the rather small step interval of 0.04g. This is feasible if one has a large number of specimens to work from. It should serve to define the shape of the histogram, and the modal value, more precisely than a larger step-interval would, by dividing the bulk of the coins between six and seven steps. The more usual interval of 0.1g would be too coarse, and would obscure the evidence. The next stage was to adjust the positioning of the central step by inspection, so as to maximize the proportion of coins falling into it, or, where small adjustments made little difference, so as to produce as 'normal' a histogram as possible. Thus, where the central step appeared to fall at 1.20–1.24g, one would try the alternatives of 1.19–1.23g and 1.21–1.25g, and so on, and choose the best. The percentage of coins falling into the central step is, of course, much smaller with an interval of 0.04g than it would be with 0.10g, and one must not allow oneself to take away the false impression that the flans of the stycas were loosely controlled in comparison with coinages for which histograms have been drawn differently. The main point is to be able to compare different categories of stycas, and for that purpose the use of the same width of step throughout is what matters—together with the presentation of the results in percentage form, so that the histograms are visually comparable, all enclosing the same area. A lower central step means less careful control of the weights of the flans.

The work of Eanred's Group A moneyers is summed up in an exemplary histogram (Fig. 1), based on 96 specimens. The modal value falls convincingly about

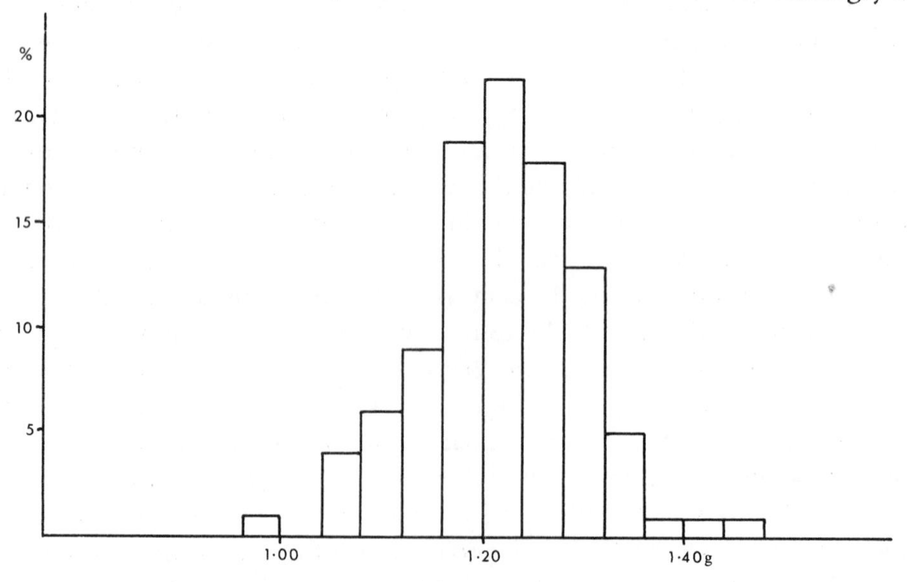

FIG. 1. Eanred, Group A moneyers.

half-way through the central step, at 1.22g. The median value is 1.223g. The shape of the histogram suggests that the mode might lie somewhere between 1.22 and 1.23g, but this is hyper-accuracy when based on only 96 specimens, especially as they have not all received uniform cleaning and conservation. The distribution is normal, with no sign of the culling of heavy flans (either by the mint or in circulation) and with no sign of a 'tail' of defective specimens—although one should remember that the sample consists of a selection of good, clear specimens. If one were in a position to draw a histogram of *all* the Group A coins in the Hexham hoard (or in some other hoard), there might or might not be rather more of a 'tail'.

Eanred's early coins were evidently all struck to a single weight-standard, of just under 19 grains. This may be presumed to derive from the traditional weight-standard of the thrymsa and the sceat in England, at best 20 grains (1.296g) or a little less. Most of the secondary-phase sceattas had fallen well below 19 grains. One should understand, therefore, that there was a theoretical standard, to which the coinage could from time to time be restored.

Eanred's Group B moneyers, taken as a whole, give a slightly less satisfactory histogram (Fig. 2). The central step contains only 17% instead of 22% of the values, and the peak is considerably flattened on its lower side. There appears to be a second

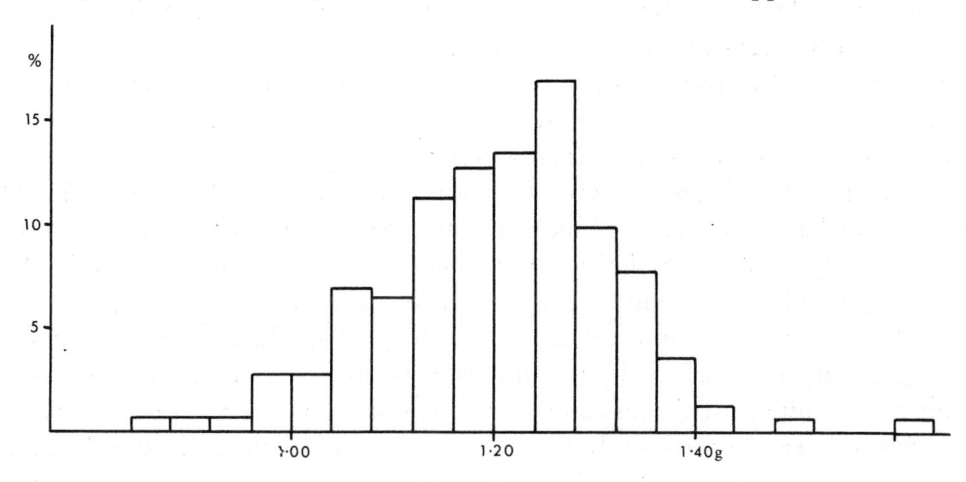

FIG. 2. Eanred, Group B moneyers.

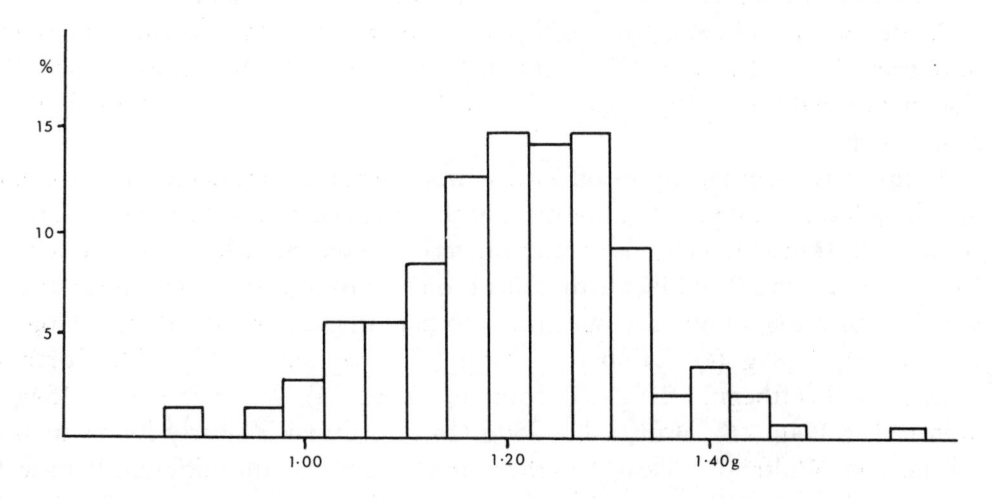

FIG. 3. Eanred, Group B moneyers (alternative position of central step).

peak at around 1.06g. The modal value of the main peak might be judged to lie close to 1.24g (that is, very slightly higher than for Group A), but the median value is 1.21g. If one attempts to confirm the pattern by shifting the position of the steps, Fig. 3 results. The central step is now reduced to 14/15%, and it is an open question whether the histogram approximates more closely to a normal distribution. The secondary peak is now no more than a shoulder. The data are, of course, exactly the same. The mode, interestingly, would still be judged to be close to 1.24g.

The group of new moneyers were working, as a whole, rather less carefully than their predecessors, perhaps under the pressure of a recoinage. The weight-standard was nominally the same. Because the histogram approximates less perfectly to a normal distribution, the accuracy of the figure 1.24g will command slightly less confidence than the 1.22g for Group A. Our ability to judge the real difference may therefore be subject to margins of error adding up to 50% of the difference or more. The best guess will be that the difference is around 15mg, or just over 1% of the weight of the styca. One possible explanation might be that this represents loss of weight by wear during circulation. Under modern conditions a coin might lose as much as 10mg a year (irrespective, it seems, of flan size);[2] and the Group A coins are perhaps on average five or ten years older than those of Group B. But the Hexham coins show very little sign of wear, and it may be that they had been hoarded for most of their lifetime. The topic of loss of weight by wear will be better left to be studied on the basis of some future hoard.

There is an obvious question to ask next, by looking at those coins which weigh less than, say, 1.10g in order to see if they seem in any way different from the sample as a whole. One notices an abnormally high proportion of blundered and retrograde coins. *BMC* 120 and 126, for example, belong to a variety reading EANHED HEX, EHRRDVVLF or similar. The six Hexham specimens in *BMC* have a mean weight of only 1.13g. Three of the light-weight coins of Forthræd (*BMC* 152, 157, 160) are similarly blundered. It seems on first inspection, then, that there may be some sort of correlation between blundered dies and sub-standard flans. The next question is whether some or all of the light coins are contemporary counterfeits, or whether they are in some sense the 'tail end' of the official output. A thorough study would need to be carried out against the background of charts of die-linkage. All that can be said at present is that Figs. 2 and 3 may conflate varieties with a more regular weight-distribution than appears, with others that tend to be sub-standard.

A large sample of coins from Æthelred's first reign yields a satisfactory regular histogram (Fig. 4, based on 303 specimens) with a modal value very close to 1.22g. The median value is 1.216g. Again, 17% or at most 18% of the weights fall into the central step.

Again, it is tempting to go off into a more detailed consideration of the coins weighing less than, say, 1.10g, but most of the irregularities of the evidence are still, at this stage, subject to margins of random variation which make them inconclusive. If one looks at the *BMC* Hexham coins moneyer by moneyer, the mean average weights, with the numbers of specimens in parentheses, are: Brother, 1.176g, (7), Cynemund, 1.181g (4), Ealhhere, 1.199g (11), Eanræd, 1.212g (47), Forthræd, 1.127g (36), Leofthegn, 1.216g (59), Monne, 1.218g (54), Wendelbeorht, 1.154g (9), Wihtræd, 1.174g (16), Wulfræd, 1.250g (14). Forthræd is clearly lower than the others, and Wulfræd is clearly higher, and in general the differences raise the question whether the flans were being cut separately for each moneyer, or at least for some moneyers. On insufficient evidence, one will nevertheless begin to suspect so.

[2] For comparative data on loss of weight by wear, see D.M. Metcalf, 'What has been achieved through the application of statistics to numismatics?', in *Statistics and Numismatics* (= *Pact*, vol. 5) ed. C. Carcassonne and T. Hackens, Strasbourg, 1981, pp. 3–24, at pp. 10–11.

Among Forthræd's coins, there are some which read EORDRED, sometimes retrograde, and these tend to be very light in weight, e.g. *BMC* 387, 1.023g, 388, 0.951g, 391, 0.614g, 392, 0.985g, 393, 0.790g, 415, 0.968g, 416, 0.931g. Study against

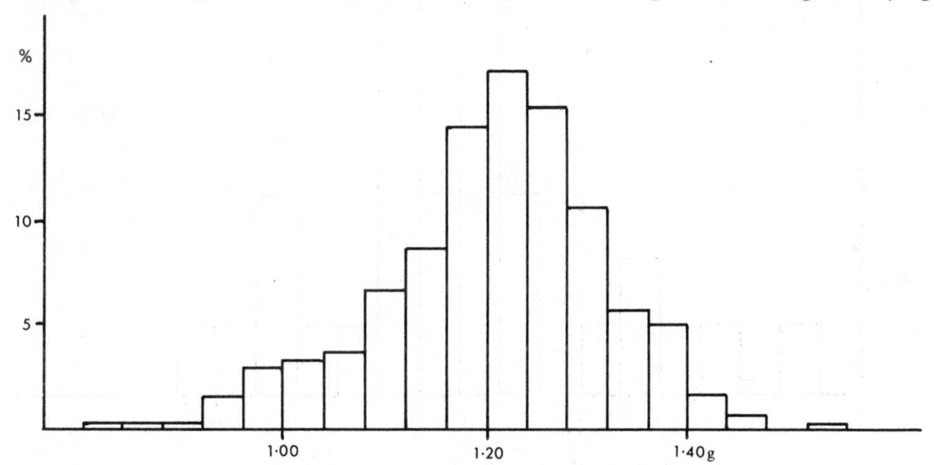

FIG. 4. Æthelred II, first reign.

the background of die-linkage is needed. There may be other, smaller groups of sub-standard coins which do not show up so well in the evidence, e.g. among those of the moneyer Eanræd. In Sugden and Warhurst's list of the Hexham coins preserved at Manchester (still, in 1979, contained in the paper wrappings in which they arrived in 1833), one's eye is caught by nos. 52–8. When two coins which share an obverse die weigh 0.99g and 0.98g, and the corresponding *BMC* coins (296 and 298) weigh 1.141g and 1.086g, one's interest is aroused. But these are questions for future research, and for large numbers of specimens.

From the reign of Redwulf, not enough Hexham coins are available to produce a good histogram. The 31 which can be used give an erratic result (as 31 specimens of

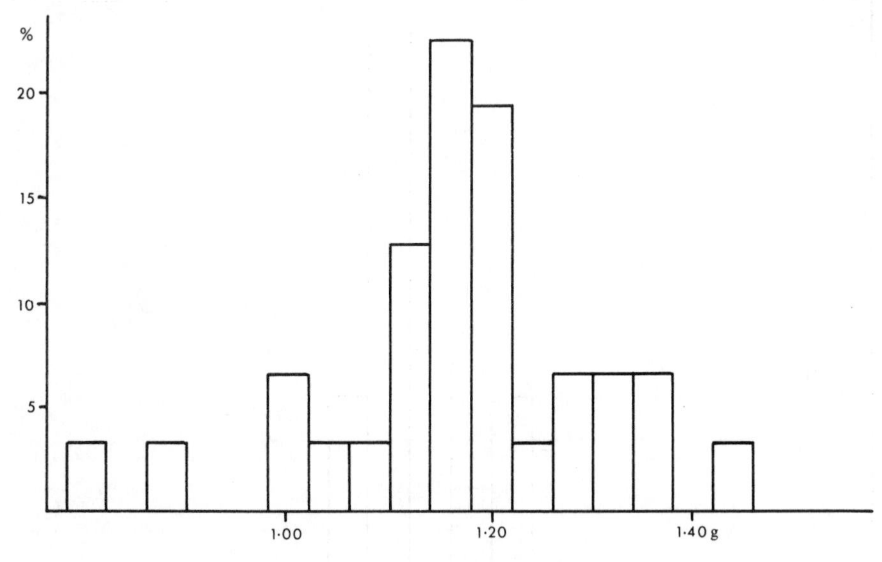

FIG. 5. Redwulf.

Eanred or Æthelred would), but with much the same dispersion as under Æthelred, and with a similar (or slightly higher) proportion in the central step (Figs. 5 and 6, alternative versions). The mode would be judged from either diagram to be about 1.16 or 1.17g. The median value is also 1.17g.

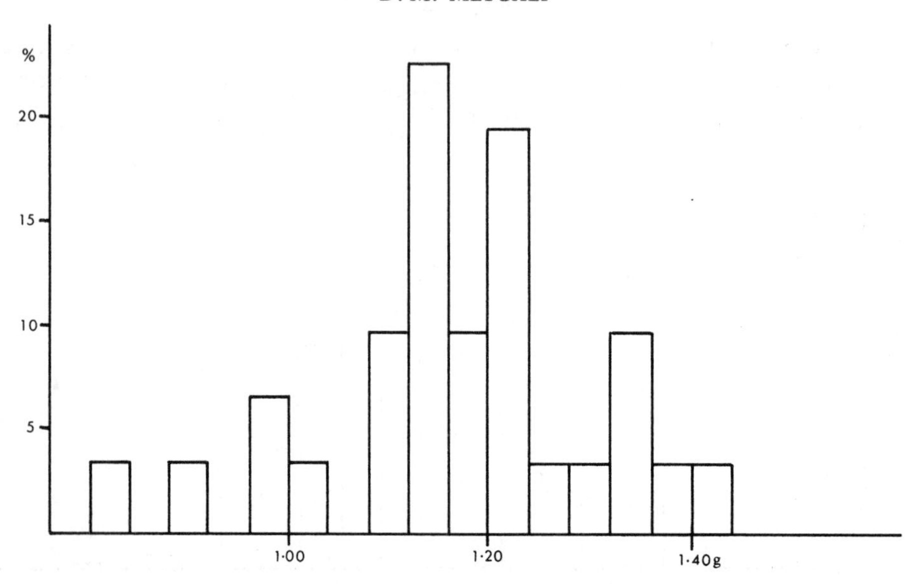

FIG. 6. Redwulf (alternative version).

The few coins of Æthelred's second reign, by Eardwulf, have a mean weight of 1.12g. (A group of 20 analysed elsewhere in the volume, not necessarily from Hexham, have a mean weight of 1.13g.) As the two mean values are close to each other, it may not be seriously misleading to work out a mode and median from a mixed group of coins with approximately the same weight as the few from Hexham. The modal value seems to work out at about 1.12 or 1.13g—a little lighter than under Redwulf, and certainly lighter than the standard in Æthelred's first reign. The reform by which coins containing no silver were introduced also lowered

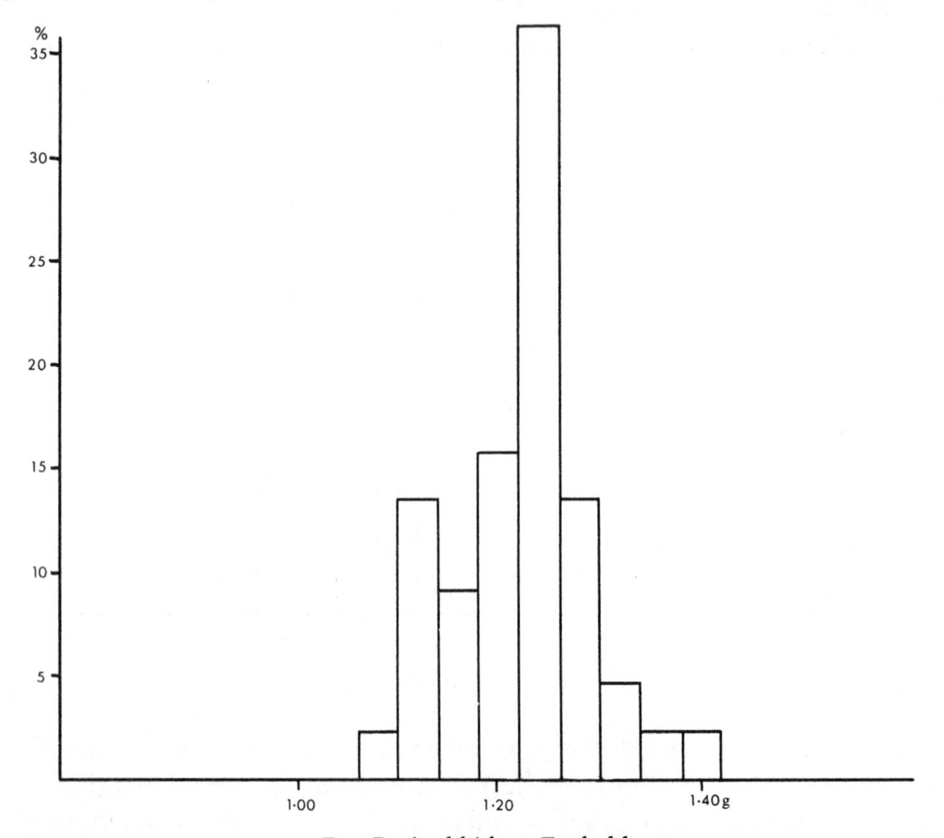

FIG. 7. Archbishop Eanbald.

the weight-standard slightly. The pattern of gradual decline will seem very familiar to numismatists, and no political significance should be read into it.

A further decline occurred in the 'blundered or derivative' issues. There were none of these in the Hexham hoard, and comparisons can therefore only be approximate. A selection of 31 specimens analysed elsewhere in the volume have a mean weight of 1.02g.

We now turn to the coins of the archbishops' moneyers. Those of Archbishop Eanbald, of which the Hexham sample may be presumed to be roughly of the same date as Eanred's Series A, show an exceptionally high proportion (36%) falling into the central step, and a modal value of 1.24g (Fig. 7, based on 44 specimens). The histogram suggests that the flans for Eanbald's coins were produced separately from those for Eanred. The median is 1.230/1.232g. Apart from their higher standard of accuracy, Eanbald's flans match those of Eanred very closely.

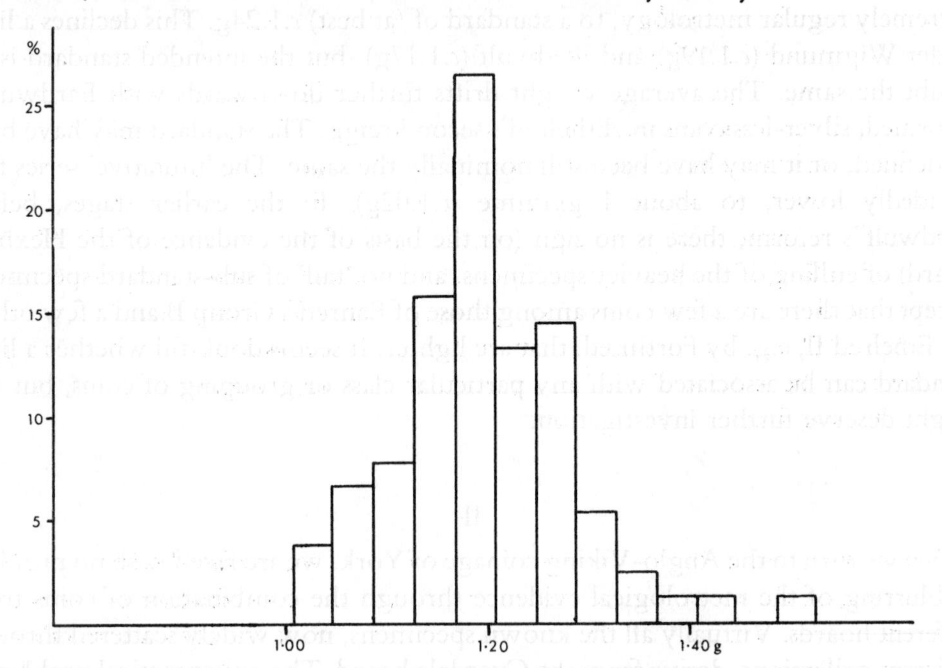

FIG. 8. Archbishop Wigmund.

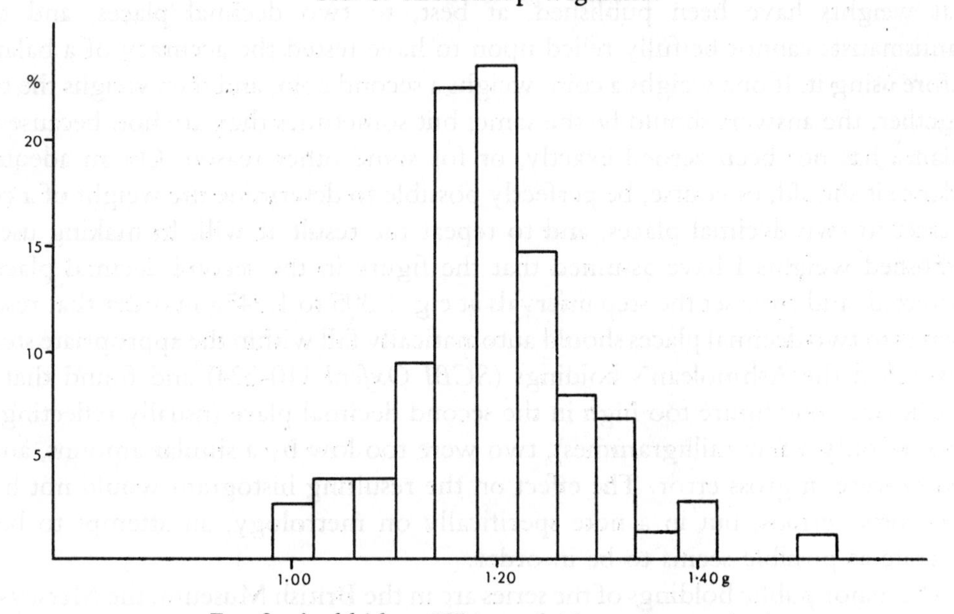

FIG. 9. Archbishop Wigmund (alternative version).

Archbishop Wigmund's coins conform a little less closely to a normal distribution. There is some positive skewness, which is visible wherever the steps of the histogram are positioned. The modal value is in any case between 1.18 and 1.20g, thus a few percentage points lower than for Æthelred (Fig. 8, with 26% of values in the central step, or Fig. 9, with 24%, both based on 76 specimens). The median is 1.192/1.193g. As with Eanbald's coins, the flans are prepared to a higher standard of accuracy than the (roughly) contemporary issues of the king's moneyers. This must raise the question whether the archbishop's coins were produced separately through the various stages of their manufacture,—in other words, whether there were two separate mints, as was the case at York later in the middle ages. Perhaps this is an anachronistic viewpoint, and one ought to be comparing the accuracy of the flans of individual moneyers.

In summary, the stycas of the first half of the ninth century reveal a uniform and extremely regular metrology, to a standard of (at best) *c.*1.24g. This declines a little under Wigmund (*c.*1.19g) and Redwulf (*c.*1.17g), but the intended standard is no doubt the same. The average weight drifts further downwards with Eardwulf's reformed, silver-less coins in Æthelred's second reign. The standard may have been re-defined, or it may have been still nominally the same. The 'imitative' series falls decidedly lower, to about 1 gramme (*c.*1.02g). In the earlier stages, before Eardwulf's reform, there is no sign (on the basis of the evidence of the Hexham hoard) of culling of the heavier specimens, and no 'tail' of sub-standard specimens, except that there are a few coins among those of Eanred's Group B and a few others of Æthelred II, e.g. by Forthræd, that are lighter. It seems doubtful whether a light standard can be associated with any particular class or grouping of coins, but this might deserve further investigation.

II

When we turn to the Anglo-Viking coinage of York, we are faced with no problem of blurring of the metrological evidence through the combination of coins from different hoards. Virtually all the known specimens, now widely scattered through different collections, derive from the Cuerdale hoard. The only practical problem is that weights have been published, at best, to two decimal places, and that numismatists cannot be fully relied upon to have tested the accuracy of a balance before using it. If one weighs a coin, weighs a second coin, and then weighs the two together, the answers should be the same, but sometimes they are not, because the balance has not been zeroed exactly, or for some other reason. On an adequate balance it should, of course, be perfectly possible to determine the weight of a coin correct to two decimal places, and to repeat the result at will. In making use of published weights I have assumed that the figure in the second decimal place is corrected, and have set the step intervals at e.g. 1.305 to 1.345g in order that results correct to two decimal places should automatically fall within the appropriate step. I reweighed the Ashmolean's holdings (*SCBI Oxford* 110-224) and found that 21 results were one figure too high in the second decimal place (usually reflecting an error of only a few milligrammes), two were too low by a similar amount, and 7 results were in gross error. The effect on the resulting histogram would not have been very serious, but in a note specifically on metrology, an attempt to be as accurate as possible seems to be in order.

The major public holdings of the series are in the British Museum, the Merseyside

TABLE 1. *Varieties of Northumbrian Viking coins, with the numbers of specimens in the metrological sample.*

			Reverse design	Coins weighed
Class I. (*Obv*. EBRAICE CIVITAS)				
a	No stops in legend, no pellets in cross	*Rev*. C SIEFREDVS REX	A	2
b	" "	*Rev*. "	B	2
c	" "	*Rev*. SIEVERT REX	D	3
d	" "	*Rev*. CNVT REX	C	23
e	No stops in legend, 3 x 4 pellets in cross.	*Rev*. C SIEFREDVS REX	A	2
f	" "	*Rev*. "	B	7
g	" "	*Rev*. SIEVERT REX	D	10
h	" "	*Rev*. SIEFREDVS REX	E	22
i	Pellet stops in legend, no pellets in cross.	*Rev*. C SIEFREDVS REX	A	3
j	" "	*Rev*. "	B	6
k	" "	*Rev*. "	C	2
l	" "	*Rev*. SIEVERT REX	B	2
m	" "	*Rev*. "	D	6
n	" "	*Rev*. CNVT REX	C	11
o	" "	*Rev*. "	D	4
p	" "	*Rev*. "	G	11
q	Pellet stops in legend, 1 or 2 pellets in cross.	*Rev*. CNVT REX	D	1
r	" "	*Rev*. "	F	16
s	" "	*Rev*. "	G	96
t	*Karolus* monogram, no stops in legend	*Rev*. CNVT REX	G	1
u	" stops in legend	*Rev*. CNVT REX	G	7
Class II (*Obv*. CVNNETTI)				
a	No pellets in angles of cross.	*Rev*. CNVT REX	C	1
b	"	*Rev*. "	G	47
c	Pellets in 2 or 4 angles	*Rev*. CNVT REX	D	3
d		*Rev*. "	F	19
e		*Rev*. "	G	263
f	*Karolus* monogram	*Rev*. CNVT REX	G	24
Class III (*Obv*. SIEFREDVS)				
a	Pellets in each angle of cross	*Rev*. REX	E	7
b	Pellet in 2 angles of cross	*Rev*. "	E	1
c	"	*Rev*. "	F	7
d	"	*Rev*. CNVT REX	G	28
Class IV (*Obv*. ALVVALDVS)				
a		*Rev*. DNS DS O REX	Ai	1
Class V (*Obv*. DNS DS REX)				
a	Pellet in 2 angles of cross	*Rev*. SIEVERT REX	G	26
b	"	*Rev*. EBRAICE C	G	7
c	"	*Rev*. CNVT REX	G	2
Class VI (*Obv*. MIRABILIA FECIT)				
a	Pellet in 2 angles of cross	*Rev*. DNS DS O REX	Aii	36
b	"	*Rev*. SIEVERT REX	G	3
c	"	*Rev*. EBRAICE C	G	44
d	"	*Rev*. CNVT REX	G	38
Class VII (QVENTOVICI) (Not Northumbrian)				

County Museums at Liverpool (essentially the collection formed by Dr Philip Nelson), the Ashmolean Museum, and the Royal Collection, Copenhagen, with smaller groups of specimens in the Hunterian Museum, Glasgow, the Fitzwilliam Museum, Cambridge, and elsewhere. These resources, published in *BMC* and the *Sylloge of Coins of the British Isles*, have been combined to create a large sample for purposes of metrology. The coins in the British Museum, published exactly a hundred years ago, were carefully reweighed by the writer using a modern balance.

The York series is numismatically complicated. It has been classified into forty varieties, nearly all of which are believed to have been struck within a period of only a few years, and at York. Some of the varieties are represented by hundreds of specimens, some by only three or four. Out of 40 varieties, 30 exist in numbers so small that one could not usefully draw a histogram for each variety separately. Nor is it likely that it would make sense to do so. There can hardly have been 40 substantive issues in only a few years, and many of the varieties are likely to have been metrologically identical or very similar. The practical question, therefore, is how to group the varieties in order to recover information about any real differences that there may have been in the average weight or in the accuracy with which the flans were adjusted.

The varieties are summarized in Table 1, which follows the scheme published by Lyon and Stewart in 1964 and used subsequently in *SCBI* and elsewhere. There are six obverse 'types' (usually a cross, with or without pellets in the angles, occasionally a Carolingian monogram) defined by their six distinctive legends (I–VI). These are variously combined with seven reverse designs (A–F), most of which, again, occur in combination variously with more than one out of a total of seven different legends. There is obvious scope, therefore, to reduce the 40 'varieties' to a more manageable number of larger groupings, on the basis of obverse legends, or reverse designs, or reverse legends.

We may make a start, empirically, by constructing a histogram for the most plentiful variety, CVNNETTI/CNVT REX (II b and II e, respectively without and with pellets in the angles of the cross). A very adequate sample of 298 pennies produces a convincingly normal distribution, with a modal value of *c*.1.32g, or possibly a shade less. This is about 7 per cent heavier than the better stycas. The same step interval of 0.04g has therefore been used. Comparisons between the stycas and the pennies will, on this basis, be slightly unfavourable towards the pennies: the latter will seem to be slightly less accurately controlled, in relation to their average weight. The central step in Fig. 10, determined by trial and error, is from 1.305 to 1.344g, allowing 19.8% of the values to fall into the step. If the central step is positioned at 1.295 to 1.334g, a slightly higher proportion of values (20.5%) falls into it, but the general fit is a little less satisfactory. This alternative has been borne in mind in judging the modal value. The median is also 1.32g.

Eleven halfpennies have a mean weight of 0.572g, and a median also of 0.57g. This is only 43% of the weight of the penny, but fractions later in the middle ages were often permitted to be made with less than the appropriate intrinsic value, in order to compensate the mint-workers for the extra trouble of coining them. A forthcoming paper by the writer and Dr J.P. Northover will show that the halfpennies are of the same fineness as the pennies.

The second block of material to examine is the plentiful EBRAICE CIVITAS/ CNVT REX issue of the same design as the first, with which it is connected by a number of die-links (Ip and Is, both with pellet stops). Lyon and Stewart envisage

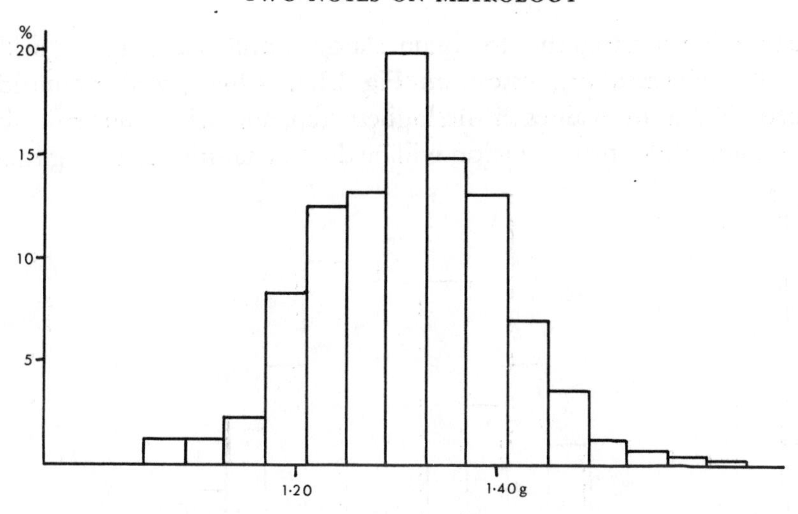

FIG. 10. Vikings of York, CVNNETTI/CNVT REX varieties.

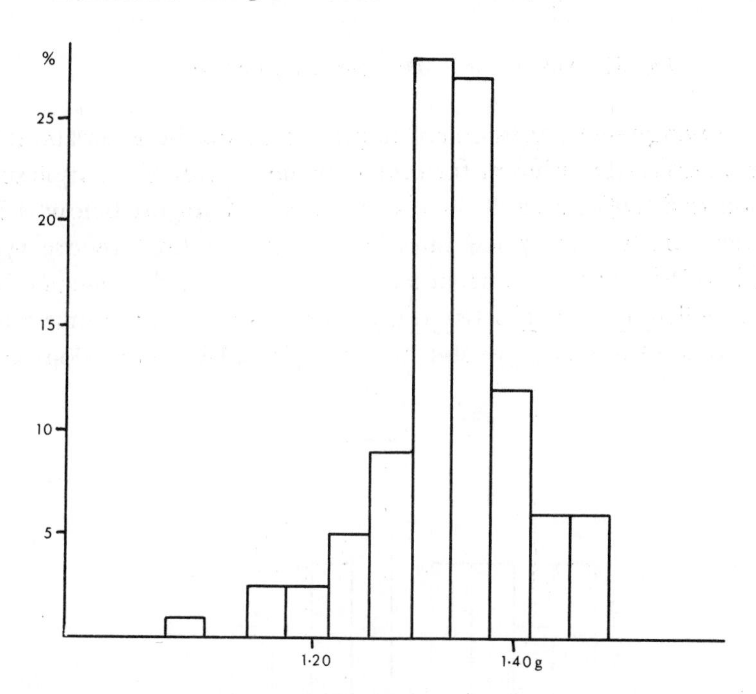

FIG. 11. Vikings of York, EBRAICE CIVITAS/CNVT REX varieties.

that these blocks—and all other types with CNVT REX reverses of design G—were in issue concurrently, but that the obverse dies were not freely interchangeable. They add that there is, however, enough die-linkage to indicate a single mint.

The histogram (Fig. 11) is less regular than for the (larger) first block of material. It is based on 81 specimens, which should have been enough to produce greater regularity. There are two central steps of almost equal height, with 28 and 27% of the values respectively. This represents a high standard of accuracy, but at the same time, the picture is blurred. The median is 1.337g.

The few halfpennies are more variable in weight than those in the first block. The mean average (5 specimens) is 0.52g.

The next exploratory move will be to compare the coins with reverse designs other than G. As there are many fewer specimens, reverse types A–F have in the first instance been lumped together to obtain a large sample (I a–o, q, r, [t, u;] II a, c, d; III a–c; IV; VI a). The resulting histogram (Fig. 12) is rather spread and untidy, with no more than 15% of the values in the highest step, and what appears to be a second peak at *c.*1.40g. One's first suspicion will be that the sample is mixing together coins

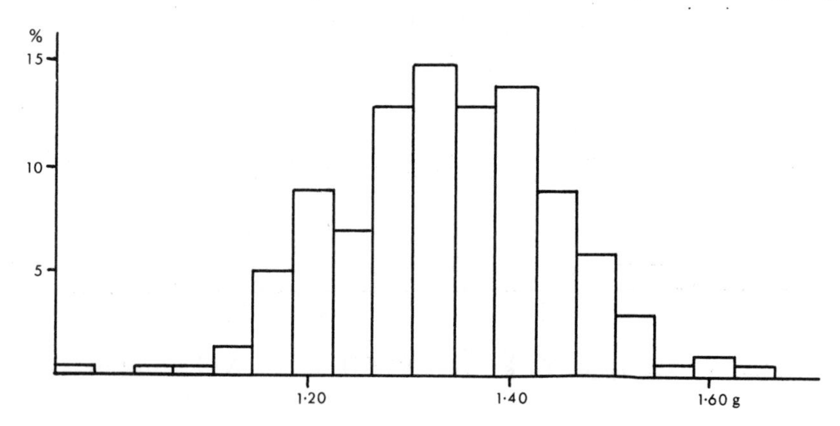

FIG. 12. Vikings of York, reverse types A–F.

on two different weight-standards, one of about 1.32g, and the other about 1.40g. It is, in any case, significantly different from Figs. 10 and 11, for the sample size is 188.

The 18 associated halfpennies show a mean and median just below 0.56g.

Many of the varieties combined into Fig. 12 are of the obverse type with EBRAICE CIVITAS, which occurs either with no stops in the legend (EC 1a) or with groups of pellets as stops (EC 1b). If this were a stylistic difference reflecting a change in the course of time, it is possible that it might reflect a metrological change.

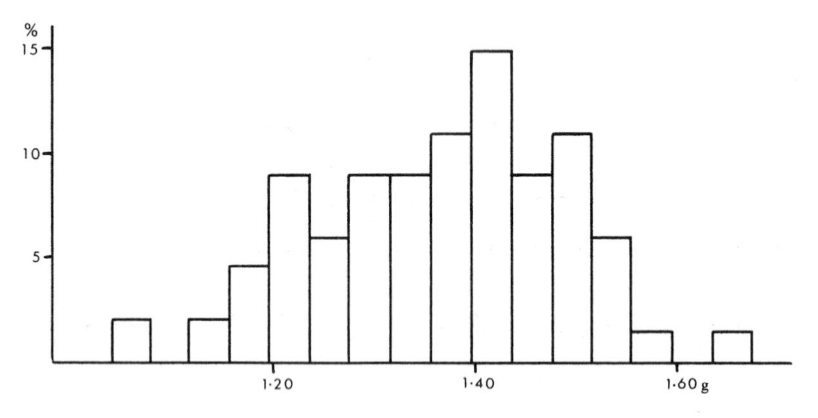

FIG. 13. Vikings of York, EBRAICE CIVITAS, variety 1a (no stops in legend).

We may look next, therefore, separately at EC 1a and EC 1b. EC 1a, with no stops (I a–h), produces an even more straggling histogram, with its main peak at *c.*1.40g, but still with only 15% of values in the highest step (Fig. 13). It is natural to ask whether some of the varieties involved are on one standard, and some on another. A quite simple inspection of the data is enough to show that this is not so: very high and very low values are found side by side whenever there are enough specimens of a particular variety for its range to be clear.

EC 1b (I i–s), in sharp contrast, returns us to a normal histogram with a good peak (24%) at *c.*1.32g (Fig. 14, 152 specimens). The pattern is dominated, of course, by variety Is, which we have already looked at in Fig. 11. but varieties I i–r show the same pattern.

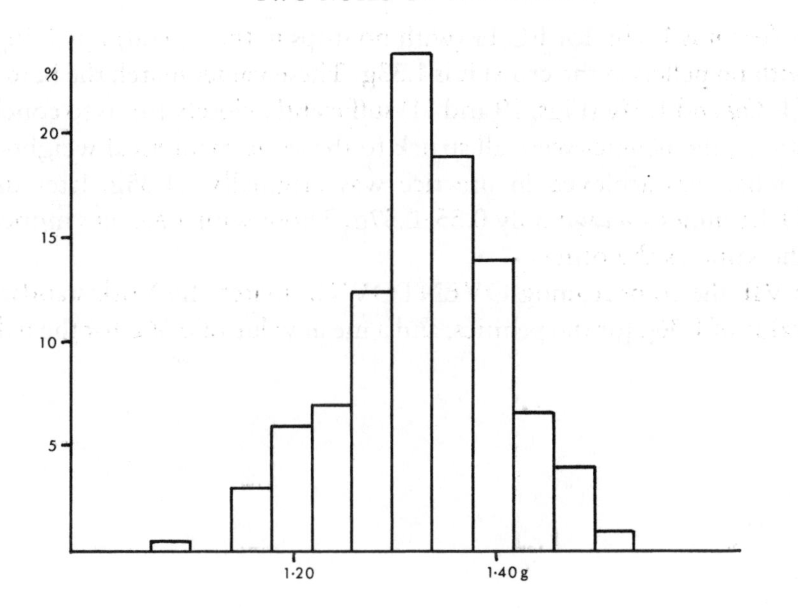

FIG. 14. Vikings of York, EBRAICE CIVITAS, variety 1b (with groups of pellets as stops in legend).

EC 1 can also be split into coins without pellets in the angles of the cross, or with pellets (EC 1a i + 1b i = I a–d, i–p vs. EC 1a ii + 1b ii = I e–h, q–s). The coins without pellets again produce a straggling histogram (Fig. 15, 69 specimens), which seems to reflect a position overlapping that of Fig. 13.

One can see by inspection that Group VI a (MF/DDOR) partakes of the same character.

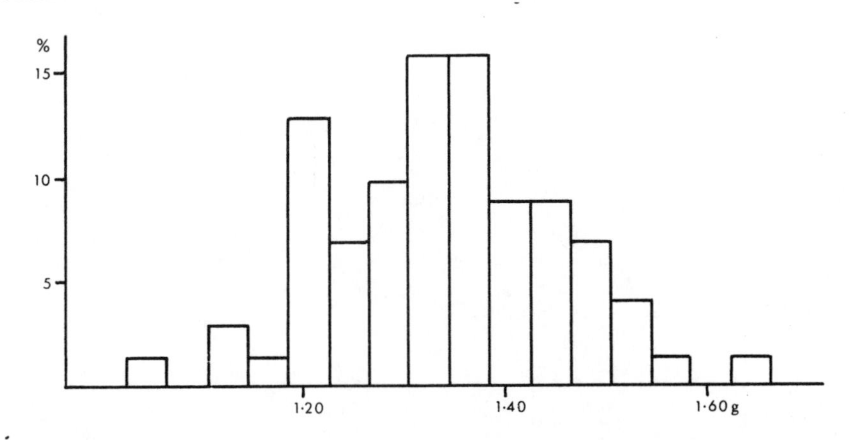

FIG. 15. Vikings of York, EBRAICE CIVITAS, varieties without pellets in the angles of the cross.

A few of the low values which are contributing to this generally muddled situation are for coins of which one or both dies are inferior in style; but it is easy to find (e.g. in the Merseyside *Sylloge*) pairs of die-linked or die-duplicate coins which are widely discrepant in weight. The appropriate conclusion therefore seems to be that there was an early phase in the Anglo-Viking coinage when the flans were less carefully controlled.

If we are led to the view that Figs. 12, 13, and 15 represent merely a rather slack attempt at a 'normal' pattern, we should go back and measure the median weight.

For types A–F it is 1.34g; for EC 1a (with no stops in the legend) it is 1.36g; and for EC 1/i (with no pellets in the cross) it is 1.33g. These values match the better attested values of 1.32g and 1.34g (Figs. 10 and 11) sufficiently closely for us to conclude that, like the stycas, the pennies were all struck to the same theoretical weight-standard, and that what was achieved in practice was originally *c*.1.35g, later drifting to *c*.1.32g. Halfpennies average only 0.55–0.57g. Those with a *Karolus* monogram are exactly the same as the others.

Group VII, the coins reading QVENTOVICI, match the York standard, with a median value of 1.36g for the pennies, and a mean value of 0.56g for the halfpennies.

Epilogue

NICHOLAS BROOKS

THE Tenth Oxford Symposium on Coinage was a richly stimulating occasion which has given birth to a volume of seminal papers; together they constitute a major advance in our understanding of ninth-century Northumbrian coinage. It was never likely that in bringing together experts in different fields—numismatics, metallurgy, philology, and history—we would immediately solve all the acute problems of interpretation that the coins pose. What did emerge in our discussions, however, was a growing understanding of the nature of the evidence upon which divergent views have been based, and that understanding is reflected in the form in which the contributions are here presented. Nonetheless since few scholars today, if any, can cope with all the different disciplines involved, it may be helpful for a historian who is very much a layman in these matters to highlight some of the principal advances and remaining problems that have emerged in these papers. It is possible too to suggest some of the directions that future work might take.

First of all we have become very aware of the relative wealth of numismatic information. Thanks to the discovery of major coin hoards [Hexham (1832/1841), York (1842), Bolton Percy (1847,1967) and Cuerdale (1840)]—each of which contained several thousands of coins and was relatively well recorded soon after discovery—our knowledge of Northumbrian coinage for most of the ninth century is far more complete than it is for other medieval issues. This is true both of the *styca* coinage of the Anglian kings and (thanks to Cuerdale) of the new silver penny coinage introduced in the closing years of the century when a Viking state had been established in the smaller southern half of the old Northumbrian kingdom. New finds (which become ever more frequent as the hobby of metal detecting grows) may in time add much to our knowledge of the rare coins of Æthelred I's second reign (790–6) and of the early 'silvery' coins of Eanred, but it seems unlikely that new *stycas* will significantly increase the total of 2,060 die-combinations already known for the 'debased' coinages of Eanred, Æthelred II, Redwulf, and Osberht.[1] Here, then, we have a coinage which we already know more fully than almost any other in the Anglo-Saxon series.

Its basic design incorporating a legend with the king's name on the obverse and the moneyer's on the reverse had, however, already been established in the late eighth century during the reign of Ælfwald I (778x9–788) and the second reign of Æthelred I (790–6).[2] At that time the coins were of silver and James Booth's fundamental reordering provides persuasive numismatic reasons for associating the

[1] Pirie, above p. 105. [2] Booth, above pp. 57 ff.

end of the Northumbrian silver *sceatta* coinage with the Viking assaults of 793 and 794 which were also responsible for the sacking of Lindisfarne and Jarrow. The abrupt ending of the Northumbrian silver coinage so that minting ceased for fifteen years or more throws a welcome light on the secular effects of raids whose impact upon the great Northumbrian churches is familiar from Alcuin's fulminating prose.

When Northumbrian coinage resumed under King Eanred, its silver contents had been drastically reduced. We now know that this coinage was not simply debased copper.[3] Instead it appears that the early *stycas* were of silver mixed with bronze (which is the alloy of copper and tin): then as Eanred's reign progressed the bronze was replaced by brass (copper with zinc) and the proportion of silver declined until in the reign of Æthelred II the Northumbrian coinage was effectively a brass coinage; finally in the derivative and apparently late series there is a reversion to bronze once more. In view of the biblical precedents for brass or bronze being regarded as a precious metal after gold or silver (an idea which recurs in the writings of Aldhelm)[4] it is clear that we should hesitate before writing of 'wretched *stycas*'. Both the shiny golden appearance of *stycas* when new and the technical accomplishment of controlling the zinc in the brass alloy whilst reducing the silver content suggest respect for the Northumbrian moneyers.[5] We still need to learn more, however, about how the metallurgy of the Northumbrian debasement compares with that of southern England and indeed with debasements elsewhere in Europe.

Moreover, until we know how much more difficult brass coins are to strike than silver, it is impossible to assess how the scale of *styca* coinage may have compared with that of pennies elsewhere in England. Even in a coinage as fully known as this, estimating how many coins may have been minted on the basis of the number of dies in use is necessarily a hazardous and controversial calculation since we know little or nothing of the circumstances governing the manufacture, supply, or use of the dies.[6] Whether we are justified in supposing the Northumbrian brass coinage to have been a massive issue of some 10 to 20 tonnes of coin designed to meet much more mundane commercial needs than was possible with the preceding silver coinage remains conjectural. An alternative view might hold that the primary function of this coinage was to serve an aristocratic elite and might use more cautious formulas to reach far smaller estimates of the total currency. What is clear is that the *styca* coinage eventually circulated widely through the Northumbrian kingdom.[7] But

[3] Gilmore, above pp. 159 ff; Metcalf and Northover, above pp. 187 ff. [4] Aldhelm, *De Virginitate* XV, XIX, ed. R. Ehwald (M. G. H., Auct. Ant., 15, Berlin, 1919), 244, 248; there is a convenient translation in M. Lapidge and M. Herren, *Aldhelm: the Prose Works* (1975), 72, 75.

[5] Gilmore, above pp. 159 ff; Metcalf and Northover, above pp.187ff.

[6] Metcalf, above pp. 6 and 350–3. For statements of the maximalist view see D. M. Metcalf, 'How large was the Anglo-Saxon currency?', *Econ. Hist. Rev*. 2nd ser., 18 (1965), 475-82; 'The prosperity of north-western Europe in the eighth and ninth centuries', *Ibid*. 20 (1967), 344-57; and 'Monetary circulation in southern England in the first half of the eighth century' in D. Hill and D. M. Metcalf (edd.) *Sceattas in England and on the Continent* (BAR, 128, 1984), 27-69. For the minimalist view see P. Grierson, 'Commerce in the Dark Ages', *TRHS* 5th ser., 9 (1959), 123-60; M. F. Hendy, 'From public to private: the western barbarian coinages as a mirror of the disintegration of late Roman state structures', *Econ. Hist. Rev*. forthcoming.

[7] Metcalf, above pp. 361 ff.

unless archaeologists can demonstrate that this distinctive brass coinage did provide a great fillip to the Northumbrian economy, there will be those who will prefer a minimalist interpretation of its function and scale. On present evidence the great leap forward in trade as in urban life appears not to come until the introduction of a silver penny coinage at the end of the century by the Viking rulers of the kingdom of York.

Acute problems remain in the fundamental numismatic work of analysing and classifying the *styca* coinage. The die-links between the coins of different moneyers are so numerous that the traditional arrangement of the *styca* coinage by reigns and pontificates and by moneyers within those categories makes it very difficult to appreciate the extent of these interrelations, let alone to comprehend how the coinage can actually have been produced.[8] It is not yet clear that classification simply by details of design or of the spelling of personal names offers any prospect of a more coherent interpretation. There would seem, however, to be a great benefit for future publications if a standard numbering of the individual dies could be achieved which was so ordered as to allow room for new discoveries whilst being arranged in terms of stylistic motifs as well as rulers and moneyers. Then it should become possible to set out the full complexity of the relationships between the coins of particular moneyers or particular reigns clearly and economically and thence to seek to understand something of the complexities of the production of the *styca* currency.

If the classification of the *styca* coinage still presents problems, the symposium did provide some glimmerings of light in the basic but thorny problem of the chronology of the reigns of the ninth-century English rulers of Northumbria. It is perhaps a curious paradox that the major attempts to reassess the written evidence should have been the work of numismatists, Hugh Pagan in 1969 and Stewart Lyon in this volume, whilst it is the historian, David Dumville, who here asks the fundamental questions about the quality of the numismatic evidence.[9] A number of general points now seem likely to command a wide acceptance. Setting aside a few nuggets of information to be found in contemporary sources from outside Northumbria, the annalistic record of Northumbrian politics comes to an abrupt end in the first decade of the ninth century. Thereafter we depend upon information found in twelfth- and thirteenth-century authors whose principal source of information is likely to have been regnal and episcopal lists. The possibility of errors and omissions in the transmission of this evidence and in the chronological calculations or guesses that were made from it is very high. Fundamental editorial scholarship on each of these works may in time clarify their authority and relationship; but it is unlikely to resolve all doubts or to determine all the erroneous calculations. In the meantime the historian must either rigorously eschew any attempt to propose a chronology for ninth-century Northumbria or make what can only be a provisional attempt in the manner that David Kirby does here, building an edifice that appears to have some internal validity from bricks of uncertain and uneven quality.[10] The numismatic evidence needs to make a full contribution to the edifice. No historian could deny that fundamental distortions with consequent knock-on effects may have occurred in the record of Northumbrian reigns and

[8] Pirie, above pp. 103 ff.

[9] Dumville, above pp. 43 ff.

[10] Kirby, above pp. 11 ff.

pontificates. The particular revisions proposed by Pagan or by Lyon, however, will only command assent if they are seen to be necessary in terms of the numismatic evidence.

In fact, however, it would seem that the coin evidence can indicate the order of the reigns of those kings who issued coins, but does not provide any foundation for conclusions about the length of their reigns. There are sufficient ninth-century hoards to establish the probability of substantial gaps in the issue of Northumbrian coinage. In particular it seems unlikely that any coins were minted in the name of Eardwulf (796–*c*.808) or of any of the English or Danish rulers between 867 and 895. Moreover, if we allow that the primary function of the *styca* coinage is uncertain, then we cannot presume that the need for coin was constant. Nor can we presume that there was a steady or sufficient supply of bullion. Shorter periods within reigns when no coins were issued and other periods when production was minimal are both likely. This means, for example, that no secure argument about the relative lengths of the reigns of Æthelred II and Osberht can be based upon the number of their moneyers or the number of dies represented in their extant coins; it also means that the absence of coins in the name of Archbishop Wulfsige is not necessarily an argument that his pontificate was short; it also means that we must be cautious how we use arguments based on die-linkage. If the coinage may have been intermittent, then individual dies may have lain for long periods in a moneyer's chest before being used once more. Some such hypotheses may prove to be the only means of explaining some of the complexities of the links within the *styca* series.

The other main evidence that has led numismatists to be dissatisfied with the traditional dating of the ninth-century kings has been the unique silver penny of King Eanred. The expert opinions of the symposiasts establish the authenticity of this coin beyond reasonable doubt.[11] But it is a difficult coin to explain whether we regard it as the only surviving 'penny' of the Northumbrian king of that name (indeed as the only penny attributable to any ninth-century Northumbrian ruler) or whether it was a coin of an otherwise unknown southern English ruler. Our knowledge of political developments in the early 850s is so slight that we certainly cannot rule out a short-lived King Eanred ruling either in Kent, or in Essex, or East Anglia or Mercia. What is clear, however, is that the legend on the reverse with its mixture of Old English and Latin is unique, and this suggests that the penny was in some sense a special issue. Given the uncertainties we cannot guess what special cicumstances may have led to its production and it would seem foolhardy to base any chronological conclusions on necessarily conjectural interpretations.

A plea to keep our options open in our historical interpretation of the *styca* coinage seems particularly appropriate since, as Elizabeth Pirie teaches us, we are only just beginning to comprehend its complexities. To a lay observer it would also seem that we should keep an open mind about the circumstances in which this coinage came to an end. In more normal times the die-links between the *stycas* of King Osberht and the numerous blundered and derivative coins would indicate that they were contemporary and would point to a significant breakdown in control of the coinage in the last years of the Northumbrian kingdom. But the circumstances

[11] See the comments of Metcalf, Pagan and Smart above pp. 36–46.

of the capture of York by the 'great army' in the autumn of 866 were not normal and dies may have fallen into all kinds of unauthorized hands then. In the South the production of imitative and blundered pennies is confidently attributed to moneyers working in the territories under Danish control in the 870s and 880s. Can we be certain that the barbarous and blundered *stycas* do not belong to the same period, given the extreme uncertainties of dating and given that their circulation was almost entirely separate from that of the pennies of the southern kingdoms? There is a natural desire to associate the main *styca* hoards with the events of 866, but it should be resisted. The 'great army' returned to York in 868–9 and came to Northumbria again in 872–3, whilst Halfdan's section of it came to Bernicia in 875 and settled the so-called 'kingdom of York' in the following year. Any of these events could have precipitated the hoarding of *stycas*, as indeed could the tortuous Northumbrian politics of the following twenty years. The only *terminus ante quem* for the Northumbrian *styca* hoards is therefore the beginning of the new silver penny coinage. The gap between the *styca* and the penny coinages in Northumbria may be more apparent than real.

THE SEVENTH OXFORD SYMPOSIUM ON COINAGE AND MONETARY HISTORY

Sceattas in England and on the Continent

The paper by Volker Zedelius, printed below, was read at the Seventh Oxford Symposium, but by an oversight which the editors regret, was not printed in the volume of proceedings of that meeting. It was held over to be included in this volume (on ninth-century Northumbria), as the best available way of repairing the omission, and in the hope that it will quickly come to the notice of the readers of the earlier work.

Eighth-century archaeology in the Meuse and Rhine valleys: a context for the sceatta finds

VOLKER ZEDELIUS

[PLATE 24]

DURING the first half of the eighth century coins still found their way into graves, and grave-robbery seems not to have been out of fashion and— one can say—so it has remained until now. The cemeteries are one important aspect of my theme. Archaeology today is—not only in Germany but elsewhere—an unmerciful race against industry and modern building operations. It was only the defect in one of four giant dredging machines which saved a Frankish cemetery from being destroyed in the Rhenish brown coal district, west of Cologne. Besides archaeology there is, as one knows, always the matter of conservation. And last but not least and even today, the archaeology of the very dark late-merovingian period and the beginning of Carolingian times is the archaeology of grave goods and single finds. Therefore it would be, even for an archaeologist, not so easy to give a satisfactory survey of this period. One can hardly do this without having a look first at the seventh century.

In the fifties a famous burial of a mighty Frankish nobleman was excavated on the church hill of Morken, west of Cologne, not far from Düren. The burial dates to the years around 600. Since then the village of Morken disappeared. The some hundred graves recently detected could have been the cemetery of the forefathers and some probably of the people of the man of Morken. But no trace of an ancient settlement to which both belonged could be found. The siliquae of the Ostrogoths and an early Frankish silver coin mark the beginning of the new (recovered) cemetery already in the Migration Period (fifth century). But there are also pseudo-imperial tremisses and gold-plated pieces from the years around 600.

From Lafaurie and other scholars we have learnt something about the so-called Magnentius type, a group of tremisses closely related in style and fabric, which occurs in the middle Meuse and lower Rhine region. The striking relationship between the tremisses from Namur, Huy, Dinant, and Maastricht continues with the famous Madelinus-type from Maastricht. Quite evidently it took the place of the former Magnentius-type. A look at the later moneyers' tremisses of the Meuse valley shows that, until the Maastricht mint was transferred to Dorestad, the Rhenish mints seem to have been closed. The Madelinus-currency, for example, can demonstrate the steady decrease of gold as early as the middle of the seventh century. Is the 'Madelinus' really the first silver coin, the first denarius, which was struck in Frisia as Prof. Zadoks-Josephus Jitta thought, the first penny, which led to the new silver currency? (I will come back to this question later.) With the most important and remarkable change from gold to silver in the second half of the seventh century, perhaps in the seventies, the touchstone for coins had fallen into disuse; it did not, of course, lose its function in testing the fineness of gold jewellery and ornaments. The distribution of this object must have been much wider than was once suggested. There are pieces in the Netherlands, for instance in Dorestad, in Belgium, France, and southern Germany too. Like the touchstones nearly all the sceattas in the Rhineland come from burials. There exists no recent map of distribution of cemeteries in the Meuse and Rhine valleys. The one printed as Fig. 1 is a combined plotting of three separate maps, which Roosens, Ypey, and Böhner published some thirty years ago. It shows a relatively dense distribution along the rivers. The vast majority of these cemeteries, however, belong to the sixth and seventh centuries. There are fewer of the eighth century. From the second half of the seventh century to the second half of the eighth century the people had no choice as to which coin to put as an offering-coin (Charon's obol) into a burial, or even the lesser choice between a merovingian denar and a sceat: that is what an excavator could expect or hope to find. The general opinion is that the custom of grave goods ended in the first half of the eighth century. In south Germany, however, it ended soon after 700; in Scandinavia it lasted until after the middle of the eighth century. But there are in the Rhineland, at least at its eastern border, few cemeteries which run up to Carolingian times.

One of these is Bislich (another is Walsum, near Duisburg). Ten years ago there on the right bank of the Rhine over eight hundred aligned (row) graves were excavated. The excavation is as yet unpublished (and will be edited by Prof. W. Janssen, of Würzburg). Nearly 30 per cent of the burials were found to have been opened and disturbed by Frankish grave-robbers. Nevertheless there were rich grave goods left. The cemetery shows Saxon influence on the eastern part of the Austrasian kingdom. The latest coins, two pennies of Louis the Pious of the XPISTIANA RELIGIO type, indicate how long people were buried there with grave goods. It seems that it was not only Christian doctrine and influence which led to a change in burial custom, but also a diminishing willingness to give up precious and valuable things as grave goods. Rather than pauperization it was perhaps also a response to robbery, or a change in the law of inheritance.

At Breberen and Doveren north of Aachen and at Rommerskirchen, some miles west of Cologne, excavations have shown a different picture: the shape of the cemeteries detected under the recent churches and the holes of wooden posts indicate that there must have been early wooden churches. The fact that people were interred with nothing else but a penitential robe made it difficult to date the burials exactly. The little pottery led some scholars to suggest that they belong to the early eighth century. Besides Breberen, Doveren, and Rommerskirchen early wooden churches have been recovered at Palenberg, Pier, and Wesel in the Rhineland, and in the Netherlands, in south Limburg, at Afferden, Buggenum, Geisteren, Gennep, and Grubbenvorst.

Soon after the beginning of the eighth century digging began in Xanten ('ad Sanctos') on the lower Rhine in an old Frankish cemetery to search for the martyr-grave of St. Victor. Not much later, when it was believed to have been found, a *cella memoriae* was built. From the excavations of Profs. Bader and Borger under St. Victor's at Xanten it is clear that the later Franks buried their people within a stone's

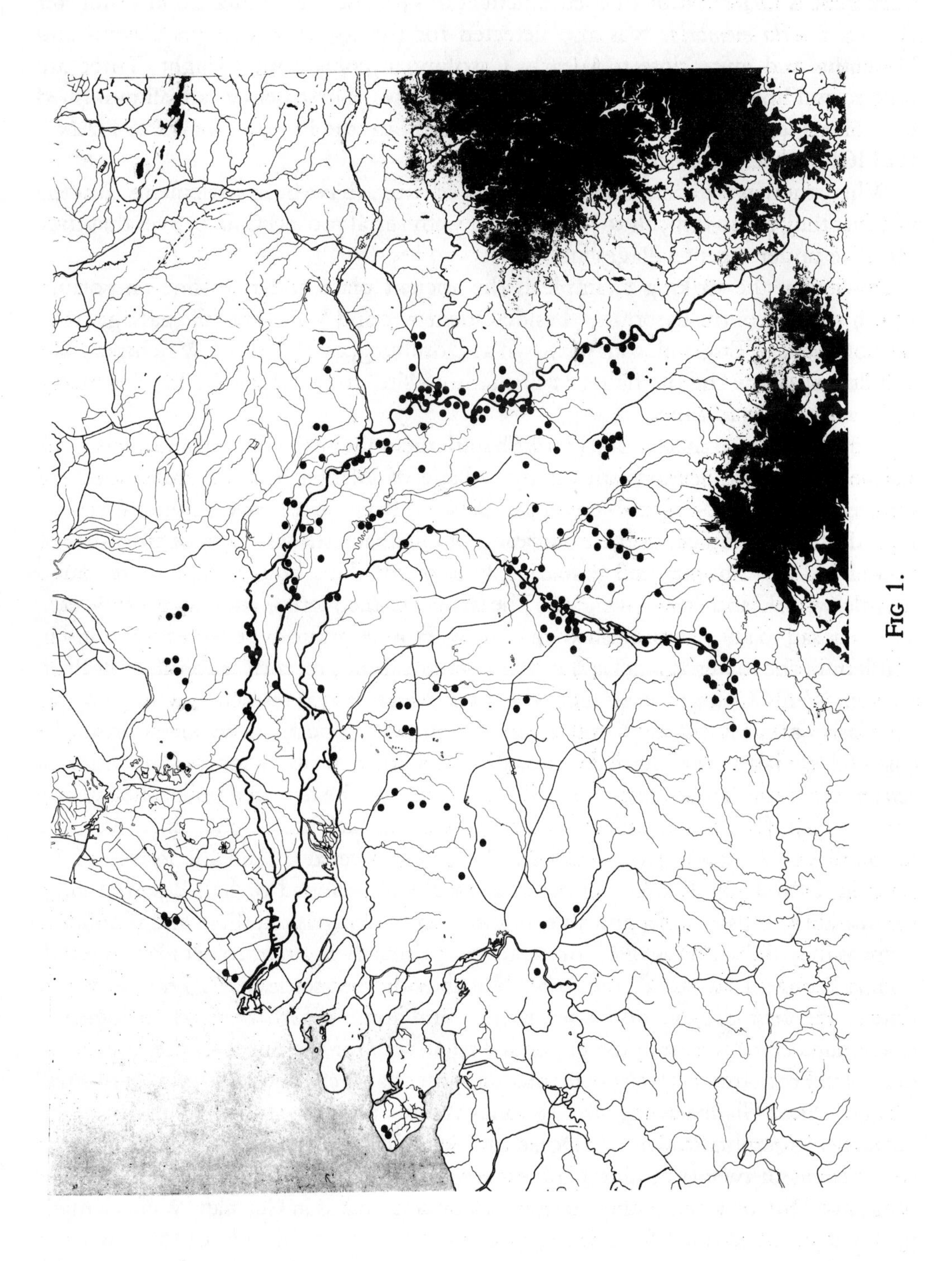

FIG 1.

throw of the first *cella memoriae*. All the sceattas found at Xanten came from the cathedral excavation and most—if not all—would seem to have been grave-obols, since there is no indication of a settlement at this precise site. Under Bonn's Münster Basilica a *cella memoriae* was also detected for the so-called martyrs Cassius and Florentius and quite close to it early Carolingian coins came to light. Three are pierced and holed (and perhaps served as jewellery). These deniers are all published by Völkers, except for one piece, the obole of Louis the Pious of the XPISTIANA RELIGIO type, excavated since 1946.

Where there were cemeteries, there must of course have been settlements. But the fact that they are so difficult to detect, even with aerial prospection, proves that they often lie under recent villages and towns.

Obviously the striking example is the ancient place and maritime emporium which was one of the harbours—beside Quentovic and Vitla—for the passage from the continent to England, today known as Domburg, on the isle of Walcheren. We still do not know the old name of this famous site, from which we have so many finds since Roman times.

In the Rhineland there is one Frankish settlement mentioned again and again in all archaeological publications: this is the village of Gladbach, some miles south of Andernach in the so-called Neuwieder Becken. It was excavated in the thirties by Prof. Böhner. The plan of the excavation of Gladbach shows traces of three-bayed houses and store-houses and granaries. In some of these houses there were found spindle-whorls and loom-weights. The artefacts recovered, such as pottery etc., are—it is sad to say—unpublished up to now. Houses of this type were also found in Haldern in the lower Rhineland and in Cologne-Porz, recently published by Prof. Janssen. While Cologne itself had been a temporary royal residence, a court of the Austrasian kings in the sixth and seventh century (Sigibert), as we know from the splendid burials under the later cathedral and from written sources, no trace of settlement of the late seventh or eighth century could be detected under the old city centre. That does not mean, of course, that there had been none, since we have cemeteries of Cologne-Müngersdorf, Cologne-Junkersdorf and the graves of St. Severin. I think the Franks did not occupy the abandoned or half-deserted *villae rusticae* (these mostly independent economic units), but visited them and plundered them as they did with the old Roman towns primarily in order to get raw materials such as bronze, lead, stone, and so on. But they did not settle there. They were, no doubt, the first diggers and after them—and long before the archaeologists—churchmen came to search (or pretended to do so?) for the burial of the martyrs to get relics. From the cemeteries we must suppose that there once existed a lot of small villages like Gladbach in the Rhine-Meuse region. As a result of their palaeodemographic studies Mr Donat and Mr Ullrich summarized: 'Settlement as single farms of twenty to thirty inhabitants at the present stage of research can be suggested.' Six or seven of these houses or hamlets, that is in German 'Weiler', made up a village, of about 125 to 150 persons or even more. In spite of the few early medieval settlements excavated by modern methods we can say that this type—like the Saxon village of Warendorf near Münster in North Rhine-Westfalia—had been the most common type of rural settlement of the seventh up to the eighth century, not only for the Franks but also for the Alamans and the Bajuvars.

Now let me turn to the Older Rhine/Lek/Meuse-region. The famous site at

Dorestad throws some light on the first half of the eighth century too: here I must pick my words carefully—shall I say 'town' or *vicus* or use the German phrase 'Fernhandelsort'?—well, the ancient settlement lies mainly under the town, nowadays named Wijk-bij-Duurstede. There are no traces of the settlement of the Merovingian period, although it could not have been far away from the modern town, nor from what Prof. van Es and Dr Verwers and their staff have excavated since 1967. The first volume, *Excavations at Dorestad. The Harbour: Hoogstraat I*, was published some years ago. From this report we learnt that the Dorestad of the Carolingian period was situated on the left bank of the Old Rhine river. From the excavation it is clear that this very site was part of the ancient harbour.

Large wooden causeways were built from the bank to the riverside. But the stream, here as in other parts of the Low Countries, did not stay in its bed, but withdrew eastward. The causeways naturally followed its movement and were again and again reconstructed. The shifting of the river should not be considered as a uniform and continuous process. On the whole the archaeologist sees a close relation between the behaviour of the Rhine and human activities.

The ground plans of the houses, not yet published, show sometimes boat-shaped walls, like the houses of Warendorf, or like the later type of Viking fortress of Trelleborg in Denmark. To each house belonged a wooden well; some had fences.

The dating—and this should be of interest for the very beginning of Dorestad—depends on C^{14}-analysis, dendrochronology, and horizontal stratigraphy. Also the finds are helpful, of course. One would expect that numismatic evidence would play an important role too, but this seems not to be so.

The archaeologists suggest that 'the occupation began sometime before 700, and around 675, and did not last long after AD 750. 'It seems,' once wrote Dr Metcalf, 'as though Dorestad was increasing in importance just at the period when Domburg was declining.'

It was again Dr Metcalf, who first pointed out, as early as 1966, that there must have been dozens if not hundreds of sceattas from the site of Wijk-bij-Duurstede. Mostly they found their way into private collections and are no longer available today. The new excavations brought only one sceatta to light, a piece in such poor condition, that the type is not certain.

Of great importance are the two Carolingian coin hoards from Hoogstraat I, both found in 1971 and preliminarily published by Prof. Enno van Gelder. The first contains twenty-five deniers, nearly all issued in the name of Pepin the Short. The second hoard consists of thirty-two coins, which fall into two sharply defined groups: seventeen light-weight coins of Charlemagne's pre-reform type, discontinued in *c*.783, and fifteen heavy pennies of Louis the Pious, with place-name on the reverse. Now it seems clear that not only coins of Charlemagne were struck and issued at Dorestad but also deniers of Pepin. The figure of a halberd-like weapon, in which Van der Chijs once saw a ship's hammer or axe, is certainly not the Frankish battle-axe or 'Franciska', as we know it from finds.

But it might be—just like the cross over the word PIPIN—a sign and symbol of Frankish power and royal authority at that very place with its port, dockyards, market, and flourishing transcontinental trade and traffic.

The finds appear to come mostly from the second half of the eighth century. And although we know as yet little—already mentioned above—not to say virtually nothing about settlement in the seventh century, there seems to be some archaeological evidence for the survival of handicraft since Roman times not only at Dorestad but elsewhere as well in the Rhine region: the production of pottery and glass, weapons, and jewellery went on. In the thirties, the famous moneyer and businessman Madelinus issued his well-known tremisses. About 650 Dorestad and the land up to the Meuse and Waal were conquered by the Frisian king. From the venerable Bede we hear that Pepin had driven out their king Redbad from Frisia citerior before Willibrord arrived in the Frankish kingdom in 690. About five years later Redbad was defeated in a battle near a so called 'castellum Dorestad'. It cannot be stated whether or not the mint at Dorestad was closed after the first Frankish occupation. The Madelinus currency, however, followed the general trend of a steady decrease in its gold contents. There is not only the evidence of colour and X-ray analysis but also a change in style and fabric: the later dies were cut with a deep grooved technique, similarly to the oldest Frisian porcupines.

Prof. Zadoks-Josephus Jitta thought that the coins of Madelinus were 'so popular that they continued to be struck afterwards in his name'. (This is possible and well known from other types.) She believed further that they were copied in a more and more barbarized form. But it is still an open question whether or not these crude imitations were struck at Dorestad or, as she suggested, somewhere in Friesland.

Mr Pol's map of Westerheem 1978 shows the wide distribution of Madelinus money in general. Over thirty pieces occur at Domburg. I think the Madelinus coins need a detailed study in which one should distinguish sharply between the tremisses (not so many), the denarii (only a few remain) and the bulk of the more or less barbarized imitations.

Although the excavator of Dorestad seems not to be fond of this phrase there is a kind of continuity at this site at least since the first quarter of the seventh century.

Among the finds recovered at Dorestad's Hoogstraat I-area, pottery takes (how could it be otherwise?) the first place. Some 87 per cent is of Rhenish provenience, from Badorf at the so-called Vorgebirge between Cologne and Bonn.

Glass should also be mentioned here. It seems that it had come partly from the Cologne area.

Wood and wine were imported from the middle Rhine region, around Mainz, and basalt-lava querns from Mayen and whetstones from Rhenish schist were shipped to the north.

We do not know exactly what the Frisian merchants brought to the south, say, in the middle of the eighth century.

There was indeed some amber, but I feel that it was not enough for trade. Later sources (of the ninth century) speak of a famous woollen coloured cloth. In 753 Frisian merchants were mentioned at the well-known market of St. Denis at Paris.

The first distribution map of sceattas in the Rhineland made by Prof. Jankuhn show a certain concentration in the Rhine-Main region.

This points to a considerable trading activity and is now supported by a lot of recently-found sceattas from Mainz. In 1981 nine ships from late Roman times were found at Mainz not far from the Rhine. With the ships a lot of isolated finds came to light, among them finds from the early medieval period. It is said, and I am sure rightly, that there were some dozens of sceattas, in particular porcupines but also the Wodan/monster type and the plumed bird type. The coins mostly disappeared into private collections. I have seen one porcupine this spring in Frankfurt at a coin dealer's.

Up to now it is not known if there had been a hoard, or single scattered finds; at least it does not look as if they were grave finds. It is a pity that these sceattas could not be studied until now, and I feel it parallels the situation with the great Carolingian hoard from Wiesbaden-Biebrich in 1921, which having just been fished from the Rhine immediately after that disappeared into the concrete of the quay-wall.

My first contact with sceattas was some ten years ago at the Münster Museum, when Peter Berghaus was so kind as to show me the old Kloster Barthe hoard, more than 750 pieces.

Many years later, while working in the Rhineland, a man from Braunschweig in Lower Saxony who used to spend his holidays on the island of Föhr on the north Frisian coast, asked me to have a look at some dozens of silver coins he had found on the shore near the so-called Goting Kliff. I saw that these were really sceattas.

These two finds are—as we have recently learnt from David Hill—the only hoards of sceattas from West Germany. Both the old Barthe deposit and the very new ones from the Goting Kliff near Wyk on Föhr are as yet unpublished. For the first I am afraid we have to wait further, while the other will be published in a year or two perhaps, by Dr Gert Hatz in Hamburg. Some coins are die-identical while some share only one die.

The impression I got at the Franekers Museum is that there is a close relation between the Barthe porcupines and the earliest porcupines in the Franenker hoard. Dr Hill, however, who had seen more differences in style showed that there are die-links between the Barthe, Groningen, and Lutje Saaksum hoards. This and the fresh condition of the Franeker and the Barthe porcupines indicates that they had not been long in circulation before being hidden in the ground. From this it has been suggested that they were produced not far from the place where they were buried.

It looks as if the discussion 'English or Continental?' has been decided in favour of Frisia. But can one exclude the possibility of an English die-cutter at the very beginning of porcupine production on the Continent, or at least English know-how?

Dr Metcalf has pointed out—and so did others—that there is likely to have been more than one mint or workshop in Frisia which issued porcupines.

The nearly uncirculated condition and the lack of imitations indicate both for the Barthe and for the Franeker hoard that a planned and well-considered selection had taken place. That makes it difficult not only to date the deposits as a whole but also the single types in themselves.

As with cemeteries with early and evidently late graves we have here—remember the Sutton Hoo purse—very old and very young issues.

The Franeker hoard contains even one piece of Metcalf's Maastricht type. It sems rather an early than a late type. There are pieces of good style as well as imitations of a flat and stiff style. From Prof. Hall's 'Isoprobe', an X-ray fluorescence analysis of the alloy, it is clear that there are pieces of good quality with over 80 per cent silver and others with only 40 per cent. It is an open question, however, where this type was struck. Menadier suggested that it was issued in north-eastern France, perhaps in Flanders. Although there might have been once a Merovingian model it is more likely that they come from Frisia.

Also the little hoard of eight silver coins—nobody knows if it is really complete—from the so-called Wittnauer Horn, a late Roman and early medieval fortress in north Switzerland, discovered in 1979, raises more problems than it solves. There are three sceattas of the 'Maastricht' type, four deniers from the Madelinus currency, crude imitation of the Type Belfort 1801, and one Merovingian denier. This hoard, or perhaps part of a hoard, came probably via the Rhine to north Switzerland.

What has been said about Barthe and Franeker seems also to be the case with the Goting Kliff hoard: a carefully selected assemblage. Nearby there are other finds which point to a settlement. There are also graves on Föhr with foreign—that means Frisian—grave goods. Thus there can be no doubt that on this island there was once a Frisian colony. Nevertheless the hoard (probably a bit later than Franeker) looks somewhat strange in this area. The individual coins can support this . One is cut into two pieces and many are scratch-marked for cutting.

In the Rhineland the sceattas come—as just mentioned and as Prof. Werner has already written—mostly from graves. Recently three new sceattas were found: one porcupine at Krefeld-Gellep and two Frisian runic types at the Frankish cemetery of Kuchenheim and at Flerzheim, some miles west of Bonn. The vast majority of sceattas from the Rhineland are, however, porcupines. Among these are many imitations including some from the mineral spring at Roisdorf, between Cologne and Bonn, in which hundreds of Roman copper coins were thrown. It is clear that one did not easily give up valuable coins as offerings or grave-obols: two of the three coins—one sceatta has been lost—are very debased and may contain only traces of silver.

KEY TO PLATE 24

1,2.	The *Madelinus* type, with *obv*. TRIECTO FIT (no. 1) or DORESTAT FIT (no. 2).
3,4.	Sceattas of Series D (the 'Continental runic' type).
5,6.	Sceattas of Series E (the so-called 'porcupines').
7.	Sceat of the 'Maastricht' or interlace type.
8.	Sceat of the 'Wodan/monster' type.
9.	'Plumed bird' variant of the 'porcupine' type.
10.	The so-called 'Herstal' or 'Star of David' type.

PLATE 24

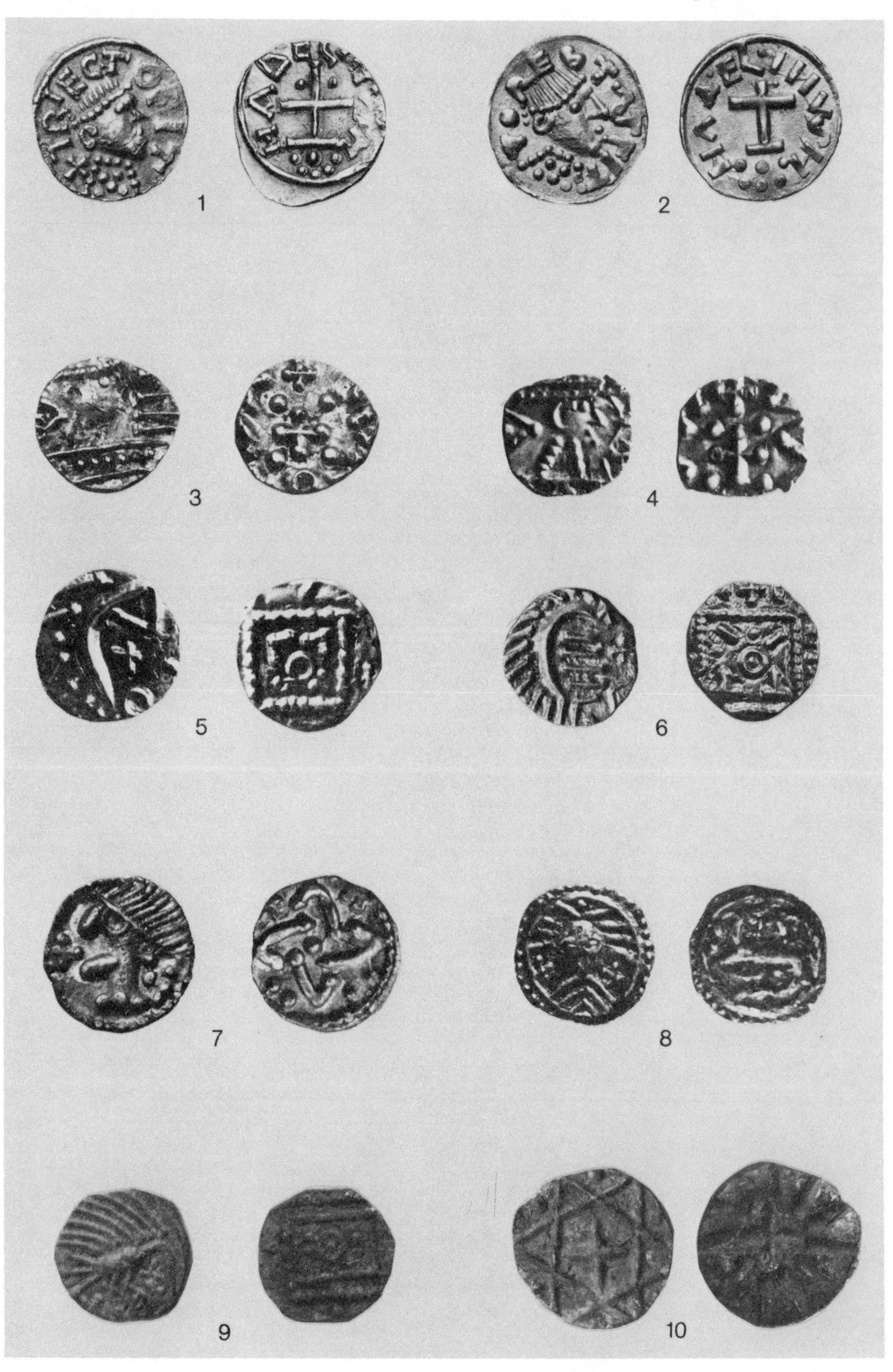

ABBREVIATIONS

Adamson, 1834 — J. Adamson, 'An account of the discovery at Hexham, in the county of Northumberland, of a brass vessel containing a number of Anglo-Saxon coins called stycas', *Archaeologia* 25 (1834), 279–310 and 23 plates.

Adamson, 1836 — Idem., 'Further account of the Anglo-Saxon coins, called stycas, recently discovered at Hexham in the county of Northumberland', *Archaeologia* 26 (1836), 346–8 and 7 plates.

ASE — *Anglo-Saxon England.*

AY — *Archaeology of York. 18/1: Post-Roman coins from York Excavations, 1971–81*, E.J.E. Pirie with M.M. Archibald and R.A. Hall, 1986.

BNJ — *British Numismatic Journal.*

Booth, 1984 — 'Sceattas in Northumbria', in *Sceattas in England and on the Continent*, ed. D. Hill and D.M. Metcalf, Oxford, 1984, pp.71–111.

Booth and Blowers, 1983 — J. Booth and I. Blowers, 'Finds of sceattas and stycas from Sancton', *Numismatic Chronicle* 143 (1983), 139–45.

EHD — *English Historical Documents*, vol. 1, ed. D. Whitelock, 1955

EHR — *English Historical Review.*

Gilmore and Metcalf, 1980 — G.R. Gilmore and D.M. Metcalf, 'The alloy of the Northumbrian coinage in mid-ninth century', *Metallurgy in Numismatics* 1 (1980), 83–98.

Hawkins, 1845 — E. Hawkins, 'An account of coins and treasure found in Cuerdale', *NC* (1842–3), 1–48,53–104.

Lyon, 1957 — C.S.S. Lyon, 'A reappraisal of the sceatta and styca coinage of Northumbria' *BNJ* 28 (1955–7), 227–42.

Lyon, 1970 — Idem, 'Historical problems of Anglo-Saxon coinage—(4) The Viking age', *BNJ* 39, (1970) 193–204.

Lyon and Stewart, 1961 — C.S.S. Lyon and B.H.I.H. Stewart, 'The Northumbrian Viking coins in the Cuerdale hoard', in *Anglo-Saxon coins*, ed. R.H.M. Dolley, 1961, pp. 96–121.

Lyon and Stewart, 1964	Idem., 'The classification of the Northumbrian Viking coins in the Cuerdale hoard', *NC*[7] 4 (1964), 281–2.
NC	*Numismatic Chronicle.*
Pagan, 1969	H. E. Pagan, 'Northumbrian numismatic chronology in the ninth century', *BNJ* 38 (1969), 1–15.
Pagan, 1973	Idem, 'The Bolton Percy hoard of 1967', *BNJ* 43 (1973), 1–44
Pagan, 1974	Idem, 'Anglo-Saxon coins found at Hexham', in *Saint Wilfrid at Hexham*, ed. D. P. Kirby, Newcastle, 1974, pp. 185–90.
Pirie, 1984	E. J. E. Pirie, 'Some Northumbrian finds of sceattas', in *Sceattas in England and on the Continent*, ed. D. Hill and D. M.Metcalf, Oxford,1984, pp. 207–15.
Pirie, 1986a	Idem, *Post-Roman coins from the York Excavations 1971–81* (The Archaeology of York, vol. 18/1), 1986.
Pirie, 1986b	Idem, 'Finds of "sceattas" and "stycas" of Northumbria', in *Anglo-Saxon Monetary History, Essays in Memory of Michael Dolley* ed. M. A. S. Blackburn, Leicester, 1986, pp. 67–90.
S	*Symeonis Monachi Opera Omnia*, ed. T. Arnold, 2 vols. 1882–5.
TRHS	*Transactions of the Royal Historical Scociety*

THE SYMPOSIASTS

David C. Axe, Esq., P.O. box 858, Index, Wa 98256, U.S.A.

Mark Blackburn, Esq., Faculty of History, West Road, Cambridge CB3 9EF

C. E. Blunt, Esq., FBA, Ramsbury Hill, Ramsbury, Marlborough Wiltshire SN8 2QJ

M. J. Bonser, Esq., Causeway End Fruit Farm, Wimbish, Saffron Walden, Essex CB10 2XP

James Booth, Esq., Dept of English, University of Hull, Cottingham Road, Hull HU6 7RX

Professor N. P. Brooks, School of History, University of Birmingham, PO Box 363, Birmingham B15 2TT

Dr. D. N. Dumville, Dept. of Anglo-Saxon, Norse, and Celtic, 9 West Road, Cambridge CB3 9DP

D. B. Feather, Esq., 14 Outward Lane, Horsforth, Leeds LS18 4JA

Dr. Gordon R. Gilmore, Universities Research Reactor, Risley, Warrington, Cheshire WA3 6AT

Dr. James Graham-Campbell, Dept. of History, University College London, Gower Street, London WC1E 6BT

Dr. N. J. Higham, Dept. of Extra-Mural Studies, University of Manchester, Manchester M13 9PL

Dr. D. P. Kirby, Dept. of History, Hugh Owen Building, University College of Wales, Aberystwyth, Dyfed SY23 3DY

Dr. M. Lapidge, Dept. of Anglo-Saxon, Norse, and Celtic, 9 West Road, Cambridge CB3 9DP

C. S. S. Lyon, Esq., 'Cuerdale', White Lane, Guildford, Surrey GU4 8PR

Dr. Melinda Mays, Yorkshire Museum, Museum Gardens, York YO1 2DR

Dr. D. M. Metcalf, Ashmolean Museum, Oxford OX1 2PH

Dr. J. P. Northover, Dept. of Metallurgy and Science of Materials, Parks Road, Oxford OX1 3PH

H. E. Pagan, Esq., 2, The Wardrobe, Old Palace Yard, Richmond Green, Surrey TW9 1PA

Miss E. J. E. Pirie, City Museum, Municipal Buildings, Leeds LS1 3AA

Dr. Veronica Smart, Centre for Advanced Historical Studies, University of St Andrews, St John's House, 69 South Street, St Andrews KY16 9AL

Dr. A. P. Smyth, Dept. of History, University of Kent, Canterbury CT2 7NZ

Dr. Ian Stewart, FBA, 2, Baldwin Crescent, London SE5 9LQ